PRACTICAL ENQUIRE WITHIN

A Practical Work that will Save Householders and Houseowners Pounds and Pounds Every Year

Volume IV

DIY

'Do It Yourself', also known as DIY, is the method of building, modifying, or repairing something without the aid of experts or professionals. It is undertaken by a wide variety of people, for many different reasons – but what links them all, is a desire to improve their material surroundings and skills.

The term 'do-it-yourself' has been associated with consumers since at least 1912, primarily in the domain of home improvement and maintenance activities. It only came into common usage around the 1950s however. Back in the mid-twentieth century, DIY referred specifically to the new trend for people undertaking home improvements and various other small craft and construction projects, both as a creative-recreational and as a cost saving activity.

In the present day, DIY can also refer to music, radio, magazines and the arts and crafts movement – in that it offers an alternative to modern consumer culture's emphasis on relying on others, to satisfy needs. It also includes crafts such as knitting, crochet, sewing, handmade jewellery and ceramics, as well as the general environmental movement towards 'Recycle, Reuse and Reduce.' Painting and decorating is also a particularly prevalent form of home and aesthetic improvement.

Aside from its appearance in 1912, DIY as a broader concept has a much longer history. Italian archaeologists unearthed the ruins of a sixth century BCE Greek structure in southern Italy that came with detailed assembly instructions. It has since become known as an 'ancient IKEA building'! The find was a temple-like construction discovered at Torre Satriano, near the southern city of Potenza; a region where local people mingled with Greeks who settled along the southern coast of Sicily from the eighth century BCE onwards. Professor Christopher Smith, director of the British School at Rome, said that the discovery was 'the clearest example yet found of mason's marks of the time. It looks as if someone was instructing others how to mass-produce components and put them together in this way.'

Much like the instruction booklets, various sections of the luxury building were inscribed with coded symbols showing how the pieces slotted together. The characteristics of these inscriptions indicate they date back to around the sixth century BCE, which tallies with the architectural evidence suggested by the decoration. Although close to the modern conception of DIY, this find cannot properly be termed a 'do it yourself' though – as the building was actually built by Greek artisans coming from the Spartan colony of Taranto in Apulia (Southern Italy).

The DIY movement is a re-introduction (often to urban and suburban dwellers) of the old pattern of personal involvement and use of skills in upkeep of a house or apartment, making clothes; maintenance of cars, computers, websites; or any material aspect of living. In the 1970s, DIY spread through the North American population of college and recent-graduate age groups. In part, this movement involved the renovation of affordable, rundown older homes. But it also related to various projects expressing the social and environmental vision of the 1960s and early 1970s. The young visionary Stewart Brand, working with friends and family, and initially using the most basic of typesetting and page-layout tools, published the first edition of *The Whole Earth Catalogue* (subtitled *Access to Tools*) in late 1968.

The first *Catalogue*, and its successors, used a broad definition of the term 'tools'. There were informational tools, such as books (often technical in nature), professional journals, courses, classes, and the like. There were specialized, designed items, such as carpenters' and masons' tools, garden tools, welding equipment, chainsaws, fibreglass materials and so on; even early personal computers. Often copied, the *Catalogue* appealed to a wide cross-section of people in North America and had a broad influence.

For decades, magazines such as *Popular Mechanics* and *Mechanix Illustrated* offered a way for readers to keep current on useful practical skills and techniques. DIY home improvement books began to flourish in the 1970s, first created as collections of magazine articles. *Time-Life, Better Homes and Gardens*, and other publishers soon followed suit. In the mid-1990s, DIY home-improvement content began to find its way onto the World Wide Web. HouseNet was the earliest bulletin-board style site where users could share information. Beyond magazines and television, the scope of home improvement DIY continues to grow online, and in the true spirit of DIY, many homeowners blog about their experiences – taking knowledge away from organisations, and into the hands of individual people.

As is evident from this short introduction to the practice of DIY, it is an aspect of human endeavour with a surprisingly long history. We will always need to make and improve the spaces in which we live and work, and DIY provides the means with which everyday people can do just this. It is hoped that the current reader enjoys this book on the subject – and it encouraged to undertake some DIY of their own.

Woodworking

Woodworking is the process of making items from wood. Along with stone, mud and animal parts, wood was one of the first materials worked by early humans. There are incredibly early examples of woodwork, evidenced in Mousterian stone tools used by Neanderthal man, which demonstrate our affinity with the wooden medium. In fact, the very development of civilisation is linked to the advancement of increasingly greater degrees of skill in working with these materials.

Examples of Bronze Age wood-carving include tree trunks worked into coffins from northern Germany and Denmark and wooden folding-chairs. The site of Fellbach-Schmieden in Germany has provided fine examples of wooden animal statues from the Iron Age. Woodworking is depicted in many ancient Egyptian drawings, and a considerable amount of ancient Egyptian furniture (such as stools, chairs, tables, beds, chests) has been preserved in tombs. The inner coffins found in the tombs were also made of wood. The metal used by the Egyptians for woodworking tools was originally copper and eventually, after 2000 BC, bronze - as ironworking was unknown until much later. Historically, woodworkers relied upon the woods native to their region, until transportation and trade innovations made more exotic woods available to the craftsman.

Today, often as a contemporary artistic and 'craft' medium, wood is used both in traditional and modern styles; an excellent material for delicate as well as forceful artworks. Wood is used in forms of sculpture, trade, and decoration including chip carving, wood burning, and marquetry, offering a fascination, beauty, and complexity in the grain that often shows even when the medium is painted. It is in some ways easier to shape than harder substances, but an artist or craftsman must develop specific skills to carve it properly. 'Wood carving' is really an entire genre itself, and involves cutting wood generally with a knife in one hand, or a chisel by two hands - or, with one hand on a chisel and one hand on a mallet. The phrase may also refer to the finished product, from individual sculptures to hand-worked mouldings composing part of a tracery.

The making of sculpture in wood has been extremely widely practiced but survives much less well than the other main materials such as stone and bronze, as it is vulnerable to decay, insect damage, and fire. It therefore forms an important hidden element in the arts and crafts history of many cultures. Outdoor wood sculptures do not last long in most parts of the world, so we have little idea how the totem pole tradition developed. Many of the most important sculptures of China and Japan in particular are in wood, and the great majority of African sculptures and that of Oceania also use this medium. There are various forms of carving which can be utilised; 'chip carving' (a style of carving in which knives or chisels are used to remove small chips of the material), 'relief carving' (where figures are carved in a flat panel of wood), 'Scandinavian flat-plane' (where figures are carved in large flat planes, created primarily using a carving knife - and rarely rounded or sanded afterwards) and 'whittling' (simply carving shapes using just a knife). Each of these techniques will need slightly varying tools, but broadly speaking, a specialised 'carving knife' is essential, alongside a 'gouge' (a tool with a curved cutting edge used in a variety of forms and sizes for carving hollows, rounds and sweeping curves), a 'chisel' and a 'coping saw' (a small saw, used to cut off chunks of wood at once).

Wood turning is another common form of woodworking, used to create wooden objects on a lathe. Woodturning differs from most other forms of woodworking in that the wood is moving while a stationary tool is used to cut and shape it. There are two distinct methods of turning wood: 'spindle turning' and 'bowl' or 'faceplate turning'. Their key difference is in the orientation of the wood grain, relative to the axis of the lathe. This variation in orientation changes the tools and techniques used. In spindle turning, the grain runs lengthways along the lathe bed, as if a log was mounted in the lathe. Grain is thus always perpendicular to the direction of rotation under the tool. In bowl turning, the grain runs at right angles to the axis, as if a plank were mounted across the chuck. When a bowl blank rotates, the angle that the grain makes with the cutting tool continually changes between the easy cuts of lengthways and downwards across the grain to two places per rotation where the tool is cutting across the grain and even upwards across it. This varying grain angle limits some of the tools that may be used and requires additional skill in order to cope with it.

The origin of woodturning dates to around 1300 BC when the Egyptians first developed a two-person lathe. One person would turn the wood with a rope while the other used a sharp tool to cut shapes in the wood. The Romans improved the Egyptian design with the addition of a turning bow. Early bow lathes were also developed and used in Germany, France and Britain. In the Middle Ages a pedal replaced hand-operated turning, freeing both the craftsman's hands to hold the woodturning tools. The pedal was usually connected to a pole, often a straight-grained sapling. The system today is called the 'spring pole' lathe. Alternatively, a two-person lathe, called a 'great lathe', allowed a piece to turn continuously (like today's power lathes). A master would cut the wood while an apprentice turned the crank.

As an interesting aside, the term 'bodger' stems from pole lathe turners who used to make chair legs and spindles. A bodger would typically purchase all the trees on a plot of land, set up camp on the plot, and then fell the trees and turn the wood. The spindles and legs that were produced were sold in bulk, for pence per dozen. The bodger's job was considered unfinished because he only made component parts. The term now describes a person who leaves a job unfinished, or does it badly. This could not be more different from perceptions of modern carpentry; a highly skilled trade in which work involves the construction of buildings, ships, timber bridges and concrete framework. The word 'carpenter' is the English rendering of the Old French word *carpentier* (later, *charpentier*) which is derived from the Latin *carpentrius;* '(maker) of a carriage.' Carpenters traditionally worked with natural wood and did the rougher work such as framing, but today many other materials are also used and sometimes the finer trades of cabinet-making and furniture building are considered carpentry.

As is evident from this brief historical and practical overview of woodwork, it is an incredibly varied and exciting genre of arts and crafts; an ancient tradition still relevant in the modern day. Woodworkers range from hobbyists, individuals operating from the home environment, to artisan professionals with specialist workshops, and eventually large-scale factory operations. We hope the reader is inspired by this book to create some woodwork of their own.

NEWNES
PRACTICAL
ENQUIRE WITHIN

A PRACTICAL WORK THAT WILL SAVE HOUSEHOLDERS AND HOUSEOWNERS POUNDS AND POUNDS EVERY YEAR

Fitting a Hatchway between Kitchen and Dining-room

IN BRICK OR PLASTER WALLS

In these days of modern devices any house falling short of the most up-to-date labour-saving equipment is incomplete. In this article it is proposed to deal with an adjunct to the house which is so often missed, namely, a "hatchway" or, to use an old term, a "buttery hatch." Now, a hatchway as we understand it for domestic use is a square hole cut through the wall which separates the kitchen from the dining-room and is used for passing through plates, trays, etc..

It will be at once seen what a tremendous amount of running to and fro with trays this simple device will eliminate.

Naturally, the conditions must be suitable, that is to say, the dining-room must obviously be next to the kitchen. This condition obtains in most small houses, but in any case we must assume that it is so.

No doubt the idea will be abandoned on the score of expense, but why not make the hatchway yourself? Here, therefore, are some practical hints as to how it can be done.

Tools required.

The tools you will require are a 2-foot rule, a saw, three chisels (1, 1¼ and ¼ inches), a cold chisel, a mallet, hammer, plane, screwdriver, gimlet, some 2½-inch brads, steel screws of various lengths (1, 1½, 2 inches), a glue-pot and glue, set square (45 degrees), 1-inch pins, punch, brace, countersinker, glasspaper (Nos. 1 and 0), and, if possible, a vice.

Making the Hole in the Wall.

First of all a hole has to be made in the wall. The wall will be of brick, either 14 or 9 or 4½ inches, or it may be lath and plaster or coke-breeze slabs.

How to find whether Wall is Brick or Plaster.

To ascertain whether the wall is solid or made of lath and plaster, tap it with a key or any other piece of metal. Should the sound be dull, the wall will no doubt be of lath and plaster; if a sharp sound, no doubt it will be of brick.

Fig. 1.—A Hatchway such as this will be found an Invaluable Labour-saver in any Home.

Dealing with a 9- or 14-inch Brick Wall.

In the case of a brick wall, great care must be taken that by cutting a hole the structure above is in no way weakened, and to set your mind at rest on this score a lintol will have to be fitted in to support the brickwork above.

How to make sure the Structure above is not weakened.

A lintol is a piece of wood, rough deal will do (4 × 2 inches in the case of a thin wall; wider if the wall is thick), a few inches longer than the width of the hole. This must be inserted as shown in Fig. 3, first having knocked a row of bricks out.

Deciding the Best Position for the Hole.

First of all decide the most convenient position to cut the opening and the size required. A hole about 2 feet 6 inches high and 1 foot 9 inches wide is a convenient size, but first satisfy yourself upon three important points: firstly, that the position decided upon for one side will prove quite convenient when cut through to the other; secondly, that there are no electric tubes or gas pipes running down and embedded into the wall at the selected position; thirdly, whether the wall is brick-nogged, that is to say, a wall composed of studding (upright pieces of wood) from floor to ceiling with courses of brickwork in between.

If the Wall is brick-nogged.

In the last case try and arrange your opening in between the uprights, if the space is sufficient, otherwise it will have to be dealt with in a similar manner to that described for dealing with lath and plaster walls (see later). Brick-nogged partitions are rarely found, however, in modern houses.

Removing the Bricks.

Mark out with a chalk line the exact position where you want to cut. Then take a cold chisel, a tool made of steel, for cutting brick or stone, and a hammer, and cut round the opening along the chalk line. Chip off all the plaster, which will be found to be of about 1 inch in thickness, until you have laid the brickwork bare.

Knock out the top course of bricks and insert the lintol (Fig. 3). Loosen the remaining bricks by striking with the chisel into the mortar joints. Once a brick or two have been removed, it will be found easy to lever the others out.

Having made a rough opening, make the square as neat as possible by chipping with the chisel (Fig. 4).

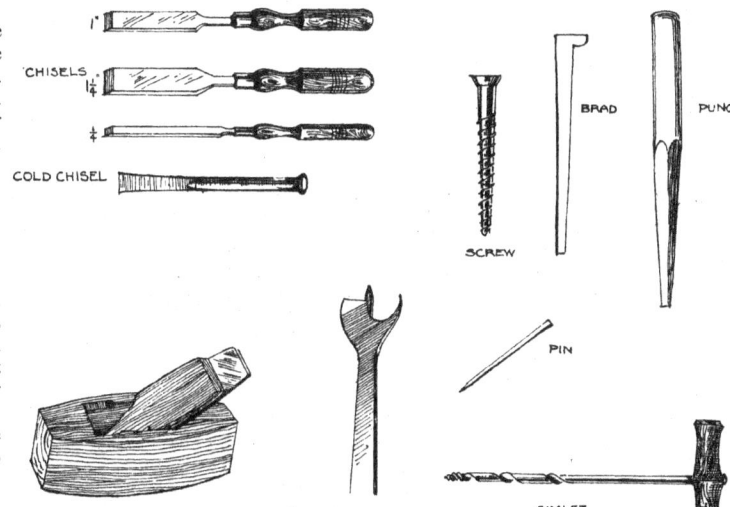

Fig. 2.—Some of the Tools required for making a Hatchway.

FITTING A HATCHWAY BETWEEN KITCHEN AND DINING-ROOM

The Framework for the Hatchway.

Now comes the framework. This may be made of deal and should be 1¼ or 1½ inches thick in order to allow for a rebate to serve as a stop for the door. A rebate (pronounced "rabbit") is made by cutting a piece out (Fig. 5), which can be done with a sharp chisel.

Plane the surfaces and rub them well down with No. 1 glasspaper, finishing with No. 0.

Dimensions.

The four pieces of deal must measure a fraction smaller than the width and height of the opening, but the depth, from front to back, should be exactly the same, including the plaster on the wall, and should finish flush with the wall face.

Now screw your four pieces of deal together as shown in Fig. 6.

How to fix a Framework into Opening.

Now you have a box without a bottom or a lid, in fact, four sides of a box. Insert this into the opening and fix it by means of 2-inch brads, and hammer the brads well in, and then by means of a punch (any blunt instrument will do) hammer the heads well below the surface of the wood. The holes thus made will eventually be filled with stopping when the painting of the woodwork is undertaken.

You can, if you like, screw the sides instead of using brads, in which case wooden plugs will have to be fitted into the wall first, into which you drive your screws.

Making the Door Frames.

Now you have a square hole in the wall lined with deal. The next step is to make two doors with frames (the latter technically known as architraves). As it would be laborious to attempt to make moulded architraves, flat ones chamfered, or bevelled off at the edges, will serve (Fig. 7). These frames should be about ¼ inch larger (inside measurement) than the woodwork which you have just fixed and should be mitred. Care must be taken to see that they are cut to the exact angle of 45 degrees, otherwise there will be an ugly gap. The angle can be determined with a set square. Well

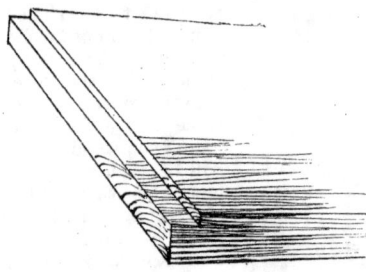

Fig. 5.—A Rebate should be cut out of the Pieces for the Framework to serve as a Stop for the Door.

Fig. 3.—To make sure that the Structure below is not weakened, a Row of Bricks should be knocked out and a Lintol inserted, as shown.

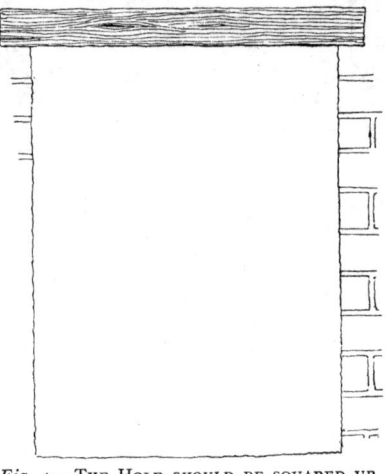

Fig. 4.—The Hole should be squared up as neatly as possible by chipping with a Chisel.

Fig. 6.—The Framework is then screwed together so that it now resembles a Box without a Bottom or a Lid.

It is then placed in the opening and fixed by means of 2-inch brads.

glue the four pieces together. The frame can then be firmly fixed to the wall by means of brads, just as you did the insides of the cupboard. It should overlap the edges as shown in Fig. 7.

Making the Door.

Now, having completed the main portion of the hatchway, the doors will next have to be made. These should consist of two uprights (stiles) and two connecting pieces (rails) (Fig. 8). This framework, 1 inch thick, will contain the panel. The rails will have to be tenoned into the mortises in the stiles (Fig. 9). The tenon can be cut out with a broad chisel, whilst the mortises may be chopped out with a ¼-inch chisel. If you have a vice to hold your wood so much the better. Chamfer the insides before fitting together (Fig. 10), and then fit the frame, well gluing the tenons before driving them home. Complete frame shown in Fig. 8.

Fixing the Door.

The panel of the door can be fixed in from the back of the frame, rebated as described above and shown in Fig. 11, fitted into the rebate of the frame and kept in place by means of small pins (Fig. 12). Fix two hinges and a knob with latch and you have your hatchway complete.

Fitting a Shelf.

Should the opening be high enough you might consider a shelf inside advisable. For this you will require to screw two cleats (narrow pieces of wood) one on either side, upon which to rest your shelf (Fig. 13).

Finishing off the Woodwork.

The woodwork will now have to be painted. Well rub down with glasspaper, finishing as before with No. 0. Fill up the holes made by the brads with stopping (made of white lead and linseed oil and a little whitening into a thick paste), put on with a palate knife; when quite hard, rub down with glasspaper.

Three coats of paint will be required. Glasspaper the surface after each coat. A final coat of enamel is good as it is so easily kept clean, and then if you really want a good job, felt it down (pumice powder rubbed on the surface with a piece of felt).

The above description applies only assuming the wall to be 9 or 14 inches thick.

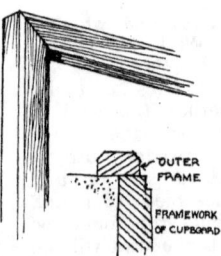

Fig. 7.—The Door Frames can be Flat Ones, chamfered or bevelled off at the Edges as shown.

FITTING A HATCHWAY BETWEEN KITCHEN AND DINING-ROOM

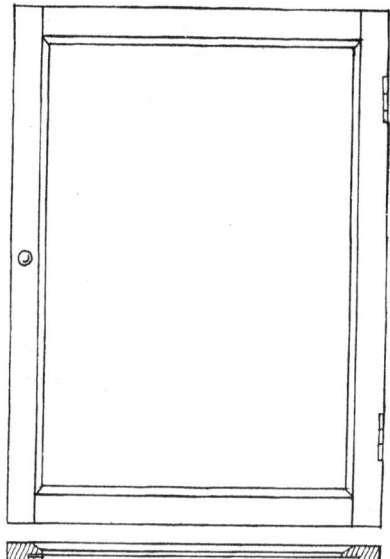

Fig. 8.—THE FRAMEWORK FOR THE DOORS.

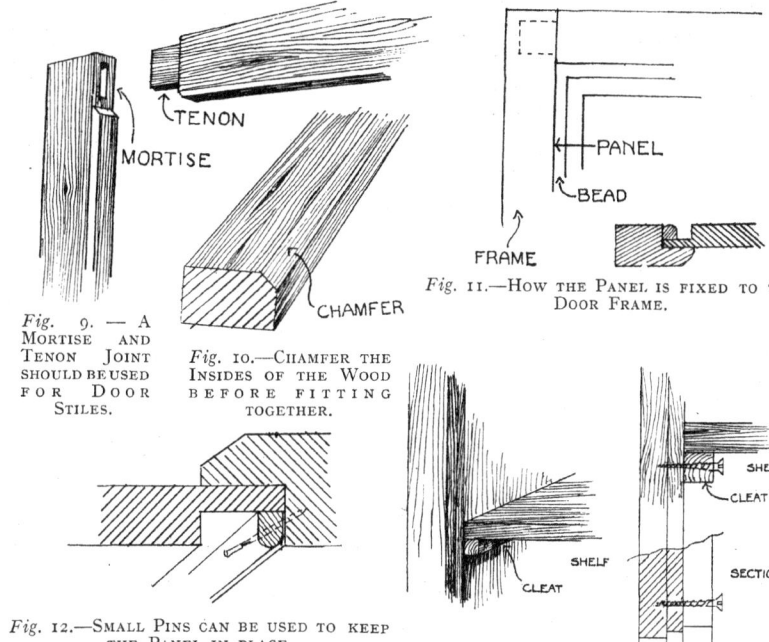

Fig. 9.—A MORTISE AND TENON JOINT SHOULD BE USED FOR DOOR STILES.

Fig. 10.—CHAMFER THE INSIDES OF THE WOOD BEFORE FITTING TOGETHER.

Fig. 11.—HOW THE PANEL IS FIXED TO THE DOOR FRAME.

Fig. 12.—SMALL PINS CAN BE USED TO KEEP THE PANEL IN PLACE.

Fig. 13.—METHOD OF FIXING A SHELF IN THE OPENING.

What to do if Wall is only 4½ inches thick.

Should the wall in question be only 4½ inches thick, then the same arrangement can be adopted, but of course the space inside between the two doors will naturally not be sufficient upon which to rest a tray of any considerable dimensions.

Build a Projecting Cupboard on Kitchen Side.

This can, however, be overcome by forming one side as a projecting cupboard, preferably on the kitchen side, and a useful arrangement would be as shown in Fig. 14, with a cupboard underneath. Thus arranged, quite a respectable piece of furniture would result.

The construction of this would be on similar lines as if only a hatchway were formed and as described above, but in this case the sides of the top part must project beyond the wall, say 9 or 10 inches, in order to give good cupboard space for the lower half.

Really, the easiest way to form the lower half would be to make a separate cupboard and screw through the floor of the top half (Fig. 15).

By the way, in all cases where screws are used they should be countersunk.

The Plinth or Base.

Now for the plinth, or base, of the lower half. This can be made out of deal, 3 × 2 inches. The top edges should be chamfered and the three pieces, front and two sides, mitred together and fixed into place with blocks for the angles secured by glue and screws (Fig. 16).

The two sides will have to be held together at the back by a piece of

Fig. 14.—IF THE WALL IS A VERY THIN ONE IT IS A GOOD IDEA TO ERECT A PROJECTING CUPBOARD ON THE KITCHEN SIDE, WITH A CUPBOARD UNDERNEATH, AS SHOWN IN THIS DIAGRAM.

A more elaborate arrangement is shown in Fig. 25.

wood 3 × 1 inches let in and screwed to the back ends of the side pieces (Fig. 17).

Fixing the Plinth.

Having made your plinth, screw it through the back plate to the skirting of the wall if there is one (Fig. 18), or if there is not and the wall is too hard to screw into, fix the plinth to the floor boards (Fig. 20). A difficulty here again may present itself for your floor may be cement, tiles or some other hard substance, and the wall be also of the same. In which case do not secure it at all, but rely upon the cupboard to hold it firmly. Screw the floor of the cupboard to the plinth as in Fig. 19.

Now the doors. These must be constructed in exactly the same way as those above-mentioned, but it will be neither possible nor necessary to fit architraves. The door will be set in the rebate as shown in Fig. 14, and fitted as before with a latch and knob for the upper part, and for the lower, no doubt, a lock with a key would be required.

Dealing with a Lath and Plaster Wall.

Now comes another question, and that is, should the wall concerned be lath and plaster, difficulties may arise, but not great, with regard to the wall construction. There will be studding, upright posts at intervals to which the laths are nailed. The space between the uprights will not be sufficient for your hatchway and so one upright will have to be cut through.

FITTING A HATCHWAY BETWEEN KITCHEN AND DINING-ROOM

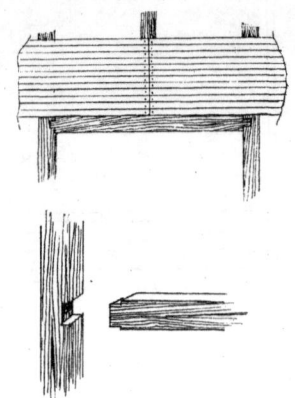

Fig. 18 (below).—How Back Plate is screwed to Skirting of the Wall.

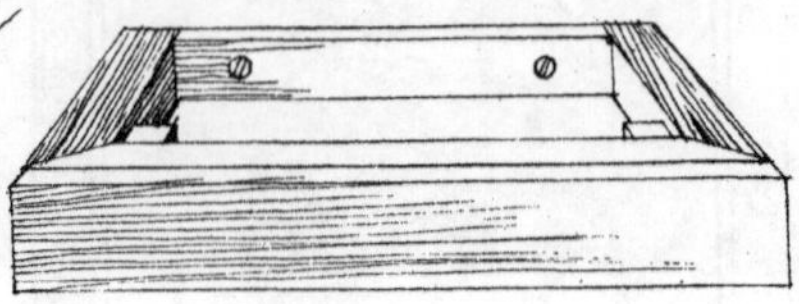

Fig. 16.—Showing use of Wood Blocks for strengthening Plinth or Base.

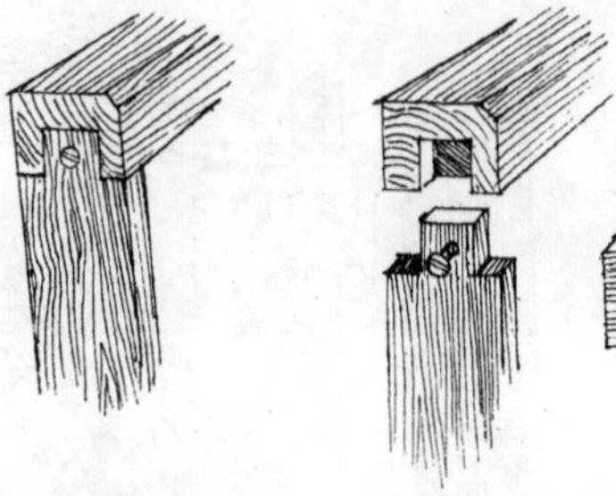

Fig. 15.—The Easiest Way to form the Lower Half would be to make a Separate Cupboard and screw through the Floor of the Top Half.

Fig. 17.—How the Two Sides are held in Place.

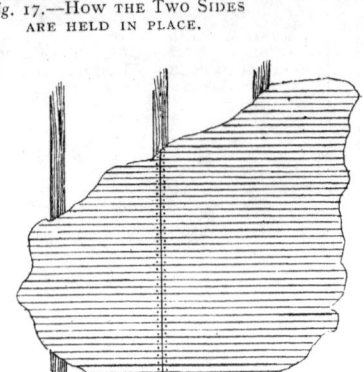

Fig. 19.—Alternative Method. Showing plinth screwed to cupboard floor.

Fig. 20.—When screwing Plinth to Floor the Screws should be Countersunk.

Fig. 21.—Showing Construction of Lath and Plaster Walls.

Fig. 22.—To avoid weakening a Lath and Plaster Wall an Additional Support, notched as shown, will be required.

Strengthening the Uprights.

This will naturally tend to weaken it somewhat and it will consequently require additional support. Fig. 22 shows how this is done. Make notches in the two uprights, into which fit two pieces of deal with the ends suitably cut (Fig. 22), allowing the centre upright which has been cut to rest upon it.

Having done this, fix the side pieces of your hatchway to the upright posts (Fig. 23), and proceed as described above, except that, as you will be dealing with wood and not brick, use screws instead of brads.

The wall will be only about 6 inches thick, so no doubt the projecting cupboard idea will suit the condition best.

Let-down Flap instead of Cupboard.

One more hint. If it is not desirable to build up a cupboard on the kitchen side or it is not convenient and the wall is of narrow dimensions, a let-down flap could be fixed to the wall which would serve as a shelf when passing through trays, etc. (Fig. 24).

The construction of this flap is simple enough. If the wall is brick, rawlplugs (these may be purchased cheaply) will have to be used. These have to be put into the wall for your screws to be screwed into.

The flap should be the length of the hatchway, viz., about 1 foot 9 inches by about 1 foot. Screw a piece of wood 1 × 1 inch × 1 foot 9 inches to the wall (Fig. 24). A, hinge your flap to this. To the right of the flap underneath, fix to the wall a piece of wood 2 × 1 inch by about 9 inches long (Fig. 24). B, to which must be hinged the triangular support (Fig. 24, C). The support is then drawn out to an angle so as to bear the weight of the flap. Fix a stop (Fig. 24, D) so as to prevent the support going over too far.

A MORE ELABORATE CUPBOARD ON THE KITCHEN SIDE

Fig. 25 shows a more elaborate cupboard built up on the kitchen side of a hatchway.

In small kitchenettes, system and

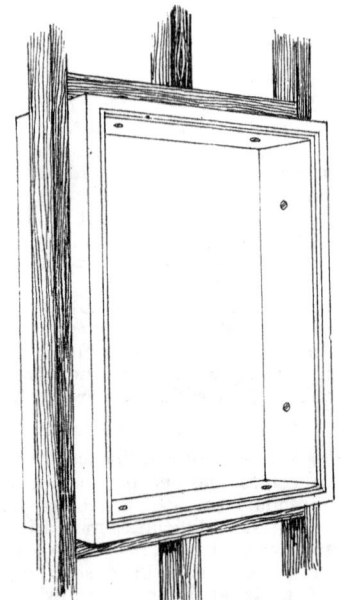

CROSS PIECES TOP & BOTTOM

Fig. 23.—How the Side Pieces of the Hatchway are fixed to the Upright Posts.

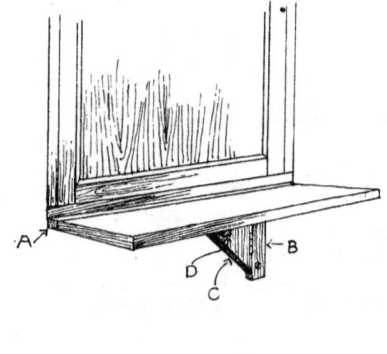

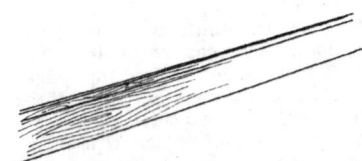

Fig. 24.—If it is not desirable to have a Cupboard on the Kitchen Side, a Let-down Flap could be fixed to the Wall as shown.

orderliness mean a great deal to the comfort of the woman who runs the home, and incidentally to other members of the household.

The space therefore should be allotted so that the things can be put away easily, without a lot of moving of other articles; in fact, "its own place" should be the easiest place to put any particular article back into.

This cupboard is divided into three distinct parts, with two doors each, and two drawers above the lower part of the cupboard (Fig. 25).

The Centre Part.

The centre part opens directly on to the hatch opening and discloses three shelves, the two upper ones being ordinary boards and the lower one the top of the lower part of cupboard. The whole is fitted quite closely to the wall, and reaches from the floor to the ceiling.

The width of cupboard is approximately 39 inches, and the width of the hatch opening about 34 inches. It is a good idea to have the doors on the dining-room side smaller; it leaves more plain wall space there—an advantage in a small room—also smells and draughts do not penetrate to the dining-room from kitchenette so readily.

The idea of having the cupboard hatchway is that various meals may be placed or "spread" in the cupboard from the kitchen side, thus saving many steps, because the housewife can get everything ready from the kitchen, and then go into the dining-room and take out everything

Fig. 25.—A Suggestion for a more elaborate Cupboard on the Kitchen Side of a Hatchway.

required for the meal from the three shelves in the hatchway without going backwards and forwards lots of times into the kitchen.

Thus meals are spread quickly and easily by one person. When the repast is finished, the plates, etc., can be piled up also by one person in a minute or so on to the empty shelves, and brought out on the other side after the guests have gone, ensuring the tidy appearance of both rooms until the time comes for washing up.

Hot food placed in the cupboard and taken out in the dining-room retains its heat better than when carried from one room to the other through the draughty passage.

Why Cupboard should go to Top of Ceiling.

The idea of having the cupboard to go right to the ceiling is to avoid as much as possible the use of un-covered shelves, which are such dust-traps. The top cupboard of the one shown is used for preserves, jams, etc., and the lower shelves in same for extra china and glass.

The centre hatchway cupboard allows space at the sides for hooks to take the cups and small jugs, and each side, on the shelves not immediately exposed to the dining-room (since the opening is some 5 or 6 inches less than the width of cupboard), is the cutlery in general use, with the fancy jam jars, sugar basins, cruet, etc.

The drawers below are used for dusters and kitchen cloths, and the lower cupboard, with its two shelves, for cooking utensils.

On the left is a narrow cupboard, also to the ceiling, which holds long brooms, sweepers, brushes, dusters in use, etc., and shelves above the various cleaning fluids, floor polishes, hearthstone and powders for cleaning.

Other Fitments.

Beyond this, against the wall, comes a small kitchen table with leaf. On the other side of the main cupboard, beneath the window, are placed the deep sink, with zinc-covered drainer on the left and a removable wooden one on the right. Below the former are two more cupboards for pails and photographic utensils.

Thus, although this kitchenette is a mere slip of a room, there are remarkably few oddments about, although all are at hand, and the room is both pleasant to look on and convenient to use.

REPAIRING AN ENAMELWARE DISH

As a general rule it is hardly worth while attempting to repair an enamelware dish if the appearance of the article is of importance. There are, however, occasions when it is desired to repair a large enamelware dish or pail which is used for purposes where appearance is not important.

Clean the Metal before repairing.

The most important point to remember if the repair is to be satisfactory is that some of the bare metal must be thoroughly cleaned to a bright finish by means of emery cloth. There must be no trace of rust or corrosion for at least ¼ inch all round the hole that is to be soldered. It is advisable to brighten the metal on both sides of the hole.

Cut Two Discs of Sheet Metal.

Having prepared the surface, cut a disc of sheet metal, preferably brass or copper, for each side. Smear a little flux on the parts and bolt the discs, one on each side of the hole, by means of a small nut and bolt and washers. Hold the nut with a pair of pincers while tightening up the bolt with a screwdriver.

Next support the patch as flat as possible on a metal plate, which should be placed on a gas ring.

Applying the Solder.

Now apply an ample supply of solder to the riveted patch so that some of the solder will be sweated right through on to the underneath piece. When this has happened, turn out the gas and allow the patch of solder to cool without moving the dish.

A Neat Finish.

A neat finish can be obtained by enamelling the patch when it has got quite cold.

Practical Notes on Varnish and Varnishing for all Purposes

Varnish may be defined as a solution, generally of gums or resins, the purpose of which is to impart protection and gloss to the surface to which it is applied.

Successful varnishing depends upon:
First, proper preparation of the groundwork.
Second, correct choice of an appropriate varnish.
Third, the utmost possible degree of cleanliness in working at every stage.

The number of varnishes made is considerable, and new types, such as the cellulose compounds, are constantly being introduced. But when we speak of varnish we generally mean the older and better-known kinds, which are technically described as oil varnishes, because linseed or tung oil enters largely into their composition.

A large part of the success of any varnishing job will depend upon the right choice of a suitable material. Therefore a brief classification may be useful.

Copal Varnish.

Probably the best known and most widely used varnishes are those in the naming of which the word "copal" is used. A true varnish of this class is made from fossil gums, which are found buried in the earth in certain Eastern countries. But, unfortunately, the word "Copal" is sometimes misused, and is applied to inferior varnishes containing what are called "false copals."

The only way of ensuring that you get a true copal varnish is to pay a reasonable price and purchase a material made by one of the well-known and reputable varnish firms of which, fortunately, there are many.

It should be noted, however, that by varying the proportions and kinds of copal gums, the linseed oil and turpentine content, and the kind of drying agent incorporated in the varnish, the material is adapted to various purposes.

Thus we have "inside copal," "outside copal," "church oak copal," "copal carriage" and a number of other descriptions.

Colour.

In addition to the classifications made necessary by atmosphere and wearing conditions, another factor enters, and that is colour.

All the types just mentioned have excellent wearing qualities, but, if the varnish is required for use over very light-coloured paint or wallpaper, these kinds would be too dark in tone.

No one has yet discovered a way of making a perfectly clear water white varnish, but it is possible to get materials which approximate to that ideal, and these are called "French Oil," "Pale Decorative," or "Pale Copal Paper" varnishes.

These are more expensive, but not necessarily of better quality, than the other types mentioned earlier. The extra cost is caused by the need for using specially selected and rarer pale gums, etc., in their composition.

Uses for Various Types of Varnishes.

A rather rough but sufficient classification would be as follows:—

Outside copal varnish is used over

Fig. 1.—Before putting a New Varnish Brush into use, Twirl it by rolling it between the Palms of the Hands.

This will throw out loose bristles and particles of dust.

exterior painted work in medium or dark colours.

Inside copal varnish is suitable over interior ditto.

Interior and exterior carriage varnishes are generally copal varnishes of an extra quality, and they are often a little paler than the ordinary copals. The word "carriage" does not, nowadays, mean that the varnish can only be used for carriages, although it may be quite suitable for that purpose.

Front Door Varnish.

Some manufacturers make a specially good quality of outside copal which they call front door varnish on the assumption, no doubt, that front doors require to be very well finished. And, obviously, a varnish which is good enough for a front door will be suitable, if the price is not a deterrent, for the rest of the exterior work.

Varnishing over Wallpaper.

For varnishing over wallpaper, a very pale varnish is necessary. In the manufacture of ready varnished papers a crystal paper varnish has to be used, as an oil varnish would be too slow drying. And crystal varnishes may be obtained for home use, but, as they are not so hard wearing as a copal oil varnish, they are not recommended. For such purposes, a white or extra pale copal paper varnish is to be preferred.

For very pale painted work, such as light cream, pale blue, pale green, pink, etc., either an extra pale decorative copal or a French oil varnish will be required. Anything darker than these qualities would definitely alter the tone of a pale surface to which they were applied.

"Floor" and "Church Seat" Varnishes.

Other varnishes that may be mentioned are those known as "Floor" and "Church Seat," which are specially intended for the purposes their names indicate. They are made so as to dry exceptionally hard and, therefore, they possess the power to stand considerable handling and friction. They are not suitable, however, for use over newly applied paint, as they might there cause cracking.

In other articles such as "Painting a Front Door" (p. 65), "Graining" (p. 111), "Varnishing Interior Woodwork" (p. 140) and "Decorating a Bathroom" (p. 673), the varnishing of various kinds of surfaces is briefly described. But there are certain general principles about which something may be said.

Varnish is very sensitive to atmospheric conditions, and particularly to changes of temperature.

Effect of Hot Weather on Varnish.

In hot weather, for instance, it becomes thinner in consistency. But this is apt to be deceptive if it leads us to suppose that it can be dallied with during application. The heat which causes it to become thinner while in bulk, also causes it to dry more quickly when it is spread on a surface, and this is particularly so if the sun is shining directly on it.

Therefore, under such conditions, the varnish should be put on and laid off evenly as quickly as possible, otherwise a satisfactory result will not be attained. It is well to so time the work as to do it when it is in shadow.

PRACTICAL NOTES ON VARNISH AND VARNISHING FOR ALL PURPOSES

Fig. 2.—This looks Simple but it must be done properly.
In pouring varnish from the container to the using vessel, care should be taken that the varnish flows gently so as to avoid aerating it, otherwise bubbles may form on the finished work.

Varnish should be acclimatised before use.

Another thing to be avoided is the sudden removal of varnish from a warm place of storage to a colder situation and its immediate use there. Far better is it to keep the varnish for at least twenty-four hours in a similar temperature to that in which it is to be applied; in other words, to acclimatise it before use.

"Blooming."

There is, however, one defect to which all varnishes are prone; and, not least, the best qualities. This is known as "blooming," which means the formation, on the dried surface, of a dull film something like the "bloom" often observable on black grapes.

The most persistent scientific research has, so far, not produced a completely satisfactory explanation of the cause of this phenomena, or devised a certain preventative of it.

It is quite common on outside varnished work during damp and muggy weather. Often its appearance is merely temporary, and the bloom disappears as the weather improves. In such cases it may be tolerated.

How to cure it.

Sometimes it occurs without apparent cause even on interior work, and remains as a lasting blemish. A brisk rubbing with a soft cloth damp with olive oil may be sufficient to remove it, but, generally, the only cure is to rub the work down with fine sandpaper, then dust it off, and apply another coat of varnish.

How to lessen the Risk of Bloom occurring.

But although no complete specific or sure preventative has yet been discovered, the observance of certain precautions will much lessen the risk of bloom occurring. It has been discovered by experience that the condensation of moisture on a newly varnished surface during the process of drying encourages the tendency to bloom. If, for instance, a front door or the walls of an entrance passage are varnished during the heat of an afternoon and this is followed by a cool evening, moisture is precipitated on to the partly dry varnish, and "blooming" is almost inevitable. Therefore,

Fig. 3.—When Cleaning Work for Varnishing always begin at the Bottom and Work Upwards.
A worn flat brush is suitable for the purpose.

during weather in which quick changes of temperature are likely, it is best to do the varnishing early in the day so that it may be practically dry before the cool air of evening strikes it.

Another frequent cause of blooming is the mopping of the floor of a room and the immediate varnishing of the woodwork while the floor is still wet. This should be avoided by allowing the floor to become thoroughly dry before varnishing is proceeded with.

Now let us consider the actual processes of application, and these will, of course, vary with the kind of surface we are working upon.

Varnishing over Painted Woodwork.

First, there is the case of woodwork which has received two or more coats of paint and which is to be varnished. It is essential to make quite sure that the paint is thoroughly dry. If the various coats are applied too soon after the earlier ones, these substances are imprisoned, only to retard proper drying and hardening and to cause trouble later.

This is especially true when a film of varnish is superimposed, for the varnish excludes air, and the oil underneath cannot dry out thoroughly.

Revarnishing Previously Varnished Surfaces.

One class of work, not hitherto dealt with, is that of the revarnishing of previously varnished surfaces.

It is often found that such work is in good condition and does not require a complete repainting, but has lost its high gloss with the passing of time and by exposure.

Cleaning down the Old Paint Work.

In such cases, the surfaces will require cleaning and otherwise preparing before a fresh coat of varnish is applied.

For cleaning down old paint work, a fairly strong solution of soda is often used, but this requires great care, otherwise the existing surface may be damaged. The dry soap powders, such as Hudson's, Compo, etc., are safer in this respect, but even with these care and a correct procedure are necessary.

The best and safest material to use as a cleansing agent is a good sugar soap (such as Mangers'). This cleans the surface without cutting into it.

When cleaning always start at the Bottom and work upwards.

One very important point to be observed in cleaning any kind of

Fig. 4.—After Washing the Surface it should be lightly Sandpapered to remove any Grits or Foreign Matter left on in previous Varnishing.

painted work is always to begin at the bottom and proceed upwards. If we begin at the top, the cleaning solution will run in streams over the lower work and, quite probably, will make marks or tracks which later cleaning of that part will not remove.

If, however, we begin at the bottom of, say, a door, a film of water is left on the bottom portion while we are washing the upper part, and this film prevents any of the solution which runs down from marking the lower parts.

Particular attention should be paid, during the cleaning, to the corners of mouldings and to those portions of doors, etc., which have been frequently handled. The slightest trace of grease left on a surface will prevent the new varnish drying at that spot.

To remove Dirt from Quirks.

In the case of work which has been neglected, a little fine brick dust is useful if scrubbed into the quirks, from which it will remove accumulated dirt.

When the whole of the surface under treatment has been cleaned, it must be thoroughly swilled down with clean water, frequently changed, so as to remove, not only the dirt loosened in cleaning, but all traces of the cleaning agent, whatever it may be.

After the actual cleaning has been done, it is advisable to rub the old work down prior to revarnishing, and this is best done by means of fine-grade waterproof sandpaper, using cold water only as a lubricant. After such rubbing, a further swill down with clean water will be required, so as to remove every trace of grit and, finally, a leathering off with a chamois leather is desirable.

The work, when cleaned, swilled, rubbed down, again swilled, leathered, and allowed to become perfectly dry, is then ready for varnishing.

When varnishing start at Top and work downwards.

In applying varnish the following procedure should be observed: Always begin at the highest parts and work downwards.

Thus, the picture mould would be done first, then the window sashes, next the window casing, followed by any cupboards there may be, next the door and, always as the last item, the skirting boards and floor surround, if any.

Fig. 6.—Start Varnishing by doing the Moulds first, using the Small Brush. Then fill in the larger surfaces with the large brush.

Scrupulous Cleanliness is essential.

As varnishing is always a final process and therefore the rectification of defects will be impossible afterwards, the most scrupulous cleanliness in working is absolutely essential.

A perfectly clean vessel must be selected for working from, and this may be either of glass, metal or earthenware. Many people prefer an earthenware jam pot to any other kind of vessel.

A Hint when pouring the Varnish from its Original Container.

Varnish should be poured from its original container quietly and steadily into the vessel from which it is to be used; and this for two reasons. First, to prevent any slight sediment there may be at the bottom of the container from being stirred up, and, second, to prevent the varnish from being aerated and forming froth or bubbles.

The last inch or so of varnish in the container should be reserved for final and less important parts of the work.

Fig. 7.—When Varnishing is completed the Work should be carefully examined.

Any surplus varnish which has accumulated at the bottom of the moulds should be carefully picked out with the tip of an almost dry small brush.

Brushes for Varnish Work.

Brushes used in varnish should always be of good quality and made with hog hair bristles. A flat 1-inch brush for the mouldings and window sashes, and a 2-inch or 2½-inch flat brush for the broad parts would be suitable.

If the brushes are new, they should be well twirled between the hands to whisk out any loose bristles or dust.

A brush is never at its best when new, but improves with use. Therefore, one that has been in use before is the most suitable, but if a new one has to be used, the less important parts of the work should be done first so as slightly to break in the brush before the more prominent surfaces, such as doors, are tackled.

Taking up the Varnish on the Brush.

In taking up varnish on the brush, just as much as the tips of the bristles will carry should be conveyed direct from the vessel to the work. And, unlike the practice in charging paint brushes, the varnish brush should not be patted against the side of the vessel.

Applying the Varnish.

The actual application of varnish also differs somewhat from that of paint. Whereas paint should be well brushed out, varnish should be applied

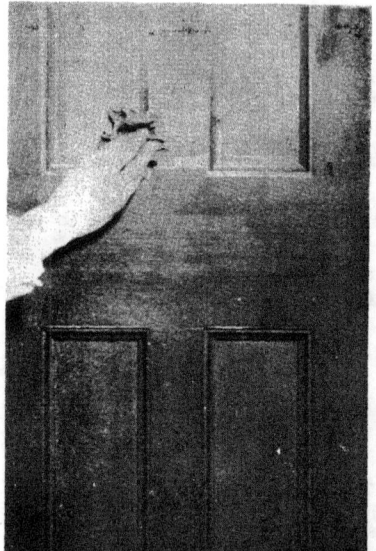

Fig. 5.—After Swilling down with Clean Water go over the Work with a Clean Chamois Leather, paying particular attention to the Mouldings and Angles.

in as full a coat as can be managed without running.

Nor should it be brushed more than is necessary to cover every part fairly evenly. It should then be left to flow out.

What to do if Varnish runs.

The varnish should be applied sparingly, however, to the quirks of the mouldings so as to prevent the running which would otherwise occur in those places, and the worker should frequently turn back to see if there is any tendency for this to occur. If there is, the surplus varnish should be picked out of the quirks with the point of the smallest brush in use.

Varnishing a Door.

In beginning to varnish a door, the mouldings should first be done, then the flats of the panels. When all the panels have been done, the surrounding stiles may be coated. In varnishing the mouldings, as little material as possible should be allowed to invade the stiles and, where this does occur, care must be taken when we come to varnish those stiles to work up any varnish already on them into that then being applied. Otherwise, such parts will have a double thickness of varnish and present an unsightly appearance.

"Cissing"—

One other point may be mentioned here. Sometimes, in varnishing, particularly over a surface which is somewhat oily or glossy, a trouble known as "cissing" is encountered.

In cissing, the varnish runs together in globules, much as water does on a greasy surface.

—and how to prevent it.

This can be prevented by vigorously leathering the work down with a damp chamois leather just before beginning to varnish. A mere trace of fuller's earth dissolved in the water with which the leather is damped will increase the effectiveness of this preventative measure.

Storing Varnish Brushes.

Whereas it is sometimes permissible to store paint brushes, when not in use, in a vessel containing water, this course should never be adopted with brushes used in varnish. These should be suspended up to slightly over the whole length of bristle in either linseed oil, varnish or a mixture of these two liquids. And the vessel should be covered with either a metal or paper lid to exclude dust.

Before being put back into varnish for use, the brushes will require well scraping on the side of the storage can, so as to remove any of the fluid in which they have been stored.

STRENGTHENING A STAIR POST

THE post at the foot of the stair banister gets a deal of pressure at times and has a tendency to get loose. The sketch shows two ways of giving it support in the direction in which it is most likely to get loose.

Fig. 1 shows the post and the bottom tread and riser of the stairs. A right-angle iron bracket, A, is strengthened against opening wider by a strengthening piece B, made of ¼-inch iron riveted to the back of the bracket and having screw holes through both bracket and strengthening piece. The bracket with the stiffener attached is sunk flush with the post and the stair tread, and a recess is cut with a mortise chisel, just the width of the

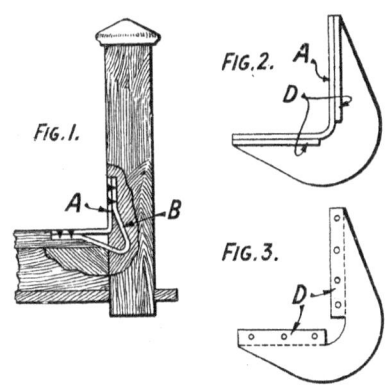

bracket stiffener, to take the latter, and the ends are then screwed firmly by good thick screws to stair tread and post.

Another method which will give a greater stiffness to the support is shown in Fig. 2. Here a flat plate of iron about ⅛ inch thick is cut to the shape shown in Fig. 3. The pieces DD are turned up at right angles and face up to the two sides of the bracket. They are shown together at Fig. 2. This has the same effect as the strengthening piece in Fig. 1, but is much stronger against bending out and takes up less width of mortise in post and stair. It is fitted in exactly the same way as is the arrangement shown in Fig. 1.

CHOPPER SHAFT LOCK

DOMESTIC coal hammers, choppers, garden hoes, etc., where the shaft or handle is driven in an open-ended socket, are generally secured by driving a wooden or iron wedge into the end of the shaft or handle after the latter has been driven into the head.

This method is more or less successful, but in the case of heavy coal hammers, and especially hatchets, there is a danger of the wood shrinking and the wedge working out and the head leaving the shaft—with the possibility of injury to the user.

In the sketch is shown an easy method of making the fastening

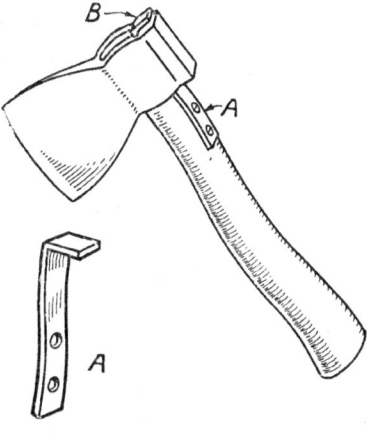

DETAILS OF CHOPPER SHAFT LOCK.

quite secure against the head coming off.

The back of the shaft is flattened with a rasp (or even a pocket knife) for a distance of about 3½ inches, and this leaves a space between the back of the shaft and the socket hole in the chopper or hammer head.

Down this space is driven the flat iron strip, A, having its head, B, turned over at right angles and also having two or three countersunk holes by means of which, when it has been driven fully down, it may be screwed to the back of the shaft.

This will prevent the head coming off, even if the wedge shrinks and head becomes a little loose.

Making a Concrete Garden Roller

A GARDEN roller is such a useful article for the ordinary householder that in most cases it is practically indispensable for garden paths, lawns, etc.

Unfortunately, however, the proprietary iron types of garden roller are often beyond the pocket of the man of small means, so that frequently he is forced to go without this very handy object.

It is possible, nevertheless, to make a very serviceable garden roller at a ridiculously low cost —as compared with the proprietary article — by employing ordinary concrete either with or without a metal exterior.

With the aid of some scrap metal and wood, the handle, stirrup-piece and bearings can be made by the amateur at a low cost.

Those who have not used concrete rollers before need have no qualms on the matter of their strength for in ordinary use it is impossible to damage them, provided that the edges are well rounded.

Sizes and Weights.

The first thing which must be decided is what weight of roller is required. This is an important consideration, for concrete is a heavy material and, without some knowledge of its weight and volume, the amateur may find himself burdened with a much heavier roller than he requires.

As a rough guide it may be mentioned that a solid concrete roller measuring 1 foot in diameter by 1 foot in length weighs about 1 cwt.

The following are some roller dimensions and weights of concrete rollers:—

Diameter.		Length.	Weight in Cwts.
Ft.	Ins.	Ft.	
1	0	1	1
1	0	2	2
1	0	3	3
1	6	1	2¼
1	9	1	3
2	0	1	4
1	6	2	4½
1	9	2	6
2	0	2	8

It will be possible, with the aid of this table to select any convenient sizes to give the required weight. In the case of long rollers, *i.e.*, where the length exceeds the diameter, it is best to make these in two or three separate sections, each free to rotate on the common axle, in order to facilitate turning whilst rolling.

USING OLD METAL DRUMS

Perhaps the simplest of all concrete-body rollers are those made from old cylindrical metal drums. Thus a 5 or 10-gallon oil drum will simplify greatly the process of making the concrete roller, for the metal casing can be utilised as the mould, and, having fitted and located the axle, all that is necessary is to pour the concrete into the drum. The general principle of construction is as follows:—

The First Stage.

Fig. 1 shows the method of making such a roller. It is first necessary to mark off the centre of each end as accurately as possible; check this by measuring from the centre to various parts of the circumference; all these distances should, of course, be equal.

Fig. 1.—An Oil Drum Roller. See also Figs. 4–15.

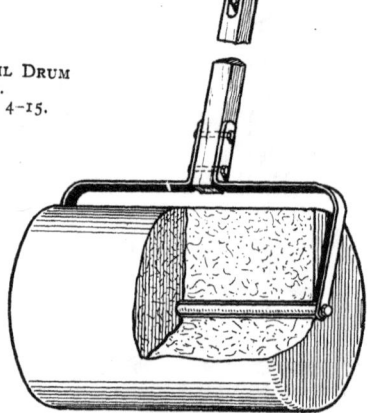

Fig. 2.—A Solid Concrete Roller with Handle and Stirrup-pieces.

Drilling out the Hole for the Axle.

Next, scribe a circle equal in diameter to the outside diameter of the tube or solid metal axle to be used. Drill out this hole, by first drilling a number of smaller holes *inside* the scribed circle, and then cutting away the metal between the circles with a chisel. File out to the required diameter to suit the axle. Alternatively adopt the method shown in Fig. 7 and described later.

Next cut out two larger holes in what will be the upper side of the drum; these holes are for pouring in the concrete mixture, tamping the latter down and allowing the air to escape.

Pouring in the Concrete Mixture.

Finally, fix the axle in position, stand the drum vertical and pour in the wet concrete mixture. At intervals during the pouring process, tamp the mixture down well, using a piece of wood, with a wide end, for this purpose.

Having completely filled the drum, and excluded all of the air by tamping the mixture, allow it to stand for several days in order to set and to harden off.

Making the Concrete Mixture.

The concrete used for making the filling mixture should not be of too coarse a constitution, as the roller must be strong for its purpose.

A satisfactory concrete for rollers is one consisting of 1 part Portland cement, 2 parts sand, and 4 parts of coarse material, or aggregate. The latter may be stones up to about 1½-inch mesh. The concrete's constituents should be thoroughly mixed before watering to a pasty consistency, and then again after watering.

SOME PRACTICAL NOTES

The series of photographs on the facing page show various stages in the construction of a roller from an old metal drum.

Materials Required.

Besides the oil drum and the cement, the other materials required are two pieces of 1-inch Tee-iron, each 4 feet long, a piece of ½-inch iron rod a few inches longer than the drum, and a piece of ½-inch gas barrel through which the rod will slide easily, and which should be about an inch longer than the total outside length of the drum. This averages about 21 inches.

The wood for handle and centre-piece can suitably be of ash or any other hardwood about 2 × 1¼ inches, and, for the first-named 2 feet, and for the second, 18 inches are required; but it is better to defer selecting the wood until the metal is made up, for reasons which are explained later.

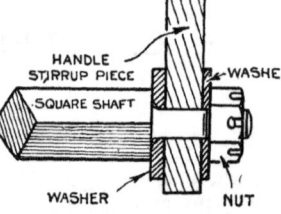

Fig. 3.—An Alternative Method of making the Bearings for the Roller.

All the screws required are Whitworth with round heads and square nuts, as follows:—

Four 2½ × 3/16-inch screws and nuts for the centre-bar.

Four ½ × 3/16-inch screws and nuts for the angles.

Three 2½ × ¼-inch screws and nuts and four washers for the handle.

Four ½-inch hexagon nuts and six ½-inch washers for the axle-rod.

MAKING A CONCRETE GARDEN ROLLER

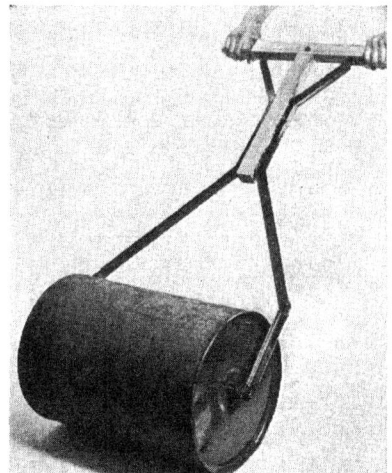

Fig. 4.—The Completed Roller made from an Old Metal Oil Drum.

Fig. 5.—The Materials required. Gas piping, rod, iron and handle.

Fig. 6.—To remove Drum Handle, bore Holes beside the Rivets.

Fig. 7.—The Centre Hole at each End can be "notched" with a Chisel.

Fig. 8.—Cutting the Holes to admit the Cement.

Fig. 9.—When filling the Drum, stand it on Three Bricks.

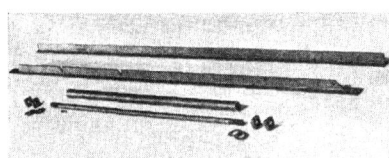

Fig. 10.—The Iron Parts for the Axle and Handle.

Note that one of the Tee-irons has been notched ready for bending.

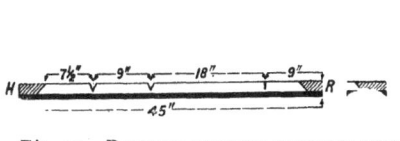

Fig. 11.—Diagram showing exactly how the Notches in the Tee-iron should be spaced and cut.

At the roller-end R it is necessary to bore a hole in each to take the ½-inch rod. Note that 1½ inches of the centre rib is cut away at both ends as shown by the shaded portion.

Fig. 12.—How to use a Gas Burner for heating the Iron while bending.

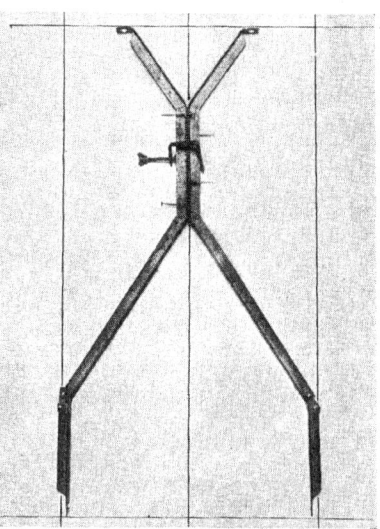

Fig. 13.—Clamp the Irons together when drilling the Holes.

Cleaning the Drum.

It is better to commence by cleaning out as much as possible any traces of oil from the drum to prevent mess, and also to allow the cement to adhere. This is easily done, fortunately, by the simple method of boiling some water in the drum, to which a generous amount of soda has been added. A good shaking before emptying the water will prove effective.

Remove the Handle.

Since the handle of the drum comes just over its centre where the axle is required to be, it is necessary to remove it. The handle is usually fixed with a pair of substantial rivets. The easiest way to remove them is to drill a $\frac{1}{4}$-inch hole through handle and drum close beside each of the rivets in turn. Then a sharp blow with a hammer sideways against the handle towards the hole will snap the rivet into the larger hole, and allow it to be levered out with the handle quite easily (see Fig. 6). It is then a simple matter to mark the centre of each end of the drum, and to drill a hole with the largest drill one happens to have. The holes thus produced are then to be notched, using preferably an old chisel which is due for grinding (for this operation will do a chisel no good). The idea of notching these holes, as shown in Fig. 7, is to produce a burred edge, which will hold the length of gas barrel reasonably firmly during the final filling of the drum with cement. Moreover, it can be done by means of tools which most people have handy and in which category a $\frac{3}{4}$-inch drill is seldom included.

Completing the Drum.

The holes left by the extraction of the handle-rivets provide a start for cutting and bending up parts of one end, as shown in Fig. 8, so as to enable one to pour in the cement and other filling easily. There is no need to remove the parts bent up, as they can be neatly hammered back into place when the cement has set.

Before the filling process, the length of gas barrel should be cut, and its ends filed reasonably square, to a length which clears by at least a $\frac{1}{4}$ inch each outside end of the drum. It is then squeezed into the notched holes, and, if necessary, it can be wedged tightly. To prevent the piece of pipe being pressed out of place, the drum is preferably stood on three bricks (Fig. 9), leaving the lower end of the gas barrel clear of the ground. A small quantity of cement should be put in to start with, so as at the same time to secure the pipe firmly in place, and to allow of its being adjusted, should it show any signs of shifting. Once the first dose of cement has set firmly, no such adjustment will be possible.

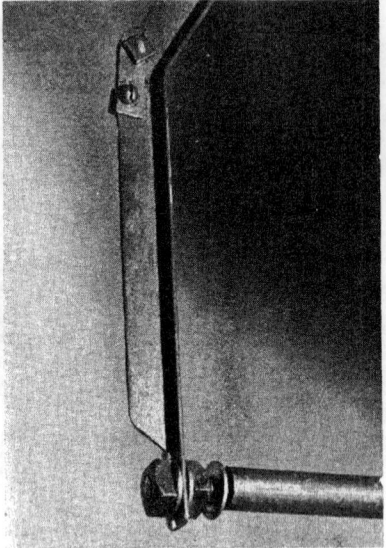

Fig. 14.—THE PRINCIPLE OF THE BEARING IS HERE CLEARLY SHOWN.

The advantage of strengthening the open angle in the framework is also made evident.

Building the Handle.

Although actually the lengths of Tee-iron required are each 45 inches long, it is better to buy 4-foot lengths because ends of this material are often twisted or bent. The few inches extra allow one to cut away faults, and to obtain in a few minutes a pair of straight, well-matched lengths. These should be laid on the bench and marked for notching as shown in the diagram (Fig. 11). At R, which is the roller-end, cut away $1\frac{1}{2}$ inches of the centre rib, and the same at the H (handle-end), as shown by the shaded lines. The various notches shown are also to be cut by a hack-saw in the centre rib, but not quite through it. The cuts should stop about $\frac{1}{16}$ inch short of the flat of the Tee. The first notch, at 9 inches from R, is just a straight cut; the other two should be V's, as indicated, to allow of bending the iron with the rib inwards. Fig. 10 shows one of the strips so cut ready for bending. Although it is much better if plenty of heat and a big vice are available, the work has been done in this instance, as the illustrations show, with the most primitive arrangements, namely, a very small vice, and a "blow-lamp" consisting of an ordinary gas-burner (Fig. 12). This has been done in order to prove that no one need hesitate to undertake the construction of this useful article.

In the bending-up, if the V notches have been made a little on the narrow side, or not quite deeply enough, this is all to the good, as a little easing out with the hack-saw, and a further application of heat, will permit of forming a close, and therefore neat, angle. Of course, the hammer can be requisitioned for final slight adjustments. Reference to Figs. 11 and 13 will show which of the lines should be parallel, and which at right-angles. It is a great help to accuracy if the two irons are laid out on the floor, as in Fig. 13, when any deviation from accuracy in the bending is at once made apparent, and can be corrected, especially if correct lines are ruled upon the piece of paper on which the irons are laid.

Angles and Ends.

The weak spot in the construction is, of course, the outward bend at the straight notch at the roller-end of the strips. It is, however, quite a simple matter to cut a couple of pairs of short strips, from any scrap metal that may be available, and to drill and bolt these across the open angles. These strengthened angles are quite clearly seen in several of the illustrations, and it is obvious that the means adopted does actually very much more than cure the weakness. It will be found best to drill and bolt the strips at one side of the gap, and then drill right through the three thicknesses together at the other side. This method ensures proper coincidence of all the holes, and makes it easy to put through the screws without trouble and without chance of any play.

At the roller-end R, of the irons, it is necessary to bore a hole in each to take the $\frac{1}{2}$-inch rod. The drill for this is rarely to be found in the outfit of the average home mechanic, but almost any ironmonger or garage will undertake this operation. At the same time, and for the same reason, it is advisable to get the ends of the $\frac{1}{2}$-inch rod screwed. The amount of the thread at each end should be enough to leave just as much plain rod in the centre as the gas barrel is long. It should be made clear that the rod put through the pipe forms the bearing on which the drum turns. Although such a long bearing might appear to be inefficient,

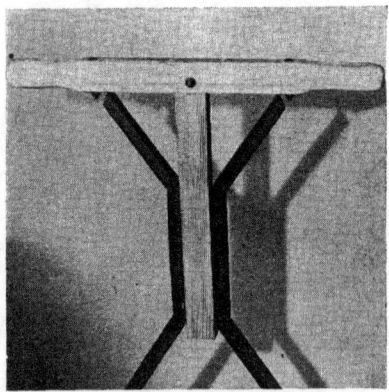

Fig. 15.—THE CENTRE-BAR IS PREFERABLY MORTISED INTO THE CROSS-HANDLE.

This picture shows the sturdiness of the whole when bolted together.

MAKING A CONCRETE GARDEN ROLLER

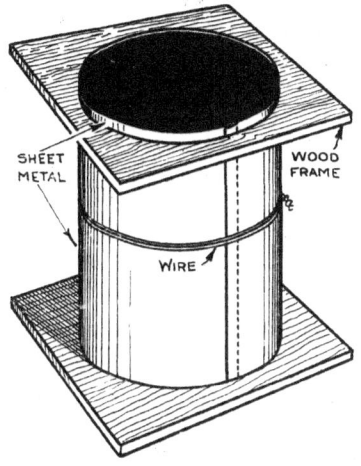

Fig. 16.—A Sheet Iron Mould

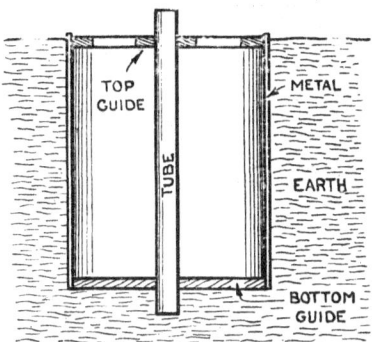

Fig. 17.—Using a Circular Hole in the Ground as a Mould.

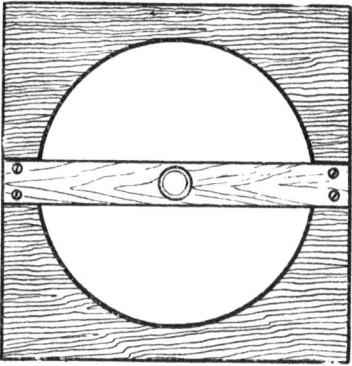

Fig. 18.—Showing Method of locating Axle.

it is not so in practice. For one thing the pipe can advantageously be filled with some thick grease before assembling the parts (together with some graphite if available) which will minimise friction, but in any case it is better to have this sort of bearing than the alternative of allowing the rod to revolve in the holes at the ends of the irons. The latter would speedily wear both the rod and the holes, and so produce an annoying wobble when using the roller, as well as provide a very weak point indeed. Naturally, more substantial forms of end-bearing can be devised, and are used, but they are scarcely within the scope of the home handyman to make.

The Handle.

This consists of two pieces of hardwood, the actual dimensions of which matter very little, with one exception. It is advisable actually to leave the making of the handle until the side-irons are ready, since it is the width of the centre-bar of the handle which may require adjusting by use of the plane. The purpose of this centre-bar is to separate the irons till the roller-ends are just the right distance apart. This distance is just the length of the gas barrel in the drum plus a washer and a nut at each end. It should be clear that it is not easy to bend the irons with extreme accuracy, and drums are not identical in dimensions, and so the width of this piece of wood permits of making any slight adjustment in separation, while keeping the bearing ends perfectly parallel. About 2 to 2¼ inches will usually be found suitable.

The handle itself, into which the centre-piece is preferably mortised, is 2 feet overall. The square centre portion comes to about 14 inches, leaving about 5 inches for each handle. I say " about," because here again the actual dimensions may be varied according to the accuracy with which the irons have been bent up.

Screw Holes.

A ¼-inch hole should be drilled in each of the handle-ends of the Tee-irons for fixing the handle on to them by means of bolts and nuts. It need scarcely be pointed out that a washer under the head, and under the nut, in the case of the screws that go through the handle, will enable a tighter grip to be obtained on tightening the nuts.

But before actually putting on the handle it is advisable to drill the holes in the irons for securing the centre-bar. These are preferably drilled, in the flat of the Tee-iron, by clamping the irons together, as shown in Fig. 13. This ensures proper coincidence of the holes, which can be drilled advantageously alternately on each side of the centre rib. There is not a great deal of room on these flats for turning nuts, and therefore it is better to drill the 3/16-inch holes in such a position that a square nut will fit closely against the rib. By using round-head screws, which have a slot for using a screwdriver, this turning difficulty is overcome.

It is a little more difficult to bore holes accurately through the wooden centre-piece, to take bolting screws right through from one iron bar to the other, than to fix them by means of ordinary wood screws, but the gain in strength is so obviously great that it seems well worth the extra trouble.

USING A SHEET IRON MOULD

If a suitable size of drum is not available, a satisfactory mould can be made by bending a thin sheet of iron plate to circular form, using two or more wooden frames or formers having circular holes of the desired size, to keep the sheet metal in position, as shown in Fig. 16.

How to prevent the Metal Bulging.

If the metal is too thin, there will be a tendency for it to bulge at the centre when the concrete mixture is poured in. This may be obviated by arranging a third former at the centre, or, better still, by placing one or two turns of soft-iron wire of about ⅛ inch diameter around the metal. The junction of the two ends should be carefully arranged by giving a slight overlap, after having bevelled the metal away with the aid of a file.

If thin sheet metal is used, a hole may be dug in the ground so as to act as a support for it, as depicted in Fig. 17. For the best results the hole should be made of larger diameter than the metal mould and, after placing the latter in position, the earth should be well rammed down the outside.

Fitting the Handle and Stirrup-piece.

The next operation will consist of fitting the handle and stirrup-piece carrying the bearings. The latter can be made from steel strip of about 1¼ to 1½ inch width by ⅜ to ½ inch thickness, according to the weight of the roller. These strips are bent to shape by first heating to redness and then hammering over a strong vice or, better still, an anvil.

The Axle.

The axle may be in the form of a solid round or square rod, with screwed ends, or a piece of gas piping may be used in the concrete, and a long rod taken through it to form the axle. In all cases as much bearing surface as possible should be arranged for, in order to reduce the wear on the bearings. An oil hole or groove should be provided for lubricating the bearings.

Simple Type of Handle and Stirrup-piece.

Fig. 2 shows a simple type of handle and stirrup-piece which will be found satisfactory. The wooden handle should be about 12 to 15 inches long by 2 inches diameter, and it should be made of ash. The straight member can be made from pine or ash of 2 × 1-inch section ; ¼-inch bolts and nuts are used for attaching the handle and straight wooden member to the stirrup-pieces.

Alternative Method of making Axle Bearing.

Fig. 3 shows an alternative method

of making the axle bearing. In this case a piece of ⅞ to 1-inch square rod is used for the axle. The ends are turned down and screwed for the retaining nuts; the latter are secured by means of holes drilled right through them and the axle end, split pins being used to hold them in position.

Locating and fixing the Axle.

The method of locating and fixing the axle is shown in Fig. 17, and also in Fig. 18. It is only necessary in the former case to use a wide strip of wood, although a circular disc will give more support to the end. The method illustrated in Fig. 18 is applicable to the form of mould shown in Fig. 16.

Greasing the Mould.

If the sheet-metal drum or mould is to be withdrawn from the concrete after the latter has set, it must be free from any dents or similar obstructions. Before pouring the mixture, the inside surface of the mould should be wiped all over with a greasy rag; it will then be found that the concrete does not stick.

Using Earthenware Piping.

It is not generally known that a good mould can be made by using a length of earthenware piping of suitable dimensions. It should be stood upon a baseboard, and its inside surface greased to facilitate the withdrawal after the concrete has set.

Using Reinforced Concrete.

In cases where rollers have to be particularly strong, in order to put up with severe buffetings, it is advisable to use a reinforcement in the shape of a cylinder of wire netting, about 3 inches smaller in diameter than that of the mould. This cylinder should be stood in its proper (concentric) position before the mixture is poured, and care taken to ensure that it is not displaced during the pouring operation.

SIMPLE COLOUR SCHEMES FOR A MODERN HOUSE

THE following colour schemes for each room in a small house have been specially prepared for execution in standard ready-mixed paints obtainable from any oil and colour merchant.

Entrance Hall.
Walls.—Dead white. Ceiling.—Pale orange, with frieze at top of walls ditto, if possible giving the effect of a scalloped edge.
Woodwork.—Grained walnut.
Floor.—Dark oak, with rugs in red, green and orange, or a linoleum with effect of bricks in a smallish pattern.
Curtains and Pelmet.—Green velvet.
Lamp Shades.—Deep rose gathered silk.
An alternative scheme would be the following :—
Walls.—Light stone water paint.
Ceiling.—White or cream distemper.
Woodwork.—Emerald-green eggshell paint.
Curtains.—Stone-coloured cretonne, with pattern in green and rose.
Lamp Shades.—Yellow or stone colour parchment, with design in green, blue and red.

Lounge or Sitting-room.
Walls and Ceiling.—Pale ivory, with picture rail pale grey.
Curtains and Upholstery.—Larkspur-blue, with sash curtains of beige net.
Cushions in various depths of rose and wine.
Lamp Shades.—Rose silk, and one or two wall brackets of cut glass.
Carpet.—Buff.
An alternative scheme would be :—
Walls.—Tan colour.
Ceiling.—Cream.
Woodwork.—Olive-green.
Curtains.—Old rose.
Upholstered Furniture.—Shades of olive-green, old rose and tan.
Mirrors and pictures with gilt frames.
Lighting Fitments.—Cut glass.
Furniture.—Walnut. Gilt enrichments or ormolu mounts would not be out of place.

Dining-room.
Walls.—Peach.
Ceiling.—Pale sky-blue.
Doors and Woodwork.—Old ivory or dark oak.
Carpet.—Deep wine colour.
Furniture.—Oak in Tudor style.
Curtains.—A bold design in printed linen in black, red, yellow and green on a white ground.
The following is an alternative suggestion :—
Walls.—Terra-cotta broken down with white, equal quantities of each being mixed together.
Woodwork and Ceiling.—Dead white.
Curtains in blue, cream, grey-green and terra-cotta.
Lamp Shades.—Cream parchment or white opalescent glass.
Carpet.—Persian, with blue and terra-cotta in the design.
Furniture.—Oak in Tudor style.

Small Boudoir or Woman's Workroom.
Walls and Ceiling.—Cream.
Woodwork and Furniture.—Plain red lacquer or cellulose enamel.
Curtains.—Pale rose net and rose silk hanging curtains, slightly darker.
Upholstery.—Black and gold damask.
Carpet.—Grey, flush with walls.

A Man's Study.
Walls.—Old-gold water paint.
Frieze and Ceiling.—Light green (Naples green).
Woodwork.—Golden-brown oak or golden-brown glossy enamel.
Furniture.—Brown leather with brown velvet cushions and one or two extra cushions in jade-green silk.
Lamp Shades.—Yellow silk.
Carpet.—Persian.

Principal Bedroom.
Walls and Ceiling.—Pale stone colour or deep cream.
Curtains.—Orange and green shot silk, or yellow and orange damask with green trimmings and lined peach.
Carpet.—Fawn.
Bedspread and Upholstered Furniture.—Green and gold.
Furniture.—Walnut.
Mantelpiece.—Blue-grey marble or scumbled paint.
Lamp Shades.—Yellow and green.
Woodwork.—Peach.

Second Bedroom.
Walls and Ceiling.—Pale emerald-green.
Woodwork.—Same as walls, but with mouldings glazed and wiped off a darker shade.
Carpet.—Moss-green.
Curtains and Bedspread.—Cretonne with cream ground and design in bright orange, red and green.
Upholstered Furniture.—Striped material in orange, red and green. Jacobean oak furniture.
Lamp Shades.—Yellow silk.

Third Bedroom.
Walls and Ceiling.—Pale peach.
Woodwork.—Jade-green glossy enamel.
Curtains.—Cretonne, chiefly in mauve with a little green and ivory. Sash curtains, soft orange gauze; and this colour should be repeated in the upholstered chair and bedspread.
Painted Furniture.—Jade-green enamel.
Carpet.—Peacock-blue.
Lamp Shades.—Ivory parchment.

Fixing a Door Lining and Architraves
WITH NOTES ON HANGING A DOOR

When the necessary opening for the doorway has been made, the door lining known in workshop parlance as "jamb" linings, the door, and the architraves, which is the moulding that fits round the door lining, should be taken in hand. Good house doors, jamb linings, and architraves of standard size are obtainable from reputable firms at such a cheap rate that it is inadvisable to consider making them. When obtaining the door lining the thickness of the wall should be stated, and if the wall is not yet plastered this must be taken into account. The finished layer of plaster on the face of a wall is usually about ⅝ inch thick.

Tools Required for the Job.

Much time is saved and trouble avoided if all the necessary tools and fittings are collected and taken at the outset to the place where the work is to be carried out. The following tools and equipment should, therefore, be collected from the workshop. A plugging chisel for seams, an axe, heavy hammer, plumb rule and plumb bob, hand saw, tenon saw, compasses, try square, bevel, spirit level, mitre block, brace, screw driver bit and ³⁄₁₆-inch shell bit, bradawl, suitable for No. 10 screws and screw driver, try plane or jack plane, smooth plane, 1½-inch paring chisel, two laths, one long enough to measure the height of the door and the diagonals of the doorway and one a little longer than the width of the door, two trestles, two 3-inch cast-iron butt hinges with suitable screws, two dozen 4-inch wire nails and about twelve pieces of wood suitable for making plugs. Some dry straight grained pieces of ordinary deal floor boarding cut about 6 inches long will be quite suitable.

Making the Holes for the Plugs.

Having placed everything in order so that operations can be carried out systematically and free from hindrance, take the plugging chisel and, beginning at a seam about 6 inches from the floor, commence chiselling the mortar out of the seams to form the plug holes. These plug holes should be made about 4 inches deep and placed about 2 feet apart on each side of the door opening as shown by Fig. 1.

Fig. 1.—The First Step is to Make the Holes for the Plugs.

Cut the Plugs to Shape.

Having chiselled out all the plug holes, take the necessary number of plugs in hand and cut them with the axe to the shape shown in Fig. 2. The black portion shows what the shape of the plug should be after cutting. The diagonal twist given to the plugs in the cutting causes them to bind into a firm position as they are driven into the seams.

Now measure the width of the door lining. This will have been supplied braced up square as shown by Fig. 3. These braces should remain in position until the lining is fixed.

Having ascertained the width of the door lining, take the plumb rule and bob and mark the ends of the plugs plumb and in line as shown by Fig. 1. Then take the hand saw and cut off the plugs to the lines, bearing in mind to keep them square across the ends. If the width of the door lining is narrower than the opening in the wall the plugs will have to protrude a little, or they may be cut off close to the wall and packing pieces put in afterwards. The thickness of these packing pieces should be obtained, and they should be nailed to the plugs before the door lining is placed in position.

Next Test the Floor.

Now take the spirit level and test the floor. If the floor is out of level from side to side in the opening, one jamb of the door lining will have to be cut so much longer than the opposite side in order to keep the head piece of the door lining square. If the floor is out of level across the thickness of the wall the ends of the jambs cannot be cut square, but the bevel must be set according to the error and the ends of the jambs marked to the bevel.

Now Mark the Cutting Length of the Jamb.

Next take the long lath and mark the height of the opening on it, then use the lath for marking the cutting length of the jambs. Be certain when setting out the lining for cutting that the rebate for the door is set for inside the room, otherwise the door would open outwards. The protruding ends of the head piece of the lining marked X in Fig. 3 should be cut off, and when this and other necessary adjustments have been made, lever the lining into position with a strong chisel. Be sure that the jambs are set plumb and that they are not twisted in relation to each other as shown by Fig. 4. Any error in this direc-

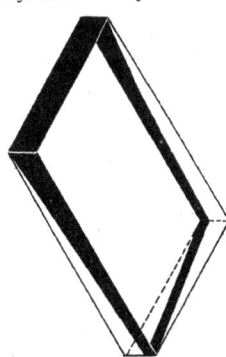

Fig. 2.—How the Plugs should be Cut to Shape.

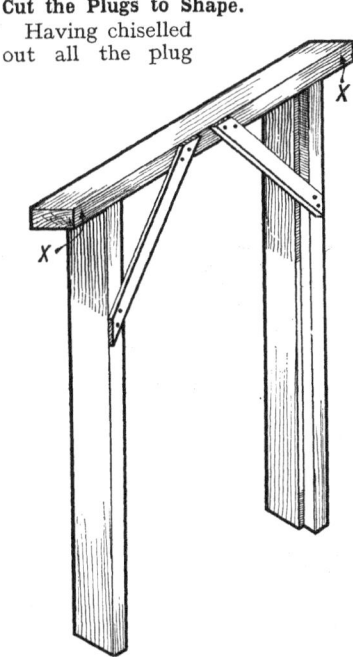

Fig. 3.—The Door Linings are supplied braced up square.

The braces should remain in position until the lining is fixed. The protruding ends marked X should be cut off.

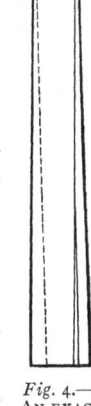

Fig. 4.—An Exaggerated Example of Twisted Jambs.

FIXING A DOOR LINING AND ARCHITRAVES

tion would cause the door not to hang properly.

Next mark the position of the plugs on the inner faces of the jambs, and with the $\frac{3}{16}$-inch shell bit and brace bore holes for the 4-inch wire nails; any danger of splitting the jambs is thus avoided. Before driving in the nails the flange formed by the head should be hammered up as shown by Fig. 5. This treatment of the head avoids large holes being made when the nails are punched down.

Now take the architrave in hand and cut the head pieces to length in the mitre block; a slight margin between the edge of the architraves and the edge of the door lining is advisable. Next take a suitable length of architrave moulding for the jamb and first fit one end to the floor.

Fitting Rough Ends of Skirting Board to Edge of Architrave.

If the door opening has not been built up, but has been cut through an existing wall, the rough ends of the skirting board will need fitting to the edge of the architrave. In such a case the architrave should be held in position and the skirting board marked for length, then cut to the mark with the tenon saw and trim off to a good joint with the paring chisel. Having carried out these instructions, mark off the mitre at the top and cut it in the mitre block. Any slight adjustment that is necessary at the mitre joint should be made with the smooth plane.

Having fitted the architraves in this manner, they should be fixed to the edges of the door linings with oval wire sprigs. If the architrave is moulded these sprigs should be driven into the narrow grooves of the mould so that when the heads are punched down they are practically hidden. Some people prefer foot blocks on architraves, as shown by Fig. 6. These add slightly to the expense of the job, but present no difficulty in fixing. Now take the lath and test the opening for being square by comparing

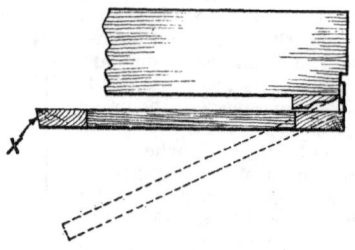

Fig. 8.—How the Opening Distance of a Door is affected by Hinge Projection.

The dotted outline shows the opening distance of the door when the hinge projection is only slight. Note the arrow pointing to the bevelled edge.

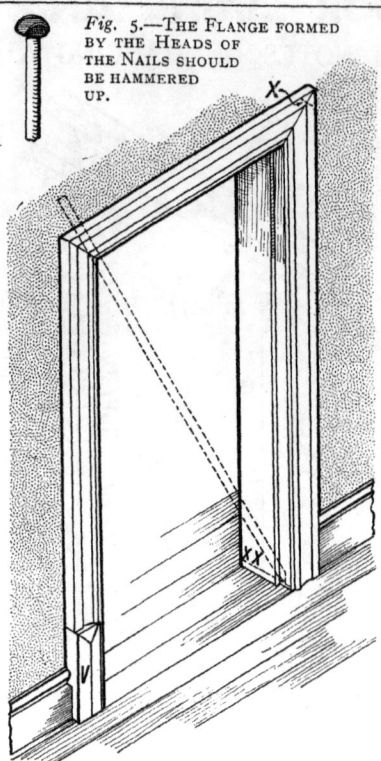

Fig. 5.—The Flange formed by the Heads of the Nails should be Hammered up.

Fig. 6.—The Door Lining and Architraves in Position.

The dotted outline shows the lath in position for testing the diagonals. Note the dotted line $\times\times$ showing the level mark on the jamb. Note also foot block V, and method of sprigging the mitre joint at $\times$.

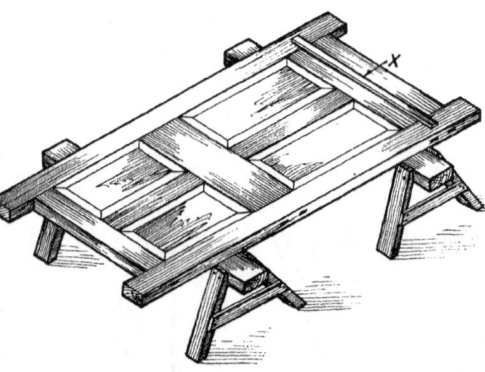

Fig. 7.—The Door laid on Trestles ready for marking to Width and Length.

Note the width lath $\times$ in position.

the diagonals. In a case where the floor is out of level from jamb to jamb, the level mark should be placed on the long jamb for this purpose of testing.

Hanging the Door.

Everything is now ready for hanging the door. This will have been supplied as shown by Fig. 7. The door should be laid on the two trestles with that side uppermost that will be inside the room. Next take the short lath and cut it to fit in between the door lining rebates; then place this lath on the door so that there is an equal margin at each end. Clearance, of course, must be allowed when marking the width of the door, and this will vary according to the time of the year. When hanging a door in winter the least possible margin should be allowed, as the door will shrink in the following summer. No further shrinkage will occur on doors hung in summer, and the usual clearance, which is not quite $\frac{1}{8}$ inch for painted doors, should be allowed, but in special cases, where the doors are polished, a bare $\frac{1}{16}$ inch is sufficient.

Bearing these facts in mind, mark the door to width at both ends, join the marks up by means of the straight edge and pencil, then proceed to mark the length in a similar manner, and if the floor is out of level or the head piece out of square the bevel must be set to the error so that the ends of the door may be marked accordingly. The clearance at the top of the door should be as for the sides, while that at the bottom varies according to the thickness of the carpet or other floor covering.

Next cut off the surplus wood with the hand saw and then shoot the edges of the door to the marks with the try-plane. The edge of the door on which the latch is to be fitted should be bevelled for shutting purposes, as shown by Fig. 8. Fig. 8 also shows how the opening distance of a door is affected by the amount of hinge projection so that if a door is required to open back to the wall the hinges will have to project just over one-half the thickness of the architrave.

Gauging the Width of the Hinge.

Having decided upon the amount of hinge projection, set the gauge accordingly, as shown by Fig. 9, and gauge the width of the hinge sinking from the inside face of the door. The correct positions for the hinges are 10 inches from the bottom and 6 inches from the top. When hanging a heavy door a third hinge is placed midway between these positions. Place the edge of the hinge flange to this gauge line and knife in the ends of the sinkings with the marking awl. Then measure the thickness of the closed hinge, deduct from this the door edge

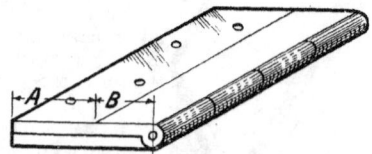

Fig. 9.—Distances for setting Gauge.

Distance A is the measurement to which the gauge must be set for the width of the hinge sinking, while distance B is the amount of projection.

Fig. 10.—The Position of the Top Hinge marked on the Hanging Jamb.

The dotted line shows a position marked for moving the hinge a little further in when the door binds on the floor in the first position.

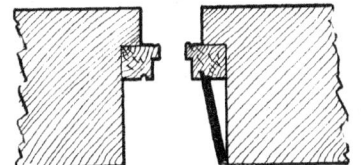

Fig. 11.—A Sectional Plan of an Outer Door Frame with One Side of the Lining and Architrave in Position.

Fig. 12.—An Iron Holdfast often used for fixing Outer Door Frames.

The holdfast is driven into a seam and a screw put through the lug into the frame.

clearance, set the gauge accordingly, and mark the depth of the sinking. The ends of the hinge sinkings should be cut in to the depth mark by means of the chisel and mallet, then carefully pare away the surplus wood. If by some mischance too much is pared away a packing of cardboard or brown paper will rectify the error.

Fixing the Hinges.

Next place the hinges in position and fix them by the middle screw. Now prepare two wedges as thick as the clearance under the bottom edge of the door. Place these wedges in the doorway, lift the door into position and carefully manipulate these wedges until the door shows the correct clearance on each edge. Two small wedges placed on each side of the door will help to hold it in position. Now mark each end of the hinges on the hanging jamb, then lift the door out of position. Next set the compasses to the width of the hinge sinking, mark this width on the hanging jamb, then continue the marks that show the hinge positions over on to the face of the hanging jamb as shown by Fig. 10. Then set the door up on the wedges in a half-open position so that the opened outer flange of the hinges coincides with the marks on the hanging jamb, then fix them by the centre screw and test the swinging of the door. If the door swings clear of the floor and shuts easily the screwing of the hinges may be finished.

What to do if Floor is not Level.

When the floor is not level some difficulty is likely to be experienced. If the door binds on the floor, the flange of the top hinge should be moved about 1/8 inch further in than its first position as shown by Fig. 10. All such faults in doors may be remedied by careful adjustment of the hinges. Only in extreme cases should the bottom edge of the door be planed, as this gives the door an uneven bottom clearance when it is closed. When the top hinge is moved further in to lift the door some adjustment is often necessary in the rebate. This, of course, is quickly effected with the rebating plane and chisel or the bull-nose plane.

These principles of door hanging may be applied with success in all cases. The fixing of an outer door frame and linings is slightly different in that the door frame is fixed first, the linings being tongued to fit in suitable grooves cut in the door frame as shown by Fig. 11. These linings are nailed to wall plugs and packing pieces in the usual manner, and the architraves are fixed as previously explained. When hanging outer doors 4-inch cast-iron butt hinges are generally used.

SINKING A SMALL WELL

A VERY cheap form of well that can be put down by almost anyone, provided water is known to be within 30 feet of the surface, is an Abyssinian or driven-tube well.

Materials required.

The following materials will be required : one well point, 1¼ × 24 inches, cost about 9s., about 30 feet of 1¼-inch well tube with sockets, in not more than 6-foot lengths, price 1s. per foot.

Tin of graphite pipe-joint combination, 1s.

Pump with piece screwed, 1¼-inch gas, cost 17s. 6d.

In addition to these materials, a monkey and cup will be needed. This can generally be hired from the firm who supply the pipe and joint at a charge of about 1s. per day.

Choosing the Site.

Select a site as near the house as possible. If no water is found, the pipe can be pulled up again and another spot tried.

Driving the Pipe into the Ground.

First make a hole in the ground and then put in the end of the well point. Put some of the graphite jointing on the threads and screw on the first length of pipe. Make quite sure that the joint is screwed right home, or else the force of the blow from the monkey will come on the threads and damage them so that it will be impossible to unscrew them again if necessary.

Now screw on the driving cap and rod on the end of the rod and slip the monkey over the tube. Lift the monkey with both hands and drive it down on the cap. Continue until the top of the tube is at ground length.

Next unscrew the driving cap, screw on another length of pipe, applying graphite compound as before.

When driving the first few feet make sure that it is going down square and vertically.

Testing for Water.

When the pipe has been screwed down about 15 feet, test to see whether any water has been struck. To do this screw the pump on the pipe and work it up and down. If water comes, continue to pump to see if the supply is maintained.

The first water to come through will be sandy and dirty, but this will clear after a time.

Presuming that you have been lucky and that a good and ample supply is obtained, then drive the pipe down so that when the pump is screwed on it, it is about 4 inches off the ground level.

Next construct a wooden frame about 18 inches square and 6 inches deep. Place this on the ground round the bottom of the pump, fill it with cement and sand (proportions 1 to 2), mix fairly wet and allow to set.

If no Water is obtained.

If, however, no water is obtained at the first test, the pipe must be driven down further until the full depth is obtained. If water is still not forthcoming, then the pipe must be pulled up and tried somewhere else. To raise the pipe, a wrought-iron clip must be fixed round the pipe, then place a motor-car jack on either side, resting on a stout beam or joist to distribute the weight on the ground, and jack the pipe up equally on both sides of the clip at once.

When the jacks have reached the limit of their travel, let them down, lower the clip on the pipe, and lift again. Repeat the process until all the pipe is withdrawn, unscrewing each length of pipe as it is reached.

Before drinking any water from a well driven down in a populated neighbourhood it should be analysed, as it may not be fit to use for drinking without first boiling.

Repairing Boots and Shoes

The handyman can save quite a considerable amount of money every year by undertaking small boot and shoe repairs at home. Although it is not advisable to attempt anything in the way of "hand-sewn" work, quite a good repair can be effected by riveting. It should, however, be borne in mind that in some types of modern machine-made footwear, especially ladies' shoes with very thin soles, it is not possible to remove the sole without altogether destroying the structure of the shoe. Some fancy heels consist of a thin block of wood in a casing of leather, and these are best repaired by an expert.

Repairs to welted shoes, *i.e.*, with two layers of leather, can, however, be safely undertaken if the following instructions are followed.

Tools required.

The following tools should be available if the work is to be carried out satisfactorily : Metal last, coarse rasp, cobbler's hammer and knife, strop for sharpening knife (this can consist of a piece of emery nailed to a piece of wood about 3 inches wide and 18 inches long), scraper, nippers, rivets, piece of leather (obtainable from a bootmaker or ironmonger), screwdriver, and finishing tool.

SOLEING
First remove the Old Leather.

The first thing to do is to remove the old leather. Place the shoe on the last and push the blade of a screwdriver in between the layers of leather and gradually lever up the sole all round.

If the shoe has been stitched it will be necessary to cut the stitches with a sharp knife as the sole is levered up. If the shoes have been riveted it will be found helpful to use the nippers, as shown in Fig. 2, the sole being pulled upwards and backwards. Having removed the old sole, shave off any stitches or bits of leather that many be sticking up and remove any nails with pincers. Then go over the surface with the rasp until it is quite smooth and level and ready to receive the new sole.

Now cut out the New Sole.

The piece of old sole that has been removed can be used as a pattern. Place it on the piece of new leather and make a mark round the outline with a bradawl or other pointed instrument. If the old sole is not in a good enough condition to act as a pattern, lay a piece of thin paper on the sole that is to be repaired and run the rasp roughly round the edge, thus forming a paper pattern.

The leather must be cut slightly larger than the pattern, so as to allow

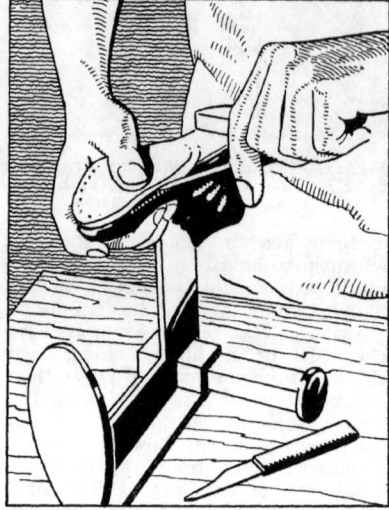

Fig. 1.—To remove the Worn Sole, prise away the Bottom Worn Layer with a Screwdriver.

If the sole is stitched, cut the stitches as you lever round.

a little margin for trimming when fitted upon the shoes, and do not forget to turn the pattern over when the first outline has been cut on the new leather, so as to obtain a correct pair.

Now prepare the New Leather.

The next step is to make a bevel on the inside of the new piece of leather. This is cut with the knife, which should be kept properly sharpened on the strip of emery cloth. Finish off with the rasp.

Now place the new piece of leather in water and leave for about ten

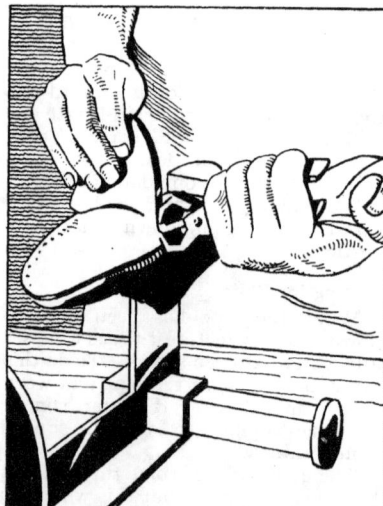

Fig. 2.—When the Leather Layers have been prised apart, the Sole can be pulled off with Pincers.

Take care not to pull the rest of the foundation apart.

minutes, so as to make it pliable. It should then be placed on the last and hammered, the leather skin side downwards. Tap quickly from the centre to the outsides. Not only will the leather be considerably compressed, but it can be given the required saucer-like shape at the same time. This will make it easier to fit over the sole of the worn shoe, which is not, of course, quite flat.

How to fit the New Sole.

The new sole is now ready for fixing to the shoe. Place the shoe on the last, lay the new sole in position and fix in position with two rivets at the toe and end.

Now take the knife and trim the edges up flush, as shown in Fig. 4, taking care not to puncture the upper with the tip of the knife.

Riveting.

Use rivets which are long enough to go just through the leather of the sole and the shoe and to clinch the in-sole when driven right home upon the last.

How to tell whether Rivets are clinching.

To tell whether the rivets are clinching properly or not, remove the shoe from the last after three or four rivets have been driven in, and look for the shiny spot inside the shoe where the rivet comes through, or by feeling with the finger. After a little practice it will be found quite easy to tell by the feel of the blow whether the rivets are clinching properly.

Rivets should be placed about every $\frac{1}{2}$ inch around in a line a $\frac{1}{4}$ inch from the edge of the sole.

How to fix Rivets in Wide-welted Shoes.

In the case of a wide-welted shoe it may be thought that it would be necessary to place the rivets more than a $\frac{1}{4}$ inch from the edge so as to get them through the inside of the shoe correctly placed for good holding. This is not so, however, and in no circumstances should the rivets be placed more than $\frac{1}{4}$ inch from the edge. The correct procedure is to use slightly longer rivets and drive them in slantwise, as shown in Fig. 5, so that the sole and welt will cling together and not let in rainwater.

Finishing-off.

Having riveted the sole in position, trim round the edge of the sole again to remove any irregularities. Then smooth over with the rasp, or sandpaper as soon as the leather is dry.

The scraper is now used to remove any wooliness left by the sandpaper. A piece of broken glass is quite suitable for scraping leather to a good finish, and either this or a proper scraper should be held as shown in Fig. 8, working with a planing action until the leather is quite smooth.

Inking and Polishing.

For details of inking and polishing, see later notes relating to heeling.

What to do if Sole is very worn.

If the soles are worn to such an extent that there is a dip in the centre, a good method of filling it is to use a bit of felt cut from an old hat or similar article.

To prevent Shoes squeaking.

Shoes that have shown a tendency to squeak can be remedied while resoleing operations are in progress. Apply French chalk liberally between the various surfaces before putting on the new sole; this will generally cure the trouble.

REPAIRING HEELS

Heel repairs are simpler than soleing; it is best to give attention to heels built entirely of leather when only the first or second layer has been worn. All that need be done is to lever up the worn part and replace with new leather. The heels of ladies' shoes, however, often consist largely of pieces of wood faced with enamel, or with a very thin cover of leather, and in such cases it is inadvisable for the amateur to attempt a repair.

Repairing a Lady's Patent Heel.

First remove the first or second layers that have become worn; then nail on the replacement of the bottom layer. Take a sharp knife and trim off any surplus leather, as shown in Fig. 6. If the shoe is held in the manner shown, it will be easy to see exactly whether the leather is being cut to the correct shape of the heel, and at the same time to give the outward bevel that is so desirable. Take care to see that the point of the sharp knife does not damage other parts of the shoe.

An alternative method to reduce the risk of damaging other parts of the shoe is to hold the shoe with the sole turned upwards, but if this method is adopted it is not so easy to see whether the correct outline is being followed.

Repairing a Badly Worn Leather Heel.

If an all-leather heel has been allowed to become worn down beyond the first or second layer it will be necessary to graft in pieces of leather to build up a new heel.

First remove the two top layers as previously. Then cut right through the remaining worn layers with a knife or small saw, so that the worn portions

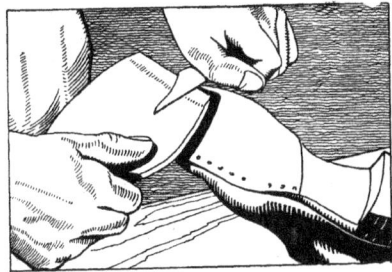

Fig. 3.—PREPARING THE NEW PIECE OF LEATHER.
Note how bevels are cut at the waist of the old sole and on the inside of the new piece of leather.

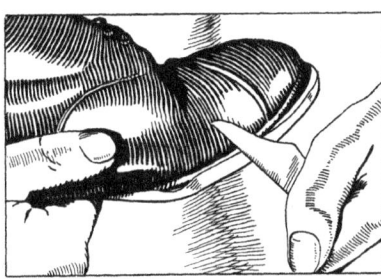

Fig. 4.—ATTACH THE NEW PIECE OF LEATHER TO THE SOLE WITH TWO RIVETS AND THEN TRIM ROUND TO SHAPE WITH A KNIFE.

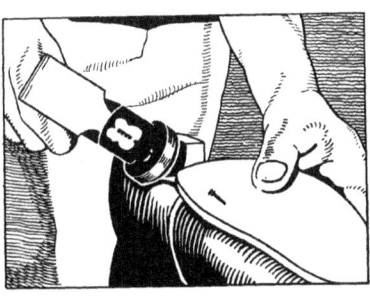

Fig. 5.—IF THE SOLE HAS A WIDE WELT, USE LONGER RIVETS AND DRIVE THEM IN SLANTWISE.
This will ensure that the edges of the shoe will not gape.

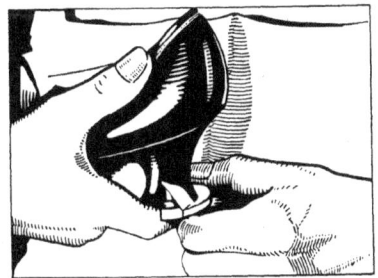

Fig. 6.—REPAIRING A PATENT HEEL.
The first or second layers that have become worn are removed and replaced with new leather, which is then cut with a sharp knife to the shape of the heel.

can be prised away. This will leave a sort of shelf or step. Use the rasp file to remove any protruding nails, and smooth out the work generally.

Now take a piece of leather of suitable size and thickness and nail this on the "shelf," as shown in Fig. 7, so that it is against the piece that was not prised away. Trim it approximately to shape.

Nailing.

The heel can now be completed by fitting on the new top layers; these are fixed with rivets about $\frac{1}{4}$ inch from the edge and at $\frac{1}{2}$ inch intervals. Use slightly longer nails for driving into that part of the heel where the additional piece has been grafted on.

The next thing is to remove any rough edges, using first the knife, then the rasp, and finally with glasspaper.

Now finish off with the scraper, as already described for soles, and the shoe is ready for inking and polishing.

Inking the Leather.

A special ink is sold for the purpose of giving the desired deep colour upon polishing, and this can be conveniently applied by means of a little sponge on the end of a wire, so as to prevent any of the ink from coming into contact with the fingers.

Polishing.

Allow the ink to become thoroughly dry before attempting to polish. A waxy substance known as heel-ball will be required, and this can be purchased very cheaply. It should be melted in a flame and applied to the edges of the leather with a rubbing movement to get a certain amount spread over the inked surface. The final finishing is accomplished by means of a finishing iron, a metal tool with a wooden handle, the metal head being shaped specially to enable a smooth and polished finish to be obtained. Heat the knob in a gas flame and then rub it around over the heel-ball, which can then be smoothed out.

Do not Polish Sole.

There is no need to polish the underneath of the sole, although this is generally done by a professional boot repairer. By sacrificing appearances, greater wearing qualities will be obtained, because a very fine finish to the underneath of the sole is generally only obtained at the expense of some of the hard skin surface that is rasped or papered away.

Treatment for Badly Worn Toe or Side of Sole.

If the toe or a side of a sole has become badly worn, a new piece should be grafted in before putting on the sole.

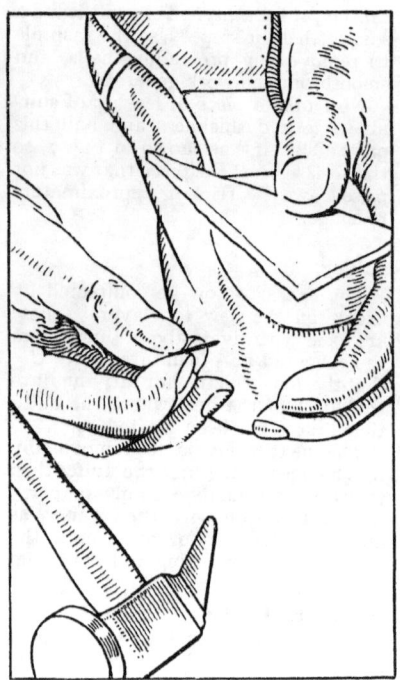

Fig. 7.—Re-heeling a Badly Worn Heel.
Remove one or two of the top worn layers. Then cut away the remaining worn part of the underlayers so that a sort of shelf is formed.

Instead of cutting a square piece, as has been described for the heel, the new piece should be bevelled or chamfered as much as possible, so that it does not produce a bump.

RUBBER HEELS AND SOLES

Rubber soles are usually secured in place by means of a special solution, generally obtainable with the pair of soles. The only point to remember is that the underneath of the shoe should be made rough and woolly with the rasp before applying the solution. The best time to apply rubber soles is when the shoes are new; for one thing it is simpler to make sure of an absolutely secure cementing job on leather before any dirt has been ground into it, while the fact that a worn sole becomes somewhat rounded at the edges tends to make the rubber sole more likely to pull away.

Fixing a rubber sole to a worn shoe is one of the main reasons why many people fail to obtain satisfactory results when using rubber soles. When fixed neatly and properly they offer a neat and good wearing finish.

Rubber heels are generally fixed with nails supplied with them, and should present no difficulty.

Fig. 8.—How to hold the Scraper when smoothing round the Heel or Sole.
A piece of broken glass can be used as a scraper.

PEPPER'S GHOST

There are many interesting illusions that can be obtained by the use of plain and also unsilvered or semi-silvered mirrors, whereby the reflected images of persons and objects appear to be in quite different positions to their actual ones. Many stage "magic" performances are based on these effects. Of these illusions, that known as "Pepper's Ghost" is probably the most striking.

In this case the audience observes an ordinary stage performance with the usual actors and scenery, but during the course of the play life-size transparent "ghosts" or spectres of persons move about the stage. These apparitions are very realistic, as they are actually the transparent images of persons, and therefore exhibit the natural physical movements of such people, but with the difference that they can, apparently, be seen through.

How the Illusion is produced.

The method whereby this illusion is produced is illustrated in the accompanying diagram. The stage confines are shown by the dotted lines F, G, H, J, the position of the stage scenery being as indicated. There is a large sheet of unsilvered plate glass MN, arranged at an angle of about 45 degrees to the front (or back) of the stage. The real actors A, B and C are seen through this glass, and as the latter is quite invisible to the audience, the latter imagine that they

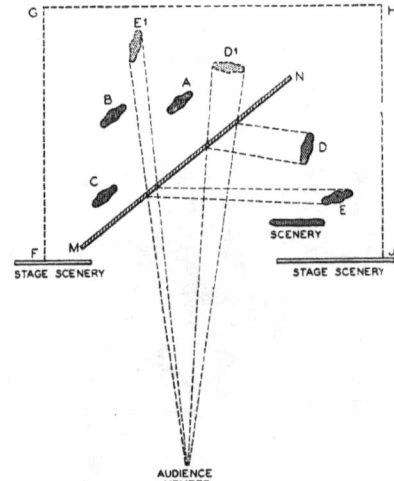

How the Stage Illusion known as "Pepper's Ghost" is obtained.

are looking, uninterruptedly, at these actors. In the wings, however, the actor or actors (D and E) who are to perform the movements of and to act as the spectres are placed in a strong illumination, against a matt-black background. They cannot, however, be seen directly by the audience, but any particular member looking directly at the stage and at the actors A, B, C will see a fainter reflected image D^1 and E^1 of the hidden actors D and E. These images, D^1 and E^1, will appear to be in the positions indicated, so that the audience sees two transparent images D^1 and E^1 moving about amongst the other actors A, B, C. These images will always be seen, no matter what are the fore and aft positions of the other actors. We thus have the striking spectral illusion previously mentioned.

It should here be explained that unsilvered glass enables objects to be seen through it, even when it is placed at angles up to about 45 degrees, but at the same time fainter images of objects on one side can be seen by reflection from the front surface; there is also a much fainter image given by the back surface, but this will not affect the illusion described.

Constructing a Useful Duplicator

Fig. 1.—The Finished Duplicator. Showing how the hinged lid is lifted.

Fig. 2.—Placing the Locking Frame in Position on Top of the Stencil Sheet.

THE duplicator described below is easily and cheaply constructed. Either hand-made stencils written with a cyclostyle pen or those cut on the typewriter can be used on this machine, and from four to five hundred copies are readily obtained from one stencil. The machine should prove of great value to secretaries, clubs, and social institutes.

The duplicator consists of the bed-plate on which the copies are printed and the manuscript stencils are cut; surrounding this is a hinged frame across which is stretched the master copy. A ply board forms the inking table, and a roller is used to spread the ink over the surface of the stencil.

Materials required.

6' × 6" × $\tfrac{5}{8}$" whitewood.
4' × 5" × $\tfrac{3}{8}$" ,, ,,
6' × 4" × $\tfrac{1}{2}$" ,, ,,
6' × $\tfrac{7}{8}$" × $\tfrac{7}{8}$" ,, ,,
6' × $\tfrac{7}{8}$" × $\tfrac{7}{8}$" hardwood.
6' × $\tfrac{5}{8}$" × $\tfrac{3}{8}$" ,, ,,
3$\tfrac{1}{2}$" × 1$\tfrac{5}{8}$" 3-ply wood.
9" × 1' 2" planished zinc $\tfrac{1}{16}$" thick.
1' × 6" sheet brass $\tfrac{3}{32}$" thick.
3" × 4" ,,   ,, $\tfrac{1}{16}$" ,,
2' dowel stick $\tfrac{3}{16}$" thick.
1 cyclostyle roller.

The Bed-plate.

Fig. 3 shows the constructional details of this. It consists of a mitre frame with hardwood tongues let into the corners as shown in the small sketch. Mounted on top of this is a framing of $\tfrac{7}{8}$-inch square material, the two central cross pieces being morticed into the long sides; this framing is glued and screwed to the mitred base. The skeleton rectangle is then covered with a sheet of planished zinc fastened to it by countersunk screws. It is important that the zinc should be *planished*, that is, rolled perfectly flat as the plates sold for engraving work; it can be purchased already "planished." Fig. 4 shows details of the hinges which are fastened to the bed-plate and carry the stencil frame; they are bent up from the brass sheet and a small rivet is used to fasten the two halves together.

The Stencil Frame.

Details of this can be seen in Fig. 5. It is made from hardwood $\tfrac{7}{8}$ inch square; a wide rebate is planed away leaving a raised lip along one side. Having prepared the rebate a frame

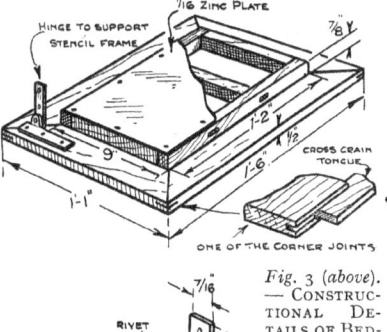

Fig. 3 (above).—Constructional Details of Bed-plate.

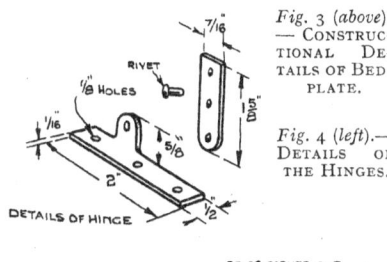

Fig. 4 (left).—Details of the Hinges.

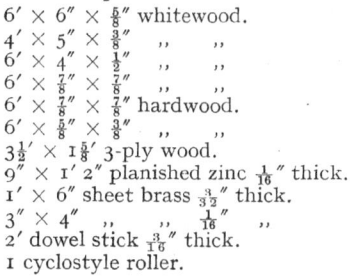

is mitred together and thin hardwood "ties" let into the corners. In the centre of the rebate and equidistant apart, lengths of thin dowel stick are glued in and cleaned off with $\tfrac{1}{8}$ inch projecting above the surrounding surface. These little pegs fit into holes bored in the underside of the locking frame thus ensuring a firm hold on the stencil sheet.

The Locking Frame.

This is shown in Fig. 6. It is a mitred frame of $\tfrac{5}{8}$ × $\tfrac{3}{8}$ inch hardwood. On the underside are a series of holes to engage with the above-mentioned pegs. Note that they are slightly larger than the diameter of the dowels. Care must be taken in setting out the centres to see that they exactly coincide with their respective pegs. Each corner of this frame is bound with a sheet brass corner piece (see Fig. 6.) This gives the slender frame added support and rigidity.

The Locking Clips.

Two kinds of clamping clips are shown in the sketches (see Fig. 7). The hook type has the moving part screwed to the side of the stencil frame; this clasps round the neck of the projecting round-headed screw in the side of the locking frame. The other pattern has a brass clip bent

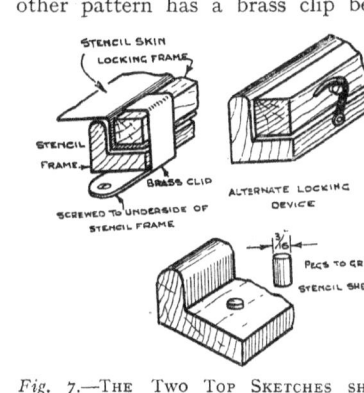

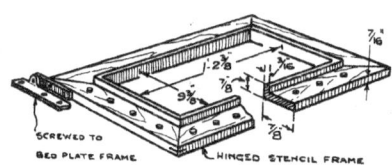

Fig. 5.—Details for Stencil Frame.

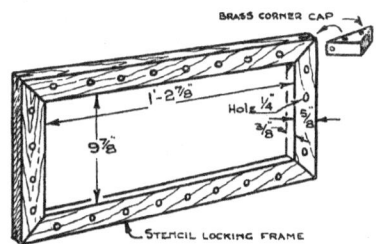

Fig. 6.—Details for Locking Frame.

Fig. 7.—The Two Top Sketches show Alternative Locking Devices. The Bottom Sketch shows the Pegs to grip the Stencil Sheet.

CONSTRUCTING A USEFUL DUPLICATOR

up from stout sheet metal as shown, and these are screwed to the underside of the stencil frame so that they turn outwards when removing the locking frame.

The Roller.

The roller should be 9 inches wide so that it coats the stencil with ink in one stroke. It is best purchased ready made from one of the proprietary firms, as they are cast from a similar composition to that used for printers' rollers. If it is desired to make one, take a piece of round wood and stretch on it a section of cycle inner tube, then support the ends of the cylinder on a bent iron stirrup in the centre of which is screwed a wooden handle. It is important with composition rollers not to lay them on the surface of the cylinder when storing, or a fatal flat will develop, rendering them useless.

The Inking Table.

The board on which the special cyclostyling ink is spread is shown in Fig. 9. It consists of a frame on top of which is glued a panel of 3-ply. Small semi-circular slots are cut from each end to facilitate handling without soiling the fingers. The raised panel prevents the ink spreading sideways to the edges of the board.

The Holdall.

A suitable containing cabinet is shown in Fig. 9. The sides are mitred together out of ⅜-inch material, and for the lid and base ply panels are recessed into rebates. The box is best made in one piece like a hollow prism, then sawn into two so that the shallow portion forms the lid; this method ensures a perfect fit between the box and the lid. The inside of the cover forms a useful place to store the unused stencil sheets which are held in position behind a sheet of cardboard by four small brass turn-buttons.

The roller is stored on the bottom of the case, and a suitable piece of quartering is screwed to the base; in the centre of this a semi-circular slot is cut which just accommodates the neck of the handle. A locking strip of brass slides across the top, securing it firmly. Note the wooden strip must be thick enough to lift the composition portion completely clear of the cabinet. Many proprietary rollers have two "horns" on the iron stirrup so that when it is turned over on its back the cylinder is off the board. The inking table which stretches the full length of the box

Fig. 8.—Rolling the Face of the Stencil with the Inked Roller.

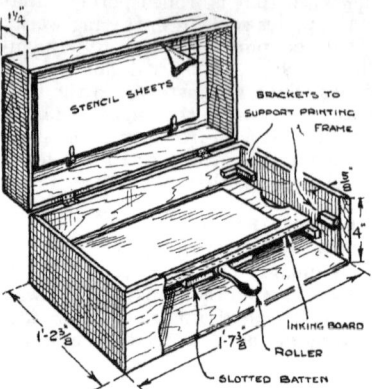

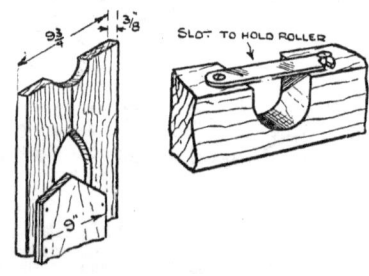

Fig. 9.—Details of Inking Board and Cabinet for holding the Duplicator.

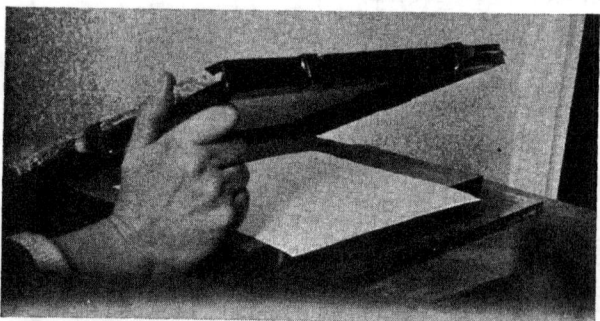

Fig. 10.—Lifting the Stencil in its Frame to remove the Finished Copy.

Note the projecting edge of the skin clamped between the two frames.

is supported on two ledges screwed to the side of the cabinet. When inking the roller the table can be held in the box with the pane uppermost; when storing it is reversed with the ink downwards, a couple of turn-buttons holding it in place. In the corners above the inking table, small wooden brackets are fixed so that the complete duplicator can be housed within the cabinet when not in use. Sufficient room will be found under the inking table to store spare tubes of ink.

Cutting the Stencils.

Hand or manuscript stencils are made in the following way. Procure a good quality stencil sheet, such as "Gestetner," remove the locking frame and place it across the stencil frame; now press the former down upon it when the *skin* will immediately tighten up like a drum; secure it by pressing home the locking clips.

Now take a cyclostyle pen which has a very small cutting wheel at the tip and write the *master copy;* uniform pressure is necessary and care should be taken to avoid tearing the *skin.* It is important that the stencil rests on the bare zinc bed while the cutting operation is carried on.

Printed stencils are cut on the typewriter by removing the ribbon so that the type slugs actually strike the *skin.* A firm uniform touch is desirable. The finished stencil is fastened in the frame as described above.

Duplicating.

Lift the frame which carries the stencil, and slip a sheet of duplicating paper on the zinc bed, then lower the skin so that it lies on the paper. Evenly ink the roller and roll *once* over the stencil, when the ink will penetrate the small holes in the skin, making a perfect copy on the paper beneath. Repeat the process with each new sheet of paper, rolling only *once* with a light pressure. It is important to see that the stencil is kept tight, otherwise it may tear prematurely.

Cleaning the Machine.

Having finished a piece of duplicating remove the stencil from the frame and destroy it, then wipe away all traces of ink from the wooden frame with a piece of rag moistened by the addition of a few drops of paraffin oil or turpentine. The importance of cleaning the machine after using cannot be over-emphasised.

HOW TO MAKE A HECTOGRAPH

Another simple method of duplicating is by means of a hectograph. The original must be hand-written, drawn or typed with " copying " or " hectograph " ink ; it is then laid face downwards on a special absorbent pad and the copies subsequently taken from the pad. Such a duplicator is capable of making an average of twenty-five good legible copies from one original.

Case.

A suitable wooden case should be prepared of a convenient size, with suitable compartments for the sponge and ink.

Metal Tray.

A metal tray will be required in which the composition is placed.

The tray is fitted into its place in the case by fixing pieces of stripwood to the lower inside angles, having previously tapered them so that the tray will fit nicely.

Preparing the Composition.

The tray has next to be filled with a suitable composition and is then known as the pad. There are several alternative compositions, choice should fall on that which can most conveniently be obtained.

Modelling Clay.

Artists' modelling clay, obtainable from any artists' material supply shop, is quite suitable ; sufficient clay will be needed to fill the tray. Probably 3 to 4 lb. will suffice.

Put the clay in the tray and press it down very evenly. Consolidate it by placing a piece of wood about 5 inches square on it and beat with a hammer or mallet to ensure a firm, uniform consistency.

Make the surface level by drawing a straight-edge across it, then warm the clay slightly and pour pure glycerine upon it. Cover the pad and leave it until the clay has absorbed the glycerine, after which it will be ready for use. Soak a piece of cloth in glycerine and lay it on the pad when the latter is not in use ; this will keep the clay moist and in good condition.

Gelatine Composition.

This composition is prepared by soaking $1\frac{1}{4}$ oz. of gelatine in cold water for twelve to fifteen hours, then pour off the water. Immediately heat $7\frac{1}{2}$ oz. of glycerine in a water bath and when it has reached the temperature of boiling water, add the gelatine. This should produce a clear solution and it should then be poured into the metal tray, which must be quite clean, be warmed and set perfectly level and firm.

Pour the solution into the tray slowly and carefully to avoid formation of air bubbles, then cover the tray so that dust cannot settle on it, and leave it for six hours to set. See that the cover is clear of the solution and that nothing comes into contact with it while drying. Cover with a dry cloth when not in use.

Using the Hectograph.

To use the clay pad, first lay a sheet of clean paper on it and smooth over the clay, then write the original with strong hectograph ink or aniline ink ; let it dry, then lay it on the pad and press it firmly into contact with the clay and leave it there for about five minutes.

Carefully peel off the original and take the copies by pressing clean white paper or card on to the pad so that it makes uniform contact, then peel it off and repeat the process.

Maintaining Alignment.

A paper guide or fence should be fixed across the tray and the stop adjusted before making the first impression with the original. Prepare the original on the paper of the same size as will be used for the copies and place it with the left hand top corner in the angle between the fence bar and stop, the top edge of the paper coming flush against the fence bar.

Place the copy papers in the same way and thus ensure that each will be in alignment and nicely centred on the paper. When finished, wipe the pad perfectly clean with the damp sponge.

Adopt a similar procedure with the gelatine pad, but in this case sponge over the surface with a damp sponge to remove dust and prepare the surface.

A roller squeegee, with a rubber roller, is a great convenience, as rolling over the paper with a firm uniform pressure ensures complete contact with the pad and conduces to the production of high grade copies.

IMITATION TILES FOR BATHROOM

THE appearance of many bathrooms is spoilt by splashings from the bath and hand-basin discolouring the walls, especially if they are covered in paper or distempered. Here is a method by which you can overcome this at the cost of a little paint, and at the same time improve the bathroom's appearance generally. You will require some patience, and the walls must not be so old that they crumble easily.

First decide how many tiles you will require and their size and shape, remembering that the larger you make them the less work you will have to do. Prepare the space you wish them to occupy by going over this very carefully and filling in all abrasions and cracks, then smooth down until a good even surface is obtained. The better this is done the more perfect will be the result.

Mark out Position of Tiles with Pencil and Rule.

Now with a long rule, a batten or lathe with one side made true will serve, mark out the tiles in pencil on the prepared area, allowing $\frac{1}{8}$ inch between each tile all round.

Now cut along Lines with a Razor.

Get some old safety razor blades, the sturdier the better, a suitable holder and your metal rule. Details for making the holder will be found on pages 230 and 231. By using a corner of the razor blade only and keeping it at right angles to the wall, cut on the lines forming the edges of each tile to a depth of about $\frac{1}{16}$ inch. The cutter should be held firmly, but not too much pressure applied, changing the blade as often as necessary. If the metal rule is held tightly against the wall it will help to prevent the edges of your imitation tiles from being torn away.

Next scrape away Plaster.

Now with a sharp instrument, such as a bradawl filed to suit the purpose, very carefully scrape away the plaster from between the cuts to a depth of about $\frac{1}{8}$ inch. These grooves, when finished, should be brushed out and all dust removed.

You will now have a raised tile effect, which can be given one or two undercoats and finished white enamel. It will look much better than if you had simply painted the wall in the ordinary way, and if big enough will take all the splashes and can very easily be kept clean.

Should you have the time and patience, all the lower half of the walls can be treated in this way. Each " tile " can be painted separately in any colour and to any design you wish. If, however, different colours are used, the channels between should be covered in a putty shade. The effect can be still further improved by putting a single line of smaller tiles all around and immediately above the larger ones to form a dado.

If you have been careful and cut all the edges fairly smooth and straight, a very pleasing imitation tiled bathroom will be the result, amply repaying you for the time and patience expended. Better still, if you had already decided to enamel the walls, it will have cost nothing extra.

A Useful Carved Chest

Where cupboard room is scanty, a chest provides a convenient receptacle for storage, and when it is made into a decorative feature, it becomes a valuable piece of furniture. The chest shown at Fig. 1 is suggestive as to the decorative possibilities, but there are many ways in which the ambitious woodworker may treat the framework and panels. Sizes for an average chest are given in the front and side views and the plan shown at Figs. 2, 3 and 4. In this design the inside capacity is 37 × 16 × 16 inches. The

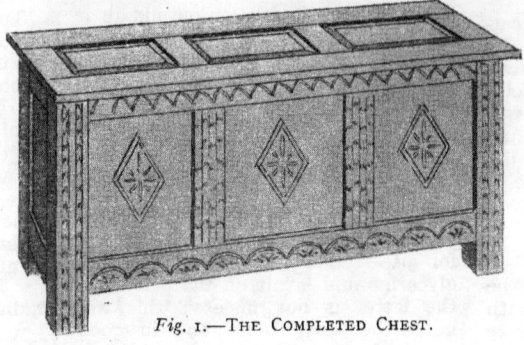

Fig. 1.—The Completed Chest.

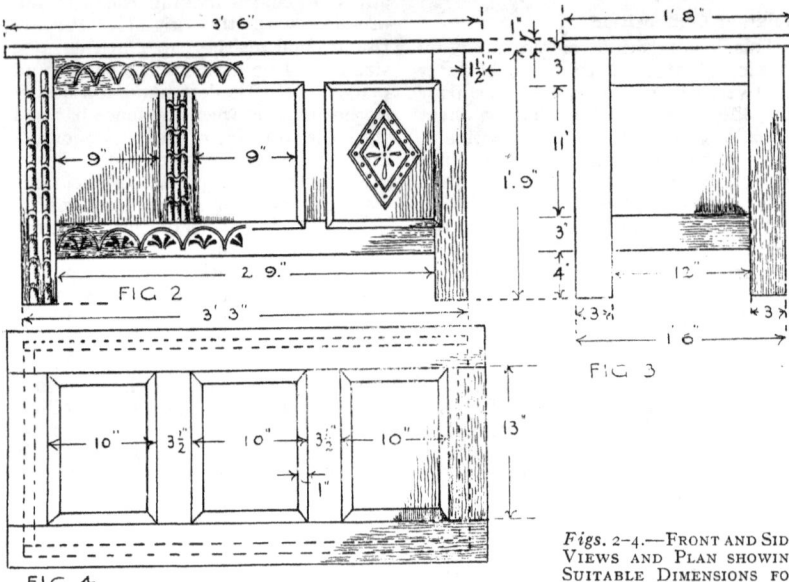

Figs. 2–4.—Front and Side Views and Plan showing Suitable Dimensions for an Average Chest.

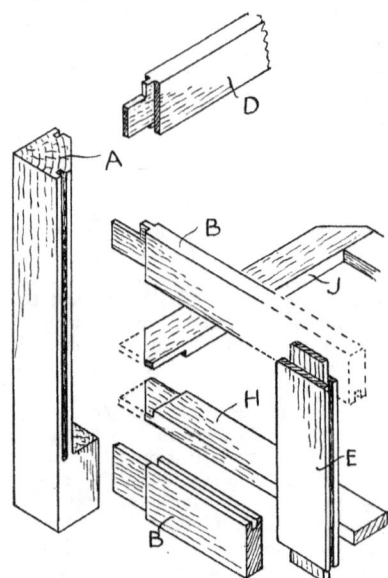

Fig. 6.—Details of Joints.

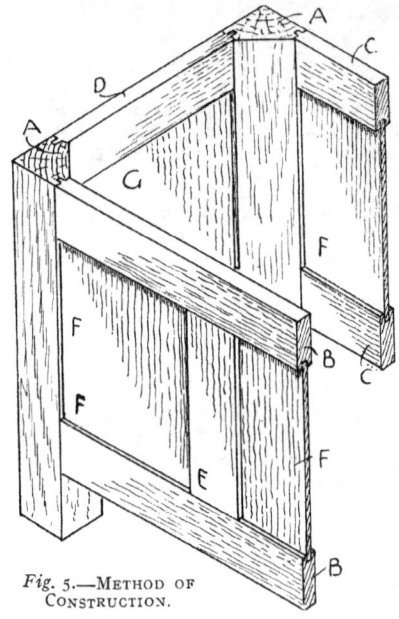

Fig. 5.—Method of Construction.

mark off the position of the haunched mortise and tenon joints on the four uprights. The top rails are 3 inches down and the lower rails 11 inches below. It will be seen that the rails are tenoned into the uprights flush with the outer sides, a mortise gauge being set to $\tfrac{3}{8}$ inch to give an inner line $\tfrac{5}{16}$ inch away. Set off 2 inches from the ends of the long and the short rails to give distances between the shoulders of 33 inches and 12 inches respectively. Gauge the lines for the

lid measures 42 × 20 inches, and the total height of the chest is 22 inches.

Materials required.

Well-seasoned oak, machine-planed to thickness should be used for the chest, the following pieces being required. For the uprights A, two lengths, 22 × 3 × 3 inches; four rails B and C, 37 × 3 × 1 inch; four rails D, 16 × 3 × 1 inch; four muntins E, 13 × 3 × 1 inch; six panels F, $11\tfrac{1}{2}$ × $9\tfrac{1}{2}$ × $\tfrac{3}{8}$ inch or thicker if desired; two panels G, $11\tfrac{1}{2}$ × $12\tfrac{1}{2}$ inches, thickness as at F; two bottom rails H, 35 × $2\tfrac{1}{2}$ × $\tfrac{3}{4}$ inch; two rails J, 16 × $2\tfrac{1}{2}$ × $\tfrac{3}{4}$ inch; two muntins, 14 × $2\tfrac{1}{2}$ × $\tfrac{3}{4}$ inch; one panel plywood, 37 × 16 × $\tfrac{1}{4}$ inch. For lid, two rails K, 42 × $3\tfrac{1}{2}$ × 1 inch; two rails L, 18 × $3\tfrac{1}{2}$ × 1 inch; two muntins M, 15 × $3\tfrac{1}{2}$ × 1 inch; and three panels N, $13\tfrac{1}{2}$ × $10\tfrac{1}{2}$ × $\tfrac{5}{8}$ inch.

The Construction.

The method of construction is shown in the detail of the carcase shown at Fig. 5, and the separated joints are shown at Fig. 6. First

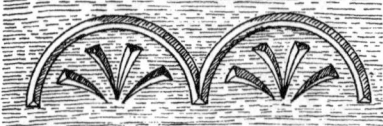
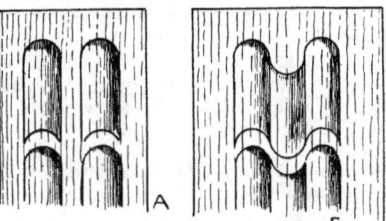

Fig. 7.—Suggested Patterns for Uprights and Rails.

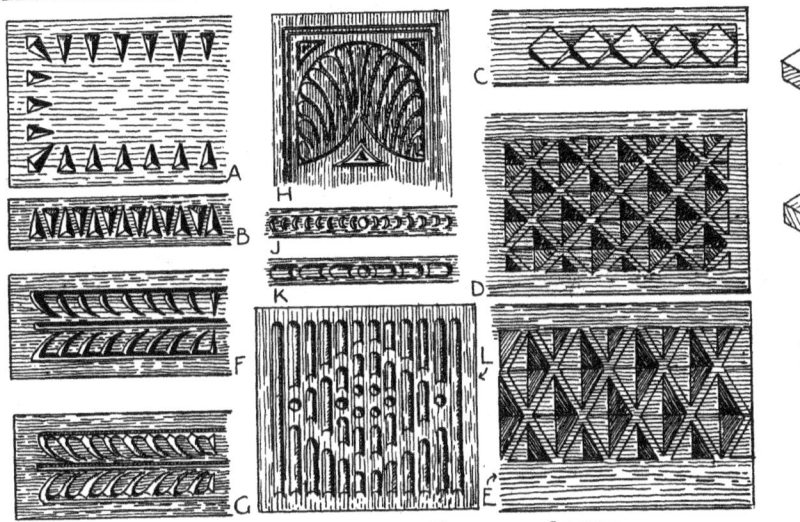
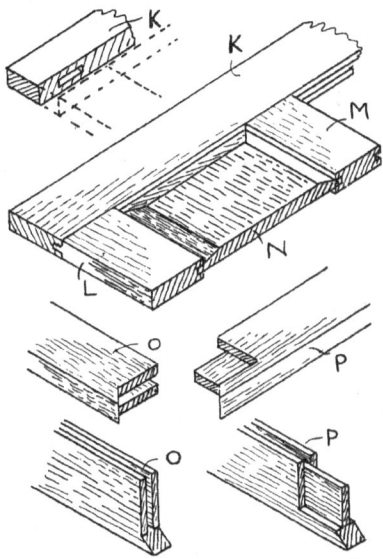

Fig. 8.—Some Alternative Methods of Carving.
The cuts at A, B, C, D and E are made with a sharp knife; those at F and G are done with a veiner or parting tool; those at J, K and L are made with a firmer gouge.

Fig. 9.—Details for Framing up the Lid.

tenons and also continue the gauge lines on the inner edges of all rails for the panel grooving.

The tenons are 2 inches wide, this allows for a ¼ inch deep groove and a ¾ inch deep haunch which should be ½ inch long. The mortises should be cut quite true to a depth of just over 2 inches and then the grooves cut in the uprights and rails; if a plough is not available, it is quite possible to cut them out with a chisel, although a long job. The muntin rails E are grooved each side, the tenons are 1 inch long and 2½ inches wide, suitable mortises being cut in the rails at the correct distances apart.

Now decide on Amount of Carving to be done.

At this stage the carving to be done should be decided on; enlarged details of the patterns suggested for the uprights and rails are given at Fig. 7. The semicircles on the rails should be set out in pencil and then cut with an ordinary carver's V or parting tool. Given a sharp edge to the tool and command over it, there is nothing very difficult in this incised carving. It will be as well, if no previous experience in the use of the tool has been gained, to practise a few cuts on an odd piece of wood. The main point to consider is to work in the direction of the grain, that is from the bottom to the top of the curve in each case. If desired, a large veiner or gouge can be used instead of the V tool, the only difference being a rounded groove. The gouge cuts on the uprights are made with a firmer gouge, the beginnings and ends of the cuts being made with the upright position. This method of decoration is a very old one and with care it is particularly effective.

The Diamond-shaped Incising.

The diamond-shaped incising in the panel is done with either a veiner or gouge or a V tool; the small round holes in the border are made by holding the veiner upright and turning it round, pressing on the handle at the same time.

A number of alternative methods are given at Fig. 8. The cuts at A, B, C, D and E are made with a sharp knife, at F and G the cuts are done with a veiner or parting tool, those at J, K and L are made with a firmer gouge. None of them are difficult and call only for sharp tools and ordinary care. Of the above patterns those at B, C, D, E, F, G, J and K are suitable for uprights, while the others are useful for panels.

Assembling the Framework.

Having completed the carving, the inner corner of the four uprights should be cut away as shown at Fig. 6 and then the bottom framework made with the halving joints as indicated at H and J in Fig. 6. The corners of the bottom framing should be cut off to fit the corners of the carcase. The framework should now be glued together; the presence of the inner bottom frame will help in keeping the whole structure quite square. It should be noted that cramps should be used in tightening up the joints; these may be made with strips of wood and suitable wedges.

The bottom of the chest, of ordinary plywood, should be screwed down to the framework. The lid is framed up similarly to the sides as indicated at Fig. 9. It should be noted that the panels are made flush with the top of the framing. A neat method of finishing the ends is shown at O and P and avoids showing the end grain on the ends of the lid. Special care must be taken in marking out the tenons and mortises for the lid, the pairs of rails being placed side by side in marking. When cutting the tenons as well as the mortises, it should be remembered that if the cutting is allowed to go over the correct marking, the lid is liable to twist and in any case it will make the gluing very difficult.

Best Methods of Finishing.

Some thought should be given to the finish of the chest and, although it is quite common, a limed finish does not suit carved work of this kind. It is better to leave the oak the natural colour and rub beeswax and turpentine into the surface with a hard brush. An antique effect can be obtained by brushing the whole of the surface with strong ammonia and then rubbing down with oil. A dark oak water stain may also be used and with care in application Stephens' ebony stain diluted provides a pleasing effect. French polish or hard glaze is equally unsuitable, but if a hard polish is desired, it is best effected by applications of linseed oil and is mainly a matter of time and elbow grease.

Fixing a Cupboard between Chimney Breast and Wall

Quite often one finds in many houses a recess, formed by the chimney breast and the wall. Such a recess may be made into a useful cupboard by working to the following directions. In cases where the floor space of the recess is needed, the cupboard should be made a single one and fixed high enough to give head clearance as shown by Fig. 1, but where the floor space is not required a double cupboard as shown by Fig. 2 may be made or, alternatively, the bottom section could be made into drawers.

Fig. 1.—A Single Cupboard fixed high enough to give Head Clearance.

Dimensions.

Dimensions will, of course, vary with each case but the wood used for the various parts should be of the following dimensions.

Battening to support the shelves, $3 \times \frac{7}{8}$ inch.

The shelves the required width and $\frac{7}{8}$ inch thick.

The door frame, $3 \times 1\frac{1}{8}$ inches.

The stiles and rails for the doors, $3 \times 1\frac{1}{8}$ inches, and grooved or rebated for the panels.

The wood should be good quality deal; the door panels may, however, be either ½-inch deal or plywood.

A rough sketch, giving the dimensions and the number of shelves, should be made of the cupboard and the necessary timber ordered accordingly.

Preliminary Work.

All the preliminary work may be done in the workshop, and first of all it would be advisable to make the frame in which the doors fit. The measurements for the doors may then be taken from the frame. Select the better side and edge of each piece of timber for the frame, plane them true and square and mark these faces with the usual sign so that they may be recognised and all square marks and gauge marks made from them.

The Mortise and Tenon Joint.

Fig. 3 shows the joints gauged with the mortise gauge and the shoulder marks squared round. Note that the width of the mortise, dimension marked x, is only about two-thirds the width of the tenon. This allows for a haunched shoulder on the tenon. Note that the stile is cut a little longer. This surplus should not be cut off until the frame has been glued up and assembled. In the case of the middle rail the mortise is, of course, made the full width of the tenon as no shouldering is necessary. When setting out mortise and tenon joints, the mortise gauge should be carefully set and always used from the trued face of the wood to ensure that all parts of the frame will coincide when the joints have been made.

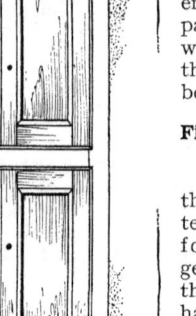

Fig. 2.—Another useful Cupboard when the Floor Space is not required.

Fitting the Mortise and Tenon.

Fig. 4 shows the mortise and tenon cut ready for fitting together, also how the joint would have to be made if a bead is worked on the inner edge of the frame. Note the wedges and the haunched tenon. These wedges are made from the surplus piece cut from

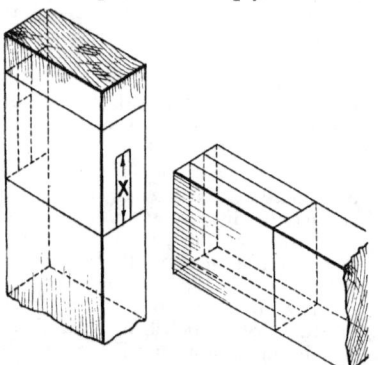

Fig. 3.—Setting out for a Mortise and Tenon Joint.

Showing the joints gauged with the mortise gauge and the shoulder marks squared round. Note that the width of the mortise, marked X, is only about two-thirds the width of the tenon. This allows for a haunched shoulder on the tenon.

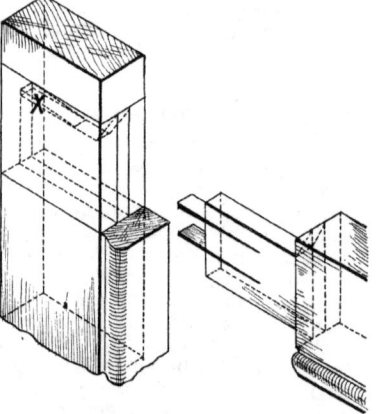

Fig. 4.—The Mortise and Tenon cut ready for Fitting together.

Showing also how the joint would have to be made if a bead is worked on the inner edge of the frame. Note the wedges and the haunched tenon.

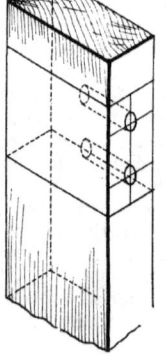
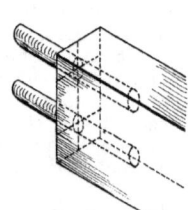

Fig. 5.—How the Frame may be Dowelled together.

Note how the centre lines for the dowels are set out so that they coincide.

FIXING A CUPBOARD BETWEEN CHIMNEY BREAST AND WALL

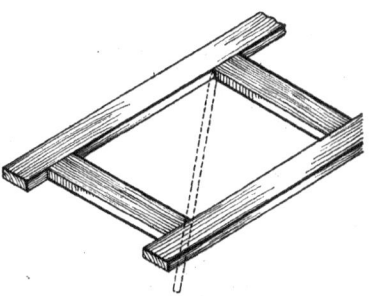

*Fig. 6.—*How to test the Diagonal Measurements with a Lath.

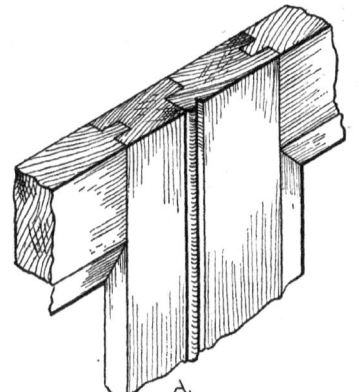
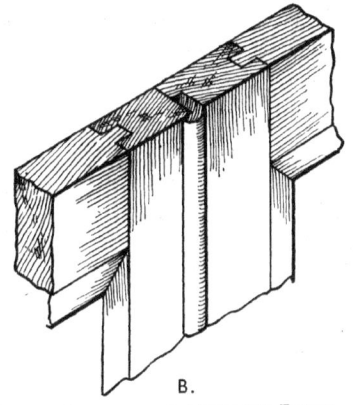

*Fig. 7.—*Two Methods of treating the Meeting Stiles of the Cupboard Doors.
In case A where the stiles are rebated after the doors are assembled, the width of the rebate will have to be taken into consideration when the doors are being set out. In case B a strip of astragal mould is applied instead of the rebate.

the tenon to form the haunch. A small portion on each side of the mortise should be cut away, as indicated by the dotted lines at x, so that the tenon swells out when the wedges are driven into the tenon saw kerfs that should be cut in the tenon before the frame is finally assembled.

Having prepared the frame ready for assembly it should be laid on the trestles, the joints glued, then cramped up with the sash cramps and wedged. As an alternative method, all these joints could, of course, be dowelled as shown by Fig. 5, but, no matter what type of joint you adopt, do not omit to test the squareness of the frame by comparing the diagonal measurements as shown by Fig. 6. Any error in the frame will, obviously, cause trouble when hanging the doors.

Setting Out the Doors.

The stuff for the doors should now be taken in hand for setting out, not forgetting, when cutting the stiles, to allow about 3 inches extra in length.

Fig. 7 shows two methods of treating the meeting stiles of the cupboard doors. In case A, where the stiles are rebated after the doors are assembled, the width of the rebate will have to be taken into consideration when the doors are being set out. In case B, a strip of astragal mould is applied instead of the rebate, a plain strip of this mould could, of course, be planted on the face of the stile and fixed with panel pins.

Again, in setting out the doors, either the dowelled or mortise and tenon joints may be used; the latter is, of course, the craftsman's joint and much stronger. In order to make a good mortise and tenon joint, the gauge marks and setting out lines should be regarded as rigid boundaries, beyond which no wood must be cut away.

Two Types of Joints for the Doors.

Fig. 8 shows two types of mortise and tenon joints that may be used for the doors. Note in type A how the tenon is shouldered on the rail to fit into the groove of the stile. When the doors are being assembled the joints should be glued and the tenons wedged as previously explained. Type B is used chiefly for fairly light doors; the tenon is not taken right through the stile. Note that a mould is worked on to the stiles and rails; this forms a rebate into which the panel may be placed after the frame is assembled.

If cheapness is the chief consideration, suitable stuff of plain section could be dowelled together as shown by Fig. 5, and moulding fixed with panels pins and glue on each side of the panel.

Door Panels.

The door panels may be of plywood or ½-inch deal. When ½-inch deal is used the back face of the panel will have to be chamfered at the edges as shown at A, Fig. 9, so that they will enter the groove. The length and width of the panels should be made as full as possible in order to cover any shrinkage that may occur.

Glass Panels can be used if Preferred.

As an alternative, glass panels could be used as shown by Fig. 10. A narrow middle rail has been inserted and the diagonal plinths marked x are sprung into position and fastened with one panel pin at each end after the glass has been fixed. These plinths give an effective diamond design on double doors. The doors should be made a little full in length and width to allow for fitting, and assembled as shown by Fig. 9.

In the case of rebated stiles and rails as shown by Fig. 8, B, the panel is inserted into the frame, after it has been assembled, and fixed in position with plinths.

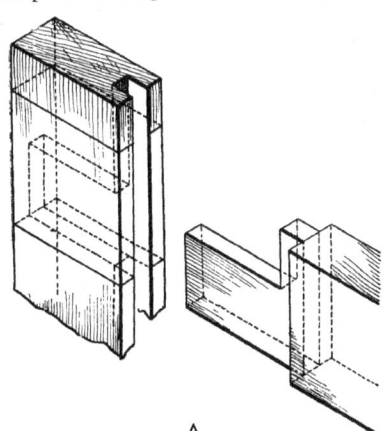
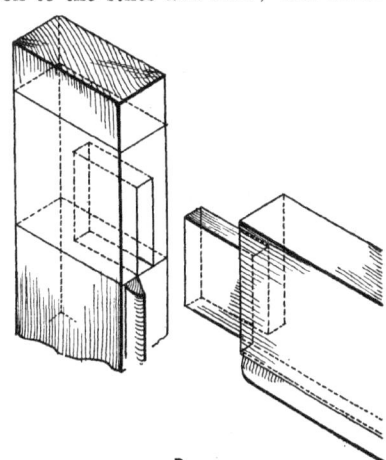

*Fig. 8.—*Two Types of Mortise and Tenon Joints that may be used for the Doors. Note in type A how the tenon is shouldered on the rail to fit into the groove of the stile. Type B is used chiefly for fairly light doors.

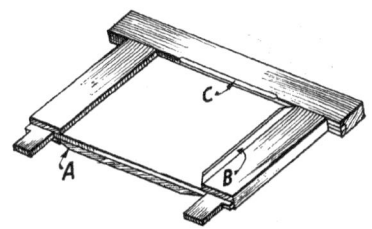

*Fig. 9.—*The Door is assembled as shown and the Panel inserted before the remaining Stile is fitted.

FIXING A CUPBOARD BETWEEN CHIMNEY BREAST AND WALL

The Moulding.

Fig. 9, B, shows how the moulding is planted on the panel. The pins should be driven through the mould on the skew so that they enter the stiles and rails. Fig. 9, C, shows how the edge of the doors may be chamfered as an alternative to the mould; this chamfer should be made before the door is assembled.

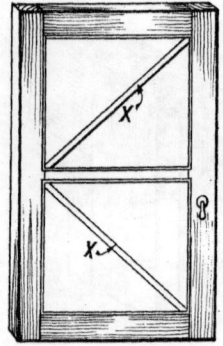

Fig. 10.—An alternative arrangement, using Glass Panels.

Assembling Frames and Doors.

Having cleaned up the frame and the doors with the smooth plane and glass paper they should be taken to where the cupboard is to be built together with the shelves, the shelf battening, some suitable wood for the plugs and the following tools and fittings, a ¾-inch drill, for drilling the walls, axe, heavy hammer, hand saw, tenon saw, spirit level, plumb rule and bob, plumb line, try square, bevel, 1½-inch paring chisel, brace and screwdriver bit, screw-driver, bradawl suitable for the hinge screws, compasses, some 3-inch wire nails for fixing the shelf battens, some 2-inch oval wire sprigs for fixing the shelves to the battens, a trestle, suitable butt hinges and screws and either knobs or drop handles for the doors.

How to ensure a Perfect Fit on the Face Side.

Having placed everything in order so that the work may be carried out methodically, take the frame work in hand and place it as near as possible in position, as shown by Fig. 11, pushing it against the skirting board and picture mould. Now, as all plaster walls are more or less wavy, take the compasses, set them to the widest point in between the wall and the frame, as shown by Fig. 11. Then starting at the top run the compasses down the full length of the frame, keeping one point close to the wall and the other marking the frame work; the mark on the frame will give the exact shape of the wall, picture mould, and skirting board, though perhaps in most cases it would be better to cut the picture mould away so that the end faces with the cupboard.

Next take the panel saw, and holding the saw slightly out of the vertical, cut to the mark on the frame; the slight bevelled edge thus produced will ensure a perfect fit on the face side. A gouge or the bow-saw may be necessary in some cases to cut the shape of the skirting board. Push this fitted edge in position against the wall and the other edge that fits to the chimney breast may then be marked from behind with a pencil. Any unevenness between the floor and the bottom edge of the frame may be covered by scribing a small plinth to the floor and sprigging it to the frame.

Having cut the frame to fit, place it in position and mark on the wall the position of the top edge of the middle rail; this mark, of course, represents the top face of the shelf.

Mark Position for Shelves.

Then place the frame work on one side, and having decided upon the number of shelves required, mark the position of them on the wall with the straight edge and spirit level as shown by Fig. 12. Next drill the plug holes about 3 inches deep, arranging two for each batten. Then cut the plugs, making them slightly bigger at the top so that they will bind into position. Having driven in the plugs and cut the ends off with the hand-saw, attach the plumb line and bob to a nail driven in the wall near the ceiling, as shown by Fig. 12. From this line mark the position of the edges of the shelves so that they will be plumb and in line. Then take the end battens, hold them in place and mark on them the position of the plugs. Now drive the nails through the battens so that the points just protrude, then hold the battens to

Fig. 11.—How to ensure a Perfect Fit on the Face Side.

The framework is placed as near as possible in position, pushing it against the skirting board and picture mould. The compasses are then set to the widest point in between the wall and the frame and drawn down from top to bottom. Note the spirit level placed on the bottom rail to set the frame square before scribing is begun.

Fig. 12.—The next Operation is to mark the position of the Shelves, using a Straight Edge and Spirit Level as shown.

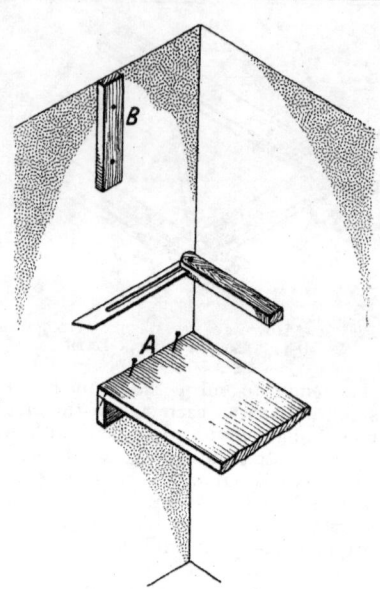

Fig. 13.—When marking the Length of the Shelves use a Bevel if the walls do not meet each other at right-angles.

Note how the nails are driven in on the skew (A) when fixing shelves to battens. When fixing door frame it may be necessary to fix battens between top shelf and ceiling as at B, so that the top of the frame may be fixed to them.

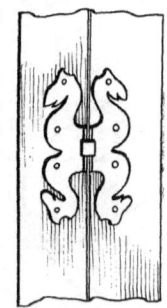

Fig. 14.—A useful type of Hinge for fitting Doors to Frame.

the lines that were previously set by the spirit level and straight edge, and drive in the nails to fix them in position. The long back batten is fixed in a similar manner and cut to fit between the two end ones.

Marking Length of Shelves.

Next mark the length of the shelves. If the walls do not meet each other at right angles, the bevel should be set and used instead of the try-square, as shown by Fig. 12. Having cut the shelves to length they should be nailed to the battens with the 2-inch sprigs, not forgetting to drive them in on the skew as shown by Fig. 13, A.

Fixing Door Frame in Position.

When all the shelves are fixed the door frame should be placed in position, and this may be fixed by either sprigs or screws driven into the edges of the shelves. In some cases where the shelves are set fairly wide apart it would be advisable to fix battens between the top shelf and the ceiling, as shown by Fig. 13, B, so that the top of the frame may be fixed to them.

Having fixed the frame satisfactorily, the doors should be taken in hand and fitted to the frame. A full $\frac{1}{16}$-inch clearance should be allowed on painted work and much less on polished work. Perhaps one of the simplest types of hinge to fix, and yet very effective in appearance, is the flat hinge as shown by Fig. 14. Knobs or drop handles, and suitable catches should be fitted to the doors according to requirements.

HOW TO MAKE A ZOETROPE

THE zoetrope, or "phenakistoscope"—as it was sometimes called—was devised about 100 years ago in order to produce the illusion of movement. It was the forerunner of the modern cinematograph projector, in principle, for it gave the same impression of motion as the present-day cinema picture. The zoetrope, or, as it was termed, "Wheel of Life," was actually introduced in 1845. It consisted of a circular drum, having a base below, but an open top. Inside the drum were pasted, at regular intervals, pictures representing different phases of movement of some animal, person or other moving body. An equal number of equally spaced vertical slots was arranged around the drum so that one picture was seen through each slot.

When the drum was rotated about a vertical axis and the eye placed near one of the slots, the pictures were seen in rapid succession, thus giving a continuous movement impression. The phenakistoscope used the same principle but employed a circular disc with radial slots, between or slightly below which the pictures were mounted. The rest of the disc was blackened. On holding the disc in front of a mirror, with the blackened side to the eye, and revolving it on its axis, a moving picture was observed on looking through the slots.

Making the Zoetrope.

The drum for the zoetrope shown in Fig. 1 can be made of tin, or cardboard bent around a circular former, the butting ends being neatly joined together by soldering (in the case of a tin drum) or by a diagonal lapped joint glued in place, for the cardboard. A wooden or metal base is attached to the cylindrical side by beading or soldering (in the case of the tin drum) or by gluing. At the centre of the base a length of brass tubing is riveted so as to be perpendicular to the base and coincident with the axis of the drum. A wooden pedestal of any convenient shape, provided with a central metal pin for forming the shaft of the tube bearing (Fig. 2), completes the construction.

Dimensions.

There is a fairly wide choice of sizes for the drum, and the amateur constructor can utilise any convenient diameter and depth. A satisfactory size is 10 to 12 inches diameter by 5 to 6 inches deep. The slots should be made about 1 inch long and $\frac{1}{8}$ inch wide. They should be equally spaced.

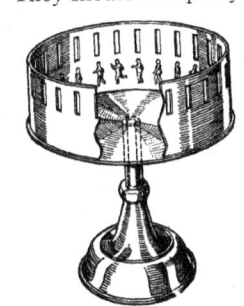

Fig. 1.—The Zoetrope.

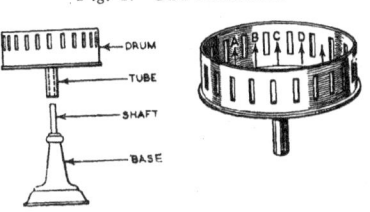

Fig. 2.—Constructional Details.   *Fig. 3.—Shallower Design.*

In regard to the spacing dimensions, these are governed by the distances between the respective pictures. If, for example, the pictures are arranged at $1\frac{1}{2}$ inches apart, then the slots should also be at $1\frac{1}{2}$ inches apart. The slots may be arranged above the pictures as shown in Figs. 1 and 2, or on the same level, as depicted in Fig. 3. In the latter case the pictures are placed between the slots, and are indicated by the lettered arrows A, B, C, D, etc., as shown in the illustration.

Speed of Rotation.

In order to obtain the correct impression of movement when the drum is rotated each picture should be seen one-tenth second after the preceding one. The slots must therefore pass the eye at the rate of ten per second. If, for example, the drum has eighteen slots at equal intervals, then the time required for these eighteen slots to pass the eye, at the rate of ten per second, will be 1·8 seconds. The drum must therefore make one revolution in 1·8 seconds, or, if we estimate the corresponding speed in minutes, this works out at about thirty-three revolutions per minute.

The operator will find no difficulty in rotating the drum by hand at this speed, or slightly faster; it is only necessary to start the drum rotating slowly and then gradually to speed it up until the figures merge from a "flickering" to a continuous effect.

The Pictures to employ.

The early zoetropes used hand-drawn figures of men, birds, animals, etc., each picture representing a slightly different phase of movement to those on either side. With a little practice line drawings of men can be made to show the different consecutive phases of running, jumping, leaping, boxing, etc. These should be drawn on paper strips to fit inside the drum, and if first made in pencil they can be examined through the slots whilst the drum is rotating. All irregularities in movement can then be rectified before inking the figures in. If one can obtain suitably sized positive prints from cinema-negative films, these will do admirably. The positive film itself can be adapted by cutting holes in the drum in order to observe the films by transmitted light. Those with artistic skill can make cartoon pictures for the zoetrope, on the lines of the Mickey Mouse ones.

An advantage of the zoetrope is that several persons can see the moving pictures at the same time, each person using a different slot.

Making a Neat Folding Card Table

A FOLDING card table is not only a useful addition to the household furniture, but it can be made quite attractive. Besides this, it can easily be modified, if desired, to form a coffee or occasional table.

The details of the table have carefully been worked out with the idea in mind of simplifying the constructional work to the greatest possible extent without in any way detracting from the utility or rigidity of the final assembly. The few joints required are of the simplest possible kind, and do not call for any great degree of skill, although they are quite as good as any others which might have been decided upon. Additionally, it is worthy of mention that two alternative joints will be suggested, so that the amateur woodworker can choose the one which he considers most appropriate to his abilities.

The Timber required.

Four lengths of timber $1\frac{1}{4} \times \frac{3}{4} \times 32$ inches (for legs).

Four lengths of timber $1\frac{1}{4} \times \frac{3}{4} \times 21\frac{1}{2}$ inches (for top frame).

Four lengths of timber $\frac{3}{4} \times \frac{1}{2} \times 8\frac{1}{2}$ inches (for braces).

One length of timber $\frac{3}{4} \times \frac{1}{2} \times 19$ inches (for stay).

One length of timber $\frac{3}{4} \times \frac{1}{2} \times 17\frac{1}{2}$ inches (for stay).

One sheet 6 mm. plywood $21\frac{1}{2} \times 21\frac{1}{2}$ inches (for top).

Four laths $\frac{3}{4} \times \frac{1}{4} \times 22$ inches (if made in deal).

Four lengths $\frac{3}{8}$-inch beading 22 inches long (if made in oak).

One piece green baize 23×23 inches (if desired).

Two coach bolts $2 \times \frac{1}{4}$ inch (for pivoting legs).

One dozen $\frac{7}{8}$-inch screws (for braces and stays).

Two dozen $\frac{7}{8}$-inch by 6's round-headed brass screws (if baize-covered).

One length $\frac{3}{4}$-inch rod 16 inches long, and short length $\frac{1}{2}$-inch dowel.

One piece springy brass or steel $2\frac{1}{4} \times \frac{3}{4}$ inch (for catch).

One dozen corrugated fasteners (if top frame is mitred).

All sizes are those of the finished members, so that in ordering, allowance should be made for planing and sawing. The wood may be either red deal (northern pine) or oak, according to preference.

A Hint when ordering the Timber.

The timber should be obtained either in 12-foot lengths or cut down to the lengths actually required. In the latter case every piece of timber should be at least 1 inch longer than the finished size, to allow for squaring-up and finishing the ends. In the same way, the plywood for the top should be at least $\frac{1}{4}$ inch longer and wider than the finished dimensions listed. It

Fig. 1.—The Completed Card Table.

will be noticed that, in order to simplify the ordering, and to effect a certain saving in cost, most of the timber required is of the same section, namely, $1\frac{1}{4} \times \frac{3}{4}$ inch (finished). Additionally, however, a small amount of $\frac{3}{4} \times \frac{1}{2}$-inch stuff is wanted for staying and bracing the legs. The timber may be bought in the rough or machine-planed as desired; the latter is advisable for those who have restricted work space or who wish to save time. In any case, the machine planing will cost no more than a few pence and will eliminate the tedium of planing by hand.

The Top Framework.

A start should be made by constructing the square framework for the top of the table, which measures $20\frac{1}{2}$ inches square overall; this is made up to 21 inches with the beading, which will be placed round later. Figs. 3 and 4 show alternative methods of jointing the corners of the framework, the former being somewhat

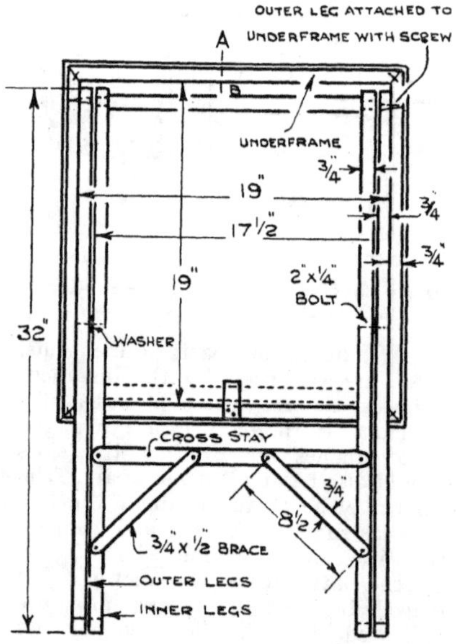

Fig. 2.—The Principal Dimensions of the Finished Table when Folded Up.

simpler, although the latter produces a more rigid job. In any case the joints are not too important because the plywood top adds considerable strength.

The Mitred Joint.

Should the mitred joint (Fig. 3) be decided upon, the four $21\frac{1}{2}$-inch lengths of material should be marked and squared off to length and the mitres marked out with a bevel, or even with a 45-degree set-square as shown in Fig. 5. Accuracy is all-important here, and it is impossible to take too much care in marking out the angles. After marking with a pencil the lines can be gone over with a scribing knife and the saw-cuts made. The sawing is obviously best done on a mitre box, but if this does not form part of the amateur's equipment an improvised sawing board can be made as shown in Fig. 6. This will provide an excellent guide for the tenon saw and should be held in the vice. In sawing, take care that all four pieces of framing are cut to exactly the same length, for otherwise there will be some difficulty later on in making the top perfectly square and firm.

Assembling the Frame.

After the ends have been sawn off, the frame can be assembled by gluing the mitred ends in turn, placing them together and driving in a corrugated fastener, both on the top and undersides. In doing this it is desirable to clamp the two adjacent members together at right-angles, and this can most easily be done by using a picture framer's clamp. When such a tool is not available, however, an almost equally effective method is to nail two short lengths of wood together at right-angles to the top of the bench and press the members against these, whilst driving in the corrugated fasteners.

Test the Frame to make sure it is Square.

The framework can be tested to make sure that it is square by the usual method of measuring the diagonals with an odd lath; both diagonals should, of course, be identical.

Next attach Plywood Top.

After this, it is a good plan to attach the plywood top before laying the framework aside, and before the glue is properly set. The top is simply attached by means of 1-inch panel pins and glue, the heads of the pins being sunk below the surface by means of a pin punch. The glue should be applied sparingly to the top edge of the frame, and the pins should be put in as quickly as possible whilst the glue is still tacky. As mentioned before, the plywood top should be

MAKING A NEAT FOLDING CARD TABLE

larger than the frame, so that it will overhang all the way round; never mind this for the present, but lay the top on a flat surface with a board and some weights over it for twenty-four hours until the glue has thoroughly set.

Setting out the Mortise and Tenon Joints.

The method just described should also be followed when using the open mortise and tenon joints detailed in Fig. 4, after the joints have been made. In marking out the joints a start should be made by measuring the correct lengths on the frame members and squaring lines round the ends. Then measure back from these lines ¾ inch and square other lines round. Next set the gauge to ⅜ inch and mark one line for each joint; alter the gauge to ⅞ inch and mark the second line. Two pieces of timber will have a tenon at both ends, the other two having an open mortise, so it is best to shade (with a pencil) the parts to be cut away in each case. The joints can then be cut out (the pieces must not yet be cut off to finished length) by holding the wood in the vice and sawing down the grain.

How to ensure a Tight Fit.

In the case of the tenons the saw kerf must be just outside the gauge lines, and in the case of the mortises, just inside the lines, in order to ensure a tight fit. Having sawn down the grain the shoulders of the tenons can be sawn off on the usual cutting board or bench hook. The open mortises may then be taken out by means of a ½-inch mortise chisel. In chiselling, start by making a cut on the shoulder line on one side of the wood, and then make a similar cut some little distance "inside" the corresponding line on the other side. After that the waste wood can be removed in a single piece by taking a few cuts with the chisel (using a mallet for driving it) and working toward the line, holding the chisel all the time with the bevelled side away from the line.

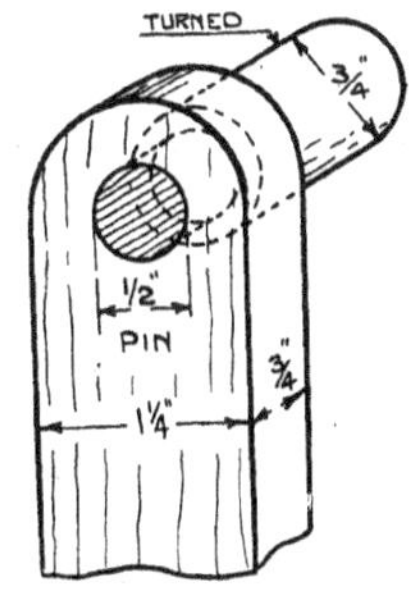

Joints can now be fixed with Glue.

After the joints have been made they can be fixed together by means of glue alone—nails should be quite unnecessary if the work has

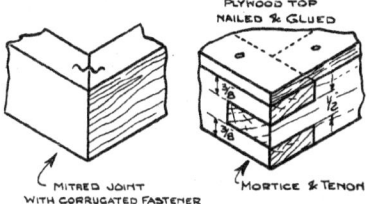

Fig. 3.—The Simplest Joint for the Corners of the Top Framework.

The pieces of framework are mitred together and secured by means of glue and corrugated fasteners.

Fig. 4.—An Alternative Joint.

The open mortise and tenon shown above is somewhat stronger than the simple mitre shown in Fig. 3, but is rather more difficult to make.

been carefully done. Once the glue has thoroughly set (this takes twenty-four hours in the case of ordinary scotch or french glue) the upper

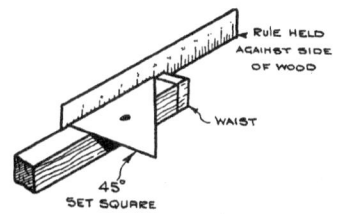

Fig. 5.—A Simple Way of Marking out the Mitres when a Bevel is not Available.

A rule is held against the side of the wood, and this serves as a guide for a 45-degree set square.

surface of the frame should be run-over with a finely set jack plane to ensure that the plywood will fit snugly against it, particularly at the

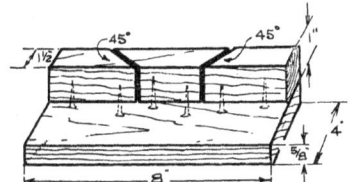

Fig. 6.—An easily-made Mitre Block which is Useful for Making the Corner Joints shown in Fig. 3.

corners. The plywood can then be attached as before.

Making the Legs.

There is not much difficulty in making the legs, and it will be seen that all four consist of 32-inch lengths

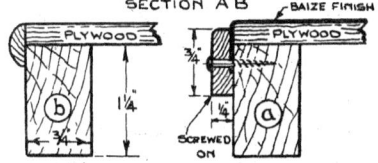

Fig. 8.—Alternative Methods of Finishing the Edges of the Table Top.

That shown at (a) is applicable when the table is made from deal and the top is covered with baize, whilst the method at (b) applies when oak-faced plywood is used for the top.

of 1¼ × 1¼-inch timber, this length giving a convenient height to the finished table. The legs are made in pairs as shown, one pair fitting inside the other. First, mark out all four to length, paring one end of each to a semi-circular shape by means of a firmer chisel. Next, saw the other ends off square and to correct length. The cross stays and braces can then be made to the dimensions shown; the stay for the "outer" legs is 19 inches, and for the "inner" ones 17½ inches long. Both ends of the stays and braces are rounded off with a paring chisel, whilst an ⅛-inch hole is made at the centre of each semicircle—by means of a brace and shell bit—to receive a ⅞-inch by 6's screws. If the table is being made in red deal, countersunk-headed iron screws will be best, but if it is in oak a better and more attractive appearance can be obtained by using round-headed brass fixing screws.

Place a Washer under the Heads of the Screws.

Fix the cross stays and braces on the "outside" legs before attaching these to the inside of the top framework by means of 1¼-inch screws. It is a good plan to place a washer under the heads of the screws and also between the legs and the framework, but the former washer should be countersunk so that the screw does not project beyond the inner face of the leg, where it would foul the other leg when the table is closed up. After the legs have first been fixed to the top they should be removed again until later.

Fix a Wooden Rod between top of Two "Inner" Legs.

A wooden rod is fixed between the tops of the two "inner" legs as shown in Fig. 7. This may be turned up to size if a lathe is available, or otherwise made from a length of broom handle or similar material, into which a short length of ½-inch dowel rod is fitted at each end; the latter will be secured to both the thicker rod and the legs by means of glue.

Now fit Two Pairs of Legs together.

The two pairs of legs should next be fitted together, and they are pivoted about their centres by means of two 2 × ¼-inch coach bolts. The heads of the bolts must be on the outside and washers must be inserted between the legs to reduce friction. After the nuts have been screwed on, it is advisable

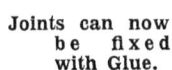

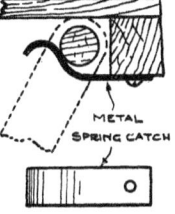

Fig. 7.—Details for the Rod which is Fixed between the two "Inside" Legs.

A turned rod is shown, but this could be built up from a spare length of broom handle or similar material, and short lengths of dowel rod.

Fig. 9.—How the Spring Catch is Shaped which holds the Table Legs in the "Open" Position.

MAKING A NEAT FOLDING CARD TABLE

to rivet the ends of the bolts over them to prevent their working loose.

Finishing the Top.

It is now necessary to return to the table top, which is ready for finishing. First of all, the edges of the plywood, and then of the framework, must be planed down, working from each corner towards the centre of each edge. If the top is to be covered with green baize this material should be cut out to a square about 1½ inches larger than the table top. It is preferable lightly to damp and iron out the material in order to avoid creases, and in doing this the iron should be worked from the centre towards the edges so as to stretch the material a little. The baize should then be laid over the table top and bent over one edge for a distance of about ¾ inch. Apply a thin smear of glue to the edge and then drive in one tack in the centre, afterwards working towards the corners, stretching the material and tacking about every 6 inches. Pull the baize as tightly as possible and repeat the process on the opposite edge, afterwards attending to the other two edges in turn.

Laths for Covering Edge of Baize.

It now remains to make the laths for covering the edges of the baize; these are of ¾ × ¼ inch in section and are mitred at the corners. They are attached by means of about six equally spaced ⅞-inch round-headed brass screws as shown in Fig. 8 (a).

When the table has been made in oak, oak-faced plywood will be used for the top, and this will not be covered with baize. Instead, a strip of ⅜-inch half-round beading will be glued and pinned round the edge to hide the plys as shown in Fig. 8 (b).

Fixing Legs to Top.

The legs can now finally be fixed to the top, and the metal spring catch (shown in Fig. 9) made from a 2¼ × ¾ inch strip of springy steel or brass. If steel is employed—and this is best—it will have to be annealed, by heating it to redness and allowing it to cool slowly, before it can be bent to shape round an iron rod held in the vice. After shaping and drilling to take the fixing screws it should be hardened again by heating it and plunging into water. It will be seen from the drawings that the purpose of the catch is to grip the rod which is attached to the two "inner" legs.

Stand the table in its "open" position and mark lines parallel to the floor across the bottom ends of the four legs; the corners can then be sawn off to the correct angles.

Finishing.

In the case of an oak table an excellent finish can be obtained by using a mixture of black enamel and ammonia, as mentioned on p. 680, afterwards polishing with wax. When the table is made in deal it is better to stain with water stain and then to apply two coats of varnish.

POLISHING INLAY WORK

This class of work is largely associated with mahogany in which genuine inlay is used to give relief and ornamentation to panels and framework as in the style known as Sheraton. Mahogany, on account of its colour, gives the correct background for the beauty of inlay work to be seen and appreciated.

Colour.

The colour of the mahogany may be from a light red brown to a dark red brown with the inlay having a brown yellow shade similar to the colour of satin walnut. Little or no difficulty presents itself in the operation or stages of polishing and can be performed by all amateurs with good results.

Applying a Protective Coating to the Inlay.

Having assured yourself that the wood is properly cleaned (see article on French Polishing) the next operation is to apply a protective coating to the inlay to obviate the danger of colouring when staining. It is necessary to apply a coat or coatings of a white or pale transparent varnish, such as white hard varnish or pale amber varnish; the varnish should be carefully applied with a camel hair pencil, making sure that the whole of the inlay is covered. Allow a few hours to harden and apply a further coat, and so on until a surface is obtained. When hard and dry it will be found that the grain of the inlay will have been filled, thus giving protection from the stain.

Applying the Bichromate Solution.

Now proceed to apply to mahogany work a solution of bichromate, and until the desired depth of colour is obtained. When the stain is dry, thoroughly paper with No. 0 grade, working with the grain including the varnished inlay. Proceed to fill the work with either plaster or woodfiller and follow the procedure as outlined in article dealing with French polishing.

STAIR CARPET HOLDERS

Very simple, neat and attractive oak stair carpet holders or rods can be made as in the sketches. They need no fastenings coming over the rod. The oak strip, A, should be 1 inch deep and 1 inch wide, and rounded at the back corner and more slightly at the top and front edge. At the back and near the end is recessed a brass plate with a keyhole slot and held by a couple of wood screws, as shown at B. At the back of the plate the rod is recessed again to take the head of a screw, as shown in section at C.

The two screws are screwed into the "riser" of the stair and placed the distance of the circular hole ends of the plates apart, and with the keyhole slots in the same direction so that when the rod is pushed up against the stair carpet the heads of the two screws enter the circular hole in the brass plate, and when the rod is pulled endways the heads of the screws are at the back of the slot in the plate and hold the rod firmly. It will be seen that no fastening is apparent when the rod is in position in the corner of the stair.

To make a neat finish a polished brass plate is screwed at the end of the rod, as shown at D. It is made of thin sheet brass turned over with a waved end to add a finish. The brass end is shown at E.

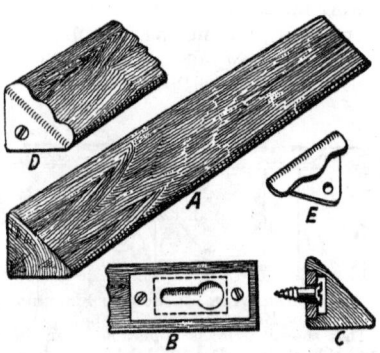

Details of Stair Carpet Holders.

Building a Brick Wall

THE various operations in building a brick wall are first to select the site; measure it, determine and order the necessary materials, then trench the ground, level it and lay the concrete foundations; lastly, lay the bricks and complete the wall.

Note particularly that a good concrete foundation is essential. Brick walls cannot be built successfully on soft soil without solid concrete foundations.

Necessary Tools.

Tools specially required are shown in Fig. 1—the line is used when setting the bricks, the trowels for spreading mortar, level and plumb rule for testing correctness of work, hawk for holding small quantities of mortar; the club hammer and bolster for brick cutting. In addition, a shovel, garden barrow, a long straight batten, and a measuring tape or rule, complete the list.

The time needed depends on the individual, but a beginner would be expected to lay about 100 to 150 bricks in a day, working single-handed. Much time is saved by having an assistant to prepare and carry mortar and bricks.

Concrete for Foundations.

This consists of best Portland cement, sand and "hard core" well mixed together. The sand should be clean, "sharp" and free from garden soil or dirt.

Hard core can be any hard clean, non-friable material, such as old bricks broken into pieces about 1½ inches diameter; "coarse ballast," that is fairly large size gravel, is good but more expensive. Broken stone can be used similarly to old bricks.

Alternatively, the concrete can be made with Portland cement and "ashes" or boiler clinker. Choice should be governed by availability and price.

Fig. 1.—The Necessary Tools.

From left to right: line pins and line, bricklaying and pointing trowels, hawk, spirit level, 1 plumb rule, mason's club hammer, brick cutter, chisel or bolster.

Bricks.

The best varieties of bricks for the purpose are called "Flettons" and "Stocks"; "First" quality should be used for greenhouse or garage walls, "seconds" when price is all

Fig. 2.—The Materials Required.

From left to right: Sand, hard core, cement, water, banker or mixing board, bricks.

important. When delivered, stack the bricks near the site as shown in Fig. 2.

Mortar.

Bricks are laid in a plastic material called "mortar" consisting of a mixture of lime and sand; it can be prepared or "knocked up" on the site, but much time and labour are saved by buying it ready for use.

Alternatively, when only a hundred or so bricks are to be laid, the mortar can consist of Portland cement and sand prepared as required in the proportion of 1 of cement to 3 of sand.

Purchasing the Materials.

Time and money are saved by ordering the required material in appropriate technical form. Prices and terms vary in different districts, but the following is the usual method.

Sand.

Sand is sold by the "yard," that is a cubic yard or a nominal quantity sufficient to fill a measure 1 yard (3 feet) long, 1 yard wide and 1 yard deep.

Bricks are sold by the 1,000, the price of say 55s. means that 1,000 bricks can be bought in the goods yard; the charge for cartage is extra, unless specially arranged. It is uneconomical to buy less than 1,000, and if a quantity around 3,000 is wanted it is much cheaper to buy a "truck"—that is—a railway truck load, nominally about 4,000.

When this is done, arrange for the bricks to be unloaded and carted immediately the truck arrives in the railway siding, otherwise "demurrage" will be charged by the railway company for use of the truck.

This may sound very formidable to the beginner—actually it is quite simple—and will save a good deal of money.

Quantities Required.

The quantity of concrete required for the foundations is found by measuring the site along

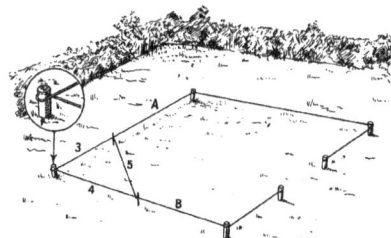

Fig. 3.—Preparing the Foundations.

Showing pegs and lines to outline the centre lines of the walls. The inset shows how the line should be put around the corner pegs.

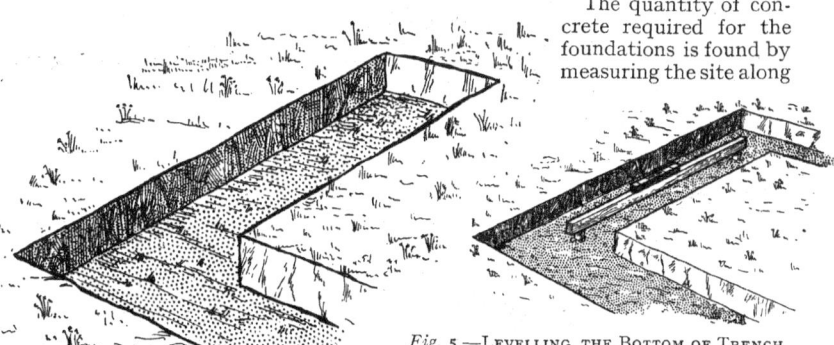

Fig. 4.—Excavating the Trench.

Remove the soil for 9 inches each side of centre line and to a depth of 6 inches.

Fig. 5.—Levelling the Bottom of Trench.

Drive pegs into the trench about 6 to 10 feet apart, place a long straight batten on them and drive one of the pegs downwards until the spirit level shows that the batten is dead level.

BUILDING A BRICK WALL

the centre of the intended wall—say it is 30 feet—then measure the width for the foundation—say 1½ feet; then the depth, which will depend to some extent on the undulations of the site, but usually will be about 1 foot. Multiply these together, thus 30 × 1½ × 1 equals 45 cubic feet. Add one third of this amount, viz., 15 cubic feet for shrinkage and waste, making a total of 60 cubic feet. As there are 27 cubic feet in 1 cubic yard, divide by 27 to ascertain the number of "yards" required, in this case 27/60 equals 2 and 6/27 yards. In other words, approximately 2¼ yards of concrete will be needed for the foundations.

If "hard core" is used obtain the calculated amount, then add to it one-third the quantity of sand; if "ashes" are used, buy one-third more than the calculated amount of "concrete." This is because the sand, or the fine ash in the "ashes," fills in the space between the pieces of hard core and makes a very solid mass. It is confusing to the novice that rather more than 4 yards of raw material will go into 3 yards of space, but it is so.

Similarly, as the cement is fine as flour it will shake down between the grains of sand until the spaces are filled and a solid mass obtained.

This point has been stressed because it is necessary to understand it thoroughly or insufficient material will be ordered.

Portland Cement.

Cement is priced by the ton and sold in bags or sacks. A bag contains 1 cwt. There are 20 bags to the ton and no charge is made for the bag. A sack contains about 200 lbs; there are 11 sacks to the ton; the sacks are returnable and are usually charged for at the rate of about 1s. 9d. to 2s. each. The most convenient way to buy is in "bags," which are strong paper bags. In some districts a sack is still called a bag, so make sure which is which when ordering. Always keep cement bone dry until wanted.

Mortar consists of lime and sand; it is bought by the yard or load. In most districts what is called "pan" mortar is very suitable; as regards quantity, a yard of mortar will suffice to lay about 1,200 bricks. Ready knocked up mortar is obtainable through any builders' merchant or direct from a mortar mill.

Determining Quantity of Bricks.

The nominal size of a brick is 9 inches long, 4⅜ inches wide, 2¾ inches thick. When actually laid there is the thickness of the mortar joint to consider. Usually the joint is about ⅜ inch thick, and therefore four bricks laid flat on top of each other, will, with the mortar joints, measure 12 inches high.

Half-Brick Wall.

A wall made with bricks is called a "half-brick" wall when it is only 4½ inches thick. A "Brick" wall is 9 inches thick and is built by arranging the bricks in a particular way called "bonding."

One horizontal layer of bricks is called a "course;" four "courses" measure 1 foot high. To find out how many bricks will be wanted, count the number in the whole of one complete course, and multiply by the number of courses. For example, a "half-brick" wall is 21 feet long, 7 feet high, how many bricks are required? There will be 28 bricks in each course, and there are four courses per foot of height, hence there will be 4 × 7 equal 28 courses in all. Multiply the number of bricks in one course by the number of courses, that is 28 × 28 equals 784.

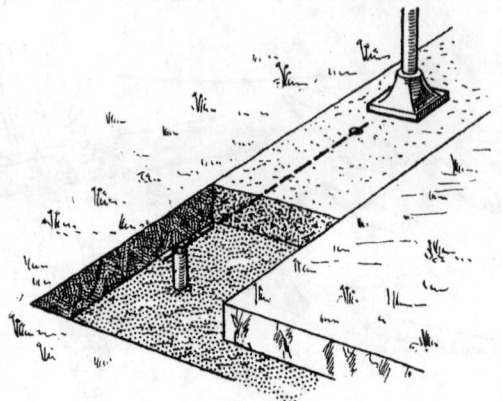

Fig. 6.—Pour and Ram the Concrete.

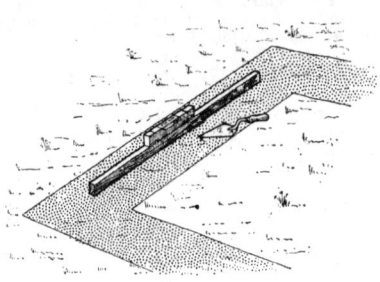

Fig. 7.—Level Surface of Concrete.
Test the level with batten and spirit level and make up any hollow places with mortar.

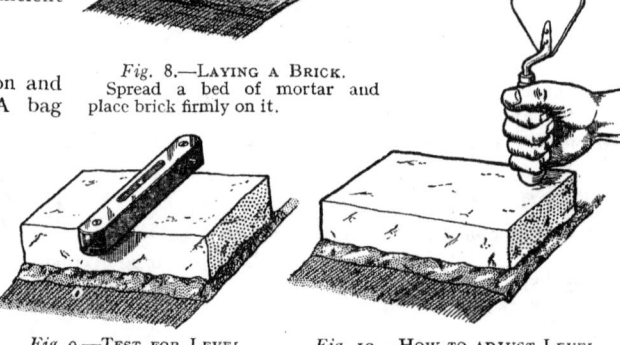

Fig. 8.—Laying a Brick.
Spread a bed of mortar and place brick firmly on it.

Fig. 9.—Test for Level.
Apply a spirit level to see brick is level.

Fig. 10.—How to adjust Level.

Fig. 11.—Laying Second Brick.
Press brick down on to mortar and slide it in direction of arrow against first brick.

Fig. 12.—Laying First Course of Bricks.
Lay one brick, then lay a half brick on top of it at each end. Put line pins in mortar joints and stretch line taut.

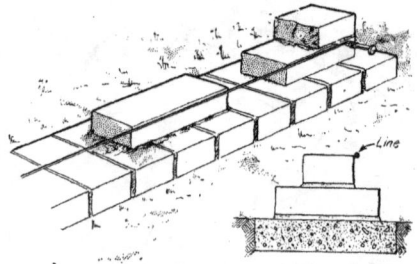

Fig. 13.—Setting Brick to the Line.
Set the top front edge of the brick flush with the line.

BUILDING A BRICK WALL

In addition there will be one course of "footings," that is bricks set directly on the concrete foundation. As this will be a "header" course and measures 9 inches wide there will be twice as many bricks for this course, that is 28 × 2 equal 56; adding this gives 840 as the number required. In practice it would be best to buy 1,000 to allow for wastage.

Rapid Reckoning.

To estimate quickly the number of bricks in a 9-inch "brick" wall, multiply the total length of wall in feet by the height in feet including the footings, plus 6 inches, then multiply by 11. For example, total length of wall 30 feet; height, including footings, 7 feet 6 inches. Add 6 inches, making 8 feet as "height," and multiply by 11; thus 30 × 8 × 11 gives 2,640 as the number of bricks. If there are several corners add 5 to 10 per cent. for cutting, or say 3,000 bricks.

TABLE OF QUANTITIES.

The following are approximate quantities of materials needed for building walls of various dimensions; others can be estimated in the same proportions.

Wall, 10 feet long, 5 feet high.	Half Brick, 4½ inches thick.	Brick, 9 inches thick.
Cement for foundations	2 cwt.	4 cwt.
Hard core foundations	⅓ yard.	⅔ yard.
Sand foundations	⅙ ,,	⅓ ,,
Bricks for wall and footings	300	650
Mortar for wall and footings	¼ yard.	½ yard.
Wall, 50 feet long, 8 feet high.		
Cement for foundations	—	15 cwts.
Hard core foundations	—	3 yards.
Sand foundations	—	1 yard.
Bricks for wall and Footings	—	2,300
Mortar for wall and footings	—	2 yards.

Fig. 14.—Building Stop Ends.
Build the ends of wall to a height of seven or eight courses.

Where to Buy.

Purchases should be made at a

Fig. 15.—Cutting a Brick.
Lay the brick on a bed of sand and cut it with the bolster and club hammer.

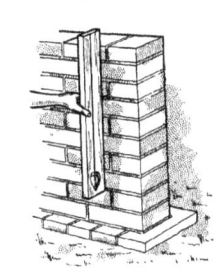

Fig. 16.—Testing Verticality.
Testing the end with the plumb rule.

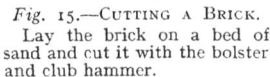

Fig. 17.—Bonding a Brick Wall.
To ensure correct "bonding" the evenly-numbered courses start with a header—shown shaded—and then two quarter length bricks. All odd number courses start with two stretchers.

builders' merchant, preferably in a railway siding or beside a canal. Cartage costs are thereby reduced. Quotations can usefully be obtained from several firms and the best price secured. A discount of 2½ to 5 per cent. for cash on delivery is often conceded.

Operative Work.

Commence operations by setting out the site with pegs and lines to indicate the centre of wall, as in Fig. 3, using the "3-4-5 angle" system to ensure square corners.

To do this, measure 3 feet along line A in Fig. 3 and put in a thin peg. Measure 4 feet along line B and put in a peg. When the corner is square the diagonal distance between these pegs will be 5 feet; but if the corner is not square adjust line until the diagonal distance is 5 feet.

Next excavate the soil to a minimum depth of 6 inches and for a width of 6 inches on each side of line for a half brick wall or 9 inches each side for a brick wall as in Fig. 4.

Level the bottom of the trench as in Fig. 5 by driving pegs into the centre of it—about 9 feet apart or as far apart as possible. Place a long straight batten on the pegs and rest a spirit level on the batten. Drive one peg down until the batten is dead level. Use the batten as a guide and remove any surplus soil until surface is level. Ram the soil down uniformly with a rammer or heavy piece of timber.

Mixing Concrete.

The quantities are measured out or "gauged" with a box or pail; the proper proportions to use are 1 of cement, 2 of sand, 3 of hard core; or 1 of cement to 3 of ashes.

Prepare a large square board, called a "banker," and put the materials in opposite corners; shovel some of the sand into the middle, then some hard core, then some cement. Turn them over with the shovel and repeat the process until the whole is thoroughly well mixed. Sprinkle with water and well mix again until a pasty mass is obtained. Shovel it into the trench

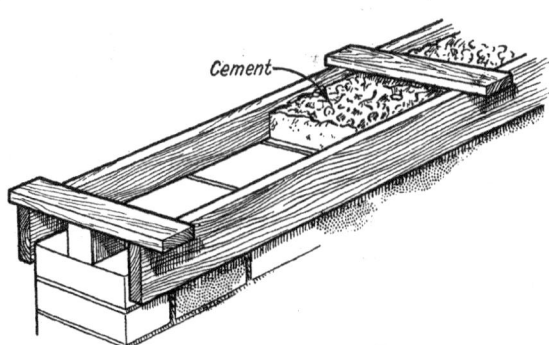

Fig. 18.—Finishing the Top.
A cement capping forms an inexpensive finish; it is held in place by timber shuttering as here shown, until set.

Fig. 19.—Turning a Quoin in a Half-Brick Wall.
The quoin or corner is formed by using all stretchers, one set longways in the face wall, then the one in course above set long ways in wing wall and so on.

BUILDING A BRICK WALL

as in Fig. 6 and ram the whole down. The levelling pegs will help as a guide to getting the top surface level, but finish off by testing with the batten and spirit level, as in Fig. 7, and fill in any hollow places.

Care of Mortar.

Sprinkle the mortar with water and turn over the whole mass with a shovel every day to prevent it setting or getting too dry. Place the mortar on a board or any clean surface and keep it covered with wet sacks.

Laying the Footings.

Lay the footings for a half-brick wall as a "header" course; that is all the bricks are laid flat with their length across the line of the wall. Spread a bed of mortar, then place the brick on it as in Fig. 8, test for level as Fig. 9, and tap the brick down when necessary to make it lay level by a sharp blow with the handle of the trowel, as in Fig. 10, then lay the next brick as in Fig. 11, pressing it sideways against the first brick so that the mortar rises into the vertical joint. Continue in this way until the footings are complete.

Laying First Course of Bricks.

All bricks are put into position in the manner just described, but in addition they must be kept in line, must be level from end to end of the course and be upright on the face or outer surface. This is accomplished by first laying one whole brick and one half brick or "bat" at each end of a straight wall section as in Fig. 12, and stretching a line from end to end.

The line is fixed to "line pins" or flattened 4-inch nails, as shown in Fig. 13, and is so placed that it comes against the top outer edges of the bricks at the ends. Intermediate bricks are then laid as in Fig. 13 and the whole course tested with the long batten and spirit level as before. Also test with a spirit level set across the line of wall to see that the top surface is horizontal.

Next build up each end of the wall for 6 or 7 courses, "racking back" as shown in Fig. 14. To start, finish and "bond" properly the first course begins with a whole brick, the second course with a half brick or "bat," the third course with a whole brick and the fourth with a "bat" and so on.

Cutting a Brick.

To cut a brick—lay it on a deep bed of sand as in Fig. 15, hold the brick cutting chisel, "bolster" or "scutch," as it is variously called, in a vertical position, as in Fig. 15, and strike it a sharp blow with a mason's "club"

Fig. 20.—BUILDING A STOP END AND BONDING A 9-INCH WALL.

A 9-inch wall is laid differently to a half-brick wall. The first course is one header (across the wall), then 2 stretchers side by side; one header, two stretchers and so on to the end.

The second course starts with two ¾ bricks set as stretchers, then one header and thence alternately two stretchers, one header and so on.

The third and all odd numbered courses set as No. 1, the even numbered courses set as No. 2.

hammer. Turn the brick on one side, repeat the operation on all four sides,

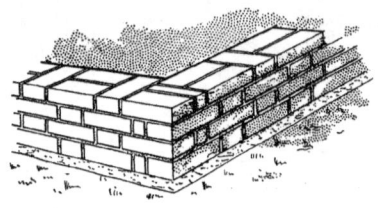

Fig. 21.—TURNING A QUOIN IN A 9-INCH WALL.

"Closers," or ¼ bricks are used in each course to preserve the "bond." The arrangement of the bricks is clearly shown above.

Fig. 22.—DAMP COURSE.
A double course of slates set in cement to prevent damp rising.

the brick will then part asunder quite neatly.

The great secret of building a wall

Fig. 23.—AIR BRICK.
Air bricks are used to ventilate the space under a boarded floor, or to allow drainage water to pass in some garden walls.

is to keep it straight, flat, and vertical; to do this test the ends with a "plumb rule," as in Fig. 16, and do not content until the ends are truly flat and vertical. If necessary, pull down the bricks and begin again. When the corners are correct, insert the line pins in the lowest uncompleted course and lay the bricks as before. The line will ensure the course being straight and level if the bricks are brought up against it but without pressing the line out of its place. When the first stage of the wall has thus been built, "level through," that is test with the long batten, and if necessary lay a bed of mortar along the bricks and trowel it off nice and level; leave it for a while to set, then continue as before.

Bonding a Brick Wall.

The bricks are bonded as shown in Fig. 17, when building a plain "brick" wall, 9 inches thick. The first course starts with two stretchers, then one header—shown shaded in Fig. 17, and continues in that order. The second course starts with one header, then come two quarter length "bats"; then two stretchers, one header, two stretchers and so on. This avoids continuous vertical joints between the courses.

The exposed top of a garden wall can be finished with special "capping bricks" or with a cement top, which can be laid between "shuttering" as in Fig. 18, that is, smooth boards held together by battens to keep the cement in place until it hardens, the surface is then finished off with cement mortar trowelled smooth.

Pointing.

Pointing is the art of neatly finishing off the faces of the mortar joints; it is done with cement mortar consisting of 2 parts cement and 3 parts sand. A small quantity is prepared and placed on a "hawk" held in the left hand, then the small "pointing" trowel is used first to rake out any rough mortar, then a small quantity of cement mortar is taken on the trowel and pressed well into the joint (see page 1001).

Turning a Quoin.

The angular corner of a wall is often called a quoin, and is turned in a half brick wall, as shown in Fig. 19, the bricks simply overlapping one another.

When building a 9-inch brick wall the stop ends or openings around doors and windows should be bonded as shown in Fig. 20, and the quoins turned as in Fig. 21, in the latter case each header appearing at the end is followed by a quarter brick, thereafter the bonding is two stretchers, one header and so on.

Two Useful Tea Wagons

The useful piece of furniture shown at Fig. 1 serves as an afternoon tea table as well as a wagon, and being fitted with two drawers will be found particularly convenient in the small house or flat. The illustration shows one of the side flaps let down, the other one, in its upright position, shows how the flaps form the side rims to the top tray.

Although the form of construction for the hinging of the flaps is designed to carry a number of light articles, increased strength can be given by fixing a couple of rule joint stays or light chains. The position of this safeguard is indicated by dotted lines at Fig. 3.

The latter illustration and Fig. 2 give the necessary dimensions and allows for 3-inch wagon castors, which should be of best quality and cost about 7*s.* 6*d.* per set. Much cheaper ones can be obtained, but they are designed only for very light structures.

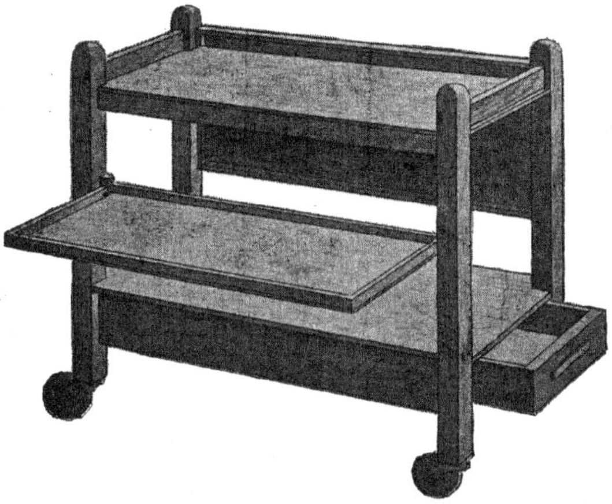

Fig. 1.—This Afternoon Tea Wagon is fitted with Two Drawers and Side Flaps and is particularly convenient in a Small House or Flat.

A design for a straightforward tea wagon is given in Fig. 8.

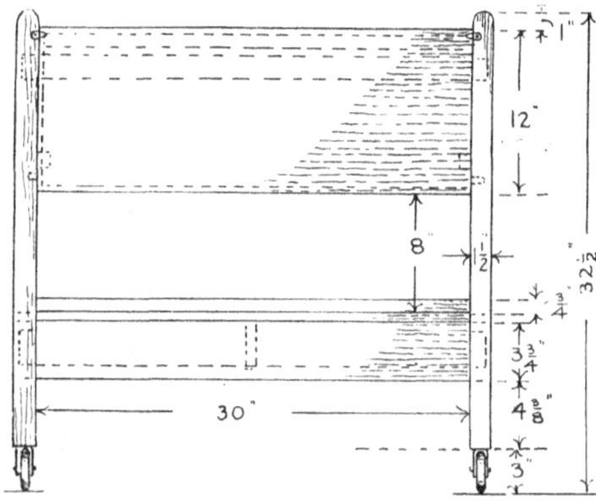

Fig. 2.—Side Elevation.

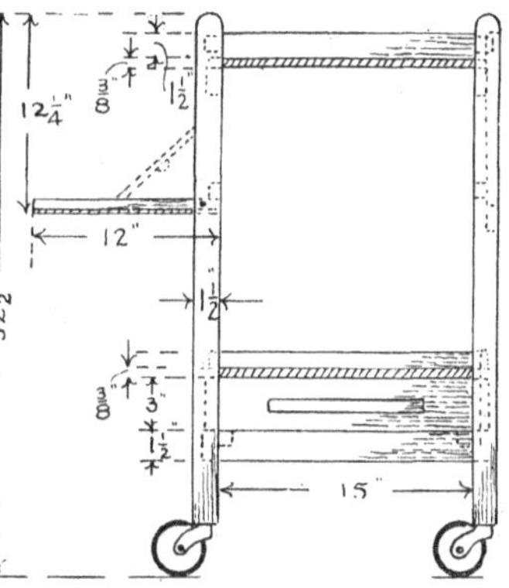

Fig. 3.—End Elevation.

Material Required.

The following material, finished sizes, machine planed oak, with oak-faced veneered panels where required.

Four legs A : $2' 7\frac{1}{2}'' \times 1\frac{1}{2}'' \times 1\frac{1}{2}''$.
Two top rails B : $2' 8'' \times 1\frac{1}{2}'' \times \frac{3}{4}''$.
Two top rails D : $1' 5'' \times 1\frac{1}{2}'' \times \frac{3}{4}''$.
One cross rail C : $1' 4'' \times 1\frac{1}{2}'' \times \frac{3}{4}''$.
Two bottom rails E : $2' 8'' \times 3\frac{3}{4}'' \times \frac{3}{4}''$.
Two bottom rails F : $1' 5'' \times 1\frac{1}{2}'' \times \frac{3}{4}''$.
One cross rail G : $1' 4'' \times 3'' \times \frac{3}{4}''$.
Two runners H : $2' 7'' \times \frac{3}{4}'' \times \frac{3}{4}''$.
One top J : $2' 9'' \times 1' 4\frac{1}{2}'' \times \frac{3}{8}''$.
One bottom K : $2' 9'' \times 1' 6'' \times \frac{3}{8}''$.

For Flaps :—

Two bottom pieces L : $2' 6'' \times 12'' \times \frac{1}{4}''$.
Four sides M : $2' 6'' \times \frac{1}{2}'' \times \frac{1}{2}''$.
Four ends N : $12'' \times \frac{1}{2}'' \times \frac{1}{2}''$.

Drawers :—

Two fronts O : $1' 3'' \times 3'' \times 1''$.
Four sides P : $1' 3\frac{1}{2}'' \times 2\frac{3}{4}'' \times \frac{1}{2}''$.
Two ends R : $1' 3'' \times 2\frac{3}{4}'' \times \frac{1}{2}''$.
Two bottom pieces (plywood) S : $1' 3'' \times 1' 3'' \times \frac{1}{4}''$.
Bottom rims, if required : Two pieces, $2' 6'' \times 1'' \times \frac{3}{8}''$.
Two pieces $1' 3'' \times 1'' \times \frac{3}{4}''$.
Two handles : $9'' \times 1'' \times 1''$.
Eight brass plates : $2\frac{1}{4}'' \times \frac{3}{4}'' \times \frac{3}{8}''$, 4 wheel castors 3″, and two pairs of rule stay joints, 8″ if required.

The Construction.

In beginning the construction, the four legs A are turned up to $1\frac{1}{2}$ inch square section and cut off to $29\frac{1}{2}$ inches long. The two top side rails at B are 2 feet 8 inches, the end rails at D are 1 foot 5 inches, a cross rail at C is 1 foot 4 inches, and all are $1\frac{1}{2}$ inches wide and $\frac{3}{4}$ inches thick. The lower front rails at E are 2 feet 8 inches × $3\frac{3}{4}$ inches × $\frac{3}{4}$ inch, the end rails F are 1 foot 5 inches × $\frac{3}{4}$ inch, the cross rail G is 1 foot 4 inches × 3 inches × $\frac{3}{4}$ inch, and the runners H are 2 feet 7 inches × $\frac{3}{4}$ inch × $\frac{3}{4}$ inch. All these parts are shown in position at Fig. 4 and the joints required to fit them together are shown at Fig. 5.

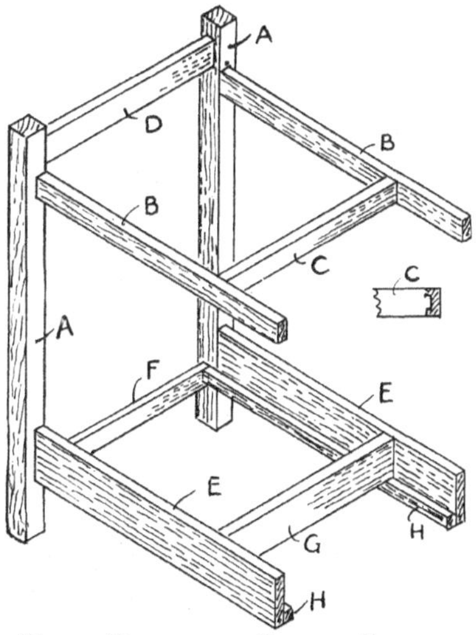

Fig. 4.—The various Parts in Position.

Marking Off Portion of Rails.

Having prepared the material, place the four legs together and set off the position of the side rails at B ; these are $2\frac{7}{8}$ inches down from the top. The lower front rails at E are $21\frac{3}{8}$ inches from the top. Number these pieces and then turn 1 and 2 and 3 and 4 inwards and mark off the position of the end rails. The top one D is 1 inch down and the lower one, F is $24\frac{3}{8}$ inches from the top. The four front rails, B and E, are placed together, and marked off 1 inch from the end, then 2 feet 6 inches along, leaving 1 inch from the end, 15 inches long, leaving 1 inch again, these 1-inch portions forming the tenons. Carry the lines on the sides with a try square and then mark off the thickness of the tenons.

Set a mortise gauge to $\frac{3}{8}$ inch and gauge lines from the face side of each of the long rails and from the inner edges of the uprights so that the marks are $\frac{3}{8}$ inch from the corner.

For the end rails the mortise gauge should be set to $\frac{1}{2}$ inch ; on the rails there will be a shoulder of $\frac{1}{8}$ inch, but on the uprights the gauging should be $\frac{1}{2}$ inch from the corner. The joints between the cross rails and the long rails are stub tenons, as shown at Fig. 4, the tenons being $\frac{1}{2}$ inch long. The runners are let into the bottom end rails $\frac{1}{8}$ inch as shown at Fig. 5. As the top board, J, must be fixed when the framing is glued up, the 2 feet 9 inches × 1 foot $4\frac{1}{2}$ inches × $\frac{3}{8}$ inch piece should be prepared, it may be plywood or $\frac{3}{8}$ inch thick material, shaped at the end with $1\frac{1}{2}$ inches × $\frac{3}{4}$ inch notches, as indicated at Fig. 6.

Gluing Up the Framework

In gluing up the framework, use hot glue; it should be thin but strong. The side pieces can be done first but a cramp of some sort should be used to pull the joints up tight. The same applies to the remainder of the gluing, and special care should be taken to see that the notches on the top piece are not too tight a fit.

Now Prepare the Flaps.

The two flaps are now prepared. The bottom pieces L are 2 feet 6 inches × 12 inches × $\frac{1}{4}$ inch, and the rim, L and M, formed by two 2 feet 6 inches and two 12-inch lengths of $\frac{1}{2}$ × $\frac{1}{2}$ inch wood, either dovetailed or notched at the corners. If a particularly neat job is desired, the bottom can be rebated into the rim; in this case the latter material should be prepared to $\frac{3}{4}$ × $\frac{1}{2}$ inch, and the bottom board to 2 feet $5\frac{1}{2}$ inches × $11\frac{1}{2}$ inches. Small screws should be used to secure the bottom to the rim.

The Lower Tray and Drawers.

The framing should now be cleaned up and the lower tray prepared and fitted. It measures 2 feet 9 inches × 1 foot 6 inches × $\frac{3}{8}$ inch, the corners being notched out $1\frac{1}{2}$ inches as indicated at Fig. 6. A rim of 1 × $\frac{1}{2}$ × $\frac{3}{8}$ inch wood can be fitted to surround the bottom tray as shown at Figs. 2 and 3; this, as shown at Fig. 1, may be omitted if desired but it adds to the safety of the wagon. The drawers, as will be seen at Fig. 6, are made with a front piece O, 15 × 3 × 1 inch, two side pieces P, $15\frac{1}{2}$ × $2\frac{3}{4}$ × $\frac{1}{2}$ inch, dovetailed to the front, one back R, 15 × $2\frac{3}{4}$ × $\frac{1}{2}$ inch dovetailed to the sides and a bottom piece S, 15 × 15 × $\frac{1}{4}$ in. rebated $\frac{1}{4}$ in. in the bottom of the front piece and secured to the sides and back with screws. This is a simple form of drawer construction and gives full depth.

The handles for the drawers are made from strips 9 × 1 × 1 in., bevelled $\frac{5}{16}$ in. each side and $\frac{1}{2}$ in. at the ends as indicated at T in Fig. 6. Care should be taken that the measurements of the drawers are correct and that the corners are all quite square, and to prevent mistakes the inside measurements of the drawer openings should be separately measured before actually cutting the joints.

Now Hinge Flaps to Uprights.

The two flaps are now hinged to the uprights and to make the action clear

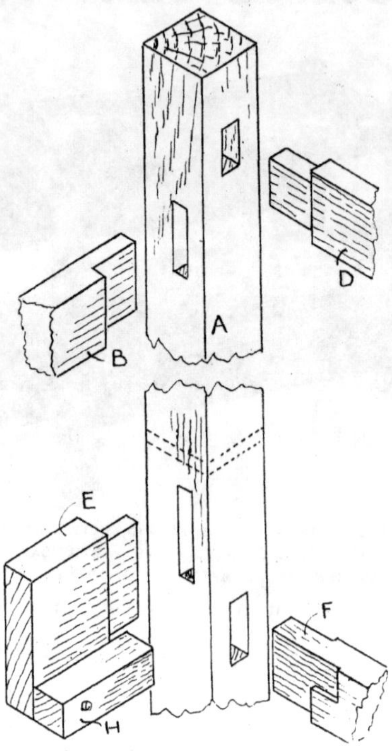

Fig. 5.—Details of the Joints.

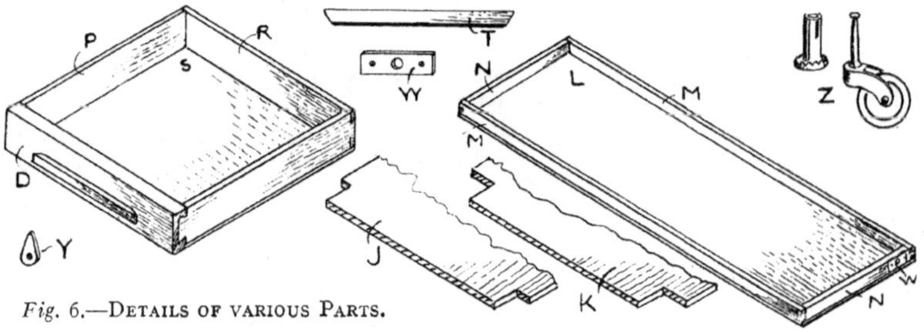

Fig. 6.—Details of various Parts.

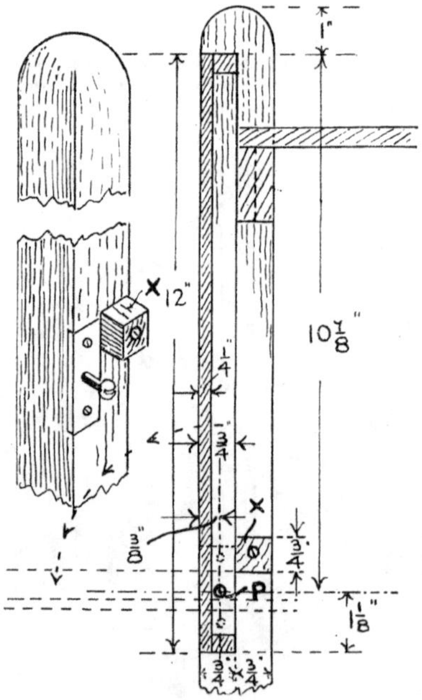

Fig. 7.—Details of Flap Hinge.

an enlarged detail is given at Fig. 7, showing a flap in its upright position. First measure down $11\frac{7}{8}$ in. from the top and $\frac{3}{8}$ in. in. This gives the position of the pivot at V. Now prepare eight brass plates as indicated at W, in Fig. 6, to $2\frac{1}{4}$ × $\frac{3}{4}$ × $\frac{1}{8}$ in. Drill a $\frac{3}{16}$ in. hole in the centre and two $\frac{1}{8}$ in. holes for screws and countersink the top of the screw holes. Two of the plates are screwed to the ends of each tray and two at each side of the framing. Holes are driven through the holes in the plates to take stout 2-in. screws. Stops of wood, shaped to $\frac{3}{4}$ in. cube are screwed on as indicated at X (Fig. 7), so that the trays are level when the back corners butt against the stop.

Strengthening the Hinge.

As mentioned above, this form of hinge can be strengthened by attaching short lengths of chain or by screwing on a pair of rule joint stays; those opening out to 8 inches will be large enough. Two brass turns, as shown at Y, about 1 × $\frac{1}{2}$ × $\frac{1}{8}$ inch, should be screwed on each side to keep the flaps upright and finally the wheel castors as indicated at Z should be fitted. These castors, fitted with rubber tyres, are provided with a steel socket as shown; they are fitted by boring a $\frac{3}{8}$ inch diameter hole in the centre of the legs, the socket is driven in tight and then the castor pushed in. This particular design has considerable strength, works freely and there is no difficulty in removing the castor should occasion arise.

When polishing, the flaps should be removed; the best means of finishing being to apply a couple of coats of hard drying glaze and a final coating of french polish. The design looks effective when made in oak with a limed finish.

A SIMPLE FORM OF TEA WAGON

An outstanding feature of the tea wagon shown in Fig. 8 is that it can be made successfully by any handyman with only the simplest tools.

The following material is required for a wagon measuring 25 inches long, 17 inches wide and 31 inches high. The design is suitable for building in mahogany or oak; the plywood should be obtained veneered on the face with wood of the selected variety.

Materials Required.

Legs.—Four tapered and grooved, $28\frac{1}{2}$ inches long with $\frac{3}{8}$-inch grooves on two faces.

TWO USEFUL TEA WAGONS

Trays.—Two pieces plywood, ⅜ inch thick, 25 inches long, 17 inches wide.

Stripwood.—1½ inches wide, ⅜ inch thick. Four pieces 24 inches long, four pieces 15 inches long.

Bracket Pieces.—One piece 24 inches long, 12 inches wide, ⅜ inch thick.

Moulding.—Astragal, ⅜ inch wide, four pieces 24 inches long; four pieces 15 inches long.

Ornaments.—Four, square 1½ inches.

Wheels.—One set of four wagon castors with 3-inch diameter rubber-tyred wheels.

All this material and needful stain and polish can be had at small cost from any handicrafts supply firm.

What to do First.

Having obtained the materials, examine them to see that they will hold up to the required sizes; timber is liable to vary slightly in thickness, so before cutting up the wood see that the piece for the brackets will fit snugly into the grooves in the legs; also make sure the four square ornaments will fit nicely on top of the legs.

The next step is to prepare all the various pieces in readiness for fitting together. The eight pieces of stripwood should be rounded on one edge by first planing off the corners to form a chamfer, as in Fig. 9, and then planing off the ridges and rounding them into one another. Finish off by sandpapering, first diagonally across the wood and then lengthways.

Preparing the Trays.

Next prepare the two trays, which at this stage should be made exactly alike for size. To do this properly necessitates the use of a shooting board, and should this handy device not be included in the worker's tool kit, it is highly desirable to make one;

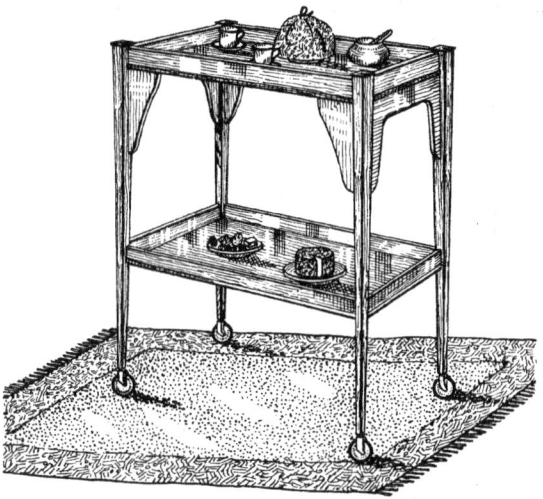

Fig. 8.—Design for a Straightforward Tea Wagon.

it will always be handy for many different jobs.

A simple shooting board shown in Fig. 10 consists of a piece of smooth, straight board, 9 inches wide, 1 inch thick, 3 feet long, with a similar board 6 inches wide, glued and screwed on top of it to form a step or L-sectioned trough. A cross-piece of batten, about 1½ inches wide and ¾ inch thick, is screwed near one end as shown.

The essential feature is that the cross batten must be at right angles to the step.

To use the board, clamp or screw it to the work bench, place the wood on the upper board with one end against the stop and the edge projecting slightly over the step. Hold the plywood firmly with the left hand and manipulate the plane with the right hand. Lay the plane on its side on the lower board so that the plane iron is vertical.

A perfectly straight square edge is speedily produced on the plywood, and, this done, cut off the extreme corner, as in Fig. 11, and plane the end square and true. The object of cutting off the corner is to check the tendency for the plane to splinter the end grain.

Plane all four edges until each piece is 24½ inches long and 16½ inches wide.

Cutting the Brackets.

The next step is to prepare two shaped end brackets, as shown in Fig. 12, which can be done by marking out a paper pattern and laying it on the plywood. Mark around the pattern with a pencil, then place the pattern for the second bracket—arranging it to cause as little waste as possible.

Prepare a pattern as in Fig. 13 for the four side brackets and mark them out on the ⅜-inch plywood, fitting them in to the best advantage to avoid waste of wood. Take care when marking out the side brackets to make two "right"-handed and two "left"-handed, to ensure the veneered face coming to the front, which can be ensured by turning the pattern upside-down for the second set pair marking out the first pair.

Plane the edges square and true, then cut the curved parts with a fretsaw and clean up the edges with a chisel or sandpaper.

Assembling the Wagon.

Inspect all four legs and, if necessary, make them exactly the same length and square at the ends, drill a hole into the lower end of each to take the shank on the castors, but do not fix the castors. Next put the end bracket into the grooves in the legs and set the top edge of the bracket 2 inches below the tops of the legs. If necessary, cut away the lower ends of the brackets or enlarge the groove a trifle to ensure a good fit.

When placing the brackets see that the veneered face is on the outside and that the remaining grooves on the legs are at the back or opposite to the veneered face.

To ensure a perfect result prepare a simple assembly jig, as sketched in Fig. 14, consisting of a few blocks of wood nailed to the work bench. Mark out the position of the legs and bracket before fixing the blocks, and see that

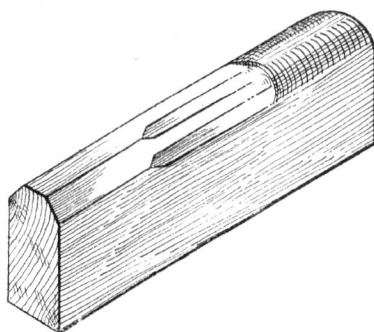

Fig. 9.—Chamfering and Rounding the Edge.

The top edges of the strip wood are first bevelled and then rounded.

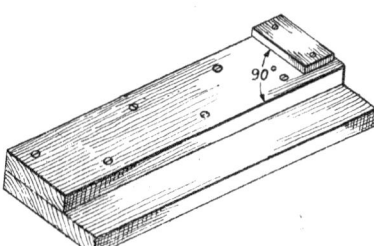

Fig. 10.—Shooting Board.

Composed of two pieces of board with a cross piece at one end as shown, indispensable for successfully carrying out the work.

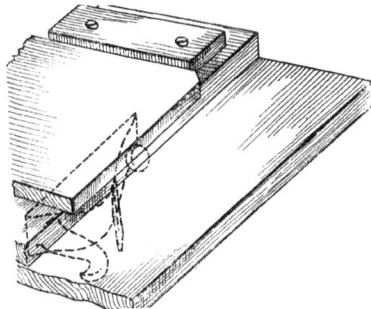

Fig. 11.—Prevent End Grain Splitting.

The corner of the ply-board is cut off prior to planing across the end-grain to prevent splitting. Plane is shown dotted.

TWO USEFUL TEA WAGONS

the outside blocks are square with the top cross strip.

Apply some hot Scotch glue to the edges of the bracket and insert it into the grooves in the legs. Tap the parts together and immediately put them into the jig, which will hold them square and true while the glue is drying. Wipe off any surplus glue with a rag steeped in hot water. Assemble the other pair of legs in the same way; the jig will ensure them being exactly the same as the first pair.

Fitting the Top.

The next proceeding is to cut notches in the corners of the top tray, as in Fig. 15, so that it will fit nicely between the legs and finish flush with the outer faces of the brackets.

Drill two screw holes through the top, near each end and each side, so that they will come central with the brackets. Countersink the tops of the holes at the end, but countersink the underside of the holes along the sides of the top tray.

Apply some glue to the joint faces, then assemble the parts and screw them together. The legs can be held by an assistant or can be kept in place by blocks of wood nailed to the floor, as in Fig. 16, and should, of course, be got ready before applying the glue.

Turn the table upside-down and glue the four side brackets into place, taking care to keep the legs parallel.

Next cut two of the long pieces of the stripwood so that they just drop into the grooves in the legs and rest nicely on the top, as shown in Fig. 17; then glue the joints and fasten them with screws driven through the holes already drilled in the top.

Fit the two cross pieces in the same way and set the work aside while the glue sets. Prepare the bottom tray in a similar way by notching the corners with a fretsaw, then secure it with glue and a screw eye, as shown in Fig. 18, in each leg. Measure the distance from the bottom of the leg to the screw eyehole to ensure each being the same height. Fix the screw eyes before fixing the

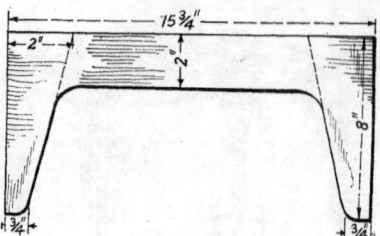

Fig. 12.—Shape of End Bracket.
Two pieces of ply-wood should be sawn to the shape here shown.

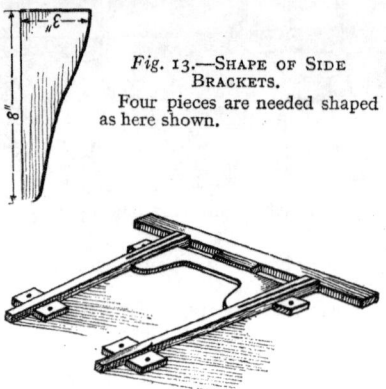

Fig. 13.—Shape of Side Brackets.
Four pieces are needed shaped as here shown.

Fig. 14.—Assembly Jig.
A strip of batten and five blocks nailed to the bench or floor will ensure the parts going together properly.

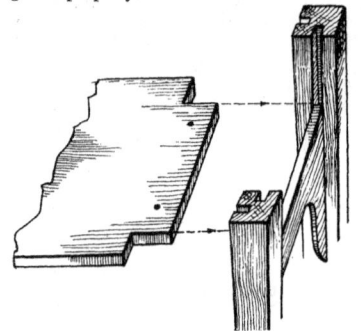

Fig. 15.—Fitting Top Tray.
Square notches are cut in the corners of the top tray so that it will fit neatly between the legs.

tray, fasten them with screws, then cut the pieces of stripwood to fit neatly between the legs, glue them into place and fasten them with screws driven upwards through the tray.

Finishing the Tea Wagon.

Rub down all the woodwork with fine sandpaper, then apply water stain to all the surfaces to bring all the wood to one uniform colour. Stain the moulding and the four ornaments at the same time. When the stain has dried, glue and pin the ornaments to the tops of the legs and fix the moulding with glue and cabinet pins to the visible edges of the trays.

Rub down the whole with old sandpaper, then give a coat of wood filler. If necessary, go over the surfaces with a rag dipped in the stain, giving an extra dose to any parts that may be lighter than the remainder. When dry, finish and polish with French polish, or with one of the specially prepared glazes sold for amateur use. Fix the castors by driving them into place, apply a spot of oil to each axle, and the wagon is finished and ready for years of arduous service.

Although a good result can be obtained by staining and polishing the work when the wagon has been completed and assembled, a better effect is obtained by first fitting together the various parts and then taking them apart and staining them all over—joint faces and grooves included. When this is done any subsequent shrinkage does not reveal tiny lines of white as might possibly happen when all the staining is done last.

In any case, if the work is stained as suggested before the final assembly of the parts, it is still necessary to finish off by rubbing down, and then apply the wood filler and stain as before described.

Very effective results are obtained when the wagon is painted and enamelled, for example, a pleasing green colour—obtained by applying at least three "undercoatings"—each allowed to dry hard and separately rubbed down before applying the final coat of glossy enamel.

Alternatively one of the "cellulose finishes" or coloured lacquers can be used with equally effective results.

Fig. 16.—Assembling the Wagon.
To prevent the legs spreading while fixing the top tray, blocks are nailed to the floor to hold the legs in position.

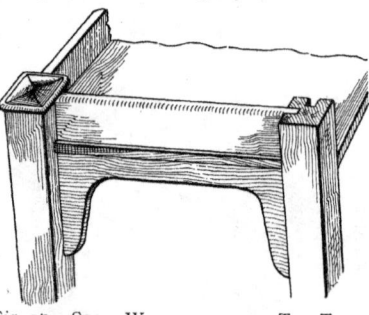

Fig. 17.—Strip Wood fitted to Top Tray.
The strips are fitted into the grooves in the legs and secured with screws through the tray. One ornamental cap is shown fitted to the top of leg.

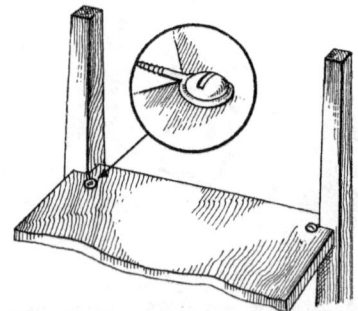

Fig. 18.—Upside View of Lower Tray.
Screw eyes are driven into the legs and screws put through them to hold the tray securely.

Pointing Brickwork Around the House

It often happens, when a house has been built some years, that the mortar which binds the bricks begins to perish, with the result that the rain is allowed to percolate through and the interior walls show signs of dampness. When this takes place, the area which will be affected first consists of the lowest ten or a dozen courses of bricks, counting from the ground level. There are many reasons why these courses wear the worst, and it is fortunate that they are the earliest to give trouble, because they are easily reached and can be repaired without ladders or scaffolding.

If the ground-floor rooms of the house begin to show damp patches low down on the walls and there is no reason to suspect a leaking pipe or a faulty damp course, it will be as well to examine the bricks and the mortar joints running between them, on the outside of the house. Should the mortar be so friable that it is possible to scratch it out with, say, a blunt stick of wood, there is every reason to suppose that it needs replacing. Even though no internal signs are visible and the mortar can be prized out in this way, the work should be taken in hand because the ill-effects are bound to follow before long.

Raking the Courses.

The work of restoring the mortar between the bricks is known as pointing and it is a job that anyone can do quite efficiently. The first step in this work is to take some blunt instrument, such as an old screwdriver of large size, and to rake out the mortar so that the spaces between the bricks are bared for a depth of about an inch. This is a dusty job and it will be advisable to wear an old suit while doing it.

When all the mortar has been loosened, a stiff yard broom should be taken and the whole of the surface swept free of the powder formed by the raking. It may be that the bricks now look very dilapidated and need cleaning. It is quite easy to clean them and give them a new appearance, but this should only be done when the cleaned area will not set up an unpleasant contrast with the parts left untouched.

Fig. 1.—First rake out the joints fairly deeply.
This can be done with an old screwdriver or special raking tool. Even a stout piece of iron, pointed and bent can be used.

Cleaning the Brickwork.

To clean the faces of the bricks obtain a new brick from somewhere — it should be yellow if the bricks in the wall are yellow and red if they are red. Rub one of the faces of the brick quite smooth and then work it over the bricks that are to be cleaned. By wearing off the outer soiled skin a new clean face is provided and the effect is the same as though new bricks were concerned.

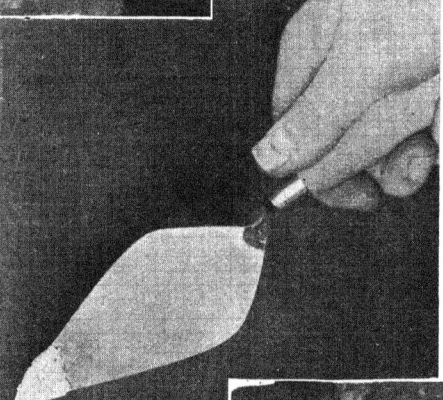

Fig. 2.—Use the back of the trowel when applying the cement to the joints.

Recolouring the Brickwork.

Some builders now apply a wash to the surface, to make the brickwork appear still more spick and span; but this is hardly necessary under the present circumstances. However, for those who may care to follow the plan, it may be stated that, for yellow bricks, they use powdered ochre and, for red bricks, any red powder, mixed up in a solution of copperas. These materials are obtained at oil-shops. The solution is applied with an old whitewash brush, for it would spoil a good brush.

Preparing the Mortar.

For the actual work of pointing, take 2 parts of Portland cement and 3 of sharp or building sand, or 1 part of lime and 2 of sand, and mix with sufficient water to make a stiff mortar. The first mixture gives a very hard and serviceable joint, but has a rather cold grey appearance; the second looks better, but is less durable.

Pointing the Bricks.

When all is ready, wet the bricks thoroughly; it is even wise to do this two or three times and to allow the wet to soak in. Then take a little of the mortar on the tip of the trowel and force it into the highest course that is to be pointed. Continue in this way until the whole of one horizontal line has been filled and follow with the next course, below it. Then treat the vertical seams, joining them, in the same way. The aim should be to level up the seams so that they are flush with the faces of the bricks, but not to get more cement on the faces of the bricks than possible.

At this point the filling process is stopped and a straight edge of wood is taken. For preference, it should be about 4 feet long. The straight edge is placed so that it exactly superimposes the higher edge of the horizontal seam, and the tip of the trowel is scored along it. Then with the straight edge still in position the mortar is scraped away where it has chanced to come above the score mark.

Next, the straight edge is placed so that it exactly superimposes the lower edge of the horizontal seam. The tip of the trowel is scored along it, as before, and the superfluous mortar is scraped away. The vertical seams are treated in exactly the same way.

When one or two courses have been pointed a few more are filled, continuing until the job is completed.

Fig. 3.—The trowel is used to give a smooth finish.
Small cracks in rough cast can also be dealt with in this way.

How to Build Small Boats

DEALING WITH A DINGHY FLAT AND PUNT

There are no doubt many people in different parts of the country who would like to possess a boat, but who cannot afford to have one built by a professional; so in this article instructions will be given for building a small boat which should be within the ability of anyone to construct successfully.

The type dealt with first is what is known as a dinghy flat, dimensions being 10 feet long by 4 feet beam, or width.

This craft can be used for fishing, shooting, sailing, etc., and, if built to the design given, is very seaworthy and safe.

The cost should not much exceed £2 in Columbian pine, while if cost is very important, good red deal might be used, reducing the figure to under this amount.

Fig. 1.—This Attractive Dinghy Flat can be made quite simply and cheaply.

Tools required.

The tools required are generally found in the amateur's kit—in any case, they are not numerous.

A handsaw, 2-inch chisel, mallet, brace and bits, screwdriver, plane, hammer and bradawl should be sufficient.

Timber required for 10 × 4-foot Dinghy Flat.

Planking.—Three 9 feet, 9 × $\frac{5}{8}$ inch ; two 7 feet, 9 × $\frac{5}{8}$ inch ; four 11 feet 6 inches, 9 × $\frac{3}{8}$ inch.
Transom.—One 3 feet, 20 × $\frac{3}{4}$ inch, English elm.
Gunwhales.—Two 11 feet 6 inches, $1\frac{1}{4}$ × 1 inch, pine or oak.
Floors.—25 feet, $1\frac{1}{2}$ × 1 inch, English elm, pine or oak.
Seats, Etc.—25 feet, 9 × $\frac{3}{4}$ inch, deal or pine.
Bottom Boards.—Approx. 20 feet, 5 × $\frac{1}{2}$ inch, deal or pine.
Seam Battens.—Two 11 feet 6 inches × $1\frac{1}{4}$ inch, deal or pine.
Oak for stem, breasthook, etc., English elm for knees.
$\frac{1}{2}$ lb. 1-inch copper nails.
1 lb. 3-inch copper nails and roves.
1 lb. $1\frac{1}{2}$-inch copper nails.
2 lb. 2-inch copper or galvanised nails.
3 lb. $1\frac{1}{2}$-inch copper or galvanised nails.
1 dozen $2\frac{1}{2}$-inch brass screws.
12 feet, $\frac{1}{2}$ × $\frac{1}{8}$-inch half-round iron (stern and keel band).

Erecting the Stocks.

The stocks on which the boat is built must first be erected, and consist of a 3 × 2-inch deal raised about 18 inches above the floor on struts and braced up quite firm (Fig. 3).

Of course, there are many other arrangements which will occur to the builder, and any of these can be used as long as it is quite firm.

The Stem.

The stem is of English oak, and can be sawn to shape at the timber yard, the grain running in the same shape (or as near as possible) to the finished part (Fig. 4).

Having shaped the stem, stern knee and transom, take a $\frac{5}{8}$-inch plank of sufficient length and draw a line down the exact centre of it.

Now fit Stem, Stern Knee and Transom to Plank.

Fit the stem, stern knee and transom to this plank, keeping them central. These should be fastened with brass screws. Turn the whole upside down and plane about $\frac{1}{16}$ inch off the bottom, or outside edge, of the plank, but do not touch the inside edge. This should be done both sides of the plank, and, when subsequent planks have been treated in a similar manner, will form a "V" joint, into which the caulking cotton or oakum will be driven.

Place Assembly on Stocks.

Now turn the assembly upright and place on the stocks, and screw the centre of the plank to the stocks, then spring the ends up about $4\frac{1}{2}$ inches

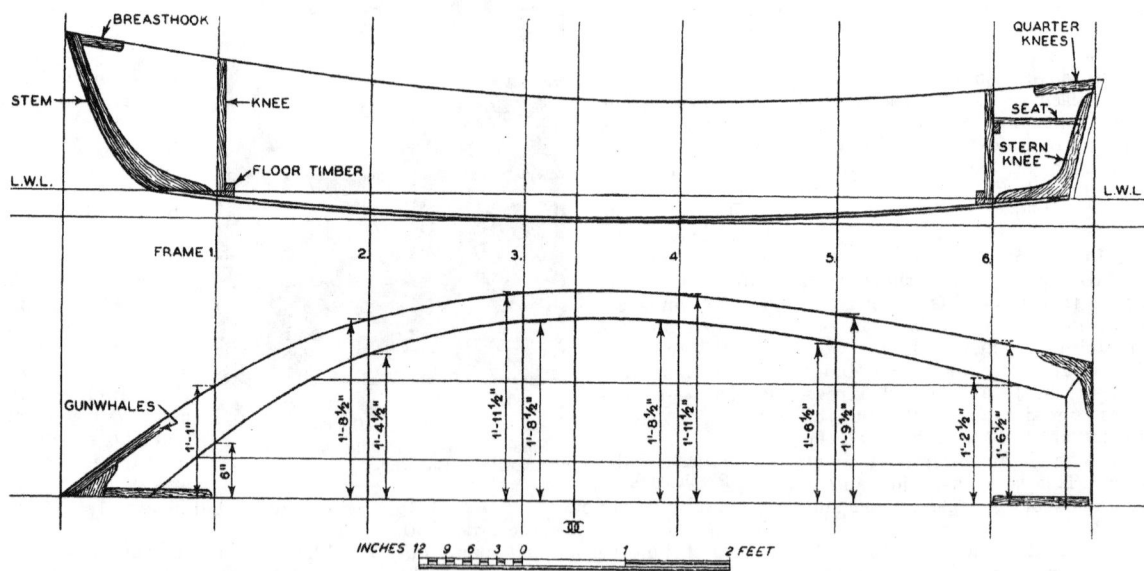

Fig. 2.—All the Principal Dimensions and Names of the Various Parts are shown in the above Diagram.

HOW TO BUILD SMALL BOATS

from the stocks, placing blocks of wood between to keep in place (Fig. 7).

Mark on the plank the positions of the "floor" or bottom frames, and square lines across at these points.

The Floors.

Take the 1½ × 1-inch timber from which these floors will be made, and cut them a little longer than shown in the drawing. When these are placed on the plank (edgeways), they will not, of course, stand upright, owing to the curve of the plank, so they must be bevelled until they do so.

Remove the plank from the stocks and fasten the frames with copper or galvanised nails (2 inch), the centre of the floor corresponding with the centre-line on the plank. This done, it can be once more put on the stocks, as before.

Using a ¼-inch bit, bore a hole in the edge of the plank half-way between each pair of floors, and insert a dowel in each, leaving about ½ inch protruding. Do this each side of the plank.

Take another ⅝-inch plank and put up alongside the first, note where the dowels come and bore to receive them. Bevel the edge of the second plank as before, and put in place after painting or varnishing the edges, then nail up.

Carry on until sufficient width is obtained in the bottom.

Now fit Temporary Side Frames.

Fix some temporary side frames to the bottom members *at the correct distance from the centre-line and at the correct angle*. These can be nailed at the bottom to the floors and stiffened by bringing battens from the top to the middle of the floors, then, with the aid of a thin batten bent around, mark off the correct curve of the outside edge of the bottom. This will be bevelled according to the angle of the sides. A shaving or two should be taken off the bottom edge for caulking.

Mark off on the temporary frames the height of the sides, then take a 9 × ⅜-inch plank and put around, with its top edge at the marks, and fit the fore end into the stem.

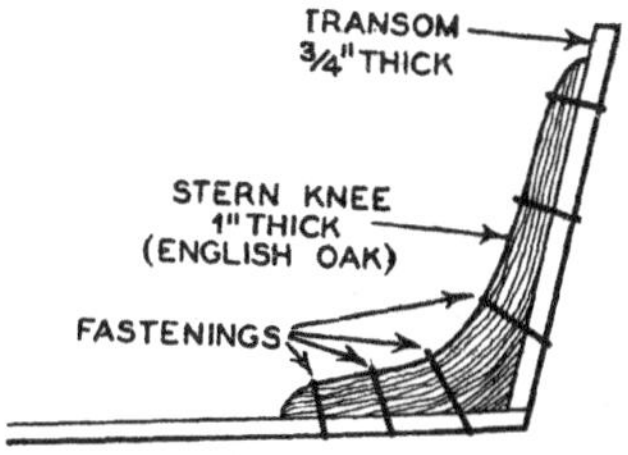

The edge of the transom will need a little bevelling to allow the plank to lie snug. When satisfactory, nail up and repeat on opposite side.

Take another plank and fit below the first, with the edges close. Fit fore and aft, and nail up, also nail round the bottom edge carefully. It may now be found that the lower edge of this plank extends below the bottom; if so, this can be trimmed off. Repeat on the other side.

The Seam Battens.

The seam battens are now to be fixed. These measure 1¼ × ½ inch, and are put around the inside, covering the seams, after which they are fastened with copper nails spaced about 2 inches apart. These nails should be rather too long, and bent over in the direction of the grain.

It will naturally be necessary to remove the temporary frames before putting these in, and pieces of wood should be wedged across the inside of the boat to prevent the top planks from springing inward.

Fitting the Gunwhales.

The next job is to fit the gunwhales, or pieces of timber, around the inside of the boat at the top.

These are 1¼ × 1 inch, and should present no difficulty, being fastened as are the seam-battens, after which the breasthook and quarter-knees are put in. These are grown to shape as with the stem. The shape and position of these can be seen in the design. They are fastened with copper nails clenched on roves, that is, the nail is driven (after a small hole has been bored for it), then a rove or dished washer is driven over the nail, and the nail cut off if necessary and riveted.

The Knees.

The next job is the knees. These are of oak or elm, also grown to shape, and carefully fitted. They are screwed at the bottom to the floors, alongside which they are placed, those forward of amidships being placed at the fore side of the floors and those aft of amidships on the after side.

The tops of these knees are about 1½ inches wide, so that they can lap over the gunwhales and are then fastened right through planking, gunwhales and knee with copper nails clenched on roves.

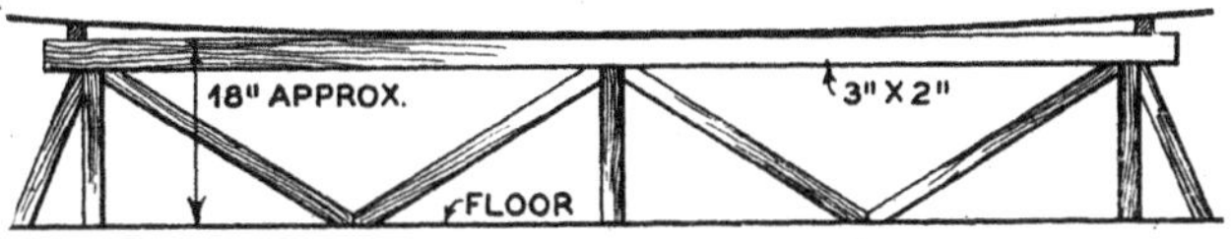

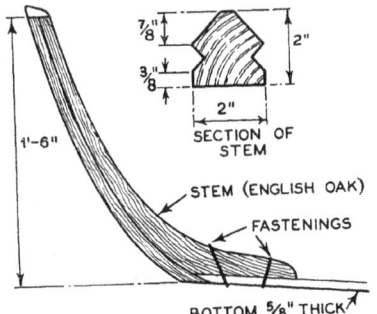

Fig. 3.—THE FIRST THING TO DO IS TO ERECT THE STOCKS ON WHICH THE BOAT WILL BE BUILT.

These consist of a 3 × 2-inch deal board raised about 18 inches above the ground on struts.

Fig. 4.—DETAILS FOR CONSTRUCTING THE STEM.

Fig. 5.—DETAILS OF TRANSOM AND STERN KNEE, SHOWING METHOD OF FASTENING.

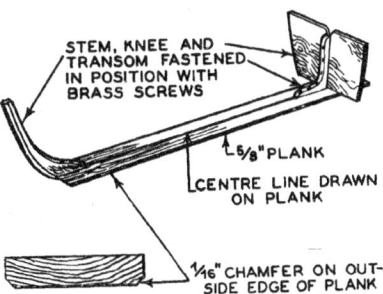

Fig. 6.—HOW TO FIT THE STEM, STERN KNEE AND TRANSOM TO THE PLANK.

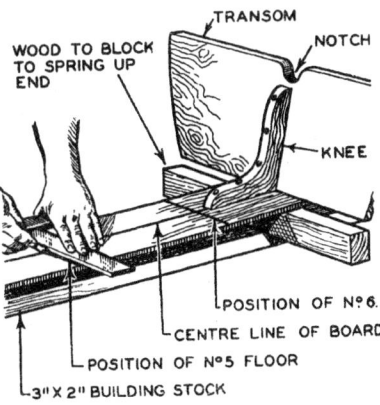

Fig. 7.—MARKING THE POSITIONS OF THE "FLOOR" OR BOTTOM FRAMES AND SQUARING THE LINES ACROSS AT THESE POINTS.

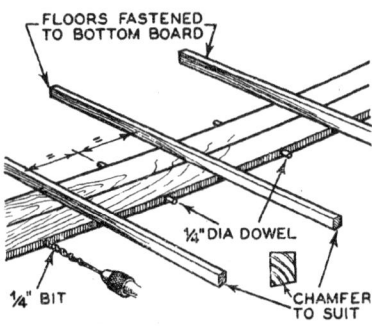

Fig. 8.—THE FLOORS FASTENED TO THE BOTTOM BOARDS.

Note how they are chamfered to the curve of the plank, also the position of the dowels.

How to Build Small Boats

The Seats or "Thwarts."

Seats or "thwarts" come next. They can rest on the seam battens, and be nailed thereto. If a locker is to be fitted aft, a support is fastened across the two frames furthest aft, after which a support is nailed across the stern on the same level as the battens, when the seats can be put in and the front filled in. A space is left in the top for a door, of course.

The other seats also rest on the battens, and are 9 × ¾-inch deal or pine; bottom boards are of the same material, 5 × ½ inch, or as convenient.

A stout galvanised ring should be fitted in the stem and stern knee, and the rowlock plates fitted as shown in Fig. 15. A notch can be cut in the transom for sculling.

Caulking.

This done, turn the boat upside down and get the caulking cotton or oakum; if oakum, pull out and twist into a suitable sized cord.

A caulking iron will be required to drive the cotton into the seam. This is something like an ordinary cold chisel, only the thin edge is about 2 inches wide and 1/16 inch thick at the edge. Before starting, prop the boat up firmly all round.

Now take some cotton or oakum, twist up hard, and get one end stuck in the end of the seam, then take a few feet and jam it in the seam again. This will leave the hands free and the caulking twisted. Now work along the seams, driving the cotton well in, but not right through. When all the seams have been caulked, give the whole bottom a liberal coat of *thin* paint or varnish, letting it run well in the seams.

When this is dry, complete the filling of the seams with putty, but do not use ordinary putty. Get some white lead and mix some whitening with this.

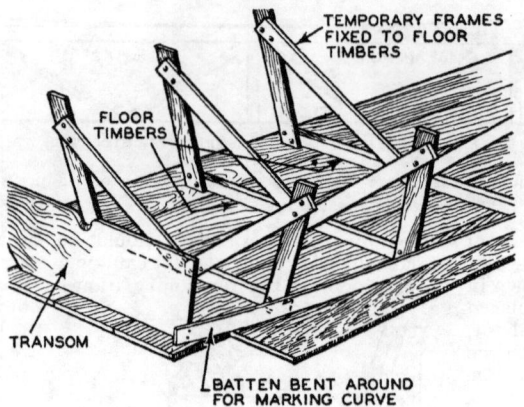

Fig. 9.—Building up the Floor.
Note the batten bent around for marking the curve.

Finishing.

The boat is now ready for finishing according to taste. Give it three coats of good paint or varnish, not too thick.

How to make the Oars.

You will, of course, require some oars. To make these, get a piece of spruce or Columbian pine, or, if cost is very important, red deal, without knots or shakes.

For a 10-foot boat, this should be obtained 8 feet 6 inches long and 4 × 2 inches. Have this sawn, as in Fig. 16, at the timber yard, then mark out as shown in Fig. 16, when it will now be seen that a rough oar is shaped.

Cut away the waste at the sides, and with a spokeshave and plane proceed to work them up to shape, the V on the blades gradually dying away to nothing. Sandpaper the oars and give three coats of varnish.

BUILDING A PUNT

A very popular type of craft for river and other calm water use is the punt, and anyone who can handle a few simple tools can build one, if these few instructions and the constructional details are closely followed.

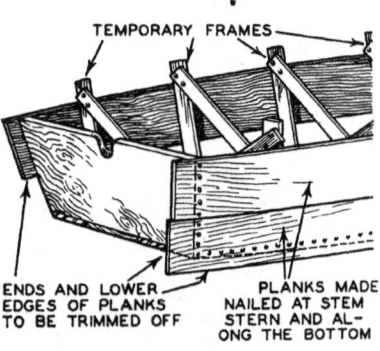

Fig. 10.—Building up the Sides.
Temporary side frames to the bottom members are fixed at the correct distance from the centre-line and at the correct angle.

Fig. 11.—Fixing the Seam Battens.
The nails are driven in from the outside and then turned over.

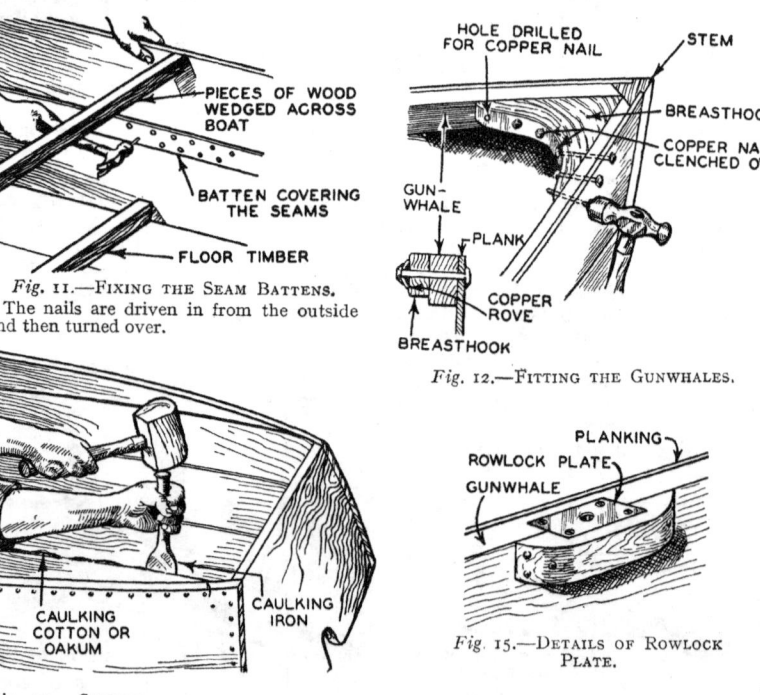

Fig. 12.—Fitting the Gunwhales.

Fig. 14.—Caulking the Boat.

Fig. 15.—Details of Rowlock Plate.

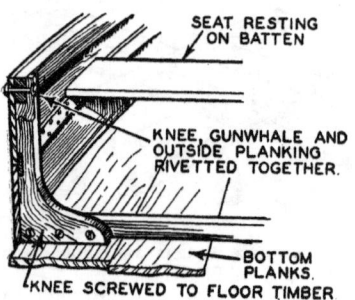

Fig. 13.—Details of Seats or "Thwarts."

Fig. 16.—Details for making the Oars.

1004

HOW TO BUILD SMALL BOATS

The Scantlings.

The scantlings will naturally depend on the size of boat to be constructed, also the usage which it will receive.

For a 10-foot punt (which is the smallest size advisable), obtain two pieces of deal or pine about $\frac{1}{2}$ inch thick, 10 feet long, and 12 inches wide, and cut to the shape shown in Fig. 17.

Put these to one side and take the planks which will be used for the bottom. These can be 9 inches wide, $\frac{5}{8}$ inch thick, and, to eliminate caulking, they can be tongued and grooved.

The Floor Timbers.

Cut the floor timbers a little longer than required. They can be of deal, pine, oak, larch or elm, $1\frac{1}{2}$ inches square and six in number, for a 10-foot boat. Place these at the correct distance apart (see Fig. 19), and quite square. Now take the bottom planking and lay on the timbers. Paint the edges well and nail in place with copper or galvanised nails (2 inch).

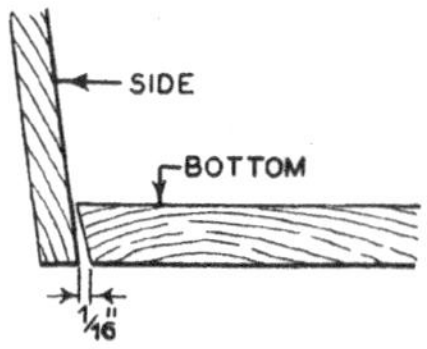

Marking off the Curve of the Side.

Draw a line right down the centre of the bottom, and, using this, mark off the curve of the sides. Keeping in mind the fact that the side flares outwards, saw off the surplus planking and timber ends. These edges can be left rough and trimmed off with a plane when the sides are being fitted.

Next fit the Chocks.

Now bevel off the ends of the planking and fit the chocks as shown at A in the drawing, and, using the same thickness of material as for the bottom, build up the sloping ends, fastening with stout screws. This done, put some 4-inch pieces of $1\frac{1}{2}$-inch square timber under the ends of the bottom, and screw the middle down to the floor, thus forming the curve as shown.

Fig. 17.—A Simply Made Punt for River or other Calm Water.

The Knees.

The knees are now fitted. They are shaped as shown, the grain running in approximately the same shape as the finished knee. When cut and cleaned up, screw to the floor timbers.

If the first part has been made properly, these knees can be all the same shape. If not, the bottom of the knee can be left a little wide when cutting, therefore allowing a certain amount of adjustment to get them in line.

The Sides.

The sides can now be trued up, and the edges of the bottom very carefully planed where necessary until there are no gaps to be seen between them and the side planks. When this is done, take off about $\frac{1}{16}$ inch from the outside edge, as shown in Fig. 18.

Having completed this properly, the sides can be nailed into place with copper or galvanised nails into the bottom, knees and ends.

Fig. 18.—When the Sides and Bottom have been planed so that there are no Gaps between them, take off about $\frac{1}{16}$ inch from the Outside Edge.

The Decks.

The decks are of $\frac{1}{2}$-inch material. Two 1 × $\frac{1}{2}$-inch battens are fastened $\frac{1}{2}$ inch below the top edge of the boat, and the decks allowed to rest on these, being nailed thereto. Another method is to lay the deck planking on top of the sides, as shown in the drawing, but the former is the neater job. In any case, the sharp edge at the extreme ends of the boat is taken off, and a half-round head put on.

The Seats.

The seats are of 9 × $\frac{3}{4}$-inch timber, resting on blocks screwed to the side of the boat. The number of these required will depend on the fancy of the builder.

Bottom boards, of course, are to be fitted, made of $\frac{1}{2}$-inch planks held together with cross-pieces underneath.

The Mooring Ring.

A ring for mooring the boat should be fitted at each end, and the whole boat liberally coated with very thin paint, especially in the seams. This dry, caulk the joint where sides and bottom meet with caulking cotton or oakum, and complete the filling with good putty, after which the boat can be painted according to taste.

There are, of course, many more elaborate methods of building such a craft, but that described is absolutely the most simple, and therefore the most suitable, for the amateur.

General Hints.

On no account be tempted to use wire nails in your boat, especially if it is to be used in salt water. They will rust out in no time. If your ironmonger does not stock copper nails they could be obtained from such firms as Pascal Atkey, Son, Cowes, who could also supply the rowlocks, caulking cotton, etc.

Knees which are not "grown to form" are also useless; they will break off short if they receive a jar.

Finally, remember to paint all surfaces before putting together.

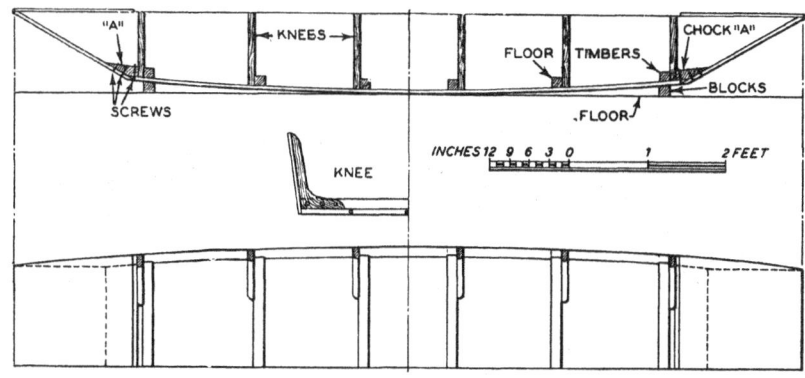

Fig. 19.—Constructional Details and Parts of an Easily Made Punt.

BICYCLE REPAIR AND ADJUSTMENT

A BICYCLE is a simple piece of machinery to keep in order. The operation and purpose of most of the parts are obvious to the least mechanical mind, and there is no need to fear that once a bicycle has been taken to pieces there will be any difficulty in reassembling.

Like most things, if the job of dismantling a bicycle is carried out in an orderly manner, much time and trouble will be saved. Have available one or two boxes into which nuts and small parts can be placed. Then proceed as follows:—

(1) Remove seat pillar and saddle.

(2) Remove the shoes of the brakes, disconnect the brakes and remove the handlebar. If cable operated brakes are used, the operating lever on the handlebar can generally be released by undoing a screw. The pull-up type brakes are released by undoing a cotter nut which keeps the rod in position. This nut for the back brake can be clearly seen in Fig. 7. The handlebar can then be removed with the brake levers attached.

(3) Take out the front wheel by undoing the two nuts at the bottom of the forks. The ends of the forks are slotted so that the wheel can be easily removed.

(4) Remove the front mudguard by undoing the screw which holds it in place at the top of the forks and by disconnecting the stays.

(5) Remove the forks by unscrewing the head screw.

(6) Disconnect the chain. With some types of chains it is an easy matter to undo a screw which keeps one of the links in place. Alternatively the chain can be forced off by holding to one side of the chain wheel so that it does not engage with the sprockets.

(7) Remove rear wheel and mudguard.

(8) Take off chain wheel, pedals and

*Fig. 1.—*TRUEING A WHEEL.

A convenient method of doing this is to place the wheel in the frame, hold a piece of chalk close to the side of the rim and spin the wheel. If any part of the wheel is out of truth it will be indicated by a chalk mark. The spokes on the opposite side where the chalk mark appears should now be tightened by adjusting the nipple.

cranks by undoing the cotter pins which keep them in place.

(9) Remove bottom bracket axle, cups and ball bearings.

The machine is now stripped to the frame and the parts ready for examination. Remove all dirt and grease by washing with paraffin. When reassembling, proceed in the reverse order.

The Bearings.

Unless the bearings are in good order, unsatisfactory running will result. Fig. 5 shows a badly worn bracket axle bearing. Note how it is pitted and uneven. It would be unwise to reassemble the bearing in this condition and the best plan would be to fit a new one. Fig. 5 also shows a wheel bearing, the cone of which is badly pitted. This, too, requires replacing.

If the machine is of a well-known make and the bearings have been regularly lubricated, there should not be a great amount of wear.

A Hint when replacing Ball Bearings.

It is a good plan to pack the ball-races with grease or vaseline before replacing the balls. They will then stay in position while the rest of the part is assembled and adjusted.

TRUEING A WHEEL

The wheels should next be tested to see whether they are slightly out of truth or not. Place the wheel in the frame as shown in Fig. 1. Hold a piece of chalk close to the side of the rim and spin the wheel. If any part of the wheel is out of truth it will be indicated by a chalk mark. The most likely cause of a wheel being out of truth is the fact that one or two spokes may be loose or bent. It is best to remove the tyre from the wheel if any trueing is found to be necessary, as there is the possibility of the spokes protruding through the nipples and causing punctures.

Now feel the tension of the spokes on the side where chalk marks appear. If they feel very tight, slacken the nipples at this place, using a special nipple spanner as shown in Fig. 1. Then tighten up the nipples on the opposite side. Only very slight adjustment is generally necessary, sometimes only about half a turn, to bring the spokes to proper tension. The tension

*Fig. 2.—*FITTING A NEW SPOKE—FIRST OPERATION.
The new spoke should be threaded through its proper hole in the hub, the screwed end being inserted first.

*Fig. 3.—*FITTING A NEW SPOKE—SECOND OPERATION.
Pull the spoke upright and push the screwed end through the appropriate hole in the rim. Attach the nipple and tighten carefully.

on every spoke in the wheel should be equal so that they all bear an equal strain.

Do not forget to make sure that spoke heads which will, after tightening, protrude into the base of the rim, are filed or ground off flush. If this is not done, continual punctures are likely to occur, even though a new rim tape is fitted.

Fitting a New Spoke.

To fit a new spoke the tyre must, of course, be removed. The broken spoke can then be taken out through the hole in the rim and the hole in the hub flange. A new spoke and nipple only cost a few pence. Place the new spoke through the hole in the hub flange and connect to the rim by screwing on the nipple. The wheel should then be tested for truth as previously described.

CRANKS AND PEDALS

Cranks should be carefully examined to make sure they are perfectly true on the bracket axle and that the pedal spindles are square with the crank face. Fig. 6 shows how a bent crank can be straightened with an adjustable spanner. The crank can be bent while cold; in fact, heat should not be used as this destroys the plating. The crank is fixed in the vice and pulled round until it is straight. To avoid damaging the plating the jaws of the spanner should be lined with brass or some other soft material.

The bearings of the pedals must be in good condition, and make sure that the ball bearings are not broken.

A mistake sometimes made when cleaning pedal bearings is to squeeze paraffin in at the end of the pedal instead of through the lubricating hole. This causes dirt and grit to be carried into the bearings. The correct method is to let the machine lean to one side while the oil is inserted in the lubricating hole. Then spin the pedal round so that any dirt will work outwards. Then tilt the machine on the other side and squirt in more oil.

When fitting the cotter pin for the cranks make sure the cranks are in line. Figs. 7 and 8 show them incorrectly and correctly fitted. Make sure that the nut for the cotter pin is facing the rear of the machine when the crank is in the upward position.

ADJUSTING THE HEAD

The correct adjustment of the head is important, both from the point of view of comfort and safety. The head ball-races must be fitted perfectly true and well "bedded down," as shown in Fig. 4, where a properly fitted and incorrectly fitted ball-race are shown. Examine the races (top and bottom) for signs of pitting before refitting and renew if necessary. The

Fig. 4.—Correct and Incorrect Methods of fitting Ball-race to Front Fork.

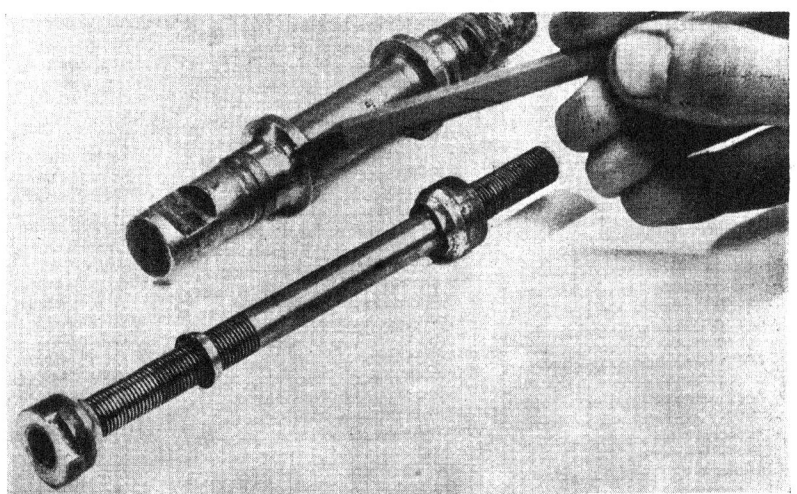

Fig. 5.—Faults to look for when examining Bearings.

Above, a badly pitted bracket-axle; below, a badly worn spindle and cone. Renewals are advisable in both cases.

Fig. 6.—How to straighten a Bent Crank.

Place the crank in a vice and bend with an adjustable spanner.

BICYCLE REPAIR AND ADJUSTMENT

Fig. 7.—Incorrect Method of Fitting Cotter Pin.
Note that the cranks are out of line.

Fig. 8.—Correct Method of Fitting Cotter Pin.
The cranks are now perfectly straight.

Fig. 9.—Testing a Chain for Wear.
A badly worn chain can be lifted from the sprockets as shown.

least distortion in this respect will cause jerky and uneven riding. If the races are not in perfect condition it may result in a broken ball and probably partial seizure of the head.

To adjust, first tighten up the head as tight as it can be adjusted. Then work it round for a time and slack out again until it works freely.

CHAINS AND SPROCKETS
To test Chain for Wear.

A simple test for wear in a chain is to see if it can be lifted from the sprockets. If it can be lifted as shown in Fig. 9,

Fig. 10.—To adjust the Cone of the Front Hub, first loosen the Nut, and then screw up the Cone sufficiently to take up any Wear.

then wear is excessive. This photo, of course, only shows the method; the test should be made when the chain is in place. Undue play can generally be taken up by undoing the two hub nuts that hold the rear wheel in position and tightening the two nuts on the adjuster which fits over the slots in the rear forks.

A new chain seldom fits well on an old sprocket that is worn to any extent, as the pitch of the chain does not conform to the teeth of the sprocket.

Care of the Chain.

It is advisable to clean the chain every 2,000 or 3,000

Fig. 11.—There is no Need to use Levers when replacing a Tyre.
The operation can be done throughout with the fingers.

Fig. 12.—Examine the Rim Tape to see if any Spoke Nipples are bared.
If left like this, continual trouble with punctures may be experienced.

Fig. 13.—In order to comply with the Law the Reflector must not be more than 1 foot from the back end of the Machine.

BICYCLE REPAIR AND ADJUSTMENT

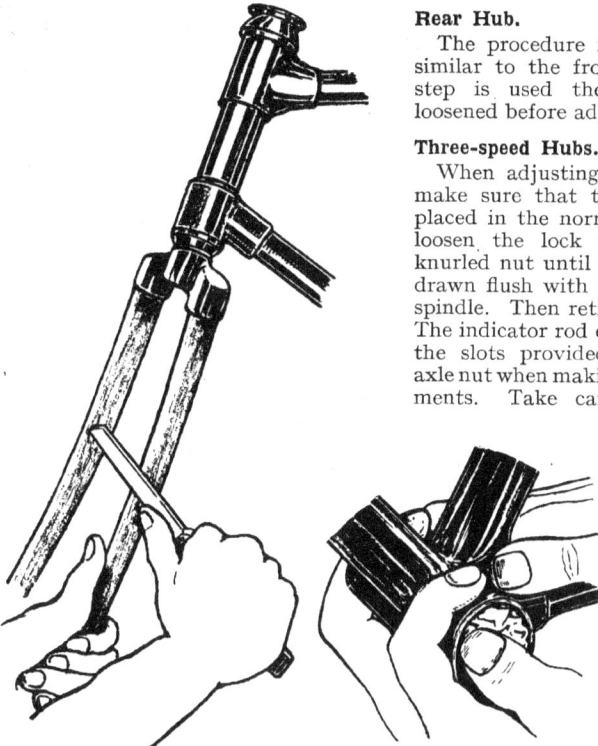

Fig. 14.—Before repainting it it is advisable to remove the old enamel.

It can be scraped off the main parts of the frame with an old knife.

Fig. 15.—When repairing and cleaning it is a good idea to stuff pieces of rag or paper into the bearings to prevent them becoming clogged with dirt and paint.

Rear Hub.
The procedure for the rear hub is similar to the front hub. If a foot step is used then this should be loosened before adjusting the cone.

Three-speed Hubs.
When adjusting a three-speed hub make sure that the control lever is placed in the normal position. Then loosen the lock nut and turn the knurled nut until the indicator rod is drawn flush with the end of the hub spindle. Then retighten the lock nut. The indicator rod can be seen through the slots provided in the rear hub axle nut when making necessary adjustments. Take care that the chain guide nut and step are perfectly tight, also that the adjusting cone is not screwed too tightly, otherwise the ball-race will get damaged and become subject to unnecessary wear.

REPAINTING A BICYCLE
Probably the most satisfactory finish for a bicycle is obtained by using cellulose lacquer. Obtain half a pint of cellulose undercoating and a similar quantity of finishing coat of the desired colour. If the machine is in a

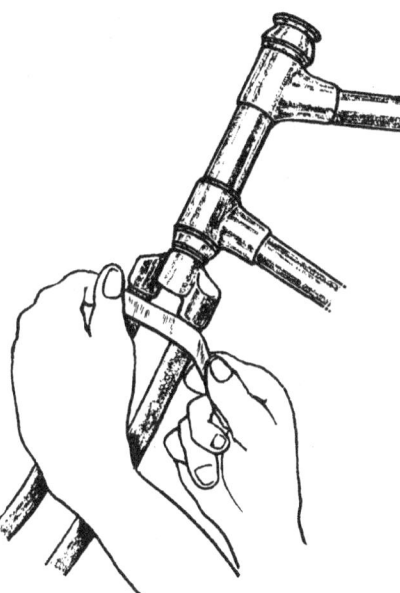

Fig. 16.—After scraping off as much enamel as possible with the knife, remove the rest with strips of emery cloth.

bad state a priming coat of stopper will be an advantage.

Brushes.
For the main part of the work use a 1-inch brush with fairly long, soft bristles, set in vulcanised rubber; for the insides of the wheel forks and other small parts use a ½-inch brush.

First dismantle the Machine.
To make a good job of repainting it is advisable to remove wheels, handlebars, brake gear, mudguards, etc. There is, however, no need to remove the front forks or cranks. To facilitate working it is a good idea to fix two stout hooks in the roof of the shed in which the work is being done and suspend the machine in the air by means of two cords. The machine can be suspended at a convenient position for working.

If hooks are not practicable stretch a temporary line across the room and suspend the machine from this.

To prevent bearings from becoming clogged with dirt or paint it is a good plan to stuff pieces of rag or paper into them (see Fig. 15).

How to remove Old Enamel.
To produce a lasting and satisfactory job the old enamel should be stripped right off. This can be done by scraping with an old knife as shown in Fig. 14. Emery paper torn into convenient strips should be used for inaccessible places. When as much of the old enamel as possible has been removed by this method give a final rub over the whole machine with fine

miles. After removing, it should be coiled into a flat spiral and placed in a bath of paraffin for a few hours. Remove any hard deposit such as grease thickened with dirt by brushing vigorously with a wire or bristle brush.

Take the chain out of the paraffin, wipe dry with a cloth and hang up for an hour of two to allow any paraffin that has found its way between the rollers and their pins to drain out. Wipe the chain again and place in a tin dish containing melted gear grease, tallow, or best of all, graphite grease. The chain should be moved about so as to work the liquid lubricant into the joints.

Remove from the bath and wipe lightly with a cloth before replacing on the machine.

ADJUSTING THE HUBS
Front Hub.
The hubs are adjusted by means of a nut on the left-hand side of the machine. A cone spanner is required for this adjustment. First loosen the spindle nut on the left-hand side and insert the large end of the cone spanner on to the flats of the cone between the hub and the cone. Screw up sufficiently to take up any wear that has taken place, but not so tightly that the wheel cannot run freely.

Fig. 17.—Use a 1-inch brush when applying the lacquer to the main parts of the frame.

Apply lacquer liberally and do not spend too much time on brushing, or brush marks may appear.

1009

emery paper. Be specially careful to remove all rust.

Cleaning the Mudguards.

First knock out the accumulation of mud from the inside and wash down with water. A curved piece of wood to fit the inside of the mudguard will be found useful for holding the emery paper when rubbing the inside. As this part of the mudguard gets whatever wet and dirt there is going, it is important to get a good lasting enamel finish on it.

Remove Oil and Grease with Petrol or Turpentine.

The next step is to remove all traces of oil, grease and dust and this is best done by wiping over with dry cotton rags and then with rags soaked in petrol or turpentine. The machine will then be ready to start lacquering.

Applying the Undercoat.

Start by painting the frame first, then the insides of the mudguards, while the first coat of the frame is drying. It is advisable to put one or two extra undercoats on the underside of the mudguards and on the insides of the wheel forks. Small parts such as lamp brackets, etc., can be hung up on wires to dry after painting.

The Finishing Coats.

The lacquer should be applied liberally, using several sweeps of the brush. Avoid spending too much time on brushing as the cellulose lacquer sets very quickly and brush marks may appear.

Using Enamel instead of Lacquer.

A good hard drying oil enamel can be used instead of cellulose lacquer if desired. It should be an enamel specially prepared for metal finishing. As enamel takes about twenty-four hours to set, it should be applied in a warm room as free from dust as possible. There is no fear of spoiling the surface if brushed several times, but once a portion of the metal has been dealt with it should not be brushed again while wet. Allow at least two days between coats to ensure the formation of a hard surface.

Lining Transfers.

The appearance of the machine will be considerably enhanced by lining transfers, which are added after the final coat has dried. They are put on with gold size or a size made up of a solution of Croid glue, one part glue to ten parts water. Gold-backed transfers give the most satisfactory results. The transfer itself is mounted on thin semi-transparent paper and has a thick protective backing paper. This protecting paper has to be pulled off the thin paper before use.

The size should be applied to the faced side of the transfer which is then applied to the frame and pressed on firmly with a rubber squeegee. When perfectly dry, wet the back of the transfer with a sponge and pull the paper off. The lining is then allowed to become quite dry before the machine is handled.

The transfers can be protected by a thin coat of clear cellulose applied about twenty-four hours after they have been put on.

AN EASY LIFTER FOR A TOOL-BOX TRAY

LIGHTLY constructed tool box and drawer trays are very difficult to handle, even when moderately filled with tools. Finger-holes drilled through the ends are of but little value due to the thinness of the average drawer stock.

Metal finger-grips or handles are also not a practical thing to put on the inside of a tray.

Procure a number of soft rubber heel tips and fasten them in place with small

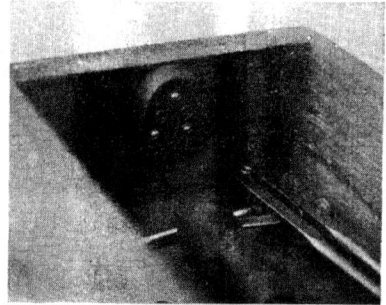

THE TOOL-BOX TRAY LIFTER.

screws as shown. The screw heads go down into the rubber, but hold it securely, not going into the wood far enough to penetrate it. These make a very good grip for the fingers in the usual and natural position the hand reaches down to lift out the tray. The soft rubber piece is thin, takes up but little tray room, and will not scratch or mar anything coming in contact with it.

REPAIRING WELLINGTON BOOTS

THE ordinary rubber-pattern Wellington boots are made from rubber to which suitable pigments and fillers have been added, by the vulcanisation process, whereby the relatively soft raw rubber and its other ingredients are subjected to the action of heat until they are converted into the hard shiny material of the finished boot. Special moulds and cores are used for this work.

When a boot of this type becomes damaged or worn there is no other satisfactory method of repair than that of re-vulcanising the damaged place. The latter is first cleaned thoroughly with sand-paper and then wiped over with benzine; the edges around the damaged place should also be included in this cleaning process.

Next the damaged surface should be covered with sufficient raw rubber. or—as it is often termed, *rubber dough*—to make up for rather more than the broken away portion A piece of oiled cloth or paper (tracing linen will do excellently) is placed right over the raw rubber and that part of the boot to be repaired is placed in the vulcaniser press.

The heat is then turned on for about ten to fifteen minutes, and ten minutes after it has been turned off again the boot can be taken out of the press. It will then be found that the raw rubber has become vulcanised solid with the material of the boot. An ordinary motor car tyre of vulcaniser is very satisfactory for this purpose. For small repairs the portable vulcaniser, known as the "Jiffy," made by Messrs. Harvey, Frost, Ltd., Great Portland Street, London, W.1, will be found most useful. This vulcaniser is very cheap to purchase, and uses as the source of vulcanising heat a small white tabloid which is placed in a cup arranged over the top of the clamp, or screw press supplied. Upon igniting the tabloid with a match it burns away and thus supplies the necessary heat required. It can be used for patches up to about one square inch area.

An Ordinary Rubber Solution is seldom satisfactory for the purpose.

Repairs made with ordinary rubber solution are seldom satisfactory for Wellington boots, although small holes can be patched with cycle or motor patches with this solution.

When the damage is serious, e.g., the heel breaking away from the upper, vulcanising is the only satisfactory method. In such cases one has to weigh up the cost of the repair against that of a new pair of boots, for, unless one is able to do the vulcanising oneself, or can persuade the local garage to undertake this work, the repair may be as expensive as the cost of new boots.

Constructing a Medical Coil

The electrical appliance described below provides a strong high frequency current so useful for the treatment and relief of such disorders as partial paralysis, rheumatism, and certain joint diseases. It is not a toy but capable of really serious work, and its strength compares very favourably with commercially made sets.

Materials required.

The necessary raw material is quite modest and need cost only a few shillings.

1 oz. copper wire, No. 24 D.C.C.
4 oz. copper wire, No. 34 D.C.C.
2 oz. annealed iron wire, No. 22.
1 foot copper tube, ⅜-inch bore.
6 inch brass rod, ¼ inch diameter.
2 × 1 inch spring brass gauge No. 24.
4 terminals and 2 screws 4 B.A.
1 sq. foot hardwood, ¼ inch thick.
½ sq. foot of 3-ply.
6 inches of cotton tape.
A supply of paraffin wax and "Croid Aero Glue."

Making the Bobbin.

Take a length of the copper tube and thinly coat the outside with a film of paraffin wax and then cut a strip of brown paper 3½ inches wide, sufficiently long to wind round the tube *four* times. Now coat this strip of paper very evenly with glue, preferably "Croid Aero," and twist it round the copper forming a paper tube; the wax will prevent it sticking to the metal. When dry slide off the paper tube, which will now be as hard as wood. Two circular ply ends are then glued on as shown in Fig. 2; leave a little of the tube projecting right through the centre hole in the ends, then, when dry, trim off flush.

Winding the Primary.

Take the completed bobbin and wind *two* layers of the No. 24 D.C.C. wire as evenly as possible and bring the ends through small holes bored in the ply discs, leaving several inches free for connecting up later. This primary winding should now be covered with a double wrapping of thin paper soaked in paraffin wax; the edge of this paper which insulates the primary from the secondary can easily be secured by running a warm piece of iron along the joint to temporarily melt the wax.

The Secondary Winding.

Instead of the No. 34 D.C.C. wire mentioned above silk-covered or enamelled wire can be used with advantage, but of course this will be more expensive. This fine wire forming the secondary can be wound on by hand or a simple bobbin winder can be fitted up as shown in Fig. 4; this consists of a spindle on which is cut a thread, the bobbin is clamped to this and the whole is supported on two wooden uprights. A handle riveted to the spindle facilitates rapid turning, while the reel of wire is best held on a rod fixed horizontally in a vice. The fine wire must be wound on as evenly as thread on a reel, sixteen layers in all are required. Between every two layers slip in a strip of waxed tissue paper sufficiently long to just lap, then stick the edges with a touch of shellac varnish and proceed to wind on top of this. The ends of the secondary should be soldered to short lengths of No. 24 wire; these being strong can be brought through the bobbin for connecting up later. Cover the completed coil with a thin piece of celluloid wound round and cemented along the joint with amyl acetate; a length of film negative does admirably for this.

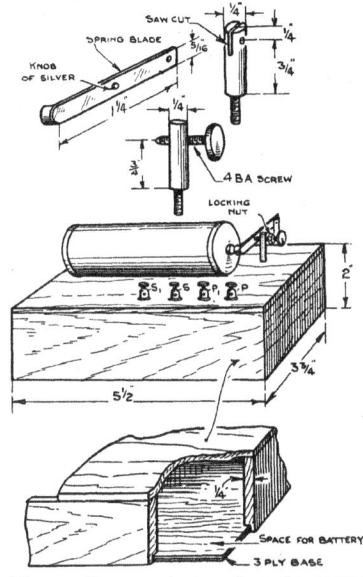

Fig. 1.—Details of the Coil Assembly.

Showing also details of the contact breaker for which two pillars of ¼-inch brass rod are required, one to carry the spring armature blade and the other for the contact screw.

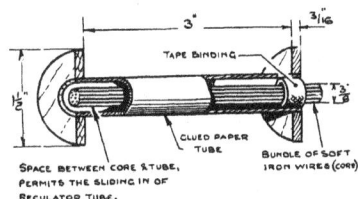

Fig. 2.—How the Core is Held in Position inside the Bobbin Tube.

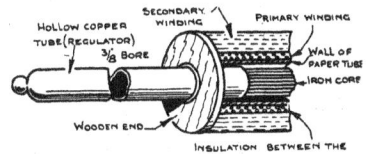

Fig. 3.—Details of the Regulator Tube.

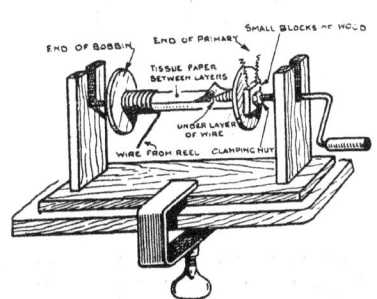

Fig. 4.—A Simply Made Bobbin Winder Suitable for Winding all Types and Sizes of Bobbins.

The Iron Core.

Take the annealed iron wire and cut it into lengths which will reach the whole way through the bobbin and project ¼ inch beyond at one end. Straighten them and make a bundle that will fit freely inside a piece of the copper tube. Bind the ends together temporarily with string, then float a coat of solder over the ends to hold the strands together permanently, afterwards removing the twine. Examine the sectional sketch in Fig. 2 and you will see how the core is held in position inside the bobbin tube. A length of ordinary cotton tape, ½ inch wide, is coated with glue and tightly bound round the wire core until it fits the hole in the bobbin. Smear the tape with adhesive and push it into place; while this is drying slip a length of the copper tube over the other end, this holds it centrally until the glue has set. Thus a channel will be left round the core permitting the sliding in and out of the regulator tube. Note that the core is taped on the end which projects beyond the bobbin.

The Regulator Tube.

Cut off a piece of copper tube long enough to slide in over the core and leave a little projecting. Block the end with a disc of sheet brass and solder on a knob or ring which can easily be grasped when pulling the regulator out (see Fig. 3).

The Contact Breaker.

Details of this are shown in the sketch (Fig. 1). Two pillars of ¼-inch brass rod are required, one to carry the spring armature blade and the other for the contact screw. The lower ends of these pillars are turned or filed down and a 4 B.A. thread cut on each; this enables them to be bolted through the top of the mounting box. The blade may be a thin steel spring or a piece of tempered brass; when using the former be careful when soldering on the armature not to "draw" the temper of the metal; for this reason perhaps a piece of spring brass is better. The fixed end of the blade is secured in a saw cut at the top of the pillar by a small rivet. The contact pillar has a $\frac{7}{64}$-inch hole bored through it and this is tapped out 4 B.A. to accommodate the contact screw. This screw is best tipped with platinum, but a piece of silver does quite well; take a small clipping from a coin if no other source is available and solder on a piece to the end of the screw; a blob should also be attached to the blade just where it makes contact.

Assembling the Coil.

Make a hardwood case as shown in Fig. 1; the sides are mitred at the corners, the top is glued and pinned in place, while the ply base fits into a rebate along the lower edge of the side pieces. Mount the coil on the top of the box, then bolt the contact breaker in position, leaving $\frac{1}{4}$-inch space between the armature and the core. Then fit four terminals in a row near the edge, as shown in Fig. 1.

Wiring-up.

The ends of the secondary winding are connected to the terminals marked S and S_1. One end of the primary is secured to the base of the contact pillar while the other end runs to the terminal P_1. A short wire connects the armature pillar to the terminal P, and a small link is fastened between S and P_1. A small $4\frac{1}{2}$-volt dry battery is housed in the box and leads from the terminals are connected to the base of P and P_1; an external battery can be used when desired by joining up to the terminals on the top of the box (see Fig. 5).

The Condenser.

Although a condenser is not absolutely necessary, it improves efficiency and greatly reduces sparking at the points; Fig. 6 shows a serviceable little condenser that can be made at home. It consists of small sheets of tinfoil cut with projecting tongues, these are sandwiched between layers of waxed tissue paper; note that the sheets of foil are slightly smaller than the insulating paper. Twelve sheets of foil, 3×4 inches, will be sufficient; six are connected up to one lead and the remainder to a second, each alternate piece being attached to the same conductor.

The sheets of the condenser are held tightly between two pieces of cardboard clipped together. The sheets of foil are best connected across the contact breaker by holding the foil ends between the jaws of two crocodile grips to which wires have been soldered. Provided it is electrically sound a disused wireless condenser of $\frac{1}{2}$ to 1 mfd. can be used in place of the one described above.

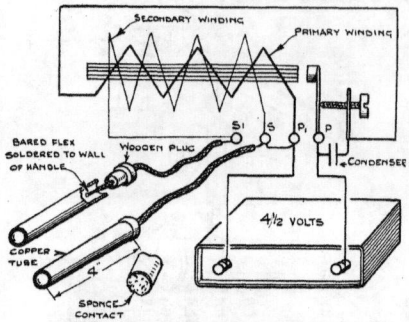

Fig. 5.—The Wiring Diagram.

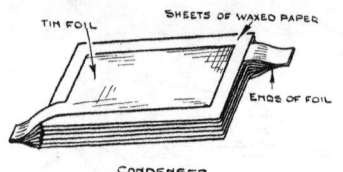

Fig. 6.—A Condenser improves Efficiency and reduces Sparking at the Points.

The Handles.

These are short lengths of copper tube fitted with wooden plugs at one end. A length of flex is brought through the centre of the wood and the bared ends are soldered to the inside of the tube.

Useful Accessories.

In addition to the handles several accessories are wanted, including a comb contact and a massage pad.

The comb is simply a metal one such as can be purchased in most shops which sell toilet requisites. This is then mounted in a wooden handle so that the operator's hand is insulated from the circuit; a length of flex is soldered to the metal back and this is attached to the coil when required (see Fig. 7).

A massage pad is made something

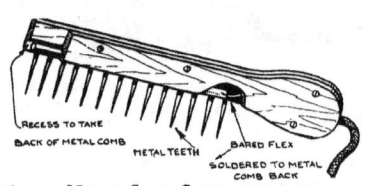

Fig. 7.—Metal Comb Contact for applying Current to the Hair.

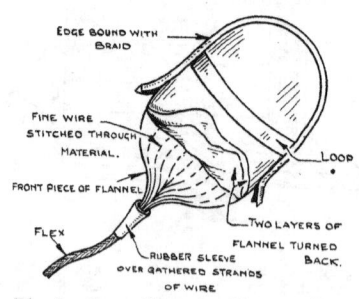

Fig. 8.—Back View of Massage Pad.

like an iron holder; several thicknesses of flannel are stitched together and a loop runs across the back to grip the hand. Darn into the outer layer of flannel a number of strands of very fine wire, the ends of which are collected up and soldered to a lead from the coil (see Fig. 8).

How to use the Coil.

To start the coil screw up the contact until the point presses against the blade, then gently tap the armature, when it will commence vibrating; adjust the circuit breaker to obtain the highest possible frequency. When the handles are connected to the terminals P and P_1 only a feeble current from the primary is felt; with the leads attached to S and S_1 the full force of the secondary is obtained, while with the wires on terminals S_1 and P the combined strength of both circuits is available. When applying the current let the patient grasp the handles one in each hand, then with the regulator pushed right *in* start the coil, when a weak current will be felt; gradually pull *out* the tube and the strength will increase rapidly until when it is fully withdrawn the power will be as much as most persons can stand.

Using the Comb.

Attach a handle to one terminal and the comb to the other, into the open end of the former press a small piece of moist sponge. Now grasp the handle with a gloved hand and make contact on the scalp with the piece of sponge, then proceed to comb the hair with the metal comb, taking care to hold it by means of the wooden handle; in this way the current will be applied to the hair without the patient feeling any discomfort.

The Massage Pad.

This is used in much the same manner as the comb. Contact is made on the limb with the little piece of sponge projecting from the handle, the skin is then gently massaged with the pad which is held in the other hand. In this way the current is localised to the area between the sponge and the pad, no effects being felt in any other part of the body; this is especially useful when treating a limb joint.

Final Hints.

Applications should be progressive and regular, commencing with a few minutes per day and gradually increasing the length of time of each successive treatment. The strength of the current must at first be the minimum and should be increased as the patient becomes stronger.

Take care to keep the points of the contact breaker clean, and when using the internal battery housed in the case always screw back the contact so that it does not touch the blade.

A Modern-type Portable Receiver

THE receiver illustrated in Fig. 1 has been designed for the latest type valves and components. With its special features of tone compensation and Class "B" output with moving-coil loud speaker, its reproduction in quality and volume is comparable with an all-mains receiver.

Class "B" Amplification.

This form of output is particularly suitable for a portable receiver owing to its economy in high tension current and the large signal output. The economy in current is due to the fact that, apart from a small idle current, the drain from the battery is proportional to the strength of the signal.

The Cabinet.

Although the majority of constructors may decide to purchase the cabinet ready made, dimensioned drawings are given in Fig. 2. Birch-faced plywood of ⅜-inch thickness can be stained and polished to resemble walnut very closely. Start by cutting the sides to the measurements given, and rebate the edges. The inside edge of the bottom section is grooved, as shown in the small drawing (Fig. 2) to accommodate the back, while the underside of the top is rebated to form a stop.

The easiest way to cut the loud speaker frets and the panel opening is to use a fret-saw, truing up the edges afterwards with sandpaper wrapped round a flat file. The top, bottom and sides are sufficiently thick to allow for rebating at the corners, but the front, of 3/16 inch thickness, is pinned and glued.

Cut the overlays to conform to the design, and glue them in position before securing the front. It is not necessary to frame the back if a straight piece of ⅜-inch plywood is used. The only operation is to rebate the bottom edge to fit the grooving.

The Frame.

Outside measurements are given in the illustration of the frame in Fig. 3. Simple butt joints are used, strengthened with fillets. Brads must be knocked well home to avoid interference with the frame windings. Round off the sharp corners where the wire is to be placed.

The Polished Panel and the Baseboard.

The baseboard is of 5-ply of ⅜ inch thickness, measuring 12½ inches bare, and 7⅛ inches wide. The panel, if not obtained in the correct size, is cut to the measurements given in Fig. 3.

The escutcheon and holes for the controls are most conveniently cut

Fig. 1.—The Completed Receiver.

with a fret-saw. A template is provided with the gang condenser for locating the escutcheon hole. Screw the panel to the front edge of the baseboard, but remove it again while fitting the components.

How to Mount the Components.

Screw the valve-holders, transformers and other parts to the chassis baseboard approximately in the positions shown in the panel and baseboard layout in Fig. 4.

Care must be taken in fixing the gang condenser in the correct position. The two holes for the front fixing brackets should be 5/16 inch from the front edge of the baseboard and equidistant from the centre. Three No. 6 B.A. countersunk screws are used for bolting the condenser. The aerial trimmer will be inaccessible when the panel is fitted, so that a wire should be connected to it and joined to the terminal of the front set of fixed plates at the present stage.

List of Materials for Class "B" Portable Receiver.

Cabinet, frame, panel and baseboard, etc. (Peto-Scott, Ltd.). (If home-constructed, see drawings.)
Loud Speaker, Rola FR5.PM 32, permanent magnet moving coil (British Rola Co. Ltd.).
Valve Holders : 1 Benjamin 7-pin ; 3 Benjamin Clearer Tone (Benjamin Electric Ltd.).
Twin Gang Condenser with Trimmers, Drive and Escutcheon (Peto-Scott Ltd.).
Iron-cored H.F. Transformer (Telsen Electric Co. Ltd.).
L.F. Transformer, 4 : 1, Model TOCO (Multitone Electric Co. Ltd.).
Driver Transformer, 1·5 : 1, Model BEPU (Multitone Electric Co. Ltd.).
Graded Potentiometer (Multitone Electric Co. Ltd.).
5-way Rotary Switch (Ormond Engineering Co. Ltd.).
Rotorohm, Volume Control and Reaction Condenser (Rotor Electric Ltd.).
1 mfd. Paper Condenser (Telegraph Condenser Co. Ltd.).
Mica Condenser, Type 665, 0·0002 mfd. (Dubilier Condenser Co. Ltd.).
3 Tubular Paper Condensers, 0·01 mfd. (Radio Resistor Co.).
3 Tubular Paper Condensers, 0·1 mfd. (Radio Resistor Co.).
1 Tubular Paper Condenser, 0·25 mfd. (Radio Resistor Co.).
1 Tubular Paper Condenser, 0·0002 mfd. (Radio Resistor Co.).
250 ohm Resistance (1 watt) (Radio Resistor Co.).
2 5,000 ohm Resistance (1 watt) (Radio Resistor Co.).
1 20,000 ohm Resistance (1 watt) (Radio Resistor Co.).
100,000 ohm Resistance (1 watt) (Radio Resistor Co.).
2 megohm Resistance (1 watt) (Radio Resistor Co.).
Fibre Panel, 5⅜ × 2 × 1/16 inches.
Fibre Backing Piece, 5⅜ × 3⅛ × 1/16 inches.
2 feet 1 mm. Insulated Sleeving (Lewcos).
30 inches Shielded Insulated Tubing (Lewcos).
Hank Glazite Wire (Lewcos).
Hank of Frame Aerial Wire (100 feet) (Lewcos).
64 yards 27/42 Enamelled Silk Wire (Lewcos).
6 feet Rubber Flex Wire.
Insulating Tape, Woodscrews, 4 B.A. Soldering Tags.
Extra Control Knob to match Rotorohm (Rotor Electric Ltd.).
2 Aluminium Brackets for G.B. Battery.
1 Aluminium Bracket for Tone Control Potentiometer.
2 6 B.A. Terminal Nuts and Screws.
5 Wander Plugs.
2 Spade Terminals for L.T. Battery.
Belling-Lee Safety Fuse Wander Plug, "Wanderfuse."
Turntable (Peto-Scott Ltd.).
Valves : Osram VS24 ; HL2 ; LP2 ; B21.
L.T. Accumulator, 20 Actual Amp. Hour Type TJT40 (Jelectro Laboratories).
H.T. Battery Pertrix, 100 volt.
G.B. Battery Drydex, 9 volt.

A MODERN-TYPE PORTABLE RECEIVER

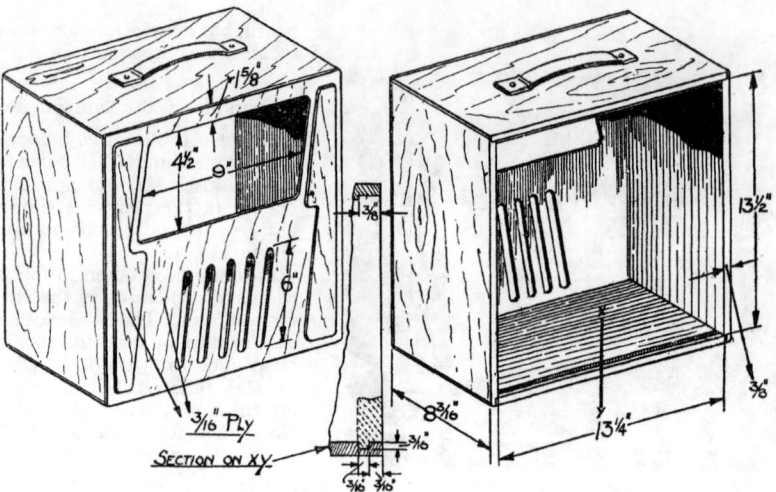

Fig. 2.—Leading Dimensions of the Cabinet.

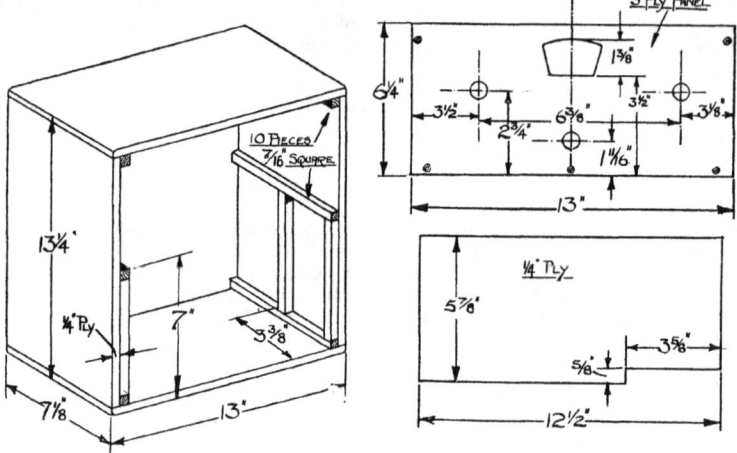

Fig. 3.—Interior Details and Dimensions of Polished Panel, Frame and Partition.

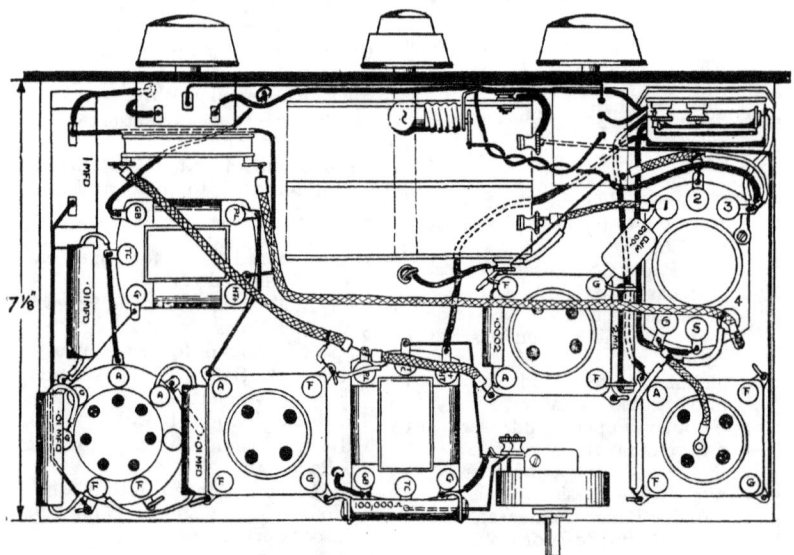

Fig. 4.—The Baseboard and Panel Lay-out.
The complete wiring to the switch is shown in Fig. 13.

Fixing Resistances and Condensers.

All the tubular resistances and condensers which are not assembled on the decoupling panel are wired from point to point by means of their own wire ends. They can be left until the wiring stages are reached.

Further Assembly.

The right-angle bracket for the support of the Multitone potentiometer is cut from a piece of scrap brass or stout aluminium, and is fixed with its spindle projecting over the edge of the baseboard. Before it is fixed, cut a slot in the end of the spindle sufficiently wide to take the edge of a sixpenny piece. Clamp the spindle vertically in a vice by means of a piece of wood on each side, and cut the slot centrally across the spindle end, using two hacksaw blades in the frame to increase the width. Bracket measurements are not important, because the hole in the back of the cabinet through which the spindle protrudes is located afterwards.

Fig. 6 shows that the grid bias battery is fixed by substantial aluminium brackets at one end of the underside of the baseboard. The brackets should be $\frac{1}{2}$ inch away from the shorter edge of the latter in order not to foul the fillets on the frame on which the baseboard rests. The battery is arranged on the L.F. side of the chassis.

Now Fix Front Panel in Position.

Now that all baseboard components are fixed, the front panel can be screwed into position. Mount the Rotorohm and the wavechange-filament switch securely with substantial washers behind the fixing nuts. The former may be supplied with a spindle longer than required. Its length can be reduced to suit the knob and the thickness of the panel. It is advisable to tighten the grub screw of each control knob on to a flat filed on the control spindle. The position of the flat must be arranged so that the knob pointer is in the correct position. The polished panel may be scratched unless the precaution shown in Fig. 7 is adopted.

Owing to the thinness of the panel, the brass strip for fixing the scale escutcheon must be bent "C" shape, as shown in Fig. 5.

Making the Decoupling Panel.

Cut the fibre panel to the sizes given in Fig. 8B, and drill the $\frac{1}{16}$-inch diameter holes shown in this drawing. The wire ends of each resistance and condenser are folded over, so that they lie side by side against the component. Now give a sharp right-angle set to the wires, at the same distance from each end, so that they extend outwards at the correct spacing to enter the holes. The method of mounting is shown in Fig. 9, where a resistance is being

A MODERN-TYPE PORTABLE RECEIVER

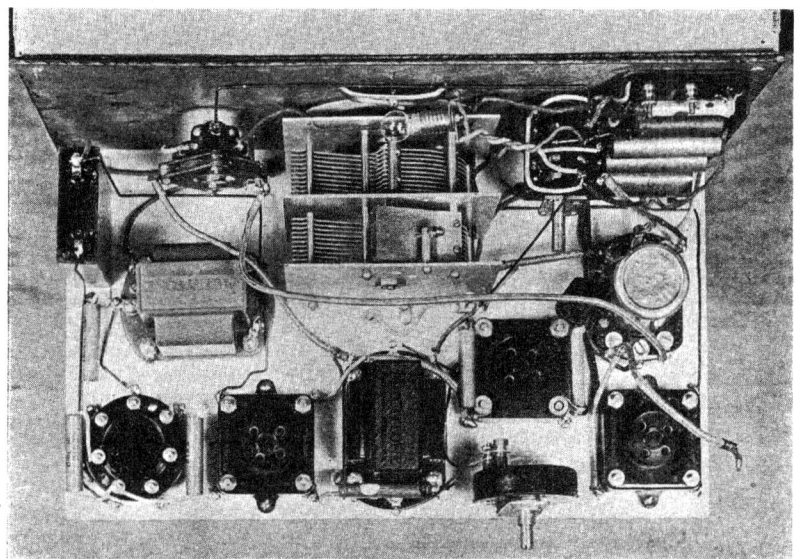

*Fig. 5.—*Plan View of Completed Wiring.
Note that the tone control potentiometer projects over the edge of the baseboard.

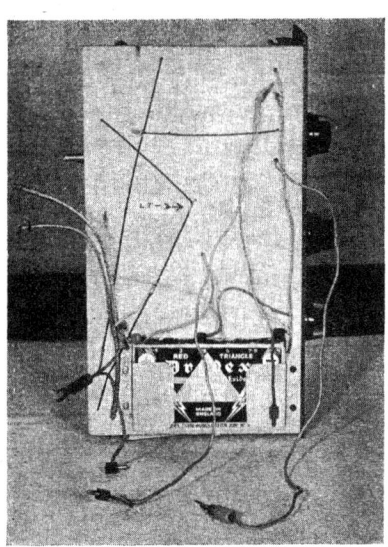

*Fig. 6.—*The Underside of the Baseboard, showing Filament Wiring, Grid Bias Battery and Leads.

pushed into position. When the resistance is close against the fibre, the wires extending at the back are bent outwards and folded over the edge of the panel. Any projecting wire ends are cut off close to the resistance.

The order of the decoupling units and the wiring is shown in Fig. 8c. In this illustration the wires are shown outside the panel, for the sake of clearness. When wiring up, a common bus-bar can be used running from top to bottom to link up all the H.T. — connections. Two No. 6 B.A. terminals are screwed to the top edge of the panel for connection of the end of the medium wave frame (the inside terminal) and the end of the long wave frame. The third hole is for the screw which fixes the fibre to the chassis panel. Rubber-covered leads are used for H.T.+1, and H.T.+2 connections, these wires passing through holes in the baseboard at the foot of the decoupling panel. They are clearly seen in Figs. 5 and 6.

The Fibre Cover.

Dimensions are given in Fig. 8D of a fibre cover into which the decoupling panel is fitted when the latter is screwed to the chassis. The cover is wider than the panel, the sides being scored with a sharp penknife from top to bottom as shown by the dotted lines and bent at right angles to form protective sides. At the top the sides are cut on the slant to allow easy access to the two frame terminals.

The Wiring of the Chassis.

Drill a $\frac{1}{16}$-inch hole adjacent to each filament tag as these wires are taken underneath the baseboard. Particular care must be taken to ensure that the L.T.— wire connects to the correct filament tag of the H.F. valve-holder. The metallic coating of a battery valve is always connected to the filament socket of the valve-holder on the right

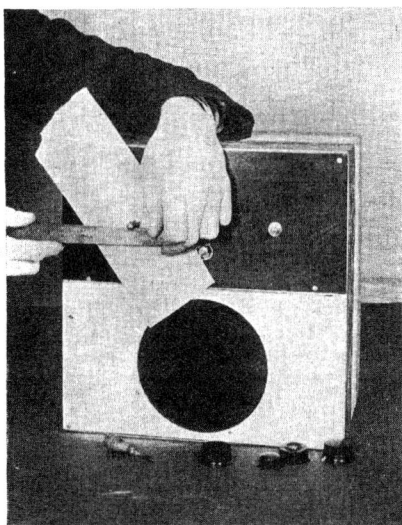

*Fig. 7.—*Place a piece of Cardboard behind each Control Spindle while Filing the Flats.

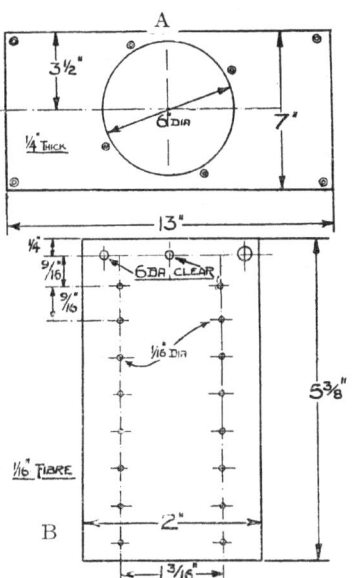

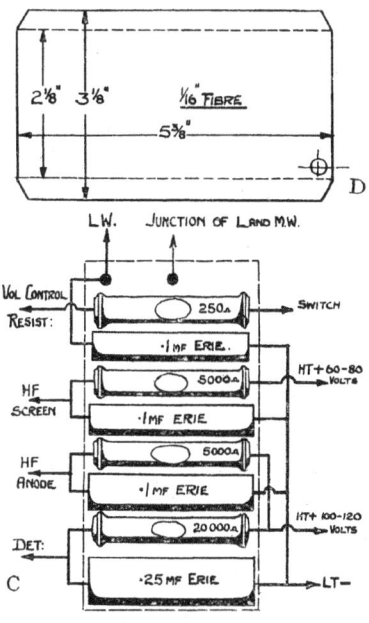

*Fig. 8.—*Details of Loud Speaker Board and Decoupling Panel.
A, measurements of loud speaker board; B, measurements of decoupling panel; C, simple wiring of decoupling panel; D, the fibre backing piece is bent at the dotted lines.

A MODERN-TYPE PORTABLE RECEIVER

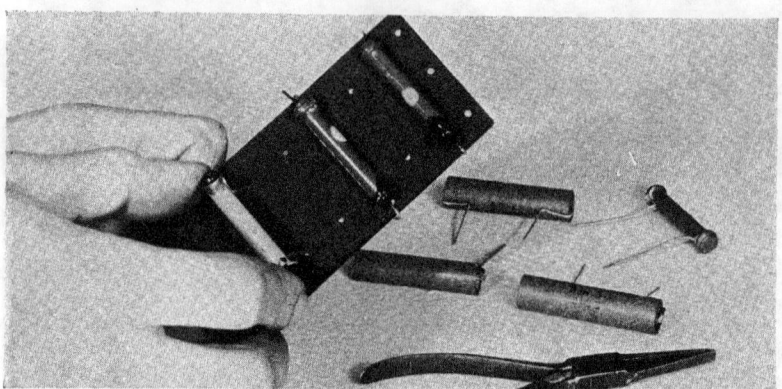

Fig. 9.—The various Resistances and Condensers are Assembled in the order given at C in Fig. 8.

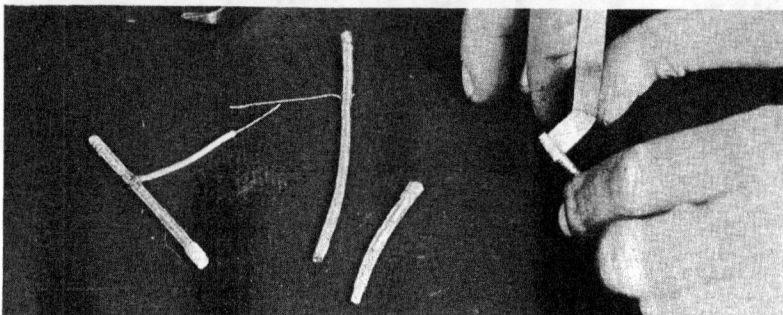

Fig. 10.—The different Stages in making the Screened Leads.

Fig. 11.—To keep the Baseboard clear of Splutterings when Soldering, cut a slot in a small visiting card and push the card under the wire.

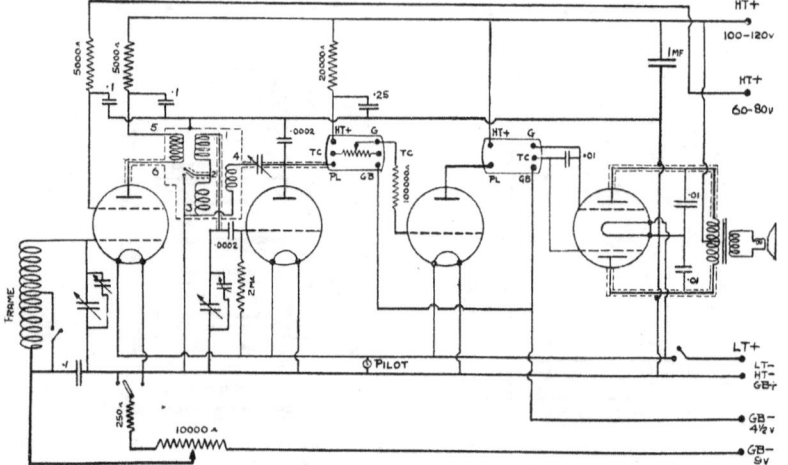

Fig. 12.—The Theoretical Circuit Diagram.

side of the grid and anode sockets when viewed from the top. If these filament wires were reversed and the flexible H.F. anode lead happened to touch the valve coating, then the full high tension circuit would be completed through the valve filaments, provided the L.T. switch was "off."

In Fig. 4 the correct filament tag for L.T.— and H.T.— is that nearest to the tone control potentiometer. This can be checked by a reference to the illustration of the underside of the baseboard wiring (Fig. 6), where the wire in question runs from the filament tag nearest the potentiometer direct to the frame of the ganged condenser. The earthing tag on the latter connects by a flexible rubber lead to G.B.+, H.T.— and L.T.—. This method of wiring should be closely followed to ensure that the H.F. return leads are at the lowest potential.

The following connections will simplify the wiring of the tone control potentiometer:—

Pot. terminal
No.
1 joins the L.F. transformer terminal TC between G and GB.
2 joins the L.F. transformer terminal G and 100,000 ohm. resis.
3 joins the L.F. transformer terminal TC between PL and HT.

Making the Screened Leads.

Certain wires in the H.F. coupling circuit are screened to prevent interaction with the frame and other wires preceding the H.F. valve. The screened wires are shown between dotted lines in the theoretical circuit diagram, where the screened H.F. transformer is also indicated in the same manner.

Eight screened leads are required, two of which are underneath the baseboard, their object being to prevent the high-pitched whistle due to low-frequency reaction. The following table gives the positions of these leads in point to point wiring:—

1. H.F. transformer, terminal No. 2 connects to wave-change switch.
2. H.F. transformer, terminal No. 1 connects to fixed plates of rear section of gang condenser.
3. H.F. transformer, terminal No. 4 connects to moving plates of reaction condenser.
4. H.F. transformer, terminal No. 6 connects to anode of H.F. valve.
5. L.F. transformer, terminal PL connects to fixed plates of reaction condenser.
6. L.F. transformer, terminal PL connects to anode of detector.
7. Anode of Class "B" valve-holder to loud speaker.
8. Anode of Class "B" valve-holder to loud speaker.

The method of making the screened leads is shown in Fig. 10. Having cut the shielded tubing to the required lengths, each end of the metallic braiding is pushed back until about ¼ inch of insulated sleeving projects. Taking care that there are no odd strands of the braiding projecting, the ends are tightly bound with insulating tape to come flush with the outer ends of the insulated sleeving. The tape is finally wiped round with "Durofix" or other suitable solution to prevent the tape from unwinding in course of time. The braiding is earthed in every instance to the nearest L.T. negative connection by means of tinned wire, about No. 22 S.W.G., wrapped round the braiding and soldered. When soldering these joints, take care not to overheat the braiding. If the sleeving is allowed to go black and carbonise, the insulation will be impaired. The trouble is indicated by crackling noises in the receiver, especially if the affected wires are moved. Do not allow screened lead No. 3 to make intermittent contact with the back plate of the gang condenser, as this may cause a crackle.

A useful hint which will prevent the discoloration of the baseboard when soldering to the valve-holder tags, is shown in Fig. 11. A small visiting card is cut to form a slot about 1/16 inch wide and ½ inch long. By means of the slot, the card can be pushed well under the wire and tag to be soldered. Any splutterings of resin or soldering compound will fall on the card and keep the baseboard clean.

Wiring to the Switch.

The method of breaking the grid bias circuit when the set is not in use has been chosen because it simplifies the wiring. A fixed resistance of 250 ohms is included in this potentiometer to keep the H.F. grid at a certain minimum negative voltage. As this resistance is adjacent to the switch, the grid bias battery is dis-

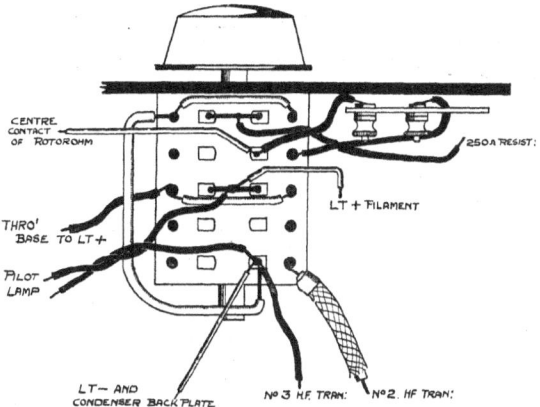

Fig. 13.—A Five-way Switch helps to avoid congesting the Switch Wiring.

connected by breaking contact between the 250 ohms resistance and L.T. negative. Fig. 13 shows the connections to the switch from which

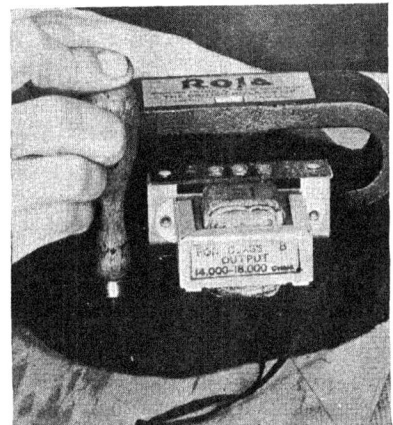

Fig. 14.—Marking the Positions for the Loud Speaker Fixing Holes with a Bradawl.

flexible leads to the pilot lamp are taken. Rubber-covered battery leads should be knotted just above the base-

board so that the strain of pulling will not fall upon a soldered joint. The screened loud speaker leads are screwed under a metal clip underneath the baseboard to take the strain off the valve-holder connections.

Mounting the Loud Speaker.

The dimensions of the loud speaker board are taken from Fig. 8A. The speaker should not be removed from the linen bag except for marking the positions for the 6 B.A. fixing screws through the holes in the rim of the speaker. This operation is shown in Fig. 14. Fix the speaker so that the magnets are on the slant, in order to clear the underside of the chassis and the bottom of the frame. If the frame and the chassis supporting fillets are correct to drawings, there should be no trouble in fitting the speaker. There is no harm in cutting away the inside bottom edge of the frame to make a little more room if this is necessary. The speaker should be arranged with the output transformer on the left as seen from the back. This will shorten the leads to the output valve.

Winding the Frame.

Screw the speaker board to the frame before winding, in order to strengthen the assembly. The long wave has forty-four turns of No. 27/42 enamelled wire with silk covering. Great care must be taken to ensure that good electrical contact is made with each strand. To ensure this, carefully scrape away the enamel at the ends for a distance of at least 2 inches. Then twist the strands together again with the fingers, and remove any insulation which remains. Solder the strands together for the whole length mentioned.

A convenient method of staging the frame winding process is seen in Fig. 15.

Fig. 15.—Stretch the Wire tightly at each Corner before turning over the Frame for the next Winding.

Fig. 16.—Tack a Sheet of Cardboard to the Frame Base to protect the Windings.

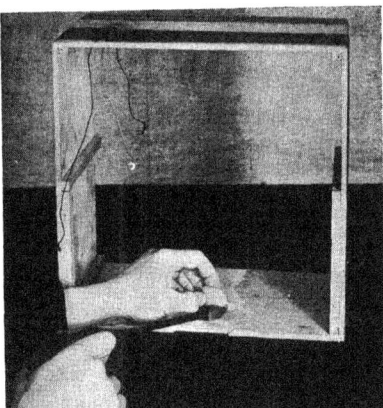

Fig. 17.—Impregnating the Bottom of the Frame as a Protection from Spilled Acid.

A MODERN-TYPE PORTABLE RECEIVER

Fig. 18.—Tilt the Chassis up on the Right so that the Grid Bias Battery will clear the Speaker Board.

Fig. 19.—The Frame Connections are made just before the Chassis Panel is Closed.

Fig. 20.—The Final Assembly ready to be fitted in the Cabinet.

In the case of the medium wave, the hank of frame aerial wire is first wound on to an empty reel. The latter is shown supported by a screw-driver driven into a piece of wood clamped to the bench. A spring is arranged under the handle of the screw-driver to prevent the reel from spinning round too easily. The extreme back of the long wave winding starts anti-clockwise as seen with the speaker board in front, so that when the two inside ends are joined together the total winding is all in the same direction. Note that the frame is rested upon a length of corrugated cardboard to protect the wires from injury when winding. The fourteen turns of the medium wave occupy $2\frac{1}{2}$ inches of space, which allows $\frac{3}{16}$ inch between adjacent turns. It is a good plan to measure and mark the corners of the frame before winding, in order to keep the spacing correct.

As a further protection to the frame windings a piece of cardboard is cut to the size of the base of the frame and tacked in position with small brads well away from the actual windings. This is shown in Fig. 16. The next illustration, Fig. 17, shows the inside of the bottom of the frame being impregnated with candle-wax melted with a soldering iron as a protection against spilled acid from the accumulator. Note that soldering tags with opened ends have been connected to the end of the long wave winding, and the junction of the end of the medium wave and the beginning of the long wave winding. The beginning of the medium wave winding, which is at the front of the frame, is joined later directly to the grid terminal of the H.F. valve.

Checking the Wiring.

Before fitting the chassis to the frame, check over carefully all the wiring, in particular that the aerial trimmer terminal has been joined to the front set of fixed plates of the ganged condenser. This wire may be easily overlooked.

Completing the Assembly.

Fit the chassis into the frame as shown in Fig. 18, first dropping the battery leads, and the, at present, disconnected speaker leads inside. Tilt the chassis up on the right side until the grid bias battery is clear. Just before closing up the panel, connect the centre tap of the frame and the end of the long wave winding to their appropriate terminals at the top of the decoupling panel. See Fig. 19. The chassis is to be fixed, after testing, by screwing the chassis panel to the frame, the completed assembly being shown in Fig. 20.

The Final Stages.

Connect the H.T.+ 2 lead to the centre tag of the loud speaker transformer by stripping the insulation at a convenient point. The screened anode leads connect to the tags on either side of the centre one. See that there is no possibility of the screened braiding touching any of these points of connection. It is a good plan to anchor these three leads with fine string to one of the spare holes adjacent to the tags.

Some distinction should be made between the two H.T.+ leads, either by knotting one of them or by the use of ivorine tablets. Fig. 3 gives the measurements of a partition which separates the loud speaker from the batteries. It is screwed to the fillets at the centre of the frame.

With these details completed, fit the valves. Viewed from the back, the screened grid valve is on the extreme right with the Osram H.L.2 detector next to it. The driver valve L.P.2 follows, with the Class " B " valve, a B21, on the extreme left. Connect up the batteries. The best H.F. screen voltage will be found between 60 and 80 volts.

Testing and Adjusting.

The receiver is tested and the trimmers adjusted before fitting to the cabinet. Pull out the chassis until the trimmer of the H.F. circuit at the top of the rear section of the gang condenser is accessible with a screw-driver. If the centre tap and the end of the frame must be disconnected to effect this, short temporary wires are fitted.

Tune in a signal on medium waves at about 50 degrees on the tuning scale, rotating both the main tuning control and the aerial trimmer until a maximum is reached. Note the setting of the latter. If it will not turn any more in an anti-clockwise direction, it indicates that the frame will not tune down to the wavelength of the H.F. circuit. The remedy is to increase the capacity of the H.F. trimmer so that the gang condenser will have a lower capacity to balance matters. While adjusting the H.F. trimmer, follow the signal with the aerial trimmer and the main tuning control. The latter is moved in an anti-clockwise direction as the H.F. trimmer capacity is increased. The reverse process is performed if the aerial trimmer gives loudest signals when turned fully clockwise.

As the constants of the frame differ from those of the H.F. coil, the aerial trimmer must be used when tuning to another station.

Fitting to the Cabinet.

Screw the panel back into position and slide the frame into the cabinet.

A hole must be drilled in the back to allow the adjusting spindle of the tone control potentiometer to project.

Using an Eliminator.

The receiver will operate successfully with an H.T. eliminator, but it must be capable of supplying the full load required by the Class " B " valve. Manufacturers specify which of their models are suitable for Q.P.P. or Class " B " amplification.

Uses for Inner Tubes

Discarded inner tubes of car tyres are of practically no monetary value, and many garages will be glad to give them away, yet the rubber in them is very good and can be turned to useful account in a multitude of ways.

Rings and Washers.

A single tube will provide a vast quantity of washers for all sorts of purposes. A couple of thicknesses are suitable for washers in taps, and similar small pieces of the rubber are useful for fixing underneath such articles as wireless sets to prevent them scratching polished furniture on which they are stood.

When cut into Bands.

Bands cut by slicing right across the tube are found even more generally useful. Tubes vary in width from about 4 to about 8 inches across the double thickness, so that rubber bands of these lengths, and of any desired width, can be cut off as required. Sleeve-bands are one suggested use, and another is shown in Fig. 1, which shows how well a band of about an inch wide will stretch.

Hot-water Bottle Cover.

A band of about 10 inches will make an excellent cover for a hot-water bottle. This acts quite as well as a flannel cover, and is much easier to clean. If the tube is rather a tight fit for the bottle, application of French chalk will help to slide it on, with a sort of massage movement of the hands.

A band will hold a couple of books together for carrying, and there is nothing like a collection of these bands for use in packing up articles for going away. They keep one's possessions tidy in the suit-case, and help to get everything in.

Cut into Strips.

Strips of various widths, cut along the tube, find all sorts of uses, too. A narrow strip fixed between two of wood becomes an efficient squeegee (Fig. 5) suitable for glazing photographic prints, or for cleaning windows. A still longer strip tacked behind a lath, which is then screwed to the bottom of a door, will stop the draught while bending over the carpet when the door is opened (Fig. 6). Bound round a screw it becomes a door stop (Fig. 4).

Making Rubber Washing Mop and Brush.

A wider strip, serrated into narrow thongs, and wound around the end of a stick, produces a washing-up mop that will be appreciated in the kitchen. Fastening is done with a piece of galvanised or copper wire (Fig. 2). A fairly thick piece, cut with broader tongues, can be bound into a brush for cleaning mud off the car or for many a household purpose (Fig. 3).

Strips on the Car, Door and Ladder.

Uses for short strips are innumerable. At the foot of a ladder strips tacked on will prevent slipping. A rattling door can be silenced by tacking a small strip of the tyre rubber in the frame, and so can a loose bonnet of a car. On the pedals a piece of the tube fastened on will give a grip that will be appreciated on a long run.

Tacked on under the oilstone case (Fig. 7), the rubber will prevent it sliding about on a smooth bench while in use.

As Mats.

As the tubes are from 4 to 8 inches wide " on the double," when cut on either fold they will naturally produce quite large sheets, which, although they will not al-

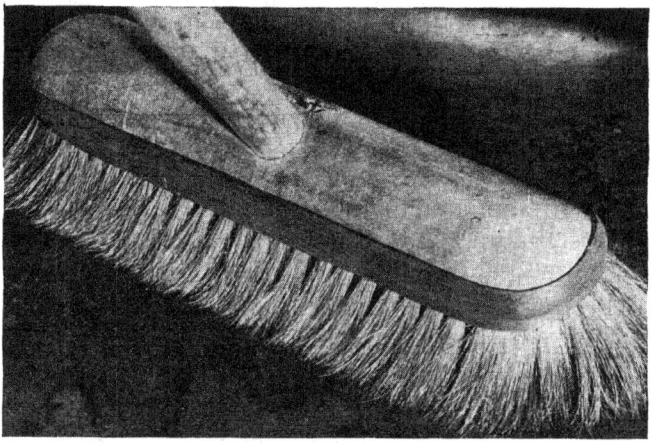

Fig. 1.—Bands cut from Old Tubes have Many Uses. This paint-guard is one of them.

Fig. 2.—An Ideal Washing-up Mop.
Make a number of cuts in a length of the rubber about 3 inches wide. Bind the rubber on to a stick with galvanised or copper wire. You will then have a washing-up mop that does not become greasy.

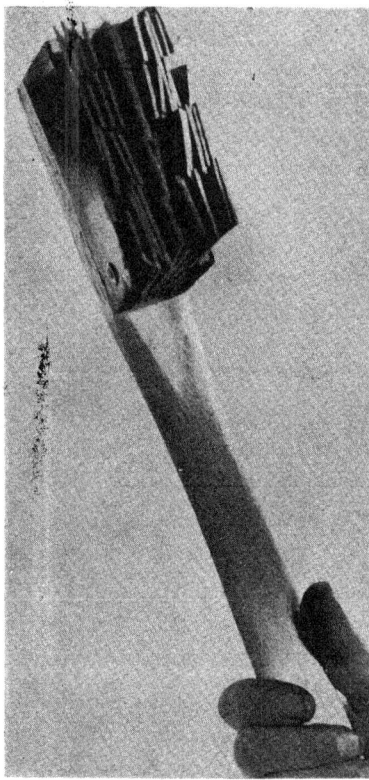

Fig. 3.—Washing-down Brush.
Slices of rubber from tubes, slit and bound together to a handle, form a strong but smooth brush which is useful to clean down the car with.

USES FOR INNER TUBES

ways lie quite flat, will answer many useful purposes. The flattest pieces seem to come when the tube is cut along the outer fold, but advantage can be taken of the dish-like shape of pieces cut on the inner fold.

Making Table Mats.

Discs cut from flat portions form quite useful mats for table use under hot plates. Quite nice shapes can be cut if the scissors are sharp. It is easy to wash off the lines of the design with soap and hot water, which also cleans up the whole tyre tube in a remarkably quick time. Further embellishment is added by punching holes with a punching tool. In using this, have a bit of cloth or card under the rubber.

Stair Treads.

Lengths of tyre tube cut along at an inch or two away from either fold are admirable to put on the edge of stairs under the carpet (Fig. 8). A springy tread and long life for the carpet result. Rubber is far better than felt for this purpose.

Fig. 5.—An Aid to Photography or Window Cleaning.
A short strip of the rubber between two strips of wood becomes a small squeegee.

Fig. 4.—A Door Stop. Screw in floor bound with strip from tyre tube.

How to make a Comfortable Kneeling Mat.

A kneeling-mat can be made of a length of tube about 16 inches long, stuffed with horsehair. One end is cemented up just as a repair is done, and is clamped while stuffing. Then the other end is cemented. Cutting the ends after cementing makes a clean edge and a securer join at the same time. It is advisable to roughen the two surfaces of the rubber well with glass-paper before applying the tyre cement, and to allow the latter to get really tacky before sticking the surfaces together. Give the article plenty of time to set thoroughly before putting it into use.

Water-wings.

Smaller sections similarly cemented up, with the addition, preferably, of a cycle valve in each, can be joined with tape bands, and form admirable "water-wings" for young swimmers. Used this way, the result is better and safer for swimming learners than using a whole tube, as is often done, as it does not raise the body so high out of the water.

Tiled Paving Squeegee.

This is made of a complete width of tubing. The rubber is sandwiched between two strips of wood about

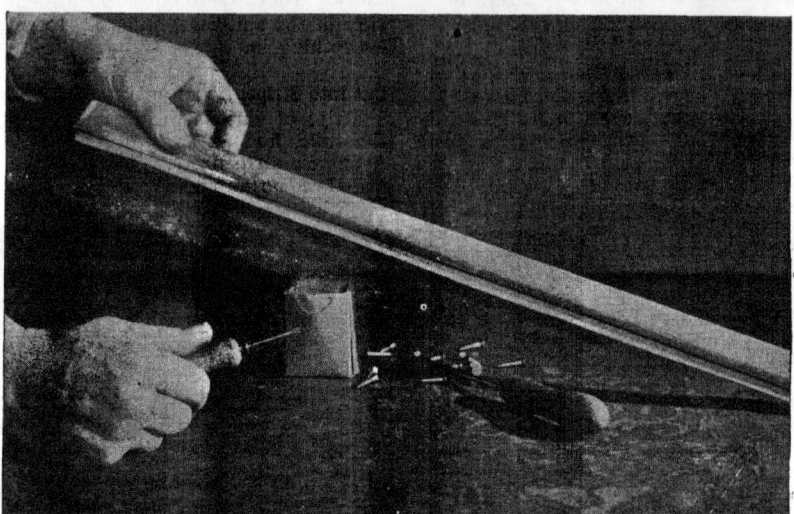

Fig. 6.—An Effective Draught Stopper.
Attach rubber strip to lath and fasten this to bottom of door.

Fig. 7.—No Need to hold the Oil-stone.
A bit of rubber tacked on the bottom of the oil-stone case prevents it slipping about on the bench when in use.

1020

USES FOR INNER TUBES

Fig. 8.—Springy Treads for the Stairs.
Cut the pieces of tube so as to leave on the fold. Place the rubber strips under the carpet.

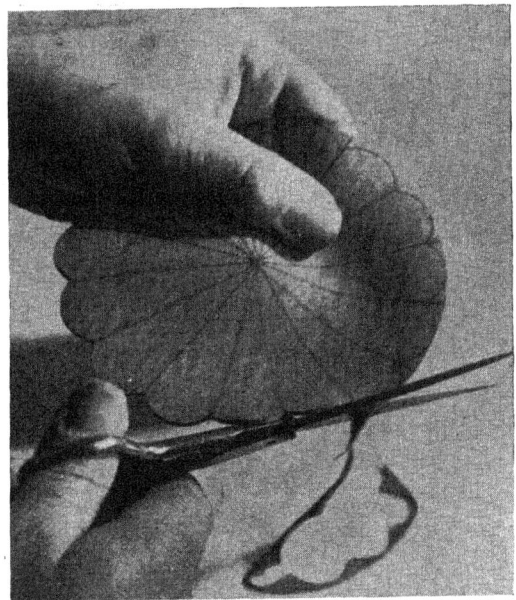

Fig. 9.—Making a Neat Table Mat.
Tyre tubes are easily cut with scissors, but they must be sharp. Wetting the rubber helps to make clean cuts.

Fig. 10.—An Excellent Squeegee for the Yard and for Tiled Paving.
Made of a piece of motor tyre tube sandwiched between two pieces of wood. When the edge is worn, the rubber can be extended by releasing the screws, as in Fig. 11.

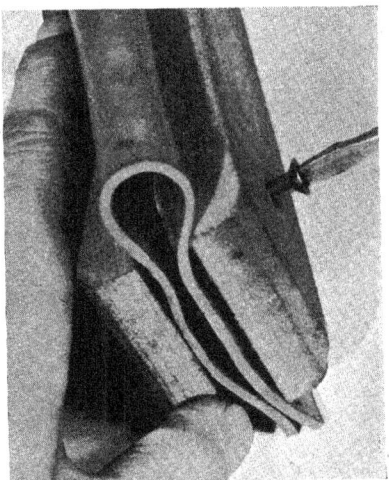

Fig. 11.—Adjusting the Squeegee.
The squeegee can be taken apart in a few minutes when the rubber gets worn. The latter can be fixed to give a new edge.

18 inches by 2½ inches by ½ inch. Figs. 10 and 11 show the construction. The advantage of this form of construction is that the squeegee can be taken apart in a few minutes by releasing the screws; when the rubber gets worn the rubber can then be fixed so as to give a new edge.

Emergency Repair to Water Pipe Leak.

Another use for a piece of old inner tube is for effecting a repair to a leak in a water pipe. After turning off the water at the main, cut one or two strips of inner tube of a size sufficient to cover the leak and extend an inch or so all round. Then on top of the rubber place a similar-sized piece of tin or galvanised iron. Finally, place an ordinary hose clamp over the rubber and piece of metal and screw it up tightly. This will provide quite a satisfactory repair.

Rubber "Shoes."

Another useful device constructed on similar lines to the kneeling-mat already described is a pair of rubber "shoes" for use when scrubbing or mopping a floor, or when cleaning a wet cellar or washing down a car, etc.

Cut out two sections of inner tube and cement the ends of each section together; then in the top of each section cut a small slit into which the feet are placed.

"Shoes" made in this fashion will not leak and will provide good protection for the feet in any damp situations.

Making Sheet Iron Ash-Pans
A SIMPLE JOB IN METAL WORK

When an ash-pan is broken or becomes too old for further use, it is often difficult to obtain one of exactly the right size to replace it. The obvious thing to do in such circumstances is to make one yourself, and this can be done quite simply out of a piece of sheet iron.

The following series of photographs show clearly the various processes in the construction of a sheet iron ash-pan. The ash-pan can, of course, be made to any size or shape required, the exact dimensions being governed by the size of the fire-place into which the ash-pan is to fit.

Tools required.

The following tools will be required for the job:—
Sharp-pointed tool.
Hand drill.
Hammer.
Block of wood.
Ruler.
Metal weight.
Shears.

Marking out the Metal.

The first thing to do is to mark out the required shape on the piece of sheet iron. This is done by using a sharp-pointed tool as shown in Fig. 1. The sketch, Fig. 5, shows the shape and dimensions of a typical ash-pan, and from this it will be quite easy to prepare a similar sketch to suit your own needs. The unwanted parts of the metal should next be cut away with shears, so that the flat outline of the ash-pan is left as shown in Fig. 2.

Fig. 1.—First mark out the Iron Plate with Ruler and Sharp-pointed Tool.

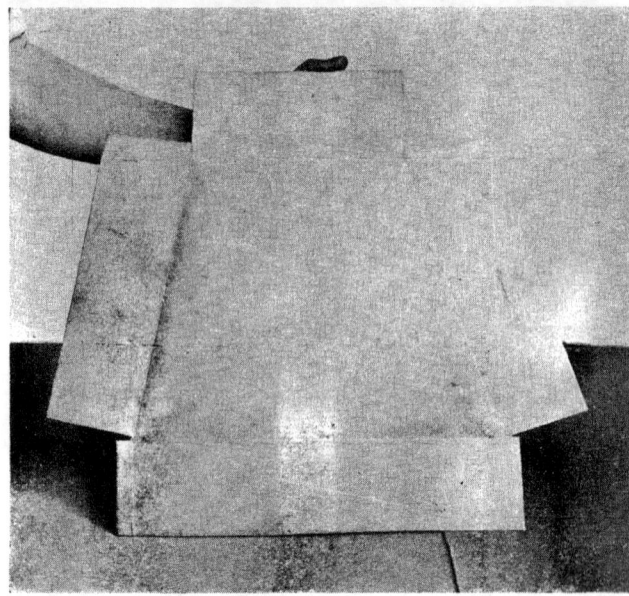

Fig. 2.—The Plate marked and cut out.

The Holes should be drilled before bending.

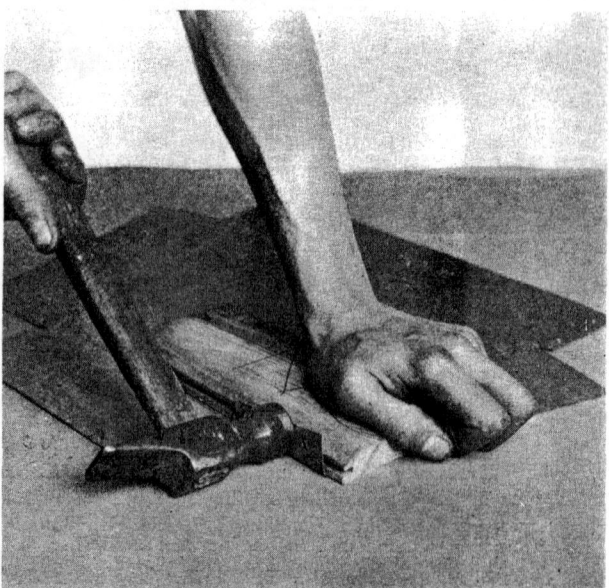

Fig. 4.—The Metal should be bent over a Wooden Block.

MAKING SHEET IRON ASH-PANS

Drilling the Holes for the Rivets.

The next operation is to drill the holes for the rivets in the edges that are to be turned up, as shown in Fig. 3. Use a $\frac{3}{16}$-inch bit. The exact position of these holes is not important, provided, of course, that they are not placed too near the edge. Approximately, the positions shown in Fig. 3 will be quite satisfactory.

Hole for the Handle.

A hole for fixing the handle in position should also be drilled in the centre of the piece of metal that will form the front. The centre can be found by drawing lines from corner to corner; these lines can be seen in Fig. 3.

Bending the Metal.

The metal is now ready for bending, and a piece of wood and a hammer will

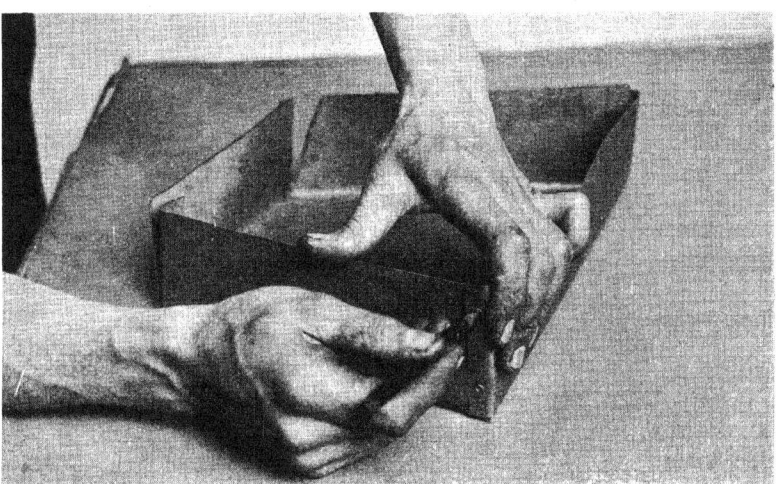

Fig. 6.—LOCATING THE HOLES WITH A PENCIL.

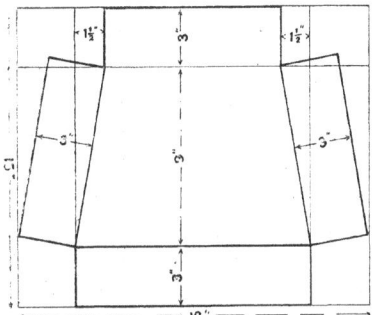

Fig. 5.—DIMENSIONS AND METHOD OF MARKING OUT.

be required. Place the wood along the line where the bend is to be made and hammer the metal up until it is at right angles, as shown in Fig. 4.

Mark through Positions of Rivet Holes.

Having got the ash-pan roughly to shape, the next step is to mark through the positions of the rivet holes as shown in Fig. 6. These holes cannot be drilled while the metal is flat, as they cannot be correctly located until the metal is bent to shape.

Riveting.

Next comes the riveting. Copper rivets, size No. 8 gauge, will be found easiest to work with. Note that the riveting is done on a metal weight, as shown in Fig. 7. When all the rivets are in place tap down any sharp edges, to ensure a clean edge. A file can also be used to clean up the edge.

The Handle.

A metal handle for the ash-pan can be bought from any ironmonger's for a few pence. It is simply placed through the hole drilled in the centre of the front and fixed with a nut as shown in Fig. 8, which also shows clearly the appearance of the finished ash-pan.

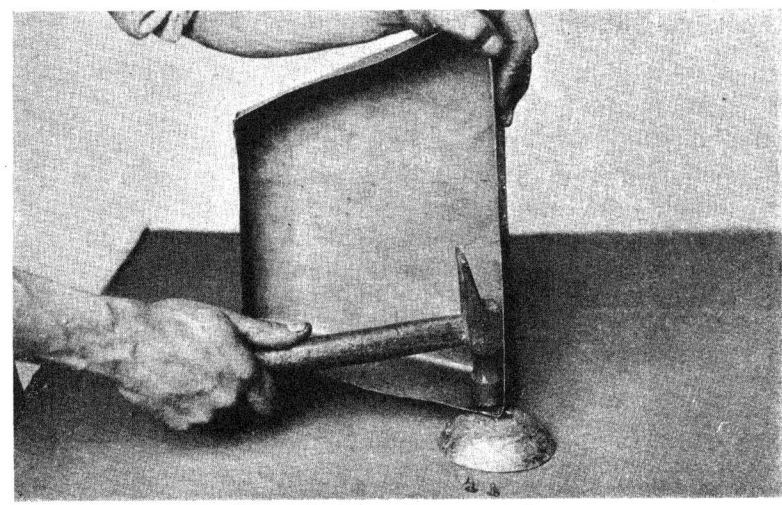

Fig. 7.—METHOD OF RIVETING UP CORNERS.
Note the weight placed under the head of the rivet.

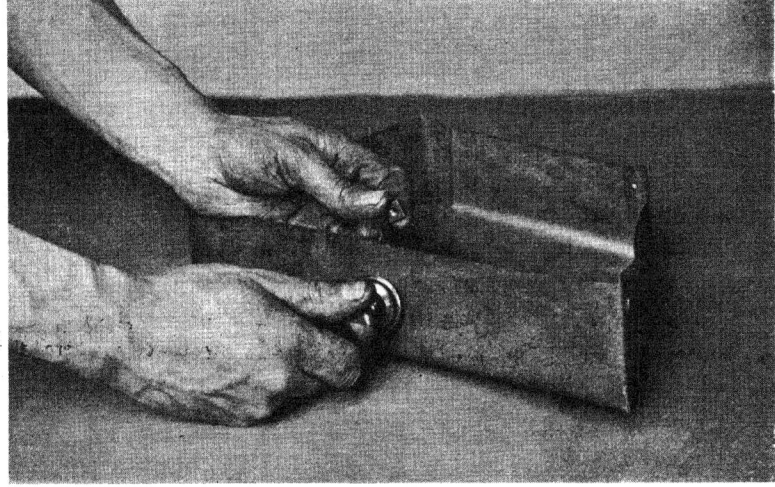

Fig. 8.—FIXING THE BRASS KNOB IN PLACE.

Revolving Fitment for Kitchen Cupboard

A USEFUL fitment for the kitchen cupboard, well within the scope of the handyman to make, is a circular and revolving one, to hold all brooms, brushes, polishes, dusters and various tins for cleaning. Usually, these are somewhat unsightly, particularly when the kitchen is on the small side, and sometimes has to do duty for a breakfast room.

The cupboard into which the example shown fitted, measured 62 inches in height, its width and depth being 21 inches. The revolving fitment was 58 inches high, and the diameter of its circular top and bottom was 18 inches (Fig. 1).

The fitment has four partitions: one, the whole length of same for brooms, the second one has three shelves, and the third and fourth five shelves to take all the smaller items.

At the centre, top and bottom, a pivot arrangement enables the whole interior to be turned easily to whichever compartment is required.

Sides and shelves are made of strong wood about $\tfrac{5}{8}$ inch thick, and each shelf has a thin edge $\tfrac{1}{2}$ inch high to prevent contents falling off.

The circles of wood, top and bottom, must be of thicker wood, approximately $1\tfrac{1}{2}$ inches thick, as they hold the sides in place.

If a fitment similar to this is being made for an already existing cupboard, make careful measurements of its interior, to ascertain if it will take one of the size described, otherwise make it smaller or larger to suit.

Materials required.

A wooden fitment of this size requires :—

2 circles of strong wood 18 inches diameter by $1\tfrac{1}{2}$ inches thick.

2 boards for sides, $58 \times 8\tfrac{3}{4} \times \tfrac{5}{8}$ inches.

2 boards for sides, $58 \times 8\tfrac{1}{2}$ bare $\times \tfrac{5}{8}$ inches.

12 feet of 1-inch square wood for runners to hold sides on to wooden circles top and bottom.

12 feet of $\tfrac{1}{2}$-inch beading for edges of shelves, and at base.

13 feet of $\tfrac{1}{2}$-inch square wood on which to rest shelves. (These supports need not be quite as long as the shelves.)

1 thick block of wood to go at top of cupboard to take the pivot arrangement. Approximately $1\tfrac{1}{2}$ inches thick,

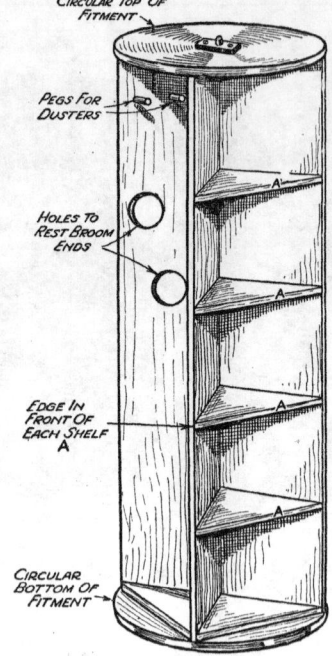

Fig. 1.—This Revolving Fitment is fixed in Place in a Suitable Cupboard.

3 inches square.

2—$2\tfrac{1}{4}$ inches iron sash clutches.

$42\tfrac{1}{2}$ inches boarding, $8\tfrac{1}{2}$ inches wide (for shelves).

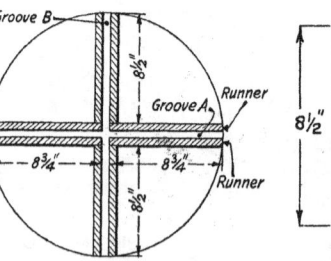

Fig. 2.—Details of Top and Bottom Circles of the Fitment. Showing how the grooves are formed by means of 1-inch runners.

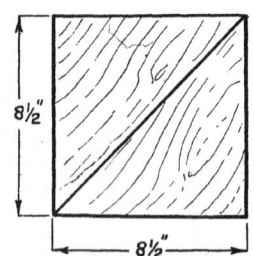

Fig. 3.—The Shelves can be cut from $8\tfrac{1}{2}$-inch Squares of Wood

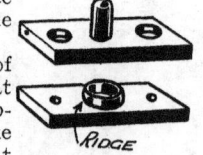

Fig. 4.—Two $2\tfrac{1}{4}$-inch Iron Sash Clutches form the Means of making the Fitment Revolve.

Buy finished wood, if possible, otherwise the job of finishing it off will take some time; 9-inch boards could be used for the sides and shelves, but a little less, as indicated, is preferable when using top and bottom circles of 18 inches diameter.

First mark Position for 1-inch Runners.

First pencil lines on the wooden circles to show exactly where the 1-inch runners are to come. These should allow space in the exact centre for the $\tfrac{5}{8}$-inch board to be slipped in. If the boards are not placed correctly in the centre it will throw the whole thing out, and make the cutting and fitting of the shelves, and various parts relating to them vary in size, and therefore more difficult to manage.

The sides of fitment are pushed or hammered into place, the $8\tfrac{3}{4}$-inch boards in groove A, Fig. 2, meet each other, and the two narrower boards, $8\tfrac{1}{2}$ inches, will fit into the B grooves, Fig. 2. The difference in the width of the boards is accounted for by the fact that the shorter ones meet the longer ones at the centre. All should be secured by screws (approximately $1\tfrac{1}{2}$ inch).

The Shelves.

The shelves are made by sawing $8\tfrac{1}{2}$-inch squares of wood from corner to corner (see Fig. 3). They are held in place by strips of $\tfrac{1}{2}$-inch square wood underneath. The strips of wood need not go the entire length of the wood in order to be effective; 6 or 7 inches would be quite long enough. Alternatively, use circles of wood $8\tfrac{1}{2}$ inches in diameter and cut to shape.

How the Fitment is Made to Revolve.

A simple way to make the fitment revolve is to fix a $2\tfrac{1}{4}$-inch iron sash clutch (Fig. 4) at the centre top and bottom, one half on the circular top and bottom of fitment, to fit into the matching halves, one of which is screwed on to a block of wood on cupboard top and the other to the floor. The half with the point is screwed exactly in centre of outside of each wooden circle (Fig. 5).

To avoid any chance of the lower pair of metal pieces jamming, owing to the weight of the fitment, slip on a thin steel washer between the two parts and when hanging the fitment in place.

The block of wood with its iron centre should exactly fill the space between the top and bottom of cupboard and the circular fitment, in order to allow the inside to revolve satisfactorily.

When assembling, the bottom of fitment must go in first, and the top of cupboard itself, with its accompanying block, be placed on last, and well screwed in place.

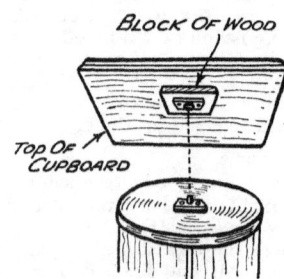

Fig. 5.—Showing how the Two Parts of the Sash Clutch are fitted.

To Prevent Rain Leaking Through Windows

It sometimes happens that although a window appears to be in perfect condition, rain water enters at the top, bottom or sides of the window. The water may enter over the top of the frame and pass to the lintol over the window, from where it drops and forms pools. It may get in the side of the window and the wall owing to loose or defective pointing, or it may trickle under the window sill to the wall, pass through it and make the plaster damp.

In nearly every case it is quite a simple matter to remedy the fault.

The most likely places for rain to enter are shown at A, B, C and D in Fig. 1.

Leakage between Wall and Head of Window.

Water entering between the wall and head of the window is probably due to the fact that the frame has shrunk, leaving a joint between it and the wall or rough-cast, as shown in Fig. 3. The correct treatment is to repoint with a mixture of cement and sand, proportioned 1 to 3 respectively. Another treatment is to place tiles, as shown in Fig. 4, to throw water off the frame, but the insertion of such tiles should not be attempted by the amateur, as there is a danger of interfering with a structural part.

Leakage between Wall and Frame.

Here again the trouble is probably due to the fact that the pointing may be loose or the rough-cast detached from the frame due to shrinkage of the latter. If such is the case, repointing or filling will overcome this trouble.

Leakage at Junction of Sash with Head of Window.

Leakage in such a case is due to faulty construction, as shown by Fig. 5. The dotted line shows how the water finds its way

Fig. 1.—The Most Likely Places where Rain may enter.
A, Between wall and head of window; B, Between wall and frame; C, Junction of sash with head of window; D, Junction between sash and transom.

Fig. 2.—A Simple Remedy for Leakage through Head or Transom.
Fix a piece of picture rail, upside down, bedding it in red lead before nailing.

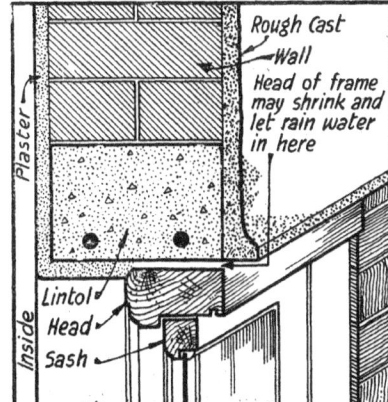

Fig. 3.—Where the Frame may shrink from the Lintol and let in the Rain.

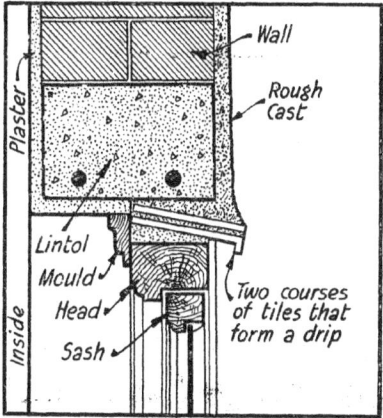

Fig. 4.—A Properly Constructed Window to prevent Water Leakage.

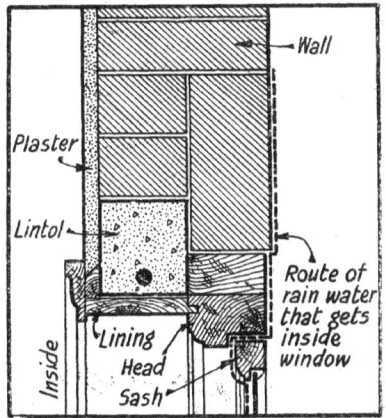

Fig. 5.—A Type of Window Construction that allows Water to enter.

TO PREVENT RAIN LEAKING THROUGH WINDOWS

through the window. If this junction had been constructed as shown in Fig. 6, there is no danger of leakage, due to the projection of the frame and the little groove or throat underneath which cause the rain to take the path shown by the dotted line.

Junction between Sash and Transom.

The same remarks as those above apply in this case.

Remedying Faults between Sash and Head or Transom.

A simple method of remedying a fault between a sash and head or transom is to obtain a few lengths of ordinary picture rail, and fix it upside down in the position shown in Fig. 2, bedding the moulding in red lead before nailing it. The groove which ordinarily takes the picture hook will act as a throat and keep the water away from the sash.

The picture rail can then be painted the same colour as the surrounding woodwork.

Leakage under Window Sill.

Fig. 8 shows a section through a typical window sill, and shows the groove which should prevent the rain water running down the wall of the house and causing the plaster to become damp. Examine the sill and if this groove is missing fix a thin strip of wood or lath along the underside of the sill, first bedding the wood in red lead. Fig. 7 shows the piece of wood being fixed in position.

Leakage at Joints at Corner of Sill.

If joints at corner of sill or other joints in the frame open and allow water to gain an entry they should be stopped with a composition of white lead with sufficient red lead to make a stiff paste.

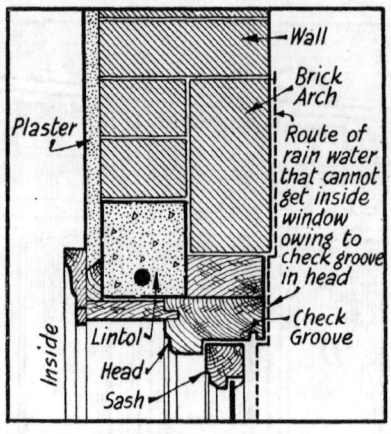

Fig. 6.—A Check Groove in the Head will prevent Water entering.

Fig. 7.—How to prevent Dampness under a Window Sill.
Nail a strip of wood along the underside of the sill, bedding it first in red lead.

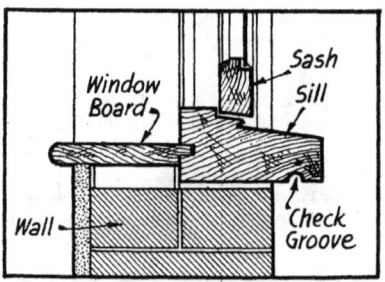

Fig. 8.—A Groove in the Sill prevents Rain Water running down the Wall of a House.

How to make a Simple Ventilator.

In bedrooms especially, a wooden-framed sliding window is left open day and night for hygienic reasons. This is apt to cause the upper member of the frame to warp or twist, so that driving rain enters the jointwork, causing it to swell and render it impossible to close the window. It is, however, quite a simple matter to make an effective ventilator to prevent this happening. It consists of a plain framework of wood the exact width of the window and any height required. The framework fits into the grooves of the upper or lower part of the window and the window closed upon it.

A single sheet of honeycombed zinc is fixed in the centre of the frame. This enables all the fresh air needed to be admitted, at the same time preventing the window frame from being exposed to the weather. Zinc is unrustable, but the wooden framework in which it is set should be painted.

Altering Window Fastenings.

In new houses especially it is often found that the shrinkage and swelling of the woodwork of the windows cause the fastenings to become out of alignment.

It may be that a casement fastener will not engage properly with its plate, or a casement stay cannot be locked over its one or two pins.

It is not difficult to overcome trouble such as this. All that is required is to take off the fittings on the sash or frame and refit them in the new or correct position.

The only trouble that may be experienced is when the fitting is let or housed into the woodwork, so that when the fitting is in its new position a part of the original sinking is exposed. It should be filled with stopping if it is small, or else pieced in with wood.

A GAS POKER FOR LIGHTING THE FIRE.

IN place of firewood and fire-lighters many fires are now lit by gas pokers. These gadgets cost from 7s. 6d., and in use effect a great saving in time, cleaning, fuel and re-laying. As the cost may be too high, the following materials assembled together give equal results, and the very moderate outlay of 1s. 2d. is quickly covered by the saving in firewood alone, the cost of gas to operate being negligible.

Materials.

Two yards (or more as required) flexible metal tubing at 3d. per yard.

Two pieces of stout rubber tube—small diameter—each 2 inches long at 1d. each.

One metal nozzle, small bore, 6d.

Assembly.

Slightly taper the ends of the metal tubing and fix on the rubbers. Fit the shank of the nozzle into one rubber, slip the other over the gas point. Test carefully for leaks.

Use.

Clear grate of clinkers, putting a small quantity of cobbles or coke in the fireplace. Turn on gas and light, inserting nozzle only through the lowest firebars of grate or if an open fireplace from underneath. The time taken to light the fire is from three to five minutes.

Constructing and Fitting Up Aquariums

The ever-popular aquarium appears in the home in a variety of forms: it may be a modest fish bowl, a rectangular tank with glass sides, or a really ambitious aquarium and stand combined. In whatever form it is found it always proves a source of interest and pleasure.

A METAL FRAME AQUARIUM

The material required for an aquarium such as the one shown in Fig. 2 will, of course, vary greatly with the size. We shall need some 18-gauge sheet iron or 16-gauge copper, a piece of ½-inch laminated board for the bedplate, a supply of 3 × ¾-inch batten for the base frame, and sufficient moulding to surround the base. In addition to the above, five sheets of ¼-inch plate glass will be required—four to form the sides, one for the base plate.

Making the Angle Iron.

The uprights have sides ¾ inch wide, while the horizontal pieces are ⅝ inch wide; thus, allowing 1/16 inch for bending, strips of sheet metal 1 9/16 × 1 5/16 inch wide should be cut to the required length. Scribe a line down the centre and place the strip along the edge of a bench and clamp it in position firmly as shown in Fig. 2A. Note the strips of iron under the foot of the G clamps; these increase the bearing surface. Now turn the free half of the strip downwards, tapping it gently with a mallet just below the bending line.

Fig. 1.—An Attractive All-wood Stand Aquarium. Dimensions and constructional details are given in Fig. 5.

Constructing the Frames.

Cut the four corner posts to length, allowing 1¼ inch extra for the foot and the ornamental top. Two rectangular frames will be needed for the top and bottom; these should each be bent from a length of angle iron so that each oblong is in one piece. Before bending the three corners, cut out small vee-shaped pieces as shown in the sketch Fig. 2, and make the join in the fourth corner. To facilitate the operation of soldering, cut out the wooden bedplate to size and carefully square; then screw the uprights to the corners, taking care to keep them vertical. The next step is to *tin* the inside surface of the posts and fit the first horizontal rectangle between the uprights with the flat side resting on the base plate. It is then quite easy to solder the horizontal frame to the uprights. The upper frame is now fastened to the top of the posts; to keep them from spreading outwards place an encircling endless cord round them and twist it tight with a short stick threaded through the loop.

Glazing the Frames.

Before attempting to put in the glass the metal frame and bed-plate should be coated first with gold size and then painted; if copper is used only the insides of the angle metal need be painted, the outside being polished and lacquered. Take a lump of plastic white lead and knead into it some dry *red*-lead powder until the whole assumes a pink colour; then generously coat the insides of the angle pieces, spreading the mixture with a putty knife. The two long glass sides are then pressed hard into place; similarly push home the two end glasses, and scrape away all the surplus lead that squeezes out. Lastly, the glass bed-plate is bedded in with the plastic white lead, spreading it thinly from the centre to the edges.

The Moulded Edge.

The mitred wooden frame can be screwed on to the bottom, leaving sufficient projecting to take the fancy moulding. The latter is glued and pinned in position later.

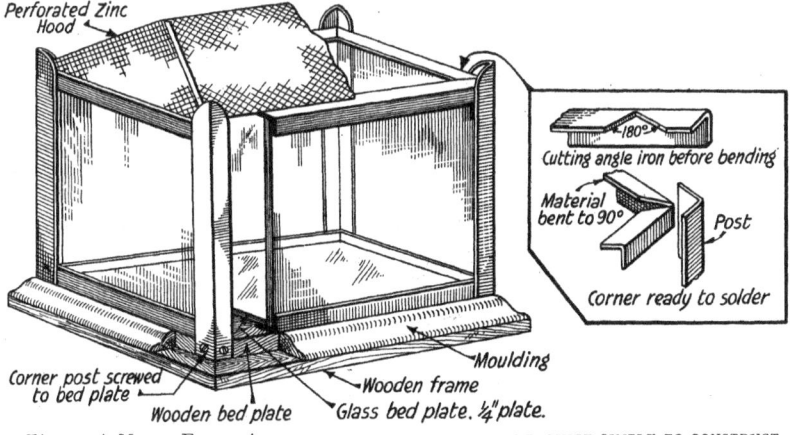

Fig. 2.—A Metal Frame Aquarium which will be found quite simple to construct. The metal used for the uprights and sides is 18-gauge sheet iron or 16-gauge copper, which is bent and soldered.

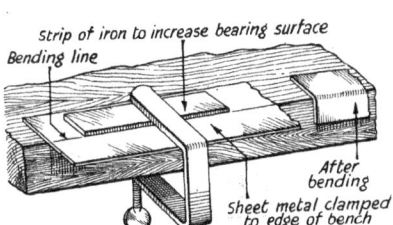

Fig. 2A.—How to bend the Sheet to form Angle Iron.

Finishing off the Tank.

Cleanse the inside of the glass and paint down the joints between the sheets with a waterproof enamel made by dissolving sealing wax in methylated spirits. The wax will readily dissolve if the spirit is warmed and the mixture is allowed to stand for some hours. This "paint" is absolutely impervious to water, is not even affected by sea water, and is harmless to the fish. The dust cover is made from a sheet of perforated zinc; it can be cut in one piece and joined with two seams along the sloping edges, or the

CONSTRUCTING AND FITTING UP AQUARIUMS

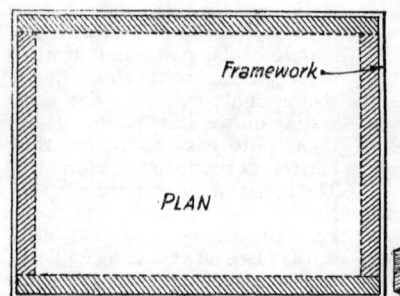

Fig. 3.—How to arrange the Glass.
Note that the glass for the sides runs the whole length of the framework. The glass is shown exaggerated for clearness.

Place a comparatively thin layer of the cement on the ironwork and then press the front and back pieces of glass into position. These can be kept fixed by means of a piece of wood wedged in between them as in Fig. 4. Next similarly put in the end pieces and

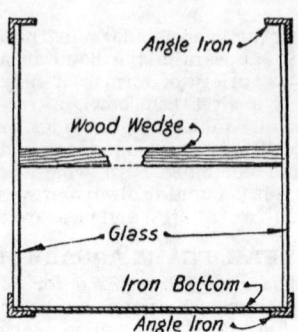

Fig. 4.—Section across a Tank, using Ready-bought Angle Iron.
The pieces of glass can be kept wedged in position by a piece of wood, when fixing in place.

triangular corner pieces can be soldered in separately.

USING A READY-BOUGHT ANGLE IRON FRAME

If preferred, it is possible to purchase a welded angle iron frame complete with a metal bottom. Give all the ironwork inside and out a good coat of bitumastic paint. This will protect it from rust, etc.

Now measure up for the glass, which should be ¼-inch plate. The front and back pieces must be the full dimensions of the framework, while the end pieces should be ½ inch less, so as to allow for the thickness of the glass. See plan, Fig. 3.

Some Useful Cements.

Although there are various formulas suggested for the manufacture of waterproof cements, the amateur may prefer to buy this from the same source as the iron framework. Some useful recipes for cements, in addition to the white lead and red lead mixture already mentioned, are as follows:—

(*a*) Make a paste of iron filings, sulphur, sal ammoniac, and boiled oil.

(*b*) Make into a paste white lead, 1 part; copal, 6 parts; litharge, 2 parts; boiled oil, 6 parts.

(*c*) Burgundy pitch, 6 parts; gutta percha, 1 part; very finely powdered pumice stone, 3 parts. Melt the gutta percha, stir in the pumice stone and then the pitch. Stir until homogeneous.

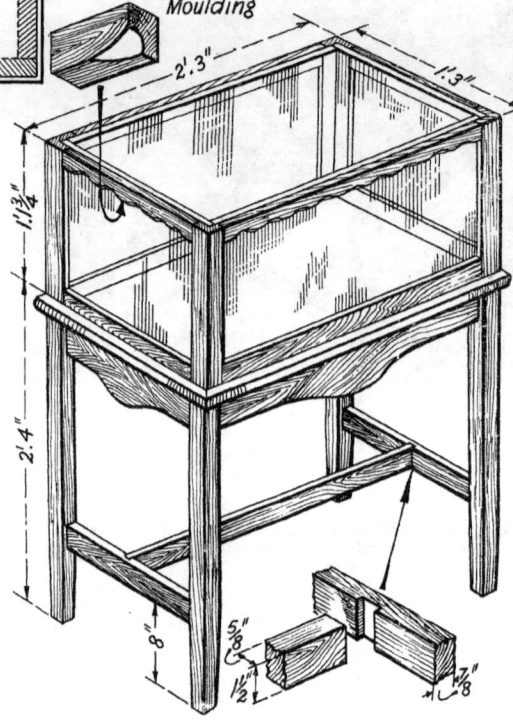

Fig. 5.—Dimensions of the All-wood Stand Aquarium.

wedge them also. The cement should be dry in three or four days.

When the cement has set wash out the aquarium by filling it with water and then emptying it at least six times, or until the water comes away perfectly clear.

AN ALL-WOOD STAND AQUARIUM

Fig. 1 shows an attractive design for an aquarium which might with advantage stand in a hall or conservatory; it is not a tank standing on a table, but is a complete unit standing on its own legs.

Materials required.

4 pieces of hardwood, 3′ 6″ × 2″ × 2″.
2 pieces of hardwood, 2′ 3″ × 6″ × 1½″.
2 pieces of hardwood, 1′ 3″ × 6″ × 1½″.
1 piece of hardwood, 3′ × ⅞″ × 1″.
1 piece of hardwood, 7′ × 1″ × ½″.
1 piece of hardwood, 3′ × ⅝″ × ½″.
1 piece of hardwood, 7′ × 1¼″ × ½″.
Laminated board, 2′ 3″ × 1′ 3″ × ⅜″.
Perforated zinc, 2′ 6″ × 2′.
Glass, ¼″ plate, 2′ 2″ × 1′ 1″ (two pieces).
Glass, ¼″ plate, 1′ 1½″ × 1′ 1″ (two pieces).
Glass, ¼″ plate, 2′ 2″ × 1′ 1½″ (one piece).

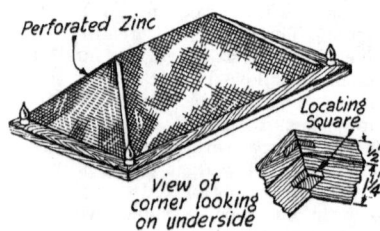

Fig. 6.—Details of Dust Cover and Frame.

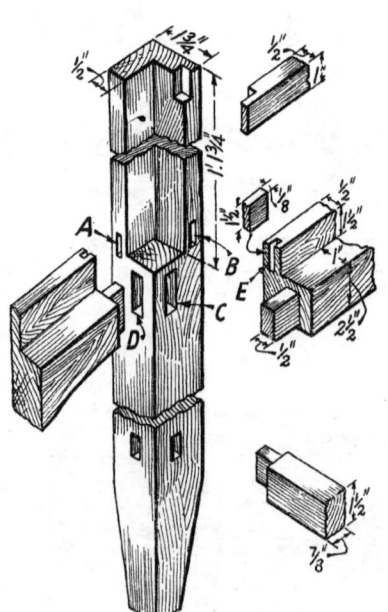

Fig. 7.—How to set out the Legs of the Stand.

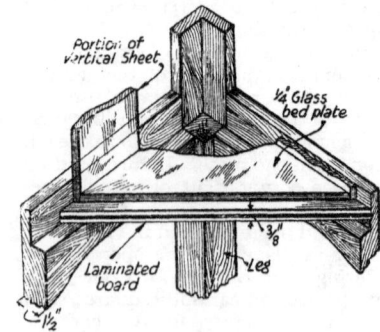

Fig. 8.—Details of One of the Corners.

CONSTRUCTING AND FITTING UP AQUARIUMS

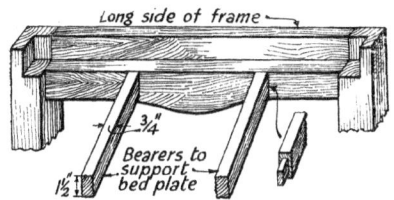

Fig. 9.—THE TWO BEARER RAILS WHICH GIVE ADDITIONAL SUPPORT TO THE BEDPLATE.

2 lbs. white lead and ½ lb. of powdered red lead.

Preparing the Legs.

Fig. 7 shows clearly how each of the four legs are set out. First note the upper portion which is cut out, leaving flanges against which the ends of the glass rest. C and D are where the main rails are mortised in. Look just above these and you will notice two long thin mortise slots A and B—these take the small tongues glued into the slots E shown at the end of the main rails (see Fig. 7). These tongues and mortises are not absolutely necessary, but add to the strength of the tank.

The Rails.

First observe the main rail in Fig. 7: the material has a very deep rebate ploughed out 1½ inches deep, and a small narrow groove E in the end into which a hardwood tongue is glued. If the reader does not possess the necessary plough, the rebate must be sawn out and then cleaned up with a bull-nosed plane. These main rails are cut from material 6 inches wide, the bottom edge being curved. The top rail which edges the glass panels has a fancy scalloped pattern along the lower side; the ends are lapped into the leg flange as shown in Fig. 7. Note the two bearer rails which give additional support to the bed-plate (see Fig. 9)—these are mortised into the two long main rails.

Gluing-up.

The framework is best glued up in two separate operations. First of all assemble the two ends, gluing in the three horizontal rails with "Croid Aero Glue," which is not affected by damp; leave it in the cramps for twenty-four hours. Now glue the two bearers into the main rails, and when dry the whole structure can be finally put together. The next step is to glue and pin the wooden bed-plate in position. A portion of this is shown in Fig. 8.

Glazing the Panels.

Before putting in the glass the bed and flanges must be painted two coats of lead colour. Then take some white lead mixed with red lead as described above and generously coat the surfaces which hold the glass. The four upright panes are dealt with first—see that the edges are clean, rubbing them on an oil stone if there are any rough places; then press them firmly into place one at a time and clean away all surplus lead that squeezes out. Lastly, fit the bottom plate—this should be bedded in with a thin layer of white lead paste, taking care not to leave any hollow spaces between the glass and the wood; this bottom sheet can be a piece of slate instead of glass if preferred. Having completed the

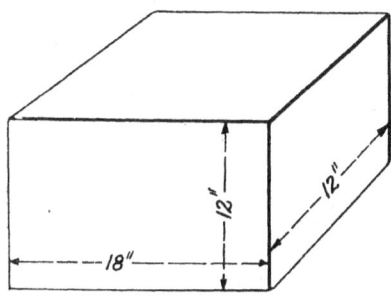

Fig. 11.—WHEN CONSTRUCTING AN AQUARIUM TO YOUR OWN DESIGN MAKE SURE THE WIDTH OF THE TANK IS NOT LESS THAN THE DEPTH.

glazing thoroughly clean away all traces of the lead from the interior and paint the joints with the sealing-wax varnish, details of which are given above. The paint should overlap the joins ½ inch on each side.

Making the Dust Cover.

Fig. 6 shows a suitable perforated zinc cover for this tank; it consists of a wooden framework with mitred corners secured by small hardwood tongues let into slots cut in the ends; details of

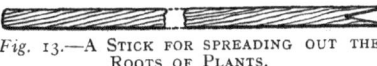

Fig. 13.—A STICK FOR SPREADING OUT THE ROOTS OF PLANTS.

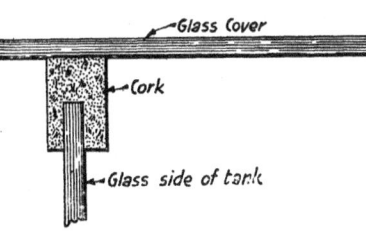

Fig. 14.—AN ALTERNATIVE DUST COVER TO THE PERFORATED ZINC IS A PIECE OF GLASS SUPPORTED ON CORKS.

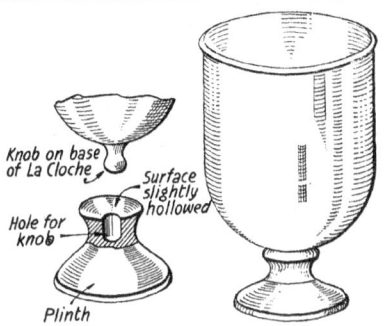

Fig. 10.—HOW AN ORDINARY GLASS *La Cloche* CAN BE CONVERTED INTO A FISH BOWL.

these corners are shown in the sketch attached to Fig. 6. The frame is covered with a sloping roof-like structure of perforated zinc. The seams can easily be soldered provided "live" spirits of salt is used for flux; difficulty is often experienced by amateurs when soldering zinc through using the wrong flux; hydrochloric acid is the only satisfactory thing to use for this metal. Four small ornamental knobs are dowelled in one at each corner to give an attractive finish. Note the four locating squares in the sketch (Fig. 6); these are glued and pinned to the underside of the frame so that they fit into the corners of the aquarium, preventing the cover from being inadvertently pushed off.

Finishing-off.

The woodwork should be stained and polished to taste, while the zinc cover may be painted to tone with the general finish. Before attempting to use the aquarium as a home for fish, it should be thoroughly cleaned and allowed to stand with water in it for several days. Although the structure is quite strong enough to support the 200 lbs. of water it contains, yet it is unwise to move it when full, as this may strain one or other of the joints. In Fig. 5 a projecting ledge is shown running round the top of the stand, giving it the appearance of a table. This is simply a moulding 1¼ × ⅞ inches, one edge of which is half-round; it is glued and pinned with oval brads to the sides of the stand. While it is not essentially part of the structure, and can be left out if desired, yet when fitted it adds greatly to the appearance.

A Fish Bowl for the Table.

Fig. 10 shows how an ordinary glass

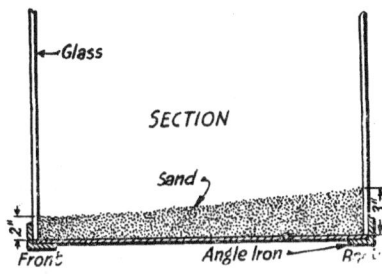

Fig. 12.—IT IS A GOOD IDEA TO HAVE THE SAND DEEPER AT THE BACK THAN THE FRONT.

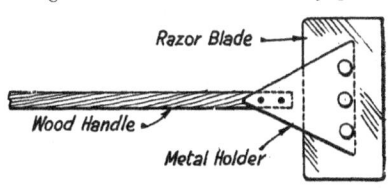

Fig. 15.—HOW TO MOUNT AN OLD RAZOR BLADE FOR SCRAPING AWAY GREEN MATTER FROM THE SIDES OF THE GLASS.

la cloche used for forcing plants in the garden can easily be converted into a fish bowl for the table or sideboard. The large round knob which forms the handle is fitted into a cylindrical hole bored in an ornamental wooden plinth. The plinth can be turned up by anyone who has access to a lathe, or an equally successful one can be fashioned from a square or hexagonal block of wood. The top surface is hollowed out slightly with a gouge so that the rounded shoulders of the glass can bed down neatly. The glass knob is secured in the hole with packing such as plastic wood or white lead putty. This type of bowl is very successful; it holds approximately 5 gallons of water and has a large surface area in contact with the air—a point which cannot be claimed for most of the globular receptacles sold in shops for the purpose of housing gold fish.

NOTES ON SIZE AND SHAPE

The tanks are usually rectangular in shape, and the following points should always be observed. The width of the tank should not be less than the depth in order to ensure a good surface for aeration per given volume of water. Thus Fig. 11 shows a well-designed tank.

The size depends on the number of fish which are to be kept. It can be taken for a rough guide that every inch of fish (exclusive of tail fin) requires 1 gallon of water. Thus a fish 3 inches long will need 3 gallons of water. A gallon of water occupies approximately 277 cubic inches, and to ascertain how many fish can be safely kept in a tank multiply together the breadth, width, and height in inches, and divide by 277. The figure obtained is the inches of fish which may be safely kept in the tank.

A useful size for commencing is 18 × 12 × 12 inches. The number of inches of fish which will thrive in this tank is

$$\frac{18 \times 12 \times 12}{277}, \text{ or } \frac{2,592}{277}, \text{ or } 9\tfrac{1}{3}$$

or (say) one 3-inch fish, two 2-inch fish, one 2⅓-inch fish.

EQUIPPING THE AQUARIUM
Sand.

Obtain some coarse sand and wash it thoroughly in running water until the latter is absolutely clear when stirred with the sand, which should then be placed in the bottom of the aquarium to an average depth of 2 inches. Have the sand deeper at the back than in the front (see Fig. 12). This is so that any decayed matter will after sinking to the bottom collect by gravity at the deepest part, in the front, from whence it can be easily periodically syphoned out. Cover the sand with 2 or 3 inches of water, and the aquarium is then ready to receive the aquatic plants.

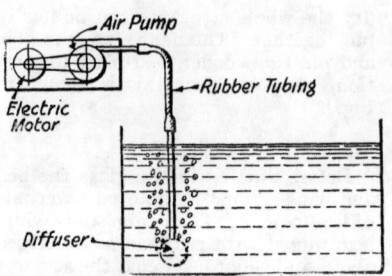

Fig. 16.—Diagram in Section of Air Pump supplying Air to an Aquarium.

Plants

The beauty of the aquarium is enhanced by growing in it aquatic plants. A further use of them is that under the action of light they absorb the carbonic acid gas expired by fishes, and, retaining the carbon, give off pure oxygen. Thus by carefully choosing suitable plants which show this property to a marked extent, it is possible to decrease the quantity of water necessary per inch of fish. It is much better to keep the water of the aquarium pure by this means than by repeatedly changing it. The water should never be changed in its entirety, but weekly (say) the decayed matter in the bottom can be syphoned off. Any decayed unused food will also give off carbon dioxide, which will be absorbed by the plants.

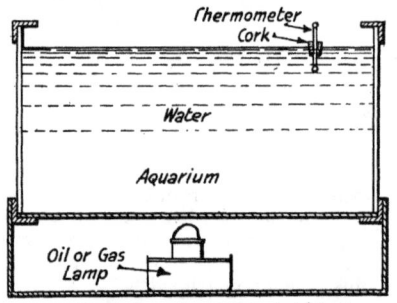

Fig. 17.—A Useful Arrangement for Heating an Aquarium when Tropical Fish are being kept.

Showing also how a thermometer can be suspended in the water.

Rooted plants should be buried in the sand with the crowns showing, *i.e.*, until the bottom of the actual foliage is just above the sand. The roots can be pushed under the sand and there spread out by means of a stick fashioned as in Fig. 13. Cuttings are planted as for land plants.

Good plants for the bottom are Vallisneria and Sagittaria, while Elodea (Anacharis) need only be thrown on the surface of the water. For the corners of the tank plant Ludwigia. Another pretty plant is the red Myriophyllum.

Shells and irregular-shaped stones are to be avoided in aquariums, since underneath they invariably provide a depression in which collects decayed matter, etc.

Cover.

In order to keep dust, etc., from falling on to the surface of the water it is advisable to provide a glass cover supported on corks, as in Fig. 14, unless the perforated zinc hood previously described is fitted.

Newts.

Newts are very interesting creatures to keep in an aquarium. They should be fed with small worms or small, thin pieces of raw meat. An island should be provided, either in the form of a piece of rock, the top of which projects above the water, or a piece of cork floating on the water. Newts hibernate on land during the winter months, so that some dark corner should be provided in the aquarium. It is essential to have a cover over the aquarium when newts are kept, otherwise they will escape.

What to do if Water gets discoloured.

One of the problems of fish keeping is that the water of the aquarium sometimes gets discoloured by reason of the growth of algæ. This may be obviated to a certain extent by not standing the aquarium in the direct sunlight. The growing of aquatic plants in the aquarium tends to keep the water clear, but should algæ form, then they can be scraped away from the inside of the glass by means of an old razor blade mounted as in Fig. 15. When the loosened algæ have collected in the bottom syphon them out.

Air Pumps.

If it is definitely decided to keep more fish in the aquarium than is permitted by the standard formula given above, then artificial aeration must be resorted to. This is generally brought about by the use of a small electrically driven air pump, as in Fig. 16.

Tropical Fish.

These require the water maintained at (say) 80° F. The tank is heated as in Fig. 17, using a gas or oil burner. Alternatively, the temperature can be controlled by an electric immersion heater or even a carbon lamp. The thermometer for measuring the temperature is kept suspended in the water by means of a cork, as shown in Fig. 17.

Cracked Glass Tanks.

These can be repaired as follows, although if the crack is in one of the sides it is rather unsightly. Empty, thoroughly clean, and dry the tank. Next put it near a fire to get warm. Obtain some bitumen of about 65 penetration and melt it in a tin can to about 300° F. Pour it on to the crack, working it on to the glass with a heated knife.

How to Line a Box with Metal
TO MAKE IT DAMP-PROOF

There are often occasions when it is desired to line the inside of a wooden box with metal in order to keep the contents damp-proof.

This is quite a simple job and one that does not call for any great metal-working skill.

Best Metal to use.

The best metal to use for this purpose is thin zinc; it is quite easy to work with and will make a neat and efficient container.

Determining the Size.

The first thing to do is to determine the size of the piece of metal required. This is done by measuring down one side of the box on the inside, across the bottom and up the other side. This will give one dimension, and the other is obtained by repeating the process with the other two sides. Fig. 2 shows the dimensions marked out for the lining of a tea-caddy, the area of the section being 5 inches square and the depth 4 inches. Note that an additional ½ inch should be allowed all round before the metal is cut out, and ¼ inch is allowed at the sides of two of the parts that are afterwards bent upwards.

Marking the Metal.

When transferring the dimensions to the zinc, they should be made with a pencil and not with a sharp-pointed tool, which would cut the thin metal. Accuracy is essential, so use a fine-pointed pencil.

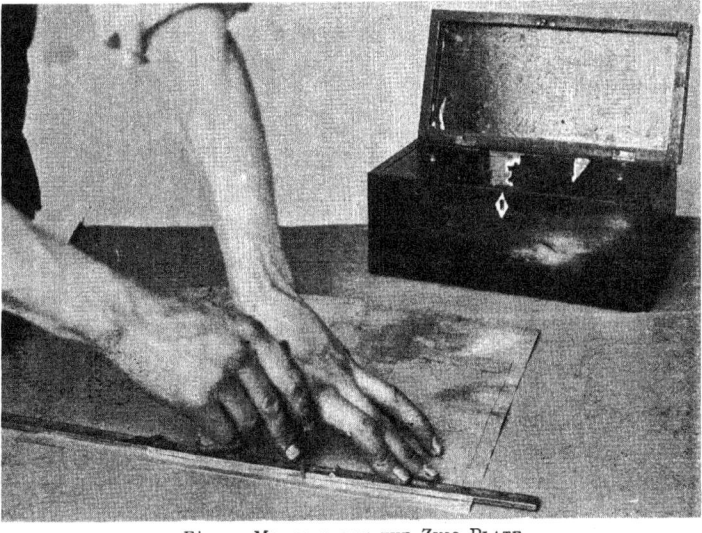

Fig. 1.—Marking out the Zinc Plate.
Note that a pencil is used and not a sharp-pointed tool.

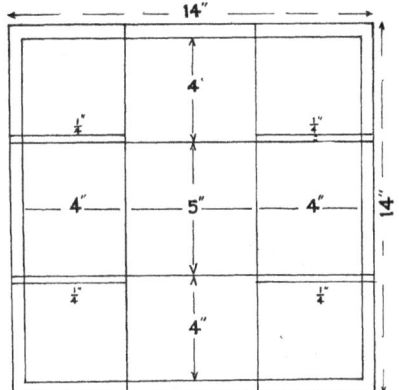

Fig. 2.—The Dimensions of the Zinc Plate.

Fig. 3 shows the zinc plate marked and cut out ready for bending.

Bending the Metal.

The best method of bending the metal is to turn it over on a wooden block as shown in Fig. 4. Bend the ½-inch edge over first until it is at right angles; then bend up the sides.

Inserting the Zinc in the Box.

The metal lining is now ready for inserting in the box. To make quite sure that it fits properly it should be " dressed " as shown in Fig. 5. Place the wooden block against the angle and knock with a hammer.

Fixing the Metal.

Fig. 6 shows why the ½-inch strip of metal was left; it is used to fix the metal into the box. Brass pins are hammered in at intervals; about three pins along each side would be sufficient for the box shown.

The next step is to clean up the edges with a file, as shown in Fig. 7. Do not use a new file if you have an old one you can use instead. A piece of emery cloth wrapped round a flat piece of wood would serve the purpose very well.

Soldering.

The final operation is to solder along the corners, as shown in Fig. 8, to make the lining absolutely damp-proof. This is simply a straightforward soldering job and should present no difficulty.

Fig. 3.—The Zinc Plate marked and cut out.
Note that ½-inch margin is left all round.

Fig. 4.—Bending the Zinc to Shape.
A wooden block is used for this purpose.

*Fig. 5.—*Dressing the Zinc into Place.

*Fig. 6.—*Fixing the Edges with Brass Pins.

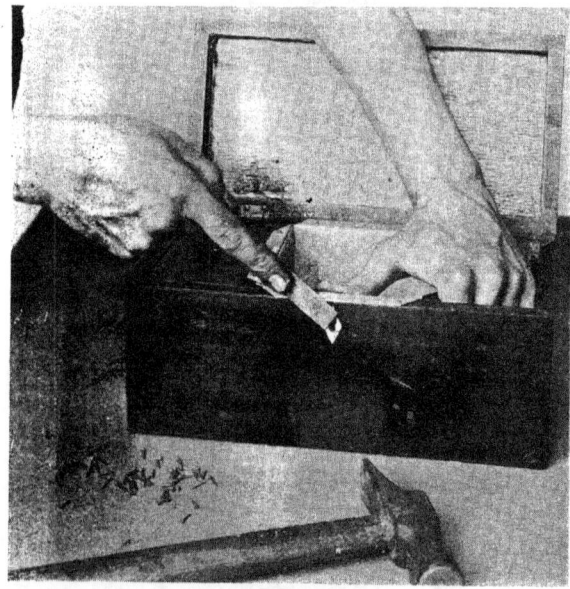
*Fig. 7.—*Cleaning Edges off with a File.

*Fig. 8.—*Soldering Corners of Completed Job.

TO COLOUR OAK AND MAHOGANY

SPIRIT stains are not recommended for work which is to be finished with polish; unless great care is taken, patchiness is the result.

Two methods are in general use: first water stains, secondly naphtha or oil.

For water, 1 lb. of oak crystals to 1 gallon of water is the standard strength; boiling of the water accelerates the solubility of the crystals. Varying shades of colour can be produced by adding more water or by increasing the amount of oak crystals.

In the case of mahogany use bichromate, strength of solution being $\frac{1}{2}$ lb. to 1 gallon of water and either strengthened or weakened to obtain the desired colour. This solution is yellow in colour, but when applied to mahogany, either one or several coatings, chemical action takes place and produces the redness which is the usual colour desired. The solution is poisonous, and care should be taken in its handling.

A Spray Painting Outfit

THE apparatus described below can be constructed by any amateur who is skilled in the use of a few simple metal-work tools. The finished outfit will apply cellulose paint, lacquer, water wash, or stain with a surface that should prove the envy of the most skilled brush worker; it can also be used to spray the expensive nicotine insecticides on the plant pests in the greenhouse with gratifying results.

Requirements.

The materials required are small, merely a square foot of copper sheet, two short lengths of ½-inch copper pipe, a foot of $\frac{3}{32}$-inch tube, a few inches of ⅛-inch brass rod, and one or two sundries including parts of a tyre valve.

How the Spray Works.

Two pieces of ½-inch tube are soldered together, forming the main barrel and the air tube. To the under side of the former are soldered the lid of the container and the handle frame, the container being fastened to the lid by means of a bayonet joint. Compressed air is introduced into the upper barrel and passes through a small hole into the lower one; this current of air is controlled by a needle valve and piston sliding to and fro at the rear of the main barrel. On entering the lower barrel the air rushes along the fine tube over the paint jet, lifting the liquid, which it breaks up into small globules and blows from the orifice in the form of a fine spray.

The Container.

This is just a plain cylindrical copper can with three lugs of rectangular section soldered to the outside near the top edge. Round the inner edge of the lid are fastened strips of square section brass with gaps just wide enough to admit the lugs. These strips slope slightly upwards towards one end so that they act as a screw thread; thus, when the container is turned the top edge is brought up tightly against the inside of the lid. A small hole is also necessary to admit atmospheric pressure.

The Main Barrel.

About 2 inches from the spray orifice a short length of screwed tubing (stem of tyre valve) is soldered to the underside of the main barrel. In approximately the centre, the air passage is partially blocked by the jet which is attached to a piece of ⅛-inch brass rod having a conical hole on one side into which the needle valve seats. The jet is held by a grub screw through the wall of the barrel. In the diagram, Fig. 1, it is shown for convenience at the bottom, but is in fact through the side of the tube. To make the jet fitting airtight, the base must be a good fit; it is bedded in with shellac. The rear end of the barrel is cut on the slope so that the needle valve and piston move backwards as the control knob is turned down; a small notch is filed at the bottom to hold the valve in the open position, a slight touch of the finger frees the lever and the needle valve is closed by the spring. Note the small plug at the end of the tube through which the stem slides; it is secured with a grub screw.

The Needle Valve.

The valve stem is a piece of ⅛-inch steel rod bent at right-angles at one end and with a cylindrical piston soldered to it near the pointed extremity. The piston must be a good fit;

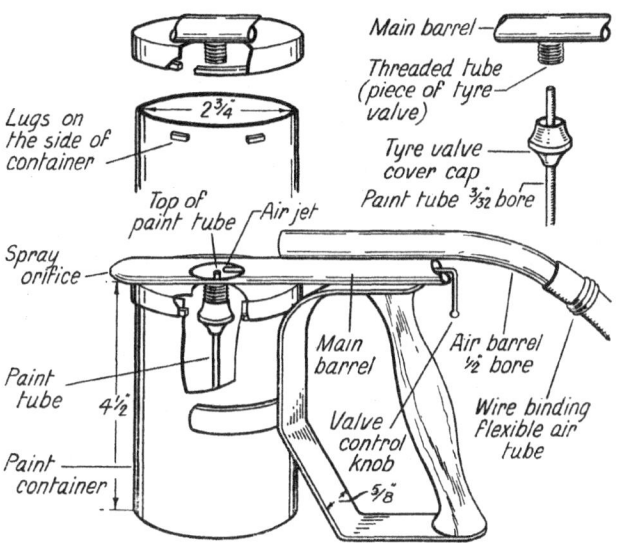

Fig. 1.—Diagram showing Details of Paint Container and arrangement of Jets.

this is ensured by *lapping* it in with pumice dust and water. The needle point should be *ground* in with fine emery and oil. Note that the piston has a circular groove near the rear which holds a few turns of greased tow packing; this prevents any escape of air at the back of the barrel when the needle valve is closed.

The Air Barrel.

This is a piece of ½-inch copper tube blocked at one end and soldered to the top of the main barrel; before joining them, small ⅛-inch holes are drilled in both and these must coincide when fixing the two tubes together. Observe that the air passage is so placed that it is covered by the piston when the needle valve is closed.

The Paint Jet.

Fig. 2 shows an enlarged view of this important part of the spray; it is a length of $\frac{3}{32}$-inch tube which passes through the centre of a tyre valve cap to which it is soldered. The completed jet which dips into the liquid screws into the main barrel, and the length of the fine tube must be such that the top comes almost level with the air jet.

It is advisable to have several spare jets, the old one being removed for cleaning after operations, and a new one fitted ready for future use. A good plan is to have an assortment of sizes with jets varying from $\frac{3}{32}$ to $\frac{5}{32}$ inch to suit liquids of different density.

The Handle.

A brass bracket is bent up as shown in Fig. 1, a semicircular band being attached at right-angles to steady the container. A metal rod with two "squares" on it to prevent turning passes through the wooden handle and is secured in two holes one at each end of the bracket. The completed handle is soldered to the underside of the main barrel.

Pumps for the Air Current.

Two ways of obtaining a continuous current of air are shown in Figs. 3 and 4. Firstly we have an ordinary pair of foot bellows as used with a blowpipe; these will maintain a fairly uniform stream of air across the paint jet, sufficient to lift the liquid and distribute it as a fine spray. Secondly we have a slightly more elaborate piece of apparatus shown in Fig. 4, comprising a motor foot pump

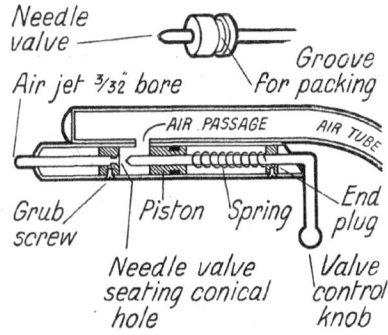

Fig. 2.—Enlarged View of the Paint Jet.

A SPRAY PAINTING OUTFIT

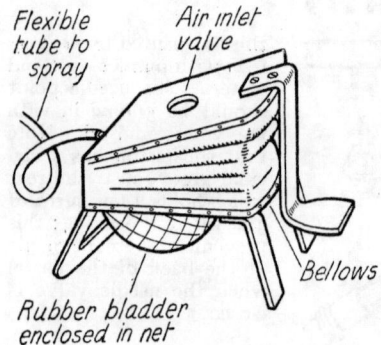

Fig. 3.—Foot Bellows used as a source of Air Pressure.

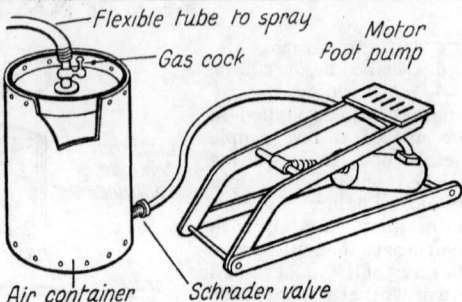

Fig. 4.—A more elaborate piece of apparatus comprising a Motor Foot Pump and a Cylindrical Air Container.

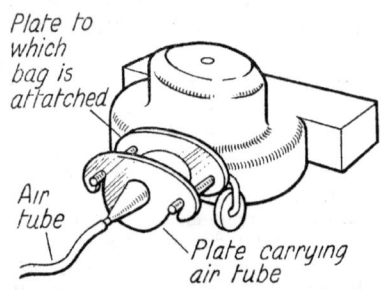

Fig. 5.—How an Electric Vacuum Cleaner can be utilised as a source of Air Pressure.

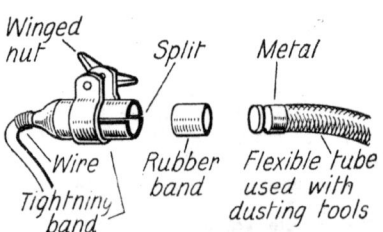

Fig. 6.—Method of attaching a Split Cylindrical Clamp to the existing Hose.

and a cylindrical air container. The reservoir is made of stout sheet metal, the ends being soldered and riveted in as shown; a suitable size for the cylinder is 6 inches diameter and 18 inches high. A complete tyre valve is sweated into the side through which the air is forced in, its escape being prevented by the valve; a turn-cock is fastened in the top and to this the flexible tube is attached. It is advisable to fit a small gauge to indicate the pressure, a Michelin tyre valve is quite suitable for the purpose. Assuming that 18-gauge iron is used for the container it is not wise to pump the air in the reservoir above a pressure of 10 or 12 lbs. With either of the above types of pump it is convenient to have an assistant to maintain the air supply, while the operator uses the spray.

Air from the Electric Cleaner.

Nearly all types of vacuum cleaner can easily be adapted to "blow" instead of "sucking," as they normally do. Most machines with an external bag can have this removed and a plate screwed over the mouth, through which the dust passes. A tube fixed to the centre of this plate as shown in Fig. 5 will receive air at a pressure sufficient to work the spray for long periods. The models with self-contained bags usually have a vent at the end remote from the hose through which the spent air is discharged; it is a simple matter to attach the hose to this end, in fact most machines are designed for this purpose. Fig. 6 shows a method of attaching a split cylindrical clamp to the existing hose; at the rear of this is a reducing cone terminating in the small rubber tubing which carries the air to the spray.

When using the electric cleaner as suggested, do not run the motor for very long periods or the machine may over-heat; it is better to run it for say twenty minutes, then rest for a few minutes.

Types of Paint to use.

It must be clearly understood that ordinary paints sold for application with a brush are much too thick to use in the spray. Most cellulose paints are made in two grades, one for use in the spray and the other for brush work. Messrs. Dockers, of Birmingham, and other firms specialise in the production of paints for the spray.

Water and thin oil stain, creosote, thin distemper, glaze, and insecticides can be readily applied with the spray. Several coats are usually necessary to obtain first-class results, but as most spray pigments dry rapidly, a second or third application can be put on almost immediately as the spray does not "rub up" the under coat as a brush will when applied to a tacky surface.

Final Hints.

Great care must be taken to keep the jets perfectly clean; the paint container should always be washed out after use and not left with a little unused material in the bottom. When working with cellulose lacquers the best solvent for cleaning is amyl-acetate. Should the spray function badly at any time the first thing to inspect is the small hole in the lid of the container; this sometimes becomes blocked with pigment, then the air current fails to lift sufficient liquid. When "tears" appear on the surface, it usually indicates that the spray is held too close to the work.

DARKENING A SOLID WALNUT BOOKCASE

THE method employed to make a solid walnut bookcase darker in colour would be first to remove the existing polish by applying the usual patent strippers or solvents, which can be purchased at any first-class stores. Having removed or stripped the work, well paper with grade No. 0, working with the grain; this operation will disturb the filling of the grain.

Now proceed to apply either a water stain or naphtha stain to the job; if water stain is decided upon, purchase some walnut crystals and dissolve in water, the proportion being 1 lb. to 1 gallon water. Crystals will easily dissolve if water is boiled. Before applying it is as well to test the colour on a like piece of wood. Add water or crystals to suit your requirements. Naphtha stains can be obtained in all shades.

Having stained the wood to the required colour, then if necessary refill the grain by using either plaster or woodfiller, after which proceed to polish the job with garnet polish.

MARQUETRY

Many attractive effects can be obtained by marquetry, which is a form of inlay in veneer just as ordinary inlay is carried out in solid wood. It is not advisable to attempt to cut your own marquetry. Sheets of marquetry, already cut, can be obtained quite cheaply at any cabinet maker's store, so that the process is reduced simply to preparing the groundwork and laying the sheets.

Tools Required.
The following tools should be available:
Toothing plane (or very coarse glasspaper wrapped round a wood block).
Chisel.
Straight-edge.
Square.
Ruler.
Hand screws and cramps.
Steel scraper.
Glasspaper, grades No. 1 and No. 2.
Glue.
Plaster of paris (for mixing with glue if small indentations have to be filled).

How to Select a Suitable Groundwork.
One of the secrets of success with marquetry lies in choosing a good groundwork. Blemishes such as knots, although planed level before placing the marquetry in position, will cause unequal shrinkage to take place and in a few weeks an unsightly mark or bulge will appear on the surface.

A reliable wood, free from objectionable knots, is straight-grained Honduras mahogany, but it is rather expensive. Yellow pine is a cheaper alternative, and, provided it is given a coat of glue size as described later, will be found quite satisfactory.

Other satisfactory grounds are plywood and the various laminated boards. If using plywood make sure there are no gaps running through the centre layer.

Two Forms of Marquetry.
Marquetry is laid either on solid grounds or else inlayed into a solid piece of wood, as in the case of a finger plate with a piece of marquetry let in (see Fig. 9).

LAYING MARQUETRY ON SOLID GROUNDS

Marquetry laid on solid grounds should always be laid on the heart side, because this side of the wood tends to become rounded owing to shrinkage taking place around the annual rings. The veneer of the marquetry, however, always pulls the groundwork hollow, so that the two forces tend to counteract each other.

The best method is to choose a board in which the annual rings pass through practically at right angles, and veneer both sides, but this is not always practicable.

It will be found that the veneer

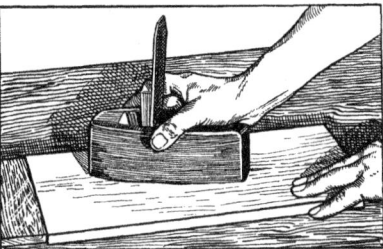

Fig. 1.—The Surface of the Groundwork should be Roughened with a Toothing Plane to provide a Key for the Glue and to remove previous Plane marks.

If a toothing plane is not available, use coarse glasspaper wrapped round a wooden block.

Fig. 2.—The Ends of the Marquetry should be Trimmed up with a Chisel. Note the straight-edge which helps to prevent the marquetry from buckling.

Fig. 3.—The Marquetry must be placed in its exact position on the Groundwork. This is done by making centre lines on both marquetry and groundwork as shown.

Fig. 4.—When Glue has been applied to both Marquetry and Groundwork, and the Marquetry placed in position, it should be fixed with two Headless Pins. This is to prevent it moving when the caul is applied.

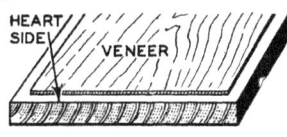

Fig. 5.—The Marquetry Veneer should always be placed on the Heart Side of the Groundwork.

Another method where possible is to place marquetry on both sides of the groundwork.

usually proves stronger than the natural twisting tendency of the wood, so, to prevent the wood pulling hollow, framework grooves should be provided when the marquetry is in the form of a panel, and adequate screwing down when it is a top.

How to prepare the Groundwork.
If you are unable to obtain a piece of groundwork entirely free from knots, they should be chopped away to a depth of about ¼ inch and in a diamond shape and a sound piece of wood inserted, glued down, and levelled. Fill any small indentations with a mixture of plaster of paris and glue.

Roughening the Surface.
To enable the glue to grip firmly, the groundwork should be roughened with a toothing plane or piece of coarse sandpaper wrapped round a block of wood. The plane has a finely serrated cutting edge, the effect of which is to cover the work with fine scratches and incidentally remove any marks left by previous planing. Work it diagonally, first in one direction then another.

Sizing the Wood.
If yellow pine or any other soft wood is being used for the groundwork it should be sized with glue. Thin out some ordinary glue until it is of a watery consistency, then apply hot evenly over the whole surface, taking care there are no lumps, hairs, shavings and such like. When hard, rub over with coarse glasspaper.

Trimming the Marquetry to Size.
It is unlikely that the piece of marquetry will be the exact size required; it will have to be cut down, if practicable, slightly smaller than the groundwork for convenience in marking out.

It can be cut by drawing a keen chisel across it as shown in Fig. 2. The main point to bear in mind is to avoid buckling the veneer, by placing a straight-edge in line with the desired cut. Place the bevelled side of the chisel against the straight-edge and incline it at an angle, to keep it tightly against the straight-edge. Do not attempt to cut through in one cut, but make two or three fairly light cuts.

Marking Out.
In marquetry work it is essential that the marquetry should be laid exactly in a given place, usually in the centre, so that both the marquetry and groundwork must be marked out. First, with a square and rule, draw the intersecting centre lines on the groundwork as shown in Fig. 3. Similar lines are then made on the back of the marquetry (see Fig. 3). Note the paper backing on the marquetry, which

MARQUETRY

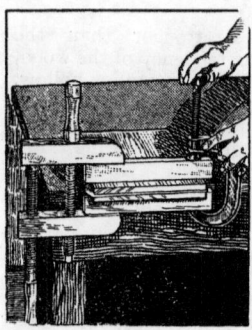

Fig. 6.—APPLYING THE CAUL. This is a flat block of wood as large as the groundwork, which is placed over the marquetry before the battens and handscrews are applied.

is glued on by the makers to hold the whole together.

Preparing a Caul.

To enable the marquetry to be pressed firmly on the ground after the glue is applied a caul should be prepared. This is a perfectly flat block of wood at least as large as the groundwork, which is heated and cramped down, so pressing out the surplus glue and bringing the marquetry into close contact with the groundwork.

Four battens should be cut slightly longer than the width of the caul and about 2 inches wide and 1 inch thick, to enable pressure to be applied properly. The inner edges of the battens should be curved slightly in their length so that as the handscrews are put on the ends the pressure is applied first at the centre, so that glue is driven out at the edges.

How to test Glue for Correct Consistency.

Bring the glue to the boil and raise the brush a few inches. If the glue runs down in a continuous unbroken stream into the pot, free from lumpiness and without breaking up into drops, it is all right to apply it to both the groundwork and the marquetry. Place the latter paper side uppermost in position, so that its centre lines coincide with those on the groundwork; then drive in two headless nails as shown in Fig. 4.

As quickly as possible lay a sheet of newspaper over the marquetry to prevent it from adhering to the caul; place the hot caul over the paper and handscrew the battens down. Speed is essential.

When heating the caul both sides should be passed over the fire or gas ring; it should be too hot to touch when applied.

After about an hour or so the caul can be taken off and the work put on one side for at least twenty-four hours.

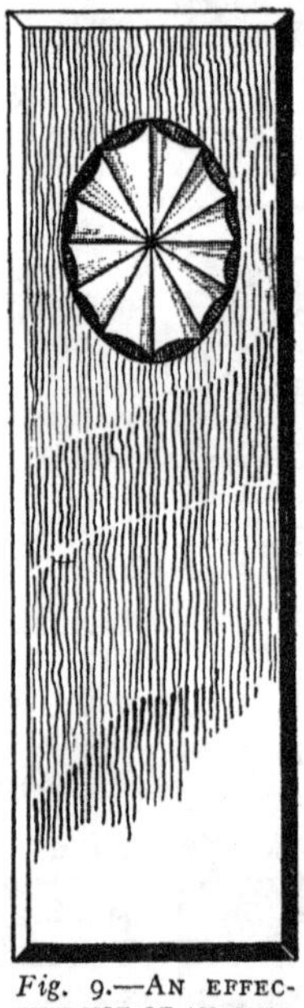

Cleaning up the Marquetry.

A steel scraper is used to clean up the marquetry as shown in Fig. 7. It removes only the finest of shavings and does not tear out the grain. Work diagonally when working over the actual marquetry and avoid digging in too deeply in any one part. Note how the thumbs are pressed in the centre of the blade at the back, making it slightly round and so preventing the corners from digging.

The work should now be thoroughly rubbed with glasspaper, using first No. 2 grade and then No. 1 grade. By wrapping the paper round a cork rubber a firm and even pressure can be maintained.

INLAYING A PIECE OF MARQUETRY

Rather different treatment is required when it is desired to let a small piece of marquetry into a piece of solid wood.

Additional Tools required.

In addition to the tools already mentioned, a mallet, gouge, router and marking awl will be required.

The wood should first be squared up and the centre lines drawn in as in Fig. 10.

Now place the piece of marquetry down on the wood and, while holding it down with the two sets of lines coinciding, draw a marking awl round the edge to mark the shape of the oval. It is not advisable to use a pencil, as the point is too thick and marks out too large an oval. Do not forget to mark both the wood and the piece of marquetry at one end so that it is replaced in the same position.

Fig. 7.—AFTER THE GLUE HAS DRIED, THE MARQUETRY IS CLEANED UP WITH A SCRAPER.

Fig. 8.—FINALLY, SMOOTH WITH GLASSPAPER HELD ROUND A CORK RUBBER.

Cutting out the Recess.

The next thing to do is to cut out the recess for the piece of marquetry. Work gradually round the entire shape as shown in Fig. 11, using appropriate gouges according to the part of the oval being cut. Tap the gouge very lightly with the mallet to avoid overrunning the line.

When gouging away the waste wood take care not to cut too deeply; the veneer is quite thin and the recess must be slightly less in depth than this thickness.

Levelling the Bottom of the Recess

The best method of ensuring that the bottom of the recess is perfectly level is to use a small router. Set the cutter so that it projects the required depth and work it back and forth in short strokes. It is impossible to take off too much with this tool.

Now place the piece of marquetry in the recess and trim if necessary with the gouge to make a good, tight fit.

Fixing the Piece of Marquetry.

Apply glue to both the recess and marquetry and place the latter in position. Then apply the caul and handscrew as previously described. As the recess was cut slightly less in depth than the piece of marquetry the caul is able to press on it firmly and ensure a good join.

Finally, clean up with the scraper and glasspaper.

INLAY BANDINGS

This is another fascinating branch of woodwork somewhat similar to marquetry. The bandings are bought

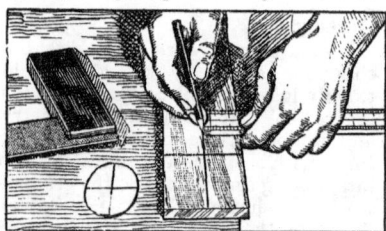

Fig. 10.—DRAWING IN LINES ON GROUNDWORK AND MARQUETRY TO ENABLE THE LATTER TO BE POSITIONED CORRECTLY

Fig. 9.—AN EFFECTIVE USE OF AN OVAL PIECE OF MARQUETRY RECESSED INTO A FINGER PLATE.

Fig. 11.—CHOPPING ROUND THE EDGE OF THE OVAL WITH A GOUGE TO MAKE THE RECESS INTO WHICH THE MARQUETRY FITS.

MARQUETRY

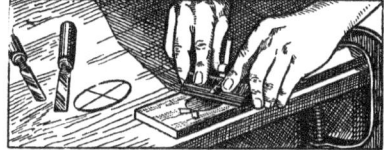

Fig. 12.—Waste Wood can be removed from the Recess with a Router.

Fig. 14.—Using the Scraper to clean up the Marquetry after the Glue has set.

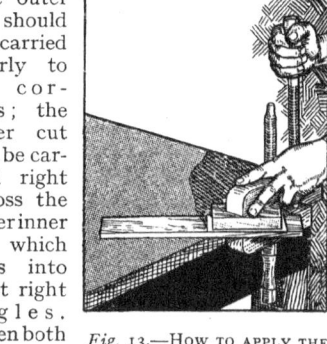

Fig. 13.—How to apply the Caul in the case of a Recessed Piece of Marquetry.

ready made, and from 1*d*. to 6*d*. per length of 39 inches are the general prices. The process of inlaying a banding consists of making a recess in the wood to be inlaid, fitting the banding to it and gluing it in. The recess may be at the edge or a little way in.

The groundwork must be planed flat and the edges must be true (see article on veneering).

Tools for making the Recess.

A tool known as a scratch is required for making the recess. A convenient size is shown in Fig. 15; it consists of two pieces of wood, each with a notch cut in it, screwed together. A cutter made of a piece of thin steel (part of an old saw blade will serve the purpose) filed to the exact width of the banding is placed between the two pieces of wood and held tightly by screws. By placing the cutter at different distances from the shoulder of the notch the position of the recess from the edge of the work can be varied. Fig. 16 shows the parts of the scratch, and Fig. 17 shows the method of using it. The cutter should project by a distance equal to the thickness of the banding, so that once it has removed the wood this amount it cannot go in any deeper.

Working the Groove.

Having filed the cutter of the scratch to the size of the banding, determine the distance in of the latter from the edge of the work. Then make a rough pencil mark all round the work, indicating the position of the outer edge of the banding. This is only for a general guide.

Next fix the panel down on the bench, using a handscrew, as shown in Fig. 17. Keep the shoulder of the scratch tight up against the edge of the wood and maintain a fair downwards pressure. It does not matter which way round the scratch is used, as it will remove wood in both the pulling and pushing strokes. If the grain of the panel runs rather definitely in one direction, the scratch should be worked one way only to follow this. Generally, however, the difference is not sufficiently pronounced for this. Do not attempt to carry the groove right up to the corners at this stage.

Working across the Grain.

Before working the groove across the grain, the sides of the groove should be cut in first with a cutting gauge.

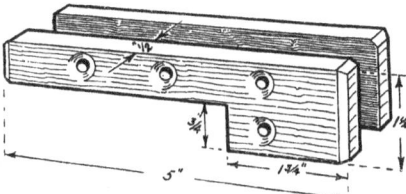

Fig. 15.—Details of the Scratch required for Inlay Bandings.

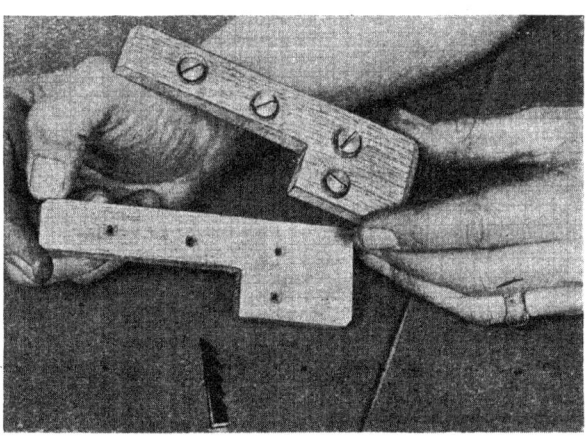

Fig. 16.—The Parts of the Scratch ready for Assembling.

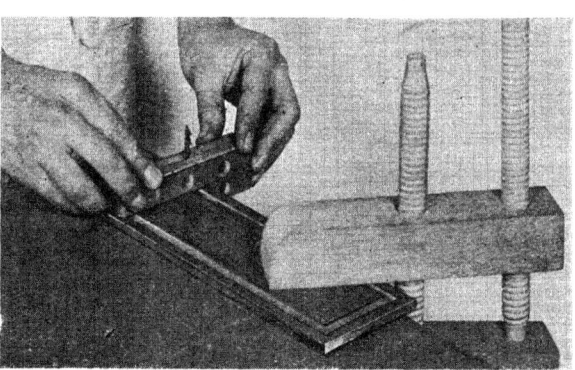

Fig. 17.—Using the Scratch.

The outer cut should be carried nearly to the corners; the inner cut can be carried right across the other inner cut which runs into it at right angles. When both cuts have been completed with the cutting gauge, the scratch can be used to complete the groove.

Finishing the Corners.

The corners are now finished off with a keen chisel, taking care not to overrun the mark.

The corners of the banding should be marked out with the set mitre and cut with a keen chisel. Start with one side and work right round the whole panel until the starting-point is reached.

Gluing.

Remove the bandings and lay them on the bench around the panel in the positions they are to be laid. Apply hot glue both to the groove and the banding and lay the latter in position, pressing the latter in with the back flat part of a hammer. Allow twenty-four hours for the glue to harden, then clean up with a steel scraper, finishing with No. 2 glasspaper, then No. 1.

Inlaying at the Edge.

When inlaying a banding at an edge, it is more satisfactory to form the rebate with either a rebate or a bull-nose plane, although it can also be formed with the scratch. First cut on the inner line with the cutting gauge, setting it to the exact width of the banding. The thickness, too, should be gauged in from the surface. Then plane away part of the rebate with an ordinary plane until it is nearly down to the line. The part of the rebate immediately against the gauge line can be cut away with a chisel to provide a start for the bull-nose plane. Take care to work down only as far as the line and keep it to the same depth throughout. The actual gluing-down process is the same as that already described.

Metal Screw Threads and How They Are Cut

SCREW threads of various kinds are in general use because of the different circumstances under which they may be used.

Screw threads which are required to hold surfaces of materials together, connect lengths of piping, etc., are triangular in section, whilst those which are used to transmit motion, for example, a worm and wheel drive, the leading screw of a lathe, are square in section.

The Pitch of a Screw Thread.

The distance between the top of adjacent threads is called the "pitch" of the thread, and it is the distance travelled by the point on a screw thread into a nut during one revolution of the screw, or the distance a nut would travel along a screw during one revolution of the nut.

The pitch is determined by the size and type of thread which is used, and is always constant for a particular type and size of thread.

Tables of screw threads generally give the number of threads per inch instead of the pitch. Taps and dies which are used for cutting screw threads generally have the number of threads per inch of the screw they will cut marked on them.

The Whitworth Standard Thread.

This thread is used for general engineering purposes. Compared with other types of threads it has a large pitch and is cut deeply, and on account of this has great strength. If it is required to use this thread when the materials will be subjected to vibration, or for use with moving parts, the nuts should be provided with a locking device.

The British Association Thread.

The thread is used for instrument and wireless constructional work and where small diameter nuts and bolts are employed.

The thread is shallower and has a

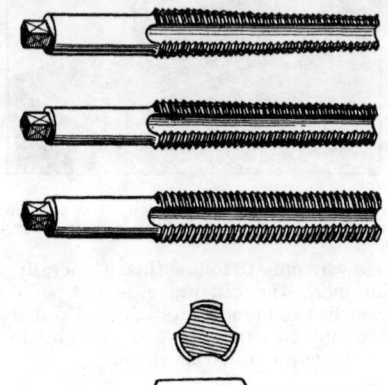

Fig. 1.—A Set of Whitworth Taps.
Showing from top to bottom, taper, intermediate or second, plug or finishing, section of tap, which is made fluted to give the most efficient cutting edge, tap wrench to take various sizes of taps.

smaller pitch than that of a Whitworth thread of the same diameter; it has not the same strength, but will not slacken off with vibration so easily as

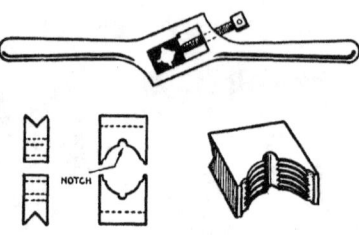

Fig. 2.—A Set of Whitworth Stocks and Dies.
The dies are split and notched, and are adjusted when cutting the thread by moving the adjusting screw fitted to the stock.

the Whitworth. It is largely used on brass screws and bolts on account of being shallow. A deep thread would materially weaken the screw or bolt.

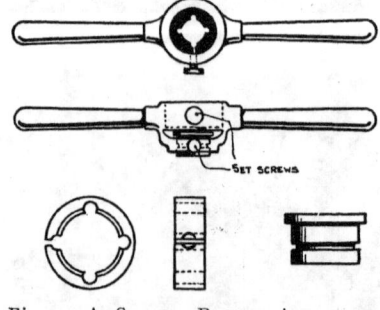

Fig. 4.—A Set of British Association Stocks and Dies.
The thread is cut in one operation, and to ensure that the axis of the tread is parallel to the axis of the material a guide tube (bottom right) is fitted to the stock. The guide tube is just a sliding fit over the material to be screwed.

British Standard Thread for Pipes.

This is a shallow thread, so as to prevent undue weakening of the pipe junctions. The size of the thread is determined by the nominal bore of the pipe, on the outside of which the thread is cut—for example, ½-inch thread pipe is cut on a gas, water, or steam pipe whose nominal bore is ½ inch.

The pitch of the thread is the same for a number of sizes, from 1 to 6 inches it is eleven threads per inch; for pipes less than 1-inch bore, the pitch is less, ⅛ inch being twenty-eight threads per inch.

Electric Conduit Thread.

A special thread is used for electric conduits and their fittings. It is shallower than the British Standard pipe thread on account of the thin walls of conduit. The size of the thread is determined by the external diameter of the conduit on which the thread is cut—for example, a ⅝-inch electric conduit thread is cut on a conduit whose external diameter is ⅝ inch.

The pitch of the thread is the same for a number of sizes—½- and ⅝-inch conduit threads are cut eighteen per inch, and ¾-, ⅞-, 1-, and 1¼-inch are cut sixteen per inch; conduits having a larger diameter than 1¼ inches are screwed with a thread of pitch fourteen threads per inch.

British Standard Fine Thread.

This is an important thread which is used for motor car construction. It is a deeply cut thread, and has a smaller pitch than a Whitworth thread of the same diameter.

Other Screw Threads.

The Cycle Engineers' Institute Standard thread is used in cycle construction.

The Sellers thread is the American Standard thread; it differs from the general Whitworth and British thread in the angle between adjacent threads. This is 60 degrees, compared with

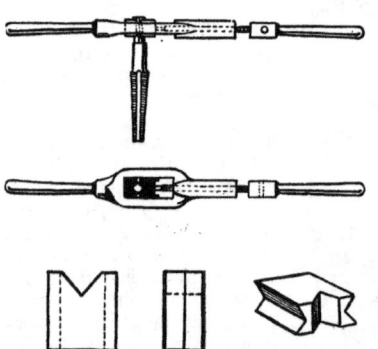

Fig. 3.—A British Association Tap and Wrench.
The wrench is fitted with movable jaws to enable various sizes of taps to be used in the wrench.

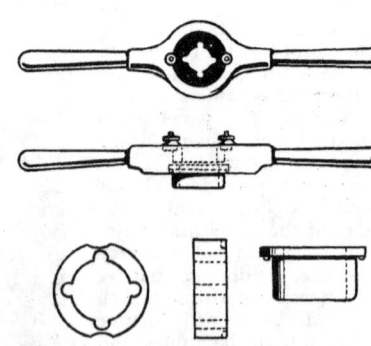

Fig. 5.—Electrical Thread Stock and Die.
The die and guide tube are held in the stock with the knurled nuts. A special shallow thread is used for electrical conduit and conduit fittings.

55 degrees adopted by British Standards.

The Standard Metre thread is in use in countries which use the metric system of measurement, and it is often used in the construction of scientific instruments in this country.

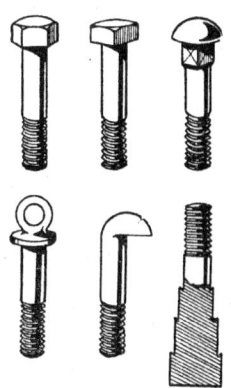

Fig. 6.—Types of Bolt.
Left to right (top), hexagon head, square head and cup head; (bottom) eye bolt, hook bolt and foundation bolt.

Male and Female Threads.

Screw threads are of two types, male and female. A male thread is cut on an exterior surface and a female thread is cut on an interior surface; for example, the thread of a bolt or screw is male, whilst the thread of a nut is female.

Hand Tools for Cutting Threads.

A male thread is cut with a die which is fitted into a stock. For small sizes and shallow threads a solid die may be used, but for Whitworth and other forms of deep threads, also pipe threads, split dies are used, the thread being cut in two or more operatious, depending on the diameter of the surface on which the thread is cut.

The die is made of hardened steel cut with a female thread of the corresponding size of the male thread to be cut. The edges of the die threads cut away the material of the screws, etc., when tracing out the male thread. The die is notched to allow the material which is being cut away to be cleared away from the surface of the screw, etc., which is being cut. The starting threads of the die have a large clearance to facilitate the starting and cutting of the threads.

Screw plates are used for cutting fine shallow threads, and for accurately finishing a machine-cut thread.

A female thread is cut with a set of taps which are fitted into a wrench. The taps used are taper, intermediate and plug.

The male threads upon the taps are themselves cut parallel throughout, the tapered form of the intermediate and taper taps being given by subsequently taking off the tops of the threads to a greater or less extent. In the former this is only done for a short distance, but in the latter it is carried to such an extent that the threads are entirely cut away from the bottom of the tap. This enables a taper tap to enter a hole of the proper size without difficulty, its first few revolutions doing little more than trace a thread of sufficient depth to lead it onwards. The intermediate tap is then entered and cuts the thread deeper, and afterwards the plug tap is entered to finish the thread to the correct depth.

Cutting a Male Thread with Split Dies.

Clear the threads of the die of any grit or metal cuttings and fit them into the stock.

Fix the rod to be screwed firmly in the vice and make a chalk mark on the rod at the point where the thread will finish. Open out the dies to allow it to pass over the end of the rod and clamp to the rod by screwing up the adjusting screw of the stock. If the rod is made of steel, wrought iron, or copper, the die should be lubricated with light mineral oil continually during the screwing process.

The first cut is made; do not turn the stock with a jerk, but apply a steady force so as keep the die cutting the metal at a steady rate until the point is reached where the thread will finish; the adjusting screw of the stock is now tightened and another cut is made, reversing the direction of rotation of the stock until the end of the rod is reached. In a similar manner successive cuts are made until the thread is completely cut; the thread may be tested for completion by a finished nut whose thread is of the same size and type. During the cutting process clear out the metal cuttings which may have accumulated in the clearance holes of the die.

Cutting a Male Thread with Solid Dies.

The thread is started at the end of the rod or pipe in this case, and in order to cut the thread parallel to the axis of the rod a guide tube is fitted into the stock before the die is fixed into position. The thread is cut in one operation and a liberal supply of lubrication is required to ensure a perfect thread and to prevent damage to the die.

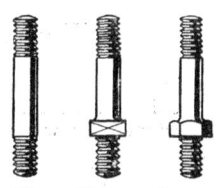

Fig. 7.—Types of Studs.

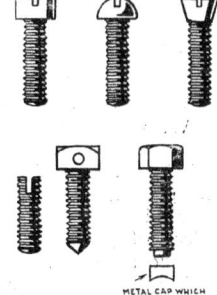

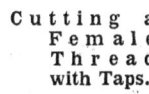

Fig. 8.—Forms of Screws.
Left to right (top), cheese head screw, cup head screw, and countersunk head screw; (bottom) grub screw and two set screws.

Cutting a Female Thread with Taps.

A hole is drilled in the material, whose diameter should

DIMENSIONS OF VARIOUS THREADS—WHITWORTH STANDARD

Diameter of Screw. Inches	Number of threads per inch.	Diameter at the bottom of thread. Inches
1/8	40	0·093
3/16	24	0·134
1/4	20	0·186
3/8	16	0·295
1/2	12	0·393
5/8	11	0·509
3/4	10	0·622
1	8	0·84
1 1/2	6	1·287
2	4 1/2	1·715
3	3 1/2	2·634

British Standard Pipe

Normal bore of pipe. Inches	Approximate outside diameter of pipe. Inches	Number of threads per inch.
1/8	13/32	28
1/4	17/32	19
3/8	11/16	19
1/2	27/32	14
3/4	1 1/16	14
1	1 11/32	11
1 1/2	1 29/32	11
2	2 3/8	11
3	3 1/2	11
4	4 1/2	11
6	6 1/2	11

British Association

Size of thread.	Full diameter over thread (approximate in inches).	Pitch of thread (approximate in inches).
0s	0·236	0·0394
1s	0·209	0·0354
2s	0·185	0·0319
3s	0·161	0·0287
4s	0·142	0·0260
5s	0·126	0·0232
6s	0·110	0·0209
7s	0·098	0·0189
8s	0·087	0·0169
9s	0·075	0·0154
10s	0·067	0·0138

Electric Conduit

External diameter of conduit. Inches	Thickness of wall conduit (B.W.G.).	Threads per inch.
1/2	17s	18
5/8	16s	18
3/4	15s	16
7/8	15s	16
1	15s	16
1 1/4	15s	16
1 1/2	14s	14
2	14s	14

METAL SCREW THREADS AND HOW THEY ARE CUT

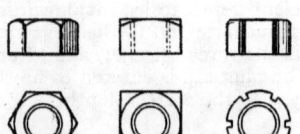

Fig. 9.—FORMS OF NUTS.
Left to right, hexagon, square and fluted, the latter being rotated with a special form of spanner.

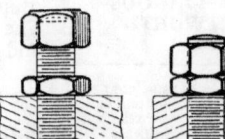

Fig. 10.—LOCKING NUTS.
A nut may be locked by a second nut, which should be twice the width of first nut. The second nut carries the load on the bolt.

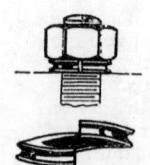

Fig. 11.—GROOVER'S SPRING WASHER FOR LOCKING A NUT.

be the tapping size for the particular thread. This is equal to the diameter at the bottom of the thread.

The tapping size of a Whitworth thread may be calculated from the rule:—

Diameter of tapping hole
$$= \text{Diameter of thread} - \frac{1\cdot 28}{\text{Number of threads per inch}}$$

For example—
Tapping hole for 1-inch thread
$$= 1 - \frac{1\cdot 28}{8}$$
$$= 0\cdot 84 \text{ inch}.$$

The quickest method is to use a drill plate which is a steel plate perforated with a series of holes, each hole representing the tapping size of a particular thread. The drill which is used should just pass through the hole which represents the tapping size of the hole to be cut. Having drilled the hole, the taper tap is entered and the tap wrench fitted on the square at the top of the tap.

Before the tap is turned with the wrench, carefully examine that its axis is at right angles to the surface of the material, so that the thread will be cut parallel to the axis of the hole; neglect of this precaution may cause the screw which is fitted into the tapped hole to be on the "skew" and also imperfectly fitted.

The tap is now slowly turned in a clockwise direction, lubrication being applied unless the material is made of cast iron or brass; occasionally ease the tap back, half a turn, especially if it appears to be binding or if the force to be applied to the wrench is excessive; attention to this detail may save the tap being broken in the hole.

When the taper tap has been through the hole the intermediate or second tap is entered; the thread will now be almost cut when this tap is used.

The plug or finishing tap is then used completely to finish the thread, which may then be tested with a screw or bolt having the same size and type of thread.

MAKING IMITATION LEADED LIGHTS

IN real leaded windows the glass consists of small pieces resting in grooved leads and the fitting up of such a window is probably not a job that the amateur would care to tackle. Fortunately it is quite an easy matter to obtain a good effect with imitation leaded windows, the lead being fixed to a pane of glass with cement.

Tools and Materials.

The only tools required are scissors, sponge, and a stiff brush for applying the cement. If a stained-glass effect is desired, a soft brush will be required. The lead used for the purpose is a substance known as "Perma-Led," obtainable in various widths and patterns, plain for ordinary straight bars and ribbed for special patterns and quick curves. For stained-glass effects, glass stains are used; these are quite permanent and waterproof, and being transparent give an effect just like real stained glass.

A Simple Imitation Leaded Window

We will assume that it is desired to make a simple imitation leaded window, with plain strips of lead laid to give a diamond pattern. It is advisable to mark out the pattern on a piece of paper cut to fit accurately behind the glass.

It is convenient to lay all the strips running in one direction first. To mark them off to length hold the lead in line with the pencil mark and with its end against the frame. Now cut the end with a pair of scissors held parallel with the frame. Hold the lead in position with the thumb and stretch the lead out until it reaches the opposite side. Then cut again with the scissors. Repeat until you have cut all the strips required for one direction. They should then be cemented to the glass.

Cementing the Lead to the Glass.

The cement should be stirred thoroughly before use. It is applied with a stiff brush over the whole length of each strip of lead. Make sure that every part is covered, but use the cement sparingly. Now leave the cement to get tacky for about a quarter of an hour before placing the lead in position. It is a good idea to wrap rags round the fingers before pressing the lead to the glass. When a long strip has been placed in position, look along the strip to make sure it is quite straight. Naturally, if the sheet of glass is a thin one, you would not apply too heavy a pressure.

When the first strips have been laid, those running across them can be proceeded with. The best plan is probably to have them in complete lengths, allowing them to pass over those already laid. This is simpler and stronger than fitting short lengths between the bars. Cut all the second strips to length and proceed to cement them as already described. Where they cross the lead should be well pressed in at the overlay, using the finger-nail with a piece of rag wrapped round. At awkward places such as where the lead ends at the framework pressure can be applied with a knife or other flat instrument.

Circular Designs.

Ribbed lead is used when circular designs are to be formed. Prepare templates of cardboard of the shape required and bend the lead round these. Bend a little at a time, continuing round until the starting point is reached. Bend about ½ inch more than required so that the two ends can be cut through with a knife to give a perfect joint.

If parts of the lead tend to spring up after being cemented, lay a piece of flat wood over the whole with a moderate weight on top.

Cleaning the Glass.

To clean off any surplus cement damp the sponge with turpentine or petrol and rub over the surface.

Staining the Glass.

If a stained-glass effect is required, the stain should be dabbed or stippled on with a brush. Stippling requires a certain amount of practice, as, after the first application, some bubbles are left on the glass. Leave for a few moments and go over again, and if necessary give a third application.

Bending Flat Lead to a Curve.

It sometimes happens that the flat lead has to be bent to a curve. First bend it approximately to shape with the fingers, a short length at a time, so that wrinkles are formed at the inner edge. Then smooth out the wrinkles by laying the lead flat on the table and pressing down with the fingers.

Basket Work
HOW TO MAKE CANE BASKETS AND CANE CHAIRS

CANE as well as osiers and willows have been used in the making of baskets from very early days, but it is only within modern times that the material known as pulp-cane has become so popular. It is the inner portion of cane drawn through a hole in a steel plate, similarly to the method employed in drawing wire, the outer portion of the cane forming the glazed cane used for chair seating and wrapping. Pulp-cane is obtainable in lengths of several feet, and in coils; the diameter varies from No. 1 (which is about $\frac{1}{16}$ inch) to No. 12 (with a diameter of $\frac{5}{12}$ inch). It can be obtained in larger sizes from 5 mm. to 18 mm., for use in framework and handles. It is available in natural or buff, as well as in a variety of colours.

Although cane is very pliable, it should be soaked in water before use, and should be kept in a damp condition all the time it is being used. This applies particularly to sharp bends, and, to ensure that the cane will not break, it is necessary to keep a wet sponge at hand so that the work can be moistened from time to time. If a piece of work has to be put away before it can be finished, it is as well to plunge it in a pail of water before working on it again.

The Wood Base.

It is much easier to begin cane basketry with a wooden base, as shown at A in Fig. 1. A large variety of shapes and sizes in wooden bases are obtainable, but, as they are not particularly cheap and not always available in just the size most convenient, it is better to make one to suit. Plywood is particularly suitable. It can be cut to shape with a sharp knife, if a saw is not available, and the edges are easily smoothed with glasspaper. The holes can be made with a bradawl or gimlet, but a more convenient tool is a geared drill and bit; the latter can be obtained to the exact diameter of the cane required for the spokes.

Mark Positions of Canes on Base.

The base, when cut to shape, should be marked out with pencil and ruler, or compasses, according to the arrangement of the spokes and the position of the holes spaced out. The distance apart of the spokes depends on the size of the basket; one with a base of 6 inches or so should have the holes spaced $\frac{1}{2}$ inch apart. In boring the holes, the plywood should be rested on a piece of scrap wood, as this will prevent undue splintering on the underside. When the holes have been made, both sides should be rubbed with glasspaper to leave the edges smooth.

Fig. 1.—A Simple Basket to begin with.
First prepare a plywood base as at A. Let in the stakes as at B, and then fill up the sides as at C.

Waterproofing Base.

As the cane must be used when thoroughly damp, it is necessary to coat the wooden base with a quick-drying varnish or with french polish. The possibility of bringing the base into a decorative scheme should not be overlooked, and, as plywood takes almost any colour, a suitable stain should be considered. The stain may be of the ordinary water stain variety, but to save time, and give greater brilliancy, a spirit stain is advisable. In any case, the wood should be coated with varnish; transparent spirit varnish is best, but a coat of size may be necessary if the plywood is very porous.

Decoration of Base.

The edges of the plywood may be finished with a coat of enamel or cellulose paint applied with a fine brush, but in this case it is advisable to use a filling in order to obtain a smooth surface. The possibility of using enamel or cellulose paint for the base is worth considering, particularly as brilliant colourings are available. It is essential before the cellulose finish is applied that the surface should be smooth and clean, and that two coats should be applied to give a lasting surface.

Putting in the Spokes.

The first stage in making a basket is to fit in the spokes. For the particular example of work shown at B in Fig. 1, the base measures 4 inches across, the holes are $\frac{5}{8}$ inch apart, and altogether seventeen spokes are required. The lengths of cane for the spokes should be cut to a length of 9 inches; this allows for a height of 3 inches and includes sufficient for the bottom and border. As a general rule, it is as well to allow more rather than the exact amount, as it is easier to finish the border with a long length.

The method of securing the spokes under the base is shown in the diagram in Fig. 2. A shows the simplest method and B a much stronger way. In this case the last spoke is threaded under the first loop made.

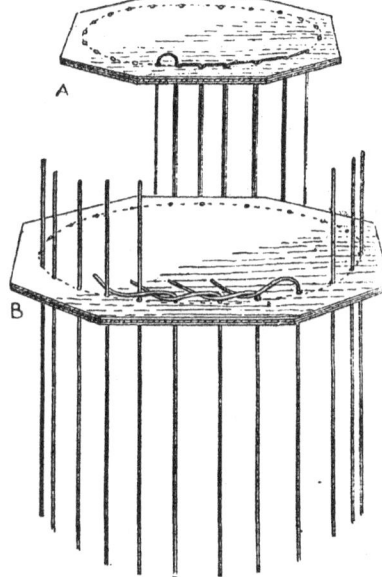

Fig. 2.—Two Methods of securing the Stakes to the Base.
A is very simple. B is more secure.

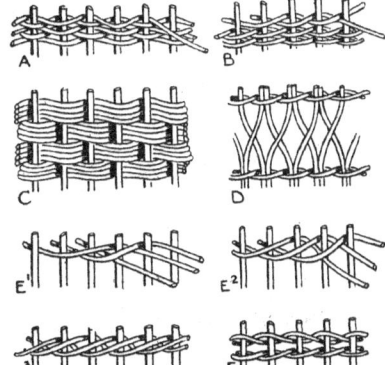

Fig. 3.—Various Methods of filling up the Sides of Cane Baskets.
A, Randing. B, Pairing. C, Slewing. D, Open-work. E, Three Stages in waling. F, Pairing in opposite directions.

Weaving.

The sides of the basket are now filled up with a weaver, that is, a long length of smaller cane woven in and out, as shown at C in Fig. 1, and also at A, Fig. 3. For a beginning it is advisable to continue this simple weaving, so that experience can be gained in manipulating the cane. It is not sufficient just to pass the cane in and out of the spokes in turn; the weaving length must be shaped with the finger and thumb, as shown in Fig. 4, and particular care must be taken to keep the spokes the correct distance apart and to avoid breaking the cane.

Beginner's Faults.

In beginning weaving, there is a tendency to pull the spokes inwards, but, as this particular basket has upright sides, the weaving length must be shaped to follow the required bend. As each round of weaving is completed, the cane should be pressed down close to the base, and if the shaping has not been done carefully the spokes will be pressed out of their upright position, and this must be avoided.

Finishing off the Weavers.

When the sides have been filled up to a convenient height, the end of the weaver can be turned down alongside the next convenient spoke. New weavers as required are secured in the same way, but the end may be left projecting inside, if desired, and cut off when the basket is finished. A simple way to finish the top is to turn the spokes down alongside the next spoke but one, but other methods will be explained when borders are specially described.

SOME WEAVING EFFECTS

Simple Weaving.

There are many different ways of filling up the sides of baskets; several are shown at Fig. 6. The example at A in Fig. 6, begun as at A, Fig. 2, is

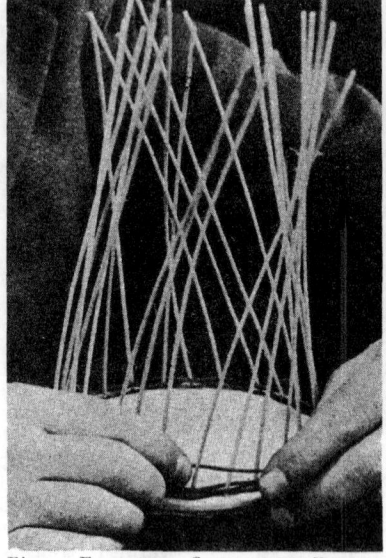

*Fig. 4.—*Filling the Sides of the Basket.
The cane should be moulded round the stakes with the fingers.

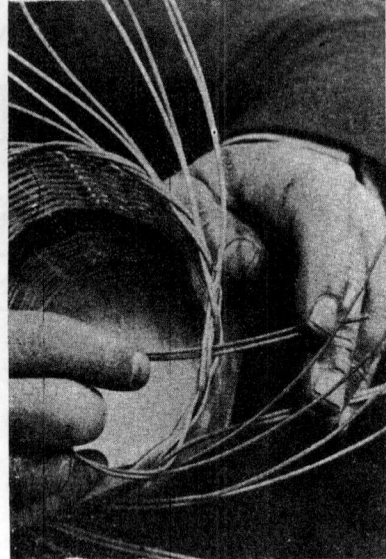

*Fig. 5.—*Forming the Border.
Care should be taken in bending the cane not to break it.

carried out with simple weaving or randing, as shown at A in Fig. 3, using No. 1 cane with sixteen No. 2 green spokes on a base, with a circle of 3½ inches diameter for the holes. There is a band of No. 1 red-coloured cane about half-way up and extending

*Fig. 6.—*Four Simple Baskets.
A shows the simple randing form of weave. B, another example of randing. C, an example of "pairing." D, the use of two colours in randing.

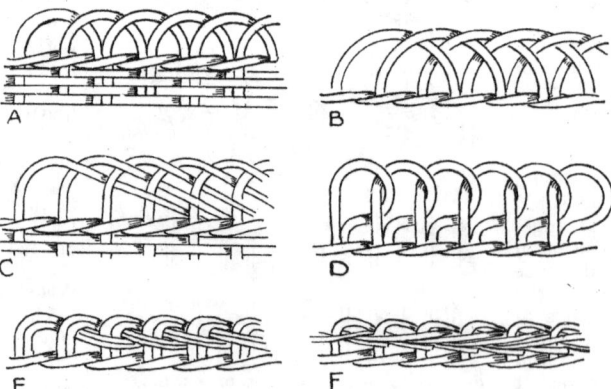

*Fig. 7.—*Some Effective Borders.
A is quite simple. B is a variation. C, the track border. D, a simple decorative border. E and F, variations of the track border.

to a quarter of the whole height, the sides being splayed out slightly.

"Pairing."

In the example at B, a similar method of weaving is used, but the twenty-five spokes on a circle of 5 inches are of blue No. 3 cane, and the sides are filled up with No. 1 cane in orange to a height of 3 inches, excepting a ½-inch band of blue about 2½ inches up. The basket at C, of the same size as that at B, has twenty-seven stakes of No. 3 natural colour, but the weaving with No. 1 cane is done with two lengths, one yellow and the other orange, as indicated at B in Fig. 3. This method is known as "pairing," and enables first one colour and then the other to come to the front. The last four rows are done in the same way, but both canes are the same colour.

In all cases the weaving should be finished with a round of pairing to keep the weaving in position and ready for the border.

Another Pairing Effect.

Another effect with similar sizes in cane is obtainable with pairing, as shown at D, by using an even number of spokes. In this example the circle is 5 inches, and the spokes in natural colour number twenty-four. One of the weavers is natural and the other orange, and, as the randing fills up the sides, the two colours are above one another. The top is finished off with two lengths of blue cane. There are several other methods of weaving, but with these two simple ones it is possible to get a considerable amount of variety when colour is used.

Slewing.

A rapid method of filling up the sides of baskets, as shown at C in Fig. 3, is known as slewing, and it is similar to randing, except that several lengths of cane are woven at the same time. The necessity of having an even or an uneven number of spokes should be considered first, as alternatives are more easily effected when an uneven number of spokes are used. Open sides in baskets, as shown at D, are obtainable by the use of double spokes, and the pairing or fitching weave or stroke, as it is called by the professional basket-maker. Another effect is obtained by using three strokes, or extra lengths placed alongside the original spoke.

Waling.

Three lengths of cane can be woven together, as shown in three stages at E; this is known as waling, and is similar to pairing. Interesting colour effects are possible when three colours are used, and waling is useful in finishing off the sides of the baskets, or for making a division between two different kinds of weaving in the same basket. Another method of effecting a division is shown at F, in which the pairing, or it may be waling, is carried in opposite directions. Here again are possibilities for the use of colour, and effective combinations can be made without difficulty.

Borders.

Of all borders, the open one shown at A in Fig. 7 is the simplest; it is formed by turning down the spokes in turn alongside the next but one. By missing another spoke and turning down the spoke alongside the third, a more decorative border, as at B, is produced. Another simple method of finishing is shown at C; this is known as the track border, and is made by weaving the spoke in front and behind those on the right or left. The spoke may be left out after the third, but four, five or even six weaves can be done before the spoke is finally run out and trimmed off when the border is finished. An adaption of the simple border at A is shown at D, and other methods of using the track border are shown at E and F.

Plaited Border.

The basket shown at A, Fig. 6, is finished with a simple plaited border; each pair of spokes is placed in turn

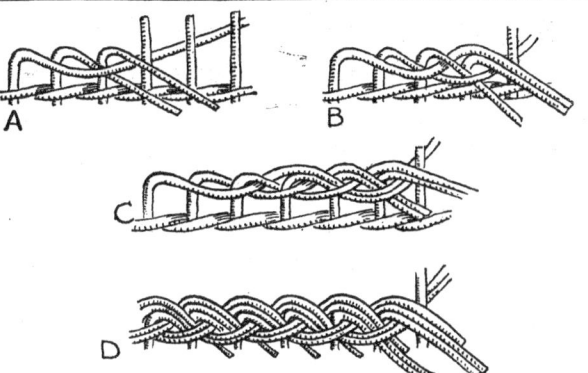

Fig. 8.—How to form a Plaited Border.
The operations necessary are shown in four stages. The plaited border effect can be seen in Fig. 10.

behind the next and in front of the next two, as indicated in the diagram at E, Fig. 7. The last lot of pairs are threaded through on the proper place, as in Fig. 5. The projecting ends are cut off neatly on the inside when the border is finished. The border at B, Fig. 6, is done similarly, but in this case there is only one spoke to turn down each time. In the examples at C, the spokes are laid down in the same

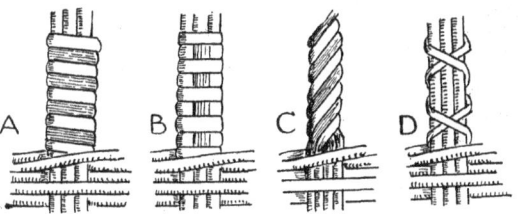

Fig. 9.—Four Simple Methods of decorating Plain Handles.
A and B show wrapping canes. C, a twisted handle with two coloured canes. D, a simple crossover wrapping effect.

way, but in the opposite direction. In the border of the basket at D, the spokes are laid down behind the next two on the right, then in front of the following two, then behind the fifth, and left in front of the sixth.

Two-three Plait Border.

One of the most effective borders is shown at Fig. 8, in four stages; this is known as the two-three plait. To begin with, two spokes are turned down to the outside, and No. 1 is

Fig. 10.—Two Examples of the Plaited Border.
Plaited borders used to finish off the rims of two wood-base trays.

carried over No. 2 to the inside of the basket, between Nos. 3 and 4, as at A. No. 3 is turned down to the outside and over the No. 1 spokes, which have been carried over to the inside; No. 2 spoke is now carried over No. 3 and to the inside of the basket between Nos. 4 and 5, but, it should be noted, No. 4 as well is turned down with it, as shown at B. The border is now continued, one group of two spokes turned in, one turned out, and a new spoke turned down as at C; and it is as well to remember that when any group contains three spokes, the short one is left behind and cut off when the border is finished, as shown at stage D. The last portion of the border is done by lifting up the spokes where necessary, so that the remaining spokes can be threaded into their correct position. The plait is suitable for finishing off the edging of trays, as shown at Fig. 10.

Handles.

Handles for baskets can be made by threading a double length of cane through the weaving underneath the border and twisting the strands together, threading the two ends alongside the weaving. Another method is to form a loop with large cane; one or more strands can be used. The loop is then covered with flat or round cane threaded underneath the border and wrapped neatly to cover the loop, and the ends are threaded alongside the spoke and the weaving. The plait may also be used as a handle when decorative treatment is specially required.

Suggestions are given at Fig. 9 for decorative handles. At A the loop is covered with flat wrapping cane in two colours. At B the wrapping is in one colour, but a second colour is threaded in and out of alternate wrappings as the latter proceeds. A simple twist is shown at C; this can be made with two or more coloured canes. For large baskets a handle can be made by looping three stout canes and wrapping them together with a pair of flat wrapping canes of a different colour, as shown at D.

A Shaped-side Basket.

A basket with shaped sides is the next step in basketry. The spokes, as shown at A in Fig. 11, are uneven in number, and are secured as shown at B in Fig. 2. Each spoke is now laid down flat, after being

BASKET WORK

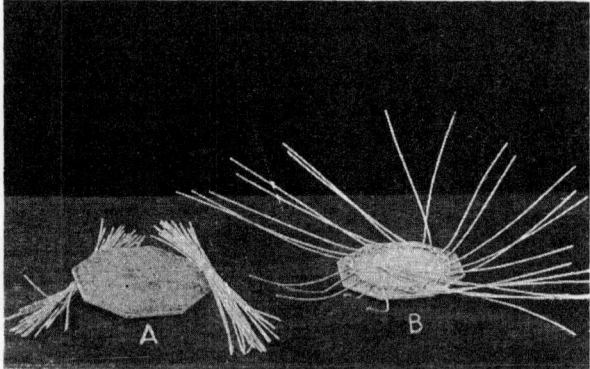

Fig. 11.—Making a Curved-side Basket.
A, the base, spokes and second spokes for a curved-side basket. The method of inserting the second spokes is shown at B.

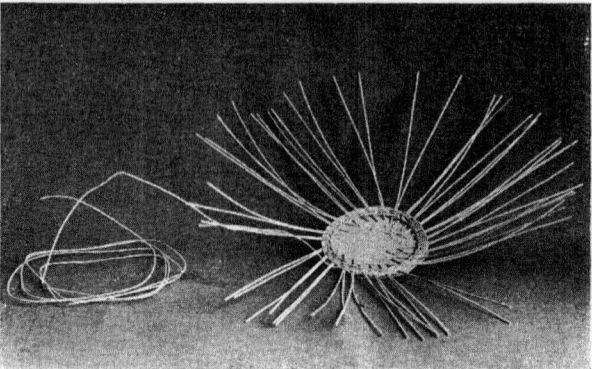

Fig. 12.—Making a Curved-side Basket.
First stage in weaving the sides of a basket.

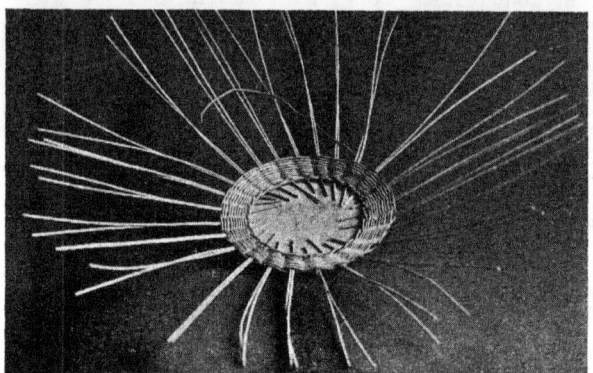

Fig. 13.—Making a Curved-side Basket.
As the weaving continues, care must be exercised to keep the spokes evenly spaced.

Fig. 14.—Making a Curved-side Basket.
The above picture illustrates a further stage in the weaving of the curved-side basket, after Fig. 13. The sides begin to assume a decided curve. This picture also shows the introduction of another colour by means of the pairing stroke, which can be seen more clearly in Fig. 15.

passed behind the next one on the right, as shown at B in Fig. 11. The next stage consists of threading a second spoke underneath the loop formed by the first; four such extra spokes are shown at B. The sides are now filled up with ordinary weaving, as shown at Fig. 12, care being taken to keep the weaves as close as possible. The work is now continued, as shown at Fig. 13, but now the sides are gradually pulled up by bringing the spokes close together. The basket will gradually assume the curved shape shown at Fig. 14, and a second colour can now be introduced by means of the pairing stroke, as shown clearly in Fig. 15. The sides are gradually drawn in as the weaving progresses, and when the required shape is formed a suitable border can be made.

MAKING A CANE CHAIR

When the principles of cane weaving and basketry have been mastered in the making of shopping baskets and trays, etc., the worker naturally turns to some more advanced cane work.

Wide Scope for Remunerative Work.
Chairs and settees of various types afford a wide scope for useful and remunerative cane work that can be executed in the home.

Fig. 15.—Making a Curved-side Basket.
Another view showing the gradual formation of the bowl shape, and also the introduction of the additional colour by means of the pairing stroke.

Tools required.
As with other forms of basketry, no expensive tools and apparatus are necessary. A simple chair frame should be attempted first, but when once the processes have been mastered, any size or shape of chairs could follow.

MAKING THE FRAME
Materials to use.
The frame itself must be constructed of stout 1-inch diameter cane or withy, or, for larger chairs, malacca cane of 1½ inch diameter is to be preferred. Cane, being more expensive than withy, might only be used for legs, seat and back, the struts and side pieces being made of withy. The front of the seat must always be of double cane.

How to bend the Cane.
A Bunsen flame or gas jet is needed to heat the cane

1044

where bends or curves occur. The bending is done with pincers and a bench vice, although an experienced worker will simply use his hands and knee.

Joining the Cane.

One and a half inch-wire nails are used to secure the cane, and, where overlapping and joining occur, the cane on the inside must be pared down so that a continuous line is maintained over the joins.

A Typical Size for a Cane Chair.

The measurements of a standard chair are given here, but these can readily be modified to meet the needs of the worker.

Width of seat, 18 inches.
Depth of seat, 18 inches.
Height of front legs to seat, 14½ inches.
Height of back legs from floor to back of chair, 33 inches.
Length of rung diagonally from leg to leg, 24 inches.
Short strut, 2 inches.
Longer strut, 5 inches.
Height of rungs from floor, 4 inches.

Putting the Frame Parts together.

Fig. 16 shows the complete frame. Three pieces of 1-inch cane are laid side by side for the arms and back.

The seat should be constructed first, next the back legs, then the front legs, arms and back.

Binding the Frame at Joints.

When the struts and rungs have been added, white ½-inch *split* cane is well damped and secured as a binding round those places in the chair where the cane meets at right angles. These are secured with ½-inch flat-headed nails. Four caps also must be fitted on the legs before any caning is begun.

CANING
Materials required.

Caning is done with either round whole cane (Nos. 4, 5 or 6), or with flat lapping cane. The round cane is stronger and finer than the flat cane, while the flat cane is quicker working and cheaper than the round. No. 6 round cane is the coarsest that is usually used for chair making.

Smooth the Framework.

Before any covering is begun, the whole frame should be lightly rubbed over with sandpaper and all knots in the cane or withy rubbed down.

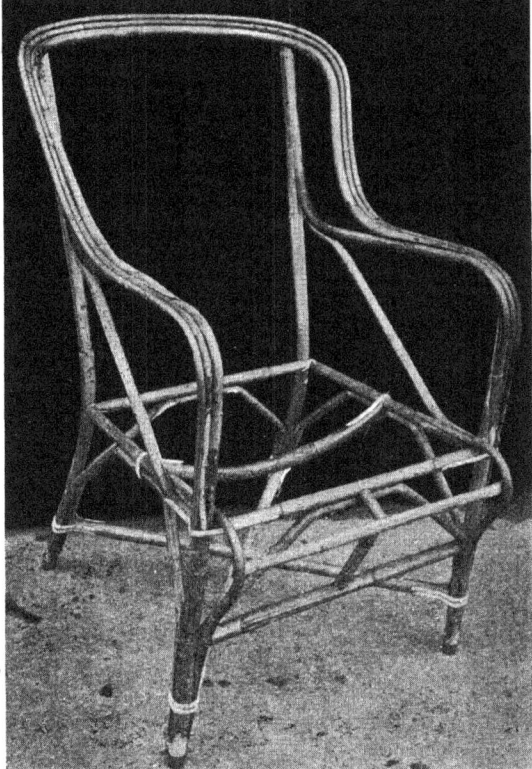

Fig. 16.—Complete Framework for a Cane Chair.

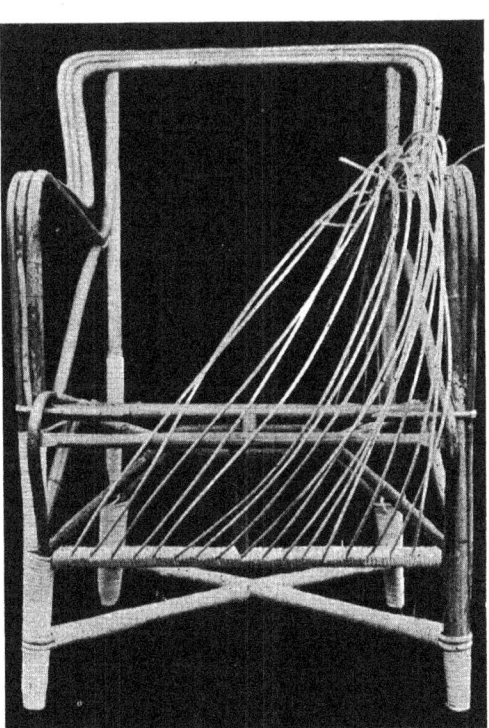

Fig. 17.—Stakes for the Seat and Back in Position. Note that the legs, struts and rungs have been covered with flat lapping cane.

Covering Legs, Struts and Rungs.

Flat lapping cane, previously soaked for five minutes in cold water, is used to cover the legs, struts and rungs. Begin on the rungs. Wire flat-headed tacks ½ inch long are used to secure the end of the cane to the rung.

This should be done about 2 inches from the end, so that the cane can be taken back and the end and head of the nail covered in the binding. Care must be taken in binding that the cane lies close and is taut—yet not pulled. In all cases of binding or wrapping, the wrapping, cane should lie as far as is possible at right angles to the frame it is covering.

To join Ends of Canes.

The end of a fresh piece of cane must be secured down in the binding (with the rounded side of the cane next to the frame) for at least 2 inches before the last of the old end is reached. Before starting with the new strand, the old and the new should be twisted once and the new piece can now be used to bind down the old end. The twisting which is the only part of the join visible should be placed on the underside or inside of the frame.

Finish covering Legs, Struts and Rungs.

The end must be securely tacked down, and, if possible, placed where it can be covered with other lapping on the inside. While it is not possible to conceal every tack used, the least number visible in the finished chair shows good working. If the chair has a square front (Fig. 18), the corner where the front of the seat joins the legs must be specially treated. This must be finished before the legs are covered. Three-inch lengths of cane are tacked down vertically and horizontally alternately until the corner is covered. When the lapping is continued up the leg the nails and ends of the corner pieces will be covered.

The whole of the frame, of whatever shape, except the seat, arms and back, must be covered before any weaving is begun.

Now stake the Seat and Back.

Nos. 10 or 12 round cane is used for the stakes for the seat and back. The stakes must be long enough to reach from the front edge of the seat, along the depth of the seat up the back, plus 2 inches. An *odd* number of lengths are necessary, arranged

1 inch or 1¼ inches apart, allowing the odd stake to be in the centre of the seat. After soaking the ends of the stakes they must be bruised and bent with pliers and secured down to the inside of the front seat bar. Even spacing is important. The bent end of the stake should reach to the next stake, the last gap being filled by an extra small bit of cane.

The whole length of the front is then securely bound, the joins in the cane being always on the underside of the frame (Fig. 17).

PUTTING IN THE SEAT
First Weave.

Whatever shape the seat of the chair may be, if round cane is used a weave termed "waling" must be done for the first inch. When flat cane is being used ordinary weaving is begun now and maintained throughout the entire chair. For "waling" three strands of cane are necessary, taking each strand of the cane in front of two stakes and behind the next. When each line is completed, all three strands are passed round the edge of the seat frame.

Inserting a Rib.

After an inch of "waling," which must be firmly done and well pressed down, an extra rib or stake the same length as the previous ones cut is inserted into the weaving alongside those already there. These extra stakes are pushed right down to the chair frame.

Second Weave.

Ordinary weaving (taking up one pair of stakes, leaving the next) is now continued across the seat, and the length of weaving cane is passed twice round the frame every alternate row. This is done if the cane used be flat *or* round. Just before the weaving reaches the centre seat strut an extra short stake, 3 or 4 inches long, is fixed to the side edge of the seat to take the weaving where the centre bar joins the side of the seat.

Fig. 19.—An Alternative Method of Lapping.

Arranging the Seat Stakes.

Should the seat be shaped in any way, the stakes must be so arranged as to be evenly spaced over the whole seat. When the weaving of the seat reaches the back uprights, another piece of staking cane must be fixed across the corner where the upright back passes the seat. Five or six rows of weaving will be passed round this cane corner. The stakes will now bend round and be vertical to form the back. Care must be taken that they do not bulge forward, as every alternate pair will be inclined to do if the weaving cane is pulled more tightly when weaving from left to right. This is a common fault with beginners.

Fig. 20.—A Cane Chair with Plain Lapping.

WEAVING THE BACK

Plain weaving is now continued until the pattern in the back is reached. This is generally two-thirds up the chair back, and can be either of the plain cane or coloured enamel cane and can be inserted over the ordinary weaving cane.

The Pattern.

The pattern is begun when the weaving cane is passed over the centre stake. This is line 1. When weaving line 2, the cane must pass *behind* the two stakes before and after the centre stake. Line 3 is plain weaving. It will now be noticed that three strands are in front of the centre stake.

Introducing a Coloured Cane.

If colour is introduced, two short lengths of enamelled cane must be inserted behind the stakes exactly to cover the weaving cane. The ends of the enamelled cane will be held tightly in place by the upright stakes. Care should be taken to ensure that these short lengths of cane are long enough to fit behind the upright stakes. In line 4 the weaving cane is passed behind the two stakes before and after the pattern. Line 5, plain weaving.

The pattern now consists of two groups of three strands in front of stakes, and two more strips of coloured cane can be inserted.

The pattern is continued to the required width and reduced again to form a diamond.

Fig. 18.—The Lapping Cane for the Arms and Back in Colour.

A variation of colour is made by a square or oblong or two small diamonds. One or two strands of coloured cane might be woven straight across the chair.

Finishing the Back.

Plain weaving is continued for the remainder of the back to within 1½ inches of the back rail. Strips of lapping cane, 5 inches in length, must be fixed over the back rail where the back joins the rail. These strips are tacked down back and front about 1 inch down, so that the remaining weaving will cover the ends of the strips, also the heads of the tacks. The gap at the top enables the binding cane to be passed round the rail. The stakes should now be cut off, leaving only sufficient to bend over at right angles and to meet the next stake underneath the back rail. Before bending, the stakes must be damped and bruised where the bend is needed, or they will probably snap. The ends of the stakes are nailed on the underside, the last gap being filled in with an odd bit of cane. This will be neatened when the lapping cane is brought round from the arms.

COVERING ARMS AND BACK FRAME

Introducing Colours with Lapping Cane.

Lapping cane is used for the arms and back, and colour can here be introduced either by lapping alternate colour and plain (Fig. 18), twisting the cane at the back when commencing the fresh colour and varying the strands of plain and coloured cane, or laying the coloured cane on top of the natural and working the two together, laying the natural cane on top of the coloured occasionally to hold it down (Fig. 19). Many patterns can be evolved, or, of course, the whole may be done in plain natural cane (Fig. 20).

Cut off and singe all Ends of Cane.

All ends of cane which must be at the back of the chair are now cut off close to the weaving. The whole must be singed either with a gas jet or methylated lamp. A taper or candle is unsuitable, as this blackens the work.

To finish the Chair.

Scrub the chair in clean cold water. The tendency of cane chairs is to go slightly darker in use, and a soaking of cold water occasionally preserves the cane. The whole chair can be dyed, painted or enamelled.

Aniline dyes in spirit or spirit stains are useful in dyeing cane, but it should be noted that brilliant colours should be chosen, as the natural colour of the cane absorbs a certain amount of the brilliancy and tones down the original tint very considerably.

In applying enamel, it is essential that the surface of the cane should be as smooth as possible. Great care should be taken to singe the cane as thoroughly as possible, so that all the loose fibres are removed.

SOME SIMPLE RULES TO FOLLOW

Chairs are simple to make provided the frame is sound and a few simple rules are observed.

Putting in the Stakes.

The stakes must be evenly spaced and kept perpendicular, the tendency will be for them to lean to the right-hand side.

Obtain materials of good quality. Dryad materials can be recommended.

Weaving.

All weaving must be as horizontal as possible. It may be that the cane which is wound round the edge of the chair becomes higher or lower than the inside weaving.

This can be remedied by occasionally omitting the double turn of the cane round the frame at the end of the rows.

A piece of garden cane across the back will help to keep the work even, and a metal rod or ruler is useful to tap down the weaving.

Care should be taken to avoid trimming the protruding ends of the cane too close to the weaving. Owing to the strain to which a cane chair is subjected, ends that are cut too close to the stakes are liable to work past them; this will spoil the effect as well as the strength of the weaving.

METHODS OF WATERPROOFING FABRICS

THE following are satisfactory methods for waterproofing fabrics such as linen, cotton, jute and hemp fabrics:—

(1) Place the fabric in a solution consisting of 1 lb. of soft soap to a gallon of water and allow it to soak for about half an hour. Next wring out the fabric and immerse in a solution of sulphate of iron (sometimes termed *copperas*), the strength of which is 1 lb. per gallon of water. Afterwards, wring out the fabric and pass once or twice through clean water.

(2) Dissolve separately 5 parts each of alum and sugar of lead (lead acetate) in just sufficient water. Heat the solutions and mix together when warm. Allow the mixture to stand quietly until a precipitate of lead sulphate is formed. The clear fluid, now containing acetate of ammonia, is then poured off and mixed with 500 parts of water containing in solution a little isinglass. Immerse the articles for twelve hours in the fluid until saturated and then dry and press them.

The fabric articles will not only be water- and wind-proof, but will also be impervious to attack from moths.

(3) First saturate thoroughly in a bath of ammonio-cupric sulphate of 10° Bé., at a temperature of 77° F., and then introduce the articles into a solution of caustic soda, 2° Bé.

A rather better second solution, instead of the caustic soda, is one of aluminium sulphate.

Oil-skin Methods.

The following are satisfactory mixtures that can be used for waterproofing linen or cotton fabrics so as to give them the familiar oilskin effect.

(1) Dissolve rosin in hot boiled linseed oil in sufficient quantity just to cause the oil to thicken.

(2) Mix chalk or pipe clay, finely powdered, with boiled linseed oil until a thin paste is formed.

(3) Melt together boiled oil, 1 pint, beeswax, 2 oz., and rosin, 2 oz.

Any of the above mixtures can be used for painting on to the fabric, an ordinary painter's brush being all that is required.

The fabric should be stretched slightly over a wooden frame in order to avoid folds and at the same time to facilitate the penetration of the mixture. To aid the latter process the mixture should be applied hot.

Make sure the Fabric is dry before Waterproofing.

It is of the greatest importance that the fabric shall not be damp when the mixture is applied to it; it is therefore advisable to warm the fabric before it is painted with the waterproofing mixture

It is usually necessary to apply more than one coat; in this case *the last coat should be perfectly dry* before the next is applied. If this precaution is not taken the fabric will be left in a sticky state. It is this stickiness which frequently results in serious damage to oilskins when they are folded and, later, unfolded again.

In any case, however, it is advisable to avoid folding an oilskin; it should always be hung up when not in use. The coated fabrics should be left to dry naturally in the ordinary air of the room; heat *should not be* applied to expedite the drying process.

TIME, LABOUR AND MONEY SAVING IDEAS

A GAS ECONOMISER

The arrangement shown in the sketch will enable two saucepans or kettles, etc., to be boiled over one gas ring of the gas stove. It is made of medium gauge sheet iron—not tin. A shows the frame, which may be 6 or 8 inches wide and long enough to take two saucepans side by side—say 16 inches (or more if desirable). The frame is 2 inches deep and riveted, one end over the other, at one end, as shown, with two iron rivets.

The bottom, B, is of fairly stout gauge iron, and is $\frac{1}{8}$ inch longer and wider than the frame A, and has six pillars (shown separately at D) made of $\frac{1}{4}$-inch round iron and filed round at the bottom ends to a shoulder, the ends being $\frac{3}{16}$ inch. The distance between

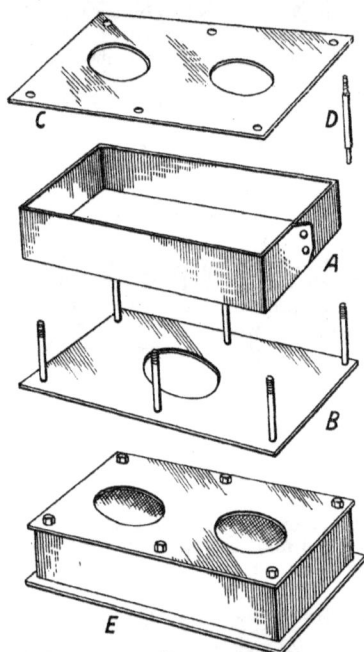

the shoulders is $\frac{3}{32}$ inch less than the depth of the frame.

In the centre of the bottom a hole 5 inches diameter is cut to let the hot flames from the gas stove ring pass up into the economiser. The top is the same size as the bottom and has two holes 5 inches diameter and spaced $\frac{1}{2}$ inch from the end.

The corners and centre of the sides are drilled to take the four pillars which locate the frame and hold the top and bottom plates and the frame firmly together when the ends of the pillars are riveted up or screwed to nuts as shown. The economiser assembled is shown at E.

TO MAKE TIN CAN COVERS EASY TO REMOVE

Small cans with screw covers con-tain many of the various prepared handy compounds used about the bench. They often stick just tight enough to be beyond the usual grip of the fingers on the bare tin. Around

the cap of each can, wind and press several turns of common electrician's adhesive tape, cut just wide enough neatly to fit the width of the cap or cover. This, of course, always stays snugly on and in place. It makes the grip very much better, and you do not have to hunt around for anything to assist it. When the can is empty, simply use the old taped cover on the new can.

TO PREVENT CEILING HOOK AND DROP CHAIN RINGS SQUEAKING

The ceiling hooks and drop chain rings of the usual heavy seat or chair porch swing invariably squeak with an exceedingly irritating noise. A drop of oil will stop it for a time, of course, but not long, especially in warm weather. Take a fairly large sheet of tinfoil. Repeatedly fold and press it firmly with a pencil or other smooth hard tool until you have a rectangular mass or pad of it somewhat wider than the ceiling hook and about an inch long. Lay this in the large hook as shown. Place the chain ring in over it

and work the inside of the ring into the packed foil. The small block of lead will quickly shape to the hook and cannot fall out. The ring will work absolutely noiselessly in its groove.

FIRE-IRON HANGER

An easily made and attractive-looking fire set pedestal or hanger is made as shown in the accompanying sketches. A shows the hanger complete.

C shows the tripod leg cut out of a piece of brass plate with a $\frac{1}{4}$-inch hole in the centre. The three legs are bent down as shown at A. D shows the four-arm hook top, also cut out of brass plate. It also will have arms bent down and hooked up as shown at A, and a central $\frac{1}{4}$-inch hole.

At B is shown the assembly of the hanger in section. A piece of polished brass-cased iron tube forms the prin-

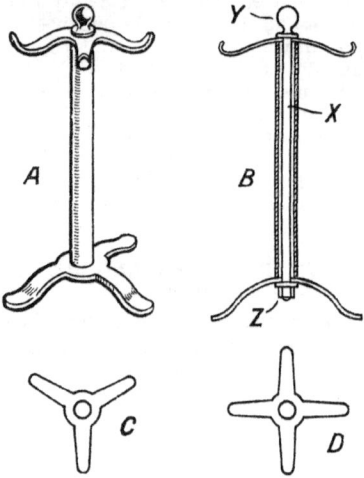

cipal part. It should be 13 inches long, and should take easily a $\frac{1}{4}$-inch iron rod screwed each end. The top end takes a brass knob, which may be screwed and then sweated to prevent its turning on the rod. The bottom end of the rod takes a hexagon nut and a washer, and, when screwed up, holds all tightly together.

The legs and the top arm should be nicely rounded at the edges and polished and lacquered; as should the knob and the brass tube upright.

A USEFUL HAND BRUSH

A very useful and lasting hand brush can be made from the end of a discarded broom, preferably of the warehouse type. A piece about 6 inches long is cut from the head, and a stout batten, say $18 \times 1\frac{1}{2} \times \frac{1}{2}$ inches, is fitted to this. Scoop a hollow in one end of this handle with the gouge—this is to enable the head to be fitted properly.

Smooth the edges of the handle with glasspaper and fix to the head by two screws.

How to Make a Small Roundabout

This consists of a stand, as shown, and a rotating member with two or four arms carrying seats. A bevel wheel fixed to the flange which forms the top of the stand, gears with a pinion carried on a shaft under one of the arms. On the end of the shaft is a chain wheel, from which a loop of chain hangs. The occupant of the seat under the chain pulls gently and the arm revolves.

How the Seats are fixed.

The seats are carried by one bolt, which allows them to swing out slightly as the arm revolves. The length of the arms can be anything within reason. Those in the sketch are 8 feet 6 inches, giving a diameter of 17 feet, or a path of approximately 53 feet per revolution, so that quite a slow speed of revolution gives a high periphery speed.

Several dimensions must be left to the choice of the builder, such as the height of the seats above the ground, etc., but the arm height should be kept about 5 feet, so that children are not likely to be hit by the revolving arms while watching those in the seats.

CONSTRUCTIONAL DETAILS

The central shaft is of 2-inch gas barrel, with a standard 2-inch gas flange screwed on the bottom end. The thread is allowed to go through the flange, and, by means of a socket, an earth tail of about 2 feet 6 inches of the same barrel is attached. The

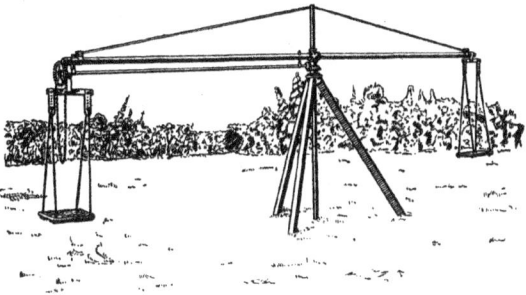

Fig. 1.—The Completed Roundabout.

flange is screwed by stout wood screws to a wood earth plate about 2 feet

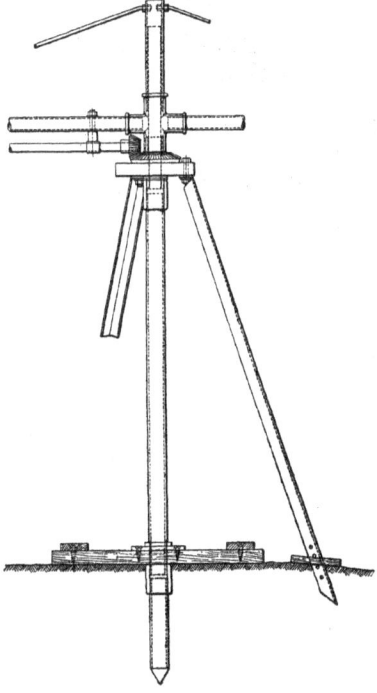

Fig. 2.—Diagram showing Arrangement of Central Shaft, Bevel Wheel, etc.

square. At the top end a socket is screwed on, and a 2-inch to 1½-inch bush is screwed into the socket. The top flange is a special size, 9 inches diameter, ½ inch, thick and has three ½-inch holes on a 7-inch circle to attach the legs.

The Bevel Wheel.

The bevel wheel is fixed to the flange, the method depending on the type of wheel. A car differential wheel and pinion make a very good pair for this job.

A length of 1½-inch barrel, about 18 inches long, is screwed through the flange into the bush in the 2-inch socket on the column. Note, the tail on the column must be driven into the ground until the wood plate rests flush. Do not dig a hole for it or the column will not remain steady.

The Angle Iron Legs.

Three angle iron legs, as per sketch, are required. Cut one end as shown, drill holes and bend piece left over. Three wood plates are required, and three lengths of ½-inch round iron for pins. The legs are bolted to the top flange on the column, and the other ends forced into the ground, the wood plates then being put round them and the pins put in the most suitable hole to support the legs. This allows for a little levelling if the ground is not quite level, as it is very essential that the column should be upright.

Details of the Revolving Arm.

The revolving arm is made up from

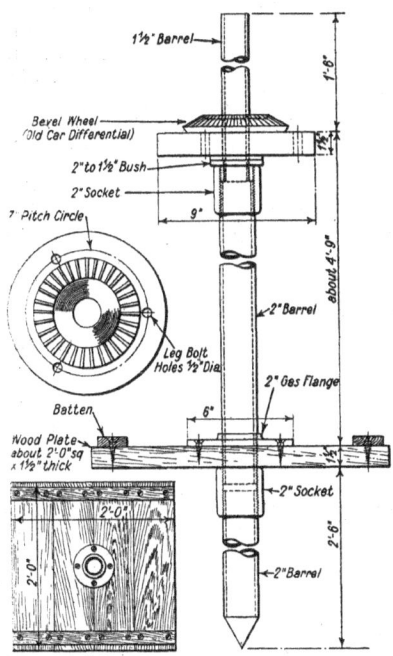

Fig. 3.—Diagram showing important Dimensions.

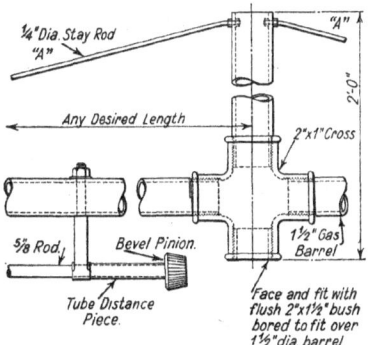

Fig. 4.—Details of the Fixing for the Revolving Arms.

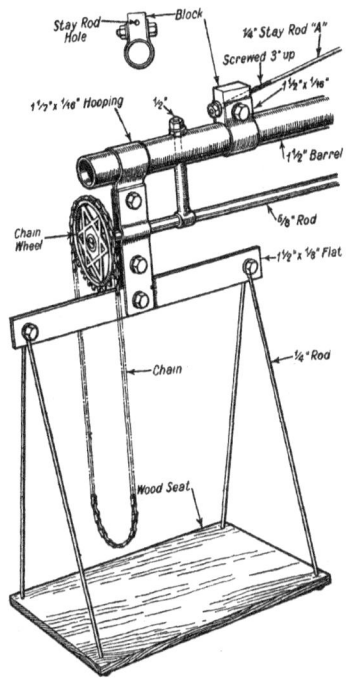

Fig. 5.—Details of the Seat and Driving Mechanism.

HOW TO MAKE A SMALL ROUNDABOUT

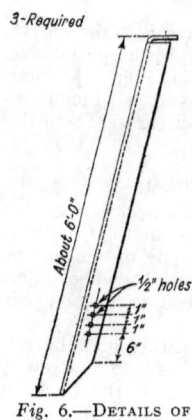

Fig. 6.—DETAILS OF ANGLE IRON LEG.

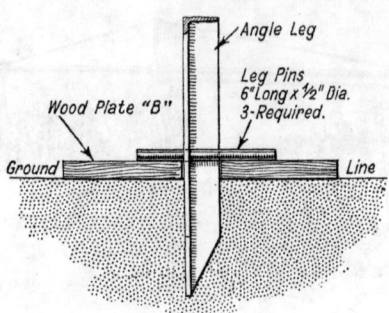

Fig. 7.—DETAIL OF FIXING FOR ANGLE IRON LEG.

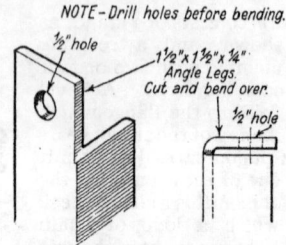

Fig. 9.—DETAIL OF TOP OF ANGLE IRON LEG.

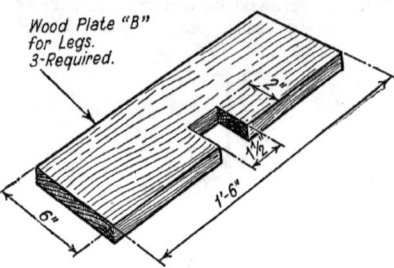

Fig. 8.—DETAILS OF WOODEN PLATES WHICH FIT ROUND LEGS.

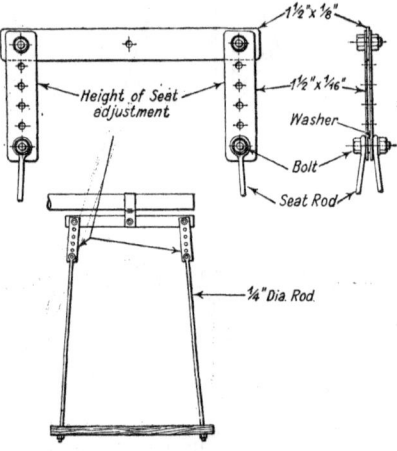

Fig. 10.—DETAIL SHOWING METHOD OF ADJUSTING SEAT.

a 2 × 1½-inch beaded malleable iron cross, a stock item, with a flush 1½-inch bush with the thread turned out screwed into the lower end. The bottom face of the cross should be faced up true, this and boring out the bush being the only lathe work required. The bush should slip easily over 1½-inch barrel. A length of 2-inch barrel is screwed into the top of the cross, and should be about 18 inches long.

The arms are made from 1¼-inch gas barrel, screwed into the cross, and of any desired length.

The pinion shaft is a length of rod carried on two arms bolted through the barrel, as shown.

The chain wheel is a cycle bottom bracket chain wheel and the chain is ordinary cycle chain, but is longer than the length on a cycle, but can be made up out of bits of worn chain.

The seats are hung on clips made from 1½-inch stout hoop steel, the top bar of the seat frame being 1⅜ inches by ⅛ inch. The seat bars are ¼-inch rod, and the two tension stays are of the same material. The pitching of the wheels can be adjusted by washers put under the cross or a tube distance piece put at the back of the bevel pinion.

Discounts off Pipe Fittings.

All pipe fittings can be got from the local ironmonger, but remind him that the discounts off these things are approximately as follows: 70, 25, 10 and 2½ per cent. for cash, a 2-inch cross priced at about 5s. coming out at about 9d. Rod, bolts, etc., can be obtained from Messrs. Buck & Hickman, Whitechapel, or Messrs. Steadall, Clerkenwell. Bevels can be obtained from any motor junk shop.

Paint the Roundabout thoroughly.

Paint very well, as the roundabout has to be in the open.

If a ball thrust race can be picked up of suitable size and cheap, it goes well under the cross above the bevel wheel.

How to adjust for Different Weights.

Adjustment for children of different weights can be made by sliding the non-driver's seat along the arm in either direction, and for this reason it is as well to leave that arm a little longer, say 6 inches. There is no danger in use, as fingers cannot be caught in either the chain or bevel wheels, and the speed can never get high enough to throw the passengers out.

Height of Seats.

The height of seats should be arranged so that the feet of the children clear the ground by about 3 inches only. It is impossible to give the total cost, as much of the stuff might be got at scrap price, and the labour will depend on the facilities available, few tools being required.

If four arms are fitted, all arms must be stayed, as shown, to central tube.

A roundabout constructed as described will be found a never ending source of amusement, and is well worth taking the trouble to erect.

FOR HOLDING BROOMS

Brooms that are continually falling down are a source of considerable annoyance. The accompanying sketch shows a very simple and inexpensive gadget that can be quickly made up from odd scraps of material and which will keep the broom from being knocked over or falling down.

First obtain a small block of wood about 2 × 5 inches and fix it at a convenient height on the wall where the broom is generally kept.

Then prepare a clip to the shape

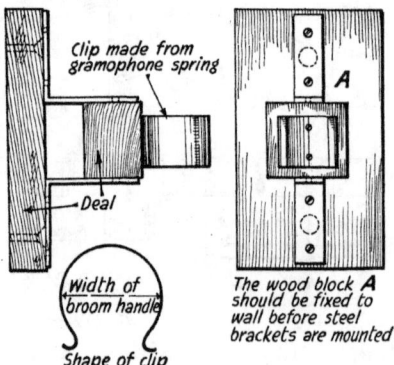

shown. A piece of an old gramophone spring will be found quite satisfactory and it should be shaped so that it is just a nice fit round the broom handle. This clip is fixed to a small block of wood by means of two screws.

Next obtain two metal angle brackets and screw them to the block of wood fixed to the wall so that there is just room for the block of wood to which the clip is attached to be screwed between the brackets, as shown.

AN ORNAMENTAL FOUNTAIN FOR THE GARDEN

IN considering the ways and means of improving the attractiveness of a garden, special attention should be given to the possibilities of the ornamental garden pool, for there are few gardens indeed that are not enhanced by such a feature. By itself, however, a garden pool with still water is not the ideal to be achieved, as it is only by the addition of an ornamental fountain that its full effects are experienced.

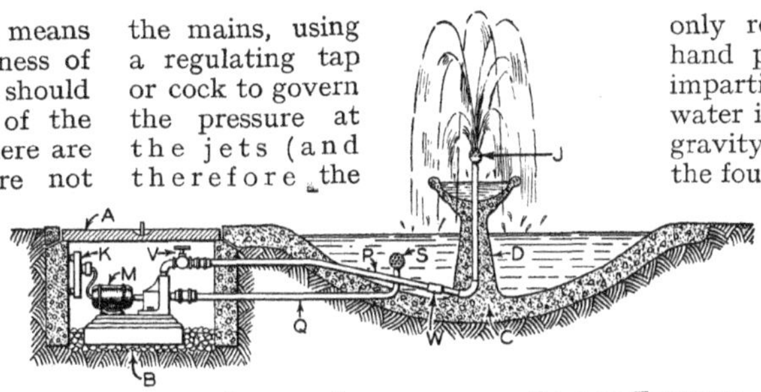

The still-water garden pool has the drawback of encouraging unwanted stagnant water growth, including both vegetation and pond life. If, however, the water is kept in a state of circulation and agitation, as when a fountain is in frequent use, it will be found to preserve its cleanliness and to discourage the growth of undesirable water plant and pond life. On the other hand, owing to the aeration of the water and to its constant circulation the garden pool is ideal for ornamental fishes, such as gold and silver fishes, ornamental pond snails and certain attractive aquarium plants.

Apart from these advantages there are few items in the garden more attractive to watch than a well-arranged fountain situated amidst the decorative surroundings of a carefully designed and located garden pool. The latter may be greatly improved with a surround of large stones or pieces of rock, with rock plants arranged in the crevices.

NOTES ON SUITABLE SCHEMES

When considering the question of installing a garden fountain the matter of first cost and of running expenses is an important one, so that the pros and cons of each alternative system must be looked into carefully before any decision is taken.

To a large extent, however, the selection of any particular system for working the fountain will depend upon the locality and also whether mains water supply and electricity are available. If neither of the latter is at hand the question of operating the fountain becomes more difficult.

Obtaining Pressure to force the Water out of the Jets.

In the case of all fountains for garden pools it is necessary to provide some means for raising the water and giving it sufficient pressure to force it out of the jets. Where mains water supply is available one can connect the fountain jets directly to the mains, using a regulating tap or cock to govern the pressure at the jets (and therefore the

Fig. 1.—SHOWING GENERAL ARRANGEMENT OF GARDEN FOUNTAIN AND HORIZONTAL PUMP IN PIT.

A, stone slab; B, coke for drainage; C, concrete bottom; D, separate concrete ornament; J, fountain jet; K, switch board; M, electric motor and pump; P, delivery pipe; Q, suction pipe; S, gauze trap over suction; V, jet delivery control cock; W, pipe connection.

height of the water that is forced out through the jets).

Electric Power.

Similarly, if electric power is available this can be utilised to operate an electric motor which in turn drives a water pump to deliver the water under pressure to the fountain jets.

Pump.

If neither mains water nor electricity is available one must seek some other source of power to lift the water through the jets.

One popular method is to pump some of the water from the pool to a storage tank placed in an inconspicuous position away from and above the fountain. The fountain will then operate so long as there is any water in the upper tank.

If the domestic water supply for the house is pumped up to a roof tank from a well or rain-water storage system, then it is an easy matter to divert a small supply of this water, by means of a pipe, to operate the garden fountain.

Windmill-driven Pumps.

In some cases a small windmill-driven pump will keep the storage tank filled, any surplus water delivered to this tank going down an overflow pipe provided for the purpose.

Hand Power.

In other cases where the fountain is only required to work occasionally, hand power provides the means for imparting the necessary pressure. The water is then pumped by hand to the gravity tank above, whence it flows to the fountain. Compressed air is sometimes used in cases where a gravity tank is not convenient; in this connection there is a very old type of fountain tank (or rather double tank) arrangement, known as Hero's fountain, that is occasionally used; this method does not necessitate storage tanks above the fountain level, the tanks being concealed beneath the fountain pedestal.

Petrol Engine-driven Pump.

A small petrol engine-driven pump is also another alternative for country districts where no other source of power is available; in this case the water supply for the fountain is generally arranged on the gravity principle, water being pumped from the house supply or from the ornamental garden pool to a tank arranged above the level of the fountain, but placed in some concealed position where it will not detract from the appearance of the garden and pool surroundings.

The bottom of the tank is connected to the base of the fountain by means of a length of metal pipe that can be appropriately hidden from view.

THE DIRECTLY SUPPLIED FOUNTAIN

Many people are of the opinion that the simplest and least expensive arrangement for a garden fountain is to connect the base of the jets directly with one's water supply from the mains. Whilst it is true that the installation work is both simple and inexpensive in comparison with, say, the electric pump method, nevertheless it is open to the following three chief objections, namely:—

(1) As the water is used for "garden" purposes an additional water charge must be paid. In many cases the water supply company will insist upon the installation of a separate water meter, the annual rental of which will be charged for in addition to the amount of water used.

(2) As the supply of water is continuous or rather accumulative at the jets, it is necessary to provide an overflow pipe to take off the surplus water; this, in turn, necessitates the provision of a length of drain pipe to

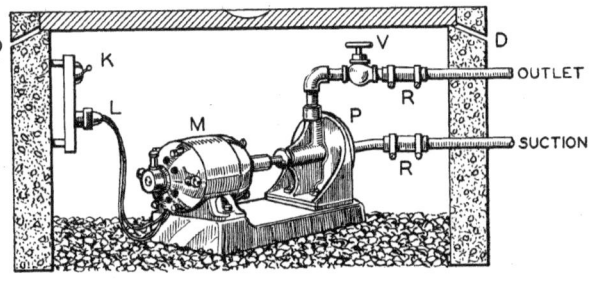

Fig. 2.—SHOWING ELECTRIC PUMP INSTALLATION ARRANGED IN PIT ON SIDE OF THE POND.

1051

AN ORNAMENTAL FOUNTAIN FOR THE GARDEN

take the discharged water to the nearest drain.

(3) Where it is desired to keep fish in the ornamental pond fed by the fountain, the low temperature of the mains water will be found to be a drawback for keeping certain kinds of fish, and for supporting the necessary plant and pond life essential to such fishes.

Advantages of using an Electrically-driven Water Pump.

For the above reasons one comes to the conclusion that, where electricity is available, the best and most convenient method of operating the garden fountain is by means of an electrically-driven water pump.

The pump is driven by a small electric motor having a low consumption, and it draws its water supply from the pool, afterwards discharging it through the fountain jets, whence it goes back to the pool again. Thus the same water is used, without loss, over and over again, the circulation and aeration effects produced being beneficial to fish and vegetable life in the pool itself.

Working Cost of Small Electric Motor.

As the fountain is not required to run continuously, the power used is certainly not excessive. Thus a small electric motor of the type used for small garden fountain pumps consumes from 60 to 100 watts. If we reckon electric power at the rate of $2d.$ per unit, then the cost of operating the fountain will work out at only $\frac{1}{8}$ to $\frac{1}{4}$ of a penny per hour. Thus it will be possible to run the fountain for eight hours daily at a cost of between $1d.$ and $1\cdot 6d.$, or, say, $1\frac{3}{4}d.$

Installation is not expensive.

Apart from the low running cost,* the installation of an electric pump is not an expensive matter, for it requires only a fraction of the piping of the other systems, and necessitates no water storage tanks. When these savings are offset against the first cost of the complete electric pump unit, the latter will usually be found to represent the cheapest proposition for working a garden fountain.

In this respect one may mention that well-designed electric motor and water-pump units suitable in every way for garden fountains cost between £4 and £5 10s. They are provided with ample bearings and, provided the lubrication instructions are carried out at regular intervals, these units have a very long, useful life.

---

* In regard to the consumption of the electric pumps, it is useful to remember that for an average fountain 1 unit of electricity is consumed for every 2,000 gallons pumped; this is about one-tenth the cost of purchasing a similar quantity of water.

CONSTRUCTIONAL DETAILS.

Before giving further particulars of suitable electric pumps for garden fountains we shall consider a typical installation, showing how the pump is arranged and connected up in the case of an ornamental fountain and garden pool.

Fig. 1 shows a convenient arrangement that has proved very satisfactory in practice.

How the Motor and Pump are mounted.

The electric motor and centrifugal pump are mounted as one unit on a cast-iron base that is placed in a pit alongside the garden pool, shown on the right. The sides of this pit are made of concrete, to a thickness of about 8 inches. The base of the pit, however, is not concreted, but consists of rammed coke-breeze or stones

Fig. 3.—An Alternative Arrangement showing the Electric Pump installed in a Cabinet on the Side of the Pool.

up to about 2-inch mesh, and to a depth of about a foot. This is for the purpose of allowing any leakages from the pump or water-pipes to soak away, and it thus obviates any risk of water getting to the electric motor. The bed of the electric pump unit is placed upon the earth (previously levelled and rammed tight with a heavy metal ram) and the coke-breeze or stones placed around and below its level. The electric pump pit is shown in more detail in Fig. 2, the electric motor being at M and the centrifugal pump at P. The suction inlet of the pump is taken to its centre, whilst the delivery is from the outside through the screw-down valve, or tap, shown at V.

Pump Suction and Delivery Pipes.

The pump suction and delivery pipes are connected to the longer pipes, Q and P, by short lengths of rubber hose (shown at R in Fig. 2). Circular clips, provided with tensioning screws, ensure that the hose makes a water-tight fit with the water pipes.

The rubber connections ensure that there is no strain on the pumping unit due to settling of the ground beneath or to any movement or expansion effects of the longer pipes P and Q (Fig. 1).

The Switch.

A small slate or ebonite panel attached to the concrete wall by means of wall-plugs or screwed rods concreted into the wall when it is first moulded serves to house the tumbler-pattern switch K for the motor and the water-tight wall-plug L for connecting the leads from the switch to the electric motor.

The pit is covered with a concrete or stone slab A, resting in a rectangular recess (made in the upper parts of the concrete walls when first moulded). Drainage holes D are provided to allow any water leaking into the recess to drain away so that the interior of the pit is kept as dry as possible. Alternatively one can procure a cast-iron manhole cover and watertight register rim of the type used by builders for covering inspection holes in external drain pipes; this particular form of cover is preferable from the viewpoint of water-tightness.

The Pipe Arrangements.

The pipes used for a small garden pool and fountain should be from $\frac{3}{8}$ to $\frac{1}{2}$-inch water pipe of the galvanised grade; the connections are made by means of standard pipe fittings arranged to suit the pool and fountain disposition.

The Suction Pipe.

The suction pipe Q (Fig. 1) should be provided with a weed trap consisting of a perforated pot S. A wire gauze cage can also be used for this purpose, a suitable mesh being one of $\frac{1}{8}$ inch.

The suction pipe should be arranged between the centre and bottom of the pool and in a position where it is accessible for cleaning; for in the autumn leaves may find their way into the pool and block the openings of the weed trap.

The Delivery Pipe.

The delivery pipe is taken to the base of the fountain pedestal D and, so far as is possible, is concealed. It is advisable to make the pipe connection, between the long member P (Fig. 1) and the pipe leading from the fountain jet J to the base of the pedestal, by means of an external screwed connection, as shown at W. This will enable the pedestal, complete with its piping, to be assembled in position independently of the pipe P; the connection W can then be made.

The pedestal D should be provided with a register or projection to locate it in the concrete at the bottom of the pool, so as to prevent any sideways movement. The weight of the pedestal will in most cases be sufficient to keep it in position permanently.

It will be seen that by keeping the pipe P external to the concrete, except where it necessarily must pass through into the pump pit, the piping arrangement is greatly simplified; moreover, the pedestal pipe can readily be disconnected at any time if required.

Arrange Pipes before concreting the Pool.

The pipes P and Q must be located in the correct positions before the pool is concreted. The pipes should be rested on wooden supports after the earth has been excavated for the pool and before the concrete is placed in position; if the concrete is well tamped around the pipes whilst it is wet a good watertight joint will be ensured.

The tap or valve at V (Figs. 1 and 2) is for the purpose of adjusting the discharge from the pump in order to regulate the height of the jet J to the desired amount.

In some cases it is usual to fit another tap or valve to the suction side of the pump in order to obviate the possibility of continuous leakage at the gland of the pump when the fountain is not used for long periods, for it must be remembered that the pump is below the surface of the water in the pool and that, otherwise, it would be in direct communication with this water by means of the pipes P and Q. Fig 3 shows an alternative scheme in which the electric pump is installed in a cabinet placed on the side of the pool.

Concrete for the Pool.

The concrete bed of the pool must, of course, be made quite watertight and strong enough to resist successfully any tendency to crack owing to minor subsidences of the ground below.

It is usual to allow a minimum thickness of 6 inches for a pool of about 10 to 12 feet diameter; for larger pools the concrete must be made of greater thickness. To be on the safe side a thickness of 8 or 9 inches should be used for a 12-foot pool.

A mixture of 3 parts aggregate (stones up to 2 to 3-inch mesh), 2 of sand and 1 of cement, will be found satisfactory. The concrete, after setting, should be faced with ½ inch of waterproof cement mixture, e.g., Pudlo. A coarser grade of concrete can be used for the sides of the pit and, further, it is not necessary to face the sides afterwards.

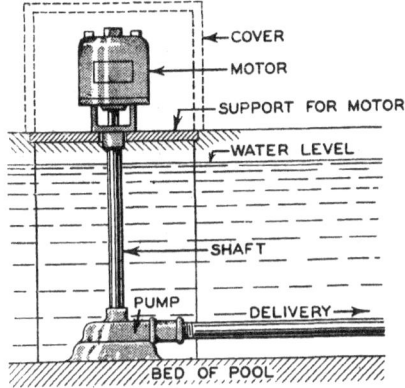

Fig. 4.—The Vertical Electric Pump Unit, with Motor placed above Level of Water.

A VERTICAL PUMP ARRANGEMENT

With the recent introduction of a vertical electric pump unit * it is possible to dispense with the pit shown in Figs. 1 and 2, and in place thereof to mount the electric motor part of the unit above the level of the water in the pool, the pump being allowed to rest on the bed of the pool, a suitable base being provided

Fig. 5.—The Whitney Electrically-driven Centrifugal Pump for Garden Fountains.

for this purpose. The drive from the motor to the pump is taken inside a metal tube, so that the water does not come into contact with the driving shaft. The motor and pump unit (Fig. 4) should be placed in a small cavity formed on the side of the pool, and a wooden cover—that can be disguised as a seat—arranged over the motor.

With this arrangement there is an

* Broadwell Engineering Co. Ltd., 42 Stamford Street, Blackfriars, London, S.E.1.

Fig. 6.—The Broadwell Small Electric Centrifugal Pump.

appreciable saving in the cost of the construction, for the suction pipe is dispensed with as the pump is now submerged directly in the water. Moreover, there is no need to fix the delivery pipe through the concrete bed of the pool as in the arrangement shown in Fig. 1. Finally, the risk of flooding, that is present with the latter scheme, is avoided in this case.

SUITABLE ELECTRIC PUMP UNITS.

As the whole success of the schemes outlined in the preceding part of this article depends upon one's being able to procure a suitable electric pumping unit, a few particulars will be given of one or two satisfactory types that are commercially available for the purpose in view.

Whitney Electric Pump Unit.

Fig. 5 shows the Whitney † electric pump unit. This consists of a substantially-designed and well-ventilated electric motor that can be obtained to suit any electric mains supply, coupled by means of a flexible coupling (shown at the centre) to an impeller type of centrifugal pump. The suction and delivery pipes are at the centre and outside respectively. Suitable lubricators are provided for the motor and pump bearings. The two units are mounted on a substantial metal base.

The pump will operate satisfactorily with a 3-foot suction, that is to say, it can be placed 3 feet above the bottom of the pool and it will deliver 3 gallons of water per minute, sufficient to supply no less than a dozen 6-foot jets for a fountain. Incidentally, this pump is particularly useful for removing unwanted water from cellar drains, wells, etc., for it will operate to a height of at least 12 feet from suction level. The price of this pump is between £4 and £5.

Broadwell Electric Centrifugal Pumps.

Fig. 6 shows one of the Broadwell‡ small electric centrifugal pumps designed for continuous work in connection with fountains and small waterfalls. The current consumption of these pumps varies from 60 to 100 watts. The pumps can be used for small suction lifts up to about 3 feet, but it is recommended that if they are placed at this height above the suction level, a foot valve or priming tank be used. These pumps are made in three different sizes, known as the MB1, MB2 and Super MB. The maximum heights to which these will pump are, respectively, 15, 25 and 30 feet and the corresponding quantities of water pumped at these heads are

† Messrs. Whitney, 129/131 City Road, London, E.C.1.
‡ Broadwell Engineering Co. Ltd., 42 Stamford Street, Blackfriars, London, S.E.1.

respectively, 85, 90 and 80 gallons per hour.

Assuming that one wishes to operate a fountain with a jet (or jets) 10 feet high, then the respective quantities of water that the three types will pump at this head are 130, 245 and 300 gallons per hour.

The prices range from £5 to £7 10s.

The pump casing is made of gunmetal, with gunmetal impeller and a non-corrosive monel metal shaft. A watertight gland is provided on the pump shaft, there being a knurled screw adjustment for this gland. The motor is fitted with ball-bearing shaft and is of the universal type for A.C. or D.C. It is coupled to the pump shaft through a flexible rubber sleeve. A screw-down greaser is provided for the pump shaft. The two units are mounted on a stiff cast-iron base plate.

A MINIATURE WATERFALL

In view of the similarity between the pumping arrangements of the garden fountain and the garden or miniature waterfall, an illustration is given in Fig. 7 of a suitable layout for such a waterfall. The latter can be fashioned in the side of any ground of suitable slope, or an artificial fall can be made as shown by first constructing a mound of suitable height, namely from 15 to 30 feet, and then arranging a series of concrete pools and sills, or steps of paving stone as shown. The steps should each be placed at a vertical distance apart of 3 to 4 feet.

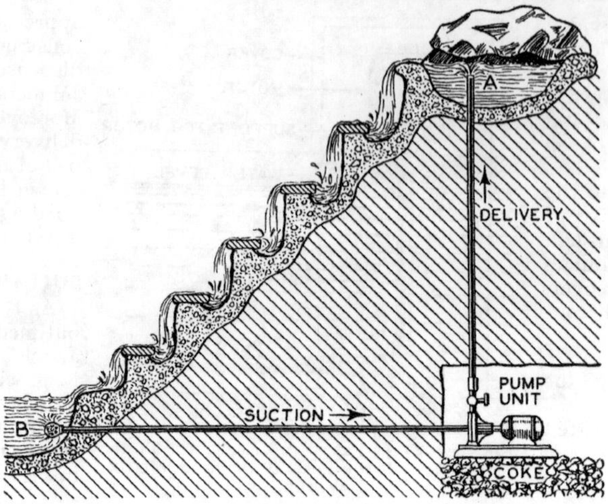

Fig. 7.—A Small Cascade or Waterfall operated by Concealed Electric Pump.

At the very top a small pool A, of about 15 to 25 gallons capacity is formed; this can be covered with a rock if it is desired to conceal the source of the water supply.

The water for this pool A is drawn from the ornamental pool B at the bottom of the falls by means of a suction pipe to an electric pump unit, and is delivered through the delivery pipe shown to A.

With a Broadwell type MB2 electric pump, costing £5 10s., a waterfall having a vertical height of 25 feet can be supplied with 90 gallons of water per hour. With a type "Super MB" pump operating at 30 feet, 80 gallons of water per hour will be supplied. For smaller heights of waterfall the quantities of water will be correspondingly greater and a bigger expanse of fall can be arranged. Thus, for the MB2 pump, working a 15 foot fall, 150 gallons of water will be delivered to the upper pool A every hour. With the Super MB pump, the delivery at this height will be no less than 250 gallons per hour.

HOW TO WAX PAPER FLOWERS

IMITATION flowers made from crinkled paper are greatly improved by being dipped in wax.

Preparing the Wax.

A suitable wax for the purpose consists of 4 lbs. of paraffin wax, 4 ozs. of spermaceti and half a plumber's candle. Place these ingredients in a fish-kettle, billycan or similar type of vessel, which is not less than 8 inches deep and 9 inches wide with perpendicular sides. The vessel should also have a swing handle over the top, or else be double handled.

Heating the Wax.

The wax must not be heated over an uncovered flame. If a gas ring is available it should be used as follows: Stand round the ring four fairly tall tins of equal height, and place a metal tray on the tins. Make sure it is quite firm before placing the wax container on the tray. Light a moderate gas and heat the wax to a temperature of between 150° and 160° F., testing the temperature with a thermometer. Stir occasionally with a metal spoon, and when hot enough turn the gas as low as necessary just to maintain the correct temperature.

Preparing the Flowers.

While the wax is being melted prepare the flowers for dipping, making sure they are nicely shaped. Then hold the flower between the fingers near the end of the stem and dip the head down into the wax for two or three seconds. Do not let the flower touch the sides or bottom of the vessel or the shape may be spoilt.

Removing Superfluous Wax.

Now raise the flower clear of the wax and gently shake it over the vessel to remove any superfluous wax. Turn the flower the right way up, separate the petals with an orange stick if they are touching one another. The flowers must, of course, be kept near the heat while this is being done, as the petals cannot be separated once the wax has hardened.

The Stem.

The part of the stem not immersed with the flower can be waxed by pouring hot wax over the stem with the metal spoon.

Storing the Wax after use.

The same wax can be used again and again. When finished with for the time being, put the lid on and allow the wax to cool. The lid must always be kept on when the wax is not in use, as dirt or dust will discolour it and spoil the appearance of any future flowers that are treated.

How to clean Wax Flowers.

Wax flowers will in time become soiled. If dusting with a camel-hair brush is not sufficient to clean them, they can be washed in warm, *not hot*, soapy water and then rinsed in clear water. Hold the flower head down in the water and gently shake it about.

What to do if Wax is cracked.

If the wax becomes cracked, it can be renovated by re-dipping. The flower should be held in the hot wax until all the wax already on has melted.

Simple Precautions.

Watch the temperature very carefully. If it falls below 150° F., the wax will coat the paper too thickly. If it rises much above 160° F., it will shrivel the paper.

Don't forget to hold the head down until it has been shaken, or the hot wax will run into the centre and settle in a lump.

Do not put waxed flowers too near a hot fire, or the wax will become soft and the flowers will droop.

A Cheap and Efficient Water Filter

FROM A GLAZED DRAIN PIPE

ALTHOUGH town-dwellers are fortunate in the matter of having their water supplies laid on from a mains source, there are still a very large number of country-dwellers, bungalow and small settlement inhabitants who have to rely upon wells and rain-water storage tanks as their only source of water supply.

This water, however, is thoroughly reliable for drinking, cooking and similar domestic purposes, although it should be filtered in order to get rid of suspended solid matter and dissolved gaseous products. In the case of town water supplies the suspended matter is extracted from the water, before it reaches the householder, by filtering it through sand and gravel beds; it is also treated chemically to reduce the dissolved mineral salts and to eliminate harmful bacteria.

Rain water, upon which so many country folk still have to rely, is a particularly pure form of water for domestic use, provided that it is collected from the roofs of houses, or bungalows, in areas where there are not too many coal-fire or factory chimneys. It must also be stored in clean tanks or reservoirs. The underground concrete-lined brick-built storage tank having a well-fitting lid is the best means of storage.

The solid matter in rain water and any gases that it may contain as a result of storage conditions can readily be eliminated with the aid of a properly designed filter, the filtered water being particularly " soft " in its character and admirably suited for drinking, washing, cooking, tea making and similar domestic purposes.

Well Water.

The standard of purity of well water depends largely upon the locality from which it is derived, but in any case, being in contact with earthy products and often contained in wells having open tops, it must contain a certain amount of suspended solid matter when drawn or pumped up from the well. It is therefore important to pass this water through a suitable filter in order to remove any solid matter before it is used for human consumption purposes, such as drinking and cooking.

The Principle of the Water Filter.

We have seen that unfiltered water contains two principal products that must be got rid of before it is suitable for domestic consumption; these are (1) Solid matter, in the form of suspended fine particles and, occasionally, sediment; the latter, after a time, settles to the bottom of the vessel which contains the water. (2) Dissolved gases derived from mineral or vegetable sources.

Getting rid of the Solid Matter.

The solid matter, including both the sedimentary and suspended, types is eliminated in the filter described in this article by passing the water through a certain thickness of fine, clean sand, such as silver sand, and then through coarser sand and small stones such as washed gravel. The latter is really provided for the purpose of retaining the finer sand above and therefore of preventing it from being carried through the filter with the water. In order to render the passage of the water through the filter beds as easy and simple as possible it is usual to allow the water to sink by gravitation through the filtering media; all that is necessary, then, is to introduce the water at the top of the filter bed and let it sink through the latter in virtue of its weight.

Eliminating the Gases.

To get rid of the gases in the water the latter should be passed through a suitable layer of charcoal, or a mixture of charcoal and manganese-dioxide. Charcoal has the property of being able to absorb an exceedingly large volume of gas in relation to its own volume. Moreover, when it can no longer absorb any more gas, most of the absorbed gases can be driven out of the absorbed carbon, merely by heating the carbon to quite a low temperature, i.e., 100° to 200° C.

The purpose of manganese-dioxide is to oxidise any mineral or vegetable impurities into harmless compounds. It is not absolutely essential in a filter of the type described, but its presence is undoubtedly an advantage and tends to make the filter rather more efficient than it otherwise would be.

Constructing the Filter.

The filter illustrated is intended for the use of the small type of house or bungalow to supply the requirements (drinking and cooking) of from three to five persons. If a larger number of persons is to be catered for it is an easy matter to duplicate the filter described.

The novel feature of this filter is that it utilises a length of ordinary glazed earthenware drain-pipe for the body, or container. This item, which is usually the most expensive part of the proprietary make of filter, is ridiculously cheap and easily obtainable from the local builder. Being glazed there need be no question of its absolute cleanliness and permanence as a filter container.

Materials required.

Whilst it is not possible to give actual quantities of the materials needed, since these will depend upon the internal diameter and length of the drain pipe available, the intending constructor can gauge these from the relative thicknesses of the strata, etc., given in Fig. 1. The following are the materials required:—

One drain pipe of glazed earthenware, about 2 feet long × 8 to 12 inches internal diameter.

One elm lid with knob or handle to fit top of pipe.

Two perforated or drilled zinc or brass plates, about 16 S.W.G. thick, to fit inside of pipe as closely as possible.

One disc of fine mesh brass or nickel wire gauze, such as petrol filter gauze, to fit inside of pipe.

Four $\frac{1}{4}$-inch diameter brass rods, screwed Whitworth or B.S.F. for about 1 inch at one end only.

Eight $\frac{1}{4}$-inch brass nuts to suit thread on rods.

Eight $\frac{1}{4}$-inch brass or zinc washers, $\frac{1}{16}$ inch thick.

One rubber or rubber-canvas washer about $\frac{1}{4}$ inch larger in diameter than internal diameter of the pipe. Thickness about $\frac{3}{16}$ to $\frac{1}{4}$ inch. Width of washer about 1 to $1\frac{1}{2}$ inches.

One tinned iron pan, such as a domestic washing bowl, about 4 inches larger in diameter than outside diameter of pipe. It should be about 4 inches deep.

Two short lengths of $\frac{5}{8}$ to $\frac{3}{4}$-inch screwed gas pipe, one elbow and one domestic type of brass tap. Two nuts and washers, $\frac{5}{8}$ to $\frac{3}{4}$-inch gas.

One wooden stool, with central hole, or slot for gas pipe clearance.

Filtering Materials.

(1) Mixture of charcoal and manganese-dioxide to give a depth of 2 to 3 inches. The charcoal should,

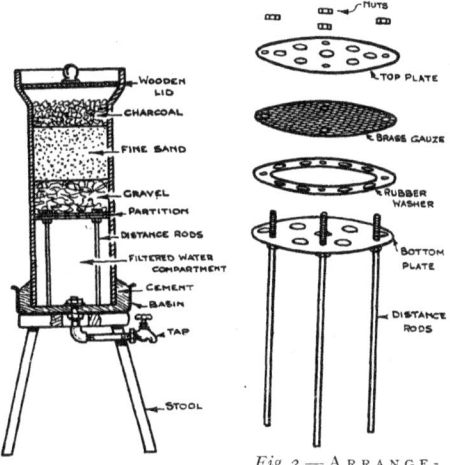

Fig. 1.—Sectional View showing Details of Filter.

Fig. 2.—Arrangement of Filter Bed Support and Distance Rods.

preferably, be in hard broken lumps of small size. Animal or gas-carbon charcoal is best for the purpose.

(2) The manganese-dioxide can be obtained at any chemists and should be about one-quarter to one-fifth of the volume of the charcoal.

(3) Fine well-washed sand such as river sand, or, better still, silver sand. Sufficient sand to give a depth of from 4 to 6 inches.

(4) Gravel. This must be well washed fine mesh gravel or small stones up to about $\frac{1}{2}$ inch maximum screen, with plenty of finer stones. It should contain no clayey or earthy matter; a thickness of 2 to 4 inches is required.

The only other item required is a small quantity of Portland cement and an equal amount of sand to make the cement for fixing the drain pipe in the basin, as shown in Fig. 1.

Constructional Details.

The construction of the filter is quite a simple matter and with the aid of the materials, and information previously given and the two illustrations, should present no difficulty.

The inside of the drain pipe should be well washed with hot soda water and afterwards rinsed off with clean water.

Next, the pipe should be placed vertically and centrally in the metal basin shown; a clearance hole to take the $\frac{3}{4}$ inch gas piping should first be drilled in the latter.

In order to form the hole in the cement base for the gas piping, a wooden plug, greased on the outside, should be fitted into the hole in the basin, so as to project about 2 inches upwards and the same distance below. The cement and sand should be well mixed and then watered a little, stirred well again, and made into a fairly stiff paste before placing in the basin.

Support the drain pipe on one or two thin pieces of wood, of 1 inch thickness, placed on their edges, with the 1 inch side vertical and then introduce the cement, ramming it well down so as to form the section shown in Fig. 1. By tamping and smoothing it on the inside a fairly uniform layer of about 1 inch depth can be made at the bottom. If one of the gas pipe washers is now placed over the wooden plug and pressed into the cement, this will ensure a flat surface for the gas pipe nut, later.

Allow the cement about two days to set and harden before placing the pipe and tap fittings in position. The bottom joint should be made with thin cork, rubber or leather washers, placed between the metal washers and the cement and bowl faces.

The partition and distance rods are shown in dismantled form in Fig. 2. The zinc or brass plates are drilled with a number of holes of about $\frac{3}{8}$ to $\frac{1}{2}$ inch. The more holes there are, the quicker will the filtered water flow through.

The rubber washer and the metal gauze are clamped between the two perforated plates by means of the nuts on the distance rods, there being one nut above and one below. By adjusting the latter the lower ends can all be arranged at the same level so that they bear on the cement base whilst the partition is at right-angles to the axis of the pipe. After assembly the partition is pushed down from the top of the pipe, the protruding rubber of the washer being forced against the side of the pipe so as to form a practically water-tight joint.

The filtering materials are then introduced to the depths mentioned in the paragraph headed "Filtering Materials," and the filter is then complete.

Using the Filter.

The first lot of water passed through the filter should be thrown away as it may contain some extremely fine particles of solid matter from the filtering materials.

It is as well to leave from 4 to 6 inches of clear space above the latter for the water to be poured in.

After the filter has been in use for a month or two the charcoal should be removed and heated on a pan or metal plate over a fire or gas flame to drive off the occluded gases. The sand should be stirred about before replacing the charcoal.

After several months of use it will be advisable to remove the sand and wash it well, finishing, if possible, with filtered water; this process will remove all the filtered solid matter from the sand. The latter can then be used again.

It will thus be seen that the cost of maintenance of this filter is neglibible; only the slight losses caused by the removal process for heating or washing need to be made up.

ENGRAVING ON GLASS

GLASS engraving, by means of emery powder and lead shot, is interesting and quite simple to carry out. In the first place a box should be secured which is rather long and deep in proportion to its width. For a piece of glass of small size a cigar box will answer the purpose. On the inside of the lid of the box glue a piece of cloth to keep the emery powder from shaking out.

The Stencil Design.

On to the sheet of glass a stencil must be fixed. This may be a design cut from paper; remember that it is the open parts of the stencil only which will stand up in relief to the rest of the glass. Attractive stencils may often be found in odd scraps of lace and these will give more delicate designs than could be easily cut from paper. The stencil is glued on to the glass, care being taken to see that, where the adhesive runs beyond the border, it is carefully cleaned away.

Clean the Exposed part of the Glass.

The exposed part of the glass must be perfectly clean, otherwise the engraving will not be satisfactory. When the stencil is in position stand the box up on end and put the glass in what will then be the bottom. It can be held securely in place by three or four drawing-pins.

The Engraving Process.

Buy a pound of emery powder and the same amount of lead shot. Put these into the box and close the lid. Then start to jerk the box violently up and down so that the emery powder and shot are repeatedly thrown against the glass. This should be continued for about a quarter of an hour, at the end of which time the box may be opened and the glass examined.

Removing the Stencil.

If the exposed parts are uniformly roughened the engraving may be regarded as finished. All that remains to be done is to take out the sheet and soak it in warm water to remove the stencil. It will then be found that the design has been beautifully worked out in a matt surface which stands up in fine contrast to the clear glass as a whole.

Uses for Small Pieces of Engraved Glass.

Small pieces of rather thick glass, treated in this way, make attractive paper weights, especially if backed with black velvet. Larger sheets engraved and then fitted into frames make handsome trays.

How to Lay Rubber Flooring

There are many house owners who at times have admired the beautiful rubber floors which they have seen and walked upon in cinemas, banks, and other public buildings, and even in the houses of friends, but have deterred hitherto from even inquiring about such a floor-covering in their own houses, fearing primarily the cost of the rubber, which has admittedly in the past been somewhat expensive, and secondly, the trouble, and again, the cost of laying.

Such fears are groundless. A good quality rubber of a suitable thickness for domestic use (about as thick as average linoleum) in very many beautiful and artistic colours and shades in both plain and marbled varieties can be purchased at prices as low as 7s. 6d. per square yard, or at practically the same as a good quality linoleum, and when it comes to the question of laying, those readers who have even the most elementary mechanical gifts can obtain excellent results by carefully studying the simple instructions given in this article.

The Advantages of Rubber as a Flooring.

Some of the chief are as follows:—
(1) It is hygienic.
(2) It is waterproof.
(3) It is easily cleaned.
(4) It is soft and resilient to the tread.
(5) Non-slipping.

These qualities alone make it of inestimable value to the nursery. The children cannot injure themselves on a rubber floor, in the bathroom it is easily wiped dry after the greatest splasher of the family has had his bath. On the stairs it is soft to walk upon, so that romping little feet do not threaten to bring down the house about our ears. In the kitchen so easily cleaned and does not allow harmful germs to be raised, as in a dusty wooden floor. In fact, the ease of cleaning it can be a labour-saving floor-covering *par excellence*.

What to decide first.

Let us suppose that you have decided to cover your bathroom floor with rubber; you must first decide whether you will lay it in sheets, as lino, or as tiles. Having done this, very carefully measure the floor space to be covered.

Provide yourself with a good 2-foot rule, as carpenters use, also a pencil or piece of chalk for marking the floor.

How to measure the Floor Space.

We will imagine the bath to be the popular panel front and built into the side of the room.

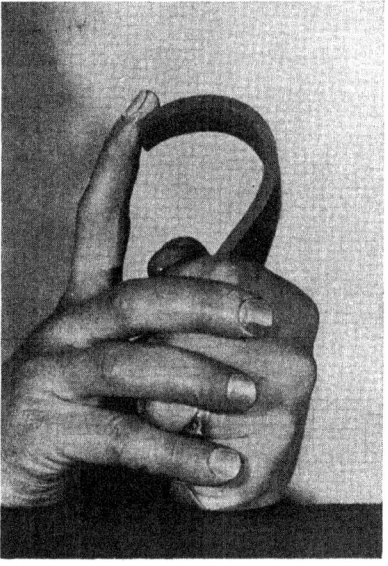

Fig. 1.—How to test the Rubber before purchasing (1).

Take hold of a corner of the sheet, bend it as shown and allow it to spring back. It should go back straight at once and not remain as shown in Fig. 2.

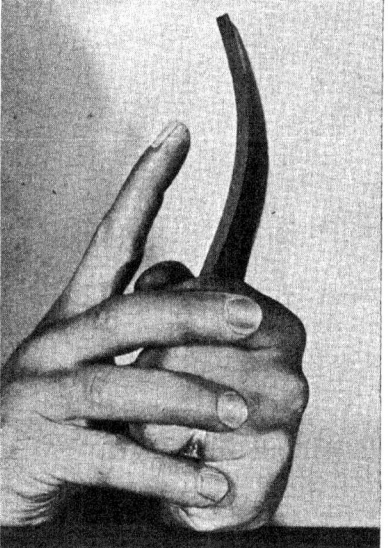

Fig. 2.—How to test the Rubber before purchasing (2).

When released after being bent as in Fig. 1 it should go back straight and not remain bent as shown above. If it remains bent it indicates that it is either beginning to deteriorate or is not up to standard quality.

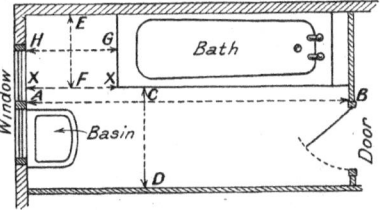

Fig. 3.—Diagram showing Dimensions required when measuring the Floor Space.

Take your measurements from A to B. Draw a chalk or pencil mark on floor at X—X, and take another dimension, C—D, you now have an oblong. Work out the yardage of this space by multiplying the two dimensions, then add the product of the piece in the corner at the top of the bath, E—F and H—G, add these together, and you have the quantity of material required.

The next question is the thickness. As most domestic rooms do not get anything like the traffic of a public space, it is generally considered that $\frac{3}{32}$ inch or $\frac{1}{8}$ inch thickness is ample. This is also governed by the condition of the floor, which is gone into later on in this article.

Selecting your Rubber.

You are now ready to purchase your rubber. We advise you to deal with firms of repute and ask to be guaranteed that the rubber is new and not been in stock a long time. Here are a few simple yet reliable ways of testing whether your rubber is good or otherwise.

Take hold of a corner of the sheet, bend it as in Fig. 1, allow it to spring back, and if it goes back at once you may be fairly sure that it is of good quality; should it remain bent over, it is either beginning to deteriorate or not up to standard quality.

Another method of testing rubber is by carefully examining the surface to see if there is "crazing." "Crazing" is fine hair-like lines running all over the surface. It will not be worth the trouble of laying. On the other hand, do not buy rubber which sticks to your hand and is soft and flabby like gelatine; this will also be in the process of decomposition.

PREPARING THE FLOOR

First examine the floor carefully, and if the floor is an old one, see that all loose boards are well nailed down, also that any lumps, bumps or knots are planed off, and fill up any cracks between the floorboards with strips of thin lath wood, fixing with glue, finally smoothing all over with a carpenter's smoothing plane.

Another method, for those who have the time, is to make a pulp of old newspapers, well soaked in water and beaten up until it is about the consistency of putty. To this pulp add a small amount of glue, previously heated in the usual way and made fairly thin with warm water. If this pulp be well pressed into the boards with a putty knife and smoothed off as the work progresses, it will be found that all the cracks have been nicely filled in. Finally, plane off as in the case of filling with laths.

Fig. 4.—THE CORRECT METHOD OF CUTTING THE RUBBER.
It should be laid out flat on the ground and cut with a sharp knife held against a straight-edge. Note how the straight-edge is kept firm by the knee.

What to do with a Floor in Very Bad Condition.

Should, however, the floor, as in many very old houses, prove to be in a really bad condition, the only thing to do then is to line it with 3-ply sheets. By this we mean to cover the whole surface of the floor, after well nailing down all loose floor-boards, with sheets of 3-plywood about $\frac{1}{8}$ inch thick. These have to be carefully fitted all round the skirting, etc., and one sheet of plywood to another with good butt joints. It does not matter how irregular they are cut, so long as they all join closely and tightly together and neatly cover the whole floor. You can easily procure this plywood from the local timber yard, and a cheap variety will do so long as it is perfectly flat and absolutely dry. Avoid any that has been standing in the open for any length of time, as the plies may have a tendency to come apart. Having fitted your 3-ply, well nail it all around each piece and diagonally from corner to corner, using a flat-head type of wire nail known as a panel pin, about $\frac{5}{8}$ inch to $\frac{3}{4}$ inch long. The better you nail down the lining the more solid will be the result.

Cutting and marking the Rubber.

You will require very few tools. Obtain a good *sharp* knife, such as shoemakers use, and which can be purchased for a few pence, although professional layers use a lino knife.

Don't think you can cut your rubber with the average penknife; you will give yourself endless trouble and probably spoil the rubber into the bargain.

Then you want a straight-edge, preferably a steel one—perhaps some engineering friend will lend you one; if not, procure a good wooden one at least 2 to 3 feet long—a 3-foot wooden measure will do provided its edges are perfectly straight and not damaged.

Using the Chalk Line.

Now lay your rubber flat and mark with a chalk line (*i.e.*, a piece of long thin string well rubbed over with chalk and held by one person at one end whilst the other end is held taut. Lift the string and let it spring back on the rubber and you will have an absolutely straight line).

Lay your straight-edge along the chalk line absolutely tight up against it and cut your rubber with the point of the knife.

Always hold the knife very slightly away from you to give the rubber a slight undercut.

Fitting round an Obstruction.

We have so far only dealt with flooring laid in sheets or panels, and that it is being laid on a floor devoid of any sort of obstruction.

Supposing, however, you have a pedestal lavatory basin or W.C. pan and towel rail.

You must make a template to fit around these. Take a sheet of brown paper, larger than will cover the foot of the pedestal, slit one edge about 6 inches at right angles.

Now cut out a portion approximately two-thirds the size of the foot of the pedestal. Take this sheet and pass around pedestal, and carefully press with a thin flat-edge piece of wood (the edge of a paper knife would do) at that edge where the foot of the pedestal rests on the floor. This pressing will show a well-defined crease. Remove carefully, trim the paper with a pair of sharp scissors and replace, and you should have a perfect job, although, if necessary, any little adjustment should be done to the template so as to make it a perfectly good fit.

Carefully measure on your rubber where the pedestal will come, mark the position, lay on top your template at the position indicated, and mark out the hole from the template, and then cut and trim to same size and the rubber should be a perfect fit when laid in position. Incidentally, any small round piece of rubber cut as this

Fig. 5.—HOW TO SQUARE THE END OF A SHEET OF RUBBER.

can be trimmed up and used for mats for jugs, glasses, etc., as fancy may dictate.

A Simple Decorative Design.

We have now dealt with the fitting of the bathroom floor, covering it completely with sheet rubber. It is, however, quite easy to increase the attractiveness of the flooring with a simple decorative design (see Fig. 8).

A Hint when laying Marbled Rubber.

In the case of marbled rubber, *always* lay with the figure or grain running towards the window or light.

One of the simplest yet probably most effective designs consists of letting in a skeleton panel.

Presuming you have a light green marble ground, a thin strip about 1 inch wide and not more than 1½ inches wide skeleton panel of plain dark green gives a fine finish. When buying the rubber procure a few feet of a much darker shade of the same colour only a few inches wide, cut this into strips of, say, 1 inch wide, set out floor as in Fig. 8, very carefully mark where these strips are to be inset, cut carefully, remove cuttings and inset the darker shade.

Unless you feel yourself very competent to cut the rubber dead straight with true right angles, don't attempt it, as it certainly requires considerable skill and practice to do this satisfactorily, and should you make a mistake and cut it badly you will be very disappointed with the result and likewise spoil your rubber.

Before going on to the cementing down, which by the way need not be done with plain sheet if not desired, *i.e.*, without panel or other adornment, we will give you a few notes on tiling.

TILING

First decide whether you want tiles of two colours, such as black and white, dark and light blue, two greens or whatever your taste may be. Further, whether you will cover the floor all over with tiles or have a border running all round the room adjoining the skirting.

Firstly, we will presume that you are dispensing with a border—it will make it easier, both to cut and lay—and that you will have your tiles all one colour in a bright marbled green.

We would like to impress upon you that the description of rubber required for tiling has to be of a thickness and finish somewhat different to that which is known as "sheet," and, due to it being thicker, will probably cost you more.

It should not be less than $\frac{3}{16}$ inch thick, should have a close and highly finished surface and be generally of tougher substance known in the trade as "press finish," having been vul-

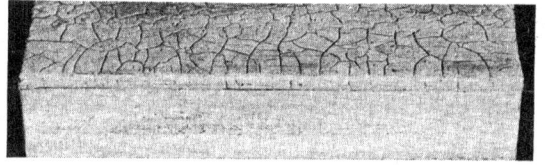

Fig. 6.—Another Method of testing Rubber is by carefully examining the Surface to see if there is "Crazing."

Here we see "crazing" showing badly on a rubber-covered step.

canized under great pressure in a hydraulic steam heated press.

Marking out in Squares.

Carefully mark out with the chalk line in squares of, say, 6 or 9 inches. To do this cut one edge of the rubber perfectly straight; now very carefully with a pencil make all along one side small

Fig. 7.—How to fit Rubber around a Pedestal Basin or other Projection.

If you do not feel capable of fitting it direct, a template should first be made of brown paper to fit round the pedestal and the rubber then cut to the exact size, as described in the text.

marks *exactly* 6 or 9 inches from each other. Then square one end of the rubber, and repeat the same operation. You will now have a sheet of rubber much like Fig. 9.

Now complete the marking on the two remaining sides, after, of course, cutting your rubber straight and squaring the remaining end.

Take your chalk line and carefully

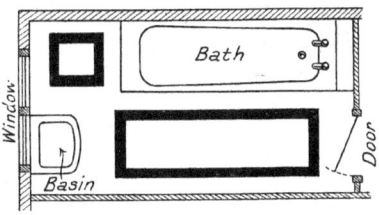

Fig. 8.—A Simple Decorative Design.

mark with the line until your sheet of rubber is covered with lines.

Next cut your rubber lengthwise in strips so that you will have a number of 6- or 9-inch wide strips with small cross lines, as in Fig. 11.

The strips of rubber should now be cut across on the lines, carefully measuring as you proceed to see that the resulting piece of rubber is a 6-inch or 9-inch square tile. The use of a carpenter's square will be a great assistance in keeping the tiles dead square.

It must be clearly understood that if your tiling is to be a success the tiles must be dead true, not varying in the slightest.

How to test whether the Tiles are square.

An easy way of testing this is to place four tiles in the form of a square. There should not be the space of a pin's point in the centre, however you mix them up or change the position of the tiles, neither should you be able to get a cigarette paper in between the joints.

If you want two colours, or black and white, don't forget when buying your rubber that you will want half your original amount of rubber in one colour and half in another. Also, if you require a border, reduce your body material correspondingly to the quantity of rubber you want for the border.

By the way, it is never worth while trying to make tiles in the border, simply use 4-inch or 5-inch wide strips, according to taste.

Fitting the Tiles.

The fitting of tiles is much the same as the sheet, except that it is essential to set out the body of the tiles first of all, then complete border, if you have one, all round. In laying marbled tiles a very charming effect can be obtained by laying the tiles with the marbling or figure running in opposite directions.

There is one point in connection with tiling—do not attempt to cut into tiles rubber of less than $\frac{3}{16}$ inch in thickness. It must be "press finish," a quality specially produced for tiling. The thinner rubber will be very difficult to fix, due to curling when the solution is applied.

Laying—the use of Solution.

Procure from the firm from whom you bought your rubber a sufficient quantity of special rubber flooring solution. Usually this is of a heavier nature and more tenacious than the usual solution sold in tubes. Allow about ½ lb. solution to the square yard.

There are two kinds of solution usually employed for rubber flooring— one has an "ether" type of solvent

HOW TO LAY RUBBER FLOORING

and the other naphtha. The first has the advantage of being non-inflammable, but against this it has a very pungent "ether" odour which is rather trying to some people, affecting their breathing. On the other hand, naphtha solution is not at all unpleasant to work with, but is *very inflammable*. Of the two, we recommend the latter as being more serviceable in the hand of an amateur, but must add a word of warning—*DO NOT SMOKE WHILE FIXING OR USING THE SOLUTION. Keep windows well open if weather is fine*, and as much as possible, if damp. Inci-

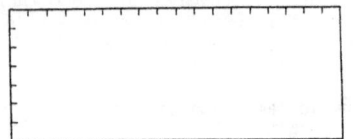

Fig. 9.—THE FIRST STEP IN MARKING OUT TILES FROM A PIECE OF RUBBER.

Make small marks all along one side exactly 6 or 9 inches from each other. Then square one end of the rubber and repeat the operation so that the sheet appears as above.

dentally, it is not overwise to attempt using solution in an extremely damp and humid atmosphere, as the solution will not " set off " overwell, and there will be a risk of the rubber coming up—but of that later on.

We cannot leave the question of smoking or the use of naked lights when employing the naphtha solution without a word of explanation. As soon as the solution is spread on the rubber and the floor it immediately begins to evaporate, and the naphtha gas given off, very readily combining with the oxygen in the air, makes a very explosive mixture which only requires a spark to cause it to burst into flames or even explode. Of course, once the solution has evaporated off and the rubber is stuck to the floor, this danger is entirely done away with, for the very simple reason that there is no more gas left to evaporate. Hence our advice—don't smoke, don't strike matches, don't use naked lights; keep doors and windows open when doing your fixing.

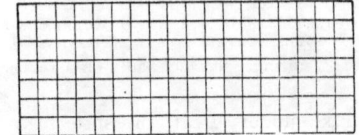

Fig. 10.—NEXT COMPLETE THE MARKING OF THE TWO REMAINING SIDES, TAKE THE CHALK LINE AND CAREFULLY MARK WITH IT UNTIL THE SHEET IS COVERED WITH LINES, AS SHOWN.

Applying the Solution.

We will assume that you have the bathroom covered all over with rubber

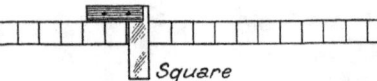

Fig. 11.—NOW CUT THE RUBBER LENGTHWISE IN STRIPS SO THAT YOU HAVE A NUMBER OF 6- OR 9-INCH WIDE STRIPS WITH SMALL CROSS-LINES. THE STRIPS CAN THEN BE CUT ACROSS THE LINES, USING A SQUARE.

nicely fitted. Take the top half of the main sheet at the end nearest the window. Turn this back half-way by

 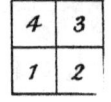

Fig. 12.—HOW TO TEST WHETHER TILES ARE SQUARE.

Place four tiles as shown on the left; there should not be the space of a pin's point in the centre. Then rearrange them as on the right: there should still be no space in the centre.

rolling back over the half at the door (Fig. 17). Take a good stiff brush about 2 or 2½ inches wide, with which spread the solution thoroughly and evenly all over the floor " A," also on the reverse side of the rubber " B." In average temperatures this should take about 20 to 30 minutes to " set off." By " setting off " we mean that the naphtha must evaporate out of the solution until it is practically dry. Test from time to time by very lightly touching the solutioned surface with the fingers and not until all but the barest feeling of stickiness is left will the two surfaces be ready for the final contact.

When you are satisfied that they are ready, very gently, carefully and evenly roll back the rubber on to the

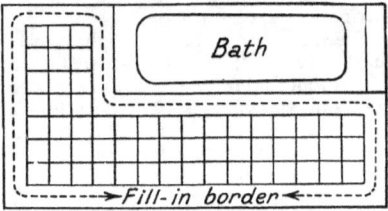

Fig. 13.—IF IT HAS BEEN DECIDED TO HAVE A BORDER, THIS SHOULD BE FILLED IN WITH STRIPS.

floor, gently rubbing in the surface of the rubber with the hands as you proceed so as to press out all the air between the floor and the rubber. Should you imprison any pockets of air you will have bad adhesion and a bubble will form in a very short time, which will cause a lot of trouble to rectify.

You will now repeat the entire operation with the other ends of the rubber, and so on with each panel until the room is all cemented down.

One benefit of laying with solution is that the floor can be used immediately, so you can walk over your floor without

Fig. 14.—A SMALL "SANDING" MACHINE WILL BE FOUND VERY USEFUL FOR SMOOTHING A WOODEN FLOOR BEFORE LAYING THE RUBBER.

Fig. 15.—IF THE TILES HAVE BEEN PROPERLY CUT, THEY SHOULD FIT TOGETHER EXACTLY.
Showing also the method of handling when laying.

waiting for it to set, as in the case of glues, casein, etc.

Make sure all Joints have stuck.

It is advisable as soon as you have your floor fixed to take a hammer with a flat smooth face and gently rub down the rubber at all joints, also around the skirtings and the bottom of pedestals, etc.

How to remove Solution that has accidentally got on the Surface.

If you should have been unfortunate enough to allow some of the solution to get on top of the flooring, now is the time to just rub it off with your fingers. It will readily come off when fresh, although it will be more difficult to remove if left for a few days, and may require the application of a little petrol on a piece of rag to dislodge it. If you have to resort to this measure, be careful not to use too much petrol, as this is a solvent of rubber, and will spoil the surface unless used with the greatest care and very sparingly.

Special Notes on fixing Tiles.

The above notes are applicable for tiles with the following modifications.

First fit and lay out the tiles and border. Take the first two rows of tiles from window-end of room. Lay them face downwards, carefully solution the underside of each tile, seeing that the solution also covers each edge of the tile, then solution the floor and wait until the floor and the tiles are sufficiently "set off." Pick up the first tile, turn over right side up and place in the top left-hand corner, see that it is exactly square and true as to position. To do this, place the fingers of your left hand at top left-hand corner of tile, holding tile very lightly with right hand, make contact and bring tile down on to the floor in one operation. Rub down with your hand, and your "key" tile is fixed. Continue in the same way for the top row, and if this is laid true and even your troubles are half over and your job should pan out all that you would desire. Do not force your tiles into place, but lay them evenly and closely side by side so that the solution on the edges will help to unite each tile to the other, and so make the entire rubber a homogeneous whole, and also, what is very necessary, give you a watertight floor.

A Word of Warning.

If you have once made a contact with the two solutioned surfaces and it is not correct, you cannot move your tiles about like the plasterer does with hard tiles in cement. You will have to take up the tile, clean the solution off the back of the tile, also off the floor, and in fact go over the whole operation again.

In other respects, as to cleaning off

Fig. 16.—When laying Marbled Tiles a Good Effect can be obtained by laying the Tiles with the Marking or Figure running in Opposite Directions.

superfluous solution, etc., the foregoing instructions given for sheet rubber applies to tiling. The warning as to naked lights naturally also applies to tiling.

CLEANING

One of the great essentials in obtaining full value out of your rubber floor, particularly when newly laid, is that the rubber be properly cleaned at frequent intervals.

Why a Whitish Bloom may appear on the Surface.

You must understand that in the manufacture of all rubber the active chemical which produces the vulcanisation is sulphur in some form or the other. In rubber flooring, ground sulphur is used, and the ideal which the manufacturers strive for is to use up entirely all the sulphur. By careful estimating and weighing, they are almost successful in eliminating what is termed "free sulphur," notwithstanding there is always a trace of this free sulphur, and this may show itself sometimes in the early days by a slight whitish bloom on the surface of the rubber, especially in the blacks and blues.

Furthermore, you may find that in the early days after laying, the rubber will show foot marks somewhat. These markings, as the rubber matures, a process which closes the open pores, will be overcome, especially if the following instructions as to frequent washing be carried out.

Cleaning with Soap.

The correct method of cleaning is as follows: dampen slightly the surface of the rubber by wringing out a house flannel fairly dry, using warm water to which has been added soap powder, well rub the floor with the flannel, well soap with a good household soap (never use soft soap), afterwards carefully rinse with clean water, and dry off with a separate cloth.

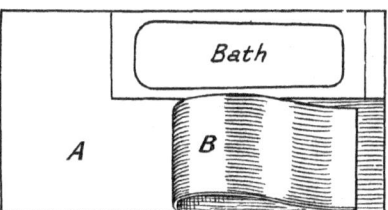

Fig. 17.—How to apply the Solution. Turn back one half of the rubber flooring, apply the solution to the floor at A and on the reverse side of the rubber B. Then roll back on the floor and do the other half in the same way.

After a few weeks of cleaning the recurrence of this bloom will have ceased.

Cleaning with a Non-abrasive Powder.

There is an excellent cleaning powder for rubber now on the market called "Lasto"; the instructions for its use may be well used as a standard method of cleaning with any reliable non-abrasive powder. Dampen the surface to be cleaned with warm water by wringing a house flannel fairly dry, sprinkle lightly with "Lasto," or other non-abrasive washing powder, well rub the floor with the flannel, afterwards carefully rinse with clean water and dry off with a separate cloth.

Cleaning a Large Surface.

For large surfaces such as halls, cinemas, etc., moisten the floor as above with a mop, lightly sprinkle with powder, and finally, when clean, rinse off by dipping mop in a separate bucket of clean water, always seeing that the mop is fairly well wrung out.

Don't use too much Water.

You will probably have observed that we specially emphasise the use of very little water. The reason is that water is the best-known lubricant of rubber, so if you swamp your rubber floor with a superfluity of water, you will never be able to make a success of your cleaning, as you will find that the flannel, instead of removing the dirt, will simply slide over the surface of the rubber without taking any effect.

ACCIDENTS TO RUBBER

Should someone spill a quantity of oil, such as castor oil, olive oil, machine oil or paraffin, at once wipe off as much as you can with some old rags. Then make up a strong solution in very hot water of common washing soda and soap powder. Well swab the portion on which the oil has been spilt and wash off with clean warm water. If the oil has been some little time on the rubber, and has soaked into the surface, you should make a paste of whiting and soap powder moistened with a saturated solution of common soda and water. To make the latter, take about ¼ pint of hot water and keep adding soda until the water will not dissolve any more soda. Moisten the whiting and powder with this solution until it forms a very thick creamy consistency. Then spread this all over the oily surface and leave for some hours. Afterwards well wash off with hot water and your surface should be practically free from oil.

In effect, what you have been doing is to turn the oil into a crude form of liquid soap. In the process you have killed the oily nature and the resulting soapy residue cleans itself. Allow the floor to dry naturally, and avoid walking across it for a day or so.

HOW TO LAY RUBBER FLOORING

Fig. 18.—Applying a Thin Coating of the Adhesive Solution to the Back of a Rubber Tile.

Fig. 19.—When the Solvent has Dried on both Tile and Floor the Tile can be Placed in Position.

You may find that this somewhat drastic process of killing the oil may affect the colour of your rubber by lightening it, particularly blues, but it should return to normal after a few days' exposure to daylight.

The rubber may also appear somewhat dull for a time, but should eventually regain its usual surface after a week or two.

It should be understood that you have had to treat your rubber rather severely, so it must of necessity require a period of time for it to regain its original condition.

POLISHING

After a period of from six to eight weeks, providing you have kept your rubber well washed with soap and water, or any of the recommended cleaners, you may, if you wish, polish the floor.

However much you polish rubber you cannot make it as slippery as polished lino or polished boards. To obtain a highly finished surface, use a water emulsion polish. It must be free from turpentine, American or synthetic, and any form of white spirit, all of which are very penetrating to the rubber.

The water emulsion polishes, by a special process, have the advantage of being hard and non-smeary, and can be readily wiped over with a flannel dipped in warm water and a little soap when the surface is dirty. They have actually very minute particles of specially suitable waxes in suspension in the water.

They do not too readily give a polish, but if carefully persevered with and used in small quantities, after several applications, produce that hard polish mentioned above, and will repay the extra labour expended in getting the rubber into condition. Once this has been obtained, it is very easy to keep the floor in good order by a light rub over with a soft cloth and the occasional application of the polish after a wipe over with a flannel and soap and water has been made and allowed to dry thoroughly. Be sure and see that the rubber is always thoroughly dry before attempting to polish, otherwise your efforts will not be successful, and will only result in a surface with a smeary mess.

There is, however, much to be said for the egg-shell type of polish which the press-finished rubber itself develops in course of time, and many readers may prefer to leave it in that condition.

A WASP AND FLY TRAP

A VERY good wasp and fly trap can be fitted up in this way. Get a fair-sized flower pot, a glass jar, a few stones, and a small saucer or tin lid. Hold the flower pot in an inverted position and place it on a table upon the stones so that it is raised up about an inch. Then put the glass jar over the hole in the pot. Fill the saucer with syrup, honey and water, or anything sweet, and place it under the pot. The wasps and flies will soon be attracted to it, and when they have had their fill they do not come out from under the pot. Attracted by the light that streams down through the hole in the flower pot the insects nearly always try to fly upwards into the glass jar, and soon it is filled with insects. You can clear a room of wasps and flies in a very short while with one of these traps. When wasps are attacking fruit trees in a garden it is a very good idea to arrange a few of these traps about the trees and bushes and the damage to the crops will be much lessened.

A Kitchen Cabinet Table

The table described below is rather unique in design and is superior to most of the ready-made articles on the market. The top of the table has a coloured porcelain enamelled surface for pastry making and cooking purposes, while the closed portion contains three compartments, a cupboard for dry goods, an airtight drawer for cakes and bread, and a refrigerator space.

This last-mentioned compartment is a zinc tunnel cooled by the principle of evaporating water soaked up by capillary action; this will not actually produce ice, but it will maintain a temperature 15 to 20 degrees below the summer heat of the kitchen. Fig. 1 shows the general appearance of the table when not in use, while Fig. 2 gives an idea of the compartments open ready to receive their contents.

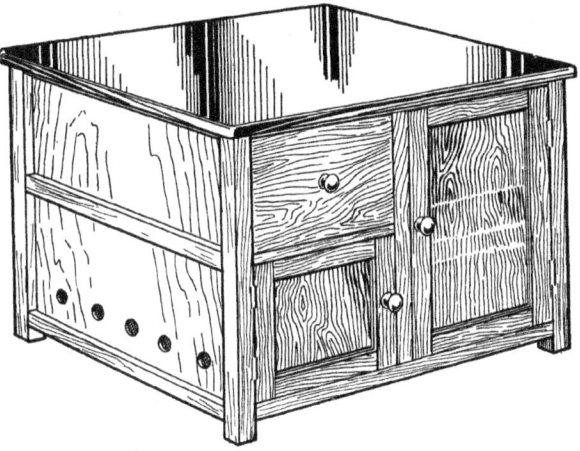

Fig. 1.—The General Appearance of the Table.

Materials required.

11 feet × 1½ × 1½ inch machined deal.
30 feet × 1½ × ⅞ inch machined deal.
8 feet × 1¾ × ¾ inch machined deal.
5 feet × ⅝ × ⅝ inch quadrant.
5 feet × 12 × 1 inch machined deal.
2 feet × 12 × ½ inch machined deal.
24 square feet of 3/16 inch birch plywood.
40 inches by 3 feet gauge 24 sheet zinc.
24 inches by 4 feet gauge 20 sheet zinc.
20 inches by 5 feet gauge 20 sheet zinc.
3 inches × 4 feet perforated zinc.
14 inches × 1 foot felt or cork.
18 inches × 4 feet flannel.
30 feet × ⅜ × ⅜ inch beading.
30 feet × ⅜ × ⅜ inch quartering and two pairs of hinges.

The Main Framing.

Fig. 3 shows details and sizes of the main framework; from this it can be seen how the horizontal rails are mortised into the four legs. The sizes of these joints are shown in the lower part of the figure; details are also given of the short front rail over which the drawer slides.

In the picture (Fig. 3) no rebates are shown in the rails for the panels, as the plywood is held sandwiched between the moulding and the quadrant as shown in Fig. 4. A vertical partition divides the dry goods cupboard from the refrigerator, and the method of fixing this is clearly portrayed in Fig. 5.

The Metal-lined Drawer.

The airtight drawer is shown in Fig. 6: the sides are 12 inches deep, and if difficulty is experienced in obtaining wood of this width then 6-inch boards must be used with the edges glued together. The two side members have a groove along the top and the bottom and also an upright one for the end-piece. Note that the back of the drawer just comes level with the top groove, permitting the plywood lid to slide into the cabinet when the drawer is withdrawn.

The front can be dovetailed to the sides if the reader wishes, but a simplified fitting is shown in Fig. 6. A half lap is sawn out at each end of the front member of the drawer and then the sides are butted in, glued and nailed with oval brads.

The lid is a piece of three-ply cut absolutely square so that it slides freely in the groove at the top of the side pieces; a small length of half-round wood is glued on the outside near the front to provide a finger-hold. The completed drawer is lined with thin zinc, gauge 24 being a very suitable thickness. The shape of this lining in the flat state before bending is shown at the bottom of Fig. 6. Carefully note the four narrow tongues at the ends of the side pieces to facilitate soldering.

Fixing the Drawer.

The bearers upon which the drawer slides are illustrated in Fig. 7. The

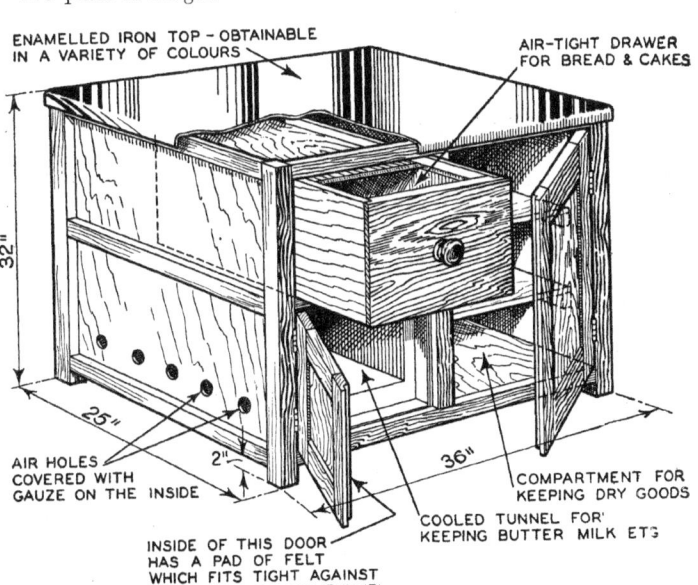

Fig. 2.—The Various Compartments of the Kitchen Cabinet Table.

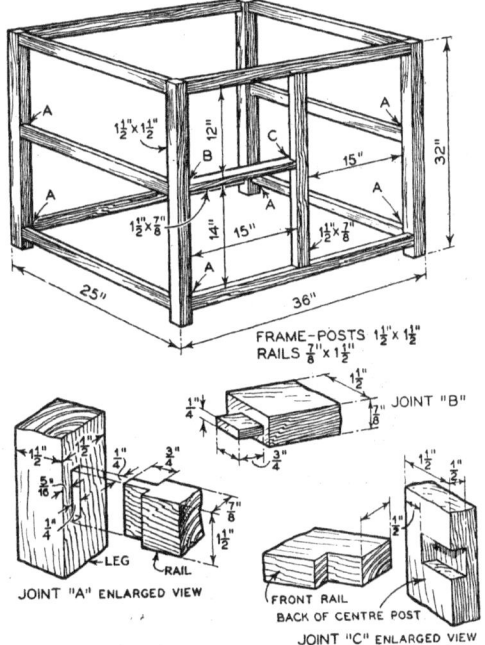

Fig. 3.—Details and Sizes of the Main Framework.

A KITCHEN CABINET TABLE

Fig. 4.—How the Panels are fixed.

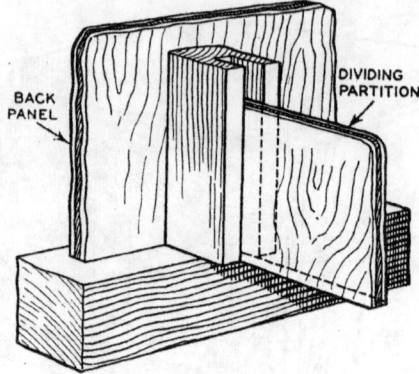

Fig. 5.—Method of fixing Partition between Refrigerator and Dry Goods.

bearers are glued to the side panel and the middle partition and are then blocked underneath with lengths of quadrant. On the top a guide is so fixed with screws as to prevent undue lateral play in the drawer.

The Doors.

The door which closes the dry food cupboard is framed up with 1¾-inch batten, down which a rebate has been ploughed to take the panel. Those readers who do not possess a plough are advised to fit the door panel the same way as the main panels of the cabinet (see Fig. 4). The door which seals the cooling tunnel is shown in Fig. 9; note how it is framed up. On the back of the panel is a pad of cork or felt, which should be just thick enough to fit tightly against the mouth of the tunnel; this pad, being a bad conductor of heat, helps to maintain a low temperature in the tunnel.

The Porcelain Top.

The enamelled iron top is purchased ready to fit. These tops are made in various sizes, one of which will just fit the table. A variety of colours can be obtained, but perhaps white with a dark edge is the best to choose. Before fixing the iron sheet in place, the cabinet is closed in with a sheet of ply stretching right across, the pressed iron top is secured by screws running through the flange, which is turned down to form the edge.

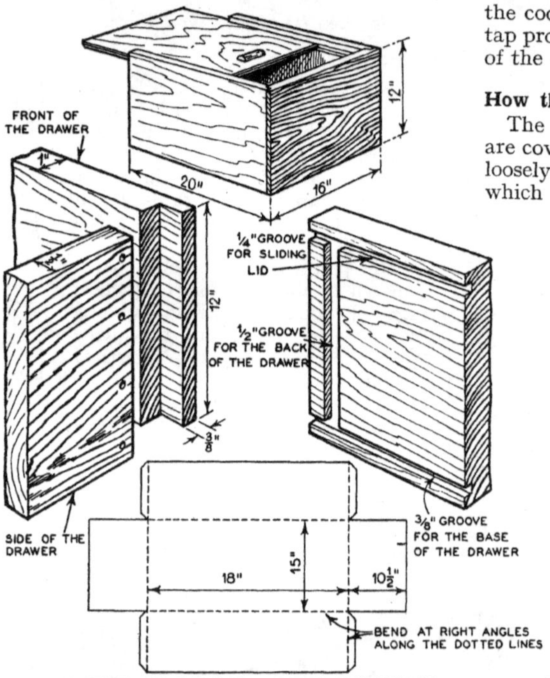

How to make the Cooling Tunnel.

Fig 10 shows the various details of the metal fittings in the cooling compartment: these are made of the stout zinc sheet, gauge 20 being used. First of all make the zinc tunnel as shown. It is in one piece, the edges being turned up at right angles to form a soldering flange; thus only one longitudinal seam is necessary.

Fig. 6.—Constructional Details of the Metal-lined Drawer.

Next observe the ends and base of the tank (see Fig. 10). It consists of one piece of zinc with two large ends bent up at right angles. One of the uprights is an unbroken sheet which blocks the end of the tunnel when this is later soldered in place. The front piece has a rectangular opening 13 × 11 inches which forms the mouth of the tunnel. Note that a 2-inch strip along each side of the base is turned up and soldered to the uprights, thus forming a tank which holds the water. The top left-hand sketch in Fig. 10 shows the tunnel soldered in place between the two end pieces. The reader will see that the tunnel is not quite so wide as the tank; thus a gap is left which permits the end of the flannel dipping into the water.

Soldering the Zinc.

Some readers may have had unpleasant experiences trying to solder zinc; no difficulty will be found, however, if "live" spirits of salt is used for the flux. Well clean the edges, apply dilute hydrochloric acid with a little piece of sponge fastened to the end of a stick, and then use a well-tinned copper bit, and no difficulty will be experienced. The free acid will slightly blacken the surrounding zinc, but this can easily be cleaned off when the work is finished. The drain cock, shown in Fig. 10, is soldered into the water tray near the front. This is useful for running off the water when the cooling tunnel is not in use. The tap projects through a hole in the base of the cabinet.

How the Refrigerator works.

The top and the sides of the tunnel are covered with a wide strip of thick, loosely woven flannel, the ends of which dip into the shallow water tank. The air-holes in the side of the cabinet are covered on the inside with perforated zinc, a similar row is arranged at the back, high up near the top, and through these a current of air is continually passing. When the warm, dry air comes into contact with the flannel, which has soaked up some of the water by capillary action, evaporation takes place. To change the water into vapour heat is taken from the metal and air in the tunnel, causing the temperature to fall many degrees below that of the room. One of the advantages of this principle is that the warmer the air in the room the more rapid the air circulation and the quicker the evaporation, with, of course, a greater degree of cooling.

Hints on Maintenance.

The water in the tank will, of course, need replenishing every few days, and

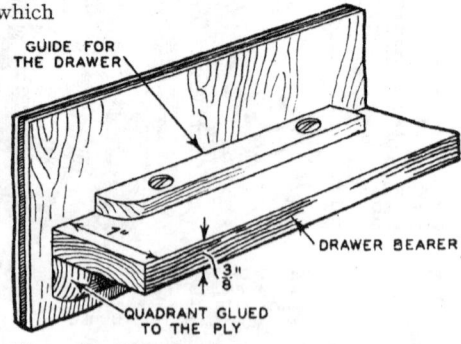

Fig. 7.—The Bearers on which the Drawer slides.

A KITCHEN CABINET TABLE

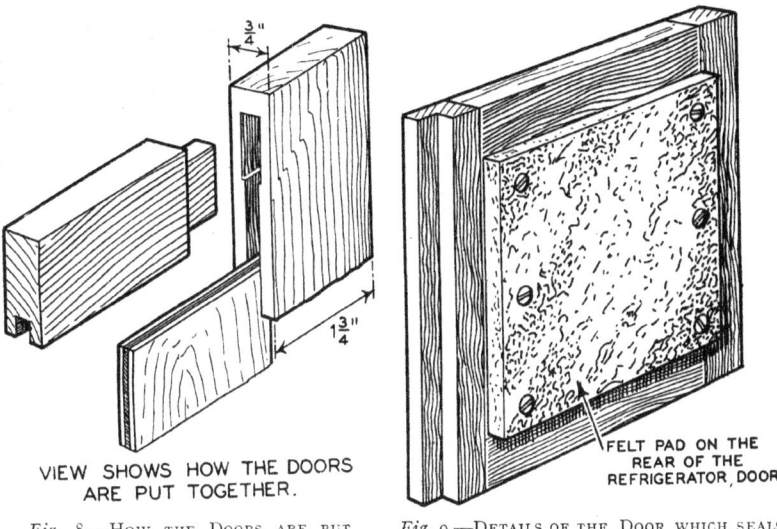

Fig. 8.—How the Doors are put together.

Fig. 9.—Details of the Door which seals the Cooling Tunnel.

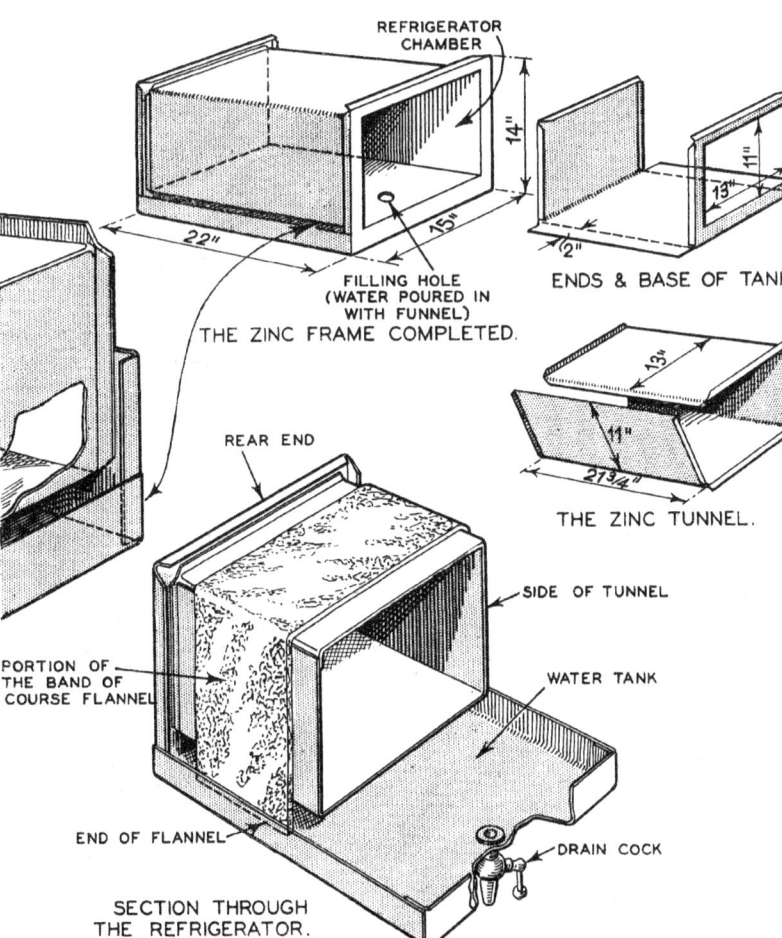

Fig. 10.—Various Details of the Metal Fittings in the Cooling Compartment.

The External and Internal Finish.

The whole of the interior woodwork in the refrigerator compartment should be painted and then enamelled white to make it impervious to the water vapour which circulates with the air currents; the dry goods cupboard is best left the natural white wood. The external finish will vary according to taste. A pleasing appearance is obtained by staining the wood with weak Solignum, using the type sold for indoor work, and then giving the whole two coats of matt varnish. When using the above-mentioned stain, it is necessary to make sure that it is absolutely dry before applying the matt varnish. This type of varnish is not as well known as it should be; it dries fairly rapidly with a beautiful egg-shell surface which stands hard wear and does not show up dust in the sunlight.

The Shelves.

Two shelves are shown in Fig. 2; these are supported on bearers $\frac{7}{8} \times 1\frac{1}{2}$ inches, screwed to the side and the middle partition. To facilitate cleaning, the shelves are not fixed, but just rest on the bearers so that they are easily withdrawn.

Space Economy.

Some readers may wish to have more space in the cooling tunnel, but it is not advisable to increase the sizes given or the degree of cooling will fall off. To make the best of the space available, construct some square zinc containers to hold the butter, cheese, and meat; these pack into a much smaller space than round and oval dishes. If these metal vessels are made with lids, then one can be stood upon another; in this case air holes must be provided in the sides to ventilate the contents.

Stand the Cabinet in a Suitable Place.

It is very important that the cabinet should stand in a position where a free current of air falls upon the ventilating holes. Thus before attempting to start work clearly picture where it is going to stand, preferably opposite a door which is frequently opened. It may so happen that when standing on the desired site the cooling chamber will not be opposite the door; in such a case the reader is advised to reverse the compartments, making the dry goods cupboard on the left-hand side instead of the right hand, as shown in Fig. 2. If any difficulty is experienced in obtaining sufficient air circulation, lift the cabinet on castors and have an extra set of air holes in the base round the outside of the water tray.

A later article deals with a larger kitchen cabinet.

a hole is provided in the bottom of the tunnel, as shown in Fig. 10, which makes this operation quite simple, provided a funnel is used. The complete metal cooling chamber is kept in place by a wooden guide surrounding the bottom tank and screwed to the base of the cabinet.

An Easily Constructed Garden Hammock

The joy of reposing in a gently swaying hammock is often denied the suburban dweller because he does not possess a stout tree under the shady branches of which he can hang this most restful of couches. The sedan described here solves this problem: it provides a stand complete with adjustable awning; suspended from this is a sprung seat which will accommodate three persons sitting, or one reclining. It can quickly be erected on the approach of sunny days, and when not in use the whole structure readily packs away into a small space.

The Legs.

The stand has two sets of sloping legs forming two triangles which support a ridge beam. Fig. 3 gives the details of these legs; note the small sketch in Fig. 2, showing how the slot is cut out to carry the ends of the ridge bar. To mark this accurately the two legs should be placed flat on the ground, the feet held 4 feet apart with a batten nailed temporarily across; bring the upper ends together so that they overlap; a line can then be scribed across the face of the wood to give a mitred joint. Saw off the unwanted material, then with edges held tightly together place a section of the ridge board centrally on the dividing line and mark round. The waste material can then be sawn out and the ends will appear as in Fig. 3.

The upper end of each leg is bound with an iron angle bracket; it is cut out to the shape shown in Fig. 2, and then bent along the dotted lines so that it takes the shape of the completed bracket (see Fig. 2). Note that there are two horn-like extensions that project upwards beyond the wood; these help to support the ridge board and the hole takes an iron peg or bolt, thus preventing any lateral movement between the bar and the apex of the legs.

The Hinges.

Those shown in Fig. 3 have very long flaps; difficulty may be experienced in tightening up the screws owing to the restricted space. The best plan is to mark the centres of the holes and put into each a screw to "tap" it out. If screws are threaded into all holes before erecting, little trouble will be experienced; a cranked screwdriver is an asset when tackling this job.

The Tie Brackets.

These four brackets are fixed between the ridge bar and one of the legs; they can be shaped up to size; the final bending of the rods is best done by trial when erecting the completed stand. One bolt can be made

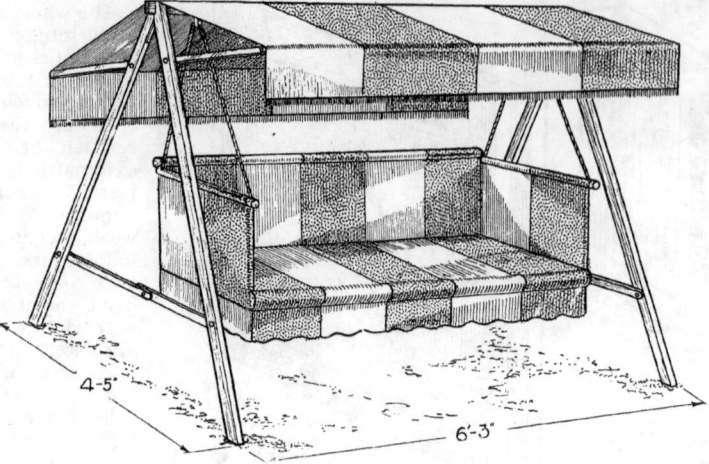

Fig. 1.—The Completed Hammock.
Easy to make and erect this hammock will be found invaluable in the garden.

Materials Required.

Wood.	Iron.	Sundry articles.
26′ × 1″ × 2¼″	6′ × 1″ × ⅛″	Sash cord (best Belfast line, 7 yards)
7′ × 1¼″ × 4″	1′ × 1¼″ × ⅛″	Fibre, 2 lbs.
5′ × ¾″ × 1½″	3′ × 2¼″ × ⅛″	Feathers, 6 lbs.
14′ × 1″ × 2″	4 rivets, ¼″ × 1½″	Webbing, 2″ wide, 4 yards
13′ × ¾″ round	2 rivets, ¼″ × ⅜″	Carpet pattern press studs, 1 doz.
4′ × 1″ round	4 bolts, ¼″ × 2½″	Braid, 4½ yards
	6 bolts, ¼″ × 2″	Tassel fringe, 4 yards
	12 washers and 4 winged nuts	Canvas, 40″ wide, 6 yards
	4 springs and hooks	
	Pair of long flap hinges	

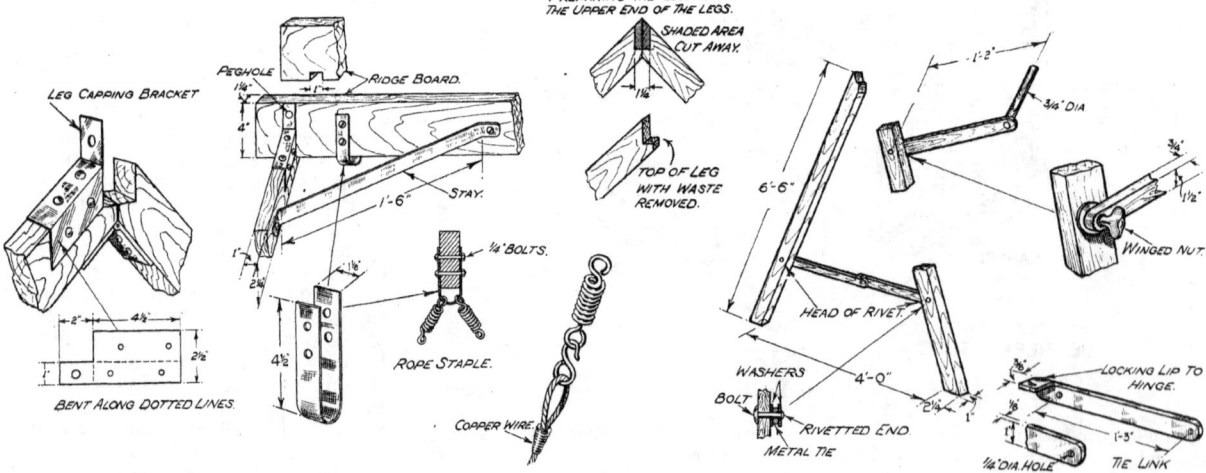

Fig. 2.—Details of Various Stages in Construction. Fig. 3.—Details of the Legs and Hinges.

AN EASILY CONSTRUCTED GARDEN HAMMOCK

to secure the ends of the two tie bars to the ridge board, but of course separate bolts must be used on the legs; winged nuts will greatly facilitate ease in dismantling.

The Hinged Tie Bars.

These are fastened between the two legs about a third of the way up. They prevent the legs slipping outwards and being pivoted in the centre close up like a hinge. Fig. 3 shows details of the two links which go to make each complete bar. Note that one link in each pair has a "lip" bent at right angles; this forms a lock which prevents the hinge folding downwards when it is open. The ends of the bar are attached to the legs with iron rivets, a washer being placed between the link and the wood; to rivet, hold an iron weight or heavy hammer against the round head and then burr over the other end, which should project $\frac{3}{16}$ inch, with the ball head of an engineer's hammer.

The Ridge Board.

A good piece of *hard* wood, free from "shakes" and knots, with perfectly straight grain, should be selected for this; two slots are cut out near each end (see Fig. 2) and two iron anchor brackets are bolted to it; these hold the supporting springs. As the adjustable awning slides across the ridge board it is as well slightly to round the upper edges to allow the free passage of the canvas.

The Awning Rails.

These $\frac{3}{4}$-inch wooden rods are supported on arms pivoted to the side of the legs; the arms are secured with bolts and winged nuts so that they can be locked in position. The ends of the rails fit into $\frac{3}{4}$-inch holes in the arms; a tight fit can be assured by making a saw cut 1 inch deep across the end of the rod and when the rail is in position, driving into this a thin tapering wooden wedge smeared with glue.

The Hammock Seat.

The frame which supports this is made up of two long lengths of batten with cross members resting on top and secured with bolts. Note that the two long pieces have a small step recessed out, into which fits the end of the cross piece; this helps to keep the frame square; metal ties can be screwed across two diagonally opposite corners should any difficulty be experienced in keeping the rectangular frame rigid.

Two lengths of webbing are then stretched full length across the frame, the canvas seat being tacked on immediately above. To get this taut, fold in an inch one end and secure this with tacks and then, using a little longer length than is necessary to cover, get an assistant to pull on

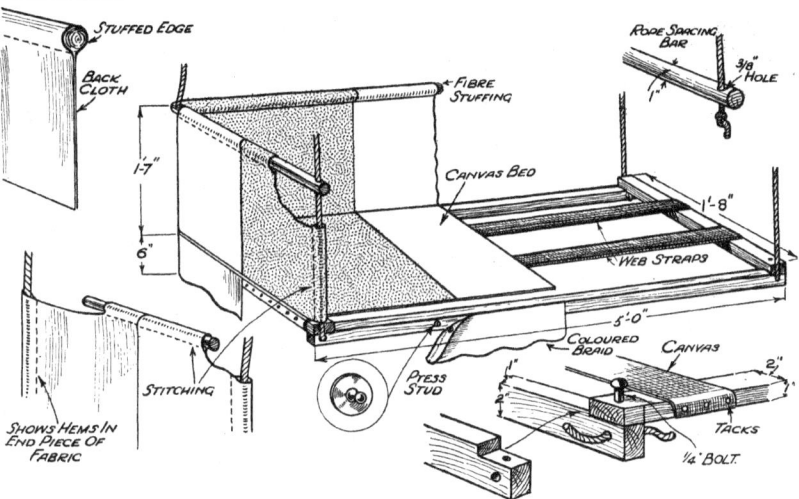

Fig. 4.—DETAILS OF THE HAMMOCK.

the other end while you fasten it down with $\frac{3}{4}$-inch tacks. The material can then be cut off to length, leaving an inch to turn in, when a second row of nails can be driven in.

Note that four holes are required in the long members of the frame so that the supporting rope may be carried through; these should be as near the end as possible. Two spacing bars are needed to keep the ropes parallel up the canvas ends. These should be made of 1-inch round hard wood, ash or oak being specially suitable. The centres of the holes in the ends must be 1 foot 8 inches apart, so that the ropes are kept vertical as they come from the seat frame.

Cutting the Canvas Sides.

Erect the stand and thread the ropes through the holes in the frame and spacing bars, tying knots under the latter so that they rest at the correct height above the seat, then temporarily fasten the four rope ends to the anchor brackets. The canvas ends can now easily be marked and cut out, allowing sufficient material to form hems round the wooden spacing rods and the vertical ropes (see Fig. 4). Note the ends of the hems are open and small holes are cut and button-stitched to permit the passage of the ropes through top hem. The lower end of the side canvas is tacked to the wooden seat frame. When the material has been stitched up it will be necessary to put the spacing rods in place before pushing through the ends of the rope. The back panel has a $3\frac{1}{2}$-inch hem along the top; this is stuffed with hair or fibre twisted into a roll pushed in from the ends with a cane. The bottom edge of this canvas panel is secured to the face of the rear wooden member of the frame with tacks. The ends of the back panel are fastened to the side panels by stitching the edges together.

The Scalloped Frill.

This is machined up from the odd lengths left over; the edge is bound with brightly coloured braid chosen to tone with the canvas. It is secured to the edge of the framing by means of brass press studs similar to those used on carpets; the stud is nailed to the frame members and the round eyelet is sewn to the inside of the frill; it is thus easily removed for packing.

The Awning.

Two widths of material sewn together provide the awning sheet, the edge of which is ornamented with a 2-inch tassel fringe of suitable colouring. The awning should project at least 4 inches below the rail, to which it is tied with loops of tape sewn at intervals along the inside edge; thus at the approach of rain it is easily removed and taken with the hammock under cover, the stand being left out without fear of damage.

The Cushions.

The hammock is quite successful without cushions, but if a real luxury is desired, two square-edged cushions should be made as shown in Fig. 5. Stuffed with fibre or flock the canvas case edged with coloured braid is quite sufficient, but when feathers are used an inner "tick" of soaped linen

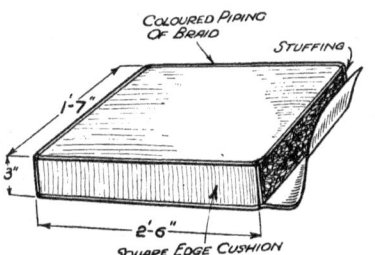

Fig. 5.—A SIMPLE SQUARE EDGED CUSHION.

casing is necessary; it is advisable not to overfill the cushions as a loosely stuffed one is more comfortable.

The Springs and Hooks.

Suitable springs as shown in Fig. 2, approximately 6 inches long, can be obtained from Messrs. Terriss, of Birmingham, and each should be capable of supporting 112 lbs. This will give an ample margin of safety.

When fastening the hooks to the sash cord the ends should be looped through the eye, and the length adjusted so that the bed of the hammock is 20 inches from the ground. The small sketch, Fig. 4, shows how the loop in the cord is secured; copper wire, gauge 20, is bound round as shown and at each third turn the wire is taken right through the two thicknesses, a hole being pierced with an awl and the wire threaded through. There should be at least eighteen turns and six wire stitches through the cord.

Finish.

The woodwork should be stained a light colour, and first of all given a coat of varnish and turps mixed in the proportion of 3 to 1—this penetrates well into the pores of the wood; finally, a coat of pure varnish should be given. The metal fittings may be enamelled to taste.

BUILDING A WOOD-LINED SAND PIT

THE main points to be considered in building a wood-lined sand pit for children are: (a) whether or not it is intended to keep the children in the enclosure; (b) size; and (c) to provide against the sand from being distributed all over the garden.

The size depends on (1) how many children will be using it at one time; (2) the space available; and (3) the type being built. A useful size for one or two children, and designed as in Fig. 1, is 6 feet wide by 9 feet long, whereas a simpler one without a guard may be as small as 3 feet by 6 feet.

Make the Framework in Sections.

We will first deal with the construction of a sand pit as in Fig. 1. Construct a framework as in Fig. 2 for the front, and as in Fig. 3 for the back. Now make two as in Fig. 4 for the ends. By making it thus in sections it can at all times be removed and erected elsewhere if necessary. Give all the woodwork a heavy coat of Bitumastic paint to preserve it.

Dig a Hole 7 Inches Deep.

Excavate for 7 inches deep in the form of a rectangle the size of the proposed sand pit. Erect these sections by bolting the sides to the front and back.

The Partition and Door.

Next construct a partition as in Fig. 5, and put it in position as on plan shown in Fig. 6. This is to prevent the sand coming out when the door is opened. This latter should now be made and erected.

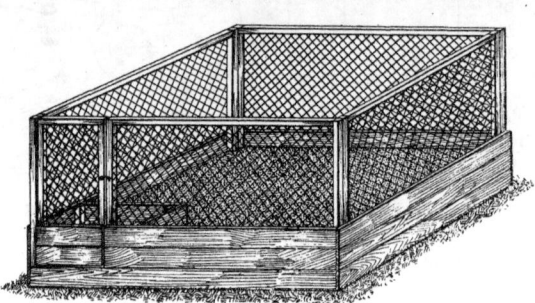

Fig. 1.—The Completed Sand Pit.

Framework and Floor.

The space between the top 7 × 1 board and the top of the framework should now be fitted in with galvanised wire netting of 2-inch mesh, fastening it with staples after straining it tightly in all directions. The floor enclosed by the partition (Fig. 6) is next covered with 2 inches of concrete.

How to prevent Mould underneath Sand being disturbed.

A point for careful consideration is that the older children while digging may disturb the mould underneath the sand, thus spoiling it. To obviate this, next put 3 inches depth of sand in the bottom and put over it a piece of galvanised wire netting, as used for the sides. Fasten the edge of this netting all round to the boards by means of staples. Now fill up with sand to the depth of a further 18 inches. The total quantity required for a 6 × 9 feet sand pit will be approximately $4\frac{1}{2}$ tons. The best type of sand for this purpose is fine sea sand of about 50 and 80 mesh.

A Simple Pit.

This has no guard and is more simply constructed. All the details mentioned above should, however, be carefully followed. The wood framework is exactly the same except the uprights need not be continued above the top of the containing boards. It is of advantage to make a small flight of steps to enable the children to get without difficulty in and out of the sand pit. Alternatively, by excavating more deeply the top of the sand pit can be brought to the normal ground level. The total quantity of sand required for one of this type (6 × 3 feet) would be approximately 30 cwts.

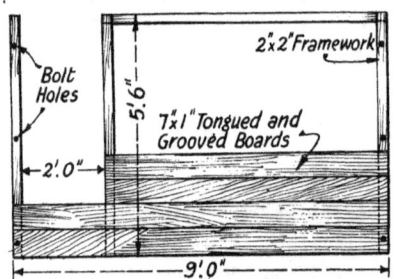

Fig. 2.—Details of Front Framework.

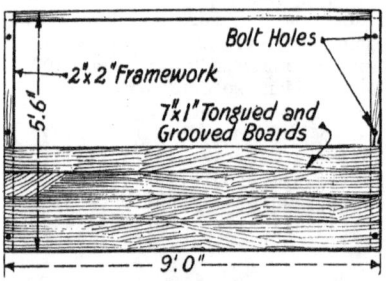

Fig. 3.—Details of Back Framework.

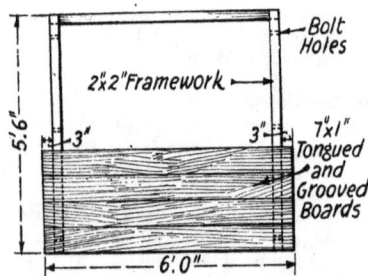

Fig. 4.—Details of End Framework.

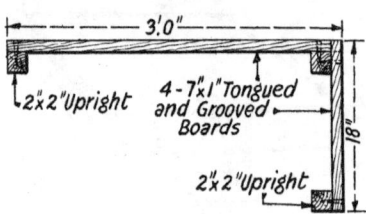

Fig. 5.—The Partition.

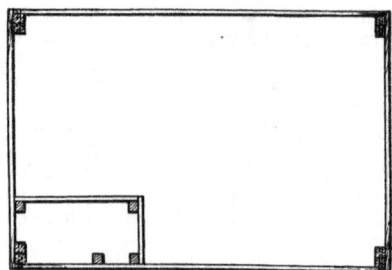

Fig. 6.—Showing Position of Partition.

Decoration by Means of Transfer Designs

Do not think that by transfers is meant nothing more than those pretty pictures you used to stick on the back of your hand when at school. Decalcomanias, or transfers, as they are more commonly called, are designs printed in oil colours, just as an artist would paint them, but face down on to specially prepared paper in such a way that they can be removed from the paper and transferred to the article to be decorated.

Fig. 1.—A Typical Example of the Use of Transfers.

A name-plate is shown here to illustrate the process of fixing transfers. Wood inlay effects and designs on furniture, lampshades, vases, walls, leatherwork, etc., can be obtained by the use of transfers.

Uses for Transfers.

If you wish to have a picture or design in colours—including wood inlay effects—on furniture, wireless or other cabinets, lampshades, vases, walls, paintwork, leather, glass, silk, parchment, etc.—in fact, on almost any surface—it can be done quickly, cheaply and with skilled effects by means of transfers. In creating new articles of any kind, the use of transfers enables them to be finished with a professional touch that means so much.

There are several different types of transfers, each specially manufactured for a particular class of surface; different methods of fixing are used, and these will be given as each type is explained. They can be obtained from Messrs. Axon, Harrison Ltd., 47 Aquila Road, Jersey, C.I.

How the Transfer is applied to the Surface to be decorated.

The most generally used transfer is printed on to a fairly stiff backing paper in reverse; the detail is only seen when the paper is held before a strong light. As a guide to correct placing on the work, however, an outline of the design is printed on the backing paper. Goldsize is used as a fixative when the transfer is to be applied to surfaces other than silk or cloth; oil varnish can be used if goldsize is not available, but a longer drying time is required for the varnish to reach the "tack point" which is necessary before fixing.

Applying the Goldsize.

Apply the goldsize to the face of the transfer very sparingly with a stiff-haired pencil brush, avoiding so far as possible going over the edge of the design. It is most important, however, that every part of the design be coated, as only that part which is sized will adhere to the surface being decorated.

Leave Coated Transfer until Goldsize becomes tacky.

Now leave the coated transfer until the goldsize or varnish becomes tacky; this may take from half to one hour with goldsize, or from two to eight hours if varnish is used. By tacky is meant partly dry, and, whilst still sticky to the touch, no size will come off on the finger.

How to test whether Transfer is ready.

The best way to test when the correct tack point is reached is to stroke the transfer lightly with the knuckle of the forefinger; if it is ready for fixing, this action will produce a squeaking sound, and if slight pressure is used, a clicking sound is produced as the knuckle is pulled away. It is most important that the correct tack point be reached, as if applied whilst the size is too wet the transfer will wrinkle and break the design when the backing paper is peeled off. Conversely, if the size becomes too dry, the transfer will not adhere to the surface of the work.

Now place Transfer in required Position.

Having reached the correct tack point, place the transfer, sticky side down, in the position required, and with a soft piece of rag rub hard on the paper backing so as to press it in close contact with the surface. With large transfers it is a good plan to use the flat side of a coin with which to rub the back of the transfer; this eliminates any wrinkles or air bubbles that are likely to occur, due to air entrapped beneath the paper.

Now take a damp sponge and rub all over the paper, pressing firmly so as to keep it quite flat on the surface; use more water as the paper becomes soaked, but not so much pressure. After soaking for about five minutes, gently lift one corner of the paper, and it will be seen that the design has detached itself from the backing paper and is firmly fixed to the surface required.

Fig. 2.—How to lay a Duplex Paper Transfer (1).

After coating the face of the transfer with gold size and leaving it to become tacky, the transfer is placed in the required position.

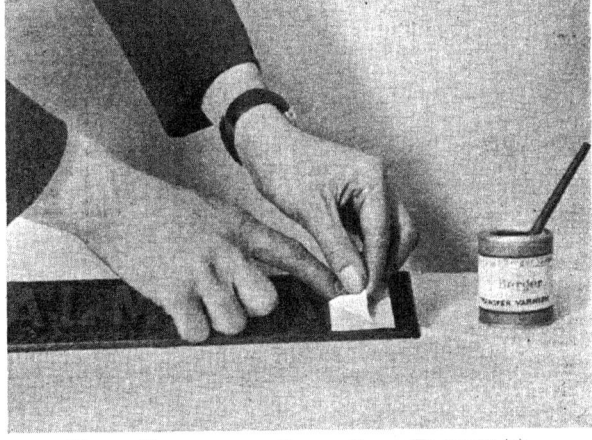

Fig. 3.—How to lay a Duplex Paper Transfer (2).

Press the transfer firmly and then peel off the stiff backing paper, the two papers having been split apart at the corner before applying by rubbing between finger and thumb.

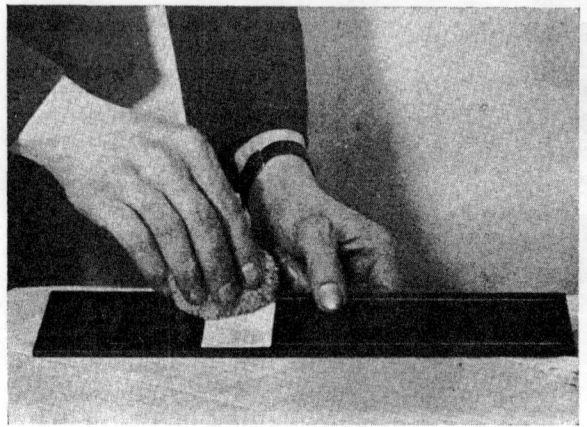

Fig. 4.—How to lay a Duplex Paper Transfer (3).
Now soak the transfer with water applied with a sponge.

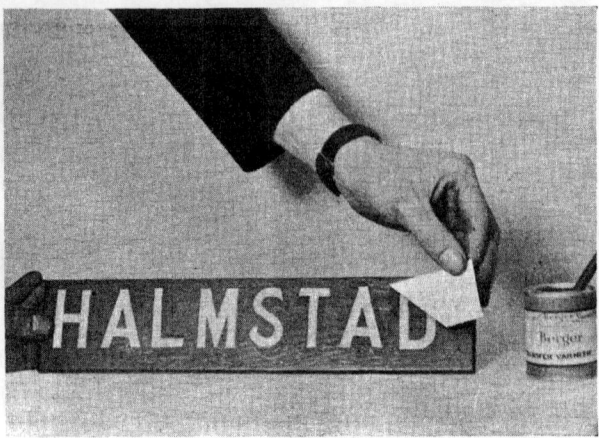

Fig. 5.—How to lay a Duplex Paper Transfer (4).
Finally, peel off the transfer paper and wipe over the design gently with a moistened sponge.

What to do if Part of Design sticks to the Paper.

If a part of the design sticks to the paper, the transfer has not been soaked enough; in such a case smooth down the paper again and allow to soak for a little longer. When the paper is peeled off, the full details and colours of the design are seen.

Wipe over Design with Soft, Moistened Sponge.

Do not omit to wipe over the design gently with a soft sponge moistened with water. This removes the gummy substance on the face of the transfer, and if this is not done the design may crack or peel off when dry. Wipe off the moisture with a chamois leather or soft rag.

Removing Surplus Goldsize.

If when sizing the transfer some of the goldsize has been applied over the edge of the design, it will show on the finished work as a dark-coloured edge. In such cases this surplus can be removed by slightly moistening a soft rag with turpentine and rubbing gently over the goldsize marks around the edge of the design until these are removed.

Polishing or Varnishing over Transfer.

If it is required to French polish or varnish over the transfer, it should be allowed to harden for twenty-four hours after fixing. When it is not desired to polish or varnish the whole surface to which the transfer is applied, the design only can be " pencil varnished " to protect it. A special type of transfer is available which is already varnished on the face of the design during manufacture, and therefore needs no protective coating after fixing. This kind costs about 10 per cent. more than the ordinary transfers.

Transfers are available in practically every kind of design, and include such as fruit and birds in natural colours, floral designs, marquetry, sign letters and numbers, Japanese and Chinese figures, nursery rhymes, both in figures and text, Dutch figures, cycle lines and crests, motor-cycle tank panels, silhouettes, etc., etc.; in a word, all those beautiful hand-painted effects that are so much admired can be obtained by the use of transfers.

Wood Inlay Effects.

Marquetry transfers will appeal particularly to the woodworker; the grain and colour of wood inlay can be reproduced so faithfully that the transfer design is indistinguishable from the actual wood. Even mother-of-pearl inlay effects can be obtained by transfers. When fixing wood inlay transfers, the work should be brought up to the "bodying-up" stage in French polishing, or the hard-drying varnish stage—which should be flatted before fixing the transfers—if varnish is used. Then, after fixing and allowing twenty-four hours to harden, the final polishing or varnishing can be carried out.

Wood inlay effects or any other transfer design can be applied over existing painted, grained, polished, or varnished surfaces equally well. Suggested uses for wood inlay transfers are wireless and gramophone cabinets, trinket boxes, wood trays, doors, mantelpieces, furniture, etc. Marquetry transfers can be obtained in lines and a large variety of wood combination strips from $\frac{1}{8}$ to $\frac{1}{2}$ inch wide, and cost only from 2d. to 3d. for a strip 23 inches long. The panel inlays, such as radial and shell designs, are equally cheap, costing only $1\frac{1}{2}d$. each for a circular radial design of shaded boxwood and ebony 2 inches in diameter.

Lining Bicycles.

With transfers it is possible to finish a bicycle in a professional manner. A set of transfer lines and crests costs only 1s. 4d. for the complete set, or crests and badges may be purchased for 2d. each. These lines are ready panelled and shaped to fit the forks, mudguards, etc., and are either single or double red, green or gold lines, or a combination of these colours. The cycle is enamelled in the usual way and, when hard, the transfers are fixed with goldsize, as described earlier in this article.

Lettering with Transfers.

For lettering house names or numbers, notices, trade names on vans, etc., transfer letters and numbers can be used to advantage. These can be purchased either in single letters or complete alphabets, in gold, white, black and red, or other colours, either plain block letters or shaded. Various styles of lettering are available and all styles are very cheap; for instance, a gold leaf block letter with red shading, 2 inches high, such as is very suitable for house names, costs only $1\frac{1}{2}d$. per letter. White letters suitable for motor-car or motor-cycle number plates cost only 1d. or 2d. a letter, and a set of plates can be done in an hour.

Decorating Painted Furniture.

With the vogue for painted furniture a decorative motif, such as can be applied with a transfer, makes a wonderful improvement. These can be natural designs of flowers, birds, butterflies or figures, or silhouettes of ships, landscapes or conventional designs. For nursery furniture in particular transfers offer the means of providing pleasing colourful pictures of amusing animals or illustrated nursery rhymes. These can be applied to polished or enamelled furniture, such as cots, play pens, toy cupboards, trays, etc. They can also be applied

DECORATION BY MEANS OF TRANSFER DESIGNS

to door panels or painted walls of the nursery, and can either be birds and butterflies placed irregularly over the wall or animal and pictorial subjects arranged to form a dado strip.

Japanese Lacquer Work.

No doubt you have often admired the beautiful designs in Japanese and Chinese lacquer work. Various lacquer work designs in transfers are available, and with these beautiful cabinet decorating work can be done. The designs are perfect examples of craftsmanship, containing all the details in gold, silver and in some cases mother-of-pearl. Applying such transfers to a well-lacquered tray or cabinet is to lift it from the commonplace to the unique.

The Use of Transfers on or behind Glass.

Very few users of transfers realise the useful and beautiful effects that can be obtained by the application of the designs to glass, either to the front of glass, as, for instance, the decoration of mirrors, etc., or BEHIND glass, so that the design shows through but is protected by the glass. Among the many uses of transfers applied behind the glass may be mentioned glass paper weights, glass-covered tea trays, table tops and teapot stands, a glass panel house name, or a house name or number applied to the fanlight over the door.

Transfers for Front of Glass.

For the front of glass, ordinary transfers are used, and are fixed with goldsize or varnish in just the same way as on a painted or polished surface. The only precaution necessary is to see that the glass is perfectly clean and free from grease.

The best way to ensure this is to polish the glass with a mixture of whiting and methylated spirit; this is rubbed on with a rag and allowed to dry, then polished off with a soft rag or tissue paper. For application to the BACK of glass a special transfer is necessary; this is printed so that the finished design is seen before application, whereas ordinary transfers are printed in reverse; that is to say, the detail and colour of the design are only seen after the transfer has been applied and the backing paper removed.

Transfers for Back of Glass.

Transfers for the back of glass cost about 25 per cent.

Fig. 6.—Two Examples of Wood Inlay Effects obtainable with Transfers.

more than ordinary transfers, and are available in the same designs. Use a very pale goldsize or varnish when fixing these transfers, as the coating of size will be seen through the glass, and, if a dark-toned goldsize is used, it will give a yellowish cast to transfers of white or pastel shades.

Great care is necessary when fixing transfers to glass, either in front or behind, to press them well down to avoid air bubbles, a slightly stronger tack point is also advisable, otherwise the method of fixing and cleaning off the surplus size is exactly the same as for ordinary surfaces. Transfers applied to the back of glass should be allowed to harden for twenty-four hours, and then either pencil varnished over the area of the design and about $\frac{1}{8}$ inch beyond the edge or the whole of the back of the glass may be painted or enamelled.

Fig. 7.—Two Examples of Decorative Work obtainable with Transfers.

Heat or Self-fixing Transfers.

With this type of transfer no adhesive, such as goldsize or varnish, is required as a fixative, consequently, they may be applied to fabrics, silk, parchment, paper and leather without fear of damaging the surface by staining. They are equally suitable for woodwork or painted surfaces if it is not desired to use a goldsize, although the size-fixed transfers are best for such work.

Fixing to Fabrics.

To apply this type to fabrics, first heat an ordinary household iron until it fizzes when lightly touched with a moistened finger. Place the transfer face down on the fabric in the desired position and iron down heavily and thoroughly. Next with a small brush wet the backing paper only sufficiently for the design to show through, confine the wetting to the design and about $\frac{1}{4}$ inch beyond; this will prevent the possibility of staining delicate fabrics. Allow to soak for about five to seven minutes, when the backing paper should peel off easily.

What to do if White Spots appear on Backing Paper.

If any white spots appear on the backing paper this indicates that it is not soaked sufficiently, and such spots should be gently rubbed with the finger nail slightly to roughen the paper.

If, when peeling off the backing paper, it sticks at all, replace and wet again until it can be peeled off without force. After the backing paper has been peeled off, moisten a piece of lintless cloth with water and gently wipe over the design to remove the gummy substance. Be careful not to allow the moisture to go over the edge of the design or it may stain the fabric. Finally, place a piece of dry white linen or muslin over the design and iron down heavily; allow to become quite cold before removing this, then peel off gently. Should it stick, do not use force, but slightly moisten the muslin and wait for a few minutes, when it can be removed without difficulty.

Fixing to Parchment, Patent Leather or Oilcloth.

Use the same method as for fabrics, but in the final operation it will be found that the muslin always sticks, and it is essential to moisten this before peeling off. Parchment very quickly blisters under heat, consequently the iron must not be so hot as for fabrics.

Self-Fixing Transfers for Painted and Polished Surfaces.

No heat is necessary when applying this type of transfer to the above surfaces. First moisten the face of the transfer by dabbing it gently with methylated spirits on a piece of lintless rag; DO NOT RUB. Allow this to dry until the design becomes tacky, then lay it face down on the work in the required position and press down thoroughly to exclude air bubbles. Next soak the backing paper thoroughly with water and again press down well; allow to soak for about five minutes, then peel off the backing paper gently, and finally wipe over the face of the design to remove the gum. If it is desired to varnish or polish over the design, allow to harden for twenty-four hours.

Duplex Paper Transfers.

Some transfers are printed on what is known as Duplex paper, that is, a thin sheet of tissue mounted on a stiffer backing; such transfers usually have the word Duplex printed on the back. To use Duplex transfers, first take a corner of the paper and rub it between the finger and thumb; this will cause the two papers to split apart just at the corner. Next apply the size in the usual way, and, when it becomes tacky, apply to the work. Press firmly and then peel off the stiff backing paper; this will leave the tissue which carries the design ready for soaking with water.

The main advantage of Duplex paper is that it requires much less soaking, as the water only has to penetrate the thin absorbent tissue; it is also much easier to fix to curved surfaces as, if desired, the stiff backing paper can be stripped off before the transfer is applied to the work. If this is done, however, it must be very carefully handled, as the tissue is easily wrinkled.

Whilst the information given in this article does not nearly cover all the uses to which transfers can be put to advantage, it is sufficient to enable the handyman to make use of transfers to give that professional touch to home-made articles or decorated and painted work.

DEALING WITH A WARPED SKIRTING BOARD

IT is sometimes found that when unseasoned wood is used for skirting boards an undesirable space results between the wall and the skirting board, as shown by the shaded portion in the diagram. This is due to the warping of the skirting board.

Foundation for the Plaster.

A good method of dealing with the fault is to point the opening with plaster. The opening should first be packed with folded strips of brown paper, preferably of the waterproof type. This paper gives a foundation for the plaster used in the pointing and prevents it from dropping behind the skirting board. In extreme cases three-ply wood could be used as a

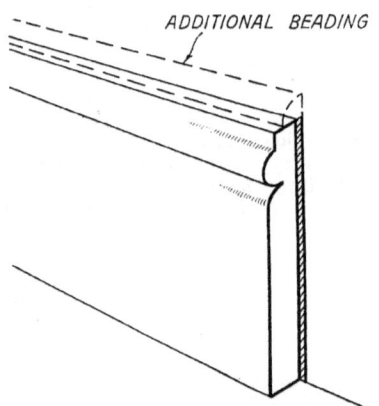

Section of Skirting Board showing Small Beading fixed to the Top Edge.

packing.

If the skirting board has a flat surface on the top edge, a small bead, or plinth, could be fixed to it with panel pins, as shown by the dotted outline in the sketch.

Gap between Skirting and Flooring.

Where unseasoned wood has been used but nailed at the top only, an unsightly gap may appear between the skirting and flooring. In such a case a small quadrant may be nailed to the floor to cover the gap.

It should be noted that skirtings should always be fixed with the heart side outwards, so that any subsequent winding will have the effect of binding the edges against the wall.

HOW TO HOLD ANIMALS

THERE is a right and a wrong way of picking up animals, and it is very important to handle them correctly. It is easy to injure a creature by holding it in the wrong way, and the following points should be borne in mind.

Rabbits often suffer a good deal from the way in which they are held. Many persons think that the proper way in which to lift the animal is by the ears. It is possible that very young rabbits might be handled in this manner without discomfort, but tame rabbits, as they grow up, become very heavy. The proper way to pick up a rabbit is to take hold of the skin just behind the shoulders. If the animal is very large its back legs might be supported with the other hand. It will be seen at once that the rabbit is quite comfortable, for it does not kick or struggle at all.

Guinea pigs are nervous little creatures, and it is wise not to handle them much. When it is necessary to lift them, do so as follows: Put the thumb just under the foreleg on one side and on the other side put the fingers. Do not press the animal more than is necessary to secure a hold.

When kittens are quite small one may follow the plan of the mother cat and lift by the skin at the back of the neck. After a month or so this method should be discarded. A cat will never struggle if you place your hand under the forepart of her body and allow the back legs to rest on the forearm. In the case of a large cat, both hands may be used in holding her up. Only small dogs and puppies can be lifted about, but in these cases one should exercise a great deal of care, and handle in the same manner as a cat. Puppies, especially, wriggle a lot, and if they are not held firmly may slip through the fingers and fall to the floor. Many young dogs have been badly hurt in this way.

Birds of all kinds must be handled now and then. With small birds in cages place the hands over the back and wings in such a way that the bird is enclosed. The handling should be very light, and be sure not to pinch in any way. Birds as large as a pigeon need special treatment. Let the bird sit in the hand with its head facing up the arm; the tail can rest between the fingers. Fowls are often treated badly, and it is not uncommon to see them lifted by the legs. The proper way is to seize the wings of the bird just behind the back. Hold the wings firmly, but not too tightly.

An Easily-made Photographic Enlarger

This enlarger, for use in conjunction with an existing camera, can be made from simple and easily-obtainable materials at the cost of two or three shillings for wood and a spare half-day for labour. The owner of a No. 2 Brownie, for example, with this easily-worked enlarger, can produce either postcard size or "whole-plate" (i.e., 8½ × 6½) prints. Almost any source of light, including daylight, can be used. The apparatus as described can easily be adapted, with a little ingenuity, for use with other types of camera.

Making the Camera Extension Box.

The first thing to make is the small plywood box seen inserted into the open back of the camera (Fig. 1). This box consists of four pieces of thin three-ply wood. Each piece is 4 inches long, one pair being 3⅝ inches wide (just a little on the full side), while the other two are 2⅝ inches wide. When joined up, they make an open-ended box 4 inches long by nearly 3¾ by 2⅞ inches. This box is the only item that needs to be constructed with specially exact care.

It is necessary that the box should slide easily, but not loosely, into the back of the camera when the spool holder has been taken out.

The "Lid-Mask."

A lid for this box consists of a mask and frame of plywood, which are glued and pinned together. The purpose of the lid is to hold the negative in place at whichever end of the box it may be necessary to use it. The little box and its lid are seen more clearly in Fig. 2, and the parts ready for assembling in Fig. 3.

Fix a rib of plywood ¼ inch thick round the box at exactly 2¼ inches from one end. The other side of the box will measure 1½ inches from the rib to the end of the box. This rib allows the box to fall only a certain distance into the body of the camera. The smaller the enlargement the longer must be the distance from negative to lens.

A couple of pieces of thin sheet glass are required, the same size as the little wooden lid between which the film negative is sandwiched, to keep the negative flat and in proper focus. Select glass free from any flaws and scratches that would certainly be reproduced in the enlargement. Two bulldog clips will serve to secure the glasses together to the mask.

Making the Paper Platform.

The next thing to tackle is the

*Fig. 1.—*The Complete Enlarger.

The only part of this simple enlarger that cannot be made at home with the greatest of ease is the camera, which probably already exists in the average home, and can be used. The example shown is a Brownie.

moving platform that carries the sensitive paper (see in Figs. 1 and 4). The piece of ply forming the flat face on which the sensitive paper is laid should be made just a shade over 8½ by 6½ inches.

The side walls attached to the movable platform have a height of 9½ inches, and can be seen in Fig. 1. A slot 3/16 inch wide runs down the centres, to allow of the position of the platform to be adjusted and secured by means of two finger nuts,

*Fig. 2.—*Details of the Camera Extension and Negative Holder.

Close view of camera extension box and the "frame-mask" which fits on top of the box. The negative, held between two pieces of glass, is clipped to the "frame-mask."

which tighten the movable walls to the outside walls of the box.

Making the Body.

The large box is made 18 inches in height *inside*. This allows a little space underneath the movable platform for keeping the packets of sensitive paper out of the way.

Fix a sheet of plywood on the inside of the door, fitting just *inside* the box. The strips forming the door framework fit *outside*. This forms a rebate which, on closing the door, shuts out all light. Provide a pair of small hinges and a couple of pairs of hooks and eyes for fastening.

The back of the box is made of one piece of plywood, 19 × 10⅛ inches (see Fig. 5).

Bore a circular hole, about 1 or 1¼ inch in diameter, in the top of the box, central with the movable platform beneath. After boring, mark out the position of the camera on the box. Then tack down four small strips of plywood to form a frame for holding down the camera, with its lens centrally looking through the hole.

Two 3/16-inch screws with fly-nuts are put through the sides of the box to engage in the slot in the movable platform. Slip washers on the screws both under the head and the fly-nuts on the inside, so that the platform can be slid up or down and secured at any point. The platform must now be moved into the correct focus. It might be preferable to stain or blacken the woodwork.

Setting the Focus.

An easy way to ensure sharp focus is to get a few odd hairs from one's head sandwiched between the two pieces of glass where the negative goes, the whole being clipped to the camera box. Insert the box into the camera, longer "half" up. Open the shutter of the lens. Stand the apparatus on the table where a strong light can shine downwards through the glasses to the lens of the camera. Place a sheet of white paper on the inside platform. A blob of light will be seen on the paper, representing the glow from the lamp. Release the fly-nuts and slide the platform up or down until the hairs are at the point of clearest definition. Then tighten up the screws again. Two strips of wood may be tacked on to the insides of the box sides, so that the platform can be brought up to that point again on any subsequent occasion without the need of refocussing. That is the setting for postcard size prints as in Fig. 1. Reverse the little camera box and replace the "hair negative" in position. Then once more adjust the platform to correct focus. This will be lower down than before, and will produce the larger picture. Tack on another pair of stops under the platform. A good plan is to fit a blank postcard in the centre of the platform in order to set the place for this size of sensitive paper when subsequently putting the enlarger into use. A piece of sheet glass laid on the platform will also be very useful to hold either size of paper in correct position during exposure. Strips of red or opaque paper stuck on the edges of this glass will mask off a white margin on the prints.

For Other Cameras.

This camera box is calculated in regard to dimensions for the popular No. 2 Brownie and its little lens of about 4½ inches focus. The box, as built, will give enlargement from almost any of the popular little hand cameras, but not necessarily in just the proportion of postcard and wholeplate.

With other cameras, to produce clear prints it may be necessary to make alterations in the dimensions of the camera box and subsequent adjustment in positions of the sliding platform, so as to compensate for variations in the various lenses. It may be added that such adjustments would usually take the form of a shorter length of the "camera-box" rather than lengthening it, but it is very little trouble to determine the actual proportions required. Although it must necessarily be done by trial and error, it is so very easy to make a box that will slide in and out easily and to be secured temporarily by means of pins.

It must be remembered that a very little movement upwards or downwards on the part of the negative will mean twice or three times the amount

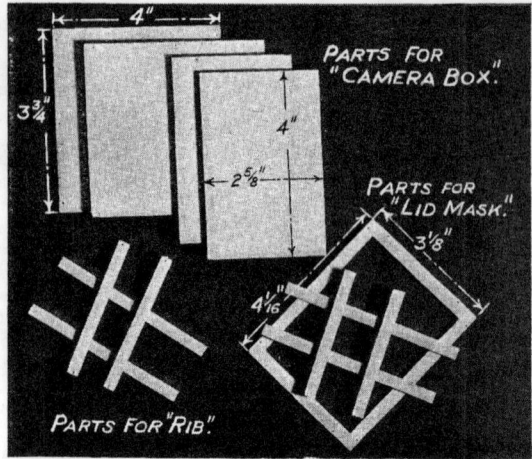

Fig. 3.—PARTS OF THE CAMERA BOX AND "LID MASK."
Sides of the thin plywood box with their dimensions are shown. The strips of wood for the rib are tacked on to the outside of the box exactly 2¼ inches from one end.

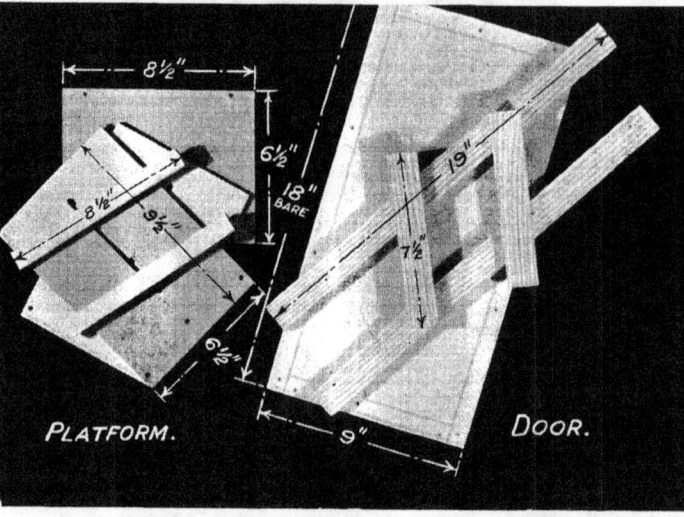

Fig. 4.—PARTS OF MOVABLE PLATFORM AND THE DOOR.
The platform consists of sheets of plywood and strips of wood. Note the ⅜-inch slot cut in each side wall. This also shows sheet of plywood and outside framework for the door.

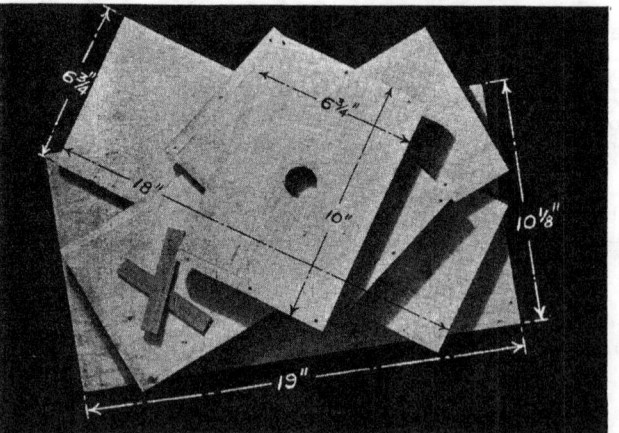

Fig. 5.—PARTS OF THE BODY OF ENLARGER READY FOR ASSEMBLING.
These consist of two pieces of board for the top and bottom ends, the top having a circular hole in its centre, two pieces of board for the sides, a piece of ply for the back, and two small strips to go inside the box.

of movement on the part of the platform where the actual enlarged image forms. Therefore such adjustments should be small ones at a time, getting a definitely sharp image each time upon the sliding platform.

Centralising the Subject.

By gumming a little black paper mask upon one of the negative holder glasses, it becomes very easy to centralise the principal part of the subject within the aperture seen, and to produce upon the finished enlargement a white margin in which the subject is correctly framed. Doing this also helps towards making the brightest possible print, because the clear margins of the film often allow light to spread around inside the box and be reflected thereupon to the surface of the sensitive paper.

How to make the best of Electric Light.

There is one valuable addition to the outfit as described—a piece of flashed opal glass. This differs from the ordinary white glass in that the whiteness is only a very thin skin on one side of the sheet. Therefore it does not intercept so much of the light, but it has the faculty of spreading light equally around the area underneath it. It is useful for placing over the negative when making enlargements by electric light, for securing perfectly even illumination. Flashed opal can be obtained from any reputable glass merchant.

In cases where it is found difficult to obtain, two pieces of ground glass, separated by, say, ¼ inch by the interposition of two strips of wood, will probably be found in most cases to be nearly as good. The best way of using either form of diffuser is to lay it over the top of the two clips, thus separating it a little way from the other glasses.

Making the Enlargements.

Within the limits for

which this instrument is designed, the results will be in every way as satisfactory as those from any professionally-constructed enlarger. It should be realised, however, that just as the Brownie lens of the camera is "slow" as compared with the equipment of the Press photographer, so also it is slower in the making of large prints. This generally matters little to the amateur, who rarely requires to make more than a few at one time. There is, however, a very simple means of enormously cutting down the time of exposure if that be found desirable. This will be described later.

If Glass Negatives are used.

Slip the film in between the two glasses clipped on top of the little box. If glass negatives are being used, just place the negative, film downwards, on top of one piece of glass.

Selecting the Illumination.

Make a choice of one of the lighting methods described that is most convenient, and *one* brand of bromide paper. *Stick to the one paper and the one method* till proficiency has been attained. Really first-rate results should not be long forthcoming.

Load in an Orange Light.

Bromide paper is recommended. This is sensitive to all forms of white light, daylight or artificial, and must be handled in a "safe light."

A special orange (fabric or glass) should be purchased for the purpose. See that the shutter is closed. Place a piece of the bromide paper with its sensitive side uppermost on the sliding platform, and place the glass on top of it. Close and fasten the box.

Exposure by Daylight.

Carry the apparatus out of doors, stand it upon a table, and open and close the shutter. After exposure, carry the box into the dark room and develop the print. If the sky is broken up by clouds there may be irregular results. To prevent this, the sheet of flashed opal should be used over the negative as before described. Perfectly even prints will be produced, but exposure time is considerably increased.

Fig. 6.—ENLARGER ARRANGED FOR DAYLIGHT EXPOSURES FROM INDOORS.
Stand the enlarger in front of window. Suspend a white sheet from the top of the window, back over a chair. The light will be reflected down into the enlarger. In fine weather exposures may, of course, be made out of doors.

Fig. 7.—ENLARGING WITH ELECTRIC LIGHT.
A 100-watt electric lamp may be used with a piece of flashed opal glass resting over the negative to diffuse the light.

Fig. 8.—USING A CONDENSER.
If a number of enlargements are required at a time, by artificial light, quick results can be obtained by using a 4-inch condenser as shown.

Another Daylight Method.

To avoid the necessity for going out of doors, it may be more convenient to arrange an artificial sky, as shown in Fig. 6. Attach a white sheet to the top of a window (preferably an upstairs one, so as to secure unobstructed light), and allow it to hang down over a chair so that it forms a reflector at about 45 degrees to the floor. The enlarger stands underneath this.

Magnesium Ribbon Lighting.

Instead of hanging the reflector over a window, it can hang from a door frame, and illuminated by means of magnesium ribbon. Using the normal No. 2 Brownie, it may be required to burn (at a distance of 2 or 3 feet) 2 or 3 yards of the magnesium ribbon to make the larger size of enlargement. This method is really more satisfactory when a camera with a more rapid lens is available. The ribbon can then be measured in inches, which will produce proportionately less smoke.

Electric Light.

Suspend a 100-watt lamp a couple of inches above the flashed opal glass (see Fig. 7). This will give an enlargement on bromide paper in anything between three and fifteen minutes, according to circumstances. Those who are familiar with the fitting up of electric lamps, and who are fortunate enough to have a radiator plug, can use a much higher-powered lamp. This would be a good investment if a number of enlargements were required.

Using a Condenser.

By screwing on a small metal tab at each corner of the lid frame, an ordinary 4¼-inch enlarging condenser can be placed centrally over the negative (Fig. 8). This has the effect of increasing the amount of light passing through the lens, and therefore divides the exposure time by something like ten. Or a smaller lamp can be used. For this purpose, one of the small opal lamps is strongly recommended in preference to the bare filament type of lamp.

The one disadvantage (apart from the cost—about 25s. for the condenser) is that it is absolutely essential to have the light correctly centred with the condenser. With this construction of enlarger it is extremely easy to arrange this. The flex from which the lamp hangs is tied in a loop, not too tightly, so that it can be moved up and down within the range of say 2 or 3 inches.

It will be noticed as the box is moved from side to side underneath the lamp that a disc of light shines on to a sheet of white paper placed on the little platform (examining this with the enlarger door open, of course). This may not be at first entirely central, but once the box has been adjusted so that the circle of light is central it is left in that position until the work is finished. Then if the patch of light is not so bright in intensity as between the centre and the margin, this can be adjusted by raising or lowering the lamp until the light over the enlarging platform is evenly bright all over. To make exposures, the shutter is left open and the light, centred as above, is switched on and off.

Exposures.

It is not possible to lay down in advance any rules whatsoever for length of exposures. There are variations first of all in the densities of negatives, and in the speeds of paper obtainable, ranging from rapid bromide papers to slow gaslight papers (with many intermediate speeds), each different brand having standards of its own.

As a result of practical tests, it can be said that the exposures from average snapshot negatives, upon the larger size ($8\frac{1}{2} \times 6\frac{1}{2}$) paper will take, with electric light, from five to ten minutes. Postcard size will take less.

With a white sheet up to a window as described, far from favourably situated, and as late as six o'clock in the evening, satisfactory enlargements were made with about the same exposures as the foregoing. Under good conditions of daylight, without obstructing buildings opposite to the window, the exposures will be much shorter. Out of doors, or in a glass-roofed conservatory, exposures will be shorter still. With the aid of a condenser exposures may be as short as fifteen to thirty seconds.

HOW TO MAKE A SKYLIGHT WEATHERPROOF

THE inaccessible position of a skylight often results in it being overlooked when the periodical house painting is undertaken. As the usual type of skylight on small houses is constructed of a timber frame and light it easily gets in a decayed state when exposed to the weather for long periods without attention.

It is, however, quite a simple matter to treat a skylight so that it is perfectly waterproof and does not require painting.

What to do first.

The first thing to do is to clean out all loose putty, then paint the rebate and fill up with new putty. Next, give the facing putty a coat of stiff paint.

Next obtain some Sheet Lead.

Now obtain sufficient 4-lb. or 5-lb. sheet lead (5-lb. lead indicates that each square foot should weigh 5 lb.) to cover the timber of the skylight. It will generally be found that the frame below is already properly weathered with back gutter, front apron soakers and flashing. The lead apron at the lower end of the window is a part of the weathering to the frame and should not need touching.

Cover the Side Rails first.

Start with the side rails and cover them with the sheet lead. Nail the lead in place with copper nails at the top as shown in Fig. 1. The enlarged section at A.A shows clearly how the lead is placed. The bottom end is usually "bossed" to shape. This means that the lead is bossed out so that the lead covers the end of the light. This is a rather difficult operation to carry out, and the amateur would probably be well advised to be content with cutting the lead, folding it to shape and soldering inside. It should then be secured in position and lightly dressed down.

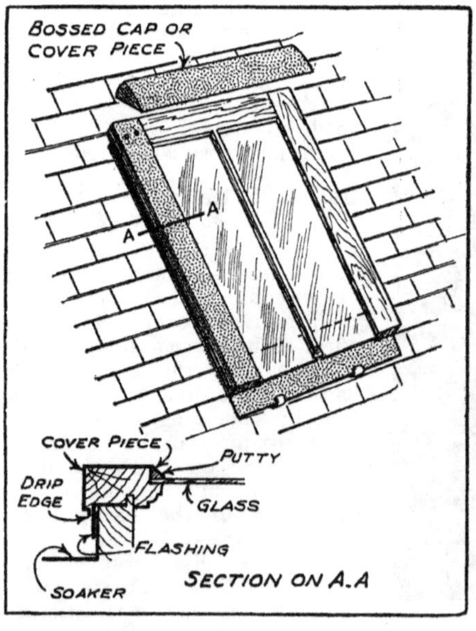

When one side has been finished satisfactorily, the other side is treated in the same manner.

Covering the Centre Bar.

After the two sides have been dealt with the centre bar should be covered with a narrow strip just wide enough to cover the bar and the putty which holds the glass in place. To secure this strip in place put in two or three $\frac{3}{4}$-inch brass round-headed screws down the centre. Before tightening up the screw-heads smear a little white lead on the shoulder so as to make them quite water-tight.

The Top Cover Piece.

The top cover piece is shown in Fig. 1. It can either be bossed or cut and soldered to the required shape.

A Safeguard against High Winds.

Although there is little danger of the lead blowing off in high winds provided the work is done properly and the lead keyed under the back edge, one or two brass screws can be inserted in the positions shown in Fig. 2 as an additional safeguard.

Rubbing Lead down to Glass.

The overhang of the lead should only be just sufficient to cover the putty, so that the maximum lighting area of the glass is not reduced. Do not attempt to get the lead edge close to the glass by beating with the dresser or you will probably break the glass. The correct way to get the lead as close as possible is to use a piece of smooth, hard wood and rub the lead down in long easy strokes until the edge of the lead touches the glass all along.

Fig. 1.—DETAILS FOR WEATHERING A SKYLIGHT. Showing one side rail covered with sheet lead, and a section on the side rail at A.A.

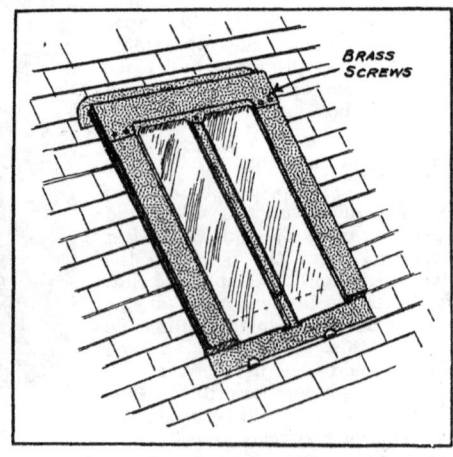

Fig. 2.—THE COMPLETED WEATHERING.

Repairing and Renovating a Piano

Before dealing with the repair and renovation of a piano, it is advisable to know something about the various parts and working of a piano. Fig. 1 shows the various parts of the casework; Fig. 2 shows the piano with the case removed.

The Back.

This consists of a wooden structure fitted with the wrest-pin plank to take the stresses of the strings, give rigidity and carry the sound board or amplifier.

The Soundboard.

This is a large board about $\frac{3}{8}$ inch thick, and is made from widths of spruce jointed either horizontally or diagonally and arched to the required degree. There are about ten or twelve shaped bars, about 1 inch wide and from $\frac{3}{4}$ to 1 inch high, and fillets or strips of wood round the edges which reinforce the board at the back. It carries the treble, tenor and bass bridges on the front surface.

The Frame.

This is an iron structure used to reinforce, or in some modern types to replace, the back and help support the wrest-plank. It should be provided with a top bridge over which the strings pass, and with hitch pins at the bottom to take the strings.

The Strings.

The strings, of course, are the producers of the sound. In the treble and tenor sections they are made of steel wire; in the bass, and sometimes in the lower tenor sections, they are made of steel wire with one or two coverings of copper wire.

The Casework.

This is the surrounding body or framework which supports the resonating structure and percussion mechanism in correct position, and also protects them from damage and dust. It is made of solid or veneered timber, decorated as required.

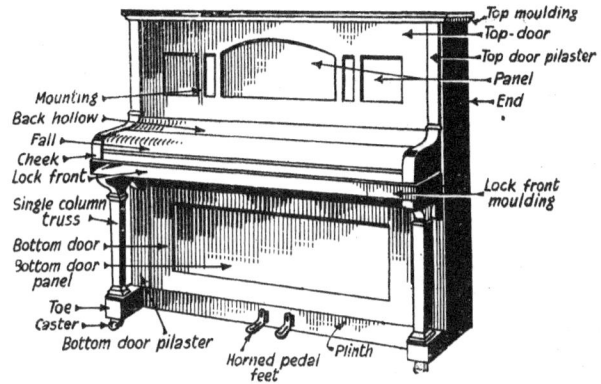

Fig. 1.—The Various Parts of the Piano Casework.

The Keys.

These consist of wooden levers covered at the front with ivory or celluloid or ebony.

The Action.

This is a delicate mechanism of finely adjusted levers and springs, consisting of wood, felt, leather and steel parts, and transmits the motion from keys to hammers.

The Hammers.

These strike on the strings to produce the sound, and consist of wooden heads covered with felt and mounted on shanks, which are in turn glued into the butts in the action.

The Pedals.

In order to enable the music to be played softly or loudly, two pedals are fitted, consisting of a combination of levers, springs and rods. When the right-hand pedal is pressed they act on the damper rail; when the left-hand pedal is pressed they act on the hammer rail or celeste movement.

CARE AND REPAIR OF KEYS

How to distinguish between Ivory and Celluloid Keys.

Ivory keys always show a joint between the "head" and the "tail," i.e., the shouldered part. A sure test is to rub the key with a little methylated spirit. If the key is a celluloid one a camphor smell will be noticed.

How to clean Keys.

After a good deal of use, the keys are likely to become grubby, due to perspiration from the players' hands causing dust to adhere to the keys. This can be removed by rubbing each from back to front, and *vice versâ*, with a clean piece of white rag moistened in methylated spirits. Use only a very little spirit, and take care that none of the spirit falls on the polished casework or a white stain may be caused.

Each key must be cleaned separately; do not attempt to clean several at a time or some of the fronts will probably be stripped off or broken at the corners. If the tops are rubbed sideways as they lie in the key frame, the cleansing material will get down the sides of the keys, and the keys themselves will be strained on the centre pins and will become so loose that they will wobble.

To clean the sides of the keys, lift one key at a time and press down the two adjacent keys, as shown in Fig. 6.

How to whiten Discoloured Keys.

If the keys are too discoloured to yield to the above treatment, mix some gilder's whiting with the methylated spirit to form a paste.

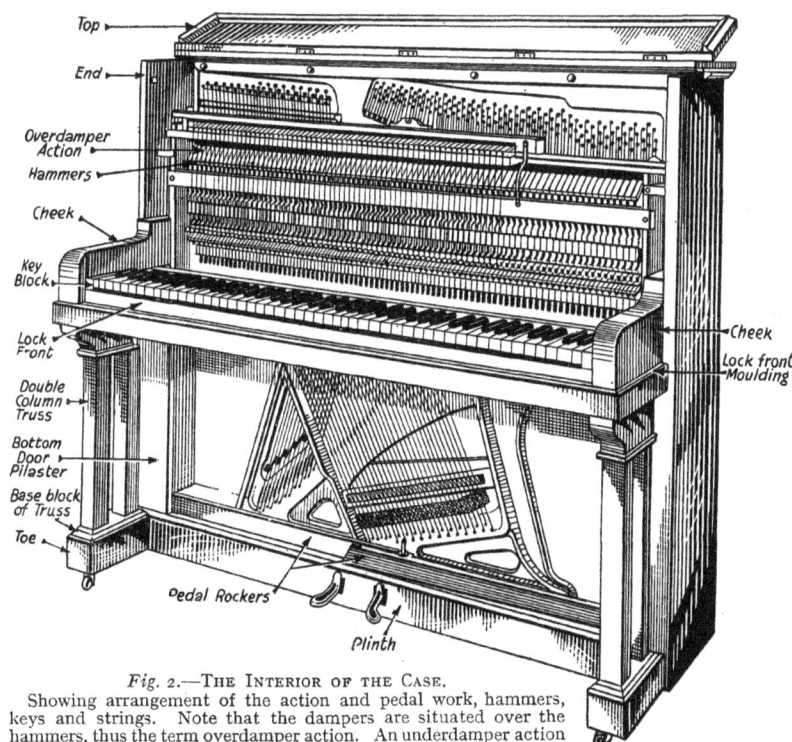

Fig. 2.—The Interior of the Case.
Showing arrangement of the action and pedal work, hammers, keys and strings. Note that the dampers are situated over the hammers, thus the term overdamper action. An underdamper action is shown in Fig. 5.

REPAIRING AND RENOVATING A PIANO

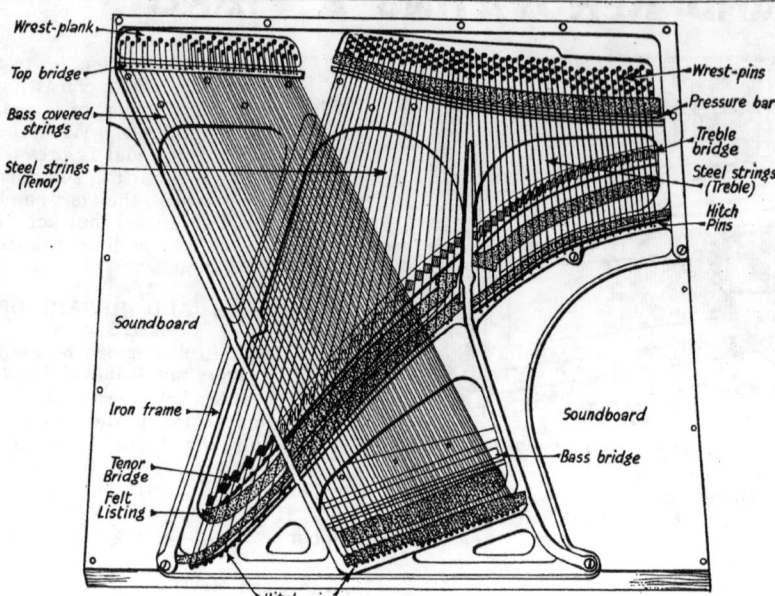

Fig. 3.—FRONT VIEW OF THE STRUNG BACK OF UPRIGHT PIANO.
Showing the arrangement of the strings and iron frame.

It will now be possible to take the keys out one by one. If not already distinctly marked, do not forget to number them in pencil on the underside.

Scraping the Keys.

Keys that have become "spooned" or hollowed will have to be scraped level. Fix the key in a vice, as shown in Fig. 7, taking care not to bend it in any way; then draw the scraper along from tail to head, easing the pressure as the front is reached so that it is not turned over. Hold the scraper quite square during the stroke to ensure equal reduction on both edges of the key. There is no need to use the scraper unless the key is hollowed.

Cleaning and Polishing.

Having removed sufficient to make the key quite flat, it can now be cleaned and polished. Sprinkle the felted wooden block with whiting and methylated spirit and rub the face of the key backwards and forwards until all discoloration has disappeared. The key should, of course, be held quite level on the block. If the edges of the key are sharp, they should be rounded by papering them with a piece of "flour" paper wrapped round a thin piece of wood in the form of a "file."

The next operation is to rub the key on the block covered with box-cloth, which should be sprinkled with dry whiting to give the key the final polish.

Cleaning Sides and Woodwork.

Dirt on the edges of the keys can be removed by rubbing the side of the key with No. 1 glasspaper wrapped round a thin piece of wood. A rag moistened in methylated spirit and wiped over the woodwork should be sufficient if it is not too

This paste is applied in the same manner as the plain methylated spirit; the key must be wiped until it is perfectly dry. Any household cleanser can be used if preferred, provided it is free from grit and does not dull the polished surface.

SCRAPING AND POLISHING A KEY

If a key is so badly discoloured that cleaning has no effect, the only thing to do is to take the key out for more drastic treatment.

Materials required.

Obtain the following tools and materials: steel scraper; two wooden blocks, 6 × 2 inches, of any convenient thickness, each with one face perfectly smooth and level, one covered with grey or white felt and the other with box-cloth; No. 1 glasspaper; "flour" paper; methylated spirits; whiting.

Removing the Keys.

First remove the top door, fall and hollow, and action. Remove the "nameboard," unless it is fixed to the back hollow. This is a rail running the length of the keyboard, screwed or fitted to the keyblocks at either end. Where screwed, undo screws first and then lift up.

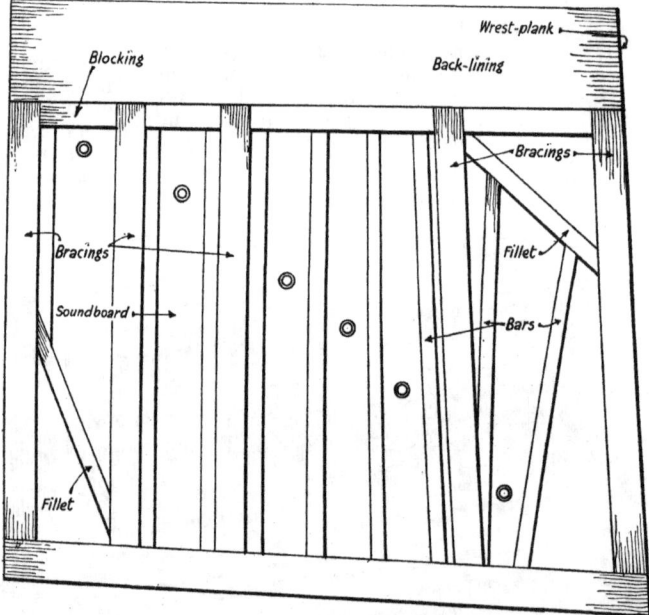

Fig. 4.—BACK VIEW OF THE STRUNG BACK OF UPRIGHT PIANO.

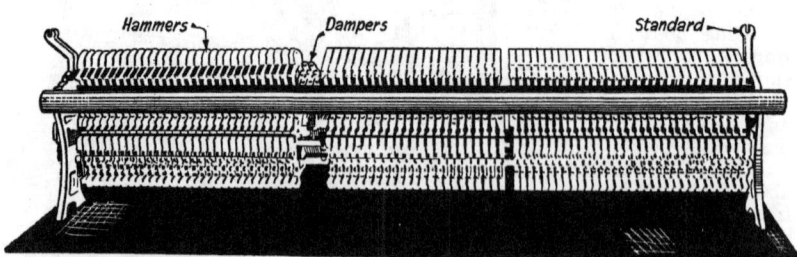

Fig. 5.—UNDERDAMPER ACTION WITH METAL STANDARDS FOR OVERSTRUNG PIANO.
In this type, springs replace gravity in returning dampers to strings.

REPAIRING AND RENOVATING A PIANO

dirty. If not, papering or scraping will be required. When using the scraper, it must be drawn with the grain and not against it.

Cleaning the Fronts.

Fix the key in the vice and clean with the "flour" paper file. Then burnish the key with the box-cloth pad held in the hand. The fronts are not so highly polished as the tops.

How to renew a Key Felt.

While the keys are out of the key-frame it is a good idea to inspect the felts. First brush over to remove any dust, then look to see if any have been attacked by moth, in which case the felt should be renewed. After removing the strip or strips of felt on the back rail of the key frame, new strips of the same thickness should be glued in their place. Replace the old baizes and centres by new sets of the same thickness. These are the felt washers on the front and centre pins respectively.

Do not disturb the paper washers on any of the pins, nor any pieces of veneer or cardboard under the frame. The paper washers make up the correct "touch," and the packing is necessary to level the frame.

The keys can now be replaced on their correct pins.

HOW TO REMOVE A BROKEN STRING

If a string is broken it is probable that the loose ends will jar on the adjacent notes, and, unless the string is removed, the piano will be temporarily out of commission.

Dismantling Front of Case.

The front of the case will have to be dismantled to remove the string. To do this, fold back the top, undo the fastening on the inside of the top door, pull the door slightly forward and lift upwards and outwards, taking care not to damage the dowels on the bottom of the door or the rest of the casework. Next grasp the back hollow with both hands and lift upwards.

Removing the Action—Overdamper.

First remove the round brass nut of the bolt passing through the wooden block on top of the damper rail. Do not touch the brass washer behind the block. Now undo the turn buttons on the standards or side blocks. Pull the action forward until the damper

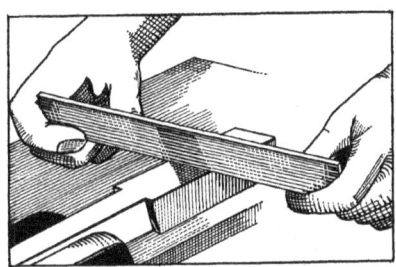

Fig. 7.—How to scrape a Key.
The key is fixed in a vice and the scraper worked from front to back.

block is clear of the bolt and lift upwards and outwards.

Removing the Action—Underdamper.

If it is an action with "wooden" standards there is no damper bolt and block to trouble with. Undo the turn buttons at each side and pull the action forward until the metal cranks—in some cases two at the bass end and in others one at each end—are clear of the side blocks. Then lift upwards and outwards.

If it is an action with "metal" standards, first unscrew the milled nuts on the bolts that pass through the slotted tops of the standards. Then pull the action forwards until standards are clear of the bolts; lift upwards and outwards as before. Note that the round knobs on base of standards rest in cupped screws instead of on blocks. Remember, too, to replace the nuts on the bolts to prevent them getting lost.

Taking out Bottom Door.

Lastly, the bottom door must be taken out; it will probably be fixed by long turn buttons at either side under the key-bottom, or by wooden or steel spring in the centre under the key-bottom.

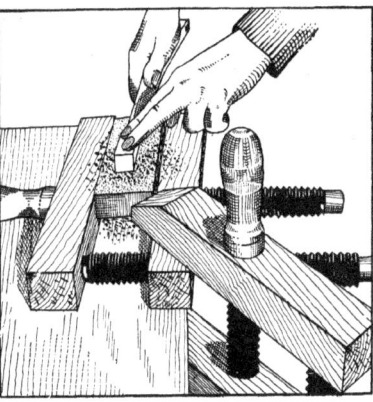

Fig. 8.—Cleaning and polishing a Key.
If a vice is not available, two hand-screws can be used as substitutes. Keep the key level when rubbing on the block.

Removing a Bass String.

If the broken string is a bass or covered one, trace this carefully downwards to the hitch pin at the bottom of the iron frame. Then ease the string off the bridge pins and raise loop off hitch pin. Pull it out gently, taking care not to scratch the varnish of the soundboard.

When the breakage has occurred above the top bridge, the process is somewhat different. The short length of wire round the wrest-pin will not cause trouble and can be left. Should there be a long strand adhering to the wrest-pin, it can be cut off with pliers as close to the pin as possible. Keep the broken pieces of string as a pattern for the new string.

Removing a Steel String.

If the broken string is a steel one, then it will be found to affect either two strings of the same note or one string of two adjacent notes. The procedure is to trace the broken strand to the hitch pin or pins on the bottom of the frame. Then trace the string up again to the wrest pin and cut off as close to the pin as possible. Then draw out the string.

REPAIRS TO THE CASEWORK

How to deal with a Crack.

If the piano has a split in the end with a gap showing, it can be repaired by inserting a piece of thin veneer into the opening.

First wedge the crack open, then cut the veneer to the approximate length and make it wedge shaped by shaving towards one edge. Insert some glue into the crack by means of a thin knife and press the thin edge of the veneer into the crack as far as it will go. Now withdraw the wedge, and the crack will close on the veneer strip.

As soon as the glue has set remove the surplus veneer with a chisel and glasspaper down the surface.

Should there be just a crack, but

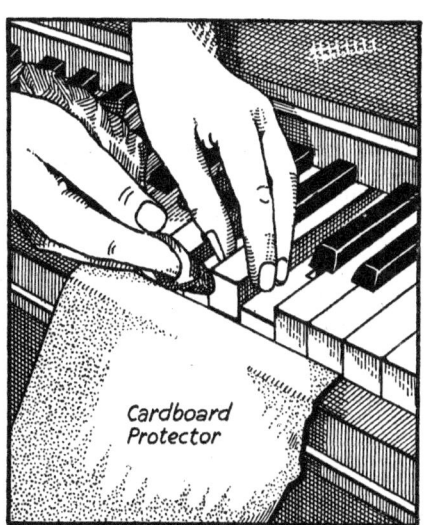

Fig. 6.—When cleaning Keys each one must be cleaned separately.

To rub the sides and front hold the key up and with the same fingers depress the key on each side of it. When cleaning tops and fronts, rub up and down and not across the key. Note the piece of cardboard placed over the rail to prevent discoloration of the rail.

1079

no gap, then pour glue into the crack and apply a cramp or heavy weight.

Broken Veneer.

If the veneer is broken in any place, it should be trimmed to an irregular shape and a new piece of veneer cut in with a penknife sharpened to a fine point. Remove all old veneer and glue, so that the new piece beds flat on the groundwork. The new piece of veneer should be slightly thicker than the original to allow it to be papered down.

To remove a Blister.

Blisters can be removed by cutting horizontally and vertically with a sharp knife and running in hot glue. Then press down the veneer, and when hard trim off any raised edges with a chisel and paper down. A knife plunged into boiling water will be found useful when running in the glue.

To cure Bruises.

A bruise or dent, if not too deep, can be dealt with by steaming. First scrape away the polish down to the veneer. Then apply hot water by means of a swab until the fibres of the wood have become swollen. Then evaporate the water with a hot iron and brown paper.

A very deep bruise is best treated with stopping, which can be purchased in sticks. Dig over the bruised part with a sharp tool to form a "key." Melt the stopping with a hot iron and drop it into the hole. Press well in while still semi-liquid with a wetted finger. When set, remove any surplus stopping with a chisel and paper down the surface.

Dealing with a Broken Moulding.

The only difficulty in gluing a broken moulding back into place is to keep the broken piece under pressure until the glue hardens. If the damage is on the front moulding, the simplest method is to undo the hinge and place the half-top on two blocks on the bench. Pressure can then be applied by a hand-screw.

If the break is on the end of the front half-top, then clamp the latter to the bench using felt and wooden blocks to protect the polish.

Place a piece of newspaper under the end to prevent glue from adhering to the bench. Screw a strip of wood about 1 inch thick to the bench parallel with the end to be repaired and at just sufficient distance from it to allow the insertion of the moulding and two wedges as shown in Fig. 9.

Glue both parts of the broken moulding and place the loose piece in

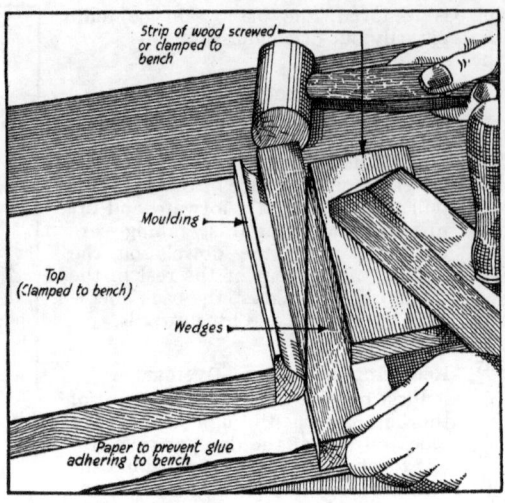

Fig. 9.—SHOWING HOW WEDGES ARE USED FOR PRESSURE IN GLUING MOULDING TO TOP.

position. Turn up the end of the newspaper over the moulding before inserting the wedges to prevent glue setting at the wedge.

Place one wedge with its straight side against the moulding and hold it in position while the other wedge

Fig. 10.—THE TURNOVER DESK.
This is fitted to the top edge of the top door.

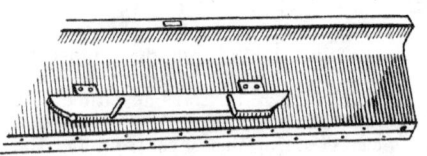

Fig. 11.—TRAY OR FALL DESK.

with its straight side against the block is gently tapped home with a hammer. The pressure should be just sufficient to keep the moulding firmly in place.

The paper and any surface glue can be removed with hot water when the job is completed.

A broken piece of moulding on the end of the back half-top is best repaired by fixing with two panel pins when the moulding has been glued in place. The pins can be sunk beneath the surface with a small punch and the tiny holes filled in with stopping.

MODERNISING AN OLD PIANO

The cost of fitting an up-to-date action and keys to an old piano would probably make the job prohibitive for all practical purposes, but there are various ways in which the appearance of an old piano can be improved. The parts that need attention are the top door panel, the moulding, pilasters, desk, cheeks, trusses and pedals.

Fitting a Modern Panel.

For instance, if a piano is adorned with an old silk, fretwork, or heavy flower marquetry panel, this should be replaced by one of modern design or by a plain panel veneered to match the rest of the case. These panels are obtainable in stock sizes, although the old type of long-shaped panel has usually to be made to order.

Remove Old Sconces.

When old sconces are removed the screw-holes should be neatly stopped up, unless electric bulbs are being fitted, in which case the plates of the new brackets will probably cover the old screw-holes.

Replace Old Pilasters by Plain Moulding.

Antiquated pilasters should be taken off and replaced by lengths of plain moulding, and top mouldings can be replaced by more modern patterns.

How to remove an Old Moulding that has been glued.

A good method of removing a glued moulding is to apply methylated spirit to the glue, which will cause it to perish, or lose its adhesive property. Once the spirit starts to act, the glued joint separates with a series of loud cracks. To get the spirit directly in contact with the glue a tiny groove should be run right along the joint and the spirit squirted into this from a clean oil-can.

Where a groove cannot be made, work a thin knife into the joint to start with and as the spirit starts to work, wedges can be introduced.

How to deal with Cheeks.

Cheeks are usually reeded and, if so, the reeding is done on a thick layer of veneer. If plain cheeks are preferred, the reeded portion can be removed with a spokeshave. The cheeks must not be reduced to the level of the fall and hollow, and the top of the cheek on which the door rests should not be reduced too much or there will be excessive overhang.

The Desk.

An old type expanding desk can be replaced by a more modern "tray" desk (see Fig. 11), which is fixed by two butt hinges. If there is no room for a "tray" desk, fit a turnover type.

The desk is fixed by cutting out of the edge of the top door just a fraction deeper than the thickness of the hinge when folded. Do not forget to allow for a piece of boxcloth or thin felt under the hinge. The fixing screws, which should be ½ inch, No. 4 brassed or blued, should have cloth washers under the heads.

Cut the side slats of the desk to the required length so that they rest on the inside of the fall when it is open. Tip the ends of the slats with boxcloth.

FAULTS CAUSED BY DAMP AND MOTH

Dampness and moth are probably the two chief causes of any faults that are likely to occur with a piano.

Dampness, for instance, is responsible for rust on the metal parts, perishing of strings and action springs, softening of glue on wooden and felt parts, and swelling of the felts in the bushings of the keys, causing sluggish action, objectionable noises and frequent breaking of strings.

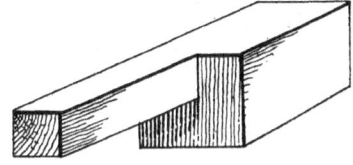
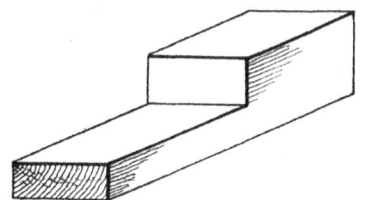

Fig. 12.—Block Toe and Ordinary Toe.

The former is for fixing above bottom board, the latter for fixing under bottom board.

What to do if Room is known to be damp.

If the room in which the piano is kept is known to be damp, then avoid placing the piano too close to the wall, stand it on insulators (see Insulators) and hang inside the top door a tin of "damp preventer" obtainable at any music shop.

How to detect Dampness in the Action.

This first becomes noticeable in the working of the keys or action. It is found that a key cannot be struck twice quickly, due to the fact that the centres being swollen do not allow the hammer to resume its original position quickly enough.

The Remedy.

The remedy is to take out the action and place it in front of a fire to dry. If you do not feel capable of dismantling the piano, then remove the top and bottom doors, take out the fall and hollow and place a stove near the piano, taking care, of course, to protect the polished part from the heat.

Rusty Springs.

It is no use attempting to clean rusty springs with emery or glasspaper, as this will reduce their diameters and put them out of tune. Unless the rust has eaten in to such an extent that the tone is affected, it is best to leave them as they are. Then when they begin to break, a new set can be fitted.

INSULATORS

Insulators are sometimes placed under the piano castors for the following reasons:—

(1) To raise a piano that is too low.
(2) To prevent wear to carpet or linoleum.
(3) To protect piano from a damp floor.
(4) To prevent sound travelling downstairs to a room below.

For purposes (1) and (2) glass, wood or vulcanite insulators can be used.

For purpose (3) glass insulators are best.

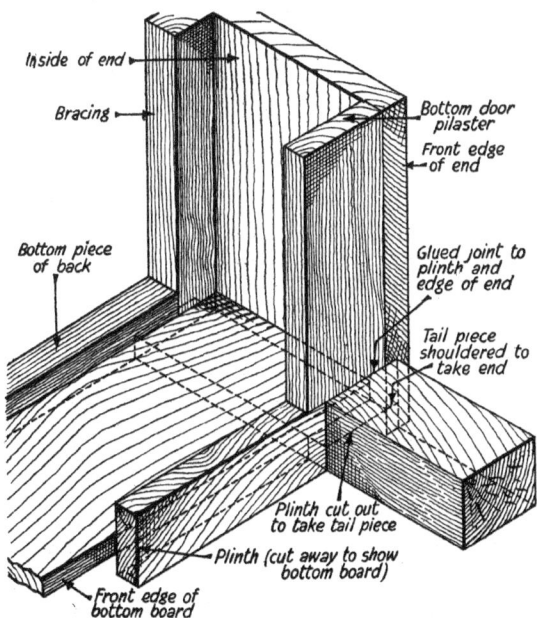

Fig. 13.—Method of fixing Toe Block underneath Bottom Board.

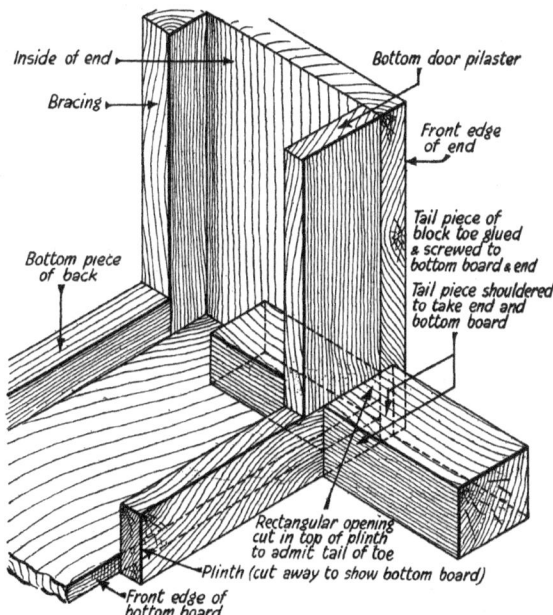

Fig. 14.—Method of fixing Toe Block above Bottom Board.

For purpose (4) vulcanised rubber insulators should be used.

Faults due to use of Insulators.

When insulators are used it may be found that the piano keyboard is raised too high, making playing awkward. The seat should be raised and a foot rest used.

An irritating jarring noise may also be caused if the castor plate rests on the rim of the insulator and allows the wheel to hang free. The remedy is to see that the castor wheel is properly bedded in the hollow. This can be done by putting the necessary thicknesses of cardboard or felt under the insulator to raise it sufficiently or place a piece of felt in the hollow of the insulator.

PLAYER PIANO FAULTS

It is not advisable to tamper with a player piano, and if anything goes wrong it is best to get the repair done by an expert player mechanic. The following notes, however, will help one to locate any faults that may occur.

Lack of Resistance during Pedalling.

If while pedalling there is a lack of resistance to the feet, this may only be due to the fact that the re-roll lever has not been thrown over sufficiently to the left, or else there may be a leak. To test for the latter cause, insert the roll as for playing and unwind it sufficiently for the blank paper to cover the holes in the tracker bar. Hold it in this position and resume pedalling. The leak is in the bottom action if there is still no resistance, but if there is resistance then the leak is in the top action.

Before testing with the roll, make sure that the main trunks and other tubes are all fitting properly on their nozzles.

Patching a Leak.

Provided the leak is found to be in an accessible part of the bellows it is quite easy to repair. Cut a patch of thin leather, slightly larger than the worn part, and fix it with seccotine round the outer edges. Allow the seccotine to harden before using the piano.

How to test the Motor for Leakage.

Motor leakage can be detected by holding the shaft to

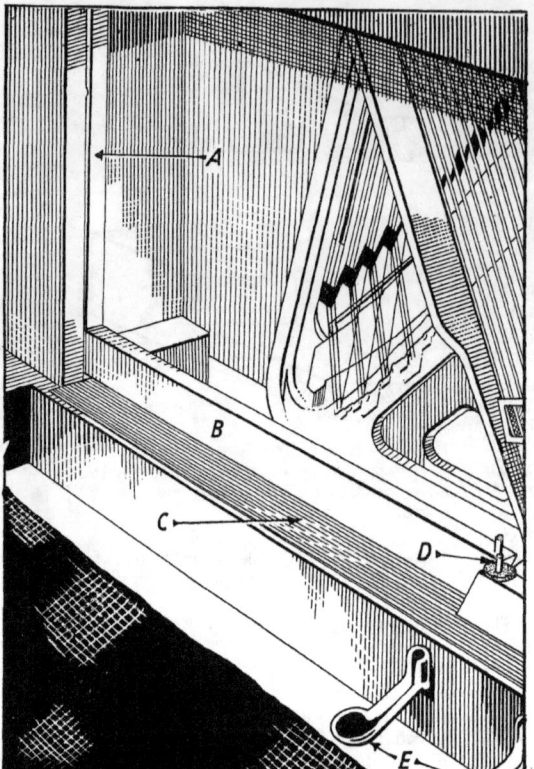

Fig. 15.—How the Pedals work.

When either pedal E is depressed it pulls down the ends of its corresponding rocker B attached to it by pedal bolt D fitted with an adjustable nut. The rocker (or lever) rests on a U-shaped spring C which acts as a fulcrum. When the pedal end is depressed the other end raises the side rod A. This engages one of the levers in action, and either raises dampers off strings or shortens hammer blow or operates celeste.

Fig. 16.—Where to Look for Moth.

If the ravages of moth are suspected the places to look are at the felt on the back, centres and baizes. Replace them if they appear moth eaten.

prevent it turning and listening for seepage due to the presence of grit or dirt under the valves or unevenness of the surface of the motor face or underside of valves.

What to do when a Note does not sound.

If no sound is obtained from a certain note, it is probably choked with dust. Set the indicator at "O" and pass a finger to and fro over the particular opening. If this does not cure the trouble, clean out the opening in the tracker bar with a wire. If still no result, the suction pump will be required. The roll is taken out and the pump used direct on the face of the bar.

Note Sounds out of Turn.

When the wrong note sounds, dirt may be keeping the valve from closing or the paper may be buckled and allowing air to enter though the note is apparently covered. Try drying the roll in front of a fire.

If a note plays once but does not repeat, either the valve has stuck or the vent is choked. If a hammer fails to return from the string, then something is interfering with the valve.

Tempo altered by Pedalling.

If when the pedals are worked, the tempo is altered, this indicates that the governor requires regulating. If the motor runs too fast, weaken the governor spring; if too slow, strengthen the spring.

How to test whether Motor is running at Correct Tempo.

If a test roll is not available, then mark off an ordinary roll in feet up to 7 feet or more, beginning from the first row of notes.

The correct tempo should be 7 feet of roll per minute when the pointer is at 70. Therefore to test take the time from a watch, pedal evenly and see whether 7 feet of roll pass the tracker bar holes in one minute. If the speed varies within half a foot either way, something is wrong with the tempo valve or governor.

What to do if Motor slows down.

If the motor shows a tendency to slow down, this may be due to lack of lubrication to the crankshaft and gear or roughness on face of motor and valves. Oil is required in the former instance, but blacklead only in the latter.

A Radio Lounge Chair

COMFORT, utility and practicability are outstanding features of the combined wireless receiving set and lounge chair illustrated in Fig. 1 and described in this article.

At first glance it might be thought that such a combination would entail some loss of efficiency, either on the wireless side or considered merely as an armchair. Neither of these fears is realised. The wireless set is built up from a "Lissen All-Wave Skyscraper 4" kit set, which provides excellent reception on the whole wave range, including the short, medium and long bands, with excellent tone and volume.

The chair itself conforms to modern ideas and proportions, and when suitably upholstered and provided with swansdown cushions becomes a truly luxurious piece of furniture.

Designed for Home Construction.

The structural features of the chair have been specially designed for the needs of the home constructor, as the normal methods of chair-making are seldom successful in the hands of the amateur. With this in view, the exterior of the chair is finished in highly polished walnut-veneered plywood, the interior is spring upholstered in the usual way, or a ready made sprung seat cushion and back can be employed. Finally, the use of a well-tested "kit set" ensures complete satisfaction on the wireless side.

Before proceeding with the actual construction, it may be pointed out that the wireless set is housed in the right arm of the chair, and the control knobs come on the top of the arm rest—conveniently to the right hand. The knobs are partially recessed, and thus are quite inconspicuous. The combined wave change and "on-off" switch knob comes at the front. Access to the set is provided by a flush fitting door in the chair side. Beneath the set are the batteries—in a separate compartment—with access from a door at the front, as shown in Figs. 2 and 3, while the loud speaker is housed in a compartment forming the rear half of the chair side; this compartment is open at the bottom, access to the speaker is provided by a door on the inside of the chair arm. The other arm

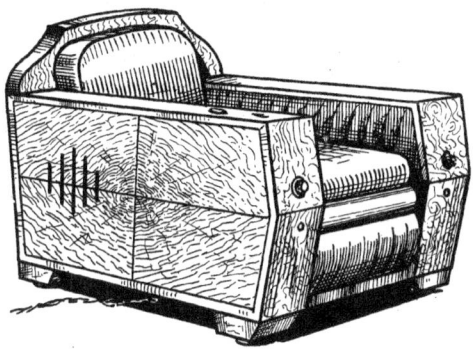

Fig. 1.—The Finished Chair.
The only evidences of the built-in radio set and speaker are the almost flush control knobs on the arm rest and the speaker fret in the side.

Fig. 2.—Doors opened for access to Radio Set and Batteries.
The cupboards seen on the right of the illustration are useful for books, smoker's kit, or other items.

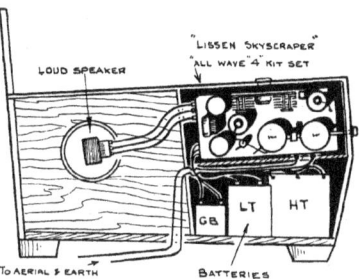

Fig. 3.—Diagram showing Arrangement of Radio Set.

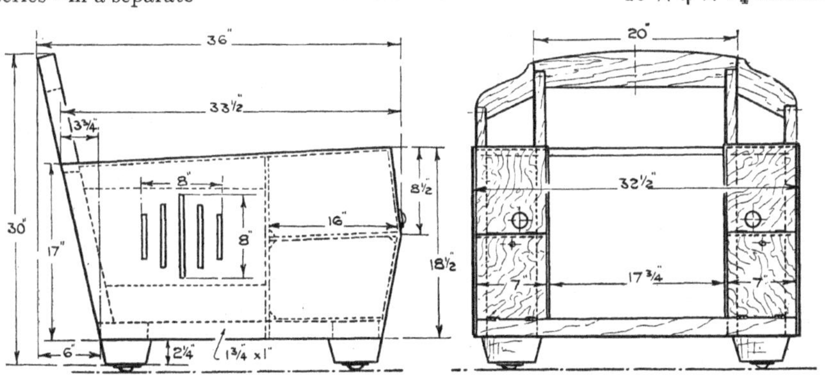

has doors at the front, providing access to compartments for books, smoking supplies, slippers, knitting wools, or whatever may be desired.

Materials required.

Wireless Set.—One complete kit set "All-Wave Skyscraper 4" with valves complete by "Lissen Ltd.," Lissenium Works, Worple Road, Isleworth, Middlesex.

Batteries.—One 2-volt L.T., No. LN2008; one 144-volt H.T. battery with G.B. tappings, No. LN3006 ("Lissen Ltd.").

Loud Speaker.—One P.M. moving coil, No. LN5324 ("Lissen Ltd.").

Wiring.—Six yards twin flexible wire for aerial and earth connections ("Lewcos"); 2 yards V.I.R. flexible wire ("Lewcos").

Chair Parts.

Sides.—Burr walnut veneer-faced plywood, two pieces $33\frac{1}{2} \times 18\frac{1}{2} \times \frac{3}{16}$ inches thick.

Back.—Burr walnut veneer-faced plywood, $32\frac{1}{2} \times 30$ inches.

Arm Tops.—Two pieces burr walnut-faced plywood, $31 \times 7\frac{1}{4}$ inches.

Arm Fronts.—Two pieces burr walnut-faced plywood, $8\frac{1}{2} \times 7\frac{1}{4}$ inches; two pieces burr walnut-faced plywood, $9 \times 7\frac{1}{4}$ inches.

Inside Arms.—Two pieces birch plywood, $32\frac{1}{2} \times 18\frac{1}{2} \times \frac{3}{16}$ inches.

Partitions and Floors.—One piece birch plywood, $40 \times 20 \times \frac{3}{16}$ inches.

Frame Rails.—Oak, 1 inch thick, $1\frac{3}{4}$ inches wide; four pieces 30 inches long; one piece 32 inches long; two pieces 26 inches long; two pieces 22 inches long; one piece 30 inches long; one piece deal or oak $28 \times 5 \times 1\frac{3}{4}$ inches; one piece deal or oak $28 \times 4 \times 1\frac{3}{4}$ inches.

Stub Legs.—Four pieces oak or deal, $7 \times 7 \times 4$ inches long.

Fillet.—"Glue block fillet" triangular section, $\frac{1}{2}$ inch; six pieces 30 inches long.

Top Back Rail.—Oak or deal, two pieces $9 \times 3\frac{1}{2} \times 1\frac{3}{4}$ inches; one piece $20 \times 4 \times 1\frac{3}{4}$ inches.

Baffle Board.—Plywood, $15 \times 11 \times \frac{1}{2}$ inches thick.

Fig. 4.—Working Drawings of Radio Lounge Chair.
The upholstery is not shown.

A RADIO LOUNGE CHAIR

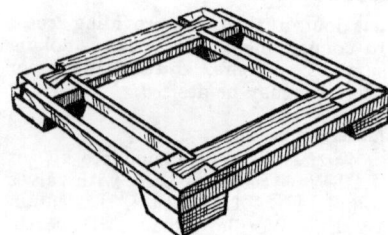

Fig. 5.—Lower Frame and Stub Legs.
Four stub legs are framed up with hardwood to form the bottom or foundation of the chair.

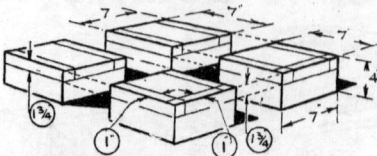

Fig. 6.—Marking out the Stub Legs.
The sketch shows the four legs in relative position as seen from the front of the chair.

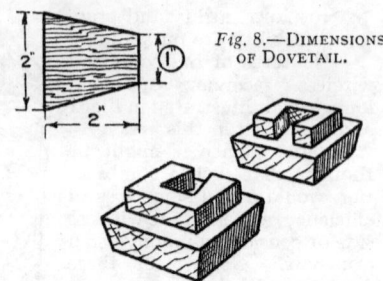

Fig. 8.—Dimensions of Dovetail.

Fig. 9.—Front Legs shaped.
Dovetail recesses cut for the cross rail of the sides and rebated for the outer rails.

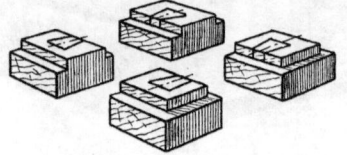

Fig. 7.—Second Stage of shaping and marking out the Legs.
After the rebates are cut, the dovetails are marked out as here shown.

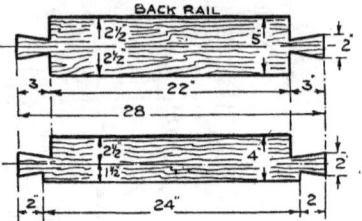

Fig. 10.—Cross Rails.
Note that the front rail is shaped differently to the back. Both are 1¾ inch thick.

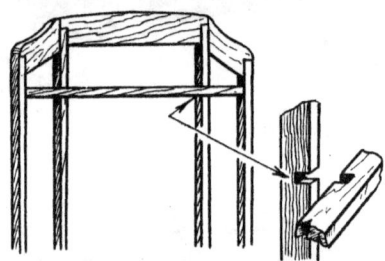

Fig. 11.—Back Framing.

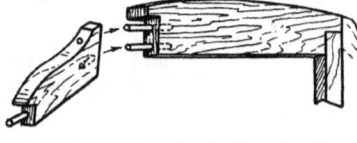

Fig. 12.—Detail of Top Frame Joint.

Fig. 13.—Right Inner Arm.

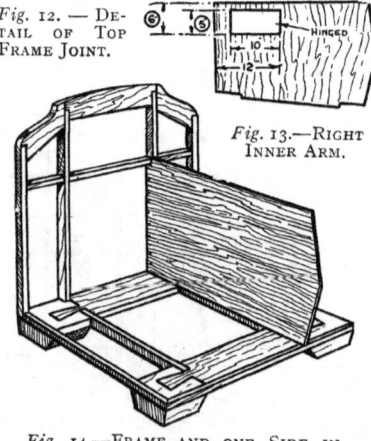

Fig. 14.—Frame and one Side in Position.

Sundries.—Five pairs small brass butt hinges, ¼ inch wide, ¾ inch long, with screws; two small, one medium, oak knobs; one "Croid" home constructor glue outfit; 2 ozs. fine cabinet pins, ½ inch long; one bottle "walnut" oil stain; one 8-oz. bottle French polish; 3 feet of ¼-inch dowel rod; four ball-bearing casters; a few screws and nails; tapestry and upholstery to choice.

What to do First.

Check over all material, then arrange to store the plywood flat under pressure to prevent it warping or buckling. Any pieces of veneered plywood that are received in a buckled state should be rejected and be replaced by perfectly flat pieces, as they cannot subsequently be flattened or pulled into shape.

The next step is to study the working drawings (Fig. 4) and other illustrations and gain a clear idea of the relationship of the various parts; then start in on the lower frame and legs.

The lower frame—shown complete in Fig. 5—consists of the four stub legs connected at front and back by cross rails dovetailed to the legs, also by four side rails glued and screwed into rebates on the legs. The dovetail joint is quite simple, and is within the capabilities of the home carpenter, if done in proper order.

First mark out the stub legs, as shown in Fig. 6, then saw away the wood at the marked edges to form rebates, as shown in Fig. 7, and then mark out the shapes of the dovetails. All four dovetails are alike, and should be marked off from a centre line drawn across the tops of the legs; the dimensions in Fig. 8 give the sizes of the dovetails.

Next drill holes about ¾ inch in diameter into the wood in the space to form the dovetail, then chisel away the unwanted wood. This done, draw a line on the underside of each leg 1 inch in from the edge and bevel the sides from the edge of the rebate to these lines, thus making the leg taper and finishing 5 inches square at the bottom.

Cut recesses to suit the casters and fit them in place, then remove them until the chair is finished; preparing them in this way is much easier than having to fit the casters when the chair is assembled and complete.

The Cross Rails.

The next proceeding is to shape the two cross rails as in Fig. 10, and then assemble the whole frame, noting that the outer side rails do not reach to the ends of the legs, but terminate 1¾ inches inwards and are bevelled to suit the angle of the back frame.

The Back Framing.

The back frame, shown complete in Fig. 11, consists of four oak uprights, 1 inch thick and 1¾ inches wide, joined by a crossbar of similar dimensions and connected at the top by shaped pieces of deal 1¾ inches thick, with simple butt and dowel joints, as shown in Fig. 12. The exact shapes and dimensions can be taken from the working drawings (Fig. 4).

The crossbar should be jointed by "halving" joints to centre uprights and glued and dowelled to the outer members. When completed, plane up both faces and the curved top; then glue and screw the frame to the bottom frame, as in Fig. 14, and follow by adding one of the shaped plywood sides.

Building the Arms.

The arms are built up with four separate pieces of plywood, which form the inner and outer faces of the arms. The two outer pieces should be walnut veneered, but the inner pair can be plain birch or gaboon mahogany stained to match.

All four are alike in main outline, but the inner pair have to be notched at front and back to fit over the cross rails. The inner piece on the left arm, as seen when seated in the chair, is solid, as shown in place in Fig. 14, but that on the right arm should have a panel cut out as in Fig. 13, to be hinged or fitted with clips, so that it can be opened to provide access to the loud speaker.

Fix both the inner pieces by gluing and pinning to the framework, then proceed to build up the various compartments by fitting the needful divisions.

The wireless set is housed in the right arm, and the various divisions are shown in place in Fig. 15, and are simply cut from $\frac{3}{16}$-inch plywood, glued and pinned in place and strengthened by triangular fillets, as in Fig. 16, to hold everything very securely.

The corresponding compartments on the left side are shown in place in Fig. 17, and are similarly made and fitted. The outer side pieces should be fitted in place and held temporarily with fine cabinet pins. The exact shape of the door over the wireless set should then be drawn with pencil and the speaker fret also marked out and very carefully cut out with a fretsaw, after the mode of fitting the top and front of the arms has been determined.

Fitting the Arm Tops.

There are two ways of fitting the arm tops; the simplest is merely to make butt joints as in Fig. 18, which is quite effective if the end grain is not objected to, or if it is subsequently obscured by a transfer " banding " to represent veneered work; the said transfers being applied after the work is otherwise complete.

If an " all walnut " finish is desired, then the arm tops and fronts should be made with walnut-veneered plywood and be mitred at all joints, or, preferably, rebated and mitred, as in Fig. 19, to ensure a strong joint and one that does not exhibit end grain. Choice is purely a matter of personal preference; the only point to watch is a slight difference in dimensions, the butted joint increasing the total height by $\frac{3}{16}$ inch; the rebated joint reducing the internal dimensions by $\frac{3}{16}$ inch.

Having prepared and fitted all the arm parts, proceed to assemble the left arm by gluing and pinning all joints, then fit a baffle board made of $\frac{3}{8}$- or $\frac{1}{2}$-inch plywood, as in Fig. 20, between the centre division and back outer frame member. Screw the loud speaker to the back of the baffle board. Drill a $\frac{1}{2}$-inch diameter hole through the centre division in the receiver compartment and then attach three insulated flexible wires to the appropriate terminals on the loud speaker, as explained fully in the " Lissen " instruction sheet accompanying the " kit set."

Leave sufficient length of wire in the wireless compartment for connection to the set, then similarly deal with the aerial and earth leads, putting these through a separate hole and drawing them out through the open bottom of the loud speaker compartment. Secure the wires by insulated staples, coil up the surplus wire and tie it up so that it does not get in the way.

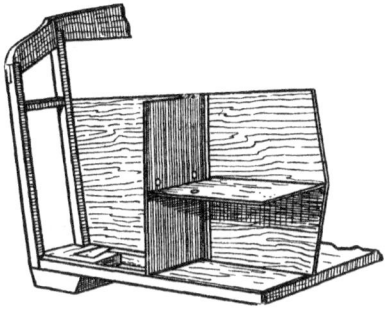

Fig. 15.—COMPARTMENTS FOR WIRELESS SET.
The right arm is built up as here shown to accommodate the wireless set, batteries and loud speaker.

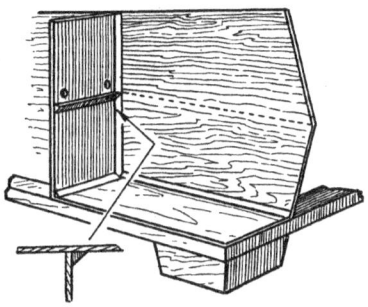

Fig. 16.—STRENGTHENING FILLETS.
Triangular moulding is glued and pinned to the angle between the division pieces, as here shown in part section.

Then fix the outer side pieces and hinge the door thereon to the arm top. A small " inside " spring catch should be fitted on the door to hold it shut; it can be opened when needed by making a thumb catch, or shallow recess, immediately beneath the lower joint.

Cover the outside of the back frame

Fig. 17.—COMPARTMENTS IN LEFT ARM.
Arranged similarly to those on the right, but spaced to form useful book cupboards.

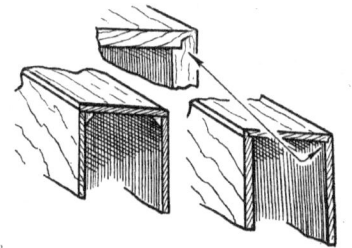

Figs. 18 and 19.—BUTT JOINT ON ARM TOP AND REBATED AND MITRED JOINT.

with walnut-veneered plywood secured with glue and cabinet pins, then fix the front arm pieces in a similar manner to the tops and hinge the remaining doors, thus completing the main structure, as in Fig. 21, leaving only the wireless installation and upholstery to be finished.

Installing the Wireless Set.

First assemble the wireless set exactly in accordance with the maker's instructions, but do not fix it in the cabinet. Make a preliminary test to see that all is in order. The cabinet parts can be used as templates to mark out the top of the arm for the passage of the tuning and volume control knobs. These can be recessed by drilling holes of sufficient size, as shown in section in Fig. 22, which reduces the projections to an absolute minimum.

The escutcheon should also be recessed to about half the thickness of the wood, but the wave change and " on-off " switch knob that comes at the front should not be recessed. Remove the valves, then insert the set into place and fix it with supporting blocks of wood and screws.

Fit the control knobs and make any adjustments necessary to ensure smooth working, then insert the valves, connect up the aerial and earth leads, also the loud speaker leads, and pass the battery cord—supplied with the set—downwards through a hole in the receiver compartment to the batteries in the lower compartment, which is reached by the lower front door. Connect them as directed in the instructions and then make a test. The improved tone and quality due to the ample baffle board area surrounding the loud speaker will be at once apparent.

Fit a dummy knob to the left arm to match the wave change knob on the right, also fit spring catches and small knobs to the lower doors.

Staining and Polishing.

Stain and polish all visible woodwork, but leave the finishing touches of the polishing until the chair has been upholstered. The wood should be lightly sandpapered, well dusted, and then fitted with a brown wood filler. When dry, rub this down with finest old sandpaper, remove all dust and apply an oil stain to darken and enrich the colour of the walnut, then apply the French polish in the usual way and as described elsewhere in " Enquire Within."

Upholstery.

There is wide choice of method of upholstery and the provision of a spring seat and back suitable for this chair. For example, a ready made spring seat can be obtained and

A RADIO LOUNGE CHAIR

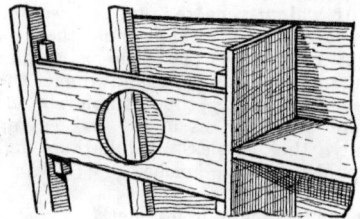

*Fig. 20.—*Baffle Board in Place.
The baffle board is glued and screwed to the outside back frame and centre division.

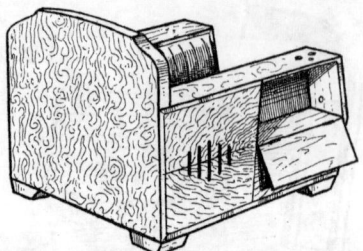

*Fig. 21.—*Frames covered ready for Wireless Installation.
Back view showing completed woodwork.

*Fig. 22.—*Receiver Tuning Knobs.
Clearance holes are provided in the arm top piece to enable the knobs to be partially sunk, as here shown in part section.

screwed directly to bearers glued and screwed to the inner side members. Alternatively, the chair can be webbed and spring upholstered in the regulation way, as described in detail on other pages of "Enquire Within"; but, in any case, this handsome chair is well worthy of really luxurious upholstery, and will then be found a delightful place wherein to rest and enjoy musical programmes from all parts of the world—a possibility well within the compass of the "All-wave" set here recommended.

GOLFING GAMES FOR THE HOME GARDEN

Many who would like to possess a private putting course do not do so because they fear that it is both difficult and expensive to make, but those who read these notes will find that all that is required is a small lawn, a little imagination, and nothing else.

Clock Golf.

If the lawn is too small to make a course with several holes it would be suitable for clock golf, which can be set out as follows:—

Place a peg in the centre of the plot, then tie a brush to one end of a piece of string, cut to a suitable length, and make a loop at the other. Put the loop over the peg, dip the brush in whitewash and paint a circle 10 or more feet in diameter.

Divide the circumference of the circle into twelve equal parts, number them 1 to 12. Sink a flower pot with a diameter as near as possible to 4¼ inches, which is the regulation size of a golf hole tin, anywhere in the circle excepting the centre, so that each hole will be of different length (see Fig. 1).

Tee the ball at one o'clock and hole out, then carry on round the clock.

The player making the smallest score for the twelve holes wins the game.

A complete outfit, with a set of iron Roman figures, a hole tin, flag, measuring chain, two balls and two putters, can be obtained for about £1.

Making a Putting Course.

On a larger area a putting course of 6, 9 or 18 holes can be constructed, or, by the use of two sets of tee plates and a little skill, the same holes can be played from two directions, thus converting a 6-hole course into one with 12 holes, 9 into 18 and 18 into 36.

If the plan is studied it will be found that quite an interesting 36-hole course can be laid out on a lawn measuring only 60 × 40 feet.

The thick lines indicate one way of playing the course and the broken lines the other, the circles indicating the position of the greens and holes (see Fig. 2).

The plan is drawn to the scale of one square to 1 foot, but if a larger area is available it can be increased to anything up to one square to 3 feet or more.

If the lawn is broken up with trees or flower beds it is quite easy to plan the course so that the holes go around them.

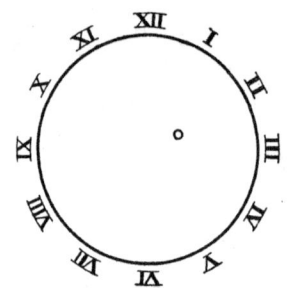

*Fig. 1.—*Arrangement for Clock Golf.

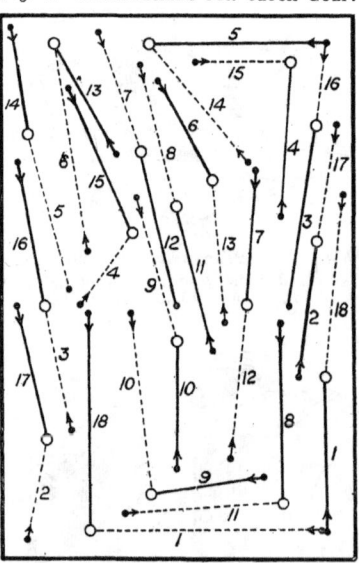

*Fig. 2.—*Arrangement for a Putting Course.

How to attend to the Turf.

Having laid out the course, the next thing is to work up the turf to as high a state of perfection as possible. If it contains any weeds take them out by hand. Kill the worms with Carter's Wormkiller. Dress once a month all through the spring and summer with dry fertiliser at the rate of 1 oz. to the square yard and water it in. Better still, dissolve 7 lbs. of soluble fertiliser in 20 gallons of water and apply it by means of a watering can to 112 square yards.

If the surface is soft dress it at the end of the season with fine coal ash or sharp sand. Mow frequently and water as necessary.

The area of a putting course is so small that it is quite easy to make the turf as good as that found on the best golf course in the country at little cost both of labour and material.

Undulating Courses.

So far the ground has been taken as it stands, and in most cases the natural contour will satisfy for the time being. In cases where it is too flat to be interesting, what is easier than to lift the turf in the autumn from one or more holes, dig the ground and contour it as desired with a rake, using the surplus soil raked out when making a hollow to form a mound; then tread and rake the ground until it is quite firm and smooth and relay the turf?

There is only one rule to remember when doing work of this sort, and that is the undulations must be so gentle and regular that when the turf is laid the mowing machine will be able to run over it and cut it to a uniform length without missing the hollows or skinning the crests.

If a rise or fall of 3 inches in 1 yard is regarded as the maximum this result will be obtained, but if it is exceeded it will probably end in failure.

MAKING A COAL CABINET

THE coal cabinet shown in Figs. 1 and 2 is a practical piece of furniture that more than repays the time and trouble involved in its construction.

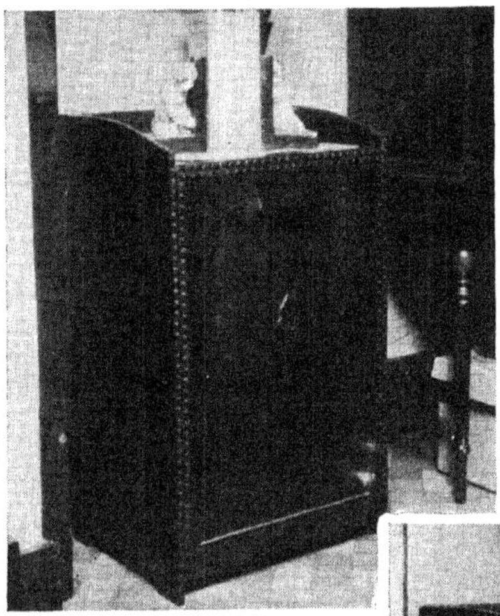

Fig. 1.—THE COAL BIN CLOSED.

Materials required.

The following comprises all parts needed for a cabinet measuring 25 inches high, 15 inches wide and 12 inches deep :—

Sides.—Two pieces oak-faced plywood, ⅜ inch thick, 25 × 12 inches.

Front.—One piece oak-faced plywood, 19⅝ × 14¼ inches.

Top.—One piece oak-faced plywood, 14⅝ × 12 inches.

Frames.—Three pieces oak-faced plywood, 14¼ × 2 inches ; two pieces oak-faced plywood, 11¼ × 2 inches.

Coal Box Sides.—Two pieces oak-faced plywood, 19⅝ × 11 inches.

Coal Box Back.—One piece birch plywood, ⅜ × 15½ × 14⅛ inches.

Coal Box Bottom.—One piece birch plywood, 13⅜ × 11 inches.

Back.—One piece birch plywood, $\frac{3}{16}$ inch thick, 24 × 15 inches.

Moulding.—No. 55 oak-carved moulding, ⅜ × $\frac{3}{16}$ inch ; four pieces 24 inches long, two pieces 15 inches long, two pieces 13 inches long.

Fittings.—One No. 888 new oak ornament ; one No. W319 embossed pull.

Glue Block Fillet.—No. D40 ½-inch deal, two pieces 11 inches long, two pieces 13⅜ inches long, one piece No. D40 1⅛ × 12 inches (Frank Romany Ltd., 52 High Street, Camden Town, London, N.W.).

NOTE. — The above are " finished " sizes, consequently the material should be obtained as recommended, specially cut and finished to these sizes, or an allowance must be made where necessary for cleaning up and finishing.

Sundries.—One gross iron wood screws, No. 4 × 1 inch long (" Nettlefolds ") ; 1 oz. No. P6 fine finishing pins (" Romany "); one " Home " outfit " Croid " aero glue ; one small tin " woodfiller " ; one small bottle Jacobean oil stain ; one 8-oz. bottle French polish (" Romany ").

Coal Bin.—One tinplate or galvanised iron rectangular coal box, 14½ inches high, 13 inches wide, 10¾ inches deep, or three sheets stout tinplate and 5 feet $\frac{3}{32}$-inch brass wire.

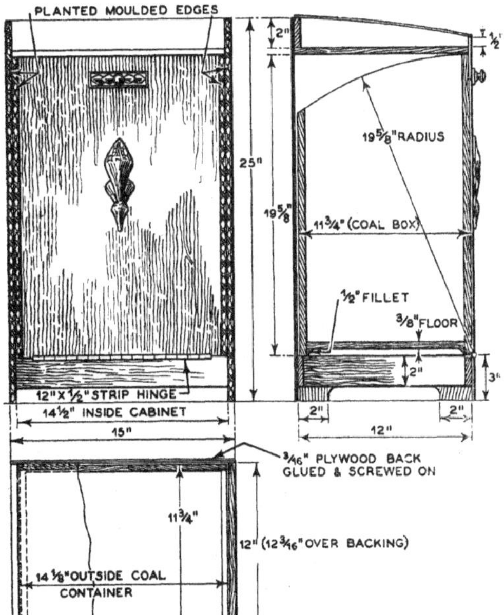

Fig. 3.—MAIN DIMENSIONS OF COAL CABINET.

What to do First.

First mark out the two sides of the cabinet as in Fig. 4, drawing the outlines on the oak-faced sides and cutting them to shape with a fretsaw before marking the position of the groove near the top.

This groove or " trench " must finish up exactly ⅜ inch wide and $\frac{3}{16}$ inch deep ; it is made by first making two parallel saw cuts and then chiselling away the wood between them. Clamp two guide pieces of wood on to the work, as in Fig. 5, using them as a guide when sawing.

The Bottom Frame.

Next make up the bottom frame as shown in Fig. 6, place the front and back pieces against the ends of the side pieces and fasten them with Croid glue applied hot. While the glue is setting, cut four pieces of 1⅛-inch glue block fillet moulding, making each piece exactly 2 inches long, and glue and screw them into the corners of the frame.

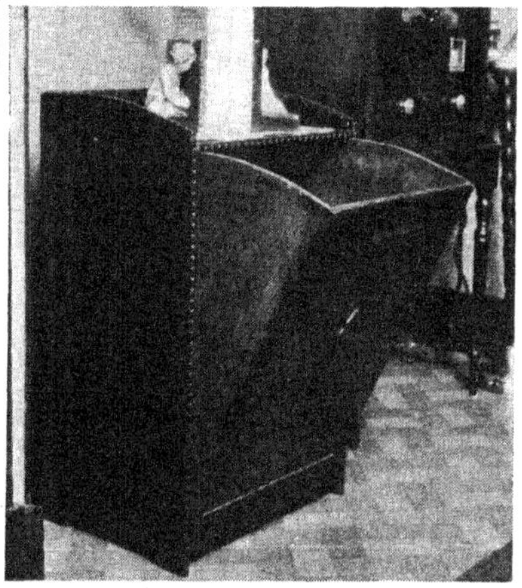

Fig. 2.—THE COAL BIN OPEN.

Next glue and screw the frame to one of the side pieces, fit the top into the grooves and see that all is correct, then glue and screw the frame to the second side piece, after having applied some glue to the ends of the top piece and fitted them into the grooves.

Fit the top back frame into place and then glue and pin the plywood backing to the back edges of the cabinet, as shown in Fig. 7 in part section.

The Coal Box.

The coal box is an entirely separate item, and is hinged at the lower front edge to the bottom of the cabinet. The construction is shown in part section in Fig. 8, and is best made by first cutting the two side pieces to shape and then gluing and screwing on the front and back pieces. Next fix the small fillets around the bottom inside the box, using glue and pins, then when dry insert the plywood bottom board, after applying glue to the joint faces and edges. When the glue has set, carefully clean up the outer edges and try the box in its place ; it should be an easy fit, with a margin of $\frac{1}{16}$ inch at each side.

The bottom hinge is fitted by laying the cabinet on its back, placing the coal box in position, and temporarily supporting it with a pile of books or in any convenient way. Fix the hinge with two screws, as near the

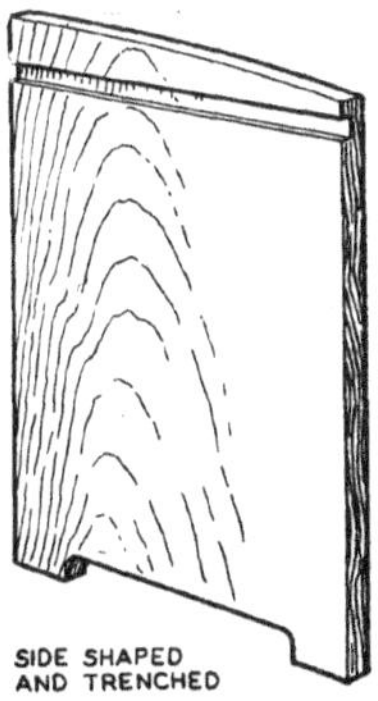

Fig. 4.—THE SIDE SHAPED AND TRENCHED.

MAKING A COAL CABINET

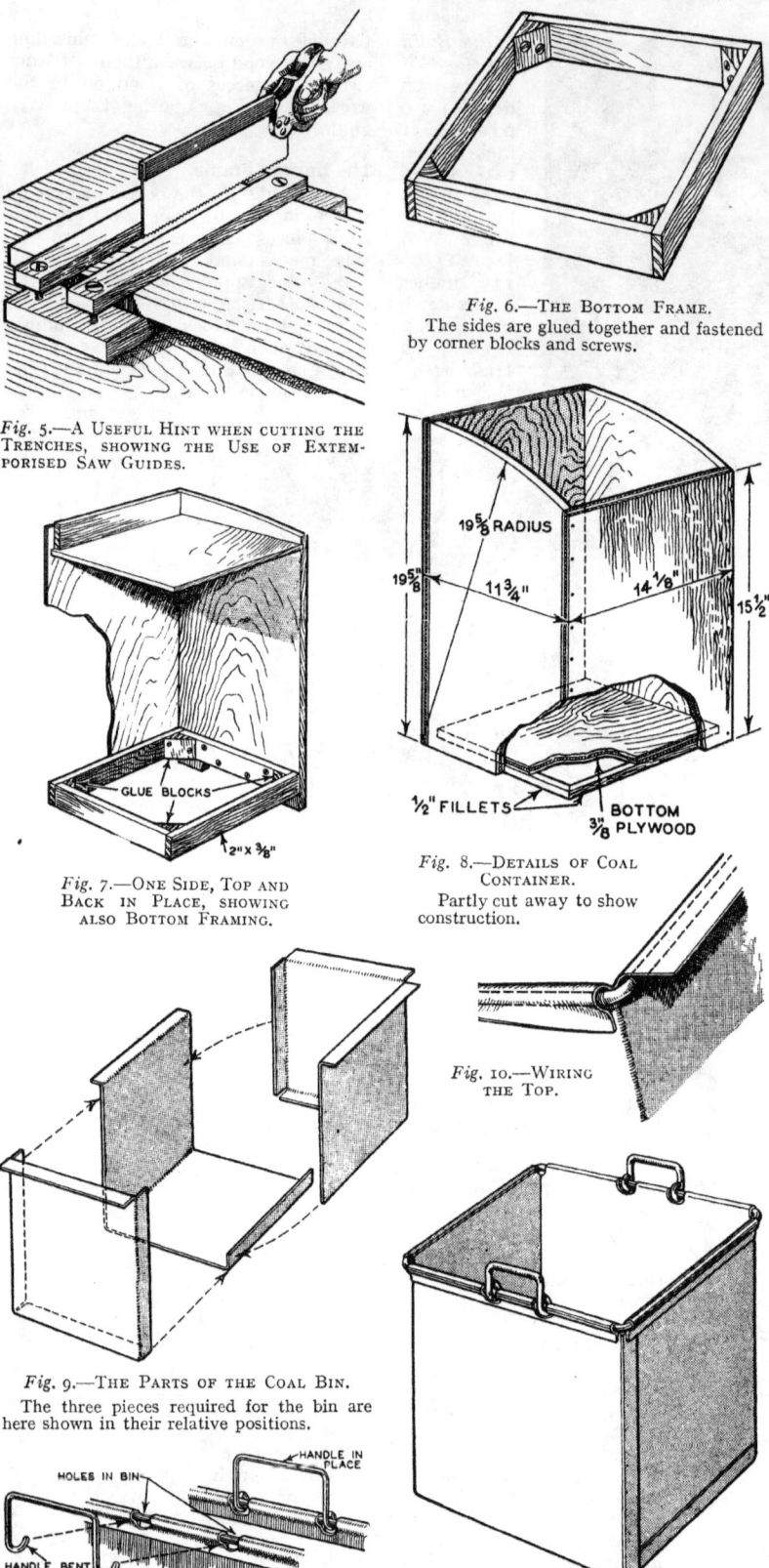

Fig. 5.—A Useful Hint when cutting the Trenches, showing the Use of Extemporised Saw Guides.

Fig. 6.—The Bottom Frame. The sides are glued together and fastened by corner blocks and screws.

Fig. 7.—One Side, Top and Back in Place, showing also Bottom Framing.

Fig. 8.—Details of Coal Container. Partly cut away to show construction.

Fig. 9.—The Parts of the Coal Bin. The three pieces required for the bin are here shown in their relative positions.

Fig. 10.—Wiring the Top.

Fig. 11.—Detail of the Handle.

Fig. 12.—The Completed Metal Coal Bin.

centre of its length as possible, then carefully close the box into the cabinet to align the hinge correctly.

A few more screws should then be driven and the hinge action again tried.

Fix the Handle or "Pull."

All being well, fix the handle or "pull" with glue and a couple of screws, glue and pin the ornament to the front panel, then cover the front and top edges of the cabinet with the embossed moulding, which should preferably be done with glue and the fine finishing pins.

Finishing the Woodwork.

Clean down the exterior with sandpaper, apply a coat of woodfiller, allow it to dry and then rub down with old sandpaper. Brush off all dust and apply a coat of stain and finish when dry by French polishing. The interior can with advantage be stained black.

Making the Coal Bin.

The metal coal bin can either be bought from a tinsmith or through an ironmonger ready made, or can be constructed at home from ordinary tinplate, in which case obtain the largest size available, and preferably about 18 or 20 gauge. It is generally possible to make the front and bottom from one piece, the back and one side can be got out of a second sheet, and the remaining side from a third sheet.

Cutting the Metal to Shape.

Little trouble will be experienced in making the bin. Simply cut the metal to shape with tinman's snips, allowing an extra for turnover at the top and at all joints. Remove all roughness from the cut edges by filing or rubbing with emery cloth wrapped around a piece of wood. Then lay the sheet on a block of wood and bend it over. Next turn over the top edge and the joint edges for a width of $\frac{1}{2}$ inch in a similar way, as indicated in Fig. 9, which shows the three pieces in their relative positions. Next put the three together and "sweat" or solder all the joints.

Wiring the Top.

Make a rectangle of wire and drop it over the bin from the bottom, so that it rests on the flanged parts. Solder it in place, then carefully bend over the top flange, as in Fig. 10, which can be done with pliers and finished by hammering. Finally solder the joint.

The Handles.

The handles are made by bending stout wire to shape, as in Fig. 11, inserting the ends through holes punched in the sides of the bin, and then twisting the handle wire around the frame wire and soldering it.

Fitting a Modern Hot Water Boiler
With Notes on Converting and Making Use of a Kitchen Range Recess

In these days the kitchen range is almost a thing of the past; in fact, it is seldom found that any are being installed in modern houses. What is more, when a house is being reconditioned and redecorated, as often as not the old range is removed, making way for a new and up-to-date pattern, or sometimes the recess is put to other purposes.

FITTING A MODERN HOT-WATER BOILER

Let us consider first the question of removing the old range and fitting a modern type boiler in its place. Figs. 1 and 2 show a small kitchen before and after the conversion has been carried out.

Turn off the Water.

First of all the range must be removed. The first thing to do will naturally be to shut down the water supply to the boiler. This is a simple matter. You will find a tap up in the roof near the cold-water tank. Turn this off, and then open the hot water taps and empty the system. Any surplus water can be gradually drained when disconnecting the boiler. There is bound to be a tap somewhere for this purpose.

Tools required.

To remove the range is a dirty, but not a very difficult matter. You will find that it will be fixed together with screws. All you will require, therefore, will be a screwdriver, hammer and chisel.

If you do not want to retain the range for any purpose, break it up if you have any difficulty with the screws, for it will be practically worthless and can only be sold as scrap-iron.

Fig. 1.—A Typical Old-fashioned Kitchen Range.
It is quite a simple matter to fit a modern type kitchen boiler in place of a range such as this. Fig. 2 shows the new boiler fitted. Another plan is to scrap the range altogether and use the recess as a cosy corner or a cupboard, as shown in Figs. 16 and 26.

Disconnecting the Pipes from the Boiler.

There will be a great deal of rubbish and mess left behind, no doubt; and, furthermore, there will be pipes to disconnect from the boiler. This should not be a difficult matter with the help of a hacksaw, or, if you can procure one, a three-wheeled pipe-cutter (Fig. 4). The pipes will be found more or less in the position as shown in Fig. 3, and must be disconnected at the nearest point just above the boiler. Remove the boiler.

Putting the Register in Position.

The register, a square piece of sheet iron, has now to be put in position in the roof of the opening. This can be done by putting two iron bearing bars, one under the front and one under the back of the register.

Having temporarily fixed the register, place the new "Ideal," "Sentry," or whatever boiler you have purchased, into the position where it is finally to stand.

Mark where New Flue Pipe will come on Underside of Register.

Now take the line of the flue pipe from the new boiler and mark correctly with chalk where it will enter on the underside of the register (the flue pipe will be bought separately).

Cut Hole for Flue Pipe.

Having marked the correct position, remove the register and cut a hole for the flue pipe. This can be accomplished by means of a cold chisel and a hammer.

Fix Flue Pipe in Position.

Now replace the register in position,

Fig. 2.—A Modern Type Kitchen Boiler fitted in Place of an Old-fashioned Kitchen Range.
Full details for making the change are given in this article

FITTING A MODERN HOT WATER BOILER

supported by the iron bars, and fix the flue pipe through the hole you have just formed in the register; it should not extend more than about 2 inches above the register. The flue pipe can be cut with a half-round file.

Connecting the Pipes to Boiler.

The pipes will now have to be connected to the boiler. By the way, these pipes will also have to be purchased separately.

The flow pipe (Fig. 3) can be fixed first, and there is one important point to remember, namely, that the pipe should not be screwed right through the wall of the boiler, but a thread or two short of the inside—see Fig. 5, showing how it ought to be done, and Fig. 6, how it ought not to be done. This precaution is not so important if the pipe tapping (hole for pipe) is on the *side* (Fig. 7) as if it is directly on the top.

Should it be in the last-named position, the pipe enters the water and a knocking will set up, owing to air in the top of the boiler.

Now connect the pipe up to the existing flow pipe. The return pipe must be fixed in a similar fashion, but to the tapping at the bottom of the boiler.

Connectors must be used.

In each case connectors must be used.

A connector consists of a piece of pipe of any length up to 24 inches, and can be purchased at any ironmongers. It is of special British standard thread. On one end of the pipe is a screw with a long thread. A socket and back nut are provided which will enable you to connect up the new pipe to the existing pipe (Fig. 8). This is a simple procedure, and is done with the help of a Stillson wrench 18 inches long.

These pipes are 1-inch galvanised steam pipes; 1¼-inch preferred in districts where the water is hard, on account of furring.

Making Watertight Joint at Junctions.

For the junction of the two pipes

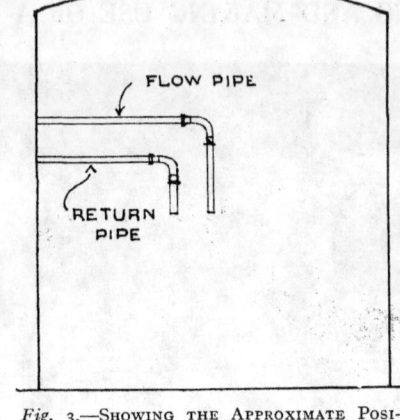

Fig. 3.—Showing the Approximate Positions of the Flow and Return Pipes when the Range is removed.

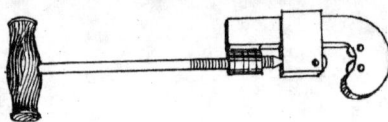

Fig. 4.—A Three-wheeled Pipe Cutter will be found useful for Disconnecting the Pipes from the Boiler.

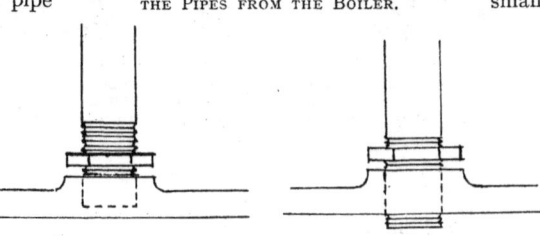

Fig. 5.—The Correct Way of Fixing the Flow Pipe.   Fig. 6.—The Incorrect Way of Fixing the Flow Pipe.

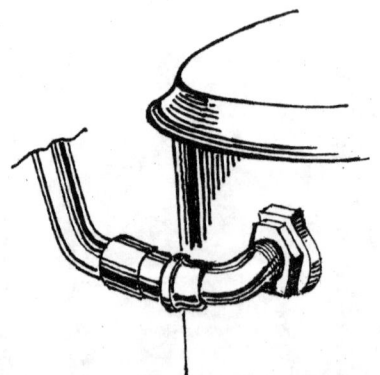

Fig. 7.—The Method of Fixing the Flow Pipe is not so important if it comes at the Side.

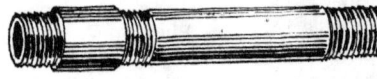

CONNECTOR

BACK NUT

Fig. 8.—Connector for Joining New Pipe to Existing Pipe.

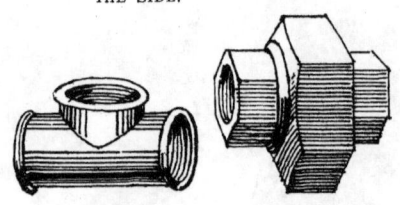

T-PIECE   UNION

Fig. 9.—T-piece and Union for Return Pipe.

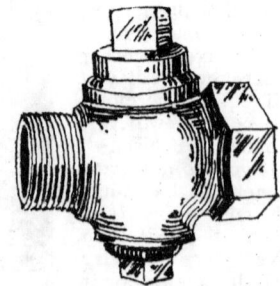

Fig. 10.—Plug Cock with Loose Key.

"pipe compound" should be used, and also hemp. Both these can be bought cheaply, and, when making the joint, paint the threads with the compound. Take three or four strands of hemp and wind them into the gutters of the thread. Then lightly paint over them again. Now screw into position until thoroughly tight, and the hemp which squeezes out can be cleaned off.

Fix a T-piece in the Return Pipe.

When connecting the return pipe, a T-piece must be fixed (Fig. 9) about 14 or 15 inches from the ground.

Get a plug cock with a loose key (Fig. 10) and screw this cock into the T-piece. This will be found useful for emptying down the system when repair work or cleaning has to be undertaken.

Now fill up the system from the tank in the roof through the return pipe into the boiler and allow the water gradually to rise to the highest point.

What to do if Joints develop Small Leaks.

See that all joints are sound. Any small leak can be stopped at any of the screwed joints by "caulking" (lightly tapping) with an ordinary chisel and hammer.

Fixing the Register.

Now the register. Seal off on the upper side in the chimney with "dry mortar" (this may be purchased), mix with it a little Keene's cement, which will help it to stand more firmly. The "dry mortar" has to be mixed with water.

Insert the flue pipe, allowing it to reach about 2 inches above the register, as stated above. This prevents soot falling down.

Seal it with a ring (Fig. 11), which is provided by most patent boilermakers, and is made in two halves and joined together with screws. This entirely seals up the hole and prevents cold air entering.

Paint all the pipes with aluminium paint or other suitable heat-resisting preparation.

Finishing the Recesses.

We have described above the method for fitting the boiler and placing it in position, but the recess itself will have to be treated in some way.

It can be simply rendered out with cement and sand and finished with a coat of Keene's cement and afterwards painted, but the neatest way of treating it is to tile it, though more costly.

For the first method mix up Portland cement—one part to three parts of sand with water—and trowel it on. When still wet, score it across to form a key for your "setting coat" of Keene's cement, give the surface a coat of sharp colour, *i.e.*, two parts turpentine, one part varnish, and a little paint. This prevents any likelihood of efflorescence.

You can now finish the recess with as many coats of paint as you may think necessary.

For tiling the sides, floor and back, proceed in the same way as described later for the floor tiling.

PUTTING THE RECESS TO OTHER PURPOSES

As previously mentioned, it is sometimes desired to do away with a range altogether, or else find other accommodation for it. The recess can, for instance, be converted into a "cosy corner" or a sideboard or buffet can be fitted into it.

The method of removing the range is, of course, the same as has already been described.

Having laid bare your opening, you will find a lot of rubble and mess behind. You will also find service pipes, flow and return (Fig. 3), to deal with, and, of course, if there is to be another boiler installed elsewhere, these will have to be connected up.

Let us suppose that an "Ideal" or other independent boiler is to be fitted somewhere else in the same room, other than that formerly occupied by the old range, or in some other room.

In this case the service pipes can be used, but will have to be turned along the back to the required position and connected up to the new boiler. They will in all probability have to run along the face of the wall, as shown on Fig. 13. The method to adopt for connecting up these pipes is similar to that already described.

Now you have an open space to deal with, you may find it formed as shown in Fig. 14, or you may find it, like Fig. 15, with a wooden beam running across.

Turning the Recess into a "Cosy Corner."

In the case of the first mentioned, what is termed a relieving arch may have been inserted as shown, and in which case a very effective treatment may be made, namely, turn the recess into a "cosy corner," as illustrated (Fig. 16) and as described below.

Chip the plaster off all round and lay bare the brickwork. Then take another brick and rub the old bricks down with it. Brush well down, scrape out the joints and point them with mortar (Fig. 17).

How to Finish the Edge.

Of course, the plaster may be thick, an inch or so, or it may be thin, but in any case some sort of finish must be given to the raw edge, which will project beyond the brickwork. This will have to be rubbed down, bevelled off and then covered with whatever you treat your general wall surface with up to the edge of the brickwork.

What to do if Opening has a Wooden Beam across.

The opening may, as mentioned, have a wooden beam across, and in which case a very effective treatment and good result may be obtained by "roughing" it. Here an adze will come in useful (Fig. 18), with which a very effective and antique looking surface can be obtained. Rub all the edges well down with coarse glasspaper and wax polish the surface. The beam may be of oak, but unless the house is old you will probably find an iron bar or a coke breeze slab, in which case remove it and insert a wood beam.

Marb-le-cote Treatment for Edge of Wall.

Now for the edge of the wall supporting the beam. Several methods can be adopted here besides the one mentioned above, but the two which seem to be most effective are marb-le-cote treatment, or what is termed sack-finished Portland cement face.

How to use Marb-le-cote.

The first, with marb-le-cote, is most attractive, and, moreover, this substance is quite easy to use. Marb-le-cote can be purchased fairly economically, considering the results which can be achieved with it, and is most fascinating to manipulate. It looks, in its dry state, more or less like plaster, and the method of using it is as follows:—

First give the surface which has to be treated a coat of oil paint or size to prevent suction. Put some marb-le-cote in a bowl or pail and add sufficient water to produce a fairly thick paste. Then take a distemper brush or a 2-inch flat painter's brush and slop it on the brickwork. All sorts of effects can be obtained; old plaster or stone, as the case may require. In this case, old stone quoins would be the finish desired (Fig. 19).

Marb-le-cote will dry as hard as cement in twenty-four hours, so when it is still soft mark out your quoins with any blunt instrument, but be

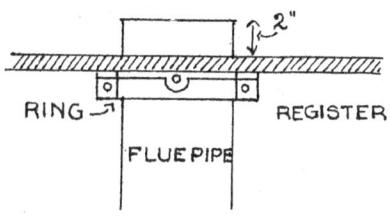

Fig. 11.—A Ring is generally provided by most Patent Boiler-makers for Fixing the Flue Pipe.

It is made in two halves and joined together with screws.

Fig. 12.—Another Method of Finishing off the Tiling when a Modern Type Boiler is fitted

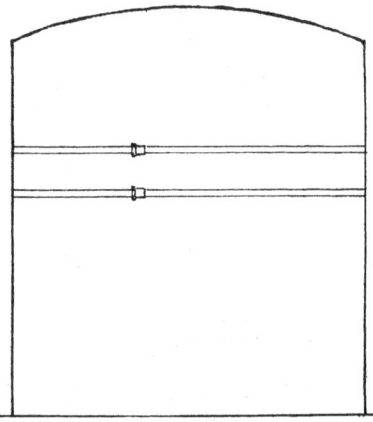

Fig. 13.—How to Deal with the Flow and Return Pipe when a New Boiler is Installed in Another Part of the Kitchen.

Fig. 14.—What you may expect to find when the Old Range has been removed.

Fig. 16.—A very Effective Treatment for a Range Recess.
The recess has been converted into a "cosy corner."

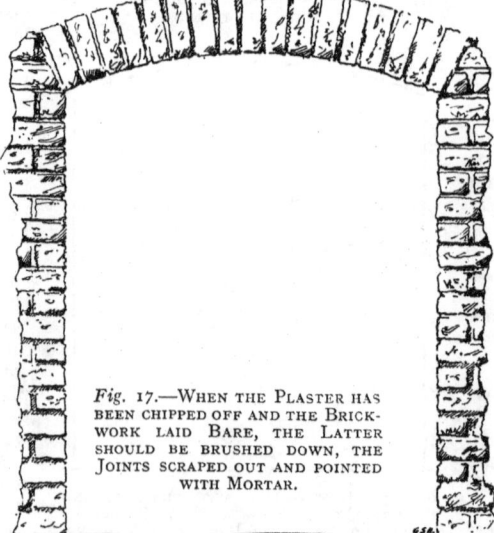

Fig. 17.—When the Plaster has been chipped off and the Brickwork laid Bare, the Latter should be brushed down, the Joints scraped out and pointed with Mortar.

Fig. 15.—In some cases a Wooden Beam may be found running across when the Old Range is removed.

wall finish as mentioned above, "sack finish," is different in that Portland cement and sand mixed together—one part cement to three of sand with water—is used and put on with a builder's trowel; when still soft, get an old sack and rub lightly over the surface. The quoins in this instance, as in the first, can be marked out. The edges (or arrises) can be rubbed down with quite sure that there are no sharp edges left.

Painting and Glazing.

Now paint the marb-le-cote a stone colour, and when dry apply a glaze, a mixture of turpentine and copal varnish, tinting it with some raw umber in order to give it an old stone effect.

Apply a Final Coat of Flat Varnish.

When the glaze is still wet, take a cloth and lightly rub over, with the result that the high lights will stand out in contra-distinction to the interstices, which will, of course, be darker. Thus a most effective result will be obtained. Then, to counteract the possibility of the surface remaining tacky, for glaze will have this tendency, give it a coat of flat varnish (this is made of turpentine, white wax, tongued oil and dryers, but flat varnish may be purchased in tins). It can then be dusted, washed and kept clean.

Treating the Interior Walls.

The interior walls of the recess can also be treated in the same manner, but in this case the effect to produce should be old plaster, and would, therefore, be left lighter in tone to the quoins on the edge and the texture finished with a different surface, but the final treatment would be much the same.

"Sack Finish."

The other suggestion for the glasspaper and finished with wax, rubbed hard.

This treatment, or the marb-le-cote treatment as above described, can be adopted for the interior wall surfaces of the recess, in conjunction with the first method of leaving the bricks around the recess bare and rubbed down as described.

The Floor of the Recess.

The floor of the recess will be found to be of concrete or cement or some other hard substance. Clear away all the rubbish and lay tiles or wood boards. For the former (red quarry tiles would be most effective) a bed of cement will first have to be made—one part Portland cement with three of sand mixed well with water and trowelled over the surface.

When still wet, score over the surface to make a key for the screed or second coat. This should be made of Portland cement and sand, though a greater proportion of cement to the sand than made up for the first rendering.

Now lay your tiles on while the cement is still wet and fill in the joint with white Atlas cement and clean off the surface. Unless the tiles are red quarry or another colour, colour the cement with Cementone.

You will require some bullnosed tiles for finishing off the front edge (Fig. 20).

Laying Floorboards.

Should it be thought advisable and artistic to lay floorboards, wooden joists will

FITTING A MODERN HOT WATER BOILER

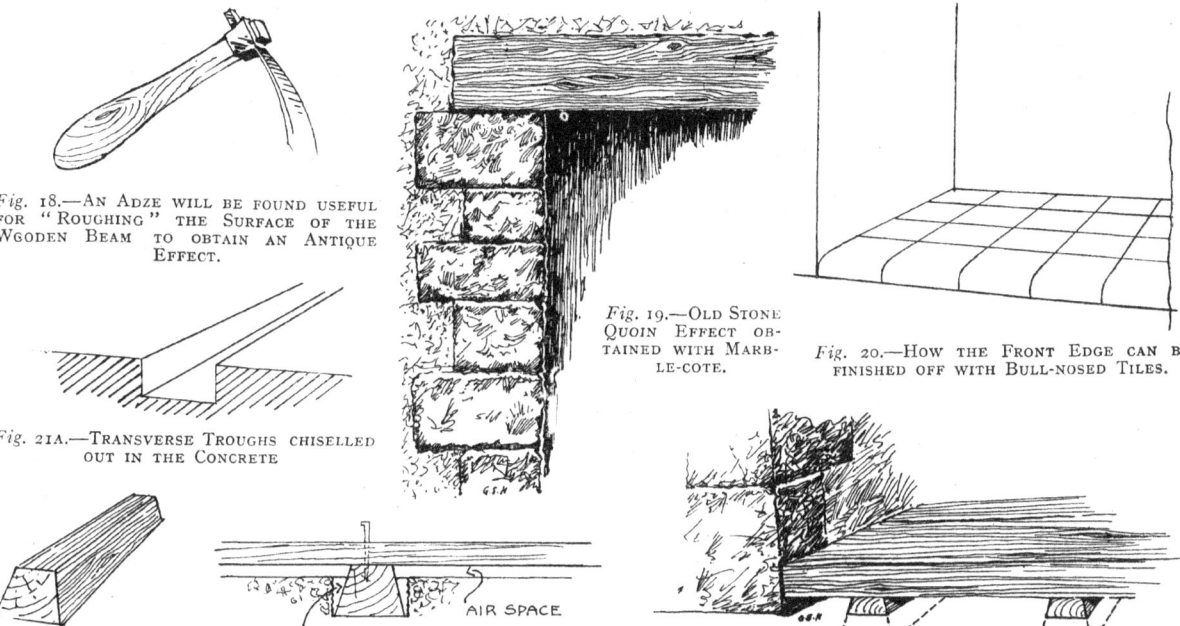

Fig. 18.—An Adze will be found useful for "Roughing" the Surface of the Wooden Beam to obtain an Antique Effect.

Fig. 19.—Old Stone Quoin Effect obtained with Marble-cote.

Fig. 20.—How the Front Edge can be finished off with Bull-nosed Tiles.

Fig. 21A.—Transverse Troughs chiselled out in the Concrete

Fig. 21B.—Shape of Joist for laying in Trough.

Fig. 21C.—Showing Floorboard in Position on Joist.

Fig. 22.—The ½-inch Gap in the Front can be covered with a Fillet rounded on the Front Edge.

have to be fixed into the concrete for nailing the floorboards to. These are fixed in the following manner: channel out two transverse troughs in the concrete with a cold chisel (Fig. 21A), into which lay your joists shaped as shown in Fig. 21B. These must be of sufficient thickness to stand about ½ inch or so above the surface of the concrete to allow of a passage of air under the boards. Having laid the joists in, fill up the space D (Fig. 21C) with cement; this forms a key to keep them in position, just in the same way as dovetails hold drawer ends together. These joists should be treated first with creosote. Now, having fixed your joists, nail down the floorboards with brads.

Covering up the Gap at the Front.

There will naturally be a ½-inch gap showing in front (Fig. 22), which can be covered with a fillet rounded on the front edge and nailed on to the edge of the floorboards and overlapping the ends of the recess (Fig. 23).

Now make a Seat of Rough Wood.

Having prepared your recess, form a seat of rough wood. This should be about 1 foot 3 inches or 1 foot 6 inches wide and slightly longer than the width of the recess (Fig. 24). Knock out bricks either side, leaving apertures to form ledges upon which to rest the seat (Fig. 25). This should have its edge well rubbed down with a file and coarse glasspaper, and then wax polished to give an antique and worn appearance.

For additional support and to give an added effect, two uprights may be inserted beneath. These would be of wood as thick as can be procured, with their edges adzed and treated in the same way as the seat (Fig. 24).

Place cushions or a squab on the wooden seat and a most cosy recess will result. Should this method of fixing the seat be adopted, be sure there is no flue on either side. This is not likely, however.

Building a Sideboard or Buffet into the Recess.

Of course, it is obvious that a recess such as is now being considered can be turned to account in many ways, but here is another way of dealing with it, namely, a sideboard or buffet. This can be made out of deal or oak, or, in fact, any wood you like, and can be as shown in Fig. 26.

Stopping up the Flue.

First of all, the flue must be stopped up. Now, supposing the head of the recess is arched, as shown in Fig. 27, proceed as follows :—

Fit a piece of wood, the thickness of the distance between the spring of the arch and the apex (Fig. 27). Let us suppose it to be 4 inches, then a

Fig. 23.—Showing Rounded Fillet in Place.

Fig. 24.—When the Recess has been prepared a Seat of Rough Wood should be fitted as shown.

Fig. 25.—Showing how Bricks are knocked out to form Ledges for the Seat.

FITTING A MODERN HOT WATER BOILER

piece of wood 4 × 2 inches the depth of the recess will be correct, and must be fixed as shown in Fig. 28 by means of Rawlplugs (these can be purchased cheaply and serve well for screwing into). Now take a board 1 inch thick, the length and depth of the recess, and screw it up to the cross piece.

If the recess is too deep for one board, two will have to be used. This " roof " will be well fixed at the centre and further supported by the sides, which must be screwed in the same way by means of Rawlplugs to the sides of the recess (Fig. 27).

The Cupboard.

Now the lower half, which is composed of a cupboard; fix a cleat (Fig. 29A) either side upon which to support the shelf (Fig. 29B). A cleat is a piece of wood, in this instance about 1½ × 1½ inches, but must measure in length about 1 inch less than the depth of the recess in order to make room for the door. If there are any pipes at the back, these can be concealed by a false back in the upper part.

Floor of the Cupboard.

The floor of the cupboard should be about 4 inches above the floor of the recess, and should be composed of a board, or boards, screwed to three joists about 2 × 3 inches, as shown in Fig. 30. These should be the depth of the recess.

What to do if Floor is Concrete.

Difficulties may be experienced in fixing the joists to the floor, as the latter may be of concrete or some other hard substance, so to obviate this let the sides of the cupboard be cut short and rest on the floorboards, and, being screwed to the sides and therefore rigid, they will keep the floor in place (Fig. 31), unless joists are let in as described above.

Fig. 26.—Another Treatment for a Range Recess. Showing a sideboard fitted into the recess.

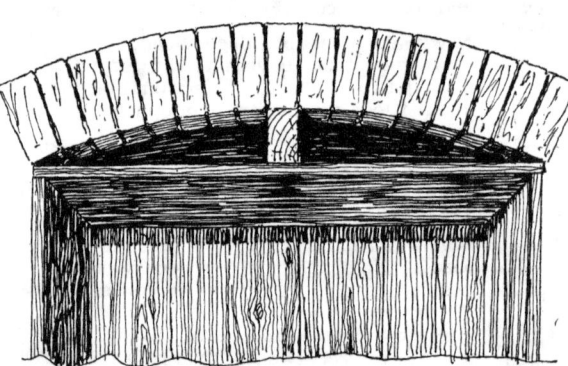

Fig. 27.—If the Head of the Recess is Arched, fit a Piece of Wood between the Spring of the Arch and the Apex.

The Frame.

Now for the frame or architraves. These should be about 1 or 1¼ inches thick, chamfered on both edges and mitred at the top (the mitre can be formed with a set square 45 degrees) and about 4 inches wide.

The Skirting.

The skirting can be formed of ½-inch wood and should be rounded off at the top edge and should butt into the architraves (Fig. 32).

The chamfer on the inside of the side pieces of the architraves should stop short of the skirting as shown (Fig. 32), as the finish will thus be neater.

The skirting will serve to cover the opening below, whilst the head of the architrave will cover the opening at the top, shown in Fig. 32.

They can be screwed in with round-headed screws or flat-headed and countersunk. The doors should be framed and chamfered on the sides. This construction is shown in Fig. 33.

Hinging Doors to Sides.

The doors can then be hinged to the sides (Fig. 26) and a "stop" should be fixed in the centre (Fig. 34), made of wood about 1 × 2 inches by the height of the cupboard. This must be rebated, i.e., the edge cut out with a sharp chisel, as shown in Fig. 34, into which the edge of the door will fit when closed.

The "stop" can be screwed through the shelf and tenoned into the floor (Fig. 34). A tenon is formed by cutting the end of the piece of wood to smaller dimensions as shown, and the mortise into which the tenon is fixed is a rectangular hole which can be chopped out with a ¼-inch chisel. Glue should be put on to the tenon and into the mortise before driving the tenon securely home.

How to finish off Top of Cupboard.

The top of the cupboard can be finished off with brackets, as shown in Fig. 26, screwed into the underside of the top, and should be about 1 or 1½ inches thick.

All screws except, of course, the round-headed variety,

Fig. 28.—How to fit the Centre Support.

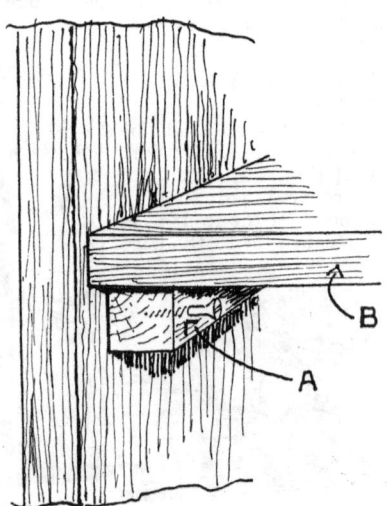

Fig. 29.—Fix a Cleat on Either Side on which to support the Shelf.

FITTING A MODERN HOT WATER BOILER

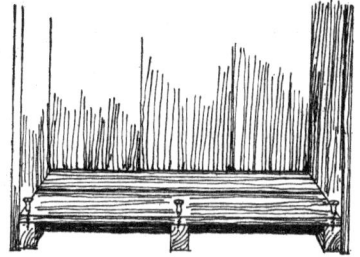

Fig. 30.—How to fix the Floor of the Cupboard.

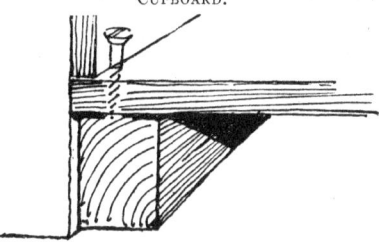

Fig. 31.—What to do if the Floor is Concrete.

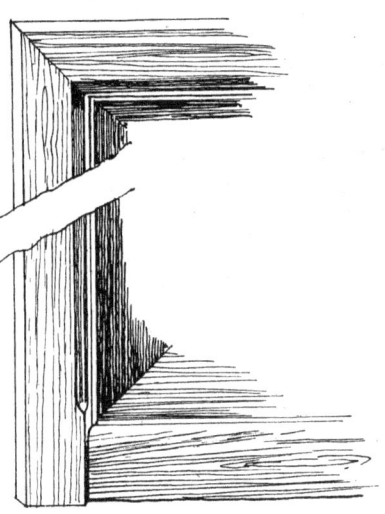

Fig. 32.—Details of the Skirting.

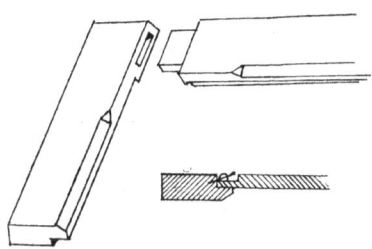

Fig. 33.—Details of Door Construction.

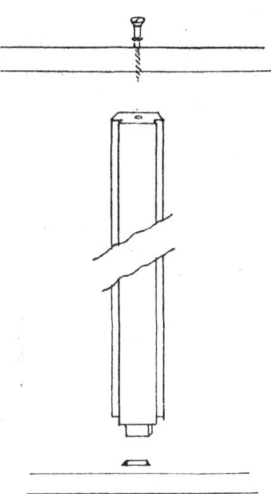

Fig. 34.—How to fix the Centre Stop for the Doors.

should be countersunk with a brace and countersinker, and all nails or brads punched below the surface of the wood with a punch (a steel tool with a blunt end) and the holes caused thereby fitted with stopping. If the sideboard is to be painted, the stopping must be made of white lead, linseed oil and a little whitening, but if stained and wax polished, your stopping must be composed of wax.

What to do if there is a Live Flue Adjacent.

The suggestion outlined herewith with regard to fitting a cupboard in the recess is given upon the presumption that there is no other live flue adjacent. If the kitchen is on the ground floor there will be no flues on either side, but it might so happen that the recess backs on to another if the house is semi-detached. In this case it would be well to omit the woodwork to the inside, with the exception perhaps of the shelf. The cupboard could be composed of doors, frame, architrave, etc., as shown in Fig. 26, but with the doors hung on battens, as shown in Fig. 35A.

The back and side in this case could be rendered with Portland cement and sand and a little "Keene's," finished in Keene's cement and then painted.

But in so many instances, if there exists a range recess to utilise in the manner described, it will be free from surrounding flues, or flues that you know are disused.

MODERNISING A KITCHEN RANGE

Apart from the added appearance, the alteration shown in Figs. 36 and 37 halves the coal consumption and improves the cooking possibilities almost to the perfection of the modern grate. The old idea was to try to pull the heat over as well as under the oven. The heat going over was expected to find its way out at the bottom, contrary to all modern practice.

When these alterations are carried out all the heat will go under the oven, unless, as the writer did, you care to go to the extra trouble and allow the heat to travel round the oven and out at the top. This, however, is a further alteration, and can be carried out afterwards without disturbing the work now under consideration.

Tools required.

Large screwdriver, hacksaw, trowel, hammer, hand drill and pointed chisel.

Materials.

One fire basket and fret, same width as existing firebars, one bucketful of sand and cement (4—1), three or four ordinary bricks.

How to proceed.

First take out the old front firebars. To do this remove the four screws, A1, 2, 3 and 4, usually located as in Fig. 36, then the bars can be freed and lifted out.

Next the Small Hob.

Remove the three screws (B1, 2 and 3, Fig. 36). The front of the hob can now be taken out, then the top must

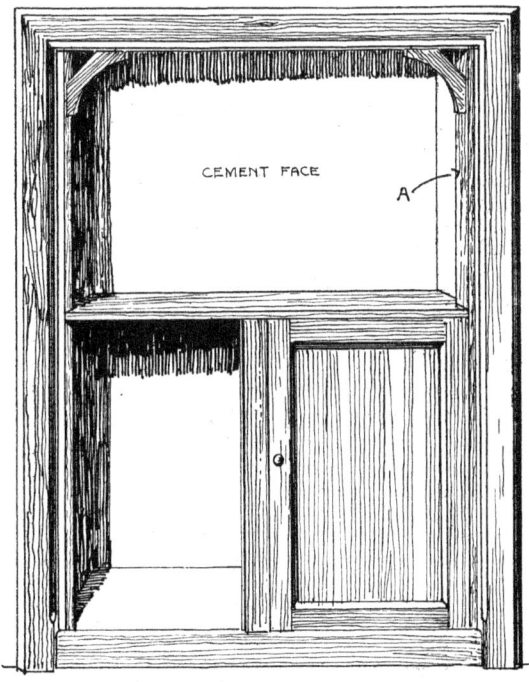

Fig. 35.—If there is Another Flue at the Back it might be advisable to omit the Woodwork on the Inside of the Cabinet.
Render the back and side with cement.

FITTING A MODERN HOT WATER BOILER

be gently moved to and fro to free it from the brickwork, in which it may be imbedded to the depth of 1 inch.

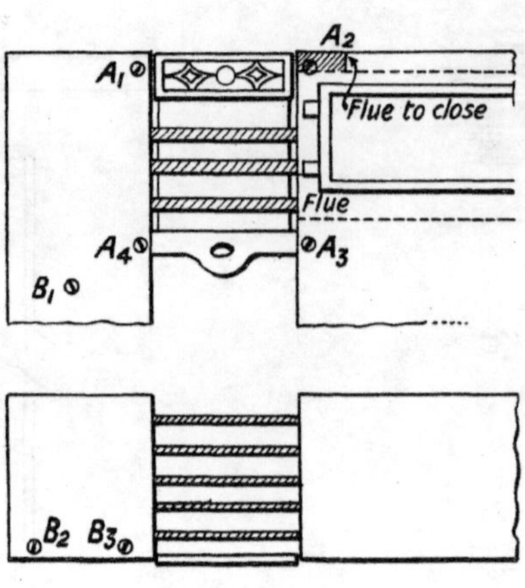

What to do if Screws are Tight.

Some difficulty may be experienced with the screws; if they are too difficult to remove with ordinary procedure, drill a small hole in the centre of the head and then gently punch the head through with a pointed chisel, and then when taken apart it is easy to remove them with a pair of pliers or in a vice.

The brick pillar exposed must now be taken down to a level a little lower than the bottom of the oven or the other side. If the top of the hole was embedded in the brickwork, a similar grove must now be made for it to fit into again at this new level. When ne, take out the old bottom bars, as they will not be required.

Now place the top in its new position and temporarily level it and measure from the underside to the floor level. At the same time measure for a new hole to replace screw B1. When the correct length is obtained, this is the length to which the front must be cut, mark a line across, first with a pencil and then with the edge of a file. Cut along carefully with the hacksaw, afterwards drill for the screw as mentioned.

To Replace Hob.

Mix your cement and sand into mortar and put a layer on top of the brick pillar, place the front in position and then the top, working the latter into the groove prepared for it until it is possible to replace the screws B1, 2 and 3. When this is done the hob is complete. All that remains to be done now is to build in the old ash-hole to receive the new firebars and fret. To fill this in use the bricks, allowing the front to protrude about 2 inches from the front of the grate. Finish over the top with a layer of cement. The height to which the hole should be filled in is governed by the depth of the new fret, the top of which when standing in position should be level with the new hob.

While using the cement, face up the side of the new hob opposite the oven, also with a thin coat the piece of brickwork left exposed over the new hob; this must be carefully done to provide a good surface for black-leading.

The flue over the oven must now be sealed along the edge nearest the fire to a depth of about 3 inches. This is best done with a suitable brick and faced with cement. When all the new work has set, the basket and fret can be placed in position, and all is ready to receive the fire.

Fig. 36.—Modernising an Existing Range (1).
Showing old-fashioned grate with front firebars.

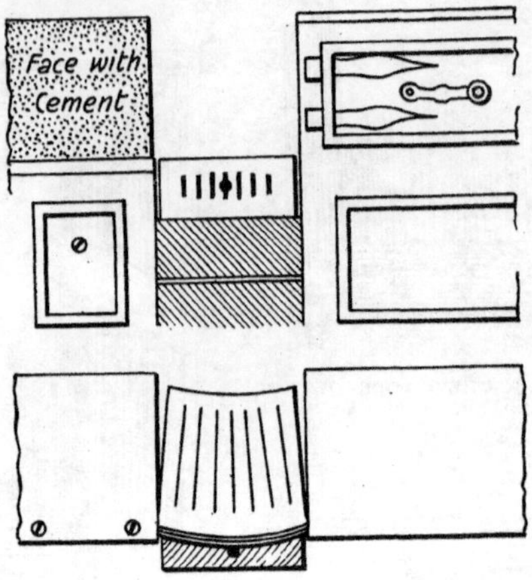

Fig. 37.—Modernising an Existing Range (2).
Showing how a fire basket and fret is fitted in place of firebars.

HOW TO MAKE SMALL DRILLS

A STOCK of small drills of various sizes form a useful part of the equipment of anyone who does much work with metal. They can quite easily be made from rods of silver steel obtainable in lengths of about 1 foot from most hardware stores.

First hammer the End out Flat.

The first thing to do is to heat the end of the rod in a gas flame until it is bright red. Then hammer the end out flat so that it resembles a screwdriver. It will probably be necessary to heat it two or three times before it is finally flattened out satisfactorily, as the steel cools fairly rapidly.

The Cutting Edges.

The next thing is to put a point on the end, and this is done with a file. The two end faces of the point should be at 60 degrees to the axis. The edges should then be bevelled in opposite directions so that they cut in the correct direction when the drill is rotated in its chuck. The backing-off angle should be about 30 degrees for the cutting edges.

Now file the two sides of the drill symmetrically until the width is equal to the diameter of the hole to be drilled. In order to give the necessary clearance when drilling, the sides should taper inwards slightly from the widest part near the point of the drill, otherwise the drill will tend to bind in the hole and will heat up in the process.

How to temper the Drill.

It will, of course, be necessary to temper the cutting portion of the drill before it is used, and this should be done as follows:—

Heat the drill in the flame until the end is a cherry-red colour, and then plunge it into lukewarm water for a second or so. One of the flat faces should now be rubbed quickly with a piece of emery paper or bath-brick, when it will be seen that a series of definite colours travel slowly towards the point of the drill. The first colour will be a whitish yellow, and this will be followed by a straw colour. As soon as this latter colour reaches the end of the drill, plunge the drill into the water.

The straw colour part of the drill will be hard enough to cut cast iron and steel without losing its edge, for a fairly long period.

If the end colour is too light, it will be found that the point will tend to be too brittle; if, on the other hand, the colour is too dark, i.e., approaching a purple or blue colour, the drill will not be hard enough to cut steel.

The cutting edges should be touched up on an oil stone after tempering, as the heating process tends to dull the edges.

Another Method of Tempering.

If preferred, the tempering process can be carried out in two definite stages. First heat to cherry-red colour, then plunge into water so as to harden it right out. Secondly, clean the end of the drill with emery or bath-brick, place it upon a piece of heated steel (black heat is sufficient) until the straw colour appears, and then plunge it into cold water, holding it there until quite cold.

Some Simple Home-made Garden Tools

Most amateur as well as professional gardeners are aware of the shortcomings of many ordinary types of garden tools which have been on the market for a very long time. Apart from the fact that these tools are by no means inexpensive, they do not provide for all the operations that the gardener has to perform.

In this article it is therefore proposed to describe a number of garden tools that are not difficult to make, and which have been proved to be extremely useful for their stated purpose. These tools include weed extractors, improved garden hoes, furrowing and seed-sowing tools, scythe and rake.

Weed Extracting Tools.

The removal of weeds of all kinds from paths, lawns and garden beds is perhaps the most important of all the amateur gardener's work, so that a description of some simple and effective devices should interest those who are confronted with this problem.

The Simplest Weeding Tool.

Perhaps the simplest of all weeding tools that have proved satisfactory in the past is that illustrated in Fig. 1. It consists of a piece of steel strip of 1 inch by ¼ inch section (⅛ inch will do in many cases) filed or otherwise shaped so as to leave a tapered end or "tang" for fixing the tool in a file handle. The other end is made with two prongs of about 2 inches length. The inside edges of these prongs are bevelled off so as to give a cutting edge.

With this tool the weeds can either be cut off flush with the ground or levered out, by placing the sharp edges downwards. If the larger weeds, e.g., dandelion, are cut off flush with the ground it is as well to sprinkle a little weed-killer over the cut portion left in the ground.

A more Elaborate Tool for Larger Weeds.

Fig. 2 shows a more elaborate and incidentally more effective tool for lifting the larger weeds. It has a tubular portion, B, for fitting to a wooden handle and pronged ends, D.

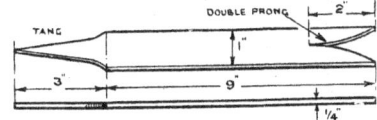

Fig. 1.—A Simple but Effective Weeding Tool.

In order to provide a suitable fulcrum for exerting the necessary leverage to lift stubborn weeds of the longer root type a tubular member, A, is arranged as shown.

The main part of this tool can readily be made from a piece of ¾-inch (inside diameter) steel tubing of about 18 gauge thickness. The tube should be about 7 inches long. Fig. 3 shows how the tube is shaped by sawing and filing first and afterwards bending the prongs out. The latter, it should be observed, are not merely left flat

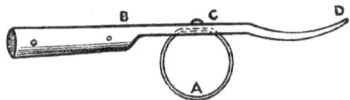

Fig. 2.—A Very Effective Weeding Tool.

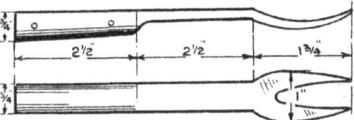

Fig. 3.—Details and Dimensions of Parts B and D.

Fig. 4.—Details and Dimensions of Part A.

Fig. 5.—Showing Method of Using the Tool.

but are inclined inwards towards the centre Vee, in order to give the necessary stiffness. If a tapered holder is required the piece of tube left plain for 2½ inches, shown on the left, can be split with a hack-saw, or a tapered section cut out. Afterwards the inner portion is hammered in so as to be of smaller diameter than the outer part.

The fulcrum, A, consists of a piece of 1½-inch diameter tube of about 16 gauge thickness, cut to the tapered form shown on the right in Fig. 4. The smaller (½ inch) end should just fit into the hollow part of the member BD. It is then riveted in place with a 3/16-inch soft iron rivet. This tool should be provided with a wooden handle about 10 inches to 12 inches long—similar to a long garden trowel handle.

In use the prongs of the fork are placed close to the weed just below the surface of the ground and the handle pressed downwards in order to lift the weed upwards, as shown in Fig. 5.

A Novel Tubular Weed Remover.

Fig. 6 shows a very useful form of weeding tool that can readily be made by the amateur. It consists of a piece of brass or steel tubing of from 1 to 1½ inch internal diameter by 16 gauge thickness. It should be about 12 to 15 inches long. A hole of ½ inch diameter is drilled near the upper end, to take a tommy bar; the latter consists of a piece of ½-inch steel rod, about a foot long. It should be a free fit in the hole of the tube so that it can be readily removed.

The only other accessory needed is a cylindrical piece of wood, about 1 inch long, provided with a stem, L (Fig. 8), and a knob or handle (an ordinary file handle will do nicely for this purpose). The plunger, P, should be a loose sliding fit inside the tube. The method of using this device is as follows: The tube—which, by the way, should be bevelled at its lower end—is placed centrally over the weed (Fig. 7) and then given a downward twisting motion by applying pressure and at the same time turning the tube with the tommy bar. The depth to which the tube is pushed will depend upon the size of the weed. Usually, however, if one goes down 6 to 8 inches, this will be found to be enough.

The tube is now pulled out of the ground and brings with it the root of the weed as well as a cylinder of earth, thus leaving a cylindrical hole in the ground. One has only to eject the weed and earth from inside the tube by pushing the plunger, P, down the tube and then fill the hole with fresh earth from any convenient nearby spot. This earth can be forced into the hole with the aid of the plunger P.

If, upon withdrawing the tube, it is found that the weed has extra long roots which have broken off at the bottom of the hole a little creosote or other form of weed-killer should be poured into the hole before filling it up with earth.

Fig. 6.—Tubular Weeding Device.

Fig. 7.—Method of Using.

Fig. 8.—Details of Plunger.

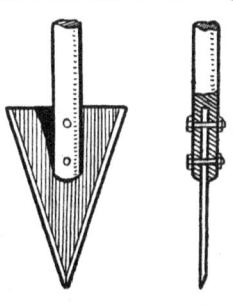

Fig. 9.—A Useful Furrowing and Weeding Tool.

SOME SIMPLE HOME-MADE GARDEN TOOLS

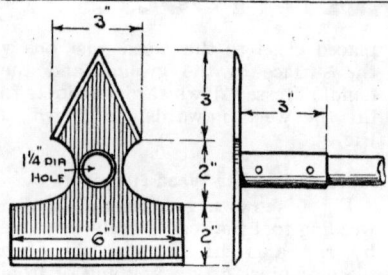

Fig. 10.—A Combined Garden Hoe and Furrowing Tool.

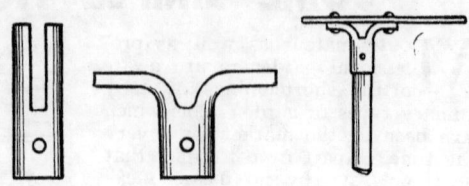

Fig. 11.—Tubular Socket for Hoe.   *Fig.* 12.—The Tube after Bending the Arms.   *Fig.* 13.—Method of Attaching the Bent Arms to Base Plate.

In the case of large-rooted weeds on lawns the hole should be filled up again with a cylinder of earth having grass roots and grass on top bored out from a spare piece of lawn. This will leave the surface of the lawn intact so that its appearance is unaltered.

Useful Combination Tools.

It is very convenient to have a tool or tools that can be used for more than one purpose; this not only saves expense but also storage space in the garden tool shed.

Fig. 9 shows a well-tried simple combination tool that has been found most useful for weeding and also for making furrows or shallow trenches for seed planting purposes. It can also be used for breaking up the earth around plants during the dry season. This tool consists of a triangular piece of steel plate of $\frac{1}{8}$ inch thickness. It should be about 3 inches wide at the base and about 6 to 8 inches long (from base to point). The edges can be filed off to a bevel, so that the tool can be used for cutting purposes as well. It is fitted into a strong ash broom handle in the manner shown, two bolts or riveted rods of $\frac{3}{16}$-inch diameter being used to secure it tightly; this must be done to prevent splitting the handle.

Combination Hoe, Weeder and Furrowing Tool.

Fig. 10 shows a combination hoe, weeder and furrowing tool. It is made from $\frac{1}{8}$-inch steel plate and should have the approximate dimensions shown in the diagram. The pointed end can be made with bevelled cutting edges if required. The flat plate portion should be fitted with a tubular socket of about $1\frac{1}{4}$-inch diameter by 3 inches long. This can be welded or brazed on or, if no local facilities are available for this purpose, an effective home-made type of socket fitted as shown in Figs. 11, 12 and 13. When making sockets of this type it is advisable to heat the split portion to a red heat before bending the arms outwards; this will give a stronger result and will, at the same time,

obviate the tendency of the metal to crack or split.

Incidentally, this form of socket can be used for any of the flat sheet metal tools described in this article.

Another Useful Tool.

Fig. 14 illustrates another useful form of garden tool having many applications. For example, the triangular end portion can be used for making trenches for seeds, as well as for breaking up the earth around plants. The toothed portions can be used for lifting weeds, and also for hoeing purposes. It can also be used in a similar manner to that of a garden rake. The width of the tool should

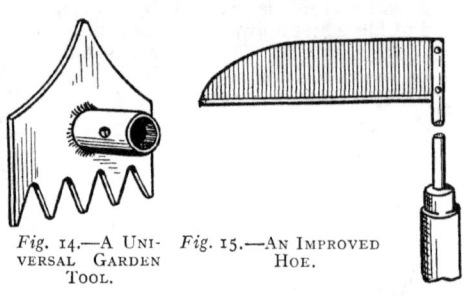

Fig. 14.—A Universal Garden Tool.   *Fig.* 15.—An Improved Hoe.

be from 5 to 8 inches, the prongs being about $1\frac{1}{2}$ to 2 inches long. It can be made of $\frac{1}{16}$- to $\frac{1}{8}$-inch steel plate and fitted either with a welded or built-up socket. The triangular portion should have an angle of 60 to 70 degrees.

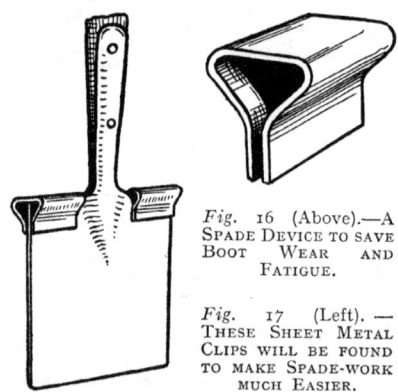

Fig. 16 (Above).—A Spade Device to save Boot Wear and Fatigue.

Fig. 17 (Left).—These Sheet Metal Clips will be found to make Spade-work much Easier.

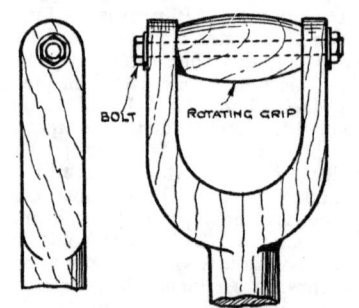

Fig. 18.—A Spade Handle Improvement.

An Improved Hoe.

The garden hoe shown in Fig. 15 is a definite improvement upon the ordinary central type, for it enables the user to get around and in between plants which the ordinary or Dutch hoe will not reach. Moreover, the pointed end is useful for hoeing up small weeds and for breaking up the soil around small plants.

The hoe in question can be made from a piece of steel plate, measuring 6 to 8 inches long by 2 to $2\frac{1}{2}$ inches wide by $\frac{1}{8}$ inch thick. A piece of $\frac{3}{8}$-inch flat or round bar is riveted to the thicker end as shown, the other end of the rod being pointed and driven into the end of a stout ash pole. A metal ferrule should be fitted to the end of the pole to prevent splitting.

Improvements to Garden Spades.

Those who use spades for digging purposes will no doubt agree that the constant pressing of the foot on the top edges of the spade is not only fatiguing but also tends to wear or spoil the soles of one's boots. In order to obviate these drawbacks simple sheet metal shields or clips can be made from 16 to 18 gauge steel plate, as shown in Figs. 16 and 17. They should be left with a tread of 1 to $1\frac{1}{2}$ inches and the lower ends closed practically together. These metal clips are knocked sideways on to the head of the spade, their natural spring being sufficient to give a good grip.

Improved Spade Handle.

Another small, but important improvement is to replace the ordinary fixed wooden grip of the spade (or fork) handle with a freely-rotating grip. The existing handle, being fixed, tends to make hands become blistered or sore, since it does not "give" to the grip. With the rotating grip, however, there is no relative movement between the hand and the handle (Fig. 18).

The existing grip can be used for this purpose. First, a $\frac{1}{4}$-inch hole should be carefully drilled centrally right through the handle. Next, with a fine saw, such as a hack-saw, cut out the handle, and, after smoothing the end faces of this part, re-assemble it, using a piece of $\frac{1}{4}$-inch rod screwed at each end to take a nut. To

SOME SIMPLE HOME-MADE GARDEN TOOLS

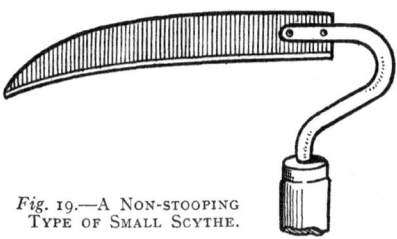

Fig. 19.—A Non-stooping Type of Small Scythe.

Fig. 20.—A Useful Rake for Grass and Leaves made from Wood with Nails as Teeth.

make a good job of this, the hole in the handle should be filed out so that it is a free fit on the ¼-inch rod, whilst the latter is a tight fit in the side portions.

A Non-Stooping Scythe.

The ordinary hand-hook used for cutting grass on banks, etc., is apt to prove fatiguing in operation, since it necessitates a constant stooping action.

In order to obviate this the blade and metal support should be removed from the existing handle and fitted into one end of an ash broom handle about 4 feet in length (Fig. 19). A metal ferrule should be fitted to the end of the wooden handle to prevent splitting when the metal support is driven in.

It will probably be found necessary to bend the metal support after fitting to the wooden handle, in order to obtain the most convenient cutting position for the blade. The new scythe is then used with a short semicircular sweeping action, somewhat in the manner of an ordinary scythe.

A Useful Rake for Grass or Leaves.

The ordinary garden rake is not a very satisfactory implement for use when removing cut grass, leaves, and similar items from the surface of the ground. In the first place the length of the toothed portion of the rake is insufficient and, secondly, the teeth are too short and too widely spaced.

An inexpensive and easy-to-make grass rake is illustrated in Fig. 20. It utilizes a long ash handle such as that fitted to garden rakes or hoes. This is screwed to a flat piece of strong timber, such as beech or ash, by means of the two screws shown. It is better to cut a flat on the end of the handle so as to obtain a good bedding surface for screwing to the cross-piece. The latter should be from 12 to 18 inches long, according to the amount of raking work to be undertaken, and of about 2½ to 3 inches in width and 1 to 1¼ inch thickness.

A series of holes of ⅛ inch diameter, spaced at about 1¼-to 1½-inch intervals, are drilled through the cross-piece (1 inch width portion). Through these holes are driven steel nails about 4 to 4½ inches long and 3/16 inch diameter. As the holes are of smaller diameter the nails will be a tight fit in them; the heads should be driven flush with the top of the timber. Before use give the cross-piece a coat of paint or creosote in order to prevent rotting.

A USEFUL TOILET COMPACT

THE unit illustrated below has the dual advantage of being simple and cheap to construct. It will also appeal to the reader as a neat and orderly method of housing those articles necessary to the toilet.

Materials required.

With one exception the whole can be made up from a strip of American white wood, size 24 × 4½ × ⅜ inch. From this the following lengths are cut:—

Backpiece, 11⅜ inches.
Tray, 6 inches.
Shelf, 4½ inches.
Side pieces, 3½ × 1 inch.

The exception mentioned above is the strut which supports the tray (see Fig. 4). This should be of ½-inch material. A dozen No. 4 wood screws complete the essentials, and after cutting the strip into the lengths required we can begin work on the tumbler shelf.

The Tumbler Shelf.

The size of this is 4½ × 4½ inches. Finding the centre of this mark off with a pencil compass the semicircular front, and cut round with a pad-saw. Finishing can be done effectively with a spokeshave. The hole taking the tumbler is central and should be about 2½ inches diameter, though the actual size is governed by the type of tumbler used. It is sufficient if the tumbler is supported about half-way down, as shown in Fig. 1. Next mark the positions for the toothbrush slots. The first two being on the centre line parallel to the backpiece (see Fig. 2). Though four slots are shown, either more or less can be used according to requirements. These are sawn back ⅝ inch and chiselled out. This member is now complete, and is secured by three screws to the backpiece.

The Soap Tray.

The size of this is 6 × 4½ inches.

The first procedure is to mark off the tapered sides. Having cut these to the dimensions in Fig. 1, commencement then should be made on the two sides or walls (see Fig. 3). These are mounted on the tray and secured by two screws from underneath. Care should be taken to ensure that the ends are vertical when the tray is secured to the backpiece.

This completed, the next consideration is the strut supporting the tray, details of which are given in Fig. 4. This is placed centrally and fastened by three screws from the top surface of the tray. The final adjustment is made on the back edge, which is planed to allow the tray to slope downwards at about 10 degrees from the horizontal.

The Finish.

All that remains now is to fix the tray to the backpiece, which is soon accomplished by fastening with two screws through the back into the strut.

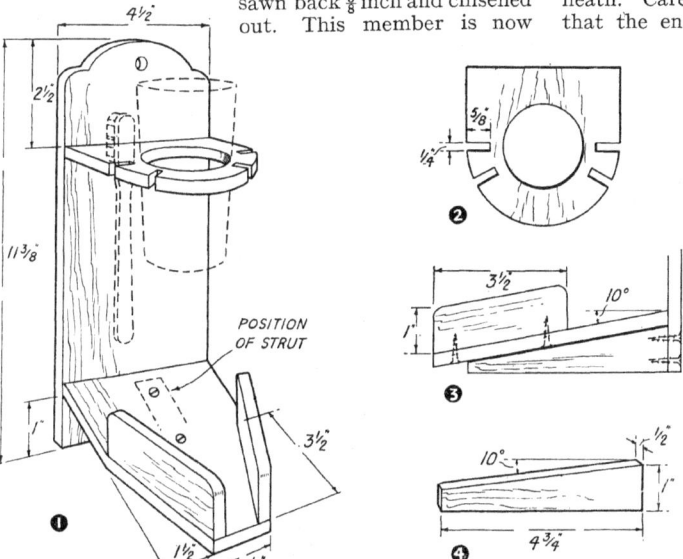

Figs. 1–4.—Details of the Construction and Assembly of the Toilet Compact.

Veneering

Fig. 1.—A Toothing Plane should be used on the Groundwork to take out the Waves and to roughen the Surface.
A piece of coarse sandpaper, wrapped round a block of wood, can be used if you have not got a toothing plane.

Fig. 2.—How to test whether the Groundwork is Smooth.
Pass the hand lightly across the grain as shown above. This will enable any waves to be detected. Make sure the surface is quite smooth before laying the veneer.

Many people think that an article which has been veneered is necessarily cheap and of poor quality, and that the veneer has only been applied to cover up bad wood and bad workmanship. This is not so, however. There are many effects which would not be practical if carried out in solid wood. Some woods are only suitable for use when they are cut thin and laid on a reliable groundwork, otherwise they would split and twist owing to their twisted and uneven grain. Good veneered work actually costs more to produce than a solid wood job.

Tools Required.

Few tools are required for veneering, and the only extras that may not be in the average householder's possession are a veneering hammer and a toothing plane. A hammer can be quite simply constructed as shown in Fig. 8, while, at a pinch, the toothing plane can be dispensed with and a piece of coarse sandpaper, wrapped round a wood block, used instead.

Types of Veneer.

Two types of veneer are obtainable, knife-cut and saw-cut, the difference being in the thickness. Knife-cut veneers are obtainable in thicknesses varying from that of brown paper up to about $\frac{1}{32}$ of an inch, and have a smooth surface. Saw-cut veneers are often $\frac{1}{16}$ of an inch or even more in thickness, and the saw marks can be clearly seen on the surface.

Choosing a Suitable Groundwork.

The groundwork on which the veneer is fixed is almost as important as the veneer itself. Suitable woods for groundwork and the method of preparing have already been discussed in the article on "Marquetry" (see page 1035).

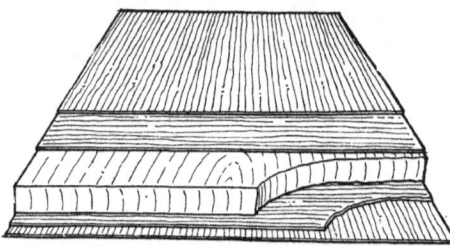

Fig. 3.—How Veneer is laid in High-class Work.
Note that the groundwork is first veneered both sides across the grain. The final veneers run with the grain of the groundwork.

A Good Method.

A method sometimes adopted is first to lay a straight-grained veneer across the grain on both sides and then lay the veneer proper over these as shown in Fig. 3. Work done in this way is absolutely reliable.

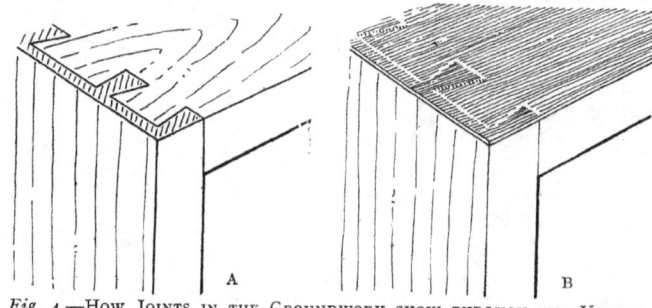

Fig. 4.—How Joints in the Groundwork show through the Veneer owing to Uneven Shrinkage.

Do not Veneer on End Grain.

It is not advisable to veneer on end grain if it can be avoided, on account of the poor grip it affords the glue. If it must be done, then thoroughly size the end grain and allow it to dry, to prevent the glue from being soaked up by filling in the pores.

Veneering over Joints.

When veneering is laid over a joint the marks of the joint are almost certain to show through eventually on the surface of the joint. For instance, Fig. 4A shows a fitment with a dovetail joint at the top, before the veneer is attached. Fig. 4B shows what the result will probably be when shrinkage has taken place. It is therefore far better to arrange a lap on the dovetails, or else use the thickest veneer possible.

How to Cut Veneer.

Veneer cannot be sawn in the same manner as ordinary wood or plywood. If knife-cut veneer, then a chisel and straight-edge should be used. The veneer should be held down on a flat surface and the cut made as shown in Fig. 5. If the veneer is extra wide the straight-edge can be held firmly by means of thumbscrews fixed at each end.

A saw-cut veneer can be cut with a fine saw, but the veneer must be laid on a flat board and the saw worked against the straight-edge.

Using a Cutting Gauge.

When several narrow strips of veneer are required it may be better to use a cutting gauge if one is available.

First "shoot" the edge of the veneer true with a metal plane, then use the gauge as shown in Fig. 7. It will be seen that the veneer is still kept flat and held down by a straight-edge (or in this case any convenient strip of wood). Cut through about half-way on one side, then reverse the veneer and complete the cut from the other side.

Laying the Veneer.

Two methods are available, caul veneering and hammer veneering, the latter being suitable only for knife-cut veneers. The process of laying with the caul has already been described in the article on "Marquetry."

HAMMER VENEERING

The process, briefly, is to glue the veneer, lay it in position, heat the glue with a flat-iron and press out with a veneering hammer. First prepare the hammer as shown in Fig. 8, then brush on the glue and lay the veneer in position while a large flat-iron is getting hot.

To Test when Iron is Hot enough.

The iron must not be used too hot; it should give a comfortable warmth when held a few inches from the cheek.

To avoid Scorching the Veneer.

A damp swab should be passed over the veneer to prevent the iron from burning it. A few dabs of glue should also be given here and there, to prevent pure water soaking through and weakening the glue.

Applying the Iron.

Now apply the iron as shown in Fig. 9, passing it lightly back and forth; this has the effect of making the glue runny. If the surface is a large one deal with about half the job at first. There will, of course, be a certain amount of steam as the heat from the iron dries up the water.

Using the Hammer.

The next thing is to apply pressure with the hammer. This should be worked with a zig-zag movement from the centre outwards, the object being to press the glue out at the edges. Pull first one side forward and then the other, keeping a firm pressure with the left hand all the time.

How to tell whether Veneer has Stuck.

To tell whether a satisfactory job has been done, go over the whole surface, tapping gently with the finger-nails. It should feel quite solid. A hollow feeling in any place indicates that the veneer has not been properly glued at that place.

What to do if First Attempt is Unsuccessful.

If this test shows that the veneer is

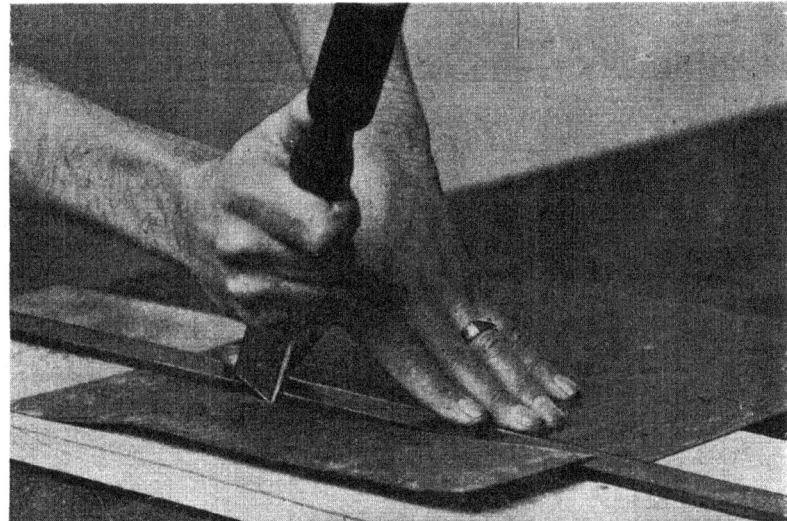

Fig. 5.—CUTTING VENEER WITH CHISEL AND STRAIGHT-EDGE.

Fig. 6.—PLANING EDGE OF VENEER ON SHOOTING BOARD.

Fig. 7.—USE OF GAUGE TO CUT PARALLEL STRIPS OF VENEER.
The piece of wood shown pressed across the veneer serves to keep the veneer flat.

VENEERING

not satisfactorily fixed, then it will be necessary to reheat and repeat the work with the hammer.

To remove a Bubble of Air near the Centre.

If, when the job has set, a bubble of air is found near the centre then a cut should be made with a thin knife through the veneer, with the grain, at the spot where the bubble is. Then heat the spot with the iron and press down with the hammer.

Cutting Overhanging Veneer.

If the veneer overhangs the edge of the groundwork it can be cut off before the glue hardens by laying it face downwards on two flat boards of equal thickness, one placed so that the edge to be cut lies in its centre as shown in Fig. 11. Then cut with a chisel. Press heavily on the work while cutting so as not to force the veneer from the groundwork.

Wipe away all surplus glue from the surface with a swab dipped in hot water and wrung dry.

Cleaning up the Surface.

The final operation is to clean up the surface of the veneer with a scraper, and follow with a thorough glass-papering, first No. 2 grade, then No. 1 grade, rubbing with the grain.

JOINING TWO PIECES OF VENEER

It sometimes happens that it is

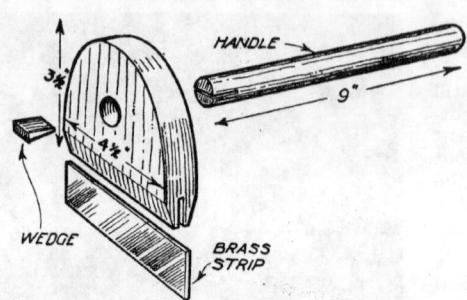

Fig. 8.—Details of Veneering Hammer.

necessary to make a joint in a sheet of veneer. First of all lay one piece as already described; then lay the second piece so that it overlaps the

Fig. 9.—Using the Flat Iron in Hammer Veneering.
The veneer is first damped with water and glue.

other piece by about 1 inch as shown in Fig. 12. Now place the straight-edge down the centre of the overlap and fix it with two thumb-screws, and cut through both thicknesses forming the joint with a chisel. The chisel will probably have to be drawn along more than once, but care should be taken not to cut into the groundwork more than possible. Now remove the two pieces of waste. The top one can simply be lifted off, the underneath one can be withdrawn while lifting up the second piece of veneer.

Next apply the iron and press down with the hammer. To prevent the joint from opening as the glue dries, glue pieces of paper over the joint as shown in Fig. 15.

CROSSBANDING

Crossbanding forms an effective piece of decoration that can be carried out in veneer.

The first thing to do is to fix the main centre part of the panel. If the crossbanding is to be, say, 1½ inches wide then the centre panel can be short of the overall size of the groundwork by about 1 inch. Then set a cutting gauge to the required depth of the crossbanding and make a cut all round the panel. Avoid cutting more deeply into the groundwork than you can help. If the glue has been allowed to harden it will probably be necessary to re-heat it before the waste can be removed, but if it is done before the glue sets it can easily be peeled off.

Cut the veneer for the crossbanding

Fig. 10.—How the Veneering Hammer is used.
A zig-zag movement is followed, the glue being driven out at the edges.

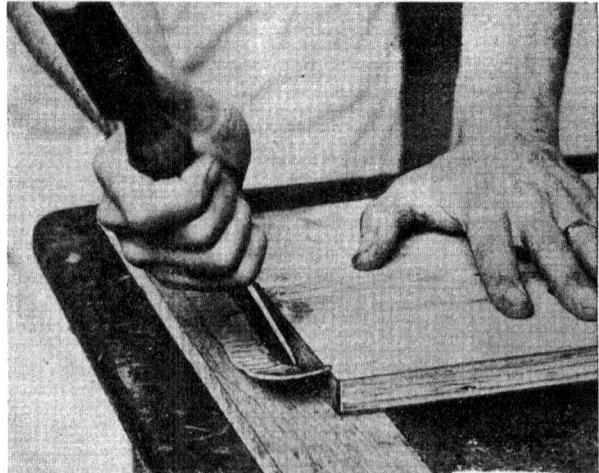

Fig. 11.—Cutting away Overhanging Veneer.
Note that the work is upside down.

VENEERING

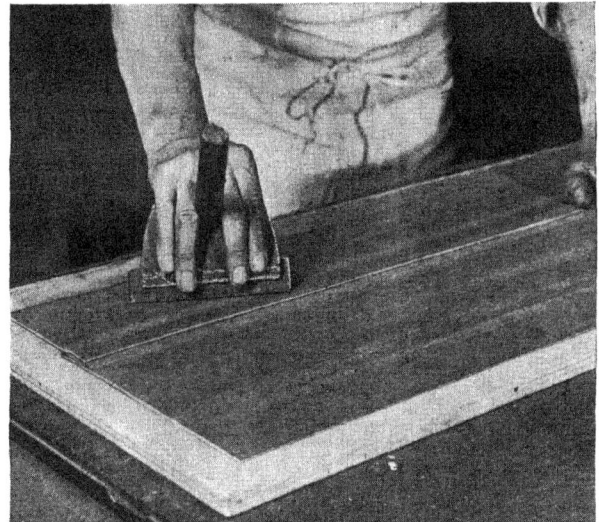

Fig. 12.—Jointing Veneers—the First Step.
The two pieces overlap about 1 inch.

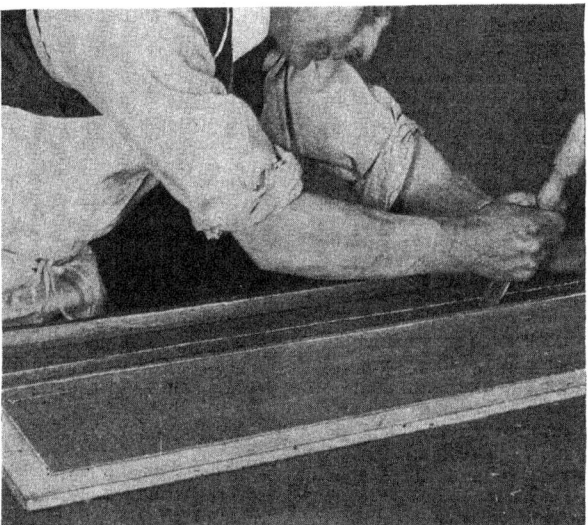

Fig. 13.—The Second Operation.
Cutting through both thicknesses in forming the joint.

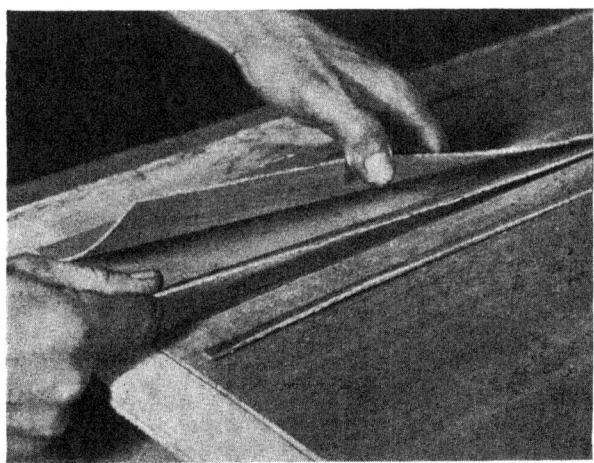

Fig. 14.—Third Operation.
Removing the surplus pieces of veneer.

Fig. 15.—The Final Stage.
Gluing pieces of paper over the joint to prevent it from opening as the glue dries out.

Fig. 16.—Crossbanding Edge of a Veneered Panel.
The main centre part of the panel is veneered. Then a cutting gauge is set to the width of the crossbanding and a cut made with it all round the panel.

Fig. 17.—Crossbanding—The Next Step.
Lifting away the waste veneer after cutting. If the gauging is done immediately after the veneer has been laid it can easily be peeled away.

VENEERING

slightly wider than required. True up the edge of the veneer on the shooting board, then cut the strips with the cutting gauge. Now make a mark across the crossbanding at one end, at 45 degrees, and cut it with a chisel. Place this piece in position, mark the other end and cut in the same way.

Repeat this process until all four strips are prepared, then proceed to fix them. Coat with glue and press down with the hammer. Provided the glue is used hot, the ironing process can be omitted. Glue a strip of newspaper over each joint, and clean up the surface when the glue has set hard, about fourteen or fifteen hours after gluing as a rule.

FORMING BUILT-UP PATTERNS WITH VENEERS

One of the advantages of veneered work is the ease with which attractive patterns can be formed, as, for example, the quartered panel shown in Fig. 19.

How to assemble Veneers.

The first step is to take a piece of paper of the same size as the panel and draw in on it the centre lines which mark the positions of the joints. Obviously, these lines must be at right angles. The veneers are assembled on this paper.

Selecting Veneers for Quartering.

It is advisable to select fairly straight grained veneers for quartering, because in a wide curly figuring the direction of the grain is not so marked, and it is the definite direction that gives quartering its value. We are not speaking of cases where the adjacent leaves are matched up, but of plain

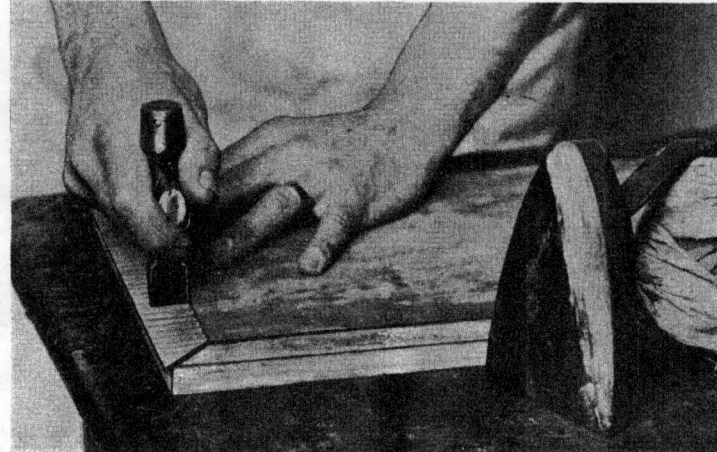

Fig. 18.—PRESSING DOWN CROSSBANDING WITH BACK OF HAMMER.

With the small strips used for crossbanding it will not be necessary to use the flat-iron, provided the glue is hot and is pressed out quickly with the back of the hammer. It is not, however, a bad idea to have the iron ready in case of accident.

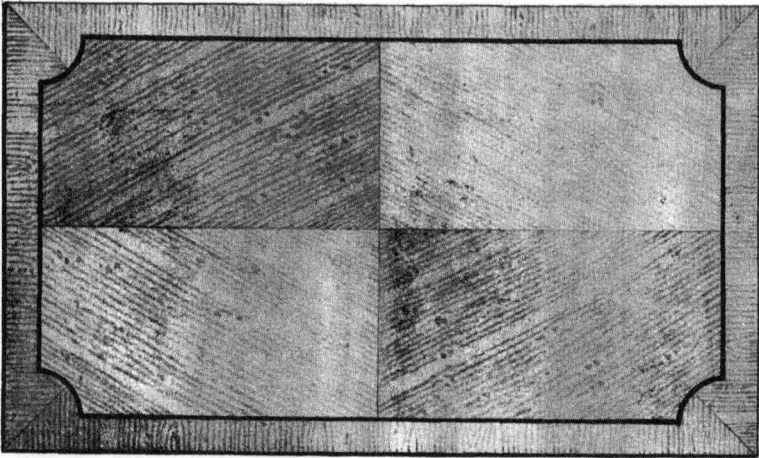

Fig. 19.—QUARTERED PANEL WITH CROSSBANDED EDGE AND INLAID EBONY LINE.

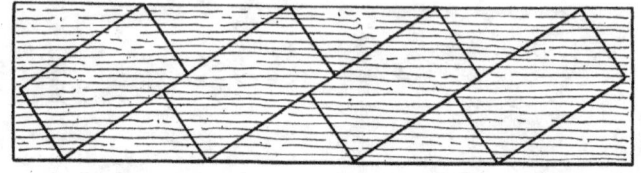

Fig. 20.—HOW QUARTERS CAN BE CUT OUT ECONOMICALLY.

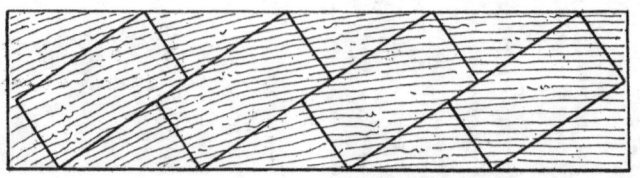

Fig. 21.—WHAT TO AVOID.

Note how the grain slopes away to the left, so that it passes through the end quarter almost parallel with the sides.

quartering, in which all four pieces can be cut from a single leaf.

The Slope of the Grain.

It is apparent that the grain must slope at the same angle in all four pieces, and this calls for care in cutting them. The actual slope depends upon the design. Sometimes it is at 45 degrees, regardless of whether the panel is square or not. Usually, however, the grain is made to run diagonally from corner to corner, as in Fig. 19. As a rule, it is possible to economise material by marking out the veneer as given in Fig. 20. This has a second advantage in that, assuming the grain to be parallel with the sides throughout, it is at the correct angle in all four pieces.

The last point has to be watched carefully. Glance at it, Fig. 21. Here the grain slopes away at one end, with the result that it is almost parallel with the sides of the quarter. In the same way it is necessary to avoid veneer in which the grain is of a different character in the quarters.

Fitting the Quarters.

The paper with the design drawn in is pinned down on a flat board. Each quarter is then fitted up in turn. Assuming the crossbanding to be 1 inch wide, the quarters should come to within about ¾ inch of the edge. Special care is needed in cutting the veneer to avoid chipping off the inner corners, the grain of which runs across, making it specially fragile. It is cut with the chisel and straightedge, and it is an advantage to begin at the corner and cut away from it.

The edges are planed on the shooting board in the way already described, and

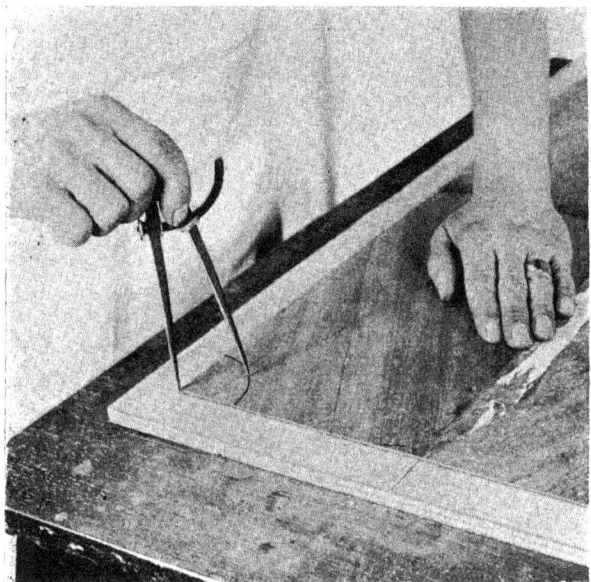

Fig. 22.—How the Rounded Corners can be Cut.
One leg of the dividers is sharpened to a cutting edge.

Fig. 23.—Laying the Ebony Line.
The ebony is bent to shape, glued to groundwork, and is held in position with veneer pins driven into the groundwork.

the first quarter placed in position and pinned down. If the pins are placed at the edges the holes will not show, as they are cut away afterwards. To enable them to be withdrawn, they should be driven in about half-way only.

When all four have been pinned down, pieces of newspaper are glued over the joints. The object of these is to hold the whole together, and to prevent the joints from opening.

Laying the Veneer.

We have already dealt in a previous article on the preparation of the groundwork. Both this and the veneer should be glued. To ensure the veneer being in the correct position, centre lines corresponding with the joints should be drawn on the groundwork. The veneer is then laid in position and two or three veneer pins driven in at the edges to prevent it from shifting when the hot caul is applied.

A Hint on Gluing.

It is a good plan to allow the glue to chill before laying the veneer in position, because otherwise it may be difficult to manœuvre the veneer owing to the glue "grabbing." A sheet of paper is laid over the whole, and the caul applied, as already described.

Adding the Crossbanding.

The caul having been removed, a cutting gauge is set to the width of the crossbanding, including the inlay line, and the edges cut in. Cut through the veneer, but do not cut unnecessarily deeply into the groundwork. The surplus is removed with the chisel.

Cutting the Rounded Corners.

To cut the rounded corners, one leg of a pair of dividers can be sharpened to a cutting edge and used, as shown in Fig. 22. Do not dig the pivoting leg deeply into the groundwork. The veneer can be raised with the chisel. Another way is to mark in the shape with compasses, and make vertical cuts with a gouge. This, however, necessitates the gouge being of exactly the same sweep as the corner, and this is not always convenient.

How the Inlay is fitted.

As ebony lines are usually rather brittle, it is necessary to make them pliable by soaking them in warm water. When many corners have to be formed it is a good plan after soaking to bend the line round and round a rounded piece of wood. When dry it will be found to have retained its shape to a great extent.

When the corner has been bent approximately to shape, the corners are mitred, a keen chisel being used to cut them. The line is then glued and pressed in position with the flat back part of a hammer. To hold it in place and to prevent it from springing, a few nails can be driven into the groundwork, as in Fig. 23. All four corners are dealt with in the same way.

The next stage is that of fitting the lines between the corners. Each mitre is fitted, and the line pressed in with the hammer. Here again veneer pins can be driven into the groundwork to hold the line in position if it shows any tendency to spring out.

The Shaped Corners.

When the glue has set the nails are withdrawn and any glue at the edge scraped away. The corners are applied first. A line at 45 degrees is drawn in at each corner as a guide. The shaped edge is cut roughly to the curve with the chisel, and is finished off with a file. The straight edges should be planed. Remember that not only the sloping edge has to make a good joint, but also that against which the straight crossbanding has to be fitted.

When all the four corners have been fitted, each is glued and pressed well down with the hammer. A piece of newspaper is glued over each joint to prevent it from opening as the glue dries out.

Gluing Down Crossbanding.

The last stage is that of gluing down the crossbanding. The veneer is cut with the cutting gauge and the jointing edge trued up on the shooting board. Fit the ends carefully against the corners, and then glue down. Once again paper is glued over all joints.

Cleaning Up the Work.

Allow as much time as possible before cleaning up. As a rule the ebony line is thicker than the veneer, and this can be taken down first with a finely set plane. The scraper, followed by glasspaper, gives the final cleaning up.

Constructing a Small Electric Motor
TO DRIVE A SEWING MACHINE, SMALL DRILL, PUMP, STIRRER, ETC.

The small electric motor described below is designed so that it can be built without the use of elaborate tools, and can be wound to suit several different voltage supplies. Its power will depend to some extent upon the excellence of the workmanship. If accurately constructed with a small clearance between the poles and the armature, it should be strong enough to drive a sewing-machine, a small drill, a force pump, a mechanical stirrer or some similar machine.

Materials required.

3½ square feet soft sheet iron, ⅛ inch thick.
6 inches steel rod, 5/16-inch diameter.
3 inches brass rod, ⅝-inch diameter.
2 inches brass tube, ⅞-inch bore.
2 square inches spring brass, gauge 24.
6 square inches copper gauze.
4 doz. armature stampings (eight slot and 1¾-inch diameter) (obtainable from The Grafton Electric Co., Grafton Street, London, W.1, at a cost of 8s. 6d. per gross).
6 iron bolts, 2 inches long, 2 B.A.
1 driving pulley.
1 oz. insulating tape.
8 oz. copper wire, gauge 18 D.C.C.
4 oz. ,,   ,,   ,,   24 S.S.C.

The total cost of the motor should not exceed 24s.

Making the Field Magnets.

Most D.C. motors are machined up from castings, but this operation demands elaborate equipment. To enable those who do not possess a lathe to make this machine, the main shell and the fields are made from

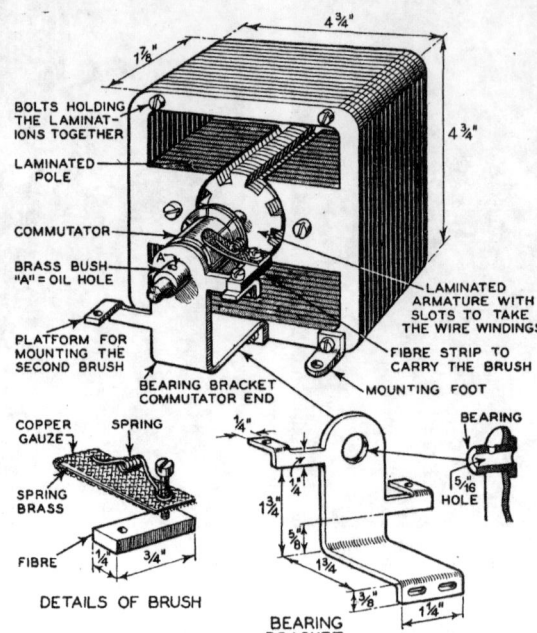

Fig. 1.—The Electric Motor assembled without the Windings.

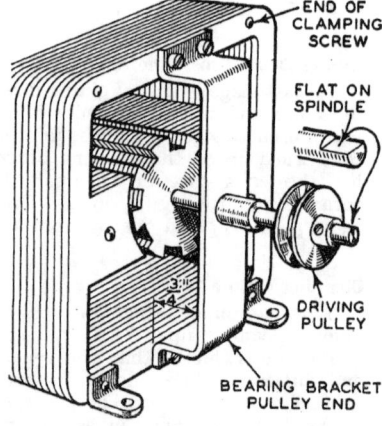

Fig. 2.—View of the Motor from the Pulley End.

laminations cut from a sheet of soft iron. Accurately set out a pattern of one of the laminations as shown in the sketch (Fig. 3) on a piece of tin and then cut it out. Using this as a template, mark out the laminations on the sheet iron and saw round with a metal fret-saw; to save time and waste, each one can be made in two pieces with joints near the corners, as shown in Fig. 3.

When adopting this method the laminations are assembled with the joints alternatively arranged on opposite sides. Do not drill the bolt holes separately, but drill one lamination as a pattern, then clamp half a dozen together with the edges coinciding and run the holes right through the batch. Repeat the process with the remainder, drilling them in sets of six, using the original one each time as a template.

Assemble the whole batch of stampings, securing them with bolts threaded into the last lamination, or, if preferred, nuts can be fitted to the ends of the bolts. It should be noted that the two lower corner bolts secure four small feet; these are made from strip iron bent up at right angles.

The Bearing Brackets.

The bracket for the pulley end (see Fig. 2) is simply a strip of 1¼-inch iron bent at right angles at the ends. In the centre is a brass bush similar to the one shown in Fig. 1. This is soldered into a hole of suitable size. The bracket is secured to the main shell with 4 B.A. screws; slots are filed out at the ends of the strip instead of holes, similar to those shown in Fig. 1; this permits a little lateral "play," so that the armature can be centred in the tunnel formed by the poles of the field magnets.

The bearing bracket at the commutator end is shown in Fig. 1; this is bent up from a single piece of sheet iron. Note that the two arms that support the brushes are not in line—one is 1⅛ inches lower than the other. The reason for this should be fairly obvious, as one brush rubs on the top of the commutator while the other bears on the under side. The brass bush in the centre is made from a piece of ⅝-inch rod. Observe the oil hole A shown in Fig. 1.

The Armature.

Fig. 4 shows details of the armature. It is composed of a number of stampings threaded on to a spindle. Each section should be coated with shellac before assembling to insulate them from one another. Should any trouble be experienced in making the stampings fit tightly on the axle, the spindle can be "tinned"; the end segments can then be secured with a touch of solder. Note that one end of the spindle has a flat to facilitate the fixing of the driving pulley.

Winding the Field Magnets.

A simple device for winding the

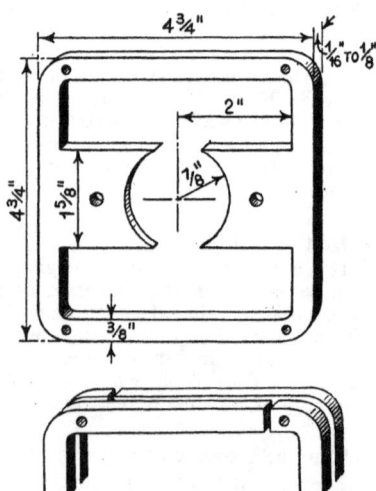

Fig. 3.—Details of the Laminations. Top, one of the field laminations; bottom, two laminations showing how the joints are assembled on opposite sides.

CONSTRUCTING A SMALL ELECTRIC MOTOR

field coils is shown in Fig. 5. The bridge and two flanges are all bent up from one piece of tin, a plate bolts on to the side of the bridge, thus forming a complete bobbin upon which to wind the wire. The plate is removed when the winding is completed, so that the coil can easily be withdrawn. Care must be taken to make the bridge exactly the same size as the pole pieces of the field magnets.

Before starting to wind the coils, cover the bridge with *two* layers of thick waxed paper, then proceed to wind on the 18-gauge wire. As each layer is completed coat it with shellac varnish; this improves the insulation and helps to hold the wire in position until the coil is taped. As many turns of wire as possible should be wound on until the depth of the winding on the coil is ⅝ inch thick. When completed, remove the side plate and slide off the coil.

Taping the Coil.

Having removed the finished coil, secure the two ends to neighbouring loops by binding round several turns of cotton thread. Now proceed to tape the coil as shown in Fig. 6, twisting it round like a bandage, each turn slightly overlapping the previous one.

The Commutator.

Details of this are shown in Fig. 7. It consists of a piece of fibre or ebonite

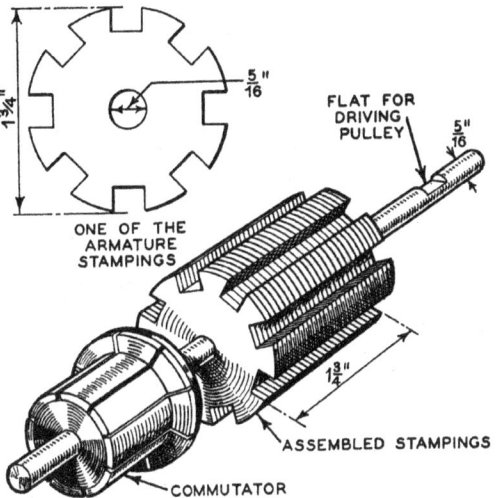

Fig. 4.—Details of the Armature, showing one of the Armature Stampings.

shaped up cylindrically with a flange at one end, and over this is fitted a piece of brass tube to which a flat ring is soldered. The round brass sleeve is then carefully divided off into eight equal segments. Before cutting them apart, two holes are drilled in each segment as shown, and corresponding centres marked on the central fibre core. The hole in the fibre is then tapped out 6 B.A. Each segment is then coated with shellac, and while wet is fixed in place with countersunk 6 B.A. screws; it is, of course, very important that there should be no metallic contact between the strips.

The above commutator will work well with a pressure of 12 to 20 volts, but if it is proposed to wind the motor for higher voltages it is advisable to buy a ready-made commutator with copper segments which are dovetailed to a mica-insulated core. This could be obtained from Messrs. Grafton Electric Co., at a cost of about 6s.

Winding the Armature.

The armature is wound in eight separate coils. Fig. 9 shows two of the coils in place. Note that in slot No. 1 there are the limbs of two coils, while slots Nos. 4 and 6 have only one limb and are only half full. Finally, all the slots will be full and half of two coils will be found in each slot. To preserve mechanical balance the slots are best wound in the following order:—

1 and 4, then 5 and 8
4 ,, 7 ,, 8 ,, 3
7 ,, 2 ,, 3 ,, 6
2 ,, 5 ,, 6 ,, 1

Thus there will be a *start* of one coil and the *finish* of another in each slot. The free ends in each slot are twisted together and soldered to their respective segment of the commutator.

The Brushes.

Two copper gauze brushes are mounted on the bracket arms, as shown in Fig. 1. A strip of fibre is

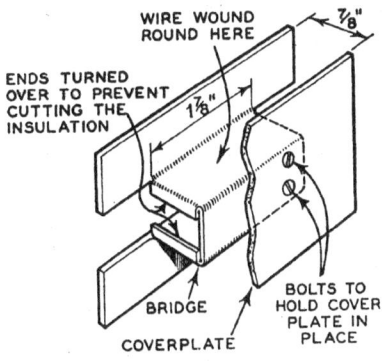

Fig. 5.—Frame on which Field Winding is wound.

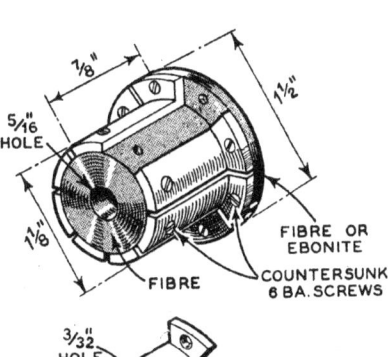

Fig. 7.—Details of the Commutator.

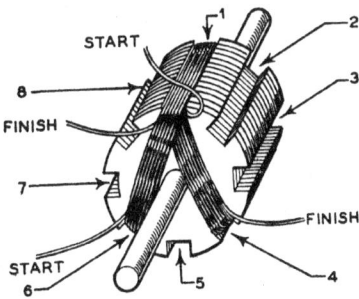

Fig. 9.—One Section of Armature Winding.

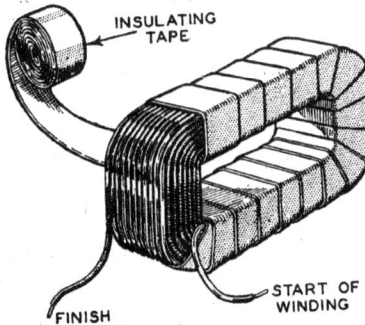

Fig. 6.—Taping the Field Winding.

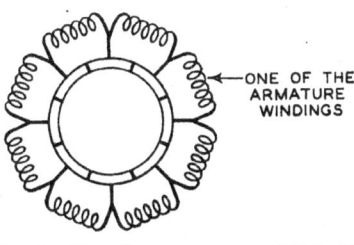

Fig. 8.—The Connections between the Commutator and Armature Windings.

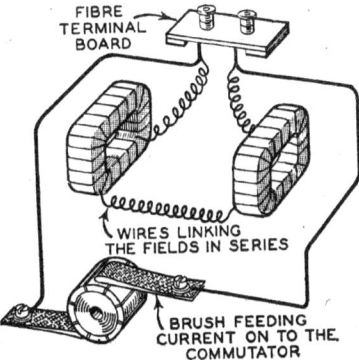

Fig. 10.—Pictorial View of the General Winding.

bolted to the projecting platform, and the brush is at right angles to this. The gauze is in the form of a loop with a piece of spring brass in the middle to stiffen it. A small coil spring with a projecting finger is held under the securing bolt; this gives additional pressure to the brush on the commutator.

How to assemble.

Having bolted together the field laminations, carefully clean up the tunnel by rubbing it down with fine emery paper held on a mandrel 1¾ inches in diameter. Mount the spindle on the bearings and slide the brackets laterally until the armature is in the centre of the tunnel; it should revolve freely within the curve at the end of the poles with as little clearance as possible. Fasten the pulley to the flat on the spindle with a grub screw, then mount the brushes in place when the motor will be ready to wire up.

Wiring-up.

Fig. 10 shows how the brushes and the field windings are connected to the supply terminals. These terminals are mounted on a strip of fibre held to the top of the main shell by two 4 B.A. screws, which fit into holes tapped in the field laminations. Use 18-gauge D.C.C. wire for these internal connections and solder all joints. Take care that the base of the terminals are not in contact with the metallic frame, and tape all joints that might rub against any parts of the frame.

Voltages and Wires to use.

A motor built to the specification given above will run on a voltage of 12, and it can be safely used on any D.C. circuit up to 16 volts. Should it be necessary to use a higher voltage, then the field coils and the armature must be wound with wire of a different gauge. Below is a simple table giving four different windings with a wide choice of voltage:—

Voltage of Supply.	Field Winding.	Armature Winding.
25 volts.	20 D.C.C.	24 S.S.C.
50 ,,	21 ,,	28 ,,
100 ,,	24 ,,	33 enamel.
200–210 ,,	26 ,,	37 ,,

When using Higher Voltages.

When using the higher voltages a ready-made commutator must be used, and duplex winding is advisable when the commutator has twice as many segments as the armature has slots, thus each slot contains the limb of four coils, making sixteen coils in all. In the duplex winding for the higher voltages the armature is wound twice, the second coil in each slot being connected one segment in advance of the first coil. When using a high voltage, an armature with sixteen slots could with advantage be substituted for the eight-slot one described above. Then, of course, for duplex winding a commutator with thirty-two segments would be required.

Running the Motor off A.C.

This little motor can be made to run off A.C., but when building the machine for this purpose the laminations of the fields must be thinner, gauge 18, soft iron, being used instead of the ⅛-inch plate described above.

A later article describes in detail the method of using this motor to drive an electric stirrer.

PREPARATIONS FOR MAKING FLY-PAPERS AND LIQUID FLY SPRAYS

PAPERS coated with certain sticky preparations are well-known expedients in fly infested rooms. These fly-papers are designed to attract the insects by virtue of some sweet-smelling or tasting ingredients and, when once in contact with the preparation, to hold the flies by means of a strong adhesive.

The latter ingredient of the coating mixture must not dry up in any way, but remain fresh and sticky for relatively long periods. The "attractive" constituents of most fly-paper preparations are honey and molasses, or treacle. The adhesive portion invariably has rosin as its basic ingredient.

Some Typical Recipes.

The following are typical recipes for the sticky preparations used to coat papers:—

By volume
(1) Rosin . . . 8 parts
　　Linseed oil . . 3 ,,
　　Honey or molasses . 1 part
(2) Rosin . . . 9 parts
　　Rapeseed oil . . 6 ,,
　　Turpentine . . 6 ,,
　　Honey . . . 1 part

Non-sticky Fly-Papers.

There is another type of fly-paper that is not sticky, but is merely soaked in water and placed in a dish or saucer.

One of these is the poisonous variety containing arsenic salts. A typical preparation is as follows:—
　Sodium arsenate . 2 ozs.
　Brown sugar . . 6 ozs.
　Water . . . 2 pints

These ingredients are dissolved together and unsized purple paper is then impregnated, dried and cut into suitable sizes of sheets. As this is a poisonous preparation, it must be clearly marked "Poison" if made for sale to the public through a registered chemist.

A non-poisonous preparation can be made in the following manner:—

Take 7 lbs. of quassia wood chips and boil with about one-half its volume of water until all of the essence has been extracted from the wood. More water may be added if there is any doubt as to the completeness of the extraction process. Continue boiling the solution, after removing the wood, until its volume is reduced to 1 gallon concentration.

Next take 12 ozs. brown sugar and 1 drachm of glucose and dissolve in this solution.

The paper—which should be the unsized coloured grade—is then dipped in this solution and after drying cut into suitable strips. When these strips are placed on a dish or plate and a little water added, the flies are attracted and are killed after drinking the water.

Spraying Fluid for Killing Flies.

A good insecticide of the liquid type that can be used with an ordinary sprayer in the house, for killing flies, is made up of the following ingredients:—

By volume
Cologne water . . 16 parts
Alcohol (90 per cent.
　strength) . . 33 ,,
Acetic ether . . 3 ,,
Bergamot oil . . 1 part
Eucalyptol . . 3 parts

This solution is used with ten times its volume of water. All windows and doors of the room should be closed and any food removed before spraying. Leave the room shut for an hour or two after spraying when the dead flies can be removed.

How to Repair a Roof Gutter

In good-class work, eaves gutters are made of cast iron, usually in 6-feet lengths. They are of three forms, as illustrated in Fig. 1, namely, the half-round, the ogee moulded, and the boundary gutter.

Half-round gutters are carried on wrought-iron stays, but moulded gutters are usually screwed on to the wall plate or facia board, wrought-iron stays being sometimes used in addition. The boundary gutter is rectangular and 4½ to 5 inches wide. It lies on the outer 4½ inches of a 9-inch wall, the outer face flush with the boundary face of the wall. It usually has an internal socket and the others external. The sockets are usually right hand, but as some firms cast them on the left it should be noted which hand is required when replacing a defective length of moulded or boundary gutter.

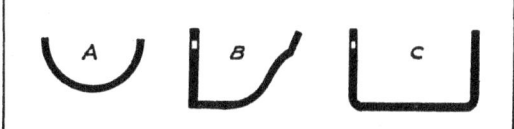

Fig. 1.—The Three Types of Cast-iron Gutter.
A, the half-round; B, the ogee moulded; C, the boundary gutter.

How to replace a Faulty Length of Cast-iron Gutter.

As considerable force and leverage has often to be used, it is important to make sure that the ladder is quite secure. It should project well above the eaves to give hand hold while at work, and the foot should be secured by spiking or by placing a heavy bag of sand at the foot.

How to unfix Gutters from Sockets.

It will often be found that the 1¼-inch gutter bolts which secure the gutter to the socket are so rusted that it is practically impossible to unscrew them. If such is the case, they should be cut with a sharp cold chisel about 4 inches long and ⅜ inch in section. Fig. 2 shows how the chisel should be held with its edge against the weakest part of the nut. It should be given a sharp blow with a small hammer along the gutter and not across it. The nut should cut quite easily and will fall off without jarring the brittle cast-iron gutter.

Naturally, care must be taken not to damage the socket of the length of gutter which is not being removed, and should the bolt get very loose, it may be advisable to get an assistant to hold a flat iron behind the nut while it is being struck.

Now remove Back Wood Screws.

The next operation is to remove the three back wood screws, unless, as is often the case, the holes in the back of the gutter are so rusted that the screws are no longer effective. In such a case, the gutter will simply have to be lifted down. Take care that the gutter does not drop suddenly and upset your balance. If two people are on the job, the ladders should be placed clear, right and left, of the length to be removed.

Cutting the New Length.

Carefully measure the length of the old piece of gutter and mark on the socketed length to be cut, then with a large three-corner file make a deep niche all along the line right round the

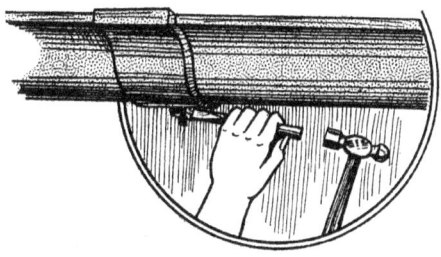

Fig. 2.—How to take down a Faulty Length of Gutter.
If the nut cannot be unscrewed it should be cut with a small, sharp chisel. Note how the chisel is held along the gutter and not across.

outside of the gutter. With a moulded gutter the end of the file will have to be used on the inner curve, and a niche may also be filed inside at that point.

Now lay a piece of stout deal quartering on a pavement, path or other solid surface, place the gutter over this, and apply light blows with a small hammer on a small, sharp, hard chisel.

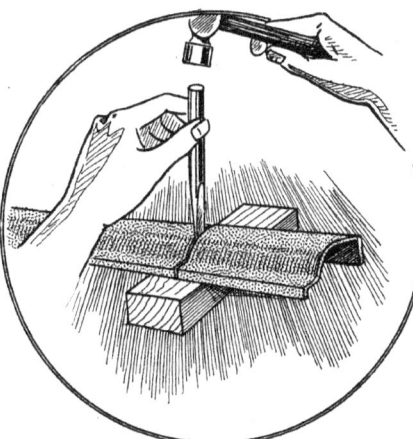

Fig. 3.—How to cut a Length of Cast-iron Gutter.
Mark out the line to be cut and file a deep niche along it with a three-cornered file. Then use a small, sharp, hard chisel and tap lightly with a hammer.

Trace the chisel all along the filed niche, vibrating all the time with the chisel. When the inner curve is reached give very light blows, so as not to fracture the gutter in the wrong place.

Keep moving along the niche with light vibrating blows until the gutter falls into two pieces. Do not strike hard in one place.

It is advisable now to try the cut length in position and mark the position for the bolt hole, which should then be drilled with the breast drill, using a twist bit for preference. No oil is required when drilling cast iron, but keep a steady pressure when drilling, taking the weight off when the drill is nearly through.

Cutting a Round Cast-iron Rain-water Pipe.

It may be mentioned that the same procedure can be followed when cutting a round cast-iron rain-water pipe. A hacksaw can be used to saw through, but it is a laborious process compared with the method just described.

Fixing the Gutter in Position.

Red lead is used for the joints in high-class work, but glazier's putty can be substituted if desired. Paint the back of the gutter before fixing, and if there are no supporting brackets screw two stout twist gimlets into the facia board for temporary support. Paint the insides of the sockets and lay in a thin bed of the putty. Now put the length in place and clear the hole for the bolt with a wire nail or other form of "feeler." Then slip in the bolt, hold the nut with pliers, and carefully and slowly tighten up, using a screw-driver in the slot inside. The reason for working slowly is to give time for the surplus putty to squeeze out.

Next screw in the three back wood screws, placing a washer and a little putty behind the heads. Then putty over and paint the back.

Inspect the Remainder of the Gutter.

It is a good idea to take this opportunity to inspect the remainder of the gutter while the ladders are available. It will probably be found that in some cases the back holes are badly rusted round the screwheads. If such is the case, remove the screws and replace with new ones, using a larger washer behind.

Do not attempt to over-tighten. Remember that cast iron is brittle and that the sockets hold the back of the gutter about ¼ inch off the facia board.

Supporting Batten for the Back.

Should the back of the gutter be found in a bad state, nail or screw a supporting batten below the gutter

HOW TO REPAIR A ROOF GUTTER

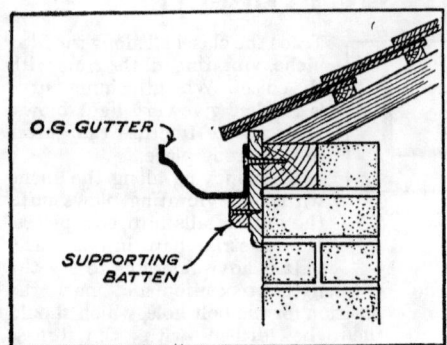

Fig. 4.—A Good Method of giving Extra Support to a Gutter the Back of which has become Weakened through Rusting.

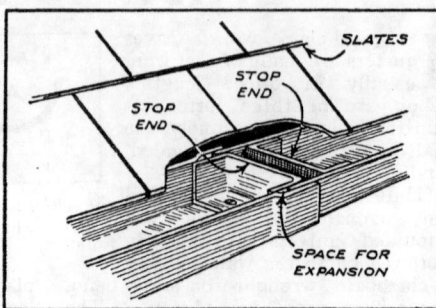

Fig. 5.—Reducing the Length of a Cast-iron Gutter.

The joint is broken and two stop ends placed as shown. The slates are only shown cut so that the stop ends can be clearly seen.

water dripping between, the piece of lead passing up the roof slope and being tucked up the eaves under the slates.

It will then be found that the space between the stop ends will allow for free movement of the gutter without imposing any strain on the joints.

NOTES ON ZINC GUTTERS

In the sulphurous atmosphere of manufacturing districts zinc gutters tend to become perforated and decompose.

A Temporary Repair.

A temporary repair can sometimes be effected by painting with a bituminous paint. This is made from a mixture of pitch, resin and tallow, the proportions being such that when cold it is still slightly pliable and elastic. The mixture is applied hot, and should only be applied when the repair is too extensive to be dealt with by soldering.

Fig. 6.—The Space between the two Stop Ends should be covered with a Piece of Sheet Lead.

Soldering a Small Crack.

It is always best to solder a small crack, and a fine solder composed of 1 part of lead and 1½ parts of tin by weight should be used. A perfectly clean metallic surface should first be obtained by scraping the surface with a shavehook or the end of a file. Then

Fig. 7.—How to solder a Crack across the Sole of a Lead Gutter.

(see Fig. 4), so as to relieve the weight off the screws and back of the gutter.

Painting Inside of Gutter.

It should be remembered that it is as important to paint the inside of a gutter as it is the outside. When the gutter has been cleaned and repaired, the inside should be given a good coat of smudge or stiff red lead paint.

What to do if Gutters drip at Sockets.

A leak at the socket of a gutter often causes a damp spot on the wall, which shows inside. Such leaks are due to the iron gutters being fixed in long stretches so that they are subject to the effects of expansion and contraction of the atmosphere. A 50-foot iron gutter at 40° F., heated by the sun to a uniform temperature of 80° F., will expand to about ⅛th of an inch longer. Although this is quite a small amount, it is sufficient to produce a see-saw movement that soon disturbs one or more of the joints.

The Remedy.

It will be obvious that if the length of the gutter between the sockets is reduced there is less risk of broken joints.

It is assumed that there is a joint about midway in the guttering at the highest point where the gutter falls to each end to the outlets. Remove the bolt from this joint, and if the joint is not already broken make it free of the jointing material.

Now drill two holes for fixing stop ends, as in Fig. 5, spacing the stop ends ⅜ to ½ inch apart and securing them with jointing putty and bolts. The stop ends should be of such a size that they fit inside the plain gutter. If the proper cast-iron type cannot be obtained, suitable substitutes can be made from hard wood, or made up from sheet lead or zinc.

Complete the job by covering the space between the stop ends with a piece of sheet lead to prevent rain-

apply a little killed spirit. Use a large well-tinned bit, hold the solder on the part to be treated and apply the bit. Gently trace a course along the crack, giving a constant feed of solder. If the solder does not unite at first, apply more flux.

Should the zinc be particularly dirty, it is best to use a weak solution of hydrochloric acid as a flux. Wash away all traces of the flux as soon as the soldering is finished, as it would tend to decompose the metal by its corrosive influence if left on.

Any difficulty experienced in heating the iron when work is in progress can be overcome by means of a blowlamp, two bits being employed, one heating up while the other is being used (see Fig. 8).

Cracks on a Vertical Surface.

If the crack is in an awkward position for soldering, such as on a vertical surface, it may be best to use one of the proprietary brands of cement, which can be spread over the defective part. These cements are usually made up from mixtures of tar, pitch and dry lime.

NOTES ON LEAD GUTTERS OR FLATS

A crack in a lead gutter requires rather different treatment.

Materials required.

The following materials will be needed :—

1 lb. stick of plumber's wiping solder composed of 1 part tin and 2 parts lead.

Petrol or paraffin blowlamp.

Wiping cloth, about 2½ inches wide, composed of well-greased fustian or moleskin folded to form 6 to 8 thicknesses. If fustian cannot be obtained, a piece of well-greased bed ticking or even thick, unglazed, brown paper will serve the purpose.

Preparing the Surface.

The first thing to do is to shave the surfaces of the lead perfectly clean, about ¾ inch on each side of the crack and the same distance beyond each end, biting right through the oxide. Tallow or mutton fat should be applied to prevent oxidation and also to act as a flux. The edges should be dressed down quite flat.

Now rub the surface all round beyond the shaved area with a cut raw potato, the acid from which prevents the solder sticking where it is not wanted.

Applying the Solder.

Next take the blowlamp, adjusted to a fairly soft flame, and gently heat the lead, applying at the same time the end of the stick of solder. Allow the flame to heat the solder and lead at the same time. As soon as the solder begins to melt rub it about until the lead surface is perfectly

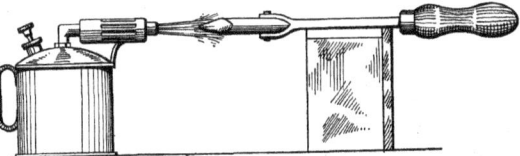

Fig. 8—Showing Method of Heating Soldering Iron with a Blow-lamp.

tinned. Do not forget to keep the flame moving about so as not to melt the lead.

As soon as it is seen that the tinning has been carried out satisfactorily, add enough solder to make a low mound all along the crack. This is done by heating the solder (starting at one end) until it is the consistency of soft butter, and then wiping it smooth with the wiping cloth, making strokes of 2 to 3 inches at a time until the end is reached. Arch the cloth slightly so that about ¼ inch thickness of solder

is left in the middle, taking care to bite down at the edges so that no solder is left projecting beyond the cleaned surface of the prepared seam.

When a repair is carried out by this method, the solder is, of course, left standing up above the surface of the lead, and if the crack extended across or nearly across the sole of the gutter, as in Fig. 7, this would obstruct the waterway and cause water to be trapped above the repair.

To deal with such a crack, the edges of the lead should be levered up until the woodwork below is exposed. Then cut a groove in the woodwork with a sharp chisel and dress the lead down into this sinking. Then proceed as already described, but instead of wiping a low mound of solder the surface should be wiped flush with the sole of the gutter, as shown in Fig. 7.

PRACTICAL NOTES ON RIVETING

RIVETING is a quick and easy method of securing two pieces of metal together, or repairing breaks in pieces of metal, etc. It has many advantages over soldering and brazing, and can be used for securing together parts that are likely to be subjected to heat, such as the handle and body of a saucepan or kettle.

Tools required.

Very few tools are required, the only essentials being a ball-pane hammer, a pair of end nippers or a hack-saw, and suitable drills. It is also a convenience to have a drill plate, which is a piece of steel containing a graduated series of holes made by either Morse drills or those of the inch fraction sizes. A supply of small copper rivets can be obtained from any tool shop.

A Simple Riveting Repair.

Riveting is not necessarily confined to the repair of metal objects. A very simple repair that can be carried out is that of mending a broken leather strap, and as this is one of the easiest repairs with riveting we will describe it first.

We will assume that a leather strap has broken away from the " D " to which it is fixed. The first thing to do is to cut off the broken part of the strap and then chamfer the end with a sharp knife. Pass this end through the " D " and fold it back on to the main body of the strap so that the

" D " is held in its correct position. Next make two holes through the leather for the rivets.

Use Washers when riveting Leather.

Now pass one of the rivets up through the hole and place a small, tightly fitting brass washer over its head. Then nip off the protruding end of the rivet so that it protrudes only about $\frac{1}{16}$th of an inch above the washer. Place the strap on some hard surface and with the rounded end of the hammer gently tap the end of the rivet. This will cause it to spread out over the washer. Finally trim up with a file if necessary.

A Metal Riveting Job.

We will assume that one of the metal legs of a iron tripod has been broken about 3 inches from the end. The best method of repairing it is to rivet on a metal plate.

First obtain a plate of mild steel of the same width and thickness as the leg, and about 2 inches in length. Mark on this a line across its middle.

Use Several Small Rivets.

As it is best to use several smallish rivets in preference to one or two large ones in a job of this nature, the next step is to make on the broken end of the leg five centre-punch marks, placing one mark in the centre and the other four at what would be the corners of a square. Suitable rivets are brass nails, just under ¾ inch in

length. Try them in the drill plate to ascertain the correct size of drill to use for the holes. It is important that the holes should be made as good a fit as possible for the rivets.

First drill the Middle Hole.

Now place the broken end on the plate, with its edge resting on the centre line marked on the plate, and drill the middle hole. When this has been done, insert one of the rivets upwards from below.

Cut off the protruding end so that only about $\frac{1}{32}$ of an inch is left standing up and then clench this over with the ball-pane hammer, tapping until the two pieces are so firmly joined together that considerable force would be necessary to produce any movement in them.

Now drill Four Remaining Holes.

Having satisfactorily finished the first rivet, drill the four remaining holes, insert the rivets and clench. You now have the broken piece of leg firmly attached to the plate.

The next operation is to make five similar punch marks in the main part of the leg and lay it on the plate so that it is tight up against the other broken piece. Then drill the middle hole and hammer the first rivet home, before drilling the remaining holes.

When all the rivets have been finished, turn the work over and file the heads of the brass nails almost flat. Then give each of them a few taps with the round end of the hammer.

A Summer-house Pavilion

Most people are familiar with the usual designs of summer-house, garden sheds and sports pavilions, and they can appreciate the uses and advantages of each of these erections. In order to obtain the advantages of all of these items combined with economy of construction the summer-house pavilion shown in the accompanying photographs was designed.

Fig. 1.—The Completed Summer-house Pavilion.
This photograph shows clearly the general construction of the building.

Although intended, primarily, as a small pavilion for use alongside a lawn-tennis court, it has served equally well as a summer-house, shelter and—in the winter season—as a store for garden furniture, *e.g.*, chairs, seats tables and stools.

It is provided with a 4-foot verandah under which chairs may be placed as a protection to their occupants against the hot rays of the sun, or, in bad weather, against the rain.

Two wide doors are provided, leading from the summer-house portion to the verandah; these can be opened right out so as to fold back flat against the front wall of the building, thus throwing the back compartment into communication with the verandah.

Inside, cupboards and lockers are provided for the use of the occupants, *e.g.*, tennis players. Garden tools are also stored in suitable cupboards in the corners of the inside room. The size of the latter (18 × 7 feet) is sufficient to enable a table-tennis outfit to be used without restriction; this has proved a useful asset in wet weather.

Finally, owing to its convenient dimensions, the building can be used during the summer months as an additional sleeping room, for it is thoroughly dry and well ventilated; moreover, it can easily be lined with matching, Insul-board, Essex-board or any other suitable composite wall-board.

There is a 3 × 2 feet window at each end, one of the lights in each case being made to open, on the lines of a casement window.

Dimensions of the Building.

The principal dimensions of the construction shown in the photographs and drawings are as follows, namely: length (overall) 18 feet, breadth (overall) 11 feet, and height (to ridge) 8 feet 10 inches.

The width of the verandah is 4 feet and of the room beyond, 7 feet.

The height to the eaves is 6 feet. The height of the front side, under the verandah, is 8 feet 1 inch.

The two doors each measure 2 feet 9 inches × 6 feet, whilst each window is 3 × 2 feet. The end shields for the verandah measure 4 feet wide × 2 feet 10 inches high. The other important dimensions are shown on the drawings.

Materials of Construction.

For the *internal framework*, 3 × 2-inch deal posts are used—700 feet will cover all requirements.

The four *verandah pillars* are of 4 × 3-inch deal or pine, each 6 feet long.

The *ridge board* measures 18 feet × 5 inches × 1 inch, and is of deal.

The *walling* consists of rebated weather board, $\frac{7}{8}$ inch thick. The quantity required is 400 square feet (four squares).

The *roofing* is of $\frac{3}{4}$ × 5-inch match-board, tongued and grooved—240 square feet of this will be required.

For the *flooring*, 6 × 1-inch tongued and grooved deal is used; 200 square feet will be required.

The *floor joists* are of 4 × 2-inch deal; 14 pieces, each 11 feet long.

The *bressemers* are of 7 × 3-inch deal; 4 pieces, each 18 feet long.

The *doors* are made of $\frac{7}{8}$ × 6-inch tongued and grooved deal, the total area required being 33 square feet. In addition, three pieces of 6 × 1-inch deal, each measuring 2 feet 9 inches in length, are needed.

For *the windows*, 3 × 2 feet frames, with one fixed and one moving light.

The *roof covering* consists of black ruberoid, two rolls being required.

Sundries include four cross

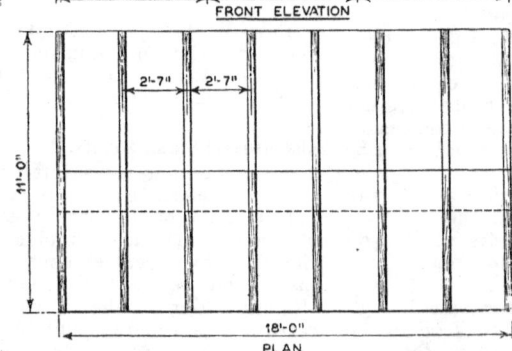

Fig. 2.—A Close-up View, showing Arrangement of Verandah, Pillars and Door.
Note how a seat can be fitted into the corner if desired.

Fig. 3.—Plan and Elevations, showing Principal Dimensions.

A SUMMER-HOUSE PAVILION

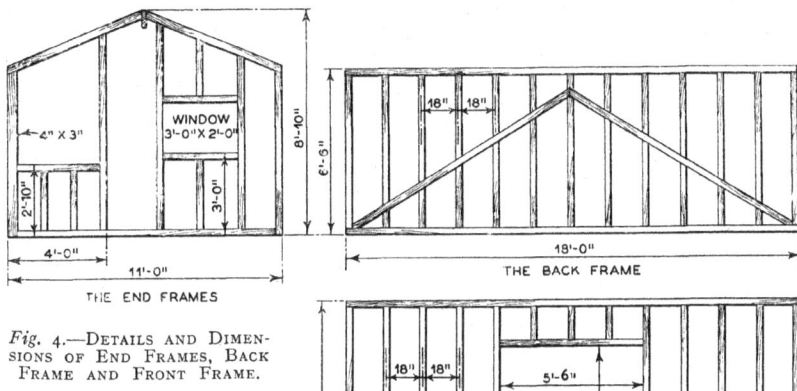

Fig. 4.—Details and Dimensions of End Frames, Back Frame and Front Frame.

garnet hinges (18 inches), about two dozen ½-inch coach bolts, nuts and washers, 3 lbs. clout nails, 7 lbs. 1½-inch French or wire nails, 7 lbs. flooring nails (2-inch), 7 lbs. 4-inch wire nails, four door bolts, lock and key.

For finishing the building, externally, about 2 gallons of creosote are required.

Finally, about five dozen bricks are required for the piers and 36 feet of guttering (if two slopes of the roof are to be drained), and the usual 2-inch sheet-metal down-pipes and angles.

Constructing the Frames.

The procedure adopted in constructing the building in question was, first, to make each of the frames separately, and then to erect these on the site, bolting the separate sections together when they were held in position by means of temporary shores, or stays.

For this purpose it is necessary to make the following separate sections, namely (1) the back frame, (2) the front frame, (3) the two end frames (these are identical in dimensions and construction), and (4) the two similar roof sections.

The Back Frame.

The back frame is made of 3 × 2-inch deal arranged as shown in Fig. 4. The outside frame members are made with half-lap joints at the corners, screwed and nailed together. The central vertical member is then placed in position and nailed through the outside timbers. After this the other verticals are placed in position at 18-inch intervals and are secured by means of nails at their ends, driven right through the two longer sides of the outside frame.

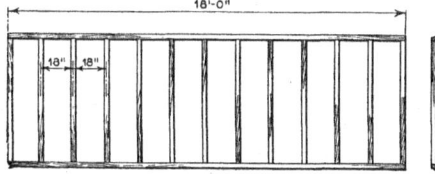

Fig. 5.—The Roof Frames (without Roof Boards).

A few of the weatherboards are then used temporarily to hold the frame in position whilst the diagonals are fitted. The latter are cut and laid on top of the verticals in their correct positions. Pencil lines are then drawn along their edges across the verticals. The diagonals are then removed and the verticals are sawn right through along these pencil lines.

Afterwards the diagonals are let into the spaces left by the sawing process in the verticals; the latter are secured by wire nails to the diagonals.

The weatherboards can then be permanently fitted and nailed down to this frame, to complete the side. The top weatherboard can afterwards be chamfered off to suit the roof slope.

The End Frames.

The outside frame is first made, the corners being half-lap joints screwed and nailed together. A temporary ridge board piece should be fitted to ensure that the slot is of the correct width and shape. Before removing this, nail a piece of 3 × 2-inch timber across the two sloping (roof) members of the frame in order to secure them in their correct position; this piece can be left on until after the ends have been erected ready for the ridge board and roof members (Fig. 4).

The verticals, window frame and verandah screen members can now be fitted in position, using 3 × 2-inch timber for everything except the front pillar (for verandah). This should be of 4 × 3-inch deal or pine and so arranged as to give a flush face on the outside, i.e., where the weatherboard is to be fastened.

The Front Frame.

There should be little difficulty in making this simple piece of framework. The outer frame is made first, and then the verticals fitted in a similar manner to those of the back frame. As will be seen from Fig. 4, a space is left for the two doors; these require an opening 5 feet 6 inches wide by 6 feet high. In order to prevent any sidewise or diagonal movement of the frame, temporary diagonal bracing members of 3 × 2-inch timber can be nailed across at two places, or the final weatherboards can be nailed in position. The same remarks apply also to the end and back frames.

The Temporary Brace Method.

The temporary brace method just mentioned is better where assistance for erecting the building is limited, for then one has only the weights of the framework to deal with, whereas if the weatherboards are in position the sections are heavy and require two or three persons to handle them.

The Roof Sections.

In this case, however, it is necessary to make the complete roof sections on the ground, and to erect them as finished members, rather than to attempt making frames, raising the latter in position and afterwards nailing the roof boarding on. The construction of the roof sections is a straightforward matter, as will be seen from Fig. 5. It should be noted, however, that the edges of the parallel timbers must be chamfered and the roofing boards given a slight overlap (½ to 1 inch) in order to accommodate the ridge board, as shown in the detail sketch given in Fig. 7.

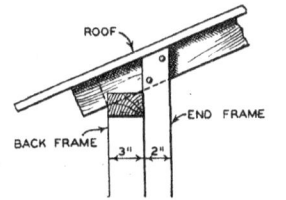

Fig. 6.—The Roof Frame and Side Joint.

Fig. 7.—Roof Frame and Ridge Board Joint.

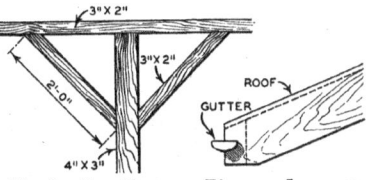

Fig. 8.—The Front Pillars and Diagonals.   *Fig. 9.—Showing Method of Fixing Gutter.*

The lower ends of the parallel members are notched, by means of two sawcuts, as shown in Fig. 6, to enable them to fit over the longitudinals of the back and front frames; this serves to locate the roof frame in its correct position.

It is advisable to set out the exact shape of the end-section on the ground, or workshop floor, in order to get the correct roof slope. The parallel members can then be marked off from this "template" with the assurance that they will be accurately to shape.

Incidentally, the parallel members of the roof sections should be spaced at 18 inches apart.

Erecting the Sections.

Before the sides, ends and roof sections can be erected it will be necessary to prepare the site for their reception.

The ground should first be roughly levelled, using a long parallel board or straight-edge and spirit-level. If a few pegs are driven into the ground these can be used to level the side, the straight-edge being placed on top of pairs of pegs and the latter driven in until the level shows them to be at the same horizontal height.

It is best to arrange for the building to rest on concrete or brick foundations, so that the floor is raised about 9 inches to 1 foot above the ground. Suitable arrangements can then be made for ventilating the support timbers and flooring, so that their lives will be practically indefinite.

Altogether eight piers were used for the building in question, each pier consisting of eight bricks arranged in two layers of four bricks. The lower bricks should be laid on top of a block of concrete, about 8 to 12 inches thick; alternatively, well-rammed earth foundations will do.

Having levelled the tops of the eight brick piers, using a long straight-edge and spirit-level for this purpose and building up the tops of any piers that are "low" with cement or concrete, the longitudinal floor beams, known in the building trade as "bressemers," should be laid. In order to prevent ground moisture from rotting these a layer of slate or damp-course bituminous strip should be placed on top of each pier before placing the bressemers in position.

The Floor Joists.

The floor joists can now be fitted in position over the bressemers. The joists should be arranged at intervals

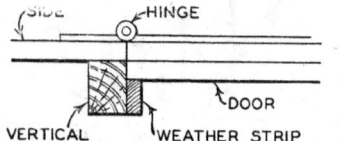

Fig. 11.—The Door Hinge Arrangement.

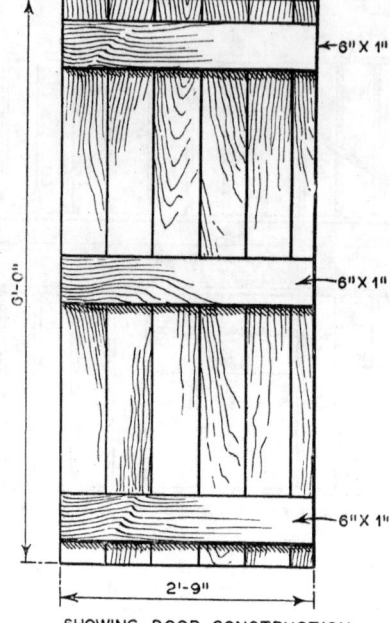

Fig. 10.—Details and Dimensions of Door Construction.

of 15 to 16 inches apart and with their longer (4-inch) sides vertical. Although it is not absolutely necessary to secure these joists to the bressemers, it is advisable to do so in order to prevent their shifting during the erection of the side sections. The joists should be positioned by means of 3-inch nails driven diagonally through their end sections into the bressemers. We are now in a position to erect the sides of the building.

Erecting the Side Sections.

Each of the two end frames should now be lifted into position on the floor joists and temporarily secured by means of braces nailed to the sides of the frames. By means of a builder's plumb line set these frames approximately vertical and at about 18 feet apart.

Next, after drilling ½-inch clearance holes at the tops and bottoms of the end verticals, lift the front frame (Fig. 4) into position, and put the shanks of the coach bolts through the holes mentioned, taking care to ensure that the rounded heads are *outside*, so that the nuts are tightened up inside, after placing the washers over the screw threads.

The front and the two end frames can now be bolted up. Next secure the bottom frame member of the front section to the floor joists, using the 4-inch nails for this purpose. Do not nail down the two end frames, as it will be necessary to adjust these when fitting the back frame in position. This latter is the next operation, and no difficulty should be experienced.

The frame should be adjusted in position so as to be correct in relation to the end frames, and then, after drilling holes at the tops and bottoms for the coach bolts, these sections should be bolted together.

The joist-resting frame members of the end and back sections can now be nailed down to the floor joists and we are then ready for the roof.

Fixing the Roof.

Before erecting the roof it is advisable to fit temporary braces to each of the four sides; usually three braces of 3 × 2-inch timber will be sufficient for each side. This ensures that the four sides will remain rigid whilst the roof sections are lifted on to them.

It is also advisable to erect the two intermediate verandah pillars and to locate these, temporarily, in their correct positions by means of 3 × 2-inch timber nailed right across from the two outside pillars.

The roof will require the aid of at least two men to lift and to adjust it into position, after having fixed the ridge board between the two end frames. The notched parallel members (Fig. 6) enable the roof sections to be located and fixed without any difficulty; moreover, these notches prevent the roof sections from slipping down before they are secured to the end frames and ridge board. With the aid of a comparatively few nails the roof can be permanently fixed to the end and side sections, although coach bolts may be employed for this purpose if desired.

Fixing the Weatherboards.

Assuming that the frames have not been covered before they were erected, the weatherboarding can now be placed in position for the walls. The tongued and grooved boards are particularly convenient to fix, as they register with one another and are thus accurately located.

When fixing these boards *commence from the bottom* of the frames and work upwards, securing them to the frame timbers by means of 2-inch galvanised or copper nails. The boards should be sawn off and fitted into position so as

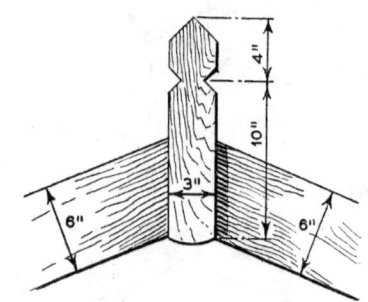

Fig. 12.—Details of End Ornaments at the Corner of the Roof.

to leave spaces for the windows, doors and the open ends of the verandah.

Finishing the Roof.

Now that the timber work of the sides and roof is finished it is best to render the building weatherproof by fixing the roofing felt in position. The ruberoid is unrolled and cut into strips of about 13 feet. Each strip, with a little to spare, will then be long enough to go right over the roof from one eave over the ridge and down to the other eave. It is secured at each eave by means of flat-headed galvanised roofing nails (sold for this purpose). Each strip of ruberoid must overlap the next by about an inch and the joint covered by means of a wooden batten of $2 \times \frac{1}{2}$-inch section.

It is advisable to creosote the outside of the roofing boards before the roofing felt is secured; the battens that secure the felt to the roof should also be creosoted beforehand.

The Flooring.

The next operation is that of laying the floor boards. This, again, is a straightforward business if one commences at one side, and proceeds to nail down each board to the joists. The next board is forced tightly against the last one fitted so that the tongue of the former is firmly fitted into the groove of the latter. If, however, a flooring cramp can be used to force the boards more tightly together, so much the better. When nailing the floor boards down it is only necessary to use two or three nails for each joist.

Completing the Details.

It is now only necessary to make and fit the two doors and the two windows, when the major part of the work will have been accomplished. Details of the construction of the doors are given in Fig. 10. The windows can be made, or sometimes a pair can be purchased from the local builder for a low figure.

The doors should be hung so that they swing clear of the ground; if a piece of $\frac{1}{8}$-inch plywood or cardboard be placed under the door whilst its hinge is being screwed into the door frame, this will give the proper clearance. Fig. 11 shows how the door and its hinge are arranged so as to fold flush with the side. The only other items remaining are the front pillar diagonals (Fig. 8), that are fitted purely for appearance purposes, the end ornaments at the corners of the roof (Fig. 12), the 6-inch weatherboards at the ends of the sloping roof members and the guttering for taking away the water collected from the roof. For this purpose the cheaper sheet-metal guttering can be used. It is located by the end boards (Fig. 9) and about three intermediate brackets; a suitable slope to one end must be arranged in order to lead the water away.

In connection with the window frames it is advisable to have a weatherboard or roofing felt strip protection at the top of the frame to prevent rain from entering the joint.

Finishing the Exterior.

All that now remains to do is to finish the exterior timber with a suitable weather protection coating. In the case of the building shown in the photographs, this was given a single coat of a mixture consisting of equal parts of coal-tar oil and creosote. This gives a brownish-black finish of great weather-resisting quality. It is cheap to purchase and can readily be applied with a distemper brush. The flooring of the verandah was given a second coat of this preparation in view of the additional wear and exposure of this portion.

The window frames were finished with two priming coats of paint, followed by a coat of a good white-lead paint.

TINTING PAINT

Although paints can be obtained ready for use in a large number of colours no manufacturer can possibly cover all possible shades, which number thousands.

Sometimes a special shade is required to match already painted work adjacent to that requiring to be done. In such cases the paint will need to be specially mixed, or ready mixed white may be tinted to the desired colour.

On pages 434 and 807 are lists of the tinting colours required in the production of a number of coloured paints, but in the case of a tint for matching purposes it is impossible to give an exact formula, if only because our English names for colours differ widely in their meaning when applied to the products of different makers.

How to match a "Putty" Colour.

If, to take one example, we are trying to match a colour of the type often called "putty," the best way to proceed is either to purchase some ready-mixed white gloss paint or mix some according to formula No. 3 on page 434, and then stain it at the scene of operations.

A small amount of golden ochre in oil, say $\frac{1}{2}$ lb., a smaller quantity of raw umber, say $\frac{1}{4}$ lb., and perhaps an ounce of oil green or oil red (not both) will be required.

Mixing.

A small quantity of the white should be placed on a small mixing board or a piece of glass. To this must be added a mere trace, first of the ochre and then even less of the umber, and the three ingredients should be well ground together on the board. The shade required may be procurable with the two colours mentioned. Or it may be too warm (which means too inclined toward red), in which case a mere suspicion of added green will cool it. Or it may be too cool in tone, which indicates that it requires a touch of red to warm it.

This small experimental mixing is for the sole purpose of finding what additions of stainers are required to produce the desired shade.

That ascertained, it is a simple matter to make the larger mixing without waste of time and material.

In the case of a colour such as "putty," the finishing gloss coat can be applied over either a flat white undercoat or a flat paint tinted to approximately the same shade as the finishing coat.

RECONDITIONING OIL LAMP BURNERS

Paraffin oil lamp burners invariably become carbonised after being in use for any length of time. This deposit is firmly attached to the metal of the burner around the edges adjacent to the flame; it is usually rather difficult to remove. If allowed to remain, this deposit may interfere with the free movement of the wick, so that it should, periodically, be removed. Although this can be accomplished by scraping with a knife or similar device, this is not entirely satisfactory, for one is apt to scrape away the metal of the burner. A better method is to make a solution of common washing soda in the proportion of 1 part of soda to 5 parts of water. Place the dirty burner in this solution and bring the latter to the boiling point. After about ten minutes the burner can be removed, when it will be found to be perfectly clean and of new appearance.

A Chair Trouser Press

A trouser press, although a necessity, often seems to be in the way. This new design obviates this and provides a permanent home for it out of sight behind the bedroom chair. The back is hinged, but is prevented from going too far backwards by means of a stop underneath the legs, and is held firm by a ball catch. A sharp forward pull frees the clip, permitting the back to fall on to the seat when the press, which is carried on the rear of the chair, is in a horizontal position ready for use.

On releasing the two bars and the pressure of the four springs, the flaps, which are held by special hinges, can be opened until they rest against the ends of the stirrups. To use the press, fold the trousers and place in position, drop the flaps, insert the bars one at a time into the holes of the stirrups, press down the free ends and slip them into the slots provided. The back of the chair can then be lifted and sprung into position, when the press is out of sight behind the chair.

Material required.

3′ × $1\frac{3}{8}$″ × $1\frac{3}{8}$″ oak quartering.
3′ × $1\frac{3}{8}$″ × 3″ oak batten.
12′ × 2″ × $\frac{7}{8}$″ ,, ,,
2′ × 3″ × $\frac{7}{8}$″ ,, ,,
3′ × $1\frac{1}{4}$″ × $\frac{7}{8}$″ ,, ,,
2′ 6″ × $1\frac{1}{8}$″ × $\frac{7}{8}$″ ,, ,,
2′ 4″ × 1′ 2″ × $\frac{3}{8}$″ multi-ply (oak faced).
1′ 9″ × 1′ 3″ × $\frac{1}{16}$″ veneer ply (oak faced).
4′ 6″ × 7″ × $\frac{1}{2}$″ oak board.
1′ × $\frac{5}{8}$″ oak dowelling.
3′ × $\frac{5}{8}$″ birch rod.
Brass strip 3′ 2″ × 1″ × $\frac{1}{8}$″.
,, sheet 4″ × $2\frac{1}{2}$″ × $\frac{1}{16}$″.
Brass sheet 8″ × $2\frac{1}{2}$″ × $\frac{1}{8}$″.
,, ,, 8″ × $2\frac{1}{2}$″, gauge 18.
,, wire 3′ × $\frac{1}{8}$″ thick.
Webbing 2″ wide, 4 yards.
Canvas 30″ wide, 1 yard.
Rexine or leather 1′ 6″ × 1′ 6″.
Fibre stuffing, 2 lbs.
Brass round-headed nails and $\frac{1}{2}$″ tin tacks.
3′ × 1″ gramophone spring.
3′ × $\frac{3}{8}$″ silver steel rod.

Making the Chair.

The seat is just a frame mortised together as in Fig. 3. X in Fig. 4 shows the shape and size of a front leg, while Z portrays a back one, which is cut with a bow saw to the curve shown, from a piece of timber 3 × $1\frac{3}{8}$ inches. W in the same figure shows the stop bar, and S gives details of the side rails, the holes in which go only half-way through.

The four legs are fixed to the seat frame with dowel pins, as can be seen in Fig. 3; the side rails A and B fit into mortises in the legs, while the two round tie pieces which carry the back stop C slip into holes bored into the pieces A and B. All the joints are glued together, while the bar C is secured in position with two pins driven through into the round rails. Before finally fixing the stop bar C, see that the ball catch in end of the press registers with the hole D.

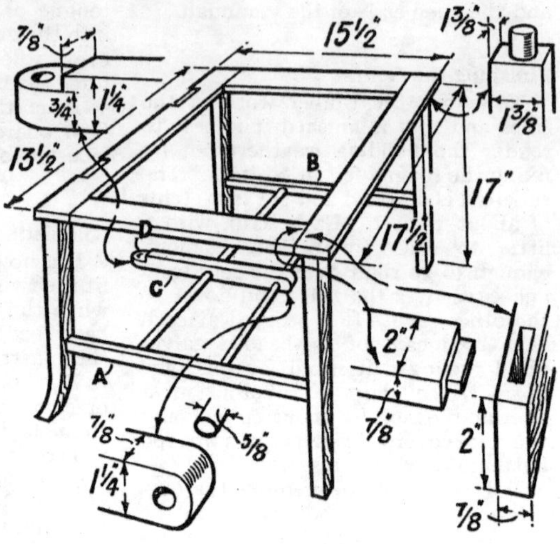

Fig. 3.—Details and Dimensions of Chair Framework.

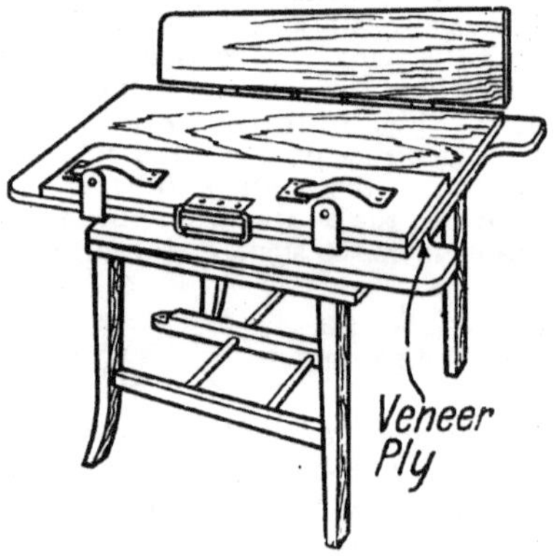

Fig. 2.—View showing Back down and Press partly open.

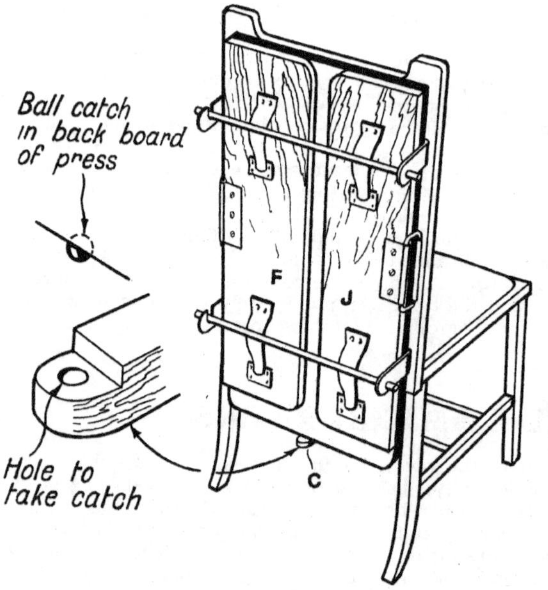

Fig. 1.—Back View of Chair Trouser Press, showing the Press in Position.

The Chair Back.

This is made up of a top and bottom rail (E and F) mortised into the two side members, and two centre slats are fitted into the pieces E and F; dowel pegs can be used if desired. The whole of this framing is covered on the rear side with a sheet of $\frac{1}{16}$ inch veneer oak-faced ply (see Fig. 5); this hides the stirrups, which are let into the main board of the press, and ornaments the front of the chair.

Two hinges are let into the bottom rail of the back, as shown in Fig. 6; these are later screwed to the rear member of the seat frame.

The Press.

Fig. 7 shows the boards which make the press; the main board is $\frac{3}{8}$-inch multi-ply, which is nearly as wide as the chair back at the upper end and tapers off towards the bottom. The two flaps H and J are made from well-seasoned $\frac{1}{2}$-inch oak board. Note the recesses cut out to take the stirrups and hinges.

Holes are bored in the back ply-board to admit the screws which secure it to the back of the chair. These must be well countersunk so that the heads are absolutely level with the surface of the board. Note that the flaps are fixed to the main board with special hinges.

Making the Hinges.

The hinges are shown in Fig. 6. They accommodate themselves to the thickness of the article in the press. The flap K is made of sheet brass, while the V-shaped piece L is soldered in to take the wire link M. The width across the link is such that when the press is empty and the flaps are closed, then the hinge leans forward, but when trousers are placed in the press the link is pulled up at right-angles to

A CHAIR TROUSER PRESS

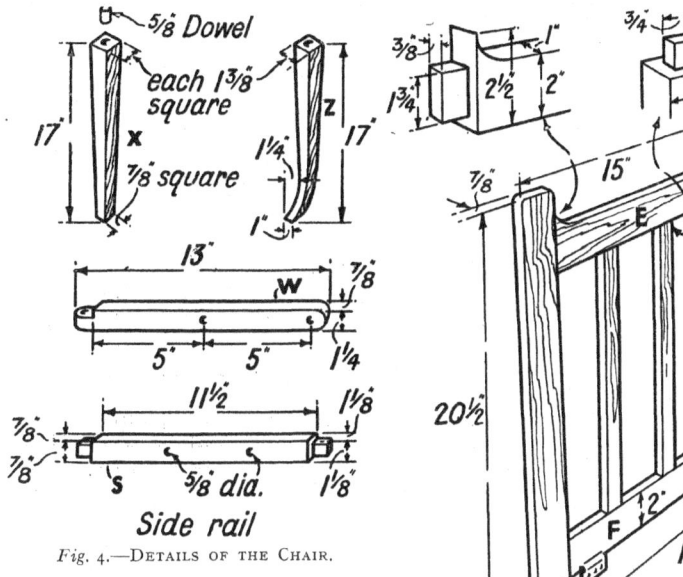

Fig. 4.—DETAILS OF THE CHAIR.

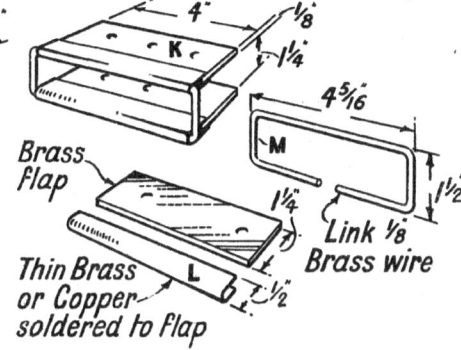

Fig. 5.—DETAILS OF BACK OF CHAIR.

Fig. 6.—DETAILS OF HINGE ASSEMBLY.

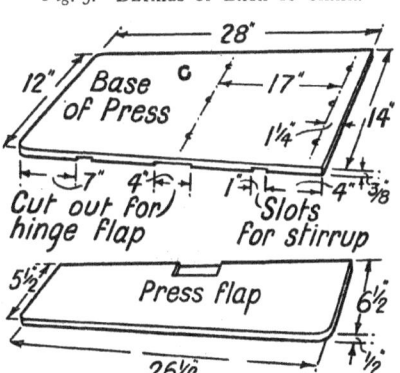

Fig. 7.—THE BOARDS WHICH MAKE THE PRESS.

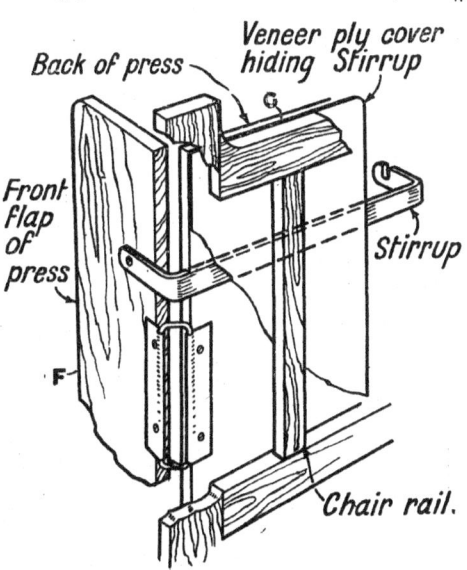

Fig. 8.—SECTIONAL VIEW AS SEEN FROM THE FRONT.

the base board. This angular movement of the link allows articles of varying thickness to be efficiently pressed.

It should be noted that the wire link M must be placed in position within the U piece L before the latter is soldered to the hinge flap K.

The Stirrups.

Each stirrup is bent up to shape, as shown in Fig. 9, out of $\frac{1}{8}$-inch brass strip; the hole N should freely take the end of the press bar, while the slot P can easily be filed out to accommodate the other end of the rod. Three holes are drilled in the stirrup to fasten it to the baseboard of the press. It should be noted that the lower stirrup is 1 inch shorter than the upper one; the sizes given in Fig. 9 are those of the upper one.

A groove top and bottom, see Fig. 7, is cut $\frac{1}{8}$ inch deep across the back of the baseboard of the press to take the stirrup; this will not be visible when the chair is viewed from the front, as the sheet of $\frac{1}{16}$-inch veneer ply covers the back of the chair.

The press bar is made from a length of $\frac{3}{8}$-inch silver steel.

How to make the Springs.

Four springs as shown in Fig. 9 are needed to screw on in pairs to the flaps. They can be made from pieces of old gramophone spring. Snap off four pieces 8 inches long by bending it over sharply while held in a vice. Soften it by heating to a cherry red and then allow to cool slowly; it can then be bent to shape on an anvil or round an iron rod. The holes which secure the spring at one end must be drilled while the metal is soft. The free end moves forward when compressed, and this point rubs on a small brass or copper plate.

Tempering the Springs.

After bending to shape, the springs must be hardened again and re-tempered. Heat again to red heat and drop into cold water; it will now be "glass" hard and much too brittle to use. To soften or "draw" the temper slightly, hold the spring in a pair of tongs over a bunsen gas flame and carefully note the change in colour in the steel as it warms up; first it turns to a pale straw colour, then deepens to yellow and rapidly becomes blue. Immediately the bluish tinge appears plunge the spring into cold water, when the temper should be correct. If too soft, that is if it does not regain its original shape when compressed, reharden and "draw" the temper again by repeating the above process.

Upholstering the Seat.

Fig. 10 shows how the seat is webbed. Note the block of wood which is pressed downwards to stretch the webbing tight before it is tacked down.

The web is then covered with a double layer of canvas, the upper piece being left a little slack to form a bag, and one side left open so that the stuffing of hair or fibre can be packed in. Push the filling in a piece at a time, poking it to the remotest corner with a length of cane. When the packing is pushed home evenly, tack down the open side of the bag. A final covering of leather or fabric is stretched on over the canvas and nailed down with ornamental brass-headed nails; if preferred, leather-covered heads can be used. Care should be taken to see that the seat does not rise more than an inch above the framing of the seat, or the press will not fold down into a horizontal position.

Fuming the Wood.

A very delightful finish can be obtained by fuming. Before upholstering or putting on the fittings

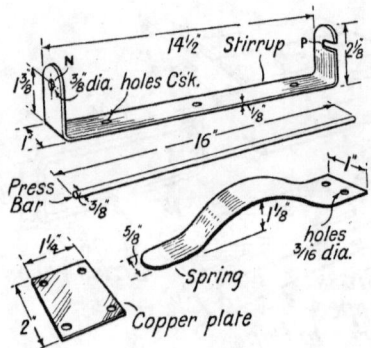

Fig. 9.—Details of Stirrup and Spring.

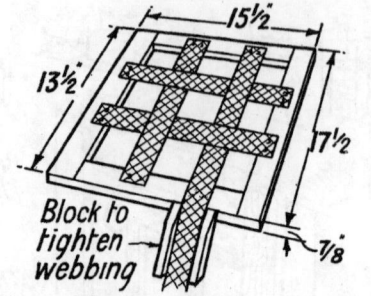

Fig. 10.—How to arrange the Webbing for the Seat.

Fig. 11.—Details of the Upholstery.

place the woodwork in a cellar and place a saucer of *strong* ammonium hydrate on the floor. Shut the door and paste paper over the cracks and leave the chemical to evaporate for eight to ten hours. On opening the door again a remarkable change will have taken place; the wood will have artificially "aged" and turned a mellow brown, a perfect replica of old oak.

The grain should then be filled by rubbing in a coating of wet plaster of paris, and finish with a rubber of french polish.

Finishing the Fittings.

Some readers may choose to have the stirrups, bars and springs electroplated at a commercial house. A very pleasing copper finish can be obtained at home. Make a saturated solution of copper sulphate, and well clean the metal parts, finally washing in methylated spirits to remove all grease. Fasten each piece to a fine copper wire, which is attached to the negative side of two Leclanché cells connected in series, and immerse in the copper sulphate. From the positive side of the battery run a wire to a small piece of copper sheet, say 3 × 4 inches, also dipped in the bath, but not touching the fittings. Let the current flow for three-quarters of an hour, when a good deposit of copper will be found on the metal fittings.

Buff them up with a chamois leather and rouge powder, warm them over the gas and finally brush on a coating of lacquer, when a pleasing copper finish will result.

CARE OF WOODEN BARRELS

WOODEN barrels and tubs, such as those used for water-butts, require a certain amount of attention if they are to be kept in good condition and also water tight.

Never leave a Water-butt empty.

In the first place a water-butt should never be left empty, or nearly so, in dry weather, as the wood then shrinks, and may actually crack in between the staves. If a wooden barrel has to be left empty for an appreciable period outdoors in dry weather, it should be placed in a shady position, *i.e.*, under trees or in a sheltered spot facing north. Further, it should be covered with sacking; it is an advantage to keep the latter damp.

Curing a Leaky Water-butt.

A leaky water-butt can often be cured by filling to the top with water, and after leaving for a day or so to enable the wood to become thoroughly moistened, the iron bands should be knocked down, using a stout strip of flat section for this purpose. Do not hammer the rings direct, or you may damage the wood.

The Bung-hole.

The bung-hole is frequently a source of constant leakage owing to the imperfect fit of the bung. The latter should be removed and, after placing a piece of wet canvas over it, driven into position again. A strip of tin screwed across the bung will keep it securely in position. This is a good plan, since bungs have a habit of coming out under the pressure of the water above.

Another Method of curing Leaks.

Leakages in wooden barrels that cannot be cured by driving the iron bands along, *can effectively be stopped* with a mixture of casein glue, powdered slaked lime and plaster, made into a paste with white of egg. The edges of the crack should be rubbed over with white of egg before applying this preparation. The latter, when it sets, becomes stone-hard.

Water-butts should have Lids.

See that your water-butt is fitted with a lid. This not only prevents evaporation, but also keeps out the water larvæ of insects, such as gnats, mosquitoes and similar creatures. The lid can be made of deal, with a few registering blocks to keep it in place. It should have a suitable size of hole for the drain-pipe that is used for conveying the rain-water.

It is a good plan, also, to stand the butt upon a footing made of bricks, thus keeping the base of the butt above the ground.

AN INDELIBLE INK FOR GLASS

IT is well known that glass is a difficult substance upon which to write; in addition, there are few inks that will remain upon glass surfaces for any appreciable length of time.

One satisfactory ink, however, is made by mixing one part, by volume, of liquid Indian ink (as used by draughtsmen) with two parts of sodium silicate (water-glass). This mixture must be kept in an air-tight bottle. The glass surface that is to be written upon should be thoroughly cleaned with hot soda water and then with hot water, afterwards drying it and polishing with a glass-cloth. Although the ink dries hard, it can, if desired at any time, be removed by scraping with a knife.

A Garden Swing

It seems hardly necessary to say that strength is an essential feature of a swing. It is not merely that it has to withstand severe strains and all kinds of weather, but that any weakness is actually dangerous. The accompanying diagram gives particulars of a reliable swing calculated to give good service and to be thoroughly safe.

From the sketch of the completed structure it will be seen that a heavy strut arrangement is sunk into the ground to give stability. This is really essential, because the movement of the swing itself tends to pull the posts back and forth, and, unless they are firmly established, they are liable to become loose in the earth, with unfortunate consequences.

The Posts.

First prepare the posts from 6 inch by 3 inch deal. This can be obtained from a timber yard ready cut to size. Cut it off to length and mark out on it the three joints. A sort of slot has to be cut at the top to take the head-piece, which is also of 6 inch by 3 inch stuff. Note that the slot is not 3 inches wide, because the head-piece is also cut away as shown. The best method of cutting the slot is to saw down the sides, and bore a series of holes near the bottom. It is then merely a matter of chopping down with the chisel.

To give a bearing for the stays or struts, a sloping cut is made at the joint. This gives a wide shoulder capable of taking considerable strain. The illustration shows how a sort of stub-tenon is cut on the strut. A corresponding hole is cut in the post to receive it. The exact position of the joints is best ascertained after the stays have been made. They can be tried in position against the bearers, laid against the post, and the length marked.

How Posts project into Bottom Bearer.

The dotted lines in the diagram show how the post projects into the bottom bearer. The latter (also 6 inches by 3 inches) is mortised to receive it. To support the stays, sloping notches are cut near the ends. They should be about 1 inch deep at the outer ends.

Assembling Main Structure.

The main structure is now ready to be assembled. It is of no use to put glue in the joints, as the damp to which the whole is exposed would soon deteriorate it. Paint is a good substitute. First fix the bearers to the uprights, and then add the stays, driving in stout cut nails to hold the joints.

At this stage the holes in the ground can be dug out and the uprights sunk in. Make sure that both are level and the correct distance apart. Ram the earth well in round the uprights, using a heavy post for the purpose. Using a pair of steps, drop

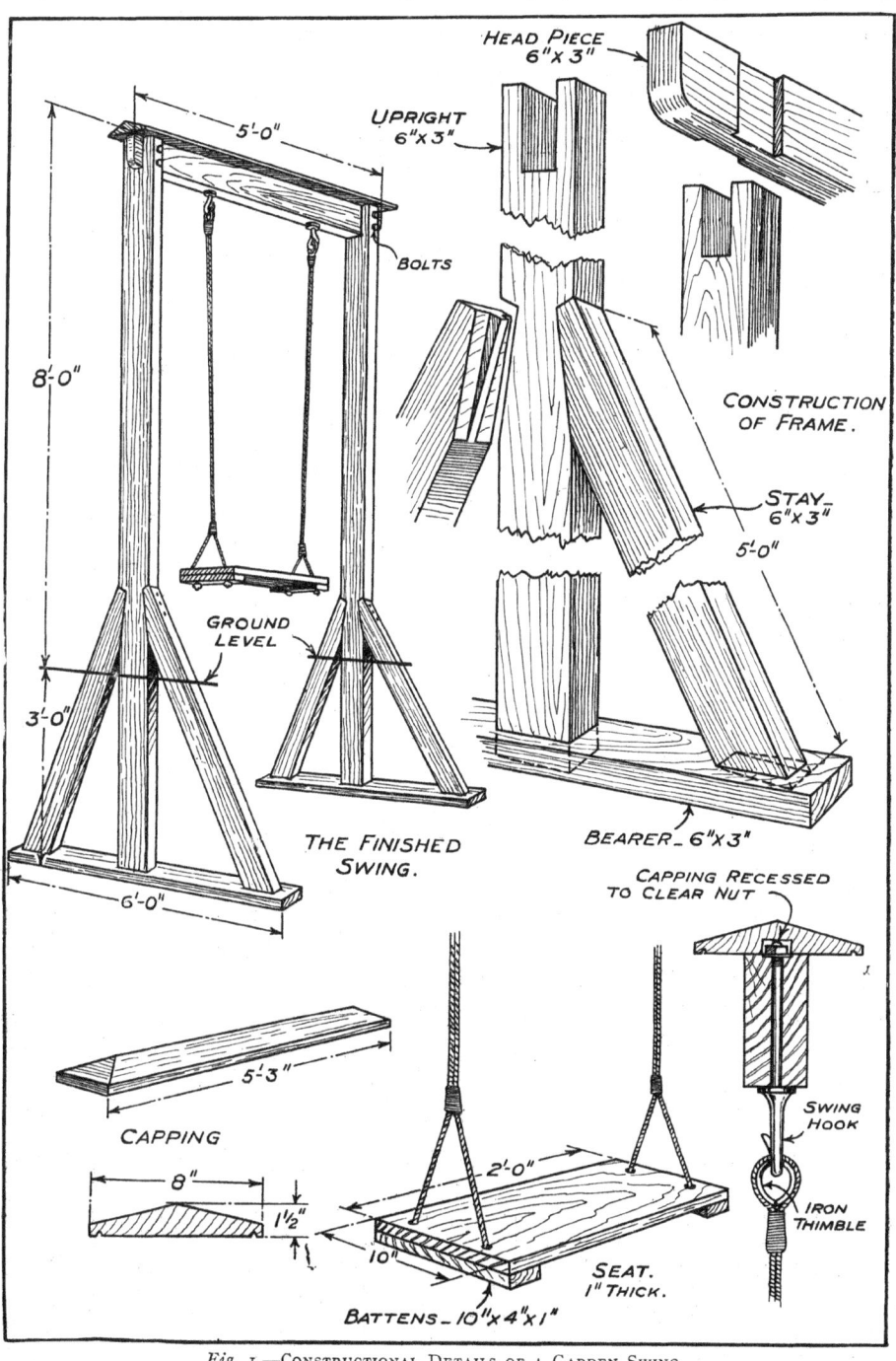

Fig. 1.—Constructional Details of a Garden Swing.

the head-piece into the notches at the top of the posts. In this case, bolts are passed through the joints. These bind the whole together and prevent any tendency for the posts to split.

The Capping.

It will be seen that a capping is planted over the whole. This is not only decorative, but also protects the ends of the uprights from damp.

Channels are cut along the underside near the edges to prevent rain from running along the underside and reaching the head-piece. The upper surface is chamfered. Small recesses have to be cut in it to take the nuts which hold the swing hooks. Remember not to fix the capping until after these hooks have been fitted in place.

The swing seat is simply a plain piece of 1-inch stuff with battens nailed to the underside. It is advisable to round over the edges. The rope supporting it is double. At the top it passes round an iron thimble and is well lashed. A further lashing is necessary near the bottom where the rope divides. Thence it passes through holes bored through the seat and battens. Large knots beneath prevent it from pulling through. Note that the iron thimbles at the top are essential, as otherwise the rope would wear through rapidly.

FOR TRAINING LOGANBERRIES

Fig. 1.—Loganberry Plants trained in the Manner described in this Article.

THE usual method of training climbers, such as loganberries, ramblers, and the like, by tacking to the fence with loops of cloth, has two disadvantages. One of these drawbacks is the time occupied, to say nothing of the discomfort from thorns in course of the work, while the other is that fixing so close to the fence does not permit of the fullest development of the plant itself.

This idea was evolved to overcome both of these objections to the old method, and has proved successful in both directions. It consists primarily in providing a simple but strong support, away from the fence, for a number of wires, to which the plant is tied by string or thin wire loops. By using thinnish galvanised wire for the loops they need only twisting very loosely around the stems of the plant to hold them without in the least restricting growth.

The supports consist of a sort of bracket of stiff galvanised wire. A coil of this is cut into lengths of about a yard each. Each of these pieces is first doubled by pulling it around a thick round upright, which can conveniently be the leg of a table which has been temporarily turned upside-down for the purpose.

These thick "hairpins" are then twisted a few turns at the loop, as in Fig. 2. With a pair of round-nose pliers each of the free ends is first bent to a right-angle, and then into a couple of small loops to take screws, as shown in Fig. 3. On screwing such a bracket to the fence, as shown in Fig. 4, it is clear that a firm support is obtained for a bean-stick which has its bottom end pushed into the earth by the fence. It is not necessary to have these supports closer together than, say, 4 feet, and when a row of them has been fixed, wires are strained from one to the next, either in lines parallel to the ground, or diagonally, according to individual inclination.

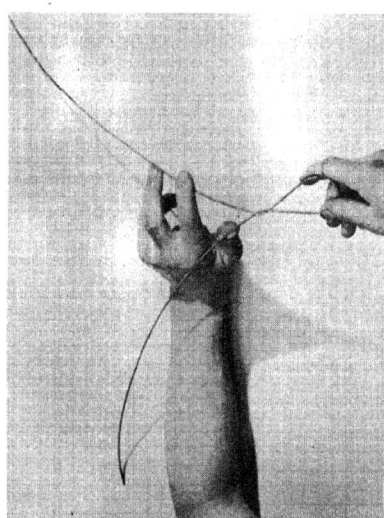

Fig. 2.—Forming the Loop for the Stick.

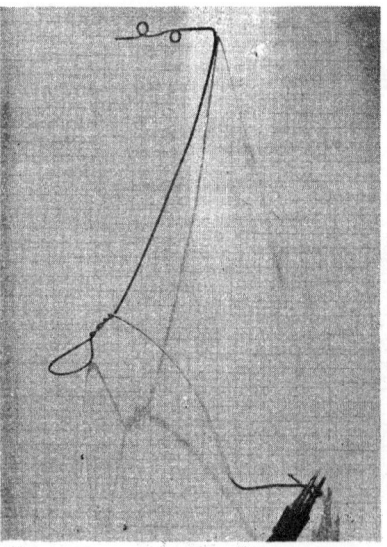

Fig. 3.—Making the small Loops for the Screws.

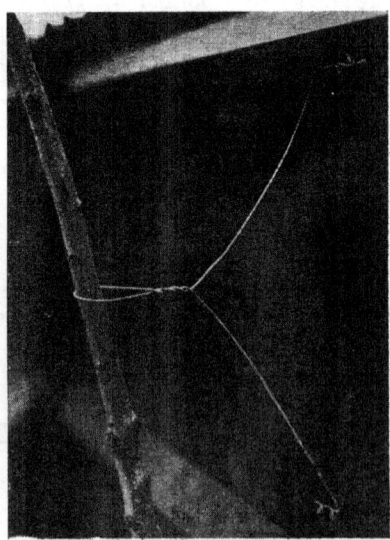

Fig. 4.—Showing how the Stick is supported away from the Wall.

Methods of Working Metal-Faced Plywood

There are sometimes occasions when one hesitates to use ordinary plywood for the panelling of outbuildings, or for doors exposed to the weather, or for other purposes where it will be exposed to severe conditions, in case it should not prove sufficiently rigid.

In such circumstances it is best to use metal-faced plywood. This is stronger than wood or plywood yet it is lighter than metal of a similar thickness. It is, in fact, ideal where a material is required of exceptionally light weight combined with strength, durability and rigidity.

An article on page 929 describes how to make the best use of plywood; in this article the best methods of working metal-faced plywood are described in detail.

Metal-faced plywood can be obtained in all such sizes in which ordinary sheet metal is sold, and in regard to the outside metal surface, the range of different materials is very wide, viz., galvanised steel, black sheet iron, aluminium, stainless steel, brass, copper, zinc and monel metal. In regard to thickness, metal-faced plywood sheets are produced in any thickness that may be required, but the standard thicknesses in which it is easily obtainable are $\frac{3}{16}$, $\frac{1}{4}$, $\frac{3}{8}$ and $\frac{1}{2}$ inch.

Application of Metal-faced Plywood.

The metal-covered surface of the plywood sheet is not affected by either damp or other atmospheric influences. It is, even in thin boards, extremely strong and, therefore, not subject to unsightly dents or similar damage through friction or pressure. The only vulnerable point about metal-faced plywood is its edge, which exposes the uncovered glue joints both between the constituent veneers of the plywood sheet as also between the plywood and the metal itself.

How to protect the Edges.

For all purposes, therefore, where metal-faced plywood may be exposed to the influences of weather it is essential to prevent humidity penetrating the glue joints on its edges. To attain this protection it is necessary to cover the edges with metal. This can be done by ordering the metal-faced plywood with protected edges, or, if preferred, the work can quite easily be done at home.

Fig. 3.—Channelling Metal-faced Plywood prior to Soldering the Joint.

Folding the Overlapping Metal over the Edge.

In Fig. 1 we see the process of folding the overlapping metal over the edge of a single-faced metal plywood sheet. The work is best done with an ordinary wooden mallet, and in order to ensure that the overlapping piece fits tightly over the edges a weight (a piece of metal as illustrated will do) is best placed upon the plywood sheet so as to keep it in position.

When dealing with double-sided metal-faced plywood it is best to trim the overlapping metal edges so as to ensure that one of them, when folded, will cover about half the thickness, whilst the other will fold about three-quarters of the thickness of the board. By this means (as shown in Fig. 2) an overlapping joint on the edges is obtained.

Fig. 2.—Protecting Edges of Plywood metal-faced both sides.
Note that some of the plywood has been cut out to shape from part of the panel.

Dealing with Corners.

As will be seen in Fig. 2, an incision is made into the overlapping metal face and by this means a straight and neat fitting corner joint can be obtained without difficulty. These joints, in order to be perfectly secure, must then be soldered down. A neater and more effective method, which can be especially recommended in all instances where large quantities of similar sized boards are utilised, is to affix a metal channel over the edge. Fig. 3 shows

Fig. 1.—Bending Metal to protect Edge of Metal-faced Plywood.
Note weight placed on sheet to ensure accuracy.

METHODS OF WORKING METAL-FACED PLYWOOD

Fig. 4.—Soldering Curved Edges and Corners of Double-faced Metal Plywood.
Note incisions of metal channel on curved edge and at corners.

the channel being affixed, *i.e.*, slipped over the edge and soldered down on both sides to the metal surfaces of the board.

When dealing with corners and round edges it is advisable not to allow the end of the channel to reach the bend but to carry it over the bend. Fig. 4 shows a case in point. On the left will be seen how an angle of 45 degrees is fitted with a channel soldered down to the board. The channel itself has an incision on both sides so as to allow for neat folding over of the corners: this enables one to bend the overlapping strip over the corner and prevent the joint falling on the corner itself.

Rounded Corners.

In regard to rounded corners, where one incision in the channel would not provide for necessary flexibility to negotiate the corner, a number of smaller incisions should be made as shown on the right in Fig. 4.

Soldering.

When soldering it must be remembered that in the case of galvanised steel metals and metals treated on their surfaces, the interfering surface material has to be removed with a scraper so as to ensure a perfectly smooth surface for the solder to hold to.

Cutting Metal-faced Plywood

When cutting metal-faced plywood an ordinary hack-saw or metal saw may be employed. For small boards it will be found that an ordinary hacksaw will meet the case, but when dealing with large surfaces it may be found that the ordinary hack-saw is difficult to manipulate because of its comparatively narrow blade. In those instances it is preferable to use a frame hack-saw (as shown in Fig. 6), or, alternatively, a triangular hack-saw.

Jointing of Metal-faced Plywood.

The jointing of metal-faced plywood may be effected in different ways. When working to framework the jointing is comparatively simple (as shown in Fig. 7). The two panels, as will be seen from this sketch, are affixed to the framework by means of nails or screws, and the joint between

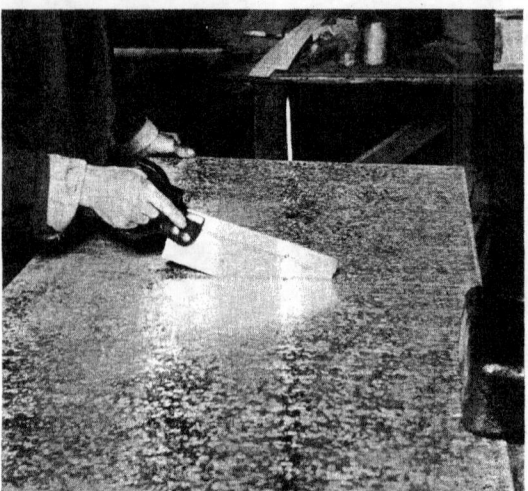

Fig. 5.—Sawing Metal-faced Plywood.
Note angle at which saw is held to allow for free passage all along the width of the board. For wire boards and where an ordinary saw cannot be conveniently used, triangular hack-saws are recommended.

them is then covered with a metal strip. If no framework is available to work to, the simplest joint is to provide a reinforced metal or wooden batten at the back of the panels and to screw the panels to this batten, covering again the surface joint with a metal strip (see Fig. 8).

A Simple Joint.

In instances where cost is an essential consideration, and appearance does not particularly matter, a simple joint can be effected as in Fig. 11. This, of course, can only be applied provided a framework can be worked to. As will be seen, in this case part of the plywood on one of the boards is removed so as to allow for an overlapping metal strip, the adjoining panel is cleaned of the galvanised surface, so as to take the solder, the two panels are placed together, and the overlap is soldered on to the adjoining board.

Joint between Two Panels.

A joint between two panels that will not be exposed to unnecessary pressure, but need not necessarily be erected against a framework, is the one shown in Figs. 9 and 12. Fig. 9 shows the preparation of the edges of the boards by filing them down so that when joined a channel is formed between them, and Fig. 12 shows how the soldering operation is finished.

The channel, as will be seen, is filled with solder and the uneven surface is then smoothed down by sandpapering or filing.

Bending Metal-faced Plywood.

The bending of plywood metal-faced on one side is an operation which cannot be conveniently performed by the operator, unless he deals with comparatively thin boards. Boards up to $\frac{3}{16}$-inch thickness can be easily bent to shape as may be required when worked to a framework and fixed to it by means of screwing or nailing.

When dealing with stouter boards, and particularly with boards faced with metal both sides, this simple operation cannot be performed without the aid of machinery. Shaped metal-faced plywood, therefore, should always be ordered in the shape required, from the manufacturers.

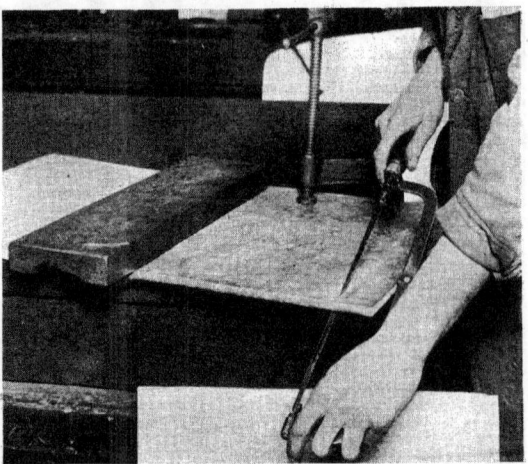

Fig. 6.—Hack-sawing Metal-faced Plywood.
For central cuts a triangular hack-saw should be used.

METHODS OF WORKING METAL-FACED PLYWOOD

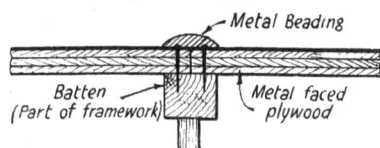

Fig. 7.—Concealed Joint of Two Metal-faced Panels supported by Batten.

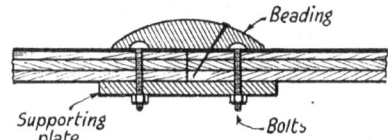

Fig. 8.—Joint of Metal-faced Panels made with the Aid of a Supporting Plate.

Fig. 9.—Preparing Surfaces of Panels for Butt-jointing.
Note that the edges of the panels are filed down to form a channel to be filled with solder.

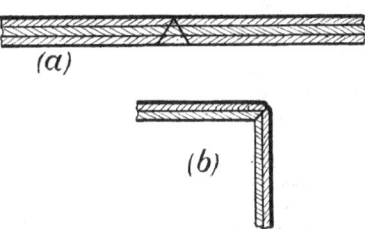

Fig. 10.—Bending Metal-faced Plywood.
Showing, A, triangular groove inserted on back of panel preparatory to bending; B, completed bend.

Simple corners, however, at different degrees can be easily made, as shown in Fig. 10.

Mark on the reverse side of the board, *i.e.*, on the plywood side, the line in which the corner is to lie, then prepare a groove carefully, so as to obtain the correct angle of the ultimate shape of the outside corner, and when folding the sheet over it will form the desired angle.

Removing Unnecessary Plywood.

If the panels are ordered in stock sizes and therefore delivered from the factory with the metal extending right up to the edge of the panel, and if it should prove necessary to solder the edges without adopting the practice of channelling, superfluous plywood has to be removed so as to provide for an overlapping metal flap. A mechanical cutter should be used if one is available, but in the absence of such mechanical means an ordinary saw or chisel will enable the same task to be performed, if not as speedily, just as accurately. Properly made metal-faced plywood should not come apart through the vibration, either brought about by hammering or the action of the machine.

Drilling Metal-faced Plywood.

Metal-faced plywood may be drilled by ordinary drillers, but it will be found easier to use the breast drill. Since most metal-faced plywood is utilised for comparatively large-sized work and the panels are obtained in uniform sizes or shapes, it will be found that the method of its affixing to battens, etc., can be also standardised, and, therefore, the necessary screwholes can be provided for in all panels alike in the same position. To simplify the work of producing these screwholes it is best to employ a template.

Nailing Metal-faced Plywood.

The nailing of metal-faced plywood is a simple operation, and in this respect it does not differ from any other material.

Screwing Metal-faced Plywood.

This is best performed by preparing the screwhole first and drilling it out. If it is necessary to countersink the screws, this matter is easily done because the metal surface is so thin that it can be easily cut away, and most of the countersunk part will lie in the wood which is easily removed.

Riveting Metal-faced Plywood.

When riveting metal-faced plywood, either to framework or to another metal-faced plywood sheet, it should always be observed that the tools are driven against the metal-face of the board and not against the wooden face, so as to ensure that no unnecessary stress is brought to bear upon the glue joint between the metal and the plywood.

Fig. 11.—Joining Metal-faced Plywood by means of an Ordinary Soldered Joint.
Showing panels being placed in position for soldering.

Fig. 12.—Applying the Solder.
Note that edges of joint are filed down to provide a channel to take the soldering tin (see Fig. 9). This and the previous photographs were staged by Messrs. Venesta Ltd.

SIMPLE STAIN FOR LIGHT WOODS

LIGHT woods such as pine, deal and birch can be stained to a permanent rich walnut colour by painting or sponging the surface with a concentrated solution of permanganate of potash in water.

It is a method that is particularly suitable for staining the floors of new houses as the stain can be polished with any ordinary domestic wax polish and will not mark as is often the case with stains containing a large percentage of varnish.

The floor should be prepared by sandpapering and then washing with warm water, which should be allowed to dry before the permanganate solution is applied.

The solution should be applied warm and each coat allowed to dry before the next is applied. The colour and depth of the stain can be readily varied by the application of successive solutions, and it will be found that the shade of the solution will vary from a faint pink to a deep blood red according to the quantity of crystals used.

To obtain a mahogany finish the surface of the wood should be brushed with a solution made up of burnt sienna dissolved in ordinary household vinegar and diluted.

How to Make a Knife-grinding Machine

THE knife grinder used to be a much more familiar sight about the streets than at present. Strangely enough this decline is not due to any lack of work; on the contrary, there is more scope for a travelling grinder than ever, as few house-holders think of having their table knives, scissors, garden shears, hatchets, etc., sharpened unless they are reminded by the appearance of an itinerant grinder that such work is necessary.

In the neighbourhood of large markets, travelling grinders usually ply a brisk trade, and every butcher's shop supplies a sheaf of knives, cleavers, etc., for his attention. The work, too, considering the time taken and the capital cost of the plant, is well paid, and many grinders did not find it necessary to take the road every day in order to make a very substantial living.

Two Main Types of Grinders.

There were two main types of grinders, the native, and the foreign, usually Italian. The former generally combined soldering with knife grinding, the cry, "Pots and kettles to mend, knives and scissors to grind," being one of the most familiar of the street cries in large towns. The foreign grinder usually specialised in grinding only, but why this was so is not clear.

The machines used by these two types differed radically. The British machine was a large and elaborate affair usually on two wheels and resembling a large skeleton baker's barrow.

The driving wheel and spindle were carried on the framework and a seat was arranged just above the handles, convenient for working the treadles. A tool box was combined in the front of the barrow, and if soldering was done, a tinker's "devil" or firepot for heating the soldering irons was slung from the front end.

Many of these machines were very elaborate, the owner letting his fancy run in decorating them with brass knobs, fancy brass-headed nails and hectic colour schemes.

The foreign machine, on the other hand, was a very plain affair, usually having only one wheel which served the purpose of a road wheel when travelling and a driving wheel when at work. A tool box was formed in the body of the machine in which the stones, driving belt, etc., were carried while the machine was travelling. The construction of the British type will be described, but it is necessary to consider the working conditions in order to see how these best can be dealt with.

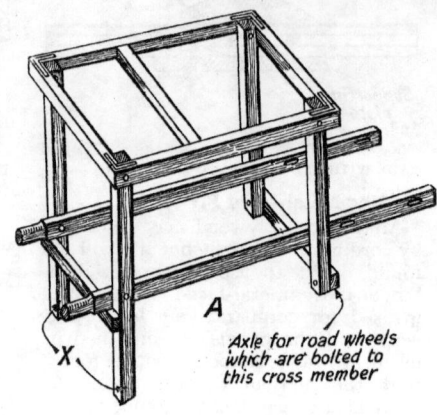
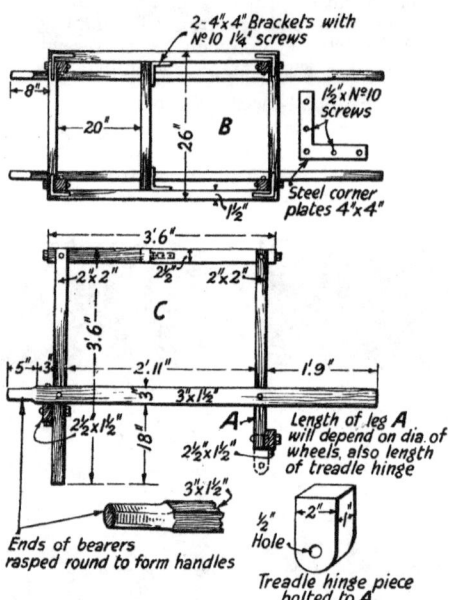

Ease of Travelling.

As long distances will have to be covered on the road, ease of travelling is essential, and it is advisable to adopt ball-bearings and pneumatic tyres for the wheels. Grinding is very hard work, as all high speed work absorbs considerable power, and for this reason friction should be reduced as far as possible, which calls for a ball-bearing grinding spindle.

As the place where the machine will have to be kept may have a narrow doorway or passage, the dimensions must be arranged to meet these as far as possible.

Cheapness and Ease of Construction.

In view of the fact that unemployed men may wish to take up this work, cheapness and ease of construction are essential, and therefore the simplest and cheapest design consistent with efficiency has been given, but this can be elaborated as desired or as the skill and means of the constructor permit. Material which is generally and cheaply available has, therefore, been chosen, the main consideration being to give a general idea rather than a rigid design.

Many dimensions will have to be made to suit the operator, as a tall man will require a much higher machine than a short. The height of the grinding spindle, for instance, is most convenient if it corresponds to the height of the operator's elbow when the arms are hanging.

The frame of the machine must be rigid and yet light and a hard wood should be used for this. Soft wood could be used, but would have to be of larger section and the joints would not keep tight under the racking of the road and work.

Why Bolted Joints are used.

Considerable experience in woodworking would be required to make joints which would stand, so that bolted joints have been described, but those capable of making mortised joints can use these if desired. Fig. 1 (A, B, C, D) shows the frame of the machine, and it will be noticed that some joints are made with steel plates and brackets which can be bought cheaply at any ironmonger's.

The two main horizontals which form the handles are continued the other side of the frame and carry a tool chest. This chest is arranged to slide along the bearers and when the machine is travelling it can be placed where it will partially balance the weight about the axle and so make the machine very light to handle. For work, the chest would be pushed back against the frame (Fig. 25).

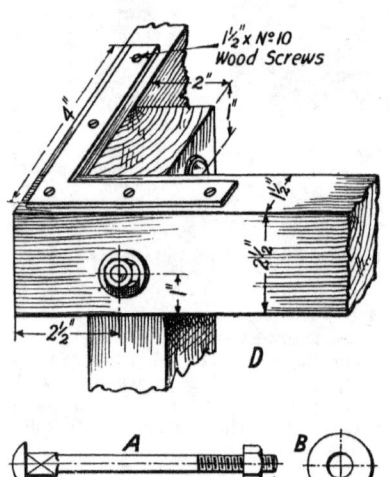

Fig. 1.—Details of the Frame of the Knife-grinding Machine.

HOW TO MAKE A KNIFE-GRINDING MACHINE

Fig. 2.—PNEUMATIC TYRED WHEELS, SIZE 24 × 2 INCHES.
Note plates on axle for bolting to cross member of frame (see Fig. 1).

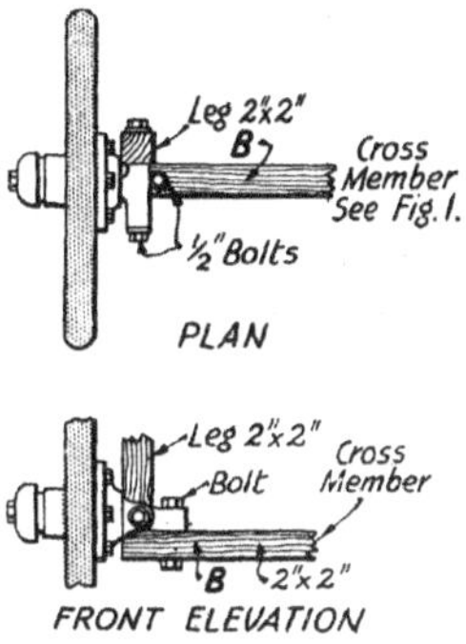

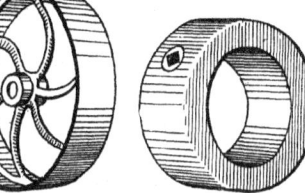

Fig. 3.—FORD MODEL T WHEEL, SHOWING METHOD OF ATTACHMENT.

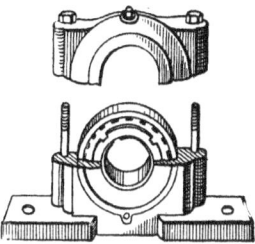

Fig. 4.—MAIN DRIVING WHEEL.

Fig. 5.—STEEL SET COLLAR.

Fig. 6.—1-INCH BALL-BEARING PLUMMER BLOCK AND HOUSING WITH CAP REMOVED.

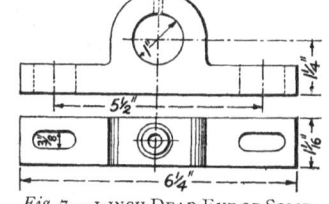

Fig. 7.—1-INCH DEAD EYE OR SOLID BEARING.
The dimensions of ¾-inch bore dead eyes are similar.

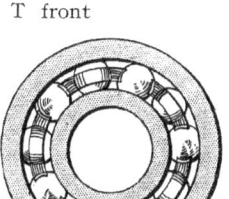

Fig. 8A.—BALL JOURNAL BEARING.

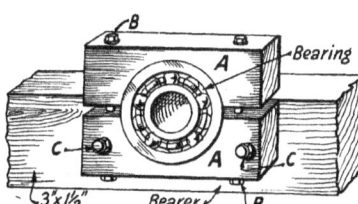

Fig. 8B.—METHOD OF MOUNTING BALL JOURNAL BEARINGS.

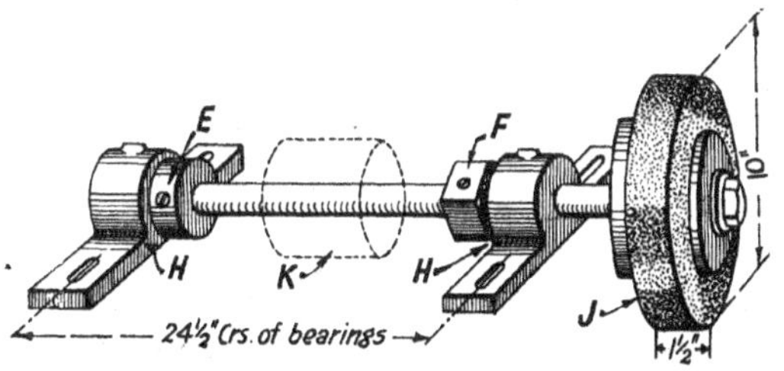

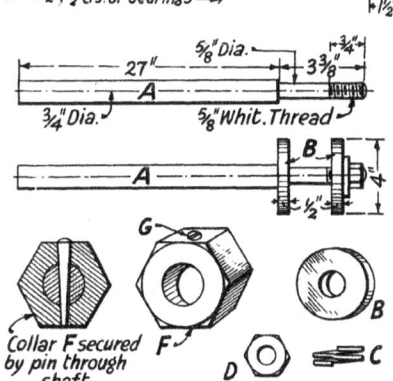

Fig. 9.—DETAILS OF GRINDING SPINDLE.
A, ¾ inch diameter bright drawn mild steel reduced to ⅝-inch diameter and screwed ⅝-inch Whitworth. BB, Flanges ½ inch thick, 4 inches diameter cast iron, ⅝-inch hole. C, ⅝-inch double coil spring washer. D, ⅝-inch bright Whitworth nut. E, ¾-inch set collar. F, ¾-inch bright nut, with thread bored out and grub screw G fitted. HH, bearings, ¾-inch bore dead eyes. J, grinding wheel. K, pulley shown dotted, 3 inches diameter, 3 inches wide.

Wheels and Axle.

The wheels and axle will have to be purchased. Fig. 2 shows a light axle with pneumatic-tyred wheels which can be purchased from Messrs. Kirkhams, Preston, for 45s., but if a firm of motor-car breakers is approached, a pair of wheels and tyres off a light car can be bought very cheaply and an axle made up for them.

As example Ford model T front wheels with tyres complete can be bought for 2s. each. These would be rather heavy for the job, but will do quite well. If these are used, the steering arms which are bought with the wheels would be bolted to the front uprights of the frame, as shown in Fig. 3, and no through axle would be used, the strip of wood B (Fig. 3) being to keep the arms rigid and in line.

Height of Wheel Centres.

The height of the wheel centres will be arranged so that when the legs XX (Fig. 1A) are on the ground the top of the frame will be level. The main driving wheel (Fig. 4) is a 30-inch diameter 2-inch face (or 2½-inch if 2-inch is not available) with a 1-inch bore, cast iron or wrought iron pulley. If one of these is bought new it will be rather expensive, but at most second-hand machinery stores such a pulley can be bought for about 2s. 6d.

Spindle or Shaft.

The spindle or shaft is a length of 1-inch diameter bright drawn mild steel costing about 6d. per foot. Two 1-inch steel set collars (Fig. 5) with countersunk set-screws at 1s. each will also be required. The bearings for the shaft should really be ball, but these, if bought new, are expensive. Two 1-inch ball plummer blocks (Fig. 6) will cost 9s. 6d. each. Plain bearings called dead eyes are much cheaper, costing only 1s. each (Fig. 7). If possible to obtain, two ball journal bearings as used in motor vehicles (Fig. 8 A and B) could be used. Worn bearings which have been removed from a car are quite good enough if undamaged, and can often be picked up at garages which have repair shops for a few pence each. The size required will have a bore of 1 inch, width ⅝ inch, outside diameter 2¾ inches; but there are several other sizes having 1-inch bore which can be used if available.

Mounting the Bearings.

The method of mounting these bearings is shown in Fig. 8B. The bright steel bar is perfectly straight and true to very fine units, so can be used as bought.

The Grinding Spindle.

The grinding spindle is of the overhung type, which is more convenient than where the wheel is mounted on the centre of the shaft (Fig. 9). With this type the wheels can be removed and changed without removing the spindle, and grinding can take place on the face of the wheel which is not convenient with a straight through spindle. The spindle consists of a length of ¾-inch diameter bright drawn mild steel. This will have to be purchased as shown in Fig. 9, unless a lathe is available, as it is important that this should run dead true. The two flanges must have the faces which touch the wheel dead true to the central hole.

To enable the spindle to be held while the nut holding the wheel is tightened or slackened, one of the two set collars (F, Fig. 9) can be made hexagonal. A ¾-inch bright steel nut with the thread bored out will do with a countersunk set-screw or a pin through the shaft (K, Fig. 9). This can be held with one spanner while the other is used on the wheel nut. Two set collars will be required; the other can be of the usual type, costing 9d. The bearings of the spindle can be either plain, using dead eyes or ball journals as for the driving spindle. The dead eyes are 1s. each.

The Pulley.

The pulley should be 3 inches diameter and 3 inches wide, ¾-inch bore. Wood pulleys can be bought of

HOW TO MAKE A KNIFE-GRINDING MACHINE

this size, or one can be made very easily. The face of the pulley should be rounded, not flat, to keep the belt on the centre of the pulley.

If the pulley has to be made, a small piece of ½-inch thick plywood should be procured and six circles, 3 inches diameter, cut out with a fret or compass saw (Fig. 10). The ¾-inch centre hole should then be bored through each disc, taking care to keep the hole central, and it is as well to mark another circle a little larger round the hole A (Fig. 10) as a guide. Drill three holes in each disc to clear a No. 6 wood screw and countersink them on one side. Mount them one by one on the spindle B (Fig. 10) and screw together.

Plate to take the Drive.

To take the drive, a plate as shown in Fig. 11 will be required and can be purchased from a blacksmith or ironmonger for a few pence. It is screwed on one end of the pulley as shown in A (Fig. 11). A drill is then run into the pulley at the keyway and the wood cleared out with a narrow chisel to form a slot or keyway.

Securing the Wheel to the Spindle.

When the position of the pulley on the spindle has been decided, a flat is filed on the spindle (C, Fig. 11), and a key which can be made from a "cut" nail is driven into the keyway in the plate D (Fig. 11) and secures the wheel to the spindle. The driving wheel being 30 inches diameter and the spindle wheel 3 inches, it follows that the latter will make ten turns to one of the former. A comfortable treadling speed is sixty per minute, which would therefore give a speed of 600 revolutions to the spindle.

Crank for the Driving Spindle.

The crank for the driving spindle is

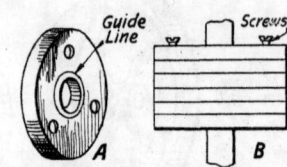

Fig. 10.—Disc of Plywood ½ inch thick, 3 inches diameter.

Six of these are required. Three holes to take No. 6 wood screws are drilled in each on a 2-inch circle and countersunk. Note guide-line round centre ¾-inch hole. (Right) Mount discs on spindle and screw together.

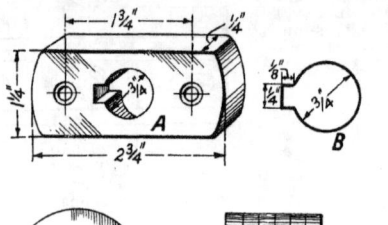

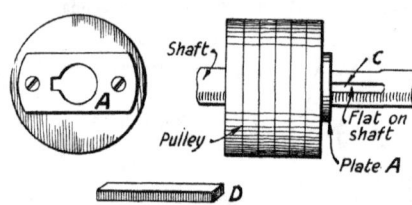

Fig. 11.—Driving Plate to Screw to one End of Pulley.

Showing also details of keyway and plate A screwed on end of pulley.

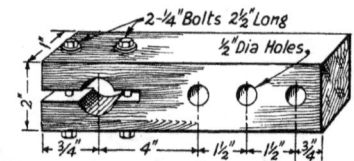

Fig. 12.—Piece of Oak 2 × 1 × 8½ inches to form Crank.

formed from a piece of oak, as shown in Fig. 12. A hole 1 inch diameter to take the spindle is bored at one end and a saw cut run down it as shown. Two ¼-inch diameter bolts with washers under both head and nut are required and holes an easy fit to the bolts are drilled one on either side of the spindle hole.

The grip given will be more than enough to transmit any power required, but to make sure that no slip occurs a strip of emery cloth, not paper, can be put round the spindle before the crank is put on and the bolts tightened up. Leg reach varies, and therefore several holes have been provided to take the connecting rod or hook, and it can be found by trial which will be the most convenient to use.

Connecting Rod.

The connecting rod is also of wood, as shown in Fig. 13. The crank pin end should if possible be fitted with a ball bearing; a small size will do for this and one with a ¾-inch bore 1½ × ½ inch can be used. It is clipped into the rod by one ¼-inch bolt as shown. The other end of the rod where it couples on to the treadle has a ¾-inch hole drilled in it and a short length of ½ × ¾-inch brass tube driven in. Very long life is possible if no bush is used, but it will not be so easy running.

What to do if Ball-bearing cannot be obtained.

If a ball-bearing cannot be obtained, both ends of the rod will be the same, as shown in A (Fig. 13). The ½-inch diameter bolts used to form the crank and treadle pins are shown in Fig. 13A. It will be noted that a length of thin brass tube ½-inch bore, ¾ inch outside diameter is put over each bolt to form a distance-piece, otherwise if the nut is tightened up it would jamb

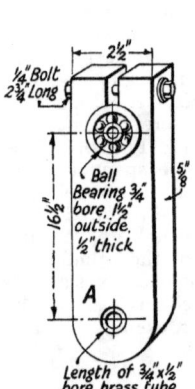

Fig. 13.—Connecting Rod.

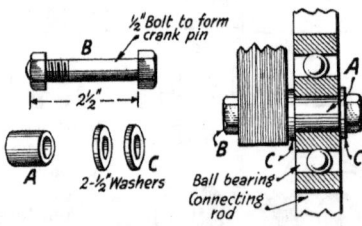

Fig. 13A.—Bolts forming Joints of Treadle and Crank.

A, length of brass tube ¾ inch long, ¾ inch outside diameter, ½ inch hole.

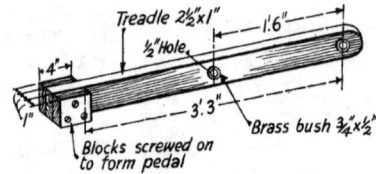

Fig. 14.—Details of Treadle.
Treadle, oak or ash.

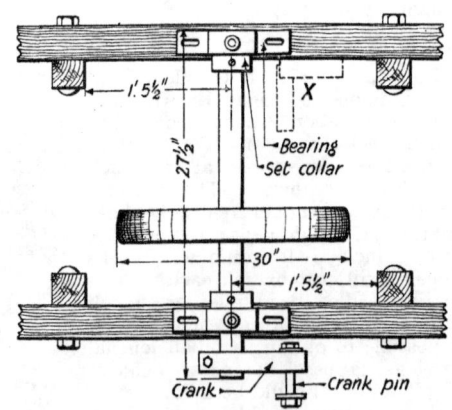

Fig. 15.—Driving Shaft and Bearings in Place on Bearers.

By means of a square, X, sight that the shaft is square with the bearers.

HOW TO MAKE A KNIFE-GRINDING MACHINE

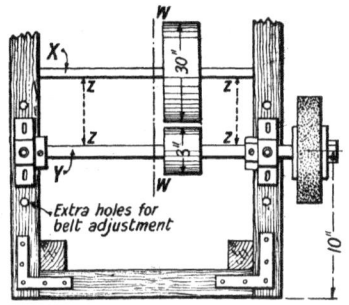

Fig. 16.—THE DRIVING SHAFT X AND GRINDING SPINDLE MUST BE PARALLEL.
Measure between points ZZ, ZZ with a wood lath cut to dead length. To ensure pulleys being in line, test by a string stretched across the faces W.

the joint. Steel tube can be used if brass is not obtainable. The tube can be cut with a hacksaw now obtainable complete with blade for 6d. at the one-price stores.

The treadle is a strip of hard wood, ash or oak, and the foot-plate is made by screwing on two short lengths of the same section (Fig. 14). The hinge joint is made in the same way as the connecting rod joint (Fig. 13A), a brass bush being used in the hole in the treadle.

Fitting up the Parts.

To fit up the parts proceed as follows: Mount the driving wheel on the shaft and then put the shaft in its bearings. If dead eyes are used, the two set collars are slipped on the shaft before the bearings. The shaft with the bearings is then laid on the main bearers and sighted to see that it is quite square with them. A square can be used if desired to check this (Fig. 15).

Boring Holes through Bearers.

Mark the bolt holes on the wood and then remove the bearings and bore the holes through the bearers with a ⅜-inch bit, taking care to keep the holes square each way. Put the shaft back and bolt the bearings down. Put a spirit level on the shaft and also on the top of the frame and see that the shaft and frame top are parallel.

Test whether Spindle is level with Driving Shaft.

Then put the spindle in its bearings and lay on the top of the frame and test by the spirit level that the spindle is level with the driving shaft. If not, shave away the wood under the high end bearing until it is level. Mark the holes, having first sighted the two shafts to ensure that they are parallel and square with the frame (Fig. 16).

Fig. 17.—ALLIGATOR BELT FASTENER.
It is hammered into belt with a hammer on a block of hard wood.

Test Shaft and Spindle for Freedom.

Bore the holes and bolt down the spindle. Test both shaft and spindle for freedom; there must be no binding. Move the set collars into place and fix. The end of the driving

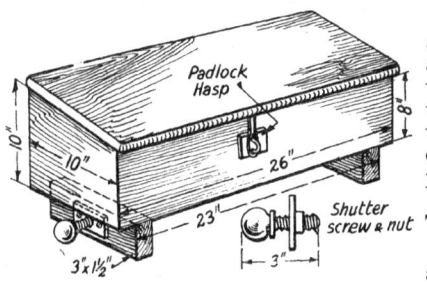

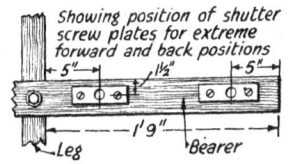

Fig. 19.—TOOL BOX OF ¾-INCH WOOD. LID TO OVERLAP ¾ INCH ALL ROUND TO KEEP OUT RAIN, SLOPING TOP FOR SAME REASON.

shaft projecting on the right side carries the crank (Fig. 12), and this should be put on and tightened up.

Next fit up Treadle and Connecting Rod.

The treadle and connecting rod are

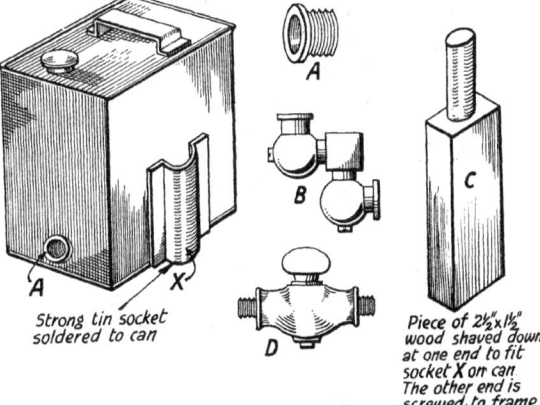

Fig. 20.—DRIP CAN MADE FROM ½-GALLON OIL TIN.
A, ⅜ to ½-inch brass bush soldered in tin. B, ¼ × ¼-inch universal gas swivel joint. C, piece of 1½ × 2½ inches wood shaved down at one end to fit socket on tin. The other end is screwed to frame. D, ¼-inch double male gas tap.

then fitted, and the driving shaft given a turn to see that all is free. Before fixing the pulleys they must be lined up or the belt will not keep on them. Fix the driving wheel about the centre of the shaft and then tap the spindle pulley along the spindle until it is in line.

How to ensure Accuracy.

To ensure accuracy, stretch a string across the driving wheel and the face of the spindle pulley and see that the distances W.W. (Fig. 16) are the same on each side. When this is correct drive in the key securing the pulley.

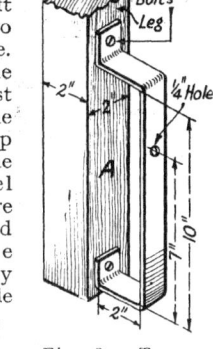

Fig. 18.—TREADLE GUIDE MADE FROM 1 × ⅛-INCH STEEL STRIP.

The Belt.

The belt must be a thin flexible one and must be of leather; it will pay well to get a good belt to start with, and a length of Tullis's 2-inch thin single orange tan belt should be obtained. To avoid the thump at each passage of the fastener round the spindle pulley an alligator fastener (Fig. 17) should be used.

What to do when Belt gets slack.

To avoid the trouble of cutting and rejoining the belt when it gets slack, several sets of holes can be bored in the top frame members. The dead eyes have slotted bolt holes (Fig. 7), and when the stretch of the belt has got beyond the adjustment of these slots, the spindle is unbolted and moved to the next pair of holes (Fig. 16).

Guide for Treadle.

The treadle will need a guide to prevent it being forced sideways by the pressure of the foot, and this is made from a strip of 1 × ⅛-inch steel which can be bent to shape round a piece of wood. The corners need not be very sharp. It is screwed to the leg as shown in Fig 18. The hole A is for a pin to go through to hold the treadle at the top of its stroke when the machine is travelling.

The Tool Box.

The tool box is shown in Fig. 19, and the method of sliding it along the bearers and securing it is also shown. A padlock should be fitted to the lid to baulk inquisitive boys

HOW TO MAKE A KNIFE-GRINDING MACHINE

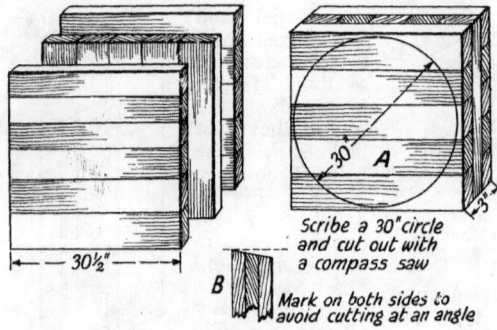

Fig. 21.—Method of making Driving Wheel.
6 × 1-inch planed floorboards cut to 30½-inch lengths. The layers are well glued and screwed together.

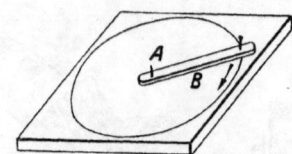

Fig. 22.—Method of scribing Circles.
A, nail with head cut off. B, lath.

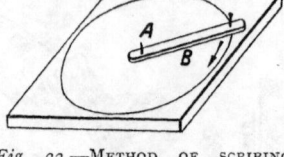

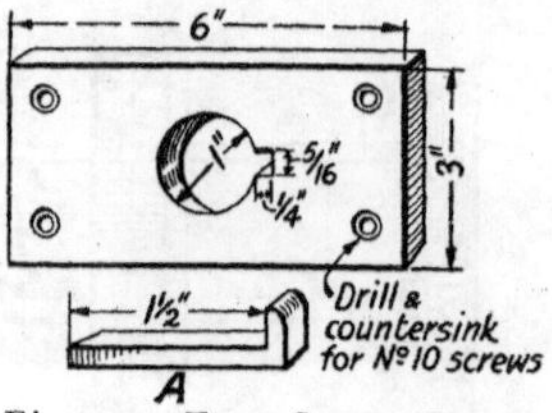

Fig. 23.—Two Steel Plates as shown of 3 × ¼-inch Plate.

while the operator has left the machine to look for or return work.

Drip-Can.

Most of the grinding will be wet, so a drip-can will be required. This should hold about ½ gallon and is fitted with a universal swivelling spout by which the water can be directed on to any desired spot. The best thing to make this from is one of the ½-gallon square tins used for motor lubricating oil (Fig. 20).

A strong socket made from stout tin should be soldered on one side (X, Fig. 20), and at the bottom of one side a brass bush or diminisher (A, Fig. 20) should be soldered on. This is called a ⅜-inch to ¼-inch reducing bush and will cost about 1½d. A brass universal swivel for gas ¼ × ⅛ inch (B, Fig. 20) is required, and a ¼-inch brass gas tap and a short length of copper tube about 6 inches long and ¼ inch outside diameter by ⅛-inch bore. Solder this tube into the ⅛-inch branch of the swivel and by means of the ¼-inch tap screw the swivel into the bush soldered in the tin. A post or stand for the tin will be required, and this can be made from a strip of the wood used for the frame, rasped down at the top to fit the socket (C, Fig. 20).

How to make up a Driving Wheel.

In some towns where little machinery is used it may be difficult to get the driving wheel at a reasonable price, and if so, a very good wheel can be made up out of 1 × 6-inch planed floorboards. The method is shown in Fig. 21. The boards are cut 30½ inches long and each layer is at right angles to the other. They should be glued together, using a good waterproof glue such as Croid, and well screwed with 1½ × No. 10 screws. When dry the circle is scribed out. It will have to be a little under the 30 inches diameter and cut round with a compass saw (A, Fig. 21). It is as well to mark the circle on both sides of the wood to ensure that the cutting is square or the edge of the pulley might appear as in B Fig. 21 and be useless.

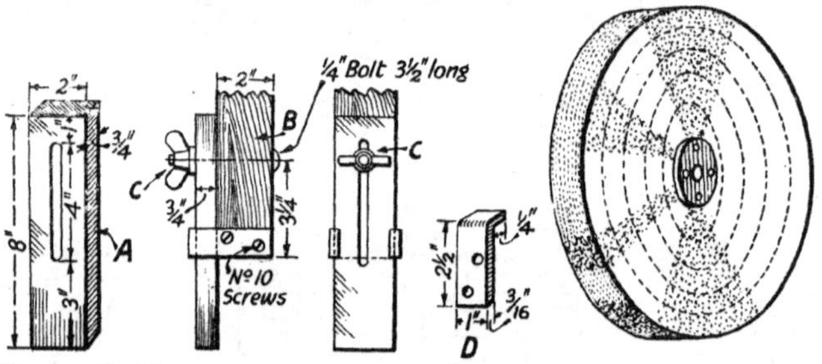

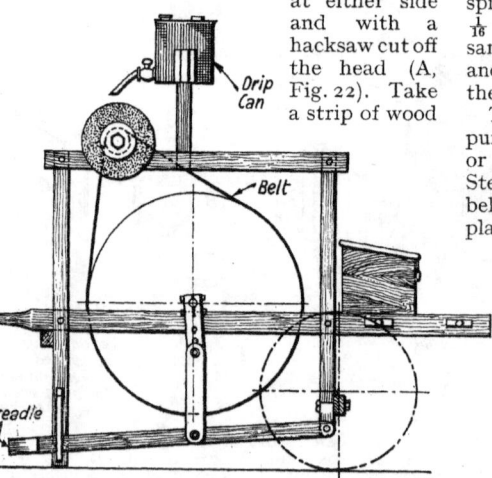

Fig. 24.—If Machine is trailed, the Legs will have to be made to clear the Ground by 2 Inches.
Extension pieces A will be required, and are secured to the insides of the legs B by ¼-inch bolts and washers fitted with wing nuts C. This allows the legs to be of varying length on uneven ground. The clips D can be bent over on a piece of iron or a weight with a hammer. On the right is a polishing mop made of calico which is a useful accessory.

How to make sure the Edge of the Circle is cut square.

To do this, mark the centre on one side and then drive a wire nail through, taking care that this is driven square. Leave the nail standing about 1 inch at either side and with a hacksaw cut off the head (A, Fig. 22). Take a strip of wood —a lath will do—and bore a hole a good fit to the nail at one end and at 15-inch centres from this screw in a wood screw so that the point just projects through the lath. Put the free hole over the nail and scribe the circle on both sides of the wood with the point of the wood screw.

Two plates will now be required similar to those in A, Fig. 11 for the spindle pulley, but with 1-inch holes. These will be as Fig. 23. Screw these to the wood as shown before the centre hole is bored, measuring from the nail to ensure the hole being in the centre. Then draw out the nail, and using the plates as a guide, bore a 1-inch hole through the wood. It should be bored half way through from each side to ensure truth. A flat is filed on the spindle to take the key, which can be bought at any engineers' stores.

Working the Machine.

The wheels used for grinding should be 6 inches to 10 inches diameter and 1½ inches wide. The spindle hole will be ⅝ inch diameter. For knife work wheels of 60 grains are suitable for the rougher work with 100 to 120 grains for the finer and finishing.

Before bolting up the wheels on the spindle, two discs of cardboard about 1/16 inch thick should be cut out the same size as the flanges on the spindle, and one of these should be put between the wheel and the flange on each side.

The materials mentioned can be purchased from the following firms or from any large engineers' stores: Steel shafts, collars, bolts, nuts, belting, grinding wheels, wood screws, plates for pulleys, mops, etc., Messrs. Burk & Hickman, Whitechapel, E.; Messrs. Melhuish, Fetter Lane, E.C.; tube, sheet metal, etc., Messrs. Smith & Son, St. John's Square, London, E.C.

Firms specialising in breaking up motor vehicles exist in all large towns. The total cost excluding labour should not exceed £3 if wheels are bought new, or less if second-hand wheels are used.

Fig. 25.—General Arrangement. Road Wheels shown dotted.

Fixing Wood Mantelpieces

Mantels are used primarily to provide an architectural finish to the more unsightly fixing of the fireplace interior to the brickwork, and secondly to enhance the beauty of the room they adorn.

Use of the Mantel.

In the more simple types of fireplace surrounds, the marble or tile slab is placed on the face of the fireplace breast to surround the opening beneath the flue. The edges of this surround in the case of those whose tiles do not return are left rough, and it is to hide these that a mantel is used. It is done by means of a rebated moulding, the face of which projects toward the centre of the surround and across the face, and this moulding also returns to the wall.

The most simple mantel need only consist of three pieces of such moulding, mitred at the angles and placed in position, as shown in Fig. 2, and it can be fixed to the wall by screws entering wood blocks for the purpose.

Style of Mantel.

In choosing the mantel, the actual fireplace interiors must be considered in relation to the mantel. In buildings embodying a definite style we often find that the rooms follow the same style. For instance, a dining-room will be panelled in a Tudor style and if of very elaborate design, a badly chosen mantelpiece and interior will upset the balance. To obviate this,

Fig. 1.—Fixing Mantels by Means of Battens.
In the above illustration the mantel is fixed by screwing two battens to the wall by wood plugs, placing the mantel in position and screwing through the sides of the mantel into the battens and covering the heads of the screws with cover pellets.

an arched interior and a mantelpiece following the same principle should be adopted.

Smaller properties, however, will not stand the expense of such a scheme as this. Further, there will possibly be no architectural features to consider, and one must be satisfied with a selection that harmonises from a decorative point of view.

To explain this, a rather appealing design of mantelpiece may be chosen in mahogany or oak, and while retaining its refined appearance in a room decorated along the same lines, would be hopelessly out of place in, say, a bedroom where the decorations were carried out in a very clashing colour scheme. In such a case the mantel could be made from one of the cheaper timbers, which would allow of its being painted or stained with the general scheme.

BUILDING REGULATIONS

The first and most important point to remember in the fixing of any mantelpiece is that there is a condition in the London Building Acts, and possibly a like condition in the by-laws of other districts, that—

Timber or woodwork shall not be placed:—

1. In any wall or chimney breast nearer than twelve inches to the inside of any flue or chimney opening.

2. Under any chimney opening within ten inches of the upper surface of the hearth or chimney opening.

3. Within two inches from the face of the brickwork or stonework about any chimney or flue where the substance of such brickwork or stonework is less than eight and a half inches thick, unless the face of such brickwork or stonework is rendered.

4. Wooden blocks shall not be driven nearer than six inches to the inside of any flue or chimney opening, nor any iron holdfast or other iron fastener nearer than two inches thereto.

The first condition does not greatly

Fig. 2.—A Simple Mantel.
The most simple mantel need only consist of three pieces of moulding, rebated to cover the surround, and mitred at the angles placed in position as shown, screwed to plugs in the wall and properly stopped and decorated.

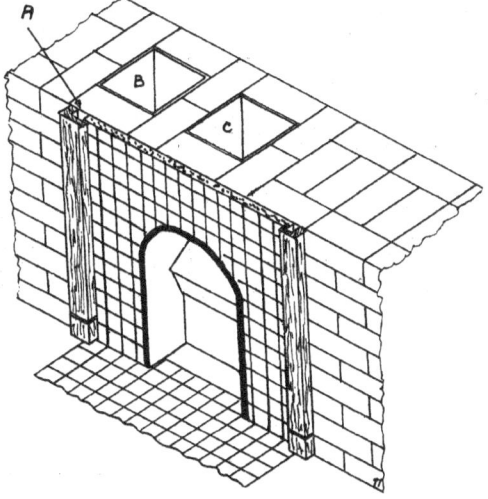

Fig. 3.—Care in the Use of Wood Blocks.
It is mentioned in the text that wood blocks must not be driven nearer than 6 inches to the inside of any flue. The above illustration is a case in which this might happen unwittingly. C is the flue of a fireplace on an upper floor, B is the flue from a lower floor, and you will note is only 4½ inches away from point A at which a fixing of a mantel would take place, and cases like this should be carefully looked for.

concern us in the matter of fixing mantelpieces, as they are not placed in the wall.

The second condition is similar; the third, however, is of vital importance, for it means that one must ascertain that the flue has been constructed with at least 9 inches of brickwork. If such brickwork were only 4½ inches thick, then it must be thicknessed to the required 9 inches before the mantel can be placed against the wall, unless the process of rendering is carried out.

The fourth condition is also very important, and unless one is very careful it cuts across the third condition, which allows, say, 4½ inches of brickwork to the flue provided it is rendered, but number four says that no plugs must be driven nearer than 6 inches to the inside of the flue; therefore, how are we to provide a fixing?

How to provide a Fixing.

Fig. 3 is intended to illustrate this and shows the mantel of an upper floor in position, the fixing plugs of which must of necessity be nearer than 6 inches to the inside of the flue from the lower floor if the 4½-inch wall shown with its rendering is allowed. The fourth condition also requires consideration regarding the iron holdfasts.

Methods of fixing Mantels.

Having studied these points we come to the actual fixing, of which there are numerous methods.

The most simple method is to fix two upright battens to the wall by means of plugs and to screw the mantel in position from the sides, as shown in Fig. 1, sinking the screws below the surface and inserting cover pellets. Occasion may arise, however, when it is not desirable to deface the edges of the mantel by the insertion of these screws, and an alternative method is to screw some caulked holdfasts to the inside edge and to build them into the brickwork, as shown in Fig. 4. This is a more costly method, as it entails a

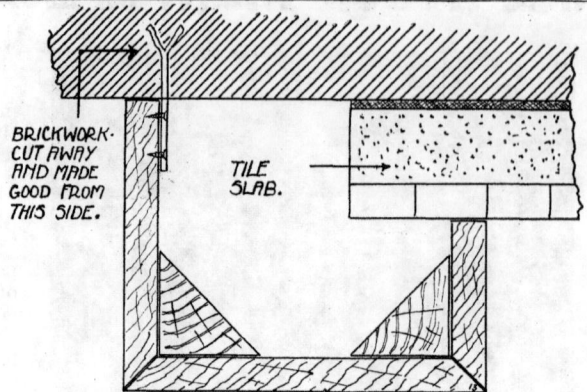

Fig. 4.—ANOTHER METHOD OF FIXING MANTELS.
The best method of fixing a mantel where it is not likely to be removed is to screw iron holdfasts to the inside and build them into the brickwork as shown. Note that the brickwork must be cut away and made good from the outsides of the mantel.

small cutting away of the brickwork for the insertion of the holdfasts and the making good.

Wood Mantelpieces fitted with Mirrors.

It is customary to find a notice attached to the backs of the majority of ready-made mantelpieces to the effect that they must not be placed in position against a damp wall. This is no idle precaution, and while in the case of specially manufactured mantels and some ready-made makes the notice may be omitted, the same precaution should be observed.

The reason for this is that the makers recognise that a newly-erected building contains a certain amount of moisture immediately after its erection, and that for a certain time this moisture exudes from the brickwork and plaster and is certainly detrimental to new woodwork placed in direct contact. With mantels having mirrors inserted in their upper panels this moisture is an added detriment, for dampness causes the silvering to peel or discolour. Both these defects can be guarded against to a large degree by giving the backs of the mantels two good coats of red-lead priming well punched into all corners and jointings.

All-tile Surrounds.

There is a general tendency to-day to use surrounds composed of tiles, marble or stonework, and to dispense with the use of the mantelpiece, with the exception of a shelf which rests upon the surrounds—in fact, in some cases, the shelf also is omitted. Where they are provided, the method of fixing them is to insert two or three iron dowels along the back edge and to pin them into the brickwork. Before doing so, examine the shelf for any irregularity or tendency to warp, for with tiled surrounds of this description there is no means of fixing them to the top of the slab, and if they should curl away, will leave an unsightly gap between the underside and the tiles.

Standard Openings.

With the use of tile slabs and their consequent unit sizes governed by the tiles, ready-made mantelpieces have come to be made in more or less standard openings, to ensure that given uniform widths of tiles are exposed to view, and due allowance is usually made for the amount of cover. Thus, for a surround composed of 4-inch by 4-inch tiles, which would be 40 inches in width and height, the opening of the mantelpiece is made 38 by 38 inches, giving 1 inch of cover along the two vertical sides and 2 inches of cover along the top. It is fairly safe to assume that similar amounts of cover are allowed for practically all types of mantels where it is required, and when ordering a mantelpiece for a tiled surround of a given size, allowance must be made for this when stating the size of the opening required.

Mantel Registers.

These are a type of combined surround and mantel and are usually made of cast iron.

Their method of fixing cannot be effectively concealed. A fault with such registers is that the continual expansion and contraction of the metal by the heat "works" the screws and lugs in their fixing.

HOW TO BRONZE A PLASTER CAST

A GOOD way to bronze a cast made with plaster of paris is first to make up a mixture of sulphate of iron and sulphate of copper in equal proportions and add this to a solution of palm-oil soap in water. This gives a green precipitate, the colour of which can be varied by altering the proportions of the sulphates. Strain the solution through a piece of butter muslin in order to collect the precipitate. The latter should be washed in clean water, strained again, and then dried. It is then mixed with a coach-painter's varnish and boiled linseed oil, or, alternatively, with linseed oil and paraffin wax. These solutions should be applied hot to the plaster cast. Upon drying the latter will be found to have an excellent bronze appearance.

Hayboxes for Cooking Purposes

EVERY housewife should have a haybox cooker, seeing that it is a piece of apparatus which can be the means of saving a considerable sum of money each year on the bill for fuel.

A haybox cooker need be nothing more than a wooden receptacle stuffed with hay; but, if full use is to be made of the advantages it offers, it is advisable to construct a special box on the lines suggested in this article. The work is quite simple and the cost very little.

What a Haybox will do.

What such a cooker will do is little short of marvellous. It will cook anything that is ordinarily prepared in a stewpan, such as boiled fish, vegetables, porridge, soups, meat stews, steamed puddings, etc., and it will never burn them. All that is necessary is to bring the pan, containing the food, to the boil by any of the usual methods and, then, to transfer it to the haybox, *while still boiling*. Shut down the lid, allow at least three times the ordinary amount of time for cooking and then the food should be properly done.

What Size is the Haybox to be?

Naturally the first consideration will be the dimensions of the cooker that is considered most suitable for one's individual needs. If it is required to hold no more than a single stewpan at a time, a cube having 15-inch sides will serve quite well; but, in practice, it will be found more advantageous to provide accommodation for two and, sometimes, three or four pans. Then, the box must be considerably larger; in fact, it might almost be said that it cannot be too large. Where space is limited and a box as capacious as one desires cannot be conveniently stored in the kitchen, it may be possible to overcome the difficulty by making the box so that it serves the purpose of a side-table, in addition to that of cooker, and doing away with some less useful article of furniture.

All things considered, a very convenient size will be 24 inches long, 18 inches wide and 16 inches high. This will provide a spacious contrivance with plenty of room for three or four pans.

Making the Framework of the Box.

Having decided on these preliminary matters, the next thing will be to obtain some strips of wood, 1 inch square in section, and to set about constructing a skeleton rectangle with them (see Fig. 2). Four pieces, 24 inches in length, will be needed for the long horizontal faces of the skeleton; four more, 16 inches long, for the width and an additional four, each of 20 inches, for the corner uprights.

Fig. 1.—THE HAYBOX COOKER COMPLETE, READY TO COOK A VAST RANGE OF DISHES WITHOUT BURNING ONE OF THEM, AND DOING THE WORK AT FAR LESS THAN THE USUAL COST.

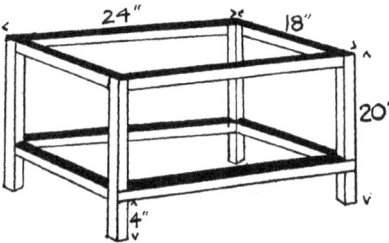

Fig. 2.—THE FRAMEWORK OR SKELETON UPON WHICH THE HAYBOX COOKER IS BUILT.

Suitable dimensions are given for a fairly large contrivance. Naturally these dimensions should be checked to see if they are suited to individual requirements.

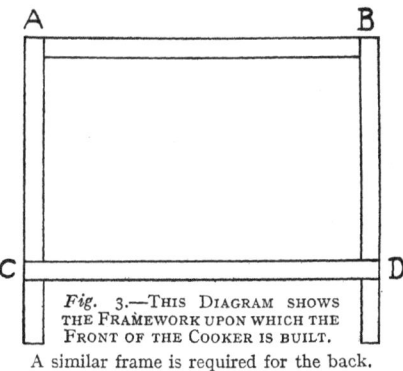

Fig. 3.—THIS DIAGRAM SHOWS THE FRAMEWORK UPON WHICH THE FRONT OF THE COOKER IS BUILT.

A similar frame is required for the back.

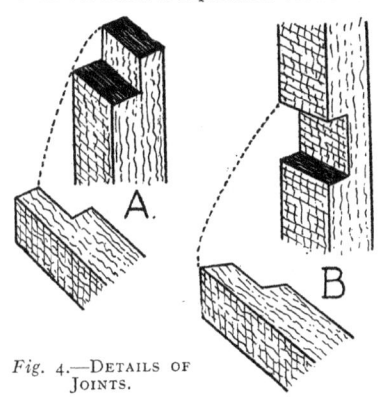

Fig. 4.—DETAILS OF JOINTS.

A represents a halved joint, suitable for the two upper corners of the frame shown in Fig. 3. B is a notched joint, such as is required at C and D in the same figure.

A glance at the figure will show that, although the height of the box is 16 inches, the corner uprights must be 20 inches long. The extra 4 inches are required to provide feet, which are needed to raise the contrivance off the ground. Of course, if the cooker is to serve as a side-table as well, the legs must be even longer. The corner strips should then be about 30 inches in length.

Why a Haybox should have Legs.

Legs should always be provided because it has been found that it is better to allow air to circulate all round the cooker than to set it down flat on some surface which may be comparatively cold. If placed, say, on a tiled floor, much of the efficiency is lost and, while dealing with the matter, it may be well to point out that the cooker should never be placed in a draught when being used.

Making the Front and Back Faces of the Box.

The simplest way to put the skeleton together will be to construct the front and back faces separately and to join them up afterwards. Of course, both faces will be exactly alike and they will each take the form shown in Fig. 3. As indicated by this figure, the strips have to be joined in four places. Those at A and B are formed by means of a halved joint (see Fig. 4A), while those at C and D by a notched joint (see Fig. 4B). Each joint will be held with sufficient strength if a 1-inch screw is put in, but it is absolutely necessary to countersink the holes and to turn the screw-heads until they are at least flush with the surface of the wood.

Filling in the Frames with Three-ply.

When the two shapes, as shown in Fig. 3, have been constructed, it is advisable to fill in the panels, A, B, C, D, with plywood before completing the entire skeleton. For this, the wood should come to the extreme outer edges of the frame and it must be fixed to whichever face of the frame is going to be used as the outside of the cooker. The fixing of the plywood is done by means of panel pins spaced an inch apart all round the edges.

Fitting the Sides.

The two frames, being filled in with plywood, the next step is to cut two more panels of ply, each 16 × 18 inches, for the sides, and to fix them so that they join up the front and back shapes. Fig. 5 explains how this work is commenced. The figure shows the right-hand edge of a side panel tacked to the front shape. The next step will be to bring up the back shape to the left-hand edge of the panel and to tack it. Following that, the second side panel will be taken and tacked in

HAYBOXES FOR COOKING PURPOSES

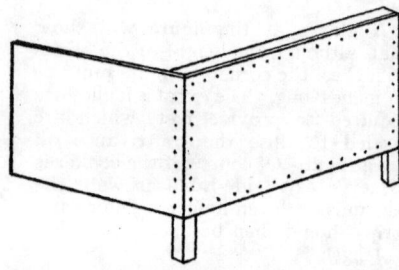

Fig. 5.—When the Front and Back Pieces of the Haybox Cooker have been made, the Sides are taken in hand.

Here a side panel is being fitted to the front piece.

the same way to the opposite upright edges of the front and back panels.

Before anything more is done it will be advisable to strengthen the upper and lower edges of both the side panels, and this is done by fixing to each of them one of the strips of 1 × 1-inch wood, 16 inches long, already mentioned. A screw should be driven through each corner upright wherever one of these pieces meets it. This will help to pull the whole contrivance together firmly.

Fitting the Bottom.

The next step is to fit the bottom panel. This should be composed of a sheet of ply 24 × 18 inches, with a 1-inch square cut out at all the four corners. This panel will rest on the strips of 1-inch wood running round the lowest edges of the vertical panels, and is fixed to the strips by means of panel pins.

Making the Lid.

The body of the haybox is now completed, but it remains to fix a lid. This can be conveniently made by constructing a skeleton frame that is exactly the same size as the upper face of the box and then covering it over with a sheet of three-ply. The frame should be made of wood, 1 inch square in section, and the corners ought to be formed with halved joints. Two hinges and a front hasp complete the constructional work.

Padding the Box with Hay.

Padding the box is the next consideration. First, put a generous quantity of dry hay in the box and ram it down so that there is a dense filling all over the bottom, from 4 to 6 inches thick. Be very certain that the corners are full and tight. Then, select the stewpans that are to be ordinarily used and stand them on the hay. Do not allow any of them to touch the sides of the box and keep them all apart from each other.

This done, pack hay around the pans and bring the material, roughly, up to the level of the lids. Try to weave or mat the hay together, much as a bird makes a nest. If the pans

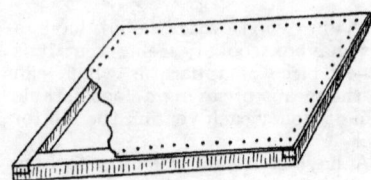

Fig. 6.—Here is shown how the Lid is constructed.

Note that a frame of 1 × 1-inch wood is first made and then a sheet of three-ply is pinned over it.

have handles, arrange where they are to lie in the hay and make depressions or grooves for them. Next, sew up a cushion cover of any clean material and stuff it with more hay. The cushion should exactly fit the box, from side to side, and reach from the top of the pans to the lid of the box. There should be no air spaces that the hay does not fill.

Now, take off the cushion, lift out the pans carefully so that the hay is not disarranged and the haybox cooker is ready for use.

Using the Haybox for Cold Storage.

It may be added that in the summer a haybox supplies an admirable storage place for ice and any cold foods that are difficult to keep cool. Naturally, they must be stored in pans or suitable receptacles.

A FLOOR SANDER

THERE are often occasions when it is desired to get a floor smooth and clean, and if the area to be dealt with is of any size at all it is a very laborious job to go down on one's knees rubbing the surface with sandpaper.

It is, however, quite a simple matter to make up a floor sander that will give results almost equal to an expensive sanding machine. The only materials needed are a milk or margarine box about 1 foot 2 inches × 12 × 10 inches, a few odd pieces of wood, a strap hinge and some large sheets of sandpaper. The sandpaper is fitted to the underneath of the box, which is filled with stones and the device is then pushed about over the floor.

The Handle.

A piece of wood approximately 4 feet × 3 inches will do for the handle. Square up one end and then screw the long arm of the strap to this end. At the other end fix a piece of wood 12 × 2 inches at right angles, as shown in the diagram. Then fix the handle to one of the sides of the box.

Fixing the Sandpaper.

There are various methods of fixing

Constructional Details of the Floor Sander.
Note the alternative methods of fixing the sandpaper to the bottom of the box.

the sandpaper to the underneath of the box. One method is simply to place the box over the sandpaper, fold up the edges and fix in position with drawing pins.

A better method is to fix the sandpaper to a separate piece of plywood through which has been driven four or five nails, so that their points are left projecting upwards. The box can then be placed on the piece of plywood and its weight will keep it in position while the device is being used. When it is desired to change the sandpaper, the box is levered off the projecting nails and the piece of plywood drawn away.

The box is filled with old stones, broken pieces of concrete, etc., until the desired weight is obtained.

It is advisable to use a fairly coarse grade of sandpaper to start with. This is fixed in position and the box is then pushed over the floor. It will soon be found that the surface is smooth and fine.

SETTING OUT DOVETAILS

THERE are three chief types of dovetail joint: the plain through joint (Fig. 1), the stopped joint as used for drawer fronts (Fig. 2), and the secret or mitre joint (Fig. 3).

Many woodworkers experience difficulty in the setting out of dovetail joints; an angle that is too acute is often used, resulting in short grain at the ends of the dovetails, as shown by Fig. 4. This short grain invariably breaks off as the joint is being assembled, thus making it rough and untidy.

Correct Angle for Greatest Strength.

The correct angle to use is 1 in 8, and generally speaking this angle gives the greatest possible strength. To obtain this angle take a short piece of board and shoot one edge true and square, then, using the try square, strike the line AB (Fig. 5) 8 inches in length, next mark the line BC 1 inch in length at right angles to AB, then join the points C and A. The line CA then gives the correct angle for the dovetails. When strength is the chief consideration, the through dovetail is invariably used, and in order to obtain a neat appearance the tails should be made much wider than the pins, as shown by Fig. 1, but in heavy work, and often in articles such as instrument cases that have to stand rough usage, the pins and tails are made equal, as shown by Fig. 6.

Setting out the Through Dovetail.

When setting out the through dovetail, say for example in making a box, the first operation is to plane the ends of the boards true and square with the smooth plane, then with the try square and pencil mark lines down each face of the board to represent the depth of the dovetails.

The distance of this line from one end of the board should be slightly more than the thickness of the stuff being used. These depth lines should

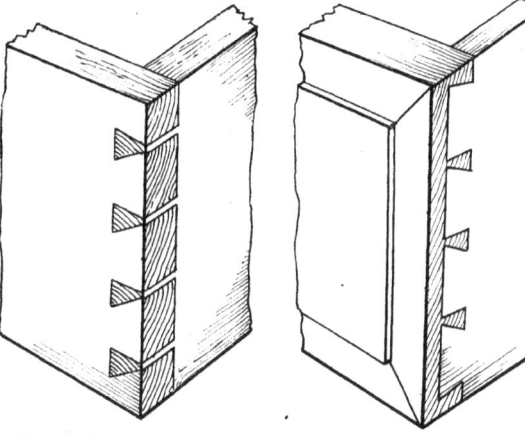

Fig. 1.—THROUGH DOVETAILING.

Fig. 2.—STOPPED DOVETAILING.

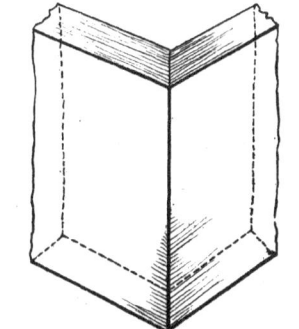

Fig. 3.—THE SECRET OR MITRE DOVETAIL JOINT ASSEMBLED.

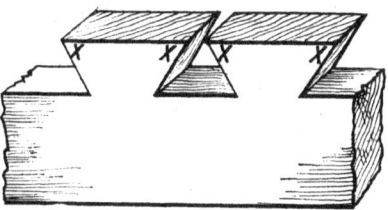

Fig. 4.—DOVETAILS THAT HAVE BEEN CUT TOO ACUTE IN THE ANGLE, RESULTING IN VERY SHORT GRAIN AT THE POINTS MARKED X.

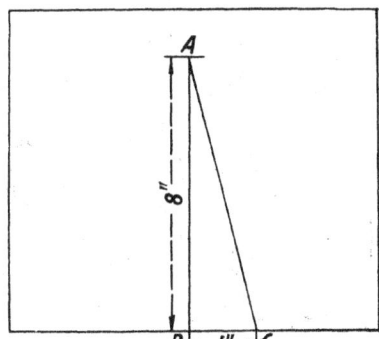

Fig. 5.—THE CORRECT ANGLE FOR DOVETAIL JOINTS.

Fig. 6.—THE THROUGH DOVETAIL JOINT, WITH THE PINS AND TAILS MADE OF EQUAL SIZE TO GIVE EXTRA STRENGTH.

not be made with either the gauge or the marking awl, as the incision thus made would be visible across the base of each dovetail on the finished work.

Dealing with the Ends of the Box.

The ends of the box should next be taken in hand and the pins spaced out on the ends of the boards to suit the width of the timber, the angle being marked to the bevel that should be set to the line CA (Fig. 5). Having marked the pins on the ends of the boards, the lines should be squared down each face of the board to the base line, as shown by Fig. 7. Any error in cutting is then more easily avoided.

A Deep Lid.

If a deep lid is to be made for the box, an excellent method of obtaining a lid the exact size of the box is to make the box full depth, assemble it, and screw on the top and bottom. The depth of the lid is then gauged all round the box, the lid then cut away with the panel saw and the sawn edges planed to a true fit. When this method is used a broad pin should be made where the joint of the lid will occur, as shown by Fig. 8, to allow for sawing and planing.

Now saw Pins to Shape.

Having set out all the pins, the ends of the box should be placed in the vice and the pins sawn to shape with the dovetail saw. The mark showing the outline of the pins should not be cut away, but left just visible on one side of the saw cut.

Removing Surplus Wood.

Then lay the boards flat on the paring block and remove the surplus wood, marked X on Fig. 7, with a suitable chisel and mallet. On no account should an attempt be made to remove all the surplus at once. An incision should be made with the

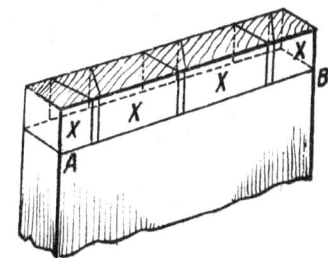

Fig. 7.—SHOWING THE PINS MARKED OUT ON THE END OF THE BOARD.

Note how the lines have been squared down on each face of the board to the base line AB.

SETTING OUT DOVETAILS

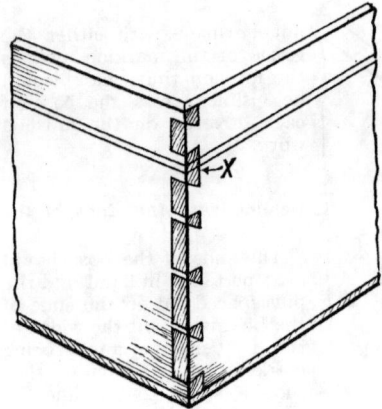

Fig. 8.—A Corner of a Box assembled with the Lid gauged ready for cutting off with the Panel Saw. Note the broad pin at X.

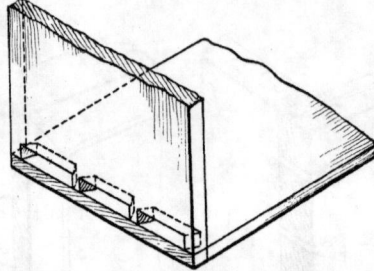

Fig. 9.—The Prepared Pins placed in Position on the Side of the Box so that the Shape of the Tails may be marked.

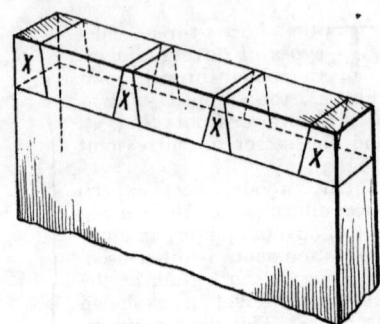

Fig. 10.—The Tails set out ready for Cutting. Note the surplus portions marked X that have to be cut away.

chisel on the base line on each side of the board to prevent splintering, and the surplus should then be carefully removed in small portions.

When all the pins are completed, the sides of the box should be laid face downwards on the bench and the pins held in turn in their respective positions, the shape of the pins being marked on the sides with a sharp pencil, as shown by Fig. 9, and each corner of the box numbered so that no error is made when the box is being assembled.

Having marked the position of the pins at each end of the sides of the box, the lines should be squared across the ends of the boards, and by means of the bevel the shape of the pins may then be set out on the other face of the board, as shown by Fig. 10.

Then in turn place each side in the vice and saw down the bevelled outline of the tail, remembering that in these pieces the tails are required and therefore making the saw kerf so that the pencilled outline of the tails is just left visible. Dovetails and pins that are sawn accurately so that they joint together without being pared and fitted are ideal, as the slightly rough surface left by the saw helps the glue to adhere more firmly than a smooth surface. A few extra saw cuts placed in the surplus wood between either the pins or tails, according to which is required, will facilitate the operation of removing it.

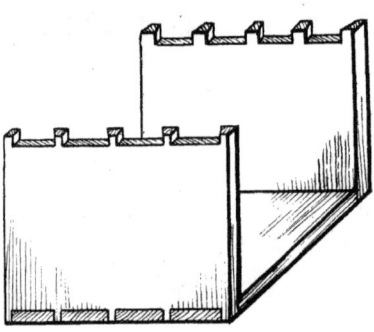

Fig. 11.—The Order in which the Box should be Assembled. Note that the ends are fixed to one side first, the opposite side then fits easily on the pins.

Gluing Box together.

When each corner of the box has been tested and fitted satisfactorily, the box may be glued together, as shown by Fig. 11. Be sure that the glue is not too thick, but preferably rather thinner than usual. Many good dovetail joints have been spoiled in the assembly by thick glue. Any slight projection of the pins and tails should be trimmed off with the smooth plane after the joints have been left to stand a suitable period for the glue to set firmly.

This open type of dovetail joint often proves useful for the jointing of framework when exceptional strength is required, as shown by Figs. 12 and Fig. 12A.

Stopped Dovetail Joint.

The stopped dovetail joint as used for drawer construction, shown by Fig. 13, presents no special difficulty in the setting out or making. The tails are, of course, made first on the drawer sides, the pins may then be marked on the drawer front, while the sides are held in position. A simple method that may be used in drawer construction is shown by Fig. 14.

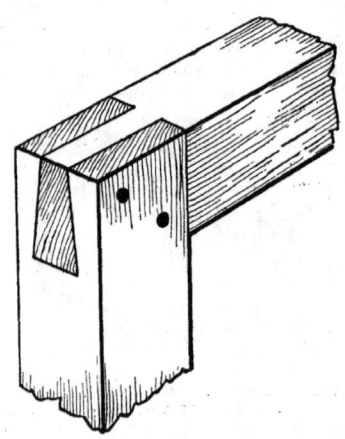

Fig. 12.—Open Type Joint for Framework.

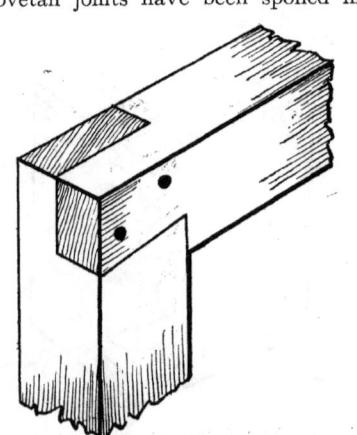

Fig. 12A.—Showing Framework Dovetailed together.

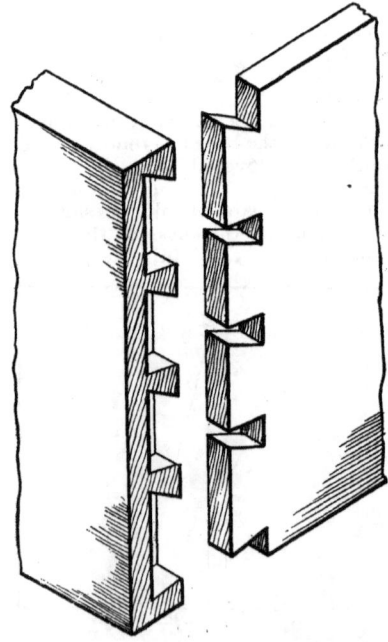

Fig. 13.—The Stopped Dovetail Joint made and ready for Assembling.

SETTING OUT DOVETAILS

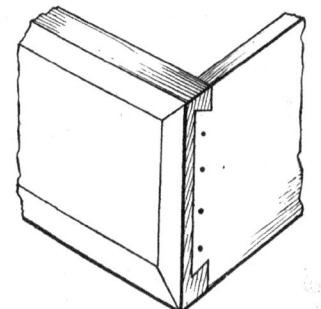

Fig. 14.—A Simple Method of Drawer Making.

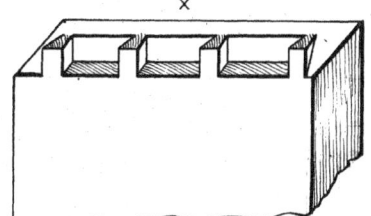

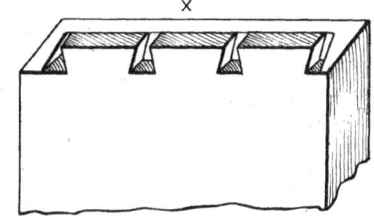

Fig. 15.—Showing the Pins and Tails of the Secret or Mitre Dovetail Joint made and ready for Assembling.

Although this method is not used in high-class work, a single dovetail proves a quick and effective method of drawer making.

The Secret Dovetail.

Perhaps one of the neatest joints used in woodworking, and yet a joint in which strength has not been given up for neatness, is the secret dovetail. The making of this joint calls for some skill in the use of tools, but is quite easily made if all operations are performed carefully and with concentration.

Fig. 15 shows the pins and tails of the secret dovetail joint made ready for assembling.

First mark off Mitre Joint.

Having planed up the ends of the wood that is to be used for the work in hand, the first operation in making this joint is to set the bevel at 45 degrees and mark off the mitre joint, as shown by Fig. 16A.

Then mark Depth of Pins and Tails.

Then, using the gauge from the trued face of the end of the wood, mark the depth of the pins and tails,

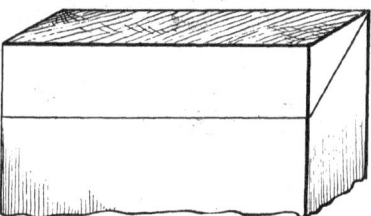

Fig. 16A.—The First Stage in setting out the Mitre Dovetail Joint.

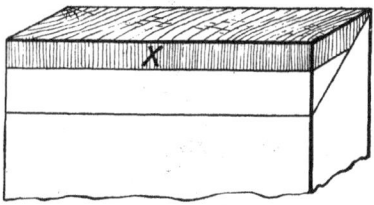

Fig. 16B.—Showing the Depth of the Pins Gauged.

Note the shaded portion marked X that is to be cut away.

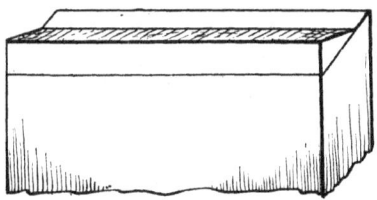

Fig. 16C.—Showing the Portion marked X in Fig. 16B cut away.

as shown by Fig. 16B. Next, by means of the dovetail saw, paring chisel and bullnose plane, carefully cut away the portion marked X so that each end appears, as shown by Fig. 16C. Now set out the pins, then pare away the surplus wood so that they appear as shown by Fig. 15. The dovetail saw could be used partly to saw out the joints, but great care should be taken not to saw the point X (Fig. 15), as any small incision made at the extreme point of the mitre would spoil the appearance of the finished joint.

Marking off the Tails.

When all the pins have been made, the tails should be marked off by holding the pins in position as previously explained. Special attention should be paid to the consistency of the glue before gluing this joint for assembly, as any tendency to lumpiness, or the presence of impurities, would completely ruin all the previous work.

Test for Squareness immediately after Gluing and Assembling.

Boxes, drawers, and similar articles that are dovetailed should always be tested for squareness immediately after they have been glued and assembled before they are finally put on one side for the glue to set.

A USEFUL MEASURING DEVICE

A PARTICULARLY useful home-made measuring device for the builder, carpenter and home mechanic is illustrated in the sketch. It is employed for making inside measurements, such, for example, as those of doorways, windows, crates and cupboards.

The device in question consists of one fixed lath member having a pair of metal guides attached to it, and a graduated sliding member; the latter can be made in several useful lengths in order to increase the scope of this article.

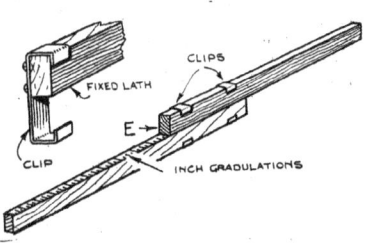

Details of the Measuring Device.

For most purposes 1 × ⅜-inch laths, planed true all over, will be found most suitable.

For the guide clips pieces of heavy gauge tinned steel will be found quite serviceable. The clips are attached to the fixed lath member by means of wood screws.

The sliding lath (shown on the left) can be graduated with pencil lines on the upper edge, so that distances are read off directly at the edge of the fixed member, marked "E" in the sketch.

A Kitchen Cabinet

Fig. 1.—The Finished Cabinet.

A kitchen cabinet is an essential in any modern home.

They are all much alike in principle and vary only in detail and arrangement. All are fitted with cupboards, shelves and drawers, so that there is little innovation possible and, consequently, nothing very striking or original will be found in the design illustrated in Fig. 1, which forms the subject of this article. A previous article deals with a small kitchen cabinet table.

Size of Cabinet.

It is of moderate dimensions, not so large as might be required for a big household perhaps, nor so small as to be liable to become suddenly inadequate when visitors are received, as some which are made might be; but of sufficient drawer and shelf capacity to allow of increasing the number and size of storage jars and vessels if required.

No fittings are shown in the drawings, except in Fig. 1, where those sketched are merely suggestions, it being presumed that these can be selected as desired.

Space for Shaker Sifter and Sugar Bin.

One item which is often found in large and elaborately equipped cabinets is a shaker sifter, and another a sugar bin, of metal, both hopper shaped, *i.e.*, conical in form.

If these are thought to be requisite, it may be found that no space sufficiently high has been provided, so that it would be well, before fitting the shelves, to purchase these things and then fix upon the position for the particular shelf which, on its underside, is to carry them.

Obviously, the best place for them is underneath the bottom shelf in the upper part of the cabinet—the portion which is closed by the flap—and this shelf, on the right-hand side, would doubtless have to be raised accordingly.

Turning now to the drawings: Fig. 3 is a front view, or elevation, of the cabinet with a cross section through the left-hand side, that is to say, through the three drawers.

Fig. 2 is a front view with all parts opened up to show the shelves and the fittings on the insides of the doors in front elevation. Fig. 2A shows a cross section taken through the right-hand side of Fig. 2 and showing the door racks in side elevation.

LIST OF MATERIALS REQUIRED

All figures given are finished sizes.

CARCASE.

Two sides ..	2 pieces	6′ 3″ × 12½″ × ⅞″ glued joint.
	2 ,,	2′ 11⅛″ × 8½″ × ⅞″
Top	1 ,,	3′ 6″ × 12½″ × ⅞″
Intermediate top	2 ,,	3′ 6″ × 12″ × ⅞″ glued joint.
Bottom shelf ..	2 ,,	3′ 4¾″ × 10¼″ × ⅞″ glued joint.
Bottom rails ..	1 ,,	3′ 6″ × 3″ × 1½″
	1 ,,	3′ 6″ × 3″ × ⅞″
Intermediate rail	1 ,,	3′ 6″ × 1⅞″ × 1⅞″

FIXTURES: LOWER PART OF CABINET.

Vert. partition	2 pieces	2′ 5⅛″ × 10¼″ × ⅞″ glued joint.
Bottom shelves	1 ,,	2′ 0⅝″ × 14″ × ⅞″
	1 ,,	2′ 0⅝″ × 12″ × ⅞″
Front drawer rails	2 ,,	1′ 3½″ × 3″ × ⅞″
Drawer side runners ..	4 ,,	1′ 6″ × 1″ × ⅞″

FIXTURES: UPPER PART OF CABINET.

Vert. partitions	1 piece	1′ 8⅞″ × 10½″ × ⅞″
	1 ,,	1′ 4¼″ × 10½″ × ⅞″
Lower shelves (2)	2 pieces	1′ 8″ × 10½″ × ⅞″
Intermed. shelf	1 ,,	3′ 4¾″ × 12″ × ⅞″
Top shelf ..	1 ,,	1′ 8″ × 7½″ × 11/16″
Partitions, etc., small drawers	1 ,,	1′ 8″ × 10″ × 7/16″
	4 ,,	2¾″ × 10″ × ⅜″

FALLING FLAP.

Panel	2 pieces	2′ 9″ × 8″ × ⅞″ glued joint.
Stiles	2 ,,	1′ 9 3/16″ × 4″ × ⅞″
Rails	2 ,,	3′ 2″ × 3″ × ⅞″

DOORS.

Lower Door, Panel of plywood ..	1 piece	1′ 8½″ × 1′ 6″ × 7 mm.
Stiles	2 ,,	2′ 2¾″ × 3½″ × ⅞″
Rails	2 ,,	1′ 9½″ × 3½″ × ⅞″
Upper Doors, Plywood panels	2 pieces	1′ 2¾″ × 10½″ × 7 mm.
Stiles	4 ,,	1′ 3⅞″ × 3″ × ⅞″
Rails	4 ,,	1′ 5½″ × 3″ × ⅞″

DRAWERS.

Bottom drawer	1 piece	1′ 3″ × 11⅛″ × ⅞″
	2 ,,	1′ 7½″ × 11⅛″ × ⅝″
	1 ,,	1′ 3″ × 10⅜″ × ⅝″
Middle drawer	1 piece	1′ 3″ × 8″ × ⅞″
	2 ,,	1′ 7½″ × 8″ × ⅝″
	1 ,,	1′ 3″ × 7¼″ × ⅝″
Top drawer ..	1 ,,	1′ 3″ × 6″ × ⅞″
	2 ,,	1′ 7½″ × 6″ × ⅝″
	1 ,,	1′ 3″ × 5¼″ × ⅝″
Drawer bottoms, plywood ..	3 ,,	1′ 7½″ × 1′ 2½″ × 7 mm.

DOOR RACKS.

On lower door ..	2 pieces	1′ 9″ × 4¾″ × 7/16″
	1 ,,	1′ 10″ × 4½″ × 7/16″
	1 ,,	1′ 10″ × 2½″ × ⅝″
	1 ,,	1′ 10″ × 3″ × ¼″
Dowel rod ..	2 ,,	1′ 10″ × ½″ or ⅝″ diam.
On top door ..	2 ,,	1′ 0″ × 4″ × 7/16″
	1 ,,	1′ 4⅛″ × 4″ × 7/16″
	1 ,,	1′ 4⅛″ × 3″ × 7/16″
	2 ,,	1′ 5″ × 2½″ × ¼″

BACK OF CABINET.

Match Boards ½″ thick, grooved and tongued, 5′ 9¼″ × added widths = 3′ 5″

SUNDRIES.

Small odd material for edges of shelves, door stops, and for making up small drawers.

A KITCHEN CABINET

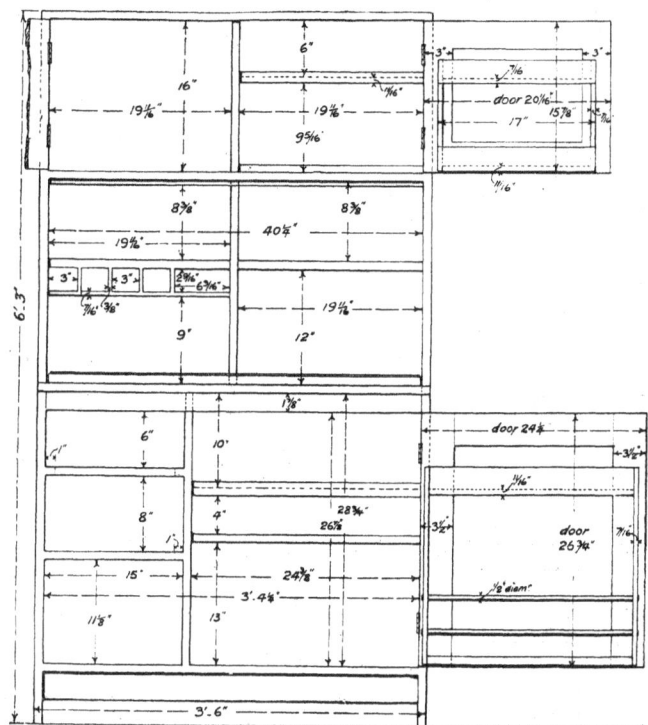

Fig. 2.—Front View of Cabinet, opened up, with Dimensions. Shelves and fittings on the insides of the doors shown in front elevation.

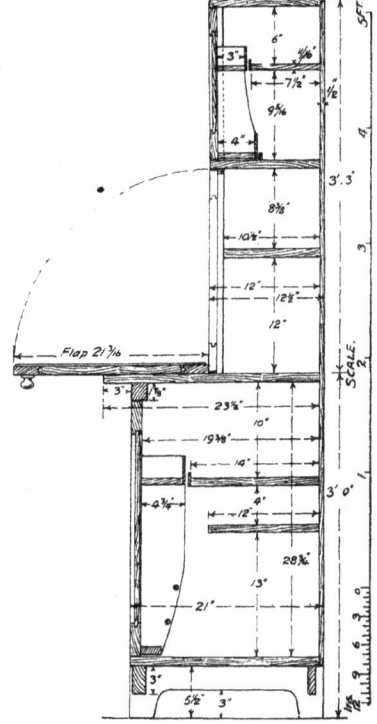

Fig. 2A.—Cross Section through Right-hand Side of Fig. 2. Door racks shown in side elevation.

Falling Flap.

From these sections it will be seen that the actual working of the food materials is done upon a falling flap similar to that on a writing bureau. The surface which is uppermost when the flap is down is best covered with a porcelain-enamelled iron plate, or, failing that, with a sheet of ¼-inch polished plate glass, which will need to have ground edges and be secured to the flap by means of metal clips.

How the Feet are formed.

Nearly the whole of the framework and shelves are of 1-inch red deal, thicknessed and finished to ⅞ inch. No corner posts or legs are fitted, supports being formed by bringing the sides down to the floor, where the centre portion, to a height of 3 inches, is cut away. The resulting feet are stiffened by rails crossing from one side to the other, serving to carry the bottom shelf, and, through the centre dividing upright, the whole middle of the structure.

Framework.

Dealing first of all with the outer framework, it should be mentioned that the back is intended to be of ½-inch grooved and tongued match-boarding, and the top of the cabinet at the back is rebated to receive this, as shown in the cross sections. The whole length of the sides should also be similarly rebated if the neatest finish is desired, though this is not imperative.

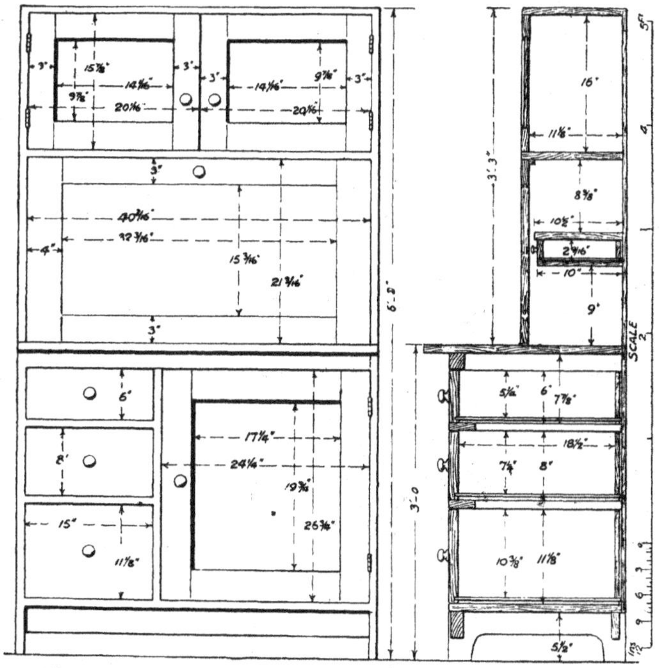

The top is dovetailed into the sides, as shown in Fig. 4. The two bottom rails will be tenoned into the sides, and to make a thorough job of these, as the sides are of only ⅞-inch stuff, the tenons and their mortises should be cut dovetail fashion and locked with wedges, as shown in Fig. 5. This will effectually prevent any tendency for the sides to spread. Of course, both tenon and wedges should be glued.

Shelves.

All shelves should be tongued at their ends and fit into grooves in main and inside uprights, as sketched in Fig. 6. The matchboards of the back should be glued at top and bottom and secured with 1¼-inch or 1½-inch oval brads.

Doors.

There are three doors

Fig. 3.—Front Elevation and Section through Left-hand Side.

1137

A KITCHEN CABINET

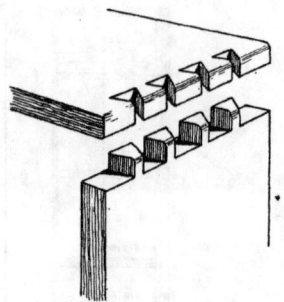

Fig. 4.—Dovetailed Top Corner of Frame.

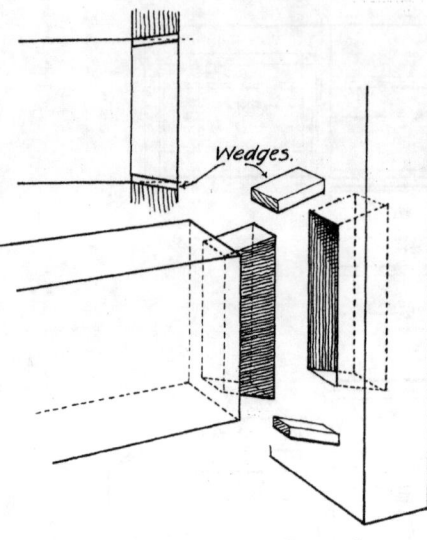

Fig. 5.—Locked Mortise and Tenon Joint of Bottom Rails.

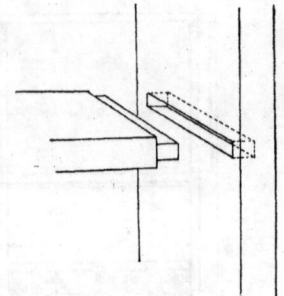

Fig. 6.—Fitting of Shelves.

in the cabinet: two at the top and one at the bottom. The top ones may be either panelled or fitted with 26-oz. sheet glass, as preferred. If panels are decided upon, the stiles and rails of each door will be grooved to receive the panel, which may be of ⅜-inch thick red deal or 7-mm. plywood. The grooves are shown in the sketch, Fig. 8. If, however, glass is used as a filling, rebates instead of grooves will require to be cut, since the glass will be put in after the door is framed up and may, at some time, need to be replaced, if broken. So separate rebate strips must be cut to hold the glass in place, and these will be mitred at the corners and simply bradded in place. The glass should be bedded on to a thin film of putty and should be inserted after the construction of the cabinet is finished and the coat of priming paint is dry.

Joints in Door Frames.

The drawing, Fig. 8, will explain the method of making the joints in the door frames. The stiles, or vertical members, should run through the full height of the door and the horizontal rails be tenoned into these. The form to which both mortises and tenons are to be cut is shown.

From the front elevation of the cabinet it will be seen that the top doors meet as do the doors of a bookcase, though this is not essential. If preferred, the partition can be brought out flush with the front of the body framing and each door will then be made ⁷⁄₁₆-inch narrower.

Making the Flap.

The flap, which is shown in the

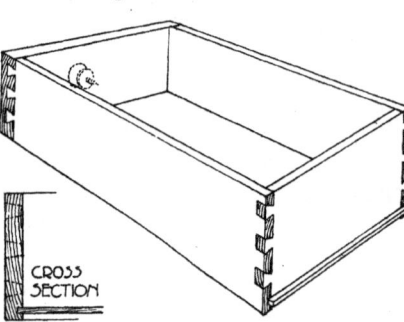

Fig. 7.—Detail Views of Drawers.

closed, or up, position in Fig. 3 and open in Fig. 2, is framed up exactly like the doors, but the panel is tongued all round to fit grooves in the framing and is the same thickness as the frame, viz., ⅞ inch. After the joining is done it should be finished with smoothing plane and glasspaper, so that the whole flap presents perfectly flush surfaces.

Fastenings.

With regard to the matter of fastenings for the doors and flap, locks can be fitted if thought necessary, but it is suggested that ball and socket latches provide all the security which may be required. Two such latches may be recessed into the top edge of the flap and one on each door. An alternative fastening would be ordinary brass or iron turnbuttons.

Drawers.

The construction of the drawers will require little explanation beyond that afforded by Fig. 7. Here it will be seen that the front and back are each dovetailed on to the sides, but the direction of cutting and fitting the dovetails is different. At the front of the drawer the dovetails are cut on the side boards, whilst at the rear they are cut upon each end of the backboard. To receive the bottom board, which may well be of 7 mm. plywood, the front and sides are grooved and the back-

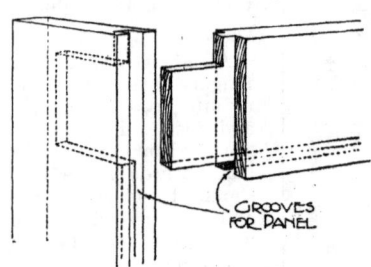

Fig. 8.—Detail of Tenoned Joint on Door Frames.

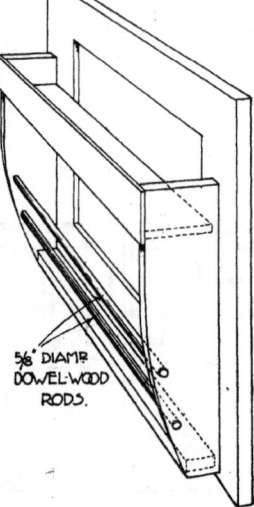

Fig. 9.—Rack on Bottom Door.

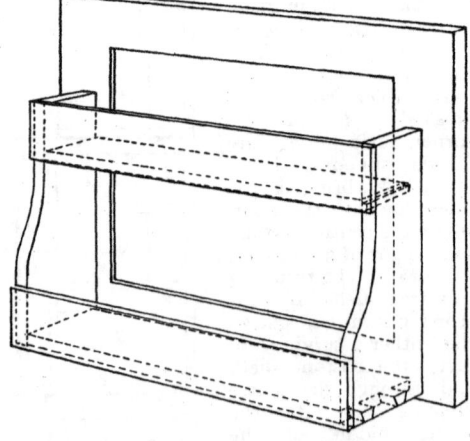

Fig. 10.—View of Rack on Top Door.

board cut away, as shown both in Fig. 7 and the cross section Fig. 3. The grooves should be cut about a ¼ inch up from the bottom edges of the boards.

The five small drawers on the left-hand side can, of course, be of very much lighter material than the largest ones and of the simplest construction, that is to say, glued and pinned together, the fronts being rebated to receive the sides.

Racks on Lower Cupboard Door.

On the inside of the lower cupboard door two useful racks are fitted. These are shown in a perspective sketch in Fig. 9. The top one is intended for either cooking utensils or for receptacles such as tins, and the lighter kinds of jars and pots; the lower one for the keeping of flat pans, trays and baking tins, etc. The side cheeks will be sufficiently well supported if they are attached to the door frames with good glued joints and bradded through from the outside; the heads of the brads punched in and the holes stopped with putty after priming.

Rack on Upper Door.

A lighter rack having two shelves, shown in Fig. 2, is fitted to the right-hand upper door. It is sketched in perspective in Fig. 10. The upper shelf will be useful for the keeping of small bottles containing sauce, extracts, and so on, whilst the lower one will support an assortment of larger articles. The blank space on the inside of the other top door, if the door is panelled, may well be utilised for recipes and charts, or a slate may be attached on which will be noted from time to time items of food and supplies to be ordered.

How to use the Drawers.

One of the drawers may well be set aside for tools, another for cooking cloths, etc., whilst the third, the largest and lowest, could, with advantage, have a detachable tin lining, with a hinged lid, for the storage of bread; such tin lining may be cross-divided and have two lids, one compartment being used for bread and the other for the preservation of cakes, etc.

The Mincing Machine.

Amongst the tools will be a meat-mincing machine, and it is suggested that to receive the clamping screw of this a metal plate of iron or brass be fitted on the outside of the flap, on the right-hand side; such a plate, if it has a thickness of, say, $\frac{3}{32}$ inch, will protect the wood from being crushed and marked by the pressure of the screw.

Use China or Glass Handles.

For the sake of cleanliness, handles to doors and drawers of white or black glazed china, or glass, are preferable, since they can be washed from time to time. Wooden knobs and brass handles of complicated patterns harbour dirt and are very objectionable where food is being prepared.

Finishing the Cabinet.

The work must be glasspapered all over, then primed and enamelled in thorough style.

A STRONG FRAMEWORK JOINT

A TYPE of joint that occasionally proves a "stumbling-block" to many amateur woodworkers is that in which three similar square section pieces of wood meet at a single corner.

This kind of joint occurs frequently in wooden framing for sheds and cupboards, the three members forming the corner of a rectangular structure to which some form of covering, e.g., plywood, matchboard or composite wall-board, is afterwards attached.

It is important to have a strong joint in most cases, so that care must be taken to ensure that all three members are securely connected to each other.

There are several methods of making such "three-piece corner" joints, but they are mostly a little difficult for the amateur to carry out.

Joint can be readily dismantled.

A simple method of making a strong framework joint that can readily be dismantled at any time for storage or portability purposes is illustrated in the sketch. It utilises a bolt and nut to secure all three members, A, B and C; these are of square section timber.

Drill a Hole right through all Three Pieces.

The two pieces A and B are half-lapped, as shown. The method of securing them to the vertical member, C, consists in drilling a clearance hole right through all three pieces and well down into the member C. A slot is cut through C so that the nut can be passed into it, and in a line with the hole drilled for the bolt.

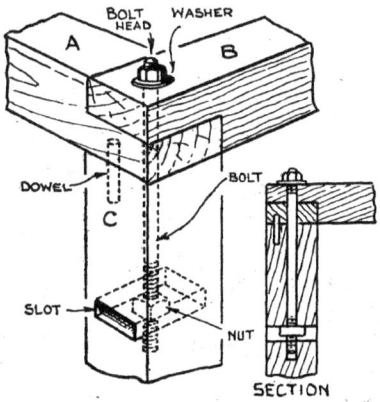

DETAILS OF THE JOINT.

Fixing the Bolt.

The bolt with its washer is then pushed down from the top and turned, whilst the nut is manipulated into position for the threads to engage. It can then be tightened up and the joint is complete.

A square nut should be used on account of the greater surface offered. The hole for the bolt should be sufficiently deep to allow the bolt to be tightened right up.

Use a Dowel Pin to locate Member C.

To locate the lower member C so as to ensure its proper alignment with the other two members, A and B, a dowel pin (as shown) can be employed.

How to Frame Pictures
WITH SPECIAL NOTES ON DISTINCTIVE PICTURE-FRAME MOULDINGS

The cost of having a picture framed is often so prohibitive that one hesitates to have the job put in hand, with the result that many people have perfectly good pictures simply stored away in any odd corner unused. Picture framing is, however, a job that any practical man can undertake himself at the minimum of cost.

Choosing a Moulding.

The first consideration is choosing a suitable moulding for the picture. Large landscape subjects will generally stand a fairly wide moulding, but light, graceful drawings and such like look their best in a narrow, plain moulding. If you are in any doubt as to a suitable type of moulding to choose, spend a few minutes looking in the window of an art dealer. The moulding can be bought in lengths of several feet. Some distinctive mouldings that can be obtained by simple carving are described later.

Tools required.

Few tools are required for picture framing. An inch rule, tenon saw, smoothing plane, vice, mitre-cutting board and plane stop, hammer, bradawl, glue-pot and a few panel nails are practically the only essentials, and will, no doubt, already be in your possession.

Preparing the Moulding.

Having determined the size of frame required, the moulding should be marked off with a pencil, the mark being made on the rebate, and an excess of about ⅛ inch allowed for cleaning up.

Next place the marked moulding on the mitre-cutting board, place the near end of the saw immediately over the pencil mark and saw through, keeping the saw as horizontal as possible. If you don't possess a mitre-cutting board already, now is a good time to make one up. All that is needed is to fix a length of wood about

Fig. 1.—The Moulding should be cut to the required Length on a Mitre Board.

3 × 3 inches and 2 feet long to a baseboard about ¾ inch thick and 9 inches wide. Then screw another piece of ¾-inch thick wood to that part of the baseboard not covered by the 3 × 3-inch stuff. Then make one or more saw cuts at an angle of 45 degrees, running from left to right and *vice versâ*. Fig. 1 shows the construction

Fig. 2.—Showing the Construction of a Plane Stop and Method of using Plane.

and method of using a mitre board very clearly.

When one end of the length of moulding has been cut, deal with the other end, but use the saw cuts on the mitre board which run at an opposite angle.

"Shooting" the Ends.

After sawing the ends of the four sides of the frame, they must be planed smooth, known as "shooting" the ends. For this purpose a plane stop is required. If you don't possess a plane stop, Fig. 2 shows how it is constructed; it is made of wood of any convenient size, and the side of the triangle against which the moulding is to be held should be at an angle of 45 degrees to the front edge of the baseboard. Note that the construction of the baseboard allows the edge of the plane to come below the underside of the moulding, the reason being, of course, that the blade of the plane does not extend right to the edge.

Make sure Pieces of Moulding are same Length.

In order to obtain a perfectly rectangular frame, the pieces of moulding forming the opposite sides must be planed to exactly the same length. To check this place each pair side by side, so that the angles correspond. Any error should be rectified.

Jointing the Frame.

The next step is to join the four sides together. Place one length of moulding in the vice, protecting it from damage by the jaws by a small piece of cardboard. Then hold the next side of the frame firmly against it, as in Fig. 3, and make a hole with a bradawl into both pieces, so that when the nail is driven in it will be guided to the right place.

Now apply a film of glue to the loose piece of moulding (using a thin piece of wood to apply the glue), place the moulding in position, put the nail in the prepared position, and drive it home.

Treat each corner in a similar manner until the frame is complete.

Using Corner Cramps.

Another method is to use corner cramps as shown in Fig. 5. These ensure the two lengths being held tightly together without slipping while being nailed. If cramps are used, join the sides of the frame in pairs; then let the pairs set hard before joining the two pairs together.

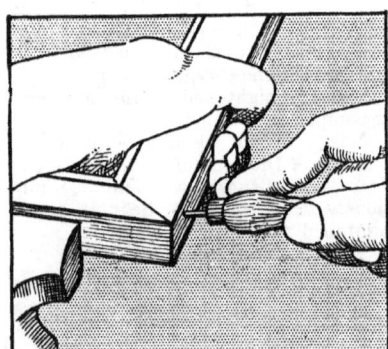

Fig. 3.—The Moulding should be gripped in a Vice and the Hole for the Nail made with a Bradawl.

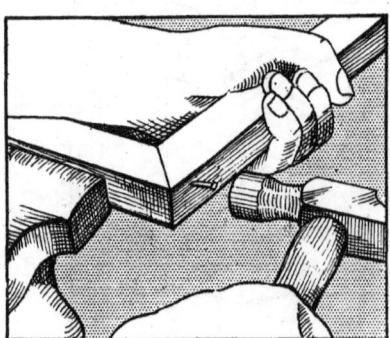

Fig. 4.—The Nail is then placed in the prepared Hole and hammered in.

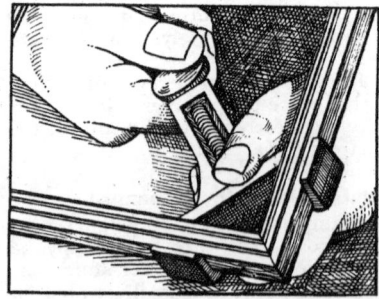

Fig. 5.—How Corner Cramps can be used for joining Mitred Corners of Mouldings.

HOW TO FRAME PICTURES

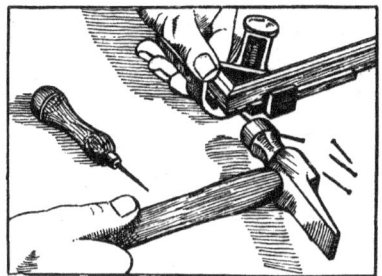

Fig. 6.—IF THE MOULDING IS NOT SQUARE ON THE OUTSIDE EDGE, SMALL STRIPS OF SQUARED WOOD SHOULD BE INSERTED WHEN USING THE CORNER CRAMP.

Leave to dry for about twenty-four hours, when the frame is now ready to receive the picture.

How to prepare a Mount.

In many cases the appearance of a picture is improved by placing a cut-out mount between the picture and the glass. It pays to use a good quality card; a poor card may quickly become discoloured.

Size of Margin.

If it is desired to leave a margin round the picture, a good rule to follow is for the bottom margin to be wider than the sides and top, say about one-third more, so that the picture looks correctly spaced.

Cutting a Bevel Edge.

The inside of the mount should be cut with a bevel edge, and the method of doing this is to run the trimming knife along a guide cut from an old piece of thick card (see Fig. 8), with the hand laid back to get the necessary angle. The forearm is pulled back straight from the elbow to ensure a smooth continuous cut. The mount is held firmly in position with the left hand.

Take particular care not to run the knife too far at the corners. It is, in fact, a good idea to cut all the sides almost to the corners and then finish off at the corners afterwards.

The Outside Edge.

The outside edge of the mount which is hidden by the moulding need not be cut bevelled. The knife can be held as in Fig. 9, and a steel straight-edge used if one is available. An old sheet of glass makes a good surface on which to do the trimming.

Fixing the Picture in Place.

Prepare a backing board either of three-ply wood or strawboard, of such a thickness that when pressed it will be slightly below the level of the back of the moulding.

Next lay the frame face downwards, and insert the glass, after cleaning both sides. Then lay the cut-out mount over the picture, placing it so

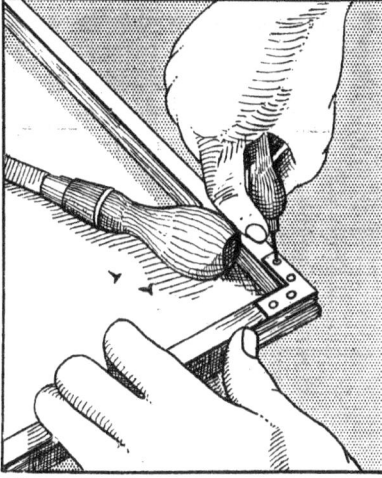

Fig. 7.—THE FRAME CAN BE STRENGTHENED BY SCREWING ON SMALL BRASS CORNER PLATES.

Fig. 9.—TRIMMING THE MOUNT.

Fig. 10.—NAILING THE INSIDE OF THE MOULDING.
Note how the hammer is held flat against the back.

Fig. 11.—A CHISEL CAN BE USED FOR DRIVING IN THE NAILS IF PREFERRED. IT WILL SLIDE FLAT ON THE BACKBOARD.

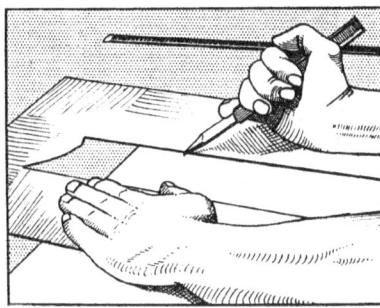

Fig. 8.—CUTTING THE BEVEL EDGE OF THE MOUNT.
Note how the knife is held at an angle.

that the margins on each side are of the same width, and place both mount and picture face downwards on the glass. Finally, place the backing board in position.

Fixing the Backing Board.

Press the backing board down against the glass and drive in a nail against the inside of the moulding as shown in Fig. 10. A small block of wood should be held against the outside of the frame opposite to where the nail is being driven in to take up the shock of hammer blows and to prevent the corners being loosened.

The head of the hammer should rest against the backing board; only two or three nails in each side will be required to keep the backing board flat. The nails are driven in about two-thirds of their length.

To keep out Dust.

Strips of brown paper should now be pasted along the four sides of the frame, the paper extending from near the outside edge of the moulding to about 1 inch on the backing board. Not only will this prevent dust being drawn into the frame round the inside edge of the moulding, but will also prevent any possibility of the nail-heads rubbing against the wall when the picture is hung up.

Eyelets for hanging the Picture.

Eyelets through which to thread the picture cord should be screwed into the two sides at the back of the moulding about one-third of the way down from the top. In the case of thin mouldings, start the holes for the screws with a bradawl to avoid danger of splitting.

Passe-partout picture framing is dealt with in a later article.

DISTINCTIVE PICTURE-FRAME MOULDING

Modern taste in picture framing favours a comparatively narrow moulding with simple decoration as well as coloured surfaces. The heavily carved frame for oil paintings has given way to the frame with a large proportion of plain surface. Water colours

HOW TO FRAME PICTURES

and pastels are framed in a variety of different ways, including coloured mouldings in greys, blues and silver, and etchings and prints are usually fitted in very narrow frame mouldings, usually perfectly plain in black or dark grey.

Carving Plain Oak Mouldings.

Individual taste now enters strongly into the framing of a picture, and although there is considerable choice in prepared picture moulding, it is possible to make use of manufactured mouldings, and turn the commonplace into the unusual with very little difficulty. The illustrations from Figs. 12 to 19 show what can be done with some plain oak mouldings by very simple carving, but the same mouldings and others equally plain may, by using cellulose or other enamels and metallic paints, be entirely transformed.

The mouldings in Figs. 12 to 14 are made from the plain spoon shape, shown in section in Fig. 20. The first example, as indicated, is treated with simple chisel or knife cuts on the rounded portions. The spacing should be carefully worked out after the frame has been made up. The curved surfaces may be smoothed with a half-round file; there should be no need for a file on the straight cuts if a very sharp chisel is used. The shape in Fig. 13 consists of plain chisel cuts only. A slight variation of the shape is shown in Fig. 21; this method is a very simple way of embellishing the plain moulding, but is very effective on narrow moulding up to ¾ inch wide.

A Simple and Effective Means of Decoration.

The shape shown in Fig. 14 is another very simple but effective

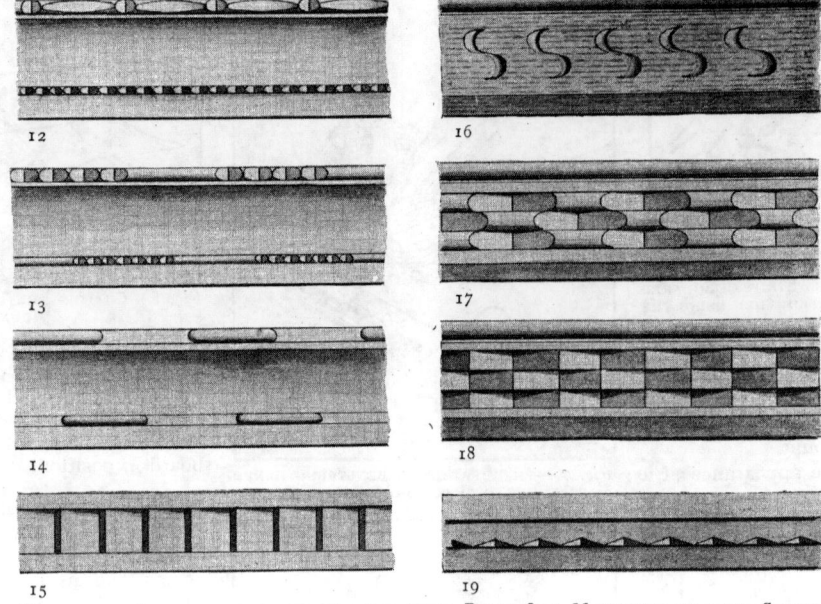

Figs. 12–19.—Showing what can be done with Plain Oak Mouldings by very Simple Carving.

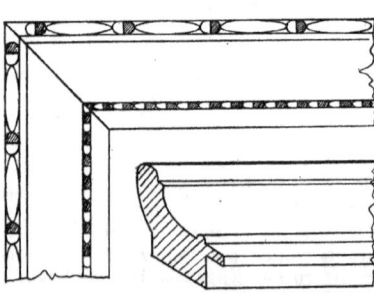

Fig. 20.—Section of Mouldings shown in Figs 12–14.

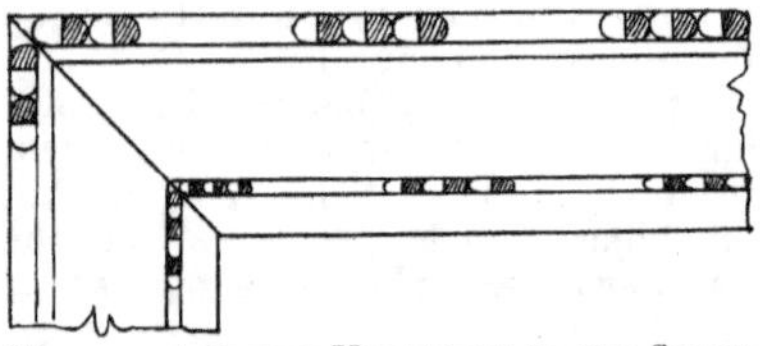

Fig. 21.—A Slight Variation of the Shape of Fig. 13.

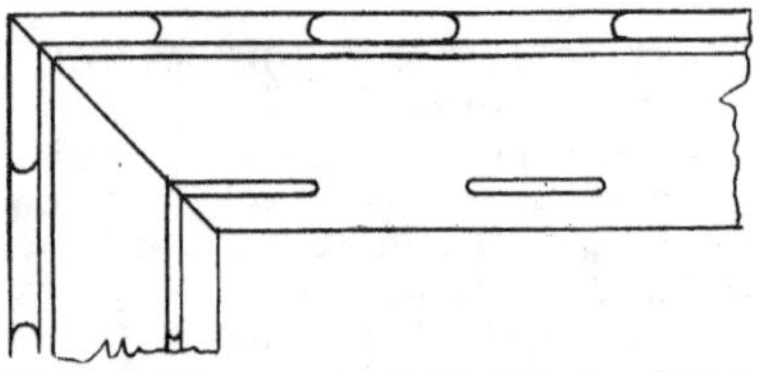

Fig. 22.—Method of marking out Shape for Fig. 14.

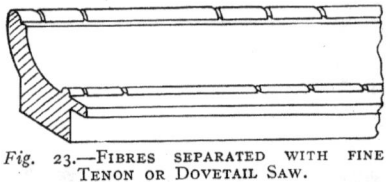

Fig. 23.—Fibres separated with fine Tenon or Dovetail Saw.

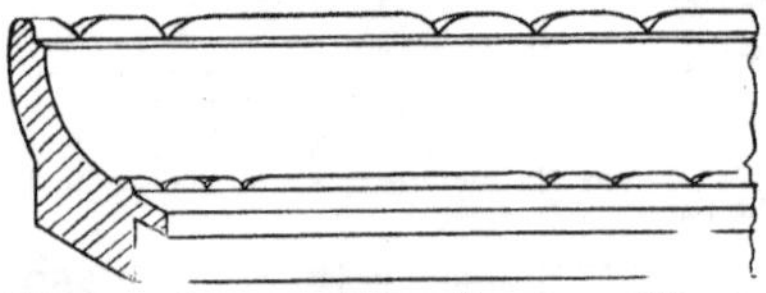

Fig. 24.—Showing Neat Finish to Edges.

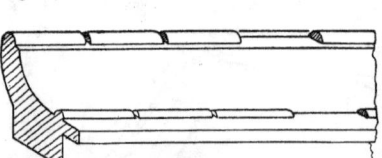

Fig. 25.—How the Rounded Portions are separated by Sawcuts.

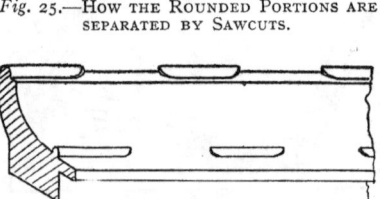

Fig. 26.—Ends worked by using a Safe-edge File.

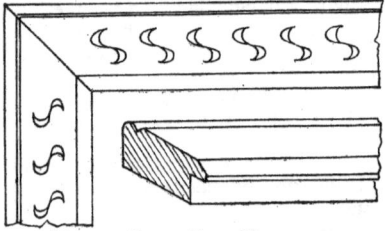

Fig. 27.—Plain Flat Moulding.

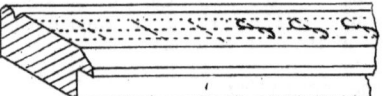

Fig. 28.—Mark out Vertical as well as Horizontal Lines.

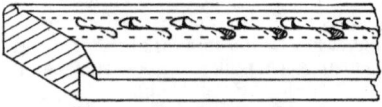

Fig. 29.—The Sloping Cuts.

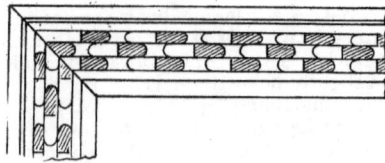

Fig. 30.—Method of planning Chisel Cuts for Fig. 17.

HOW TO FRAME PICTURES

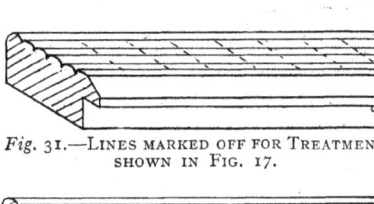

Fig. 31.—Lines marked off for Treatment shown in Fig. 17.

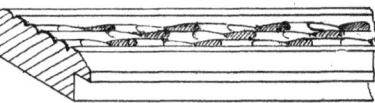

Fig. 32.—Showing Sloping Cuts made with a Narrow Chisel.

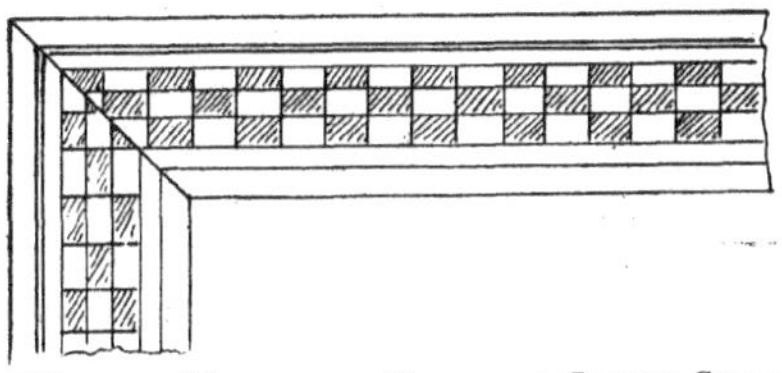

Fig. 33.—Method of Planning Chisel Cuts for Fig. 18.

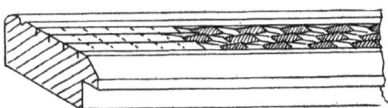

Fig. 34.—Method of Marking out for Moulding in Fig. 18.

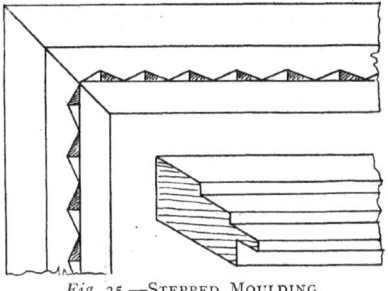

Fig. 35.—Stepped Moulding.

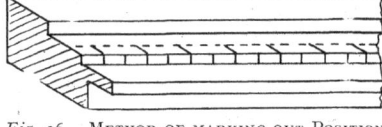

Fig. 36.—Method of Marking out Position of Cuts.

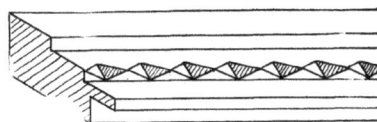

Fig. 37.—A Variation of the Stepped Moulding.

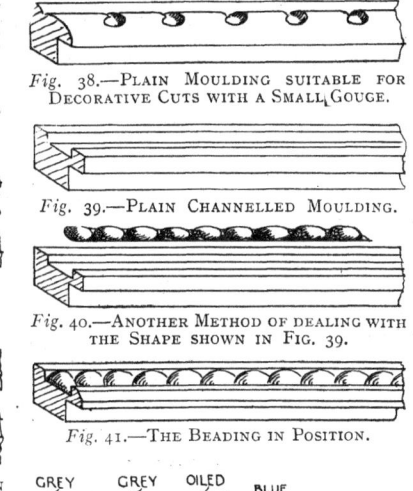

Fig. 38.—Plain Moulding suitable for Decorative Cuts with a Small Gouge.

Fig. 39.—Plain Channelled Moulding.

Fig. 40.—Another Method of dealing with the Shape shown in Fig. 39.

Fig. 41.—The Beading in Position.

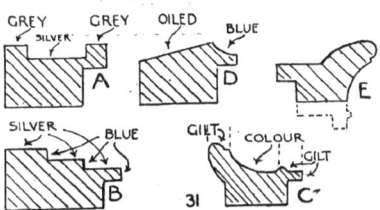

Fig. 42.—A Pleasing Effect with Channelled Moulding.

means of decoration, but owing to the rounded ends of the projections, considerable care is needed to avoid damage to the flat surface below. A fine tenon or dovetail saw, or a fret-saw, can be used to separate the fibres, as indicated in Fig. 23. The saw-cut should not be taken down close to the flat surface of the moulding, but sufficiently near to enable a file to finish the edges neatly as shown in Fig. 24. In working out the shape in Figs. 14 and 22, the rounded portions of the moulding are separated by saw-cuts as shown in Fig. 25. The waste is cut away with a chisel, and the surface smoothed down with a fine flat file. The ends can be worked as shown in Fig. 26 by using a safe-edge file, or rounded as in Fig. 14.

Altering the Appearance of a Plain Flat Moulding.

The plain flat moulding shown in section in Fig. 27 can be altered in appearance in many ways. The simple gouge cuts as shown in Fig. 16 are easily made. Care should be taken in marking out the position of the cuts, vertical as well as horizontal lines as shown in Fig. 28 being advisable. The method of making the gouge cuts is quite simple, and consists in first making vertical cuts with the gouge, a mallet being necessary in order to drive the cut deep enough. Sloping cuts are now made on opposite sides as indicated in Fig. 29. Care should be taken to make all sloping cuts at the same angle.

Improving an Old Type Reeded Beading.

The shape in Fig. 17 requires a beaded surface, and although the beading can be done with a scratch beading tool, the example is included, as it shows a method of dealing with manufactured reeded beading.

The method of treatment is quite simple, and consists of marking off lines as indicated in Fig. 31, and then making sloping cuts with a narrow chisel as shown in Fig. 32. Another method of dealing with flat moulding, and one that is particularly effective, is shown in Fig. 18. In this case the moulding is marked out as indicated in Fig. 34, and four deep gauge lines cut into the surface as shown in the section. A narrow chisel is used to make the cuts.

Stepped Moulding.

The stepped moulding, as shown in Fig. 35, provides many opportunities for decorative treatment, the simplest method of treatment being shown in Fig. 19. Care should be taken in marking out the position of the cuts, as shown in Fig. 36. The cuts may be made the same distance on the top and down the edge, as shown in Figs. 19 and 35, but a variation is possible by increasing the distance on the top, as shown in Fig. 37.

The plain moulding, as shown by the end section in Fig. 38, provides an opportunity for decorative cuts with a small gouge. Mark out equal spaces along a line drawn along the centre of the wide curve, make hollow cuts by revolving the gouge, and then cut back to the outer edge with a veiner. Instead, the smaller round on the outside of the moulding can be treated with chisel cuts similarly to Figs. 12 and 13.

The plain channelled moulding shown in Fig. 39 contains several possibilities, one of the most effective being shown in Fig. 15. In this example the inner flat surface is marked out to give approximately square divisions, and either vertical or slightly sloping cuts are made with a sharp chisel. The long sloping cuts need not be more than $\frac{1}{8}$ inch deep.

Colouring Oak Moulding.

Oak moulding can be treated by means of colour and gilding. An example of a pleasing effect with channelled moulding is suggested at A in Fig. 42. The inner surface is covered with a silver or aluminium paint and a pale grey or pale blue paint or enamel applied to the remaining surfaces. Cellulose finish serves admirably.

Another suggestion is given at B for dealing with stepped moulding, and at C for the treatment of the ordinary spoon moulding. The parts to be gilded or silvered should be done after the colour is applied, the latter portion being covered with paper. Another form of moulding as at D can be improved by filling in the hollow with a colour to suit the picture. The example at E shows a method of using the spoon moulding to provide an entirely different shape.

Some Useful Ideas for Cushions

Much of the comfort and beauty of any home depends upon its cushions. They are the easiest way of providing a soft surface to rest against, or of changing or accentuating any particular colour note in a room.

Cushions are much cheaper, of better materials and more suited to a particular room if they are made at home than if bought ready-made.

It is best to make the cushions themselves separately, permanently enclosing them in cheap, durable covers of unbleached calico, and then to slip on over these the ornamental cushion covers. To stuff an ornamental cover direct means that it is a great deal of work to change the cover if it goes out of fashion or no longer suits the room.

Also a light cover should be easily washable, which is not the case if it is filled.

Stuffings used for Cushions.

Two different stuffings are used for cushions. In most cases kapok or vegetable down, costing about 1s. 6d. per pound, is employed. It is cheap, easy to make up and very comfortable when new, but tends to get lumpy after a certain amount of wear.

Owing to their higher price, feather cushions are scarce. However, although the first cost is distinctly more, such cushions should be afforded if possible. Cushions with this filling must have a featherproof lining.

How to make and stuff a Kapok Cushion.

To make and stuff a kapok cushion, decide on the shape and size required (this will be discussed later) and cut the pieces of the case from unbleached calico accordingly. Seam them together with ½-inch seam turnings, leaving an opening for filling.

Stuff the empty case with kapok, as in Fig. 2, which shows a bolster shape being made. Fill the case well, but not tightly, or it will be too hard. From 1 to 2 lbs. of kapok will be required, according to the quality of the stuffing and the size of the cushion. Afterwards sew up the open end.

To make and stuff a Feather Cushion.

To make and stuff a feather cushion, make the case of waxed cambric. (Further details about this material were given in the article, "How to Make an Eiderdown," on page 553.) Seam the case with ½-inch turnings (if worked by hand use backstitch) and overcast the turnings together as a further safeguard against feathers escaping.

Fill the case by sewing its open edges to the edges of the bag containing the feathers and then pumping these through the tube so formed, as is described more fully in the eiderdown article.

Fig. 1.—A Bolster-shaped Cushion is particularly suited to lie along the End of a Couch.

SUGGESTIONS FOR SHAPES AND SIZES

There is a wide variety of cushion shapes and sizes. The following are the most popular and the easiest to make.

The Square Shape.

This looks well, comes economically out of the material and is very comfortable. It is made from two equal-sized squares of stuff, the most usual size being 18 inches square, so that the whole cushion is cut without waste from only ½ yard of 36-inch material.

The Oblong or Pillow Shape.

This is a better shape than the square for use along the length of a couch or divan. It lends itself to many types of trimming. It has also the asset that if made pillow size (30 × 20 inches) as is the patchwork cushion in Fig. 5, and provided with a detachable ornamental cover fastened with press studs, it may be taken out of this in a moment and put into a pillowslip for emergency bed use.

For this reason every house should possess one pillow-sized cushion, preferably filled with feathers. A useful smaller size for oblong cushions is 24 × 16 inches.

To make this shape, cut two oblongs of the desired size, and seam as for square cushions, leaving one end open for stuffing.

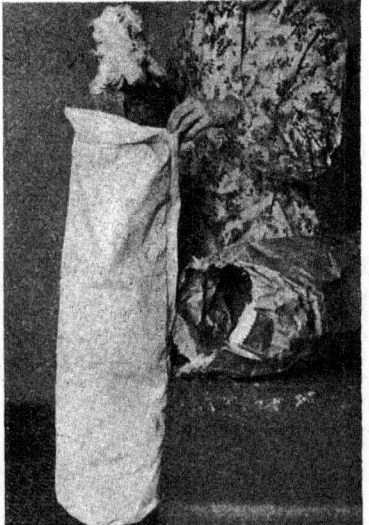

Fig. 2.—Stuffing the Calico Case for a Bolster Cushion with Kapok.

The Bolster Shape.

This is particularly decorative and Fig. 1 shows how ideally suited it is to lie along the end of a couch or chesterfield. A usual size is 30 inches long and about 28 inches round the thickness; but if it is being made for use on any particular couch, it should be constructed the same length as the depth of the couch from back to front, as in Fig. 1.

To make a bolster cushion the size mentioned above, 1 yard of 50-inch wide unbleached calico will be required. Cut from this an oblong 31 inches long by 29 inches wide and two circles, each measuring about 8 inches across. An easy way to obtain the shape for these, if you have no compasses, is to draw round a plate of suitable size.

Form a cylinder by seaming each short edge of the oblong round a circle, leaving part of one circle open for filling, which process is shown in Fig. 2. Stuff a bolster rather more firmly than an ordinary cushion.

Round Cushions.

These are a little more troublesome to make than those with straight edges. Round cushions are usually made rather large, about 21 inches across.

Cut two circles this size, seam them together most of the way round, but leave enough open for filling. Circles stretch out of shape very easily, so care must be taken when seaming to keep the shape correct. For the same reason, the open part of each circle should have a taut gathering thread run along it, so that it will not stretch during stuffing.

Tuck-in Cushions.

These may be either oblong, as in Fig. 1, or square. Their distinctive point is not shape but their specially small size, to enable them to tuck comfortably into the small of the back, for which the ordinary cushion is too large. An oblong tuck-in should measure 15 × 10 inches, and if made in sturdy material not easily soiled and provided with a carrying strap, may also be used as a travelling cushion. A good size for a square tuck-in is 12 inches.

Make these cushions exactly like the larger ones of the same shape, but stuff them rather harder, as they are intended to give definite support rather than softness.

The Fan Shape.

This type is more wasteful of material than most other shapes and rather more difficult to make. It resembles a fan opened only to a right angle and lends itself to particularly pretty trimmings, so it should be a " best " rather than a workaday cushion.

To make it, mark out on doubled unbleached calico a right angle which measures 21 inches along each arm. From the corner, using a pencil pivoted on string secured at the corner (as explained more fully in " How to Make an Eiderdown," page 553) describe a quarter-circle from one 21-inch point to the other.

Seam together the two shapes so secured along the curve and one straight side, leaving the other open for filling. Take care to preserve the curved shape accurately when seaming. For effective trimming of the ornamental cover and to preserve the illusion of a fan, a cushion this shape should only be rather flatly filled.

Boxed Cushions.

There are cushions of any shape—square, oblong or round—which have the top and undersides joined by a thickness strip instead of to each other, to give a flat effect like a box. Such cushions are particularly comfortable, but as they are rather severe-looking they are generally only used where comfort is more important than decoration. The upholstered loose cushions of chairs and couches, which are always boxed, are an example of this.

For ornamental purposes, round and tuck-in cushions are the shapes most often boxed, as the circular outline takes away from the hardness of the style, and boxing gives a tuck-in cushion the necessary firmness.

For the making of boxed cushions refer to the end of " Fitting Loose Covers " on page 257. Piping, however, should only be used on the ornamental cover, not on the inner calico case.

Pads.

These are a special flat form of cushion used to soften a hard seat or to make it a little higher and at the same time to add an ornamental colour note. Use pads rather than cushions for the tops of wooden dressing-table stools or on wooden dining-room or kitchen chairs. They are made with one cover only, though this is more or less decorative, as in Fig. 3.

As pads are to be sat upon, they should not be trimmed except with piping, as shown. Make the pad like a square cushion, but the exact size and shape of the seat it is to cover.

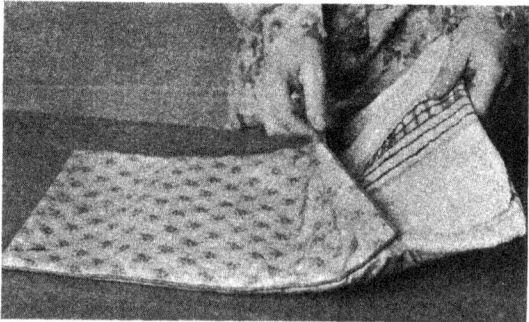

Fig. 3.—Several Thicknesses of Terry Towelling folded together form good Padding for a Flat Form of Cushion.

Fig. 4.—A Plain Square Cushion with Corners of Floral Cretonne button-holed on.

Fig. 5.—A Crazy Patchwork Cushion Cover.

It is not stuffed, but padded with several layers of thick material cut to size and slipped in, as Fig. 3 shows. These layers should be tacked together before being inserted.

Cheap felt, such as that made for laying under carpets, may be used for the padding. Better, because washable, are several thicknesses of cheap terry towelling, folded together as in Fig. 3.

CUSHION COVERS

There is hardly any material which cannot be used for the making of ornamental cushion covers to slip over the plain cushions. Well-made and well-chosen covers can easily make all the difference to the look of a room.

Often the most successful ones are those that in some way match the apartment in which they are placed. The square cushion in Fig. 4 is an instance. One small square of cretonne was left over from making the curtains in the room. It was not large enough for a cushion, but when cut across into two different-sized triangles, which were mounted corner-wise on plain material the colour of the leaves in the design, a pleasantly harmonious effect was obtained.

A diagonal treatment of this sort also breaks up the right angles which predominate among cushions. An open buttonhole stitch decoratively joins the corners to the main material.

If a cushion cover is made entirely of patterned material, a plain piping is often the only trimming needed. This may well be of cotton bias binding. For details of how to pipe see the article, " Fitting Loose Covers " on page 257.

Crazy Patchwork.

A cheery cushion cover which will look well added to any colour scheme may be made at practically no cost by means of crazy patchwork (Fig. 5). A look through the family piece-box will reveal ample bits of all sizes and hues, either of silk and velvet, as in the cushion illustrated, or cotton. Do not mix silk and cotton pieces.

Foundation for Patchwork.

As foundation for the patchwork use a piece of unbleached calico or any firm cotton, which need not be new, as it will be completely covered. Arrange the pieces more or less haphazard, as their shape and colours dictate, on the foundation, turning in and tacking down some edges, while others will be covered by neighbouring patches overlapping them.

Home-Made Incinerators for Garden Use

The disposal of garden refuse is one of the problems that invariably confront the householder or gardener. In certain seasons of the year this rubbish is apt to accumulate and become a nuisance, unless one takes steps to dispose of it by burning or burying. There is little doubt that the method of getting rid of this rubbish by burning is the most convenient of any, for the relatively large bulk of the combustible matter is reduced to a few ashes in a very short period of time.

In this way such items as leaves, twigs, weeds, paper, roots and all similar material can be burnt up, for once a well-designed incinerator has been lit in the proper manner, so great is the heat that even green wood and vegetation is quickly dried and burnt therein. Household refuse such as vegetable parings and refuse, paper, cardboard, and similar combustible material can also be quickly disposed of in the garden incinerator; moreover, the ashes left from the burning of this vegetable refuse are good fertilisers for the garden.

Incinerator Requirements.

The first essential feature of an incinerator is that it shall provide sufficient space to hold a good quantity of the refuse, so that it will not require too frequent re-charging or similar attention.

Secondly, it must provide sufficient draught to supply the necessary air (or oxygen) to burn the material quickly. The draught should be arranged near the bottom of the refuse container so that the whole of the contents are burnt from below in an upward direction. The draught orifices should be so arranged that they can take full advantage of any wind that is blowing, as within certain limitations the increased draught caused by such wind will expedite the burning process.

Thirdly, it should be of a more or less permanent character as it has to stand out in the open for long periods in all weathers, and other corrosive influences. Moreover, it must be made strong enough to withstand the heat, for the metal—in the case of metal incinerators—frequently becomes red-hot. In this condition it is not nearly so strong as when the metal is cold.

Finally, it is an advantage—although not always essential—to make the incinerator portable.

If the incinerator is to be definitely located in the garden it is a good plan to arrange a screen of shrubs, such as privet, near it, in order to shield it from view—as an incinerator is usually an unsightly affair from the garden-lover's viewpoint.

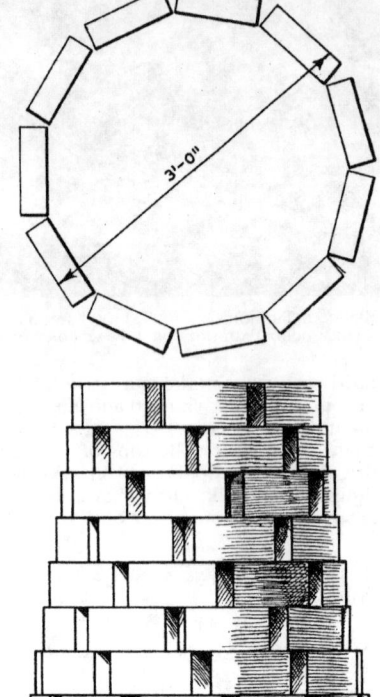

Fig. 1.—The Brick Incinerator.
This is very simple to make, and is both permanent and very effective in use.

Types of Incinerators.

Of the various kinds of receptacles for burning rubbish, the three most interesting and, at the same time, useful varieties are (1) the brick type, (2) the metal container type, and (3) the perforated or wire type. Typical examples of each of these types are described in this article. Before proceeding, it may be of some utility to mention the most appropriate capacities for garden incinerators; this will enable those who are about to make these items to select the most

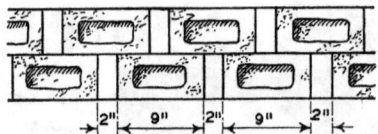

Fig. 2.—Showing how the Bricks are arranged in Staggered Fashion.

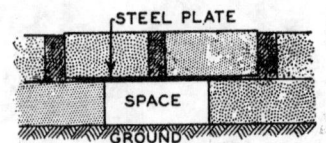

Fig. 3.—Showing Use of Steel Plate for Supporting Bricks.

suitable sizes for their own particular requirements.

For the small garden one would suggest a size of receptacle having a capacity of about 5 to 6 cubic feet. A cylindrical container measuring 1 foot 8 inches internal diameter by 30 to 36 inches in length will be about correct.

For large gardens the capacity can be from 6 to 12 cubic feet. A cylinder of 2 feet in diameter and 4 feet long will give a capacity of about 12 cubic feet.

THE BRICK INCINERATOR

This is a particularly convenient form of receptacle for burning garden refuse. It is very easy to construct and is absolutely permanent in character.

For this reason it is particularly useful for seaside houses and bungalows, where the salt air generally causes quick corrosion of the usual galvanised iron incinerators.

Another advantage of the brick incinerator made in the manner we are about to describe is that it gives regular air openings all the way round, thus greatly improving its burning properties. Its only disadvantages are that it is liable to be accidentally knocked so that some of the bricks become dislodged, and that it is not portable; these, however, can only be considered as being drawbacks of a minor nature.

Method of Construction.

The method of construction is illustrated in Fig. 1. The upper diagram shows how the first layer of bricks is arranged in circular fashion upon a piece of level ground. If seven or eight bricks are used for this ring or layer, the air spaces being about 2 inches, a base circle of about 3 feet diameter will be obtained.

The bricks are stood on their 3-inch faces so that their $4\frac{1}{2}$-inch faces are vertical and the 9-inch ones are horizontal.

The next layer of bricks is staggered so that their air spaces come over the centres of the bricks in the first layer; and so on for each successive layer of bricks.

About every third or fourth layer upwards one brick should be removed from the ring in order to obtain a tapering shape. Thus, the fourth layer will have seven bricks and the eighth layer six bricks.

Height.

The usual height for an incinerator of this type is from 3 feet to 3 feet 6 inches. It will be found that from fifty to sixty bricks are required to make an incinerator of the dimensions mentioned.

To make a more permanent job

the bricks can be cemented or mortared in position, using a mixture of two or three parts of sand to one part of cement, made to a stiff paste with water.

At the base one brick should be removed in order to provide a space for lighting the rubbish and for removing the ashes from the burnt rubbish afterwards. As the two bricks above this space would otherwise not have any support, a piece of 16-gauge steel plate should be placed across to form a bridge for supporting these two bricks as shown in Fig. 3. After the fire has been started this space can, if required, be blocked, temporarily, by means of a loose brick. This form of incinerator gives a fierce heat and will operate equally well, no matter what the direction of the wind.

METAL INCINERATORS

The sheet-metal incinerator is undoubtedly the most popular type, as it is both neat and simple in construction. It is generally made cylindrical in shape and is provided with air spaces for the draught below, and special feet to keep the base above the ground, and a lid; the latter serves to keep the contents dry until they can be burnt.

The usual galvanised iron incinerators are often made of too thin a gauge of metal. When the refuse is burnt the sides often become red-hot and the zinc coating melts and runs down the side. The steel surface then loses its rust-preventing coating and is thus liable to corrode more readily. This type of incinerator seldom lasts more than a season or two.

Using Old Cistern as Incinerator.

Perhaps the simplest and cheapest form of incinerator is that shown in Fig. 4. It utilises an old water storage tank of about 30 to 40 gallons capacity. Builders occasionally have to replace these hot or cold cisterns in houses, so that the old ones can often be picked up for a mere song from builders' yards. They will usually be found to have one or two holes in their sides, but this is no drawback, for they will assist as draught orifices.

The tank should be set on a few bricks in order to keep the bottom off the ground. Several holes can be punched through the bottom and larger ones made through the sides. A special cutter-bit should be used to make the latter holes; alternatively, a series of small holes can be drilled around the periphery of the larger hole and the surplus metal cut away with a cross-cut cold chisel. An old tank fixed up in the manner indicated will be found to give quite a lot of efficient service as an incinerator.

The cylindrical pattern hot-water tank can also be used in a similar manner; there is no need to block up the holes made for taking the hot-water pipes, as these will provide extra draught orifices. The gauge of metal used on domestic water cisterns is generally much heavier than that used on the usual garden incinerator, so that a much longer life can be anticipated for the cheap second-hand cistern incinerator.

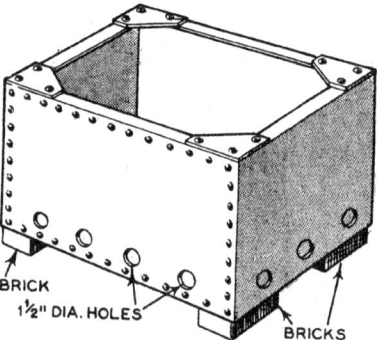

Fig. 4.—The Cistern Type Incinerator, utilising a Disused Water Cistern.

Making a Cylindrical Pattern Incinerator.

Perhaps the simplest method of making a cylindrical incinerator is to utilise a new or used dustbin. Even a new receptacle of this kind is not too dear to employ, where a small pattern incinerator is required.

All that is necessary is to fit four legs to the dustbin, to support the base a few inches above the ground, and to puncture a few holes around the periphery near the base, to provide the necessary draught. The holes can be made by driving a cold chisel right into and through the metal; this leaves a burr inside, but a smooth funnel-shaped opening when viewed from the outside. Fig. 5 shows the sectional elevation and plan of a home-built incinerator that is within the capabilities of the home handyman. It can be made in any convenient dimensions, according to the wishes of the constructor.

A good size for average use would be one having a diameter of 20 to 24 inches and height of 2 feet 6 inches to 3 feet. The cylindrical portion can be made by rolling a sheet of 16-gauge metal and making a butt or lap joint where the two ends of the sheet meet. If there is a garage handy, equipped with an oxy-acetylene welding plant, it will be a simple matter to butt-weld the seam as shown in Fig. 6; the edges of the metal are bevelled with a file so as to form a vee between the ends for the welding rod to deposit its molten metal.

Alternatively the cylinder may be completed by lapping the ends and riveting or bolting them together.

If a disused cylinder, such as that of a large (20-gallon) oil drum or of a dustbin are obtainable, this will save a good deal of trouble, although the metal will probably not be so thick as in the preceding case. In order to provide the necessary amount of draught, instead of the somewhat laborious method of drilling or punching large holes in the sides, or base, a sheet-metal disc about $1\frac{1}{2}$ inches smaller in diameter than the internal diameter of the cylinder is used. This will leave an annular air space of about $\frac{3}{4}$ to 1 inch between the side and the disc; the latter, of course, forms the bottom of the container.

The feet, of which there are four in number, are made from steel strip of $1\frac{1}{2} \times \frac{1}{8}$-inch section metal, with one

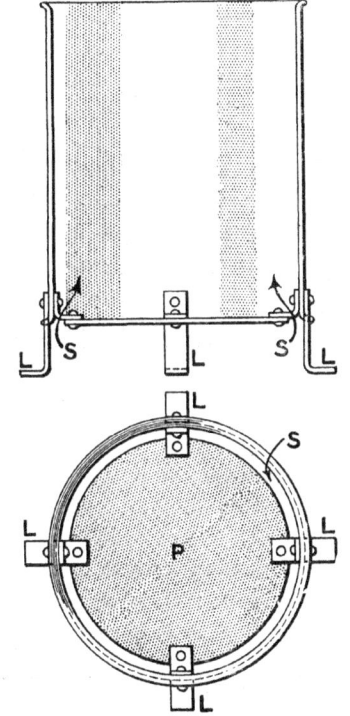

Fig. 5.—Sectional Elevation and Plan View of Cylindrical Type Incinerator with Annular Draught Space at Base.

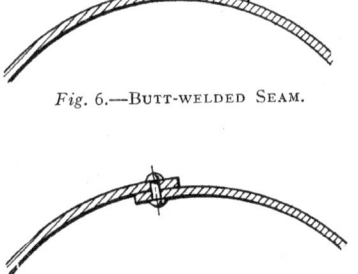

Fig. 6.—Butt-welded Seam.

Fig. 7.—Lapped and Riveted Joint.

end bent at right angles in order to form a foot, or support. These feet are bolted or riveted to the lower part of the cylinder. They are shown at L (Fig. 5). The air spaces are denoted by the letters S and the base-plate by P. The latter can be attached to the cylinder by means of flat steel strips similar to that employed for the feet. These strips are bent at right angles and the arms are riveted or bolted to the base and side of the cylinder respectively. By careful arrangement the same rivets or bolts can be used to secure these as for the feet. Fig. 8 shows the method of attaching the feet and the base support members.

This type of incinerator will be found to give a good draught and will burn practically any type of refuse. To protect it against corrosion it should be painted with bituminous aluminium paint such as Bowrenite.

A WIRE-CAGE TYPE INCINERATOR

In order to overcome the drawbacks of the usual cylindrical type of incinerator, namely, of rusting and burning through, after a certain period of use, a wire-cage incinerator can be used.

This type is not open to the same objections as the sheet-metal cylindrical pattern. It need not be scraped when the container is rusted or burnt away. In this case there is a permanent strong metal framework and a detachable and removable wire cylinder fitting inside the former.

Fig. 9 illustrates the metal framework of this type of incinerator. It is made from $2 \times \frac{3}{16}$-inch or $2 \times \frac{1}{4}$-inch metal strip, built up and riveted as

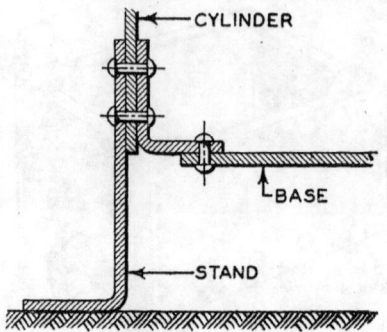

Fig. 8.—SHOWING HOW THE LEGS AND BASE ARE CONNECTED TO THE CYLINDER.

shown. There are two cylindrical "hoops" H that can be made by

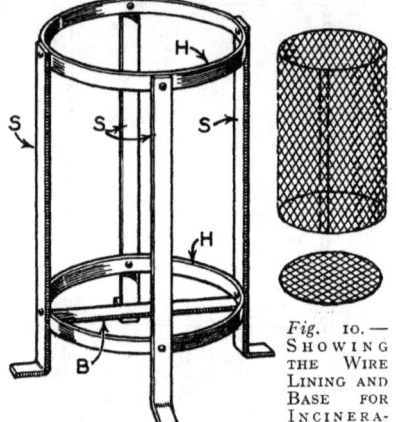

Fig. 9.—THE BUILT-UP FRAMEWORK FOR EXPANDED WIRE TYPE INCINERATOR.

Fig. 10.—SHOWING THE WIRE LINING AND BASE FOR INCINERATOR.

rolling the strip to cylindrical form and then riveting or welding the ends.

The hoops are located and fixed by means of the four straight members S, rivets being used to connect these parts together. The lower ends of the members S are bent over at right angles for a distance of about 3 inches each, in order to form the feet.

Across the base of the lower hoop H, two pieces of strip metal are arranged so as to form two diameters of the hoop H. One of these strips is shown at B in Fig. 9. These members serve to support the wire lining and the base (shown in Fig. 10).

The wire cage should be made from a thick gauge wire netting or, much better, from a sheet of expanded steel netting such as that used by builders for reinforced concrete. If the metal has a thickness of about $\frac{1}{8}$ inch, this will give a strong and durable cage. The two ends of the steel netting are connected by means of 14-gauge iron wire, or by spot-welding. The base consists of a circular disc of the same netting cut to fit the interior of the framework.

When the wire cage and its base have been assembled in position, they should be secured to the framework in a few places by means of soft iron wire.

This type of incinerator should not be used in very exposed places, as the draught may be too strong. When arranged in a protected spot, however, it gives a fierce burning action, which is quicker and more effective than most sheet-metal incinerators.

A NOVEL PORTABLE LAMP GUARD

WHEN a portable electric light is used in the workshop or garage, it is necessary to protect the lamp bulb against fracture by enclosing it in some form of strong guard. The latter, whilst obviating any risk of damage to the bulb from outside sources, should not obstruct the light from the lamp. Further, it is an advantage to provide the lamp guard with some ready means of support on the bench or ground.

A simple but effective type of lamp guard that fulfils all of these requirements is illustrated in the accompanying sketch. It is made from an ordinary upholsterer's conical spring

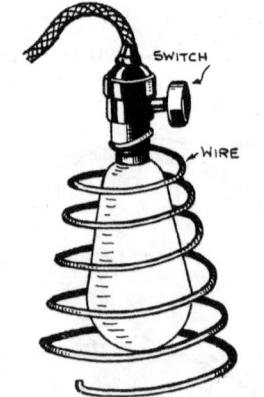

SHOWING HOW AN UPHOLSTERER'S SPRING CAN BE USED AS A LAMP GUARD.

similar to that employed for springing mattresses or seats.

The top end of the spring is pinched in so as to form a circle rather smaller in diameter than the lamp-holder sleeve. It can then be sprung tightly on to the latter as shown.

With such a guard the lamp can be protected and at the same time allowed to give practically its full outside illumination.

The complete unit will stand on any flat surface, and having a springing action the lamp itself is protected from shock when it is stood on a bench or the ground.

A Pole Lathe

The pole lathe represents one of the earliest forms of turning lathe, but in the modernised form shown at Fig. 1 it is possible to carry out comparatively large pieces of work such as chair and table legs. The action is slow compared with that of the modern treadle lathe, as the cutting tool is effective only during a few revolutions at a time. The origin of the lathe can be seen in the simple form of bow lathe shown at Fig. 2, and with this simple appliance, spindles and small knobs, etc., can be turned without difficulty by securing the bottom of the framework in a vice. The disadvantage of this form of lathe is that it is very difficult to use it single-handed and help is required in moving the bow to revolve the wood.

The pole lathe, which retains the same principle as the bow lathe, can be worked by a treadle, thus leaving both hands free. The bow can still be used as indicated by dotted lines in the side view shown at Fig. 4, but it will be found more convenient to use a large check spring as shown at Fig. 1 and also at Figs. 3 and 4. The latter illustrations show all the parts as well as the main dimensions.

Materials required.

The construction of the lathe is quite simple and the materials are inexpensive. The following lengths of wood and other materials will be required.

Pole AB, 7 to 8 feet $\times$ 2 $\times$ 2 inches; end upright C, 34 $\times$ 2 $\times$ 2 inches; base D, 42 $\times$ 4 $\times$ 1 inch; four rails E, 42 $\times$ 1$\frac{1}{2}$ $\times$ 1 inch; treadle R, 24 $\times$ 4 $\times$ 1 inch. Tailstock FG, 21 $\times$ 2 $\times$ 2 inches; HJ, 24 $\times$ 1 $\times$ 1 inch; K, 4 $\times$ 2 $\times$ 1 inch. Tool rest L, 6 $\times$ 4$\frac{1}{4}$ $\times$ 2 inches; M, 8 $\times$ 6 $\times$ 1 inch; N, 3$\frac{3}{4}$ $\times$ 2 $\times$ 2 inches; O, 4 $\times$ $\frac{1}{2}$ $\times$ $\frac{1}{2}$ inch. One 7-inch and one 6 $\times$ $\frac{1}{2}$ or $\frac{3}{8}$-inch bolt with flynuts and washers. Two bolts for centres 5 inches or 4$\frac{1}{2}$ $\times$ $\frac{1}{4}$ or $\frac{5}{16}$ inch. One hook with nut, 4$\frac{1}{2}$ $\times$ $\frac{3}{8}$ inch. Two G cramps. Backflap hinge. One 6-inch check spring or strips of ash or hickory, 48, 30 and 15 $\times$ 1$\frac{1}{4}$ $\times$ $\frac{1}{4}$ inch. Raw hide strip and cord to requirements.

A hardwood such as birch or beech will make the best job, but it will do if the parts E, F, G, H, J, L, M, O and P are made of hardwood, the remainder may be of deal.

Preparing the Pole.

The pole at A should be at least 6 feet long, 1 foot longer if a wood bow is used instead of a spring. The portion B is cut to 10 inches long, the lower end bevelled and screwed to the top of the pole. The end piece C is 34 inches long and both uprights are tenoned into the base piece D; the latter is 42 inches long and allows of a projection of 1 inch at the pole end and 2 inches at the other. The tenons are 1$\frac{1}{4}$ inches square and the mortises are cut centrally in the base.

The lathe bed is formed by four rails E, each 42 inches long; these are screwed on as indicated to leave $\frac{1}{2}$ inch between. The hook at the top of the pole should be about 4$\frac{1}{2}$ $\times$ $\frac{3}{8}$ inches. Anything lighter than this will not stand the strain. The pole centre is 38 inches from the ground, but this can be adjusted to meet individual requirements, and if the height suggested should be too high, the position of the rails should be adjusted so that a distance of 4 inches is allowed between the centre and the top of the rails.

The Tailstock.

The tailstock indicated at F in Fig. 3 and shown separately in Fig. 5, is composed of eight parts. Front and side views with a plan are given in Fig. 6. The two uprights F and G are 10$\frac{1}{2}$ $\times$ 2 $\times$ 2 inches, the outer piece being bevelled off. The runners H and J are 6 $\times$ 1 $\times$ 1 inches and the small pieces K are 2 $\times$ 2 $\times$ 1 inch.

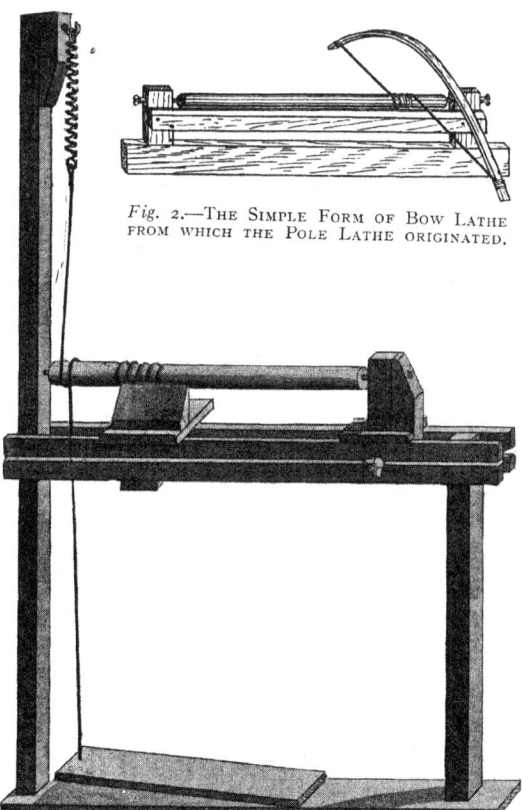

Fig. 2.—The Simple Form of Bow Lathe from which the Pole Lathe originated.

Fig. 1.—A Pole Lathe suitable for turning comparatively large Pieces of Work, such as Chair and Table Legs.

First screw on the top runners H with a piece K between and place the head on the bed. Slide it along to the projecting centre secured to the pole. Mark off the position of the fixed centre on the face of the headstock and then remove it so that the hole for the other centre can be bored and the bolt driven in place. Replace the headstock, mark the space between the side rails, then bore the hole for the bolt and finally place in position so that the two bottom runners J with the remaining piece K can be screwed on. These pieces should allow of easy movement, but no slackness. Fit in bolt and washers and attach flynut to complete.

The Tool Rest.

The tool rest shown at L in Fig. 3, in two parts in Fig. 5, and in elevation and plan in Fig. 6, is composed of an upper part of hardwood 6 $\times$ 4$\frac{3}{4}$ $\times$ 2 inches, end grain uppermost, is tenoned into a base M, 8 $\times$ 6 $\times$ 1 inch with a $\frac{1}{2}$-inch wide slot about 3 inches long. The lower portion has four parts, an upright 3$\frac{3}{4}$ $\times$ 2 $\times$ 2 inches with a central hole $\frac{1}{2}$ inch diameter bored through it. Two runners O, 2 $\times$ $\frac{1}{2}$ $\times$ $\frac{1}{2}$ inch, are screwed on 1$\frac{3}{8}$ inches from the top. The bottom piece P is 4 $\times$ 4 $\times$ 1 inch; it has a hole $\frac{1}{2}$ inch diameter in the centre and a recess 2 $\times$ 2 $\times$ $\frac{3}{8}$ inch. The lower part should be screwed to the upright and then it can be sprung into place between the rails of the lathe bed. The tool rest is now placed on top, the bolt and washers fitted and the flynut attached to complete.

The Check Spring.

The check spring is now secured to a length of raw hide strip, but instead of a complete length of hide from the spring to the treadle, the centre portion only need be of leather, the remainder being of stout strong cord securely fastened to the leather; a short length of stout gut can be used instead of leather, but owing to the wear and strain on that portion of the cord which goes round the wood to be turned, ordinary cord will not last very long. The actual length of the cord from the spring to the treadle depends on the diameter of the wood to be turned and the height at which the treadle can be conveniently moved.

The Treadle.

The treadle as shown at R is a 24 $\times$ 4 $\times$ 1-inch strip hinged to the bottom piece D. It will be found convenient to fit a

A POLE LATHE

length of wood in the lathe, wrap the cord once round the wood and tie to the spring. Fasten the other end to the top of the treadle and discover a convenient position. Use this string for determining the length of the hide strip.

Hints on using the Lathe.

In using the lathe, apart from the fact that the cutting tool operates on each down stroke of the treadle, there is no difference from the continuous turning lathe, both as regards tools and method of using them. In Fig. 7 the cord is shown wrapped round the wood, and it will be seen that the square wood is roughly planed down to an octagonal shape as indicated in three stages, 1, 2 and 3. The end on which the cord is wrapped should be rounded as indicated at S, but it

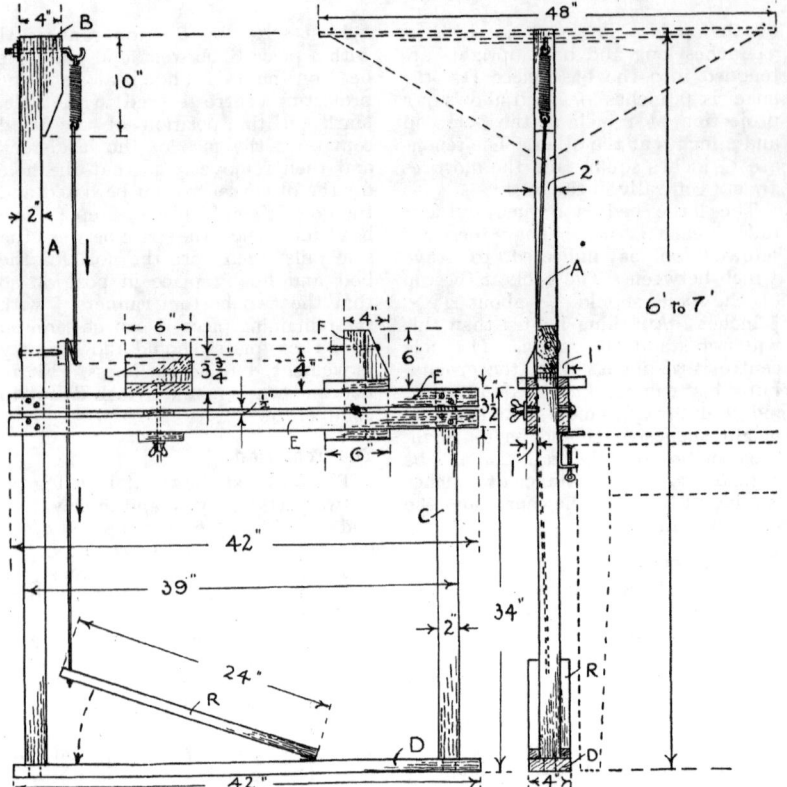

Fig. 3.—FRONT VIEW, SHOWING MAIN DIMENSIONS. Fig. 4.—SIDE VIEW.

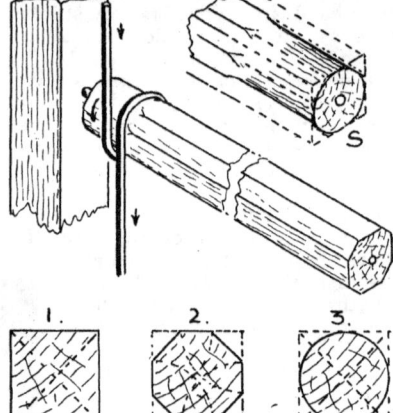

Fig. 7.—HOW THE POLE LATHE IS USED.

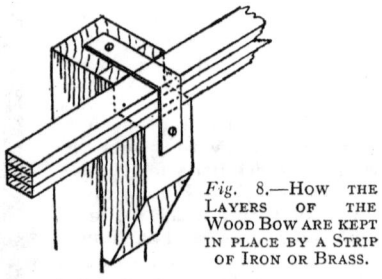

Fig. 8.—HOW THE LAYERS OF THE WOOD BOW ARE KEPT IN PLACE BY A STRIP OF IRON OR BRASS.

should not be smoothed; the facets left help to grip the cord.

If a wooden spring bow is used, as shown by the dotted lines in Fig. 4, the strips should be rested on top of the projecting piece B and kept in position by a strip of iron or brass, as shown in Fig. 8. If it should be desired to make the lathe to take apart easily, bolts and flynuts should be substituted for the screws used to attach the rails at E. In attaching the lathe to a table, holes should be drilled in small G cramps as shown at T in Fig. 5, and then they are screwed to the pole and the end upright.

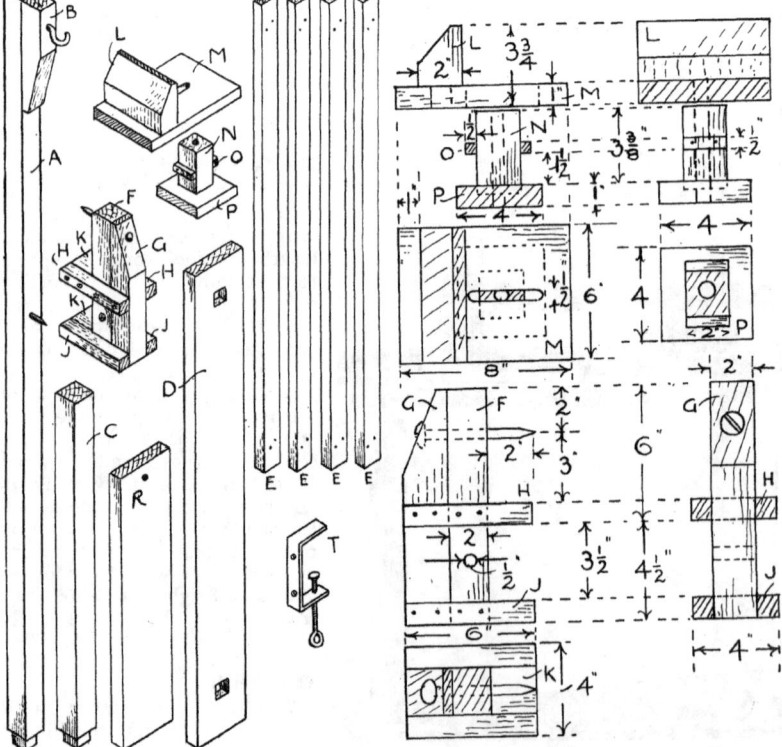

Fig. 5.—THE PARTS OF THE POLE LATHE.

Fig. 6.—FRONT, SIDE VIEWS AND PLAN OF TAILSTOCK AND TOOL REST.

1150

Two Useful Leatherwork Articles

THE making of two useful articles for smokers is described in this article. The first is a cigarette case; the second, a companion match holder. The case for cigarettes is made of a limp kind of leather and is contrived to hold twenty cigarettes, including the carton in which they are purchased. Thus, there is no need to unload the cigarettes, as there is with all other kinds of cases; the carton is merely slipped into the leather covering after the cardboard flap has been torn off. The match case almost speaks for itself. It is little more than a strip of leather folded to take a packet of book matches.

Selecting the Leather.

There are several kinds of leather that may be used for making these articles, but whatever is chosen, it is advisable to select the same material for both, in order that they may be complementary to each other.

(a) The actual examples shown in Figs. 1 and 2 were made of a brown composition leather costing 1s. per square foot. It had a pimple-grained surface and the substance, while being limp and easily folded, was not too pliable.

(b) If a real leather is preferred, a calf-finished Persian of light substance may be selected. It can be obtained in various shades of brown and also black. The usual price is 1s. 6d. per square foot.

(c) When it is desired to make the articles of the same colour as, say, a lady's handbag, then a velvet Persian leather should be chosen. It can be obtained in almost any colour and, therefore, has obvious uses. It is too limp by itself for the present articles, but may be suitably stiffened by pasting a fancy paper or piece of silk to the flesh side. Then it serves admirably. Cost, about 1s. 6d. per square foot.

(d) Other leathers, such as crocodile and morocco, are suitable, but the cost is greater. These run to about 2s. 6d. per square foot. All the above may be obtained at craft shops or from fancy leather dealers.

Cutting a Paper Pattern of each Article.

The first step in the construction is

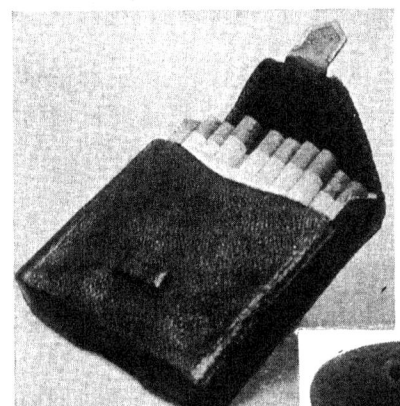

Fig. 1.—The Leather Cigarette Case.

Fig. 2.—The Match Case.

to make a paper pattern the full size of both the articles. Figs. 3 and 4 provide all the necessary measurements. It will be seen that in Fig. 3 the two side pieces are cut separately from the body strip, although it would save a little of the stitching if they were planned to form part of it. This is done because the stitching affords a more

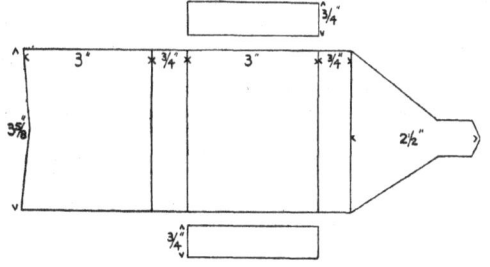

Fig. 3.—The Cigarette Case, showing the necessary Shape in the Flat, with Dimensions in Inches. The cross lines show where the leather is to be creased.

shapely edge than if the leather is merely creased along this line.

When the paper patterns are cut, place them flat on the leather and

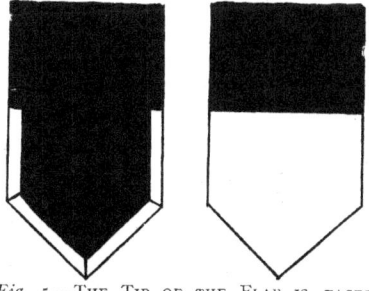

Fig. 5.—The Tip of the Flap is faced with a Thin Plate of Metal in order to make it Rigid.

Here, the back view and the front view are shown.

decide where they should go so as to cause the least waste. Often, a little scheming results in a considerable saving of material. Mark the outline of the patterns on the leather with a pencil, then place the leather on a sheet of glass and cut with a ruler and pocket-knife. If the cutting is done with scissors, continuous straight lines are almost impossible.

Stiffening Leather that is Limp.

Should it be necessary to stiffen the leather, as suggested above for velvet Persians, the material must be cut ⅛ inch larger all round before the pasting. The final trimming is then done when the two thicknesses have been given time to dry together.

Pasting is effected with any ordinary photo-mountant or by using flour and water. No kind of glue is advised. Coat both materials and leave them for a few minutes; then coat again and place the backing material on to the leather. Immediately cover over with a sheet of clean blotting-paper and press out the creases. Never try to flatten out the wrinkles by working on the actual materials; always have a sheet of something in between. This avoids stretching on the part of one of the substances.

When the pasting has been done, place the materials under pressure for a whole day, to dry flat. For small pieces, there is nothing to equal the pages of a large book to keep them from unsticking. When they have dried, cut them to the actual shape, as already described. If the leather is trimmed to the proper dimensions before the pasting, there is always a fear that the edges may be smeared or that the paste may soak through at the edges and cause a glazed streak.

Folding the Leather.

The next step is to fold the leather along the lines indicated in Figs. 3 and 4. This may be done by drawing

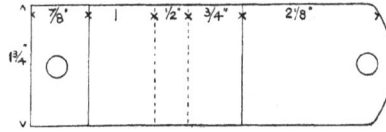

Fig. 4.—The Match Case, showing the Shape in the Flat, with the Dimensions in Inches.

The dotted lines indicate where the band is to be stitched on to the main portion of leather. The other cross lines show where the material is to be creased.

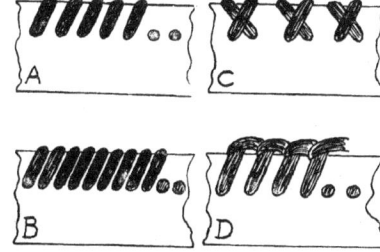

Fig. 6.—Various Kinds of Thonging Stitches.

A is single whip; B, double whip; C, crossed whip; and D, blanket stitch.

The Work of Stitching.

Turning now to the cigarette case, it will be necessary to stitch up the sides. With material as light in substance as is now being used, a needle is sufficiently strong for the work, but the holes must be pricked first. Here the main difficulty will be to get the holes equally spaced. If a pricking iron is possessed (cost 1s. 6d.), the work is simple enough, but failing one of these implements, the best plan is to spread a piece of tracing paper on a ruler, divided off in tenths of an inch, and mark the divisions on the paper. Then place the paper on the edges of the leather and prick through them with a fine-pointed awl.

Whatever method is chosen to space the holes, it is advisable to pierce each hole with the awl so that it is large enough to take the needle. For sewing material a saddlers' silk should be used if a very strong stitch is desired, but any of the Dorcas threads ought to be sufficiently stout for the cigarette and match cases. Naturally, a thread will be chosen that harmonises with the colour of the leather.

The sewing, in this instance, will be done so that the threads lap over the edges and show on the outside of the case. It will not be a bad plan if two needles are used and if the threads of both needles pass through the same hole. This gives strength and makes a neater row of stitches.

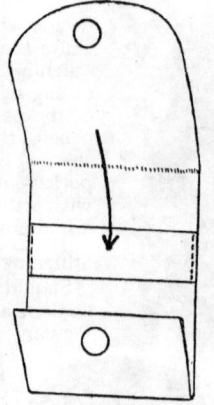

Fig. 7.—The Match Case, illustrated in Fig. 2. Showing the ½-inch band of leather, marked by an arrow.

Making the Loop for the Closing Flap.

In addition to the side seams, it is necessary to sew on a loop of leather, into which the tip of the closing flap is slipped. Fig. 1 shows approximately where this loop should come, but it will be advisable to finish off the flap first and to slip a packet of cigarettes into the case before deciding exactly where the loop should be fixed. This plan ensures a perfect fit, which no amount of measuring can provide.

Tipping the Flap with Metal.

Now regarding the flap. In order that it shall be rigid, a piece of metal is folded over the tip. Fig. 5 shows how it is fitted on to the leather. The left-hand sketch gives the back view and the right-hand sketch the front view. Very thin sheet metal should be used for this. If nothing better can be found, cut the necessary shape out of the inner circle of metal found in a hermetically sealed tin of fifty cigarettes. Do the cutting with ordinary scissors and flatten down the turned-over edges with a light hammer.

Thonging the Flap.

The two tapering edges of the flap are ornamented as well as strengthened by the provision of a thong. For this, a strip of material, such as a leather or mohair bootlace, is used or special thongs can be purchased from leather dealers. A third plan is to cut a long strip, ⅛ inch wide, from the leather used for making the cases and to employ it for the binding. Fig. 6 shows four different kinds of thonging. In each case, the run of stitching is begun and ended by merely making a knot in the material, while the holes, through which the thongs pass, are made by the aid of a fairly stout awl. Regular spacing is, of course, imperative. The method, already suggested, of using a marked piece of tracing paper, should be followed.

Finishing off the Match Case.

Turning now to the match case. Two operations remain to be performed. The first is to sew a band of leather across the middle panel; it serves to hold the paper flap of the book of matches. This band, which should be about ½ inch wide, does not appear in Fig. 2 because the matches hide it; but it is given in Fig. 7. Naturally, the band is only sewn along the two short ends.

The second operation is to fit a press stud. Before beginning this work, insert a book of matches in the case and then fit over the closing flap. See that it folds properly; prick a hole through the upper piece of leather and continue on to the underfold. The two marks, made in this way, show exactly where the centre of the stud pieces are to come. If a press-stud punch is available (cost 9d.), the fitting of the stud is easily done, but when one is not possessed the work is a little fidgety. Then the necessary holes should be made with a pocket-knife and the sections forced together by means of a hammer blow. Look at the stud on an old glove if there is any doubt as to how the pieces are put together.

A METAL TENT PEG

THE ordinary beech-wood tent peg is not altogether satisfactory for its purpose as it frequently splits at the top when driven into the ground with a mallet. Moreover, it makes an ugly hole if used on a lawn, and, further, it cannot be inserted or withdrawn by hand alone.

An improved and cheap form of metal tent peg is that illustrated in the sketch. It can usually be pushed into the lawn by hand and withdrawn in the same manner.

It is made from 1 × ⅛-inch steel strip. The curved end can be bent cold in the vice over a piece of ¾-inch rod or strong steel tubing, whilst the point is made by sawing off the two lower corners.

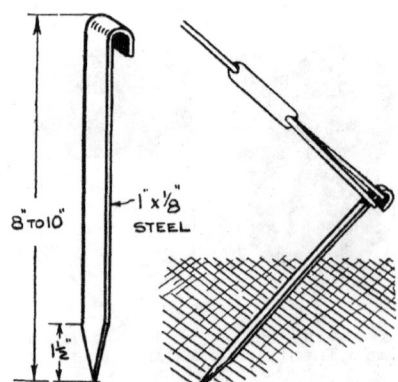

The Dimensions of the Peg and the Angle at which it should be Inserted.

Coat with Bitumastic Paint.

The metal peg should be given a coat of bitumastic or aluminium paint to prevent rusting.

If the peg is required to be inserted well down into the earth it can be knocked down with a hammer, but for most purposes it can be inserted by hand.

Having the broad surface opposed to the pull of the cord it offers the maximum resistance.

The approximate angle at which the pegs should be inserted in the ground to obtain the maximum benefit is clearly shown in the accompanying sketch, which also shows suitable dimensions.

CELLULOSE PAINTING

The advent and development of colour finishes having a cellulose base have opened up many fresh possibilities to the decorator which are worthy of his attention.

Some Advantages of Cellulose Finishes.

In the first place, the rapid drying qualities of this type of finish make it invaluable for use in "rush jobs," since each coat is thoroughly dry and ready to receive the next coat within an hour or so from the time of application, the speed of application being also assisted by the fact that this material lends itself particularly to spray application.

Hardness.

Secondly, the nature of the material from which cellulose finishes are made renders the finished surface one of exceptional hardness which, if anything, improves with age.

Strength.

Thirdly, each coat applied actually becomes permanently welded to the previous coat, forming a perfectly homogeneous covering of great strength and tenacity.

Flat or Glossy Finish as desired.

Fourthly, cellulose finishes provide considerable control over the nature of the finished surface which can be left flat or may be polished, whichever is desired. Indeed, it is possible to attain finishes on high-class work equal to that of the best Japanese lacquer work if necessary.

Durable.

Fifthly, cellulose finishes by their very nature have the strong attractions of great durability and retention of their original quality of finish for an infinitely longer period than ordinary paints.

Sixthly, cellulose finishes are quite unaffected by water and most corrosive agents, and are thus particularly suited for use in bathrooms, etc., where they are called upon to resist considerable moisture.

Lastly, owing to its quick drying properties, dust does not menace the work to anything like the same extent during the application period as it does in the case of enamels where work of high quality is involved.

Two Distinct Types of Finish.

Remember that there are two distinct types of cellulose finish—one, fast drying and specially prepared for spray application, the other being specially

Fig. 3.—THE PULL-OVER METHOD OF FINISHING WOODWORK WITH CELLULOSE LACQUER (3).

The pull-over operation, using a cotton-wool pad covered with chamois leather. The pull-over solution is a cellulose solvent somewhat less drastic in action than thinners and cleaners.

Fig. 2.—THE PULL-OVER METHOD OF FINISHING WOODWORK WITH CELLULOSE LACQUER (2).
Take care to apply an even coating. This will minimise subsequent handwork in the pull-over operation.

Fig. 1.—THE PULL-OVER METHOD OF FINISHING WOODWORK WITH CELLULOSE LACQUER (1).
First apply a stain filler with a coarse rag, wiping off excess across the grain. The use of stain filler often obviates the necessity of initial staining and does not raise the grain.

developed for hand application and taking a considerably longer time to set, although it can still be classed as quick drying by comparison with oil paints.

Cellulose finishes intended for spray application are particularly suited to covering large areas, where full advantage can be made of the superior speed of application and finish offered by the spray.

There are many cases, however, where spray painting ceases to be practicable owing to the large amount of masking entailed—where there are many windows with small panes, for instance—in which case it is advisable to employ the special finish for brush application.

SPRAY PAINTING

Equipment required.

The equipment required for spray painting is a suitable gun and a suitable air-compressing device to feed this gun; some air hose capable of withstanding a pressure of at least 80 lbs. to the square inch will be needed to connect the compressor with the spray gun, and a supply of thinners or cellulose solvents will be necessary to clean the spray and perhaps adjust the viscosity of the cellulose medium to suit the work in hand. The recommendation of the manufacturers should be carefully followed.

Spray Guns.

Spray guns are obtainable in great variety. There is a small size suitable for working at low pressure from a small reservoir maintained by manual effort, the whole plant costing approximately 45s. inclusive of compressor. Then there are sizes ranging upwards to those employing some 6 cubic feet of air per minute, which are used in conjunction with mechanical compressors and large paint storage vessels. Full details for making a spray painting outfit are given on page 1033.

In the smaller guns the paint container forms part of the gun and usually holds about a pint of spraying medium. In the case of the larger guns it is preferable to use a separate large paint container to avoid too frequent filling.

Spray guns also vary greatly in design so that no definite general instructions can be laid down regarding their setting and maintenance in these pages. Such instructions are always supplied by the makers of the gun with each instrument, and should be closely followed. It can be laid down, however, that the use of a relatively high air pressure is desirable to obtain the best results, something in the region of 50–60 lbs. per square inch.

Masking Paper and Tape.

When using a spray gun it is essential to protect areas it is not required to paint by masking them with sheets of paper. These may often be retained in position by the simple expedient of wetting them and laying them in position. The water will hold them in position long enough to enable the part to be sprayed successfully once. The better plan, however, is to use some of the special masking tape obtainable for this purpose, which is treated with an adhesive on one side and sold in rolls of 50 yards, in widths up to 18 inches, at a modest figure.

When to use Respirator.

It may be advisable, particularly if much work is to be undertaken in small confined spaces, to make use of a respirator to avoid excessive inhaling of the spray which is unavoidable without such protection. Suitable respirators are obtainable from most suppliers, such as Brown Brothers Ltd., and usually cost about 12s.

BRUSHING
Brushes required.

For the application of brushing cellulose finishes a suitable range of *rubber set* brushes with soft bristles are required and these should carefully be cleaned in cellulose thinners after use.

Other Materials and Equipment.

In addition to the cellulose finishing colour, special priming material will be required for the first coat, and a cellulose putty to fill up cracks and blemishes in the surface.

A supply of waterproof sandpaper of the "wet-or-dry" type will also be needed, some No. 280 grit for rubbing down the priming coats, and some No. 400 grit for dealing with finished surfaces.

If the work is to receive a high finish, a supply of suitable rubbing polish recommended by the makers of the finish employed is also called for.

Undercoatings and how to apply Them.

Like ordinary paint finish the cellulose variety needs to be applied upon sound foundations if lasting and satis-

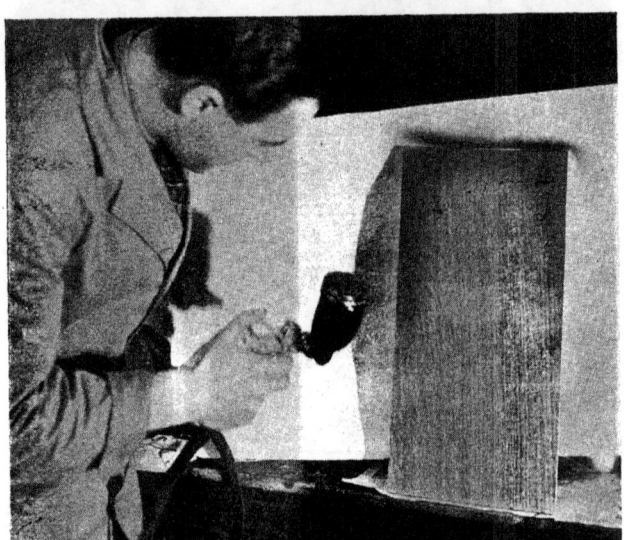

Fig. 4.—Obtaining Jacobean Effects by spraying Cellulose Solvent Stains, which do not raise the Grain as a Water Stain, and are Faster to Light than Spirit Stains.

factory results are to be obtained, and, by reason of their peculiar nature, special care must be used for selecting the undercoating for cellulose finishes. Where the work to be treated is new and devoid of finish or priming of any sort, it is a relatively easy matter to apply the necessary undercoatings successfully.

Telling whether Surface needs Stripping.

In the case of old work, however, special conditions arise from the fact that cellulose finishes are to a certain extent solvents of ordinary paint, and varnishes and enamels in particular, so that when applied to certain work it will behave very much in the same way as the usual commercial paint stripping liquids. This is particularly so in the case of paint which has been fairly recently applied, but it is usually quite safe to apply cellulose finishes to paintwork which has stood for twelve months or more.

The wise operator will apply a small quantity of the cellulose finish to an area of, say, 3–4 square inches where it will not readily be seen should it spoil the work, before proceeding with the bulk of the work. If this small area dries off quite smooth and hard it may be taken as an indication that it is quite safe to proceed. If, on the other hand, examination of the small patch reveals surface cracks or, in severe cases, peeling, or if the cellulose finish shows a reluctance to dry and remains tacky, it may be taken as a definite indication that the existing covering material is unsuitable for the application of a cellulose finish.

STRIPPING

The only thing to do under such circumstances is to strip your work completely, preferably by the blowlamp method.

With Paint Remover.

If a caustic or similar type of paint remover is used it is essential to neutralise its effects by carefully washing the surface after stripping with a solution of 5 per cent. acetic acid and water, followed by a careful washing with copious quantities of fresh water. A simple method of testing the neutral condition of the surface is to apply small pieces of litmus paper (obtainable from chemists) at various points, and while the surface is still wet after washing. Should the blue litmus paper turn just slightly pink after about five minutes, this is a clear indication that the surface is just slightly on the acid side and therefore safe to work on.

—With Cellulose Thinners.

If a liquid stripping medium must be used, then by far the safest thing to employ for the purpose is cellulose thinners. This material is quite effective and has the advantage that it ensures the proper adhesion of subsequent application of cellulose material.

PREPARATION OF WORK
Smoothing.

Whether the surface be old or new, it is first necessary to render it as smooth as possible. To this end all surfaces about to be cellulosed should be carefully smoothed off with sandpaper, remembering that old paint work is best dealt with by using one of the waterproof types of paper, with plenty of water to prevent clogging and assist cutting. When you have smoothed the surface to a sufficient extent attention must be given to its proper cleaning.

Cleaning.

One of the most important features in the successful application of cellulose finishes is that the surface should be absolutely free from grease, oil, dirt, wax, alkalis and acids. Any of the foregoing are liable seriously to affect the primary coat and either prevent it from drying off properly or prevent it from adhering and uniting to the surface of the work. Removal of the alkaline group of impurities, such as oil, grease, etc., is readily effected by wiping the surface carefully with a rag soaked in naphtha, methylated spirits or cellulose cleaners, taking particular care to clean out all crevices. *The use of dirty or greasy rags must be avoided at all costs.*

Wax is not dissolved by naphtha or methylated spirits and, when its presence is suspected, it is essential further to clean the surface with rag soaked in benzole.

Priming.

Having thoroughly cleaned the work it should be given a *thin* coat of one of the special primers prepared for this purpose. *Ordinary primers as used for oil colours are definitely not suited for use with cellulose finishes and should on no account be used.* There are a number of cellulose primers on the market as it is usual for the manufacturer of cellulose finishes to market suitable primers to use in conjunction with their product. Whenever possible use should be made of these since good results are more likely to be attained by their use than by an indiscriminate selection.

Primers for Cellulose Finishes.

It should also be remembered that there are two distinct types of primers for use with cellulose finishes. Firstly, one having an oil base—perhaps the most satisfactory to use on work previously treated with oil paints, and secondly, a primer having a cellulose base. The oil primer is a relatively slow drying medium and in cases where quick work is essential the cellulose base primer should be used, as this enables successive coats to be applied in almost immediate succession when necessary.

The number of coats of primer to be applied depend of course on the nature of the surface, so that no hard and fast rule can be applied. The operator must be left to judge for himself

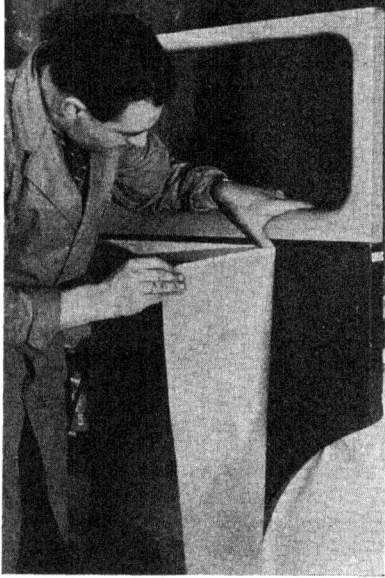

*Fig. 5.—*Masking when Spraying Cellulose (1).

Showing how to mask a car door after the bottom panel has been sprayed. It is carried out with 1-inch wide adhesive tape previously affixed to paper. This leaves a good clean edge. Curves in the beading can be easily negotiated and the masking tape can be used several times.

whether the surface has attained the desired standard of smoothness.

Priming Coat should be thoroughly dried.

Thorough drying of the priming coat is an essential or the cellulose finish will tend to disturb it and thus spoil the finished work. Primers should be left to dry over-night whenever possible,

*Fig. 6.—*Masking when Spraying Cellulose (2).
Applying colour to top half of door panel after masking. The tape should be removed by pulling away at right angles to the work, and the final operation, that of colouring the beading, is done by means of a small round mop or lining brush according to the width of the bead.

particularly if an oil base primer has been used, and no convenient method is available for keeping the work reasonably warm. The best drying temperature for primers is usually in the neighbourhood of 75° Fahrenheit. When oil base primers have been used on somewhat rough surfaces the attainment of a really smooth surface can be accelerated by the use of an oil base cellulose surfacer as the next coat or coats, but its use is to be avoided on economical grounds whenever possible.

Filling Cracks and Holes.

When the priming coats are thoroughly dry, carefully examine the surface for blemishes, and fill any abrasions, such as scratches, nail holes, etc., with the special putty manufactured for the purpose. Here again, there are two types available; oil base glazing putty for use in conjunction with oil base primers, and cellulose base putty for use with the cellulose base primer.

When dealing with the holes remember that the putty will shrink slightly when drying, and if the very best work is required it will be necessary to reputty such places several times to ensure a perfectly level surface. Remember also that it is always better in the case of large crevices to fill them by several sparing applications of putty to enable the hole to dry thoroughly, rather than employ a single application which will merely dry on the surface and remain soft beneath.

When dry, the areas puttied should be well smoothed down with glasspaper to present a smooth and unbroken surface with the surrounding work. On the quality of the surface at this stage depends to a large extent the degree of excellence of the finished work.

Rubbing Down and Sanding.

When really high-class work is required, rubbing down or sanding will be necessary. This may be carried out either by the old pumice stone method or by the more modern waterproof sandpaper method, utilising papers of the "wet-or-dry" type. It is important that sanding should not be indulged in until the priming coats and putty are thoroughly dry and hard. When carrying out the sanding operation remember that plenty of water is essential to prevent clogging of the sanding material and facilitate its cutting. It is also of some importance to rub, as far as possible, in the same direction as the final polishing of the finished cellulose surface will take place, except in the case of large flat surfaces, such as panels, where a circular motion should be employed.

Sanding should be continued until the surface presents a perfectly smooth appearance free from scratches and blemishes. This may in certain cases entail removing the surfacer or priming to a large extent, but this need cause no anxiety, the important point being the attainment of a sufficiently smooth surface.

When satisfied with the quality of the surface you should thoroughly clean the work with a sponge and water to remove all traces of the minute particles left by the sanding operation. If this is not done a high quality finish will not be possible.

THE FINISHING COATS
Spray Gun Application.

The final result attained depends very much upon the correct application of the finishing coat, and it is therefore of importance to make quite sure that it is applied in the proper manner. If the spray gun method of application is employed great care should be taken to see that the correct air pressure is utilised at the spray. For light-bodied colours, such as black and blue, a spray pressure of 60 lbs. per square inch is permissible and economical, while for colours of heavier body, such as white, cream and yellow, a spray pressure of 50 lbs. per square inch should be utilised.

Spray at Right Angle to Surface.

It is of the utmost importance to keep the spray striking the work at right angles. Should the spray be directed obliquely, uneven application is bound to result. Keep the spray gun constantly at right angles to the surface, moving it to and fro at the same distance from the work by a combined motion of the arm and wrist. *Do not stand at one spot and swing the gun round as from a pivot or oblique spray direction will be inevitable.*

Distance of Gun from Work.

The gun must not be held too far from the work or the spray will not strike with sufficient force. On the other hand, the spray must not be held too close to the work or rings will be formed where the spray impinges on the work.

The best distance to hold the gun from the work under normal conditions is from 8–10 inches, depending on the weight of the colour. A light colour, that is to say, light in weight, such as blue or black, can be applied 8 inches from the work successfully, while heavier colours, such as white, cream, yellow, etc., should be applied some 10 inches from the work.

Employ Slow Even Strokes.

The operator should employ slow even strokes extending the full width of the panel whenever possible. *Never use a spray with a circular motion or move it about jerkily.*

It must be realised that the covering power of the spray is greatest at the centre, tailing off to the edges, so that a certain amount of overlapping must take place between adjacent strokes if an even coat of the finishing medium is to be applied. It must also be remembered that it is essential to keep the edges of overlapping strokes wet if they are to flow freely and smoothly into each other.

Test Gun before applying to Work.

Before attempting to apply the

Fig. 7.—Applying Cellulose Lacquer to a Wireless Cabinet.

Note how the spray is held at right angles to the work. When dealing with an object of this nature, it is an advantage to mount it on a suitable turntable, so that all the work can be carried out without altering the direction of the light shining on the object. (*Photos by courtesy of Messrs. Cellon, Ltd.*)

finishing coat to the work it is advisable to regulate the spray delivery on to a special panel of wood to avoid the possibility of spoiling the finished work. This applies to experienced operators as well as to operators new to this method of paint application, since there is always the possibility of the gun delivery being defective.

Not until you are satisfied that the gun is delivering a satisfactory spray for the work in hand should you apply it to the surface to be finished in the manner just indicated.

Temperature of Room.

Spraying is best carried out with the room warm and well ventilated and yet free from draughts. To obtain the best results it is important to prevent the cellulose finish from chilling when it is applied, which would prevent adjacent applications from flowing into each other. The best temperature is approximately 75° Fahrenheit, and the room should be warmed to this temperature before application, whenever possible.

All naked lights should be avoided, however, during the spraying process.

BRUSH APPLICATION

There are many circumstances where spray application is neither economical or convenient, and to meet such cases a type of cellulose finish has been developed by manufacturers suitable for brush application. The main difference between such cellulose finishes and those employed for spray application rests in their slower drying characteristics, which give brush marks more time to spread and smooth out.

There is little difference between the procedure to be adopted with brush-applied cellulose finishes, the important thing to remember being the fact that this type of finish does not stand " working "; it must be applied with deliberate directness and without subsequent smoothing out, otherwise it will drag on the brush and produce an extremely poor finish.

The brush should be well loaded and of ample size for the work, and, as previously pointed out, should be of the rubber set type with soft bristles.

Covering Large Panels.

When covering large panels the first brush stroke should be started at the edge of the panel and tail off towards the centre, running parallel to one edge all the time. The next stroke should start along the same edge but at the opposite side of the panel and should tail off to meet the previous stroke. If the brush is of sufficient size and sufficiently well loaded, these two strokes will overlap to the desired extent, producing a painted strip of panel which is evenly coated. While the first is still wet continue with the next strip, slightly overlapping with the first so as to make the two flow freely into each other and continue in this manner until the panel is completed. One of the secrets of successful application of brushing cellulose finishes is speed, since the too tardy workman allows the edge to set before he can apply the next strip, with consequent poor results.

Brushes used on cellulose work should be thoroughly cleaned out with thinners before being put away or they will set hard and be extremely difficult to reduce to a working condition again.

POLISHING

Cellulose finish applied by the spray process possesses a semi-matt finish of the " egg-shell " variety, and in many decorative uses is best left in this condition. If, however, a decoration scheme would be improved by a high finish to the surface, a mirror-like finish can easily be obtained by polishing with one of the rubbing polishes specially marketed for the purpose, after the surface has been given some twenty-four hours to dry thoroughly hard.

First sandpaper lightly.

First of all the surface should be lightly rubbed over with some No. 400 grit waterproof sandpaper, using plenty of water to remove any small blemishes or runs. The surface may then be polished with the rubbing polish applied on a pad of soft material, such as flannel or felt, and finally finished off with a dry soft rag, using, perhaps, a trace of wax polish. In this way a finish superior to the best enamel work can be obtained which has the advantage of improving each time it is subsequently polished.

Brush-applied cellulose finish, by the nature of its constituents, dries with a more glossy surface than the spray-applied variety; nevertheless, it can readily be polished to the same high finish in precisely the same way.

USE OF CLEAR CELLULOSE LACQUERS

These clear transparent lacquers are suitable for finishing woodwork where the colour and grain effects are to be retained. It can be applied directly to new work, but where the wood has already been treated with varnish or polish, all trace of this must be removed by rubbing down or stripping with cellulose thinners. The thinners should be applied liberally with a stiff brush and well worked in. After a short time the old varnish will be softened and should then easily be removed by scraping. When dry, the surface should be carefully sandpapered, and finally washed with methylated spirits and allowed to dry thoroughly before applying the clear cellulose lacquer. Two or more coats may be applied, as desired, and finally polished when thoroughly dry, in the manner indicated for ordinary cellulose finishes.

SOME USEFUL RECIPES FOR JAMS

FRUIT should be bought at the height of the season, when it will be at its cheapest. It should be ripe, fresh, firm and sound, and must be as dry as possible to get perfect results. Do not use fruit that has become soft; it is not economical and may spoil the flavour. Always use enough preserving sugar, as jam made with insufficient sugar will not keep. Care, however, must be taken not to use too much, as it is liable to make the jam sickly and destroy the full flavour of the fruit. When fruit has to be washed, and this is generally advisable, it should be drained so as to get it as dry as possible.

The Preserving Pan.

A copper preserving pan is best, but a stout aluminium one can be used. Enamel pans are not advised, as they are liable to become chipped. The pan should always be greased with butter to prevent burning, and ½ oz. of butter added during the last ten minutes is a great improvement to either jams or marmalade. It makes it bright and clear and more easily turned out of the jar.

In making strawberry, raspberry, blackberry, red and black currant jam, hull and wash the fruit. Cook quickly to preserve the colour, stir constantly while cooking, and to test if it is done, cool a little on a cold plate; if it sets quickly it is done.

Always label and date each jar, and store in a dry, cool place. The following recipes have proved satisfactory:—

Strawberry Jam.

Hull and drain the fruit, and add equal quantities of sugar, bring to the boil, and continue boiling for about ten minutes, or until a skin is formed, when a little is cooled on a plate to test.

Raspberry Jam.

Pick the fruit over carefully, and to every 1 lb. add 14 ozs. of sugar. Bring up to boil, and boil about ten minutes. Test in the usual way to see if it is sufficiently cooked.

Dried Apricot Jam.

This is an excellent jam made with the dried fruit, and quite equal in flavour to that made with fresh. Soak 1 lb. of apricots in 3 pints of cold water for twenty-four hours, stew gently until quite tender, then add 3 lbs of sugar, and boil until it sets; test as usual on a plate. It is improved by the addition of 1 oz. of bitter almonds. These should be blanched and shredded and added to the final boiling.

Plum Jam.

Take equal quantities of plums and sugar. Wash and pick the plums, allow to drain, place in preserving pan with a little water, simmer for twenty minutes, add sugar, and boil for fifteen or twenty minutes. It is a good plan to skim off the stones as they work to the top. Test in usual way to see if it is ready. Victoria plums are always the best for plum jam, as they can be stoned before using.

The jam must be put into warm jars and covered.

Black Currant Jam.

3½ lbs. of black currants, 3½ lbs. of sugar, ½ pint of water, ½ oz. of butter. Pick currants carefully, wash and drain them. Cook the currants alone slowly in the water for twenty minutes, add sugar and butter, boil rapidly for fifteen or twenty minutes until nicely set. Pour into warm jars and cover.

Another Way.

Another recipe for this jam is prepared as follows. Prepare half a dozen sticks of rhubarb, cut them up and cover with water. Gently simmer for half hour, and strain through muslin. Return the liquid to the pan, and when nearly boiling, add 3 lbs. of black currants and simmer for half hour. Add 3 lbs. of sugar. Gently boil mixture until it sets. Test in the usual way. The liquid from the rhubarb is used in this recipe instead of water. It enriches the flavour of the jam and makes it set much more firmly.

Black Currant Jelly.

Wash the fruit carefully and drain thoroughly.

It is not necessary to pick the fruit off the stalk in preparing it. Cover with water and gently boil until all juice is extracted from the fruit. Pour through a fine strainer, and then strain a second time through butter muslin. Return the juice to the preserving pan, add sugar, 1 lb. to 1 pint of juice, boil gently until it sets, and test in the usual manner. A small knob of butter or a little salad oil, stirred in well, will thoroughly clear the jelly. When finished, care must be taken to pour the jelly into hot jars.

Blackberry Jelly.

A very good way to make this jelly is to put the fruit in a stone jar and place it in a saucepan of water. Bring the water up to boiling point, and as soon as the juice is drawn, pour the contents of the pot into a bag made of flannel, the latter being previously well washed. Press the contents of the bag to drain out all the juice into a pan. Then add 1 lb. of sugar to each pint of juice. Stir in a nob of butter. Boil for twenty minutes and pour into warm jars.

Modernising a Dining-room Fireplace

When introducing a modern style of decoration into a room of older type, the fireplace is nearly always a problem which gives concern. It is, however, possible to effect a complete transformation at small cost, as shown in Figs. 1 and 2.

The first operation was to knock off with a hammer and chisel the mantel-shelf, and the smaller shelf below it, followed by sawing off the upper projecting portions of the scroll-shaped brackets supporting the mantel. This left the two pillars reasonably flush-fronted from top to bottom.

Fig. 1.—A Fireplace with excessive Ornamentation does not fit in very well with modern Styles of Decoration.

It is, however, quite an easy matter to effect a transformation by covering with plywood, as shown in Fig. 2.

Building the Casing.

A pair of troughs were next built of ½-inch boards (AA in Fig. 3, and seen in Fig. 4), to fit snugly over the foregoing pillars, but about 1 inch taller, from floor to top. This extra height is required to cover a possible gap in the plaster of the chimney-breast. These were glued and nailed, and plenty of small blocks were glued in the angles for added strength. At the same stage a thick block was glued and nailed inside the upper end of each trough at such a height that they nearly, but not quite, rested upon the flat top of the pillars between the scroll brackets. By leaving a little clearance between these blocks and the flat on which they are finally to be screwed, the latter operation causes the bottom end of each trough to bear tightly on to the floor, and thus assists rigidity.

An Important Point that may be Overlooked.

A point of construction that might very easily be overlooked here is that the dimensions of the two pillars being cased in did not by any means tally. Each of the troughs had to be made separately, and in fact each side of each trough had to be of a different width, and required final planing on the inside edges for a nice fit. This was quite easy, of course, only taking time, but it is pointed out that no measurements should be taken for granted when dealing with old fixtures.

Next Fix Troughs in Position

The troughs were then screwed into position (not permanently) while the front board, B, 1 inch thick and the same width as the trough fronts, was carefully cut to fit between them. A firm job was assured by two substantial blocks CC, screwed and glued into place. The whole was given a day or two for the glue to set very hard. Then the securing screws were temporarily removed, for the casing to be covered.

Covering the Casing.

Oak-faced three-ply was used to cover the casing. It will be obvious that if cut and fixed on with square edges, the layers of ply would be visible at each angle. Therefore each edge was first planed quite straight and then planed on the back to a bevel.

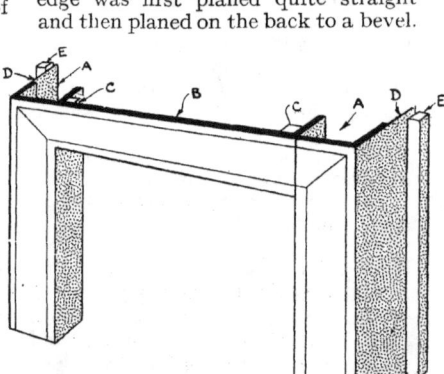

Fig. 2.—An older Type Fireplace covered with a Plywood Casing.

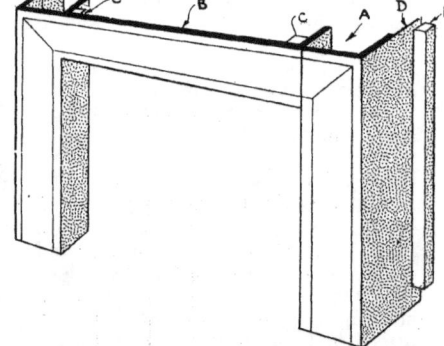

Fig. 3.—Details of the Plywood Casing.
AA, troughs of ½-inch board; B, front board 1 inch thick; CC, blocks; DD, outside pieces of plywood; EE, strips of 1 × 1½ inch oak to prevent warping.

The first attempts to make a perfect 45 degrees bevel proved that a close joint would not result. A much flatter angle was used, and with a sharp plane it was found fairly easy to leave the oak veneer with a feather edge. Slow-drying glue of the Croid class was used, owing to the large areas to be glued, and it was found necessary to fix one side at a time, cramping it in place with boards and screw-cramps. This was because the moisture of the glue tends to make the ply curl outwards, away from the casing.

Use Fine Panel Pins for Holding Edge of Plywood.

Plenty of very fine panel pins were driven in to hold the extreme bevelled edges of the ply down. These were put in slanting, but only part way in, with the twin objects of holding the ply down, and affording a means of subsequent withdrawal. The two adjacent bevels, when well fixed, tended to make a knife edge projection in parts, but that was easily corrected with glass-paper when dry, and clearly was better than leaving gaps to be filled in. The piece of ply covering the centre-board was bevelled at its ends in the opposite direction so that they lay under the bevel edges of the upright pieces, and not only cannot spring away should the heat of the fire affect the glue, but the joins are rendered much more inconspicuous. It will be noted that the two outside pieces of ply, DD, are wider than the troughs, thereby covering the whole of the old woodwork back to the wall.

The Front Board.

Although the final effect suggests a square moulding cut from the solid, actually it was obtained by fixing pieces of inch oak board, selected as having an uncommon figure, above the ply. This front board was built in the form of three sides of a square, and is turned back-to-front in Fig. 4 so as to show how the mitres were strengthened with angle plates. The recesses for these were chiselled out, and the boards laid flat, with glue put in the mitres while the plates were screwed in. Then this front frame was fixed to the casing,

Fig. 4.—THE PLYWOOD FRAME READY FOR FITTING.

also with plenty of glue, by screwing from the inside of the casing. This method permitted of obtaining a very close fit between the boards and the ply face, in spite of the hardness, and a slight tendency to warping here and there of the construction. The result naturally is a fixture of quite unusual rigidity. The original backboard where the small shelf was, was also covered with oak ply.

Fixing the Casing.

Having taken care in the preliminary stages to ensure good fitting of the parts over the old mantel, the new casing slid tightly but easily over into position. The same screws as before held the upper blocks firmly, and pressed the whole tightly to the floor. It needed only a few screws through the back edges of the outer pieces of ply DD to prevent any chance of shift. To prevent still further the chance of subsequent warping, a strip of 1 × 1½-inch oak was screwed against each of these outer edges right through the ply and into the old woodwork, as shown at EE in Fig. 3, a small piece of the skirting moulding near the floor being sawn out to accommodate it.

The Shelf.

This consists of a board of ¼-inch oak, on which is fixed 1 inch thick board of the same wood. The latter is 1 inch shorter at each end, and sets back the same amount from the front edge, so as to give the step effect, but both are flush to the wall at the back. It was found necessary to plane and then to glass-paper the top of the understructure very carefully to ensure the board lying snugly upon it, and even then to insert a judicious screw here and there, in addition to the same glue and panel-pin method which was used for the ply. By boring the countersunk holes for the long but thin screws fairly deeply, they were easily filled in flush with a little paste made of some glue and oak sawdust, and so made indetectable after the final glass-papering.

Staining and Polishing.

Staining was done, after plenty of careful and energetic smoothing with glass-paper, by means of spirit stain. This was bought in the form of powder, and dissolved in spirit as required. Two powders were obtained for a reason which will be made plain. One was that usually sold as "oak" stain, the other being "Jacobean oak," and which gives a colder colour. This was done because the actual colour which results on oak depends as much upon the wood itself as upon the stain. An old, hard variety, such as the figured board used for the front, tends to absorb less stain, and is inclined to look too red, whereas the oak used for plywood is more spongy, absorbs stain greedily, and becomes dark and cold. Therefore the colder stain was brushed over the old, hard, boards, and *vice versâ*, using successive dilute washes, and allowing each application to dry.

By this means a reasonably even colour was obtained throughout, especially as fine glass-paper was also applied occasionally between stainings.

Polishing was merely an application or two of ordinary wax floor-polish, which not only brings out the grain of the wood effectively, but is so easy to apply as often as may be desired by means of a shoe brush (see Fig. 5), which, however, should be kept specially for this purpose. The reliability, both of the construction described, and of the simple method of polishing, is proved by the two winters of regular fires which the work has withstood without deterioration.

Improving a Fireplace that Smokes.

A fireplace which is merely sluggish, or which has a tendency to send smoke out into the room, can sometimes be improved by building up the throat more steeply with concrete at the base of the flue. Sometimes this can be done without

Fig. 6.—AN OLD-FASHIONED FIREPLACE CONCEALED WITH PLYWOOD, WITH AN ELECTRIC FIRE STANDING BEFORE IT.

Fig. 5.—AN ORDINARY WAX FLOOR POLISH APPLIED WITH A SHOE BRUSH GIVES AN EFFECTIVE FINISH.

removing the mantel and surround. Remove all soot and dirt and see that the existing surface is sufficiently rough for the new concrete to key on to it. Then apply sufficient concrete to build up the throat by perhaps an inch. The back of the fireplace below the flue should generally slope out toward the room at an angle of about 75 degrees from the horizontal.

INSTALLING A GAS OR ELECTRIC FIRE

A good way to effect a complete modernisation is by installing a gas or electric fire, and the latter is in most instances simplest of all. If the house is already wired for electricity, the old-fashioned mantel and surround, and also the existing coal fireplace, can all be boxed in with plywood, so that a simple modern background for the electric fire is obtained.

Masking Fireplace Opening with Plywood.

An even simpler method is to mask the fireplace opening with a single rectangle of plywood as shown in one of our photographs. In this case no attempt need be made to conceal the mantelpiece, and the old coal fireplace is always available at any time simply by removing the plywood. With plywood at, say, 1s. 3d. a square foot, the entire cost of concealment will only be a matter of shillings.

Wooden Fireplace.

This method of transformation should present little difficulty if the mantelpiece is of wood. First measure the width and height of the fireplace aperture, taking care to get the measurements strictly accurate. Then construct a rectangular frame of 1 × 1-inch deal to fit the aperture. This frame could be butt-jointed and perhaps strengthened with chamfer blocks. It should then be placed in position and screwed to the sides of the mantel.

Metal or Stone Mantelpiece.

If, however, the mantelpiece is of metal or stone, it will be necessary to

Fig. 7.—A Typical Victorian Fireplace.
By concealing the mantelpiece with plywood and fitting a gas or electric fire this ugly old-fashioned fitment is easily transformed.

Fig. 8.—The Ugly Victorian Fireplace effectively concealed.
The painted wood surround conceals the old Victorian mantelpiece shown in Fig. 7.

remove some of the tiling from the inner surround and plug the plaster beneath with wood to receive the screws.

The plywood should now be sawn to the exact size required, and finally it should be nailed into position on the deal frame, using brass or silver-headed nails. The plywood could be finished with a coat of gold-bronze or silver paint, or cellulose lacquer.

All that then remains to be done is for the electric fire to be placed in a centre position in front of the plywood, a convenient plug-point, of course, being fitted in the adjacent skirting.

Hot-water Radiators.

A similar treatment could be followed if one is installing hot-water radiators. It frequently happens that when an out-of-date kitchen is modernised the new boiler or stove provides sufficient hot water for one or two radiators, and as this is an economical form of heating if the hot water is available, it is good policy to instal the radiators in the bedrooms and perhaps the entrance hall. A good position for them is often in front of the old fireplace, if the latter is masked with plywood in the manner suggested.

Gas Fires.

The installation of a gas fire, if it is done well, is somewhat more complicated than putting in an electric one, for in order to obtain the best results, there should be direct communication between the back of the fire and the chimney. Any fumes given off will then be sure of a proper outlet, and there will be no danger of their finding a way into the room.

With gas fires it is found that best results are obtained if the fire is raised about 6 inches from the ground, to ensure that the heat is thrown out into the room as far as possible. A surround which would be suitable for a gas fire could be constructed with either deal or plywood, as shown in Figs. 7 and 8, and it tends to simplify matters if the existing mantelshelf can be left to form the top of the new fitment. This has been done with quite good results in the case of the examples shown.

Fig. 9.—The Hearth is a Suitable Position for a Hot-Water Radiator if the Fireplace is masked with Plywood.

Modern-type Coal Fireplace.

If, however, you should decide after all in favour of a modern-type coal fireplace you will do well to make a careful preliminary inspection of the different types now available. They are very numerous. From the artistic point of view you may select a fireplace with a surround of tiles, brick or wood, and many of the smartest nowadays have a narrow rim, or inner surround, of stainless steel. Tile fireplaces are often excellent for bedrooms, a brick fireplace would be suitable for the sitting room or dining room, and a figured timber mantel for the drawing room. But there is no hard and fast rule, and brick or tile fireplaces, which cost from about £4 upward, can be used quite well in almost any room of the house.

"Hot Air" Fire.

From the practical point of view there are several fires with unusual features which are worth considering. For example, one of the newest models is known as the "hot air" fire, and is designed to keep the room warmed throughout at the same level temperature. Cold air from near the floor is drawn through two vents, resembling grilles, on each side of the hearth. Passing into a cavity or heating chamber beneath and behind the fireplace, the cold air is warmed and then passes into the room through two more vents at the top of the fireplace. This keeps the room at a level temperature, and even after the fire has gone out the heating chamber will remain warm for several hours and will continue to warm the room.

There are also coal fires fitted with a gas jet for lighting the fire. All you have to do after laying the fire is to light the gas jet and leave it for perhaps a quarter of an hour, after which the gas can be turned out.

There is also a small convertible fire which can be used either as a gas fire or for burning coal.

Two-way or Back-to-back Grates.

Another excellent idea is a two-way or back-to-back grate fitted in the wall between two rooms, such as dining room and sitting room. With a grate of this kind one fire is made to do double duty, for it supplies heat to both the rooms. This means that there is only one fire to lay and light and keep clean instead of two, and half the quantity of coal is burned.

A point to remember is the fact that smokeless fuel of various kinds is now obtainable and is likely to be used increasingly in the future. An existing fireplace can generally be adapted for burning smokeless fuel without much difficulty.

Several types of the enclosed anthracite or smokeless fuel stoves which keep burning day and night are not nearly such an extravagance as they may at first sound. There is a stove, for example, which will burn anthracite, coke or ordinary house coal, and which keeps in day and night at a cost of sixpence per twenty-four hours. The fire needs practically no attention beyond stoking twice a day, from autumn to spring, and there is no scattering of dust and ash throughout the house as with an ordinary open fireplace.

WALLPAPER SCHEMES FOR BEDROOMS, NURSERY AND BATHROOMS

BEDROOMS with a sunny aspect will present fewer difficulties than those facing north and east, which require colour to suggest warmth and brightness during the greater part of the year. A south room can have a white wall without fear of seeming cold and uninviting, whereas white in rooms of other aspects has a cheerless appearance. In such rooms if light walls are desired, yellow (but not lemon yellow), cream and deep cream will be effective.

Chintz Papers.

Chintz papers in all probability will always be popular for bedrooms on account of their familiar and homely associations with comfort and cleanliness. Chintz designs are printed on tinted backgrounds as well as on white, which extends their usefulness to rooms where white backgrounds are undesirable but the bright colours of their patterns are needed.

The choice of wallpapers for bedrooms, as for other rooms, is frequently governed by the style of the furniture, so that the wall covering shall be related to the scheme not only in colour and appropriate texture but also in pattern treatment.

Papers to Suit the Furniture.

White enamelled furniture can have walls with the brightest colours. Grey walls should be reserved for sunny rooms. Grey furniture needs a contrasting wall paper, a dull rose pink or old rose, both are pleasant, as also are patterns with these tints.

The guest's bedroom can be treated with greater freedom than is desirable in rooms continually in use. Patterns or schemes which are more than ordinarily arresting can be adopted as the occupants are not likely to lose interest by familiarity and such differences add interest to the house and to the pleasure of visitors.

NURSERY

The first thought in connection with a nursery will be the desire for a bright room. If possible the choice of aspect would be towards the south, and in any case the walls should be light but not glaring. If the aspect of the room is due south, fawn, parchment, pale green or blue can be adopted, but if toward either east or west the warmer colours, yellow and maize, should predominate.

Should it be objected that a light paper is easily soiled, a dado can be arranged by a border or rail at a height of about 3 feet from the floor and below this a paper of darker shade. A part of the dado or even the whole of it can be painted with a flat black paint to give a surface for children to amuse themselves with chalk drawing.

Immediately above the dado is an excellent position for a nursery frieze or panels instead of under the cornice or ceiling as still frequently done, but which is far too high for children.

Friezes.

There are a number of very attractive friezes now produced for nurseries, some of these are in the form of a border, about 10 inches wide, having some simple features, such as trees at certain intervals; between these animals and other cut-out objects can be placed where they may be considered most effective. There are also friezes which are sufficient to go completely around the room without repetition.

Naturally, the subjects of these decorations include such children's favourites as Christopher Robin, Fairies, Mickey the Mouse, Noah's Ark, and a number of nursery rhymes.

BATHROOMS

It is of the first importance that the surface of the walls should be unharmed by steam condensing and water splashing. Immediately around hand-basins and baths walls are frequently tiled, an excellent treatment. Some such treatment is desirable especially above the hand-basin, but the space so covered need not extend beyond the width of the basin and a foot above it. A filet of wood makes a suitable finish.

Lincrusta.

Apart from this the walls can be covered with paper or, at a rather increased cost, Lincrusta. Of this material a variety of tile patterns are available and are made in many tints finished with a hard enamel. Papers offer a wider range, though simple tile designs are as effective as any, and as popular. For those who prefer the unusual there will be found a series of papers which form a background of clouds or atmospheric effects on which seagulls or other motifs made especially for bathrooms can be superimposed. These decorative materials are prepared for varnishing after they are hung, needing two coats of good size before varnish is applied. There is also a splendid series of marble papers obtainable.

The Dado.

For the dado a colour different from that above the dado rail but in harmony with it or a good contrast, is very pleasing. The dado and the exterior of the bath should have a definite colour relationship and the paintwork of the skirting should either match the dado or be a shade deeper.

Bathrooms are usually small, so the floor should be considered, in conjunction with bath exterior and the dado colour. If this is a strong colour the architrave of the door and window can be treated in the same manner as the skirting and the door and window frame in lighter tints to harmonise with the walls.

RESTRINGING A TENNIS RACKET

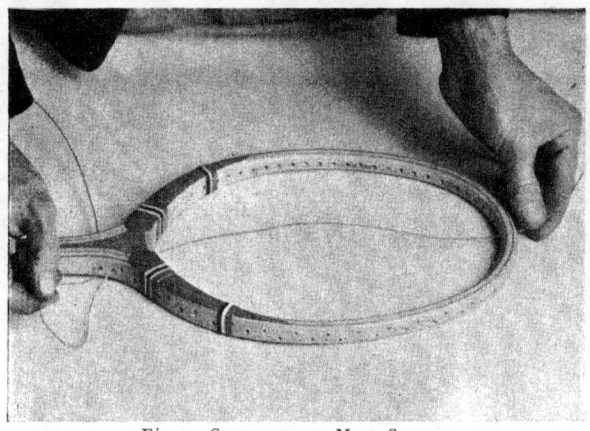

Fig. 1.—STARTING THE MAIN STRINGS.
Showing how the first main is placed in position.

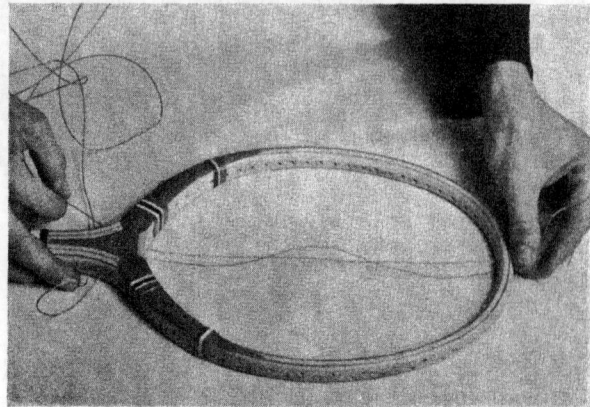

Fig. 2.—THE OTHER END OF THE GUT IS PULLED THROUGH PARALLEL TO THE FIRST STRING.

AFTER one or two seasons of use the strings of a tennis racket tend to become slack and inclined to break. The most satisfactory treatment is to restring the racket entirely, and this can be done cheaply and efficiently at home by anyone by following the instructions given in this article.

As the method of stringing varies slightly with different makes of rackets it is a good idea to make a rough sketch of the arrangement before cutting away the old threads.

The stringing is done in two sections, first the main (vertical) strings, and then the crossings (horizontal) strings. Finally, the job is finished off with trebling; three lines at the top and three lines at the bottom.

Materials and Tools required.

Lamb gut is the best material to use for the mains and crossings, and two lengths of about 21 feet will be needed. The trebling is done with a tough

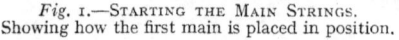

Fig. 3.—HOW TO BEGIN THE MAIN STRINGS.
A, when there is a hole through the throat of the handle, and B when there is no such hole.

string. These materials can be obtained from any sports dealers, or a supplier of fishing tackle could procure them if he has not some already in stock.

A number of pegs will be required and ordinary matches will serve the purpose quite well. An awl will be needed, and if a vice is available for holding the racket it will facilitate the work.

Preparing the Gut.

The gut will probably require stretching before it is used, and this can be done with the aid of two broom-handles or similar articles. Wind two turns round one handle and then about a yard along the gut wind two more turns round the other handle. Then fix one handle in a firm position, or get someone to hold it, and pull tightly with a few sharp jerks. Repeat this process yard by yard until the whole length of gut has been stretched. This will ensure that the gut does not sag after it has been threaded in the racket.

Fig. 4.—SHOWING NINE MAINS IN POSITION ON EITHER SIDE OF THE FIRST TWO.

Fig. 5.—TIGHTENING THE MAINS, WORKING FROM THE CENTRE TO THE OUTSIDE.

Threading the Mains.

You can now start threading the mains. Start by inserting one end of the gut through the throat-hole. Then through the hole immediately above the throat-hole so that it comes out on the inside of the racket. Pull it through and insert through one of the holes in the top of the racket, as shown in Fig. 1.

Now take the other end of the gut, insert it through the hole immediately above the throat-hole on the opposite side, and pull it through up to the top of the racket, as shown in Fig. 2. Then take hold of both ends and pull the whole length of gut tight so that you now have the centre of the gut in the throat-hole and two long ends of gut at the top of the racket.

What to do if there is no Hole in the Throat.

The above instructions only apply in the case of a racket that has a hole in the throat of the handle. If there is no such hole then the method shown at B, in Fig. 3, should be adopted. Here it will be seen that the two ends of the gut are inserted from the top of the racket and then through the holes nearest to the handle. The method of completing the mains is, however, the same, and is as described below.

Completing the Mains.

Having got the first two mains in position the next operation is to complete nine more mains on either side of the first two, as shown in Fig. 4. Each end is then passed under the existing mains on the outside of the frame, to hold the gut in position.

Tightening the Mains.

The next operation consists of tightening the mains to get sufficient tension. Before this is done obtain a narrow strip of wood as long as the inner length of the racket and wedge this in position, as shown in Fig. 5. This is to preserve the shape of the racket when it is subjected to the strain of tightening.

Start tightening from the centre of the racket and work outwards. The method of tightening is shown in Fig. 5. As soon as the gut has been pulled up sufficiently to get the gut previous to it tight enough, fix a peg in the hole so that the gut is kept in this position.

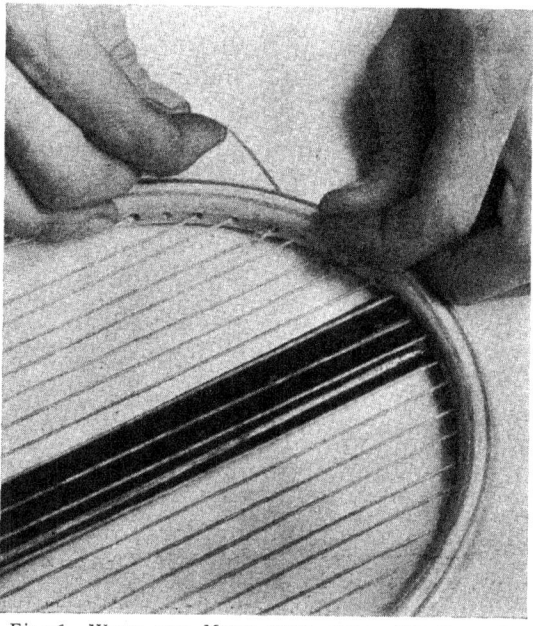

Fig. 6.—WHEN THE MAINS HAVE BEEN TIGHTENED THE CROSSINGS ARE STARTED BY MAKING A KNOT ON THE FOURTH MAIN AS SHOWN.

Repeat the process with each of the strings in turn.

Threading the Crossings.

When the mains have been tightened up a start can be made with the crossings. Begin by making a knot on the fourth main from the outside, as shown in Fig. 6. Then thread the gut through the next hole towards the

Fig. 7.—THE GUT IS THEN THREADED THROUGH THE NEXT HOLE, PROCEEDING OVER AND UNDER THE MAINS TO THE OPPOSITE SIDE OF THE RACKET.

handle and proceed to take it across to the other side of the racket, passing over and under the mains, as shown in Fig. 7.

When the opposite side is reached thread the gut through the hole and hold it tight in position with an awl, as shown in Fig. 8. The gut is then threaded through from side to side until twenty crossings have been completed. Then finish off with a knot round the mains similar to the start of the crossings. The crossings can be straightened and regulated with the point of a blunt instrument such as a pencil.

The Trebling.

The racket is now complete except for the trebling. This is begun by tying a knot round the last crossing and then working to the opposite side of the frame in the manner shown in Fig. 9. This is repeated for three rows at the top and bottom of the racket.

A Gut Strengthener.

It is a good idea to give both faces of the gut a coat of shellac, dissolved in methylated spirit. This preparation strengthens and protects the meshing, and it is a good plan to apply it two or three times every season.

The above notes should enable anyone to make a thoroughly satisfactory job of restringing a tennis racket.

HOW TO PRESERVE A TENNIS NET

Tennis and garden netting, like rackets, require a certain amount of attention if they are to last more than a season or two. Tennis netting should be treated with some form of preservative, and a good solution is ordinary tar oil or creosote, the nets being soaked in a bath of this liquid and then hung out in the open to dry.

Another Method.

Another good method of treating the nets is to dress them in a solution made by boiling about ½ lb. of powdered oak bark in 1½ gallons of water. The bark solution should be allowed to boil for about half an hour. Place the net to be preserved in a wooden trough and pour the hot dressing over it, making sure that the net is well covered.

Leave the net in the solution

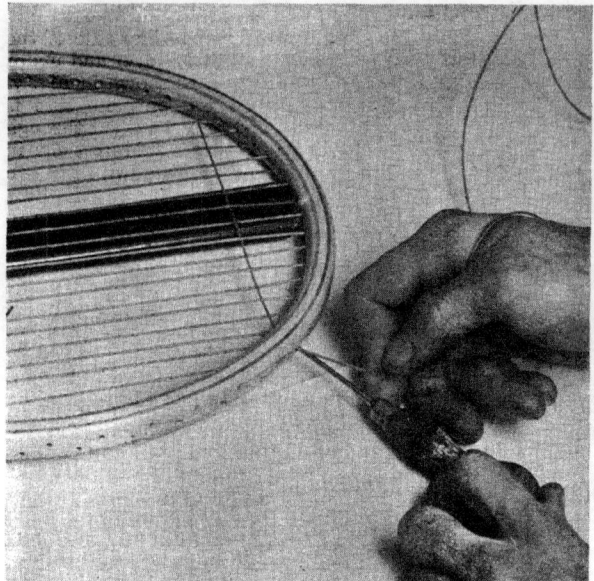
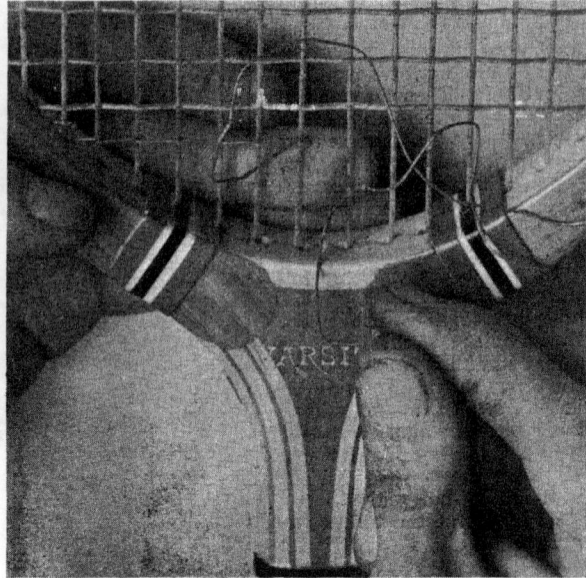

*Fig. 8.—*Tightening the Crossings. This is done as each crossing is threaded until twenty crossings have been completed.

*Fig. 9.—*The Trebling is begun by tying a Knot round the Last Crossing and working to the Opposite Side as shown.

for about forty-eight hours, occasionally turning it over and agitating the liquid. Then remove it from the trough and hang it up in order to allow the surplus liquid to drip off. The net should then be well rinsed in cold water and dried in the open air, when it will be found that the strings have a leatherlike colour and are quite impervious to all weather influences.

Attention should be drawn to the fact that a metal bath or trough must not be used, as the oak bark solution will attack the metal, the liquid turning black in the process.

Don't forget the Usual Precautions.

Although the above treatment will render a tennis net much more resistant to the effects of the weather, the usual precaution of slackening the top rope of the net during a shower of rain should still be observed. It is also a very good plan to take in the nets each evening.

Thanks are due to Messrs. A. G. Spalding Bros. (British) Ltd., 317, High Holborn, W.C. 1., for the photographs which accompany this article.

SOME USEFUL METAL WORKING HINTS

Straightening Bent Wire.

Kinks in a piece of wire are difficult to straighten out with ordinary tools. A good plan is to take a block of hardwood and screw into it four or six steel wood-screws having cheese-heads. First draw a straight line with a pencil along the block of wood, then place the screws at equal distances alternately on either side of this line. To use the device thread one end of the piece of wire through the projecting screws and fix it in a vice; then draw the device along the wire when all bends and kinks will be quickly smoothed out.

A Simple Steel Bronzing Method.

When steel parts are required to be bronzed they should first be polished to a fine finish, then dipped in olive oil and allowed to drain. Now expose the oil-coated steel parts to the action of steam issuing from a kettle of boiling water, rotating them so as to allow the steam to act on all parts of the surface. They will then assume a bronzed effect.

How to remove a Broken Drill.

If a drill breaks below the surface of the metal during drilling operations it can be removed by filling the hole with paraffin and leaving for a few hours. This will loosen any dirt that may have caused the fracture and the broken drill will generally fall out after a little shaking.

To soften Brass or Copper.

When it is required to soften brass or copper a method that is just the reverse of that employed to harden steel is used. Heat the parts to be softened in a flame or oven of even temperature, to a temperature that is equivalent to a dull red colour. Then plunge into cold water. Do not heat the metal to a full red colour or it will disintegrate.

Brass and copper cannot be hardened by heat-treatment, but only by hammering, rolling or extruding through steel dies.

A Hint when filing Soft Metals.

When soft metals such as copper, lead, solder or aluminium are being filed, the file quickly clogs and the particles of metal adhering to the file tend to scratch the surface of the metal. A good plan to avoid this is to keep the file wet by dipping it in a jar of water or paraffin.

Filling Holes in Castings.

Small holes or pits, known as "blowholes" are sometimes left in castings made in various metals, for example, cast iron, brass or lead. Such holes detract from the good appearance of the casting and should be filled up.

A method that is quite satisfactory for iron castings is to mix together cast-iron turnings and powdered sal-ammoniac, moistening the mixture with water and then ramming some of it into the hole to be filled. This composition sets very hard.

Another method of filling holes in iron castings is with alloys having the same colour as cast iron. A suitable alloy for the purpose and one that fuses much more readily than iron is made from antimony, 65 parts; copper, 16 parts; and lead, 13 parts (by weight).

In the case of brass or gun-metal castings, spelter or tinman's solder can be used for filling purposes. The casting should be heated to about the melting-point of the filling alloy.

Making Concrete Garden Steps

STEPS made in concrete are often required for a garden where the lawn or flower beds slope away from the house, and the following article describes the best method of carrying out this work.

First excavate the Site.

The first thing to do is to level the site lengthwise, as shown in the sectioned view in Fig. 1. It will probably be necessary to consolidate the ground by ramming it with a suitable rammer to make it quite firm so that there is no danger of it sinking. A suitable rammer can be made at home by getting a heavy piece of wood about $12 \times 8 \times 3$ inches and nailing to it a handle shaped from a piece of 2×2-inch timber.

The Design.

The concrete steps shown in Fig. 1 consist of steps 6 feet between strings (sides) with 5-inch risers and 10-inch treads. To ensure that water does not lay on the steps the treads should have a $\frac{1}{4}$-inch fall from back to front. As the strings are 6 inches thick with pre-cast coping attached, it will be possible to stand pots or other garden ornaments at the foot and head.

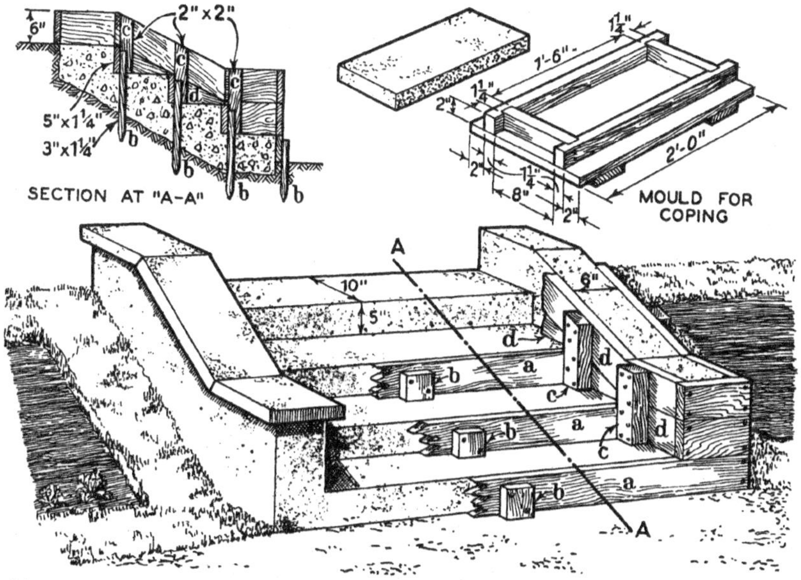

Preparing the Shuttering.

A suitable arrangement of shuttering or framework will be required to keep the concrete in position while it is setting, and ordinary $1\frac{1}{4}$-inch deal wood will be quite suitable.

The various sizes required are shown in Fig. 1. The timber need not necessarily be planed, but the smoother the surface of the timber the better looking will be the final job.

As the actual width and depth of the steps required will vary in almost every case, it is impossible to give actual dimensions, but the details given below should enable anyone to prepare suitable shuttering to suit their needs.

The first thing to do is to make up the shuttering for the strings. This should be strengthened with 2×2-inch battens, as shown at c in the sectional view. Screws should be used for holding the shuttering together and a little grease should be placed on them before assembling, so that the shuttering can be easily dismantled.

When the shuttering is being fixed in position, stumps marked b should be placed on the outside of the strings and in the centre of the timbers which act as risers. Fix them securely with screws. Additional stumps can be temporarily fixed wherever required by nails, leaving the heads projecting so that they can be easily withdrawn.

Check the levels very carefully with the spirit level when assembling the shuttering, and use temporary braces to ensure that the whole set of shuttering is quite rigid. If any parts are not made quite secure trouble will be experienced when the concrete is added.

Fig. 1.—Details of the Method of Erecting the Shuttering for the Concrete Garden Steps.
Showing also details of mould for the coping.

Preparing the Concrete.

Having got the shuttering in position the next step is to mix the concrete. A suitable mix for a construction of this nature consists of four parts $\frac{1}{2}$ to $\frac{1}{8}$-inch graded ballast, two parts clean washed sand, and one part of cement. It is essential to take particular care over the mixing. Every particle of ballast and sand should have a coating of cement, and this can be ensured by thorough mixing. First mix together three times in the dry state and then four times in the wet state.

The concrete should be used in a fairly plastic state, but not sloppy.

Coloured Cements.

Coloured cement can be used if it is desired to have the work in keeping with the natural surrounds. A buff-coloured cement would probably be quite effective.

Inserting the Concrete.

As soon as a batch of concrete has been suitably prepared, it should at once be placed in between the shutters and well tamped into position. Leave the top more or less rough to form a key for the next batch.

Continue this process until the work is completed, and leave the face of the treads more or less smooth.

When placing the concrete which forms the steps it will, of course, be necessary to undo the screws in the stumps marked b and withdraw them before the work is completed. The cavity left after withdrawing the stumps is filled with concrete.

If desired, pockets can be left in the strings to hold sufficient soil to enable flowers to be grown. These pockets can be formed by inserting balls of clay which can be raked out when the shuttering is dismantled.

Leave Shuttering in Place for Seven Days.

For a really satisfactory job, the shuttering should be left in place for about seven days. The nails and screws can then be removed and the shuttering taken away.

The Coping.

The coping is done in a separate mould. It is quite a plain affair, 2 inches thick, the edges being left square. A suitable size for a mould is shown in Fig. 1. The side forms can be either screwed or clamped together and fixed temporarily to a baseboard. It is a good idea to have the coping of such a width that it overhangs the strings by about 1 inch on either side.

How to fix the Coping.

When the coping has hardened it can be fixed to the strings of the steps by using cement and sand mixed one part of cement to four parts of sand.

If a concrete floor is required at the foot of the steps, erect a wooden structure round the site to be filled. First drive in wooden pegs at each corner. Set one peg to the level of the concrete surface required and level the other pegs to this. Then nail suitable boards to the pegs. Make sure the boards cannot move when the concrete is poured in.

How to Make a Washing Machine

Much of the drudgery of wash-day can be minimised by the use of the simple home-made washing machine which forms the subject of these notes.

The washer is built into an ordinary gas-heated copper such as that shown in Fig. 1, and consists essentially of a fixed inner frame built into the interior of the copper—as shown in the sectional view in Fig. 2—and the hollow rotor or dolly which is actuated by the handle outside the machine.

The dolly and its bearing are attached to the hinged lid of the copper and when this is raised free access to the copper is obtained.

Action of Washer.

Clothes are placed into the warm or boiling water in the copper, together with such soap or washing powder as is necessary; the cover is then closed, thus bringing the dolly into the copper. The handle is then worked steadily from side to side and occasionally raised and lowered bodily; these actions force the clothes to and fro in the soapy water as well as raising them, and thus simulate the actions of scrubbing and effectively remove all dirt, a process which is completed by boiling all appropriate materials in the usual way.

Materials and Tools.

Necessary tools are only those which are normally found in any householder's tool kit, nor is there any difficult work involved in making and fitting the woodwork.

As regards materials, it is assumed that a gas-heated copper is available, but in any case one of these handy contrivances can be purchased for £1 or less. This will have a capacity rating of about 8 gallons and will be large enough to deal with all the usual washing for a normal household.

The wood used for the washer should be good, clean, hard wood such as birch, elm or oak; soft wood is not suitable on account of its tendency to develop splinters and roughness under the action of water. The following are the quantities required for a washer suitable for a normal 8-gallon size copper; exact dimensions must be adjusted to suit the size of any particular copper:—

Fig. 1.—The Washer in Use.

Hard work is greatly reduced on washing day by the use of the home-made washer described in the text.

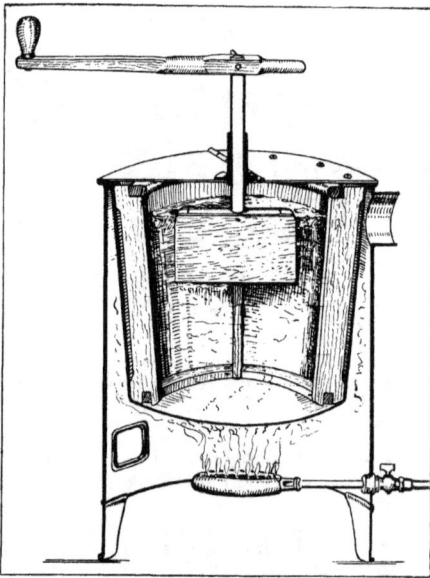

Fig. 2.—Sectional View of Washer.

This cut-away view shows the fixed bars within the washer and the dolly which does the work of a scrubbing brush.

Framework.—Hardwood, 4½ inches wide, ¾ inch thick, 10 feet run.

Uprights.—Hardwood, 1½ inches wide, ¾ inch thick, 6 feet long.

Dolly.—Hardwood, two pieces 8 inches long, 4 inches wide, ½ inch thick. Two pieces 4 inches long, 1½ inches wide, 1 inch thick. One piece 6 inches long, 1½ inches wide, 1 inch thick.

Handle.—Hardwood, 2 inches wide, 1 inch thick, 18 inches long.

In addition, there will be required one brass bush with flange, 1 inch bore; one piece galvanised iron pipe, 1 inch outside diameter, 14 inches long, to turn easily in the bush.

One hardwood knob; one ¼-inch coach bolt and flynut; ½ dozen round-head brass screws, 2 inches long; 1 dozen countersunk head brass screws, 1¼ inches long; a few feet of ¼-inch hardwood dowel rod.

Commencing the Work.

The first thing to do is to measure the inside of the copper and, if necessary, adjust any of the dimensions given in this article; then proceed to prepare two hardwood rings as shown in Fig. 3 and four upright pieces as there shown.

It is seldom possible to find a suitable piece of wood wide enough to enable the rings to be sawn from the solid, and plywood is not suitable as the constant heat and steam would cause it to disintegrate, consequently it is necessary to build them up from four separate pieces, those for the top ring being shown in Fig. 4.

One of these quadrants can be cut from a piece of board ¾ inch thick, 4½ inches wide and 14 inches long. Mark out the wood by striking arcs of circles with radii of 8½ inches and 7 inches respectively, as shown in Fig. 4, then mark off the angle of 90 degrees and on either side of this line draw a radial line.

Preparing the Quadrants.

Cut the wood to shape with a keyhole or bow-saw, then make a halved joint at each end by making a saw-cut down the middle of the thickness of the wood and sawing across on the radial line at the top of the left-hand end and across on the underneath of the right-hand end.

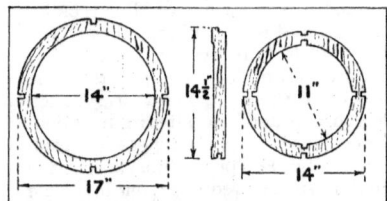

Fig. 3.—The Parts of the Fixed Framework.

Two rings and four vertical bars constitute the structure of the inner framework.

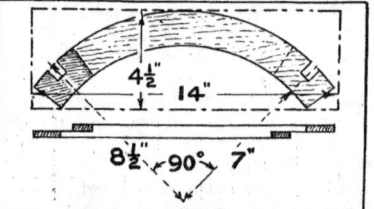

Fig. 4.—Setting out the Top Quadrant.

The top ring is built up of four pieces sawn from flat wood and jointed together. The dimensions here given enable the wood to be marked out properly.

Fig. 5.—Joints of Top Frame.

The joint between two quadrants and that at the top of an upright are here shown.

HOW TO MAKE A WASHING MACHINE

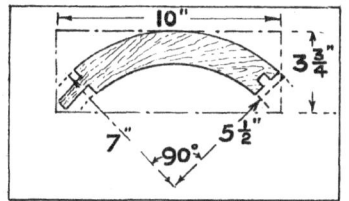

Fig. 6.—SETTING OUT THE BOTTOM QUADRANT.
The bottom ring is made with four pieces of flat wood cut to the shape shown and jointed at the ends.

Fig. 7.—JOINTS OF BOTTOM FRAME.
Here is seen the joint between the ends of two bottom quadrants and that of the lower end of the upright.

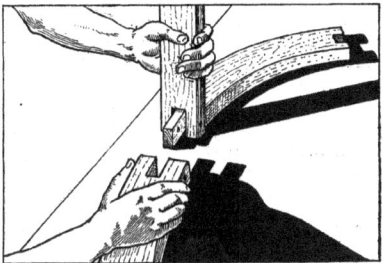

Fig. 8.—ASSEMBLING THE BOTTOM FRAME.
The parts of the lower frame joints are assembled as here shown.

Cut and shape four pieces in the same way and screw them together temporarily while four notches, ¾ inch wide and ¾ inch deep, are cut in the outer edge. These notches must be equally spaced and should come to 90-degree lines already drawn and thus come in the middle of the halved joint. This is clearly shown in Fig. 5, where the corresponding notch that has to be cut in the top ends of the uprights is also shown.

These notches can be cut with a tenon saw, but should be done neatly and the joints made to fit nicely.

After the joints have been made the surfaces of the ring should be planed flat, the outer edge bevelled to fit into the top of the copper and the inner edge neatly rounded off.

The halving joint is connected by four dowel pins—visible in Fig. 5—and these should fit nicely and may be secured with a trace of red lead and gold size; glue must not be used. The uprights are held to the ring by brass screws countersunk into the top surface of the ring.

Making the Bottom Ring.

The bottom ring is made with four pieces somewhat similar to the top, but differently jointed. The mode of setting out the four pieces is shown in Fig. 6, where it will be seen that the ends are connected by a long tenon and a short slot. This, as can be seen in the close-up Fig. 7, leaves notches on the inside and the outside into which the forked end of the upright piece is fitted.

Apart from this variation, the lower ring is prepared and finished in the same way as the top ring.

The length of the upright pieces and the inclination of their ends should be adjusted to suit the copper; they should reach from the underside of the cover to the turn of the bottom, or that

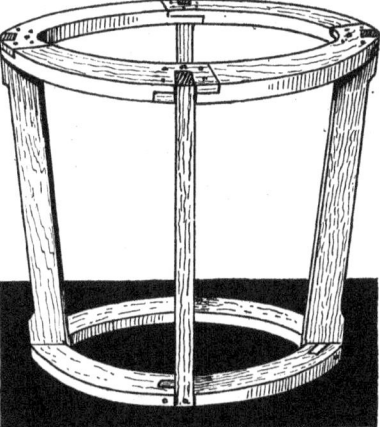

Fig. 9.—COMPLETED INNER FRAME.
The inner framework is here shown, assembled for test purposes.

Fig. 10.—ASSEMBLING FRAMEWORK IN WASHER.
The various parts of the inner framework are put together piece by piece inside the washer and then secured by wooden dowels.

part where the sides begin to curve inwards to form the bottom. Only the

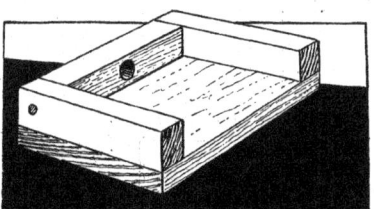

Fig. 12.—THE DOLLY DURING CONSTRUCTION.
The narrow pieces of wood are dowelled and screwed to one of the flat pieces as here shown, and then covered by the second flat piece of wood.

top and bottom of the outer edge should bear against the copper, the intermediate part should be "backed off" or planed off to a depth of about ⅜ inch to allow the water to circulate, as can be seen in Figs. 2 and 3.

Assembling the Framework.

The framework should now be assembled by inserting the lower ends of the uprights into the notches between the lower ring—as shown in Fig. 8—then placing the upper ring in position as shown in Fig. 9, which illustrates the work at this stage.

This frame cannot, however, be inserted bodily into the copper because the fixed part of the cover is in the way, consequently the frame is taken apart and re-assembled as shown in Fig. 10, inside the copper, but is easily accomplished if the parts have been fitted as described.

The uprights should be so placed that two of them come under the fixed cover, so that round headed brass screws can be put through holes drilled or punched through the cover and can bite into the uprights. Two or three other screws should be similarly driven into the top ring to prevent any chance of its moving. If necessary, insert a thin slip of hardwood to fill any gap between the cover and the top ring.

Making the Dolly.

The dolly is, practically speaking, a box with the lower end open; it is made with five pieces of wood of the sizes given in Fig. 11, the three pieces of 1½ × 1 inch wood being screwed and dowelled to the face of one of the

Fig. 13.—THE DOLLY FIXED TO THE SPINDLE.
Here the dolly is shown permanently affixed to the main spindle.

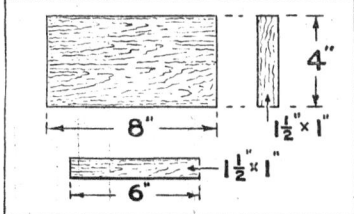

Fig. 11.—PARTS OF THE DOLLY.
Shapes and dimensions of the parts for the dolly.

HOW TO MAKE A WASHING MACHINE

flat pieces as shown in Fig. 12, and then covered by the other flat piece. A hole is drilled at the top to take the iron pipe, and this can be fitted—as shown in Fig. 13—directly all the outer edges of the dolly have been neatly rounded off. The pipe should be a tight fit in the hole and be secured by a screw passed through the dolly and through a hole drilled at right angles through the pipe. The ends of the tube should be plugged with hardwood and a small hole drilled through the pipe just below the top plug.

Fitting the Bearing Bush.

A suitable brass bearing bush can generally be had second-hand or from an ironmonger's, or can be built up by brazing a brass ring, about $2\frac{1}{2}$ inches diameter and $\frac{3}{16}$ inch thick to the outside of a thick brass tube about 5 inches long.

This bush must be fitted to a hole drilled through the hinged part of the cover, as near the centre of the copper as possible. The easiest way to make this hole is to drill a series of $\frac{1}{8}$-inch diameter holes with a small hand drill, spacing them equally around the circle, then breaking out the solid part in the middle and filing it to shape. The flange part of the bush is then bolted to the hinged cover—as

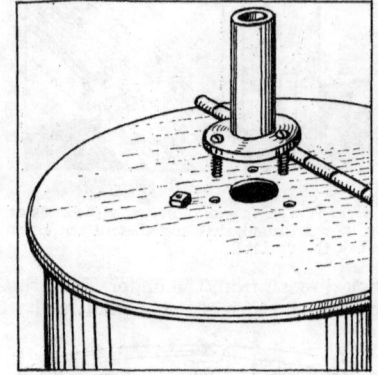

Fig. 14.—Main Bearing Bush.

A brass bush with flange piece is bolted to the hinged cover of the washer; the dolly spindle rotates in this bush.

shown in Fig. 14—and the spindle of the dolly put through it from the underside.

If everything is correct the hinged cover can be opened and closed with the dolly in place if the latter is raised to the top.

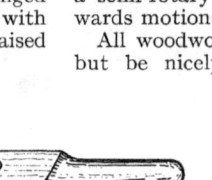

Fig. 15.—Details of Handle.

The driving handle is detachable, and when not in use is stored within the washer. It is used to rotate and to raise and lower the dolly.

The Operating Handle.

The handle is easily shaped with a plane and spokeshave, and is provided with a suitable hardwood knob or hand grip on the outer end—as shown in Figs. 2 and 15. A hole is drilled at a distance of 12 to 14 inches from the hand grip into which the top end of the dolly spindle should fit nicely and to which it is secured by a coach bolt and flynut.

The projecting part of the handle beyond the spindle hole should be rounded off, as this and the corresponding part on the opposite side is used when working the dolly up and down.

A little vaseline or oil should be put on the spindle where it turns in the bush and the machine operated while it is dry, to see that everything is correct. The dolly should be capable of rotating completely without striking against the uprights, even when in its lower position, although it is used with a semi-rotary or backwards and forwards motion.

All woodwork should be left plain, but be nicely sandpapered and be absolutely free from any suggestion of splinters or roughness. The bush may be painted black and the handle stained and varnished, as this gives a finished workmanlike appearance to the completed washing machine.

RENOVATING RUSTY TOOLS

ENGINEERS' and carpenters' tools that have become rusty owing to lack of use, or to storage in a damp place, can readily be cleaned by rubbing them with a piece of felt or cork that has been dipped into a mixture consisting of ordinary vaseline and fine emery or carborundum powder.

For measuring instruments that have rusted ordinary knife machine powder and machine oil mixed to the consistency of a thin paste and applied with a cloth or felt wad will be found effective.

A HOME-MADE BEADING TOOL

IT sometimes happens that the amateur woodworker has not a beading plane amongst his tools. In such a case a very good makeshift tool can readily be constructed from a block of wood and a countersunk screw of suitable dimensions.

Use a Piece of Hard Wood.

The block of wood should be about $3 \times 3 \times 4\frac{1}{2}$ inches, and should have one face finished quite flat and smooth. If a piece of oak, or beech is available, this will give much longer service than any of the softer woods.

Cut away a Portion of the Screw.

The countersunk screw should have a small portion cut away, as indicated

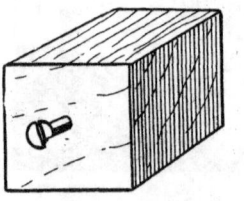

Fig. 1.—Showing Position of Screw in Wood Block.

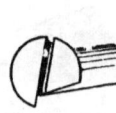

Fig. 2.—Showing Portion cut away from Screw.

in Fig. 2. This can be done by filing it right across so as to leave a flat. The screw is then screwed centrally into the flat face of the wooden block, making sure that it goes in quite squarely. The cutting edge should be arranged in the position shown in Fig. 1.

This tool will be found to cut beadings very quickly, in soft woods, the grooves thus made being finished off by sand-papering.

If much beading work is to be done the block of wood can be shaped and rounded off so as to give a convenient shape for handling.

How to Make Gramophone Records at Home

It is really surprising to note that of the numerous hobbies which present-day science offers to the amateur enthusiast, so little interest is taken in the art of making one's own gramophone records at home.

The actual thought of being able to produce gramophone records usually strikes the uninitiated as being far beyond his reach, both with regard to expenditure and skill. Actually, however, the cost of making records at home is infinitely cheaper than the usually associated hobbies of wireless and photography.

Fig. 1.—A Typical Home Recording Set in Operation.

How Sound Recording takes place.

Before dealing with the components required, perhaps it would be well to give the reader an approximate idea of how sound recording really takes place. The artiste or person who is making the record is placed in front of a recording microphone, the instrument which turns the musical or voice vibrations into electrical vibrations. The output from the microphone, however, is very weak, and has to be applied to the second stage of the apparatus, viz., the amplifier, which, in operation, is very similar to an ordinary wireless set. Instead of applying the output from the amplifier to the customary loud speaker, it is taken to the third and final stage of the equipment, the cutting head, which is situated on the tracking device, or the part of the apparatus which runs the grooves on to the blank discs.

Components required.

The two main essentials are a gramophone and a wireless set. Any gramophone capable of playing a 12-inch record will suffice, together with a wireless set, either battery or mains driven, and capable of filling an average room with good undistorted volume. Should it be desired, a special amplifier may be built for the job, although if the reader possesses a reasonably good radio receiver, this additional expense can easily be saved.

Next we need a recording microphone, a tracking device, a recording head, some blank aluminium alloy discs, and a few tools. It is interesting to note that an apparatus, known as the "Cairmor" Electrical Home Recording attachment manufactured by Cairns and Morrison Ltd., contains all these required essentials, whilst the total cost is only in the region of £4 10s.

The Microphone.

The connections of the "Cairmor" microphone, complete with internal matching transformer, a 3-volt dry cell, and controlling switch, are clearly depicted in Fig. 2.

How to connect the Microphone to the Wireless Set.

This is a very simple operation and calls for little or no technical knowledge. The connections of the output from the microphone consist of two terminals, which, on again referring to Fig. 2, will be seen to come from the secondary windings of the microphone transformer. If the radio set is fitted with sockets for adapting a gramophone pick-up, then it is merely a matter of connecting the microphone terminals direct to the pick-up sockets, as the secondary windings of the microphone transformer will be of similar impedance to an average gramophone pick-up, which one would normally use with the receiver. When switching on the microphone, the output will be amplified and reproduced by the loud speaker of the wireless set.

If the set has a volume control for the gramophone position, then matters are further simplified, as the volume from the microphone may be varied at will. If not, a volume control in the form of a 50,000-ohm variable resistance may be connected across the microphone terminals.

What to do if a Radiogram is available.

If the reader is fortunate in possessing a radiogram, he has the most perfect combination for his experiments, and if this is the case, it is recommended that a D.P.D.T. change-over switch be fitted for putting in circuit either the microphone or the pick-up. This procedure is extremely simple, and should require no further explanation. In the case of a battery-operated wireless receiver, the grid filament circuit of the detector valve may be broken by a switch for throwing the microphone into circuit, as will be seen by the simple diagram in Fig. 3.

It should be noted that the microphone must be connected to a room apart from where the wireless set is situated, in order to prevent what is known as "back coupling" from the loud speaker, resulting in a continuous howl, completely blotting out all trace of speech.

Having reached a stage where good quality and volume is being reproduced on the loud speaker, with someone speaking in an adjoining room, we must now consider a method of utilising this sound for recording.

The Recording Head.

For amateur use a recording head can consist of an ordinary gramophone pick-up. It is advisable to operate the recording head through either a 1-1 output transformer or simple form of choke filter, in order to protect the delicate pick-up coil windings from the continuous

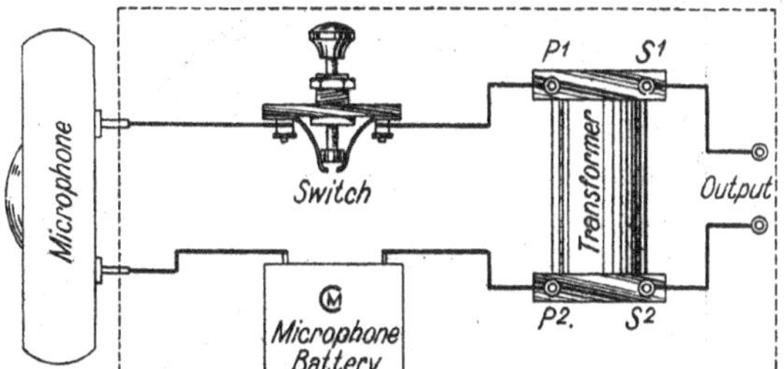

Fig. 2.—Diagram of Connections of the "Cairmor" Microphone Unit.

flow of D.C. current which would otherwise pass directly through its windings. This, however, will apply only to a fairly small battery-operated receiver or amplifier, where the anode impedance of the output valve is in the region of 4,000 ohms, thereby directly matching the impedance of the recording head.

Importance of Matching Output.

This is extremely important, as complete success or failure will depend largely upon this point. If the "Cairmor" recording head, with its impedance, as stated above, of approximately 4,000 ohms at 1,000 cycles, has to be connected to the output of an average radiogram, then a special matching transformer will be necessary, as usually this output is designed especially for matching the speech coil of a modern moving coil loud speaker having an impedance often as low as 10 ohms. This difficulty can easily be overcome, however, by using a matching transformer between the amplifier and the recording head, and the Ferranti O.P.M.6 Transformer is recommended for this position. It must, of course, be connected the reverse way round, so that the high resistance winding is connected to the recording pick-up.

The Recording Stylus.

The blank records, being made of a special alloy of aluminium, have to be cut by some form of cutting stylus. The "Cairmor" outfit contains a sapphire point for this operation, and although this is quite satisfactory for the preliminary experiments, sapphires have the disadvantage of only being able to cut about fifty discs, whilst the depth which they produce is extremely shallow. The most satisfactory form of stylus is a real diamond, and although this is expensive, for a real diamond stone costs 20s., it well pays for itself, inasmuch that with careful use it will last almost indefinitely, whilst it is capable of producing a most amazing depth of cut.

The "Cairmor" Tracking Device.

This instrument performs the operation in an extremely simple, and yet most efficient manner. It consists essentially of a threaded spiral about 4 inches in length, connected at one end to a pair of bevelled gears, and a socket for adapting to the centre of the turntable spindle. The recording head is provided with a hook which engages with the tracking spiral, and when driven by the revolving turntable spindle, gradually feeds the recording head across the disc. A better idea of the arrangement can be seen in Fig. 4, which shows

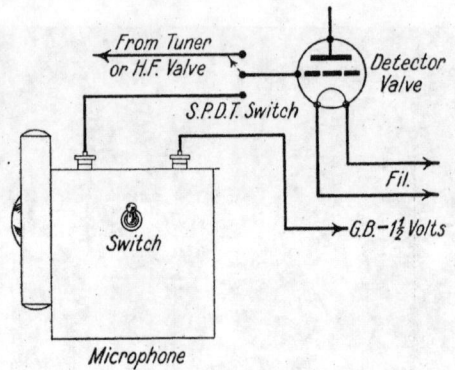

Fig. 3.—How an Existing Battery-driven Wireless Set could be adapted for Use with the "Cairmor" Microphone Unit.

the attachment adapted to an ordinary portable gramophone.

If, as sometimes may be the case, it is desired to make records with the grooves running from the inner to the outer edge of the disc, then the tracker can be supplied with the thread on the tracking spiral turned in the opposite direction.

Balance and General Operating Practice.

Before attempting to record, the operator should "balance up" his artistes, in order to produce the desired amount of voice and piano. For example, nothing sounds worse, either on radio or record, than when the speaker is completely drowned by a heavy accompaniment. This balance can be effected by careful placing of the microphone and listening on the loud speaker in an adjoining room.

Fig. 4.—The "Cairmor" Tracking Device fitted to a Portable Gramophone.

When satisfactory volume and quality have been obtained, a blank disc should be placed on the gramophone turntable, smeared with a thin film of oil to assist the cutting stylus, whilst the recording head should be gently lowered on to the outer edge of the blank disc. The output from the amplifier may then be disconnected from the loud speaker by a simple D.P.D.T. switch and applied to the recording head. The record may be replayed immediately it has been recorded, provided only a fibre or Burmese Colour needle is employed, as a steel needle would, of course, immediately ruin the relatively soft alloy from which the discs are made.

Volume and Sound.

The volume of the finished record will depend entirely upon the output from the amplifier, whilst the depth of cut is, to a large extent, dependent upon the type of recording stylus used, and also the weight of the recording pick-up. If the gramophone motor has sufficient power, then it is often advisable to add a few ounces of extra weight, in order to obtain a better depth of cut in the aluminium alloy, as success depends entirely upon these two factors. The general rule to be adhered to is to regulate the volume of the output of the amplifier according to the depth of cut which it is possible to obtain, for if too much volume is applied to the recording head when only a very shallow groove is being made, then it will be found impossible to accurately track with a Burmese Colour needle. Aim, therefore, for as deep a cut as possible, and load it with as much undistorted volume as the amplifier will permit.

Recording a Broadcast Programme.

It is an extremely simple matter to take records direct from any broadcast programme, merely by following the procedure described above, apart from the fact that the microphone in this case is, of course, totally unnecessary. It is great fun making up a recorded catalogue of your favourite radio stars, but it cannot be over-emphasised that this is for private and individual use only, and that the experimenter would be liable to very heavy penalties if any attempt were made to commercialise the use of his home-made records.

Making the Records Permanent.

It is possible to have records made permanent by sending them to the makers of the "Cairmor" apparatus for a special electro-chemical treatment. This procedure, however, is rather costly and must necessarily be regarded as a luxury.

Cardboard Modelling

THE model of a Tudor cottage, shown in Fig. 1, is a typical example of work that can be carried out in cardboard. Full details are given in this article of the methods to employ, and it will be realised that it is quite a simple matter to adapt the instructions given for making a model of your own house in preference to the actual design given.

Materials that can be used.

The materials used for cardboard modelling are few and inexpensive, the very best material is known as Bristol Board, but there are many kinds of card that can be used successfully. There are different trade names for various brands of card, but so far as the amateur is concerned, any smooth white card of appropriate thickness for the work in hand can be considered as usable.

For some purposes a slightly grained card is very helpful, for example, to represent a rough cast wall, while for others a coloured card is preferable, for instance, a grey card for the slate roof of a model house.

Marbled and enamelled cards can be utilised in a like manner whenever their surface is appropriate to the purpose.

Strawboard should not be used except under special circumstances, as it quickly absorbs moisture and buckles readily whenever the weather turns damp.

Cardboard is made in a wide range of thicknesses, and is generally classified by the "sheet" or "ply," a single ply being the thinnest; usually a three-ply card is amply thick enough for all general work, two-ply can be used for small "folded" pieces, but four-ply, or thicker card will be required for base plates and other foundation pieces.

Adhesives and their Use.

A good adhesive, such as Croid glue, is absolutely essential.

Some of the recently introduced cellulose adhesives are very useful, as when dry they are quite waterproof.

In all cases only a smear of the adhesive is required, and it should be allowed to become tacky before putting the parts together.

Fig. 1.—Model of a Tudor Cottage.

Ordinary flour paste or a ready-prepared paste such as "Stickphast," "Gloy," or any photo-mountant, should be used whenever two sheets of card are to be stuck together. In such cases the thinner of the two pieces should have the paste brushed lightly and evenly over it, and then the piece is laid upon the other, and, if possible, rubbed into firm contact, well pressed down and then allowed to dry under uniform pressure. A usual and convenient method is to place the cards upon a piece of newspaper spread on a flat surface, another piece of clean paper is laid over the cards, then a piece of thick card, and, finally, sufficient books or other weighty objects.

Fig. 2.—Cutting with the Knife.

Take care, however, that the cards are completely covered by the weights, or, if necessary, a piece of board or very thick card should be used to distribute the weight evenly.

Accessories.

A few items are desirable as aids to successful model making; the chief is a selection of pins of all kinds and sizes; they are invaluable for temporarily fastening parts together or for steadying them while drying, and so forth.

A few drawing and paper clips are also useful on occasion. A large sheet of thick strawboard to lay on the table while at work is most useful, as also are a few small tin boxes with lids to retain small parts while the work is in progress.

Tools.

The most necessary tool is a really keen cutting knife; some workers prefer a print trimmer's knife, others prefer safety-razor blades in a special handle, but the most popular and generally serviceable is a strong pocket-knife with choice of two blades, one with a sharp angular end, the other being the usual curved shape. The latter is used when making long clean cuts; the sharp-pointed blade when cutting into angular corners.

Sometimes a very sharp chisel is helpful, especially when cutting out small rectangular apertures.

Beautiful effects are possible by carving in low relief, for which purpose a small selection of ordinary wood carver's tools will be required, but they are not essential for all ordinary work.

Tool Sharpening.

Good work can only be done when the cutting knives are absolutely keen and sharp, hence a fine oil-stone is essential. It should always be at hand so that the knife can be sharpened at any moment. Also keep a piece of rag handy so that the oil can be wiped from the blade. Chisels and

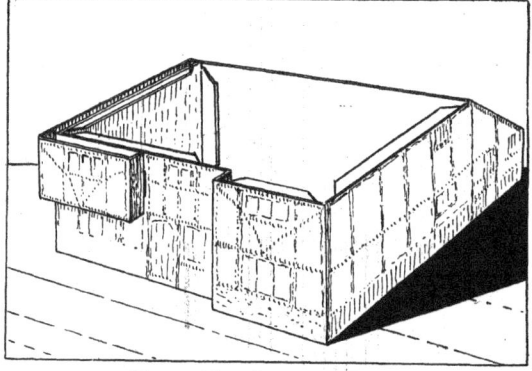

Fig. 3.—Main Walls in Place.
The projecting course is here shown fixed in position.

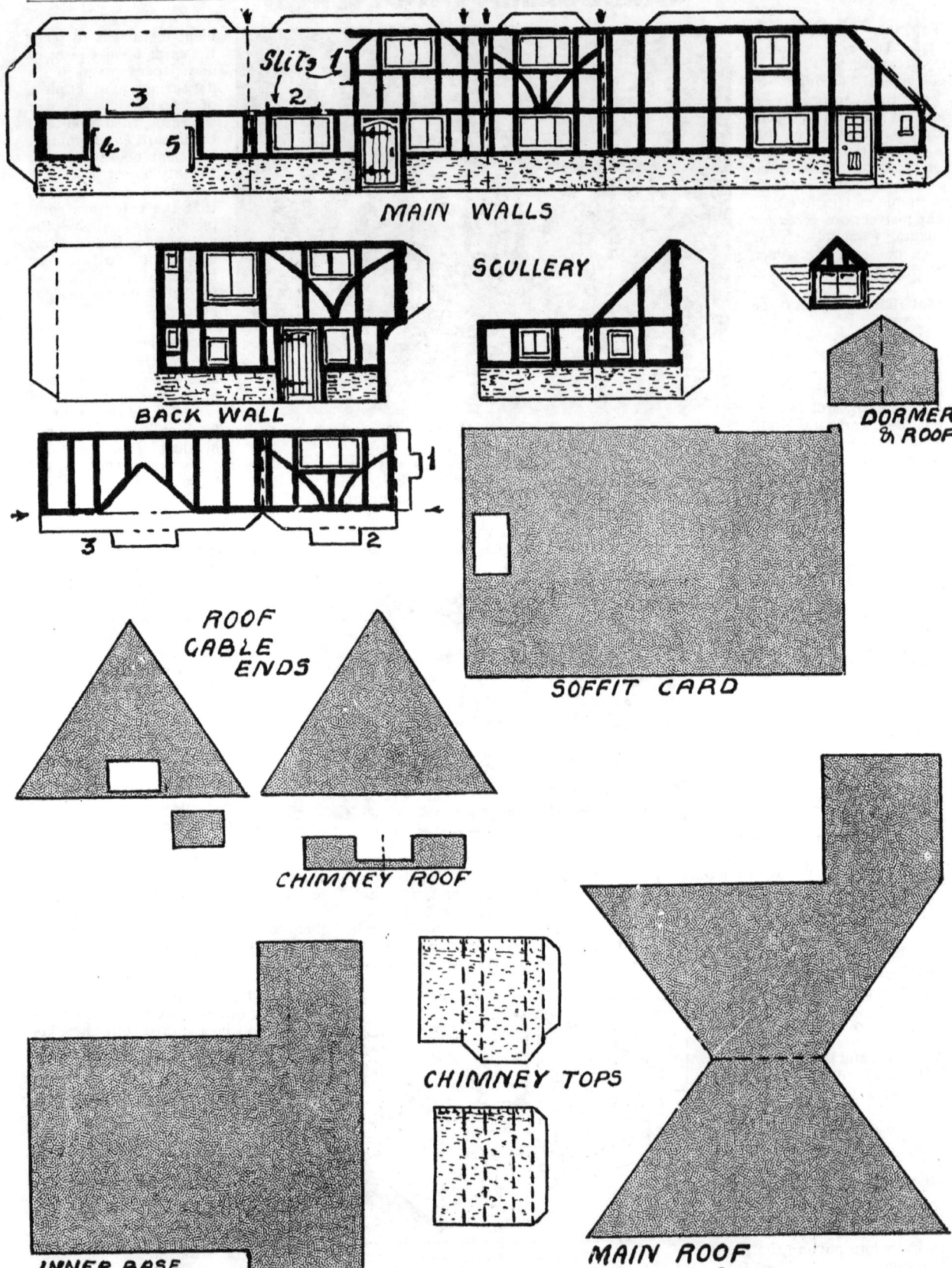

Fig. 4A.—Trace the Patterns on to Tracing-paper, and then transfer them to Cardboard.

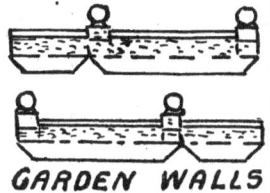

Fig. 4B.—PATTERN FOR GARDEN WALLS.

carving tools must likewise be kept absolutely keen and sharp; they are preferably stored in a baize roll when not in use.

Using the Knife.

The method of handling the knife to make a clean cut is shown in Fig. 2; the handle is grasped in the right hand with the first finger extended along the back of the blade.

The card to be cut is laid upon a piece of plate-glass when the card is very thin, or upon a sheet of thick strawboard or evenly grained wood when the card is of three-ply or greater thickness.

Guide the knife blade with a boxwood rule, or a steel straight-edge, and take care to hold it very securely. Keep the finger-tips behind the guide edge to avoid accidents.

Endeavour to sever the card with one clean cut. This cannot always be done, but it is the ideal, and every endeavour should be made to attain sufficient dexterity to do so.

Always keep the blade square with the surface of the card, otherwise the edge will not be square.

When the card is too thick to cut with one stroke of the knife, take the greatest pains to go over the same track, otherwise the edge of the card will be serrated or be in a series of steps, and will have to be trued up.

Scissors can be used successfully when the card is thin enough to cut cleanly, but the resulting cut is never quite straight, consequently scissors should only be used in curved work or quite unimportant pieces.

Working Drawings.

The majority of cardboard models are made from working drawings of the desired object, and it is necessary that the outline of every separate part shall be drawn full size and absolutely accurately upon the surface of the card. There is no need to draw every minute detail on the card, the essentials are accurate outlines, to which the card is cut, and sufficient of the important features to enable the work to proceed.

Tracing the Designs.

The drawings reproduced in this article can be traced directly on to the card by the simple process of putting a piece of ordinary typewriter carbon paper face downwards underneath the printed page. Place the sheet of two-ply card under the carbon paper, the face of the carbon paper will thus be on the card, then, with a blunt-pointed instrument, such as a wooden meat skewer sharpened at the end like a pencil, trace over all the main outlines of the drawing.

Having traced the main outlines, trace in the windows and other features with as much detail as desired. Any minor detail can be added later on directly on to the card.

Alternatively, trace the outlines of the patterns first on to tracing paper and then transfer to the card. This is perhaps preferable, as it does not spoil the pages of the book.

Very thick cartridge paper or any two-ply white card will be suitable for any of the designs in this article.

There are two ways of making most things with cardboard, the first and most widely useful is known as the folded system, and an example of this method will now be considered.

THE FOLDED SYSTEM

On the folded system, the bulk of the object is cut out of one piece of card and then folded to shape.

Bending the Card.

To make a clean angular bend, lay the scored card flat on the work table, press a straight-edge on to it with the edge over the part to be bent, then press the card upwards and run the thumb nail along the bend. If the card is at all springy it will have to be

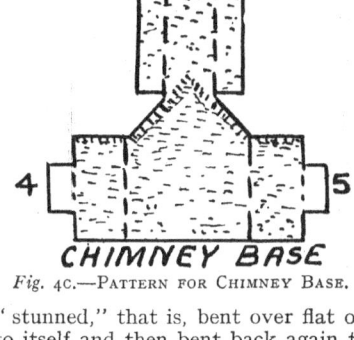

Fig. 4C.—PATTERN FOR CHIMNEY BASE.

"stunned," that is, bent over flat on to itself and then bent back again to its proper place.

Make all the bends in this way, then apply a trace of adhesive to the tab and press it into contact with the starting end of the card.

Take care to keep all bends perfectly square and true, then leave the piece untouched while the adhesive sets hard.

Meanwhile, cut out the base card, mark the outline of the structure upon it, and then fix it by smearing it with adhesive on the back on to a flat piece of board or thick card, securing it with the heads of four or more drawing-pins. Use sufficient pins to keep the card quite flat; do not put them through the card, but grip it with the head part only.

Erecting the Structure.

Directly the adhesive has set on the tab joint, apply a smear of adhesive to the bottom edges, brushing it on from the inside parts towards the outside, as this tends to reduce the risk of the adhesive showing on the face of the work.

Press the structure firmly into place and hold it for a few moments while the adhesive bites, then leave it untouched, but look at it occasionally to make sure it is firmly in place and has not lifted, but, if so, then press it down again and put a very light weight on to it to keep it all in place.

A good plan is to make the base card in two pieces —one thick piece for the outer or lower base, and the other a trifle thinner for the inner base. The latter card is carefully cut to fit exactly within the structure, but it is pasted on top of the lower base before the walls are erected.

In all such cases allow the inner base card to dry under pressure, and do not fix the structure until the base is quite dry.

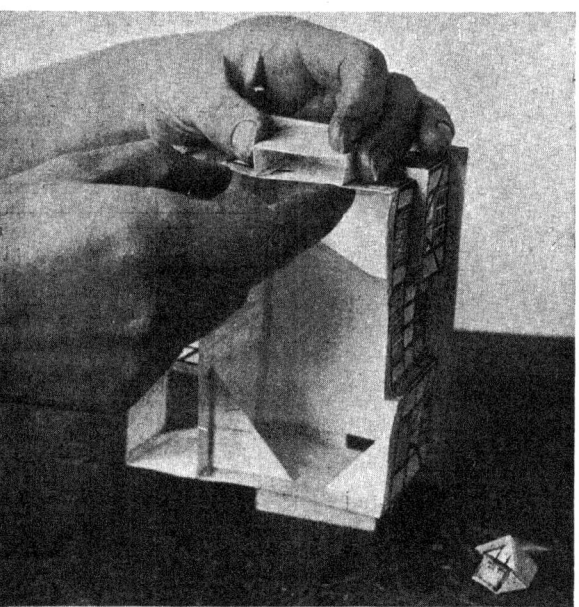

Fig. 5.—BUILDING THE TUDOR COTTAGE.
Fixing the chimney base below the projecting course.

CARDBOARD MODELLING

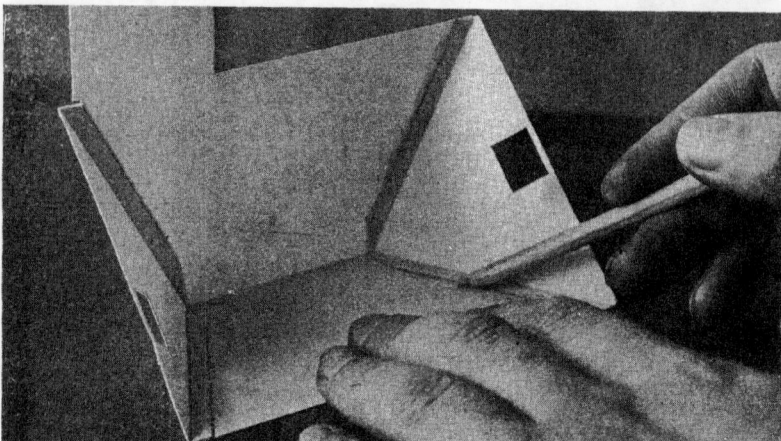

*Fig. 6.—*Finishing the Roof.
The joints are made with angle strips of thin card gummed into the corners.

*Fig. 7.—*Fitting the Roof.
The pyramidal roof is fixed on to the under or soffit card.

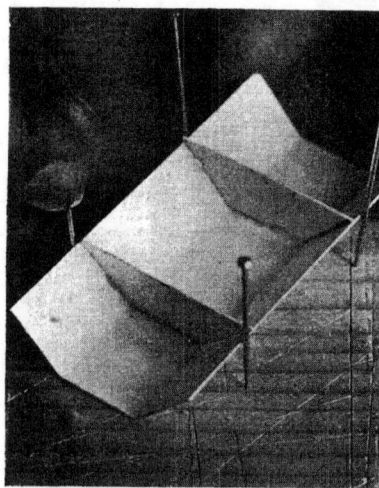

*Fig. 8.—*Use of Steadying Pins.
Small parts should be held in place while drying by means of pins driven in the base.

*Fig. 9.—*Trueing up the Edges.
Sandpaper block in use to level the edges of a built-up piece.

Attaching the Roof.

The next thing to do is to fix the roof. The adhesive is therefore applied to the upper edges of the walls by means of a paper brush, and the folded roof card pressed upon it and allowed to set in the same way as before.

Fixing the Chimney.

The chimney is folded in the same way as the walls, and is then applied to the ridge of the roof. The bottom of the chimney is cut to a V-shape to fit snugly upon the roof.

The model is completed by sticking the porch brackets into place, and after the adhesive has set the front V-piece and the roof are added.

The model is then painted in realistic manner with poster-colours or ordinary artist's water-colours.

The colours are used in exactly the same way as if painting a picture, but in all cases work the colours as dry as possible, avoid getting the card wet all through, and use good bright colours and boldly applied lines of shadow.

Much can be done by shading to represent moulded work and other details which are not otherwise modelled.

Poster-colours are preferable to the ordinary water-colours, because they have more body, and therefore have better covering power.

One important point to watch is that none of the adhesive gets on to the surfaces to be painted; if it unfortunately does so, it should be very carefully removed by rubbing with very fine old, but clean, sandpaper. Water-colours will not take on adhesive and will always crack and peel off, hence the need for great care when applying adhesives.

BUILT-UP WORK

The second group of constructional methods come under the general category of built-up work, because all the parts are cut out separately and the structure built up piece by piece. This is undoubtedly the very best method, and one which should always be adopted for good work. The angle joints can be butted, or the card, if thick, can be mitred.

The first stage in building up is to cut out sufficient of the pieces, then to assemble the four outer walls, steadying them with pins driven into the work table or board.

The inner angles are strengthened with angle pieces of card gummed on the faces and carefully pressed into position.

Stiffeners.

Angle pieces or webs are used at all corners to impart stiffness and strength, they should also be used to steady and support any large flat area of card which might otherwise buckle or go out of shape.

Another form of stiffener consists of a flat card cut to fit on to all available surfaces and to butt against any others. When such a card is fixed be sure that all work beneath it has been completed.

Modelling the Tudor Cottage.

The model Tudor cottage shown finished in Fig. 1, with patterns in Figs. 4A, 4B and 4C, is built on a composite system, being partly folded and partly built-up.

Full details of every process involved are given in this article, to which reference should be made. The order in which the work should be done is as follows:—

Trace out the design and cut out all the parts, fold the main walls, noting carefully the small fold in the front wall.

Stick the back wall in place, then add the scullery, which is stuck to the projecting end of one of the main walls and to the face of the back wall.

Add the projecting course to the left-hand end of the building, inserting the straight tabs on it into slits cut on the main walls. Put some adhesive on the tabs and bend them over on the inside, the result will then be as shown in outline in Fig. 3.

Add the under card by sticking it to the top of the walls and fix webs in the inner corners, then fold up the main chimney base and fit it to the end walls as shown in the photograph (Fig. 5), but note that the top of the chimney base goes through the hole in the under card and that the roof piece fits on to the lower part.

Now fold up the roof and stick the triangular ends into place, put the one hole in it at the left-hand end, and strengthen the joints with angle pieces of paper gummed in place, as seen in Fig. 6, then fix it on top of the soffit card, as in Fig. 7, and add the chimneys and dormer, which have only to be gummed in place. The tops of the chimneys are completed by narrow bands of paper.

Now mount the base card on a shaped block of wood, stick the walls on to it and add the garden walls, complete the work by painting the building, garden paths and walls, and representing the lawns with green cloth gummed on to the base.

Tapered Work.

An excellent but simple example of tapered work in Figs. 6 and 7, is the pavilion roof of a house model such as the Tudor cottage. Any two opposite sides of the pyramid are cut from one piece of card, and then scored and bent along the ridge. The ends are then filled in with "hip" or gable-end pieces, triangular in shape, secured with gummed angle strips which can be pressed firmly into place with the blunt end of a piece of round wood about the size of a lead pencil.

Such a roof is then fitted on to a "soffit" card—which is a flat piece of card—fitted across the whole of the walls so that it projects to form the underside, or soffit, of the eaves.

Built and Folded Work.

A combination of folded and built work is shown in Fig. 8, which shows the inside of a small bow window. The walls are formed by folding the card, but are retained in shape by gumming two web pieces to them. Such parts should be held in place, while the adhesive sets, by pins driven into the work board and then pressed against the card so as to hold it in place.

Fixing Clamps.

When building up any card structure it is often difficult to keep the pieces in place while the adhesive dries; one way to overcome this is with an odd piece of card with a slightly tapered notch cut in it to act as a cramp. The card is merely pressed into position and left there until the adhesive is dry.

Guide Pins.

When assembling any intricate flat pieces, which have to be set vertically, it will be found helpful to put a series of pins on either side of the card and at bends and corners to keep them temporarily in place.

Laminated Parts.

Excellent effects are obtained by laminating, that is, superposing one card upon another, each being cut to appropriate shape. An example is the porch in Fig. 9, where the sides and front are made in three layers, cleaned up flat on the edges by holding them vertical, as shown, and rubbing on a smooth piece of sandpaper glued to a flat block.

FIXING SCREWS IN HARD WOODS

It is more difficult to fix wood-screws in hard woods such as oak and ash than in the soft woods, and one sometimes finds that screws are broken off in the attempt to force them into the wood.

First drill a Pilot Hole.

The best procedure in such a case is to drill a pilot hole with a hand-brace, the diameter of this hole should be slightly less than that of the screw shank.

Next take a steel wood-screw of the correct size similar to the screws that will eventually be used.

File away one-half of the Screw.

File away one-half of this wood-

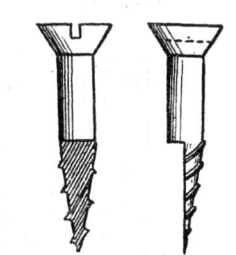

SHOWING HOW ONE-HALF OF THE SCREW IS FILED AWAY.

screw as shown in the sketch and then screw it down very nearly to the same depth as the final screw is to go.

The sharp edges of this wood-screw will be found to cut away the wood on the side of the hole, giving a true thread impression similar to that of a tap.

The wood-screws will then readily enter these holes and can be tightened down as much as required. If this method is employed there will be no risk of breaking off, even brass wood-screws.

If much screwing work is to be executed the cut-away wood-screw should be soft-soldered on to the end of a brass rod having a slot to engage with that of the screw.

Constructing an Ultra-violet Ray Lamp

Artificial sunlight is used to-day on a very wide scale to combat disease and tone up the body.

What are Ultra-violet Rays?

Most readers know that when you view sunlight through a prism or a three-cornered piece of glass the light is split up into the seven primary colours, starting with RED and ending with VIOLET. Although not visible to the human eye, because their frequency is too high, we know that there are rays *beyond* the violet, and it is these which are the much sought after ultra-violet rays. They are sometimes called the actinic rays, and under this name they will be familiar to photographic enthusiasts.

Below the red there are the heat rays, some of which are known as the infra-red; these have a frequency too low to be perceived by the human eye.

The Electric Arc is the Best Method of producing Ultra-violet Rays.

Although the amateur is not advised to treat specific maladies without medical advice, yet he can use a sunlight lamp with very beneficial results to tone up and improve general health. Many lamps have been devised such as the mercury vapour type and high-frequency vacuum tubes, but without a doubt the electric arc is the best way of producing these desirable rays. The small arc described below is easily and cheaply constructed; it has a unique feature in so much that resistances are part of the lamp system, and their glow gives forth radiant heat and infra-red rays, so useful when mixed with the ultra-violet emitted by the carbon pencils.

Materials required.

Sheet copper, gauge 24, 2 × 2 feet.
  ,, iron, 7 × 20 inches.
Iron rod, $\frac{3}{8}$ inch diameter, 2 feet.
  ,, ,, $\frac{3}{8}$,, ,, $\frac{1}{4}$,, 2 ,,
  ,, strip, $\frac{7}{8} \times \frac{1}{32}$ inch × 4 feet.
  ,, tube, $\frac{3}{8}$-inch bore, 4 inches.
Brass rod, $1\frac{1}{2}$ inches diameter, 3 inches.
Sheet tin, gauge 22, 1 square foot.
  ,, fibre, 6 × 3 × $\frac{1}{2}$ inch.
  ,, fibre 7 × 6 × $\frac{1}{8}$ inch.
1 doz. brass screws, 4 B.A.
1 ,,   ,,   ,, 2 B.A.
1 element wire, 750 watts.
Ebonite tube, 1 inch diameter, 1 feet 9 inches.
Asbestos tube, $\frac{3}{4}$ inch diameter, 1 foot.
Flex, 5 ampere, 2 yards.
2 winged nuts, 2 B.A.

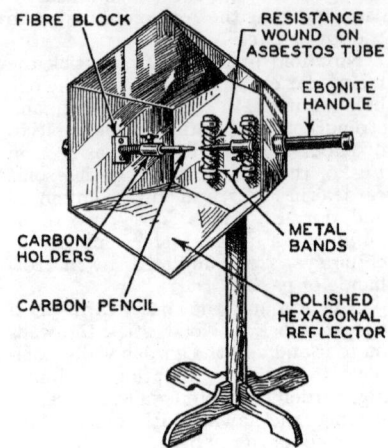

Fig. 1.—The Front of the Lamp. Looking into the mouth of the hexagonal flare.

Making the Reflector.

The hexagonal reflector is shown in the flat in Fig. 9. Note that tongues are left for soldering on the back, and similar narrow strips are arranged round the outer edge; these are rolled back to give a curved appearance to the outside of the reflector. Two $\frac{5}{8}$-inch holes are drilled in two of the panels as shown to admit the rods which carry the carbons; these holes are later backed with blocks of fibre, so that there is no electrical contact between the reflector and the arc.

How the Lamp is mounted.

The completed reflector is supported in a strip metal U-shaped bracket, details of which are given in Fig. 8. Slots are cut in the tops of the vertical arms, and into these drop two bolts with square heads which are soldered to the outside of the reflector. The heads of these bolts must be packed up when fastening to the hexagonal panels so that their stems are in a straight line. Spring washers and winged nuts are fitted to the bolts, so that the lamp can be tilted to the desired angle and then locked in position.

The Pedestal.

The U-bracket to which the lamp is pivoted is supported on a pillar fitted with feet. Fig. 6 shows how to make the sheet-metal type of foot. Two pieces are cut out as shown and vertical slots filed out half the width of the material. Note that one slot starts from the top while the other commences from the bottom. This allows the two pieces to be assembled at right angles when four feet are formed. A fillet of solder is then run down the four angles, making the whole perfectly rigid. The small sketch shows the end of the pillar with two longitudinal cuts at right angles; these are made with a hacksaw fitted with two blades to give a slot wide enough to slip on to the cross formation at the centre of the feet. The pillar is secured in place at the foot with solder. Fig. 10 shows an alternative type of foot weighted with lead. In this figure will be seen the top fitting to which the lamp bracket is fastened. It is a short strip-metal stirrup riveted and soldered into a wide saw-cut running down the pillar. The two horizontal arms of the stirrup are bolted or riveted to the base of the lamp bracket, as shown in Fig. 8.

The Ebonite Handles.

The handles are made from 1-inch ebonite tube, each one being 8 inches long. Fig. 3 shows a section of the complete handle and feed mechanism.

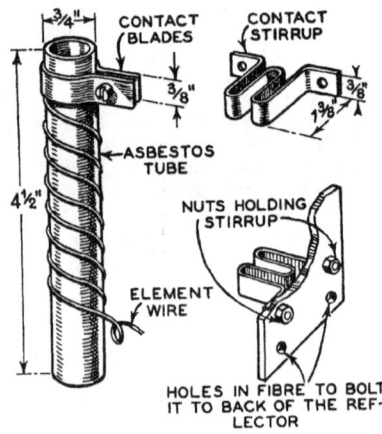

Fig. 2.—Details showing Assembly of Resistance Tubes.

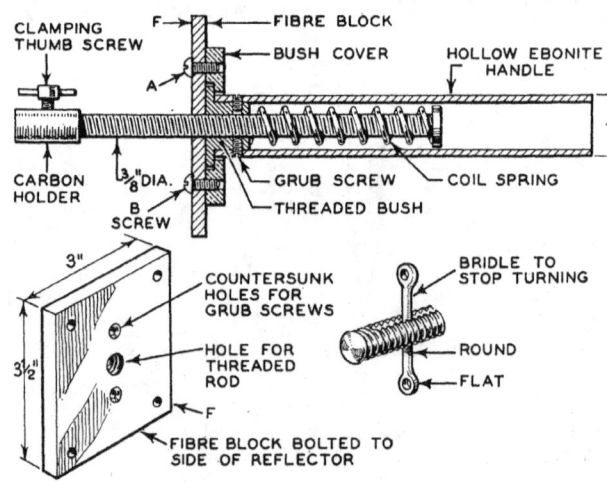

Fig. 3.—How the Ebonite Handles are constructed.

1176

CONSTRUCTING AN ULTRA-VIOLET RAY LAMP

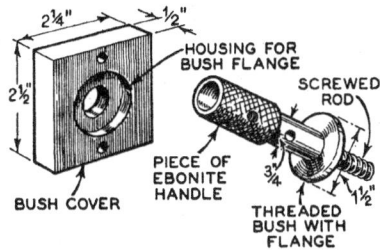

Fig. 4.—SHOWING THREADED BUSH WITH WIDE FLANGE, WHICH IS FITTED INTO ONE END OF THE HANDLE.

From this it will be seen that the threaded rod, which carries the carbons and is "alive," slides within the handles and is gradually fed out as the carbons burn away. Into one end of the handle is fitted a threaded bush with a wide flange (see Fig. 4). The bush is tapped out with a $\frac{3}{8}$-inch Whitworth thread; it should be a tight fit in the ebonite tube to which it is secured with a countersunk grub screw. The head of this screw can be covered with a layer of black wax, if desired, as, of course, it is "alive." The open ends of the handles are plugged with ornamental knobs of ebonite or wood, as shown in Fig. 1.

The Carbon Holders.

These are composed of pieces of rod, 9 inches long and $\frac{3}{8}$ inch in diameter on which a Whitworth thread has been cut. The collar which holds the carbon pencil screws on to the rod, a tight fit being obtained by cutting a shallow thread in the collar, so that it is difficult to screw on. A 2B.A. screw with a steel pin through the head fits into a hole tapped in the side of the collar; this grips the carbon pencil. The other end of the rod has a small head fitted to it against which the coil spring presses. A slot $\frac{1}{8}$ inch wide runs for a distance of 5 inches down the centre of the feed screw (see the small sketch in Fig. 3). This slot starts 1 inch from the collar and carries a pin or bridle with eyelets at each end. The ends of the bridle are secured by the screws A and B, which also hold the bush cover in place. This slot and pin prevents the rod turning when the handles are revolved, yet permits the rod sliding in and out of the handles. To cut this slot drill a series of $\frac{3}{32}$-inch holes, then open them up, and finally clean the slot with a thin ward file; it is advisable to make the slot before cutting the thread.

How to mount the Carbon Holders.

The threaded rod goes through the central hole in the fibre block F (Fig. 3) and the flange on the handle bush is held against the fibre by the bush cover, details of which are shown in Fig. 4. The cover is made from a block of fibre $\frac{1}{2}$ inch thick; a hole right through just admits the handle, while another larger one halfway through accommodates the flange on the bush; this latter cavity must be only paper thickness deeper than the thickness of the bush flange.

Thus, when the bush cover is screwed to the fibre block F, the handle with its flanged bush revolves freely, but no perceptible "shake" can be felt; the cover thus forms a bearing as well as an insulating case. Note that the hole in the panel of the reflector is $\frac{1}{4}$ inch larger than the one in the fibre block F; thus the rod cannot touch the metal.

The Resistance Tubes.

Details of these are shown in Fig. 2. To the two lengths of asbestos tube are clamped bands of copper, the ends of which form the contact blades. Round each tube is wound *half* a length of a 750-watt element, as used for electric fires, the ends of the resistance wire being fastened to the

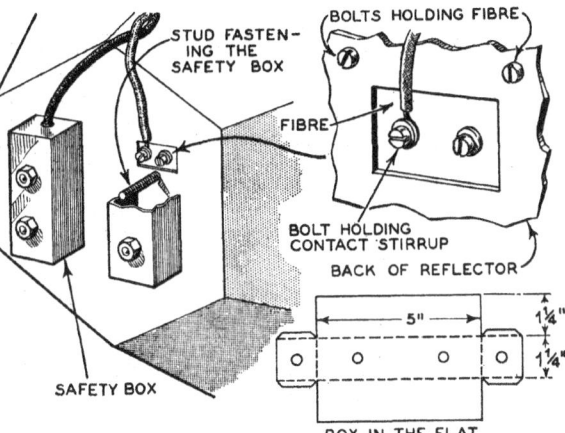

Fig. 5.—HOW THE LIVE PARTS OF THE CONNECTIONS ARE SHIELDED WITH SMALL RECTANGULAR BOXES MADE OF TIN.

copper bands by the small bolt. Four contact stirrups are required to carry the ends of the blades (details of these are shown in Fig. 2). Each stirrup is fastened to a block of fibre, which in turn is bolted to the reflector, as shown in Fig. 5. Note that a hole is cut in the copper back so that no portion of the resistance is in contact with the metal part of the reflector.

The Safety Boxes.

Fig. 5 shows how the live parts of the connections are shielded with small rectangular boxes made of tin. A plan in the flat is given in the picture, and the method of fixing is also shown. Two bolts come through holes in the reflector, and these are soldered firmly in position with the stem sticking out at the back. Holes in the safety boxes permit them being placed on these fixed studs and secured by means of nuts, as shown in Fig. 5.

Wiring up.

Fig. 7 gives a pictorial view of the wiring suitable for a D.C. supply; in this case one resistance is connected in series in each lead. The flexible connections to the carbons are insulated with glass or porcelain beads. Fig. 11 shows a different method of wiring suitable for A.C. circuits. In this case one resistance is in series while the other is *shunted* across the carbons. The flex connecting the

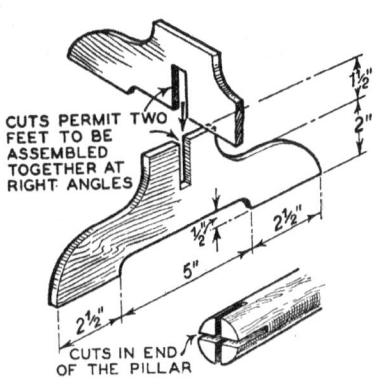

Fig. 6.—HOW TO MAKE THE SHEET-METAL TYPE OF FOOT.

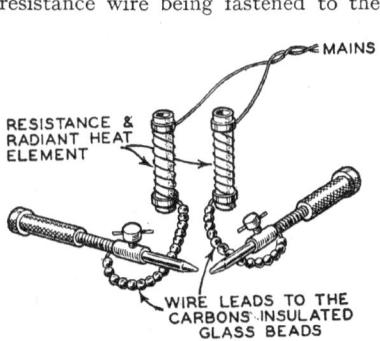

Fig. 7.—PICTORIAL WIRING DIAGRAM FOR USING THE DEVICE FROM A DIRECT CURRENT SUPPLY.

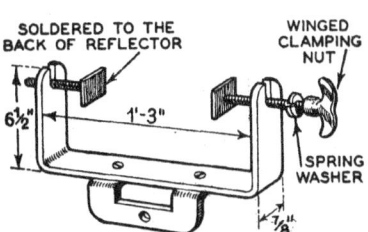

Fig. 8.—DETAILS OF DEVICE FOR TILTING THE LAMP.

CONSTRUCTING AN ULTRA-VIOLET RAY LAMP

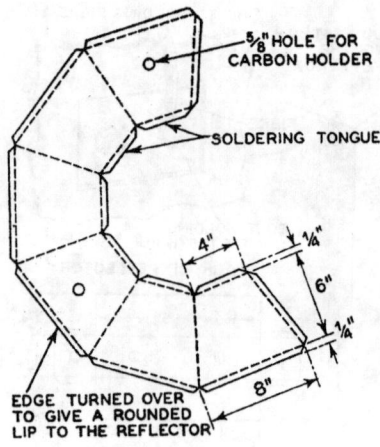

Fig. 9.—The Hexagonal Reflector.
Note that tongues are left for soldering on the back, and that similar narrow strips are arranged round the outer edge.

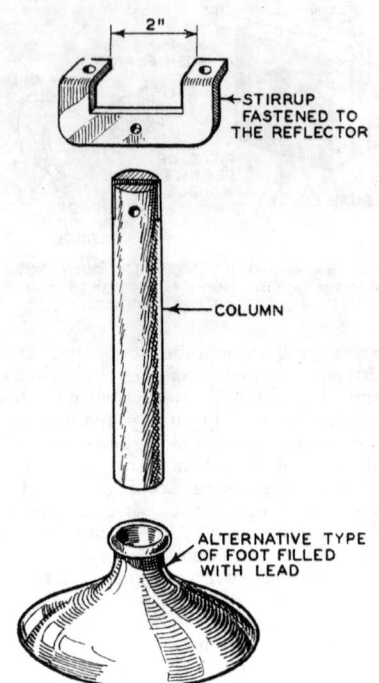

Fig. 10.—An Alternative Type of Foot.

ideal for this lamp, although quite good results can be obtained with the carbons taken from the small dry cells used in H.T. batteries. Screw back the feed rods and fix the pencils in place, then with the pencils apart switch on the current. Now touch the carbons together for a moment, when the ends should splutter and glow; quickly screw back the handles so that the points are slightly parted. If the arc dies out, shorten the element wire on one of the resistance tubes to suit the carbons in use. When adjusting the resistance for A.C. supply, it is best to leave the shunting coil alone and make the alterations to the series coil. In no circumstances attempt to make any adjustments to the resistances while the flex is plugged into the supply socket. When using carbons larger than 6 mm. the lamp must be used on a power circuit and 10 to 15-ampere flex should be used. It should be noted that when D.C. is used, one carbon will burn away twice as quickly as the other, but on A.C. both pencils waste at the same rate.

How to apply the Rays.

When using the lamp the patient must wear blue glasses, as the rays are

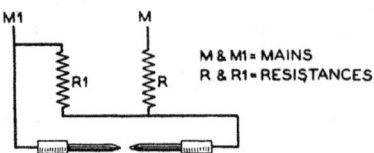

Fig. 11.—A different Method of Wiring, suitable for Use when the Mains Supply is Alternating Current.

harmful to the eyes. The body must be either uncovered or clad in artificial silk to gain the full benefit, as cotton and woollen garments restrict the passage of the rays. The periods of treatment should be progressive, starting with six minutes and gradually increasing the time up to twenty minutes per day. After a month's treatment have a period of rest and then start again.

lamp to the mains should be capable of carrying at least 5 amperes.

The Finish.

The copper reflector should be well polished and then lacquered. The pillar and feet, unless made of brass, are best enamelled a dark colour suitable to the taste of the reader; the safety boxes and lamp bracket look well treated in the same way. The ebonite handles are improved if the ends are milled with a chaser. A wire guard to fit over the front of the lamp is a useful addition, and prevents children from touching the arc.

Operating the Lamp.

Carbons, 6 mm. in diameter, are

A WOOD PANEL-CUTTING DEVICE

THE home carpenter is occasionally called upon to cut large holes in panels, such as plywood members, but it is seldom that the relatively expensive panel-boring tools are found in the home tool kit. Indeed, so seldom does one require to use such a tool that it is hardly worth purchasing.

The usual method of cutting a circular disc out of a panel, if the latter is thin, is to drill one or two holes, cut away the intervening wood, and insert the blade of a pad saw so as to saw away the disc. For thicker and harder woods the method generally employed is to drill a number of contiguous, or "touching," holes, just inside the circle, corresponding to the size of the larger hole required, and afterwards to saw or cut away the wood between the holes, finally filing or cutting the hole smoothly to shape.

A method that can be used to cut a hole accurately and much more quickly than that just described is to make a disc-cutting tool. This has a steel rod (a stout nail answers quite well) at one end, to act as a pilot, or guide, and a steel cutter made from a nail, filed up to shape after driving through the wood. It is important to make the wooden member from a piece of hardwood, *e.g.*, oak or ash, otherwise the nails will work loose.

The cutter may, if one desires, be fastened more tightly with an ordinary metal screw tapped into the hole. It is necessary, of course, to space the two holes in the wooden block so that the distance between the centre of the pilot rod and the outside of the cutter is equal to the radius of the hole to be cut in the panel.

To use this device, first mark out the centre of the hole to be cut, and drill a pilot hole for the pilot or guide pin of the cutter to fit without any play or slackness. Fix the panel to the bench and rotate the cutter, applying pressure so that it cuts away a circular groove. When the latter is just over half-way through, reverse the panel and apply the cutter on the other face; this will prevent splintering when the disc is cut through.

This method will be found satisfactory for cutting holes in aluminium, plywood and ebonite sheets for wireless purposes, etc.

Hiding-Places for Valuables

Most of us leave our houses unattended occasionally in the evenings or during week-ends, and we all have valuables that burglars would certainly appropriate if they broke in and found them. The thing that concerns us is where to hide such possessions as money and jewellery so that they will be comparatively safe during our absence.

Where Burglars usually search.

Burglars are not wonderfully original, and, when they break in, there are definite places to which they turn instinctively. They are sure to ransack the drawers in dressing-tables, the chests and wardrobes in bedrooms, and the writing-desks in living-rooms. Accordingly, these places are danger-spots and nothing of special value should be stored in them. In addition, burglars have the habit of looking under rugs and carpets in bedrooms and dining-rooms, because many householders have the erroneous belief that these are safe places for storing banknotes.

The Value of Original Hiding-places.

The best way to outwit burglars is to construct one or two hiding-places in positions that nobody would ordinarily dream of. Naturally, the more original the position the better and, it may be added, the chosen place should not be of a makeshift character. If it is, it will be very easy to forget about it, with the result that the articles may be lost. Legitimate access to the secret place should be a simple matter. One does not want to move a stack of dusty articles to put away a handful of treasures just before setting out for a dance or a dinner.

A Door provides a Capital Hiding-place.

An excellent hiding-place can be constructed in almost any door. Look round the house and select one that leads into a room that is seldom used; it should open inwards and the top edge must not be visible from some adjacent flight of stairs. Open the door wide and stand on a step-ladder; then cut out a hole in the thickness of the wood large enough to take a 2-oz. tobacco tin, standing on its side. Into such a tin, a considerable amount of money and jewellery can be stored, and no burglar would ever find it, as long as the contents do not rattle, should the door be thrown open.

To construct such a hiding-place, mark out the requisite space on the upper edge of the door, fairly close to the hinge. It should be slightly wider than the tin that is to be used and about an inch longer. The cutting is, perhaps, fidgety, but if a brace and bit is employed for boring a hole at each corner and then the holes are

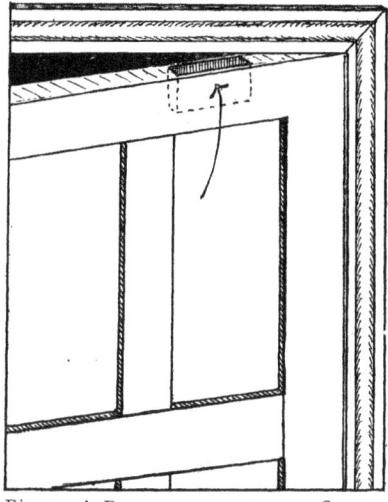

Fig. 1.—A Door provided with a Secret Storage Place.

A well has been cut in the position shown by the arrow, and into this well an ordinary 2-oz. tobacco tin, filled with valuables, can be housed.

enlarged by the aid of a chisel, the bulk of the wood can be got away fairly easily. The greatest difficulty is to keep the sides of the opening parallel with the outer faces of the door, but this can be done if care is

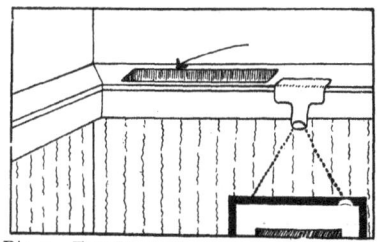

Fig. 2.—This Diagram shows how a Hiding-place may be easily constructed in an Ordinary Picture Rail.

taken to see that the chisel-cuts are vertical.

When such a hiding-place has been constructed, it will be no more than the work of a moment to stand on a chair, to reach up for the tin, to lift it out and to place in it anything that is to be left behind when the house will be unattended.

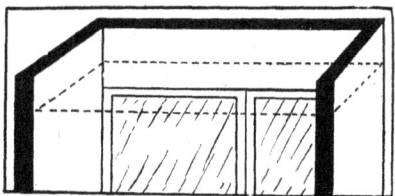

Fig. 3.—Bookcase with Back and Top removed to show the Space above the Glass Doors which can be utilised as a Secret Storage Place.

The dotted lines show where the beading should be fixed so that the two pieces of three-ply may be supported.

A Dummy Switchboard.

A second idea is to construct an unobtrusive box and to mask it with a dummy switchboard. This can be set up in the cupboard under the stairs or wherever the real switchboard is fixed. The box should not stand out more than 3 inches from the wall, and the other two dimensions may be about 9 × 6 inches. For preference, the wood used for the purpose should not be fresh or new, and the front ought to be a hinged door with a snap and ball fastener or, if desired, a small lock. The front panel should be made to imitate the service switchboard by fixing on to it several china bridges and, if it is thought desirable to simulate the real thing minutely, there is no reason why dummy cables should not be run from the box to an obscure corner of the cupboard. The contrivance will then appear to be a superseded switchboard which has not been taken down or a subsidiary one to the board actually in use.

This box can be fitted with a shelf or two, or divided into compartments; it will then be sufficiently roomy to store a considerable quantity of valuables. And it will be a place in which no burglar would think of looking.

Hiding-places in Picture-rails.

Another original idea is to make a kind of well in the picture-rail of one of the rooms. The rail chosen for the purpose should be fairly substantial. All that is necessary is to scoop out the wood with a chisel and mallet for a distance of about 8 to 10 inches and a depth of 1 to 1½ inches. Care must naturally be taken to see that the outer face of the rail is not perforated nor in any way altered by the work done in forming the well. If felt desirable, it will be a good idea to line the sides of the space with pieces of velvet, which can be stuck down by means of tube glue.

This hiding-place will be quite out of sight, and nobody entering the room would suspect its existence, yet it will serve admirably for storing a considerable quantity of jewellery and small amounts of cash, though not notes nor papers.

Secret Chambers in Bookcases.

Bookcases can often be fitted with secret chambers that defy discovery. With some, a false back, constructed on the inside, provides a capacious place for storage, but an even better situation is available if there is a wide pediment running across the top of the front which forms an internal space rising above the uppermost edges of the glass doors.

By tacking a narrow beading all round the inside of this space about an inch or more below the roof and fitting two pieces of three-ply to rest on this

HIDING-PLACES FOR VALUABLES

edging, one piece being fixed and the other hinged at the side, it is possible to make an admirable secret chamber.

Access is gained to this space by pushing up the hinged flap, and a considerable quantity of valuables, such as documents, notes, cash and jewellery can be hidden away on the fixed sheet of three-ply. Of course, it will be necessary to stain or otherwise treat the new wood so that it matches the rest of the internal construction.

A Jewel Case made from an Old Book.

Burglars do not, as a rule, take much notice of books, seeing that they have little time to examine things closely. Thus, if a jewel case is needed for storing personal ornaments, there is no better form for it to take than that of a book. Select a fairly large bound volume that has grown out of date. Sixpence or less will buy one in a second-hand bookshop. Then stick down the first

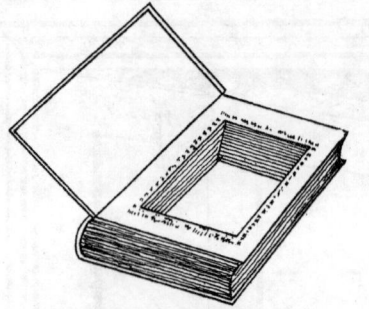

Fig. 4.—Here is a Thick Book that has been Transformed into a Jewel Case.

dozen pages to the front cover and, with the remaining pages standing one above the other, cut a well out of the centre of the pile, as shown in the diagram. Use a sharp pocket-knife for the purpose and leave a good margin of paper all round the edges.

When the well has been cut out, paint the sides with glue and stick a piece of card all round. Thus the pages will be held together, yet there is nothing to show on the outside of the volume that anything has been done to it. If desired, cover the walls and bottom of the well with velvet and fit a piece of ribbon to each flap of the cover to permit of the book being fastened.

A jewel case made in this way may be stored on a bookshelf with other volumes. It will look perfectly innocent and will, certainly, not attract any attention.

Naturally the best hiding-places are those that each householder originates for himself. The examples mentioned here are given in the nature of suggestions to show what can be done, but anyone seeking for novel ideas should not overlook the possibilities of fitting secret plywood panels to unsuspecting pieces of furniture, of false backs to picture-frames, and the construction of compartments situated under the floorboards.

TWO USEFUL CLOTHES AIRERS

An essential to a wife who does some of her washing at home, especially in the winter, is a Clothes Dryer, and Fig. 1 shows one which, although light in weight, is very strong and has stood the test of several years' constant use.

Its cost is but a few shillings and its construction so simple that any handyman could make it.

The length can be made to suit any room, and the essential feature is its girder-like construction which makes it very strong. The spreaders are cut out of three-ply wood and the rails passed through holes cut to shape and secured with small blocks of wood about $\frac{1}{4}$ inch square and $\frac{3}{4}$ inch long on either side, secured with panel pins and a touch of glue.

The galvanised wire is fastened to the middle rail at one end, drawn tightly under the notched pieces on the centre spreaders and then fastened securely at the other end as shown.

Some ordinary spring clothes pegs fixed with a small brass screw through the plywood and a spot of glue, are very useful for handkerchiefs, collars, socks, etc., and some brass hooks in the lower rails are also useful.

The dryer is hung through two galvanised pulleys on hooks in the picture rail and window moulding and

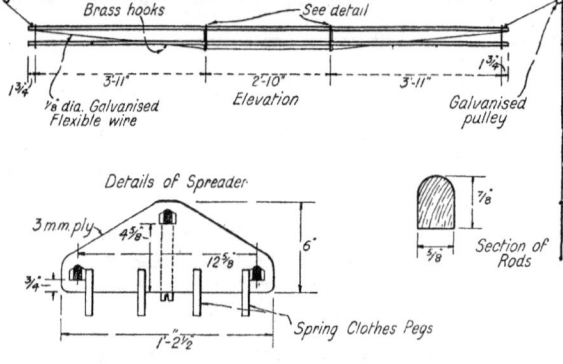

Fig. 1.—A Cheap and Useful Clothes Airer that will last for many years.

by means of two knots at suitable intervals in the double cord, can be lowered to a suitable height for filling

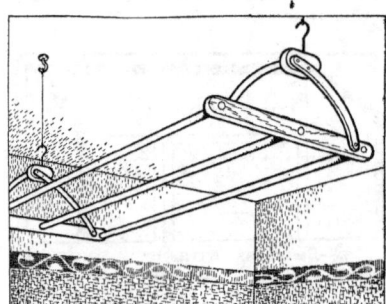

Fig. 2.—A Simple Clothes Airer made from Coat-hangers, Three Rods and some Odd Pieces of Batten.

then raised to the high level for drying.

Another Design.

Another type of clothes airer, even simpler, is shown in Fig. 2. This is constructed from four coat-hangers, three rods of the desired length, about 4 feet of 2×1-inch batten, and a few screws. First of all the batten should be cut in two 20-inch lengths, the remainder being cut in halves, each 3 to 4 inches in length, to form the small blocks through which the hanging wires go. The coat-hangers are cut off to the required length, and their wire hooks withdrawn for insertion in the small blocks. Holes are then bored for the rods in the long pieces of batten, and the whole assembled as shown in Fig. 2.

The airer is suspended from the ceiling by the wire hooks. These fasten into screw-eyes about $\frac{1}{2}$ inch in diameter driven into the ceiling so that they bite into one of the joists. The position of the joists can be found by tapping on the ceiling, a more solid or dead sound being heard when the joist is tapped. Another method is to drive a very thin steel awl into the ceiling until the joist is found. The small holes left by the awl can be filled in with a spot of moist whiting. Alternatively the airer can be suspended from pulleys and lines.

A Glass Canopy

A GLASS canopy fixed to the back of a house above the French doors makes an ideal cover under which to sit and have meals out of doors. Often, too, the erection of such a canopy enables the coal box and dust bin to be visited in wet weather, but this depends, of course, on the layout of the house.

There are two methods of constructing a glass canopy, and these are shown in Figs. 1 and 2. It will be seen that in one case the canopy is supported by wooden posts, while in the other case iron cantilever brackets are used. The method to be adopted depends entirely on personal taste.

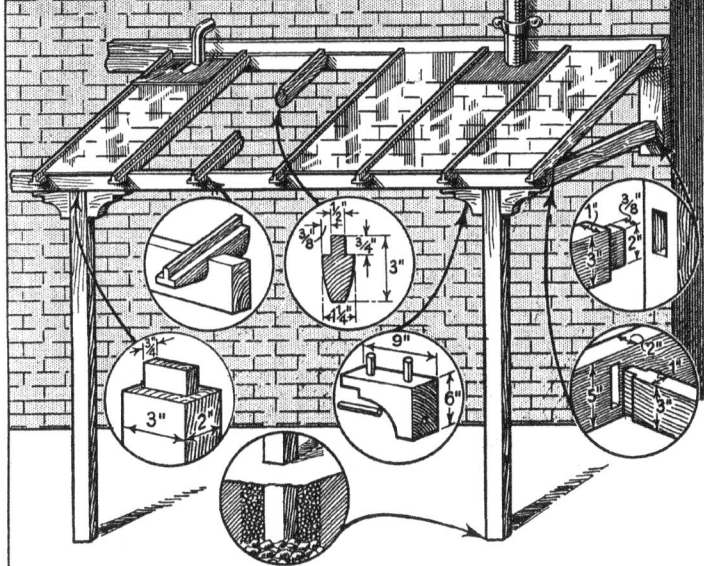

Fig. 1.—Portion of a Typical Glass Canopy.
The small diagrams show how the various joints should be prepared.

Materials required.

For the canopy supported by wooden posts the following materials will be required, assuming that the width to be dealt with is 21 feet.

Main Front Bar.—One piece yellow deal, 21 feet × 5 × 2 inches.

Wall Board.—One piece machined board, 21 feet × 6 × 1 inch.

Horizontal Distance Pieces.—Two pieces deal, 4 feet × 3 × 1 inch.

Vertical Wall Boards.—Two pieces deal, 2 feet 6 inches × 3 × 1 inch.

Glass Pane Supports.—Fifteen pieces 3-inch sash bar, 5 feet long.

Upright Supports.—Three pieces yellow deal, 9 feet × 3 × 2 inches.

Angle Brackets.—One piece deal, 4 feet 6 inches × 6 × 2 inches.

Glass.—Fourteen pieces, 1 foot 6 inches × 5 feet.

Sheet Zinc.—1 foot × 1½ feet for each pipe which penetrates the canopy.

In addition, 3 lbs. of putty and a supply of 2-inch oval brads and 3 and 4-inch cut nails will be required.

If the cantilever bracket canopy is being made, three such brackets will be required; they cost about 5s. each. The vertical posts, distance pieces and angle brackets will not, however, be required.

Preparing the Posts.

The first thing to do is to prepare the posts. These need not necessarily be equally spaced if this would result in one of the posts coming in front of the windows. The distance between any two posts should not, however, exceed 12 feet. First cut the tenons on the top end of the posts and then creosote or char the end which is to be placed in the ground.

Now make the Angle Brackets.

The next thing to do is to make the three pairs of angle brackets. These should be marked out on the timber in pairs and sawn out with a pad or bow saw. Finish the curved surface off with a spokeshave, drill two ¾-inch holes 4 inches apart in the top edge and glue in two dowel pegs as shown in the enlarged section in Fig. 1.

Fig. 2.—Diagram showing the Arrangement of an Iron Cantilever Bracket Canopy.
Only one half of the canopy is shown here.

Now assemble and erect Posts.

The next operation can consist of assembling and erecting the posts. Place the front bar on the ground with the posts at right angles and opposite the mortise slots. Then drive in the tenons and pin them with an oval brad. Now fit the angle brackets by driving the pins into the holes already prepared for them. Bore a hole through the bracket into the side of the post and drive in another dowel peg. This will hold the structure secure.

Holes for the Posts.

The three holes for the posts should be dug about 2 feet deep. Some assistance will probably be required to lift the structure vertical and drop the posts into the holes. Check that each post is equidistant from the wall and make sure the top bar is level with a spirit level. Half fill in the holes with old bricks and stones.

The Wall Board.

The wall board can now be fitted. It will probably be sufficient to hold it in place with 3-inch iron cut nails driven into the mortar between the bricks, but if a secure hold cannot be obtained three or four wooden plugs let in as in Fig. 3 will provide a sound hold into which to drive the nails.

A groove ½ × ¼ inch, 2 inches from the upper edge of the board will be required. If no rebating tool is available it will probably save a lot of time to

The Main Bar.

The main bar should next be prepared. First mark the position of the three mortises on the edge of the bar into which the upper ends of the posts are to fit. The slots should be cut 2 inches deep. Then cut two more mortises in the wide faces of the bar at the ends for the distance pieces.

The next thing to do is to bore the two holes each side of the three mortises, for the dowel pegs which have been inserted in the angle brackets. The best method of locating the positions for these holes on the main bar is to hold the angle brackets against the bar and square the holes across.

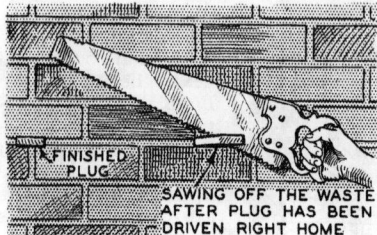

Fig. 3.—PLUGGING THE WALL FOR NAILING UP THE WALL BOARD.

have this groove made by the timber merchant from whom the wood is obtained. The board should be fastened 9 feet from the ground.

When the wall board has been fixed, the two vertical wall boards can be dealt with, first cutting a 2 × 3/8 inch mortise slot in the lower end for the tenon on the distance bar.

The Distance Bars.

The tenons should now be prepared on each end of the distance bars, as shown in Fig. 1. The bars can then be slipped into place by forcing the top of the posts forward while the ends are pushed into the mortises on the wall board. Then force the front bar on to the tenons by pushing the posts back into an upright position, after which the top bar should again be tested with the spirit level, and the posts trued with a plumb line.

Provided everything is in order, fill in the holes with concrete, which should be allowed to set before further work is proceeded with.

The Sash Bars.

The fixing of the sash bars can then be put in hand. Take one of the 5-feet lengths, hold it in position and make a mark at the end parallel to the wall board to give the necessary slope. Cut off the waste, and again hold the bar in position, this time with the end flush against the wall board. Then mark out the position of the groove which fits over the front bar, as shown in Fig. 4. Saw down the two marks and chisel out the waste.

This bar can then be used as a template for preparing the remainder of the bars.

Fixing the Sash Bars.

At the wall board end the sash bars are nailed with three 3 or 4-inch cut nails, as shown in Fig. 5. At the front, the bar can be held to the front bar with a single oval brad.

To keep the sash bars parallel and the correct distance apart, cut a piece of batten 18 inches long, i.e., the same distance as the width of the sheets of glass, and use this as a gauge.

When all the sash bars are in position give them two coats of lead paint. The glass can then be placed in position.

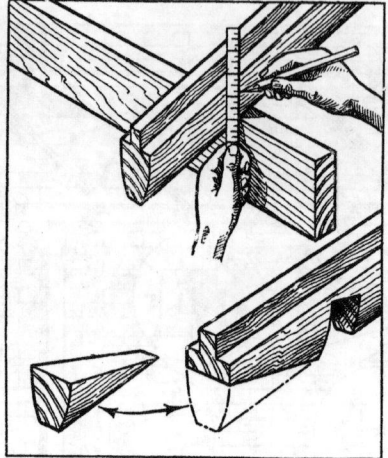

Fig. 4.—HOW TO MARK OUT THE SASH BAR FOR FIXING TO MAIN FRONT BAR.

Fixing the Glass.

Take a lump of putty, knead it in the hands until it is quite soft, place a layer of about 1/4 inch in the rebates. Place a sheet of glass in position and press the edges well down into the putty, cleaning off with a knife any surplus putty that is squeezed out.

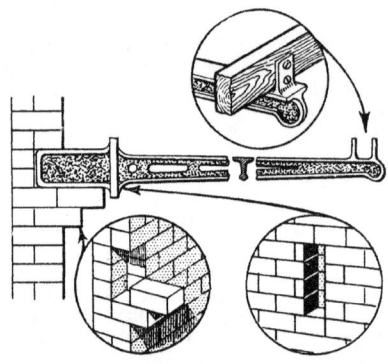

Fig. 6.—DETAILS FOR FIXING THE CANTILEVER BRACKETS.

What to do if there are Pipes running down the Wall.

If there are any pipes running down the side of the wall it will, of course, be impossible to fit the glass round them. Small sheets of zinc must be used instead. The first sheet of glass to be fixed should be placed so that it

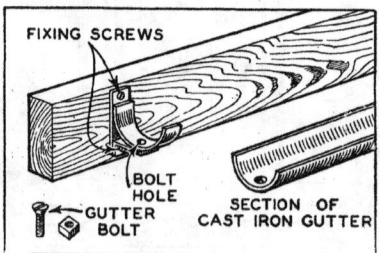

Fig. 7.—IF A GUTTER IS REQUIRED THIS CAN BE FIXED TO BRACKETS SCREWED TO THE FRONT BAR.

Fig. 5.—SHOWING HOW THE SASH BAR IS FASTENED TO THE WALL BOARD.

comes to within about 4 inches from the pipe. A piece of zinc 1 foot 6 inches wide and long enough to reach from the wall to the glass and overlap it for at least 1 1/4 inches, should then be cut to fit round the pipe and puttied in.

IRON CANTILEVER TYPE CANOPY

As there are no posts to interfere with the doors, the cantilever brackets should be placed equidistant from each other. A convenient height is 7 feet from ground.

First of all remove four half bricks as shown in Fig. 6. This can be done with a cold chisel and hammer, but care must be taken not to cut deeper than 4 1/2 inches. When the hole has been cut out, take two bricks and place them in the form of a step, as shown in Fig. 6. They should be held in place with a two-to-one mixture of cement and sand.

When these bricks are firmly in place fit the end of the bracket into the hole above the steps. The outer end of the bracket should then be temporarily supported with a wooden strut while the space in the wall is filled in with cement, which should be allowed to harden before the support is removed.

The other two brackets are fixed in a similar manner, care being taken to see that all the ends are the same distance from the ground.

Fig. 6 shows how the front bar is held in position at the outer end of the brackets. The fixing of the sash bars is the same as already described.

Final Operations.

The iron cantilevers should be coated with Brunswick black, while the woodwork of both structures should be given two coats of a good lead paint, which should be run 1/2 inch over the joint between the sash bar and the glass.

If it is desired to fix a gutter this can be done by means of small brackets screwed to the main front bar, as shown in Fig. 7. A slight fall in the gutter to a waste pipe leading to an existing drain should be arranged.

How to Make an Ice Chest

In every home there should be an ice chest for the storage of foods of a perishable nature. Chests of various types may be bought, but, as a rule, they are expensive. However, the home-worker can construct a very efficient example at no great outlay; it will not be hard to make and it will save whatever it costs in a very short while, seeing that the wastage on such items as milk, meat, fish and butter will be reduced to practically nothing.

There are two points to remember when designing an ice chest. The first is that a dry atmosphere within the chest is essential. Therefore, the melting ice must be kept apart from the foods. And the second is that cold air descends; thus, the ice compartment should be situated above and not below or at the side of the food chamber. A chest embodying these features is dealt with here.

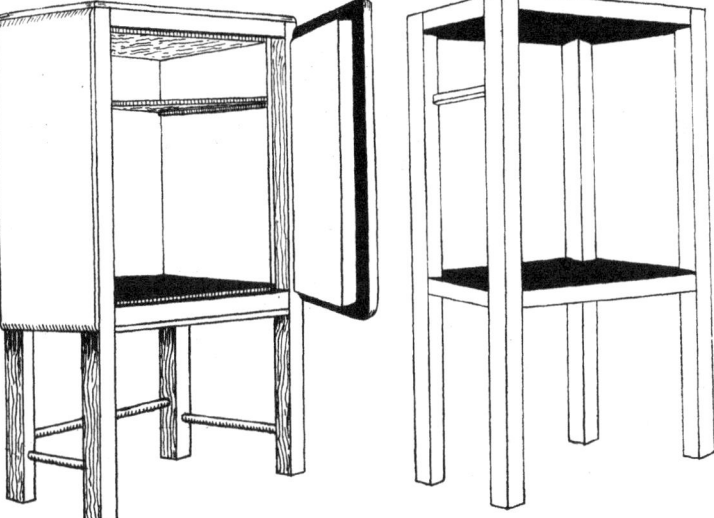

Fig. 1.—THE COMPLETED ICE CHEST.
Note the separate compartment at the top for the ice.

Fig. 2.—THE FRAME OF THE ICE CHEST.
The roof and bottom of the chamber are shown in black.

The Ice Chest described.

A glance at Fig. 1 will help in understanding how the chest is planned. Standing on four legs, there is a large zinc-lined chamber which is divided into two portions. The upper and smaller compartment is intended for the storage of the ice, but bottles of milk, covered butter dishes and other articles that are either sealed or wrapped may be kept there as well.

The larger and lower compartment is intended for storing joints awaiting to be cooked, dishes that have been partially consumed, supplies of butter, eggs and other perishable foods. In fact, it is the place where nearly all the foods, cooked and uncooked, that enter the house should be kept while they are awaiting consumption.

The chest, being made in two compartments, can house both fish and delicately flavoured foods in separate spaces. The fish may be stored in the ice chamber and all the other articles in the lower compartment.

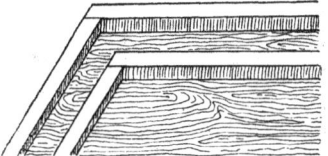

Fig. 4.—ONE CORNER OF THE DOOR.
The outer and inner frames have been fixed to the plywood base and the next step is to pack the slag wool into the recesses.

Although the diagram does not show it, the walls of the chest are of double thickness, with a cavity between. The internal spaces are stuffed with slag wool, which is a poor conductor of heat. Thus, the cavity walls, lined on the inside with sheet zinc, and the

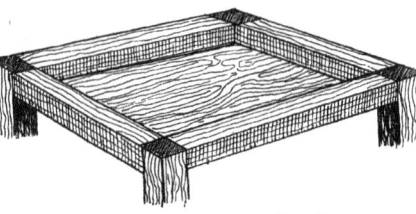

Fig. 3.—THE TOP OF THE ICE CHEST.
At this stage the slag wool should be packed into the recess and the upper sheet of plywood fixed.

ice within the chest, all help in the scheme of providing a beautifully cool chamber for the food.

The Frame.

The first step in the construction is to make the frame, shown in Fig. 2. For the uprights and cross pieces, strips of wood 2½ inches square in section are advised. They provide a very solid foundation for what will eventually prove to be a rather heavy piece of furniture. The uprights should be about 4 feet high; the front horizontal strips about 20 inches long, and the side ones about 15 inches. The chamber should take up about 2½ feet of the height, the uppermost dozen inches of which are reserved for the ice compartment.

Joints can be butted.

There is no real need to mortise or halve any of the corner joints; they will be quite safe if butted and held together with two or three long nails.

Supports for the Shelf.

When the frame has been put together, the next step is to fit two side lengths of wood, 1 × 1 inch. These are intended for supporting the shelf within the chest. One of these lengths is shown on the left of Fig. 2. For preference, they should be recessed for ½ inch within the upright at either end and they must come flush with the inner edge of the uprights.

The Inner Walls.

That done, it will now be convenient to make the inner walls of the chest. For them, plywood ⅜ inch thick is needed. First fit the floor and roof, as shown blackened in Fig. 2. Note that the plywood in these two cases comes to the extreme outer edge of the horizontal rails, and that a piece of the plywood has to be cut out at each corner in order to make the sheets fit.

When the floor and roof are done, fit the two sides, making them extend to the outer edges of the upright posts.

Fixing the Back.

All that now remains of this part of the work is to fix the back. It will be found that there is nothing on which to nail this panel; therefore, run a strip of wood, 1 × 1 inch in section, along the floor and another along the roof of the chamber, arranging the inner edge of both flush with the inner corners of the upright posts. When these are fixed, nail the back panel on to them.

The next step is to cut five panels of plywood to fit under the bottom, over the top, along the sides and across the back of the frame. In each case the panels should reach to the outer edges of the supports to which they are to be nailed, and it will provide a neat finish if all the edges are

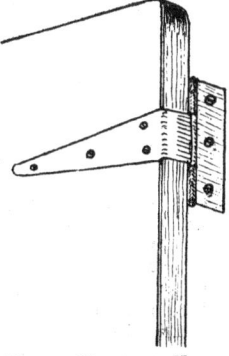

Fig. 5.—HOW THE HINGES ARE FIXED TO THE DOOR.

bevelled, as shown in the side panel (Fig. 1).

Packing the Cavities.

Before these panels are fixed, it is necessary to fill the cavities which they form with slag wool. This is easily done if the frame is appropriately turned about as each space is filled.

Fixing the Zinc Lining.

It is necessary, now, to fit the zinc ining to the chest. There are many ways of doing this. The worker who is not happy with a soldering iron will cut the five faces in one piece and reduce the soldering to a minimum. But the best plan is to start with the two side walls and the back, cutting them in one long strip and allowing ½ inch for turning over, both top and bottom. The folding should be done by placing a stout strip of wood, with a straight edge, on the inside of where the fold is to be made and beating with a hammer on the opposite side. Note that a piece must be snipped out of the zinc edging at each place where a fold is made.

When this sheet of zinc has been shaped, it is nailed in position and, then, a floor and a roof of zinc are cut to the exact size and, also, nailed. The joins are, finally, soldered, and it is as well to put a touch of solder over every nail head.

The Door.

Fig. 4 helps to show the way the door is made, but, first, it is advisable to look at Fig. 1 and note how its outer edge closes over the front of the chest. Having determined the "all over" dimensions by measuring the front of the chest, a piece of plywood is cut and edged with strips of wood, 1 × 1 inch in section. Next, an inner frame of similar strips of wood is nailed in position, as shown in Fig. 4. This frame should be slightly less in size than the front opening of the chest. Slag wool is spread over the plywood up to the level of the frames and, then, another sheet of plywood is fixed over the first. This is followed by a sheet of zinc.

Now, another frame of 1 × 1 inch wood is nailed to fit exactly over the inner of the two lower frames, slag wool is again packed in the space so made, a piece of plywood is nailed over it, and this is followed by a sheet of zinc.

The door is now made, but it will be necessary to round off the corners and generally smooth the edges.

How the tee hinges are fitted is shown in Fig. 5. The only point to note regarding them is that the long arm of each hinge must be bent to fit round the thickness of the door.

Any strong catch may be used to fasten the door.

The Inner Shelf.

Now that the door is fixed, it will be advisable to take in hand the inside shelf of the chest. This should be made of a frame of wood, covered with a piece of perforated zinc and supported on the two sides by a strip of 1 × 1-inch wood. Nails are driven through the strips to the corresponding lengths in the frame and, thus, the shelf is held firmly in position.

In determining the length of the shelf, from back to front, it is important to see that the door shuts against it without leaving any space.

Finishing off.

The ice chest is now practically finished, but two or three minor details require attention. There are three dowel rods to fit into the legs, the whole of the surfaces and edges of the chest need smoothing, and two coats of a light paint should cover the whole of the outside. If desired, a box for containing the ice may be made of sheet zinc.

A later article deals thoroughly with the construction of an electric refrigerator.

RECIPES FOR CIDER, CLARET AND HOCK CUP

In entertaining, one of the principal items to be considered is that of suitable drinks. It is not always possible to have coffee or soft drinks, and in this case the best thing to have is either cider, claret or hock cup. Most people like these cool and refreshing drinks, and they are inexpensive.

Cider Cup.

A good cider cup is as follows. Cut up about eight or nine slices of cucumber very thinly, and place them in a large jug, add 1 oz. of castor sugar, and a sprig of mint. Pour over these ingredients a wineglassful of sherry and a quart bottle of sparkling cider. Lastly, add a siphon of soda-water. Cover all well, and leave for about two hours before using. Take out the mint and cucumber and serve.

Some currants or small fruits in season (just sufficient to float on the top) give it a dainty and appetising appearance.

Claret Cup.

This is usually a favourite with everyone, and the following is a good recipe. It can be made with more expensive claret, but made as stated below it is quite satisfactory.

To 1 bottle of claret add 1 siphon of soda, 1 glass of sherry, the peel of ½ lemon, 9 slices of cucumber cut very thin, sugar to taste, and a large lump of ice. The sugar should not be added until just ready to serve.

The claret used for this cost 2s. 6d., and the sherry 4s. A little more sherry than the amount stated above can be used with advantage to the flavour.

Claret cup is greatly improved if brandy is used instead of sherry. Many prefer using a siphon of lemonade with the claret instead of soda, if made in this way the lemon peel and sugar is omitted, cucumber only being used.

Keep in cool place until ready to serve.

Hock Cup.

Many people prefer hock cup to claret cup, and it certainly makes a change; but it should be remembered it is more expensive to make. The least expensive method of making it is as follows:—

One bottle of hock to a siphon of soda, to which add 1 tablespoonful of castor sugar, 3 large slices of pineapple (fresh if possible, if not, a good tinned brand can be used), and a lump of ice.

The pineapple is added to give it the required acidity.

A Richer Hock Cup.

A richer one is made as follows, and is delicious. It is best made in a large jug, in which place a large lump of ice, add a liqueur glass of curacao, and a wineglassful of brandy. One bottle of hock and a siphon of soda. Stir thoroughly, adding a few slices of cucumber cut very thinly, and a bay leaf. The latter adds greatly to the flavour.

Sparkling Hock.

This is sometimes preferred, and is made as follows. To a bottle of sparkling hock, add a lump of ice and a liqueur glass of pineapple syrup. Also add a few slices of thinly cut cucumber and a siphon of lemonade.

Another Recipe.

Still another recipe, which is richer than the one above, is made with the juice of lemons.

To the juice of 2 lemons (which must be strained thoroughly), add 1½ oz. of castor sugar, and a wineglassful of maraschino. Mix well, until the sugar is dissolved, then pour in 2 bottles of sparkling hock, and 1 siphon of soda. Add a few pieces of ice, and keep in a cool place until required.

Practical Notes on Lawns
PREPARING, LEVELLING AND DRAINING

PROBABLY the most satisfactory way of producing a lawn is by sowing seed.

Preparing a New Lawn from Seed.

For general purposes a sowing of 1 to 2 ozs. of seed for every square yard should produce a good lawn. It is advisable to divide up the ground into squares with pegs or string, then divide up the seed into as many squares as you have to fill. This will ensure that you don't use too much seed on the first squares and leave insufficient seed for the final ones.

Always choose a dry, calm day for sowing, and do not cover the seed more than ¼ inch. This is done by lightly raking the surface in two directions.

When to cut New Grass.

New grass should not be cut until it is about 2 inches high, although a light roller can be used on it when it is about 1 inch high. Any coarse grass or weeds should be pulled out as soon as they appear, and to avoid damaging the grass, place a plank on the ground and work from this.

When to sow.

The ideal time to sow a new lawn is probably in the autumn when the soil is warm and there is plenty of rain about, but it is not always possible to delay sowing until this season. Perfectly satisfactory results will be obtained by sowing in spring or even in summer, when the weather is showery, or the grass can be watered frequently.

Before sowing, dig the surface to a depth of about 1 foot, break up any large lumps and rake out stones and weeds. If levelling is necessary this should be carried out as described in detail later. Heavy soil will be improved by digging in sand, etc.; light soil by applying a 2-inch layer of good loamy soil.

Laying Turves.

Another method of producing a lawn is by laying turves. This method has, of course, the advantage that the lawn is roughly finished at once, but unless really good turves are obtained it may be found that it requires a great amount of weeding and working up before it can be got into decent condition.

A turf is generally 3 × 1 foot in size, so that it is quite a simple matter to estimate the number required. Presuming the site to be turfed is 60 × 30 feet, then this is equivalent to an area of 1,800 square feet. As each turf is 3 square feet, then the number required would be 600.

They should be laid close together, leaving no space whatever between them as shown in Fig. 2. They should then be beaten with a wooden beater to ensure a firm, even surface.

Fig. 3.—When Turf has been laid it should be beaten with a Wooden Beater to ensure a Firm, Even Surface.

Fig. 2.—Turves should be laid close together with no Space whatever between them.

How to get a Straight Edge to Grass.

A useful hint when trimming grass round the edges of flower beds is to place a plank along the edge when trimming with the edging iron. This will ensure a perfectly straight line, and is more convenient and accurate than stretching a string along the edge.

LEVELLING A LAWN
Dealing with Mounds and Hollows.

If a lawn is already in existence and there are only a few unsightly mounds and hollows, it is not necessary to level the whole site. The mounds and hollows can be dealt with locally by removing the turf from an area slightly larger than the fault to be corrected so as to provide a margin of solid earth on which the ends of the straightedge can be placed.

If the fault is a hollow, then fill it up with good soil well trodden and rammed into position. If a mound, then after reducing it to the desired level, remove about 3 or 4 inches more soil and fill up with good soil.

When the turf has been replaced, keep it well watered until it roots.

Using a Plank.

Another method of levelling small hillocks and hollows is by using a plank. Place this edgeways on the lawn; hillocks cause the plank to rest unsteadily, while hollows are revealed by daylight being seen beneath the plank. The defects can be remedied by removing or adding soil as described.

Fig. 1.—Before sowing Grass Seed, any Stones or Weeds should be raked out.
Heavy soil will be improved by digging in sand; light soil by applying a 2-inch layer of good loamy soil.

LEVELLING A LAWN

There are two methods of levelling a lawn, the method to be adopted depending largely on whether the site is already more or less level, or has a definite slope. If the former, then it will probably be best to level the site in a true horizontal plane, like, for instance, the top of a table. If the latter, then reducing the site to a level in the general plane will probably be most satisfactory. This can be compared to making the surface like a table tilted in one or two directions.

A site that has not received any previous attention should be trodden in with the heels as shown in Fig. 4 to make the soil quite firm before any attempt is made to level it.

Fig. 4.—Before any Levelling Operations are started on a Site that has not had Previous Attention, it should be Trodden quite Firm with the Heels.

Levelling in a Horizontal Plane.

The first operation is to mark out the site with pegs to get the site level, and a quantity of pegs 1 inch square (rose stakes cut down will suit) will be required. Prepare these by making a mark 6 inches from the top. Then take one of the pegs and drive it into the ground as far as the mark at what seems to be the highest corner of the ground, taking no notice of any small mounds or hillocks which may be higher. This first peg is the master peg from which the remainder of the measurements will be taken, and is shown in Fig. 7, which represents levelling operations on a site 100 × 50 feet.

Now take another peg and drive it in at the position marked A1. Pay no attention to the mark on the peg for the moment, but get the top of the peg level with peg A by placing a straightedge and spirit level across the top and adjusting peg A1 until the bubble in the level remains stationary in the centre. It is a good idea to tie the spirit level to the straightedge so that it will not fall off every time it is moved.

Next drive in peg A2, and level the top with peg A1 as already described. Continue this process until you have a row of pegs right across the lawn, with their tops all level.

Now drive in the side pegs from A to B, from B to C, and from C to A5. Then fill in as many centre pegs as you think necessary.

You now have the site pegged out and will probably find that the pegs are all standing out different amounts from the ground. Where the pegs have had to be driven in past the mark it shows that the site is higher at this point, and *vice versâ*, and it will therefore be quite easy to ascertain the

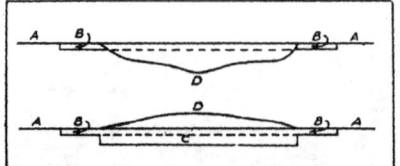

Fig. 5.—How to deal with Mounds and Hollows when Turf is to be Replaced.

The line AA shows the finished level. BB are margins of solid earth to take the ends of the straightedge. The dotted line shows the finished level of soil, sunk to allow turf to be replaced. C is the subsoil replaced with good soil, and D the original surface (exaggerated).

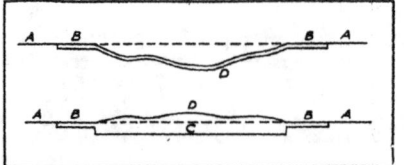

Fig. 6.—How to deal with Mounds and Hollows when Seed is to be Sown.

Note that the surface is finished flush with the line AA.

Fig. 7.—How to level a Lawn by adding Additional Soil.

The peg A is the master peg. The tops of the remaining pegs are all made level with it by means of a straightedge and spirit level. It will then be seen where additional soil is required.

fall of the ground by measuring the distance they stand out of the ground.

Referring to the example in Fig. 7, if peg A5 stands 12 inches out of the ground, peg B, 18 inches, and peg C, 20 inches, it will be obvious that the site falls 6 inches from A to A5, 12 inches from A to B, and 14 inches from A to C.

Using Boning Rods.

If a large area is to be dealt with, it may be quicker to use boning rods as shown in Fig. 8. When an even fall of ground is required, pegs are inserted in the ground at each end and others at intervals between. These are then hammered down until when looking over the boning rods they are seen to be level one with the other.

Having got the pegs in correctly, you can now see the various places where soil must be removed or be added to get the site level. There are two methods of carrying out the work:—

(1) Using additional soil.
(2) Without using additional soil.

Using Additional Soil.

Method 1 is probably the simplest, and all that has to be done is to put down earth on the ground and tread, rake and roll it until the surface is quite firm and flush with the marks on the pegs. It is advisable to check the work as you go along with the straightedge and level as shown in Fig. 9.

Spread the earth in thin layers, not exceeding 2 inches deep, in order to prevent the surface sinking later.

Levelling without Additional Soil.

Method 2 is rather more involved, as the actual levelling must be done with the subsoil and not with the top layer. The first thing to do then is to remove the top soil to a depth of about 6 inches and wheel it clear of the site.

Provided the site is more or less level, the next thing to do is to drive the master peg up to its mark somewhere about the centre of the site to be levelled, as in Fig. 10, preferably at a point slightly below the centre, as this will ensure that a surplus of soil will be left and not a deficiency if we do not get it quite right.

Now from the master peg fix the line of pegs AB in the downward direction, levelling the tops with the master peg as already described. Then dig straight into the hill, throwing

Fig. 8.—WHEN A LARGE AREA IS TO BE DEALT WITH IT MAY BE QUICKER TO USE BONING RODS, INSTEAD OF USING THE STRAIGHTEDGE AND SPIRIT LEVEL METHOD.

Fig. 9.—WHEN ADDING THE ADDITIONAL SOIL, CHECK BETWEEN THE PEGS WITH A STRAIGHTEDGE AND SPIRIT LEVEL AS SHOWN.

the earth as it is dug behind you and so build up the low area to the marks on the pegs. It is, of course, not possible to fix the pegs A to C until some of the earth has been removed.

It will be necessary to have a slight slope at either end as indicated in Fig. 10, and this slope should be made at an easy angle so that there is no difficulty in cutting the grass with the mower.

Now bring back the top soil and spread it evenly over the levelled surface, testing as the work proceeds. A true finish can then be obtained by one of the following methods.

How to obtain a True Finish.

In many cases, the site is already in a fairly level condition, and all that is required is to get a perfectly true surface.

One good method is to fix two laths about ½ inch deep to two sets of pegs, parallel with one another and work a straightedge across them, pushing a little fine dry soil before it as shown in Fig. 11. This will fill up any little hollows that may exist. The laths must, of course, be fixed true to the tops of the pegs, and as one square is finished they must be moved on to another square until the whole area is finished.

Another method is to put in short pegs about 6 feet apart so that the end of a straightedge can be placed on each and swung round in a full circle. Place a little dry, finely-sifted soil down in front of the straightedge before it is swung round (see Fig. 12).

Levelling in the General Plane.

This is perhaps not quite so easy as the method of levelling already described, but when dealing with a site that has a very definite slope, is probably the best method. It is necessary to rely largely on the eye.

We will assume for the purpose of describing the method that it has been

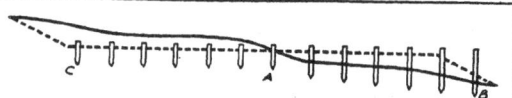

Fig. 10.—HOW TO LEVEL WITHOUT USING ADDITIONAL SOIL.
Fix the master peg A about or a little below the centre of the ground. Fix pegs downhill level with it. Then build up low area with earth from the hill, fixing pegs A to C as the area is dug. Note slopes at each end.

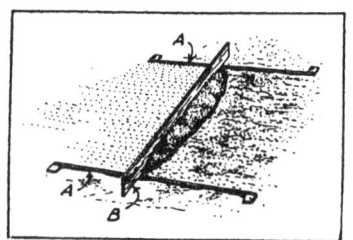

Fig. 11.—ONE METHOD OF ACCURATE LEVELLING.
Fix two parallel laths about ½ inch deep to two sets of pegs and work a straightedge across them, pushing a little fine dry soil before it.

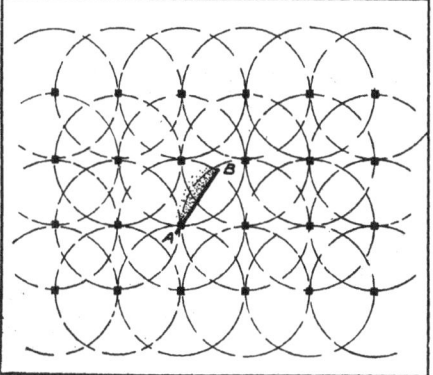

Fig. 12.—ANOTHER METHOD OF ACCURATE LEVELLING.
Showing a series of pegs in a surface which has been approximately levelled. The end of the straightedge is placed against each peg in turn and swung round in a full circle, driving before it some finely sifted soil.

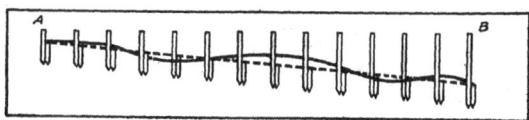

Fig. 13.—THE METHOD OF LEVELLING IN THE GENERAL PLANE.

found that the site falls 30 inches from A to B in Fig. 13. This is equivalent to a fall of 3 inches every 10 feet, so that if the master peg A is driven in up to its 6-inch mark, then the second peg must be marked 9 inches from the top, the third 12 inches, and so on, until when the last peg is reached it is marked 30 inches.

In cases where the marks on the pegs come below the surface, when the tops are levelled with the master peg, then sufficient earth should be dug away to expose them. When all the pegs are in position the top soil must, of course, be removed before levelling, as already described.

DRAINING A LAWN

An excess of moisture in lawns is highly undesirable. It makes the soil soft and muddy, encourages the growth of moss, and is harmful to the grass which in order to thrive demands that the soil shall be firm, porous and airy. Therefore, if pools of water accumulate it is advisable to consider the possibility of arranging some form of drainage.

Unless, however, there is some means of disposing of the water collected by the drains, i.e., a ditch or existing land drain, then there is little that the amateur can do, as it would be unwise to tamper with any of the house drains.

We will, however, assume that some means of disposing of the water is available, and will describe the method to be adopted in laying the drains.

How to arrange the Drains.

Drains for this type of work are generally laid on the herring-bone principle as shown in Fig. 15, which shows the method of laying the drains for various slopes. It will be seen that the main idea is to lay the pipes as much as possible diagonally across the direction the water in the soil is likely to flow so as to catch as much water as possible. Another point to remember is the position of the outlet which should always be in the same direction as the water flowing in the existing drain, never against it or at right angles to it. For instance, in example A the existing drain should be flowing from C to D. This point does not arise, of course, if the new drain is discharging into a ditch and is well above the normal water line of the ditch.

Type of Pipe to use.

Agricultural drainpipes are made in lengths of 12 inches, and pipes 3 inches in diameter will be satisfactory for the main drain of a small area, and 2 inches for the lateral drains. These latter should be 10 or 15 inches apart, according to the nature of the soil—closer for very heavy and wet soil and wider apart for less heavy soil.

Cutting the Drains.

Having chosen an outlet for the drain, peg out the route of the main drain and its outlets, then cut to the width of a spade to a regular depth if the ground is on a slope of 12 or 18 inches. If the ground is level, then start at about 12 inches and allow a fall of about 1 inch in every 10 feet. Make sure that the branches where they join the main are on the same level or a little higher.

Testing the Slope.

Having cut the trenches, remove the loose stuff with a trowel and then slide a straightedge with spirit level fixed at its centre down each trench and note whether the bubble is always at the top end, as it should be, and that there are no hollows in the trenches where water might accumulate.

Now lay the Pipes.

The pipes should now be placed in the trenches in a straight line and the junctions fitted close and tidily; if the joints are bad, soil will work in and perhaps choke the drain. It is advisable to test the drains before filling in the soil by pouring a can of water at the head of them and getting someone to watch that it all runs freely out of the outlet.

Fig. 14.—A Useful Tip for getting the Edge of a Lawn Straight.
Place a plank along the edge when trimming with the edging iron. This will ensure a neat edge.

Filling in the Trenches.

Having got the drains nicely laid, the next thing is to fill in the trenches, and here a word of warning is advisable. It is useless to dig trenches in impervious clay; place the pipes and cover them with the same impervious clay. The trenches must be filled to within 3 inches of the surface with clean breeze, and the surface finished off with the top-spit soil.

Draining an Excavated Lawn.

When an excavation has been made for the purpose of obtaining a level lawn, the excavated end will always be the wettest, due to the surface water running from the hill and oozing out of the banks. In such cases it is advisable to cut trenches as shown in Fig. 16, making them 12 inches or more deep at B and allowing a good fall to the ends A and C. Then a similar trench BD can be run diagonally across the lawn.

Pipe the drains as already described.

Getting Rid of Worms.

Worms can do a lot of damage to a lawn. It may in fact be found almost impossible to renovate a bare place in a lawn with grass seeds, because the movements of the worms keep the soil loose and cause the young plants to die. In any case the worm casts are unsightly.

The proper time to deal with worms is during the breeding seasons, *i.e.*, from the end of August to the beginning of December, and from the end of September to the end of May. On a day that is dull and the ground moist apply a pound of a substance such as Carter's worm killer over two square yards, and water it in. The first worm should be up in within one minute, and after five minutes about twenty worms should be up. If some such result as this is not obtained, delay the work for a few days and try again. When conditions are found to be satisfactory, and the worms are coming up freely, continue spreading the worm killer over the ground at the rate of ½ lb. to a square yard, watering it in immediately.

We are indebted to Messrs. W. H. Gaze & Sons Ltd., High Street, Kingston-on-Thames, for the photographs which accompany this article.

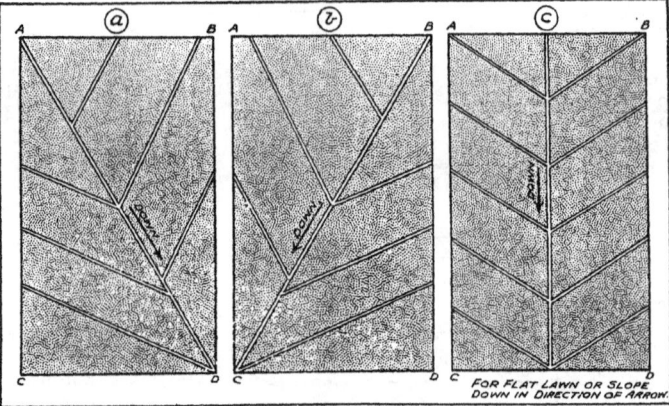

Fig. 15.—How to arrange the Drains.
The best form is the herring-bone principle and the above diagram shows their arrangement relative to the slope of the ground.

Fig. 16.—The Method of arranging the Draining of an Excavated Lawn.

A Welsh Dresser

THE dresser is a popular piece of furniture. It combines usefulness with an attractive appearance. Nothing looks nicer than a dark oak dresser with a display of blue and white plates, and it provides excellent accommodation with its long shelves, cupboards, drawers, top, and wide lower shelf.

Size.

That shown in Fig. 1 is 4 feet 6 inches long, a convenient size for the average modern house. For a small room the length could be cut down to 4 feet or even 3 feet 6 inches, but it is better to make it as large as can be conveniently arranged.

Wood to use.

Oak should be used throughout—or, at any rate, for all "show" parts. A less expensive wood such as deal can be pressed into service for inner rails, drawer sides, and so on, if it is necessary to cut down the cost. The legs can be obtained ready made, and it should be noted here that it is advisable to obtain these before any actual work is begun, because, although the design is fairly representative, there may be a slight difference which may necessitate the sizes being adapted.

THE LOWER STRUCTURE

This may be taken in hand first. It consists in the main of four legs, of which two are turned, joined together by a series of rails. We advise readers who have had a fair experience in woodwork to cut mortise and tenon joints for fixing the rails to the legs. It is the most satisfactory way, though a quite good alternative is to use dowels. The latter method is simpler, since it is only necessary to bore holes and glue in the dowels. It is a point for the reader to decide for himself.

Mark out Positions of Joints on Legs.

In either case the first step is to mark out the positions of the joints on the legs. To do this they should be fixed together side by side temporarily with a cramp, with the ends level. The marks are then squared across the whole, thus ensuring all being marked alike. They are afterwards separated and the marks squared round each individually.

The Leg Joints.

Fig. 3 shows what the joints are like. Notice that in all three rails a small "set back" is allowed at the top. This necessitates a third line being squared across between those which mark the over-all width of the rails. If dowels are used, the over-all marks are made, and between them are drawn the dowel positions. Two dowels should be used to each joint.

Sides and Back are panelled.

It will be seen that both the sides and the back are panelled.

Fig. 1.—This Welsh Dresser is a Convenient Size for a Small Average House, being 4 feet 6 inches long and 6 feet 6 inches high.

Preferably these panels should fit in grooves worked in the rails and legs, and this means that the mortises must be set back also on the panel side. They should be set back by a distance equal to the depth of the grooves, say $\frac{1}{4}$ inch. This grooving calls for the use of a plough or router, and if one is not available the only alternative is to fix little strips of wood all round to form a rebate in which the panel can fit. By fixing round a small moulding afterwards on the outside, the whole is kept firmly in position. In this case, of course, there is no need to set back the mortises.

The Mortises.

These should be $\frac{5}{16}$ inch or $\frac{3}{8}$ inch wide, and the width is marked by means of a mortise gauge. There are two markers on this, and these should first be set to the width of the chisel being used. The fence is then set so that the markers will mark the centre of the rails. (The last-named should be 1 inch, finishing $\frac{7}{8}$ inch.) Mark each joint with the gauge, and proceed with the chopping out. A great deal of the waste wood can be removed by boring. Select a bit a trifle smaller than the mortise width, and bore a series of holes along the mortise close to one another. When chopping with the chisel, cramp the legs over a firm part of the table (over one of the table legs) and, starting at the middle, work along to one end, taking care to hold the chisel upright. Reverse the chisel and work towards the other end. A piece of paper can be stuck to the chisel to mark the depth. The mortises should be deep so that the mortise on the adjacent side meets it in the thickness of the wood.

The Rails.

As in the case of the legs, the rails can be fixed together in sets when being marked out. It is advisable to square the marks across with a chisel. This gives a very definite shoulder mark. Afterwards the marks are squared round each independently. In the case of the front and back rails, the centre must be marked out for the upright between the drawers. Notice that the lower front drawer rail is shaped. The most satisfactory way of dealing with this is to cut away the rail where required. Alternatively, the rail can be made to the thinnest part, and small pieces glued on at the ends and centre. The decoration in the middle is an applied fret. This can be glued on after the whole thing has been put together.

ASSEMBLING

To save having to deal with many joints in one operation, the two sides should be glued up independently and the glue allowed to set. They can then be regarded as complete units in themselves. If the panels are grooved in, they should be inserted whilst the gluing-up is being carried out. If being beaded in, they can be added afterwards. A cramp will prove useful in making tight joints.

When adding the front and back rails, put the centre upright between the drawer rails first. The ends and stretchers are then added. Test for squareness in both elevation and plan before setting aside for the glue to harden.

Levelling the Joints.

Any levelling of the joints is now carried out, and the drawer runners added as in Fig. 4. These are notched to fit around the legs, and are glued and skew-nailed in. Guides are placed on top as shown. To prevent the drawers from dropping when opened, a centre kicker is added (Fig. 4).

The Top.

The top can be a solid piece of oak with the moulding worked around three edges. A simpler method is to make the edges square and apply a ready-made moulding. It is necessary to cut the shelf around the legs. It is fixed either with screws driven upwards through the stretchers, or by means of corner blocks glued in the angles.

The Drawers.

For the drawers the most satisfactory construction is dovetailing. A simpler method is to cut rebates across the side edges of the front and fix the sides in these. To hold the back, the sides are grooved about ½ inch from the back. A special drawer bottom moulding can be obtained. This is grooved to hold $\frac{3}{16}$-inch plywood, and is glued and nailed around the inside.

THE UPPER STRUCTURE

Either $\frac{3}{4}$-inch or $\frac{7}{8}$-inch oak is used for this. The shelves fit in grooves cut across the ends. The top, however, fits in rebates as shown in Fig. 6. It does not matter about the grooves running right across, because a moulding is planted on the front edges all round (see Fig. 7). It is certainly simpler to cut them right across. The depth is marked with the gauge, and the sides sawn across. The waste is removed with the chisel, and if possible finished off with a router.

When cutting the shelves to length remember to allow sufficient length for them to enter the grooves. The top is a trifle longer as the rebate is deeper than the grooves. It is a simple matter to calculate the length of the short shelf and the intermediate uprights by marking out on the ends and long shelves, and laying the short ones on them.

Glue the whole thing together, and drive in nails. The simplest way is to drive them through the sides into the shelves, punching them in and filling in the holes. They should slope

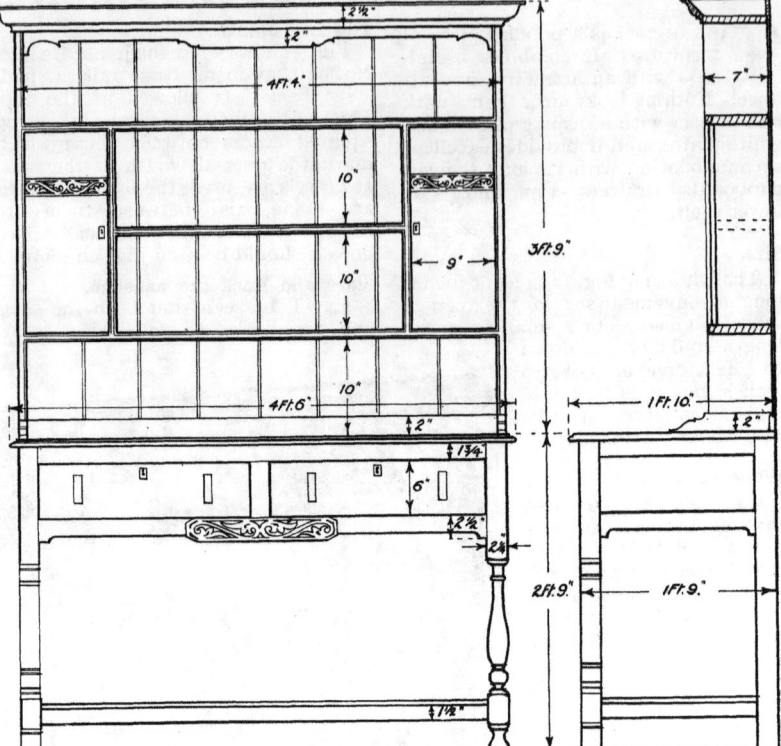

Fig. 2.—The Principal Dimensions for the Welsh Dresser.

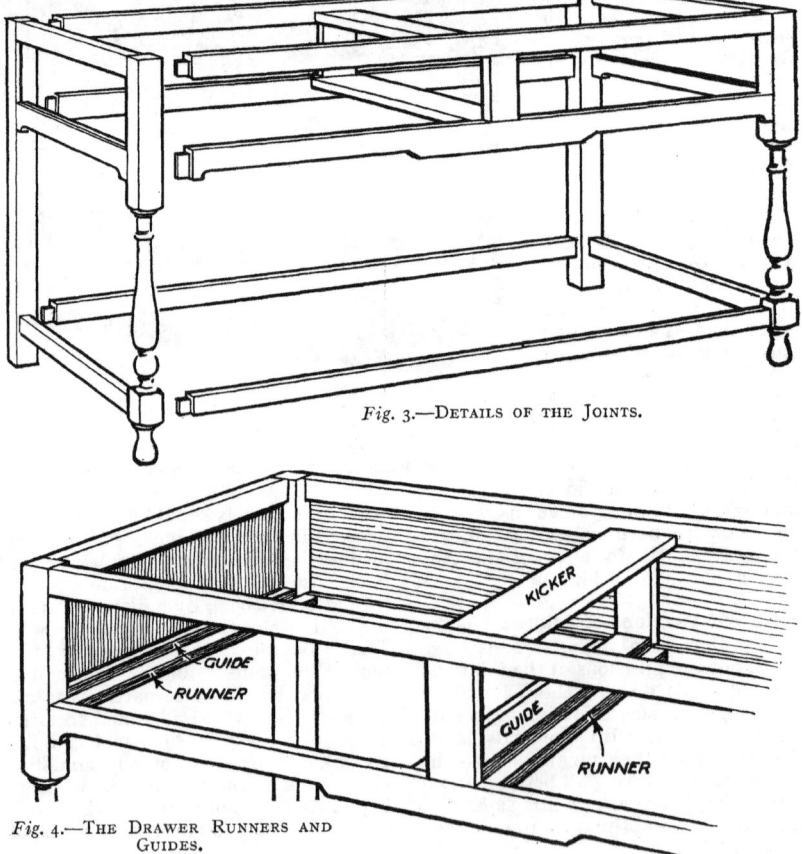

Fig. 3.—Details of the Joints.

Fig. 4.—The Drawer Runners and Guides.

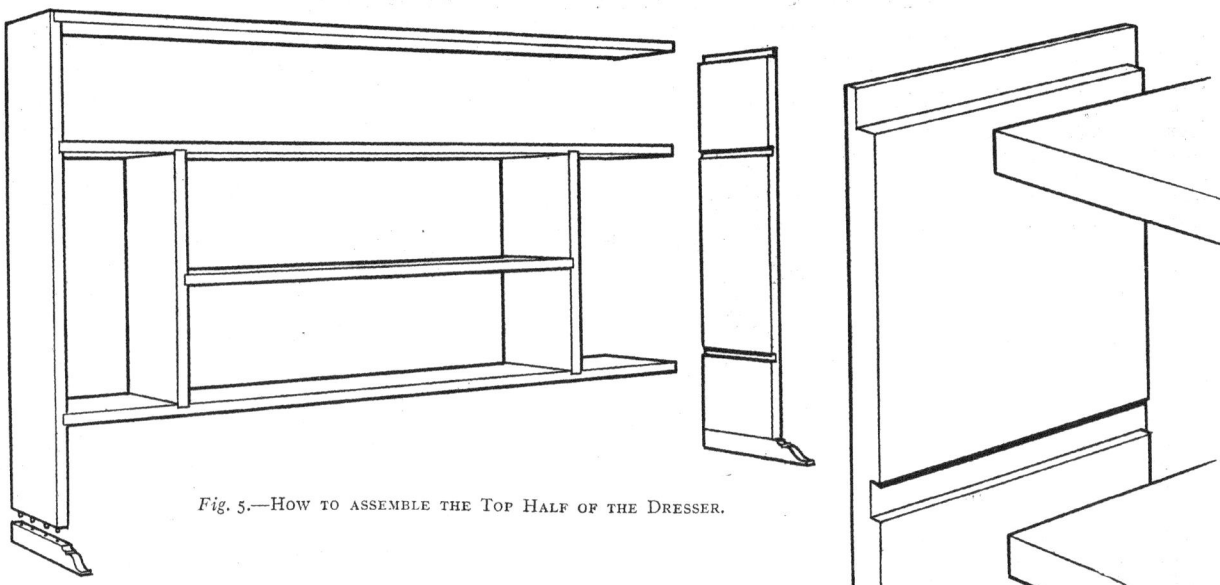

Fig. 5.—How to assemble the Top Half of the Dresser.

Fig. 6.—The Joints in the Upper Structure.

towards each other so that they have a dovetail grip. To avoid the nails being seen, they can be driven in at the inner corners underneath at an angle. This necessitates the whole thing being held together with cramps.

To prevent the Dresser toppling forward.

Notice from Fig. 5 that cross-pieces are fixed beneath the sides. These prevent any tendency for the structure to topple forwards. They are fixed with dowels. It is desirable to work rebates along the back edges of the sides to hold the back. In this case the shelves reach only to the rebate depth. If rebating offers a difficulty, a thin back can be used, this being nailed directly on to the back edges.

To prevent Plates slipping forward.

Notice from Fig. 7 that a shallow groove is worked about 2 inches from the back edges. This is to prevent plates from slipping forwards. Here, again, grooving may be awkward, and an alternative is to fix little strips of wood about the same distance from the back.

Cornice Moulding.

The cornice moulding is mitred around level with the top. Above it a

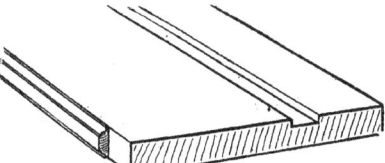

Fig. 7.—A Section through the Dresser Shelf.

dust-board of thin plywood is nailed. The shaped edging is of $\frac{3}{8}$-inch or $\frac{1}{2}$-inch oak. It is fixed by means of glue blocks rubbed in the angle at the back. The front edging moulding should be mitred where it intersects.

The Doors.

Either well-seasoned solid oak can be used for the doors, or oak veneered plywood. The decoration is an applied fret. A back rail is fixed between the sides at the bottom. Preferably it should be rebated to take the back. The latter is nailed or screwed on.

The whole thing should be finished with a dark stain. Walnut stain gives a good colour. It is then lightly polished with french polish, and finally waxed.

CLEANING CEMENT AND TERRA-COTTA SURFACES

CEMENT and concrete are now largely used for parapet copings, wall cappings, railing pillars, etc. After a time these may become dirty, and cleaning may be necessary. The best method is to first scrub the surface as clean as possible and then apply a coat of cement wash. Ordinary cement is first made into a thick paste with water, and then thinned down with more water.

This is brushed over the surface to be treated and will make it look like new. While the cement wash has considerable enduring quality of its own, this can be largely increased if a small quantity of waterglass (silicate of soda) is mixed with water separately and then added to the cement wash.

The terra-cotta coping stones on garden walls and other ornamental work made from the same material often gets very dirty with the passage of time, particularly if it is adjacent to a main road and therefore subjected to fumes from motor traffic.

If it is desired to clean terra-cotta, the following procedure is best. First soak an old stiff bristled brush in coal tar naphtha and scrub vigorously with this. Then brush over with petrol to expedite the drying off. Not less than twelve hours later scrub the surface with a solution of Manger's sugar soap in hot water. Finally, wash down with clean water.

If there are any particularly black patches, these may be scrubbed with a piece of fine pumice stone during the application of the naphtha.

Watch Cleaning and Repairing

In the following article will be found some useful hints on taking an ordinary wristlet watch to pieces for cleaning or repair. Studied in conjunction with the series of photographs on this and the following pages, no difficulty should be experienced by those readers who like to do this sort of work at home.

Tools required.

All the operations described in this article can be carried out with the aid of a penknife, tweezers and small screwdriver.

First unwind the Mainspring.

It is always advisable before starting to dismantle a watch to make sure that the mainspring has been unwound. In the majority of cases this is done by slowly lifting up the click and gently holding the winding shaft. Let it slide round until there is no power left in the mainspring.

The watch shown in Fig. 2 is a typical example of a well-known make of watch. The bezel has been unscrewed from the case, and the case has been opened. The next operation is to remove the winding shaft, and this is done by unscrewing the small screw near the edge of the movement. This can be seen just by the side of the first finger.

To remove Movement from Case.

To remove the movement from the case it is necessary to unscrew the two case screws. In most watches these screws are on the top plates, or there may be one in the bottom of the hole. In the latter case this will have to be removed by a screwdriver of the same diameter as the screw so as not to spoil the brass plate. After this the movement can be slipped out.

Removing the Minute Hand.

Having got the movement out of the case, the next thing is to remove the minute hand. Hold the movement as shown in Fig. 3, and place a sharp penknife between the hour and minute hands. Then lift up the latter, pressing the other end of the hand against the dial with the finger so that it does not flick away and get lost.

Removing the Dial.

Then unscrew the dial screws and lift the dial very gently. This will cause the second hand to come off, leaving the hour hand with wheel on the dial as shown in Fig. 4. The dial screws are in the majority of watches on the bottom plate, which is easily found by the feet of the dial. It is of copper in all cases, and protrudes between the top plates. In other watches the dial screws are placed in the outside of the bottom plate.

When removing the dial make quite sure that the dial screws are free of the feet; if the dial is forcibly lifted the dial will probably break.

Removing Balance Cock.

The next operation is to remove the balance cock, and this is shown in Fig. 5. Unscrew the balance cock and insert a fine pair of tweezers into the small undercut in the cock. Hold the cock lightly with the tweezers and lift the balance carefully off the movement. Take great care not to bend or twist it.

Removing the Pallet Cocks.

Fig. 7 shows how the pallet cocks are removed. This has to be done even more carefully, as the pallets might fly away if the mainspring has not previously been unwound, as already advised.

Taking out Mainspring Barrel.

The next step is to lift off the top plate to enable the barrel containing the mainspring to be taken out. The barrel is the part shown still in the bottom plate next to the thumb. To remove the top plate look for two screws alike in size and undo these. Then unscrew the large-headed screw holding the click. It is also necessary to unscrew the large-headed screw holding the rachet wheel to the barrel. As this screw may have either a right- or left-hand thread, do not try to force it. Try to loosen it first by unscrewing one way and then the other, or else the screw may break in the arbor, which would require a highly skilled man to repair.

Removing the Spring.

In Fig. 9 the barrel housing has been taken off the plate. Insert the tweezers in the small opening of the barrel cover, lifting it in order to remove the barrel arbor, and insert a sharp-pointed knife under the coiled spring and lift it out.

How to repair a Spring.

If the spring is broken at the end held by the tweezers, a new one will be required; if, however, it is broken at the far end, it is quite easy to make another hook in it by passing it over the flame of a small spirit lamp until red hot, when the end can be bent about $\frac{1}{8}$ inch outward. Repeat this three or four times until a hook is formed.

Replacing Spring in Barrel.

To replace the spring in the barrel,

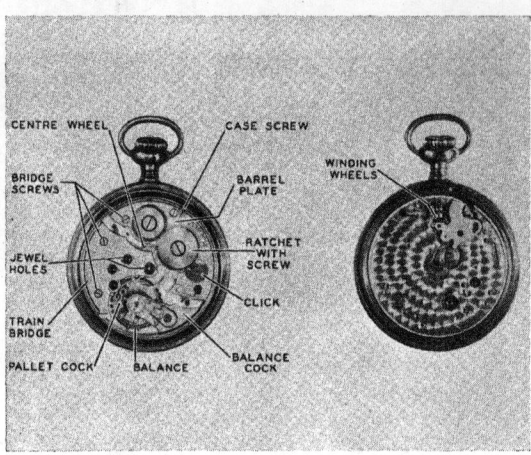

Fig. 1.—The Main Parts of a Watch.

Fig. 2.—Removing the Case Screws so that the Movement can be slipped out.
The winding shaft must first be removed.

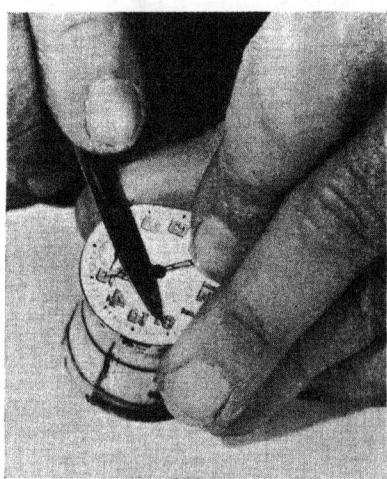

Fig. 3.—Removing the Minute Hand by lifting it with the Edge of a Penknife.
Note how the end of the hand is pressed against the dial to prevent it flicking away.

WATCH CLEANING AND REPAIRING

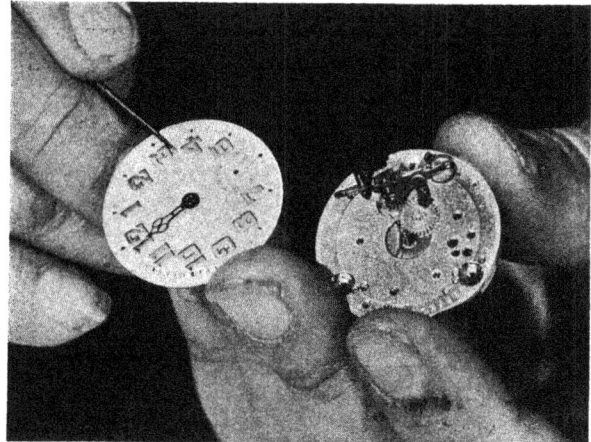

Fig. 4.—Lifting off the Dial with Tweezers after removing the Dial Screws.
The dial screws may be either on the side or top of the plate.

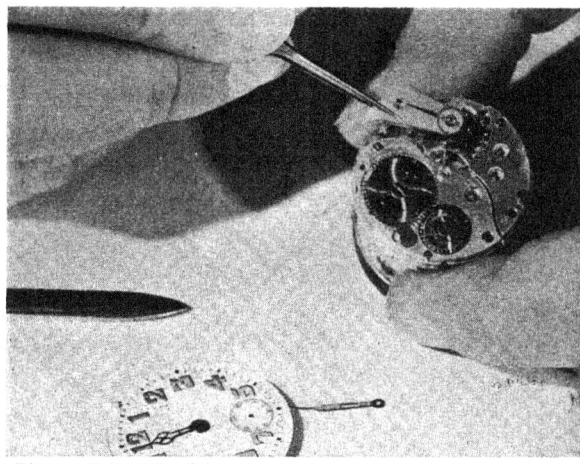

Fig. 5.—The Next Operation is to remove the Screw holding the Balance and lift out the Balance Cock as shown.

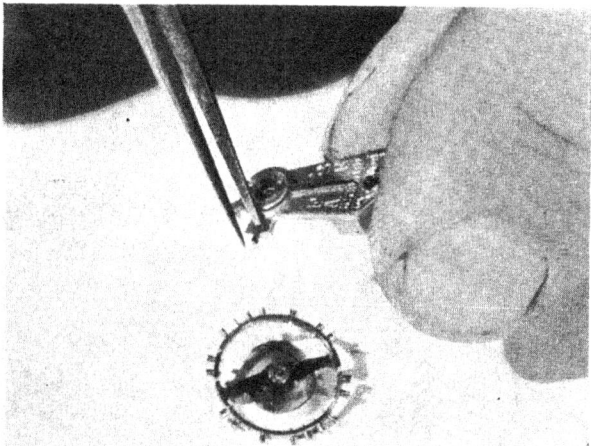

Fig. 6.—Removing the Balance from the Balance Cock.
Loosen the screw and push out the hairspring stud with the point of the tweezers. The balance will then fall free from the balance cock.

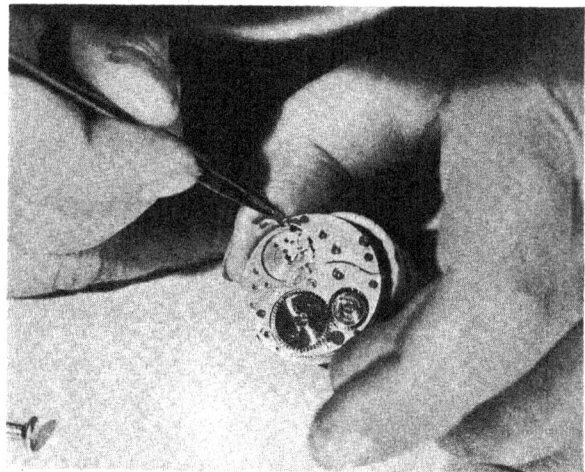

Fig. 7.—Now remove the Pallet Cock as shown after taking out the Screws which hold it in place.
This will reveal the pallets, which can then be lifted out.

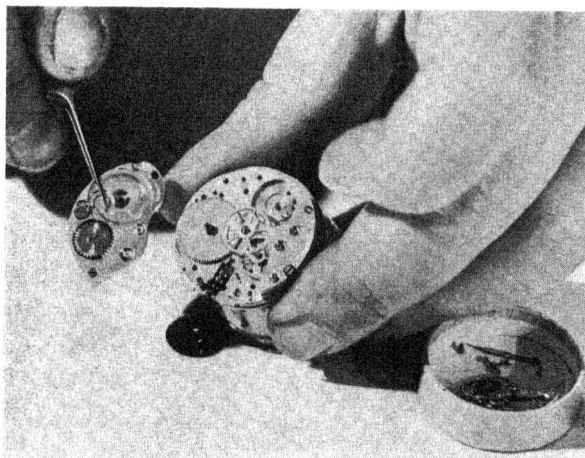

Fig. 8.—The Top Plate should now be removed to enable the Barrel holding the Main Spring to be taken out.

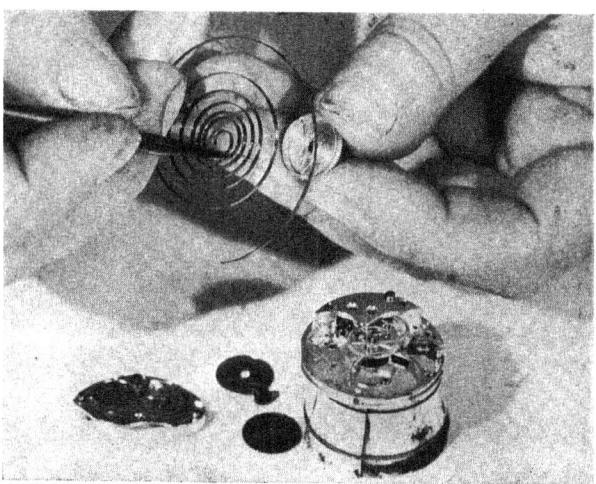

Fig. 9.—Insert the Tweezers in the Small Opening of the Barrel Cover, lift it off in order to remove the Barrel Arbor, and lift out the Spring.

WATCH CLEANING AND REPAIRING

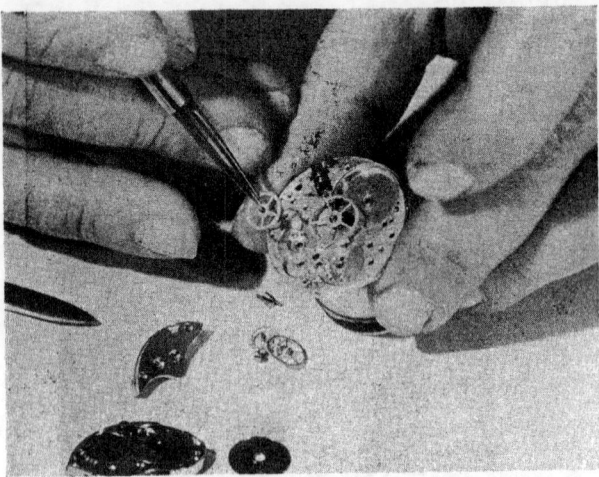

Fig. 10.—When lifting out the Train, one Wheel should be removed at a time.

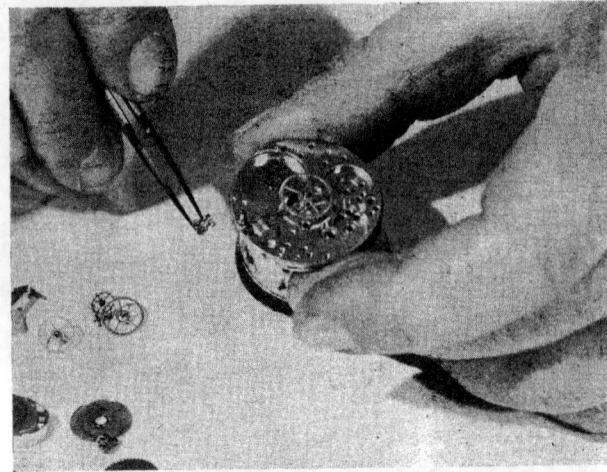

Fig. 11.—Removing the Winding Wheels. Note that only the centre wheel now remains.

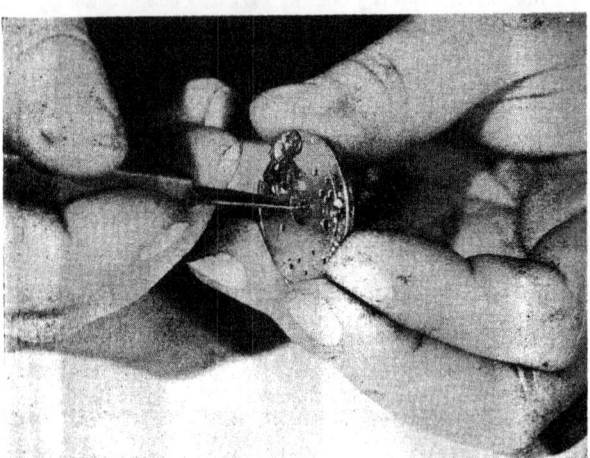

Fig. 12.—Pushing the Centre Wheel out of the Canon Pinion. The centre wheel is on the side opposite to that shown in the photograph.

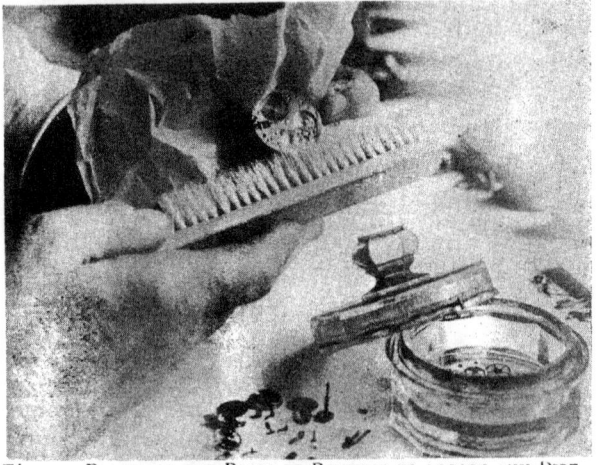

Fig. 13.—Place all the Parts in Benzene to loosen any Dirt. Then brush each part, holding it in tissue paper.

hold the latter as shown in Fig. 14, then put the end of the spring in position. Turn the barrel round in the fingers and gently press the spring in until the whole has been wound into place. Make quite sure that the barrel arbor is hooking on the inside of the spring. When fixing the cover make sure that it snaps sharply into place.

Removing the Train.

Fig. 10 shows the method of removing what is termed the train, *i.e.*, the going wheels, which, in most cases consist of four, the centre, third, fourth and escape wheels. This is done by removing the screws which hold the plate in position and lifting off the plate so that the wheels fall out, leaving only the centre wheel.

When these have been removed, the winding wheels should be lifted out.

To remove Centre Wheel.

To remove the centre wheel, insert a pair of fine tweezers or piece of hard thin steel in the centre of the bottom

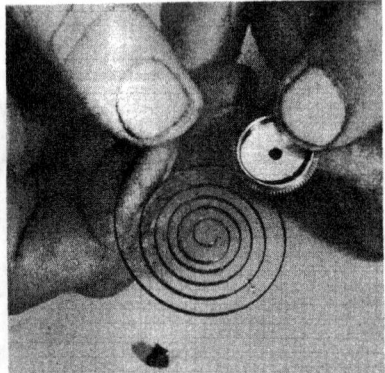

Fig. 14.—Replacing the Main Spring into the Barrel.

Hold the barrel firmly in the left hand and place one end of the main spring into the barrel. Slowly turn round while pressing main spring into place.

part of the wheel as shown in Fig. 12.

Removing old Oil and Dirt.

Place the parts in clean benzine for a few minutes to remove the old oil and dirt. After taking each part out of the benzine they should be put to dry on a piece of clean cloth. Then brush every part of the watch with a clean watchmaker's brush, holding the pieces in clean tissue paper.

Reassembling.

Start by putting each wheel, *i.e.*, escape, fourth, third and centre wheels, in each of the jewel holes or brass holes, taking care not to bend or force the pivots in the holes. When they are properly in position, hold the bottom plate firmly and put one train plate on top, finding the top holes of each wheel by pressing the top plate gently. Make sure all the wheels are in position and running freely before screwing the plate down.

An Old-World Ingle Nook

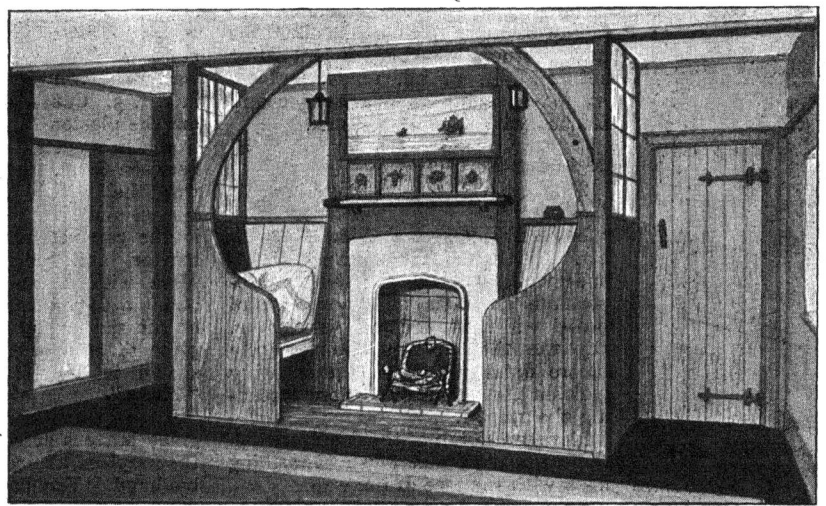

Fig. 1.—This Delightful Fireside Retreat will appeal to all Lovers of the Old-world Type of Home and to Everyone who appreciates the Delights of a Cosy Fireside Seat.

IMAGINATION fails to provide a more cosy picture than that of an old-world ingle nook with comfortable settles beside a glowing wood fire. No matter how cold and boisterous the elements may be, there is placid contentment and comfort in the warm shelter of this typical old English fireside fitment which cannot be equalled by any modern advancement of the builder's art.

Such a homely fireside structure as that depicted in Fig. 1 has been built within the last few years by an amateur in a modern house and has proved to be the most attractive and popular feature in the home.

The duplication of this delightful scheme in practically any house is possible and is not beyond the powers of the home craftsman, although at first sight it might appear to be a formidable task.

Structurally the scheme embodies a low platform or dais, with a stout post at each corner, connected at the top by dummy beams. A settle with sloping back and glazed panel above is built into the gaps between the posts and the wall at each side of the fireplace. The recesses are partly enclosed and have a narrow shelf at the level of the seat back, while the fireplace itself is treated in a style in keeping with the general scheme.

Electric lights set within old-world lanterns are provided for illumination of the settles, and can preferably be controlled by pull-switch lamp-holders.

Dimensions and Materials.

The general features and constructional details of the ingle nook are clearly shown in Figs. 2 and 3, which are drawn to scale, and show respectively a front view, side view and a plan.

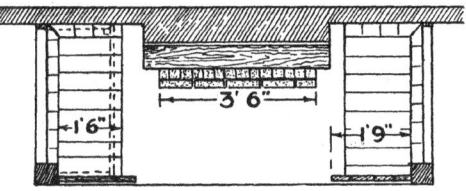

Fig. 2 (above).—Front and Side View of the Ingle Nook, giving all important Dimensions.

Fig. 3.—Plan View showing the Relative Positions of the Settles, Fireplace, Hearth, and Front of the Dais.

Fig. 4.—Building the New Brick Hearth. Showing the proper arrangement of the bricks for this purpose.

Assuming that the ingle nook to be built is substantially the same size as that shown, the following materials will be required:—

Floor Joists.—3 × 1½ inches 30 feet, deal.

Corner Posts.—Two pieces, 6 inches square, 8 feet long, or eight pieces of board 5½ inches wide, ½ inch thick and 8 feet long, oak or deal.

Seat Framing.—3 × 1 inch, 30 feet, deal.

Seat Boards.—6 × 1 inch tongued and grooved boards, 28 feet.

Seat Backs.—75 square feet of 5 × ½ inch matchboard.

Dummy Beam.—6 × 1 inch × 16 feet, deal or oak.

Dummy Posts.—6 × ½ inch × 32 feet, deal or oak.

Curved Braces.—Two, 4 feet 6 inches long, 11 inches wide, 1¼ inches thick, deal.

Seat Ends.—6 × 1 inch tongued and grooved boards, 32 feet, deal.

Dais Floor.—6 × ¾ inch floorboard, 35 square feet.

Fillets.—1 × 1 inch, 100 feet.

Picture Moulding.—2 × 1 inch, 12 feet for mantel picture.

Mantel Board and Beam.—6 × 1½ inches, 12 feet.

Beading.—⅝ × 1 inch for leaded light panels and general use, 40 feet.

Batten.—2 × 1 inch for general use, 50 feet.

Other requirements are about 56 lbs. of cement and 1 cwt. of sand for making the mortar for use in the fireplace; about 100 red bricks for the hearth; a firebrick about 18 × 24 inches; about 30 red flooring tiles; a pair of wrought-iron fire-dogs and a fireback.

A quart of dark oak water stain; a quart tin of pale oak varnish; about 25 feet of lead-covered twin-lighting cable; two ceiling roses; two switch

AN OLD-WORLD INGLE NOOK

Fig. 5.—A Tudor Effect is obtained by a Stonework Surround made by forcing Cement Mortar into a Framework fixed temporarily to the Wall.

or coal; while it is safe to say that if a mantel register stove is present and cannot be removed the result would be so incongruous that the ingle had better not be built at all, unless perhaps treated in a more modern style and finished with coloured enamel.

Beginning the Work.

Start operations by taking away the fire grate, removing the loose brick rubble at the back and tiling the opening. Set the tile in mortar made with one part cement, two parts sand; support the tiles with battens or pieces of board while the cement is setting. Dip the tiles in water immediately before fixing them; also thoroughly moisten the brickwork before spreading the mortar.

Render the top of the fireplace with cement mortar and finish everything flush with the face of the wall.

Spread a bed of mortar about 1 inch thick over the hearth and set the bricks thereon, placing them upon their long edge as shown in Fig. 4, continuing until the hearth is covered or coal; while it is safe to say that if fitments, then nail some 2 × 2 inch battens to the wall, as shown in Fig. 5. Cut out the plaster from the space between them, wet the wall surface and fill

Fig. 6.—A "Horse" or Template used to form the Moulding on the Cement Mortar.

in the gap between the battens with mortar and press it firmly into place with a trowel. Leave it for about a day, then mould the surface of the mortar by scraping it with a piece of zinc or tinplate, shaped as shown in Fig. 6, and known as a "horse."

The horse is traversed between the guide battens at the sides and top of the fireplace, the corners being shaped by hand. The battens are then removed and any rough places on the mortar made smooth by trowelling.

The Chimney Breasts.

The outer corners of the chimney

lamp-holders; 2 lbs. of 1½-inch oval brads; and a few oddments in the way of longer nails and screws.

Preliminary Work.

If the existing fireplace is one of the old pattern cast-iron register type with a canopy it will have to be removed and the fireplace opening faced with red tiles, but if the stove is of modern type, with barless grate and a large firebrick back, it could be left untouched except for the removal of the wooden mantel and surround, and the substitution of the dummy beams, posts and plain mantelshelf.

This matter of the fireplace must be settled by personal taste and inclination, but there is no doubt that the best appearance and greatest comfort are attained by the open wood fire; the next best is a barless fire burning logs

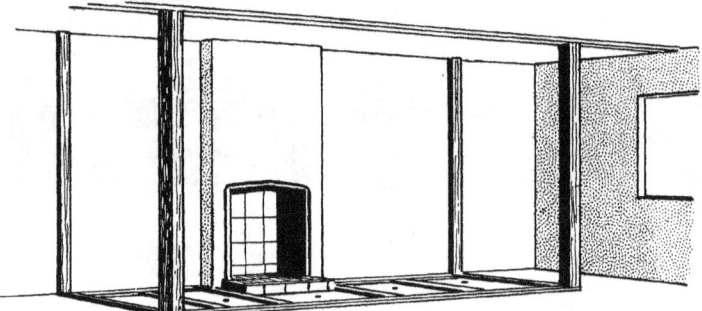

Fig. 7.—The Corner Posts and the Floor Joists for the Dais are here shown in Place.

and the brickwork extends for 6 to 9 inches on each side of the chimney breasts and is 12 to 15 inches into the room, all as shown in Fig. 4.

This completes the work on the fireplace proper, because the fire-dogs, firebrick back and ornamental iron fireback stand in place and are not fixed in any way.

The Front of the Fireplace.

The front of the fireplace has, however, to be dealt with on the following lines:—

First remove any existing mantel breasts are then faced with 6 × ½ inch deal boards, and the dummy chimney beam and mantel board fixed. All these parts can be nailed directly to the wall surface.

Corner Posts and Dais.

When the work on the fireplace has been completed the joists for the dais floor should be nailed to the floor of

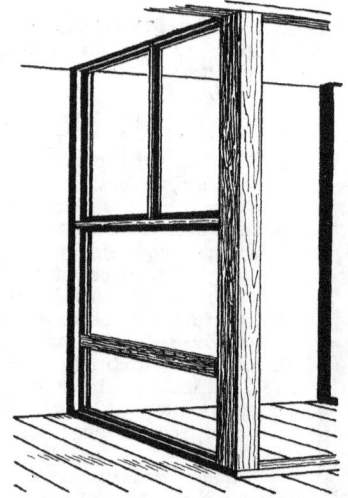

Fig. 8.—Here are shown the Various Partition and Seat Rails fixed in Place between the Corner Post and the Upright Piece attached to the Wall.

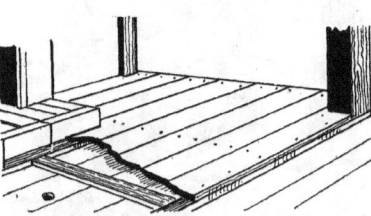

Fig. 9.—How the Dais Floor is covered with Boarding, together with Some Details of the Joists and Bearers.

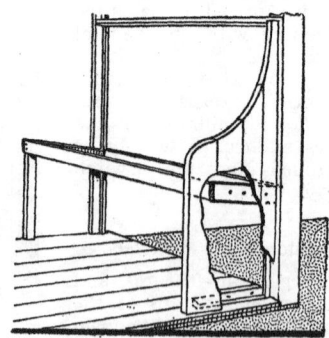

Fig. 10.—The Pew End and Seat Frames are built up as here shown.

AN OLD-WORLD INGLE NOOK

the room and be arranged as shown in Fig. 7. The timbers are laid flatways and are only butt jointed.

The corner posts, if solid, should be notched on the outside corners so that they fit into the angle of the joists—but if built up with four boards glued and nailed at the corners only the inside pair need be cut away.

The dummy beam should be cut to length to fit between the side walls of the room and be fastened to the ceiling by screws driven into two of the ceiling joists. The posts are then set up and held in place by cross nails until the other parts of the framework are completed.

Now fix an upright of 3 × 1 inch deal to the walls opposite to the posts and then nail a fillet to them, terminating it 1 inch from the ceiling and setting it 1 inch from the face of the post and the upright as shown in Fig. 8. Fix a piece of 3 × 1 inch deal at ceiling level between the post and the upright and secure it with cross nails.

Cut out a part of the fillet so that the seat rail will fit nicely into it, and cut other notches for the top rail of the seat back, but set this piece flatways and flush with the edges of the upright and post. Then fix a fillet to the top and to the underside of this rail and other fillets to the underside of the ceiling rail.

Cut out the fillet where necessary and fix an upright of 2 × 2 inch deal to the centre of the upper opening, placing this crossways of the opening and projecting equally on each side of the fillets.

Finally, fix a fillet to each side of the upright, placing them in line with the other fillets, fixing all of them with oval brads driven slantwise and punched well below the surface. The framework will then appear as in Fig. 8. A similar framework is to be built on the opposite side of the fireplace.

Dais Floor.

The floor of the dais should next be fixed and should be fitted neatly around the corner posts on fillets nailed to the inner faces; the edges of the side planks should finish flush with the outer face of the fillets as shown in Fig. 9.

Ventilation holes, about 1 inch diameter, should be drilled through the floor of the room before the dais floor is fixed. Bearing pieces must be nailed to the floor around the hearth to support the ends of the floor boards.

Making the Seats.

The settles or fireside seats each consist of a shaped pew end, a simple rail and bearers and the solid seat boards. The pew end and frame are clearly shown in Fig. 10, the former being

Fig. 11.—Fixing the Sloping Back which adds so much to the Comfort of the Seats.

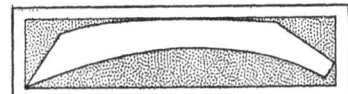

Fig. 12.—How the Curved Bracket can be marked and cut from a Single Wide Board.

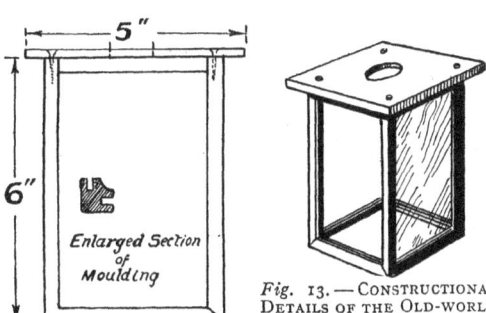

Fig. 13.—Constructional Details of the Old-world Type of Electric Lamp Case.

Fig. 14.—The Fresco in its Oak Frame and Some Other Details of the Space above the Fireplace.

Fig. 15.—Sectional View showing how the Glass Panels above the Seat Back are fixed and the Ornamental Lead Strips fixed to the Glass with Cement, sold for that Purpose.

made from 1-inch tongued and grooved boards, held together with a batten at the bottom and by another at the seat level, both being screwed to the inner faces of the boards. The outline of the pew end is then marked upon the boards and sawn to shape with a keyhole saw and rounded off with a spokeshave and sandpaper.

They are fixed in place by screwing the batten to the floor and the vertical edge to a fillet nailed to the corner post.

A bearer of 2 × 1 inch batten is then screwed to the back upright. The outer end of the bearer is supported by a short vertical strut, to the face of which, and to the end of the bearer on the pew end, the horizontal seat rail is glued and screwed.

The seat is then made by cutting and fitting short lengths of floor board to the two horizontal rails, keeping the back ends flush with the back rail but overhanging and rounding off the front ends.

The rectangular space at the back of the seat is then filled in with the matchboarding, and after this the sloping seat back is fitted. This is nailed to the fillet on the underside of the top seat rail and to another fillet nailed to the seat boards, as shown in Fig. 11.

The space in the recess beside the fireplace can be filled in to the level of the top seat rail by fitting a sloping seat back in a similar manner, and finishing it at the top with a shelf about 4 inches or so in width. The junction between the two seat backings must be bevelled and the ends of these pieces should be supported by a batten fixed diagonally for that purpose.

Finishing the Ingle Nook.

The whole of the woodwork should now be carefully stained, allowed to dry, then rubbed down with sandpaper, given a coat of wood filler, again rubbed down and stained; after which the whole should have one coat of varnish.

While this is drying the ornamental curved braces which span the space between the pew end and the beam should be sawn to shape, finished with spokeshave and sandpaper and then stained and varnished. These pieces are sawn from a single piece of plank as shown in Fig. 12. They should fit nicely into place and be secured with long thin screws driven into deeply countersunk holes, which can afterwards be stopped with plastic wood.

Wiring the Electric Light.

The electric light wires should be run in the usual way and be connected to the nearest convenient point on the house-wiring system.

AN OLD-WORLD INGLE NOOK

Details of the wooden lamp cases are given in Fig. 13, and are readily constructed with the aid of angle moulding—as shown—for the corner pieces and bottom edging. The top piece is sawn to shape from $\frac{3}{16}$-inch plywood and has a hole through the centre by which it is clamped to the lamp-holder. The panels can be glazed or be filled in with cellastoid or other non-inflammable translucent material.

The glass panels are simply inserted into the grooves in the woodwork and held in place by gluing the bottom rails into position. The whole of this woodwork should be painted dull black to represent iron work.

The space above the fireplace is filled by a fresco or painting framed in oak, somewhat as shown in Fig. 14, which also shows detail of the timbering.

The spaces over the seat backs should be glazed by bedding the glass in putty and securing it with a beading fixed with sprigs or fine nails—as shown in Fig. 15—which also illustrates the lead strips attached to the glass to represent old-fashioned leaded light panels.

Clear or coloured glass can be used as desired. The kind known as Cathedral glass is particularly effective; a pale amber colour is generally the most satisfactory choice.

The whole of the structural work being now completed, the woodwork should be lightly sandpapered, given a final coat of varnish which should have several days to harden before the seats are used. A generous supply of cushions in gay colourings complete a fascinating feature of a cosy home.

SOME USEFUL RECIPES FOR SANDWICHES

Scrambled Egg and Tomato Sauce.

Place a piece of butter the size of a walnut in a saucepan, let it melt but on no account brown, beat two eggs, add pepper and salt and pour into the melted butter, stir over the heat until the egg is firm, but do not allow it to boil. Leave the scrambled egg to cool and then add tomato sauce to taste, mixing it well in. When quite cold make sandwiches.

Scrambled Egg and Cheese.

Scramble two eggs to which have been added 1 oz. of grated cheese. Tomato sauce may be added or omitted as preferred.

Hard-boiled Eggs.

To cook the eggs place them in a pan of cold water, bring them to the boil and boil for ten minutes, then stand them in cold water; this will prevent discoloration and enable the eggs to be easily peeled. When cold shell the eggs, chop them up, place them in a basin, add butter (1 oz. to two eggs), and beat the mixture till it becomes a paste, add black pepper, salt and tomato sauce to taste. The filling is now ready for use. A lettuce-leaf will be a great addition to this sandwich.

This filling may be varied by using anchovy instead of tomato sauce, also by spreading a little chutney on the bread before the filling.

Cream Cheese.

Brown bread should always be used when cream cheese is the basis of the filling. The cheese can be simply flavoured with salt and black pepper and spread on the bread.

Cream Cheese and Finely Chopped Olive.

Flavour only with black pepper, the olive being salt.

Cheese and Walnut.

One cream cheese, 2 ozs. finely chopped walnuts, marmite and black pepper to taste, add a little cream and beat to a paste. If a double cream cheese is used, butter can be used instead of the cream.

Cheddar or Cheshire cheese mixed with the same ingredients makes a slightly heavier and more satisfying meal.

Cheese and Celery.

Take 3 ozs. grated cheese, 3 ozs. finely chopped celery, a *soupçon* of vinegar and cayenne pepper, enough olive-oil to bind, mix to a paste, use brown bread.

Cheese and Mushroom.

Take 3 ozs. grated cheese, $\frac{1}{4}$ lb. mushrooms fried in butter and finely chopped, mix to a paste with cream and flavour with black pepper. White bread should be used for this variety.

Cheese and Onion.

Fresh or pickled onions may be used according to taste. 2 ozs. of Cheddar cheese, one onion (small) very finely chopped, a pinch of mustard, $\frac{1}{2}$ oz. butter, mix to a paste, and spread on brown bread.

Potted Cheese.

This is very useful to keep in a house where sandwiches are frequently required. It is prepared as follows: $\frac{1}{4}$ lb. butter, $\frac{1}{4}$ lb. grated cheese, two well-beaten eggs, pepper and salt. Melt the butter, but do not make it too hot, add the cheese and flavour with pepper and salt, let it get very hot but do not let it boil, stir in the eggs and well mix, pour into small jars and cover with melted butter.

Salmon.

Take $\frac{1}{2}$ lb. of salmon (tinned or fresh), 1 oz. of butter, 1 teaspoonful anchovy sauce, 1 teaspoonful of lemon-juice, $\frac{1}{2}$ teaspoonful black pepper, a few slices of cucumber. Pound all the ingredients except the cucumber, peel and cut the cucumber into very thin slices and lay in oil and vinegar for a short time, then drain. Both the slices of bread for this sandwich must be buttered, lay the cucumber slices on one piece, spread the salmon filling on the other and put together.

Sardine.

Take one tin of sardines, vinegar, sharp pickle, black pepper, cayenne, mustard, celery salt, marmite or bovril ($\frac{1}{2}$ eggspoonful). If the sardines are large remove the tails and bones, put them in a basin or mortar and add the flavourings according to taste. Beat the mixture to a very smooth paste. The filling is now complete, and both pieces of the bread (either brown or white) should be buttered.

Sardines and Hard-boiled Eggs.

One tin of sardines, two hard-boiled eggs, vinegar, cayenne, curry-powder and celery salt to taste. Pound all together to a smooth paste and use as directed in previous recipe.

Haddock.

Remove the skin and bones from a cooked smoked haddock, place it in a basin with two well-chopped hard-boiled eggs and 2 ozs. of butter and beat it to a cream. Flavour with celery salt, cayenne or paprika and anchovy sauce to taste. Be careful not to use too much anchovy sauce or it will obscure the flavour of the haddock. Use white bread, buttering both slices.

Lobster.

Tinned or fresh may be used, the former is easier to deal with, though, of course, the latter is much nicer. Pound the fish with 2 ozs. of butter, season with cayenne, powdered mace and a little salt. This is not an easy filling to make as it requires a lot of pounding before it can be worked into a nice smooth paste. Use white bread, and butter both slices.

Crab.

Treat as for lobster, but add a little vinegar or lemon-juice to the flavouring.

Marmite.

This mixed with butter, flavoured with black pepper and a little celery salt and spread sparingly on very thin bread is a very palatable dainty to offer anybody as a first meal after tooth extraction with gas.

How to Collect Butterflies and Moths

This fascinating hobby appeals to both young and old who are interested in the natural sciences. It forms a pleasant recreation on country outings and summer holidays. The knowledge gained is not without its practical advantages. The capturing and location of specimens or their caterpillars trains the eye to be alert and teaches one to be patient. One learns also the habits of some of the insects and their larvæ which infest our gardens. It is essentially a hobby for the spring and summer months, although the enthusiastic collector may use his spare hours in the winter reading up the subject and visiting the natural history museums, in which comprehensive British collections are displayed.

Life Story of Butterflies and Moths.

The life of a butterfly or moth starts with the eggs laid by the female insect on the leaves of the particular plant to which the species is addicted. After some days the eggs hatch out to tiny caterpillars (also called larvæ or grubs), which feed on the leaves of the plant. As the caterpillars grow they become too big for their skins, so that after a day or so of fasting they shed their coats for new and larger ones which have formed beneath. This process is continued until the caterpillars are fully grown. The life of the caterpillar stage varies from a fortnight to several months, depending on the species and the climate.

The Chrysalis or Pupa.

When the caterpillar is fully grown it spins a cocoon round itself, or bores into the ground and sheds its skin for the last time. The imperfect insect now resembles the body of a butterfly or moth, and, if examined, the underside will show distinct markings in relief of the wings and feelers of the insect which is to emerge later. Some caterpillars, particularly those of butterflies, when they turn to the chrysalis stage do not spin a cocoon, but simply suspend themselves on any suitable object by means of a silk thread. The caterpillars of a large number of moths bore a few inches in the earth to spend their time in the chrysalis stage.

A chrysalis does not feed; it is apparently lifeless, but will move its tail when held between the fingers.

The Perfect Insect.

The chrysalis or pupa stage of the insect lasts anything from a week to a year, depending on the weather and the species. When the insect emerges from the chrysalis case, its wings are folded and not fully grown. Butterflies usually emerge in the early morning; the moths after midday. The newly born insect can

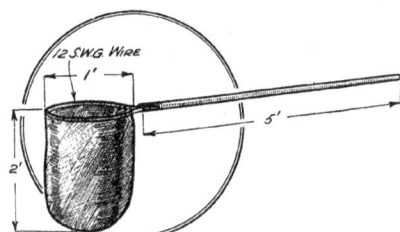

Fig. 1.—A Net of simple construction which the Collector can make for himself.

crawl, but not fly. It attaches itself to the nearest convenient object so that its wings are free. In a very short time, generally not more than an hour, the wings are fully grown and dry. The insect then takes to the air, after a little wing exercise on the fence or tree to which it is attached. After this the insect does not grow any more and feeds chiefly on the honey of flowers until it is eaten by the birds or dies a natural death. In most species the sex of the insect is easily distinguishable. Either the size, shape or markings differ. For example, the female orange tip butterfly does not have the characteristic orange tips on the wings, while some female moths have no wings at all.

Collecting Equipment.

The essential equipment required by the collector consists of a net, killing bottle, setting boards and storing boxes. A suitable box is also required, in which to keep the dead insects when they are caught away from home and cannot be set immediately.

How the Specimens are preserved.

Unlike the collecting of stuffed birds and animals, no special preserving process is required with butterflies and moths. After the insect is caught, either in a net or at rest on a tree, it is killed in a bottle by the fumes of potassium cyanide. Finally, it is pinned through the thorax and its wings set into position and allowed to dry. The various items of the equipment and the methods of using them are now described in more detail.

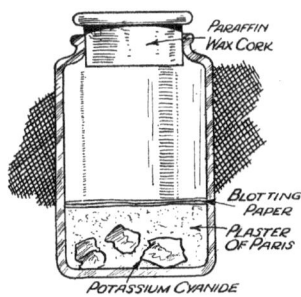

Fig. 2.—The Killing Bottle.

The Net.

The construction of a suitable net is shown in Fig. 1. For the net itself 1½ yards of 30-inch wide green gauze or white mosquito netting is required. If green gauze is used, it is soaked in warm water and dried before use, so as to remove the dressing and some of the colouring matter. The hem at the top of the net is made 1 inch wide. The supporting frame is made from 12 S.W.G. galvanised iron wire, and it is secured to the stick by means of copper binding wire. To enable the net to be threaded on to the circular frame, the top half of the vertical seam of the net must be finished off by hand afterwards. The handle consists of ½-inch cane 5 feet long. A longer handle is required on occasions, for captures over hedges, but for most purposes the length shown in Fig. 1 is sufficient.

The Killing Bottle.

Although special glass jars with screw tops are available for this purpose, an ordinary cork-stoppered bottle with a 2 to 2½-inch neck will answer just as well. The best substance for killing the specimens is potassium cyanide. It is a deadly poison and must not be handled with bare fingers; even to inhale the fumes from it is dangerous. Obtain 1½ ounces of the pure substance and cover it in the bottle with some freshly mixed plaster of paris. The plaster must not be made too wet or the cyanide will dissolve and its effectiveness be destroyed. The bottle tends to become wet inside owing to the affinity of the cyanide for water. It is kept in a dry condition by means of layers of blotting paper on the surface of the plaster. In order to render the bottle as airtight as possible the cork is soaked in paraffin wax.

When the bottle is fresh butterflies and small moths are killed in less than a minute. Make sure that the insect is dead by leaving it in the bottle for a quarter of an hour. The large moths may be left in for half an hour.

Substitute for Cyanide.

A useful substitute for potassium cyanide is ordinary laurel leaves. Variegated laurel is not suitable. The leaves are chopped, after the style of mint for mint sauce, and placed in the bottle with a covering of blotting paper. The leaves must be renewed every day if in regular use, because the amount of poison which they contain is small and soon evaporates.

Locating Butterflies.

The different species have their particular habits and haunts. Since honey forms their principal food, the wild flowers in the hedges and fields are a fruitful source of specimens.

HOW TO COLLECT BUTTERFLIES AND MOTHS

1. **Swallow Tail.** Male. The female is larger. Yellow in colour with black markings. Blue patches with one red spot on the lower wings. Rather scarce.
2. **Black-veined White.** Female. The male has similar markings, but the enlargement of the veins at the wing tips is not so marked. Usually rare, it is a visitor from the continent.
3. **Large White.** Female. In the male the black spots are absent and the blackish tips less pronounced. Usually common.
4. **Small White.** Female. The black dots are absent in the male, and the black tips, faint or absent. Common.
5. **Green-veined White.** Female. The veins, of greenish black, are less distinct in the male. The spring brood of this butterfly is less heavily marked, and whiter in colour. Common.
6. **Wood White.** Male. The blackish tip is almost absent in the female. Not very common and rather local.
7. **Orange Tip.** Male. The orange tip occurs only in the male. Both sexes are mottled with green on the underside. Common.
8. **Pale Clouded Yellow.** Female. The blackened wing tips of the male are smaller and more broken up. The male is pale yellow and the female white. Common in some years, it is a visitor from the continent.
9. **Clouded Yellow.** Male. The black border of the wings is somewhat broken up with yellow in the female. A deep chrome yellow with the underwings slightly suffused with black. Common in some years.
10. **Brimstone.** The male is sulphur yellow, while the female is a very pale yellow. Both sexes have four orange spots as shown. Not uncommon.
11. **Comma.** Warm brown colour with a distinct white comma on the underside. The female is generally larger than the male. Rather scarce and local.
12. **White Admiral.** Male. The female is larger and lighter in colour than the male. It is blackened brown, lighter brown on the underside. Rather local.
13. **Purple Emperor.** Male. The central portion of the wings of the male are dark purple on dark brown. The purple colour is absent in the female, which is larger and lighter in colour. Rather scarce.
14. **Small Tortoiseshell.** Blackened on the inner portions of the wings, the principal colour is reddish-brown, with a number of bright blue crescents in the outer black margins of the wings. A common butterfly. The large tortoiseshell, not shown, is very similar in markings, but is larger and not so common.
15. **Pearl-bordered Fritillary.** Male. Brown with black markings. The undersides of the lower wings have a number of silvery crescents, hence the name of the butterfly. Common around woods. The black markings of the female are slightly larger.
16. **Peacock.** Very dark red ground colour, with blue patches in the eyes. Almost black on the underside. Common.
17. **Camberwell Beauty.** Deep chocolate colour with blue spots in the black borders. Pale yellow outer borders. Rare. The drawing is taken from a male caught at Dover in 1890.
18. **Painted Lady.** Male. The female is smaller and has more blackened markings on the lower wings. The principal colour is light brown, which is shown shaded with single lines. Common.

HOW TO COLLECT BUTTERFLIES AND MOTHS

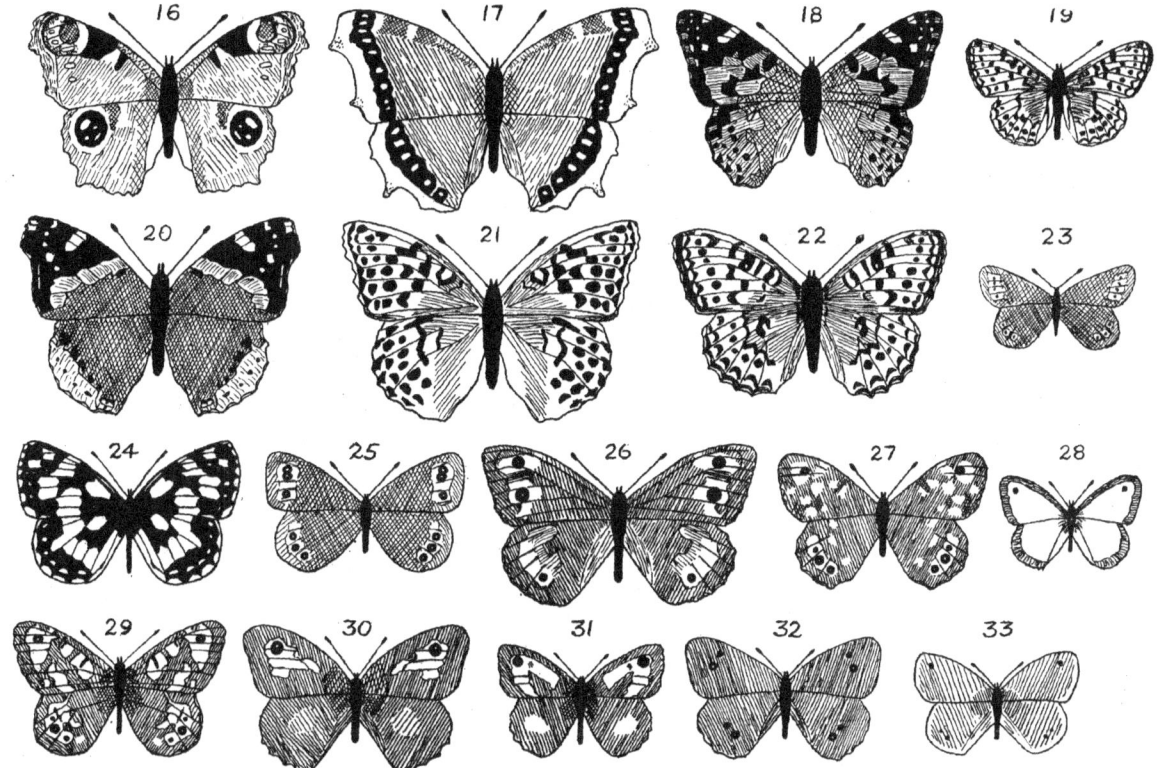

19. **Small Pearl-bordered Fritillary.** Very similar to its larger cousin in colour and occurrence.
20. **Red Admiral.** Female. The bright red bands (lightly shaded) are narrower in the male. Inner portions of the wings have the appearance of black velvet, suffused with red. Common.
21. **Silver-washed Fritillary.** Female. The male is a darker brown than the female and black markings on the inner portions of the forewings are more elongated. Green with silvery patches on the underside. Not uncommon.
22. **Dark Green Fritillary.** The male is a darker brown than the female. Green, studded with silver on the underside. Rather local.
23. **Small Mountain Ringlet.** Male. The female is larger and lighter in colour. Both sexes are a dirty brown with lighter brown patches surrounding the black dots. A north country species.
24. **Marbled White.** Male. The female is larger and the black markings are less definite. Common in some districts.
25. **Scotch Argus.** Female. The lighter brown patches of the forewings are smaller in the male. The principal colour is dark brown. Confined to Scotland and the north of England.
26. **Grayling.** Female. The male is somewhat smaller, with the light brown patches more suffused with black. Fairly common.
27. **Speckled Wood.** Female. The yellow spots of the male are generally smaller than those of the female. The ground colour is dark brown.
28. **Small Heath.** Pale straw to light brown with blackened borders, which are frequently very faint. Very common on heathlands.
29. **Wall.** Male. In the female the blackened bands of the forewings are sharper and narrower. The colour is brown. Common.
30. **Meadow Brown.** Female. The light brown patches of the forewings are much smaller, or practically absent, in the male. Very dark brown in colour. Very common.
31. **Gatekeeper.** Male. The central blackened lobe of the forewings is absent in the male. The bright patches are light brown. Common.
32. **Ringlet.** A very dark dead-leaf brown, the female is somewhat lighter than the male. Not uncommon in the north.
33. **Large Heath.** Light brown to blackened brown. Varies in depth of colour a good deal. Rather local, it occurs only in the north and in Scotland.
34. **Brown Hairstreak.** Female. The orange patches on the forewings are smaller in the male. Very dark brown on the upper sides of the wings, golden brown with white hairstreaks underneath. Rather local.
35. **Purple Hairstreak.** Female. Purple patch of the forewings is shown shaded with single lines. The purple of the male is more suffused. The underside is grey. Not very common.
36. **Black Hairstreak.** Female. The orange patch of the forewings is absent in the male. Dark brown in colour. Rather uncommon and local.
37. **White Letter Hairstreak.** Male. The pale spot of the forewings is absent in the female. Nearly black in colour with white "W" on the underside.
38. **Green Hairstreak.** Male. The white mark is absent in the female. Dark brown in colour, green on the underside. Not very common.
39. **Small Copper.** Central portion of forewing and bands of the lower wings burnished copper in appearance. Common in fields. Aberrations are not uncommon.
40. **Silver-studded Blue.** Male. The male is a blackened blue colour, while the female is dark brown with orange crescents at the edges of the wings. Rather local.
41. **Brown Argus.** Not unlike the female silver-studded blue, but darker, with more prominent orange crescents in the forewings.

1201

HOW TO COLLECT BUTTERFLIES AND MOTHS

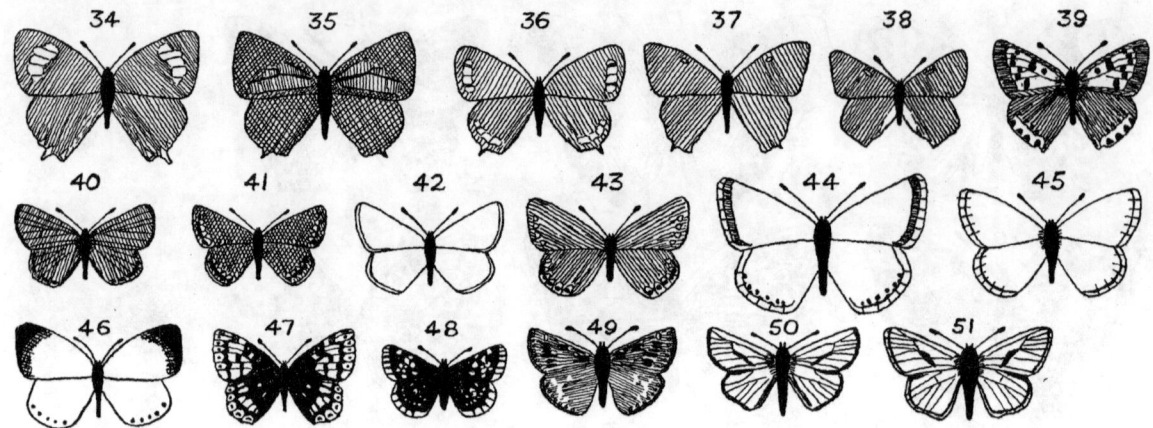

42. **Common Blue** Male. Bright blue in colour, with white silky fringe to wings.
43. **Common Blue.** Female. Brown suffused with blue. Orange crescents, round the black spots. The proportion of blue to brown varies considerably.
44. **Chalk Hill Blue.** Male. Grey-blue satin appearance with white silky fringes to wings. The female is brown with orange crescents at the wing tips. Fairly common in chalk hill districts.
45. **Adonis Blue.** Male. Bright blue with white fringes. The female is brown with orange crescents, principally on the lower wings. Occurs in the south of England. Rather local.
46. **Holly Blue.** Female. The blackened fringe of the male is less marked. Pale blue on the upper side, paler blue with black specks on the underside. Common.
47. **Duke of Burgundy Fritillary.** Female. The lighter patches of brown are smaller in the male. Rather uncommon.
48. **Grizzled Skipper.** Female. The male is lighter in appearance. Very dark brown, mottled with white. Fairly common.
49. **Dingy Skipper.** Very dark brown with borders of white specks on both wings. Fairly common.
50. **Small Skipper.** Male. The oblique black mark on the forewings is absent in the female. Brown with blackened border. Not uncommon in England.
51. **Large Skipper.** Male. The oblique black mark on the forewings is absent in the female. Brown in colour. Common.

Valuable catches are also possible in parks and gardens. The flowering weeds on the fringe of rubbish dumps are also worth a visit.

The partialities of some butterflies are remarkable. For example, the Red Admiral is fascinated by rotten apples, so that it is often to be found feasting on the decaying windfalls in orchards. The Purple Emperor is fond of decaying flesh, and, in fact, it is such a lofty flier that it is difficult to net it by other means.

The Fritillary butterflies are found in and around woods. The varieties such as the Silver Washed and the Dark Green Fritillaries are fast fliers and difficult to net. These butterflies are generally found in the clearings of the wood and not in the shade of the trees.

May to September is the best period of the year for catching butterflies, although if the spring is forward the early species—for example, the Holly Blue, the Whites and Orange Tip—are on the wing in April.

Butterflies are fond of warmth and the sunshine. It is practically a waste of time to go out with the net in dull weather.

Local Species.

Apart from the normal attractions of butterflies, some species are confined to certain localities. The handsome Swallow Tail butterfly is confined to the Norfolk Fens, while the White Admiral is found in the New Forest. Stray specimens are also to be taken elsewhere. The New Forest is the happy hunting ground of collectors. The Purple Emperor and most of the Fritillary butterflies are to be found there in addition to the more common species.

Number of Butterflies.

There are less than sixty different butterflies native to this country. Some are very scarce and difficult to obtain, and the diligent collector may be justly proud if he obtains even thirty-five different British species with his own net.

Netting.

When catching an insect on the wing care must be taken not to frighten it, but to follow it at some distance in the hope that it will settle. The net is brought across the path of the specimen, so that it is forced into the net. The net is then given a sharp turn so that it folds over the frame and traps the butterfly or moth. Do not allow the insect to struggle longer than necessary or it will damage itself, but, if worthy of the collection, close a portion of the net round it and introduce the capture into the mouth of the killing bottle. The bottle is capped while it is still in the net so as to avoid the possible loss of the specimen.

Difference between Butterflies and Moths.

Moths differ from butterflies in several ways. Moths hide and are stupefied in the daytime and fly only at dusk and at dawn. Their anatomy is also different. In contrast to butterflies, moths have, generally speaking, larger bodies and are not so brilliant in colour. The most noticeable differ-

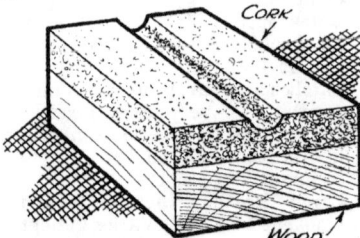

Fig. 3.—THE CORRECT POSITION OF PINNING THE INSECT THROUGH THE THORAX WHEN IT IS MOUNTED FOR SETTING.

Fig. 4.—A SETTING BOARD.
The surface of the board is sometimes saddle-shaped, but a flat board, as shown, is preferable. Three widths are required: 2, 3 and 4 inches. A specially wide board will be occasionally necessary for a goat moth or a death's head hawk moth.

ence is in the feelers, or two horns, which are attached to the head. All butterflies have the feelers distinctly club-shaped, while those of moths end in a point. There are a few exceptions to these rules. Some moths fly by day. The most notable example, likely to be mistaken for a butterfly, is the Six-spotted Burnet, which is a day-flying moth with feelers somewhat club-shaped.

Catching Moths.

It is almost impossible to catch the large moths on the wing, because they dart about rapidly. In the daytime moths are found resting on tree trunks and fences. When located they may be tipped straight into the killing bottle without the use of the net. Moths at rest are not easy to locate. They always choose the shade and a background which artfully mingles with their colouring. After sunset a number of moths can be caught in the net. Flowers are the chief natural attraction. They prefer the dull calm weather, and are found in fields, lanes, woods and gardens. A large number of moths are attracted by a strong light. They will fly in through the open window, and can also be netted round the street lamps. Moths do not fly all through the night. An hour or so after dusk they rest again. Certain moths are more evident just before dawn.

June to September is the best period of the year for catching moths.

Sugaring.

By applying a special sugar mixture to the trunks of trees, a number of moths can be attracted at night-time. The mixture consists of sugar " foots " and rum, mixed with sufficient treacle to make it adhesive. The sugar mixture is smeared on two or three trees in a quiet spot. Do not be disappointed if the catch is small at the first attempt. Sugar the same patch several nights running. Some of the moths are overcome by the rum and fall to the base of the tree. The moths feasting on the sugar patch may be taken without the net after they have settled there for a few minutes. It is worth while to visit the spot early the next morning, in order to collect any remaining stupefied specimens.

Setting.

The material required for setting the specimens consists of setting boards, silvered pins and tracing paper. The silvered pins are used for mounting. Ordinary pins are unsuitable because they corrode.

After removal from the killing bottle the insects must be set as soon as possible, otherwise they will become too stiff. They must not be left overnight.

Of the several methods of setting the wings into position, the band method is recommended. The first step towards setting is to mount the specimen on a silvered pin. The pin is passed through the thorax of the insect, slightly at an angle, as shown in Fig. 3. Next select a setting board large enough to contain the wing span of the butterfly or moth. If the specimen is a small one, a setting board with a small groove is necessary, otherwise the major portion of the wings will not rest on the surface of the board. The mounted specimen is now pinned into the middle of the board groove and its body adjusted for height, so that the underside of the wings are level with the top of the groove. If the wings are closed they are carefully bent down with one of the fine silvered pins and a strip of tracing paper held over them. The wings are arranged into position by means of the same pin or one of the special setting bristles which are sold for this purpose. The wings can be moved into the correct position without injury if the point of the pin is applied to one of the larger veins of the wing at a point near the body. Do not allow the pin to pierce the wings. The colouring matter of the butterfly or moth is due to a large number of minute scales which easily rub off, so that great care is necessary when manipulating the wings under the tracing paper. With the wings in position the paper is pinned in a taut condition. The feelers are set into position by means of ordinary pins.

Setting Upside-down.

It is usual to set specimens with the legs on the underside, but, owing to the beauty of the undersides of some species, many collectors may prefer to set some varieties to show both sides of the wings, when sufficient specimens are available.

Time on Setting Board.

In dry, warm weather the small species are safely dry in a week, but the large specimens must be left on the board for at least a fortnight.

Storing.

The specimens are stored in airtight glass-topped boxes, preferably away from the light. As the collection advances, a cabinet will be necessary if moths and butterflies are kept. Moths are far more numerous than butterflies, and it is not difficult to obtain over 200 different species of them.

HOW TO DEAL WITH IRONMOULD

IRONMOULD or rust spots on material are often very difficult to treat. By far the best plan is to go through a small series of experiments until the mark yields. Often, if one treatment is not successful, another will be. After each method has been tried, wash thoroughly so as to get rid of all traces of the substance used before applying anything fresh.

Lemon Juice and Salt.

Lemon juice and salt may be applied and the article then placed in the sun for a few hours.

Rhubarb or Begonia Leaves.

If this does not act, cut up a stalk of rhubarb and boil in a cup of water for about an hour. Then steep the marked place in the solution. Begonia leaves boiled in a little water will also give a rust-removing liquid.

Hydrochloric Acid and Water.

If none of these plans clear away the mark, hydrochloric acid should be tried. Get a chemist to make up a solution of equal parts of the acid and water. In just a few cases the mixture might affect coloured stuff, and it is well to apply a little of the solution by way of a test on some out-of-the-way part of the material. If the result is satisfactory try the mixture on the rust stain.

How to use the Acid.

The best way to do this is to spread the material over a bowl of steaming water and then drop on to the stain the diluted acid. When the mark turns a bright yellow colour dip into hot water and rinse thoroughly. In all probability the mark will disappear. Rinse several times so as to get away any acid that may be in the fabric. In the case of very delicate fabrics it is a good plan to add a little borax to the last rinsing water so as to neutralise any acid that might be on the cloth.

Making a Settee from a Motor Seat

When a large private car is converted for other purposes, the rear seat, that is the cushion and the upholstered back or squab, are no longer required. These two items, being of little value to the coachbuilder, may be purchased cheaply, but they are usually luxuriously made, and will make a comfortable settee for home use if a frame is made for them.

General Description.

The settee shown in Fig. 1 is made from a motor cushion and back. The only upholstery to be done consists of padding and covering the two arms, one of which is hinged so that the settee may be used as a lounge. Figs. 2 to 5 show the general arrangement and leading dimensions. The dimensions may be varied to suit the size of the motor seat available. In this instance the cushion is 4 feet long, 11 inches thick in front, and 1 foot 9 inches wide. The seat back is 4 feet long and measures 2 feet from top to bottom.

Types of Cushions and Backs.

The framework is designed for a cushion and back which is already made up on a wooden foundation or framework. If the cushion is not so made, that is, it has a linen or other flexible foundation, then a seat board is required to cover the bottom of the settee. When the cushion has a wooden base, boarding is necessary at the back of the cushion in order to make up the difference in width of the cushion and settee. In some cars the back or squab is made up into the framework of the body, and it has no boarded foundation. In this instance the webbing, to which the back springs are attached, is fastened to the framework of the back of the settee.

Timber required.

The settee frame is made of birch or other available hardwood with boarding of selected deal. The following is a list of the timber required:—

One front leg: $3'' \times 1\frac{1}{4}'' \times 2' 6''$.
One front stump leg: $3'' \times 1\frac{3}{4}'' \times 1' 1''$.
Two back legs: $3'' \times 1\frac{3}{4}'' \times 3' 4''$.
Two top arm rails: $2\frac{1}{4}'' \times 1\frac{1}{4}'' \times 2' 8''$.
One bottom arm rail: $2\frac{1}{4}'' \times 1\frac{1}{4}'' \times 2' 5''$.
One top end rail: $2\frac{1}{4}'' \times 1\frac{1}{4}'' \times 2' 5''$.
One bottom arm rail: $2\frac{1}{4}'' \times 2\frac{1}{2}'' \times 2' 5''$.
Two bottom end rails: $2\frac{1}{4}'' \times 1\frac{1}{4}'' \times 2' 3''$.
One front seat rail: $2\frac{1}{4}'' \times 1\frac{3}{4}'' \times 4' 10''$.
Three bottom cross rails: $1\frac{3}{4}'' \times 1\frac{1}{4}'' \times 2' 3''$.
One top back rail: $3\frac{1}{2}'' \times 1\frac{3}{4}'' \times 4' 10''$.
One middle back rail: $2\frac{1}{2}'' \times 1\frac{3}{4}'' \times 4' 10''$.
One bottom back rail: $2\frac{1}{2}'' \times 1\frac{3}{4}'' \times 4' 10''$.
One centre back batten: $3'' \times 1'' \times 2' 8''$.
Three arm posts: $3'' \times 1\frac{3}{4}'' \times 1' 6''$.
Two end platform boards: $2\frac{3}{8}'' \times \frac{3}{4}'' \times 2' 5''$.
Two end platform boards: $5\frac{1}{4}'' \times \frac{3}{4}'' \times 2' 5''$.
Two end platform boards: $7\frac{1}{2}'' \times \frac{3}{4}'' \times 2' 5''$.
Two end panels: $8\frac{1}{2}'' \times \frac{3}{8}'' \times 2' 5''$.
Two front panels: $6'' \times 2'' \times \frac{3}{8}''$.
One seat board: $5'' \times \frac{1}{2}'' \times 4' 10''$.

Front Legs and Arm Posts.

There is one front leg 2 feet $5\frac{1}{4}$ inches long when finished for the fixed end (Fig. 6) and one stump leg, also three arm posts for the hinged end of the settee (Fig. 7). The stump leg which is a continuation of the arm post is 12 inches long and the arm posts are 1 foot $5\frac{1}{4}$ inches long. These five pieces are planed to the finished cross section of $3 \times 1\frac{3}{4}$ inches, and have a rebate $\frac{3}{8}$ inch wide and $\frac{7}{8}$ inch deep, which runs around the top of the leg and arm posts, and is continued to within $3\frac{3}{4}$ inches of the bottom of the legs (Figs. 6 and 7).

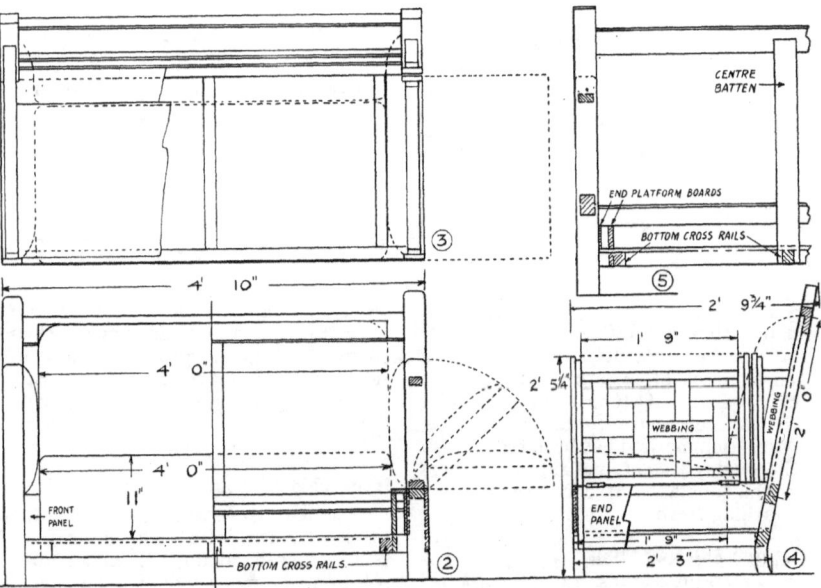

Fig. 1.—This Comfortable Settee, which seats Three Persons, is made from a Motor Car Cushion and Upholstered Back.

After making the wooden frame, the only upholstery required is for the arms, one of which is hinged so that the settee may be used as a lounge.

Figs. 2–5.—Details and Dimensions of the Framework.
(2) Front of settee. The left-hand half shows the upholstery in position, and the right-hand half the framework with dotted lines indicating the position of the upholstery and the adjustment of the arm; (3) plan of settee framework; (4) end view of framework; (5) portion of back framework.

MAKING A SETTEE FROM A MOTOR SEAT

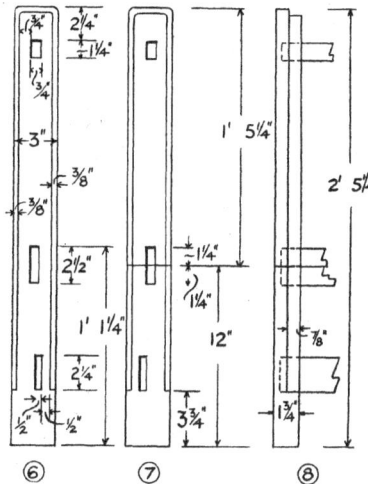

Figs. 6–8.—DETAILS OF FRONT LEGS.

(6) Position of leg mortises; (7) position of mortises in stump leg and hinged arm; (8) end view of stump leg and hinged arm.

of all the end rails, also the correct angle for the bevelled shoulders of the tenons where they enter the mortises of the back legs. Top arm and bottom arm rails, also a bottom end rail are required for the fixed end. For the hinged end the top arm rail is cut into a long portion tenoned into the two arm posts, and a short portion tenoned into the fixed arm post and back leg. At the bottom of the hinged arm there are two rails which together are the same size as the bottom arm rail of the fixed end. The upper of these two rails is tenoned into the hinged arm posts and the lower one is tenoned into the front stump and back legs.

Fixed End Assembly.

With a supply of glue ready to hand, drive the tenons of the three rails into the front leg (Fig. 15), and then drive on the back leg (Fig. 16). When assembled it will be found that the rails are recessed $\frac{3}{8}$ inch on the inside from the full width of the legs. Into the outer recess is fitted a $\frac{3}{8}$-inch panel which extends from the centre line of the bottom arm rail to the lower edge of the bottom end rail (Figs. 15 and 16).

Hinged End Assembly, First Stage.

The fixed portion of the hinged end assembly is made up first (Fig. 17). To make up the substance of the bottom arm rail a piece of wood is butted between the arm post and back leg and screwed to the rail below it. The top end rail is marked and cut out for the flaps of a pair of $2\frac{1}{2}$-inch butt hinges.

Hinged End Assembly, Second Stage.

The hinged end assembly is completed by making up the hinged frame of two arm posts with their top and bottom rails (Fig. 18). The bottom arm rail is recessed for the hinges to correspond with the rail of the fixed portion. Allow $\frac{1}{4}$ inch between the

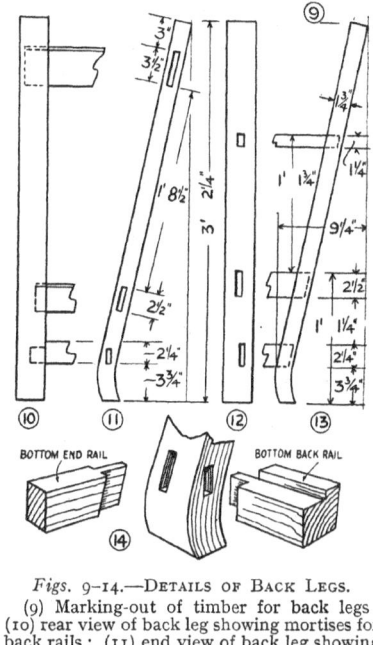

Figs. 9–14.—DETAILS OF BACK LEGS.

(9) Marking-out of timber for back legs; (10) rear view of back leg showing mortises for back rails; (11) end view of back leg showing mortises for back rails; (12) front view of back leg showing mortises for end rails; (13) end view of back leg showing mortises for end rails; (14) back leg mortises for bottom end and bottom back rails.

fixed and movable arm posts as working clearance.

Front and Back Rails.

The two end assemblies are connected by one front and three back rails. All these rails are the same length between the shoulders and all are rebated for the seat and backboards. The middle of each back rail is cut for the lap of the centre batten.

Front Seat Rail.

The front seat rail is finished $2\frac{3}{4} \times 1\frac{3}{4}$ inches with the larger dimension placed vertically. The back of the rail is rebated $\frac{3}{4}$ inch wide and $\frac{1}{2}$ inch deep. This provides a bearing for the seat board, the edge of which is concealed from the front of the settee. The back of the rail is also lapped underneath for the three cross rails, which are the full depth of the front rail below the rebate. The position of the cross rails is shown in Fig. 2.

Back Rails.

The top back rail is framed in square with the slope of the back leg, and is rebated on its lower front edge for the top of the back-board. This rebate is $\frac{1}{2}$ inch deep and $2\frac{1}{4}$ inches wide (Fig. 4).

Leg and Post Mortises.

The legs and posts are now marked out for the mortises of the arm and end rails. The position and dimensions of these are shown in Figs. 6 to 8. With the fixed end the bottom arm rail and the top end rail are combined in one piece. At the hinged end there are two separate rails. When marking the mortise for the bottom end rail in the leg and stump leg, it should be remembered that in each instance the mortise is $\frac{1}{2}$ inch from the outside rebate. The top mortise of the stump leg and the bottom mortise of the arms are open on their top and bottom surfaces respectively. Mark out the leg, Fig. 6, first, and then mark out the stump legs and arms from it, afterwards cutting them to their finished length.

Back Legs.

The two back legs with their curved feet are cut out from a piece of timber 3 inches thick and 4 inches wide, as shown in Fig. 9. Each requires three mortises for the end rails, and three mortises for the back rails. The position and size of these mortises are shown in Figs. 10 to 13. The position of the mortises of the bottom end and bottom back rails is shown in Fig. 14. Mark out the two back legs together, also mark for the inside face on each leg so that the mortises are cut on the correct face.

End Rails.

Make a full size drawing of the end of the settee as shown in Fig. 4 in order to ascertain the exact length

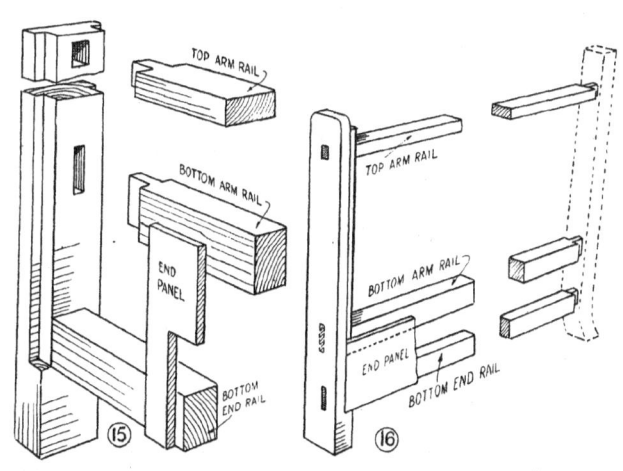

Figs. 15 and 16.—CONSTRUCTIONAL DETAILS AT BACK OF FRONT LEG AND FIXED END ASSEMBLY.

MAKING A SETTEE FROM A MOTOR SEAT

The middle back rail is framed in square with the slope of the back leg (Fig. 4), and has a rebate ½ inch deep and 1½ inches wide for the lower edge of the backboard. The bottom back rail is bevelled at the back flush with the leg, but the other surfaces, also the mortise and tenon, are square with the horizontal line of the bottom rails. The front of the bottom rail has a rebate ½ inch deep and 1½ inches wide for the back edge of the seat board.

Main Assembly.

The main framework of the settee is now assembled. The tenons of the front and three back rails are inserted in their respective leg mortises of one end assembly, after which the other end assembly is secured. The settee frame is turned over on its front face so that the three cross rails may be lapped in position from underneath to the front and back rails.

End Platforms.

The surface at the hinge line of the movable end is extended inwards by means of a small platform. This platform is wide enough to accommodate the thickness of the arm padding, and keeps the cushion in position endwise. A similar platform is made at the other end. Each consists of two boards ¾ inch thick stood edgewise. The outer board is rebated at each end and fastened to the legs (Fig. 20). The inner and wider board is secured to the adjacent cross rail (Figs. 2, 19 and 21). The space between these two boards is covered with a top board and a front panel (Figs. 2, 4 and 21).

Seat Board.

The woodwork is completed with a ½-inch board 5 inches wide, the full length of the cushion placed at the back to make up the difference between the width of the cushion and that of the settee.

Fittings for the Hinged Arm.

When open, the hinged arm is supported by a stay (Fig. 22). This consists of a ⅞ × ¼-inch rod pivoted at its upper end where it is screwed to the fixed arm post. This stay has two or more holes as required for adjustment. The holes in the stay are made to register with the hole in a plate let in flush into the hinged arm post where it is held by a fly-bolt. A small catch (Fig. 23) holds the hinged arm in the closed position.

Polished Wood.

Any parts which are to be finished

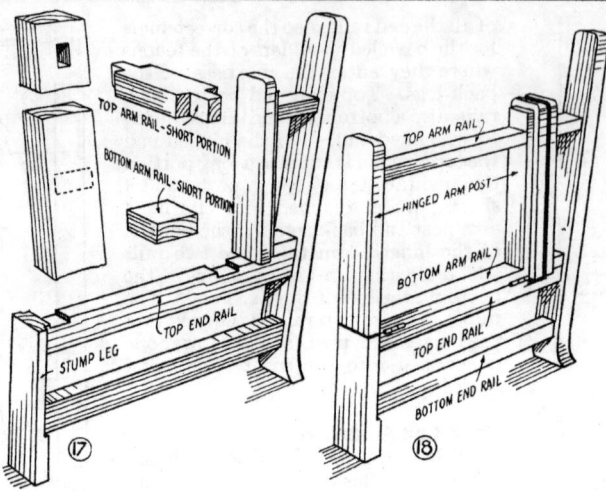

Figs. 17 *and* 18.—Hinged End Assembly; (17) First Stage; (18) Second Stage.

in polished wood, such as the legs, the small front panels and the front seat rail, should be dealt with before beginning the upholstery of the arms.

Webbing the Arms.

Strain two lengths of webbing on the inside of the fixed arm between the top and bottom arm rails. One is close against the back leg and the other is placed centrally (Fig. 24). Fold the end of the webbing and tack it at the bottom, strain at the top and insert two tacks, then fold over the web and add two more tacks (Fig. 25). Fix a web against the leg in a similar

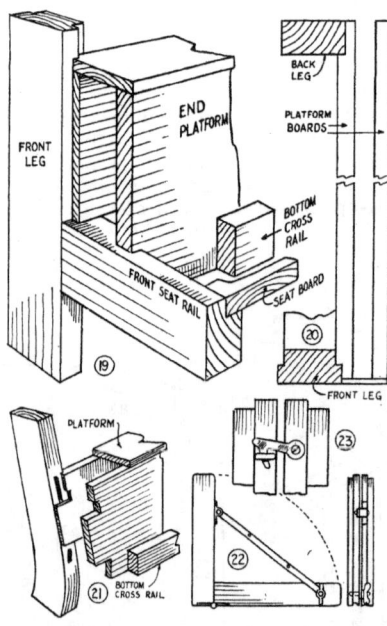

Figs. 19–23.—Details of End Platform, etc.

(19) Constructional details of front of end platform; (20) plan of end platform; (21) constructional details of back of end platform; (22) adjustable stay of hinged arm; (23) catch for hinged arm.

position at the short fixed end, while for the hinged arm three rows of webbing are fixed between the arm posts and four between the top and bottom rails (Fig. 4). About 5½ yards of webbing are required altogether, and the work is facilitated if a web strainer is available.

Canvas Foundation.

The inside of the arms is now covered with hessian canvas. A piece 36 × 18 inches is required for each arm, so that if the material is 72 inches wide, only ½ yard will be necessary. Tack the hessian on the inside of the rail at the bottom of the arm, draw it over the top arm rail and fasten it on the outside. Also tack it in the ⅞ × ⅜-inch recess of the front leg of the fixed arm and in the similar recesses of the arm posts. At the back leg the hessian is sewn to the webbing (Fig. 26).

Stuffing Bridles.

A ball of buttoning or tacking twine is now required, also an upholsterer's bent or curved needle. With the twine and needle, make a series of loops in the hessian along the top rail. Each loop should be just large enough to accommodate the fingers of one hand. Continue with the loops downward parallel with the back leg, then along the bottom, up by the front leg and then add three rows in the centre (Fig. 26). Tie the end of the twine. These loops or bridles help to hold the padding in place. Make loops in the hessian of the hinged arm and one central vertical loop in the small fixed end.

Scrim Covering, First Stage.

Before inserting the hair or other padding its covering of scrim is partly fixed in position (Fig. 26). Scrim is a lighter canvas than hessian, and two pieces about 4 feet × 2 feet 9 inches will be sufficient. The padding, when finished, is about 2 inches thick on the inside and top of the arms (Fig. 27). The scrim should be both long and wide enough to allow for the fullness of the padding. Fold the edge of the scrim and tack it to the rail at the bottom of the arm (Fig. 26). After fixing it at the bottom of the arm, turn it over so that it lies on the seat.

Padding.

Each arm takes about 3 lbs. of fibre or 2½ lbs. of hair. Insert the hair or other padding in the bridles of the hessian (Fig. 28). Arrange the hair so that it is evenly distributed, and have about three times the bulk necessary for the thickness of the padding so as to allow for compression. Now lift the scrim, pull and fasten it temporarily with a few tacks in the centre of the top rail. Then add temporary tacks at each end of the rail. If the fullness is uneven, insert a skewer, or, better still, an upholsterer's regulator, in order to adjust the hair or insert additional material.

Scrim Covering, Second Stage.

In order to keep the stuffing in place, the covering is stitched and tied. A straight needle is required. This is 9 inches long, and has a point and eye at one end and a point at the other, so that it may be used in either direction. With the straight needle and twine insert the needle eye-end first into the scrim and right through to the hessian. Without reversing the needle, insert it in the hessian about an inch away from the first hole and bring it again through the scrim. Make about a 3-inch stitch in the scrim, then take the needle again for an inch stitch in the hessian, and make a series of stitches, working towards the centre as with the stuffing bridles. The first stitch is knotted and then the twine is drawn taut through the series of stitches and fastened with another knot at the end.

Scrim Covering, Third Stage.

The sides and top edge of the scrim are now fastened in the same position as

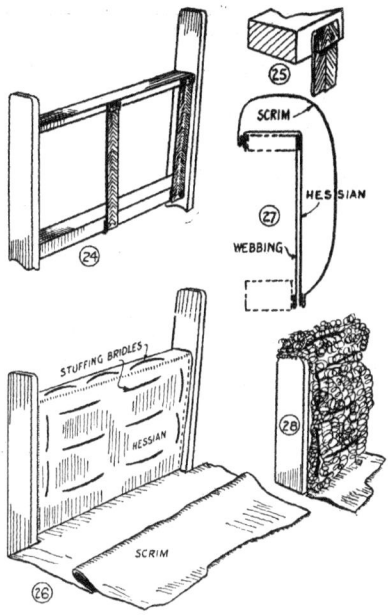

Figs. 24–28.—Final Details.

(24) Position of webs for fixed arm; (25) top end of web folded and tacked after straining; (26) fixed arm covered with hessian and looped for padding. The lower edge of the scrim has been tacked to the bottom arm rail; (27) diagram showing the relative position of webbing, hessian and scrim on the top and bottom arm rails; (28) padding inserted in loops (shown also in Fig. 26) ready for covering with the scrim.

the hessian foundation, that is, tacked in the leg and arm recesses and sewn to the web at the back leg. The work is done by stretching the material evenly parallel with the threads and removing the temporary tacks as the final ones are inserted.

Top Cover.

The final shape is given to the padding by spreading over it a layer of sheet wadding. The material to be used for the cover will depend on that of the existing cushion and back. The cover extends over the top of the arm and down the outer side to the top line of the end panel, or this may be covered also. The tacks holding the edge of the cover are concealed with gimp, or a banding of leather cloth fastened with nails, having covered heads to match.

Covering the Back.

A piece of the covering material is stretched each side of the seat back to cover the space between it and the leg. The whole of the back of the settee is covered with a piece of leather cloth.

A settee constructed on the lines described in this article will make an attractive and useful piece of furniture. No difficulty should be experienced in obtaining a suitable seat from any firm of carbreakers, and the cost of the whole job will be extremely reasonable.

HOW TO USE TRANSFER GRAINING PAPER

A USEFUL form of decoration for walls, doors, etc., consists of using transfer graining papers.

The principle of this type transfer graining method is the printing of the grain pattern with a mixture of colouring matter and glue or other binder, which is soluble in water, so that when the graining paper is moistened with water the glue is softened and allows the colouring matter to be transferred to a prepared surface.

Preparing the Surface to be Grained.

The surface to be grained should be brought up to a suitable colour (light stone colour for oak) with an oil paint, and this should be quite dry and hard before graining is attempted.

Using the Graining Paper.

The method of using the graining paper is to first cut to the size required, then lay on a clean flat surface, pattern side down, and moisten the back of the paper with a damp sponge.

Rub Painted Surface with Mixture of Whiting and Water.

Leave for three or four minutes for the paper to become soft. Whilst the paper is soaking, rub over the painted surface with a mixture of whiting and water; only a thin film of whiting should be left on, and this will provide an even dampness on the painted surface.

Apply the Paper.

Now take up the graining paper, which will appear to have sweated slightly, indicating that the pattern colour has begun to soften, place it carefully on the painted surface, avoiding wrinkles, and brush into close contact with the surface by moderate pressure on the brush.

Peeling off the Paper.

Leave for three or four minutes, then lift one corner to see if the pattern has been transferred; if so, peel off, taking care not to smudge the grain pattern. Should the grain pattern be smudged or otherwise unsatisfactory, it can be sponged off with water, and after applying more whiting the same graining paper used again. Good transfer graining papers can be used four or five times.

"Softening."

Whilst the graining colour is still damp, take a soft paint or duster brush and gently stroke the surface in the direction of the grain; this is called "softening," and considerably improves the result.

Varnishing.

Allow the graining to dry thoroughly, then varnish with a glaze made from varnish tinted with a little burnt umber or other suitable staining colour, according to the type of wood imitated.

This will give a richness and depth to the finish, and provide the correct shade, as the graining papers only produce the dark grain markings and in the intervening spaces the ground colour retains its original shade. The work should preferably be given a final coat of clear varnish.

In the transfer graining method used by craftsmen years ago for hand graining, stale beer was used for "binding" water-colour graining, the sugar in the beer acting as a binder or fixative; modern graining colours, however, are supplied ready bound.

Printing on Fabrics
With Lino or Wood Blocks

In principle, the process of wood or lino printing is neither more nor less than that of ordinary "stick-printing," or of taking an impression from such an improvised surface as the end of a cotton reel dipped in printing-ink or dye, and applied to the fabric.

Making the Printing Block.

In practice, it is possible to use quite large printing surfaces if the substance employed be lino mounted on plywood, or even moderately large-sized blocks up to, say, 12 × 10 inches if the blocks be wood, usually either sycamore, plane or maple, which are cut plank section.

The Design.

Actually an "outline" is first made upon the wood or lino with pencil or brush; it is then sharply cut all round with a knife on the outside or on both sides of this outline, taking care that the cutting *slopes away* from the outline, ordinary wood-carving tools being afterwards used for clearing away the background.

Size of the Block.

Always the size of the block is governed by the width of the material; if, for instance, the cloth is 50 inches wide, then the horizontal repeat will divide into 50 inches, while the vertical repeat may be any convenient measurement.

The process of block printing is one that dates back to the dawn of history, having been used by the Chinese at a very remote period, and later penetrating to the western nations.

Selecting a Suitable Fabric for Printing.

Coming now to the selection of a suitable fabric on which the print may be made; this will prove to be a matter of great importance as the final effect will depend so much on its inherent surface qualities. Material should be chosen for its appropriateness of texture, rough and canvas-like say for a hanging, fine and smooth for a scarf. It is quite likely the same design may look equally well on either texture, but it will certainly look entirely different. It is also possible to print on practically every material from georgette to velvet, including linen, cotton and silk of every quality.

Fig. 1.—Lamb Design printed on a Nursery Hanging.

Balloon fabric is good for trial printing, and takes the dye quite readily. It is also cheap. Russian crash is suitable for work of a bolder description. Casement cloth is pleasant to use, and looks successful when the printing is complete. Perhaps linen is the most used of all. It wears well, looks well, and can be used for almost any finished article, for hangings, summer frocks, bedspreads and table runners. Of the silks crepe-de-Chine is perhaps the most effective; velvet or velveteen gives a very rich effect.

Wash the Material before Printing.

It should be noted in this connection that all material other than velvets should be washed before printing in order to remove all dressing and to flatten the fibres of the cloth.

SETTING OUT THE DESIGN

It has already been noticed that the character of the material and the use to which it is to be put will determine the most appropriate "subject" for the pattern. Yet even more, it will determine the *direction* in which the pattern is to run.

How to run the Pattern.

If for dress material, the pattern would run up and down, so that it may appear the same when inverted; if for hanging spotted, bordered, or sprayed, the pattern will be an "all-over" of a bolder description.

Adopting a Suitable Design.

A sense of richness can be obtained even if the unit be very simple; and at all times the simplest possible design that will satisfy the requirements should be adopted. Remembering that this design is obtained by "repeating" a simple unit by means of a lino or wood block, it is essential not only that that unit should be simple, but that it should be lively and interesting. Above everything else, it should link on properly in a natural manner, where it is repeated. There should be no jerks or breaks.

A Concrete Example.

In order to illustrate these points let an actual case be taken (see Fig. 1). The size of the block was 7 × 4¾ inches. The various stages which led up to its final appearance and the "motifs" which guided the designer were somewhat as follows: first, it was decided the hanging was to be for a nursery, therefore its nature to be gay. Secondly, it might be repeated all-over by one of two methods, viz., by making the block "self-contained" and hence, merely repeating side by side; or repeating as a "drop" alternately, like bricks in a wall, allowing portions of the design to "run over" the edges here and there, into the

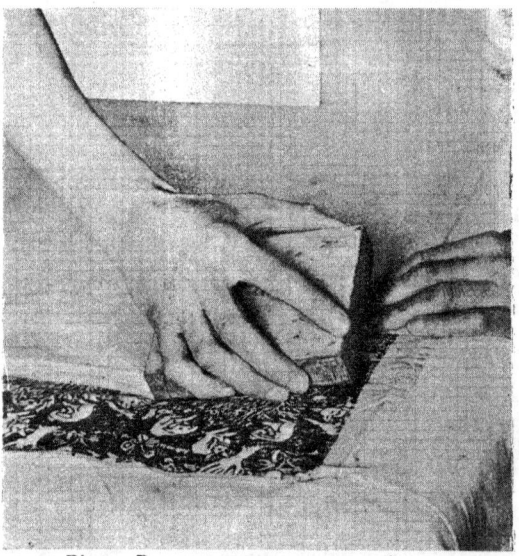

Fig. 2.—Pattern being printed on Silk.
Note the padding on which the fabric is placed for printing.

PRINTING ON FABRICS

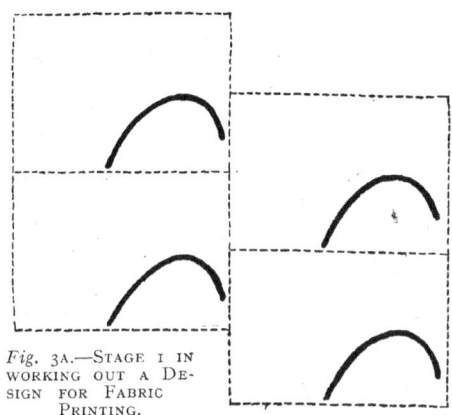

Fig. 3A.—Stage 1 in working out a Design for Fabric Printing.

next repeat, if this were felt to be desirable. This makes the design somewhat more involved, and requires the most careful "linking up" with the next repeat. In the end the latter method was adopted.

Designing a Nursery Hanging.

As it was essential for the design to be gay and attractive for children, lambs sportively frisking about were chosen as the theme. To give expression to this idea of leaping motion in line, an "upward curve" was adopted as the first "action line." (see Fig. 3A).

Stage 2.—This curve by itself would, by running only in one direction, have been too insistent. The eye must be attracted slightly away from the main theme by "opposing" lines (Fig. 3B).

Stage 3.—The attention will now be apt to stray out and away from the main theme, so must be brought back by a "returning line" (Fig. 3C).

Stage 4.—Next there is need for repose, so a "steadying" line is added, which later can be translated into the lamb resting on the grass (Fig. 3D).

Stage 5.—Finally the design is worked out in its details, using definite forms to replace single guiding lines: the lambs now become a group, and in order to prevent the overlapping parts being displaced, most careful "registering" was needed (Fig. 4).

Stage 6.—The design is now ready for tracing (Fig. 5).

CUTTING THE BLOCK

The all-important matter of the cutting of the block will now be described. First, there is the "transferring," by means of tracing paper.

Transferring the Design to the Block.

Having completed the design, a tracing is then prepared from the drawing to transfer to the block. The drawing may, in order to give an idea of its final appearance, have been executed in white on black paper, or the blacks filled in solidly on a white ground.

The most convenient way of transferring the drawing to the block is : (1) to make a good accurate tracing of the outline ; (2) Put a carbon paper or tissue paper rubbed over with red powder between the tracing paper and the block, which are securely fixed down to the corners, care being taken not to injure the surface of the block in any way ; (3) Go over the lines with a hard pencil. Then when the tracing paper is removed, the design will be seen to show up black or red. If necessary the block

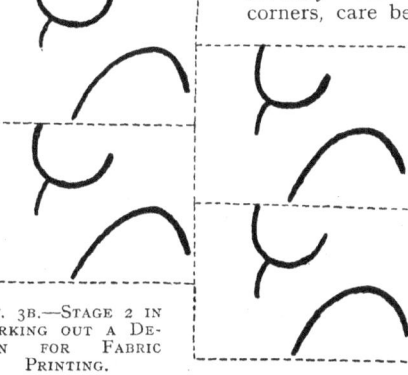

Fig. 3B.—Stage 2 in working out a Design for Fabric Printing.

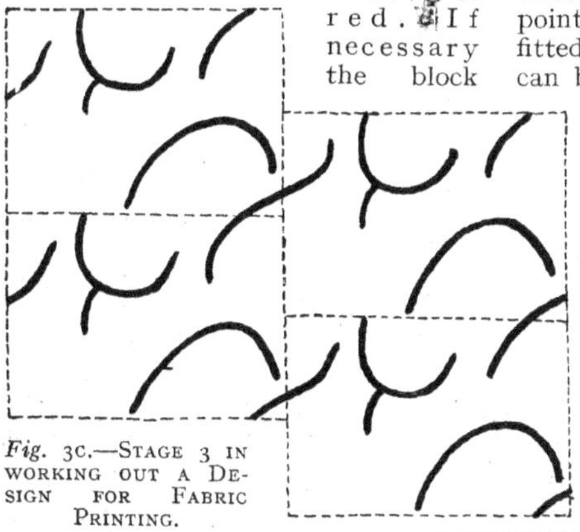

Fig. 3C.—Stage 3 in working out a Design for Fabric Printing.

could first be covered with a thin coating of white paint, so that the tracing is more apparent ; or with a coating of black, in which case the transfer paper would have to be a white one, using powdered chalk for the purpose.

It follows from the above that the design will be either in the form of a black silhouette on a white ground, or a white design on a black ground, or a combination of the two methods, or merely a design in outline, but in any case it should be *bold* and *definite* in character. It is ap-

parent therefore that in the first instance the *surface* of the block is lowered in every part not intended to print, and in the second that the *pattern* is cut away, leaving the background to print.

Cutting the Block.

With the "cutting" knife an incision is first made all round the outlines and any other portion to be left standing. This deep cut will slope *outwards away* from the line. This forms a buttress and protects the design. from the force of the mallet-stroke in the printing. This cut is next met by one sloping in the opposite direction, so that there will be a V-shaped channel all round the design. The low parts are then cleared away with a gouge and mallet, and such parts should be cut *deeply* so that the white parts of the design may print cleanly.

When the printing is done, these low parts must be carefully watched to see that the dye does not collect in them, or splashing will result. To remedy this the block must either be wiped each time with a rag, or be cut away more deeply. It is necessary when planning and cutting the design to see that the extreme corners are left standing to form *points of "Registration."* Though forming *parts of the pattern* they should be quite unobtrusive ; otherwise artificial points or metal pins will have to be fitted at the corners. This, however, can be avoided by adopting the first method.

Flocking the Block.

When the block has been cut and is ready for printing, an adhesive mordant or anything in the nature of a varnish may be painted over it, or rolled over it by a squeegee. A thin layer of wool dust is then sprinkled over it with a sprinkler (*e.g.*, a pepper-pot), and then left to dry. The next day the process is repeated ; surplus flock is brushed off, and the block is ready for the dye

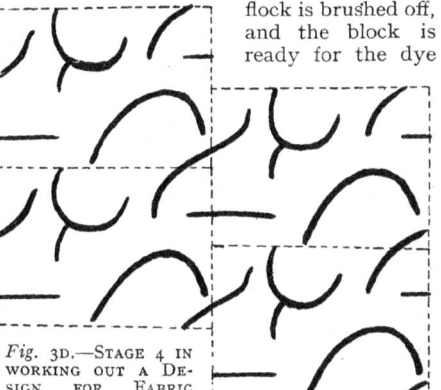

Fig. 3D.—Stage 4 in working out a Design for Fabric Printing.

printing to begin. Should printers' ink known as "Fabric Ink" be used instead of dye, flocking is unnecessary.

In Fig. 6 will be seen two sets of blocks from different points of view. The one on the left has its ground cut deeply away, and is of wood. The one on the right has more shallow grooves and is in lino.

Tools for Cutting and Their Use.

The tools for cutting comprise mallet, clamp for holding block to table, various chisels and gouges, and cutting knife. Two small lino cutting tools, and a "pen" lino tool, with detachable nib, which cannot be sharpened. Tools are kept keen by an oil-stone (India, Turkey, Arkansas, Washita or Carborundum), and should be kept well-oiled in a baize tool-case with separating divisions. The tools consist, therefore, of the following.

Knife.

Usually *pushed* rather than *dragged*, and is bevelled to allow for the production of the "buttress."

Gouges.

These are hollow, deep, and V-shaped and vary in size according to the treatment desired. Those for lino are set in a short handle, so that the ball of the handle can be forced along by the palm of the hand; and those for wood are set in a longer handle, as the tool is usually forced along by the blows of a mallet.

Chisels.

These are used with the mallet for deep indentations and clearing. The fan-shaped tool is used as a chisel with the mallet for outlines, in place of the knife, when the wood is hard.

Mallet.

That for the block cutting is usually entirely of beech-wood; that for the printing has a head of steel (covered sometimes with felt), and *shaft end* padded with leather. It is this padded end (and not the head), which is used for tapping the block, so that all the weight of the force of the blow comes from behind the hand. The mallet itself weighs 2 lbs. To strike with the head would cause vibration, and a double impression would occur.

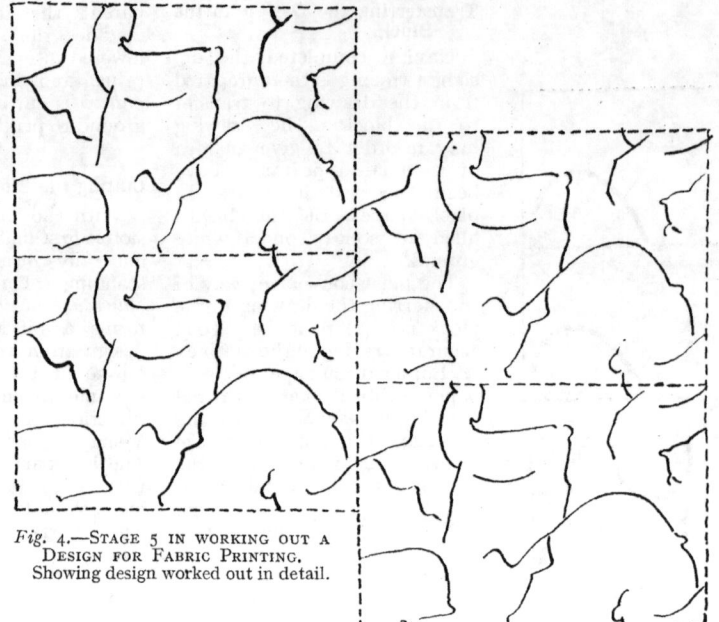

Fig. 4.—Stage 5 in working out a Design for Fabric Printing. Showing design worked out in detail.

Dye Recipes for Printing.

Dyes differ according to the material to be printed upon; a different dye would be used for cotton from that used for silk. Below are the recipes:—

For silk, artificial silk, crepe-de-Chine or velvet, mix :

Dye	1 part.
Glycerine	1 ,,
Gum trag	18 parts.
Acetic acid (40 per cent.)	4 ,,
Water	9 ,,

Boil until smooth, thoroughly cool, then add :—

Tartaric acid	1 part.
Water	2 parts.
Acetic tannic	4 ,,

For cotton :—

Dye	1 part.
Starch (wheat)	1 ,,
Gum trag	5 parts.
Acetic acid (30 per cent.)	3 ,,
Water	20 ,,

Boil, cool, and add :—

Tartaric acid	½ or ¼ part.
Acetic tannic	2 parts.

PRINTING

Everything is now in readiness for the actual process of printing to begin. The first essential is a good solid table.

Preparing the Table.

This must be firm and level or the block will print unequally in some places, and it is an advantage if the foundation be of stone or slate. There are two successful methods of setting up the table.

Padding the Table.

Upon any ordinary kitchen table place the padding, which is to consist of four or five thicknesses of felt or blanket. Household blankets will do. This padding is to give a spring to the printing, and to help to drive the dye into the fibres of the material. Over this place the backing cloth. The surface of the table is now ready to receive the material, the padding being movable. As each length of material is printed, the felt is moved along, so that repinning is obviated.

Another Method of Padding.

Pad the table top with felt or blanket, or horsehair, so that the padding is the same size as the table top. Stretch a piece of American cloth tightly across the felt, and pin to under-edge of table. Sometimes a wooden beading runs all round the table. The American cloth has the advantage of being washable, and it makes a good smooth surface. In this case the backing cloth is pinned upon

Fig. 5.—The Design is now ready for Tracing.

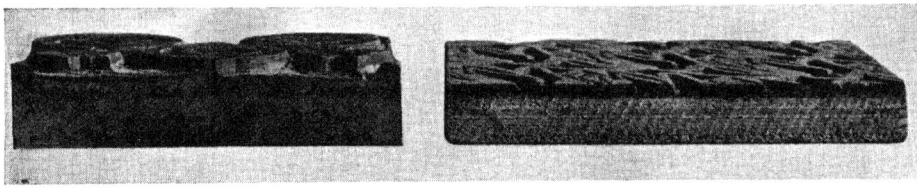

Fig. 6.—Designs cut on Blocks for Printing on Fabric.
On the left is a wood block deeply cut; on the right a lino cut, the lino being attached to a wood block.

the table and, lastly, the material to be printed. If the table be a large one the material will not have to be repinned many times, though with a small one, of course, it will need constant repinning. The two methods are equally popular.

It is necessary also to be very accurate in pinning the material on to the "backing," and through a thickness or two of blanket. The folds in the material or the selvedge should be used to get a straight edge, and it is advisable to mark with a "T" square a faint pencil line at right angles to the selvedge. The material which is about to be printed will already, if it is not a velvet, have had the dressing first washed out of it. Other preparations will include on a small table near by a dye-pad made of blanket or absorbent material if dye be used, or a tube of fabric-ink, roller and glass slab, if ink be used. As already mentioned the actual "banging" of the block is accomplished by two or three sharp strokes with the leather-padded end of the mallet.

Making the Printing Pad.

A large block of wood, about 9 inches × 1 foot 6 inches long, should be covered with several layers of blanket or felt, over which a piece of American cloth has been stretched and fixed, and outside this again a piece of coarse-grained absorbent cloth or blanket carried well over and down the sides. The dye is brushed over this in all directions by a large flat brush, about 2 inches wide, and the block is charged from this surface by pressing it well, face downwards, first in one direction and then in another. Not too much dye should remain on the surface of the block (see Figs. 7 and 8).

Printing on Cotton—Special Treatment.

When printing on cotton, after washing and drying it as usual, it is generally necessary to soak it further in oleine oil, then thoroughly dry and iron before commencing to print.

Methods of Printing.

In passing it is worth while taking note of the four chief methods of printing. These are known as:—

Direct Printed Style.

The colour is applied directly to the fabric by printing, then steamed and fixed.

Dyed Style.

A thickened mordant is applied by printing the fabric after receiving its colour by dyeing.

Discharge Style.

The cloth is printed with a substance capable of removing a dyed ground, or mordant, leaving the natural cloth in its place.

Resist Style.

This is the reverse of discharge. It consists of printing some substance that prevents the fixation of any colouring matter or mordant, subsequently applied to the cloth.

Trial Experiment with the Block.

Mark the top of the block "top," charge it with dye and try it out two or three times on a spare piece of material or newspaper, to get it into good working order.

Printing—The Process in Detail.

This will be most usefully followed by studying Figs. 2 and 7 to 10, while reading the descriptive notes.

The process is continued at each repeat, taking the greatest care to get the "registering" correct, until the whole surface is covered.

Printing in Two or More Colours.

Should the design be in more than one colour and therefore made up of several blocks (one for each colour), the first print must be allowed to dry thoroughly before adding the next.

AFTER PRINTING

Drying the Fabric.

The fabric is dried by pinning it to a wall, or hanging it in the open. It may then be folded.

Making the Dye Permanent.

A dyed material will not be fast to light or resist wet unless it is first "steamed" and "fixed." Let the printed material be rolled in a cloth in such a way that no two parts of the article are exposed or touch one another. An outer cloth is wrapped round the bundle, which is placed on a wire sieve or any gadget that will raise the bundle several inches from the bottom of a dustbin-shaped steamer, or even of a covered pail (for small things), containing a sieve. The underside of the sieve may be covered with

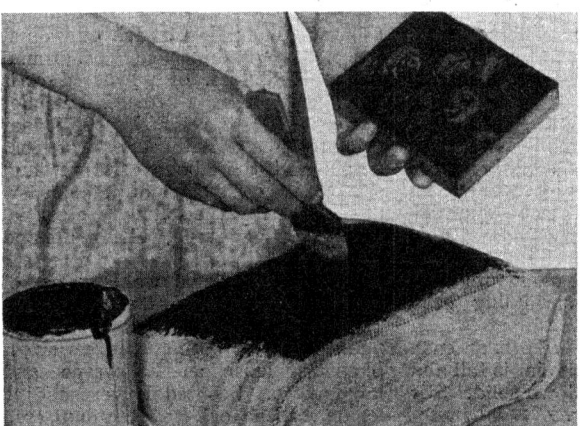

Fig. 7.—Charging Pad with Dye.

Fig. 8.—Charging Block with Dye in Readiness for Placing on Fabric.

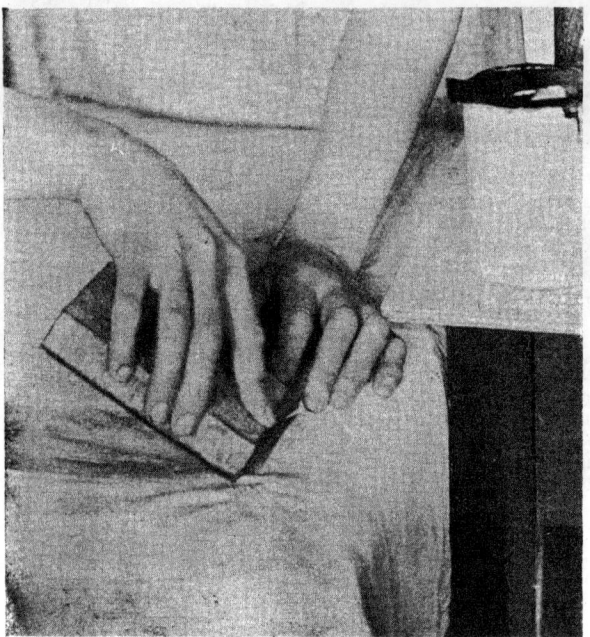

Fig. 9.—Block being placed in Position on Fabric.
Make sure the block is correctly registered before placing on the material.

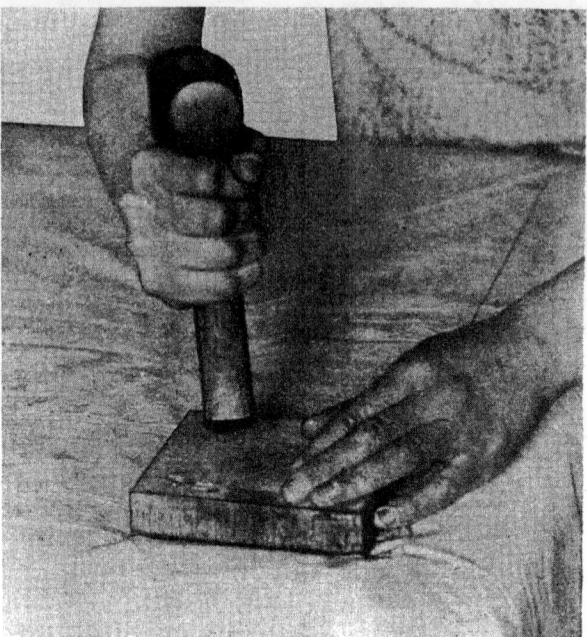

Fig. 10.—Block being struck by Two or Three Sharp Taps on the Back.
The lifting of the block revealing the printed impression is shown in Fig. 2.

felt; and a piece of felt or grease-proof paper may be placed on top of the bundle to protect from condensation. The water in the bottom of the steamer must be well away from the article, so that none of the bubblings splash up; and on no account must the bundle touch the sides of the steamer, also on account of condensation.

The material may be steamed for an hour or more, and at the end of that time it is taken out and shaken briskly and quickly. The final airing should be given in the open, if possible.

Final Process—Fixing.

This is the final process immediately following the steaming as given above. The reason for "fixing" is to make the soluble lakes of dye insoluble.

Fixing Bath.

First, the material is wetted in cold water and then plunged into the fixing bath, as follows:—

1 oz. tartar emetic (dissolved in hot water).
10 pints cold water.
1 oz. calcium carbonate.

It is the tartar emetic that makes the dye insoluble and penetrates the fibres of the cloth. The material should be well moved about in the bath and then rinsed in cold water. It is next washed in hot soapy water, 60 per cent., causing the surface dye that has not been made fast to the fibres of the cloth to come out, together with the remainder of the gum. When no more dye appears to be coming out it is rinsed in several changes of cold water, and dried without too much wringing. It should be dried out of doors in warm air if possible. The dyeing is now quite permanent. A gloss may be given to silk by adding a little glycerine to another rinsing of water; and to cotton by adding starch, the material afterwards being ironed.

All the materials required can be obtained from Messrs. T. N. Lawrence, 1–3, Red Lion Passage, London, E.C.4.

HOW POT POURRI IS MADE

THIS is a very simple but effective Pot Pourri to make. Select the best petals of about one dozen roses or more, as desired, and add any other flower petals that are scented. Place them on an old tray, and sprinkle with table salt; leave them in the sun to dry, turning them over occasionally.

When quite dry, place the mixture in a box with:—

3d. of powdered orris root.
3d. of lavender flowers.
The peel of a lemon chopped quite fine.
1 teaspoonful of mixed spice.
1 dozen cloves.
6d. of eau-de-Cologne.

This mixture will be greatly improved with the addition of a few drops of attar of roses.

Keep well mixed, and preserve in a box, keeping the lid tightly fixed. Take out small quantities of the Pot Pourri as required, to freshen up the existing supply.

Another Mixture.

Another mixture, slightly more elaborate, which has a delightful perfume, is as follows: Select a quantity of rose petals, place them on a table in the shade for an hour or two. Arrange them in ½-inch layers in a large covered jar, sprinkling each layer with salt. Add fresh petals each day, with a sprinkling of salt on each layer of ½ inch, until the jar is full and the contents pressed down solid. Stir thoroughly every day.

Leave for ten days after the last addition, and then mix together in a separate dish: ¼ oz. each of ground mace, cloves and allspice, ½ oz. ground cinnamon, 2 ozs. of powdered orris root, and ¼ lb. of dried lavender flowers. Fill the Pot Pourri jar or dish with alternate layers of rose petals and the above mixture, and sprinkle on each layer of petals a few drops of one of the following essential oils—rose, geranium, bitter almond and orange flower.

Sprinkle over the whole 1 oz. of any good lavender water or eau-de-Cologne. Its strength may be maintained by adding various sweet blossoms such as heliotrope and mignonette. Scented leaves such as lemon verbena, oak-leaf geranium, etc., may be added and are a welcome addition.

Making a Lady's Workbox

THE trend of modern furnishing design is such that not even "my lady's" workbox can be allowed to detract from the general appearance of a room, and to meet this tendency a handsome lady's workbox can be made in polished oak. The finished box stands 5¾ inches high, is 16 inches long and 9 inches in width. Inside is a tray 1½ inches deep and divided into eight sections. This tray fits into the top of the box and leaves ample room underneath for the larger articles and materials necessary for the woman's sewing work.

Wood Lengths required.

Oak, 4 feet 6 inches × 5½ × ⅜ inches; 6 feet × 1½ × ¼ inches; 15 × 2½ × ¼ inches.
Two fillets, 8½ × ½ × ⅜ inches.
Oak-face ply, 16 × 9 inches.
Ply, 16 × 9 inches; 15 × 8 inches.
⅛-inch beading, 4 feet × ⅝ inch.

Sundries.

Two chromium-plated case clips, two designed (or plain) brass back-flap hinges, one chromium-plated bar-pull and four domes or rubber feet.

Preparing Front, Back and Sides.

Cut two lengths of oak for the front and back (16 inches) and two lengths for the sides (9 inches), dovetail-joint the corners and glue. Next fix the oak-faced plywood to the top and the ordinary plywood to the bottom, using ¾-inch fine pins, which must be punched slightly below the surface, and glue. The corners can then be rounded off with a small plane and cleaned with glasspaper.

The Lid.

To cut the lid, set a gauge to 1¼ inches, gauge from the top and saw off with a fine saw. If no gauge is available, the box should be marked 1¼ inches from the top before the corners are rounded. After sawing,

Fig. 1.—The Completed Workbox with Lid Closed.

plane the rim of the body in order to level and thus ensure that the lid fits evenly, then glue and pin the beading along the inside so that it overlaps the top by about ⅛ inch.

Making the Tray.

Now we come to the making of the

Fig. 2.—The Workbox open, showing the Tray.

tray which is to form the top of the box, and for this purpose the strip of oak is used. Cut this into lengths to fit the inside of the box (approx. 15 × 8 inches) and dovetail the corners. Cut grooves in the sides to divide the width into two and the length into four even sections (see Fig. 4) and then pin the plywood to form the bottom.

Halving Partition.

Cut three lengths of oak 8¼ inches; cut each away in the centre to form groove (see Fig. 4) for halving partition and glue into their respective positions. For the centre partition, take the piece of oak 15 × 2½ inches, reduce to 14¾ inches, shape it to the centre and cut to give shaped hand grip, also making three grooves in bottom edge to fit corresponding grooves on the cross partitions (see Fig. 4).

Fillets for the Tray.

Now screw the two fillets, using ⅝-inch screws, on the inside ends of box and 1½ inches from the top. These will carry the tray.

Staining and Polishing.

The box now is ready for staining and polishing, after which screw the back-flap hinges on to the box, using ⅜-inch brass screws. Place the lid in position—the beading will hold it firm—and attach hinges to the back.

Fixing the Clips.

The clips can then be screwed on the front, about 2 inches from edge, using ⅜-inch nickel-plated screws. Bore holes in front centre of lid for the bar-pull, place this in position and fix with the nuts as supplied with the pull. To complete the box, fix a dome in each corner underneath the box.

If the box is to stand upon a polished surface, rubber feet should be used instead of domes.

A workbox such as this will form an extremely useful adjunct in the home, besides being attractive in appearance. Especially useful is the tray in which all the smaller sewing requisites can be kept in separate compartments.

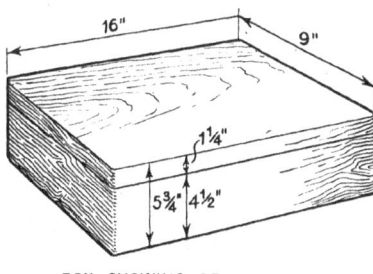

Fig. 3.—Constructional Details for Workbox.

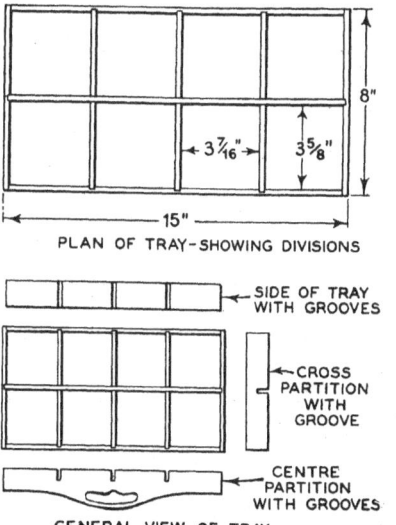

Fig. 4.—Details of the Tray.

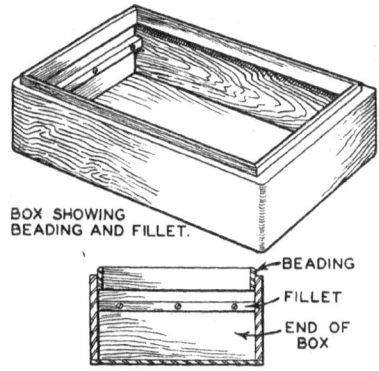

Fig. 5.—Diagram showing the Beading and Fillet.

Making a Motor Trailer Caravan

THE best way to make a caravan to be towed behind any motor car is first to acquire a trailer chassis with wheels, tyres and brake gear complete. There are several types. One known as the model CC8, supplied by Messrs. F. Boddy & Son, Engineers, Boroughbridge, Yorks., is inexpensive, but especially adapted to the purpose. It is supplied with wheels shod with Dunlop 27 × 4·00-inch tyres, the framework measures 5 feet long, 3 feet 6 inches wide, and is made throughout of channel and angle steel.

Automatic brakes—working when the car is slowed down—and a compensated spring-leaded coupling gear are also provided.

The First Step.

First bolt the coupling gear to the rear of the car frame, then couple up the trailer and give the whole outfit a short trial run. Note particularly the forward limit for the caravan body to allow an adequate turning circle for the car; this naturally varies a little with different makes of car.

Light Caravan Body.

Individual requirements will no doubt determine necessary accommodation, but a serviceable caravan giving ample sleeping accommodation for two adults is shown finished in Fig. 1, the working drawings are given in Fig. 2. The main frame bolts directly to the steel chassis and measures 7 feet long, 5 feet 6 inches wide. The body is 5 feet high at eaves, but a little more headroom is obtained at the centre where the roof is upwardly curved. The body could be higher, but then tends to become unwieldy. The lower part is lined inside with ⅛-inch plywood, the upper part is covered with waterproof canvas. The roof is covered with 1/16-inch plywood and canvas; the rear portion of the body is hinged and swings upwards and outwards to form an awning.

A small window is provided at the fore end, two trestle beds are fixed — one each side of the body — while at the front are capacious storage lockers. An electric lighting equipment is also incorporated.

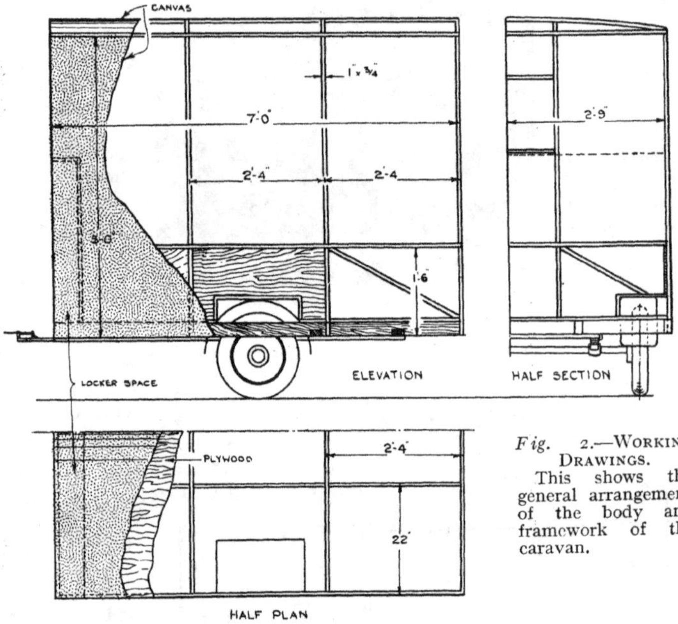

Materials required.

Materials for the caravan body only:—

Main Frame.—Oak, 3 × 2 inches, 3 pieces 5 feet 6 inches long; oak, 3 × 1¼ inches, 4 pieces 7 feet long.

Floor.—Deal, tongued and grooved, 4 × ¾ inch, 23 pieces 5 feet 6 inches long.

Body Framing.—Oak or ash, 1 × ¾ inch, 13 pieces 5 feet long; 8 pieces 7 feet long; 4 pieces 6 feet long, 5 pieces 5 feet 6 inches long; 8 pieces 3 feet long; 2 pieces 3 feet 6 inches long.

Sides.—Birch plywood, ⅛ inch thick, 6 pieces 28 × 16 inches; 2 pieces 33 × 16 inches.

Roof.—Three pieces plywood, 1/16 inch thick, 68 inches long by 28 inches wide.

Covering.—Waterproof canvas, 24 square yards.

Frame Plates.—Steel, 48 "Angles," 18 "Tees."

Bolts and Nuts.—Steel, 3/16 × 1 inch, countersunk heads.

Making the Main Frame.

The main frame consists of three cross members, 3 inches deep, 2 inches thick, which must be securely fastened to the steel chassis by means of steel bolts with "castle nuts" and split pins. The four long members—as

Fig. 1.—The Finished Caravan.
The whole structure is light but strong; easy to make, and is admirable for summer and other holiday making.

Fig. 2.—Working Drawings. This shows the general arrangement of the body and framework of the caravan.

Fig. 3.—Main Frame on Chassis.

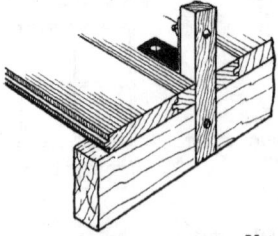

Fig. 4.—Joint between Upright and Frame.

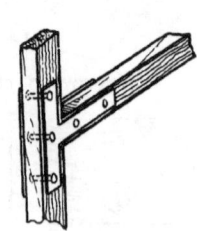

Fig. 5.—Plated Tee Joint.

MAKING A MOTOR TRAILER CARAVAN

Fig. 6.—Brace Joint.
The brace is cut to fit dead tight and is held by thin screws.

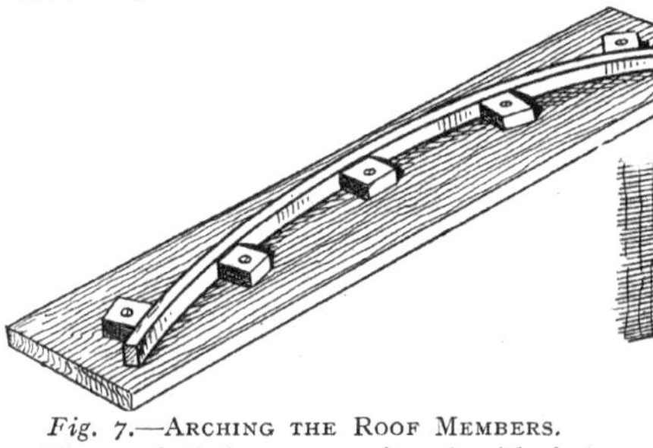

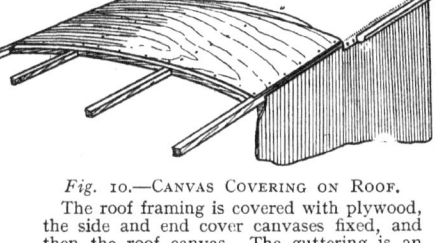

Fig. 7.—Arching the Roof Members.
The roof timbers are softened with hot water, forced into position on the board, and held by the blocks until dry.

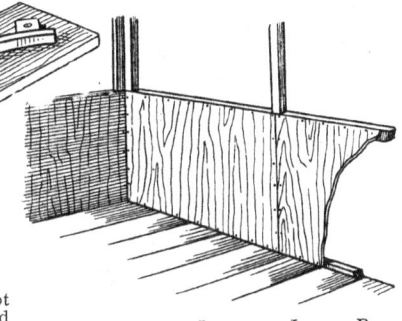

Fig. 8.—Plywood Lining of Lower Body.
Thin plywood sheets are glued and pinned to body framework and to fillets fixed on the floor.

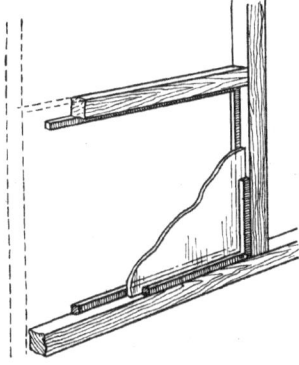

Fig. 9.—Detail of Window.
The opening formed by the body framework is "beaded" and the glass secured by inner beadings—as here shown in part section.

Fig. 10.—Canvas Covering on Roof.
The roof framing is covered with plywood, the side and end cover canvases fixed, and then the roof canvas. The guttering is an optional fitting.

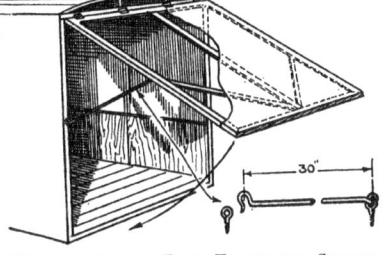

Fig. 11.—Hinged Back Frame and Struts.
A separate canvas-covered frame hinged at the back forms an awning when camping. Iron struts with hook and eye ends act as stays.

seen in Fig. 3—are 3 inches deep, 1¼ inches thick, and are halved to the cross members, glued securely, and strengthened by steel angles screwed in the inner corners.

Next screw or securely nail the floorboards to the main frame, set the boards across the frame; smear all joints with red lead paint before fixing, and leave spaces for the wheels and mudguards.

Building the Body Framework.

All the needful joints must be prepared before the body framework is assembled, but for clarity and conciseness the various joints are here described and illustrated in their order of assembly. There are four uprights at each side, spaced 28 inches centre to centre; the lower ends are glued and screwed, as in Fig. 4, to notches cut in the main frame and floor. The inner angle is then strengthened by a steel angle plate bolted to the upright and screwed to the floor.

The horizontal member, 18 inches up from the bottom, is butted against the end upright members and secured with two steel tee plates bolted on as in Fig. 5. The intermediate joints in the same member and the uprights are halved, glued, screwed and strengthened by a single internal tee plate bolted on. The upper horizontal rails are halved to the uprights, glued, screwed and tee-plated on the inside. The joints on the ends are similarly made. The diagonal braces, shown in Fig. 6, should be a dead tight fit and be glued and screwed.

The roof cross rails are arched

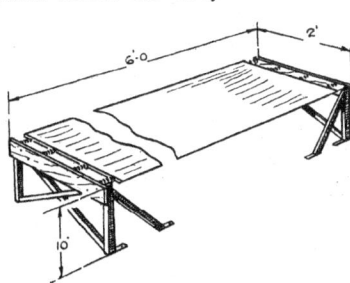

Fig. 13.—Trestle Bed Frames.
The wood framework is bolted to the floor and furnished with a stretched canvas or wire spring mattress.

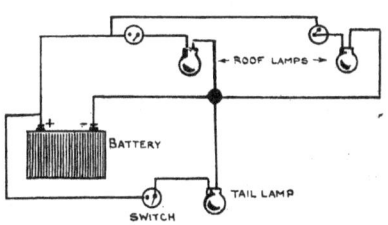

Fig. 14.—Lighting Circuit.
The battery can be recharged from the car lighting dynamo. The circuit provides two internal lights and one tail lamp.

Fig. 15.—Supporting Legs.

Fig. 12.—Locker Construction.
Sectional sketch showing one useful arrangement of lockers built with plywood in the forepart of the caravan. The side compartment covers hinge upwards to form table tops; in the centre are three drawers.

by first thoroughly wetting—preferably with boiling water—and then leaving to dry on a board with blocks, as in Fig. 7, to impart a permanent curvature to them. The roof joints are similar to those at the side; when completed the lower part of the body is covered on the inside with plywood, as in Fig. 8, glued and pinned in place. The window, if required, is then provided with narrow beads around the opening, as in Fig. 9, and glazed when all else is completed.

The whole exterior is then covered with waterproof canvas fastened with rosehead rails, or with clout nails and washers. First cover the sides, then the front end, and finish by covering the roof as in Fig. 10, after having glued and nailed on the thin plywood covering.

A metal "guttering" at each side, arranged to discharge at the front, is a welcome refinement, and has only to be screwed in place at each side of the roof.

The back frame can be built up as a single piece, hinged at the top, as in Fig. 11, and provided with two bolts or staples and hasps to keep it closed and two hook and eye struts to hold it open, when it forms a useful awning.

Making the Lockers.

The lockers are most conveniently built up with ⅜-inch plywood as in Fig. 12, all joints being butted and all internal angles having a triangular fillet glued and pinned in position.

The trestle bed frames can be made of oak, $1 \times \frac{3}{4}$ inch, with 2×1-inch end top cross bars, arranged as in Fig. 13, screwed at all joints and fixed to the floor with angle plates. The wheel openings should be enclosed by light plywood panels.

Electric light is a desirable feature. The best way is to use an accumulator of 6 or 12 volts—corresponding to that on the car—so that it can be charged by the car system. A suitable circuit is given in Fig. 14.

If the caravan is to be used for some time on the same site a set of four struts, as in Fig. 15, should be provided and be bolted to the main frame when needed; they relieve the chassis and body generally of a good deal of strain and ensure complete stability when in camp.

SILVER EFFECTS IN DECORATION

THE increasing use of shining silvery metals, such as stainless steel, for furnishing accessories, door plates, etc., has led to a demand for colour schemes which include elements of silver.

A scheme of silver interior decoration can be carried out by several means. Silver walls or ceiling can be obtained by using silver leaf, aluminium leaf, aluminium paint (made with aluminium powder), or silvered wallpaper.

It should be remembered that real silver leaf, although more expensive than aluminium, is not so satisfactory, because the silver has a tendency to tarnish and turn black. If real silver leaf is used it should be finished with a coat of varnish, but even if this is done it may be found to grow darker in tone and may lose something of its lustre in course of time.

Paint or Foil?

The nature of the surface to be decorated should be the deciding factor in determining whether to use paint or foil. If the wall is rough, consisting of plastic paint, a coarse wallpaper, or other textured surface, aluminium paint will probably give the best result, as the unevenness will cause the paint to catch the light, thereby increasing its brilliance. For smooth surfaces, aluminium leaf applied to a basis of gold size is more suitable.

Materials required.

The materials required for gilding—whether with gold, silver or aluminium foil—are firstly the metal leaf, secondly the oil size referred to later, and lastly a gold-cutting knife, a gilder's tip and cushion, brushes and cotton-wool.

The metal leaf is obtainable in books containing twenty-four sheets or in packets containing fifty extra large sheets, and the prices of the books range from 8d. each upwards.

The gilder's cushion is of leather, and is fitted with a parchment shield or screen, which keeps the draught from the leaf and prevents it blowing away before it is applied.

The gilder's tip is for picking up the finer kinds of leaf, and consists of a piece of cardboard to which hairs are attached in a wide flat shape.

The gold-cutter's knife is characterised by a projecting edge at the back of the blade. When used for cutting metal leaf the knife is used flat, as though to hold the leaf down in position, and a slight pressure on the edge at the back of the blade cuts the leaf.

Lastly, a black camel-hair mop is used for dusting off when the leaf has been applied to the size. This mop is generally set in a quill.

How to apply Aluminium Leaf.

At least two coats of silver-grey flat paint should be used for the groundwork, whether on woodwork or plaster. Allow the paint to dry, then brush on thinly and evenly a coat of oil size, which may be obtained ready mixed at the gold-beater's where metallic foil is purchased. Allow about twenty-four hours for the size to become tacky.

A special gold size known as "French oil size," which dries more rapidly than ordinary oil size, can be used if the work is to be done in a hurry.

When applying gold size evenness is essential. Do not let pools of size form in the crevices of mouldings or in corners or irregularities of the surface. Do not gild too soon before the size has become tacky, or too late when it has nearly dried off.

The aluminium leaf will be obtained in books and should be applied direct to the tacky surface. Hold the book in the left hand, open it and keep the pages back with the thumb of the left hand, the binding of the book being upwards. Then press the metal lightly on to the sticky surface.

Cover a fair surface roughly in this manner and then press the remaining unattached pieces of aluminium on to the work with a large camel-hair mop. A final polish with a wad of cotton-wool should fill up any small missed places and give a nice burnish to the surface.

After about twenty-four hours apply a coat of good varnish, which will give a richer colour to the metal and prevent it looking too grey.

Obtaining a Silver Effect with Aluminium Paint.

Aluminium paint is really one of several metallic bronze powders now used for paintwork and applied in a solution of either gold size and turpentine, or varnish and petrol. It can be sprayed or stippled as well as applied with a brush, and it is possible to get handsome shot or flossed effects.

A new idea in the use of silver-bronze paints is to mix one-third of gold-bronze with two-thirds of bright aluminium. This gives a white golden effect which is both unusual and beautiful, and the resulting mixture also covers better than ordinary coarse aluminium paint.

Choosing and Furnishing a Flat

THE choice of a flat must always depend, in the last resort, on two things: the district in which one wishes to live, and the amount of rent one is prepared to pay. In many parts of the country recent years have seen the erection of numerous and extensive blocks of flats, planned and fitted on progressive modern lines; and at the same time, in every town and suburb, there are older houses which have been converted to accommodate two, three or more families.

If the flat is in a recently built block, one has the advantage of up-to-date planning, perhaps a small roof-garden, central heating, and a communal restaurant. But flats of this up-to-date kind are naturally expensive, and even for a flat consisting of two rooms and a kitchenette, one often has to pay anything from £100 to £150 per annum.

Flats in old houses which have been converted are, as a rule, much cheaper. Often it is possible to get a suite comprising three or four rooms for £50 or so a year, and this fact alone is generally a conclusive argument. Moreover, many flats in converted nineteenth-century houses are extraordinarily comfortable; everything depends on how they are fitted up.

Points to look for when choosing a Flat.

When looking over a flat the following are among the most important points to make sure of:—

(1) Is the flat free from draughts, and do the various rooms get enough sunshine?

(2) Is it quiet? If there is a danger of noisy neighbours, are the walls, floors and ceilings sufficiently insulated against sound?

(3) Are there plenty of cupboards?

(4) Is the kitchen conveniently placed, well fitted and sufficiently light?

(5) Is the flat entirely self-contained, or does one only have the use of a communal bathroom, etc.?

Doorways and Cupboards.

There are flats which seem to be all doorways and no cupboards, and this is certainly a kind to beware of. One has a right to expect reasonable cupboard accommodation in kitchen and bedrooms, and another great advantage is a sitting-room facing south and bedrooms with east windows.

Fig. 1.—The Kitchenette forms an Important Part of a Flat.

Here is a small kitchenette which is really a large cupboard or closet with a small window. Such an arrangement goes a long way to making the smallest flat convenient. (Bowman Bros. Ltd.)

One of the commonest causes of draughts is too many and badly placed doorways, as, for example, where there are old-fashioned folding doors between rooms in addition to the ordinary entrance doors. Sometimes, too, shrunken floor boards or beaver board panelling to walls and ceiling which has shrunk sufficiently to leave cracks between the boards and mouldings, will enable currents of air to enter the room from between floors or from cavity walls.

Any defect of this kind should be made good by the landlord before occupation. If, in addition, the carpet is fitted right against the walls instead of being laid with a surround of bare floor boards, any tendency to draughts will be minimised still further.

Sharing the Bathroom.

It sometimes happens that in an old house which has been converted there is only one bathroom, which is shared by all the tenants. This is an arrangement which is usually found to work satisfactorily if there are not more than three families in the house, but, of course, it is to some extent a disadvantage and should make a difference to the rent.

Practical Notes about the Agreement.

The agreement with the landlord should be for a period of one year or three years, with the option of renewal at the end of the term. A five- or seven-year agreement is rarely desirable, and it is important to make quite sure that the landlord will be responsible for all reasonable repairs, maintenance and redecorations. Unless the premises are in A1 condition, he should redecorate before you take possession, and should allow you to select the colour schemes for each room. In no circumstances is it wise to sign what is called a repairing lease, because this makes one liable for the redecoration and perhaps even the partial rebuilding of the premises on the expiry of the tenancy.

Make sure also that there is no possibility of the rent being increased at any time before the expiry of the lease, and that there are no unreasonable restrictions as to the tenants having children or keeping pets.

Do not forget to find out whether the rent asked includes the rates. If the rent is, say, 25s. a week *exclusive*, then you may reasonably expect to have to find about another 5s. a week for rates. If, however, the rent is *inclusive*, then the question of rates need not worry you.

FURNISHING THE ROOMS

The first step is to decide on the use to which the various rooms may best be put, and this must naturally depend on the position of the kitchen or kitchenette. The dining-room, which need not necessarily be large, should adjoin the kitchen, next should come the sitting-room, and lastly, the bedroom. A plan which is illustrated shows a very convenient arrangement where the flat consists of just a bedroom and a living-room with an adjacent kitchenette. If, however, there is also a child to accommodate, you will need two additional small rooms, each approximately half the size of the big living-room. One of these rooms should be equipped as a night nursery, and the other as a dining-room.

Furniture should be as small as possible.

When selecting furniture for your

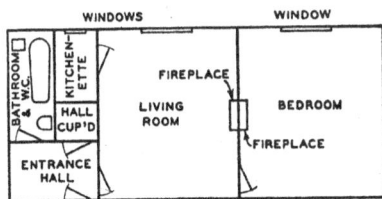

Fig. 2.—Plan of a Well-arranged Small Flat, the Windows of which face South.

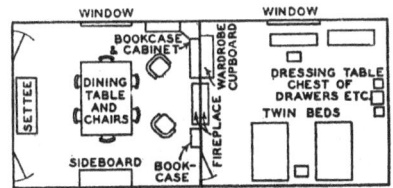

Fig. 3.—Suggested Arrangement of Furniture for Living-room and Bedroom.

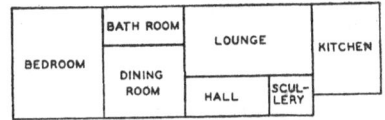

Fig. 4.—A Flat such as this should be Avoided.

The kitchen and dining-room are too far apart; the scullery is too near the hall. It will probably be cold and draughty.

Fig. 5.—Unit Furniture is ideal for the Lounge or Sitting-room. (*Bowman Bros. Ltd.*)

Fig. 6.—Modern Space-saving Furniture in the Bedroom of Small Flat. (*Bowman Bros. Ltd.*)

flat it is important to remember that a bigger home may be desirable after a few years, and the equipment chosen should therefore be such that it would also be suitable for use later in a suburban house. It is very much easier to use small-scale furniture in a large house than bulky furniture in a small house, and for this reason the furniture should all be as small in size as possible. It should be of a kind which could be added to later on, as one's requirements increase, without having to refurnish completely.

The Combination Unit Principle.

Quite a lot of furniture brought out recently is specially intended for this purpose. Much of it is definitely designed on the combination unit principle, and almost all of it is for placing round the walls of rooms in groups which can be added to from time to time and where as little space as possible is occupied. Obviously, if this kind of furniture is chosen, all one has to do when moving into a larger home is to purchase one or two extra units or pieces for adding to the groups already in existence.

It is possible, for example, to equip an entire home with units comprising shelves, drawers and cupboards which are equally appropriate in sitting-room, dining-room or bedroom. It is quite easy to change the pieces round if it ever becomes necessary, and furniture previously used in a dining-room or sitting-room could be transferred to a bedroom, so that only one living-room need be refurnished.

It is also a mistake to suppose that this furniture is necessarily expensive. It is possible to equip a small flat for well within £100 if cost is a prime consideration, and, of course, almost any furnisher nowadays will readily arrange deferred terms to suit one's income.

Concerning the Kitchenette.

Kitchen arrangements are of great importance, and go a long way toward making a small flat comfortable and livable. Occasionally in converted houses the sink is placed in a corner of the dining-room, and in cases of this kind a screen should always be kept round it. You can get a special box screen for this purpose, the inside of which is fitted with shelves where every kind of kitchen requisite can be kept without being visible. It is far better, however, if the flat includes a compact kitchenette similar to the example in Fig. 1 installed in a goodlysized cupboard.

With a kitchenette of this kind the most important thing to make sure of is a window giving access to the outside air, because without this feature the kitchenette will almost inevitably get damp and musty. If there is no window in the kitchenette, the landlord should be persuaded to instal one, for it should not cost him more than about £5. Alternatively, however, the cooker may help to keep the kitchenette dry and an electric lamp should be installed as near the sink as possible. It may be so fitted that it is switched on and off by opening and closing the cupboard door. This arrangement ensures that it is impossible for the lamp to be left burning when the cupboard is closed, and, of course, the door will only be opened when the kitchenette is being used.

Fitments in the Kitchenette.

The most essential items in a kitchenette are the sink and draining boards, which, of course, should be just beneath the window. There must also be shelves for china, earthenware, saucepans, etc., and a place for saucepan lids, the frying-pan, and so forth. There should be a bracket fitment on which to hang the egg-whisk, tea-strainer and spare skewers. The shelves for china and earthenware are best treated, so to speak, as small cupboards within the cupboard, and another item which will go a long way toward the success or failure of the whole flat is the cooker. This may by heated by gas, oil or electricity, for special bijou models are available nowadays using any of these fuels. For several reasons, however, an electric cooker may be preferable; no fumes of any sort are given off, and a small electric cooker is simple to operate and reliable in use.

Dining Table with Reversible Top.

With a very small kitchenette, it is assumed, of course, that much of the work done ordinarily in the kitchen, such as pastry-making and the preparation of most kinds of foodstuffs, will be done in the living-room. With this in view, it would be well to include a dining-table with a reversible top. There are several models now available which have been specially designed for this purpose. One side of the table-top is of stained and polished oak, and the other is of porcelain enamel. If the kitchenette is a little bigger, however, it may be possible to include in it a small kitchen cabinet or table-dresser.

Redecorating or Reconditioning.

Should you wish to do anything in the way of redecorating or reconditioning the flat for yourself, it is important to get the landlord's consent first. In at least one instance a tenant has been known to decorate his rooms with mural paintings, only to be sued by the landlord for defacing his property! In most instances the decorations are undertaken by the landlord rather than by his tenants.

Avoid Built-in Fixtures.

In equipping the flat it is also important to avoid installing anything in the nature of built-in fixtures, because these, being part of the structure of the building, become the legal property of the landlord and may not be taken away when moving.

REMEDYING A DEFECTIVE PLASTER CEILING

A CEILING that has been damaged by the effect of vibration set up by heavy motor traffic is generally recognisable by the large number of cracks that appear on the surface.

It is, however, also possible for a ceiling to be weak and yet not show any cracks. Such weakness can be tested by mounting a step-ladder and pressing against the ceiling with the open hand. If any up or down movement can be felt, this is a sign that the material has left the laths to which it is keyed, and there is danger of the ceiling falling.

Immediate attention should be given if a ceiling is found to be weak; do not wait until some of the plaster begins to fall.

Methods of Remedying a Defect.

There are three methods of remedying a defective ceiling, the method to employ depending largely on the extent of the damage. They are as follows:—

(A) If the fault has been detected before any plaster has fallen, the surface should be panelled with laths which are screwed to the joists above the ceiling and so support the weight of the plaster.

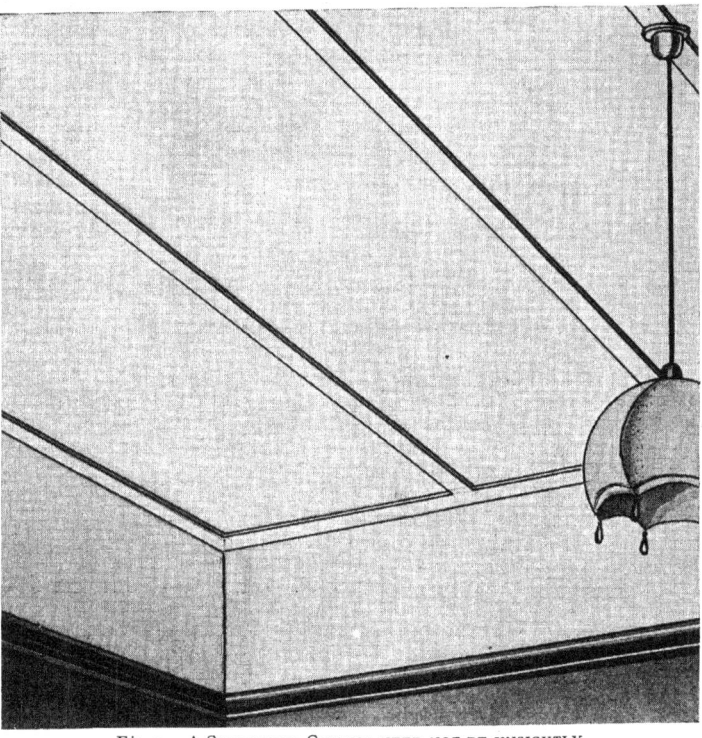

Fig. 1.—A SUPPORTED CEILING NEED NOT BE UNSIGHTLY.
This shows a ceiling provided with parallel laths to support the plaster which had begun to bulge.

(B) If the ceiling is badly cracked in small areas and some of the plaster has already fallen, the ceiling should be covered entirely with sheet asbestos, three-ply wood or pulp boards, and then panelled with laths.

(C) If the ceiling is in a very bad state and most of the plaster has fallen, then the remainder of the plaster and all the keying laths should be cleared away and asbestos, wood or pulp used to form a new ceiling.

STRENGTHENING A CEILING WITH LATHS

We will deal first with the method of remedying a ceiling by means of laths. The first thing to do is to examine the ceiling and find out where the joists come.

How to locate a Joist.

The best method of locating a joist is by means of trials with a gimlet. Force the gimlet through the plaster and then on through the keying laths. If no resistance can be felt when they have been penetrated, then it is obvious that no joist exists over that spot. Try again elsewhere until when the gimlet has passed through the plaster and keying laths considerable pressure is required to make it go farther upwards. This indicates that a joist has been located. Remember that all the joists run one way and are equally spaced apart.

Mark Position of Joists on Ceiling.

When the joists are located, mark their position in pencil on the ceiling.

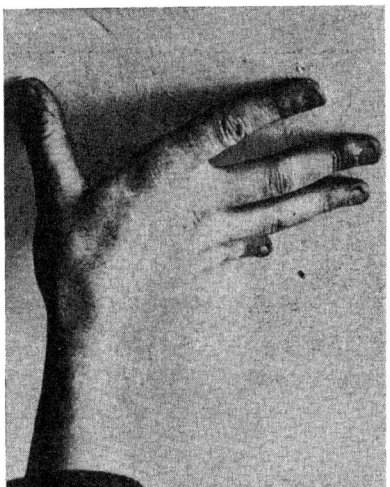

Fig. 2.—IS YOUR CEILING SAFE?
To find out if any slackness exists in a ceiling, press against it with the open hand. If there is the slightest movement up or down, it is a sure sign that the plaster is weak.

Fig. 3.—PREPARING THE CEILING SUPPORTS.
Before the cross laths are fixed to the ceiling halve the cross-over joints, so that the latter will lie flat over the plaster.

Fig. 4.—MAKE SCREW-HOLES IN LATHS BEFORE PUTTING UP TO CEILING.
Here the holes are being countersunk so that the screw-heads will not show.

REMEDYING A DEFECTIVE PLASTER CEILING

It will then be possible to see exactly where the laths should be placed, the position of the cracks or bulges naturally being taken into account.

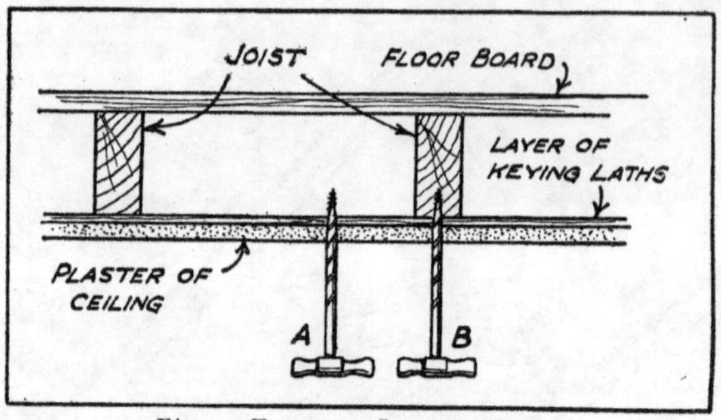

Spacing the Laths.

If the damage is only slight it will probably be quite sufficient to fix the laths parallel to each other, as shown in Fig. 1, but if additional strength is considered advisable, it will be better to place half the number of laths at right angles to the remainder.

This will have the effect of forming squares or rectangles; and, provided the spaces are not made too small, the result will be quite pleasing, and will not detract from the appearance of the room. At least a yard apart can be allowed quite safely; even more when the damage is not serious.

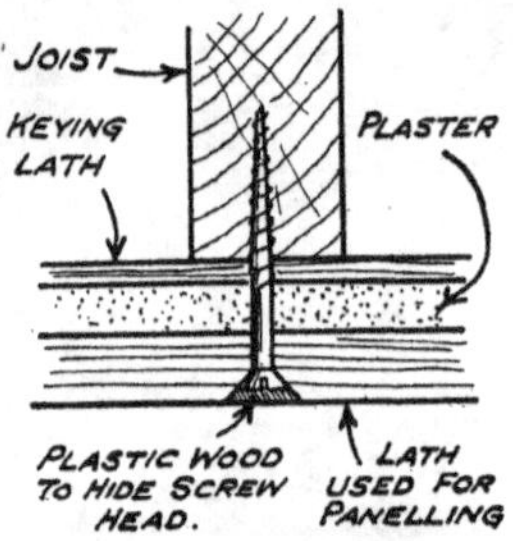

Fitting Parallel Laths.

The laths for the purpose can consist of ordinary deal strips 2 inches wide and ½ inch thick. Make holes with a gimlet at intervals of about 18 inches. Then countersink the holes. Use 2¼-inch screws for fixing the laths to the joists and drive the screws well home so that the heads can be covered with plastic wood or other suitable filler.

Fixing Laths across Joists.

If the laths are to be fixed across the joists and not parallel with them, then the holes for the screws should, of course, be arranged accordingly. It is sufficient if a screw is put in where the lath crosses each alternate joist.

Crossing Laths.

When it is decided to run the laths both parallel and across the joists, a halving joint should be made at each place where the laths cross each other. Screws are then inserted at each crossing.

Finishing off the Job.

A pleasing effect can be obtained by staining the laths or painting them a deep brown, the effect of which will be in keeping in Jacobean furnishings and other styles. Alternatively the laths can be given two coats of flat white paint. It is not advisable, however, to distemper over the wood, as it is liable to flake off in a short while. Fill up any cracks in the ceiling with

Fig. 5.—Finding a Joist by Trial. In A, the gimlet has not found the joist, but has been successful in B.

Fig. 6.—How each Screw is fitted.

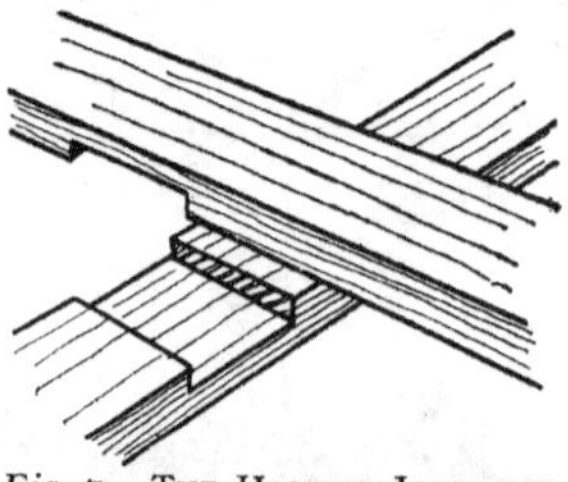

Fig. 7.—The Halved Joint for Laths crossing over each other.

Keene's cement, and rewhiten the ceiling if necessary. The holes made by the gimlet when locating the joists can be filled in with moistened whiting.

Fig. 1 shows the appearance of a ceiling supported by laths.

COVERING THE SURFACE WITH ASBESTOS, ETC.

We will now deal with ceilings which are too badly damaged for laths to form a satisfactory repair. The treatment then should consist of covering the whole surface with asbestos or other sheeting. The fact that asbestos is fireproof makes it a more suitable substance than plywood or pulp board, but it is, of course, more expensive and is liable to crack if handled clumsily.

The first thing to do is to locate the joists and mark out their position on the ceiling, as already described. As asbestos sheets can be obtained in a number of different sizes, this will enable the least wasteful size to be selected.

Fitting the Asbestos Sheets.

Place one of the asbestos sheets flush against the edge of the wall and cut the further edge of the sheet so that its boundary line runs along the centre of a joist, the idea being to give a footing on the same joist to the next piece of sheeting. As the joists are all spaced the same distance apart, when one sheet of asbestos has been cut to the required size it can be used as a template for the remainder.

Fig. 8.—Ceiling supported with Sheet Asbestos. The edges of the sheets are hidden by narrow battens.

When fitting the wall and corner pieces supporting screws should be run into the joist which comes nearest to the wall.

As far as possible the asbestos should be supported all round the edges by means of screws, placed 1 foot apart. When a joist is not available near an edge, the one nearest to the edge should take the screws.

Covering the Joins between Pieces of Asbestos.

The joins between the pieces of asbestos should be covered over with laths, which need not, however, be as stout as those used in the previous case, about 1 inch wide and ¼ inch thick being quite sufficient. The laths should be held in position by long, thin panel pins, passing between the edges of the sheets, into the joists.

BUILDING MODEL BOATS

DEALING WITH DECORATIVE MODELS, SAILING BOATS AND POWER-DRIVEN CRAFT

SHIP MODELLING is at once the most fascinating and the oldest known hobby. The cost of materials is small, elaborate tools are not needed, while the variety of subjects is so great that everyone can find something to meet personal taste and inclination.

Comparative Costs.

Practically speaking, all ship models can be grouped into three classes; first, the "showcase," or decorative variety, that are never put into water; secondly, all types of sailing models for use on ponds or the seacoast; thirdly, all types of power-driven craft, using clockwork, steam or electricity as motive power.

Decorative ship models cost practically nothing for materials, require only simple tools, and result in handsome decorative pieces, for example, the *Ark Royal*, Fig. 1, which has been built entirely by an amateur.

The second group costs a little more for material—the average 36-inch sailing boat costs about 22s. 6d., but when nicely finished is worth five or six times that amount. Readers who desire to take up model sailing yachts as a hobby will find there are clubs and numerous open prize competitions which can be entered or competed for.

Power-driven models are the most expensive, the cheapest cost about 35s. for materials, but the resulting model could not be bought for less than £6 or £7.

Methods of Construction.

There are several distinctly different methods of building any of the before-mentioned ship models; those most suited to amateur construction are the "solid block," the "laminated" and the "rib and plank" or "built" systems.

The solid block method is generally used for decorative and show models and for working models about 30 inches or less in length.

The laminated system is appropriate for show models, and is by far the best method for any model of 24 inches or greater length.

Rib- and plank-built hulls of 36 inches or greater length are very desirable for high-class racing models; and a modification of the system known as "built" is one of the best for the smaller power-driven models.

Fig. 1.—The "Ark Royal."
Despite the elaborate appearance of this fine model, it can be duplicated by following the instructions given in the text.

Representative examples of each are progressively dealt with in the following pages.

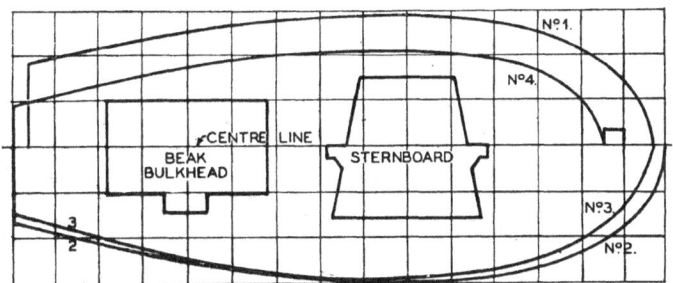

Fig. 2.—The Shapes of the Four Hull Planks.
One half only is shown; the other half is drawn as explained in the text. The beak bulkhead and sternboard are complete. Each square represents ¼ inch.

Fig. 3.—The Hull Parts assembled with Sternboard and Beak Bulkhead in Place.

Methods applicable to any Model.

It should be noted that various phases of model boat building are common to any type of boat; hence in this article such methods are detailed when they first arise, and only mentioned briefly in later models. Readers should therefore refer back for fuller particulars; for example, the method of building a hull for a sailing ship model can be adapted for a steamship—the only practical difference is the shape or "lines" of the hull and the proportions of its parts.

MODELLING THE "ARK ROYAL."

The *Ark Royal* is generally assumed to have been the flagship of the Earl of Effingham at the time of the Spanish Armada. The model now to be described is based on old prints and other data, and is a fair representation of the British ships of that period. It forms an agreeable decorative piece for any room, but should not be too big, something about 12 inches long and 10 inches high overall is most suitable.

Materials required.

The following comprises the materials for a model of *Ark Royal*, measuring 12 inches long overall.

Hull.—One piece pine or satin walnut, 30 inches long, 3 inches wide, ¼ inch thick; 1 piece $\frac{1}{16}$-inch fretwood, or 1 piece 1-mm. plywood, 12 × 12 inches.

Masts and Spars.—One piece "dowel rod," ⅛ inch diameter, 24 inches long; 1 piece dowel rod, $\frac{1}{16}$ inch diameter, 24 inches long.

Sundries.—One tube seccotine, 1 reel thin black cotton, 1 reel thick black cotton, 1 postcard, 1 long pin, 1 box water-colour paints or preferably a small bottle of each of the following "Poster" colours: Vandyke brown, vermilion, Prussian blue, 1 small bottle gold paint, 1 piece soft thin buff-coloured paper 24 × 12 inches for sails.

Making the Hull on the Laminated System.

The first step is to make the hull on the laminated system, consisting in this case of four flat pieces of wood sawn to a boat-like shape,

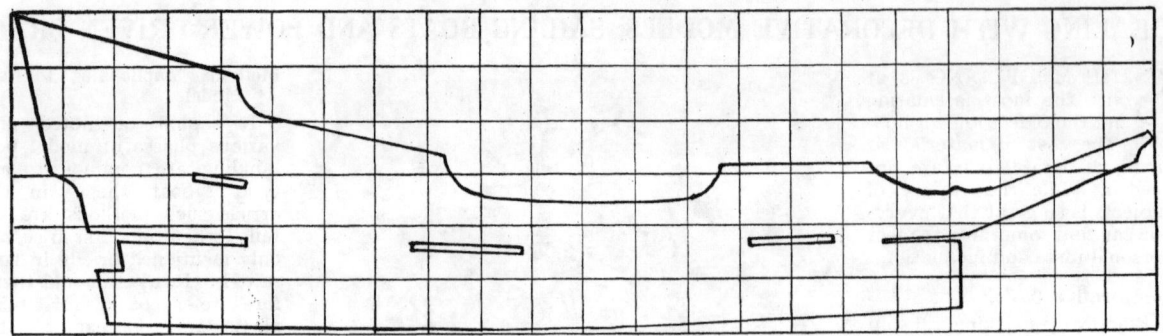

*Fig. 4.—*The Shape of the Side Planks.
Two are required, cut from plywood or fretwood 1/16 inch thick. Each square represents 1/2 inch.

and then glued one on top of each other.

The shapes of each piece are given in Fig. 2, and for convenience are shown on squared paper. To enlarge this drawing, first draw on a sheet of paper the same number of squares as shown in Fig. 2, but make each square 1/2 inch each way. Then draw on the paper the largest outline, that of plank No. 2.

Next draw a centre line along the length of the piece of 3 × 1/4-inch wood, lay a carbon paper face downwards on the wood, and put the paper on top of it, with the centre line thereon in register with that on the wood. Trace the outline, then turn the paper upside-down, and trace the same curve on the opposite half of the wood, thus getting the full-sized piece. Draw each of the remaining curves, one at a time, and trace them on to the wood as before. Cut out these pieces with a fretsaw and clean up the edges with sandpaper or a small plane, so that their shapes agree exactly with the original lines.

Note that the top plank (No. 1) is 1/16 inch smaller at the sides than the plank beneath it, also that it terminates 1/4 inch from the back or "stern."

Glue all four together and leave them to dry under pressure from a heavy book, if proper clamps are not available.

Similarly, draw and cut out the sternboard and the beak bulkhead—as shown in Fig. 2—then place one at each end as in Fig. 3, but do not fasten them at this stage.

Shaping the Hull.

The hull or body of the boat is now

*Fig. 5.—*Shaping the Hull.
The layers of wood are shaped by cutting away the steps or angular corners.

in a series of flat steps, and to shape it proceed to carve away the outer corners, either with a chisel—as indicated in Fig. 5—or with a sharp pocket-knife.

Do not make "flats," but simply round off the wood; it will be found to assume a pleasant boat-like shape if the angles are carved away, until the whole is smoothly curved.

To hold the hull while carving it, make use of the waste wood from the top plank, which, if nailed to the work-bench—or to a block of wood—forms a recess in which the hull can be rested. Note particularly that the recess or rebate formed by the top and second planks must not be carved away.

Finish off the hull with sandpaper, then glue the beak bulkhead into place at the front or "bows," and glue the sternboard into place at the stern, but make it incline outwards as shown on the general arrangement drawing (Fig. 6).

The Bulwarks.

The upper part of the hull—often called the bulwarks—and the upper decks are constructed on the "built" system, and consist of a single piece on each side of the hull which fits into the rebate on No. 1 plank and is fastened to the back bulkhead and sternboard. The shape of these side-pieces is shown in Fig. 4 on squared paper, and is to be similarly enlarged. Cut two pieces from 1/16-inch fretwood or preferably plywood, try them in place, and, if necessary, clean up the edges with sandpaper to make a good fit. Mark the outside face of each, then proceed to build thereon the

*Fig. 6.—*General Arrangement of the "Ark Royal" Model.
The positions of rigging and other details are here clearly shown.

"wales" or strengthening pieces shown clearly on the general arrangement drawing. These are narrow strips of card cut from a postcard and have only to be fastened in place with seccotine, as shown in Fig. 7; it is helpful to hold down the thin plywood with drawing pins while fixing the strips to prevent the thin wood "pulling" or becoming distorted. Any amount of detail can be built up in this way, but the smaller parts can be represented by paint-work if preferred.

Fixing the Decks.

The shapes of the various decks and "bulkheads" or vertical partitions are shown on squared paper in Fig. 8, and after enlargement as before should be cut out and then fixed in place. The larger deck pieces have projections on them which fit through slots cut in the bulwarks, and it is necessary to assemble them in proper order.

First fix one bulwark to the hull with seccotine and fine pin points, then insert the main deck —as in Fig. 9—next fix the bulkheads, and then the upper decks, finally fixing the second side-piece.

A projecting piece called the "stem" has to be made and fixed centrally at the bows, as shown on the general arrangement drawings, then a triangular piece fitted on top of it; and the extreme front ends of the side-pieces bent around the top piece and fastened together at the extreme front of the boat to form the "beak."

The sides and back of the main deck where it projects at the stern are then provided with little walls or bulwark rails to form the "gallery" or stern-walk for the use of the admiral. The four side "castles" can be shaped from odd pieces of soft wood—or very easily from an hexagonal lead pencil. When shaped they are glued to the bulwarks where shown on the drawings. If a pencil is used the coloured exterior should be scraped off and the bare wood exposed.

Masts and Rigging.

The masts and spars are made from thin round sticks; the main mast is in three pieces, the foremast in two pieces, the other masts and all the yards or spars which support the sails are made of single pieces.

All the masts should taper a little towards the top end, the yards should taper from the middle towards each end. The tapering can be accomplished by rapidly rotating the wood between the folds of a piece of sandpaper.

Circular platforms with tapered rims called "top castles" are fixed on each mast; they are made of cardboard—as shown in Fig. 10—the rims being gummed to the circular platforms, and when dry they are fixed in place on the mast with seccotine.

The masts should be stuck into holes drilled in the hull and should be in line and upright when viewed from the end, but should incline backwards when seen from the side of the boat.

The principal rigging is called the "shrouds"—which consist of six strands of thick cotton, brought together at the mast and splayed out at the bottom; the best way to make them for a small show model is shown in Fig. 12, and consists of threading the cottons over a card to hold them in place while the "ratlines" are fixed.

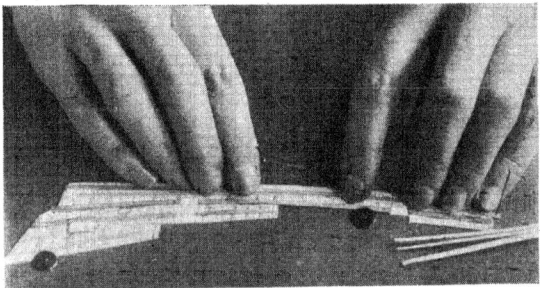

Fig. 7.—BUILDING UP THE SIDE PLANK.

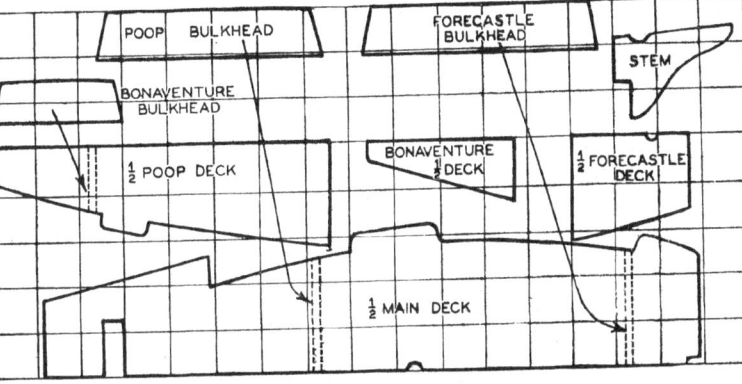

Fig. 8.—SHAPES OF HULL PARTS.
The bulkhead and stern are shown in their entirety; the decks are shown in half from the centre line. They should be completed by reversing the drawing as described in the text.

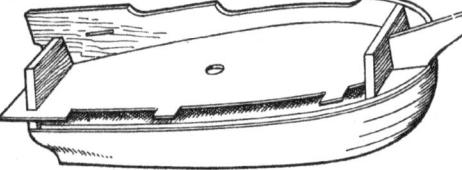

Fig. 9.—ASSEMBLING THE HULL.

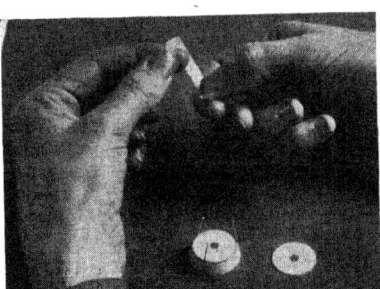

Fig. 10.—MAKING THE TOP CASTLES.
Note use of pins to hold rims in place while gum is drying.

Fig. 11.—FIXING THE RIGGING ON THE MODEL OF THE "ARK ROYAL."

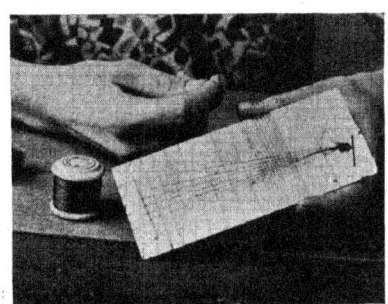

Fig. 12.—MAKING THE SHROUDS.
The card keeps the cottons in position while the ratlines are fixed with gum.

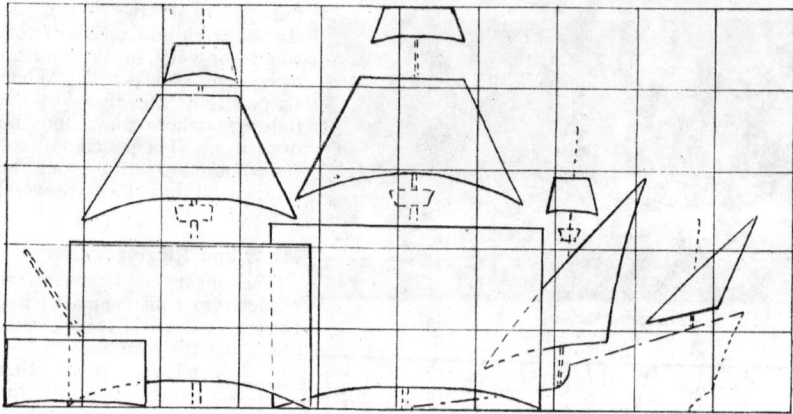

Fig. 13.—The Shapes of the Sails.
All the sails are here shown in correct relative positions as if set flat and lengthways of the ship. The squares represent 1-inch spaces.

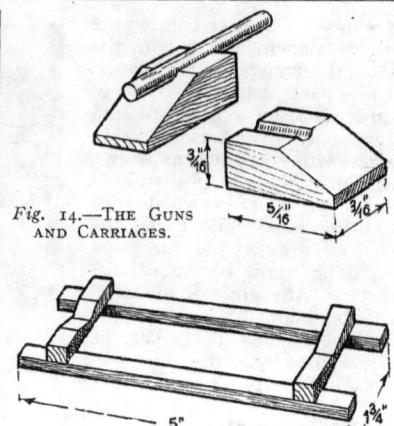

Fig. 14.—The Guns and Carriages.

Fig. 15.—Stand for the Model.

The ratlines are thin cottons fastened across the main strands and can easily be fixed with diluted glue. When dry, the cottons are released from the card and fastened in place on the model. The next step is to fix the top masts and then gradually add all the rigging as shown in Fig. 11, and the general arrangement drawing (Fig. 6). The sails are then drawn out full-size—following the outlines in Fig. 13 as before. When shaped, the sails should be decorated in colours with red crosses, yellow "lions"—or, more properly, "leopards rampant," on the lines shown in the various illustrations.

When painted, stick the top edge of each sail to its yard and fasten them in place with cottons, following the arrangement shown clearly in Fig. 6, the general arrangement drawing. The hull should then be painted in bright colours, the part below the water should be a deep green, the various wales and other raised timbers should be a darker brown than the hull, the upper works generally should be decorated in bright green, red and yellow, and picked out with gold lines.

The guns on deck should be made up with shaped blocks of wood for the "carriages," and small pieces of round wood for the guns — as shown in Fig. 14 —but the guns on the hull sides can be like pegs, tapered towards the outer end and then glued into holes drilled in the hull.

A neat stand on the lines shown in Fig. 15 will complete an attractive model.

Fig. 16.—Racing Yachts lined up ready for the Start of a Race.

BUILDING A 36-INCH RACING YACHT

The first model shown in Fig. 16 is rightly named "Speedwell," as it is one that will sail fast and well, it is a good all-round serviceable boat, and will give general satisfaction."

Materials required for 36-inch Model Yacht.

Hull Planks.— Good clean yellow pine.
Top plank : 37 inches long, 8 inches wide, 2¼ inches thick.
2nd Plank : 30 inches long, 8 inches wide, ¾ inch thick.
3rd Plank : 25½ inches long, 8 inches wide, ¾ inch thick.
4th Plank : 22 inches long, 7 inches wide, ¾ inch thick.
5th Plank : 19 inches long, 5 inches wide, ¾ inch thick.
6th Plank : 16 inches long, 2½ inches wide, ¾ inch thick.
7th Plank : 14 inches long, 1¼ inches wide, ¾ inch thick.
8th Plank : 8 inches long, 1⅜ inches wide, ¾ inch thick.
9th Plank : 14 inches long, 2 inches wide, ¾ inch thick.
Deck.—Yellow pine, 37 inches long, 8¼ inches wide, ⅛ inch thick.
Spars.—Mast, 48 × ½ inch diameter pine, boom 30 × ⅜ inch diameter, fore-boom 14 × ¼ inch diameter.
Rudder.—Mahogany, 10 × 1½ × 5/16 inch thick.
Sail-cloth.—1½ yards striped sail-cloth, 4 yards binding.
Keel.—3½ lbs. scrap lead.
Fittings.—Automatic tiller, sliding mast tube, hatch cover, boom socket, spreader, 2 round plates, foresail plate and socket, 1 piece brass tube 5/16 inch bore 10 inches long, 2 dozen small screw eyes,

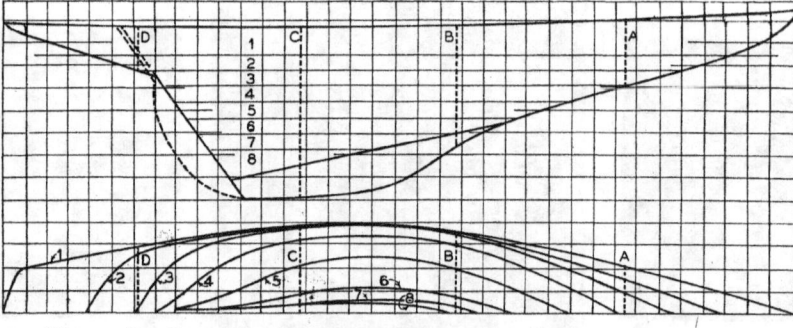

Fig. 17.—The Shapes of the Planks required for the Model Racing Yacht.
The letters show positions of cross-sections shown in Fig. 21. The squares represent 1-inch spaces ; the lines on the lower part of the drawing are ½ plans of the separate layers.

BUILDING MODEL BOATS

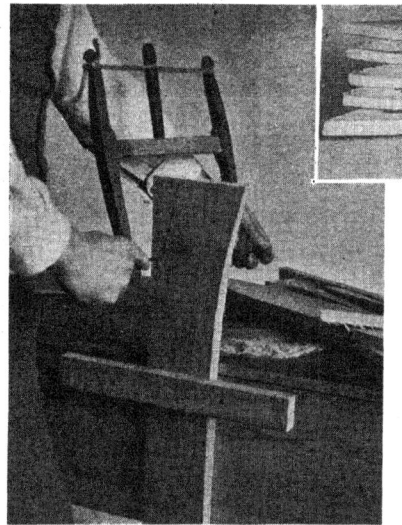

Fig. 18.—Cutting out the Planks with a Bow-saw.

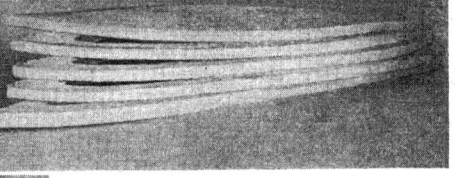

Fig. 19.—The Planks cut to Shape.

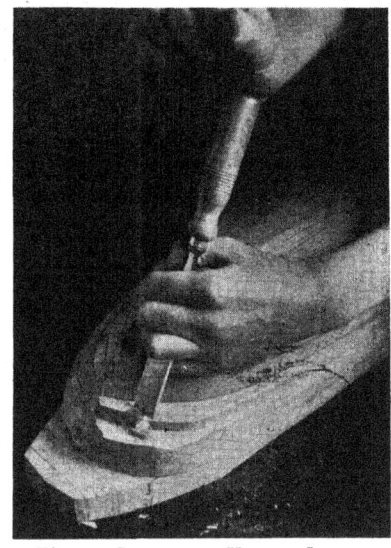

Fig. 20.—Carving the Hull to Shape.

12 bowsies, 8 oz. bottle shellac varnish, 1 tin undercoating, 1 tin enamel, 1 hank "Lowko" thin rigging cord, 1 hank thick rigging cord. (Bassett-Lowke Ltd.)

What to do first.

The hull can be carved from a solid block, but is preferably built on the laminated system.

The hull lines or shapes of the separate planks or layers are clearly shown in Fig. 17, and should be enlarged as already described and the lines transferred to the wood, as before. The squares represent 1-inch spaces. The planks are then sawn to shape—either with a keyhole-saw or preferably with a bow-saw, as shown in Fig. 18—which, incidentally, shows how the wood can be clamped to a bench or table by screwing a batten to the bench front, and so clamping the wood in a vertical position.

Hollowing the Interior.

Having sawn the exterior to shape, plane the edges, so that they follow exactly the curves on the original drawing; next proceed to mark out the shaped planks for the internal shaping.

To determine the amount that can be cut out, lay the planks on top of each other in correct order—as in Fig. 19—bring all centre lines into register, and then run a pencil line around the steps, thus drawing on the wider or upper plank the shape of the narrower lower plank. Now draw another curved line inside the first line, and about $\frac{3}{8}$ to $\frac{1}{2}$ inch away from it at

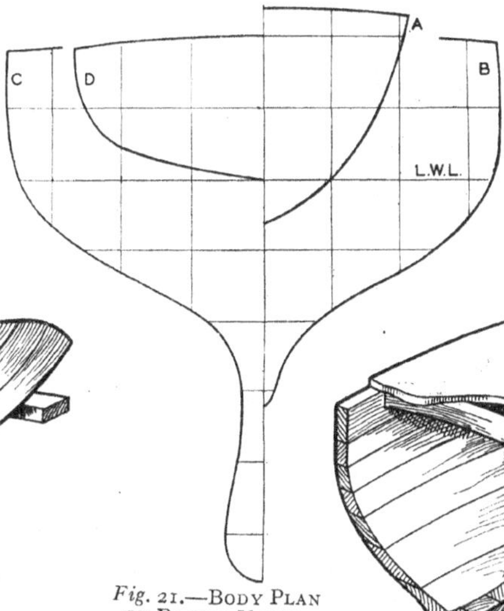

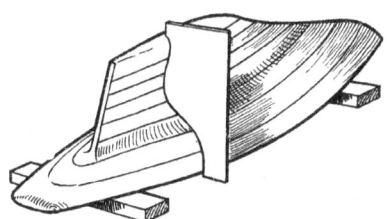

Fig. 22.—Template in Use.

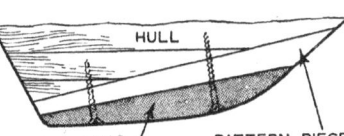

Fig. 23.—Lead Keel in Place.

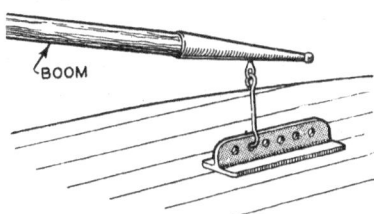

Fig. 26.—Foresail Plate.
The boom is fixed in the socket which hooks to the plate screwed on the deck.

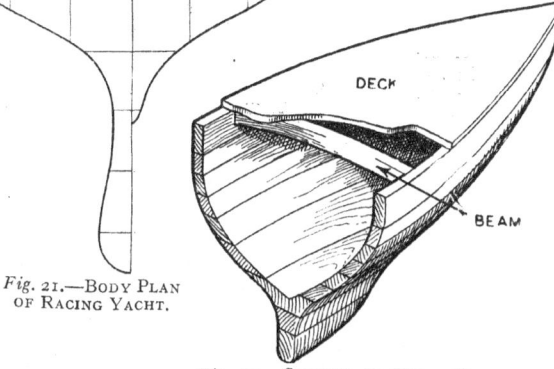

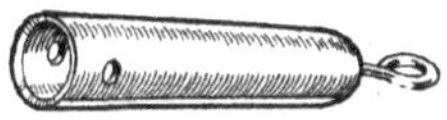

Fig. 21.—Body Plan of Racing Yacht.

Fig. 24.—Section of Hull, Beam and Deck.

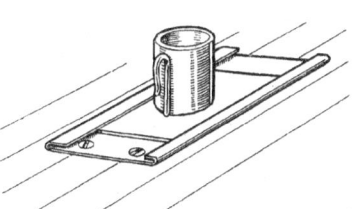

Fig. 27.—Main Boom Fitting.

Fig. 28.—Adjustable Mast Tube.

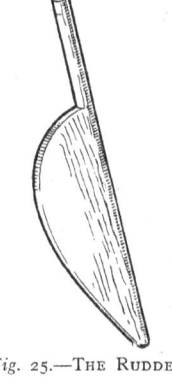

Fig. 25.—The Rudder.

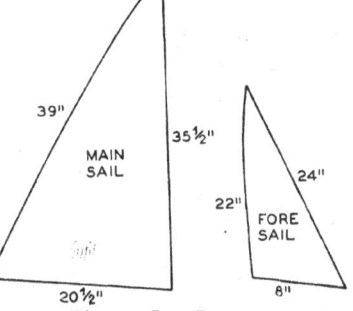

Fig. 29.—Sail Plan.
The figures are the lengths of the sides of the actual sails.

BUILDING MODEL BOATS

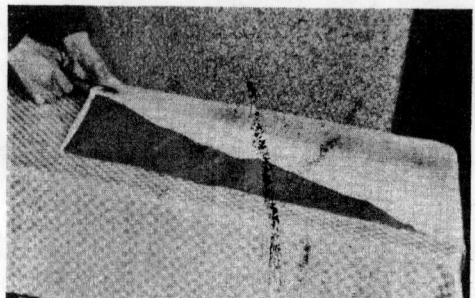

Fig. 30.—Cutting out the Sails.

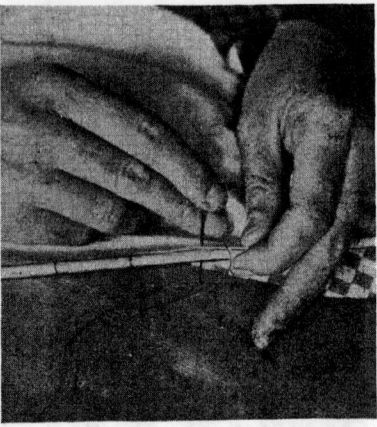

Fig. 31.—Sewing Sail to Spar.

the sides and rather more at each end.

This last line represents the amount that can be sawn out of the plank, which is accomplished by drilling a hole through the plank and sawing away the wood with a keyhole saw.

Replace the planks in proper order, and it will be seen at once that the outside is shaped correctly from end to end, but is in steps from top to bottom; furthermore, most of the wood from the interior has been sawn away, thus enormously reducing the labour of internal and external carving.

Shaping the Hull.

Glue the layers of wood together first in pairs, and let them dry under pressure to keep them flat, then glue together these pairs of planks and leave the whole to dry under pressure. Then carve the exterior by chiselling diagonally across the steps, as in Fig. 20, taking care, however, to keep the exterior nicely curved. The cross-sections of the hull are shown in the body plan (Fig. 21), and if an exceptionally nice hull is wanted, cut card templates to these shapes and apply them to the hull—as in Fig. 22—at the appropriate places; the templates are a guide to the proper shape—the procedure is to carve the hull locally until the template fits snug against it.

Carve away the angles inside the hull, then cut the deck to shape and nail it temporarily in place.

Making the Keel.

The best way to make the lead keel is first to fasten the bottom piece of the hull by gluing it in place with a piece of paper in the joint, then, when it has been carved, the wood can be removed by splitting the paper. The shaped piece is then used as a pattern, and the lead cast in a plaster mould in the usual way. The approximate weight of the lead keel is 3½ lbs., but a little more can be used if the hull is exceptionally light. The correct weight and position of the lead is proved by floating the hull in water, when—if all is correct as it should be—it will float on the line marked L.W.L. and be quite level and true, but if not, adjust the weight by adding or removing lead, and

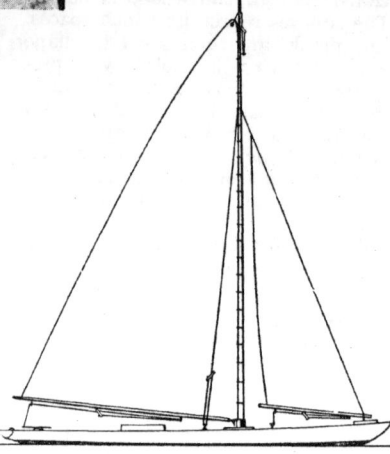

Fig. 32.—Rigging Plan.
A general arrangement drawing showing the whereabouts of all the cordage and gear.

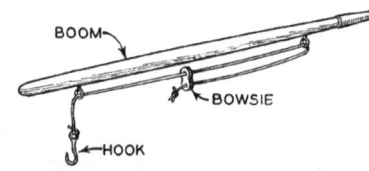

Fig. 33.—Rigging Detail.

Fig. 34.—The "Scootalong" Model Speed Boat.

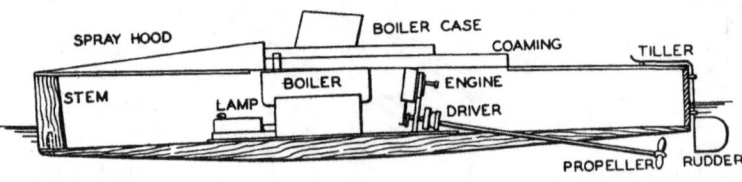

Fig. 35.—General Arrangement of the "Scootalong."

adjust the position by moving the lead forwards or backwards. When correct, screw the lead to the hull with long thin brass screws.

The wooden pattern is used to fill in any deficiencies between the lead keel and the hull—as shown in Fig. 23—to ensure the boat having its proper profile or shape, as seen from the side.

Fitting out the Hull.

Paint the hull inside and out with several coats of shellac varnish, then cut out the shape of the hatchway opening and cut the slot for the sliding mast tube. Fix the deck to the hull—after curving the top edges of the hull to the "sheer" line shown on the side views.

Fix a "beam" or cross-piece of wood about ¼ inch wide, ⅜ inch deep, just clear of each end of the hatch opening, the end of the beams being glued and screwed to the hull, as in Fig. 24, before the deck is fixed.

Cut the rudder to shape as in Fig. 25, and round off the "stem" so that it will turn easily in the rudder tube, which should be fixed with plastic wood in the hull, and let it project a little beyond the deck.

The foresail plate and boom-socket is shown fitted up in Fig. 26, the main boom end in Fig. 27, and sliding mast tube in Fig. 28—all of which can be made of brass, or, preferably, purchased ready-made.

Making the Sails.

Dimensions and shapes of sails are given in the sail plan (Fig. 29) and should be made by first cutting paper patterns to exact size, pinning them on the sail-cloth, as in Fig. 30, and cutting to shape with sharp scissors. Allow about ⅜ inch extra on all edges

BUILDING MODEL BOATS

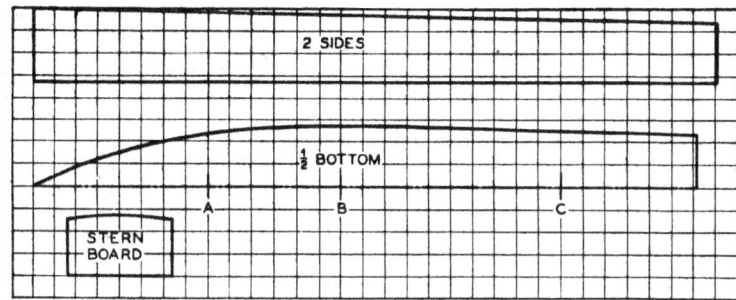

Fig. 36.—SHAPE OF THE HULL PARTS FOR THE "SCOOTALONG."
Squares represent 1-inch spaces.

Fig. 37.—SECTION OF MOTOR BOAT HULL.

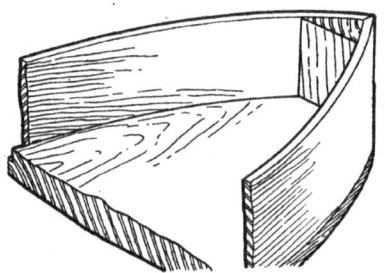

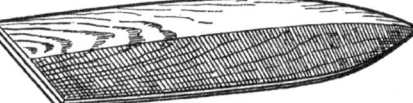

Fig. 39.—SHAPE OF THE BOTTOM BOARD.
The bottom is sawn from one piece and carved on the exterior only.

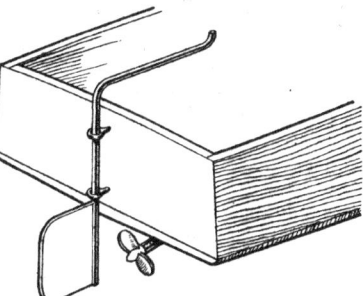

Fig. 40.—RUDDER AND TILLER.

Fig. 38.—STERN IN PLACE.
The stern is a solid block, shaped to fill in the angle between the hull sides and bottom plank at the bows or front.

for hemming and binding. Next make the mast and booms—tapering them as before described—give them a coat of varnish, and, when dry, sew the sails to the booms as in Fig. 31, using good stout waxed thread and fastening off securely. Rings are to be sewn on the edge of the sail—about 4 inches apart—to slide on to the mast.

Next rig up the boat, following the details shown in the rigging plan (Fig. 32), using hooks and screw-eyes to secure the rigging cord. Adjustments for length are made with a "bowsie" or miniature tent runner—as shown in Fig. 33.

The hull should be enamelled in the usual way in any desired colour scheme. The boat is then ready for use. It may be pointed out that this boat can be used with the rudder set in the central position, but the best results are obtained by the use of an "automatic tiller," which can be bought ready-made and should be fitted in accordance with the maker's instructions.

MODEL SPEED BOAT

"Scootalong," shown in Fig. 34, is a speedy but quite inexpensive power-boat that will prove entirely satisfactory when used on smooth waters.

The hull is built on a combination of the "built" and "carved" systems, as can be seen by the general arrangement drawing, Fig. 35, and other illustrations.

The following material is required for this boat.

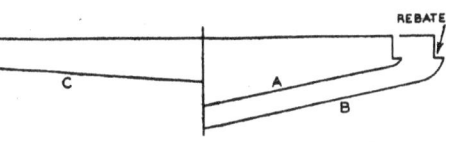

Fig. 41.—BODY PLAN OF THE "SCOOTALONG."
Showing ½ scale cross-sections of the bottom board.

Hull.—One piece pine or deal, 5½ inches wide, 30 inches long, 1 inch thick; 2 pieces ⅛-inch mahogany fretwood, 31 inches long, 3½ inches wide; 1 piece ⅛-inch mahogany fretwood, 5 inches long, 2¾ inches wide; 1 piece

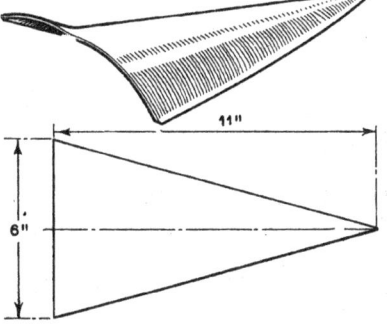

Fig. 42.—THE SPRAY HOOD.
A triangular piece of tinplate is compressed to form a conical-shaped cover for the bows as here shown.

pine for stem, 2 inches wide, 3½ inches long, 1½ inches thick.

Engine and Boiler.—One complete

Fig. 43.—THE FUNNEL AND BOILER COVER.
Built from tinplate and soldered together.

power plant consisting of boiler, lamp, and engine on base. (Bassett-Lowke Ltd.)

Propeller and Shaft.—One 3-blade propeller 1¼ inches diameter, 1 steel shaft and tube for same, 8 inches long.

Deck.—One piece pine, 30 inches long, 5½ inches wide, $\tfrac{3}{32}$ inch thick.

Sundries.—One piece tinplate for hood, rudder and funnel; 8-oz. bottle shellac varnish; 1 tin enamel; a few fine brass screws about ⅜ inch long.

Building the Hull.

The shapes of the hull planks are reproduced on squared paper in Fig. 36, and should be redrawn full-size as before and transferred to the wood. The squares represent 1-inch spaces.

Next, saw the bottom plank to shape and work the rebate along all outside edges as in Fig. 37, which also shows one side plank fitted in place.

Cut the side planks to shape and fasten them with glue and screws to the rebates. Next glue and screw the sternboard into place at the back of the hull, then proceed to carve the wood block for the stem so that it will fill in the triangular space at the bows, and enable the side planks to be glued and screwed to it, as shown in Fig. 38, then drill a hole through the bottom plank into the stem and glue a wooden dowel pin into this hole.

Carving the Hull.

Next carve the outside of the bottom plank to shape as indicated in Fig. 39, using templates taken from the body plan (Fig. 41), as previously described. The hull form is quite simple, and is easily shaped by first carving the hull to the profile or side view and then rounding off the angular edges.

Very little carving is required on the interior—that needed can be seen by first putting the power plant into the hull in its proper place—as shown in Fig. 35—then running a pencil around the outer edge of the base; the wood between this line and the sides of the hull can then be carved away as much as possible.

Fitting the Propeller Shaft.

The propeller shaft is a steel rod which turns freely in a brass tube; it is fitted to the hull by drilling a hole from the outside, inclined somewhat so that the inner end of the hole will be in line with the crankshaft on the engine. The hole will probably run "out of truth" when first drilled, and it should be corrected by "drawing over," that is, filing or burning out the hole until it is correct.

Next put the tube in place and line it up nicely with the engine, so that when the propeller shaft is in place it will just touch the end of the engine shaft. Fill in all gaps in the hull around the tube with plastic wood.

Cut the propeller shaft to correct length, fix the "driver" or fork on the inner end and screw the propeller to the outer end. Put plenty of oil on the shaft and in the tube before assembling it finally.

Making the Rudder.

The rudder should be cut to shape from tinplate, and then soldered to a piece of $\frac{1}{16}$-inch brass wire, which should be bent to shape as in Fig. 40, to form the tiller. The rudder is fitted to the hull by putting the wire through two small screw eyes in the stern board before finally bending the wire to shape.

Next screw the power plant to the bottom of the hull after well oiling the engine; connect the engine to the propeller shaft by adjusting the "drivers," and see that the whole works perfectly freely—any trace of stiffness or binding anywhere must be removed or the boat will be a failure. The whole power of the engine is needed to drive the propeller; the less energy wasted on overcoming useless friction the faster the boat will travel.

Testing and Trimming.

The boat should be given a couple of coats of shellac varnish inside and out before fixing the power plant. A trial run in the domestic bath is desirable at this stage. If the hull floats level, well and good—if not, it must be "brought into trim"—by adding small lead weights inside the hull to make it float correctly, and then screwing the weights in place. Next give the engine a run under steam—following the instructions supplied with the power plant. All being well, clean the boiler and engine and fit the deck, spray hood and other small details.

The deck should first be fitted to the hull, noting that a large part of the deck has to be cut away to allow access to the power plant. Next make the spray hood from a triangular piece of tinplate, as in Fig. 42, which should be curved by squeezing it sideways, which makes it take a conical form.

Paint the inside, and when dry, screw the spray hood to the front part of the deck. Then cut some strips of wood about $\frac{1}{8}$ inch thick and $\frac{1}{8}$ inch wide, round off the top edges, and fasten them around the deck opening to form the "coaming" or rim.

A slightly curved tinplate cover for the boiler should next be made, as in Fig. 43, an opening cut in it for the funnel uptake on the boiler to pass through, and any necessary holes made to clear the safety valve or other fittings.

A piece of tinplate is then cut to a length of about 7 inches and height of 2 inches, and rolled up to form an oval tube or funnel, which can then be soldered to the boiler cover.

Painting and Finishing.

The hull should then be enamelled or painted and varnished in any bright colours, the deck should be varnished, and the funnel and boiler cover painted dead black, as any other colour soon tarnishes with the heat. The spray hood looks best if enamelled white, but can be the same colour as the hull, according to personal fancy.

"Scootalong," if nicely made and finished as here described, will travel at a respectable speed and will run for twenty minutes or more on one filling of water and methylated spirit, but more elaborate models can be built much on the same lines.

PAINTING A CANVAS CANOE

As many of the canoes seen on our lakes and rivers are made of canvas stretched over a wood framework, a few notes on how to paint them may be useful.

Removing Old Paint.

If the old paint is badly cracked, flaked or perishing, it is a sign that it needs removal. This can be effected by the use of a paint-removing compound of the wax (not alkali) type, which can be purchased in small tins at any paint store.

The exposed surface of the canvas will then require wiping over with a rag soaked in turpentine so as to remove all traces of wax, and then a light sandpapering should follow.

Priming Coat.

A first priming coat of fairly stiff paint must next be applied, and this can be made up from :—

Stiff genuine paste white lead	4 lbs.
Turpentine.	1 pint.
Outside copal carriage varnish	$\frac{1}{3}$ pint.
Liquid driers	2 ozs.

This will make about a quart of paint, sufficient to coat once an average-sized canoe. The paint should be very well brushed into the canvas.

Second and Third Coats.

When this first coating is thoroughly hard and dry, second and third coats may be applied. The paint for these coats requires to be rather thinner in consistency than the first, which may be achieved by slightly increasing the varnish content.

Coloured Paint.

If a coloured paint is required, the right quantity of staining colour should be added during mixing, and while ordinary colours ground in oil will serve, colours ground in turpentine are preferable as reducing the amount of oil in the paint. It will be noted that in the formula given above varnish takes the place of the oil used in other kinds of painting. Further particulars regarding the tinting of paint will be found if reference is made to page 434.

Hole in Canvas.

If when examining the canvas before beginning to paint it is found that there is a hole in it, this can be repaired by inserting a piece of new canvas behind the torn part.

The patch should be considerably larger than the hole, and it should be pasted down with a mixture of thick paste white lead and japan gold size. Each end of the patch may also be fastened to the two nearest wooden ribs by means of copper or brass tacks.

If the canoe is in good condition and the old paint is fairly intact, the latter need not be removed and the priming coat mentioned may be omitted.

Final cautionary notes are that no painting should be begun until the canvas has been thoroughly dried, and that following coats must not be applied until earlier coats are completely hard.

How to Make a Flight of Straight Open Stairs or Steps

THE handyman is sometimes faced with the problem of making and erecting flights of straight open stairs or steps for outbuildings or warehouses. The two principal points that govern the setting out and construction of any staircase are shown in Fig. 1. From the "rise" or height to which the stairs ascend, and the "going," which is the horizontal distance from the face of the first step to the face of the last one, may be ascertained the pitch of the stairs and all necessary dimensions. Fig. 2 shows the principles on which stairs are set out.

No definite dimensions can be given for the setting out of stairs, as these vary considerably according to circumstances. The following examples will, however, show the method by which all the required dimensions may be determined. Generally, no straight flight of stairs should contain more than twelve steps without a landing. A landing is, of course, also useful where a change of direction is necessary, and two flights of steps and a landing, as shown by Fig. 3, are much better than one very steep flight.

Fig. 1 gives, for reference, the names of the three chief parts of a flight of stairs.

In the type of stair being dealt with the risers are, of course, not necessary, but a method of obtaining the width of the tread and the height of the rise will be useful as a help to the setting out of the strings.

Determining the Tread and Riser Dimensions.

There are many methods of ascertaining the tread and riser dimensions, but a useful and common rule is to let the width of the tread plus twice the rise equal 24 inches. Two feet is assumed to be the average length of a step taken in walking on a level surface, and by assuming that it is twice as difficult to climb upstairs as it is to walk on the level, the given rule is determined. This rule gives for an 8-inch tread an 8-inch rise, for a 9-inch tread a 7½-inch rise, for a 10-inch tread a 7-inch rise, and so on, always keeping

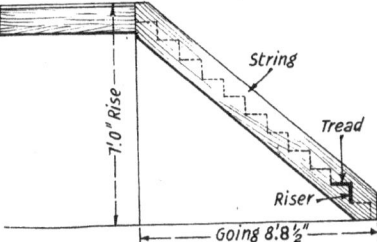

Fig. 1.—Showing the Principal Points that govern the Setting Out of Stairs. Note the three chief parts named for reference.

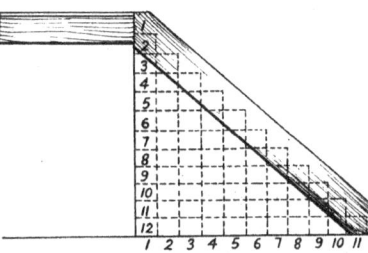

Fig. 2.—Showing the Principles on which Stairs are set out.

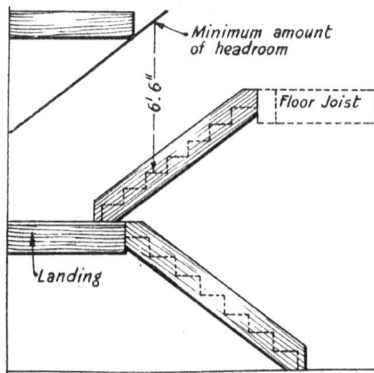

Fig. 3.—How the Head Room is obtained and a Landing used in preference to one Steep Flight.

the ratio the same; generally, however, the rise should not exceed 8 inches or be less than 4 inches.

An Example.

As an example, take the dimensions given by Fig. 1. The rise, 7 feet, should be obtained by a lath or rod about 1 inch square. Then it is necessary to determine the going, 8 feet 8½ inches, and in order to obtain the point on the floor directly underneath that end of the stairway opening to which the head of the stairs will fit, a plumb line should be dropped as shown by Fig. 4, and the position indicated by the plumb bob marked.

From the point thus obtained the length of the going should be measured and marked on the floor. The length of the going is, of course, chiefly determined by the amount of room available at the foot of the stairs and the head room. In most cases a minimum height of 6 feet 6 inches should be allowed for head clearance, as shown by Fig. 3. It will readily be seen that in certain cases the length of the going will be restricted by obtaining the necessary head clearance where the stairway opening is already made.

Assuming that twelve risers are to be used, divide the rise 7 feet by twelve. This gives 7 inches. Then divide the going 8 feet 8½ inches by eleven, because there is always one more riser than treads in a flight of stairs. This gives the width of the tread as 9½ inches.

Slight Variations are permissible.

According to the given rule, that the width of the tread plus twice the rise should equal 24 inches, these dimensions, 7 inches rise and 9½ inches tread, are not correct as they give 23½ inches, but slight variations such as this are often necessary according to circumstances, as the amount of rise and going always depend upon the available space. The treads and risers should, however, always bear as near as possible this certain ratio to avoid having stairs that are too awkward or too fatiguing to climb. In cases where the going is very short the steps have to be made so steep that they have to be used more as a ladder than stairs.

Setting out the Pitch Board.

When all the required measurements have been obtained, and the height of the rise between the treads and the width of the treads ascertained, the

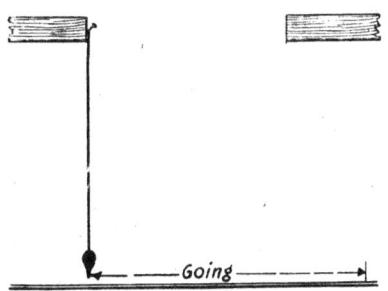

Fig. 4.—How to Mark the Length of the Going on the Floor.

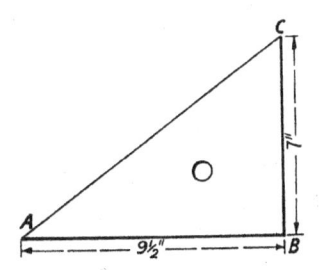

Fig. 5.—Showing the Pitch-board.

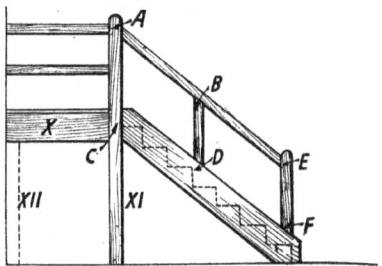

Fig. 6.—Handrail and Landing Supports in Position.

HOW TO MAKE A FLIGHT OF STRAIGHT OPEN STAIRS OR STEPS

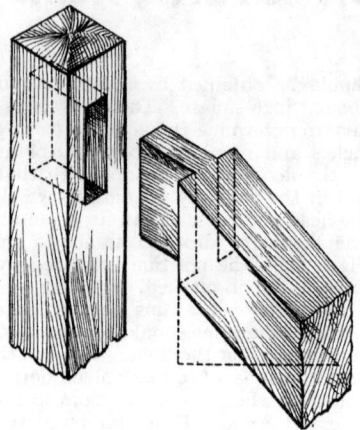

Fig. 7.—THE TYPE OF JOINT USED AT JOINTS A AND E ON THE HANDRAIL.

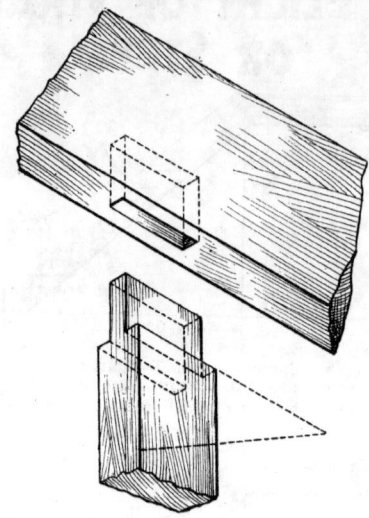

Fig. 7A.—THE TYPE OF JOINT USED AT JOINTS B, D AND F ON THE HANDRAIL.

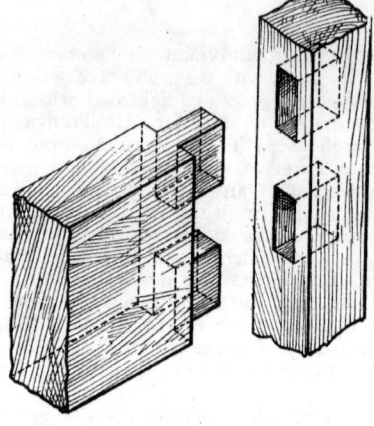

Fig. 7B.—HOW THE LANDING BEARER JOINTS INTO THE SUPPORT AT C.

pitch-board should be set out. Great care should be taken in the setting out and making of the pitch-board, shown by Fig. 5, as everything depends upon its accuracy. The lines AB and BC are at right angles, while the line AC varies according to the length of AB and BC. The board could be made of three-ply, and all the edges should be made true and square with the try-plane.

The length of the string may be obtained approximately by multiplying the longest edge of the pitch-board by one more than the number of steps in the stairs, and about 1 foot should be added to allow for possible bad ends of timber to be cut away.

Strings are usually 9 inches or 11 inches wide and 1½ inches or 2 inches thick in the type of stair being described, according to the strength required, and the treads should be 1¼ inches thick.

Having decided upon the width of the stairs (this is governed chiefly by the amount of space available), the amount of timber necessary for the treads may be ascertained, not forgetting when giving the measurements that each tread will be housed into the strings ½ inch. This means that the tread will be 1 inch longer than the width between the strings.

Handrails.

Handrails, as shown by Fig. 6, are often required. Figs. 7 and 7A show the different joints of the handrail in detail, the dotted outline of the pitch-board showing how to utilise the pitch-board to obtain the required angles.

Timber for Landing.

When a landing is required, as shown by Fig. 6, the bearers of the landing marked X should be made from timber of ordinary floor joint dimensions, while the upright marked XI should be of suitable strength according to what is required for the stairs under construction. Usually timber about

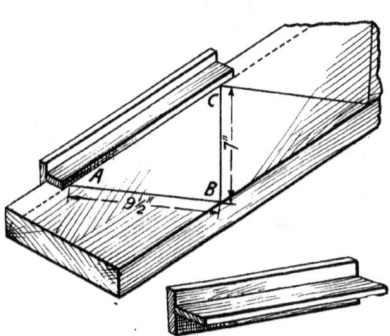

Figs. 8 AND 9.—THE PITCH-BOARD AND MARGIN TEMPLATE IN POSITION ON THE STRING.
Showing how margin template is made out of two pieces of wood.

Fig. 10.—THE TEMPLATE IN THE POSITION FOR SETTING OUT THE WIDTH OF THE HOUSINGS.

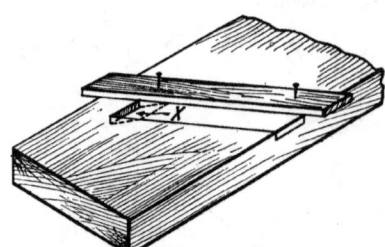

Fig. 11.—THE PIECE OF WOOD IN POSITION TO GUIDE THE TENON SAW.
Note the place marked X, where a portion has been cut away to give clearance for the end of the tenon saw.

3 inches to 4 inches square will be found suitable.

Supporting the Landing Bearers—Brick Walls.

One end of the landing bearers may be supported by being fixed in the wall. This is only advisable, however, if the wall is of brick or stone.

A sufficient number of bricks should be removed. Most inner walls are only two bricks thick, so great care should be taken when removing bricks from one side of a wall not to disturb the bricks on the opposite side.

Having formed a cavity to receive the bearer, the bricks that have been removed should be cut to fit round the wood and then cemented into position.

Lath and Plaster Walls.

In cases where the walls are lath and plaster, or coke breeze slabs, it would be advisable to support the landing by means of an extra upright fixed close to the wall, as shown by the dotted outline marked XII in Fig. 6.

When all the leading dimensions have been ascertained and the required timber obtained, the setting out and construction of the stairs may be carried out in the workshop.

Tools required for Constructing Stairs.

The following tools should be at hand to carry out the work: Jack plane, smooth plane, old woman's tooth plane or router, hand-saw, tenon saw, 1-inch firmer chisel, mallet, heavy hammer, gauge, marking awl, brace and $\frac{3}{16}$-inch shell bit, nail punch, together with a quantity of 4-inch wire nails.

Set out the Strings as a Pair.

In order that the strings may be set out as a pair, they should be laid edge to edge on the trestles and the position of the treads set out with the pitch-board as shown by Fig. 8.

If the treads are not being housed

HOW TO MAKE A FLIGHT OF STRAIGHT OPEN STAIRS OR STEPS

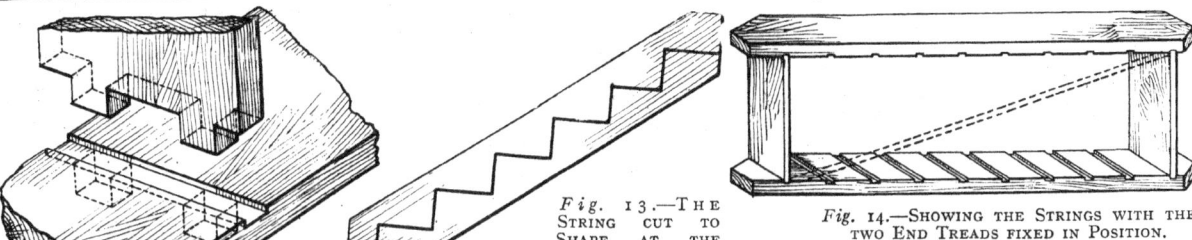

Fig. 12.—Showing how the Treads may be Tenoned through the Strings to give Extra Strength.

Fig. 13.—The String cut to Shape at the Ends.
Note that the two faces which form each end are respectively parallel with the treads and the risers.

Fig. 14.—Showing the Strings with the two End Treads fixed in Position.
Note the dotted outline showing how the diagonal measurements may be compared as a test for squareness.

through the full width of the strings, a margin template should be made to use in conjunction with the pitch-board, as shown by Fig. 8.

Fig. 9 shows how the margin template is made.

Template for setting out Width of Housings.

When both strings have been marked off to the pitch-board, a template should be made as wide as the thickness of the treads. This template is used for setting out the width of housings for the ends of the treads, as shown by Fig. 10.

Fix a Guide for the Tenon Saw.

Having set out the width of the housings, the depth of them, ½ inch, should be gauged on each edge of the strings so that no error is made by cutting them too deep. Then take a piece of wood, about 2 inches wide by ½ inch thick, and fix it so that one edge just leaves visible the line that marks the width of the housing, as shown by Fig. 11. This piece of wood will act as a guide for the tenon saw when sawing down the sides of the housings, and it should be moved and refixed for each edge of the housings.

When all the saw-cuts have been made, the bulk of the wood that is to be removed from between them may be chopped out by means of the mallet and chisel and finished to an even depth with the old woman's tooth plane or router.

If the treads are not being housed through the full width of the string, a portion of wood should be cut away from one end of the housing to allow clearance for the end of the tenon saw when making the saw-cuts, as shown by Fig. 11.

Where extra strength is required each alternate tread could be tenoned through the string, as shown by Fig. 12.

The ends of the strings should then be cut off according to the lines marked from the pitch-board, as shown by Fig. 13. These ends should then be planed true and square with the smooth plane.

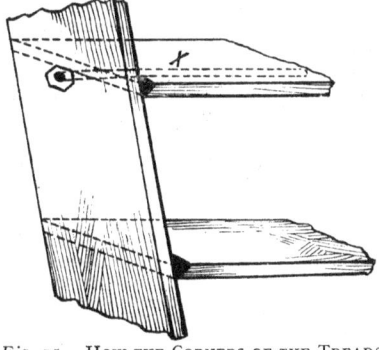

Fig. 15.—How the Corners of the Treads may be treated.
The black portion should be cut away. Note the dotted outline marked X, showing how the rods are fixed.

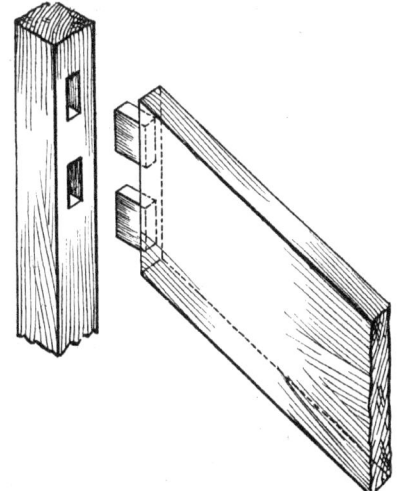

Fig. 16.—How the Ends of the Strings may be Tenoned for Fixing.

Assembling the Stairs.

When the treads have been cut to length and planed true and square at the ends, the stairs are ready for assembling.

Before assembling the stairs in the workshop an inspection should be made of the place where the stairs are to be fixed in order to make sure that the doorways will allow for the entrance of the constructed stairs. Where an entrance is not possible, the stairs will have to be built up in the place for which they are intended.

First fix Two End Treads in Position.

When assembling the stairs the two end treads should be fixed in position first. The strings with the two end treads fixed in position should then be tested for squareness by comparing the diagonal measurements with a lath, as shown by Fig. 14.

If Ends of Treads are not tenoned through Strings.

If the ends of the treads are not tenoned through the strings they may be fixed in position by driving 4-inch wire nails through the strings into the ends of the treads. Holes should be bored for the nails through the strings with the brace and the 3/16-inch shell bit in order to avoid splitting the timber.

Dealing with the Corner of the Treads.

Fig. 15 shows two methods of treating the corner of the treads that stand out from the string in this type of stairs.

When the stairs have been assembled the back could be matchboarded, or, alternatively, a three-ply back could be fitted.

To give Strength and Rigidity.

In order to give strength and rigidity to these stairs, three long bolts should be obtained, long enough to span the full width of the stairs. Rods of iron, threaded at each end for a nut, will, of course, be quite suitable.

Fixing the Rods.

These rods should be fixed so that they pass directly underneath a tread, as shown by Fig. 15. A rod should be fixed under the first and last tread and one somewhere about the middle.

The Ideal Method.

The ideal method of fixing stairs is to tenon the ends of the strings into the newel or trimmer, as shown by Fig. 16. This type of stairs is, however, usually fixed by means of iron brackets. If one string fits close to a wall, plugs could be driven into the wall and the string fixed by nails.

The methods and principles explained may be applied with equal success to a short flight containing only two or three steps.

Some Useful and Attra[ctive]

Layout No. 1.

FEATURES of this plan are the masking of the workshop or shed by a timber pergola, flanked by clipped privet hedges, which shut off the vegetable garden from the general picture.

A curving stone-flagged path leads across the lawn; at the right is a small rose garden with surrounding path. A lilac or other flowering tree or shrub and a stone bird bath on the lawn complete a pleasant layout.

Recommended suppliers.—Shed: Rayners, Meadrow, Godalming, Surrey; Pergola: A. Turrell & Sons, 65 Stanstead Road, Forest Hill, London, S.E.; Garden Ornaments: Scoffin & Willmott Ltd., Barking Bypass Road, Barking, Essex; Stone Paving: Vint Bros., "Idle," Bradford, Yorks.; Flowering Shrubs: G.F. Letts & Sons, 39 Hadleigh, Suffolk; Incinerator: Lostoch Iron Basket Co., Lostock Gralam, Nr. Northwich.

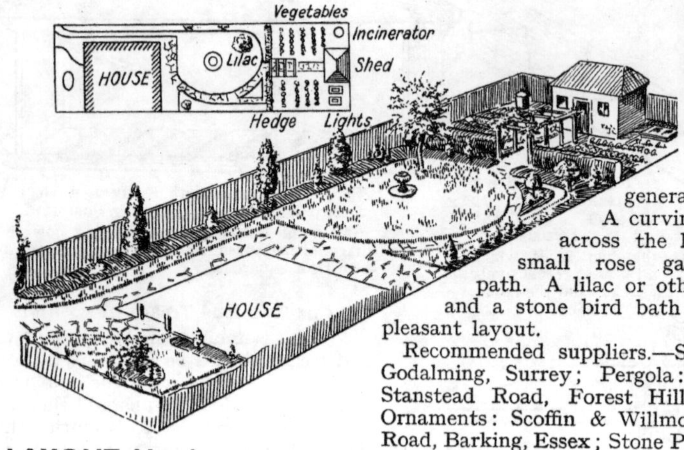

LAYOUT No. 1.

LAYOUT No. 4.

Layout No. 2.

This plan gives the maximum possible impression of breadth to what in fact is a long narrow garden. Steps from the house terrace lead to a "stepping stone" path and to a sheltered seat. An oval bed for roses is disposed at the right, while further along on the left is a clump of evergreen flowering shrubs and a lilac tree.

The beds are irregular in form, the "heads" serve to break up the monotony of the long garden, and this is enhanced by the quadrantal pergola and off-set sundial. At the bottom a privet or evergreen hedge screens a garden frame and small vegetable or salad garden.

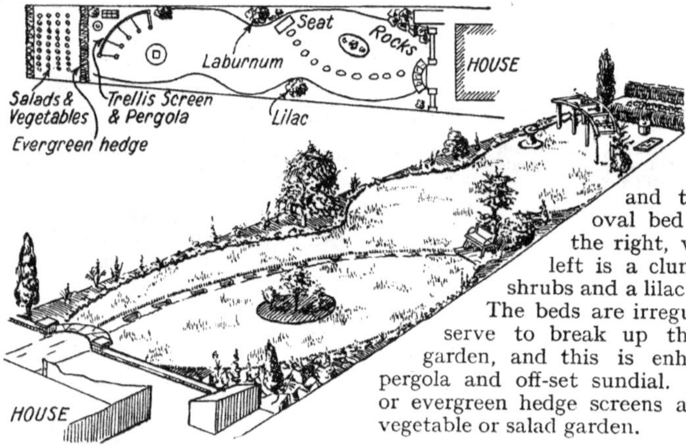

LAYOUT No. 2.

LAYOUT No. 5.

Layout No. 3.

This plan makes the most of a relatively small garden. A single path leaves the stone-paved house area and branches at about one-third the length of the garden, where a sundial is erected. Two beds for roses, surrounding a cement garden statuette or bird bath, add interest and enhance the apparent size of a pleasant little garden. Note the value of a few well-placed trees and evergreen shrubs.

Recommended suppliers.—Trees and Shrubs: Taylors' Nurseries, "Trelawny," Tilehurst Lane, Bexley, Kent.

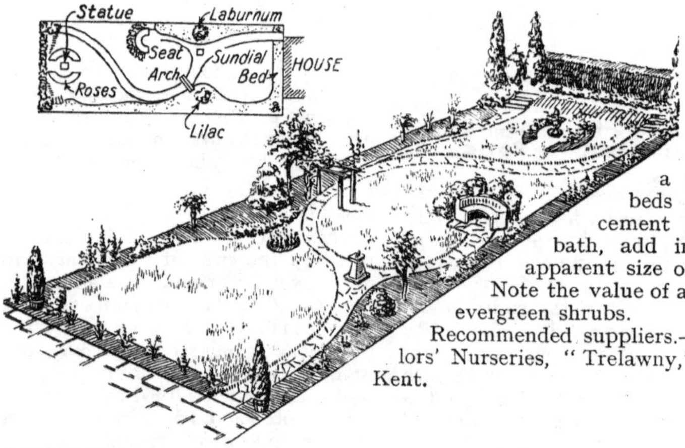

LAYOUT No. 3.

LAYOUT No. 6.

LAYOUTS FOR GARDENS

Layout No. 4.

A simple stone step, flanked by two low walls and guarded by slow-growing cupressus, lead by a crazy paved path through a timber pergola to a semi-formal rose garden with a sundial, and thence to a stone or wooden seat. The picture is completed by a background of evergreen shrubs, azalias, rhododendrons and cupressus—which are pleasant all the year round. The right foreground is filled by a rock garden, which separates the existing cement path from the flower bed, with sinuous edge on the ht.

A lilac or laburnum on the lawn breaks up the erity of line and adds an early touch of colour.

Recommended suppliers.—Sundial: Carters Ltd., ynes Park, S.W. 20; Pergola: T. Bath & Co., Riley orks, Herne Hill, S.E.24; Seat: Western Forestry , Haverfordwest; Evergreens: Willin Bros., Rearsby, cester.

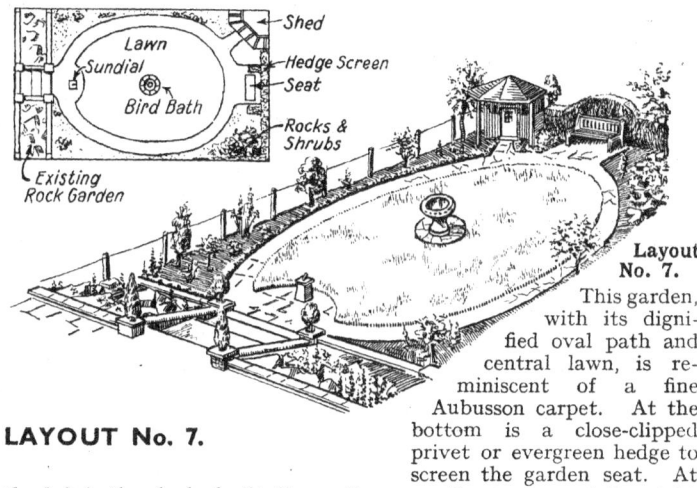

LAYOUT No. 7.

Layout No. 7.

This garden, with its dignified oval path and central lawn, is reminiscent of a fine Aubusson carpet. At the bottom is a close-clipped privet or evergreen hedge to screen the garden seat. At the left is the shed—built diagonally across the corner; at the right is a cluster of flowering evergreen shrubs and a Rowan or other tree.

Layout No. 5.

A lych gate forms a distinctive feature at the entrance and is set back from the path about 3 feet. At the rear of the house a low wall with central semi-circular steps lead to a grass lawn, with paths and flower beds on each side. At the bottom is a raised terrace with flower beds in front, a trellis screen at back and a pergola along the terrace. A few well-placed trees add to the charm of this somewhat formal but very pleasant garden.

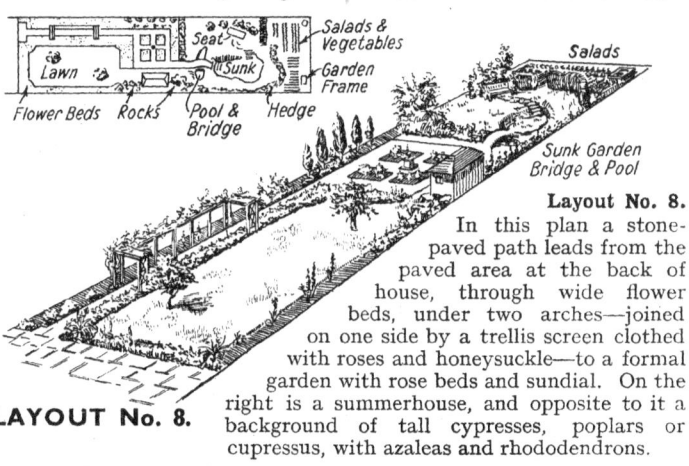

LAYOUT No. 8.

Layout No. 8.

In this plan a stone-paved path leads from the paved area at the back of house, through wide flower beds, under two arches—joined on one side by a trellis screen clothed with roses and honeysuckle—to a formal garden with rose beds and sundial. On the right is a summerhouse, and opposite to it a background of tall cypresses, poplars or cupressus, with azaleas and rhododendrons.

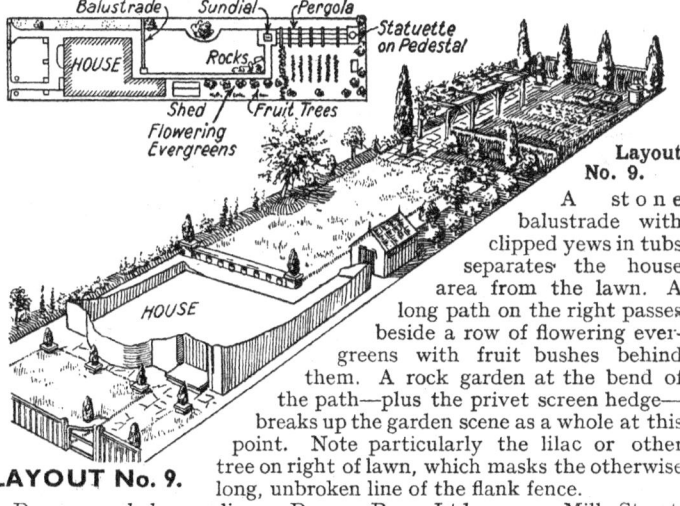

LAYOUT No. 9.

Layout No. 9.

A stone balustrade with clipped yews in tubs separates the house area from the lawn. A long path on the right passes beside a row of flowering evergreens with fruit bushes behind them. A rock garden at the bend of the path—plus the privet screen hedge—breaks up the garden scene as a whole at this point. Note particularly the lilac or other tree on right of lawn, which masks the otherwise long, unbroken line of the flank fence.

Layout No. 6.

The existing concrete flat is here used with advantage as a foundation for the shed or workshop, which is backed and surrounded by a trellis screen. Brick "baskets" at the front corners of the concrete are used for flowering plants. Vegetables are arranged for at the back and end of the shed. A narrow enclosed garden beside the house would make a delightful old-world flower garden.

Recommended suppliers.—Roses: Bees Ltd., 175D Mill Street, Liverpool; Hedges: Barnum Nurseries, Barnham, Sussex; Trees and Shrubs: Chas. Daborn & Sons, Nurseries, Bisley, Surrey; Trellis: A. E. Caseley & Sons, 35 Merridale Road, Wolverhampton; Flowering Shrubs: Willin Bros., Rearsby, Leicester; Seats, etc.: J. Cheal & Sons, Ltd., Crawley, Sussex.

CHINA AND POTTERY DECORATION

There are several methods of china and pottery decoration that can be carried out at home by the amateur, but the choice of those most suitable depends on the facilities that are available. The potter employs principally two methods, known as underglaze and overglaze painting, but in both cases it is necessary to fire the decorated ware in a kiln before it can be used. Overglaze painting can be done quite easily by the amateur, and it is generally possible to send the decorated work to a local pottery where it can be fired at a small cost.

Using Enamel Paints.

The alternative to overglaze painting is to use enamel paints which may be applied to biscuit ware as well as glazed and partly glazed pottery. This method, although not so permanent as kiln firing, is quite satisfactory, provided that the decorated articles are carefully handled and do not need frequent washing in hot water. The unglazed ware will be found more satisfactory, as any kind of paint or enamel is liable to chip off highly glazed surfaces.

Where to obtain the Pottery.

China and pottery in its unglazed state is known as biscuit ware, and can be obtained from pottery firms and many art shops in large variety. After the clay has been moulded or cast into shape it is placed in a kiln, subjected to great heat and thus transformed into pottery. At this stage it is porous, but quite hard, and in order to render it waterproof, a glass-like surface is burnt on it—this is known as glazing. The decoration can be applied at the same time as the glaze, or it can be applied after the glaze—the materials used in this case are designed to run on the glazed surface when the ware is sufficiently heated.

NON-FIRING METHOD OF DECORATION

The non-firing method of decoration can be applied to all unglazed biscuit ware as well as glazed and partly glazed pottery, and is particularly suitable for all sorts of cases, bowls, jars, ornamental pots, etc., as well as jam pots, white china articles, plain

Fig. 6.—Simple Geometrical Pattern suitable for Decorating China or Pottery.

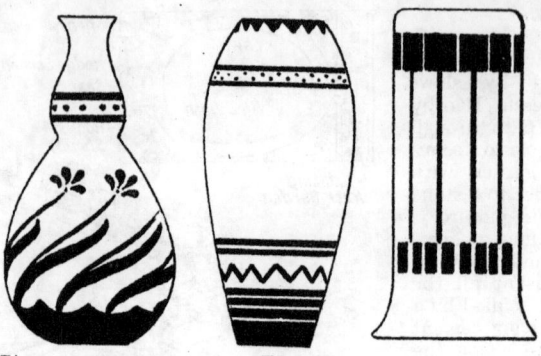

Figs. 1, 2 AND 3.—Decorative Treatment for Various Shapes.

Fig. 1 illustrates the effect obtained by a combination of simple paint brush forms. For the bands and curves the brush is applied while the ornament is revolved on a stand (see Fig. 9). Fig. 2 shows simple geometrical forms, the bands being painted on while the piece is revolving. The third method is illustrated in Fig. 3. This shows an example of the effect obtained by the use of stencils. All these simple methods can be used to obtain striking effects if one or more colours are used on a coloured ground.

Fig. 4.—Suitable Scheme of Geometrical Patterns for a Plain Pot.

earthenware and objects made of plaster of Paris. There is considerable

Fig. 5.—You can practise on an ordinary Flower Pot.

First put on a coating of colour. Then practise mottling and shading effects by means of stippling with different spots of colour as described in the text.

choice in the materials to be used in the decorative work as well as in the methods of applying the colour.

Treating Unglazed Pottery before Painting.

Unglazed pottery of any kind, being porous, will soak up a considerable amount of paint unless it is treated first of all with a priming medium. Even the coarse earthenware flower pot may be prepared for decorative work and provided with a smooth surface with a suitable filler.

The cheapest filling medium is made by adding finely powdered whiting to best size. A small packet of powdered concentrated size, together with a pennyworth of whiting, will make a large quantity of filler. First dissolve the size in just sufficient hot water for the work in hand, making a thin syrup, and then while still hot add sufficient finely powdered whiting, a little at a time, to form a fairly thick syrup. The filler should be kept quite hot while it is being used, being well brushed into the surface. With fine biscuit ware the liquid can be thinner with less whiting. When quite dry the surface should be rubbed over with fine glasspaper. Another filler suitable for biscuit ware is ordinary shellac varnish, which dries quickly and leaves a hard waterproof surface, suitable for articles intended to hold water.

Suitable Paints.

The prepared pot is now ready for the first coating of paint, the most suitable material being a hard quick-drying enamel. There are two kinds that can be used, the ordinary enamel paint with an oil basis requiring a considerable time to harden, and the lacquer enamels which dry very rapidly but require greater care in use. The lacquers known as newinlac, luc, etc., are typical of the quick-drying mediums. The best brush to use is a good-quality flat squirrel hair or "wash" brush; the rather coarse fibre brush usually sold for enamelling is not so suitable. A new brush should be placed in hot water for some time before use, and then stroked between the fingers before drying to make certain there are no loose hairs.

Choice of Colours.

The choice of a suitable colour for the groundwork depends on the particular style of decoration to be employed or the appropriateness of the colour scheme to the surroundings of the object. It is an advantage to know

Fig. 7.—Examples of Simple Geometrical Patterns that can be Selected for Decoration.

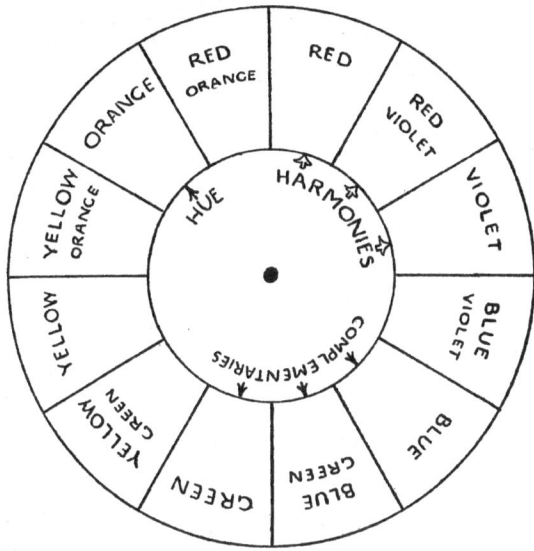

Fig. 8.—This Chart will help you to select Suitable Colour Schemes.

To make up the chart, paint where indicated in tempera or gouache colours on a sheet of drawing paper. Attach a small disc of cardboard in the centre of the paper with a paper fastener and mark it as shown. This gives the colours in harmony and those complementary with the colour you select.

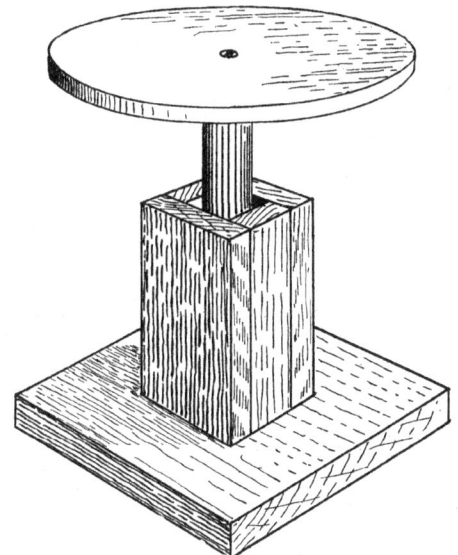

Fig. 9.—A Simple Home-made Revolving Stand for China Painting.

Made with short length of broom handle encased in a box with a piece of plywood screwed down as a pedestal.

something about colour harmonies and, if possible, a colour chart, as shown at Fig. 8, should be prepared. Draw a circle on a piece of smooth drawing paper or Bristol board and divide it into twelve parts. Fill in every other one in order with the six primary colours—violet, blue, green, yellow, orange and red—using tempera or gouache colours. In between each of the six hues paint a mixture of the two in equal quantities. In the centre attach with a paper fastener a small disc of cardboard, marked as shown in the diagram. The arrow heads in black indicate the colour and its complementaries, those in outline show the colours in harmony.

Decorating.

To take a simple piece of work as an example, the ordinary flower pot shown at Fig. 5, after being treated with the filler and carefully smoothed down with glass-paper, can be coated with white lacquer; at least two coats, probably three, will be needed to obtain a perfect surface. Each coat should be allowed to dry and is then rubbed down with pumice powder applied with a piece of thick felt before the next one is applied. Better results are obtained by several thin coats treated in this way than one thick coat; the surface will be much smoother and harder. The brush strokes should be light and laid on evenly so that the colour spreads smoothly over the surface.

Mottled or Shaded Effects.

For many purposes the pot will be found sufficiently decorative when painted in one colour, but by means of stippling, another colour can be introduced to give a mottled or shaded effect.

With an orange ground a stipple of green is very effective, or the main stippling can be done with a shade of violet with green spots here and there. The stippling should be done with a poster colour, using a sable brush with the hairs spread as much as possible. It may be noted here that shades of a hue can be obtained by mixing it with black; tints are obtained by adding white.

Putting on a Coloured Groundwork.

If the decorative effect is to be obtained by means of a pattern or by bands of colour, it is still necessary to give the pot a ground of some suitable colour, even if lacquer is used to form the pattern. A good sable hair brush, about No. 6 round, will do for ordinary use, but a selection of brushes is advisable, especially if several colours are used. It is also convenient to work with the article on a revolving stand; a simple stand can be made with a short length of broom handle encased in a box with a piece of plywood screwed to the top of the upright, as shown at Fig. 9.

Mapping out Pattern—Simple Brush Forms.

Bands and border lines can be painted on the articles more accurately and easily when it can be turned round against the brush, but in any case it is advisable to make chalk lines as a guide—ordinary white chalk is used. Suitable patterns can be built up with simple brush forms, as shown at Fig. 10, and when they are arranged with lines a large variety of attractive patterns can be evolved, as shown at Figs. 1, 11 and 15. All pattern work should be mapped out first with chalk lines so that correct spacing is obtained. If the pattern is painted on with poster colour, mistakes do not matter very much, as the paint can be wiped off, but with lacquer it is almost impossible to remove a mark once applied to the article, as the medium dries so quickly.

Designing the Decoration.

Attractive patterns can be made with simple geometrical forms—a selection of suitable shapes is shown at Figs. 6 and 7, and when they are arranged as a border, as shown at Figs. 2,

Fig. 10.—Simple Brush Forms suitable for Decorative Painting on China.

CHINA AND POTTERY DECORATION

Fig. 11.—Bowl decorated with Simple Brush Forms.

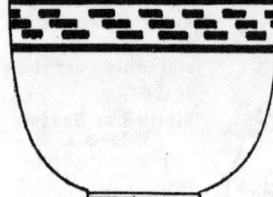

Fig. 12.—Very Simple Treatment for a Cup.

Fig. 13.—A Suggestion for Bold Colouring.

4 and 12, especially if more than one colour is used, the decorative effect is usually very pleasing. As a rule it is better to keep to simple brush shapes or geometrical and conventional forms rather than attempt naturalistic treatments of flowers, fruit, etc. Much more really decorative work is obtained by the use of colour in forming simple patterns with the brush or a stencil, as at Figs. 3, 13, 14 and 16, than in elaborately detailed floral ornament.

Using Coloured Varnishes.

For the non-firing decoration of white china, white or cream grounds, the coloured varnishes used in glass painting are eminently suitable. In the form of "vernis gras" it is possible to obtain the six spectrum colours and, being transparent, it is possible to obtain a brilliancy impossible with opaque colours. These colours can be blended together to form tints and shades, and they are easily applied with camel hair or siberian hair brushes, which should be kept specially for use with the vernis gras. The medium can be thinned with ambro-naphte. The latter colours do not require any further treatment after the decoration is finished, but all work done with poster colours must be coated with transparent spirit varnish, applied with a flat sable or wash brush.

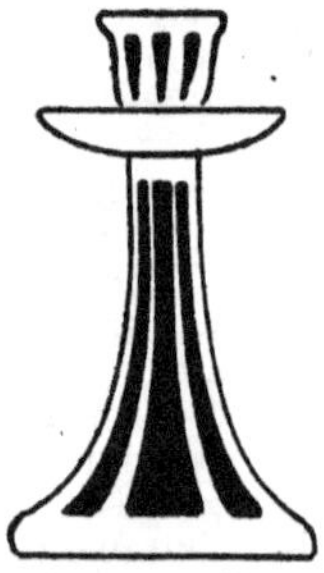

OVERGLAZE PAINTING

The suggestions for decorative effects outlined above are equally suitable for overglaze painting, but owing to the smooth surface of the glazed china, much more delicate treatment is possible. Special colours are required which, mixed with fluxes, adhere to and become one with the glaze when the article has passed through the kiln, or has been "fired," as it is called. Some little alteration is bound to take place in the colours, and therefore some experience is necessary before accurate colouring effects can be obtained.

The Colours.

For overglaze painting the special colours can be obtained in tube form ready mixed, or in powder very much cheaper. With a rich blue, middle green, egg yellow, rose pink, red, brown and black it is possible to obtain a considerable range. Other colours are available, but the above selection is given because they fire well with little alteration. The powder colours have to be mixed with a little turpentine and "fat oil," the method being to place a little of the powder on a white glazed tile, and about two drops of the fat oil and about six drops of turps to a saltspoonful of powder colour. Mix thoroughly with a palette knife and apply with a fine sable brush.

Applying Colours to China.

The china for overglaze painting should be thoroughly clean and wiped over with turpentine and then dried immediately before the painting is done. Any mistakes can be wiped out with a soft rag dipped in turps,

Fig. 14.—Vertical Lines are pleasing on a Shape like this.

Fig. 15.—Border Patterns from Brush Strokes.

but care must be taken not to leave any finger-marks on the completed work in case a little of the colour happens to be left. As most of the colours come out paler than when applied first, a deeper colour scheme can be worked out with the paint in the first place. Too much fat oil mixed with the colours has the effect of dulling them.

UNDERGLAZE PAINTING

Underglaze painting, although not quite so simple as overglaze, can be carried out on biscuit ware, but after the painting has been done it will have to be sent to the potter to be glazed as well as fired. The same kind of decoration as suggested for non-firing and overglaze is suitable, but mistakes cannot be rectified once the underglaze paint has been applied to the ware.

Paint for underglaze decoration is obtainable in powder form, and is mixed with a little gum water and a drop or two of glycerine. As far as possible the colour should be used in its pure state and not mixed with others; a sufficiently large range is available, but it should be noted that the colours alter much more in underglaze painting than with overglaze work.

Applying Paint.

The ware to be painted is first coated with gum water; gum arabic is the best. One coating is generally enough because the pores of the ware must not be entirely filled up or the paint will not adhere. About ½ oz. of gum arabic to ½ pint of hot water gives the best consistency. With ordinary care in selecting and mixing the colours and arranging the decoration, both overglaze and underglaze painting is quite easily done at home with little expense apart from the cost of the ware.

Many pottery firms supply biscuit ware of all household china utensils and, providing that facilities exist for the firing, a useful home craft can be carried out. All ware for the pottery should be marked at the bottom with a distinguishing mark and carefully wrapped

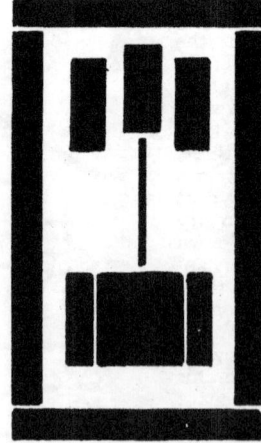

Fig. 16.—Suggestion for a Stencil.

in clean tissue paper. If sent any distance the ware should be packed in straw, or it can be surrounded entirely with granulated cork or wood shavings.

General Remarks

The designs shown in this article have purposely been confined to the simplest patterns. Once the amateur has attained some little skill in using the process it would be an easy matter for him to procure a great variety of designs. It should, however, be remembered that it requires much more skill to obtain a really pleasing effect with a highly intricate design or with a design which attempts to depict scenes or landscapes as apart from conventional patterns.

Redecorating China which has been repaired

It will be remembered that an earlier section explains the methods of restoring broken china and pottery. The reader who has acquired a little skill in pottery decoration will be able to apply this in matching up the design on broken or chipped pottery which is being repaired.

The original pattern should be matched by means of artists' tube colours, and after the colours have dried two or three coats of spirit varnish should be applied to give an imitation of the original glazing. If it is merely a part of the edge of, for example, a bowl which has been chipped off, the missing portion can be moulded in position and afterwards painted.

Providing the article is chiefly used for show, as in the case of an ornamental bowl plaster of Paris may be used for this purpose. After the plaster is set, the surface is rubbed down smooth and treated with a filler.

HOW TO MAKE COOKED MEATS

Brawn.

This is quite simple to make and very cheap. Take half a pig's head and a knuckle of veal. Wash thoroughly and put into a saucepan with sufficient water to cover. Add salt, peppercorns or herbs, or any other desired flavouring. Boil from 2 to 3 hours, or until the meat is easily removed from the bones. Skim off all fat from the top, chop the meat and put into moulds, covering it with the liquor.

Press a plate over the top to keep the meat down. When quite cold dip the mould in boiling water for a minute and the brawn will turn out ready for use.

Galantine of Beef.

This is very nice and makes a welcome change. It is quite inexpensive. Take $\frac{1}{2}$ lb. of lean stewing steak, $\frac{1}{4}$ lb. of bacon, $\frac{1}{4}$ lb. of breadcrumbs, with a flavouring of herbs and pepper to taste and one egg. Mince all together, mix in the egg, then place into a greased jam jar and steam in boiling water for $1\frac{1}{2}$ to 2 hours. Allow to get cool, then, if it sticks at all, dip the jar in hot water to turn it out; allow to get perfectly cold before serving.

German Sausage.

This is very nice when made at home, and is far superior to that bought and quite as cheap. Take 1 lb. of beef steak, $\frac{3}{4}$ lb. of streaky bacon, $\frac{1}{4}$ lb. of breadcrumbs, pepper, salt and nutmeg to taste, and two eggs. Mince the meat and the other ingredients together. Then break and mix in the two eggs. Flour a board and roll into a large sausage. Tie in a pudding cloth and boil for 2 to 3 hours. Turn out when partly cold, allowing it to get quite cold before serving.

Brine for Salting Meat.

For salting beef, pork, etc., this is a very old but excellent recipe and is quite infallible. It is a much better plan to salt your meat at home. If the salting is carried out in the way suggested, it will taste much better than if done at the butcher's.

You will require :—

2d. block of common salt.
2d. saltpetre.
2d. salt of prunella.

Crush these ingredients together and mix thoroughly. Place the mixture in an earthenware pan. Rub it in well all over the meat. Turn the meat over daily. The brine will keep fresh for some time, but will gradually become liquid. A week is usually long enough to salt a joint, but this, of course, depends upon its size.

Sheep and ox tongues are much better salted in this way.

For a Cold Meat Meal.

Savoury balls make a welcome addition to a cold meat meal. Take equal parts of breadcrumbs and mashed potatoes, add two hard-boiled eggs chopped very finely. Add a finely chopped onion or two, some chopped parsley and flavour with a little thyme, pepper and salt to taste. Finally add a small knob of butter, which should be melted. All these should be thoroughly mixed together. Then a beaten egg should be added to bind them together. The mixture should now be formed into balls, dipped into egg and breadcrumbs, placed into a pie dish and baked in a fairly hot oven.

This dish is often served alone as a vegetarian dish, to which is added a brown gravy made from a good stock.

REPAIRING STONEWARE JARS

Stoneware jars are often put on one side because it is thought that they will no longer be of any good service. In the cracked state the jar is likely to leak, but here is a plan by means of which the jar may be made fit for use again. Make a weak solution of cement and water which is about the consistency of a batter. Now pour this into the jar and turn the whole thing about so that the cement runs all over the inside. Allow time for the cement to dry and then repeat the process. Again allow a short period for drying and then put water in the jar. In nearly all cases it will be found to be perfectly watertight, owing to the fact that the thin cement has worked into the crack and filled up the opening. On occasion it may be necessary to give a third application of the cement, and even the three coatings will not make the jar appreciably heavier. This treatment will not only stop leakage, but it will also prevent the crack spreading to such a degree that the jar is not likely to break. Of course, jars repaired in this way should be handled with reasonable care, and not be banged down on a hard surface.

Making a Triangular Summer House

IF a garden is bounded at the back and sides by a brick wall, high enough to form two sides to a summer-house, it will only need front, roof, seats and uprights to make a very effective structure. If, however, fences bound the garden instead of brick walls, it is possible to bring the house away from the fence, and to put in wooden sides, with trellis at the top to form part of the house (Fig. 1).

A triangular house does not occupy much room, and it can be built in the corner of the garden away from the house.

Prepare the Site.

Level it and, if possible, put in a concrete foundation with 6-inch walls (Fig. 2).

The timbers should be above the ground. It is poor economy to let the uprights into the earth, as the wet will rot the wood.

Making the Foundations.

Mark off 4 feet 6 inches on each side. Dig out the foundations 6 inches deep 6 inches wide. When the trenches are dug drive in some pegs, which should be levelled, and be a guide for the height of the concrete.

Concrete Walls.

Concrete walls, 6 inches high, can be used for the house. Make the shuttering for them out of 6-inch boards, 6 inches apart. On each side let in two 6 × ½-inch bolts, with an iron plate on the square of the bolt. The top of the bolts should project 2½ inches above the concrete.

Brick Walls.

A brick wall of three courses can be used to support the house if preferred. It does not take many bricks, and it is not a difficult task to place them.

Put down a layer of cement mortar (mix six of sand and one of cement), then place the bricks in position. Use a short piece of floor board to true up the bricks. Tap back any which may be out. Put a spirit-level on the board when it is resting on the tops of the bricks. Place the first brick on the second course so it breaks the joint at the angle. Do the same with the third

Fig. 1A.—A useful Triangular Summer House erected at the End of a Garden.

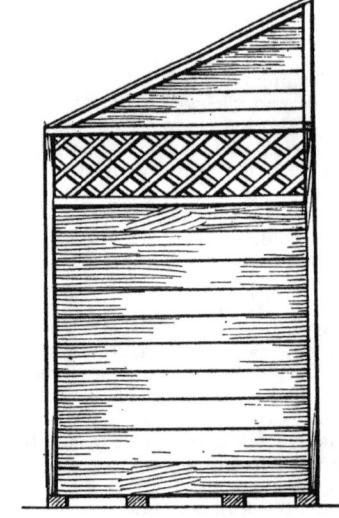

Fig. 1B.—One of the Sides of a Triangular House.

course. Cut the end bricks with the trowel so they will not project beyond the front of the house (Fig. 3).

Timber Foundation.

If brickwork is too expensive a timber foundation could be made from some short pieces of 3 × 4-inch. These should be tarred and let into the ground 1 foot 6 inches, and should be 6 inches above it. They should be placed one at the back, two on each side, and three between the two front ones—eight pieces in all. They should be lined up and a level used so they are the correct height. Place them so the 4-inch side supports the floor (Fig. 4).

Preparing the Framework.

The uprights and sides and other sections are made from pieces of 2 × 3-inch, which should be planed.

Cut off six side pieces and two for the front and place them on the brickwork where they will overlap; then mark the places with a pencil. Two sets require marking in this way. Saw half way down the mark with a tenon saw, then divide the 2 × 3-inch with a rip saw (Fig. 5).

Each piece is halved, and when placed on the brickwork, or 3 × 4-inch uprights, should lie level. The timbers should be at the outside of the brickwork.

Fastening the Woodwork.

Mark the centre of each halved pieces, then bore a ¾-inch hole through them. With a jack plane take the corners off a 3-feet piece of ¾ × ¾-inch, and these should be cut 4 inches long. They should be put in the holes to hold the pieces together and to fasten the uprights to the framing (Fig. 6).

On the front piece mark the position of the doorway. If the front is equalised into three parts it will leave sufficient space for an entrance.

Mark out the position for the uprights for the door and cut recesses 2 inches wide and ½ inch deep for them. A piece is needed for the top. Cut this and recess it for the uprights (Fig. 7).

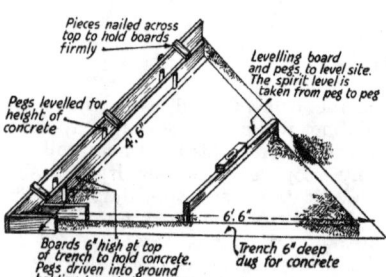

Fig. 2.—The Site should be levelled and a Concrete Foundation prepared.

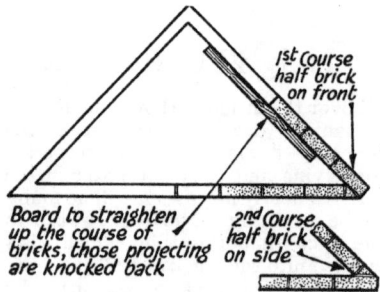

Fig. 3.—Laying the Bricks for a Brick Foundation.

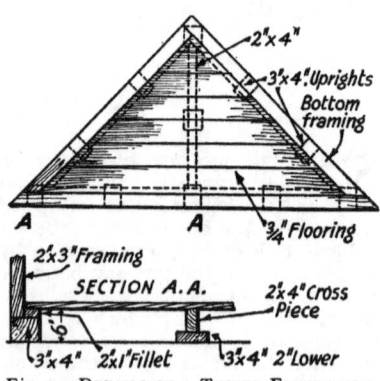

Fig. 4.—Details of a Timber Foundation.

MAKING A TRIANGULAR SUMMER HOUSE

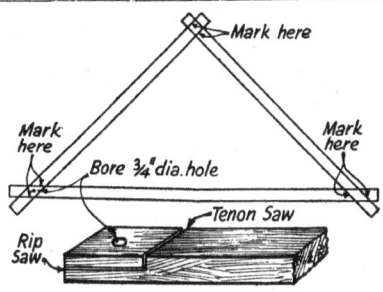

Fig. 5.—Details for preparing the Framework.

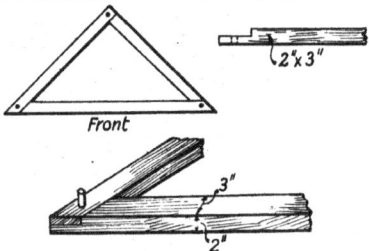

Fig. 6.—Showing Position of Pegs placed through Framework.

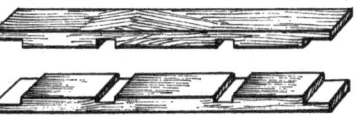

Fig. 7.—The Recesses for the Uprights.

Place it on the bottom piece so it is exact in position, then mark on it the position of ¾-inch pegs. Bore a ¾-inch hole at each end.

The Outside Uprights.

Two outside uprights are needed; they should be 1 inch less than the door frame uprights. Place them in position at the outside of the long piece at the front and mark the position of the pegs. Bore out the holes. The front can now be put together. The outside uprights can go on the pegs at the end, the door uprights in the recesses. Do not fix them; just a nail in the door frames to hold them in position. See the joints are correct. Place the frame in position, then mark in the two outside uprights for a recess for the two seats. This should be 1 foot 7 inches from the bottom of the frame. A piece of 2 × 3 inches should be let into the outside uprights and in the upright which goes at the junction of the two side pieces (B, Fig. 8).

The back piece of 2 × 3 inches should be equal in height to the two side uprights (A).

The pieces for the top should be cut and halved and bored for the ¾-inch pins. The top front piece should be halved; so the side pieces go on to the front piece (Fig. 8).

Assembling the Framework.

The framework is easily put together and nailed, then the two uprights for the doorway are put in and nailed. It can then be fastened to the 3 × 4-inch

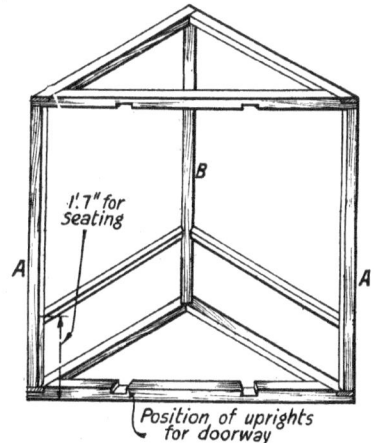

Fig. 8.—The Framework assembled.

uprights. Drop a line with a small weight on it from the top piece and correct any error with regard to the framing should it be out of square or leaning out of the straight.

If it is decided to board up the sides, before fastening the house to the timber foundation, bring it forward about a foot, having a piece of 2 × 4-inch to take the weight at the back, then the boards can be put on from the inside.

Covering the Sides.

Planed weather boards will make the best covering for the sides. Nail the bottom boards first and bring them over the outside of the brick, concrete, or the timber foundation. They should be at least 3 inches from the ground. The boards should be cut at an angle for the back so they make a tight joint. Should it be desired that the top part should be covered with trellis, carry the boards up at least 5 feet, then cut pieces of 2 × 2 inches for each side and nail this between A and B (Fig. 8) to take the top boards of the weather boardings. This 2 × 2 inches will stiffen the boards and will be strong enough for trellis.

The Roof.

In the centre of the front piece nail a strip of 1 × ½-inch wood, 2 feet 6 inches high. Use the square to see it is upright, then put a piece of 2 × 3 inch against it, one end at the top of the 1 × ½-inch strip, the other outside of the top of the house. Mark the piece and this will give the correct angles for the span at the top. Cut two pieces to these angles. A short piece of 3 × 3-inch arris rail is needed for a ridge to go from the top of the span to the back of the house. Nail the two pieces for the span to the front of the house, then measure with 2 × ½-inch strip the length for the ridge. Get the exact measurements with this strip and cut the angles before cutting the arris rail. Nail this to the span in the front and to the back piece.

With a small-sized house planed weather boards will not need any support between the back and front of the house. With a house twice the size, two 2 × 2-inch rafters should be put in on each side to support the weather boards.

Be careful about the joints at the ridge or the roof will leak. Capping out of ½ × 2½-inch and ½ × 3-inch can

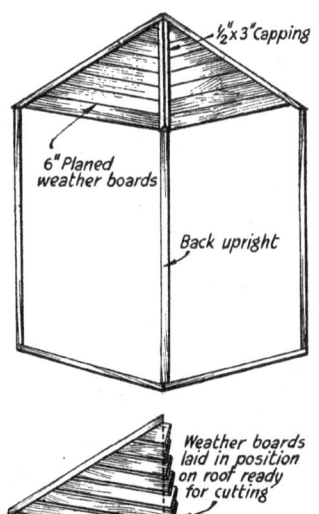

Fig. 9.—Details for erecting Roof.

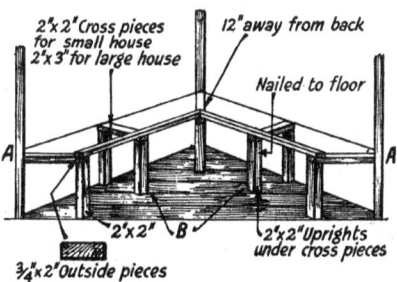

Fig. 10.—Details of the Seats.

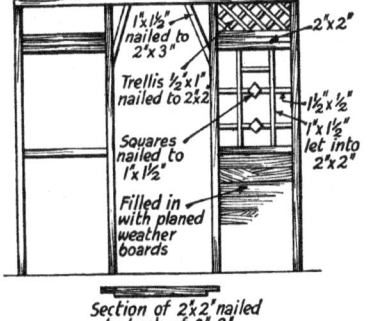

Fig. 11.—One Method of finishing a Small Triangular Summer House.

MAKING A TRIANGULAR SUMMER HOUSE

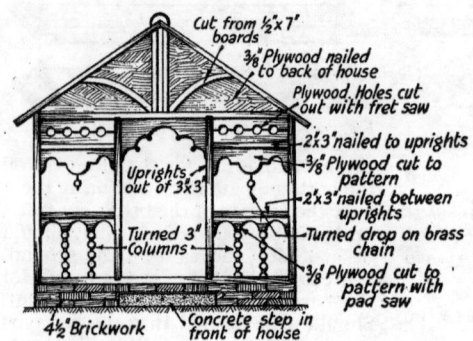

Fig. 12.—An Ornate Design for a House in which extensive use is made of Plywood for Decorative Purposes.

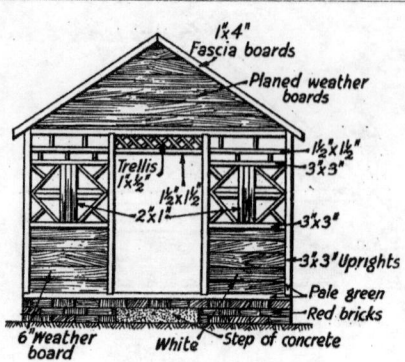

Fig. 13.—Another Method of finishing a Larger Triangular House.

be used. Nail the $2\frac{1}{2} \times \frac{1}{2}$-inch on to the 3-inch. Cut it to the length of the ridge and nail it to the ridge and weather boards.

The Floor.

A recess is left on the bricks or the timber foundation for the floor boards. A piece of 2×4-inch is carried from front to back to take the weight of the floor. The back and front pieces of 3×4-inch uprights are 2 inches lower than the others to allow for this joist (see Fig. 4).

A piece of 2×1-inch is placed on each side of the house. It rests on the bricks or the 3×4-inch and is nailed to the sides.

Cut the long lengths of floor boards first. These should be 1×6-inch tongue and grooved. Use a gauge to get the correct angle, $\frac{3}{4}$-inch floor boards for a small house. Nail the boards down with 2-inch floor brads.

The structure is finished; still it is advisable to put up two zinc gutters to take the rainwater from the sides of the house.

Inside the House.

In the small house seats on each side are sufficient. Make these of 2×2-inch and of $\frac{3}{4} \times 1$-inch strips. Five pieces of 2×2-inch are required for uprights (marked B on Fig. 10). These should be cut the same height as the pieces which go from front to back (A to B, Fig. 8). Five cross-pieces are required, 13 inches long, and these are nailed to the uprights with 4-inch oval brads. These are nailed to back pieces at the side, and the lower part of the uprights are toe-nailed to the floor.

Two pieces of $\frac{3}{4} \times 2$-inch are planed, so the two top edges are taken off and are nailed to the outside edges of the seats. The remainder of the space is filled with $1 \times \frac{3}{4}$-inch strips. These should have the top edges taken off with a plane. They are nailed the wide side on the cross-pieces and are put $\frac{1}{2}$ inch from each other. Punch the nails down so they do not tear any clothes, and after priming them fill up with putty.

Finishing the House.

The finishing of the house is an opportunity of self-expression in design. Four examples show what can be done with simple materials.

In the small one which has been described the effects have been obtained by planed weather-boards, 2×2 inches, cut at the ends so as to fit between the framework, planed $1 \times 1\frac{1}{2}$-inch stuff, nailed to the door framework, $1 \times 1\frac{1}{2}$-inch stuff with a $4\frac{1}{2}$-inch square out of $\frac{3}{4}$-inch boards being nailed in the centre and trellis at the top made out of planed $\frac{1}{2} \times 1$-inch. The sizes are in Fig. 11.

The other houses are larger, twice the size of the one described. The uprights and other timbers should be larger, at least 3×3 inches; and should the house be put on wooden supports the spacing of these should be the same as those described in the small house.

In making the front, the large timbers should be cut so they are a tight fit between the uprights. This can be done easily. Mark them in position with a pencil, then cut outside the marks. This extra amount will be sufficient to make tight joints. Then they can be nailed to the uprights without any trouble. Some of the smaller sections, such as the $1\frac{1}{2} \times 1\frac{1}{2}$ inches forming squares and oblongs, should be nailed up before they are fastened to the house.

Using Plywood.

The ornately designed house (Fig. 12) can be made with plywood for decorative purposes.

The advantage of plywood for this class of work is that it can be cut to any design and still be strong, whereas ordinary wood would break. Ordinary 3×3-inch could be used for the columns. If the edges were taken off they would be more effective.

Such an ornate house can be painted in very gay colours; still it is not every person's taste. When making a large house, if this is placed on three courses of brickwork do not forget to make a concrete step (Fig. 13).

Should plywood be used for outside decorations of the house, this must be painted at least four coats. Special attention should be given to the sawn edges, so the pores are completely closed with paint, otherwise the three-ply will not stay in condition.

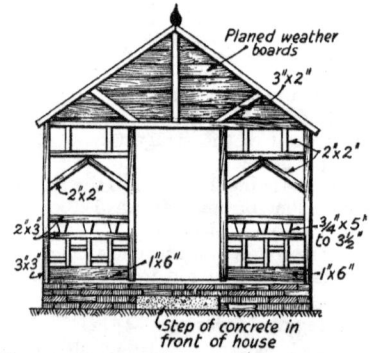

Fig. 14.—Another Design suitable for a Larger House.

CHERRY-STONE CHAINS

LITTLE chains which make pretty necklets, etc., can be made from cherry stones. Get a good number of the stones and rinse these well in water. Each stone will provide one link for the chain. To make the link, put the stone on its side on a hard surface, and then, with a sharp pocket-knife, cut down first on one side and then on the other of the slight ridge which is round the stone. The stone is not so difficult to cut as might be imagined. When the two cuts have been made, you will have a nice little ring from the centre part. Make a good number of rings in this way. When these have been cut, smooth down the sides and edges with medium glasspaper.

The rings are easily linked together. With a knife make a cut right through the ring to open it up, then slip in another ring. The rings are elastic and, after opening the gap, the parts close together at once. To form the chain it is only needful to cut a slit in every other ring.

The cherry-stone chains can be dyed any desired colour.

Sewing Buttons to Stay On

THE craftsman tailor has a special way of sewing on buttons so that they will usually remain on the garment for at least the greater part of its life. When buttons do come off and are resewn at home, it is not uncommon to find them quickly becoming loose again. Many people will be glad to know the proper tailor's method.

Materials.

A tailor never uses cotton for sewing buttons. He uses linen thread, and prefers the kind sold in skeins to that on reels. He keeps a lump of beeswax at hand for waxing the thread. The needles used for sewing buttons are of a stumpy shape with a round eye. At the tailor's trimming shop they are called "ground-downs," but the draper sells them under the name of "betweens."

Making the "Four-cord"

The tailor sews buttons with four threads at once. This serves two purposes. Not only does he save time by having to make fewer stitches, but by waxing and twisting the four threads together first, he produces a cord that is unbreakable. To make this "four-cord," take two lengths of thread from the skein, or, say, 2 yards from the reel, and thread the two through the eye of the needle. If any difficulty is found in doing this, bite the ends and twist them, making a point that will give a start. Pull the needle to the middle of the lengths, so that the four ends are about equal. Then take the lump of beeswax, and drag the thread over it three or four times, as illustrated in Fig. 1. A last pull between finger and thumb will leave the thread hanging straight and almost stiff. Then tie a knot at the end of all four together.

The necessary twisting is done by holding the knot between the teeth,

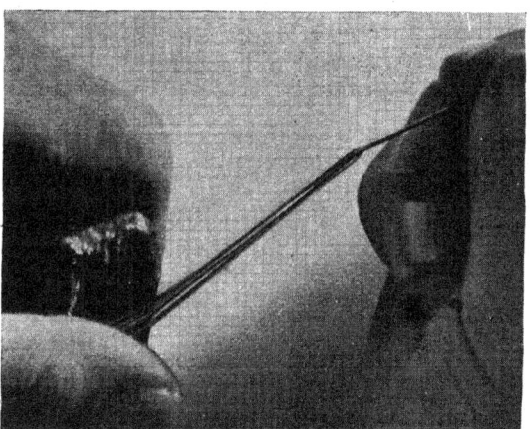

Fig. 1.—Preparing the Thread.
Thread two equal lengths of linen thread in the needle and rub them with beeswax.

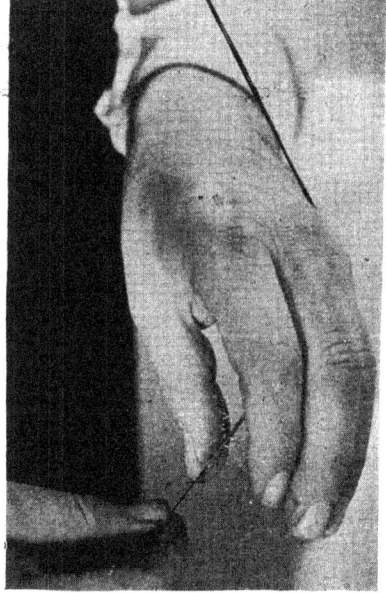

Fig. 2.—Preparing the Thread.
Knot the four waxed strands at the end and hold the knot in the teeth. Twist the needle round and round, keeping the thread taut. This produces the "four-cord."

keeping the threads taut, as shown in Fig. 2, and rapidly turning the needle until the whole of the thread is tightly twisted. Again pull the thread through finger and thumb, and it will remain in the form of a single thick thread with the needle at one end and a knot at the other.

Put Stop Knot on Button Side.

On reference to Fig. 3 it will be apparent that the first stitch, instead of being made from underneath the cloth, has been made downwards, and the second stitch is the first to go up through the button. The reason for doing this will be apparent on reference to the next illustration (Fig. 4), where the stitching has been carried a stage further. The knot will be noticed in the middle of the stitches, right under the button. Under the cloth, in the ordinary domestic fashion of sewing, it would be exposed to all the intense rubbing against other surfaces that occurs in normal wear of men's clothing, and would soon wear away and release the hold of the thread, and so of the button. Safely stowed away like this, amongst the stitches, the knot is now immovable.

Only Four Stitches needed.

Only four stitches are put through the button, two across each pair of holes. As this produces a total of sixteen actual threads, obviously it is a sufficient number. The wax and the twisting help to strengthen the job also. In Fig. 4 only one pair of stitches has been made, and when the next pair are done, the knot is almost hidden. The apparent looseness of the stitches in these photographs is intentional, and has been exaggerated for clearness, along with the size of the button and the thickness and colour of the thread.

In the case of buttons on coats, jackets, and waistcoats, it is useless to

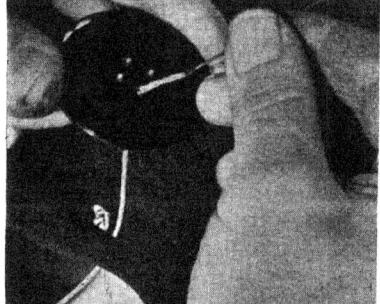

Fig. 3.—The first Stitch.
The first stitch is made *downwards* through the cloth, leaving the knot where the button comes.

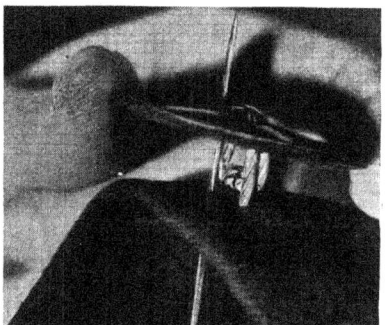

Fig. 4.—First two Stitches.
The stitches enclose the knot, which can never be worn away. Size of button and thickness of thread are exaggerated for the sake of clearness.

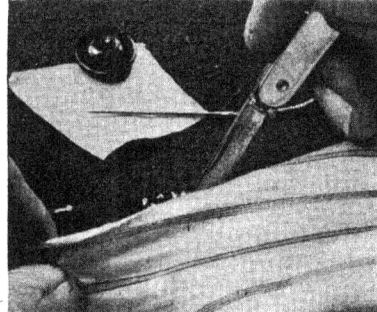

Fig. 5.—To strengthen the Material.
Insert a bit of canvas between cloth and lining. This prevents clothes being torn by pull on the button.

SEWING BUTTONS TO STAY ON

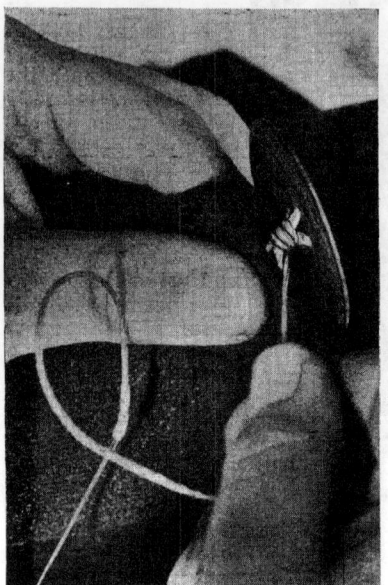

Fig. 6.—Winding the Stitches.
When two stitches each way have been made, the cord is wound tightly round them. For coat buttons the stitches are made loose in order to form a "neck."

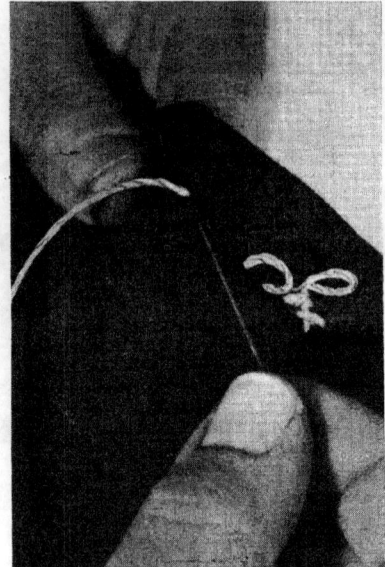

Fig. 7.—Finishing Off.
Three "back-stitches" on the underside provide a firm anchorage for the cord. They are shown loose only for explanation. Each should be pulled tight as made.

buttons, the button is stitched close.

Finishing Off.

Just as the knot has been secured at one end of the stitching, so is it just as necessary to fasten off the final end of the thread, or the pull on the button would very soon undo all the strong stitches. This is done by three "back-stitches" on the underside of the garment, as seen in Figs. 7 and 8. In Fig. 7 the stitches have been left loose, so as to show how they are formed, but actually each one should be pulled very tight before making the next. These stitches are made well away from the button, so as to take some of the strain away from the spot at the middle of the button, where most of the pull comes. When pulled tight, they can hardly be seen, and on making the third back-stitch, cut the thread, and the button is on to stay.

When the Material is weak.

In men's clothing there is usually a layer of canvas between cloth and lining where the buttons go. Sometimes this is found to be absent, and in such cases, as well as where the outer material is of a soft character, it is advisable to add a piece of canvas at the spot where the button is to be resewn. The best way to insert the canvas is to cut the stitching between cloth and lining with a small sharp knife. The method shown in Fig. 5 is quicker, and actually safer, than using scissors. The bit of canvas is slipped in between, the button sewn on with the four-cord, and then the opening can be stitched up again, leaving no trace of the operation.

Summary.

First make your four-cord, with two doubled lengths of thread in the needle, and wax it. Then twist the cord tightly and knot it.

Make the first stitch *downwards*, leaving the knot on top where the button is to come. Sew the button with four stitches, loosely for coat buttons, tightly for trouser buttons.

Wind cord tightly round the neck under the button two or three turns for trouser buttons, but to cover the "neck" in others. Pass the needle and thread down through the cloth to secure.

Fasten off by three back-stitches well apart.

sew the buttons close down to the cloth. A "neck" has to be left under the button to allow for the thickness of the material of the buttonholes on the opposite side to button up properly. The slack stitching is for this purpose. When the four stitches have been made through the buttons, pull hard on the button, if necessary twisting it too, to get the four loops equal. They will then divide the strain and wear equally. Push the needle up through the cloth, but not through the button, and very tightly twist the cord around the stitches (see Fig. 6). Then pass the needle down through the cloth again to prevent any chance of loosening. The winding around the stitches is done with fewer turns when, as in trouser

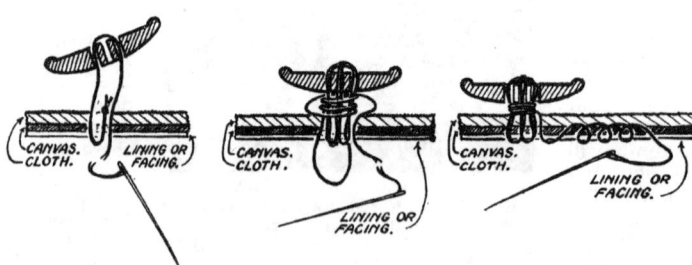

Fig. 8.—Explaining the Whole Process.
The first picture on the left shows the first stitch. Note the knot *between* button and cloth. The centre sketch shows how the "neck" is formed. Finishing off is illustrated in the right-hand sketch, the stitches being placed well apart.

KEEPING MILK IN HOT WEATHER

EVERYBODY knows how quickly milk goes sour in hot weather, especially if there is thunder about. Here is a good way of keeping milk sweet without the use of a refrigerator. In some position, where no direct sunshine can fall, place a rather deep tub or bath. A good place would be on the tiled floor of a larder. Then fill the vessel with water. The milk is put into bottles, which must have closely fitting corks so that no leakage is possible. Immerse the bottles in the tub, taking care that each is completely under the water. If only a little of the top of a bottle projects, the chilling effect will not be so complete. The milk will be almost as cool as if it had been iced when stored in this way. Naturally, the bottles must be kept scrupulously clean inside.

Simple Designs for Garden Gates

A SIMPLE gate can be formed of a few palings and two pieces of arris rail with a paling put aslant to form a strut (Fig. 1).

It is very easily made. Buy some palings ¾ × 3 inches and plane them. Save a piece of arris rail which will make two lengths to reach across from post to post. The arris should be planed. While it does not look out of place in a fence, two sawn pieces of arris rail upon a gate give it a crude appearance, which does not add to one's self-esteem as the owner of the house.

Place them so that the paling projects above the top rail, and 6 inches below the bottom one. Nail two pieces of the 3 × ¾ inches on the outside, then mark off on the inside space the position of the other palings. They should be divided equally, and as far as possible the space should be about the width of the palings. It must be remembered that the arris rail is almost a triangle, and it would be difficult to put on hinges at the back. It is best to put the long part of the garnet hinges on the arris rail before putting on the palings.

Finishing off the Tops of the Palings.

The simple gate has the palings left square at the top, but to point them gives them a better finish. They can be rounded with a pad saw, and the corners could be cut off. A gate with only two lengths of arris rail to support the palings should not be higher than 3 feet. When the palings have been nailed on, then put a piece from the hinge side of the top side of the arris rail to the under side of the rail close to the latch. Make it a tight fit, as it prevents the gate from sagging.

A Simple 3 feet 6-inch Gate.

A gate 3 feet 6 inches high and upwards should have at least three rails to support the palings. It is possible to design a gate of these dimensions

Fig. 1.—A Very Simple but Effective Gate can be constructed from a few Palings and Pieces of Arris Rail.

so that it will be attractive. A simple gate similar to the first one can be made. The design can be varied by using long and short palings (Fig. 2), placed alternatively.

The gate is made by placing the three cross pieces on a bench, or a flat surface. Mark off with a rod the positions of the cross pieces. Nail the first paling on the lower, the centre, then the top cross piece. Take the rod to the other end of the arris rail and mark off the position of the palings. It is as well to make this the hinged side, and to put the hinges on before nailing the outside palings. Mark the position of the long palings and nail them on. The short ones should then be nailed between the long ones.

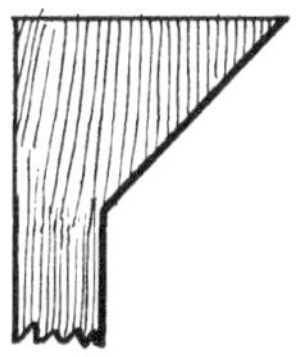

How to obtain Varied Effects.

It is surprising the varied effects which can be made in the appearance of a gate of this simple design. The wood can be tapered at the end. The best method of marking the wood is to cut a piece with the correct angle upon it, then to put it against the paling, and then to mark each side (Fig. 1A).

For 3-inch palings make the depth of cut at least 1⅝ inches. The two lines will intersect at the top. Mark the palings, cut off these pieces, then plane the top.

If a rounded top, make a similar pattern with a half-round space, then mark off the palings. They should be cut out with a pad saw.

Using 2-inch Palings

While 3-inch palings are the usual size for these gates, they can be made attractive if 2-inch ones are used. Use a tapered or a round top. With these palings the space should be lessened in proportion to their width.

Using 1-inch Strips.

A gate made of 1-inch strips looks serviceable and is strong. It is less trouble to taper these 1-inch strips. A gate with the 1-inch strips close together at the lower part makes a very strong gate.

Another way of making this simple gate is to use 1-foot strips put on with a 1-inch space (Fig. 5). The top bar should not be put too high. The strips should be put on the gate with a nail so that they can be taken off very easily. When in position the strips, which are all one height, are marked according to a desired design. They can be cut alternately long and short, a difference of 3 inches.

Another plan is to use a curved design on the top of the pieces of wood. They should be marked with a pencil, then sawn either pointed or rounded.

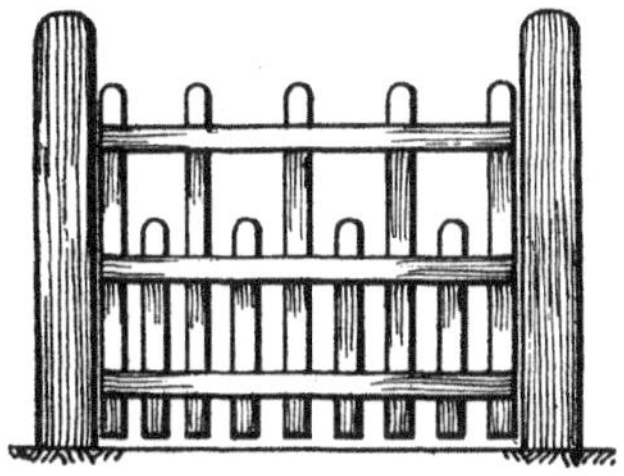

Fig. 1A.—A Simple Template for Marking Tops of Palings when Tapered Effect is Desired.

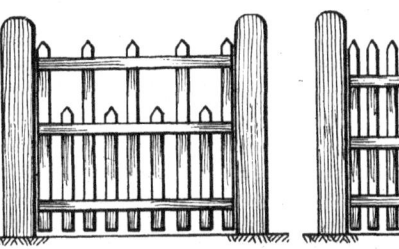

Fig. 2.—A Simple Design, using Long and Short Palings Alternately.

Fig. 3.—The Design shown in Fig. 2 but with Tapered Tops.

Fig. 4.—Gate constructed with Palings all the same Length.

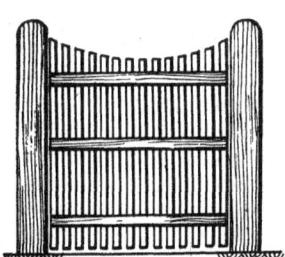

Fig. 5.—An Effective Gate formed with 1-inch Strips.

Fig. 6.—A Simple Closely Boarded Gate. Front View.

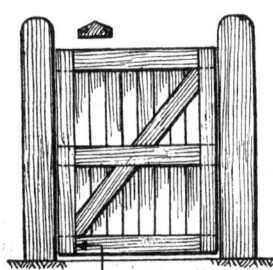

Mortise and Tenon Joint.
Fig. 7.—Back View of Closely Boarded Gate showing Simple Construction.

SIMPLE DESIGNS FOR GARDEN GATES

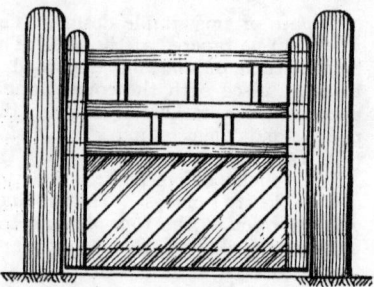

Fig. 8.—A More Elaborate Gate built of Heavier Timbers and Panelled at the Bottom.

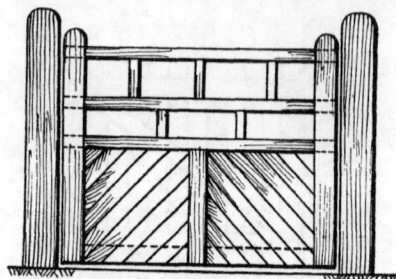

Fig. 9.—Alternative Arrangement of Panelling for More Elaborate Gate.

Fig. 10.—Design for a Larger Gate. The spacing is made with ¾-inch rounds.

It is as well to number them with a pencil before removing them, so that they can be put back in the proper position.

Closely Boarded Gates.

A gate used a great deal is the closely boarded one (Fig. 6). This is built more massively than those previously described. These gates average 3 feet 6 inches to 4 feet high and from 3 feet to 4 feet 6 inches wide. They consist of two stout uprights usually 2 × 3 inches, one top rail of the above size rebated on one edge and two rails of 1¼ or 1-inch stuff.

The two uprights are put side by side and the position of the cross pieces marked upon them.

A gauge is necessary for marking the position of the mortises. Mark the wood on the smooth side, and take all measurements from it. For 2-inch uprights make a ⅝-inch mortise, marking the two uprights on each edge.

Cutting the Mortise.

Use a sharp chisel and take upright cuts across the mortise, then turn the chisel and force it with the mallet against the cuts which have been made. This will take out the parts cut with the chisel. Next, cut with the chisel the other way to the line, turn the piece over and proceed as before. When a cut has been made through the piece it is easy to get out the rest of the mortise.

The pieces which have to be tenoned should be marked on each side. A firm stool should be used, if a vice is not available, to hold the wood while it is being sawn. Use a ripping saw for cutting the tenons. If not sure of sawing correctly, cut down the lines on one side, then turn the piece over and cut down the lines on the other. Cut all the lines making the tenons, then crosscut them with a tenon saw.

Top Piece.

The top piece of the gate is the same thickness as the two uprights. If possible it should be rebated on the lower part, to take the thickness of the boards to be used for making the gate. The two lower parts which should be used should be level with the bottom of the rebate of the top piece. When the tenons and the mortises have been made, they should be tried and should make a tight fit without cramping.

Glue joints are of little value for outside joints, though casein glue will hold them, even when they are exposed to damp atmospheres.

Paint the Tenons with Priming Colour.

The tenons on the cross pieces should be painted with a good priming colour, then put into the upright rails. They should be cramped up, the square used for correct position, then each tenon should be held tightly by a wedge.

Peg the Tenons in Position.

A hole should be bored through the tenons and the outsides of the mortises,

Fig. 11.—Some Typical Forms of Hinges.
Remember that when arris rail is being used it may be advisable to fit the hinge during assembly.

Fig. 12.—Some Useful Forms of Latches.

then an oak peg driven through them to hold the tenons in position.

The matching weather boarding or oak pales can be used for filling up the space. Two struts should be used, one from the lower to the middle rail, and one from the middle to the top. They should go from the hinge side at the bottom to the latch side at the top.

If no Rebating Tool is available.

If it is impossible to rebate the top rail for want of a tool, then use a piece the thickness of the lower rail for the top one. Put the gate together. Square up the gate before driving in the wedges. Measure the top rail and cut a piece of wood, ½ inch less in width, and the width of the space between the two uprights. Nail this on the top rail level with the top. This will form a rebate on the top rail for the matching. Nail this on, then cut a piece of wood 1 inch thick, and 1 inch wider than the top rail and matching. Put a chamfer or a bevel edge on each side, then nail it on the top of the gate.

A More Elaborate Gate.

A more elaborate gate is one which is built of heavier timbers and is panelled at the bottom. Gates can be made so that they can express the maker's sense of beauty. They are mainly built out of 2 × 3-inch timbers, with light boards, squares or rounds for either the top or the bottom of the gate.

A Larger Gate.

Fig. 10 shows a gate built of 2 × 3 inches, with top and centre rails 2 × 3 inches. Rounds are used for the spacing. These can be either ¾ or 1 inch. Space out the top and middle bar and drill holes ⅝ inch deep. Cut the rounds ¼ inch less than the space between the bottom of the holes in the top and bottom rails. These can now be fixed in. The shaped pieces at the bottom are nailed to two pieces of ¾ × 2 inches, and then nailed to the bottom and middle rail.

HOME-MADE EQUIPMENT FOR A SMALL WORKSHOP

However well equipped the amateur's workshop, there are always times when some additional appliances are needed to carry through a piece of work. The purpose of this article is to show what can be done with extemporised apparatus, and how to make sundry useful and practical devices which will enable an otherwise impossible job to be carried through successfully.

Turning a Large Wheel.

Wheels considerably larger than the " throw " of the average small lathe can be turned successfully if the headstock has a hollow mandrel. First remove all change wheels and the quadrant from the end of the headstock, then turn a special bush to fit over the end of the mandrel. Turn a shoulder and cut a thread on the shank —as in Fig. 1—to accommodate the faceplate, then bore as large a hole as possible through the bush. Fix the bush to the mandrel with a long steel bolt and nut with a large washer to bear on the face of the faceplate. Mount the wheel on the faceplate with dogs or clamps, set the work as true as possible, then rig up a very rigid wooden tool rest—as sketched in Fig. 2—placed as near as possible to the work as practicable. Strip steel or ordinary timber about 2 × 1 inch will answer very well for this tool rest.

The lathe can now be run at a slow speed and the work turned with hand turning tools. If the wheel is of metal a " hook tool," as in Fig. 3, is the best. It can be made from an old square file and is used as in Fig. 4, by resting the heel or bottom part of the tool on the rest—which in this case ought to be of metal or at least faced with metal. A long handle must be

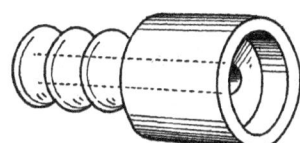

Fig. 1.—Faceplate Bush.

Details must be arranged to suit the particular lathe—the essentials are the screw thread and shoulder; recessed part to fit one mandrel and hole for clamping bolt.

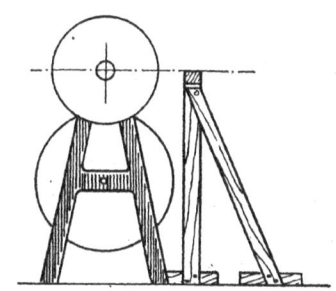

Fig. 2.—Work in Lathe with Extemporised Tool Rest.

The large wheel is mounted on back end of mandrel; a temporary tool rest is used to steady the tool.

Fig. 3.—Hook Tool.

A special tool for turning metal by hand can be made from an old file.

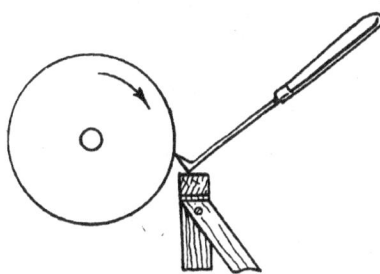

Fig. 4.—Using the Hook Tool.

This diagram shows correct angles of tool when turning metal.

fixed securely to the tool and should rest against the worker's shoulder. The cut is made by holding the tool down firmly on the rest with both hands and pressing the handle upwards with the shoulder.

Alternatively the left hand can hold the tool and the right can manipulate the handle; the former method is the best and safest.

Holding Irregularly Shaped Objects.

Curved work, such as a model boat hull or some kinds of carved woodwork, and many other jobs of a like nature, are often difficult to hold. In most cases a rig-up, such as that in Fig. 5, will overcome the trouble and can be rigged up in a few minutes.

A piece of thick board of suitable size is used as a base, and to it are screwed specially shaped cross-pieces, which for use with delicate work should be padded with cloth or leather to prevent bruising.

The work is rested in the cross-pieces—after the base has been screwed to the bench. The work is held firmly by a leather strap fixed securely to the base at one end. The free end has a stirrup or loop, and the worker puts his foot in it and so tightens the strap and holds the work firmly, both hands being free to manipulate the carving tools.

Extemporised Pipe Vice.

Gas and other heavy pipes cannot be held successfully in an ordinary bench vice unless provided with special " chains," but a serviceable substitute is to rig up a large pair of " footprint " grips, as indicated in Fig. 6. The grips are held upright by means of two angle plates or blocks screwed or clamped to the bench. The ends of the handle part should project beyond the bench to the right. The pipe is

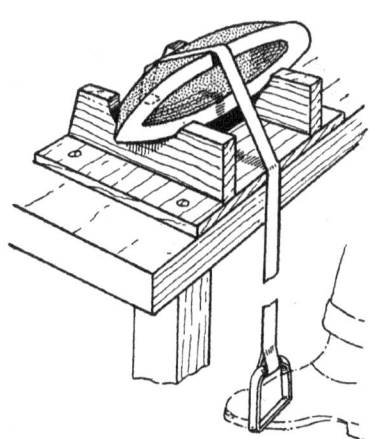

Fig. 5.—Holding Irregularly Shaped Work.

A strap, tightened by the foot, draws the work down into shaped pieces on a baseboard fixed to the bench.

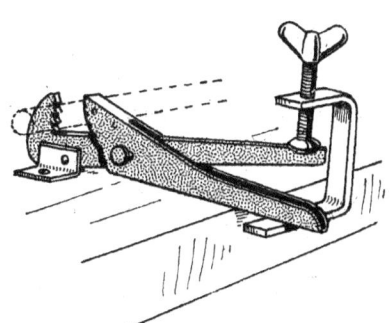

Fig. 6.—Extemporised Pipe Vice.

A pair of " Footprints," two angle plates and a cramp combine to make an effective pipe vice.

Fig. 7.—Supporting Long Work.

This simple device will hold lengthy pieces of metal or wood and is readily adjustable for height.

HOME-MADE EQUIPMENT FOR A SMALL WORKSHOP

then placed in the jaws and gripped by exerting pressure on the handles with an ordinary "G" cramp. The "footprint" must be bolted or otherwise firmly held to the angle plates. This rig-up will be found very useful when dealing with stubborn pipe joints.

Supporting Long Work.

When planing or working on long pieces of material it is necessary to support the free end. One simple and effective way of doing this is to take two pieces of batten about 3 feet 6 inches long, 2 inches wide and 1 inch thick, drill a ¾-inch diameter hole near the lower end of each, and put a screw through the two pieces about 6 inches from the top. This makes a scissor-like arrangement, shown in Fig. 7, which will stand up by putting a piece of rod through the holes in the lower ends. The height of the support is adjustable by opening or closing the legs, and can most readily be held securely by a piece of cord tied across the bottom. The work to be supported rests in the V-shaped opening at the top.

Illuminating the Work.

However well lighted the workshop, it is often difficult to illuminate odd corners of small work. A good tip is to mount a small mirror on a stand as in Fig. 8, and place it so that an adjacent light is reflected directly into the dark corner.

There is no need to make anything elaborate—a block of wood, two pieces of soft iron or copper wire about No. 16 gauge and a piece of mirror, about 6 × 8 inches or any handy size, are all that is needed. First bend the wires into loops, then open out the ends and bend them to form claws to clip the glass, as in Fig. 9, then screw the other end to the wood block. The mirror can be set at any desired angle by bending the wires.

Handling Heavy Objects.

The single-handed worker faced with the task of handling a very heavy object, for example, an electric motor, or some massive castings, should always remember that much assistance can be obtained from a simple block and tackle. One way to arrange it is to place a strong timber or bar of iron on the collars or cross-members of the roof. Next lash a

Fig. 8.—Light Reflector.
A simple thing that is invaluable for throwing light into a dark corner.

Fig. 9.—Shaping the Wire Arms.
Successive stages in bending the wire arms for the mirror are here shown. The wire is looped at A, ends turned up at B, clips formed at C, and arm bent down at D.

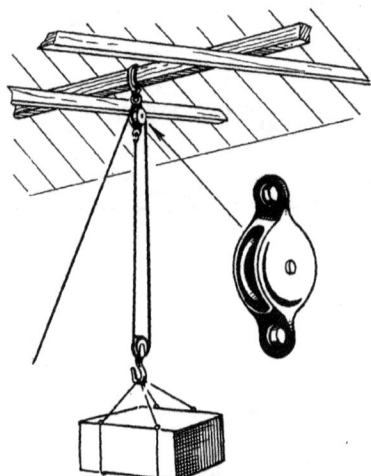

Fig. 10.—Simple Lifting Tackle.
Two small galvanised iron pulley blocks and a stout rope arranged as here shown make a "purchase tackle" that will raise heavy weights.

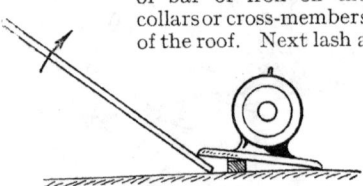

Fig. 11.—First Stage of Raising Heavy Weight.
The object is tilted up at one side with a crowbar and a block of wood inserted.

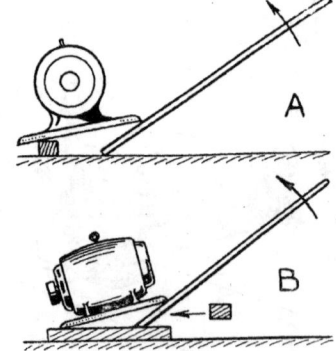

Fig. 12.—Second Stage of Elevation.
The opposite side is raised as before and another block inserted, as at A; the object is then lifted at right angles and a cross block inserted as at B.

pulley block to the bar, reeve a stout rope through the block, reeve it through a second block, and bring the end up to the eye on the first block, as in Fig. 10, or fasten it to the overhead beam. The work is next hooked or slung on the lower block, and the free end of the rope hauled on until the object is raised a few inches off the floor. By grasping the rope it will be found easy to move the object some distance with one hand, because the bulk of the weight is carried by the tackle.

Raising a Heavy Weight.

When it is necessary to raise a heavy weight, the best procedure when working single-handed—or with amateur assistance—is to elevate the object in successive stages, keeping the object as nearly vertical as possible during the process. Successive stages are shown in Figs. 11, 12 and 13. In the first sketch the object is being levered up and a block of wood inserted under it; in the second the opposite side is being raised to twice the height of the first "lift"; in the third sketch the weighty object has been raised on to a strong box or other support, whence it can be moved by inserting a crowbar or "pinch-bar" under one end and gradually levering it forward. It is far better to work slowly but surely in this way than hastily to lift the weight and then have nothing with which to support it.

If rollers are used to move heavy things, several rollers should be prepared, and in many cases it is best to lay on the floor two parallel boards for the rollers to traverse, also always put some boards, a strong box lid or something of that kind under the object for the rollers to bear upon. Endeavour always to have two rollers under the object, as in Fig. 14, and work forwards from them on to the third, then bring the released roller forwards and progress on to it as before. If the rollers are set at an angle the object will always roll in the direction of the rollers.

Cramping Large Areas.

The woodworker is often faced with the problem of exerting pressure upon or "cramping" a large area, for example, when veneering, or when gluing up a large panel. In such cases

Fig. 13.—Weight Raised.
The process is repeated and further blocks added until the object is raised and can be pushed into position.

HOME-MADE EQUIPMENT FOR A SMALL WORKSHOP

Fig. 14.—Use of Rollers.
Any heavy object can be moved in the workshop with the aid of rollers, as here shown.

the amateur can rig up an effective cramp on the lines sketched in Fig. 15, by temporarily nailing a piece of stout board on the roof rafters over the centre of the bench on which the work is set up. The working surface must be covered by stout cross-pieces of wood.

Four battens about $2 \times 1\frac{1}{2}$ inches are then disposed between the work and the ceiling and drawn inwards with cords, which, when twisted with a wooden lever, act as a tourniquet, and by drawing the struts together cause great pressure to be exerted. The only risk with this scheme is that the roof if very light may be forced upwards.

Ripping Long Boards.

Novices who try to "rip" or saw lengthways along a long board will speedily find it a difficult job because the board springs up and down violently. A quick and simple rig-up that overcomes the difficulty—especially when only one sawing trestle is available—is sketched in Fig. 16, and consists of laying the board in loops of rope, one near each end; other loops of rope are then passed over the board and fastened down tightly to the workbench legs, or if need be to screw eyes in the floor.

The saw-cut should be started for a foot or two so that the saw can be worked freely inside the suspended part. The sawing trestle should be moved progressively as the sawing progresses.

Work under the Drill Press.

The usual type of pillar drill, for example, that shown on page 606, has

Fig. 15.—Cramping a Large Area.

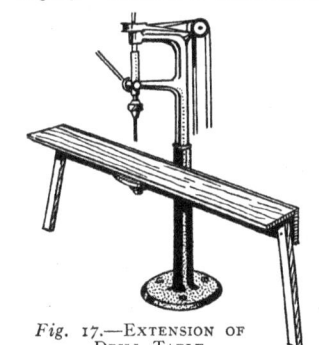

Fig. 17.—Extension of Drill Table.

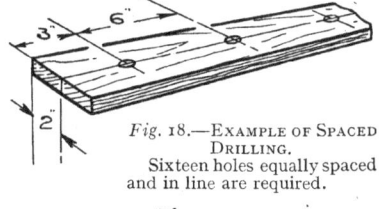

Fig. 18.—Example of Spaced Drilling.
Sixteen holes equally spaced and in line are required.

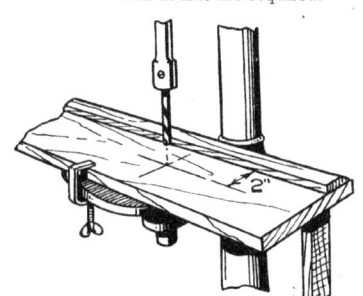

Fig. 19.—Guide or Fence.
The batten is located at the required distance from the drill centre, in this example 2 inches.

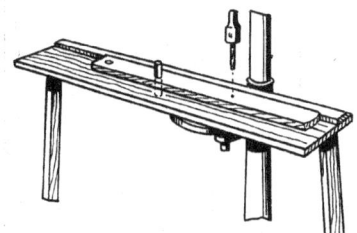

Fig. 20.—Locating Pin.
A pin is inserted through the last hole drilled and into a spacing hole drilled in the board.

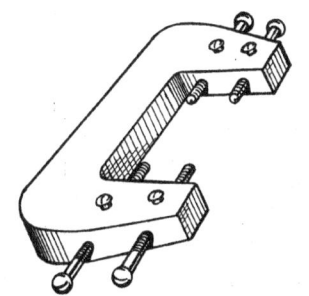

Fig. 21.—Home-made Limit Gauge.

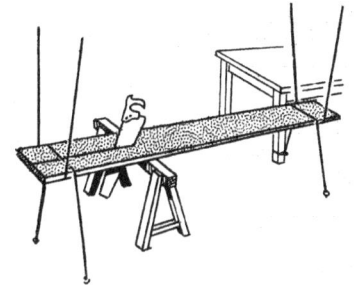

Fig. 16.—Sawing Long Board with Single Trestle.

a small circular work-table which is inadequate as a support when drilling a series of holes in a long piece of work. One simple way of overcoming the difficulty is to take a suitable length of smooth board about 9 inches wide and nail to one edge another piece of board about 6 inches wide, as in Fig. 17, and if necessary cut a slot through it to allow the edge of the drill table to pass. A couple of wooden struts nailed to the floor will make all secure, and incidentally this rig-up paves the way to a species of semi-automatic drilling.

Spaced Drilling.

With the foregoing rig-up it is possible to undertake spaced drilling; for example, the job sketched in Fig. 18 consists of a row of sixteen holes spaced 6 inches apart and all being 2 inches from one edge.

In the ordinary way this job would need careful marking out, centring and drilling, but by the following method it is only necessary to measure off the first two holes and set up the "fence" properly.

To do this, screw or nail securely to the long board on the drill table a piece of smooth batten, as in Fig. 19, then set the board on the drill table, and if practicable cramp or screw it in position so that the centre of the drill

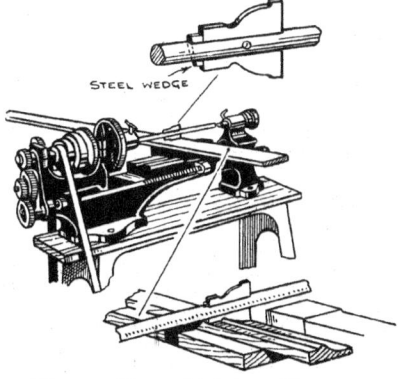

Fig. 22.—Using Lathe as Moulding Machine.

A flat steel cutter shaped to the converse of the moulding is mounted between centres, run at fastest speed and the work fed gently against the revolving cutter, preferably from the back of the lathe.

is just 2 inches away from the face of the batten. Drill the first and second holes in the work, and while the drill is still in the work, drill through the first hole into the fixed board. Prepare a metal or wooden pin—a nail will often answer the purpose. Withdraw the drill, move the work forwards until the pin—when put through the hole last drilled in the work—will slip into the hole in the board. This, as shown in Fig. 20, locates the work, and it only remains to drill the next hole, remove the peg, slide the work forwards and peg in as before. This simple system takes longer to describe than operate, but ensures a remarkable degree of accuracy. This scheme is adaptable to work in wood or metal of any size, and leads naturally to the use of all kinds of home-made spacing and gauging jigs.

A Practical Gauge.

One example of a practical gauge, costing practically nothing to make is given in Fig. 21, and can be made in hard wood or metal; it is suitable for measuring the diameter of circular work or the length of straight work.

Moreover, it acts as a limit gauge and ensures the work being correct to size within very small limits of error. The body can be of hardwood, plywood or metal, and through it are driven four screws with the points filed off. Small screws are driven at right angles to act as set screws and prevent movement of the gauge screws. To set the gauge, adjust the inner pair until the distance between their ends exactly corresponds with the required dimension—say 3 inches. Fix the screws in this position, then adjust the front pair so that the end of one of them is in line with one of the first screws. Then adjust the fourth screw so that the distance between it and the third is 3 inches plus or minus any desired limit of error. In practice the best way to do this—without a micrometer—is to take a piece of material of the required length—say 3 inches—and grip it between the inner pair of screws, then when adjusting the outer pair use the same piece of material, but with a little bit of very thin notepaper between it and one screw. Tighten the screw to just grip the paper, then secure the screw and remove the gauge material.

The outer pair of screws will now be 3 inches plus about three-thousandths of an inch; the inner pair will be almost exactly 3 inches apart. To use the gauge, turn or shape the actual work until it just slips past the outer pair of screws, but will not pass the inner pair. Always use the gauge gently, as it could readily be forced open a few thousandths of an inch, but if used with ordinary care it is quite possible to turn out work within three or four-thousandths of an inch of exact size. Moreover, its use saves repeatedly measuring or calipering.

Using Lathe as Moulding Machine.

Any reasonably good small lathe can be used for making lengths of moulding in wood. The method is to mount a "fly-cutter," as shown in Fig. 22, on a mandrel run between centres. The lathe should be run at top speed and the work fed carefully against the cutter. A guide with fence is desirable, and if the work is at all coarse a roughing cutter should first be used and then be followed by a very sharp finishing cutter. For small jobs the cutters can be mild steel, case-hardened. In some cases it is desirable to feed the work from the back of the lathe so that the cutter revolves towards the work.

MENDING STOCKINGS WITH THE SEWING MACHINE

A LADDER in a stocking can be quickly mended by folding it together on the wrong side and running a pin tuck along. This does not show as it would if darned.

As most stockings are liable to wear at the heel, especially at the point where the top of the shoe rubs against it, ordinary darning, however well it is done, cannot fail to show. In this case the stocking can hardly be used, except in the house. By using the sewing machine a perfect repair can be carried out without darning.

Turn the stocking inside-out and sew along inside the back seam, beginning about 3 inches or so above the hole. Gradually work the stitching inside the seam, leaving the hole on the outside, and finish the sewing near the bottom of the heel. Remove from machine, place the left hand inside, and then cut off the material rather close to the stitching, as shown in the illustration, and then oversew. This method will not be so satisfactory if the hole is a large one, but generally the fabric will give sufficiently for the reduction to be made.

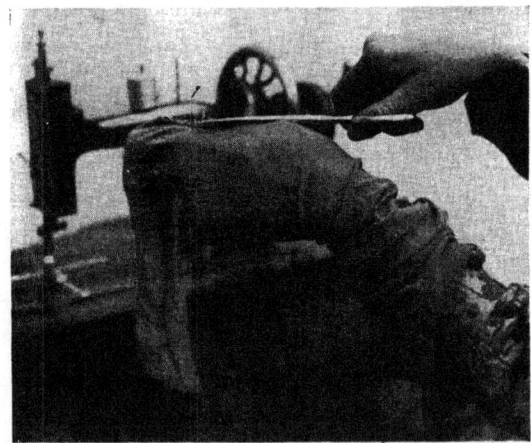

*Fig. 1.—*Trimming the Seam.
The surplus fabric is cut away close after sewing.

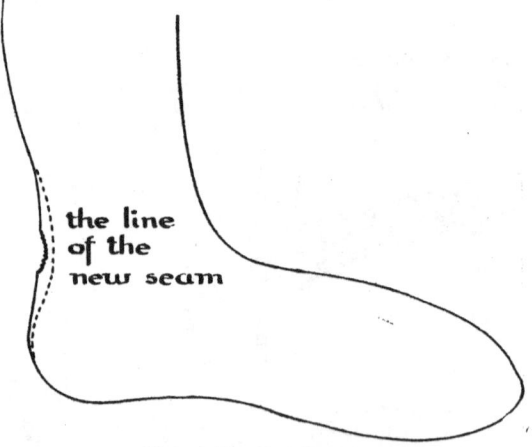

*Fig. 2.—*Mending Stockings.
Showing where to run the stitching.

When and How to Use Enamel

The two main functions of an enamel are to impart to the surface to which it is applied both colour and gloss. Enamels have to be applied over suitable undercoatings, which supply the density of colour the enamel itself cannot completely provide.

Several methods of obtaining high gloss coloured effects by means of paint and varnish have already been described in this work, notably in the articles " Painting a Front Door," on page 65, " Graining," on page 111, " Painting a Kitchen," on page 208, and " Painting Interior Woodwork," on page 705.

When to use Enamel.

Although both methods produce a full gloss, the quality of the respective glosses differs in a way quite apparent on actual examination, but not easy to define in words. That of enamel is more porcelain-like than the brilliant lustre of a good varnish. For that reason it is preferred by many people.

Pure Pale Tints can be obtained.

Another reason for the considerable use of enamel is that purer pale tints can be obtained with it than by the paint and varnish method.

It has not yet been found possible to produce a perfectly water-white varnish. Therefore the very palest varnishes procurable impart, when applied over a very light coloured, and particularly a white, paint, a creamy tone to the finished work, and this tone is apt to deepen as time goes on.

Therefore, when a very pure delicate tinted, or a perfect white, gloss finish is required on interior work, it is often good policy to choose an enamel for the final coating.

Tools required.

The tools required in enamelling, including the preparatory processes, are :—
Fine and medium waterproof sandpaper ;
A rubbing block ;
A painter's putty knife ;
A filling knife with a thin and flexible blade ;
A paint strainer with a fine mesh ;
A painter's duster ;
Three flat hog-hair brushes ; one 2½ inches, one 1 inch, and a ½ inch.
A flat fitch for the narrow quirks.

Brushes are never at their best when quite new, those part worn or " broken in " being far preferable. If the worker does not possess such brushes, new ones can be purchased and " broken in " during the application of the undercoatings.

Cleaning " Broken-in " Brushes.

After the final undercoating has been applied, however, these brushes

Fig. 1.—When all Old Paint has been burned off by means of a Blowlamp and Scraper, any Small Traces of Paint still left on can be removed by first slightly warming the Surface and immediately wiping it over with a Coarse Rag.

will require thorough cleaning before being put into the enamel.

This cleaning can be effected by first washing out the accumulated paint from the bristles in turpentine, white spirit or petrol, and then thoroughly washing again in warm soapy water.

When, but not until, all traces of paint have been removed, the brushes are cleared of soap by twirling them round in clean water.

They should then be taken out of the water, twirled between the hands to remove as much moisture as possible, and laid aside on a flat surface to dry.

Fig. 2.—Any Hollows in the Surface should be filled with Stopping applied with a Knife as shown.

The stopping should consist of equal parts of paste white lead, dry red lead and ordinary putty, and should be well mixed on the handboard shown in the above photograph.

Great care should be taken to see that they are completely dry and free from the slightest trace of moisture before being put into the enamel. Otherwise, disaster will ensue.

Preparing the Surface.

The preliminary stages of the work preparatory to enamelling are the same (except for the last two coats) as for a paint and varnish job.

Wherever there is old paint present which is cracked, crazed or soft, that paint will require removal. In this, as in other matters, it is always a false economy to build on unstable foundations. The processes of removal are fully described in the article " Painting a Front Door," on page 65, to which the reader is referred.

The old paint having been removed, the surface must then be smoothed, knotted, and primed with white lead paint, also as described in the article just mentioned. This priming, when thoroughly hard, should be well sandpapered to render it perfectly smooth.

Enamelling over Old Paint.

If, however, the old paint is quite hard and shows no sign of cracking or blistering, it will not be necessary to remove it. But it will require a thorough cleaning down with water in which a little good soap (preferably a sugar soap such as Manger's) has been dissolved.

Then a thorough smoothing, with waterproof sandpaper, of the surface, which is moistened with a sponge, should be carried out. The sludge so created should then be swilled off with clean water and the work be left to dry.

From this stage onward, the processes are the same whether the old paint has been removed and a coat of priming has been applied, or the old paint has been merely washed and rubbed down.

Further treatment will consist of two coats of undercoating and one coat of finishing enamel. Nothing less will produce a perfect job of enamelling, and, where a very great change of colour from dark to light (such as black to white) is required, three coats of undercoating may be necessary to get that complete purity of colour which must be obtained before the actual enamelling takes place.

First Undercoating.

Assuming, however, that two undercoatings are to be applied, the first should be of a white lead paint made according to the following formula :—
28 lbs. white lead paste ;
2¾ pints raw linseed oil ;
2¾ pints turpentine ;
1 lb. paste driers, or 4 ozs. liquid driers.

It may be mentioned here that the

Fig. 3.—Preparing a Brush for Enamelling.
After washing the brush in soapy water, clean it by twirling it round in a vessel of clean water. Then twirl it again after taking it out of the water.

paint for every coat preparatory to enamelling must be absolutely free from lumps, grit or skins, and this can be achieved by straining it through either a paint strainer with a fine mesh or through a piece of fine muslin tied over the top of a suitable container, such as an earthenware jar or a paint kettle.

This first white lead undercoating must be allowed ample time (two days is a suitable period) to dry, and must then be smoothed down with fine waterproof sandpaper, the surface being damped with a sponge so that the water acts as a lubricant to the sandpaper. A clean sponge dipped in clean water should be used to wipe away the sludge created.

We are now ready for the final undercoating.

Second Undercoating.

Some makers of enamel state that the best results can only be obtained by the use of their specially prepared undercoatings. The manufacturers of that well-known enamel "Ripolin," for instance, prescribe the use of their undercoating "Fletto," which can be obtained in all the colours in which the finishing enamel is made. And the same is true of many other proprietary enamels.

In the absence, however, of a special final undercoating, a suitable one can be made to the following formula:—

21 lbs. white lead paste;
7 lbs. finishing enamel;
4 pints turpentine;
4 ozs. liquid driers;

together with sufficient oil staining colour to produce a shade similar to that chosen for the finishing enamel. For a white result, of course, no staining colour will be required.

Quantities required.

It is to be noted, also, that the quantities given in the above formulas are for the sole purpose of giving the right proportions, and do not represent the quantities required for any particular job. For the woodwork of an ordinary room, probably one-quarter the quantities mentioned would be more than ample.

In getting work up for enamelling, it is not enough to smooth well the successive dried coatings. Each of the coats should be brushed on as evenly as possible, so as to avoid, as far as possible, the formation of either brush marks or unevenness in the thickness of the coating itself.

"Stopping."

Three factors enter here. One is

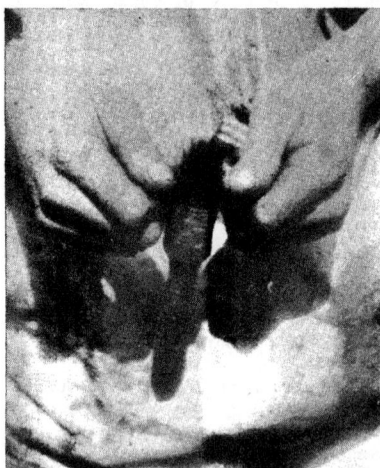

Fig. 4.—Before putting the Brush into Enamel, examine it by dividing the Bristles as shown.
Make sure that all traces of paint or other foreign matter have been removed and that the brush is scrupulously clean.

the choice of suitable tools and brushes, and another is the correct use of them. A third point to be observed is the proper "stopping," as it is called, of all holes, cracks, open joints and other inequalities in the surfaces under treatment.

In the case of burnt off and primed work, at least the major portion of the stopping should be done after the priming and before the first undercoating, and only minor blemishes that have been overlooked in the first stopping should be done after the first and before the second undercoating.

In the case of work which is not burnt off, all the stopping must be very carefully done between the first and second undercoatings, and, after the stopping has been applied, it must be given at least a few hours to harden before it is sandpapered smooth.

On no account must any stopping be left until the last undercoating has been applied, for any filled-up places left until then would inevitably show through the final enamel.

Ordinary glazier's putty is often used for stopping holes and cracks during painting work, and, although on rough jobs a passable result may be obtained with it, it is by no means the best kind of stopping for enamel work. Here we require something harder setting and more capable of being rubbed down to absolute conformity with the rest of the work.

Several admirable formulas for good stopping are available, but one of the best is a mixture of equal parts of paste white lead, dry red lead and ordinary linseed oil putty.

The mixture should be firmly pressed into the holes or cracks with a stopping knife, the end of which is used for cutting off the superfluous material and levelling off that which remains.

"Filling."

If the whole surface of the woodwork is not very smooth, perhaps owing to roughness of grain, and a very high-class finish is required, a further process besides the stopping, and known as "filling," is often adopted.

The "filling" itself is a semi-liquid composition which is spread over the whole surface with a broad thin flexible knife. The knife forces the composition into all the hollows and roughly levels the surface. After the filling has set, there follows a thorough

Fig. 5.—To make a Complete Success of Enamelling, it is imperative that the Paint used for the Undercoats is thoroughly strained.
This can be done by pouring it through muslin or silk in the manner shown.

smoothing with sandpaper, folded over a cork or wood block.

If these two processes of "stopping" and filling are carefully done, a perfectly smooth surface should be obtained.

Fillings are purchasable, ready made, at most paint merchant's stores, but if any difficulty is experienced in obtaining one, a suitable compound can be made by thoroughly mixing equal parts of paste white lead and dry whiting and reducing this to a workable consistency with equal parts of Japan gold size and turpentine.

All the preparatory processes described having been completed, we are ready for the actual enamelling—but first the work should be lightly sandpapered and thoroughly dusted down.

Applying the Enamel.

A sufficient quantity of the chosen enamel is obtained in a sealed tin, and some of this may be poured into a perfectly clean vessel (a 2-lb. earthenware jam jar is suitable). The general principle in applying all the coatings, and particularly this final one, is to do the upper work first and work downward. The procedure is similar to that described for the application of varnish in the article "Practical Notes on Varnish and Varnishing for all Purposes," on page 966.

Care should be taken to apply a fairly full coat of the enamel; indeed, to put on as much as possible without danger of it running. It should not be brushed more than is necessary to lay it on evenly over every part of the surface. It should then be left to flow out, which, if it is a good quality enamel, it will do without leaving brush marks.

Mouldings, however, should be coated rather more sparingly than the broad flat parts, and careful watch must be kept of any tendency for the enamel to run in the narrow quirks. Should this occur, the surplus may be carefully picked out with the tip of an almost dry small brush kept apart for this purpose.

When the work is completed, every possible precaution should be taken to see that no dust is created in the vicinity for at least twenty-four hours, at the end of which time the enamel will be dry, if not absolutely hard. Indeed, if the apartment in which the enamelling has been done can be left empty and undisturbed for from thirty-six to forty-eight hours, it is all to the good.

Flat Enamel.

Finally, it may be mentioned that, sometimes, a flat or dull finish is required on enamel work, either on the whole or parts (such as panels) of it. The process of doing such flat enamelling is exactly the same as already described, except that, for the final coating, a special " flat " enamel must be obtained instead of the usual gloss variety.

USING VEGETABLE DYES

THE use of vegetable dyes is valuable in preparing wool for the handloom and other decorative work, such as rugs, in which delicate harmonies are preferable to brilliant hues. Another advantage of vegetable dyes is to be found in the fact that they are not so liable to fade as the chemical dyes, and when fading does occur it is not inharmonious.

For Wool.

It is essential that the material to be dyed should be scoured by placing it in a bath containing about 1 ounce of cloudy ammonia, two teaspoonfuls of ordinary washing powder and about half a small packet of Lux mixed with about six quarts of water. The mixture should not be too hot, just sufficiently so to enable the hands to be placed in it without discomfort. The wool is left in the water for about a quarter of an hour and moved about from time to time; it is then rinsed in at least two changes of warm water.

Fixing.

The next step is to place the wool, after lightly wringing it to squeeze out the water remaining in it, in a fixing solution known as the "mordant." For the ordinary dyes it is usual to use alum in the proportion of 2 ounces to 1 gallon of water, but there are other mordants which must be used with certain dyes.

As it is usually necessary to boil the liquids used both for the mordant and the dye, a galvanised or enamel bath or bowl will be required, care being taken that all receptacles are perfectly clean, with no trace of grease.

VEGETABLE DYE RECIPES.
Madder Red.

The mordant is alum, 2 ounces; ½ ounce cream of tartar and one gallon of water. Bring up to the boil, and then place the wool in the liquid, and then boil for half an hour, take it out and allow it to drain and cool off, then replace and boil again for another half an hour.

The dye bath is prepared by dissolving ¼ lb. of madder in one gallon of water, and place the vessel over a gas ring. When it is warm place the wool from the mordant bath, after rinsing it in warm water, into the dye and bring up to boiling point slowly. The dye water should not be allowed to boil, but kept just under boiling point, and the material should be moved about as often as possible. The usual time for a madder dye is one hour, and then the wool is taken out and thoroughly washed until there is no trace of colour in the rinsing water, a little Lux may be placed in the first rinsing water to help in the washing.

Orange Red.

An orange red is obtained by using the same kind of mordant, but the dye is varied by adding 1 ounce of fustic powder to the 4 ounces of madder. A small teaspoonful of stannous chloride is now dissolved in hot water and added after the first two ingredients have boiled for about a quarter of an hour. The colour of the dye is now fixed by adding to the boiling mixture ¼ ounce of flavin, which is a deep yellow and should be dissolved in hot water first. This dye will give a range from light orange to brown, depending on the time the wool is allowed to remain in the bath.

Yellow.

A pale yellow dye is made by dissolving 2 ounces fustic powder in a gallon of water, the alum mordant being used first. Care must be taken not to boil too quickly, or the colour will be patchy.

A deeper yellow dye, following the alum mordant, can be prepared by taking the same amount of fustic powder and adding to it half the amount of flavin previously dissolved in warm water.

Reds.

A range of reds, from pink to crimson, can be obtained by using cochineal following an alum mordant bath, and boiling the wool for about half an hour. About 1 ounce of cochineal should be pulverised and then placed in a small quantity of water to boil. The liquid is now poured into a bath, and about 1½ gallons of cold water added. The material is now placed in the bath and boiled for about an hour. A good scarlet dye can be made by adding muriate of tin, about 2 ounces of the liquid preparation will be sufficient.

A further selection of recipes for vegetable dyes appears in a later article.

Making a Projection Screen for Home Use

One of the main considerations in home cinematography is to have a suitable projection screen. The following article shows how anyone who is handy with tools may make his own projection screen.

The first point to decide is the size; this should be according to the capabilities of one's projector. If the illuminant is strong enough—say, a 200-watt projection type lamp—then the screen may be about 50 × 40 inches or smaller or slightly larger in proportion. Remember when working out proportionate sizes that 1 inch of the length equals ⅘ inch of the height, so that if a screen is to be 20 inches long, the correct height will be 20 × 4 ÷ 5 = 16 inches. Thus, the screen would be 20 × 16 inches. Another way is to project on to the blank wall, mark the edges of the illuminated space and then take the measurements from this.

Base.

A rolling screen may be made to roll up if desired, so that where there is little space to spare it may be packed out of the way when not in use. Apart from this consideration, however, it is better to have a rigid screen base, since with canvas or other material there is always the difficulty in a home-made screen of getting it to stretch perfectly taut. If it does not do so, the edges curl and slight "rolls" appear, which are anything but conducive to good projection results.

Plywood makes an excellent base, for it has the advantages of being light, level, strong, and workable. Three-ply is quite suitable and may be purchased in large sheets at a reasonable price. A small screen should have no joins in it, and this alone is an adequate reason why plywood is good for the purpose.

Surfacing.

It is well to smooth the surface with glasspaper—first coarse and then fine—before applying the screen surface paint. This may be that sold as "silver" or aluminium, either of which should be applied carefully and evenly, finishing off by brushing one way all over in straight firm strokes running the whole length of the screen. This prevents any brush-marks showing. It is always best to surface the screen before doing anything else, so that if it does not turn out satisfactorily the first time, then a minimum of labour will have been spent.

Fig. 1.—The Finished Projection Screen.
Note the black surround which helps to give a sharp edge to the picture.

There is a preparation on the market known as "Extralite" cine screen coating solution, sold by Photo-Trading Co. Ltd., Change Alley, Sheffield, and this is readily applied with a brush to any surface of wood or metal without previous preparation. Canvas or other material should be given a coat of size before applying the solution.

When the silver surface has been completed satisfactorily, it is a good plan to paint a black surround as shown in the illustration of the finished screen. This helps to give a sharp edge to the picture, and it imparts a finishing touch to the appearance of the screen itself. A dead black matt paint should be used for this. The corners should be rounded, as shown, to coincide with the picture frames. The correct curve may be obtained without damaging the surface of the screen (as may be the case with compass points) by tacking a long piece of card to each edge of the screen. The pointed foot of the compass may then rest on this card without doing any harm. The corner should be drawn in lightly with pencil and afterwards followed closely with the brush—for which, of course, a steady hand will be necessary. The black margin need not be wider than 3 or 4 inches.

Construction.

Perfect rigidity is essential to ensure sharpness of the projected picture, and this may be obtained in plywood by means of battens. These should be about 3 × 1 inches and should be strongly glued and lightly tacked to the edges of the back of the screen and also across the centre, as shown in the constructional sketch. Care should be taken to see that the tacks are not long enough to pierce through to the front of the screen or the surfacing will be ruined. These strengthening strips may be morticed and tenoned to give extra stability, if desired.

Naturally, to hold a large screen, there must be a substantial base or plinth. This may be cut from a board about 2 inches thick, so that there shall be no danger of the screen toppling over if it receives a jog. A double plinth as illustrated not only adds to the base weight but also gives a better appearance. To hold the screen to the base, two strong iron stays should be screwed to the side battens, shaped over the plinth, and screwed to this also.

Useful Details.

Should one wish to give the screen an extra smart finish, it is a good plan to make side and corner pieces as shown in the illustrations. These should be cut to a modern shape and with a rebate at the rear, so that they may be affixed to the edges of the screen as shown in the detail or section drawing.

Rubber feet should be fixed to the underside of the plinth.

If desired, the screen may be "recessed" by the simple process of making a false surrounding edge, with curved corners and affixing the screen to the back of this, thus preventing a flat aspect.

Finish with a dark oak matt stain, followed by a coat of clear varnish. This completes a highly satisfactory home projection screen.

Finally, place a length of black cloth on the table and then stand the screen on this, as shown in the drawing.

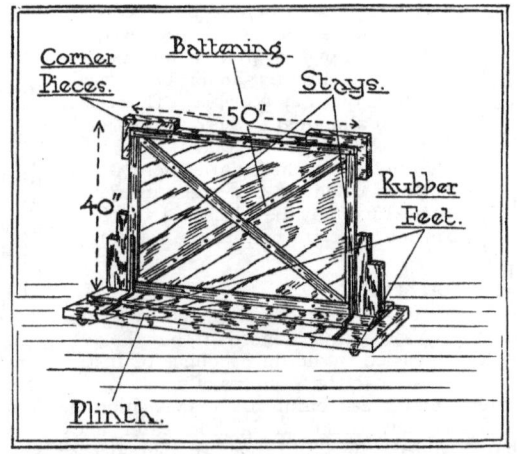

Fig. 2.—Constructional Details for the Projection Screen.

Making a Radio-gramophone Cabinet

WITH NOTES ON FITTING A MOTOR AND RECEIVER

THE handsome walnut radio-gram cabinet seen in Fig. 1 can be made by any handyman, and does not call for special tools nor technical skill. All the wood parts are supplied ready machined, thus eliminating most of the difficult and arduous work. This does not mean that the pieces of wood have only to be fastened together without doing anything to them; on the contrary, they have to be properly fitted, assembled, stained, polished and completed; all of which is, however, relatively easy, as the parts have already been machined to size and shape.

The finished cabinet measures 38 inches high, 21 inches wide, 17 inches deep, and provides ample space for a clockwork or mains-driven gramophone and almost any kind of battery or mains-driven receiver. The lower part of the cabinet forms the loud speaker chamber, above it is a shelf for the receiver. The gramophone motor is fastened beneath the motor board; access to the turntable and tone arm is afforded by the hinged lid at the top. The first part of this article deals with the construction of the cabinet, the second portion deals with equipment, and gives specifications of various suitable receivers and gramophone motors.

Materials for the Cabinet.

One complete kit of machined parts in walnut, No. 259, for a "Modern" radio-gram cabinet ("Charles Osborn Ltd.," Regent Works, Arlington Street, London, N.1).

One self-supporting stay with screws ("Frank Romany Ltd.," 52 High Street, Camden Town, London).

One pair needle cups.

One 12 × ½-inch strip hinge with plated screws.

One bottle black stain.
One bottle walnut stain.
One small tin wood filler.
One bottle French polish.
One small tin "Croid" aero glue.

On receipt of the kit of wood parts, carefully unpack and examine them; if any parts have been damaged see to their replacement at once. Next place all the plywood sheets on a flat surface and keep them flat under pressure until wanted, as this will check any latent tendency for them to warp or become distorted.

Commencing the Work.

First assemble the plinth or stand, shown in Fig. 2, by merely putting the four pieces in position, testing to see they are square, and applying glue

Fig. 1.—The Finished Cabinet.

to the mitre joints and securing them with panel or cabinet pins.

This done, take the plywood bottom

Fig. 2.—Plinth, Bottom Board and Bearers.

board, also seen in Fig. 2, and plane the edges so that it will fit easily but without much shake into the plinth,

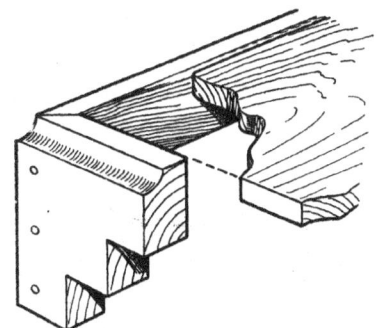

Fig. 3.—Section of Plinth, showing Position of Bottom Board.

The bottom board fits inside the plinth but is fixed to the bottom of the cabinet, not to the plinth.

as shown in section in Fig. 3. This piece does not fix in the plinth, but later on is fixed on the bottom of the main body.

Assembling the Body.

The body consists of the front panel, two side panels, four corner posts, two back crossrails with machined joints, front crossrail and two side liners for the motor space and necessary glue block. The arrangement of these parts is shown in Fig. 4; the corner posts and crossrails with their machine-made joints are shown in Fig. 5, and will serve in identifying the parts.

First clear out the machined slots with a small chisel, or alternatively round off the corners of the tenons with a pocket knife. The essential thing is to ensure the machined joints fitting nicely.

The arrangement of the top back rail and corner post, as seen from the back, is shown in Fig. 6; the rebate at the back is intended for the removable plywood back panel. The bottom crossrail and joint is shown assembled in Fig. 8. The two back rails should be fitted to the back corner posts, then glued together and preferably cramped up, but if proper cramps are not available, the parts should be assembled on a flat table, the joints pressed tightly together, and the whole left untouched while the glue is drying. Be very careful to have this frame perfectly square and true.

Next take the front panel. Clean up the edges of the speaker fret with a file or sandpaper, round off the side edges with sandpaper, then apply glue to one of the side edges and force it home into the groove in the front corner post. Take care to fix the correct post; all four are variously machined, and the correct posts can be seen by placing them temporarily in position. Fix the opposite post to the front panel; see that it is all square and true. If all is correct, the front pair will exactly correspond with the back pair. When dry, round off the edges of the two veneered side panels and glue them one at a time to the grooves in the front posts, then glue the back edges of the side panels and press them into their grooves in the back posts.

The front panel with one post and side temporarily assembled is shown in Fig. 7, with one post separated to show the machine-cut grooving.

Fixing the Bottom.

The next step is carefully to true up the bottoms of all four corner posts and the ends of the three plywood panels, then fix the bottom board on to the bottom of the posts and secure

MAKING A RADIO-GRAMOPHONE CABINET

it on the inside with glue blocks, as shown in Fig. 9 in part section.

The arrangement of the motor space at the top of the body is shown in Fig. 10, the linings are glued to the side panels and fit snugly between the posts. A similar lining is fixed across the front, but the back rail itself forms the inside liner at the back.

The projecting corners of the posts can now be cut away with a chisel to carry on the line of the interior (as shown in Fig. 10), or they can be untouched as desired.

The motor board is a stout plywood panel with a walnut veneered face. The corners must be notched, as in Fig. 11, to allow it to fit up against the underside of the liner and back rail. Two oak bearers are then screwed to the corner posts beneath the board to keep it in place, but allow of its easy removal.

The shelf for the radio set is then fitted and is supported on bearers screwed to the corner posts, as shown in Fig. 12, in section. The baffle board (Fig. 13) should be fitted so that it can be screwed to the corner posts; it is beneficial to cover it on the face side with thick felt to absorb vibration and improve the tonal qualities.

Making the Moulded Lid.

The lid, which is hinged to the body, consists of four moulded pieces rebated at the top to receive the walnut veneered top board.

The joints are mitred and have slots in them into which fit thin plywood strips called "feathers," as shown in Fig. 16, where one assembled corner with the top board in place is seen at the upper part of the picture and one joint with the feather partly in place in the lower portion of the same illustration.

To assemble the frame, first round off the edges of the feathers so that they will slide easily into the slots, then see that there are no "burrs" or roughnesses to prevent the joints closing properly. After this remove the feathers; keep the pieces in correct order and reassemble them, but this time apply hot glue to the joints and press them firmly together. Assemble the frame on a flat surface and see that all corners are square. When

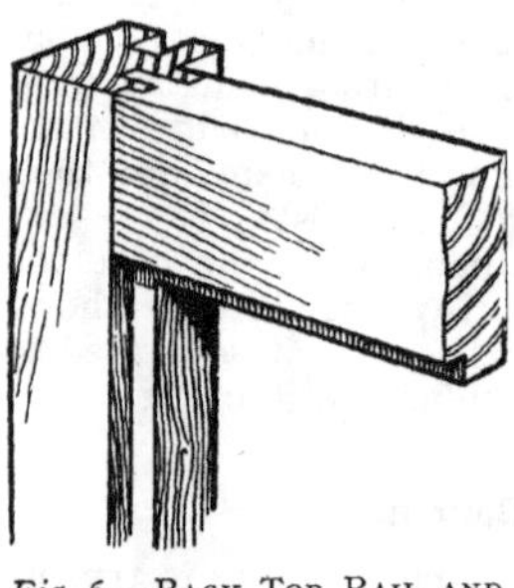

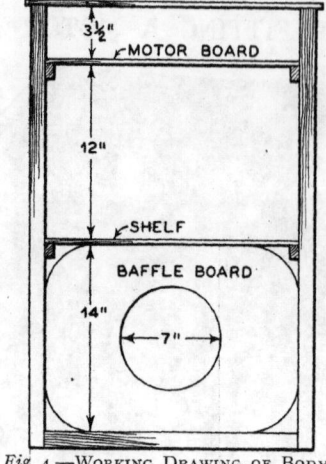

Fig. 4.—Working Drawing of Body.
The main case fits on to the plinth; the hinged and moulded lid is a separate item.

the glue is dry and hard clean off the projecting ends of the feathers,

Fig. 5.—Corner Posts, Cross Rail and Machine-made Joints.

Fig. 7.—Panels and Posts Assembled.

remove any glue that may have squeezed out—preferably with a rag steeped in hot water before the glue has dried—otherwise use a sharp chisel or knife.

Next plane up the edges of the top board so that it will just fit nicely into the rebates, as in Fig. 14, and fix it there with glue and a few cabinet pins driven from the underside.

Complete the constructional work by mitreing the ends of the four narrow strips of wood that still remain from the kit set and glue and pin them around the top edges of the body, as seen in Fig. 15, then fix the long strip hinge to the lid and to the back of the body.

Screw the adjustable stay into position, as shown in Fig. 17, taking care to fix it so that when closing the lower end just clears the motor board. The two needle cups can be screwed one at each front corner of the motor board.

Staining and Polishing.

The reader may feel a little disappointed at this stage of the work because the veneered panels, with their nicely figured graining, are different in colour to the other parts, and the whole thing present a somewhat piebald appearance. This, however, all disappears when the work is properly stained and polished. First, however, rub down all surfaces with fine sandpaper, then remove all dust and apply a coat of wood filler. Leave this to dry, again rub down with fine sandpaper, and this time remove every trace of roughness. Again remove all dust and proceed with the staining. The plinth should be stained dead black; Johnson's ebony wood dye is excellent for this purpose. Stain all the remainder—inside and out—with walnut stain, apply a second coat where necessary to bring the colour to a uniform tone, but do not apply too much to the veneered front panel or some of the beauty of the veneering and the figure and grain may be lost. If the stain causes any part of the grain to "lift" or swell up, rub it down with fine sandpaper moistened with a few spots of linseed oil and bring up the colour with stain if necessary. Then finish off with the French polish in the usual way; full directions for

Fig. 6.—Back Top Rail and Post.
The back rail fits into machined joints in the post; the rebates are for the removable back.

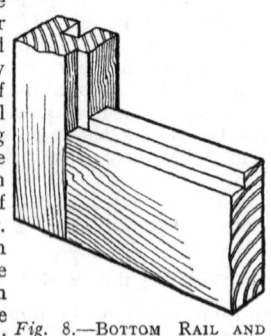

Fig. 8.—Bottom Rail and Post.
This back cross rail completes the rear framework.

MAKING A RADIO-GRAMOPHONE CABINET

Fig. 9.—BOTTOM BOARD IN PLACE.
Glue blocks are used to hold the bottom board to the cabinet sides.

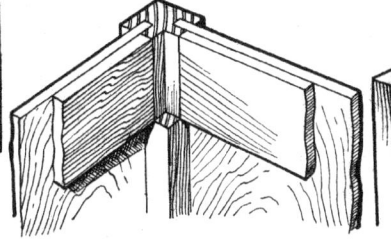

Fig. 10.—INTERNAL ARRANGEMENT AT TOP.
The corners of the posts can be cut away flush with the inside linings to present a neat appearance.

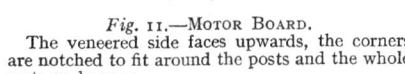

Fig. 11.—MOTOR BOARD.
The veneered side faces upwards, the corners are notched to fit around the posts and the whole rests on bearers.

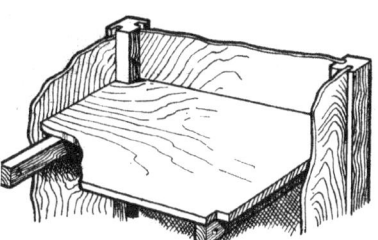

Fig. 12.—RECEIVER SHELF AND BEARERS.
The shelf is fitted around the posts and supported by bearers screwed to the case.

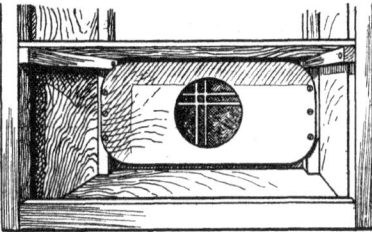

Fig. 13.—BAFFLE BOARD.
This fits beneath receiver shelf and is screwed to the posts.

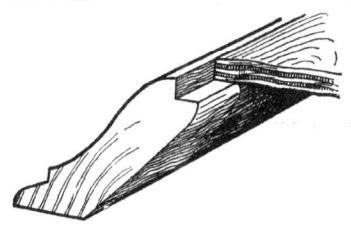

Fig. 14.—SECTION OF LID.
The top fits into the rebate and is fixed with glue and cabinet pins.

this work are given elsewhere in ENQUIRE WITHIN.

The lid and motor board should be removed for the polishing process. Reassemble the parts, fit the back cover into its rebate and secure it with a couple of turn buttons, then glue the gauze, supplied with the kit set, over the inside of the speaker fret after the edge of the fret openings have been stained or enamelled black.

These fretted edges should be stained or enamelled after the rest of the work has been polished, because if any stain appears on the face it can be wiped while wet from the polished surface without discolouring it.

The Motor.

The type of motor to use for driving the turntable will depend on the source of power. In most cases, if electric power is available, a motor for use on A.C. mains will be suitable, but if a battery receiver is used a clockwork motor with crank handle winding gear will be needed.

In either case the general procedure is the same except that when a spring motor is used a hole for the winding spindle must be drilled through the side of the case.

Materials for Gramophone Equipment.

The following materials are needed for a spring-driven, hand-wind machine :—

One "Garrard" spring-driven gramophone motor unit and turntable complete ("Garrard Engineering Co.").

One B.T.H. Junior tone arm and pick-up, complete with volume control ("B.T.H. Ltd.").

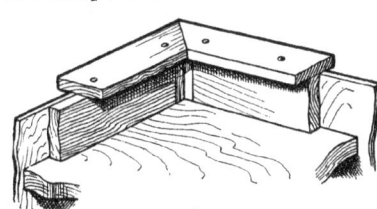

Fig. 15.—COVER STRIPS AT TOP.
The top edges of cabinet are covered by separate strips of wood glued and pinned in place.

For use where A.C. electric mains are available, the following materials and components are needed :—

Fig. 16.—ONE CORNER OF LID ASSEMBLED IS SHOWN AT THE TOP. BELOW ARE THE TWO MOULDED EDGES AND THE FEATHER JOINT SHOWN PARTLY ASSEMBLED.

One B.T.H. "Truspeed" motor unit with turntable complete.

One B.T.H. "Senior de Luxe" pick-up and tone arm, complete with volume control ("B.T.H. Ltd.").

One mains disturbance suppressor unit ("Belling Lee Ltd.").

Fitting up the Motor.

A template is supplied with the motor unit, and this should first be fastened to the top of the motor, either with small nails through the fixing holes or by means of a few dabs of paste.

Drill the holes for fixing bolts and other parts, and then cut out the motor opening with a fretsaw; the shape of the opening can be transferred to the motor board by "pricking through" with an awl, as shown in Fig. 18, which avoids destruction of the template, which generally includes the maker's fitting instructions—all of which should be followed implicitly.

Bolt the motor in place, then fix the tone arm and see that it tracks properly, as it will do if placed in accordance with the template.

The leads from the tone arm should be connected to the "pick-up" terminals on any receiver fitted with them. The volume control is generally shunted across these leads.

In the case of A.C. sets the use of the mains disturbance suppressor unit, connected across the leads to the motor as in Fig. 19, will be found distinctly beneficial, as it generally cuts out a good deal of extraneous "mush" and background noise.

MAKING A RADIO-GRAMOPHONE CABINET

Fig. 17.—The Lid Completed and in Place.

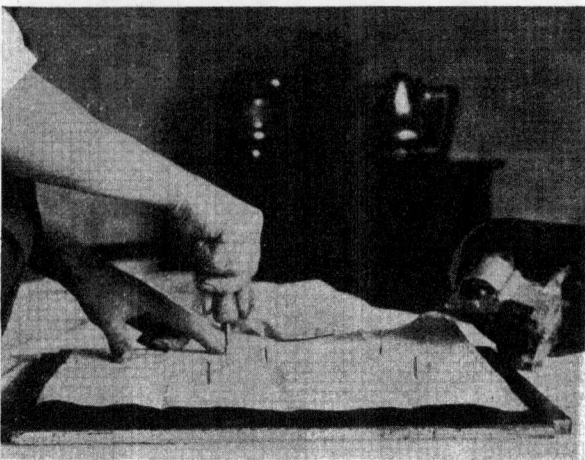

Fig. 18.—Marking out Motor Board.

Assembling the Receiver.

The cabinet as here described is suitable for practically any receiver, but for the benefit of readers who wish to assemble a set specially the following circuits with lists of specified components will be found extremely helpful, a choice of several types of receiver is given, together with brief notes on the class of reception to which they are best suited.

In all cases it is desirable separately to "earth" the gramophone motor frame and metal parts; the pick-up leads should preferably be run in metal-braided and earthed wires, while the L.F. amplifier section, and especially the transformers, ought to be as far away from the pick-up leads and the gramophone motor as circumstances allow. In the case of A.C. mains sets the "mains" transformers ought to be well shielded and as far away from the gramophone motor and pick-up as is convenient. The control spindle holes should be drilled through the cabinet front to suit the template supplied with the components.

Simple Battery Set.

A three-valve set with Pentode output valve and "Westector" economy circuit (Fig. 20) gives excellent tone and quality for local station radio reception and ample volume for record playing.

Recommended Components.

Coil.—Ferrocart F.5 ("Colvern Ltd.").

Tuning Condenser.—·0005 mfd. ("Utility," "Wilkins and Wright Ltd.").

Reaction Condenser.—·00015 mfd. ("Utility," "Wilkins and Wright Ltd.").

Valve Holders.—Two 4-pin, one 5-pin ("Clix").

Panel.—14 × 7-inch ebonite ("British Ebonite Ltd.").

Baseboard.—14 × 9 × ¼-inch plywood ("F. Romany").

Brackets.—Two panel brackets ("Bulgin").

L.F. Transformer ("Multitone").

H.F. Choke ("Wearite").

Fixed Condensers.—One each, 1 mfd.,

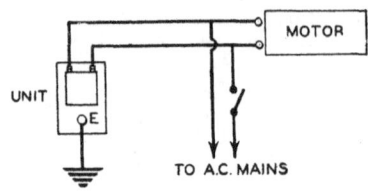

Fig. 19.—Connections of Mains Suppressor Unit.

This is connected across the mains leads and cuts out much of the "mush."

·0003 mfd., ·00001 mfd., ·01 mfd.; two ·0002 mfd. tubular ("T. C. C.").

Metallised Resistances.—One each 20,000 ohms, 500 ohms, 1 megohm ("Dubilier").

Terminals.—One each marked A.E. PU1, PU2, HT +, HT + 1, LT −, LT +, LS +, LS − ("Belling Lee").

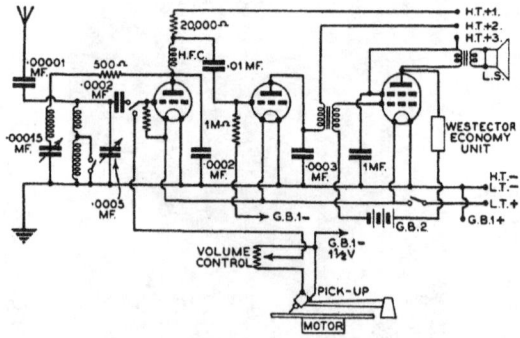

Fig. 20.—Simple Battery Receiver.

For use with spring-driven gramophone motor. The "Westector" economy unit greatly reduces H.T. battery current consumption.

Change-over Switch.—One type GCO ("Wearite").

On-off Switch.—One type GWC ("Wearite").

Loud Speaker.—"Multex" ("R. and A. Ltd.").

Batteries.—H.T., 120-volt "Drydex," type H1012; L.T., 2-volt "Exide," type HZ4; G.B., 9-volt "Drydex," type H1007 ("Exide").

Economy Unit.—One with "Westector" ("Wearite").

A.C. Superhet Receiver.

This is one of the most powerful types and will receive practically any European station. The circuit incorporates separate oscillator and detector valves, a "Westector" second detector and Westinghouse metal rectifier in the mains equipment. By an ingenious system devised by the "Westinghouse Co." the gramophone pick-up feeds to the I.F. amplifier, and thereby gives majestic volume for record playing.

A simple form of automatic volume control is incorporated as well as manual control of the two variable-mu valves.

Components required.

Tuning Condenser.—Three-gang ·0005 superhet type with slow motion dial ("Jackson Bros., Ltd.").

Coils.—One set H.F. band pass and oscillator coils, type WFR3 ("Wearite").

Intermediate Frequency Coils.—Three type WF1P ("Wearite").

Potentiometer and Mains Switch.—10,000 ohms ("Wearite").

Valveholders.—Five 5-pin ("Benjamin").

Fixed Condensers.—Two 4 mfd., type 87; four 1 mfd., type 65; seven 0·1 mfd., tubular, type 250; three ·0001 mfd.; one electrolytic 4 mfd., type 801;

one electrolytic 7 mfd., type 801; one electrolytic 25 mfd., 25-volt, type 511 (" T. C. C. Ltd.").

Metallised Resistances (1 watt type).—One 300 ohms; three 500 ohms; two 10,000 ohms; five 100,000 ohms; two 5,000 ohms; one 20,000 ohms; one 30,000 ohms; four 50,000 ohms (" Dubilier ").

Mains Transformer.—Type W33 (" Heayberd ").

Metal Rectifier. — Type HT.9 (" Westinghouse ").

Second Detector. — " Westector," type W4 (" Westinghouse ").

Pre-set Condenser.—One ·002 mfd. (" Igranic ").

Loud Speaker.—" Magnavox," with 2,500 ohms resistance field coil (" Benjamin Electric ").

Terminals.—One each marked A.E., PU1, PU2 (" Belling Lee Ltd.").

L.F. Choke (" Wearite ").

L.F. Transformer. — " Parafeed " (" R. I. Ltd.").

Valves.—Two type VMS4, metallised; one each type MS4B, metallised; MPT4; MH4, plain (" Marconi-Osram ").

Baseboard.—⅜-inch plywood 18 × 11 inches (" F. Romany Ltd.").

Full size layout diagrams and full details for making a similar receiver can be had at small cost from Messrs. Westinghouse Co., 82 York Road, London, N.1.

A back view of the cabinet with radio receiver in place is shown in Fig. 21.

As already mentioned the radio-gramophone cabinet described in this articl provides ample space for a clockwork or mains-driven gramophone and for almost any kind of battery or mains-driven receiving set. When assembled the result will be a very attractive piece of work that will amply repay any trouble taken in making it.

Fig. 21.—Finished Cabinet with Radio Set and Loudspeaker.

HOW TO MAKE MERINGUES

MERINGUE is used for making tasteful cakes and biscuits, and can be served as an added attraction with hot and cold puddings. Knowledge of how to make and serve it is, therefore, very useful.

Utensils required—

1 medium-sized shallow bowl.
1 large knife or wire egg-whisk.
1 tablespoon.
1 flat baking tin.
Grease-proof paper.

Ingredients required—

The whites of new-laid eggs.
1 tablespoonful of icing sugar to each egg.
Flavouring essence.
Whipped cream.
A pinch of salt.

Method of Making.

Place the whites of the eggs in a shallow bowl, add a pinch of salt and, with a large knife or egg whisk, beat briskly until a froth is obtained which is firm enough to keep in shape; then, lightly fold in the sugar, a tablespoonful at a time. Add a few drops of whatever flavouring essence is preferred and whisk again, until the mixture is thick enough to stand firmly when heaped up.

Lay a sheet of white, well-greased paper upon a flat baking tin, and on it arrange the meringue in egg-shaped heaps, using a tablespoon for moulding purposes; leave a space of one inch between each meringue and sprinkle the surfaces with sugar.

In the Oven.

Place the tin in a very slow oven for about an hour. The heat must be just sufficient to dry the meringues slowly; do not try to hasten the process by increasing the heat, as they quickly change to a brownish colour if care is not taken, and their appearance is thus spoilt.

When set, remove them from the oven and wait while they cool, then lift them from the paper with the aid of a knife. If the undersides have not set, stand them, inverted, on a wire tray or mat and return them to the oven for a few moments until quite dry.

As Biscuits.

Spread the flat sides with whipped cream and place them together in pairs. If preferred, a small portion may be scooped from the centre of the flat side of each and the cavities thus formed may then be filled with whipped cream. They are then placed together in pairs.

Preparing Meringue Fingers.

Meringue fingers are prepared in the same way as the above, but a forcing bag, instead of a tablespoon, is used for shaping purposes. To make a bag of this kind, take a square of grease-proof kitchen paper, the sides of which are about 4 inches long, and roll it to form a cone; keep the sides in place by means of a pin or a piece of gummed paper. From the point of the cone cut a portion sufficient to leave an opening ¾ inch wide. Take a teaspoon, and with it pack the egg mixture into the bag, forcing it through the wide end, but leaving enough space at this end to enable the paper to be folded over and thus close the bag. With the left hand, hold the cone in such a position that the smaller opening just rests on the greased paper lining the baking tin and, with the right hand, press the wide end, thus forcing the meringue from the narrow end on to the paper on the tray. Slowly draw the cone backwards until the finger of egg mixture is as long as is required. Repeat this process until all the meringue has been converted into finger shapes, each one inch from the next. If desired, the tops may be sprinkled with desiccated coco-nut.

After they have been dried in the oven, they may be spread with whipped cream on the flat sides and placed two together, or the cream may be dispensed with and the meringues may be served as they are.

The white of one egg with one tablespoonful of sugar will make four or five egg-shaped meringues the size of a large tablespoon. It may be preferred, however, to form much smaller cakes. Twelve little meringue biscuits can be made from one egg; for these, heap the mixture on the tin by means of a dessertspoon, instead of a tablespoon, and with it form them into neat rounds.

Meringues to serve with Sweet

It is a good plan to keep a store of meringue cases in an air-tight tin. Then, when required, they may be served as a sweet, either on a bed of ice-cream, or filled with a mixture of mashed bananas and cream and decorated with shelled walnuts.

Beaten white of egg is frequently used for the purpose of decorating baked puddings, or cold sweets. A hot pudding should be cooked first. The beaten white of egg should then be spread on and the pudding returned to a slow oven until the meringue has set.

Useful Hints for Watering the Garden

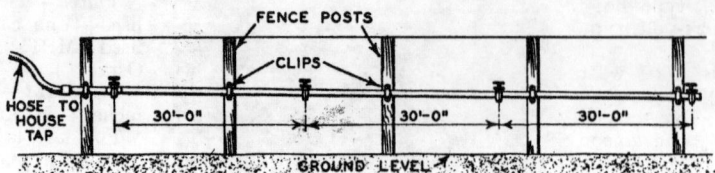

Fig. 1.—Typical Layout of Piping to avoid Long Lengths of Hose.
Showing water main with four cocks spaced 30 feet apart. Note how the pipe slopes down to the end for draining purposes.

In the case of extensive gardens, or gardens long in proportion to their width, the watering by means of a long length of rubber hose is liable to be a troublesome process. The long hose tends to kink and tangle up, and when dragged over the ground fouls plants, shrubs, etc., and damages them. The coiling up of a long hose also is a troublesome and weary process and one liable to be neglected, so the hose soon suffers in condition and becomes leaky and troublesome.

How to avoid Long Lengths of Hose.

In such cases it is better to instal a water main along one or both sides of the garden and use a comparatively short length of hose which is easy to manipulate and cheap to replace when worn. The cost of such a main is small, and it can be fitted up easily and without special tools. Up to 100 feet in length $\tfrac{3}{4}$-inch pipe should be used. Over this, to 200 feet, 1-inch pipe.

Choosing Suitable Piping.

The best pipe for the purpose is known as galvanised water barrel, but this is hardly warranted unless the job is to be a permanent one. Good second-hand gas barrel of the size required can be purchased for less than 1d. per foot, and will last for many years if given a coat of bituminous paint before fitting up. This bituminous paint, by the way, is invaluable for painting all exposed ironwork that can be black in colour, and also any wood it is desired to preserve, but no other paint except bituminous can be used over it. It is sold as Bitumastic Paint and costs 5s. per gallon, a quantity which goes a long way.

The iron pipe or barrel is sold in various lengths; each length when new being supplied with a socket or screwed coupling (Fig. 2). Second-hand barrel has generally been cut out of its previous use with a hack-saw and the ends may not be screwed. The pipe should be run along the fence or wall, and be highest at the house end, sloping gradually to the other end to allow it to drain to avoid damage by frost (Fig. 1).

Fixing Piping to Wooden Fence.

If fixed to the

Fig. 2.—Length of Barrel as purchased with Screwed Coupling or Socket.

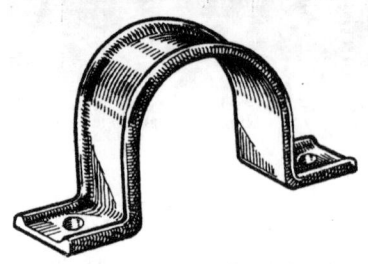

Fig. 3.—Wrought-iron Pipe Clips for screwing to Fence Posts.

Fig. 4.—The Tail of this Clip is cemented into a Hole cut in the Wall.

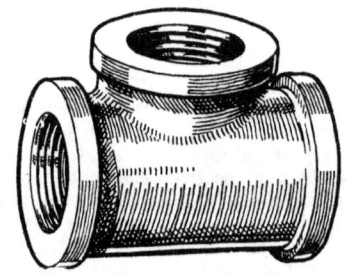

Fig. 5.—T-piece for Iron Pipe.

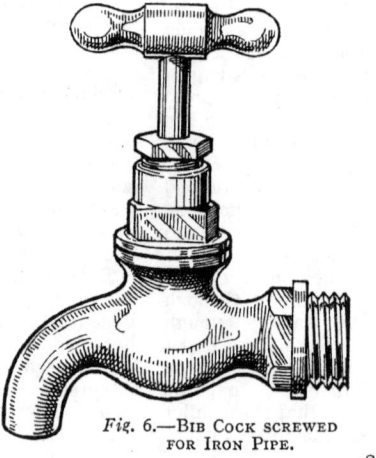

Fig. 6.—Bib Cock screwed for Iron Pipe.

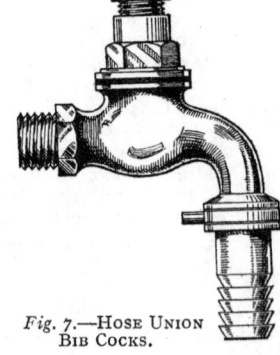

Fig. 7.—Hose Union Bib Cocks.

wooden posts of a fence, clips shown in Fig. 3 can be used and which cost a few pence per dozen. If a brick wall is available for support, clips as shown in Fig. 4 should be cemented into a hole chipped in the wall with a cold chisel. Both types of clips are sold to suit the sizes of pipe, $\tfrac{3}{4}$-inch barrel is $1\tfrac{1}{16}$ inches outside diameter and 1-inch barrel $1\tfrac{1}{4}$ inches outside diameter, but in ordering the clips the inside size of the pipe is given. It will be necessary before fitting up the pipe to decide how many points are to be fitted to attach the hose.

Suggested Layout.

In Fig. 1 is shown a suggested layout for a garden main with points at every 30 feet, or four in all. At each point a tap will be required and a T or branch piece, except for the end point, where an elbow or bend can be used.

Taps.

Fig. 5 shows a T-piece, which can be bought for a few pence each at many ironmongers'. The taps are known as bib cocks (Fig. 6). These should be bought new for 2s. 6d. to 3s. 6d. each, but for a few pence extra hose union bib cocks (Fig. 7) can be obtained. As only one, or at the most two, hose nozzles would be required, a reduction in the price could no doubt be obtained by not taking these. The sizes are known by the size of pipe to which they are screwed; a $\tfrac{3}{4}$-inch cock is screwed to suit $\tfrac{3}{4}$-inch barrel.

If New Pipe is bought.

If new pipe is bought it can be ordered in the correct lengths to bring the cocks where required, but if second-hand barrel is bought it may have to be cut to suitable lengths and then there will be no threads to connect it.

In the latter case, when the T-pieces are purchased, get the ironmonger to supply short pieces of barrel of the size required screwed at one end only. Every firm which does any pipe fitting has large quantities of these pieces, which are ends cut off lengths of barrel in fitting work to bring them to some dead length, and are regarded as waste.

Joining-up.

The method of join-

USEFUL HINTS FOR WATERING THE GARDEN

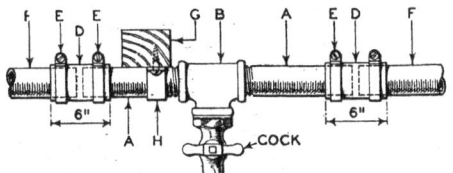

Fig. 8.—METHOD OF JOINING UP TEES WITH THE MAIN LENGTH OF BARREL.

AA, odd short lengths of barrel screwed one end only; B, T-piece; DD, lengths of rubber hose; EE, hose clips; FF, main lengths of barrel; G, fence post; H, clip.

Fig. 9.—WORM TYPE HOSE CLIP.

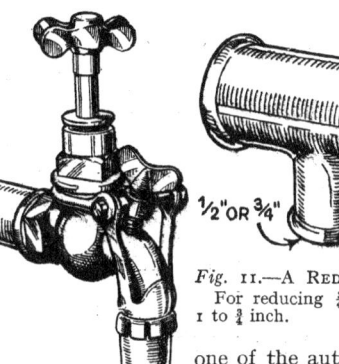

Fig. 10.—A HOSE UNION WHICH WILL NOT BLOW OFF OR LEAK.

Fig. 11.—A REDUCING T-PIECE. For reducing ¾ to ½ inch or 1 to ¾ inch.

ing up the T-pieces and the barrel by means of these short lengths is shown in Fig. 8. The rubber joint should be a good fit to the tube and the clips of brass to avoid rusting. The best form of clip is that shown in Fig. 9, as it can be taken on and off several times without trouble if necessary.

Screw the tap into the T-pieces and also the short lengths of tube, using graphite mixed with oil for jointing, which will enable the parts to be unscrewed readily when required. See that there are no ridges or burrs on the ends of the pipes before joining up.

Clip the pipes up firmly in the pipe clips, arranging one clip to come on one of the short lengths of pipe fitted to a tee, in each case to hold it firm (H, Fig. 8). If the clip does not clip the pipe tightly pack it with a piece of old inner tube and then screw up, seeing that the tap is horizontal before finally tightening the hose-clips.

At the House End.

At the house end of the line there may not be a tap on the outside, and in any case this tap may be required for purposes at times other than for the garden water. A length of hose will therefore have to be fitted to allow the main to be connected to this tap. The length will depend on the position of the tap in relation to the pipe line.

A good, quick, detachable hose union will have to be fitted to this hose. Fig. 10 shows the best type for this, as it avoids the annoying blowing off and leaking common to the usual types of hose-tap unions. If ordinary bib cocks (Fig. 6) are used on the pipe line, a union of this type will be required on the garden hose also. Its cost is about 1s. 6d.

There is one important point: if the line is long enough to require 1-inch pipe the cocks need not be more than ¾ inch and the T pieces ordered will be 1 × ¾ inch (Fig. 11).

For small gardens the taps, in the case of a ¾-inch pipe, need not be more than ½ inch, and the tees will then be ¾ × ½ inch (Fig. 11). This will give a corresponding reduction in the cost of the taps, but the tees will not be any cheaper.

If a T-piece is fitted at the end of the hose the free end must be closed by a plug, which can be bought with the other fittings (Fig. 12).

Where to purchase the Fittings.

New pipe, pipe fittings, cocks and clips can be purchased at Messrs. Walworth Ltd., 69 Union Street, Southwark, London, S.E.1, or any large ironmongers' or engineers' supply stores. Hose clips, hose unions, etc., Messrs. E. P. Kinnel and Co., 65 Southwark Street, London, S.E.1.

Second-hand iron pipe and fittings, Messrs. Fred Watkins, Coleford, Gloucester, and Acme Works, Grove Road, Balham, London, S.W.

Paint the whole of the pipes, clips, etc., well when fitted up. At the end of the summer drain the pipe and leave all the cocks full open during the winter to avoid frost damage. The iron pipe can be cut easily with a hack-saw, purchasable with blade for 6d. at the one-price stores.

HOW TO MAKE GARDEN SPRINKLERS

The problem of keeping lawns and flower-beds watered during long spells of dry weather is one with which every householder is concerned at times. The method of using a watering-can for this purpose is a long and tedious one where larger sizes of lawn or flower-beds are concerned. If, however, a hose-pipe and watering-rose type of nozzle is employed the labour of watering is greatly reduced, although to soak a lawn thoroughly with the aid of a hose-pipe is often a fairly lengthy process.

Fig. 12.—A PLUG FOR CLOSING THE END OUTLET OF T-PIECE.

Advantages of the Sprinkler Devices.

A much better method is to employ one of the automatic forms of garden sprinklers, when one can supply the lawn or flower-bed with water in the minimum of time and with little trouble.

With a properly designed sprinkler the moisture can be deposited in a fine spray over a relatively large area. The advantage of this method over that of the garden hose is that the extremely fine drops of water do not damage the grass or flowers. Further, the water is supplied at such a rate that, unlike the results given by the watering-can or hose-nozzle it sinks into the ground and does not run off the surface. Thus by leaving the sprinkler in one spot for twenty minutes to one or two hours the water penetrates right down into the soil. The sprinkler is undoubtedly the next best alternative to continuous fine rain. By moving the sprinkler at intervals the whole of the lawn or bed can be thoroughly watered; moreover, no harm is caused by leaving it in one position for a long period.

A Simple Sprinkler.

Most of the really effective garden sprinklers on the market are relatively expensive for the ordinary person, and as it is only during limited periods of the year that such a sprinkler is required, many people prefer to go without them.

It is possible, however, to make a simple and effective device that will produce the same results as some of the more expensive proprietary articles. All that is necessary for this purpose is the fine rose fitting of an ordinary garden watering-can and a piece of metal gas-tubing bent through a right angle, as shown in Fig. 13. Such a piece of tubing can be obtained for a few pence from a plumber. It should be screwed to take the thread of the nozzle, or that on an old garden watering-can taken off and soldered to the end of the pipe.

The bent pipe can be held in a vertical position by means of a block of hard wood, such as oak, ash or beech, a hole being bored to take the vertical part of the tube and a groove made for the horizontal branch. The

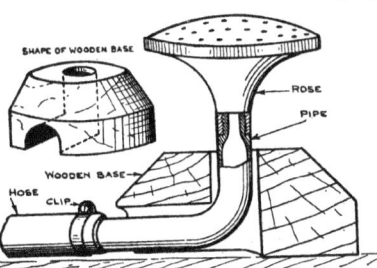

Fig. 13.—A SIMPLE SPRINKLING DEVICE UTILISING A WATERING-CAN ROSE.

1259

USEFUL HINTS FOR WATERING THE GARDEN

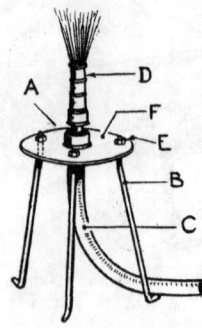

Fig. 14.—Showing one Method of fixing the Variable Spray Nozzle shown in Fig. 15 to make a Garden Sprinkler.

tube should be placed in the position shown, first, and the rose screwed on afterwards. The horizontal end of the metal tubing is connected to the rubber hose in the usual manner; it is best to use a water-pipe clip to hold the hose securely to the pipe, since there is a fair amount of water pressure to withstand.

The wood should be given two or three coats of paint, preferably of the cellulose type, since this is waterproof and will withstand a good deal of exposure without allowing the wood to deteriorate.

An advantage of this simple sprinkler is that it can be moved about the lawn to different positions merely by manipulating the hose-pipe at a safe distance from the sprinkler itself; there is therefore no need to turn off the water supply before moving the sprinkler.

Another Variable Spray Device.

Another simple sprinkler is illustrated in Fig. 14. It utilises an inexpensive proprietary make of nozzle, sometimes known as the "Boston spray," which is sold at most hardware or garden requisite shops for about 2s. 6d. This nozzle is shown separately in Fig. 15. Its principal feature is that it can be adjusted by rotating the upper part relatively to the lower, or fixed part, so as to give a fine, medium or coarse spray. It has two internal cone fittings and the water supply can be completely shut off by tightening the two parts on to each other. It is made with tapered connections for $\frac{1}{2}$, $\frac{5}{8}$ or $\frac{3}{4}$-inch bore hose-pipe, or can be supplied with a union joint in these sizes.

Fig. 15.—This Nozzle gives a Variable Angle Spray merely by rotating the Upper Part.

How to use the Nozzle.

One method of using this nozzle for garden sprinkling purposes is to mount it on a metal plate, A (Fig. 14), provided with three legs made of $\frac{1}{4}$–$\frac{1}{2}$-inch steel rod, having nuts, F, to hold them to the metal plate. The latter should be of $\frac{1}{16}$ brass and of about 3–6 inches diameter, in order to give stability to the nozzle. The base of the latter should, preferably, be soft-soldered to the brass plate. The nozzle is shown at D and the rubber hose pipe at C, in Fig. 14.

An alternative method of mounting the variable spray nozzle is shown in Fig. 16. This utilises a cheap fitting, known as the "Mysto," which is provided with a metal spike for holding it in the lawn. The hose connection in this case is taken off at the side. Incidentally, the combination shown can be used for car-washing purposes.

Methods of fixing the Hose.

In the case of home-made sprinklers, where plain pipes are used for the water supply, the rubber hose should be slipped over the plain end of the pipe and then clamped tightly by means of a metal clip. An efficient clip for this purpose is shown in Fig. 9. A screwdriver is all that is required to tighten this clip. The clips are obtainable in a wide range of diameters.

Considering, next, the attachment of the rubber hose-pipe to the ordinary house tap, there are several alternative methods, three of which are shown at A, B and C in Fig. 17.

That illustrated at A consists of an (upper) fitting that is soldered on to the tap. It has a screw thread (below) with which the internal thread on the lower hose-pipe fitting engages. The hose is pushed over the tapered serrated portion shown at the right in the diagram. The fittings shown at B and C are of the push-on type, having rubber liners inside that are expanded tightly against the tap by the water pressure. If the hose-pipe is heavy it is best to use an adjustable chain device, as shown at C. This takes the weight of the hose and thus prevents the fitting in question from being dragged off the tap.

A More Elaborate Sprinkler.

Those of our readers with the necessary mechanical knowledge and a small workshop, with lathe available for making the turned parts required, can construct an inexpensive and serviceable sprinkler of the reaction type in which there are two or four arms mounted on a central fitting having a vertical bearing. The arms are attached radially to this central boss, their outer ends being bent at right angles and provided with small nozzles. The arms rotate automatically when the water emerges from the jets.

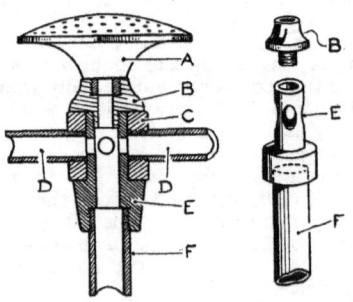

Fig. 16.—Sprinkler with Metal Spike.

In the design shown in Fig. 18 and the accompanying detail sketches, a watering can or hose type of rose fitting is shown mounted on the top; this gives a better watering action over the central area not covered by the rotating jets.

How to Mount the Rotating Arms.

The method of mounting the rotating arms and their cylindrical boss is illustrated in Fig. 19. In this diagram the perforated rose is shown at A. It is screwed to a cone fitting B. This in turn is screwed into a brass member, E, made hollow and provided with holes to supply the water to the boss C and tubular arms D. The boss, C, is made a good running fit on the smaller diameter of E. The latter is attached, by means of a piece of about 1-inch (outside diameter) gas-pipe of about 2 feet 6 inches to 3 feet 6 inches length, to the metal base, G.

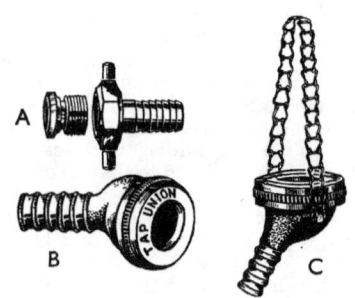

Fig. 17.—Three Types of Adaptors for connecting Rubber Hose Pipe to Tap.

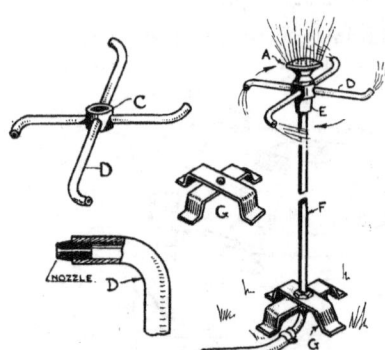

Fig. 18.—Details of a Home-made Reaction Sprinkler.

Fig. 19.—Sectional View through Sprinkler.

USEFUL HINTS FOR WATERING THE GARDEN

The Base.

The base in question is made from two pieces of strip steel about 2 × 3/16 inch, arranged in cruciform fashion and provided with feet, as shown. The pipe is screwed externally with a gas-thread, and is attached to these foot members (G) by means of two nuts; in this way both the vertical pipe and the metal base are rigidly attached.

The Rotating Unit.

The rotating unit (Fig. 18) has four arms made from any convenient size of metal tubing, preferably about 5/8-inch bore, screwed tightly into the boss C. The outer ends of these arms are bent at right angles in the manner shown. The arms should be from 15 to 20 inches in length. At their outer ends brass nozzles are screwed into position, as shown in Fig. 18. They should be drilled with 1/8–3/16-inch holes, countersunk at the front, or open ends, in order to give a diverging spray. It may be necessary to experiment a little with different sizes of hole, commencing with the smallest size and then opening these out with a fluted drill or reamer until the best spray effect is produced.

It is not a difficult matter to fit variable jets at these ends so as to be able to regulate the size of the sprinkling area to suit the lawn on which it is used. Another alternative is to flatten the ends of the arms at their outlets so as to leave narrow horizontal slits instead of using the nozzles mentioned.

The rotating boss, C, should have very little clearance at its two ends between the parallel faces of B and E; this will ensure the absence of water leakages at these faces.

Finally, all of the steel parts should be given a priming coat of paint followed by one or two coats of green paint or enamel.

A TABLE TOP OVER THE STAIRCASE

How provoking, after having carried an armful of things upstairs, to find all the doors shut and no place available for putting down the load.

A table on the landing is really a necessity, but often there is no room for one. And yet, generally the very place is there to hand, upon the balustrading over the descending flight of stairs.

Fig. 1 shows a table top at the head of a staircase where the landing was too restricted for a separate table. Such a table top could be made by an amateur, or it would be inexpensive if a joiner was employed. It should be well made and properly finished off, as it will occupy a prominent position in the home. It must not look like a makeshift.

Fig. 1.—A Useful Table at Top of Staircase.

Watch the Headroom.

Two points may be noted, though they will probably occur to most readers at once. The table must not be placed where it will curtail the headroom required by anyone passing up the staircase, and unduly restrict the height required for moving in furniture. If the latter contingency arises, the table could be screwed in such a manner that it could be lifted off when occasion requires.

Also there must be a skirting or guard along the edge over the stairs to prevent articles placed on the table from rolling or sliding off and falling down the staircase.

How it is Made.

Figs. 2 and 3 show how the table top is made and supported, and give suitable sizes and thicknesses of materials.

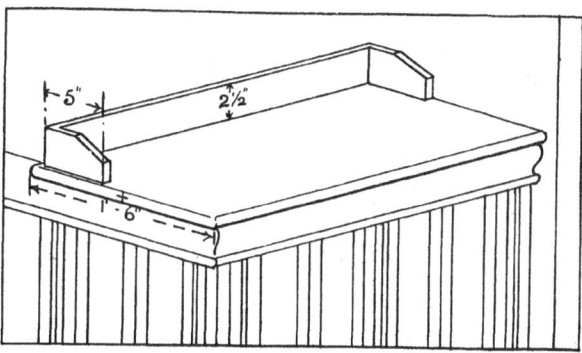

Fig. 2.—Suitable Sizes and Thicknesses of Wood for Table Attached to Balustrading.

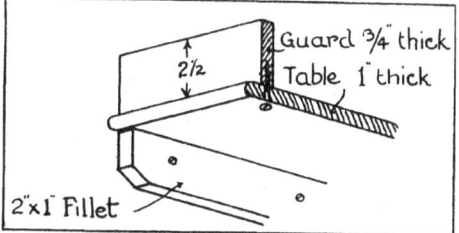

Fig. 3.—Details of Guard and Fillet. See that fillet is securely fixed to the wall.

The balustrade will almost assuredly be strong enough to carry the front edge or two edges if the balustrading returns at the end, as in Fig. 1. There remains the support against the wall. A fillet of wood about 2 inches by 1 inch should be fixed to the wall perfectly level, and at the exact height of the top of the handrail. Do not trust to nails driven direct into the plaster for supporting the fillet, but use wood plugs or, better still, Rawlplugs, and screw the fillet to them.

It will be much easier and stronger to fix the guard to the table top before the latter is put in place. A return end to the guard will strengthen it, and the angles should preferably be dovetailed.

The table top will not be obtainable in one piece of wood. Probably two widths will be required. They should be cross-tongued together. This is perhaps beyond the powers of most amateurs, but the table top could be obtained already cross-tongued and fixed together from the merchant supplying the wood.

In a methodical household known to the writer, a table was provided at the foot and another at the head of the staircase. If any member of the family had something to go up or down and was not at the moment going to the next floor, she placed the article on the table, and the next person going empty handed would carry it and place it on the other table. Many an unnecessary journey was saved, to the housewife at any rate, by this simple system.

Things You Can Do with Mirrors
SOME PRACTICAL HINTS FOR IMPROVING THE APPEARANCE OF A ROOM

MANY small houses and flats nowadays are improved almost beyond recognition by the skilful use of mirrors to reflect the light in dark corners and create an illusion of greater spaciousness. In dealing with a very small room, a professional decorator will sometimes line the whole of one wall with looking-glass, thereby doubling the *apparent* size of the interior, or he will run a broad frieze of mirrors all the way round the room, so that you seem to be looking through on to an adjacent interior, and in one or two instances there have even been successful looking-glass ceilings which have removed the oppressive sense of confinement usually felt in rooms which are too low.

How the Mirrors are fixed.

Without adopting complicated and expensive schemes, however, it is quite easy for any home lover with a practical bent to profit by the wisdom of the expert decorator and improve his home enormously by the use of mirrors. In a small room it would not be difficult to line one of the walls entirely with looking-glass if you took accurate measurements and had the mirrors made to fit, and there are many and varied uses for the unframed, unbevelled and comparatively inexpensive mirrors now fashionable for modern furnishing which are available in standard sizes. These mirrors can be simply plugged and screwed to the wall like any other fixture, using crystal or coloured glass-headed screws, and there are very few rooms in the home that cannot be improved by their use.

Fig. 1.—This Mirror is carried up Flush with the Ceiling and increases the Apparent Loftiness of the Room. A second mirror is on the opposite wall, and can be seen in the photograph.

Have a Mirror over the Fireplace.

In a small lounge or dining-room, for example, one should have a mirror instead of a picture over the fireplace, and there should also be a second mirror occupying a midway position on the opposite wall. If these two mirrors are exactly facing each other, and if the room is a true rectangle so that the mirrors are parallel, the picture seen in one looking-glass will be reflected again in the other, and the result will be two apparently endless vistas. There is no more certain way of getting rid of an impression of restricted space.

Mirrors to give a Heightened Effect to a Room.

If, in addition to being small, the room is rather too low, both mirrors should be carried up past the picture rail, so that their tops finish flush with the ceiling. A portion of the picture rail corresponding to the width of the mirror should, of course, be removed before the mirrors are placed in position, and it will be found that this treatment goes a long way towards making the room seem loftier.

To make a Room look Lighter.

As a guiding principle, it may be said that when it is desired to create an illusion of space, mirrors should be placed opposite one another, in pairs, and they should be carried up flush with the ceiling. If a room is too dark, and light rather than spaciousness is the problem, the looking-glasses should always be placed *in the darkest corners of the room*. They will then pick up the light from other parts of the interior, and if rightly placed they will almost have the effect of doubling the amount of daylight.

Mirrors between Two Windows.

One very good place for fixing a full-length mirror is on the wall space between two windows. This is always liable to seem a dark spot, through contrast with the light thrown on the other walls of the room, and a mirror here is often just what is required. For a soft, well-diffused reflection, however, the ideal arrangement is for mirrors to face each other on the walls at right angles to the windows. Mirrors should never be placed facing

Fig. 2.—Mirrors placed on the Walls of a Dark Landing or Staircase will increase the Light.

Fig. 3.—A Door panelled with a Mirror can be set at any Angle to give a Different Reflection.

the windows, because there should be light enough on this wall already, and the effect is likely to be harsh and glittering. Moreover, this arrangement tends to make the wall space between the windows seem darker than ever.

Improving an Entrance Hall.

No entrance hall, of course, should be without its full-length wall mirror, for this is a practical necessity when adjusting outdoor clothes, and if the hall is inclined to be dark, the mirror will again be useful in increasing the light. On a dark landing, or half-landing, too, a mirror is the best alternative to an extra window and will often produce the desired effect of light, cheerfulness and space.

Uses for Mirror Splash-backs.

In addition to wardrobe and dressing-table mirrors, a small bedroom should have a looking-glass splash-back on the wall behind the wash-stand or lavatory basin, but if this arrangement is chosen there may be no necessity for a mirror on the chimney-breast, for if too many mirrors are used in the bedroom the effect will seem cold.

Yet another use for a mirror splash-back is in the dining-room, where glass is necessary as a wall protection behind sideboard and side-table. Mirrors in the dining-room have another great advantage, for they greatly increase the effectiveness of a well-appointed table. As far as possible, they should be placed so as to give a good reflection of the dining-table from various angles.

Fig. 4.—A Good Position for a Full-length Mirror is on the Wall between Two Windows.

Getting a Glimpse of the Garden.

Another use for looking-glass which has not been exploited nearly so fully as it deserves is as a means of bringing the pictorial fascination of the garden within doors. If the garden includes any unusually picturesque features, such as a well-designed vista, or formal and decorative features of any kind, it is often possible to place a mirror in the lounge or dining-room so that a glimpse of the garden is reflected within doors. One way in which this can sometimes be done is by fixing a full-length mirror to the sitting-room or dining-room door. This is especially practicable if the door is of the laminated, flush and unpanelled type, and by moving the door one gets a different picture in the mirror.

How Mirrors can be used in a Colour Scheme.

Of course, there is no necessity nowadays for mirrors to be of the ordinary "silver" type unless this is really preferable, for instead of being silvered at the back, there are many beautiful mirrors now available which give a reflection tinted either gold, peach, smoke-grey, sapphire blue or green, the colour being either in the backing or in the glass itself. Consequently, mirrors can play a very effective part in the room's colour scheme, or if ordinary silvered looking-glass is used, it may have a coloured border of perhaps blue or green. Peach-tinted mirrors, for example, could be used in a blue room or a room in which pink predominates, while if the room were principally in light or medium green, gold-tinted mirrors would look remarkably well. Smoke-grey, however, being neutral, can be used almost anywhere, and it looks particularly effective with light, bright colours, for the restrained contrast which results shows up both the looking-glass and the colours which surround it to greater advantage.

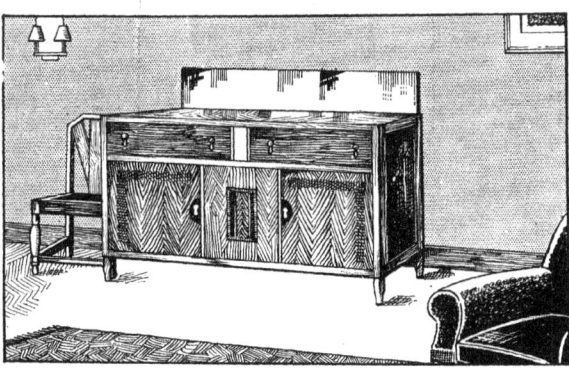

Fig. 5.—A Mirror Splash-back behind the Sideboard will protect the Wall and at the Same Time reflect the Dining-table Appointments.

CLEANING INSIDE GLASS VESSELS

THE illustration on the right shows a useful method of cleaning vases, lamp glasses and other articles of a similar form. The device consists of a piece of springy wire coiled in the middle of its length so that the two ends expand. When it is inserted in a duster, the latter is pressed firmly against the glass and can be easily rotated inside.

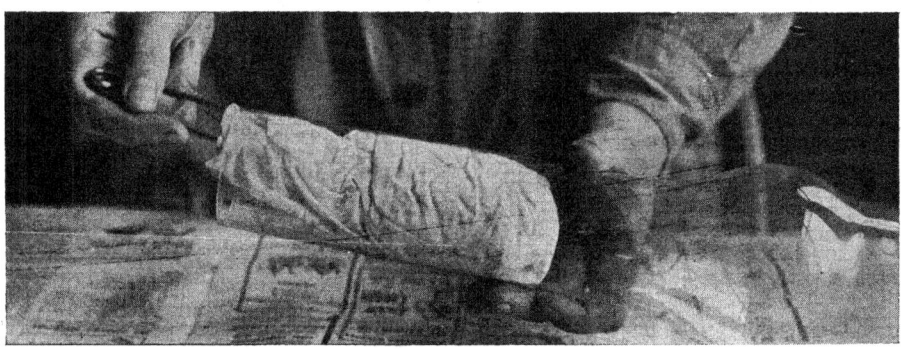

NOTES ON MODERN UPHOLSTERED FURNITURE

There is a general impression that a three-piece upholstered suite is invariably expensive; this, however, is far from being the truth. The cost of a Chesterfield set is necessarily affected by several factors—the timber used for the showwood parts, the material in which the suite is covered, and the size of the settee. The largest settees have three removable cushions along the seat with three corresponding loose cushions along the back. But a settee of this type, which would probably be about 5 feet 6 inches long with a depth of 2 feet 6 inches or 2 feet 9 inches from front to back, is too large for an ordinary sitting-room of average size. It takes up far too much space and is almost impossible to accommodate in a room less than 12 feet by 15 feet. A room of nearly twice these dimensions would be more suitable.

Choosing the Right Size.

For the average sitting-room a settee with a two-cushion seat is to be preferred, because the existence of only two cushions will mean that the settee is very nearly one-third smaller. Cheapest of all are the suites with settees consisting of a long box seat and a cane bergere back. There are no loose cushions with the cheapest models, but, of course, it is better to pay more and obtain something with rather better quality if it is possible to do so.

As a matter of fact, the Chesterfield suite loses noticeably in comfort if too small a model is chosen. While it is a mistake to select furniture too bulky for one's sitting-room, the easy chairs should be, if possible, so deep that the edge of the chair comes just to the knees when one sits down. A chair answering this requirement would have a depth from front to back of 27 inches. The smaller models have a depth of 22 inches, but are decidedly less luxurious in use. It is a principle which applies to every kind of chair that an upright back is less comfortable than one slanted at an angle. By lowering and increasing the depth of the seat and increasing the inclination of both seat and back, a chair of correspondingly greater restfulness is obtained.

Covering Materials.

Regarding the material with which a lounge chair may be covered, the most durable it is possible to obtain is hide. Brown hide is especially suitable for a man's den or study, a smoking-room, or a living-room with oak-panelled walls. But its effect is certainly sober. This, however, may be largely overcome by choosing a hide suite which has been dyed another colour, such as blue or green.

Fig. 1.—An Alternative to the Old-fashioned Antimacassar.
Loose detachable cover for top of chair back, as a protection against hair oil. The cover should be of the same material as the permanent chair cover.

At present cretonne is exceptionally popular both for curtains and chair coverings, and there are also many handsome damasks and moquettes. Plain woven material in light grey and biscuit shades is also frequently used.

Fig. 2.— Easily-made Reading- and Writing-board to go across Arms of Chair.
Its construction will be made clear by referring to Fig. 3. Note hinged centre flap.

Chairs covered in this way should be selected to tone with the walls, and the necessary contrasts should then be provided by ornaments, flowers, pictures and books, and, of course, the woodwork of occasional tables and bureaux.

Fig. 3.—Reading- and Writing-board for Armchair.
Board shown with centre flap raised for use as a book-rest. A suggestion for those who like to read at meals.

Loose covers, although not quite so neat in appearance as fixed covers, are useful and convenient in that they save the permanent cover from wearing and are removable for cleaning; and if the housewife cares to keep two or three sets of differently coloured covers in her linen cupboard, she can vary the colour scheme of her sitting-room at will. Making and fitting loose covers is a task calling for a certain amount of skill and the method of procedure is described on pages 257 to 264.

A Hint on Testing Springing.

When buying an upholstered chair or settee it is important to make sure that the furniture is really well sprung. Sometimes an attempt is made to conceal indifferent springing by the use of extra thick loose cushions. When one sits down on these cushions the effect is very pleasant and luxurious, but if the chair is sprung as it should be, there is no need for the cushions to be more than 3 inches thick. Take the precaution of removing the cushions and sitting in the chair without them. Test the springs thoroughly by moving your weight from one side of the chair to the other. Also, have the chair turned right over and feel the springs through the bottom, making sure that they are set on a proper metal foundation.

A Home-made Easy Chair Writing-Board.

For those who like to write or read in a comfortable chair instead of sitting at a desk or table it is quite easy to construct a home-made writing-board to rest across the arms of the chair, just above one's knees when seated. The board could be made of ordinary deal finished with oak or mahogany stain, and should be from 2 feet 6 inches to 3 feet wide according to the width of the chair, and about 14 inches or 15 inches deep. Hollows could be made at the sides of the board for pen, pencil, inkwell and ash-tray. There could also be a hinged centre-piece which would lie flat when closed, providing a slightly raised area for the writing-pad, and when opened and secured with a hasp and staples, would provide a useful book-rest.

CARE OF UPHOLSTERED FURNITURE

Loose Covers.

A few words on the care and cleaning of upholstered furniture should prove of practical assistance. Reference has already been made to the use of loose covers, which will save the permanent covers from going threadbare and will conceal the worn places if it has already done so. Loose covers should be removed periodically for cleaning, and in the case of chintz, for re-glazing, and they are best entrusted to one of the well-known cleaners specialising in this class of work.

To prevent Moth Ravages.

One of the greatest enemies of upholstered furniture, as of fabrics generally, is the several species of clothes' moth familiar to almost everyone. Naphthalene in the form of crystals, flakes, powder or "moth-balls" is helpful as a *preventive*, but it is useless where moths have already laid their eggs and the destructive *larvæ* are at work. The best and most efficient re-agent is paradichlorbenzene, a compound which destroys both eggs and grubs. Paradichlorbenzene should especially be used at spring-cleaning time—in April or May—for if this precaution is neglected there is danger of the moths making their appearance and becoming numerous during the summer.

Cleaning Upholstery.

The first step in cleaning upholstered furniture is a preliminary brushing and a few smart blows on cushions and upholstered areas where dust is likely to settle. Upholstered furniture should be kept in good condition by the regular use of a vacuum cleaner; and when a chair or settee becomes greasy or stained with hair oil it should be cleaned by applying first benzine and then clean water.

Antimacassars to protect the backs of chairs are now unpopular, but so long as men use hair oil, antimacassars will have their uses. As an alternative, one could use a piece of the same material as that used for covering the chair. The piece of material could be cut and sewn so as to fit like a cap over the back of the chair. It will then be hardly noticeable and is easily removed for cleaning.

MATTRESSES

With modern beds, as with upholstered furniture, there has been an immense improvement in standards of comfort, and these improvements have resulted from the same cause: the use of spiral springing. As with chairs, so with mattresses. The mattress of to-day is far superior to its forerunners of comparatively few years ago.

Modern Spring Mattresses and their Uses.

The ordinary woven wire mattress has now been improved upon by means of various forms of spiral spring mattress, the most widely known of which is probably the box-spring mattress. Mattresses which contain springs instead of one of the usual soft fillings are now of many different types. There are spring mattresses which look like an ordinary overlay mattress stuffed with hair, only rather thicker. A spring mattress of this kind may be placed either on a box mattress or on a special base support which is upheld with spiral springs and is really a simpler alternative to a complete box mattress. There is then no need for a hair overlay mattress. Another good suggestion is a box mattress with a hair mattress or a mattress containing wool and hair in alternate layers on top. Any of these combinations should result in a comfortable bed which would remain in excellent condition for many years.

Care of Spring Mattresses.

If you decide in favour of a spring mattress other than a box mattress, the following points should be borne in mind.

A spring mattress should never be rolled, or the ticking may be badly strained and the springs become interlocked. A spring mattress should be kept flat.

The mattress should be reversed occasionally, from head to foot of the bed, and if it is double-sided it should be turned over every few weeks, so that all parts have equal wear and equal rest.

A spring mattress other than a box mattress should not be used for sitting on. It is only designed to take one's weight when lying down, and the concentrated weight when sitting may affect the mattress adversely.

Expose all bedding to fresh air and sunshine at least once a week.

Uses of the Box Mattress.

A box mattress, however, is so stoutly constructed that it can be used on french castors, or may be raised 6 or 9 inches from the ground on short legs. A complete bedstead is no longer necessary. Many box mattresses are set on a shallow frame or plinth so that they are equally suitable for use as beds or divans. They have a graceful headboard which may be either fixed or detachable, but no board at the foot. A bed without a foot panel is said to have a "stump end," and it is

Fig. 4.—A Home-made Upholstered Divan.

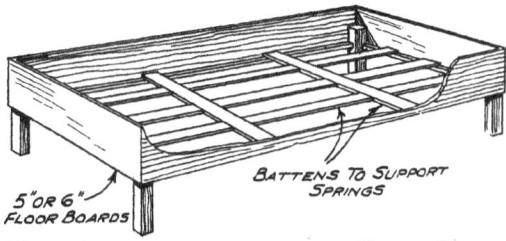

Fig. 5.—Illustrating how to make a Modern Divan
The box base and how it is formed.

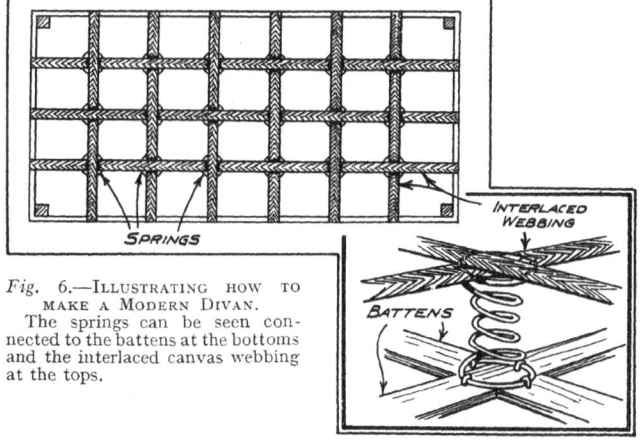

Fig. 6.—Illustrating how to make a Modern Divan.
The springs can be seen connected to the battens at the bottoms and the interlaced canvas webbing at the tops.

Fig. 7.—Packing the Mattress Case with Rugging.
Take care to keep the corners square.

found that the stump end is a great convenience in small bedrooms, for the bed then seems to take up less space in the room. It is also possible to use the end of the bed as a seat during the day, especially if the bedroom is equipped for occasional use as a sitting-room.

Fitting Box Mattress to Existing Bed.

When it is desired to fit a box mattress to an existing bed which was originally intended for a woven wire mattress and a hair overlay mattress, the box mattress, being 9 inches deep, will make the bed seem too high.

One should ask for a *sunk* box mattress, which will fit within the frame of the bedstead and drops from 4 to 6 inches. As an alternative one could have the legs of the bedstead shortened, but this may have a practical disadvantage if it becomes difficult to sweep and clean beneath the bed.

An Economy Hint when furnishing the Bedroom.

Elimination of the bedstead is a sound, practical economy when furnishing, because the money thus saved may be spent on better bedding. The wisest course is to spend as little as possible on the bedstead, because an elaborate bedstead is unnecessary, and to spend as much as one can possibly afford on a really good box-spring mattress, all-wool blankets, and good quality sheets, perhaps of the new coloured linen in pale blue, peach or apricot.

How to make a Divan at Home.

A simple box mattress or divan can be quite easily made at home. A typical divan is shown in Fig. 4. The following materials should be obtained :—
Floorboarding, 6 × 1 inches.
Wooden slats and stretchers.
Spiral springs.
Staples.
Canvas webbing.
Unbleached calico.
Rugging or other filling material.

The method of forming the box base is shown in Fig. 5. The floorboarding should be butt-jointed to form the sides of the mattress. Two parallel wooden slats should run the full length of the mattress and these should be intersected by two stretchers across the width. These carry the spiral springs which should be placed in position on the slats and stretchers, each spring being held down with three small staples. Interlaced webbing should be used to hold the tops of the springs in position, and each spring should be secured firmly to the webbing with string.

The next step is to make a stuffed mattress or mattresses to go on top of the springs. For a divan 6 feet by 2 feet 6 inches, the easiest course will be to make three small mattresses, each 2 feet 6 inches by 2 feet and with a thickness of about $3\frac{1}{2}$ inches.

The mattress should be made from unbleached calico. There must be a piece for top and bottom, and a strip long enough to go right round between them. This strip should be about $4\frac{1}{2}$ inches wide, thus allowing $\frac{1}{2}$ inch for turning in at top and bottom.

Filling the Mattress.

A good material for filling the mattresses and also for any loose cushions is rugging or blanket flock, which is a waste product from new blankets, and should be easily obtainable from any house furnisher. When filling the mattress, take care to keep the corners square. It is advisable to tuft or button the mattresses and details for doing this are given on page 475.

AFTER A ROOM HAS BEEN REDECORATED

LET us suppose that a room has been redecorated—the ceiling whitened, the walls papered and the woodwork painted, or it may be that no more than one or, perhaps, two of these three jobs have been effected. It is only in very rare instances that there is still not a great deal to do to give the room a really finished appearance.

The Paintwork of the Window.

However well the paint may have been applied to the window sashes, there are always places where the brush has run too far over the glass and caused an unsatisfactory edge. If it is left, it will be a perpetual eyesore. Therefore, take the blade of a pocket-knife or, better still, a safety razor blade, fitted into a patent holder, and scrape away the surplus paint. Two or three minutes spent in this way will make a great deal of difference to the appearance of the window.

When all the edges have been cleaned up, look critically over the panes of glass. It would be very unusual if there were no paint splashes on them. Carefully scrape all of them away and, if necessary, rub the parts with a dab of turpentine.

The Hinges of the Door.

Now go to the door. More than likely, the hinges have received an over-generous coating of paint and, when the door has been opened and closed a few times, the paint will rough up. Take a pocket-knife and scrape away any excesses. Correctly speaking, there should be no paint on the barrel of a hinge at all. Therefore, it will not be wrong to scrape it until the metal is bared. This done, put a drop of lubricating oil on each hinge and wipe away any of the oil that is likely to run down on to the paint.

The Door Handle.

The next step is to examine the door handle. Usually, the collar of the handle has not entirely escaped the paintbrush. If it is made of brass or other metal, the surplus paint should be cleaned off with turpentine; it must not be scratched away with a pocket-knife or the lacquer will be removed as well. Naturally, none of the turpentine may be allowed to run over on to the door, so it will be helpful to cut a template of thin card and to fit this round the collar while the rubbing is done. In the case of a polished wooden handle, a dab of furniture polish should take the place of the turpentine.

It will be as well to see if the handle of the door turns properly, now that we are dealing with such matters. The tiny screw that holds it to the cross bar often works loose. Therefore, tighten it up. Should it have worn so that it will no longer hold, replace it by a larger screw and, if you have not such a thing and the handle keeps falling off, just run a strip of adhesive tape round the part where the screw head comes, while you are arranging to get a larger screw. It cannot fall out now and the handle will not be able to pull off.

The Finger Plates.

Probably the finger plates were removed before the painting was done. If so, replace them, but clean them thoroughly first, and do not forget to rub up the heads of the screws, if the same ones are to be used again.

Painting Wall Blocks.

In most rooms, there are several wall blocks which serve as mountings for electric-light switches, bell pushes, etc. These should not be overlooked, and if they are covered with paint, they may as well be renewed. A good plan is to give them two or three coats of a suitable cellulose lacquer. The lacquer will dry quickly and there will be less inconvenience than is caused when an ordinary slow-drying paint is applied.

Then it will be a good plan to go round the edges of the floor in the proximity of the skirting board. Here there may be splashes of paint or overlapping streaks of the same material. If the floor is covered with linoleum, turpentine will be useful for cleaning away the spots and streaks and, where a polished surround is concerned, some furniture polish will do the work.

Fitting a Light on a Newel Post

The appearance of a hall can be considerably enhanced by fitting an electric light to the newel post or main upright at the foot of the stairs, as shown in Fig. 1. This light is controlled by a separate switch recessed into the post. Not only does such a light look attractive, but in many cases it serves the dual purpose of lighting the hall and landing in place of two separate lights.

Materials required.

As the fuses and main switch will probably be situated in the cupboard under the stairs, only about 5 or 6 yards of lead-covered twin lighting cable (5 amps.) will be required. Obtain the following fittings:—

1 plain batten lamp-holder, with flat base.
1 wooden fixing block to fit newel post.
1 solid brass gallery, about $3\frac{1}{4}$ inches in diameter, to fit on to lamp-holder.
1 flush-fitting switch.
Some small staples or saddles for fixing the lead-covered wire.

Tools.

The only tools required for the job are a small hammer, screwdriver, brace and bit, chisel, gimlet or bradawl, and a pocket knife.

Running the Wire.

The first thing to decide is where the lead-covered cable is to run from the fuse-box to the top of the newel post. Choose a route that is simple and direct without being too conspicuous. It will probably be possible to run the wire underneath the staircase handrail, as shown in Fig. 2.

Having decided on the most con-

Fig. 1.—The Appearance of a Hall is considerably enhanced by fitting a Light to the Newel Post.

venient run, fix one end of the cable underneath the handrail close to the post, leaving about 1 foot of cable to spare for connecting up to the light. Then follow the route you have planned, fixing the wire in place at regular intervals with staples.

A hole of about $\frac{1}{2}$ inch in diameter will have to be drilled to enable the wire to be passed through the stairs into the cupboard where the fuses are fixed, unless, as in some cases, the fuses are fixed somewhere on the wall in the hall. Fix the wire firmly up to about a foot away from the fuse-box.

Removing Surplus Cable.

Any surplus cable can be removed by making a nick in the lead covering with a pocket knife and bending the wire over. Allow ample for making the connections to the fuse-box, then score along the covering with the knife, and open it out like the leaves of a book.

Strip Insulation from Wires.

The next step is to remove the insulation from the ends of the wires to the extent of about 1 inch. This can be done either with a pocket knife or by holding a lighted match to the ends of the wires until the insulation is sufficiently burnt or charred to enable it to be easily scraped off.

Wiring the Newel Post.

At this stage it is advisable to leave the fuse-box and complete the wiring at the post end before connecting up to the fuses.

Fitting the Wooden Fixing Block.

The first thing to do is to prepare the underside of the wooden fixing block so that it fits neatly on to the top of the post, which will probably be moulded. Remove as much wood as necessary with a chisel.

Next place the lamp-holder in the centre of the fixing block and mark through with a piece of wire or scriber the positions of the holes that are to be drilled through the block for the wires. The block is secured to the post by two thin screws placed about $\frac{3}{4}$ inch from the centre and well clear of the holes drilled for the wires.

Drilling the Holes in the Newel Post.

The next thing to do is to drill passages in the newel post through which the wire is to pass. First drill a hole about $\frac{1}{2}$ inch in diameter at the

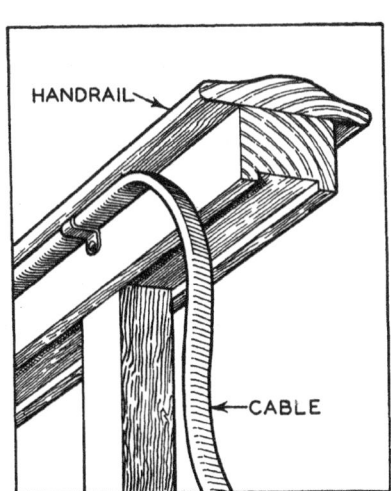

Fig. 2.—Showing how the Cable can be concealed underneath the Staircase Handrail.

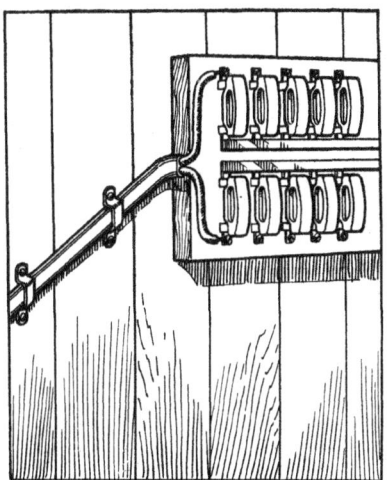

Fig. 3.—How the Wire is connected to the Fuse-box.

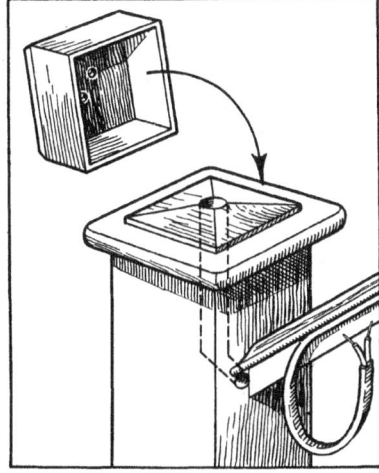

Fig. 4.—Showing the Fixing Block and Holes drilled in Post.

FITTING A LIGHT ON A NEWEL POST

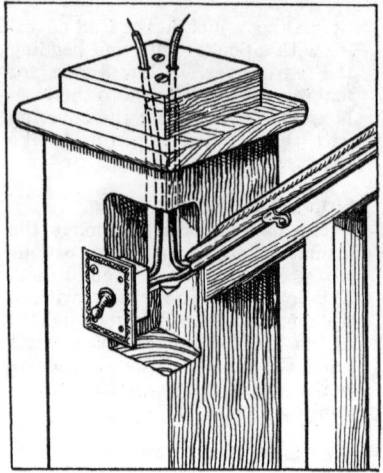

*Fig. 5.—*The Wiring at the Switch.

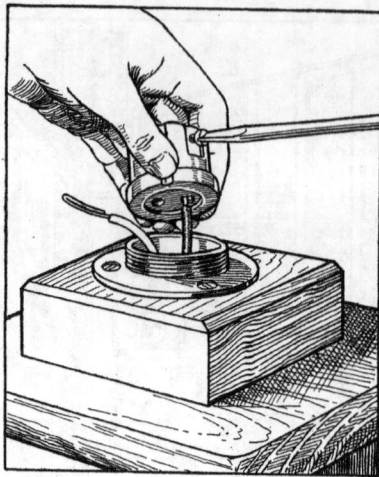

*Fig. 6.—*Fixing the Wire to the Lamp-holder.

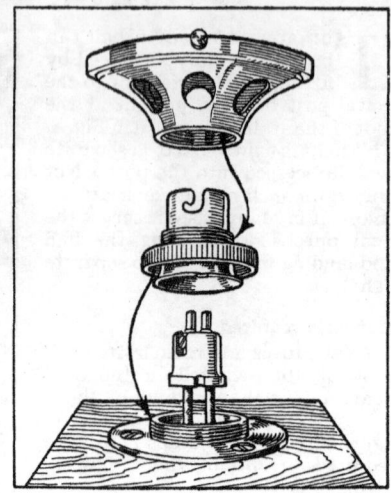

*Fig. 7.—*Method of Assembling Lamp-holder.

point where the cable is to enter, and continue it upwards and inwards to the centre. Then drill a second hole downwards from the centre of the post until it joins the first hole.

Recess for the Switch.

Now cut away a recess on the face of the post until the switch fits into it and is flush with the surface. Then drill holes from the recess to communicate with those already drilled.

Inserting the Wire.

Now insert the wire from the outside of the post and twist it about until it comes out at the switch recess. The lead sheathing should now be removed as already described, until two fairly long ends of wire are uncovered. Lead one of the wires through the centre hole until it comes out at the top of the post. Then cut the second wire, leaving just sufficient to connect to one of the terminals of the switch after the end has been bared for a short distance.

This will leave one short piece of wire over, and one end of it is connected to the other terminal of the switch, and the other end passed through the centre hole and out at the top of the post.

Make sure the wires are firmly connected to the switch before screwing it in place, and that there are no exposed places on the wire. If the metal is visible at any parts of the wire, either shorten the wires or cover with insulating tape.

Now bare the two ends of wire that are sticking out of the top of the post and screw the flange to the fixing block. Then connect the two ends of wire to the lamp-holder, as shown in Fig. 6.

Assemble the remaining parts of the lamp-holder, as shown in Fig 7, and insert a bulb ready for testing when the connections have been made to the fuse-box.

Joining Wire to Fuse-box.

Before connecting the wires to the

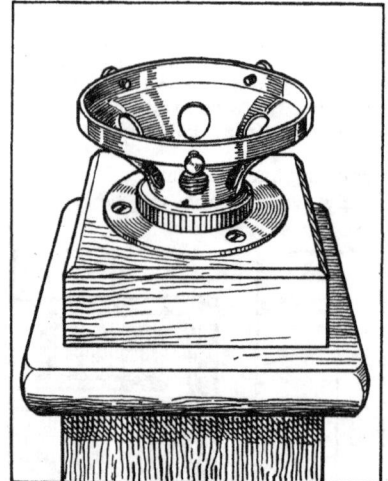

*Fig. 8.—*The Completed Job ready for the Glass Shade to be fitted.

fuse-box it is necessary to find out which are the correct terminals. First of all see that all the switches in the house are off; then turn off the main switch, remove one of the fuses, turn on the main switch again, then go round the house, switching on the lights until you trace the ones that do not light, due to the fuse having been removed.

Note which they are, return to the fuse-box, switch off the main switch and replace the fuse. Now remove the fuse immediately opposite (above or below) the one you have just removed, switch on the main switch again, and see if the lights that were previously off are still off. If, however, they are on this time, then it will be necessary to repeat the test until the correct fuse is located.

With the main switch off, connect one of the wires to the outside terminal of the first fuse that was removed and the other wire to the terminal of the other fuse that you have located by testing. Fig. 3 shows the connections quite clearly.

Switch on the main switch, return to the stairs and switch on the light. If everything is in order, switch off, remove the lamp and screw the gallery on to the holder, as shown in Fig. 8. Replace the lamp, and put a flambeau or other form of shade on to the gallery and secure it with the screws or clips provided for the purpose.

A USEFUL BRONZING SOLUTION

THE following is a good recipe for a bronzing liquid that can be rubbed or brushed on to brass, for bronzing or restoration of worn bronzed surfaces. Mix together the following substances:—

Fuchsin . . . 2 parts
Aniline purple . . 1 part
Alcohol (95 per cent. pure) . . . 20 parts

When dissolved add 1 part of benzoic acid. The mixture should be heated to the boiling point until the colour changes to a bronze-brown. The solution, when cold, should be applied to the previously cleaned brass surface. It is important to eliminate any trace of oil or grease from the latter.

Converting a Victorian Wardrobe into Two Modern Fitments

Flats and small houses are so much the vogue nowadays that the Victorian wardrobe, however well made or however commodious, has become a very cumbersome piece of furniture.

In many cases when a removal takes place from a house with large rooms to a more compact one with smaller rooms this piece of furniture becomes a problem.

How the actual conversion of a fine mahogany wardrobe was effected and the wardrobe fitted with two recesses with a chest of drawers left over as a separate piece of furniture is described below.

Fig. 1 shows it as it was, with the interior as Fig. 2. The two recesses to be fitted are shown in Fig. 3.

This wardrobe, as large wardrobes always are, was made up of several pieces. Fig. 2 shows its component parts and Fig. 3 shows the completed fitment.

Additional Material required.

The only new pieces of mahogany required were two pieces (6 feet × 8 inches in Fig. 3 A and B), and two pieces of skirting (Fig 4 A and shown in Fig. 3), some odd pieces and some pieces of plywood.

The Right-hand Fitment.

Let us take the right-hand fitment first. It so happened that the part marked A in Fig. 2 nearly fitted (on its side) into the recess.

Making up any Deficiency in the Width.

First of all a piece of wood the depth of the wardrobe is screwed to the wall on the left side (Fig. 5). Plywood was used because it can be obtained in wide pieces. This piece was the height of the wardrobe and finishes to the point where the lowest line of the cornice is to come.

This piece serves to make up the deficiency in the width as the part of the wardrobe concerned fell short, by 1 inch, of the recess.

The plywood pieces shown in Fig. 6 were then screwed to the sides and back. These are fixed for the upper part above mentioned to rest upon.

Framework for Floor of Cupboard.

Next, a framework of deal 2 inches by the height of 1 inch less than the skirting, viz., 5 inches had to be fixed at floor level, the back and sides being screwed in, but the front is fixed as shown in Fig. 4 B, box pinned-jointed, glued and screwed. The floor of the cupboard is fixed to this framework.

The right-hand end (polished mahogany) of the original wardrobe was cut down the centre, from top to bottom, half of which was used here and screwed to the left-hand side, from the inside (Figs. 7 and 8).

The Upper Part and Back.

The upper part now rests upon its fixed supports (Fig. 9) and is screwed through the sides and back. The back is composed of the original panelled back of the wardrobe.

A piece of deal, 5 × 1 inch by the length of the front is fixed in front (Fig. 10).

On the right is now fitted a polished mahogany upright which serves as a hanging stile for the right-hand door, glued and screwed top and bottom and resting on the front batten. The bottom screws are countersunk and filled with stopping before being polished, the bottom tenoned into the batten (Figs. 3 and 9).

The Skirting.

Then the skirting of polished mahogany (Fig. 4 A and C) is fixed by screws from the inside of the framework and through the piece of wood first mentioned and is mitred on the left front angle, butting into the chimney breast on the left and the wall on the right. The skirting projects above the framework 1 inch, this being the thickness of the plywood floor which is dropped in and scribed round the end (Fig. 4 C) and screwed down.

Fig. 1.—An Old-fashioned Victorian Wardrobe.

A piece of furniture such as this is unwieldy in a modern house, but can quite easily be converted into the two modern fitments shown in Fig. 3.

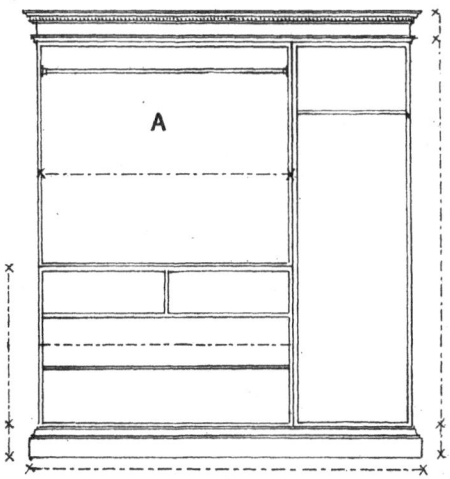

Fig. 2.—The Component Parts of an Old-fashioned Wardrobe.

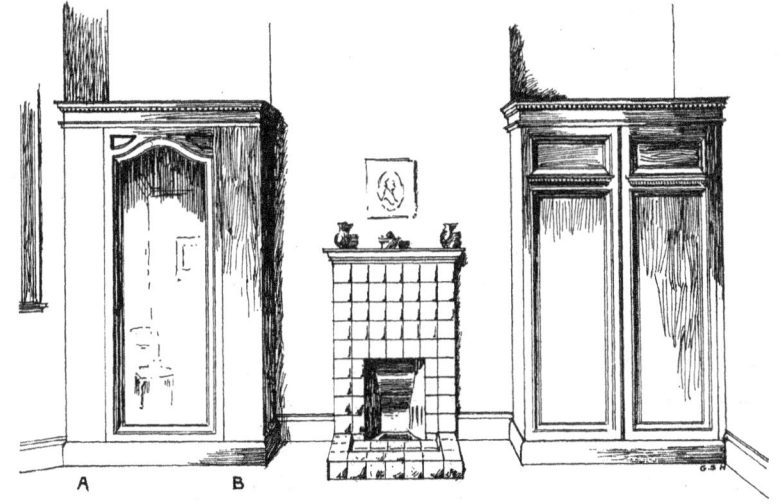

Fig. 3.—The Completed Conversion.

CONVERTING A VICTORIAN WARDROBE INTO TWO MODERN FITMENTS

The Cornice.

Now the cornice, the one from the original wardrobe, was nearly long enough for the two fitments, allowing for the two return ends (Figs. 3 and 11), and to make up the few inches deficiency the cornices were cut in the centre and the lengths fixed, butting into key blocks (Fig. 11).

The cornice is arranged so as to overlap the front about 1 inch, the thickness of the doors, in order that the finish may be more or less flush.

The cornice is fixed by means of screws into the back and side walls. Battens are fixed on to the inside through which the screws are driven. The battens finish about ¾ inch below the top of the cornice to allow of a piece of plywood to be screwed in from the top and finish flush with the top of the cornice. This serves as a dust board (Fig. 11).

Fixing Battens to Inside of Cornice.

The method of fixing the battens to the inside of the cornice in order to secure them properly is shown in Fig. 11, the back box-pin jointed into the sides and sides rebated into the back of the cornice (Fig. 11 A). The front batten is screwed into the back of the cornice.

The Doors.

The two doors A and B, Fig. 1, are hung as shown in Fig. 3. A rod for hanging is fixed inside.

The original wardrobe lock existed on the left-hand door and was arranged to latch into the right-hand door, a

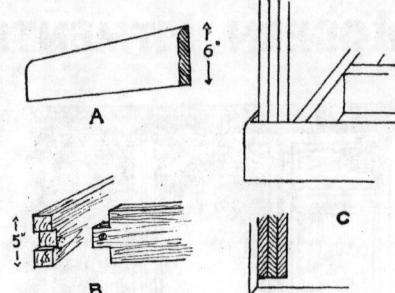

Fig. 4.—Details of Pieces of Skirting, Box-pinned Joint and Method of Fixing Skirting.

bolt being fixed inside to stop on to the floor of the upper part.

Green cut-glass handles completed the appearance.

The mahogany was, of course, french polished originally, and needed only reviving, whilst the bare wood was stained with permanganate of potash diluted in water, and then french polished to match the other work.

The Left-hand Fitment.

The fitment for the left-hand recess was a more simple matter than that on the right.

A skeleton framing was first fixed up against the wall (Fig. 12.) Four pieces of deal 2 × 2 inches at floor level screwed to the floor. Four upright 2 × 2 inches screwed to the wall and secured at the top by a piece of plywood the depth and width of the fitment, 1 inch thick. This framework is constructed as shown in Fig. 14, the centre and bottom pieces being morticed and tenoned, the joints being well glued. The top board is screwed in from the top with additional transverse rails at the top.

The framework having been fixed, two pieces of polished mahogany, 8 inches wide, 1 inch thick, were fixed to the front, as shown in Fig. 3, to form the width for the mirror door (Fig. 3). These pieces are fixed at floor level and screwed through the front rail of the bottom framework from the front and at the top secured by screws from the back of the top rail.

Three-ply is used for the inside back and sides, and the skirting is fixed from the inside through the framework by means of screws, mitred at the right-hand side, butting into the chimney breast and scribed into the angle wall on the left (Fig. 16). The floor, made of three-ply, is screwed to the transverse rails.

The right-hand return end is formed with the other half of the original wardrobe end, half of which was used for the other recess, as described above, and screwed through the inside at the top and through the front at the bottom as shown (Fig. 13), covered by the skirting.

The cornice is placed in position and is formed exactly as on the other cupboard, but mitred on the right-hand side, butting into the chimney breast and scribed into the angle wall on the left. This is secured in the same way as on the other cupboard.

The mirror door, the centre one from the original wardrobe, is hung on the right and had a lock already fixed, which served well here. The top

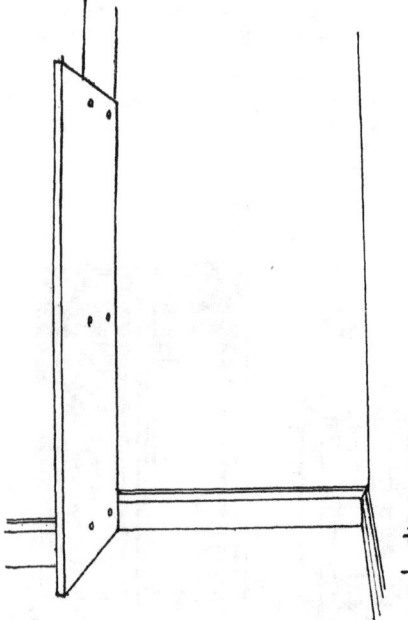

Fig. 5.—The First Operation is to screw a Piece of Plywood the Depth of the Wardrobe to the Wall on the Left Side.

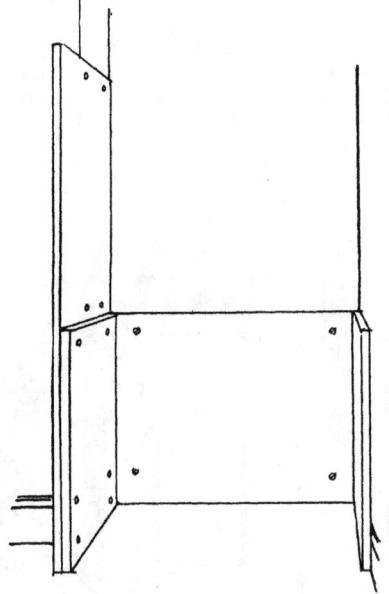

Fig. 6.—Showing Pieces of Plywood added to the Sides and Back.

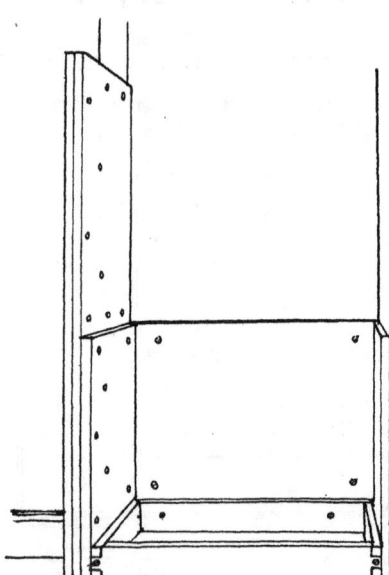

Fig. 7.—The Framework for the Floor of the Cupboard.

CONVERTING A VICTORIAN WARDROBE INTO TWO MODERN FITMENTS

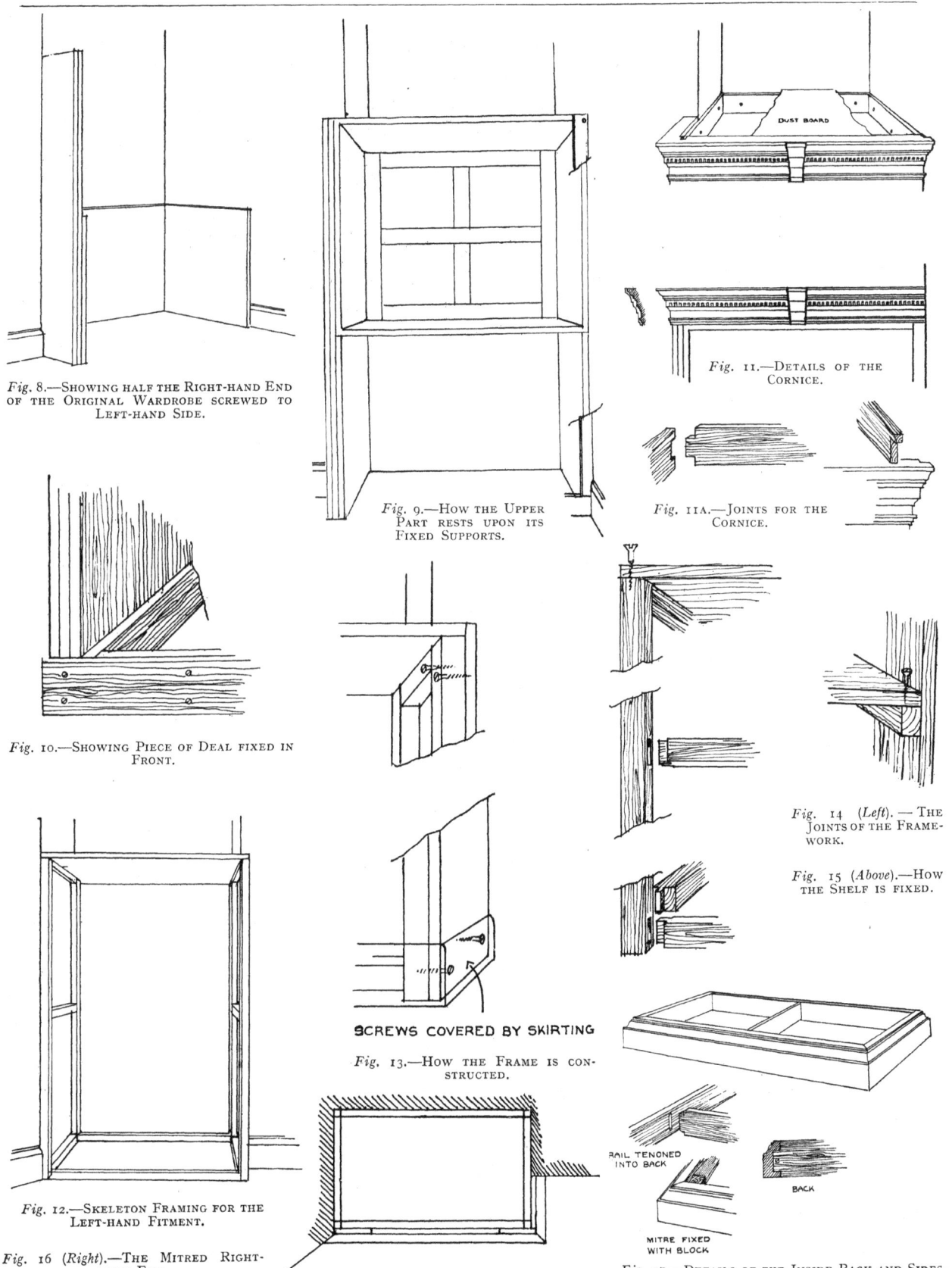

Fig. 8.—Showing half the Right-hand End of the Original Wardrobe screwed to Left-hand Side.

Fig. 9.—How the Upper Part rests upon its Fixed Supports.

Fig. 10.—Showing Piece of Deal fixed in Front.

Fig. 11.—Details of the Cornice.

Fig. 11A.—Joints for the Cornice.

Fig. 12.—Skeleton Framing for the Left-hand Fitment.

Fig. 13.—How the Frame is constructed.

Fig. 14 (Left).—The Joints of the Framework.

Fig. 15 (Above).—How the Shelf is fixed.

Fig. 16 (Right).—The Mitred Right-hand End.

Fig. 17.—Details of the Inside Back and Sides.

...rd which was fixed to the deal uprights served as a "stop" for the door. A cut-glass knob is fixed on the front as on the other doors and the polishing dealt with in the same way as described above.

This fitment is used for hanging and has a rod fixed across, underneath a shelf, which is fixed on cleats, about 1 foot from the top (Fig. 15).

Converting the Drawer Part into a Chest.

The part composed of drawers, as shown in Fig. 2, came out separately. The part which was originally above the drawers was used, as explained, for the right-hand recess and was separate from the bottom part, including the polished mahogany end.

On top of the chest were four stub tenons into which the top part originally fitted. These had to be cut off and the top of the chest covered with thin three-ply, screwed on.

The plinth, or skirting, removed from the original wardrobe was used for this chest and had, of course, to be cut down to the required length and depth. One end was already mitred, but the other end had, of course, to be cut and mitred accordingly to fit, and framed up as shown on Fig. 17.

Fig. 18.—How the Drawer Part of the Wardrobe is converted into a Useful Chest.

The Handles.

Now came the question of the handles. As the doors of the wardrobe closed practically tight up against the drawers, flush handles had been fitted to the drawer fronts. These were removed and green cut-glass handles substituted, and to cover up the ugly holes which existed flat pieces of polished mahogany were fixed over and the handles fitted with spindles put through and fixed by means of nuts on the inside.

One end, being the original carcase end of the wardrobe, was already polished, but the other bare wood. The difficulty was, however, overcome by first rubbing it well down with glasspaper, then staining and french-polishing.

The top could also have been polished, though as a matter of fact, in this instance, it was covered with a piece of brocade (Fig. 18).

There were found to be quite a number of odd pieces over after and original wardrobe was dismantled and pieces which could be cut up the adapted for the new fitments.

PAPIER MACHÉ BOWLS FROM OLD NEWSPAPERS

MANY people may be unaware that old newspapers can be made into attractive bowls of papier maché for bulb planting or other uses, by proceeding as follows: Any rough or spongy surfaced paper as well as newspapers will do.

Paste.

You will need in addition to the paper, paste made up by mixing one full teacup of flour with sufficient cold water to bring it to consistency of thick cream, to which must be added a teaspoonful of powdered alum. Then add two cupfuls of boiling water, stirring to remove all lumps and place vessel containing paste in a saucepan of water, which should be boiled for ten minutes, stirring all the time, as this will make the paste thicker, and hasten drying. Any bowl or basin— an ordinary kitchen mixing bowl or enamel bowl, if clean—will do. *Do not use* a bowl with a top smaller than the bottom, as you will not be able to remove the papier maché when it has dried hard.

Smear the Inside of the Bowl with Grease.

Before starting, remember to smear the inside of the bowl, or whatever you are using for a mould, with grease or oil to prevent the papier maché sticking when dry.

How to Proceed.

The paper should be torn—not cut, as the cut edges will cause ridges in the finished article—into pieces about 3 or 4 inches square and soaked in water for about an hour. While this is going on you can leave it and make the paste, as directed, in the meantime.

Take the paper out of the water and squeeze as much water out of it as possible; a rolling pin is very useful. Lay a layer of paper in the mould to about the desired depth and all over the bottom, and with a soft pad— cotton wool for instance—press the paper well down so as to be certain that no air bubbles are left, and ensure entire surface of the mould is covered. Be very careful about this.

Now give this first layer an even coat of paste, and lay another layer over the first, and continue with the pasting between each layer until eight or ten layers, according to thickness desired, have been completed. Press as heavily as possible between each layer, for reason given above, and be careful that no paste gets on the mould, or difficulty will be found in removing the finished bowl when dry. The edges should be trimmed with sharp scissors.

Leave for Two or Three Days to Dry.

On no account hurry the job. It will take two or three days to dry, and leaving it in a fairly warm place will help. The bowl will slip out quite easily when fairly dry, but it should be left until it is absolutely bone-dry before proceeding to paint it. It must be rubbed all over with glasspaper, inside and out, to give an even smooth surface, and given a coat of shellac, to make it waterproof.

Allow to dry and again glasspaper it, and having chosen the colour, according to the colour schemes of the rooms in which you intend using the bowls, apply two or three coats of Darkaline Japanese lacquer, which will give a fine professional finish. You can get small sizes and therefore you need not buy large pots of paint with the possibility that the colours will be too bright for other purposes.

Glasspaper between each coat—but *not* of course the last one, and be certain each coat is dry before proceeding with the next.

These are cheap and interesting to make, and square ones can be made— certainly with a little extra trouble— by using small wooden boxes, greasing as much as possible before starting. These wooden moulds can moreover, be soaked in water again and/or pulled apart if necessary to loosen article made therein.

The main secret is, of course, to press (or pulp) the paper firmly together so as to merge it into a complete whole, but success is reasonably certain.

Practical Notes on Hire Purchase and Credit Trading

THE Hire Purchase and Credit Trade to-day is every bit as respectable, fair dealing and satisfactory as the cash trade. Moreover, it has opened up for thousands the means of obtaining the necessities for comfort and well-being, as well as a few of the luxuries, previously denied them.

To-day these systems of instalment trading are simple, whether it be the hire-purchase system for furniture and the like, or the credit buying of soft goods, etc.

Buying Furniture on the Hire Purchase.

Let us first take the application of hire purchase to furniture, for this is an important matter to those who desire to set up housekeeping.

With the keen competition between firms to-day, one is able to compare values, prices, terms, etc., very thoroughly, and there is not the slightest need for anyone to say that they have bought any goods or signed any agreement under a misapprehension; provided, of course, that they possess ordinary common sense.

$2\frac{1}{2}$ per cent. added for Deferred Payments.

Whatever the firm, the procedure is more or less the same. One can visit the showrooms—many of them extensive and containing a variety of goods of the most artistic and up-to-date design—and select whatever furniture is desired. The total value of this is ascertained, and in the majority of cases an addition of $2\frac{1}{2}$ per cent. is added for deferred payments. This covers all costs as to collection of accounts, etc. The total figure is then divided into a number of equal payments to be made monthly.

Cases when a higher Percentage is Charged.

In the case of some firms, no deposit is asked; in others a certain percentage is asked. The monthly payments commence usually a month from the date the agreement is signed.

It should be mentioned, however, that in the case of vacuum cleaners, motor cars, etc., and other articles where deterioration is likely in a comparatively short time, a far higher percentage is charged for deferred payments than in the case of furniture—often as much as 7 to 10 per cent.

The Agreement.

The gist of the Agreement, whatever the firm, is usually the same. There is a more or less standard agreement used by all. In it the vendor agrees to sell to the buyer goods to a certain value, to be paid for by so many equal monthly payments until the total sum is paid, when the goods become the absolute property of the buyer, *but until the whole of the payments are completed they remain the property of the vendor.*

If Payments are not maintained.

There is, however, in most agreements, a clause to protect the buyer if for some reason or other from unforeseen circumstances it is found impossible to maintain the payments. This clause enables the buyer—or rather the hirer, as he is called in the agreement—to return the goods after a nominal period if circumstances force the issue, without further liability.

The whole of the time, until the last payment is made, the goods are deemed to be "on hire" to the signatory to the agreement.

A Concession that is sometimes made.

Although no clause appears in agreements, it is the policy of most of the reputable firms to allow a person, forced through circumstances to ask for cancellation of the agreement, to keep a portion of the goods in return for the money they have already paid in instalments; provided, of course, that it is a genuine case of inability to continue and that a sufficient number of instalments have been made to warrant such an action on the part of the vendor.

But this is merely a concession on the part of the vendor, and is not a part of any agreement.

When buying furniture, it is best to deal with a house which advertises its CASH values rather than its terms. For here you know the value you are getting and can reckon safely that there will be about $2\frac{1}{2}$ per cent. added for terms. If you are more interested in the length of time given you to pay, then you must expect to pay more.

Points to remember when purchasing by Hire Purchase.

Here are a few words of advice in regard to the purchase of furniture by hire purchase.

(1) Read any agreement carefully before you sign it, and don't sign any paper without understanding its meaning.

(2) Remember that the goods remain the property of the vendor until the last instalment is paid.

(3) Every hire-purchase agreement should contain a clause enabling the hirer to return the goods and terminate the agreement, after a given number of instalments have been paid, without any further liability. (Thus it will be seen that the instalments paid have been regarded as the rent of hiring the goods.)

(4) That the goods must on no account be sold *under any conditions.* This is a criminal offence, and the seller is liable to 6 months' imprisonment. They can, however, sometimes be transferred with the agreement, provided the permission of the vendor is obtained.

(5) If you are visited by a traveller from a firm, do not on any account accept his very kind (*sic*) offer to pay the first instalment out of his commission.

(6) Do not allow any clause to be inserted or deleted by a representative, without first getting confirmation from his employers. Do not sign any agreement which has been altered, unless so confirmed.

CREDIT TRADING

Here is a different form of instalment trading. Commonly known as the "Tally System," it goes back, I believe, for thousands of years, when the trader cut notches on sticks as a means of keeping "tally" of the purchases of his customers.

This system differs to some extent, though fundamentally the same, from the hire purchase. The difference lies chiefly in the fact that the credit trader, dealing as he usually does in goods of a more *personal* nature, *i.e.*, soft goods and clothing, cannot easily repossess himself of the goods if the buyer does not pay the full amount.

Again, there is no agreement signed between the vendor and the buyer. A person orders certain clothes, bed linen or other soft goods and arranges to pay for them in *weekly* instalments, using them while paying.

For example, what would be the use of a credit tailor, after supplying a suit of clothes to a man, trying to repossess himself of the suit after the man had worn it for three or four months. It would not be of the slightest value to the trader, for he could not sell it to another customer.

So here we have a definite sale; and, though the price is to be paid in weekly instalments, the goods are the property of the buyer immediately the first payment is made.

In the case of the default of the buyer the trader has no redress except through the County Court.

Value for Money.

It is often said that by purchasing goods on either the hire-purchase or credit system, one "pays through the nose." This statement can, however, be flatly contradicted. Take furniture for example. It is true that the hire-purchase firms charge a bit more than the cash trader, but when one thinks for a moment of the fact that they may have to wait anything up to four years to get the full purchase price of the goods, surely it is only to be expected. The actual value of the goods is more or less the same, except for the extra charge made for deferred payments.

Another charge sometimes made is that the goods are of shoddy materials or badly made. How can this be the case? Would it be to the advantage of any particular firm if it were to sell inferior goods? Very soon the news would travel around and the bottom would drop out of their trade. The general public is too cute in these days to be put off with inferior goods.

The same applies to the credit trader. More often than not he sells *branded* goods, which are sold in the cash traders' shops, and it would be useless for him to try and make his customers take inferior goods, even if they do pay for them by weekly instalments.

Advantages of these Systems.

This system of paying for goods by instalments, though still decried by some people, has distinct advantages to many who, but for its operation, would either have to wait a long time or probably deny themselves altogether, even some of the necessities of clothing, furniture, etc.—not to mention the small luxuries which make life worth living—were it not for the possibilities it has opened up.

Buying a House.

Here again we come to instalment selling, for there is no question but that the property is definitely *purchased*.

The procedure is more or less simple, and the same, whether one buys direct from the vendor or through a Building Society. In each case the property is mortgaged until such time as the total purchase money is paid.

But there has crept into this business of house buying of recent years a new factor, that of including in the instalments the various rates, taxes, road charges, legal fees, etc. By this means the purchaser pays a monthly (or other periodical) amount, and this not only pays off the capital amount of the purchase price, but also frees the purchaser of all worries as to rates, taxes, etc., during a definite period. This has the great advantage of allowing the purchaser to know his total commitment in regard to his house for a number of years, with the exception, of course, of repairs.

Herein lies an unknown factor, for in most agreements it is definitely laid down that the property must be kept in such a state of repair that it would be in a fit condition for resale, should circumstances deem this compulsory.

Of course, when the capital sum has been paid, the question of rates, taxes, ground rent, repairs, etc., are a matter purely for the buyer, for it has then become his property absolutely.

A Final Don't.

When purchasing *anything* on hire-purchase or deferred payments, always summarise your income and expenditure and see if it is safely possible to pay "just that shilling or so a week more."

If your income is a fixed figure and you want to get a new dining-room suite on terms of another 2s. 6d. or 5s. weekly and you are doubtful if you can manage it, *don't get it*. Be content with the old suite until you are *certain* that you can find that extra each week or month with safety.

Something happens unexpectedly one week or month and an instalment is left unpaid; which means that it will be double to pay when the next period comes around, and before you know where you are you are "in arrears."

It does not matter whether it is clothing, furniture, vacuum sweepers or anything, **don't do it!** "Safety first" always.

A Square Deal.

But whatever you buy on hire purchase or credit, you can safely rely upon the fact that if you deal with reputable firms and use your own common-sense you have nothing to fear. The systems are fair and the people fair dealing. You can be certain of a square deal.

WASHING CHAMOIS LEATHER

LIKE every-thing else, there is a right and a wrong way of washing chamois leather if it is to be kept in the best possible condition.

When it is washed in the usual way it generally dries stiff and harsh. This can be prevented by making a nice soapy lather in water that is not too hot,

Fig. 1.—To Wash the Leather.

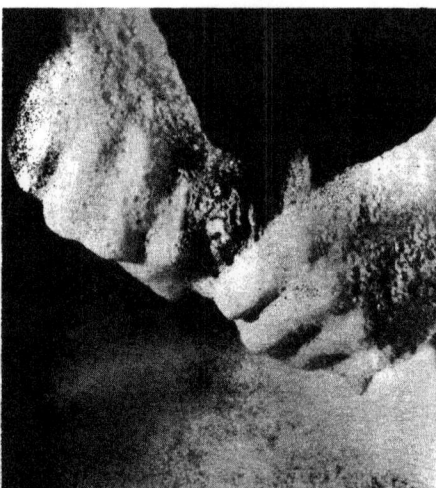

Fig. 2.—It will Dry out Soft.

placing the leather in the lather and washing it by squeezing as shown in Fig. 1.

When all possible dirt has been removed, squeeze out as much of the lather as you can, as shown in Fig. 2, but do not rinse the leather. Simply hang it up to dry as it is. The effect of leaving the soap in the leather will be to make it beautifully soft, even when it is quite dry.

COLOURING BRUISES ON FURNITURE

THE appearance of furniture is frequently marred by little knocks, which remove the polish and display the bare wood underneath. To cover these places a little colour and a brush are all that is required.

Take as much Bismarck brown as will go on a sixpence and the same quantity of spirit black, and add a quarter of a pint of methylated spirits. Leave these to soak for half an hour. Then take up a little of the resulting colour on a pencil brush and paint the damaged part to the required shade. With these ingredients practically any of the colours used on furniture can be reproduced merely by varying the proportions.

HOW TO IDENTIFY MARKS ON SILVER

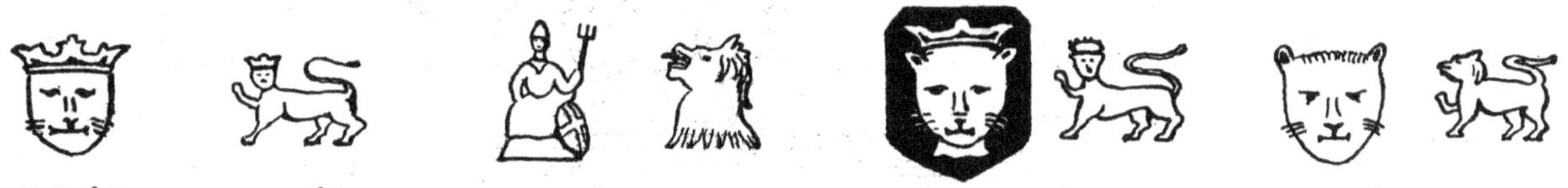

1307–1697 | 1544–1697 | 1697–1720 | 1721–1822 | 1822–1931

LONDON HALL-MARKS AND FINENESS-MARKS

Edward I. granted the privilege of assaying to the Goldsmiths Company in 1300. The first mark is a Leopard's Head crowned. The fineness-mark was the Lion Passant used first in 1544. The figure of Britannia was used from 1697 to 1720 with the Lion's Head erased as the fineness mark. The other hall and fineness-marks in use from various dates are shown side by side.

The hall-mark indicates the town, the fineness-mark that the silver is up to the specified standard of quality.

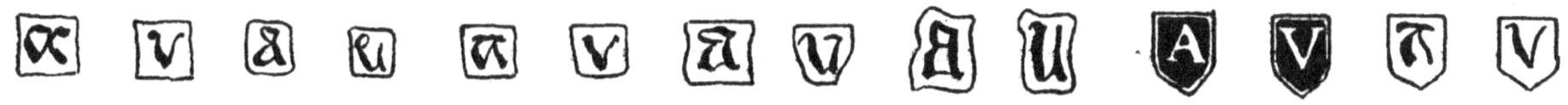

1478–1497 | 1498–1517 | 1518–1537 | 1538–1557 | 1558–1577 | 1578–1597 | 1598–1617

1618–1637 | 1638–1657 | 1658–1677 | 1678–1696 | 1697–1715 | 1716–1735 | 1736–1755 | 1756–1775

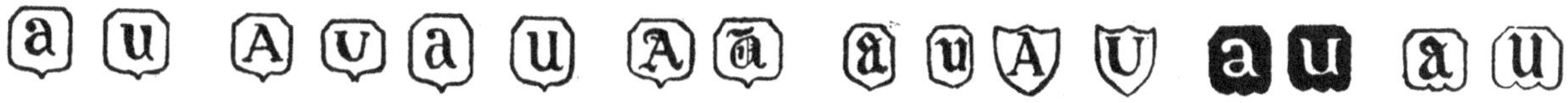

1776–1795 | 1796–1815 | 1816–1835 | 1836–1855 | 1856–1875 | 1876–1895 | 1896–1915 | 1916–1935

LONDON DATE-MARKS FROM 1478–1935

The year letter or assayer's mark is an alphabet; one letter is used for each year, commencing at A, omitting the letter J and concluding the twenty-year cycle with the letter U. Provincial offices use a similar system, but differently arranged—with different letters in any one given year. The marks thus show: *(a)* the town; *(b)* the fineness; *(c)* the date.

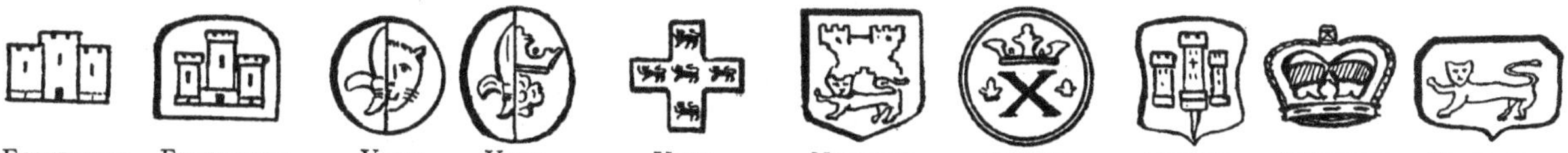

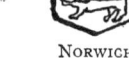

EDINBURGH 1485 | EDINBURGH 1782 | YORK 1562–1631 | YORK 1632–1698 | YORK 1700–1856 | NORWICH 1565–1697 | EXETER 1570–1650 | EXETER 1701–1882 | SHEFFIELD | SHEFFIELD

PROVINCIAL HALL-MARKS

In addition to the London assay offices, a number of provincial towns were authorised. The town-marks of several are shown above, with their dates. The Edinburgh fineness-mark is a Thistle. The York, Norwich and Exeter assay offices are now closed. The Sheffield fineness-mark is also shown.

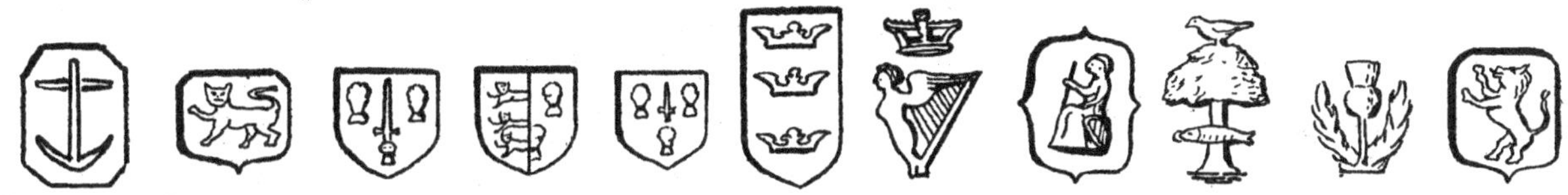

BIRMINGHAM | BIRMINGHAM | CHESTER 1687–1692 | CHESTER 1701–1778 | CHESTER 1779–1918 | HULL | DUBLIN | DUBLIN | GLASGOW 1681 | GLASGOW 1913 | GLASGOW

PROVINCIAL HALL-MARKS

A further selection of hall-marks are shown above, the Birmingham fineness-marks—a Lion—is also shown. The changes in the Chester mark are interesting. Prior to 1807 the Crowned Harp was used by the Dublin office as a combined town and fineness-mark, but since 1807 the figure of Hibernia has been used as a town mark only. The Glasgow fineness-mark, a Lion Rampant, is also shown.

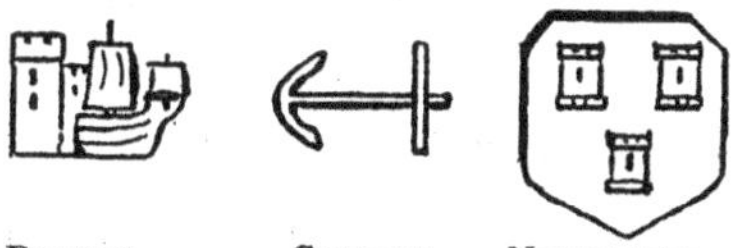

BRISTOL 1730 | GALWAY 1650–1730 | NEWCASTLE 1672–1886

PROVINCIAL HALL-MARKS

The Bristol mark is exceedingly rare. The Galway Anchor must not be confused with the Birmingham mark.

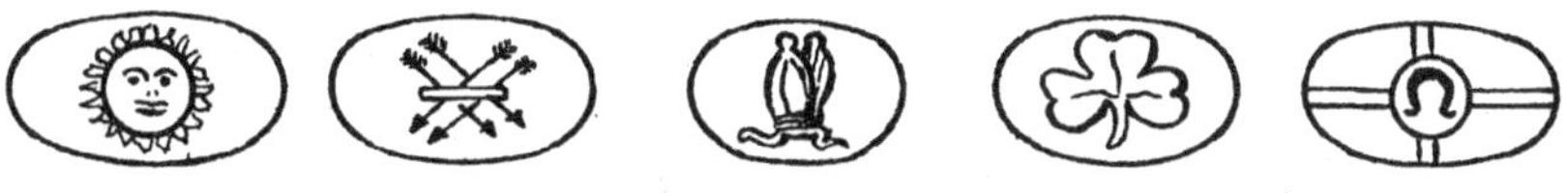

LONDON | SHEFFIELD | GLASGOW | DUBLIN | LONDON

MARKS IMPOSED ON FOREIGN SILVERWARE

These marks were used by the English assay offices on silver imported from abroad; the first four were imposed in 1904 and revoked in 1906.

HOW TO IDENTIFY MARKS ON SILVER

| SHEFFIELD | CHESTER | EDINBURGH | GLASGOW | DUBLIN | BIRMINGHAM | FINENESS |

MARKS IMPOSED ON FOREIGN SILVERWARE

Further town marks; the last example is the fineness-mark impressed by the foreigner. The date and other marks are also used by the assay office as usual.

| 1784 | 1786 | 1821 | 1831 | 1837 | 1612 | 1718 | 1734 | 1782 | 1821 | 1900 |

DUTY-MARKS   MAKERS' MARKS

During the period 1784–1890 a duty was imposed and a profile of the reigning sovereign was stamped on the silverware to indicate the duty had been paid.

Imposed by statute since 1363, initials were generally—and since 1720 exclusively—used. From left to right the makers' names are: Edward Antony, Thomas Bolton, Thomas Farrar, Patrick Robinson, Philip Grierson, John Round & Son Ltd.

| BLUE WREN | NEW SOUTH WALES | VICTORIA | QUEENSLAND | SOUTH AUSTRALIA | DATE MARKS | | FINENESS |

AUSTRALIAN HALL-MARKS

The growing importance of Colonial silversmithing was the reason for the formation of the Australian Hall-Mark Company in 1923.

The emblem is a Blue Wren, the fineness-mark is shown in numerals, and the branches of the Hall-Mark Company by the clipping of the corners of the punch, as shown above.

The date-mark is a Roman Capital Letter.

HOW TO MAKE A WILL

To make a will disposing of your property in the event of death, you must be over twenty-one; not an idiot, a lunatic, or of unsound mind through old age or infirmity.

A will must be in writing. If you propose writing your own will in preference to consulting a solicitor write it in the plainest, simplest possible language. Do not attempt to imitate technical phrases. It is of the utmost importance that your meaning should be made plain, and that can only be done if you use words whose meaning you thoroughly understand.

A will must be signed by the person making it *in the presence* of two witnesses present at the same time. The witnesses must sign their names in the presence of the person making the will. A person entitled to benefit under the will, or the husband or wife of any person entitled to benefit, must not be a witness. An executor may be a witness, however.

A will requires no stamp or seal.

If you wish to alter the will after it has been signed and witnessed, it is generally better to avoid confusion by having a new will made. But if this course is not considered necessary (a mere addition, for example), a codicil may be added. A codicil is very much in the nature of a postscript. It must be written, signed, and witnessed exactly in the same manner as the original will. The witnesses to the codicil, of course, need not be the same persons as the witnesses to the will.

If you wish to alter the will after it has been drafted but before it has been signed, the alteration should be initialled in the margin by the maker of the will and the witnesses.

A simple will might follow this form:
" Revoking all former Wills, this is the last Will and Testament of me (*here state full Christian and surname of person making will, and his or her address and description*, e.g., *butcher or baker*). I give, devise and bequeath all my real and personal estate whatsoever and wheresoever unto (*here state name of person to whom property is to be given*) absolutely, and I appoint the said (*or, as the case may be*) sole executor of this my Will (*or in the case of a woman 'executrix'*). In witness whereof I have hereunto set my hand this   day of   one thousand nine hundred and   .

" Signed by the testator as and for his last Will and Testament in the presence of us both present at the same time, who at his request, in his presence, and in the presence of each other, have hereunto subscribed our names as witnesses,

} (*Signature of person making the Will.*)

(*Signatures of the two witnesses, with their addresses, and descriptions,*)

Trustees.

You cannot compel anyone to act as a trustee. If any person does not wish to act in such a capacity he can disclaim the trust when he knows that he has been appointed. The Public Trustee may be appointed as an executor or a trustee.

How to Prove a Will.

A will should be proved by the executors as soon as possible after the death of the testator. It can be proved, if desired, without the assistance of a solicitor by attending at the Principal Probate Registry, Somerset House (Room 44, Personal Application Department.), or at any of the district probate registries. Where the *gross* estate does not exceed £500 it can also be proved through the local Officer of Customs and Excise.

In cases of intestacy, letters of administration are issued through the same channels.

When the application for a grant of probate of the will or letters of administration is made the amount of the Estate Duty is assessed, and this duty must be paid before the grant is issued.

Some Useful Designs for Bookcases

In the following article will be found details for constructing four simply-made bookcases. It will, of course, be realised that it is perfectly simple to alter the sizes given to suit any particular space available.

Hanging Wall Bookcase.

The wall bookcase shown in Fig. 3 is very simple, practical, and efficient; it is particularly useful for anyone living in rooms, and has the merit of easy portability.

The parts required are as follows:—

Shelves.—Three pieces oak, 24 inches long, 5½ inches wide, ⅜ inch thick.

Cords.—8 yards of coloured cord about 3/16 inch diameter.

Hooks.—Two ornamental wall hooks.

Draw pencil lines across the faces of each shelf, ½ inch from each end, then bore four holes on each line, spacing them ½ inch from each edge, and the others 1½ inches apart.

Remove any roughness on the wood by rubbing it with fine sandpaper, then cut the cord into four equal parts and

Fig. 1.—Simple Standing Bookcase.
An easily-made article of furniture suitable for the dining-room.

pass the two ends of one piece through the outer holes on one of the shelves, pass another cord similarly through the other end of the shelf, then similarly put the ends of both cords through the holes on the remaining two shelves.

Space the shelves about 12 inches apart, then fix the cords tightly in the holes with wedges of match-stick. Tie a loop in the end of one cord; fix the wall hooks into place by means of Rawlplugs.

Adjusting the Shelves.

The shelves are adjusted in the following manner. First slip the loop on to one of the wall hooks, then tie a loop in the second cord and slip it over the second wall hook so that the shelves hang level or parallel with the floor. Now take the cords from the front of the shelves, put them over the hooks, and then tie loops so that the front edges of the shelves are slightly higher than the back.

Put the remaining cords upwards through the middle pairs of holes in the bottom shelf, draw them tight, then cross them, put the ends up through the middle shelf, cross them again and then pass them upwards through the top shelf, and over the

Fig. 2.—Bureau Bookcase.
Home-made bureau bookcase with drop-down fall closed.

wall hooks. Bind the ends of the cords together, then unfasten the knots of the first pair of cords, put them over the wall hook from opposite sides and bind the ends together with coloured thin string. Bind together the whole of the loops with the fine string, cut off any surplus ends, then fix the cords permanently in the shelves by driving fine nails through the end of the wood so that they pass through the cords.

Small Standing Bookcase.

The bookcase shown finished in Fig. 1 measures 24 inches wide and 48 inches high, and can be made with the following pieces of oak:—

Sides.—48 inches high, ⅞ inch thick, 11¼ inches wide at foot.

Shelves.—Four, each 23 inches long, 7½ inches wide, ⅜ inch thick.

Top.—22¼ inches long, 4 inches wide, ⅝ inch thick.

The suggested positions of the housing grooves for the shelves in Fig. 5 will be found suitable for most requirements, but they can be varied if desired to suit any particular size books.

Round off the front edges of the shelves, either with sandpaper or with a small plane, and then glue them into the grooves, as shown in Fig. 6, and glue the shaped top piece into its place.

Fig. 3.—Hanging Wall Bracket.
Simple and inexpensive to make, this bookcase will accommodate a number of volumes and is always useful in the home.

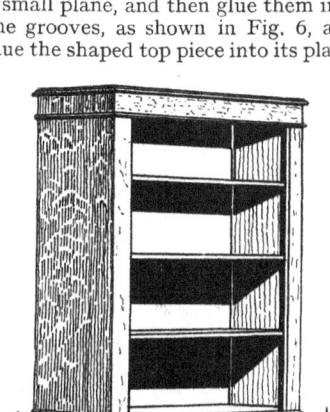

Fig. 4.—Standing Bookcase.
This bookcase measures 4 feet high and 3 feet wide.

SOME USEFUL DESIGNS FOR BOOKCASES

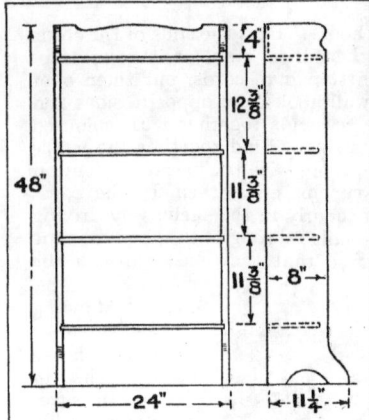

Fig. 5.—DIMENSIONS OF THE STANDING BOOKCASE SHOWN IN FIG. 1.
The disposition of the parts and their relative sizes are here given. The distance between the shelves can be altered to suit individual requirements.

Fig. 6.—FITTING OF THE TOP SHELF.
The housing groove and shelf which fits into it are here shown with the shelf nearly fitted.

Fig. 8.—SHOOTING THE EDGES.
To ensure a perfect joint the edges of the divisions can be planed up on a shooting board as here shown.

Fig. 9.—DETAILS OF THE DRAWER.
This composite picture shows the dovetail joint between the side and front of the drawer, above it is the drawer and bottom ready to put together.

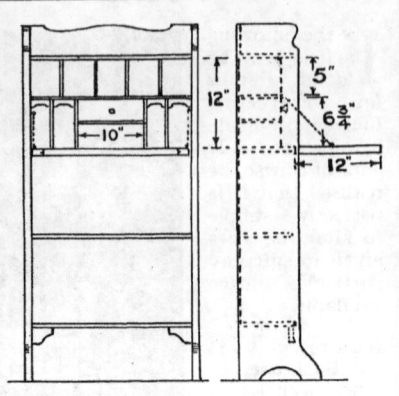

Fig. 7.—DIMENSIONS OF THE BUREAU BOOKCASE SHOWN IN FIG. 2.
The fall is here shown opened in the writing position and to reveal the arrangement of the internal divisions and drawer.

The wood can be left plain or be stained and polished as described later.

Bureau Bookcase.

The bureau bookcase illustrated in Figs. 2 and 7 is a development of the simple standing bookcase, and is made of similar parts, with the addition of the drop-down fall and internal divisions.

Materials Required.

Sides.—Two, each 48 inches long, $\frac{7}{8}$ inch thick, $11\frac{1}{4}$ inches wide.

Shelves.—Three, each 23 inches by $7\frac{1}{4}$ inches by $\frac{3}{8}$ inch; one only, 23 inches by $7\frac{1}{8}$ inches by $\frac{3}{8}$ inch.

Top.—One only, $22\frac{1}{4}$ inches long, 4 inches high, $\frac{5}{8}$ inch thick.

Fall.—One piece 20 inches long, 12 inches wide, $\frac{5}{8}$ inch thick.

Clamps.—Two, each $1\frac{1}{2}$ inches by $\frac{5}{8}$ inch by 12 inches long.

Drawer.—Front, 10 inches by 2 inches by $\frac{5}{8}$ inch. Sides, two each 6 inches by 2 inches by $\frac{3}{8}$ inch. Back, 10 inches by $1\frac{1}{2}$ inch by $\frac{3}{8}$ inch. Bottom, plywood, $9\frac{1}{2}$ inches by 6 inches by $\frac{1}{8}$ inch.

Divisions.—Four, each 5 inches by 7 inches by $\frac{1}{4}$ inch; four, each $6\frac{3}{4}$ inches by 7 inches by $\frac{1}{4}$ inch. Drawer shelf, 10 inches by 7 inches by $\frac{1}{4}$ inch. Division shelf, $22\frac{1}{4}$ inches by 7 inches by $\frac{1}{4}$ inch.

Spacer Blocks.—Four, each $3\frac{1}{2}$ inches by $1\frac{1}{4}$ inches by $\frac{3}{8}$ inch.

Corner Blocks.—Two, each $3\frac{1}{2}$ inches by $2\frac{1}{4}$ inches by $\frac{7}{8}$ inch.

Plywood Back.—$23\frac{3}{8}$ inches by 35 inches by $\frac{1}{8}$ inch thick.

Moulding.—3 feet half-round ball moulding.

Sundries.—Hinges, one pair, 2 inches long, $\frac{3}{4}$ inch wide, four screw eyes, 2 feet light brass chain. One drawer knob, one lock and key, or spring ball catch as desired.

The first thing to do is to assemble the framework, noting, however, that the widest of the four shelves is set at the top and that the front corners must be notched. Next glue and pin the plywood back into its place, taking care that everything is quite square.

Assembling the Drawer.

The drawer has dovetail joints at the front corners and is tooth-jointed at the back, as shown in Fig. 9, while the bottom is fitted into grooves machined in the front and side pieces.

The joints are put together with glue and the bottom glued into place. Drive the joints together tightly, and test all corners with a set-square to make sure they are true.

The next proceeding is to prepare and fit the various parts for the internal divisions of the bureau, for which purpose it may be necessary to plane up the edges. This can be done with a plane and

Fig. 10.—ASSEMBLING THE INTERNAL DIVISIONS OF THE BUREAU BOOKCASE.
The pigeon holes and drawer are built up separately and then inserted into the bureau

SOME USEFUL DESIGNS FOR BOOKCASES

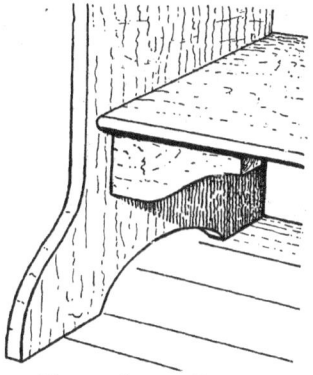

Fig. 11.—CORNER BRACKETS.
Detail showing one of the brackets glued into place at the corner of the bottom shelf.

Fig. 12.—CLAMPING THE FALL.
The writing-flap or "fall" is prevented from warping by the grooved end pieces, called clamps, which are fitted as here shown.

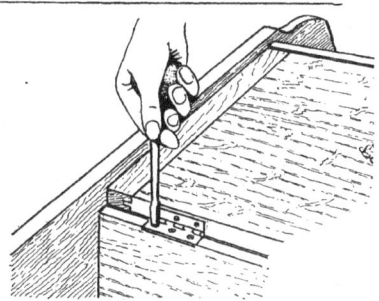

Fig. 13.—HINGING THE FALL.
The fall is hinged to the second shelf, as here shown, with long narrow hinges screwed to the joint edges.

Fig. 14.—FALL SUPPORTS IN PLACE.
Light chains are fixed, as here shown, at each side of the fall to support it when lowered.

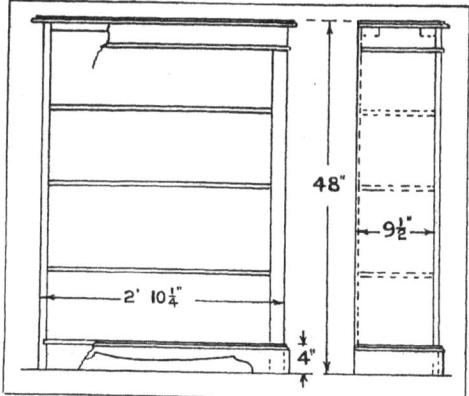

Fig. 15.—DIMENSIONS OF BOOKCASE SHOWN IN FIG. 4.
The arrangement and leading sizes of the parts are here shown.

Fig. 16.—DOVETAIL JOINTS.
The sides are held together at the top by two tie-bars with dovetail joints, which are fixed in position with glue.

Fig. 17.—CHISELLING THE TOP FRAME JOINT
The inner end of the groove has to be squared out with a chisel—as here shown.

shooting board, as shown in Fig. 8, the work being rested against the stop piece, which is fixed accurately at right angles to the groove in which the plane is worked.

Commence by placing the drawer in the middle of the division shelf, then rest the drawer shelf upon it and place one of the longer divisions at each side. Glue and pin the divisions to the shelves, taking care that the drawer can move easily, then fit the spacer blocks, as shown in Fig. 10, and the two remaining long divisions.

Fit the four short division pieces to the top of the long shelf—then place the whole in position between the top and the second shelf; fix them with glue and with a few fine cabinet pins driven through the plywood back. Finally fix the remaining spacer blocks between the divisions and the sides of the bureau, then glue the corner brackets to the underside of the bottom shelf, as shown in Fig. 11.

Preparing and Fitting the Fall.

The fall has a tongue at each end which fits into a groove in the clamps or end pieces, as shown in Fig. 12. Apply hot glue to the joints and drive the clamps firmly into place. After the glue has set, plane off any inequalities on the top and bottom edges and hinge it to the second shelf, as shown in Fig. 13, then support it with the chains and screw eyes, arranged as shown in Fig. 14.

The outside of the fall should be ornamented with a diamond or other shape, made up with half-round moulding, this being cut to length and merely glued and pinned in place.

Staining and Polishing.

If a light oak finish is preferred, it is only necessary to sandpaper the wood and finish it with a white wax polish, but if a dark oak finish is wanted, the wood should first be sandpapered, then given a coat of wood filler and again sandpapered. Next apply a dark oak water stain with a linen pad rubber, and when this is quite dry, finish it by french polishing. Apply the polish with a linen pad rubber, use brisk, light, circular strokes of the rubber and continue until a high polish is attained.

Standing Bookcase.

The imposing bookcase shown in Figs. 4 and 15 is from oak. The following is a list for an oak bookcase, 4 feet high and 3 feet wide:—

Top.—36 inches long, $\frac{7}{8}$ inch thick, 12 inches wide, moulded on front and ends.

Sides.—Two, each $9\frac{1}{2}$ inches wide, 3 feet 11 inches long, $\frac{7}{8}$ inch thick.

Shelves.—Three, each 2 feet $8\frac{1}{2}$ inches long, $\frac{5}{8}$ inch thick, 9 inches wide.

Tie Bars.—Two, each 2 inches by $\frac{7}{8}$ inch by 2 feet $9\frac{1}{2}$ inches long, with dovetail ends.

Bottom.—One piece 2 feet $9\frac{1}{4}$ inches

SOME USEFUL DESIGNS FOR BOOKCASES

Fig. 18.—Corner of Bottom Shelf.

The outer corner of the bottom shelf is notched to fit around the side frame.

Fig. 19.—Details of Plinth.

The corners of the plinth are mitred like a picture frame, then glued and pinned to the front edge of the bottom shelf and to the sides of the case.

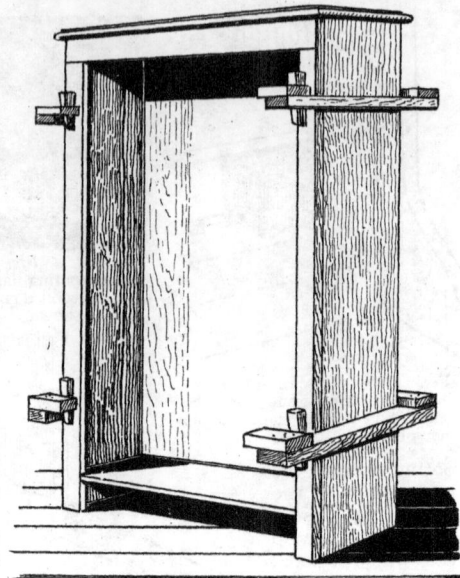

Fig. 20.—Cramping the Sides and Front.

Home-made cramps with wedges are used in this way to hold the front firmly to the sides while the glue is drying.

long, 10½ inches wide, ⅝ inch thick.

Plinth.—One piece—shaped and moulded—2 feet 11 inches long, 4 inches deep, ⅝ inch thick, 2 pieces ditto 11 inches long.

Front.—Top rail, 3 inches by ⅞ inch by 2 feet 10¼ inches long; two sides, each 2 inches by ⅞ inch by 3 feet 8½ inches long, tongued at one end.

Moulding.—10 feet Astragal Moulding, ½ inch wide.

Back.—Plywood, 2 feet 9¾ inches wide, 3 feet 7½ inches high, ⅛ inch thick.

Assembling the Case.

Commence by fitting the top tie-bars, so that the dovetails fit into the top edges of the uprights, as shown in Fig. 16, and glue them into place. Then insert the bottom shelf into the housing grooves and cut the front corners away, as shown in Fig. 18, so that the plinth and side members will fit nicely, then fit the plywood back and secure it with small nails.

Next clear out the groove in the top rail and chisel the end or "shoulder," as shown in Fig. 17, so that the tongue on the side piece fits square and true. Next screw the outer top to the two tie-bars, then glue the joints of the front frame; fit them together and glue and cramp them to the edges of the case. An extemporised cramp and wedges, as shown in Fig. 20, will answer perfectly if regular carpenter's cramps are not available. Remove any surplus glue while it is wet by wiping it off with a hot wet rag, then when the glue is dry, fix the moulding around the top, mitre the ends of the plinth and glue and pin it in place, as shown in Fig. 19.

Finish off with a rub down with sandpaper and by waxing or staining and polishing as preferred.

The book shelves should be supported at suitable levels by means of round-headed screws, with one part of their heads filed to a flat surface so that the shelves will lay flat upon them.

A WINDOW PAINTING HINT

WHEN painting window frames it is by no means an easy matter to avoid painting the glass where it joins the wooden parts of the window frame.

If the glass is thus inadvertently dabbed with paint the operation of window painting is apt to become a lengthy one, since all the paint on the glass must be removed before it dries and without wiping any of the paint off the window frame itself.

To overcome this

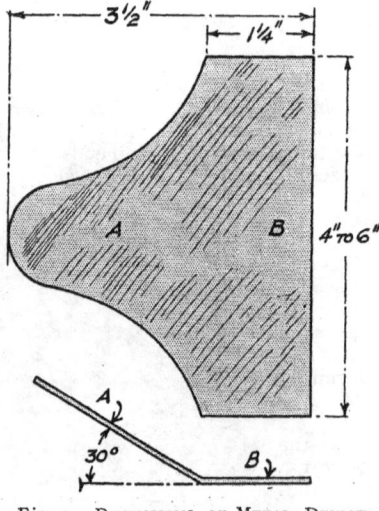

Fig. 1.—Dimensions of Metal Device and How it is Bent for Use.

Fig. 2.—How Window Painting Device is Used to Prevent Painting the Glass.

difficulty a piece of sheet zinc or tin of about 20 to 24 gauge thickness should be cut to the shape and dimensions shown in the sketch. The part marked A should be bent to an angle of about 30° with the part B.

With this device held against the corners between the glass and the window frame, during the painting process no paint will find its way on to the glass and window frames can very quickly be painted in one operation.